Learning SolidWorks® 2013

Randy H. Shih
Oregon Institute of Technology

ISBN: 978-1-58503-769-8

SDC
PUBLICATIONS
Mission, Kansas

Schroff Development Corporation
P.O. Box 1334
Mission KS 66222
(913) 262-2664
www.SDCpublications.com

Publisher: Stephen Schroff

Trademarks

SolidWorks is a registered trademark of Dassault Systèmes Corporation.
GeoGebra is a trademark of International GeoGebra Institute.
Microsoft, Windows are either registered trademarks or trademarks of Microsoft Corporation.
All other trademarks are trademarks of their respective holders.

Shih, Randy H.
Learning SolidWorks 2013/
Randy H. Shih

ISBN 978-1-58503-769-8

Printed and bound in the United States of America.

Preface

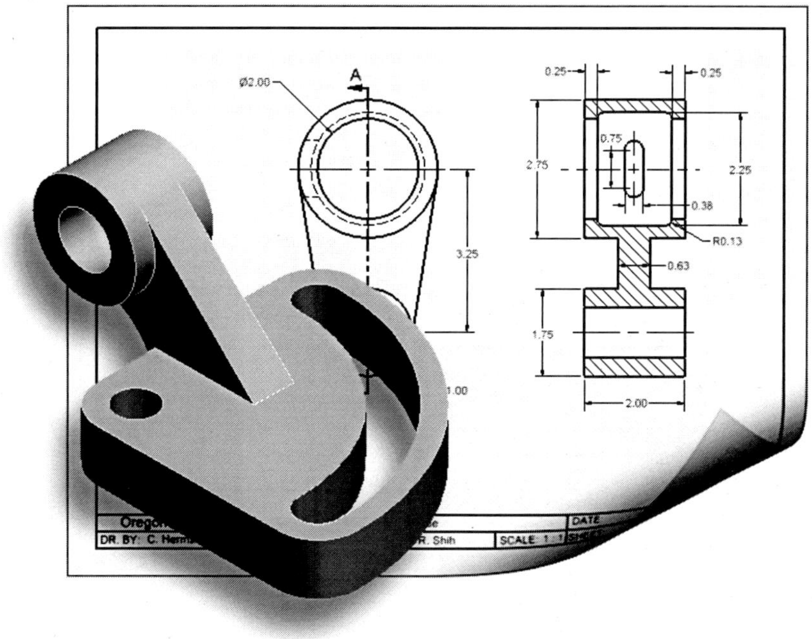

The primary goal of ***Learning SolidWorks 2013*** is to introduce the aspects of designing with **Solid Modeling** and **Parametric Modeling**. This text is intended to be used as a practical training guide for students and professionals. This text uses *SolidWorks 2013* as the modeling tool and the chapters proceed in a pedagogical fashion to guide you from constructing basic solid models to building intelligent mechanical designs, creating multi-view drawings and assembly models. This text takes a hands-on, project-based approach to all the important *Parametric Modeling* techniques and concepts. This textbook contains a series of twelve tutorial style lessons designed to introduce beginning CAD users to ***SolidWorks***. This text is also helpful to *SolidWorks* users upgrading from a previous release of the software. The solid modeling techniques and concepts discussed in this text are also applicable to other parametric feature-based CAD packages. The basic premise of this book is that the more designs you create using *SolidWorks*, the better you learn the software. The book presents the basics to parametric modeling by modeling the *Tamiya Mechanical Tiger* kit. Additional engineering analyses are also performed in both *SolidWorks* and the dynamic geometry software, *GeoGebra*. With this in mind, each lesson introduces a new set of commands and concepts, building on previous lessons. Majority of the main parts of the *Tiger* design are modeled in the chapters. This book does not attempt to cover all of the *SolidWorks's* features, only to provide an introduction to the software. It is intended to help you establish a good basis for exploring and growing in the exciting field of **Computer Aided Engineering**.

Acknowledgments

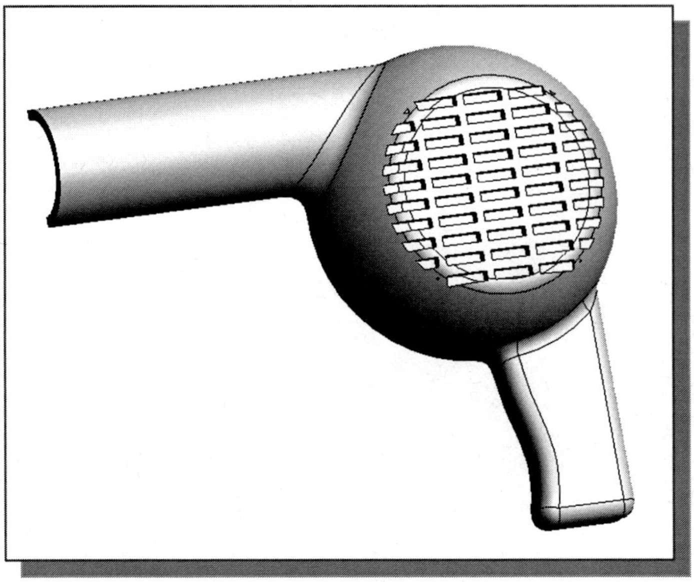

This book would not have been possible without a great deal of support. First, special thanks to two great teachers, Prof. George R. Schade of University of Nebraska-Lincoln and Mr. Denwu Lee, who showed me the fundamentals, the intrigue, and the sheer fun of Computer Aided Engineering.

The effort and support of the editorial and production staff of Schroff Development Corporation is gratefully acknowledged. I would especially like to thank Stephen Schroff and Mary Schmidt for their support and helpful suggestions during this project.

I am grateful that the Mechanical Engineering and Technology Department of Oregon Institute of Technology has provided me with an excellent environment in which to pursue my interests in teaching and research.

Finally, truly unbounded thanks are due to my wife Hsiu-Ling and our daughter Casandra for their understanding and encouragement throughout this project.

Randy H. Shih
Klamath Falls, Oregon
Fall, 2012

Table of Contents

Chapter 3
CSG Concepts and Model History Tree

Chapter 4
Parametric Constraints Fundamentals

Chapter 5
Pictorials and Sketching

Chapter 6
Symmetrical Features and Part Drawings

Chapter 7
Datum Features in Designs

Chapter 8
Gears and SolidWorks Design Library

Chapter 9
Advanced 3D Construction Tools

Chapter 10
Planar Linkage Analysis using GeoGebra

Chapter 11
Design Makes the Difference

Chapter 12
Assembly Modeling and Motion Analysis

Chapter 1
Introduction – Getting Started

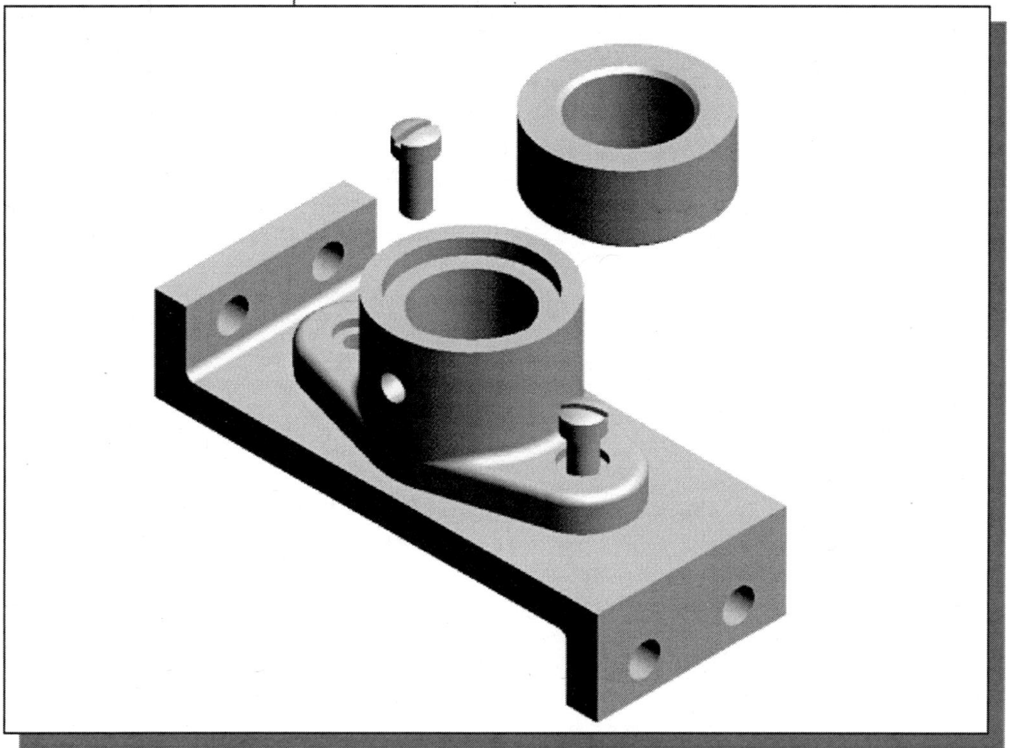

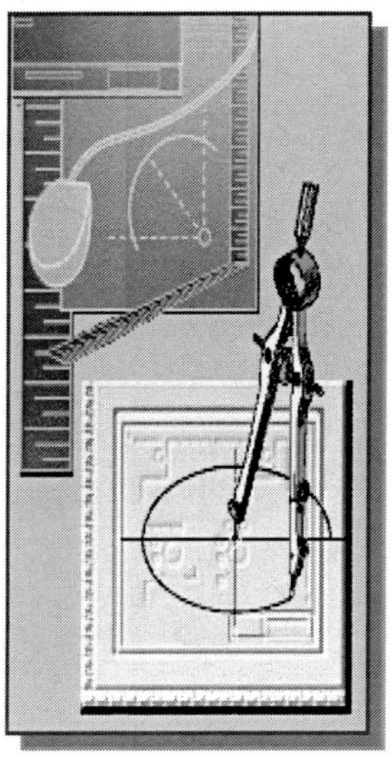

Learning Objectives

- ♦ Development of Computer Geometric Modeling
- ♦ Feature-Based Parametric Modeling
- ♦ Startup Options and Units Setup
- ♦ SolidWorks Screen Layout
- ♦ User Interface and Mouse Buttons
- ♦ SolidWorks On-Line Help

Introduction

The rapid changes in the field of **Computer Aided Engineering** (CAE) have brought exciting advances in the engineering community. Recent advances have made the long-sought goal of **concurrent engineering** closer to a reality. CAE has become the core of concurrent engineering and is aimed at reducing design time, producing prototypes faster, and achieving higher product quality. ***SolidWorks*** is an integrated package of mechanical computer aided engineering software tools developed by *Dassault Systèmes*. ***SolidWorks*** is a tool that facilitates a concurrent engineering approach to the design and stress-analysis of mechanical engineering products. The computer models can also be used by manufacturing equipment such as machining centers, lathes, mills, or rapid prototyping machines to manufacture the product. In this text, we will be dealing only with the solid modeling modules used for part design and part drawings.

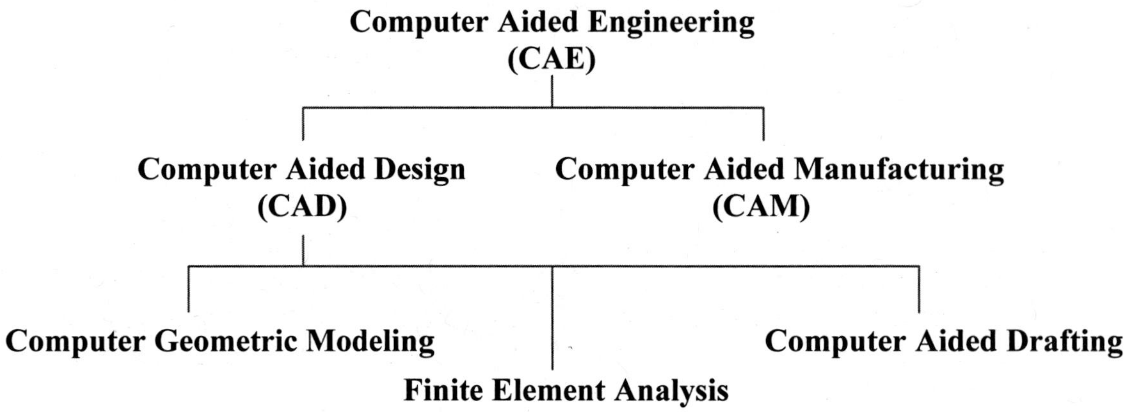

Development of Computer Geometric Modeling

Computer geometric modeling is a relatively new technology, and its rapid expansion in the last fifty years is truly amazing. Computer-modeling technology has advanced along with the development of computer hardware. The first generation CAD programs, developed in the 1950s, were mostly non-interactive; CAD users were required to create program-codes to generate the desired two-dimensional (2D) geometric shapes. Initially, the development of CAD technology occurred mostly in academic research facilities. The Massachusetts Institute of Technology, Carnegie-Mellon University, and Cambridge University were the leading pioneers at that time. The interest in CAD technology spread quickly and several major industry companies, such as General Motors, Lockheed, McDonnell, IBM, and Ford Motor Co., participated in the development of interactive CAD programs in the 1960s. Usage of CAD systems was primarily in the automotive industry, aerospace industry, and government agencies that developed their own programs for their specific needs. The 1960s also marked the beginning of the development of finite element analysis methods for computer stress analysis and computer aided manufacturing for generating machine tool paths.

The 1970s are generally viewed as the years of the most significant progress in the development of computer hardware, namely the invention and development of **microprocessors**. With the improvement in computing power, new types of 3D CAD programs that were user-friendly and interactive became reality. CAD technology quickly expanded from very simple **computer aided drafting** to very complex **computer aided design**. The use of 2D and 3D wireframe modelers was accepted as the leading edge technology that could increase productivity in industry. The developments of surface modeling and solid modeling technologies were taking shape by the late 1970s, but the high cost of computer hardware and programming slowed the development of such technology. During this period, the available CAD systems all required room-sized mainframe computers that were extremely expensive.

In the 1980s, improvements in computer hardware brought the power of mainframes to the desktop at less cost and with more accessibility to the general public. By the mid-1980s, CAD technology had become the main focus of a variety of manufacturing industries and was very competitive with traditional design/drafting methods. It was during this period of time that 3D solid modeling technology had major advancements, which boosted the usage of CAE technology in industry.

The introduction of the *feature-based parametric solid modeling* approach, at the end of the 1980s, elevated CAD/CAM/CAE technology to a new level. In the 1990s, CAD programs evolved into powerful design/manufacturing/management tools. CAD technology has come a long way, and during these years of development, modeling schemes progressed from two-dimensional (2D) wireframe to three-dimensional (3D) wireframe, to surface modeling, to solid modeling and, finally, to feature-based parametric solid modeling.

The first generation CAD packages were simply 2D **computer aided drafting** programs, basically the electronic equivalents of the drafting board. For typical models, the use of this type of program would require that several views of the objects be created individually as they would be on the drafting board. The 3D designs remained in the designer's mind, not in the computer database. Mental translations of 3D objects to 2D views were required throughout the use of these packages. Although such systems have some advantages over traditional board drafting, they are still tedious and labor intensive. The need for the development of 3D modelers came quite naturally, given the limitations of the 2D drafting packages.

The development of three-dimensional modeling schemes started with three-dimensional (3D) wireframes. Wireframe models are models consisting of points and edges, which are straight lines connecting between appropriate points. The edges of wireframe models are used, similar to lines in 2D drawings, to represent transitions of surfaces and features. The use of lines and points is also a very economical way to represent 3D designs.

The development of the 3D wireframe modeler was a major leap in the area of computer geometric modeling. The computer database in the 3D wireframe modeler contains the locations of all the points in space coordinates, and it is typically sufficient to create just one model rather than multiple views of the same model. This single 3D model can then be viewed from any direction as needed. Most 3D wireframe modelers allow the user to create projected lines/edges of 3D wireframe models. In comparison to other types of 3D modelers, the 3D wireframe modelers require very little computing power and generally can be used to achieve reasonably good representations of 3D models. However, because surface definition is not part of a wireframe model, all wireframe images have the inherent problem of ambiguity. Two examples of such ambiguity are illustrated.

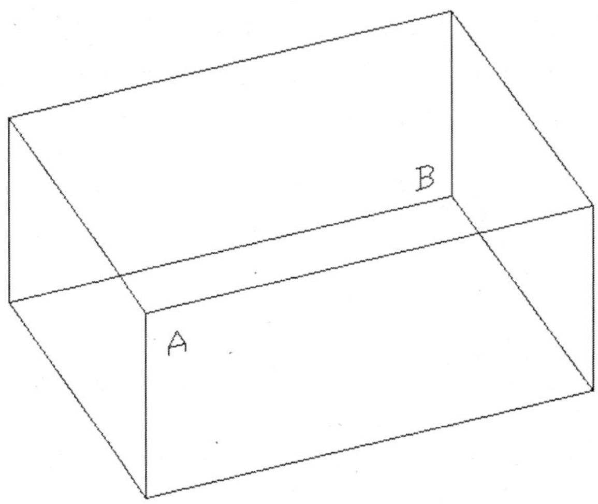

Wireframe Ambiguity: Which corner is in front, A or B?

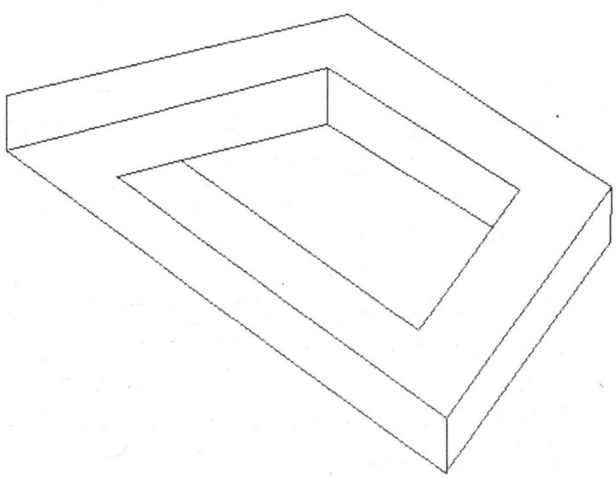

A non-realizable object: Wireframe models contain no surface definitions.

Surface modeling is the logical development in computer geometry modeling to follow the 3D wireframe modeling scheme by organizing and grouping edges that define polygonal surfaces. Surface modeling describes the part's surfaces but not its interiors. Designers are still required to interactively examine surface models to insure that the various surfaces on a model are contiguous throughout. Many of the concepts used in 3D wireframe and surface modelers are incorporated in the solid modeling scheme, but it is solid modeling that offers the most advantages as a design tool.

In the solid modeling presentation scheme, the solid definition includes nodes, edges, and surfaces, and it is a complete and unambiguous mathematical representation of a precisely enclosed and filled volume. Unlike the surface modeling method, solid modelers start with a solid or use topology rules to guarantee that all of the surfaces are stitched together properly. Two predominant methods for representing solid models are **constructive solid geometry** (CSG) representation and **boundary representation** (B-rep).

The CSG representation method can be defined as the combination of 3D solid primitives. What constitutes a "primitive" varies somewhat with the software but typically includes a rectangular prism, a cylinder, a cone, a wedge, and a sphere. Most solid modelers also allow the user to define additional primitives, which are shapes typically formed by the basic shapes. The underlying concept of the CSG representation method is very straightforward; we simply **add** or **subtract** one primitive from another. The CSG approach is also known as the machinist's approach, as it can be used to simulate the manufacturing procedures for creating the 3D object.

In the B-rep representation method, objects are represented in terms of their spatial boundaries. This method defines the points, edges, and surfaces of a volume, and/or issues commands that sweep or rotate a defined face into a third dimension to form a solid. The object is then made up of the unions of these surfaces that completely and precisely enclose a volume.

By the 1980s, a new paradigm called *concurrent engineering* had emerged. With concurrent engineering, designers, design engineers, analysts, manufacturing engineers, and management engineers all work together closely right from the initial stages of the design. In this way, all aspects of the design can be evaluated and any potential problems can be identified right from the start and throughout the design process. Using the principles of concurrent engineering, a new type of computer modeling technique appeared. The technique is known as the *feature-based parametric modeling technique*. The key advantage of the *feature-based parametric modeling technique* is its capability to produce very flexible designs. Changes can be made easily and design alternatives can be evaluated with minimum effort. Various software packages offer different approaches to feature-based parametric modeling, yet the end result is a flexible design defined by its design variables and parametric features.

Feature-Based Parametric Modeling

One of the key elements in the *SolidWorks* solid modeling software is its use of the **feature-based parametric modeling technique**. The feature-based parametric modeling approach has elevated solid modeling technology to the level of a very powerful design tool. Parametric modeling automates the design and revision procedures by the use of parametric features. Parametric features control the model geometry by the use of design variables. The word ***parametric*** means that the geometric definitions of the design, such as dimensions, can be varied at any time during the design process. Features are predefined parts or construction tools for which users define the key parameters. A part is described as a sequence of engineering features, which can be modified and/or changed at any time. The concept of parametric features makes modeling more closely match the actual design-manufacturing process than the mathematics of a solid modeling program. In parametric modeling, models and drawings are updated automatically when the design is refined.

Parametric modeling offers many benefits:

- **We begin with simple, conceptual models with minimal detail; this approach conforms to the design philosophy of "shape before size."**
- **Geometric constraints, dimensional constraints, and relational parametric equations can be used to capture design intent.**
- **The ability to update an entire system, including parts, assemblies and drawings after changing one parameter of complex designs.**
- **We can quickly explore and evaluate different design variations and alternatives to determine the best design.**
- **Existing design data can be reused to create new designs.**
- **Quick design turn-around.**

With parametric modeling, designers and engineers can maximize the productivity of the design and engineering resources to create products better, faster, and more cost-effectively. The tools available in parametric modeling are designed to cover the entire design process; from design and validation to technical communications and data management. The intuitive design interface and integrated software work together and provide designers and engineers the freedom to focus on innovation.

Getting Started with *SolidWorks*

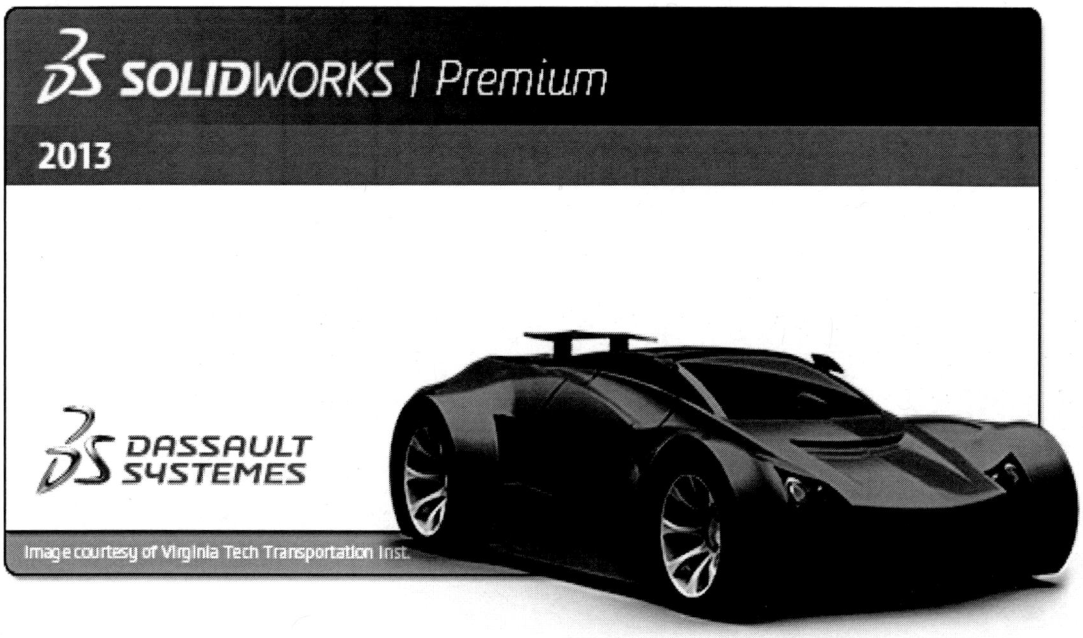

- *SolidWorks* is composed of several application software modules (these modules are called *applications*), all sharing a common database. In this text, the main concentration is placed on the solid modeling modules used for part design. The general procedures required in creating solid models, engineering drawings, and assemblies are illustrated.

Starting *SolidWorks*

How to start *SolidWorks* depends on the type of workstation and the particular software configuration you are using. With most *Windows* systems, you may select **SolidWorks** on the *Start* menu or select the **SolidWorks** icon on the desktop. Consult your instructor or technical support personnel if you have difficulty starting the software.

- ❖ The program takes a while to load, so be patient. The tutorials in this text are based on the assumption that you are using *SolidWorks'* default settings. If your system has been customized for other uses, some of the settings may appear differently and not work with the step-by-step instructions in the tutorials. Contact your instructor and/or technical support personnel to restore the default software configuration.

Once the program is loaded into memory, the *SolidWorks* program window appears. This screen contains the *Menu Bar* and the *Task Pane*. The *Menu Bar* contains a subset of commonly used tools from the *Menu Bar* toolbar (**New**, **Open**, **Save**, etc.), the *SolidWorks* menus, the *SolidWorks Search* oval, and a flyout menu of *Help* options. By default, the *Menu Bar* menus are hidden. To display them, move the cursor over or click the *SolidWorks* logo.

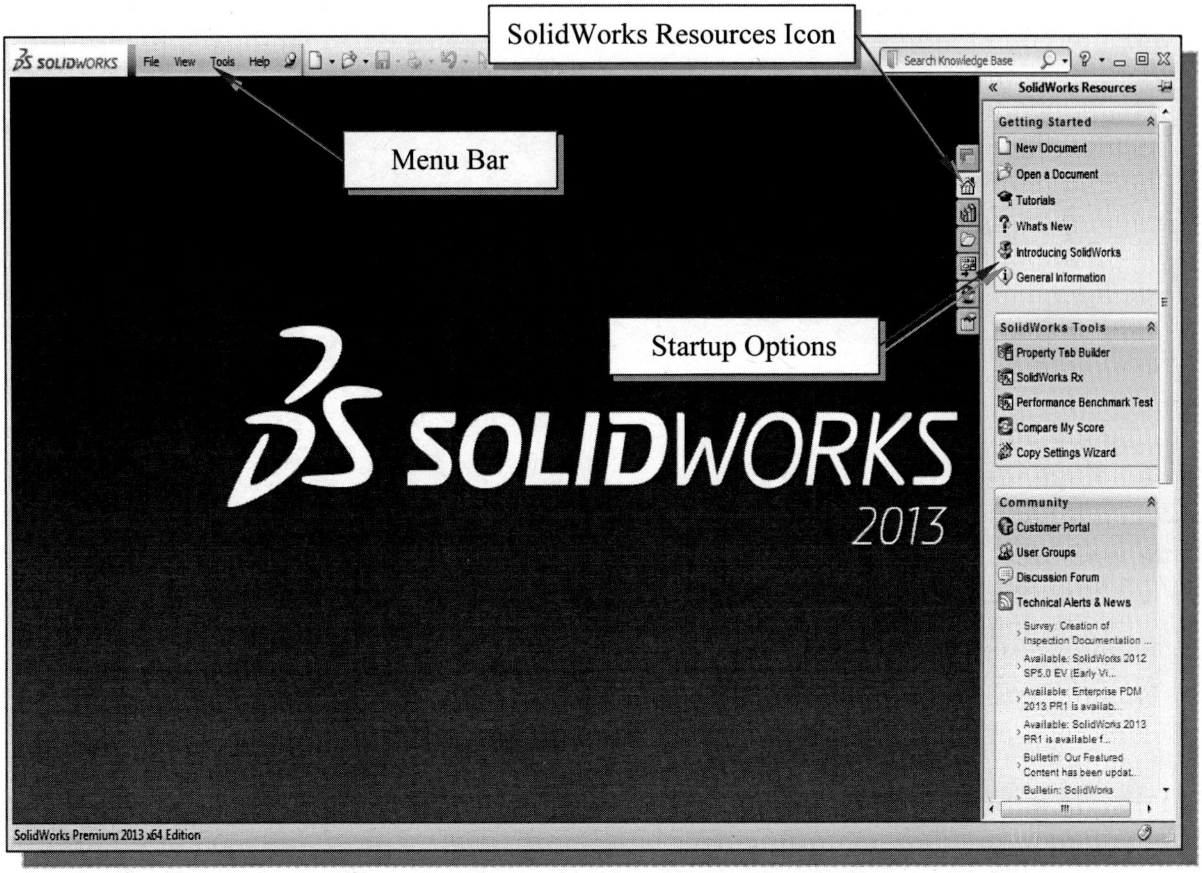

If the *task pane* does not appear to the right of the screen, click the **SolidWorks Resources** icon on the right side of the window. Other options for the *task pane* are the *Design Library* and the *File Explorer*. The icons for these options appear below the **SolidWorks Resources** icon. To collapse the *task pane*, click anywhere in the main area of the *SolidWorks* window.

The following two startup options are available: **New** and **Open**. The **New** option allows us to start a new modeling task. The **Open** option allows us to open an existing model file. These two commands can be executed in the *Getting Started* dialog box in the *SolidWorks Resources task pane* or on the *Menu Bar*. The *Getting Started* dialog box also contains a **Tutorials** option which provides some quick helps that illustrate the features and general procedures of using *SolidWorks*.

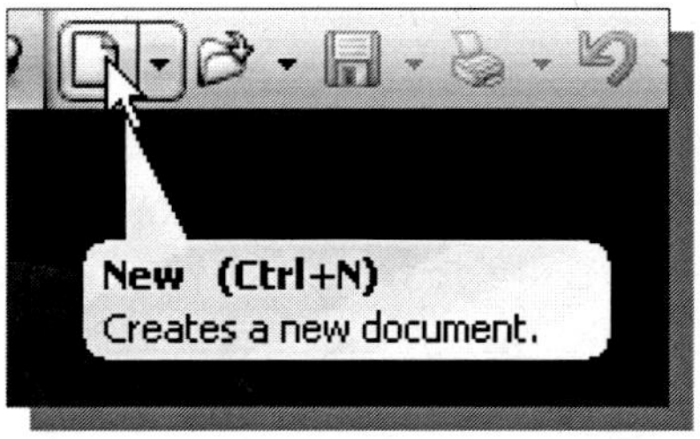

➤ Select the **New** icon on the *Menu Bar* with a single click of the left-mouse-button. The *New SolidWorks Document* dialog box appears.

Three icons appear in the *New SolidWorks Document* dialog box. Selecting the appropriate icon will allow creation of a new **Part**, **Assembly** or **Drawing** file. A part is a single three-dimensional (3D) solid model. Parts are the basic building blocks in modeling with *SolidWorks.* An assembly is a 3D arrangement of parts (components) and/or other assemblies (subassemblies). A drawing is a 2D representation of a part or assembly.

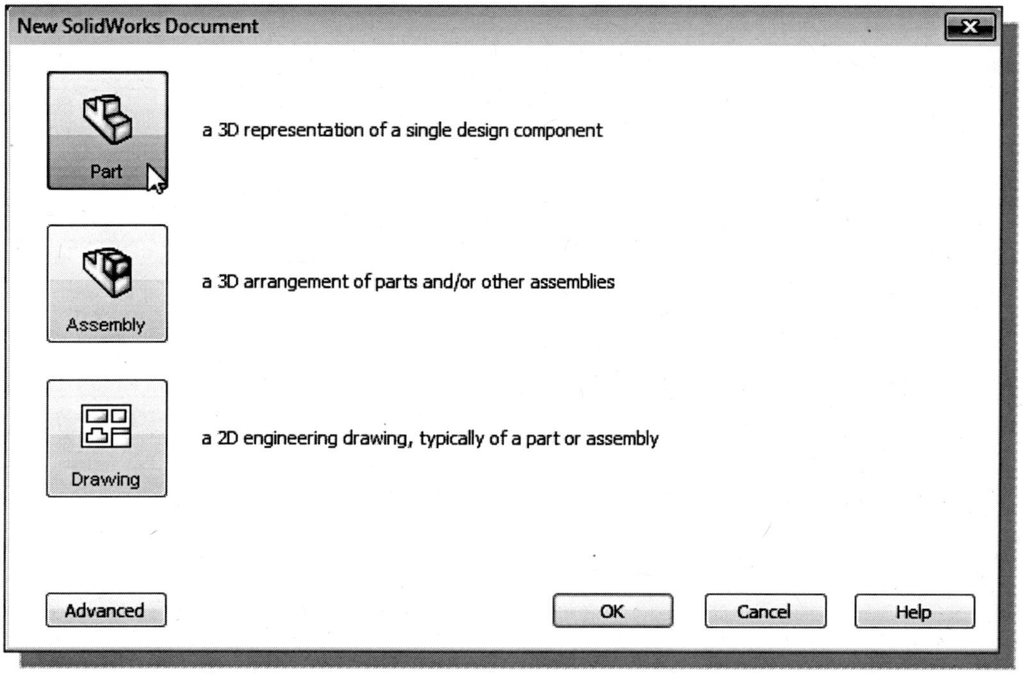

➤ Select the **Part** icon as shown. Click **OK** in the *New SolidWorks Document* dialog box to open a new part file.

Units Setup

When starting a new CAD file, the first thing we should do is to choose the units we would like to use. We will use the English (feet and inches) setting for this example.

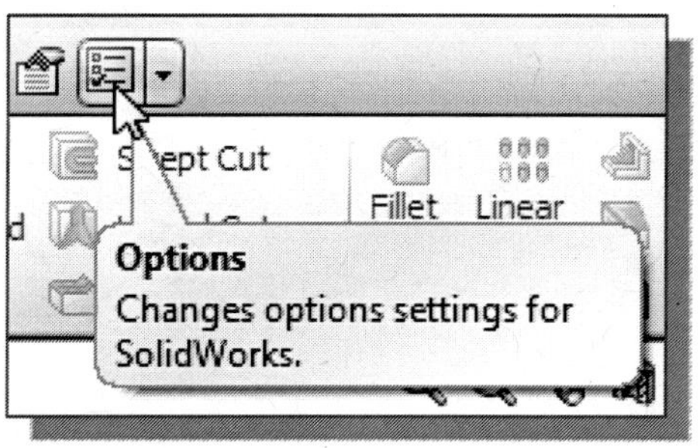

➤ Select the **Options** icon from the *Menu Bar* as shown to open the *Options* dialog box. (The *Options* dialog box can also be opened from the *Tools* pull-down menu.)

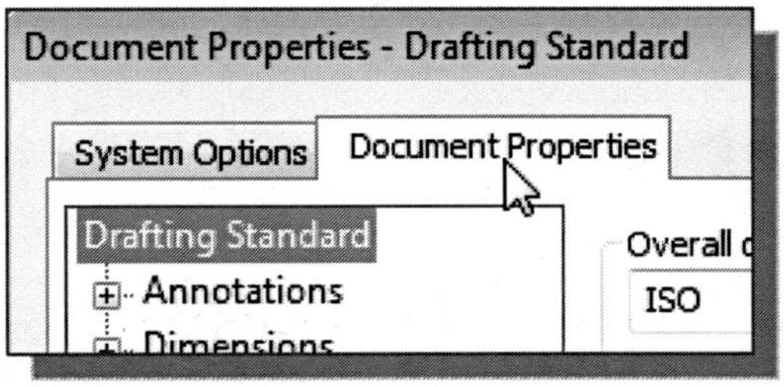

➢ When the *Options* dialog box opens, the **System Options** tab is active. The units setup is located under the Document Properties tab. Select the **Document Properties** tab as shown.

➢ Select **Units** on the left menu as highlighted below. Select **IPS (inch, pound, second)** under the *Unit system* options. Select **.123** in the *Decimals* spin box for the *Length* units as shown to define the degree of accuracy with which the units will be displayed.

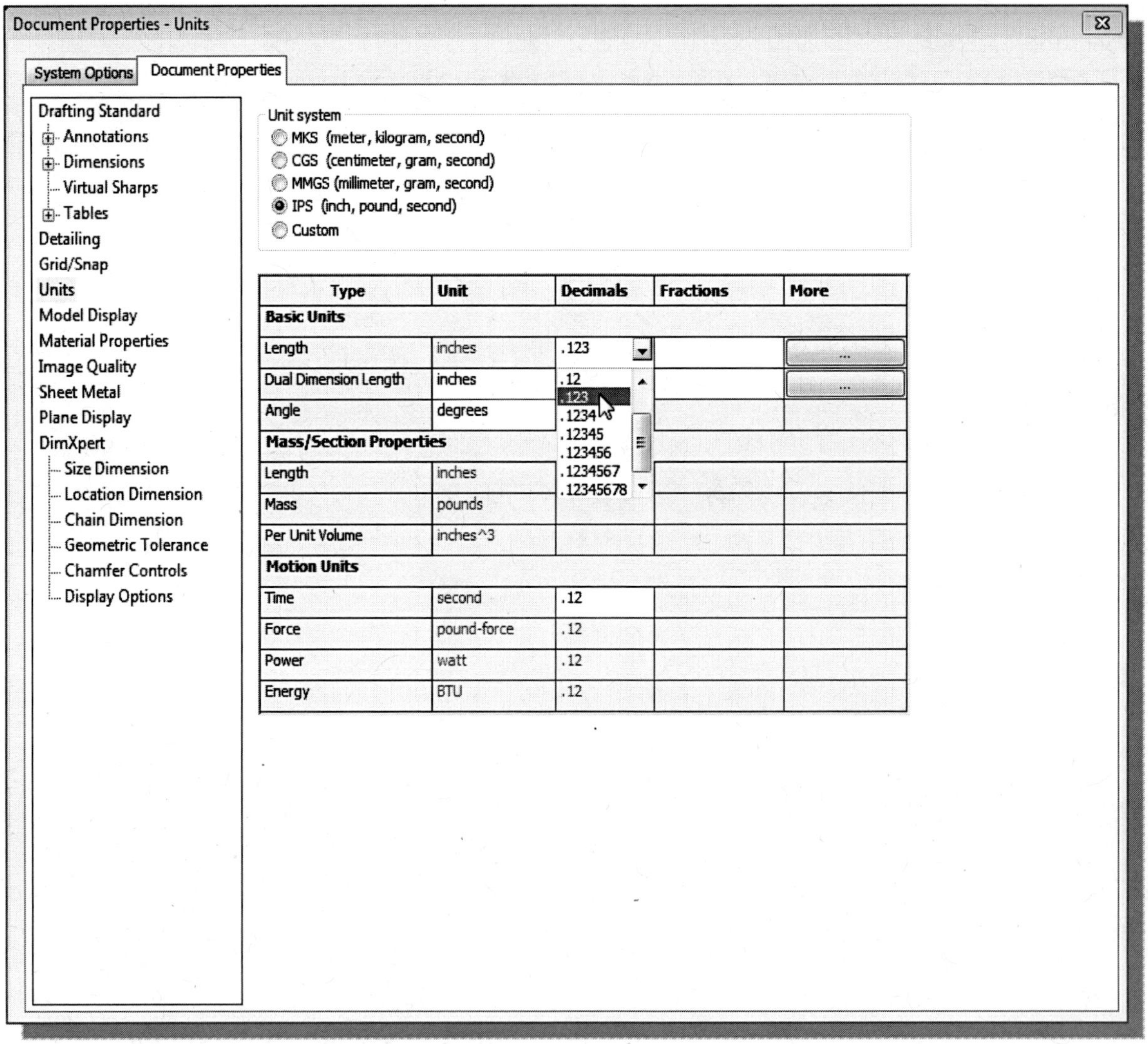

➢ Click **OK** at the bottom of the *Document Properties - Units* window to set the units.

SolidWorks Screen Layout

The default *SolidWorks* drawing screen contains the *Menu Bar*, the *Heads-up View* toolbar, the *Feature Manager Design Tree*, the *Features* toolbar (at the left of the window by default), the *Sketch* toolbar (at the right of the window by default), the graphics area, the *task pane* (collapsed to the right of the graphics area in the figure below), and the *Status Bar*. A line of quick text appears next to the icon as you move the *mouse cursor* over different icons. You may resize the *SolidWorks* drawing window by click and drag on the edge of the window, or relocate the window by click and drag on the *window title* area.

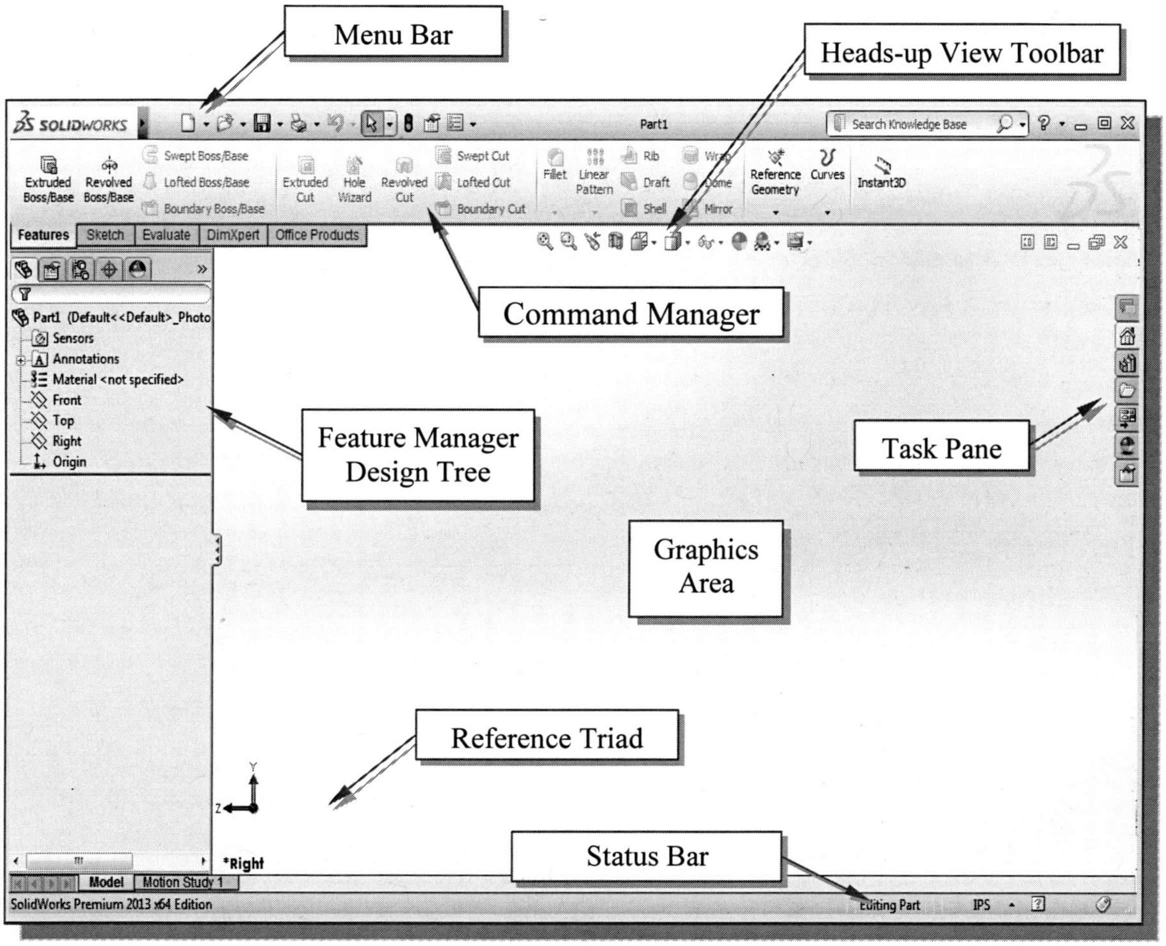

- **Menu Bar**

In the default view of the *Menu Bar*, only the toolbar options are visible. The default *Menu Bar* consists of a subset of frequently used commands from the *Menu Bar* toolbar as shown above.

- **Menu Bar Pull-down Menus**

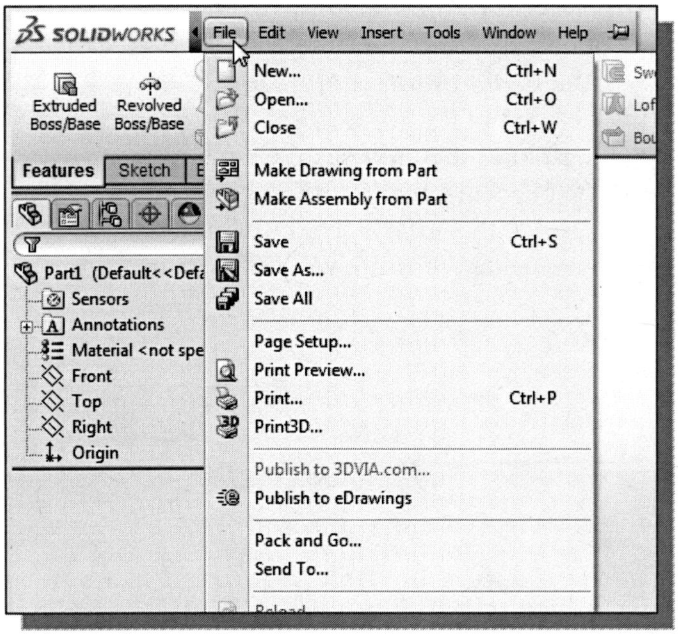

To display the *pull-down* menus, move the cursor over or click the *SolidWorks* logo. The pull-down menus contain operations that you can use for all modes of the system.

- **Heads-up View Toolbar**

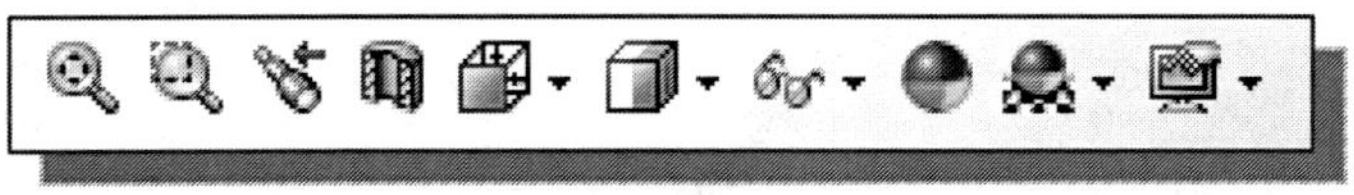

The *Heads-up View* toolbar allows us quick access to frequently used view-related commands, such as Zoom, Pan and Rotate. Note: You cannot hide or customize the *Heads-up View* toolbar.

- **Features Toolbar**

By default, the *Features* toolbar is displayed at the top of the *SolidWorks* window. The *Features* toolbar allows us quick access to frequently used feature-related commands, such as Extruded Boss/Base, Extruded Cut, and Revolved Boss/Base.

- **Sketch Toolbar**

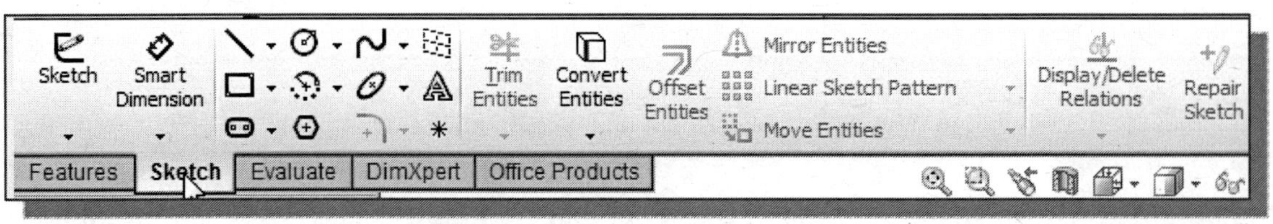

By default, the *Sketch* toolbar can be accessed by clicking on the **Sketch** tab in the *Ribbon* toolbar area. The *Sketch* toolbar provides tools for creating the basic geometry that can be used to create features and parts.

- **Feature Manager-Design Tree/Property Manager/Configuration Manager/ DimXpert Manager/Display Manager**

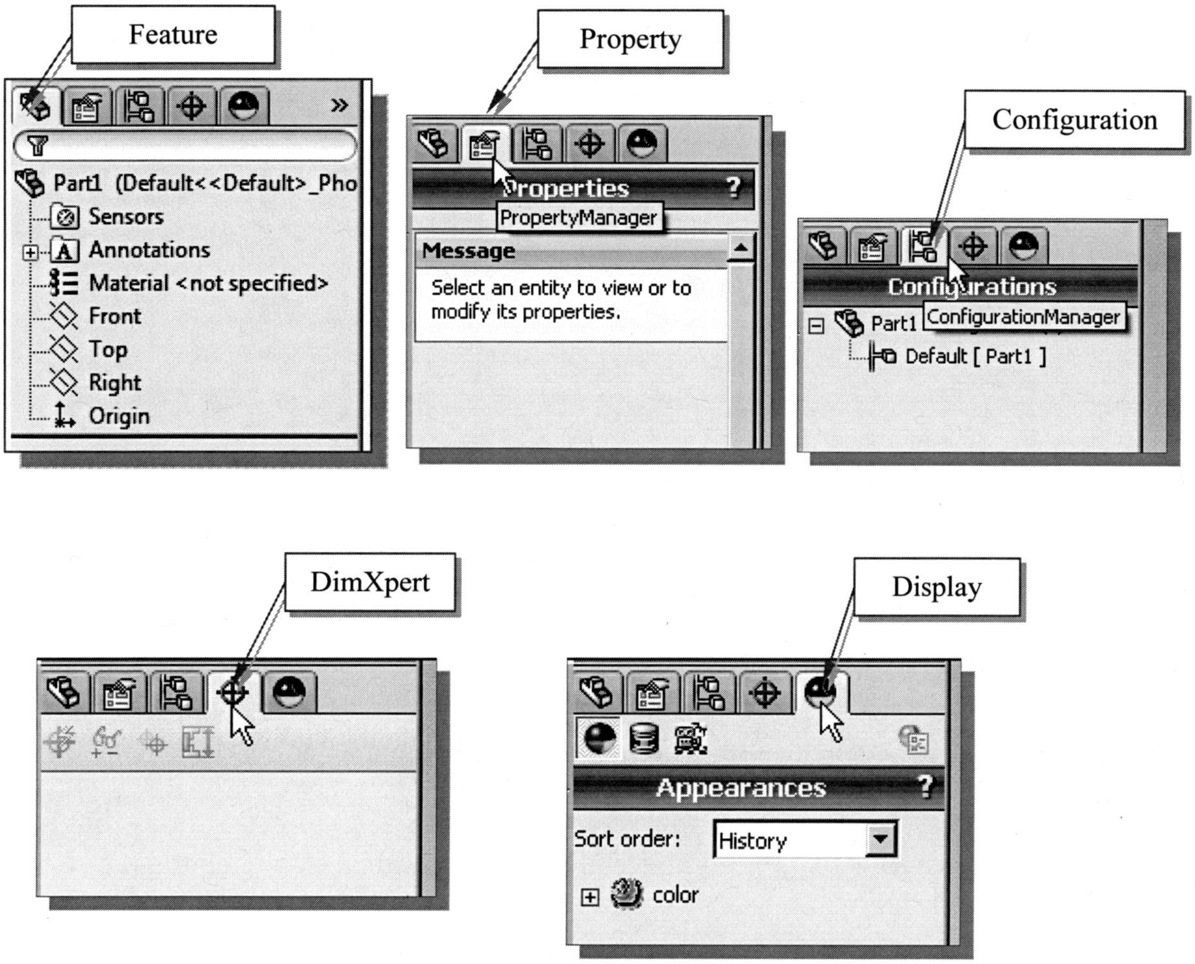

The left panel of the *SolidWorks* window is used to display the *Feature Manager-Design Tree*, the *Property Manager*, the *Configuration Manager*, and the *DimXpert Manager*. These options can be chosen by selecting the appropriate tab at the top of the panel. The *Feature Manager Design Tree* provides an overview of the active part, drawing, or assembly in outline form. It can be used to show and hide selected features, filter contents, and manage access to features and editing. The *Property Manager* opens automatically when commands are executed or entities are selected in the graphics window, and is used to make selections, enter values, and accept commands. The *Configuration Manager* is used to create, select and view multiple configurations of parts and assemblies. The *DimXpert Manager* lists the tolerance features defined using the *SolidWorks* '*DimXpert for parts*' tools. The *Display Manager* lists the appearance, decals, lights, scene, and cameras applied to the current model. From the *Display Manager*, we can view applied content, and add, edit, or delete items. The *Display Manager* also provides access to *Photo View* options if the module is available.

- **Graphics Area**

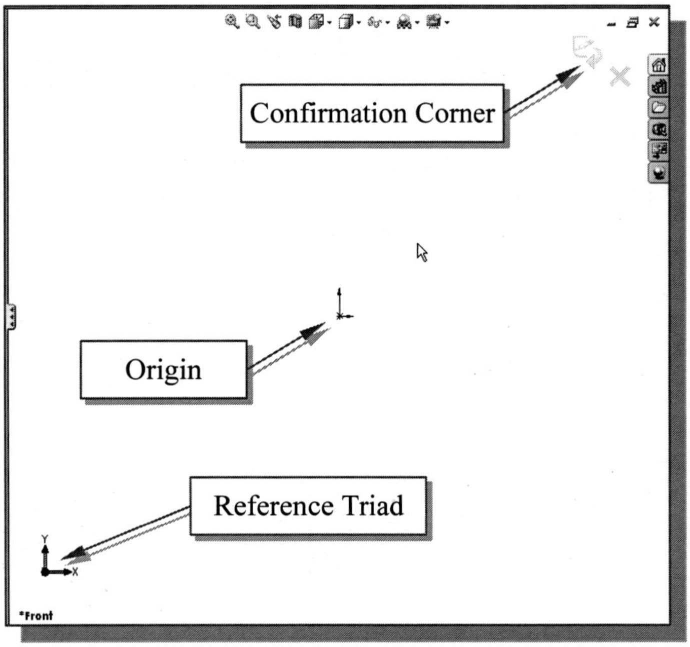

The graphics area is the area where models and drawings are displayed.

- **Reference Triad**

The *Reference Triad* appears in the graphics area of part and assembly documents. The triad is shown to help orient the user when viewing models and is for reference only.

- **Origin**

The *Origin* represents the (0,0,0) coordinate in a model or sketch. A model origin appears blue; a sketch origin appears red.

- **Confirmation Corner**

The *Confirmation Corner* offers an alternate way to accept features.

- **Graphics Cursor or Crosshairs**

The *graphics cursor* shows the location of the pointing device in the graphics window. During geometric construction, the coordinate of the cursor is displayed in the *Status Bar* area, located at the bottom of the screen. The cursor's appearance depends on the selected command or option.

- **Message and Status Bar**

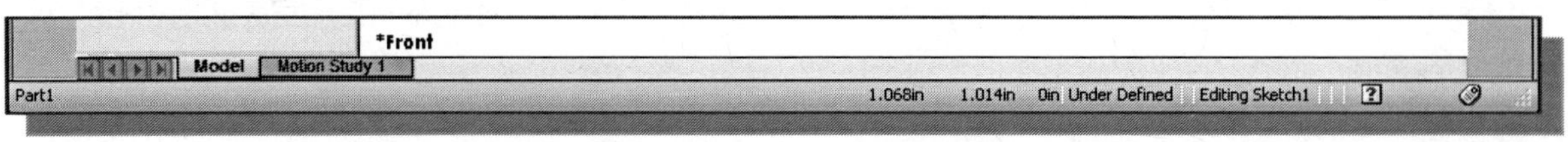

The *Message and Status Bar* area displays a single-line description of a command when the cursor is on top of a command icon. This area also displays information pertinent to the active operation. In the figure above, the cursor coordinates are displayed while in the *Sketch* mode.

Using the *SolidWorks* Command Manager

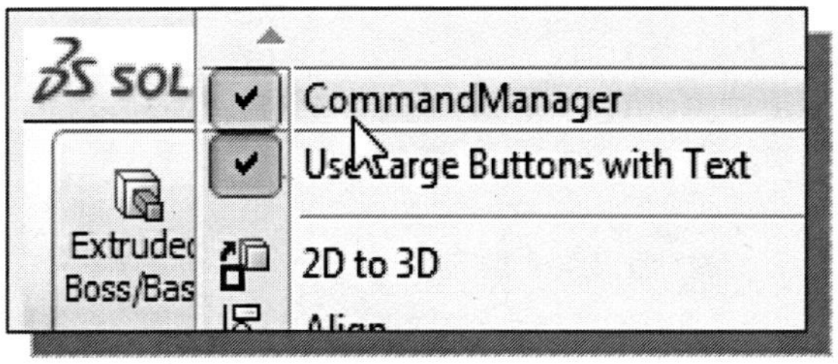

The *SolidWorks Command Manager* provides a convenient method for displaying the most commonly used toolbars. To turn on/off the *Command Manager*, **right click** on any toolbar icon, then select **Command Manager** from the top of the pop up menu list of toolbars.

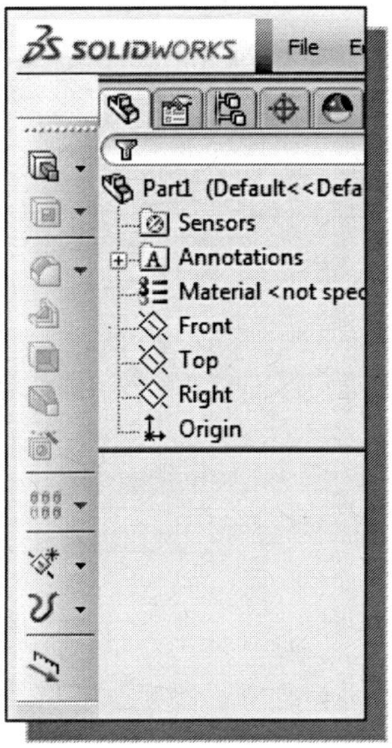

You will notice that, when the *Command Manager* is turned off, the *Sketch* and *Features* toolbars appear on the left and right edges of the display window.

To turn on the *Command Manager*, right click on the *Command Manager* (or any other) toolbar and toggle the *Command Manager* on by selecting it at the top of the pop-up menu.

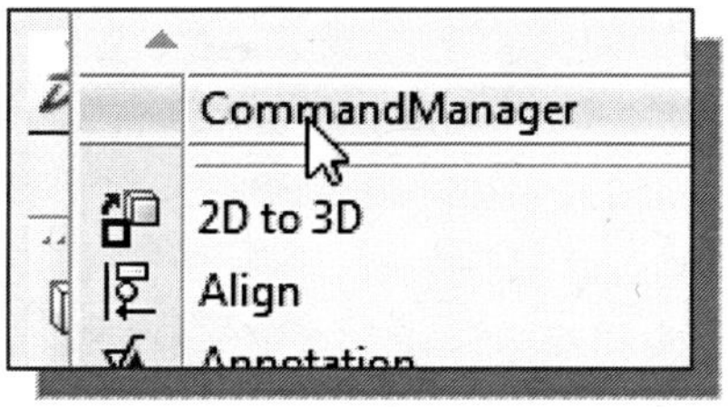

The *Command Manager* is a context-sensitive toolbar that dynamically updates based on the user's selection. When you click a tab below the *Command Manager*, it updates to display the corresponding toolbar. For example, if you click the **Sketches** tab, the *Sketch* toolbar appears. By default, the *Command Manager* has toolbars embedded in it based on the document type.

The default display of the *Command Manager* is shown below. You will notice that, when the *Command Manager* is used, the *Sketch* and *Features* toolbars no longer appear on the left and right edges of the display window.

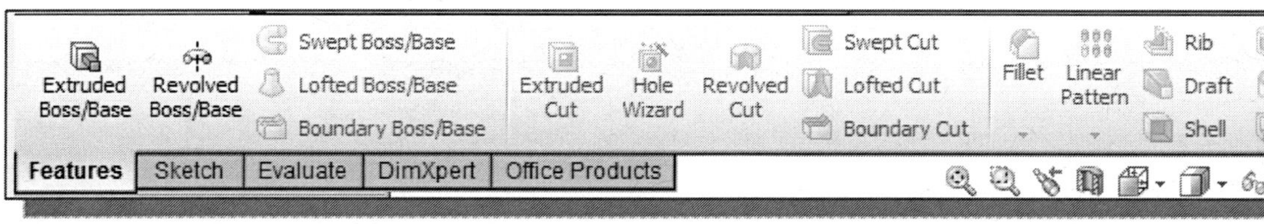

Important Note: The illustrations in this text use the *Command Manager*. If a user prefers to use the standard display of toolbars, the only change is that it may be necessary to activate the appropriate toolbar prior to selecting a command. For example, if the instruction is to "select *Extruded Boss* on the *Command Manager*" it may be necessary to first display the *Features* toolbar through the **Customize Toolbar** command.

Mouse Buttons

SolidWorks utilizes the mouse buttons extensively. In learning *SolidWorks'* interactive environment, it is important to understand the basic functions of the mouse buttons.

- **Left mouse button**
  The **left-mouse-button** is used for most operations, such as selecting menus and icons, or picking graphic entities. One click of the button is used to select icons, menus and form entries, and to pick graphic items.

- **Right mouse button**
  The **right-mouse-button** is used to bring up additionally available options in a context-sensitive pop-up menu. These menus provide shortcuts to frequently used commands.

- **Middle mouse button/wheel**
  The middle mouse button/wheel can be used to Rotate (hold down the wheel button and drag the mouse), Pan (hold down the wheel button and drag the mouse while holding down the [**Ctrl**] key), or Zoom (hold down the wheel button and drag the mouse while holding down the [**Shift**] key) realtime. Spinning the wheel allows zooming to the position of the cursor.

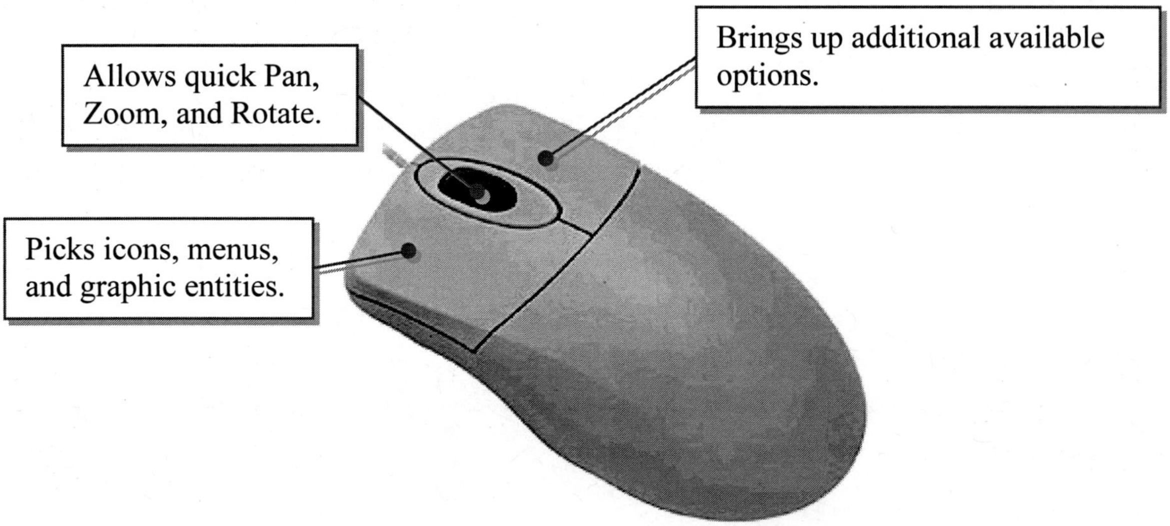

[Esc] – Canceling Commands

The [**Esc**] key is used to cancel a command in *SolidWorks*. The [**Esc**] key is located near the top left corner of the keyboard. Sometimes, it may be necessary to press the [**Esc**] key twice to cancel a command; it depends on where we are in the command sequence. For some commands, the [**Esc**] key is used to exit the command.

SolidWorks Help system

❖ Several types of on-line help are available at any time during a *SolidWorks* session. *SolidWorks* provides many on-line help functions, such as:

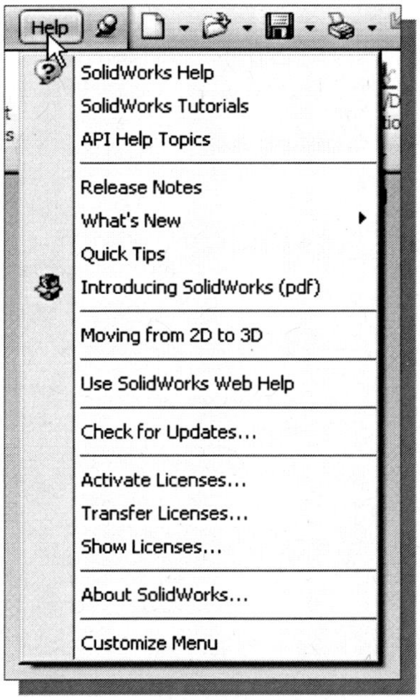

- The **Help** menu: Click on the **Help** option in the *Menu Bar* to access the *SolidWorks Help* menu system. (Note: Move the cursor over the *SolidWorks* logo in the *Menu Bar* to display the pull-down menu options.) The **SolidWorks Help** option provides general help information, such as command options and command references. The **SolidWorks Tutorials** option provides a collection of tutorials illustrating different *SolidWorks* operations.

- The SolidWorks Tutorials can also be accessed from the *SolidWorks Resources task pane* on the right side of the screen by selecting **Tutorials**.

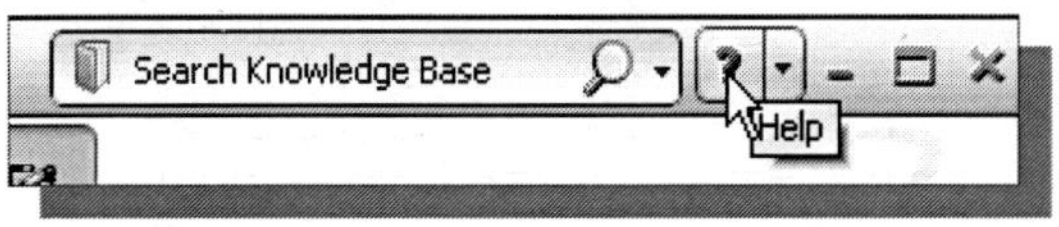

- The **SolidWorks Help** option can also be accessed by clicking on the **Help** icon at the right end of the *Menu Bar*.

Leaving *SolidWorks*

➢ To leave *SolidWorks*, use the left-mouse-button and click on **File** at the top of the *SolidWorks* screen window, then choose **Exit** from the pull-down menu. (Note: Move the cursor over the *SolidWorks* logo in the *Menu Bar* to display the pull-down menu options.)

Creating a CAD files folder

It is a good practice to create a separate folder to store your CAD files. You should not save your CAD files in the same folder where the *SolidWorks* application is located. It is much easier to organize and back up your project files if they are in a separate folder. Making folders within this folder for different types of projects will help you organize your CAD files even further. When creating CAD files in *SolidWorks*, it is strongly recommended that you *save* your CAD files on the hard drive.

➢ To create a new folder in the *Windows* environment:

1. In *My Computer*, or start *Windows Explorer* under the *Start* menu, open the folder in which you want to create a new folder.

2. On the **File** menu, point to **New**, and then click **Folder**. The new folder appears with a temporary name.

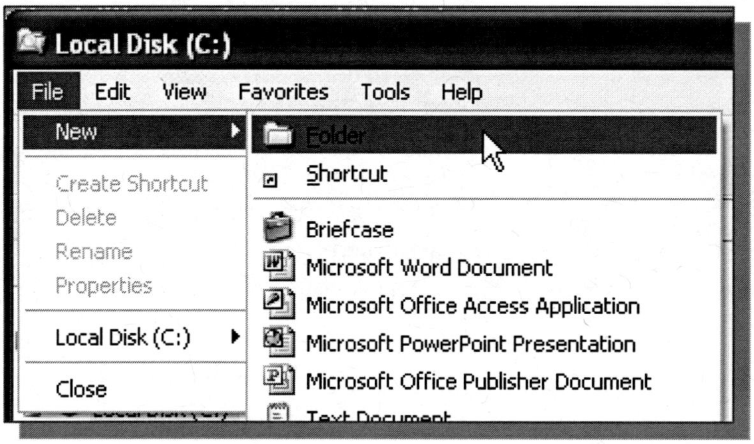

3. Type a name, such as ***Mechanical-Tiger*** under the ***SolidWorks Data*** directory, for the new folder, and then press [**ENTER**].

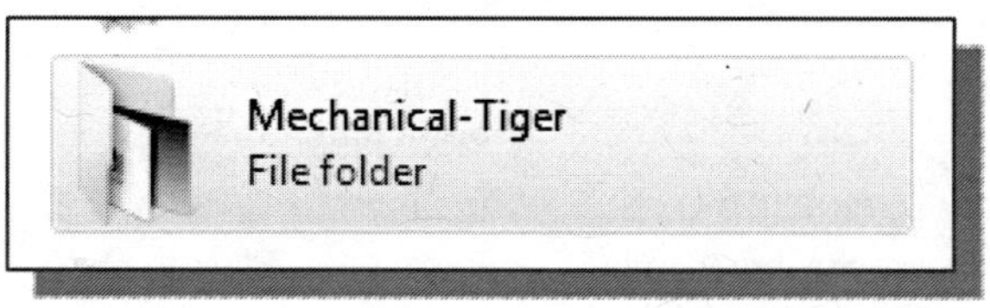

Chapter 2
Parametric Modeling Fundamentals

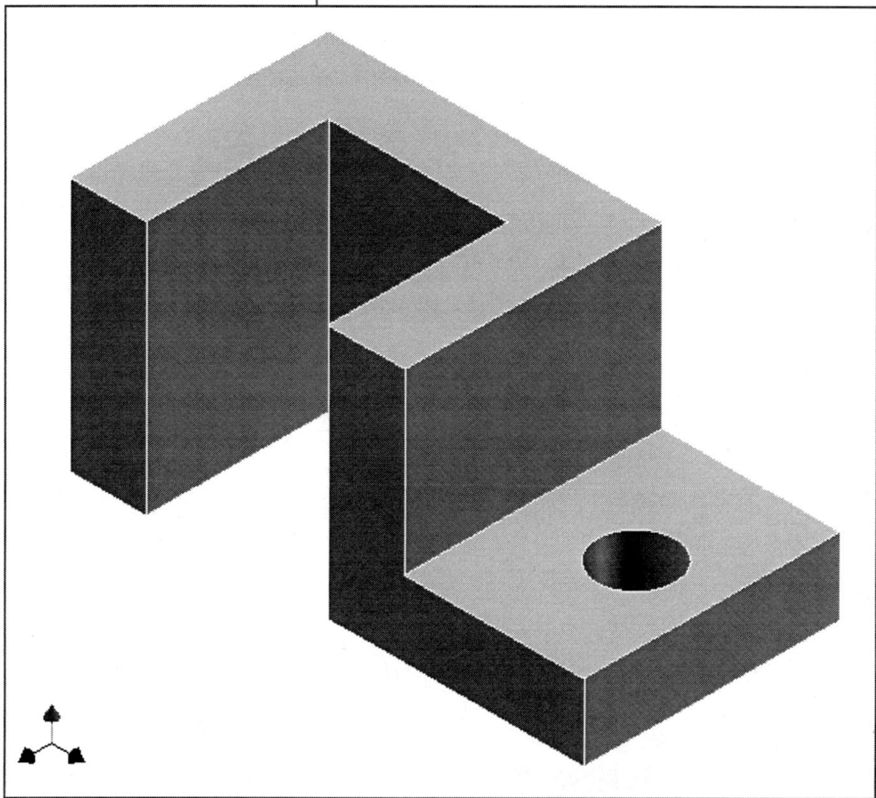

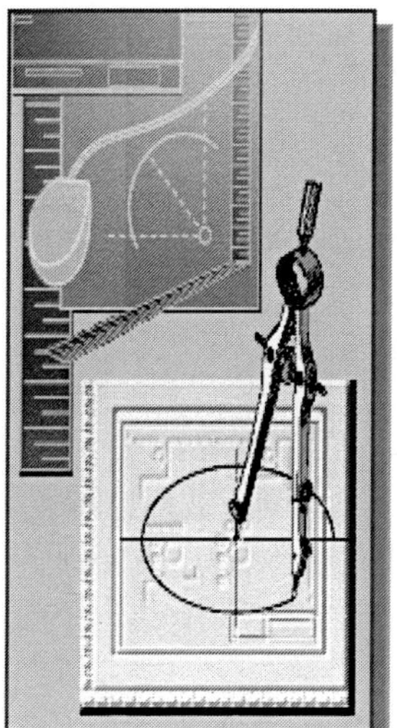

Learning Objectives

- Create Simple Extruded Solid Models
- Understand the Basic Parametric Modeling Procedure
- Create 2-D Sketches
- Understand the "Shape before Size" Design Approach
- Use the Dynamic Viewing Commands
- Create and Edit Parametric Dimensions

Introduction

The **feature-based parametric modeling** technique enables the designer to incorporate the original **design intent** into the construction of the model. The word ***parametric*** means the geometric definitions of the design, such as dimensions, can be varied at any time in the design process. Parametric modeling is accomplished by identifying and creating the key features of the design with the aid of computer software. The design variables, described in the sketches and described as parametric relations, can then be used to quickly modify/update the design.

In *SolidWorks*, the parametric part modeling process involves the following steps:

1. **Determine the type of the base feature, the first solid feature, of the design. Note that *Extrude*, *Revolve*, or *Sweep* operations are the most common types of base features.**

2. **Create a rough two-dimensional sketch of the basic shape of the base feature of the design.**

3. **Apply/modify constraints and dimensions to the two-dimensional sketch.**

4. **Transform the two-dimensional parametric sketch into a 3D feature.**

5. **Add additional parametric features by identifying feature relations and complete the design.**

6. **Perform analyses/simulations, such as finite element analysis (FEA) or cutter path generation (CNC), on the computer model and refine the design as needed.**

7. **Document the design by creating the desired 2D/3D drawings.**

The approach of creating two-dimensional sketches of the three-dimensional features is an effective way to construct solid models. Many designs are in fact the same shape in one direction. Computer input and output devices we use today are largely two-dimensional in nature, which makes this modeling technique quite practical. This method also conforms to the design process that helps the designer with conceptual design along with the capability to capture the ***design intent***. Most engineers and designers can relate to the experience of making rough sketches on restaurant napkins to convey conceptual design ideas. *SolidWorks* provides many powerful modeling and design-tools, and there are many different approaches to accomplishing modeling tasks. The basic principle of **feature-based modeling** is to build models by adding simple features one at a time. In this chapter, the general parametric part modeling procedure is illustrated; a very simple solid model with extruded features is used to introduce the *SolidWorks* user interface. The display viewing functions and the basic two-dimensional sketching tools are also demonstrated.

The *Tiger Head* Design

Starting *SolidWorks*

1. Select the **SolidWorks** option on the *Start* menu or select the **SolidWorks** icon on the desktop to start *SolidWorks*. The *SolidWorks* main window will appear on the screen.

2. Select the **New** icon on the *Menu Bar* with a single click of the left-mouse-button. The *New SolidWorks Document* dialog box appears.

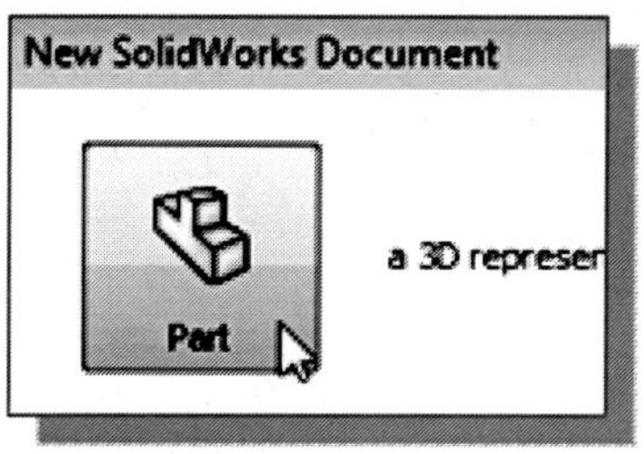

3. Select **Part** by clicking on the first icon in the *New SolidWorks Document* dialog box as shown.

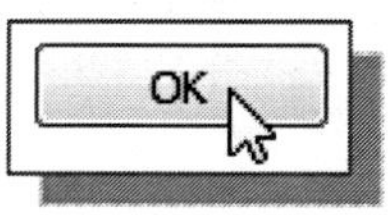

4. Click on the **OK** button to accept the settings.

SolidWorks Screen Layout

The default *SolidWorks* drawing screen contains the *Menu Bar*, the *Heads-up View* toolbar, the *Feature Manager Design Tree*, the *Command Manager* toolbar the graphics area, the *task pane* (collapsed to the right of the graphics area in the figure below), and the *Status Bar*. A line of quick text appears next to the icon as you move the *mouse cursor* over different icons. You may resize the *SolidWorks* drawing window by click and drag on the edge of the window, or relocate the window by click and drag on the *window title* area.

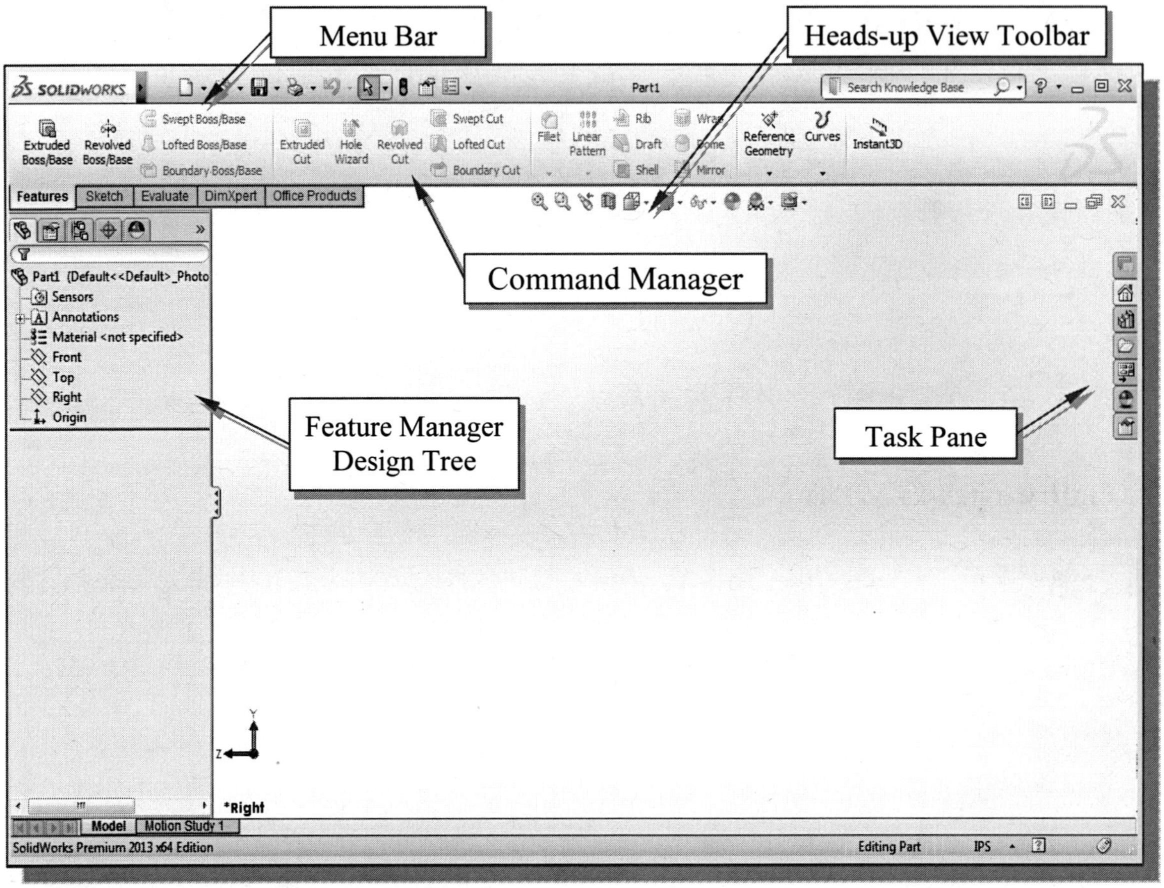

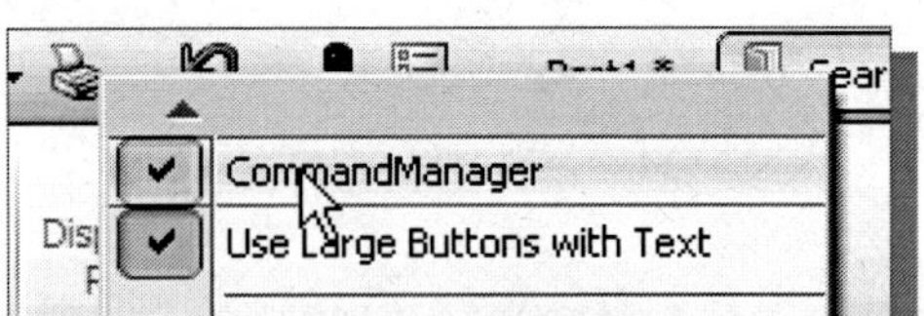

5. In the *Standard* toolbar area, **right-mouse-click** on any icon and activate **Command Manager** in the option list if necessary.

6. Select the **Options** icon from the *Menu* toolbar to open the *Options* dialog box.

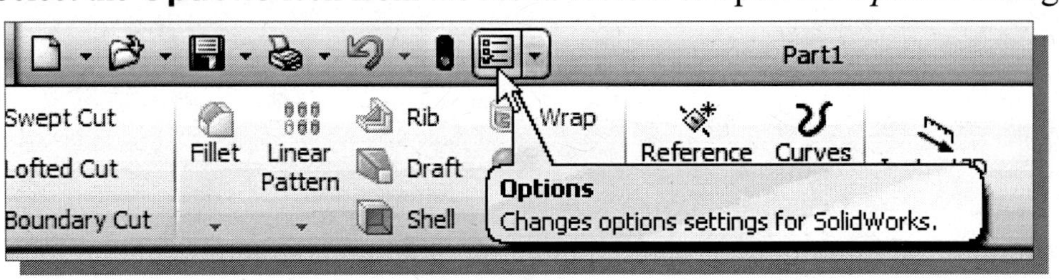

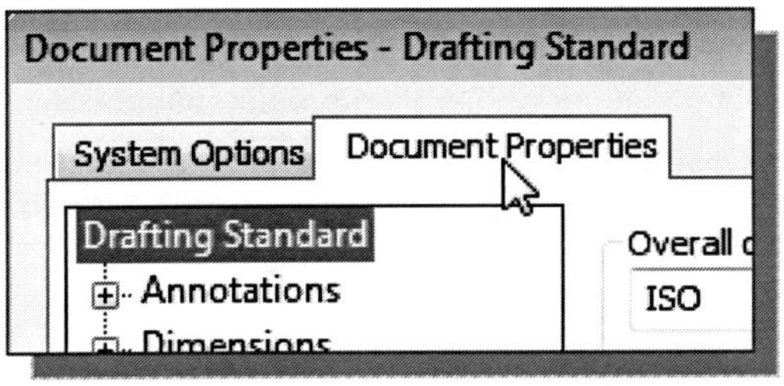

7. Select the **Document Properties** tab as shown in the figure.

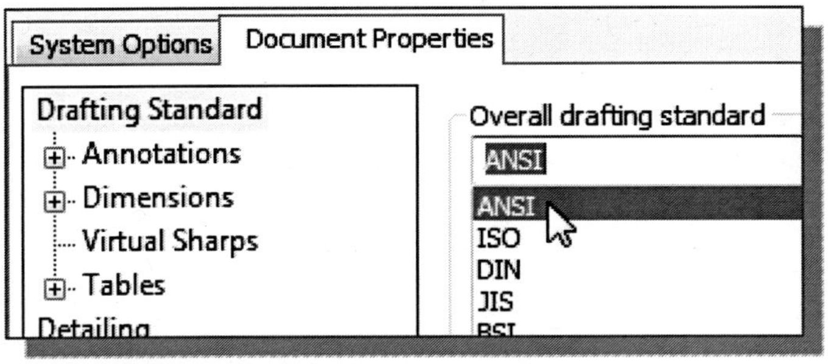

8. Set the *Overall drafting standard* to **ANSI** as shown.

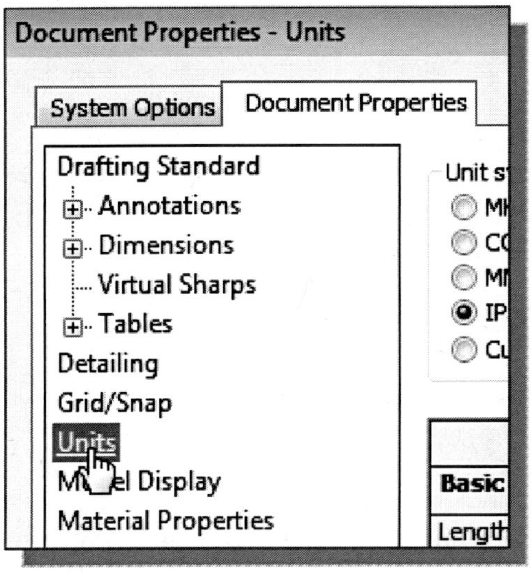

9. Click **Units** as shown in the figure.

10. Select **IPS (inch, pound, second)** under the *Unit system* options.

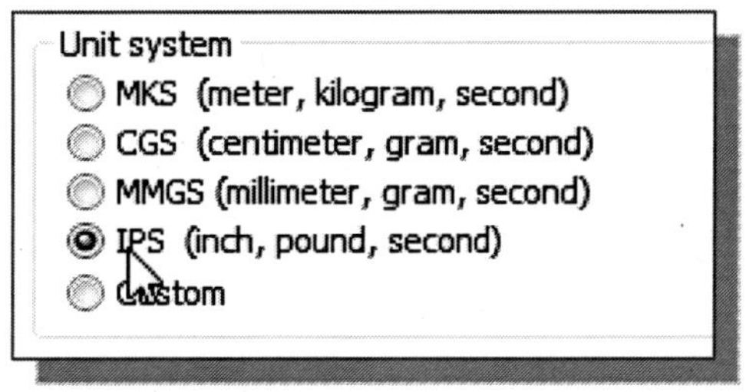

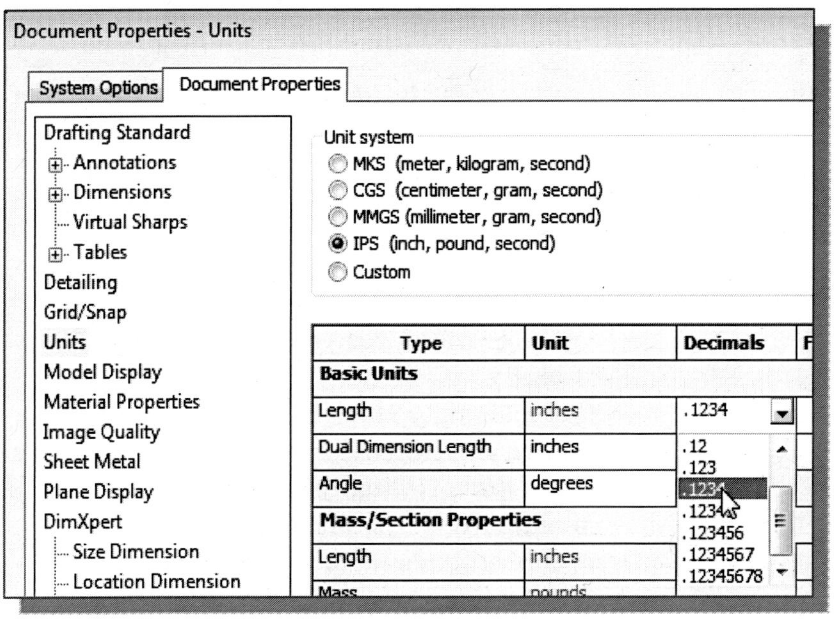

- Note the different options available to set/adjust the display of the selected units set.

11. Click **OK** in the *Options* dialog box to accept the selected settings.

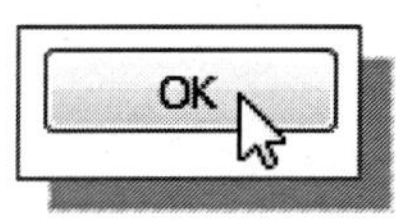

Step 1: Determine/Setup the Base Solid Feature

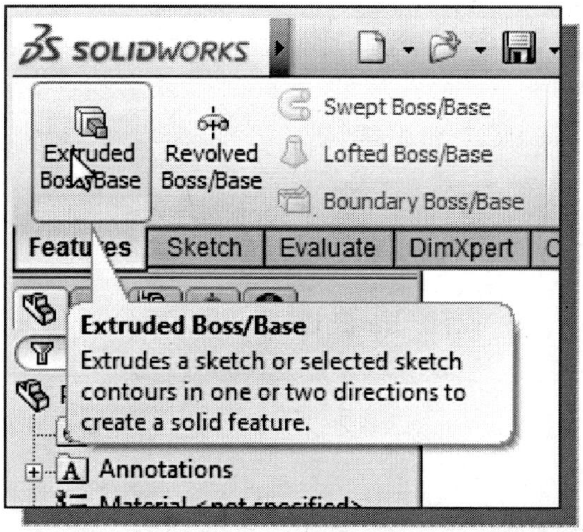

1. In the *Features* toolbar select the **Extruded Boss/Base** command by clicking once with the left-mouse-button on the icon.

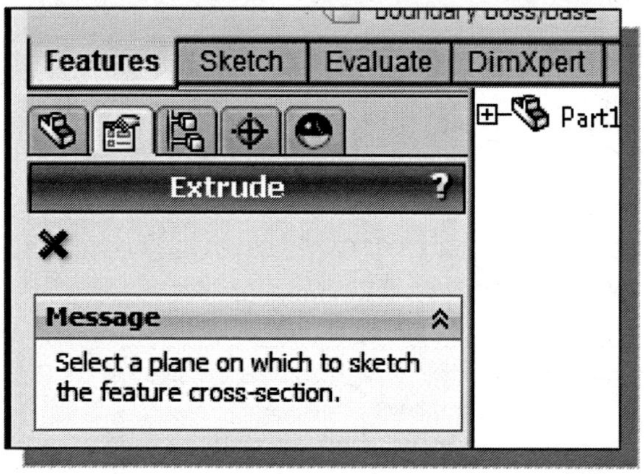

- Note the *Extrude Property Manager* is displayed in the left panel. We have activated the extrude feature; *SolidWorks* requires the use of an existing 2D sketch or the creation of a new 2D sketch.

Sketching plane – It is an XY CRT, but an XYZ World

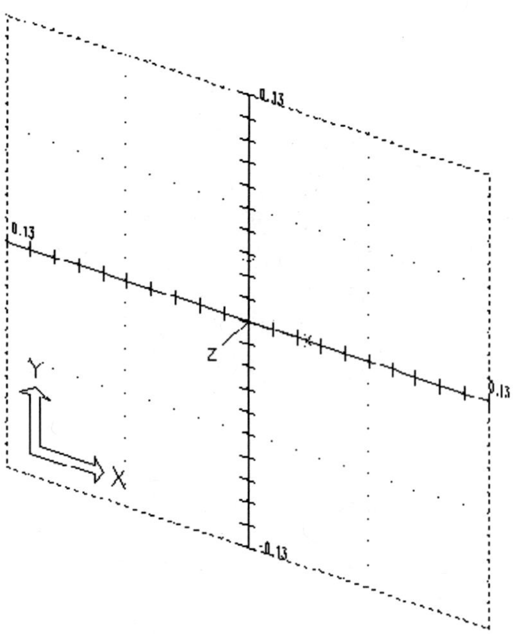

Design modeling software is becoming more powerful and user friendly, yet the system still does only what the user tells it to do. When using a geometric modeler, we therefore need to have a good understanding of what its inherent limitations are.

In most 3D geometric modelers, 3D objects are located and defined in what is usually called **world space** or **global space**. Although a number of different coordinate systems can be used to create and manipulate objects in a 3D modeling system, the objects are typically defined and stored using the world space. The world space is usually a **3D Cartesian coordinate system** that the user cannot change or manipulate.

In engineering designs, models can be very complex, and it would be tedious and confusing if only the world coordinate system were available. Practical 3D modeling systems allow the user to define **Local Coordinate Systems (LCS)** or **User Coordinate Systems (UCS)** relative to the world coordinate system. Once a local coordinate system is defined, we can then create geometry in terms of this more convenient system.

Although objects are created and stored in 3D space coordinates, most of the geometric entities can be referenced using 2D Cartesian coordinate systems. Typical input devices such as a mouse or digitizer are two-dimensional by nature; the movement of the input device is interpreted by the system in a planar sense. The same limitation is true of common output devices, such as CRT displays and plotters. The modeling software performs a series of three-dimensional to two-dimensional transformations to correctly project 3D objects onto the 2D display plane.

The *SolidWorks* ***sketching plane*** is a special construction approach that enables the planar nature of the 2D input devices to be directly mapped onto the 3D coordinate system. The *sketching plane* is a local coordinate system that can be aligned to an existing face of a part, or a reference plane.

Think of the sketching plane as the surface on which we can sketch the 2D sections of the parts. It is similar to a piece of paper, a white board, or a chalkboard that can be attached to any planar surface. The first sketch we create is usually drawn on one of the established datum planes. Subsequent sketches/features can then be created on sketching planes that are aligned to existing **planar faces of the solid part** or **datum planes**.

1. Move the cursor over the edge of the Front Plane in the graphics area. When the Front Plane is highlighted, click once with the **left-mouse-button** to select the Front Plane as the sketch plane for the new sketch. The *sketching plane* is a reference location where two-dimensional sketches are created. The *sketching plane* can be any planar part surface or datum plane.

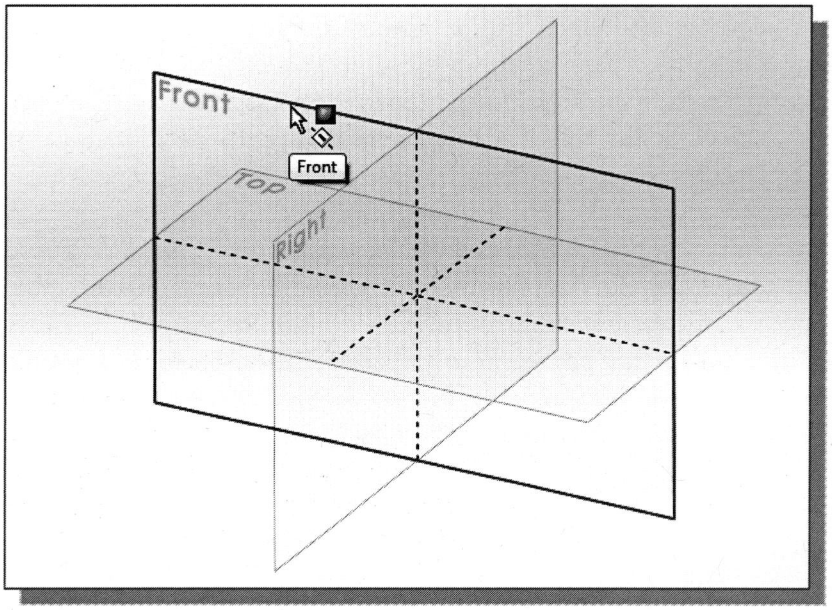

Creating Rough Sketches

Quite often during the early design stage, the shape of a design may not have any precise dimensions. Most conventional CAD systems require the user to input the precise lengths and locations of all geometric entities defining the design, which are not available during the early design stage. With *parametric modeling*, we can use the computer to elaborate and formulate the design idea further during the initial design stage. With *SolidWorks*, we can use the computer as an electronic sketchpad to help us concentrate on the formulation of forms and shapes for the design. This approach is the main advantage of *parametric modeling* over conventional solid-modeling techniques.

As the name implies, a ***rough sketch*** is not precise at all. When sketching, we simply sketch the geometry so that it closely resembles the desired shape. Precise scale or lengths are not needed. *SolidWorks* provides us with many tools to assist us in finalizing sketches. For example, geometric entities such as horizontal and vertical lines are set automatically. However, if the rough sketches are poor, it will require much more work to generate the desired parametric sketches. Here are some general guidelines for creating sketches in *SolidWorks*:

- **Create a sketch that is proportional to the desired shape.** Concentrate on the shapes and forms of the design.

- **Keep the sketches simple.** Leave out small geometry features such as fillets, rounds and chamfers. They can easily be placed using the Fillet and Chamfer commands after the parametric sketches have been established.

- **Exaggerate the geometric features of the desired shape.** For example, if the desired angle is 85 degrees, create an angle that is 50 or 60 degrees. Otherwise, *SolidWorks* might assume the intended angle to be a 90-degree angle.

- **Draw the geometry so that it does not overlap.** The geometry should eventually form a closed region. *Self-intersecting* geometry shapes are not allowed.

- **The sketched geometric entities should form a closed region.** To create a solid feature, such as an extruded solid, a closed region is required so that the extruded solid forms a 3D volume.

➢ **Note:** The concepts and principles involved in *parametric modeling* are very different, and sometimes they are totally opposite, to those of conventional computer aided drafting. In order to understand and fully utilize *SolidWorks's* functionality, it will be helpful to take a *Zen* approach to learning the topics presented in this text: **Have an open mind and temporarily forget your experiences using conventional Computer Aided Drafting systems.**

Step 2: Creating a Rough Sketch

➢ The *Sketch* toolbar provides tools for creating the basic geometry that can be used to create features and parts.

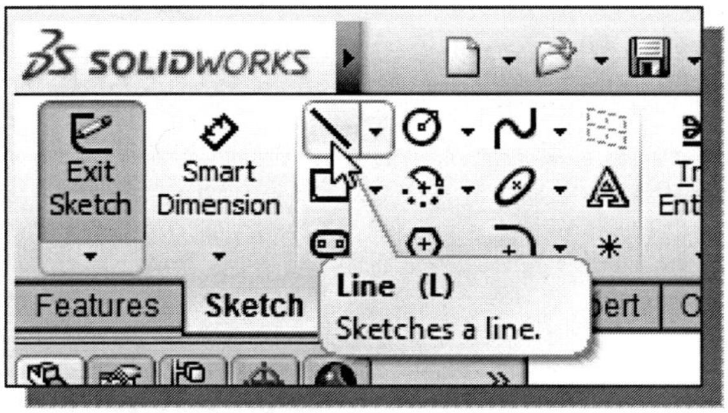

1. Move the graphics cursor to the **Line** icon in the *Sketch* toolbar. A *Help tip* box appears next to the cursor and a brief description of the command is displayed at the bottom of the drawing screen: "*Sketches a line.*" Select the icon by clicking once with the **left-mouse-button**.

- Note the *Insert Line Feature Manager* is displayed in the left panel with different options related to the active command.

Graphics Cursors

➢ Notice the cursor changes from an arrow to a pencil when graphical input is expected.

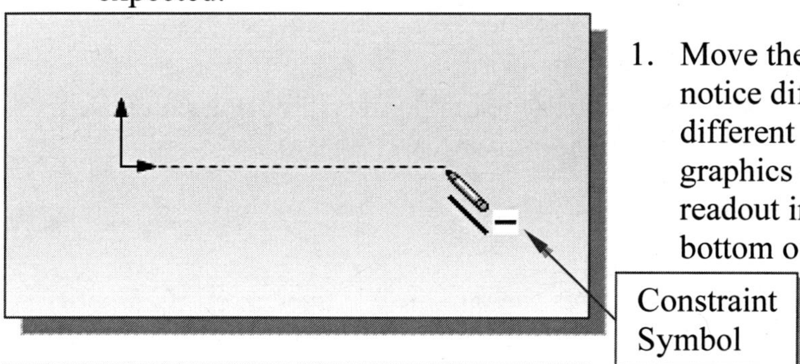

1. Move the cursor around and you will notice different symbols appear at different locations. As you move the graphics cursor, you will see a digital readout in the *Status Bar* area at the bottom of the window.

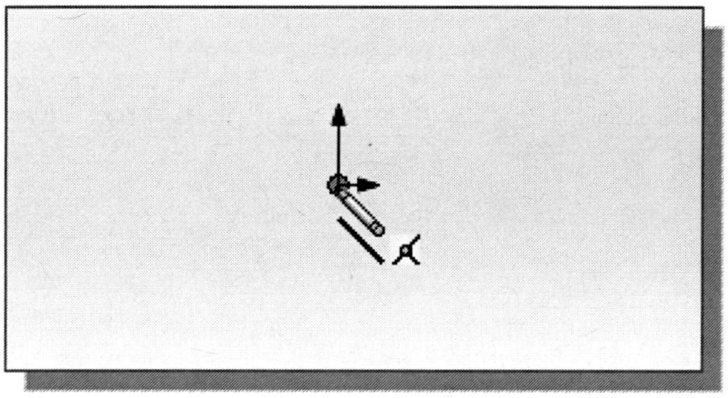

2. Move the cursor on top of the *Origin*, the little coordinate system near the center of the graphics area, and notice the constraint symbol as shown.

Geometric Relation Symbols

SolidWorks displays different visual clues, or symbols, to show you alignments, perpendicularities, tangencies, etc. These relations are used to capture the *design intent* by creating relations where they are recognized. *SolidWorks* displays the governing geometric rules as models are built. To prevent relations from forming, hold down the [**Ctrl**] key while creating an individual sketch curve. For example, while sketching line segments with the **Line** command, endpoints are joined with a **Coincident** relation, but when the [**Ctrl**] key is pressed and held, the inferred relation will not be created.

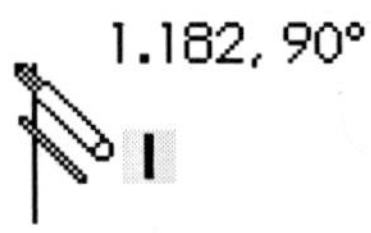	**Vertical**	indicates a line is vertical
	**Horizontal**	indicates a line is horizontal
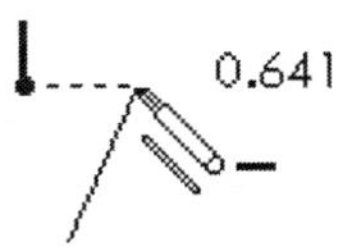	**Dashed line**	indicates the alignment is to the center point or endpoint of an entity
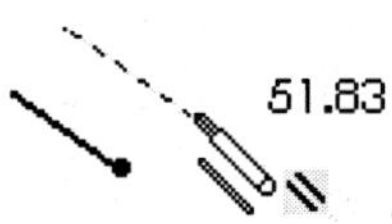	**Parallel**	indicates a line is parallel to other entities
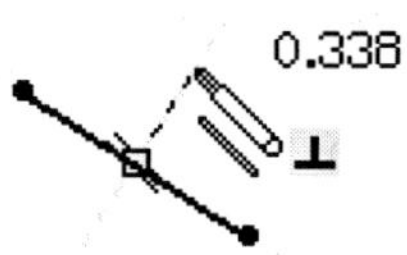	**Perpendicular**	indicates a line is perpendicular to other entities
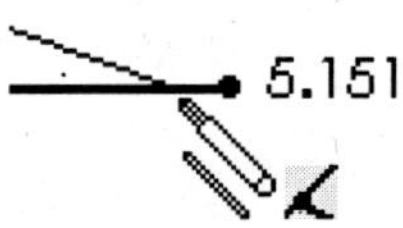	**Coincident**	indicates the endpoint will be coincident with another entity
	**Concentric**	indicates the cursor is at the center of an entity
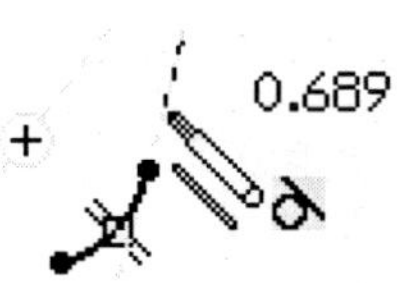	**Tangent**	indicates the cursor is at tangency points to curves

1. Create the sketch as shown below, starting at the *Origin*, and create a closed region ending at the starting point (**Point 1**). Do not be overly concerned with the actual size of the sketch. Note that the **four inclined lines** are sketched **not perpendicular or parallel** to each other.

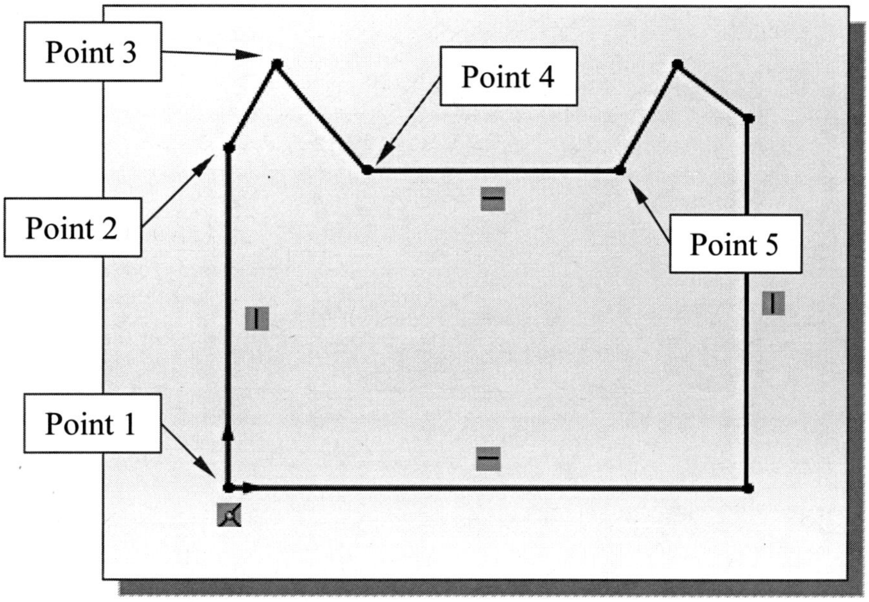

2. Click the **OK** icon (green check mark) in the *Property Manager* to end editing of the current line, then click the **OK** icon again to end the Sketch Line command, or hit the [**Esc**] key once to end the Sketch Line command.

Step 3: Apply/Modify Constraints and Dimensions

➢ As the sketch is made, *SolidWorks* automatically applies some of the geometric constraints (such as horizontal, parallel, and perpendicular) to the sketched geometry. We can continue to modify the geometry, apply additional constraints, and/or define the size of the existing geometry. In this example, we will illustrate adding dimensions to describe the sketched entities.

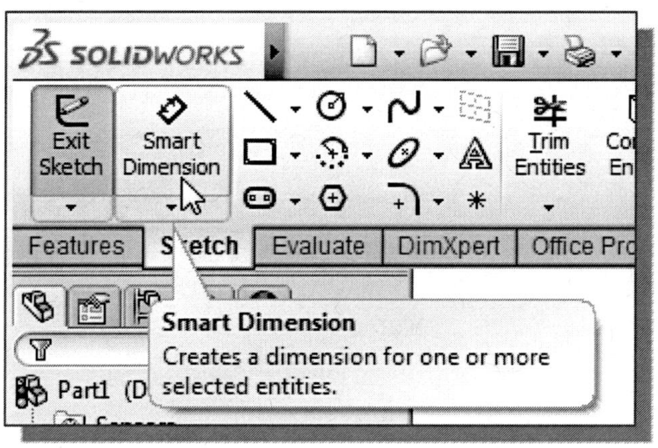

1. Move the cursor to the second icon of the *Sketch* toolbar; it is the Smart Dimension icon. Activate the command by left-clicking once on the icon.

2. Select the left vertical line by left-clicking once on the line.

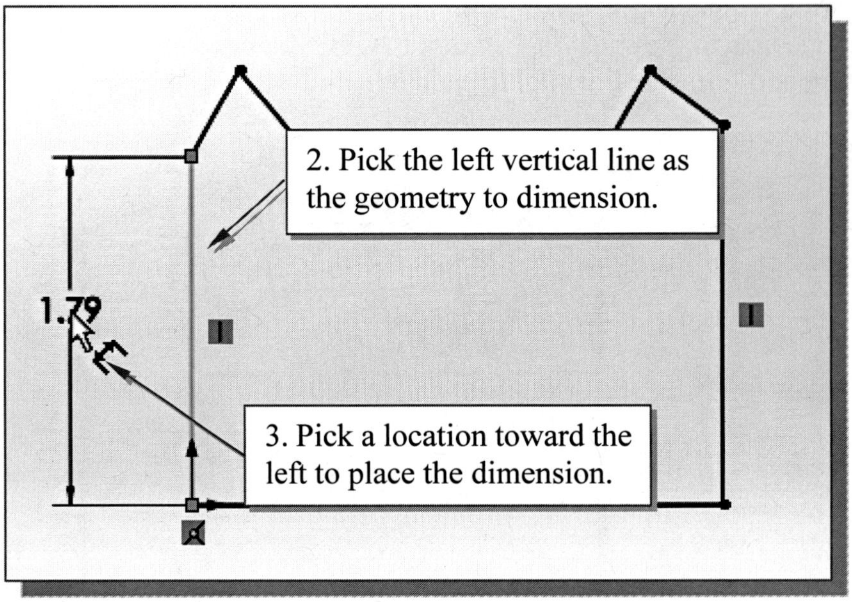

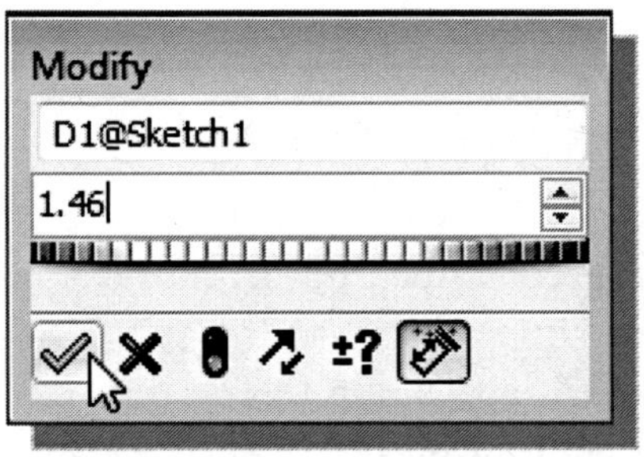

3. Enter **1.46** in the *Modify* dialog box.

4. Left-click **OK** (green check mark) in the *Modify* dialog box to save the current value and exit the dialog. Notice the associated geometry is adjusted.

5. On your own, repeat the above steps and create another length dimension on the right as shown.

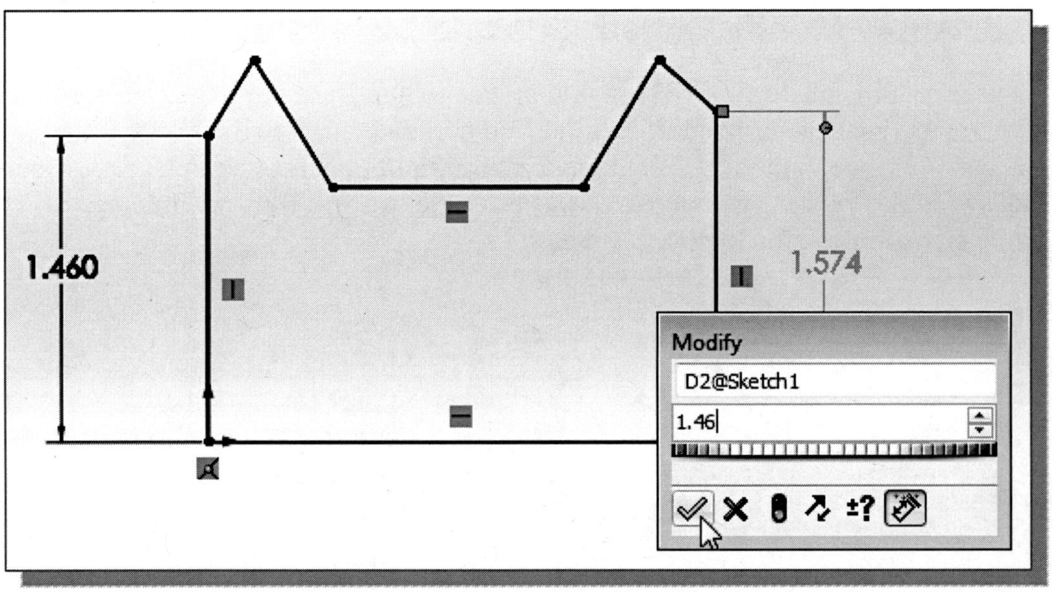

❖ The Smart Dimension command will create a length dimension if a single line is selected.

6. Select the left-vertical line as shown below.

7. Select the right-vertical line as shown below.

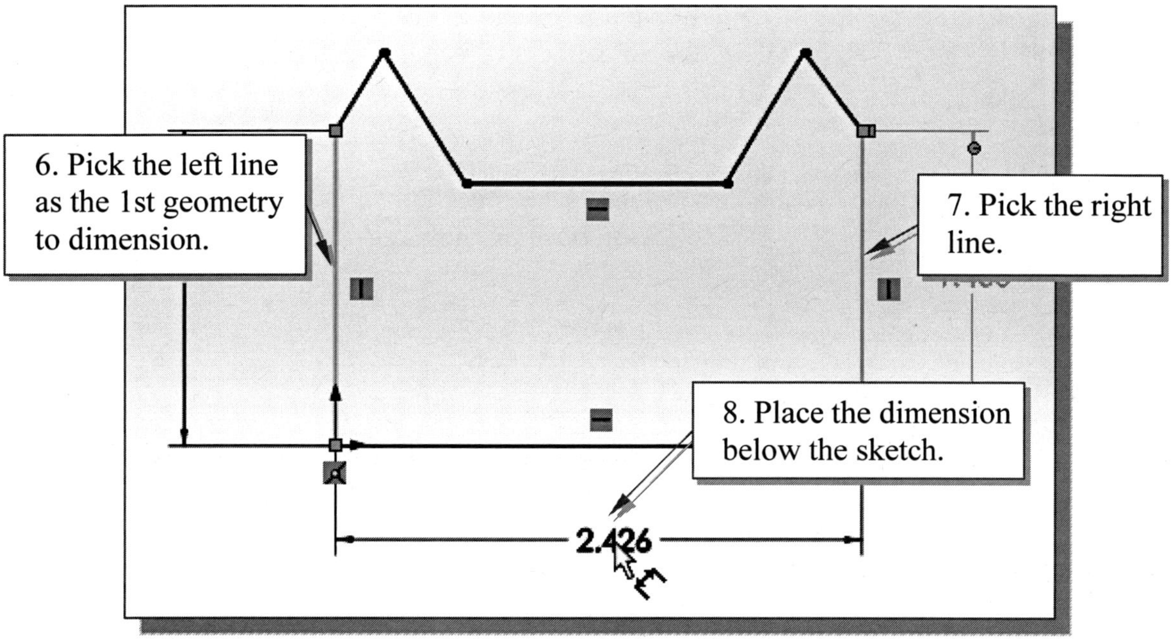

8. Pick a location below the sketch to place the dimension.

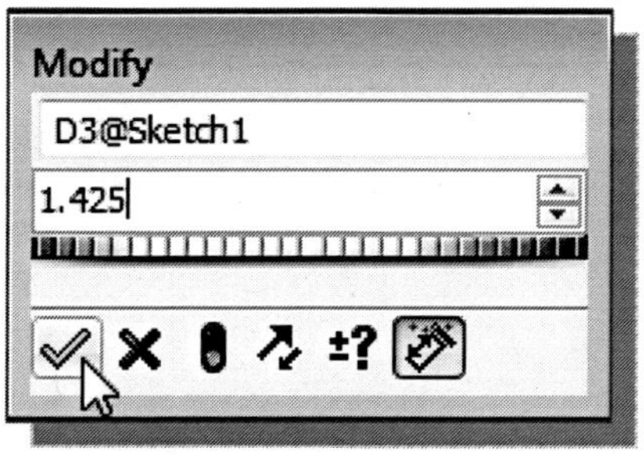

9. Enter **1.425** in the *Modify* dialog box.

10. Left-click **OK** (green check mark) in the *Modify* dialog box to save the current value and exit the dialog.

- Notice the sketch is adjusted, but the shape is twisted since several dimensions are still needed to fully define the sketch.

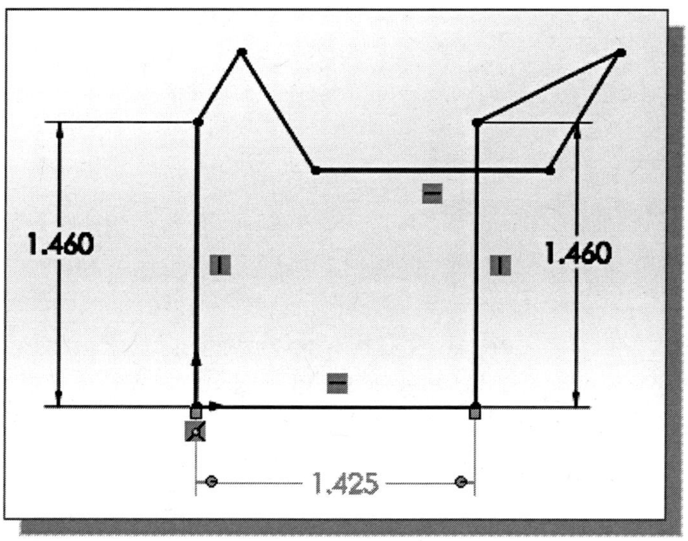

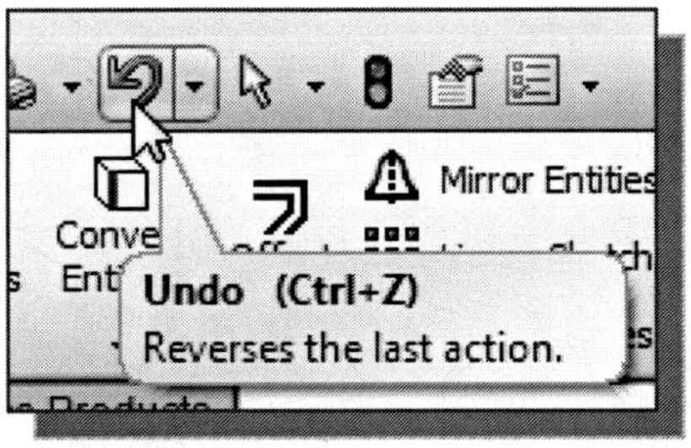

11. Click **Undo** in the *Quick Access Menu* as shown.

- In parametric modeling, it may be necessary to delay the adjustment of some dimensions.

12. Activate the **Smart Dimension** command by left-clicking once on the icon.

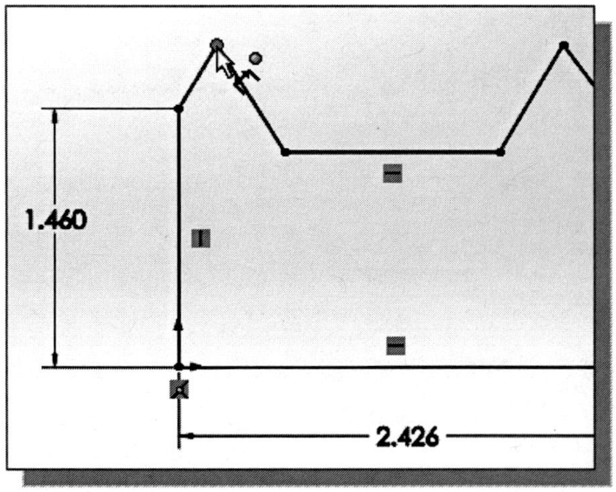

13. Select the top left corner as shown.

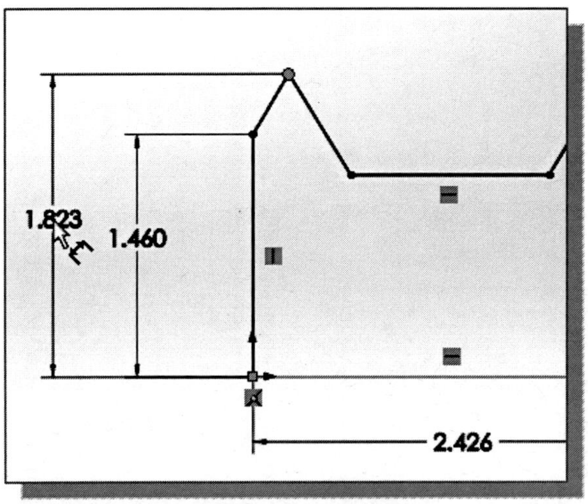

14. Select the bottom horizontal line as the 2nd geometry to dimension.

15. Place the dimension toward the left of the sketch as shown.

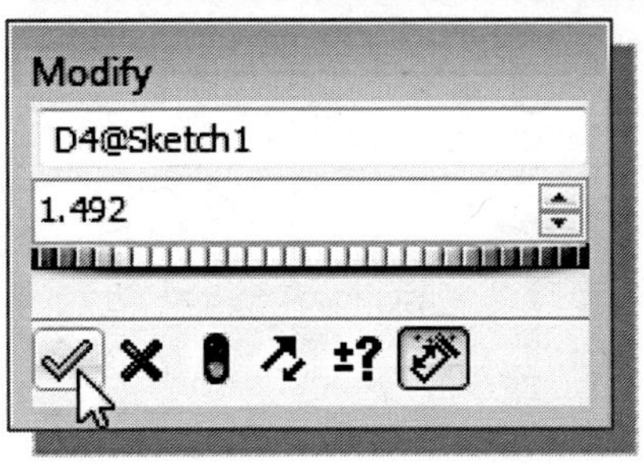

16. Enter **1.492** in the *Modify* dialog box.

17. Left-click **OK** (green check mark) in the *Modify* dialog box to save the current value and exit the dialog.

18. Select the left vertical line as shown.

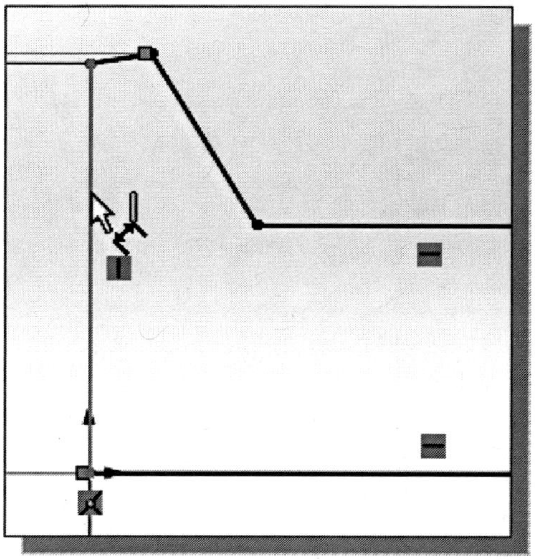

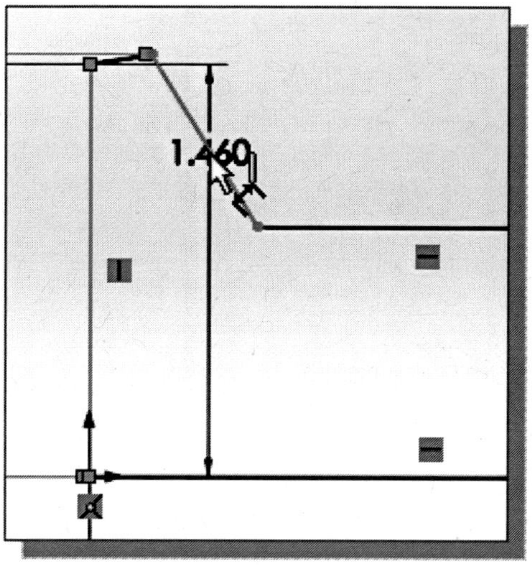

19. Select the longer inclined line on the left as the 2nd geometry to dimension.

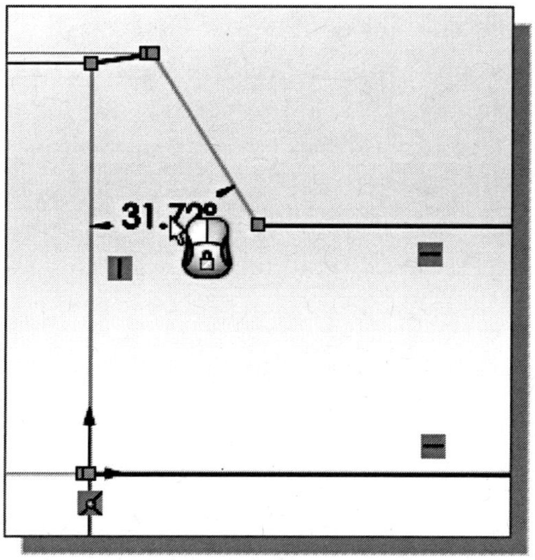

20. Place the angular dimension in the middle of the two selected lines as shown.

21. Enter **50** in the *Modify* dialog box.

22. Left-click **OK** (green check mark) in the *Modify* dialog box to save the current value and exit the dialog.

❖ Based on the selected entities, the Smart Dimension command will create associated dimensions; this is also known as **Smart dimensioning** in *parametric modeling*.

23. On you own, repeat the above steps and create additional dimensions so that the sketch appears as shown.

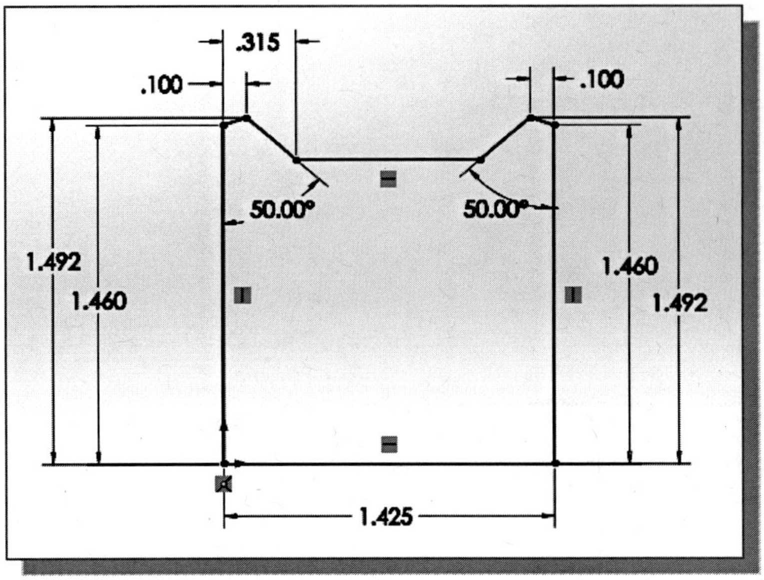

Viewing Functions – Zoom and Pan

- *SolidWorks* provides a special user interface that enables convenient viewing of the entities in the graphics window. There are many ways to perform the **Zoom** and **Pan** operations.

1. Hold the [**Ctrl**] function key down. While holding the [**Ctrl**] function key down, press the mouse wheel down and drag the mouse to **Pan** the display. This allows you to reposition the display while maintaining the same scale factor of the display.

2. Hold the [**Shift**] function key down. While holding the [**Shift**] function key down, press the mouse wheel down and drag the mouse to **Zoom** the display. Moving downward will reduce the scale of the display, making the entities display smaller on the screen. Moving upward will magnify the scale of the display.

3. Turning the mouse wheel can also adjust the scale of the display. Turn the mouse wheel forward. Notice the scale of the display is reduced, making the entities display smaller on the screen.

4. Turn the mouse wheel backward. Notice scale of the display is magnified. (**NOTE:** Turning the mouse wheel allows zooming to the position of the cursor.)

5. On your own, use the options above to change the scale and position of the display.

6. Press the **F** key on the keyboard to automatically fit the model to the screen.

Delete an Existing Geometry of the Sketch

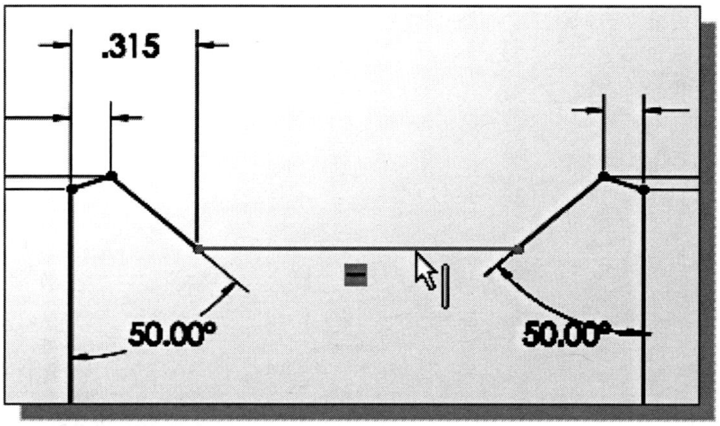

1. Select the top horizontal line by **left-clicking** once on the line.

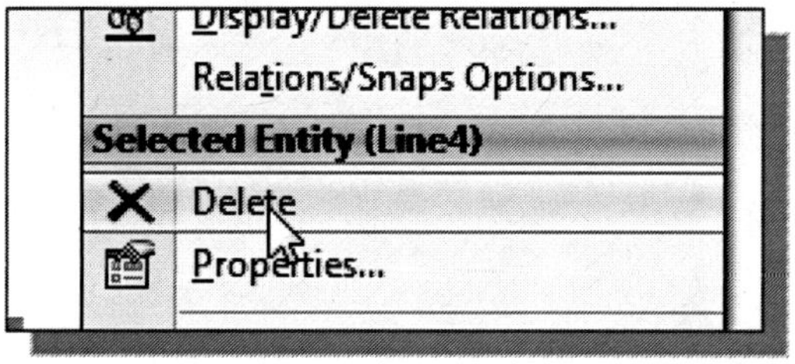

2. Click once with the right-mouse-button to bring up the **option menu**.

3. Select **Delete** from the option list as shown.

➢ Note that any dimension attached to the geometry will be also deleted.

Using the 3-Point Arc command

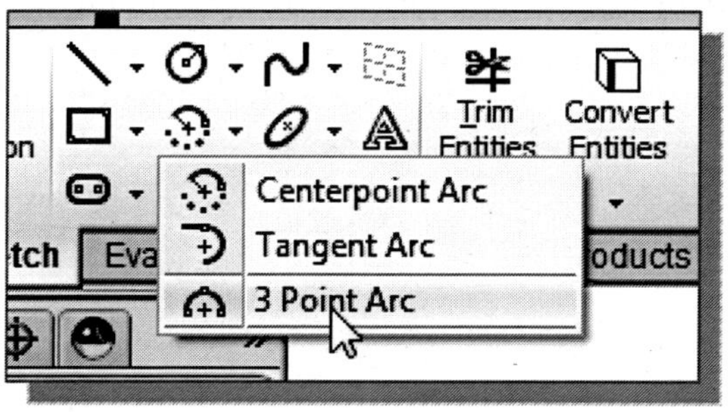

1. Select the **Three Point Arc** command in the *Sketch* toolbar as shown.

   ➢ Note the **Three Point Arc** command requires defining the end point locations first.

2. Select the **left endpoint** of the long inclined line on the left as shown.

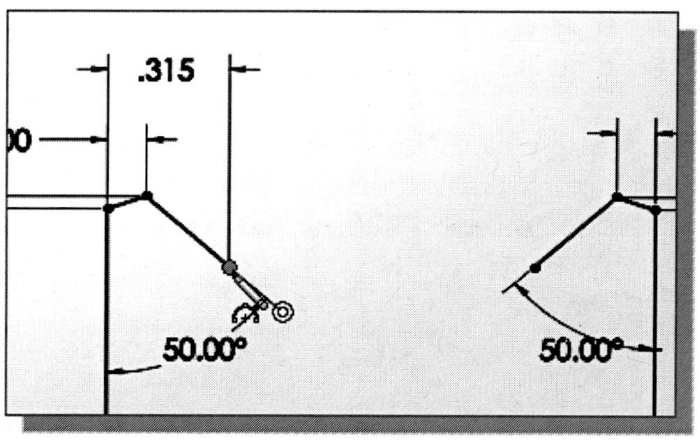

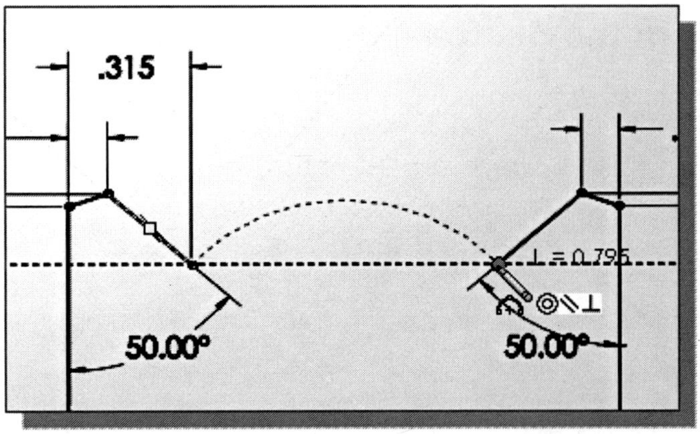

3. Select the endpoint of the longer inclined line on the right as shown.

4. Move the cursor above the two selected points to set the curvature of the arc, **left-clicking** once when the radius is roughly *0.9* inch as shown.

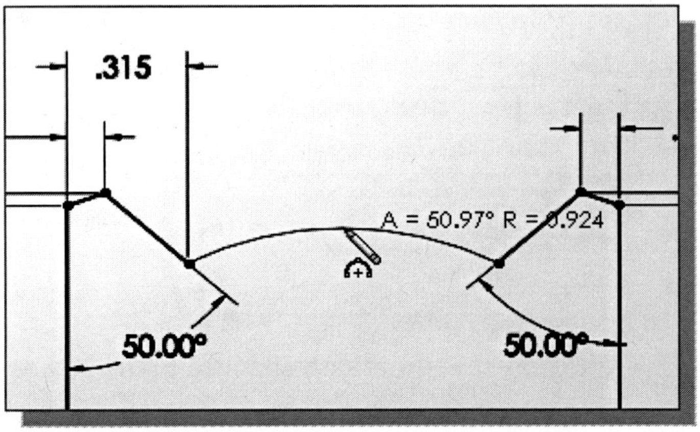

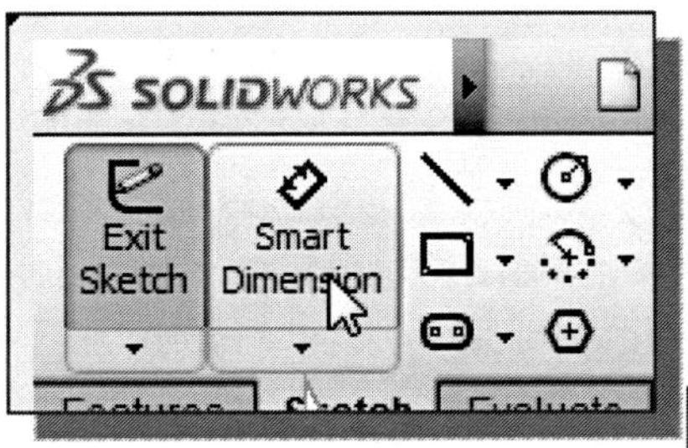

5. Activate the **Smart Dimension** command by left-clicking once on the icon.

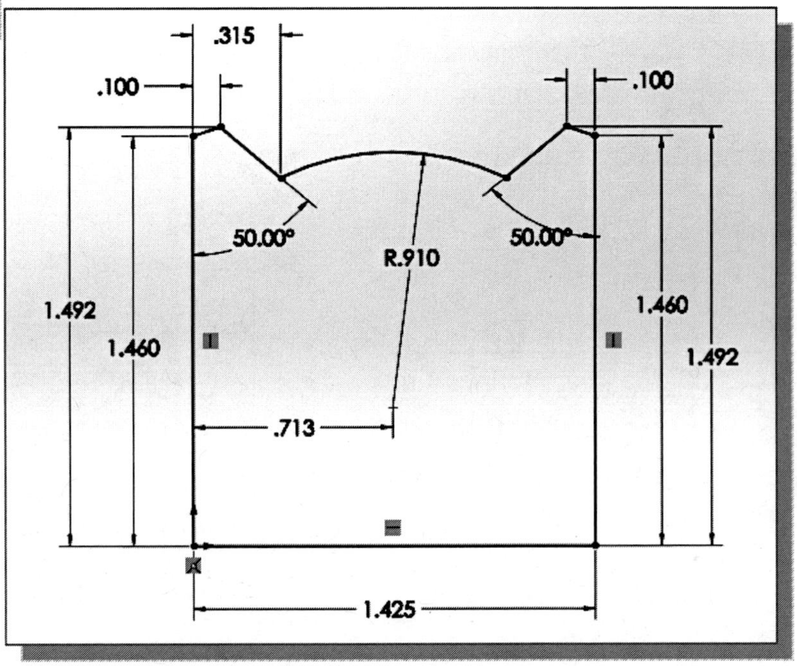

6. Select the arc we just created, and enter **0.91** as the radius dimension as shown.

7. Also create the horizontal location dimension, **0.7125**, for the arc center as shown.

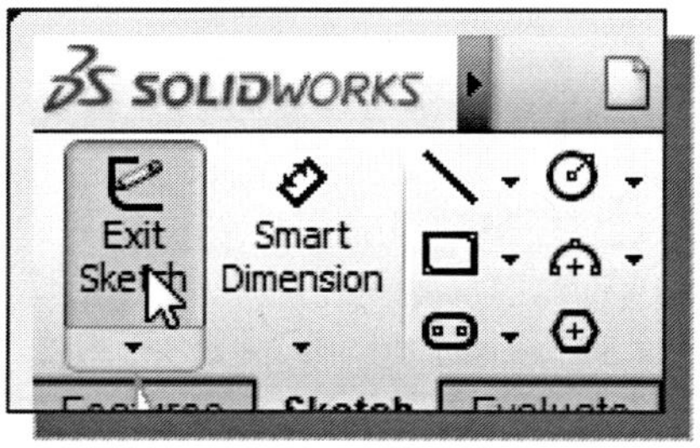

8. Click **Exit Sketch** in the *Sketch* toolbar to end the **Sketch** mode.

Step 4: Completing the Base Solid Feature

Now that the 2D sketch is completed, we will proceed to the next step: creating a 3D part from the 2D profile. Extruding a 2D profile is one of the common methods that can be used to create 3D parts. We can extrude planar faces along a path. We can also specify a height value and a tapered angle. In *SolidWorks*, each face has a positive side and a negative side, the current face we're working on is set as the default positive side. This positive side identifies the positive extrusion direction and it is referred to as the face's ***normal***.

1. In the *Extrude Property Manager*, enter **0.1** as the extrusion distance. Notice that the completed sketch region is automatically selected as the extrusion profile.

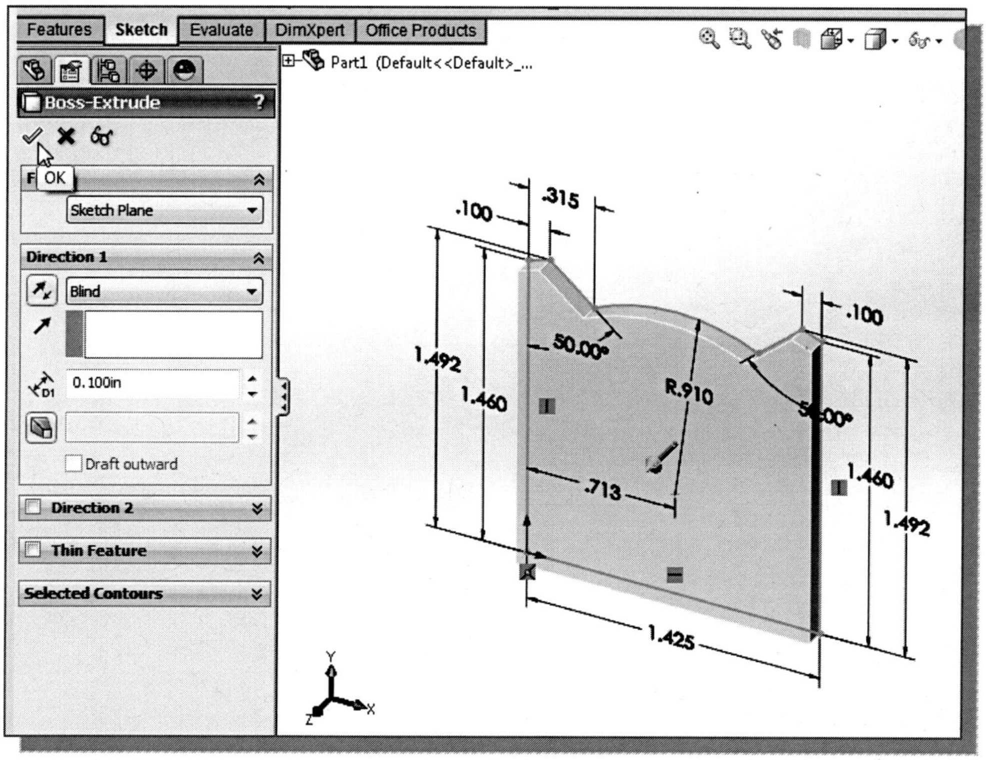

2. Click on the **OK** button to proceed with creating the 3D part.

➤ Note that all dimensions disappeared from the screen. All parametric definitions are stored in the ***SolidWorks* database** and any of the parametric definitions can be re-displayed and edited at any time.

Isometric View

❖ *SolidWorks* provides many ways to display views of the three-dimensional design. We will first orient the model to display in the *isometric view*, by using the *View Orientation* pull-down menu on the *Heads-up View* toolbar.

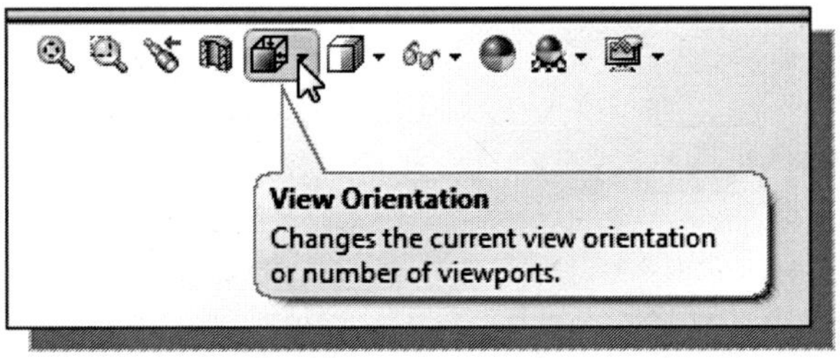

1. Select the **View Orientation** button on the *Heads-up View* toolbar by clicking once with the left-mouse-button.

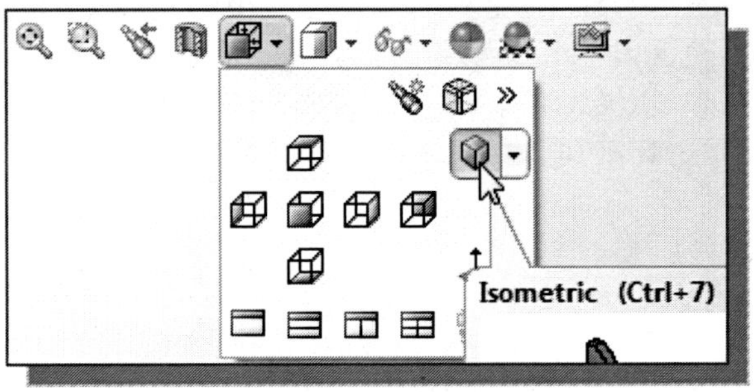

2. Select the **Isometric** icon in the *View Orientation* pull-down menu.

❖ Note that many other view-related commands are also available under the **View** *pull-down menu.*

Rotation of the 3D Model – Rotate View

The Rotate View command allows us to rotate a part or assembly in the graphics window. Rotation can be around the center mark, free in all directions, or around a selected entity (vertex, edge, or face) on the model.

1. Move the cursor over the **SolidWorks** logo to display the pull-down menus. Select **View** → **Modify** → **Rotate** from the pull-down menu as shown.

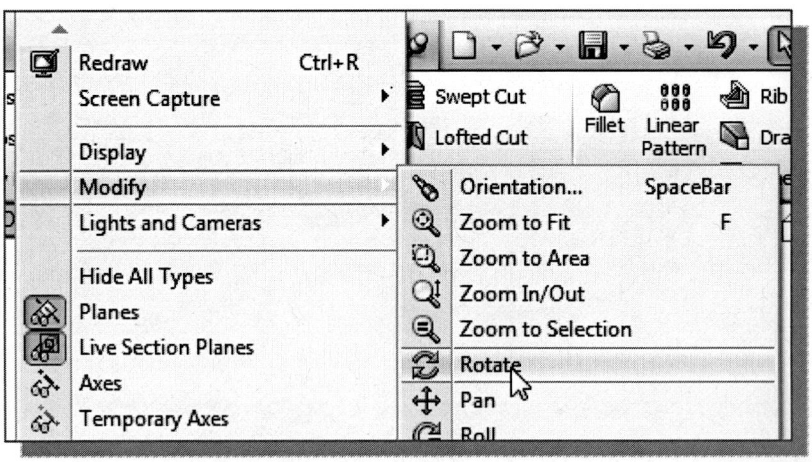

2. Move the cursor inside the graphics area. Press down the left-mouse-button and drag in an arbitrary direction; the Rotate View command allows us to freely rotate the solid model.

- The model will rotate about an axis normal to the direction of cursor movement. For example, drag the cursor horizontally across the screen and the model will rotate about a vertical axis.

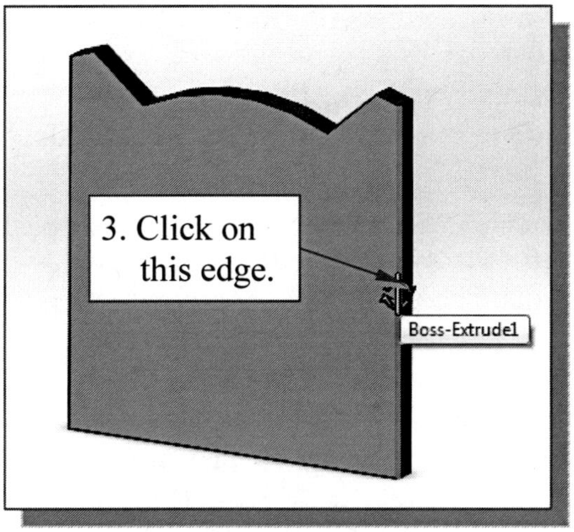

3. Move the cursor over one of the vertical edges of the solid model as shown. When the edge is highlighted, click the **left-mouse-button** once to select the edge.

4. Press down the left-mouse-button and drag. The model will rotate about this edge.

5. Left-click in the graphics area, outside the model, to unselect the edge.

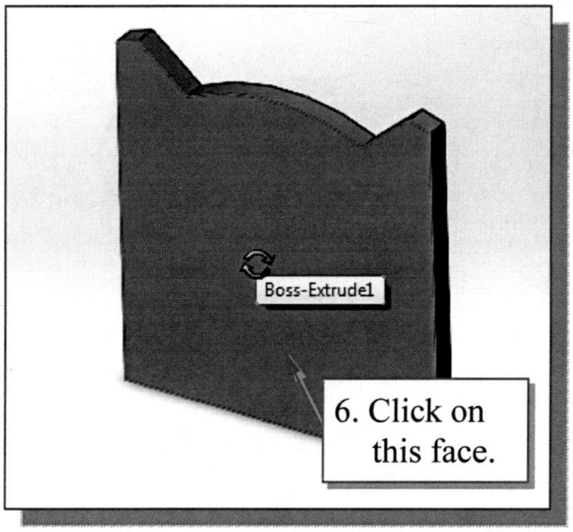

6. Move the cursor over the front face of the solid model as shown. When the face is highlighted, click the **left-mouse-button** once to select the face.

7. Press down the left-mouse-button and drag. The model will rotate about the direction normal to this face.

8. Left-click in the graphics area, outside the model, to unselect the face.

9. Move the cursor over one of the vertices as shown. When the vertex is highlighted, click the left-mouse-button once to select the vertex.

10. Press down the left-mouse-button and drag. The model will rotate about the vertex.

11. Left-click in the graphics area, outside the model, to unselect the vertex.

12. Press the [**Esc**] key once to exit the Rotate View command.

13. On your own, reset the display to the *isometric* view.

Rotation and Panning – *Arrow Keys*

➢ *SolidWorks* allows us to easily rotate a part or assembly in the graphics window using the **arrow** keys on the keyboard.

- Use the **arrow** keys to rotate the view horizontally or vertically. The **left-right** keys rotate the model about a vertical axis. The **up-down** keys rotate the model about a horizontal axis.

- Hold down the [**Alt**] key and use the **left-right arrow** keys to rotate the model about an axis normal to the screen, i.e., to rotate clockwise and counter-clockwise.

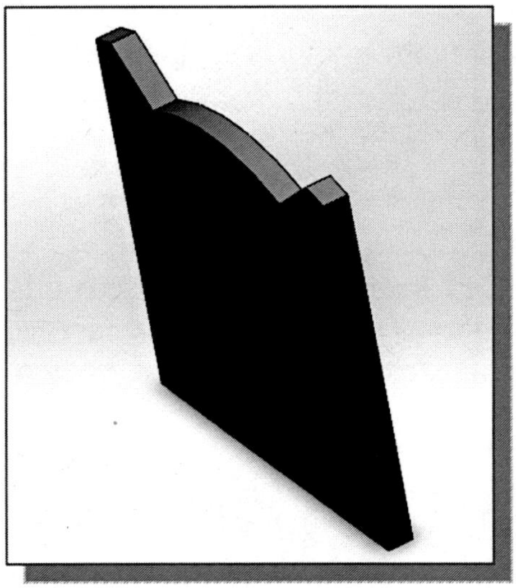

1. Hit the **left arrow** key. The model view rotates by a pre-determined increment. The default increment is 15°. (This increment can be set in the *Options* dialog box.) On your own, use the **left-right** and **up-down arrow** keys to rotate the view.

2. Hold down the [**Alt**] key and hit the **left arrow** key. The model view rotates in the clockwise direction. On your own use the **left-right** and **up-down arrow** keys, and the [**Alt**] key plus the **left-right arrow** keys, to rotate the view.

3. On your own, reset the display to the *isometric* view.

- Hold down the [**Shift**] key and use the **left-right** and **up-down arrow** keys to rotate the model in 90° increments.

4. Hold down the [**Shift**] key and hit the **right arrow** key. The view will rotate by 90°. On your own use the [**Shift**] key plus the **left-right arrow** keys to rotate the view.

5. Select the **Front** icon in the *View Orientation* pull-down menu as shown to display the **Front** view of the model.

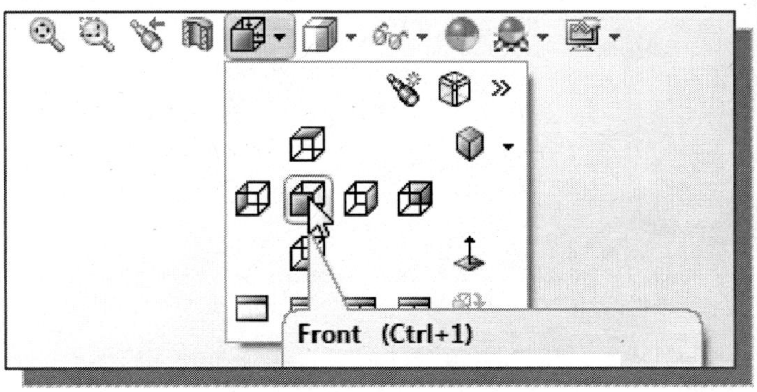

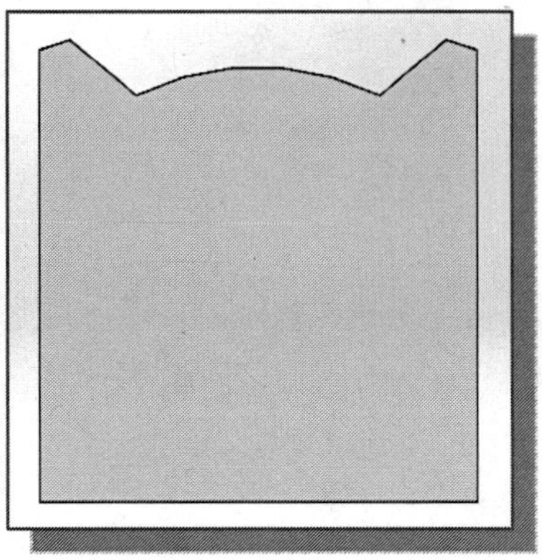

6. Hold down the **[Shift]** key and hit the left arrow key. The view rotates to the Right side view.

7. Hold down the **[Shift]** key and hit the down arrow key. The view rotates to the Top view.

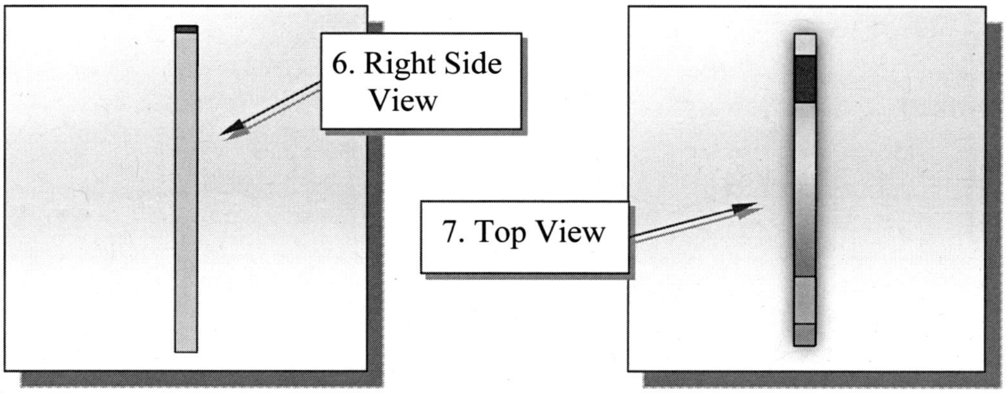

8. On your own, reset the display to the **Isometric** view.

- Hold down the **[Ctrl]** key and use the left-right and up-down arrow keys to Pan the model in increments.

9. Hold down the **[Ctrl]** key and hit the left arrow key. The view Pans, moving the model toward the left side of the screen. On your own use **[Ctrl]** key plus the left-right and up-down arrow keys to Pan the view.

Dynamic Viewing – Quick Keys

We can also use the function keys on the keyboard and the mouse to access the *Dynamic Viewing* functions.

❖ Panning

(1) Hold the Ctrl key; press and drag the mouse wheel

Hold the **[Ctrl]** function key down, and press and drag with the mouse wheel to **Pan** the display. This allows you to reposition the display while maintaining the same scale factor of the display.

Pan

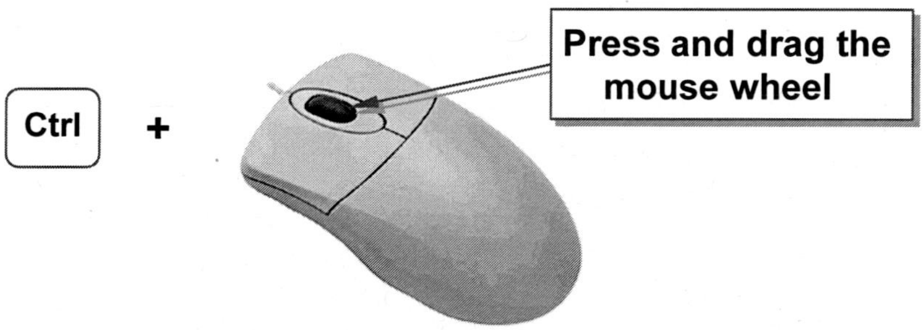

(2) Hold the Ctrl key; use arrow keys

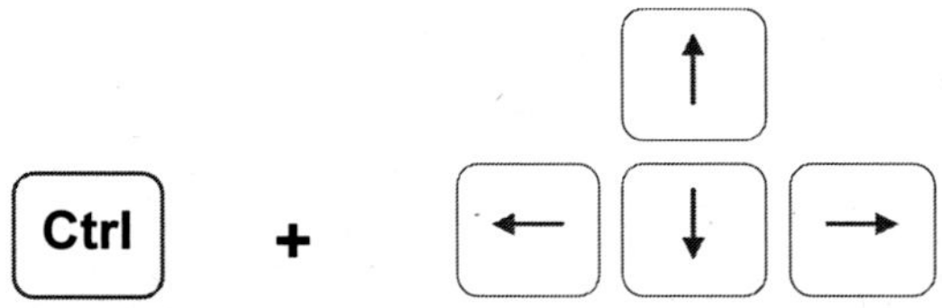

❖ Zooming

(1) Hold the Shift key; press and drag the mouse wheel

Hold the [**Shift**] function key down, and press and drag with the mouse wheel to **Zoom** the display. Moving downward will reduce the scale of the display, making the entities display smaller on the screen. Moving upward will magnify the scale of the display.

Zoom

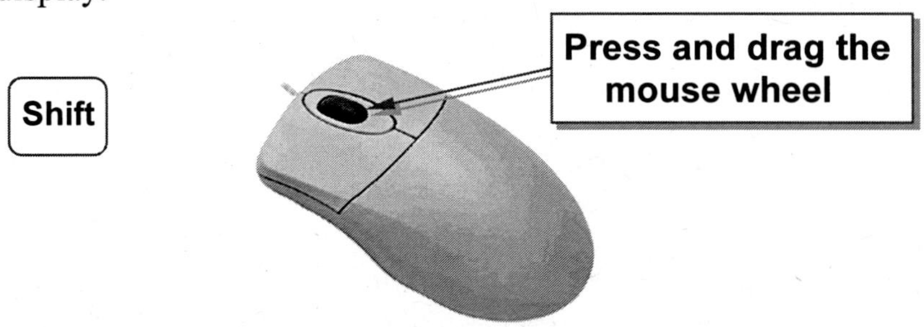

(2) Turning the mouse wheel

Turning the mouse wheel can also adjust the scale of the display. Turning forward will reduce the scale of the display, making the entities display smaller on the screen. Turning backward will magnify the scale of the display.

- Turning the mouse wheel allows zooming to the position of the cursor.
- The cursor position, inside the graphics area, is used to determine the center of the scale of the adjustment.

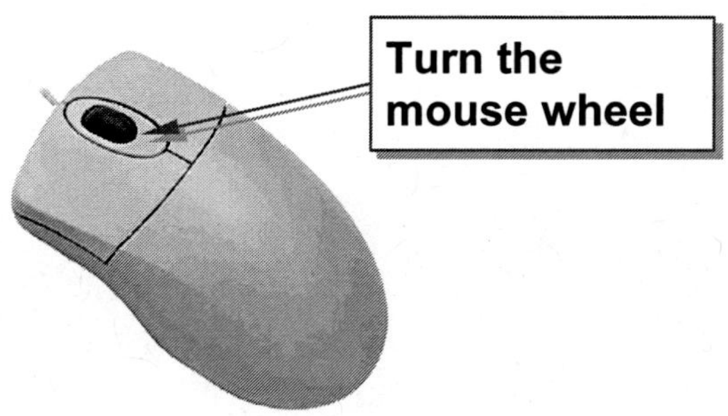

(3) Z key or Shift + Z key

Pressing the [**Z**] key on the keyboard will zoom out. Holding the [**Shift**] function key and pressing the [**Z**] key will zoom in.

3D Rotation

(1) Press and drag the mouse wheel

Press and drag with the mouse wheel to rotate the display.

Rotation

(2) Use arrow keys

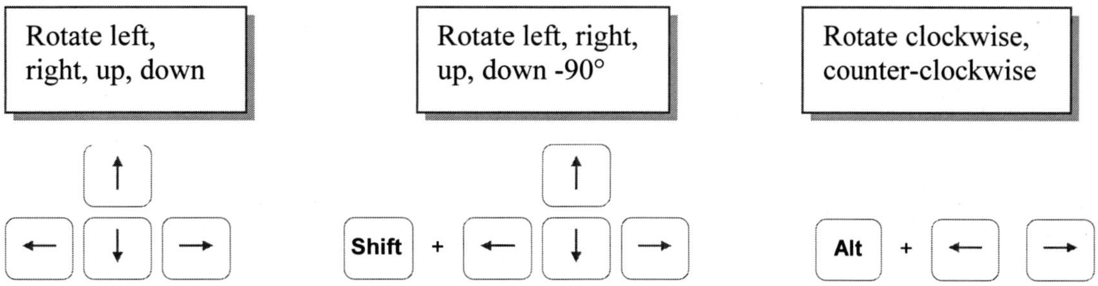

Viewing Tools – Heads-up View Toolbar

The ***Heads-up View*** toolbar is a transparent toolbar which appears in each viewport and provides easy access to commonly used tools for manipulating the view. The default toolbar is described below.

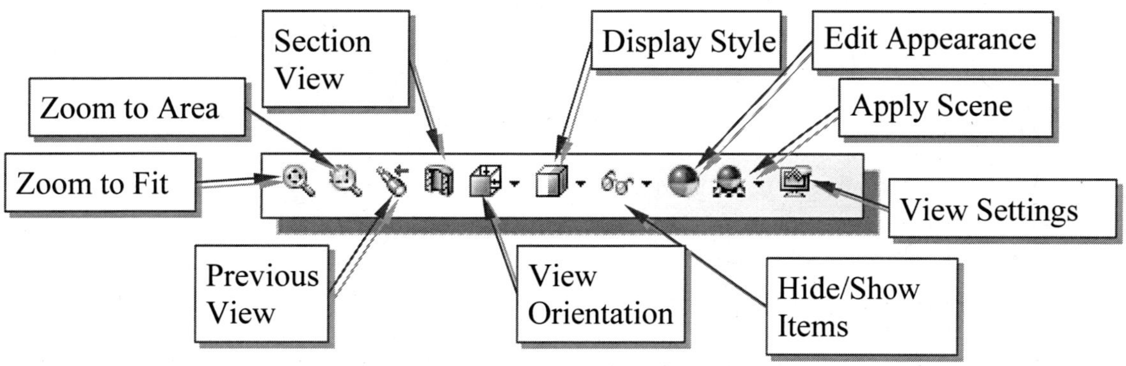

Zoom to Fit – Adjusts the view so that all items on the screen fit inside the graphics window.

Zoom to Area – Use the cursor to define a region for the view; the defined region is zoomed to fill the graphics window.

Previous View – Returns to the previous view.

Section View – Displays a cutaway of a part or assembly using one or more section planes.

View Orientation – This allows you to change the current view orientation or number of viewports.

Display Style – This can be used to change the display style (shaded, wireframe, etc.) for the active view.

Hide/Show Items – This pull-down menu is used to control the visibility of items (axes, sketches, relations, etc.) in the graphics area.

Edit Appearance – Modifies the appearance of entities in the model.

Apply Scene – Cycles through or applies a specific scene.

View Settings – Allows you to toggle various view settings (e.g., shadows, perspective).

View Orientation

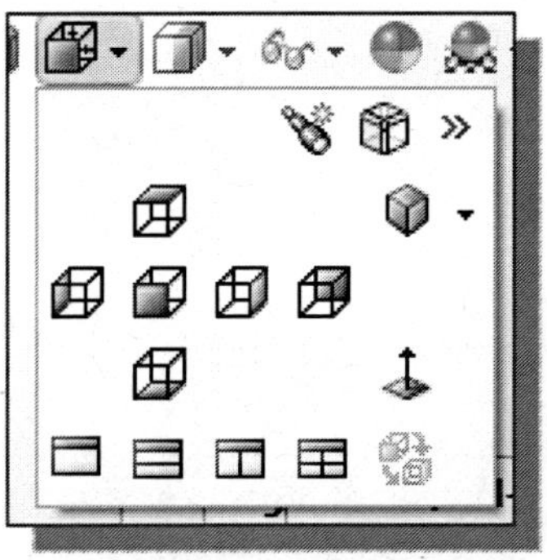

1. Click on the **View Orientation** icon on the *Heads-up View* toolbar to reveal the view orientation and number of viewports options.

Standard view orientation options – **Front**, **Back**, **Left**, **Right**, **Top**, **Bottom**, **Isometric**, **Trimetric** or **Dimetric** – icons can be selected to display the corresponding standard view. In the figure to the left, the Isometric view is selected.

Normal to – In a part or assembly, zooms and rotates the model to display the selected plane or face. You can select the element either before or after clicking the Normal to icon.

❖ The icons across the bottom of the pull-down menu allow you to display a single viewport (the default) or multiple viewports.

Display Style

1. Click on the **Display Style** icon on the *Heads-up View* toolbar to reveal the display style options.

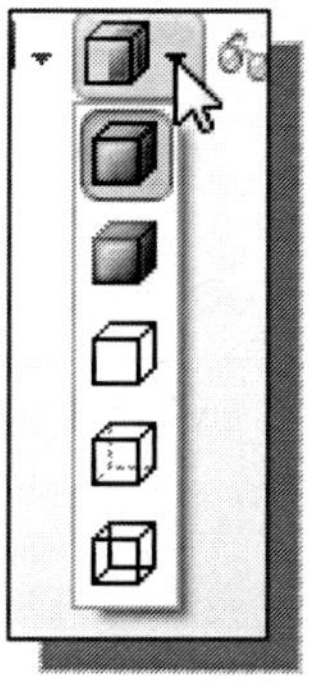

Shaded with Edges – Allows the display of a shaded view of a 3D model with its edges.

Shaded – Allows the display of a shaded view of a 3D model.

Hidden Lines Removed – Allows the display of the 3D objects using the basic wireframe representation scheme. Only those edges which are visible in the current view are displayed.

Hidden Lines Visible – Allows the display of the 3D objects using the basic wireframe representation scheme in which all the edges of the model are displayed, but edges that are hidden in the current view are displayed as dashed lines (or in a different color).

Wireframe – Allows the display of 3D objects using the basic wireframe representation scheme in which all the edges of the model are displayed.

Orthographic vs. Perspective

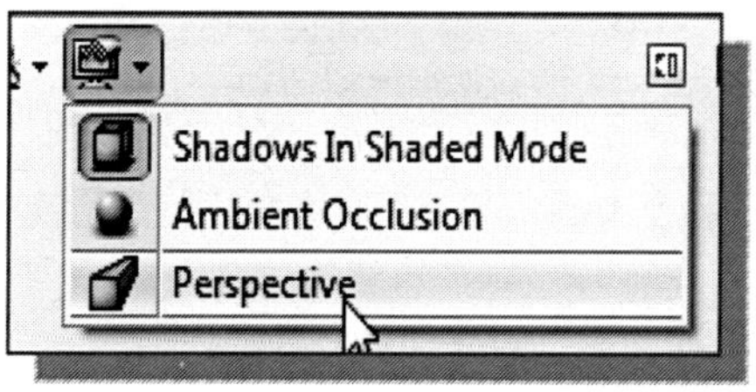

Besides the basic display modes, we can also choose an orthographic view or perspective view of the display. Clicking on the **View Settings** icon on the *Heads-up View* toolbar will reveal the **Perspective** icon. Clicking on the **Perspective** icon toggles the perspective view *ON* and *OFF*.

Customizing the Heads-up View Toolbar

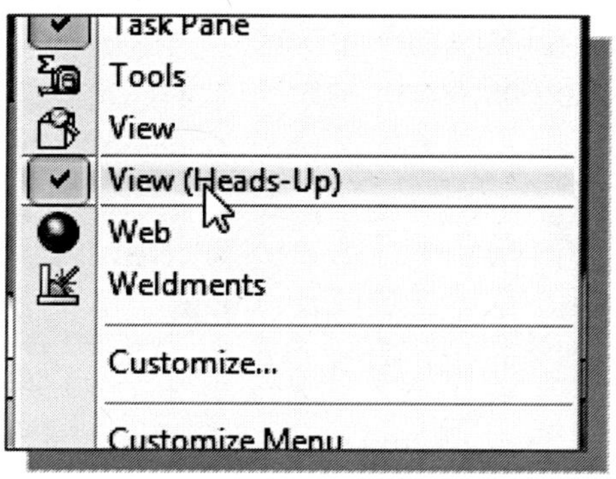

The *Heads-up View* toolbar can be customized to contain icons for user-preferred view options. **Right-click** anywhere on the *Heads-up View* toolbar to reveal the display menu option list. Click on the **View (Heads-up)** icon to turn *OFF* the display of the toolbar. Notice the **Customize** option is also available to add/remove different icons.

➢ On your own, use the different options described in the above sections to familiarize yourself with the 3D viewing/display commands. Reset the display to the standard **Isometric view** before continuing to the next section.

Step 5-1: Adding an Extruded Feature

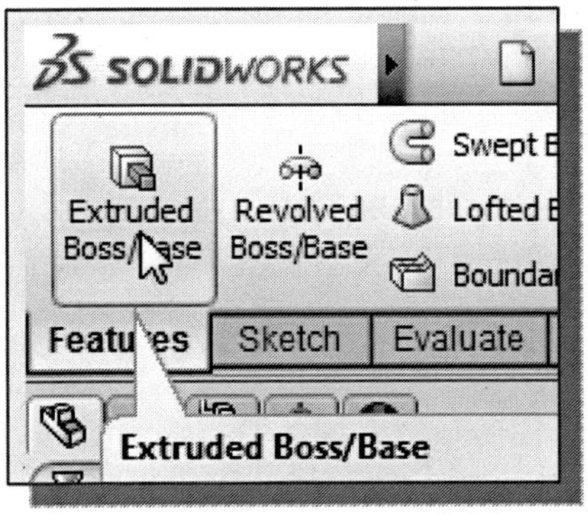

1. In the *Features* toolbar select the **Extruded Boss/ Base** command by clicking once with the left-mouse-button on the icon.

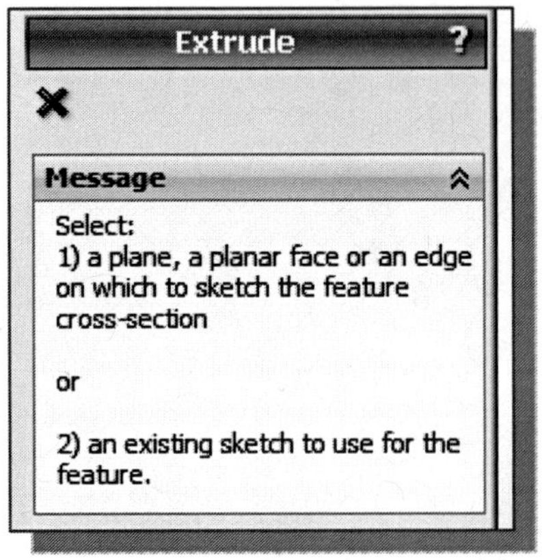

- In the *Extrude Manager* area, *SolidWorks* indicates the two options to create the new extrusion feature. We will select the back surface of the base feature to align the sketching plane.

2. On your own, use one of the rotation quick keys/mouse-button and view the back face of the model as shown.

3. Pick the back face of the 3D solid object.

- Note that *SolidWorks* automatically establishes a *User Coordinate System* (UCS), and records its location with respect to the part on which it was created.

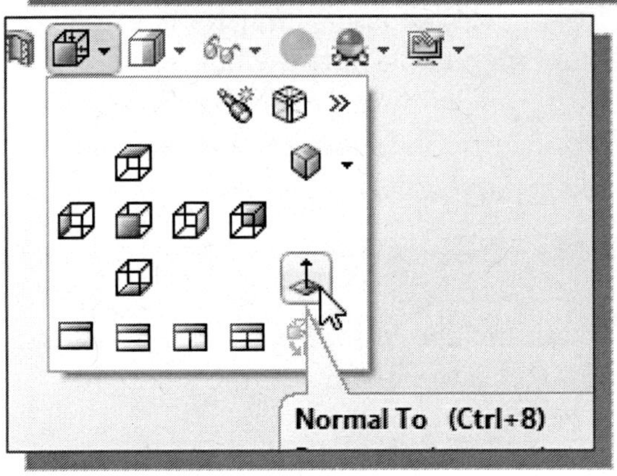

4. Adjust the display by using the **Normal To** option in the *View Orientation* panel as shown. (Quick Key: **Ctrl + S**)

- Next, we will create and profile another sketch, a rectangle, which will be used to create another extrusion feature that will be added to the existing solid object.

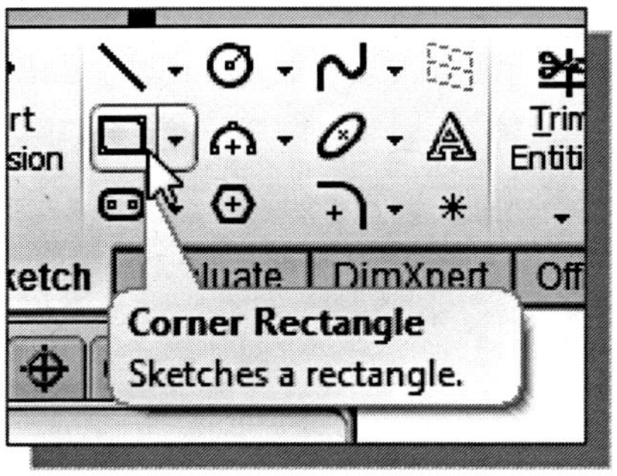

5. Select the **Corner Rectangle** command by clicking once with the **left-mouse-button** on the icon in the *Sketch* toolbar.

   ➢ To illustrate the usage of dimensions in parametric sketches, we will intentionally create a rectangle away from the desired location.

6. Create a sketch with segments perpendicular/parallel to the existing edges of the solid model as shown below.

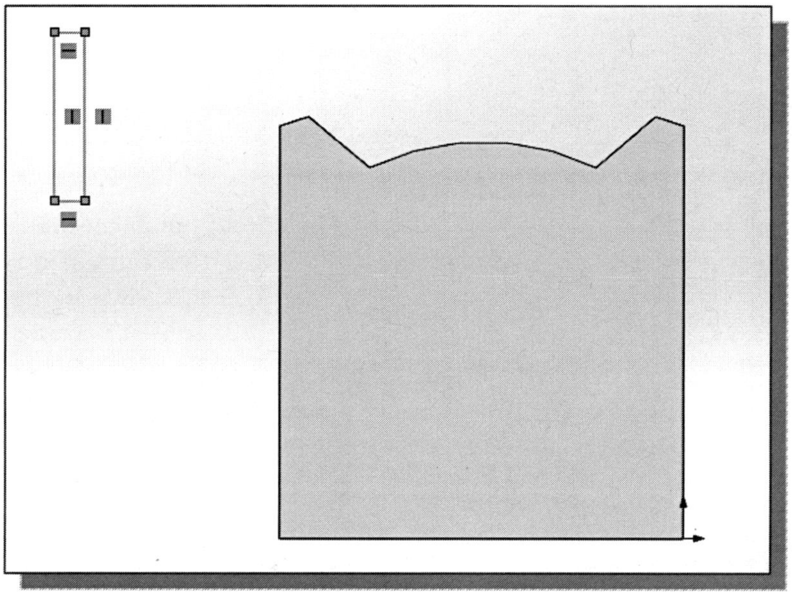

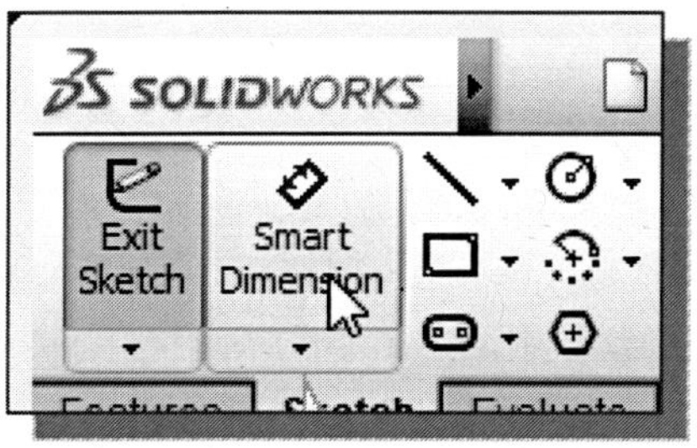

7. Select the **Smart Dimension** command in the *Sketch* toolbar. The Smart Dimension command allows us to quickly create and modify dimensions.

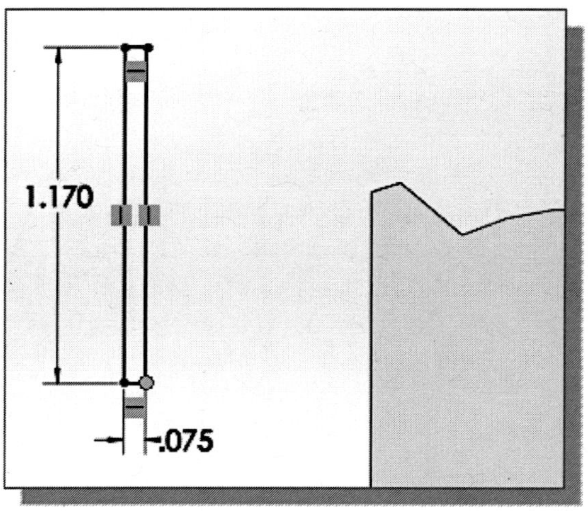

8. On your own, create and modify the size dimensions to describe the size of the sketch as shown in the figure.

9. Create the two location dimensions, accepting the default values, to describe the position of the sketch relative to the top corner of the solid model as shown.

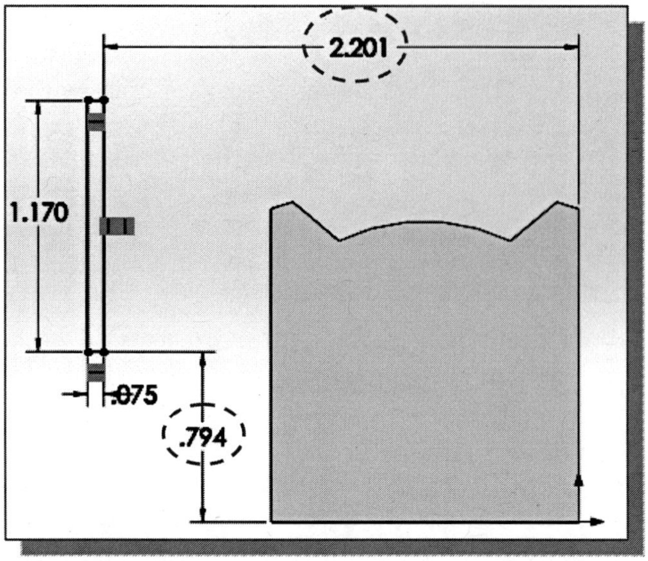

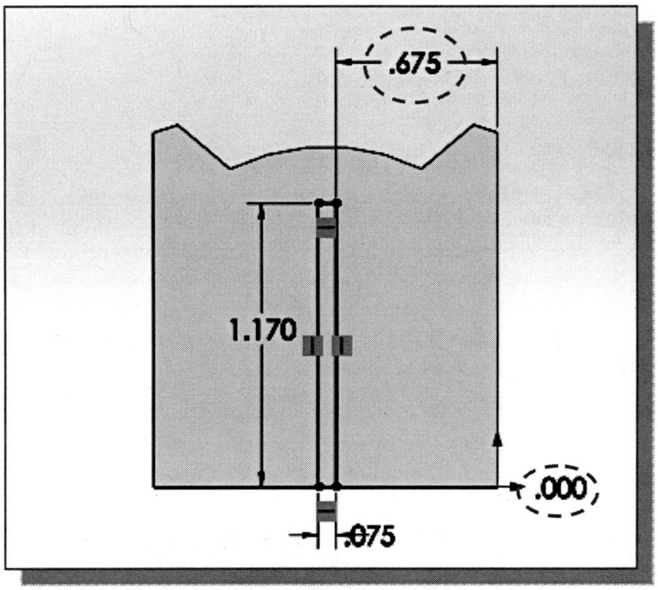

10. On your own, modify the location dimensions to **0.675** and **0.0** as shown in the figure.

➢ In parametric modeling, the dimensions can be used to quickly control the size and location of the defined geometry.

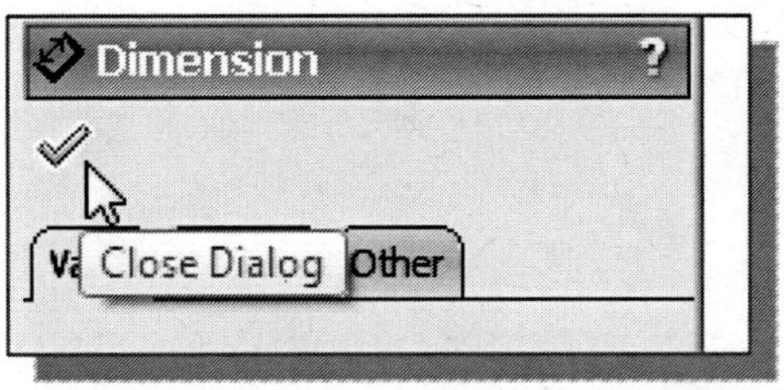

11. Select **Close Dialog** in the *Dimension Property Manager* to end the Smart Dimension command.

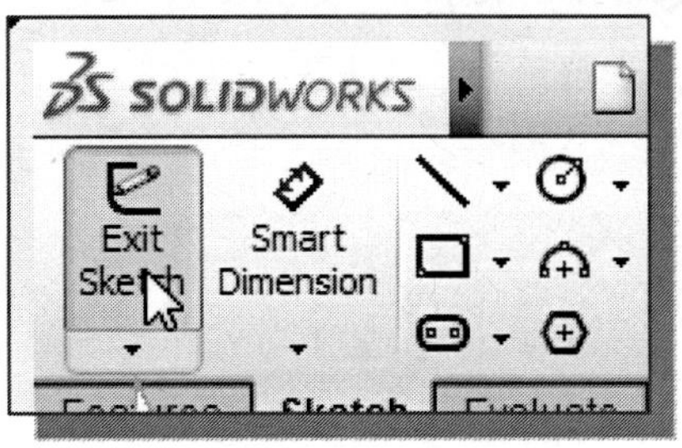

12. Click **Exit Sketch** in the *Sketch* toolbar to end the Sketch mode.

13. In the *Boss-Extrude Property Manager*, enter **0.45** as the extrude *Distance* as shown.

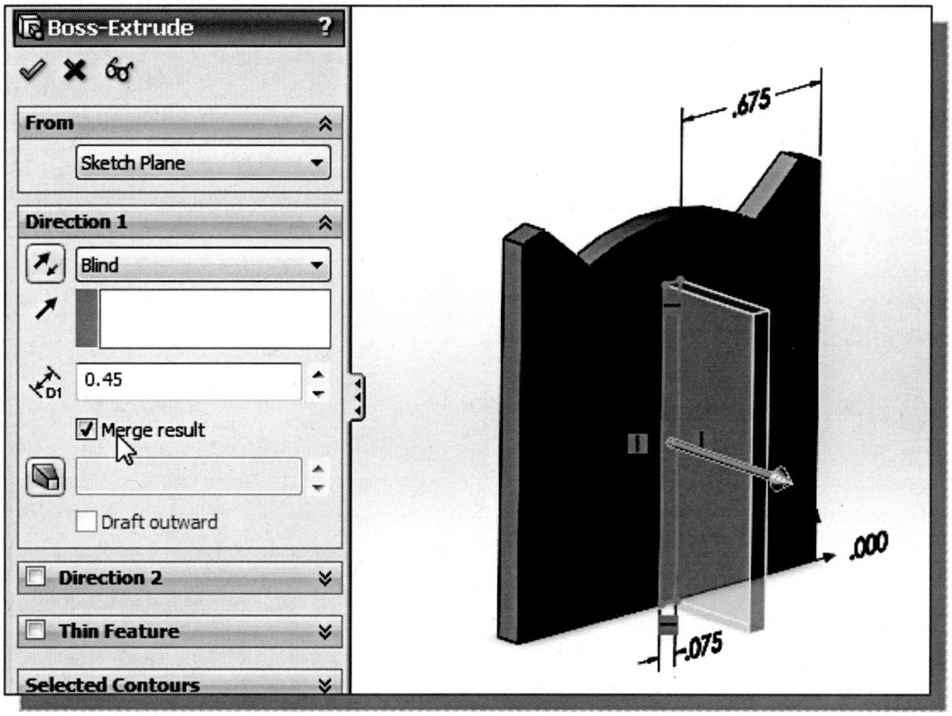

14. Confirm the **Merge result** option is activated as shown.

15. Click on the **OK** button to proceed with creating the extruded feature.

Step 5-2: Adding a Cut Feature

- Next, we will create a **cut** feature that will be added to the existing solid object.

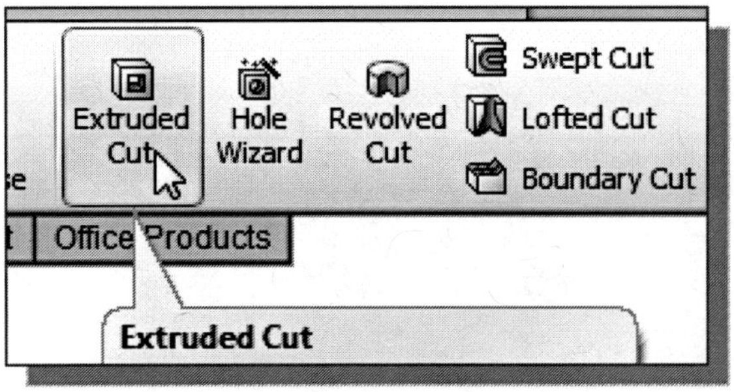

1. In the *Features* toolbar select the **Extruded Cut** command by clicking once with the left-mouse-button on the icon.

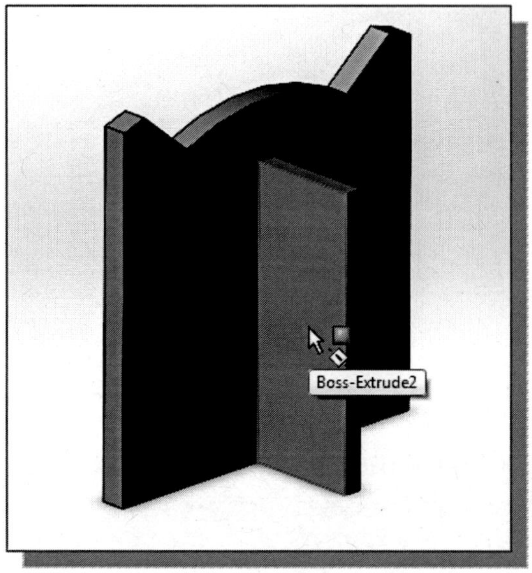

2. Pick the vertical face of the last feature we created, as shown.

3. Select the **Line** command by clicking once with the **left-mouse-button** on the icon in the *Sketch* toolbar.

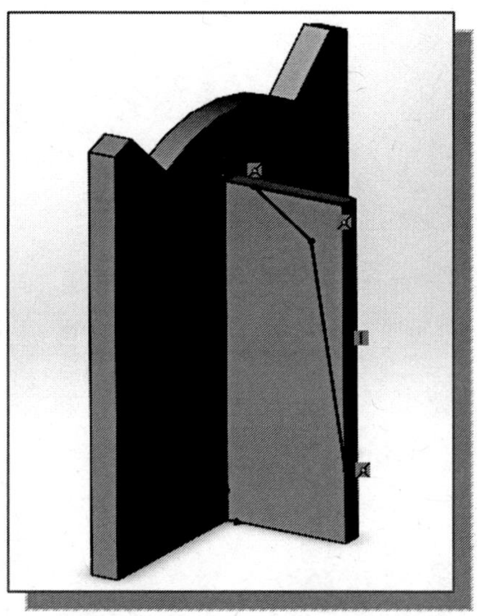

4. Create a closed region consisting of four line segments aligned to the upper right corner of the second solid feature as shown. (Hint: Start the line segments at the top corner.)

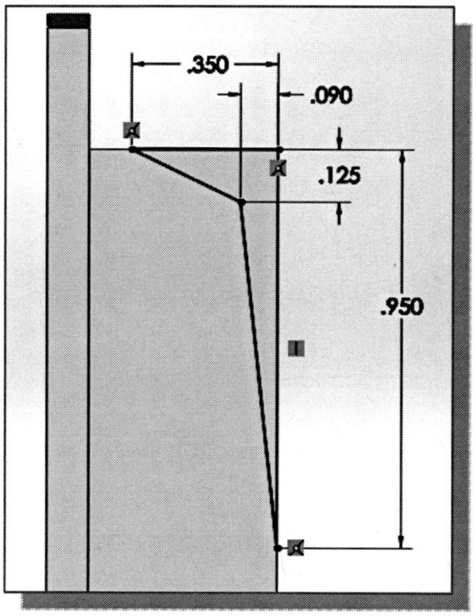

5. On your own, create and modify the dimensions of the sketch as shown in the figure.

6. Click **Exit Sketch** in the *Sketch* toolbar to end the Sketch mode.

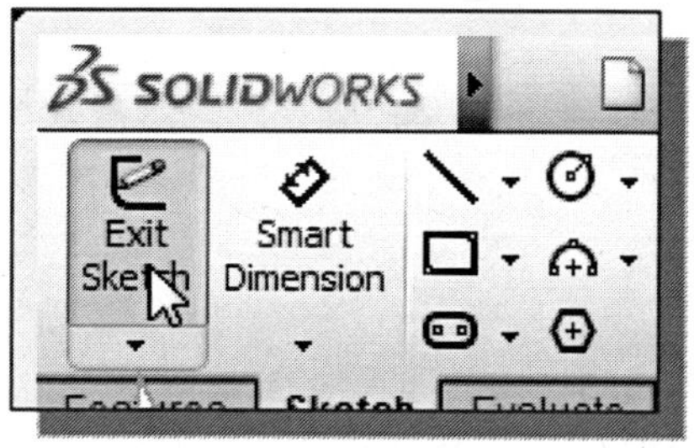

7. Set the *Extents* option to **Through All** as shown. The *Through All* option instructs the software to calculate the extrusion distance and assures the created feature will always cut through the full length of the model.

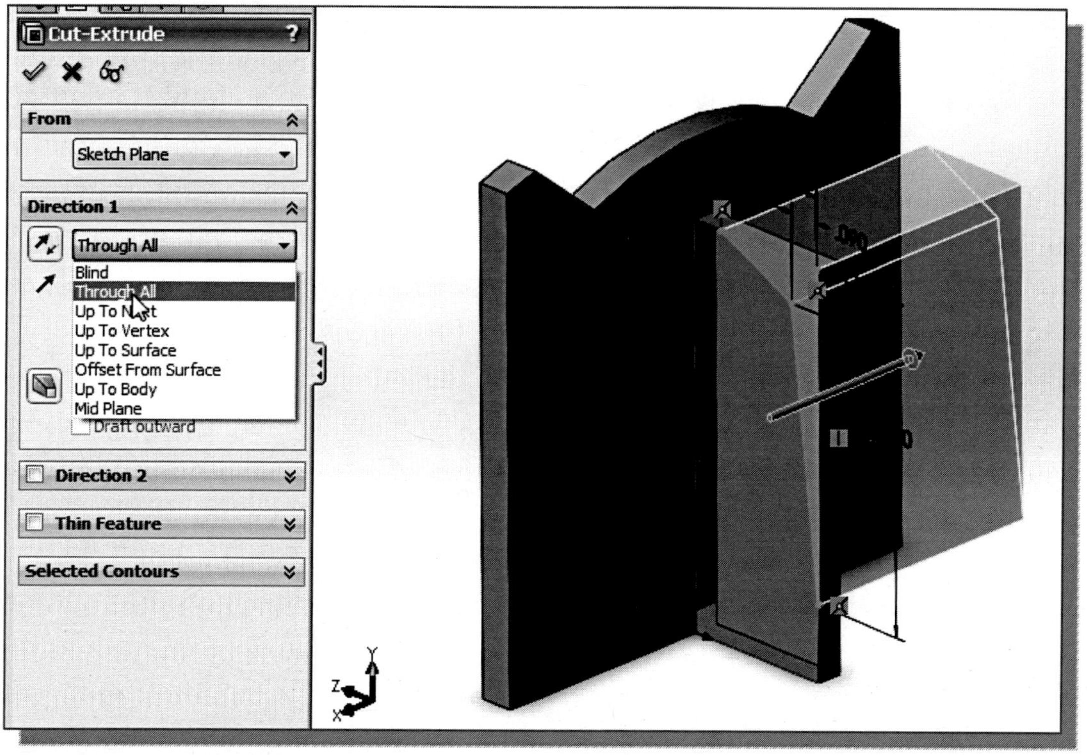

8. Click on the **OK** button to proceed with creating the extruded feature.

Step 6: Adding Additional Features

- Next, we will create and profile another sketch, a circle, which will be used to create another extrusion feature that will be added to the existing solid object.

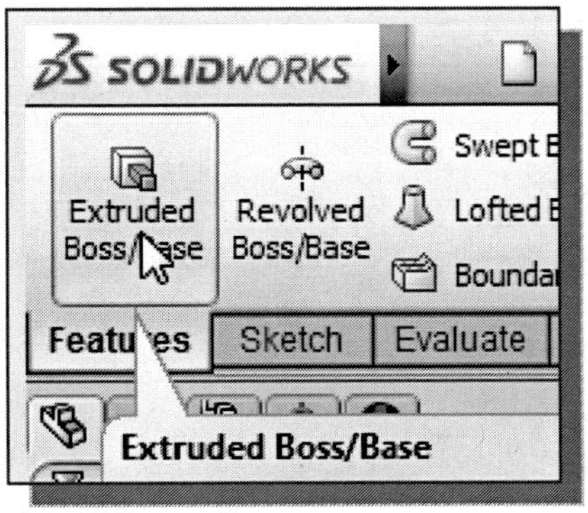

1. In the *Features* toolbar select the **Extruded Boss/ Base** command by clicking once with the left-mouse-button on the icon.

2. Pick the bottom horizontal face of the 3D solid model as shown.

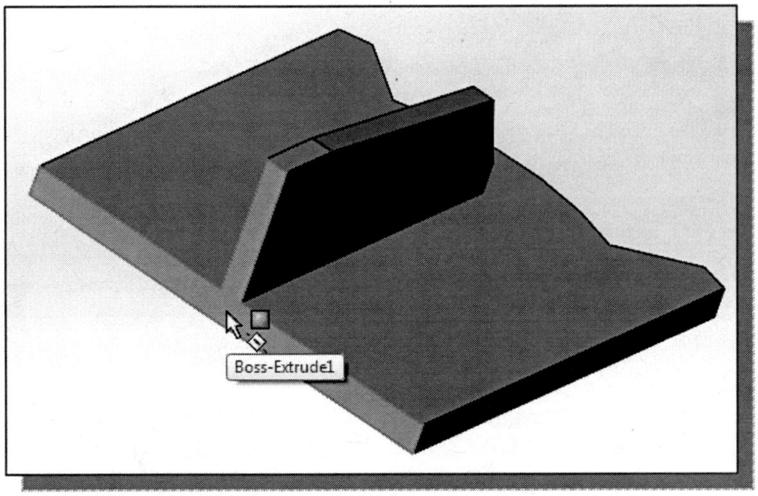

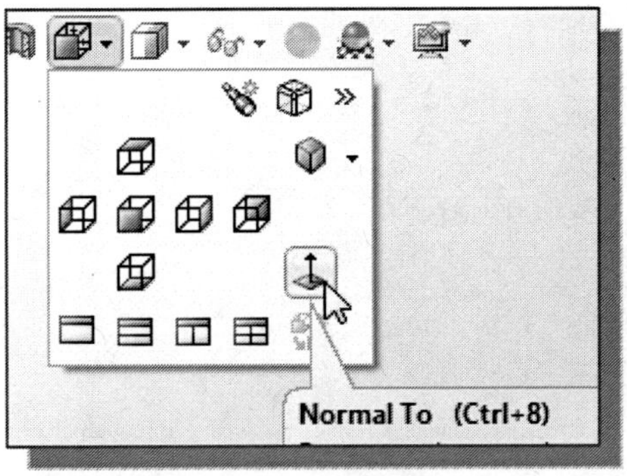

3. Adjust the display by using the **Normal To** option in the view orientation panel as shown.

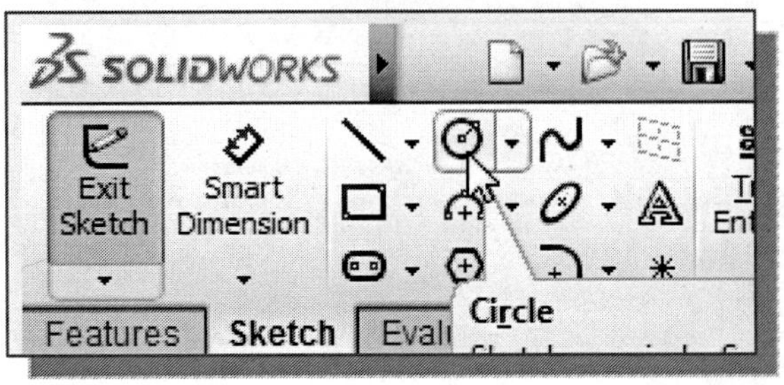

4. Select the **Circle** command by clicking once with the **left-mouse-button** on the icon in the *Sketch* toolbar.

5. Create a circle near the right edge of the bottom surface as shown.

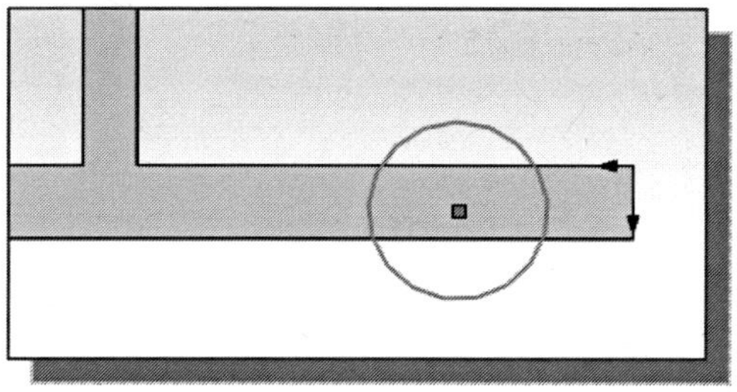

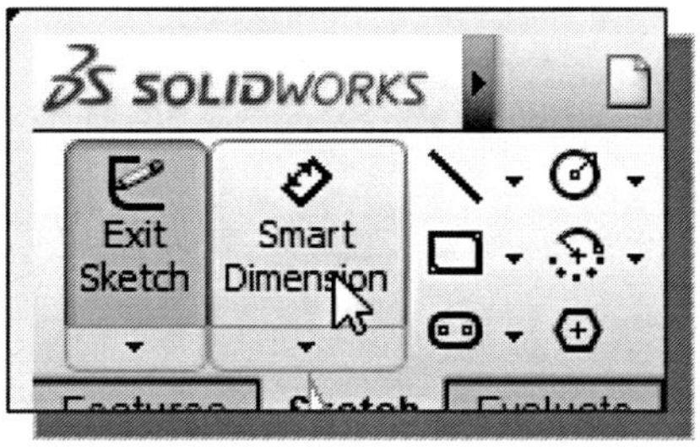

6. Select the **Smart Dimension** command in the *Sketch* toolbar. The Smart Dimension command allows us to quickly create and modify dimensions.

7. On your own, create and modify the three dimensions as shown.

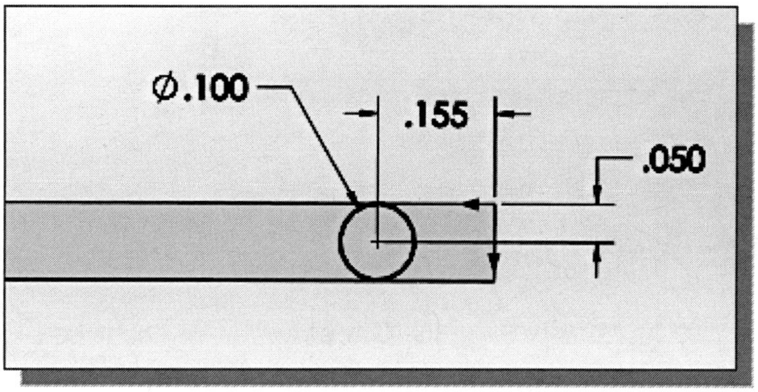

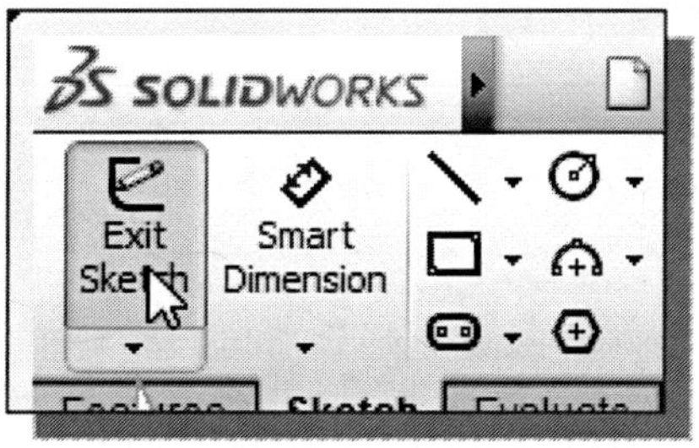

8. Click **Exit Sketch** in the *Sketch* toolbar to end the Sketch mode.

9. On your own, complete the **0.32** the extrusion as shown.

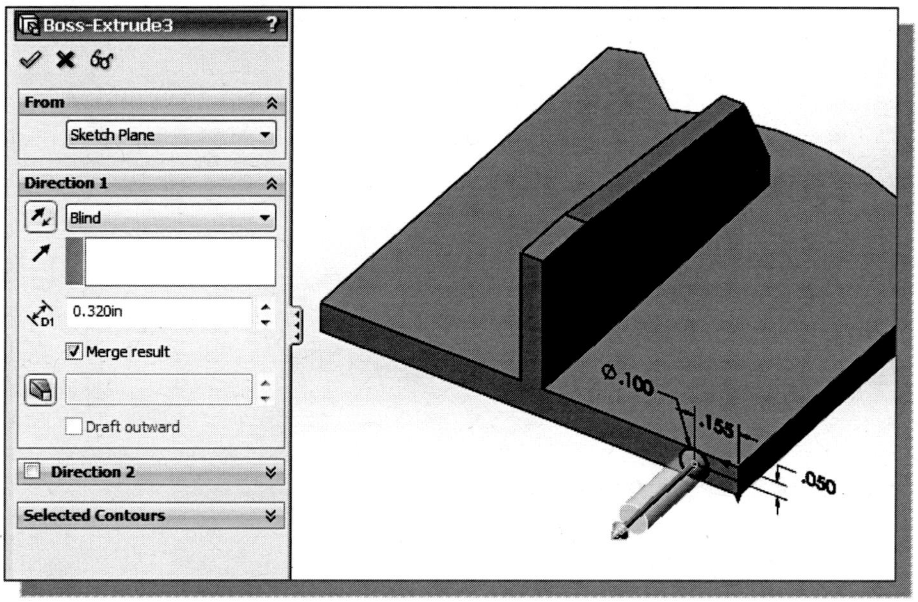

10. On your own, repeat the above steps and create another extruded feature on the other side.

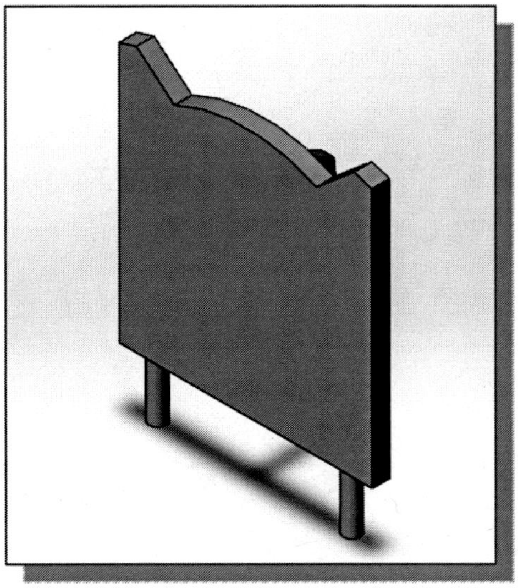

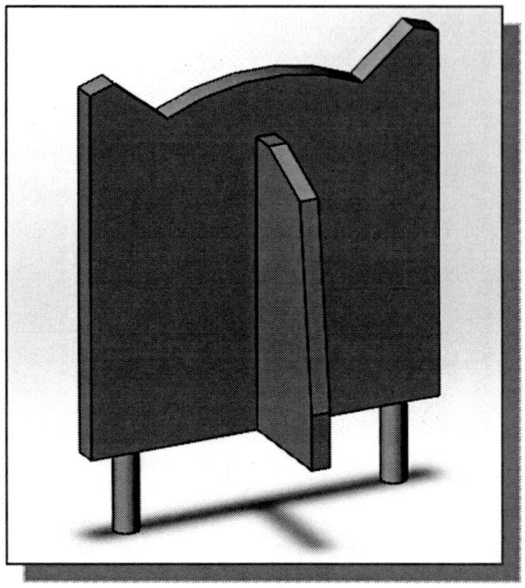

Adding a Decal

❖ In *SolidWorks*, the **Decal** option can be used to apply a bitmap image on a surface to obtain a more realistic three-dimensional model.

1. Download the *TigerFace.bmp* file and save it to the *Mechanical-Tiger* project folder. (URL: http://www.schroff.com/SolidWorks/TigerFace.bmp)

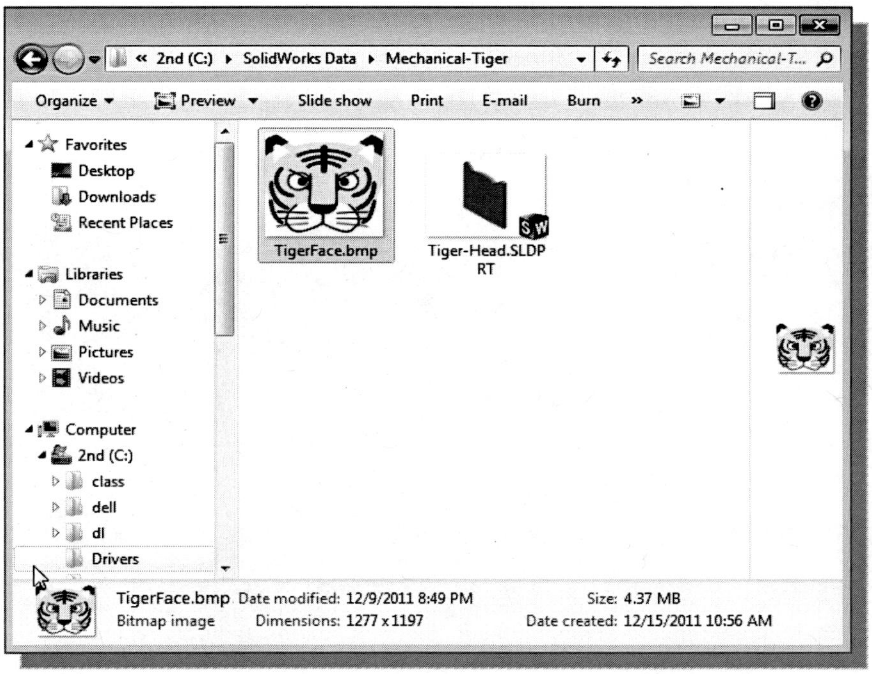

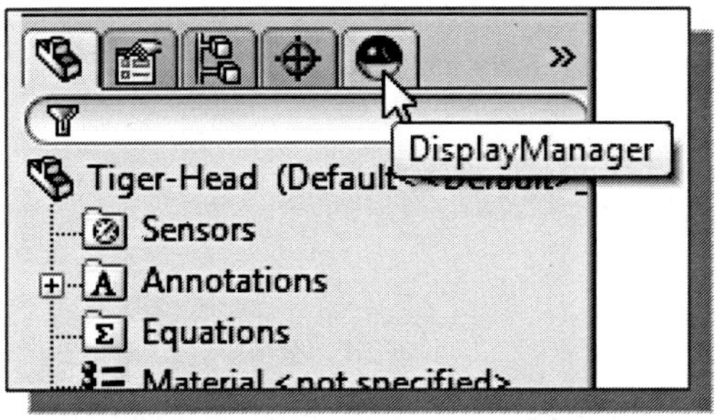

2. Activate the **Display Manager** by clicking on the associated tab as shown.

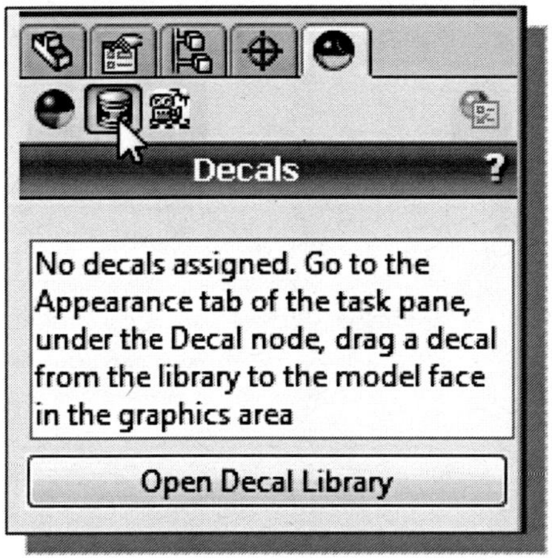

3. In the *Display Manager*, select the **Decals** command by left-clicking once on the icon.

4. Click on the **Open Decal Library** button to view the existing decals available.

- In *SolidWorks*, a decal can be applied to a surface by **drag and drop** from the *Decal Library*.

5. Select one of the decals in the *Decal Library* and drag it to the front surface of the *Tiger* model as shown.

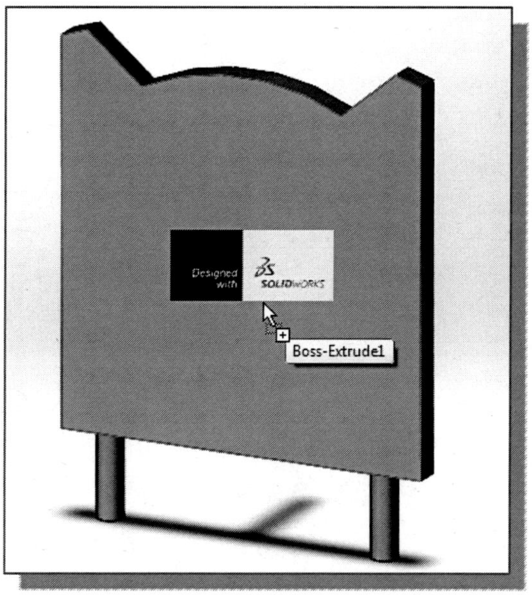

- Note that the selected decal is used to access the *Decal Editing Manager*, which will allow us to import the *TigerFace.bmp* file.

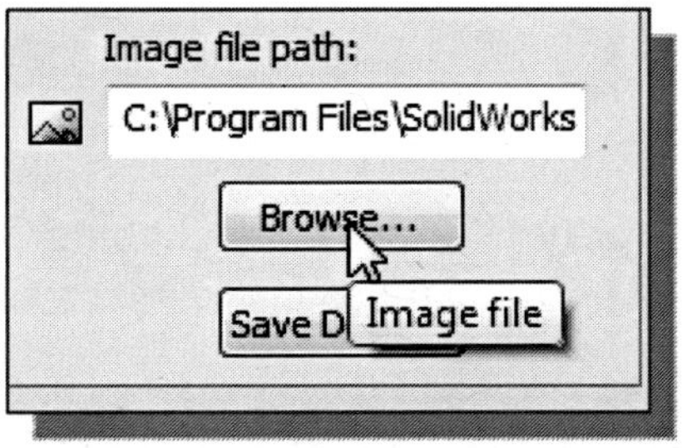

6. Click the **Browse** button in the *Decal Editing Manager* as shown.

7. Select the ***TigerFace.bmp*** in the *Mechanical-Tiger* project folder.

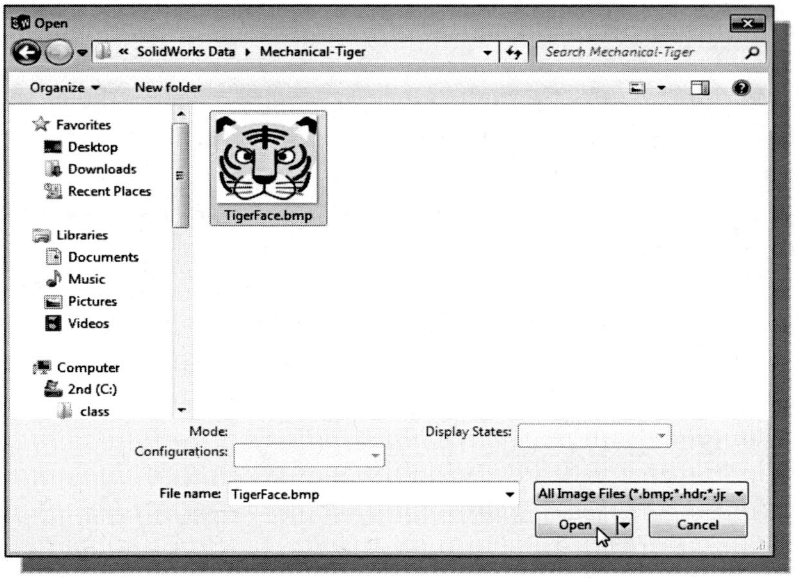

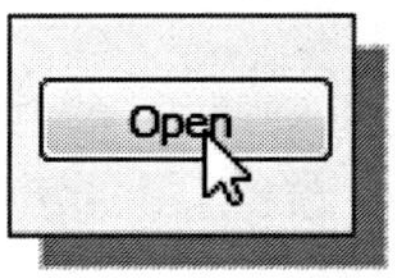

8. Click **Open** to import the image into the current model.

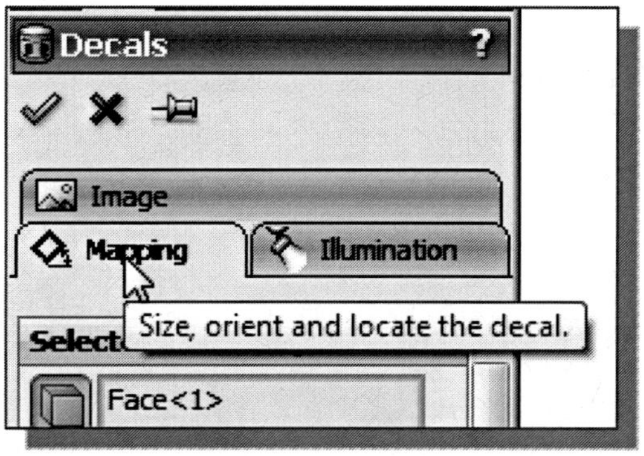

9. Switch to the **Mapping** options by clicking on the associated tab as shown.

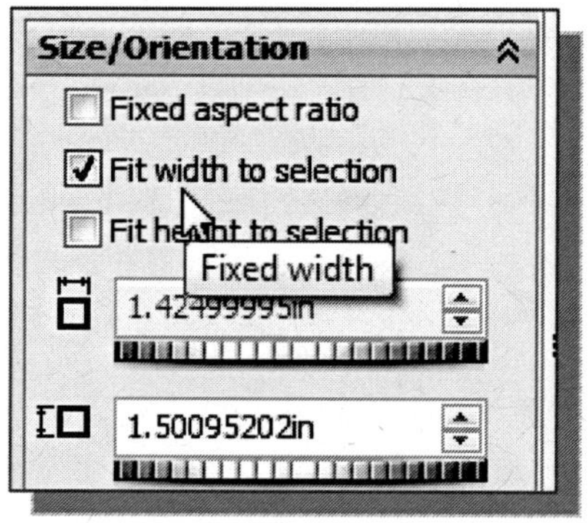

10. In the ***Size/Orientation*** section, turn ***OFF*** the *Fixed aspect ratio* option, and turn ***ON*** the *Fit width to selection* option as shown.

11. On your own, adjust the height of the decal by dragging one of the control-points using the left-mouse-button as shown.

12. Click **OK** to end the **Decals** option.

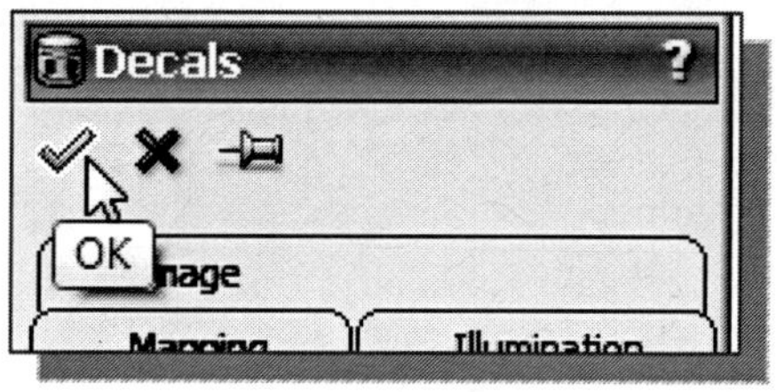

Save the Model

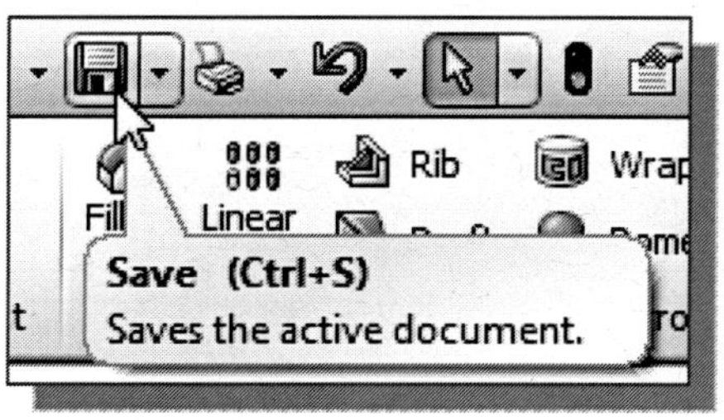

1. Select **Save** in the *Quick Access* toolbar, or you can also use the "**Ctrl-S**" combination (hold down the "Ctrl" key and hit the "S" key once) to save the part.

2. In the *File name* editor box, enter **Tiger-Head** as the file name.

3. Click on the **Save** button to save the file.

❖ You should form a habit of saving your work periodically, just in case something might go wrong while you are working on it. In general, one should save one's work at an interval of every 15 to 20 minutes. One should also save before making any major modifications to the model.

Questions:

1. What is the first thing we should set up in *SolidWorks* when creating a new model?

2. Describe the general *parametric modeling* procedure.

3. Describe the general guidelines in creating *rough sketches*.

4. List two of the geometric constraint symbols used by *SolidWorks*.

5. What was the first feature we created in this lesson?

6. How many solid features were created in the tutorial?

7. How do we control the size of a feature in parametric modeling?

8. Which command was used to create the last cut feature in the tutorial? How many dimensions do we need to fully describe the cut feature?

9. List and describe three differences between *parametric modeling* and traditional 2D *computer aided drafting* techniques.

Exercises:

1. **Inclined Support** (Thickness: **.5**)

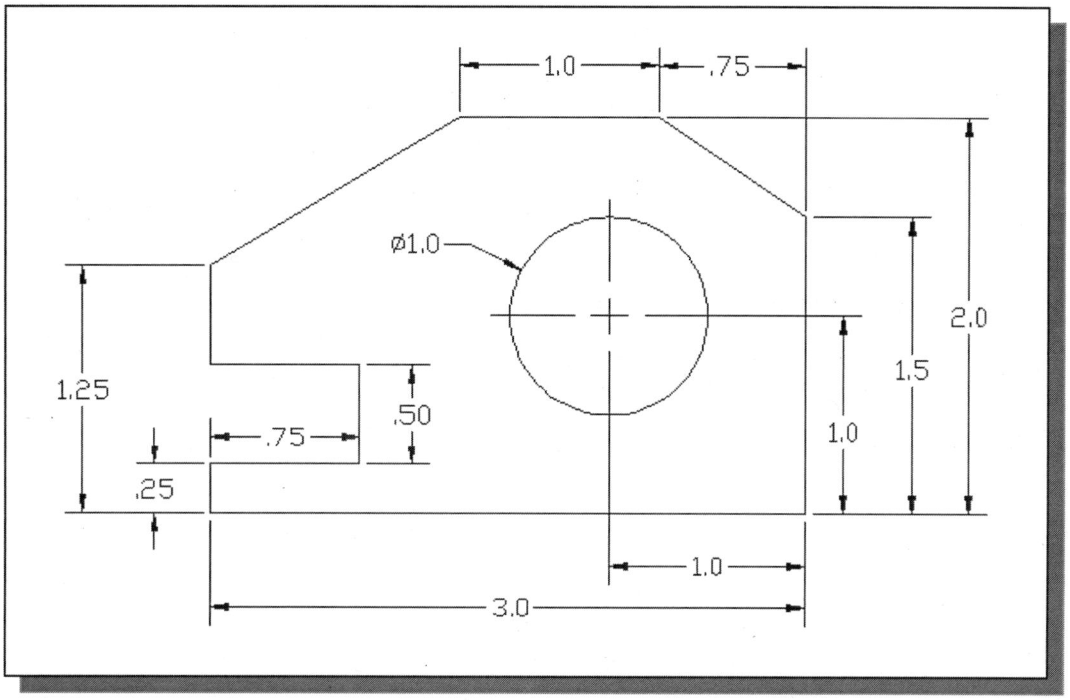

2. **Spacer Plate** (Thickness: **.125**)

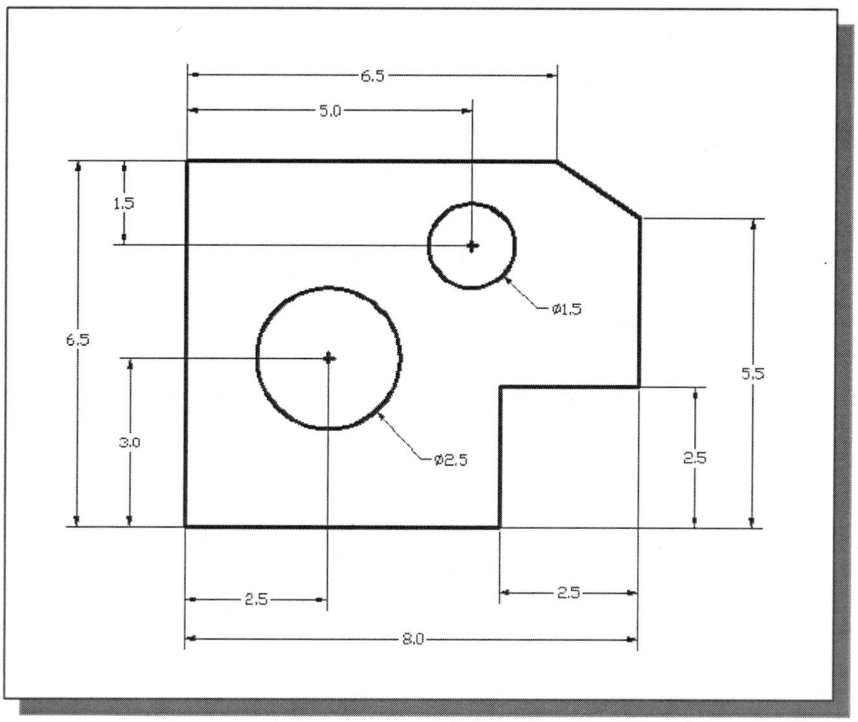

3. **Positioning Stop**

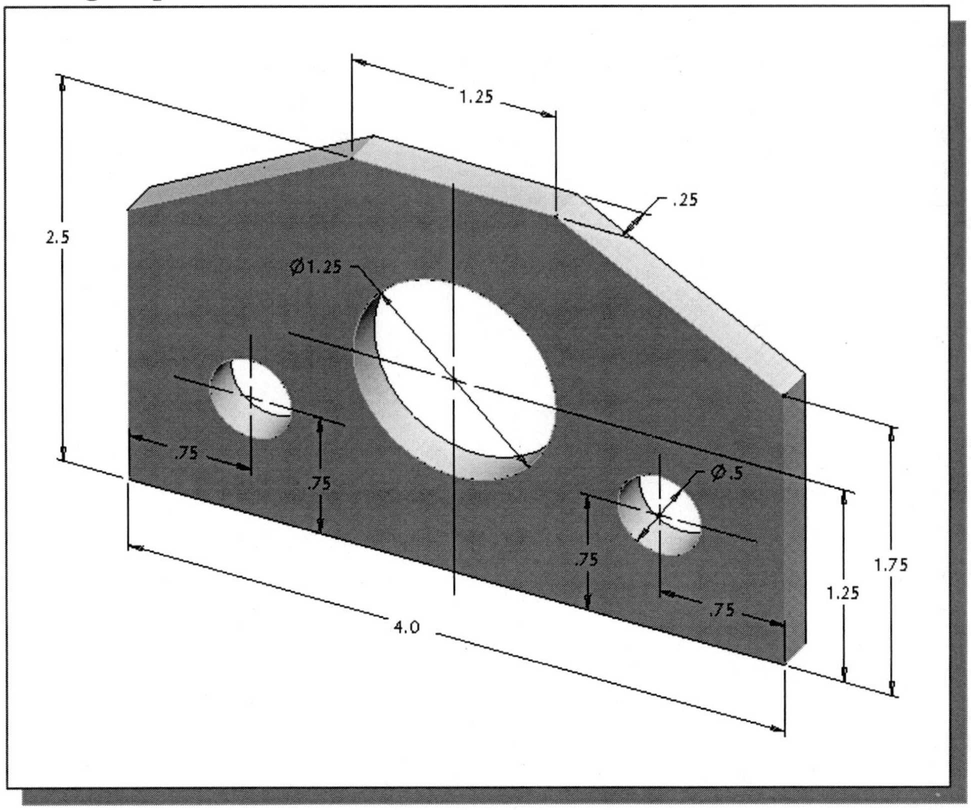

4. **Guide Block**

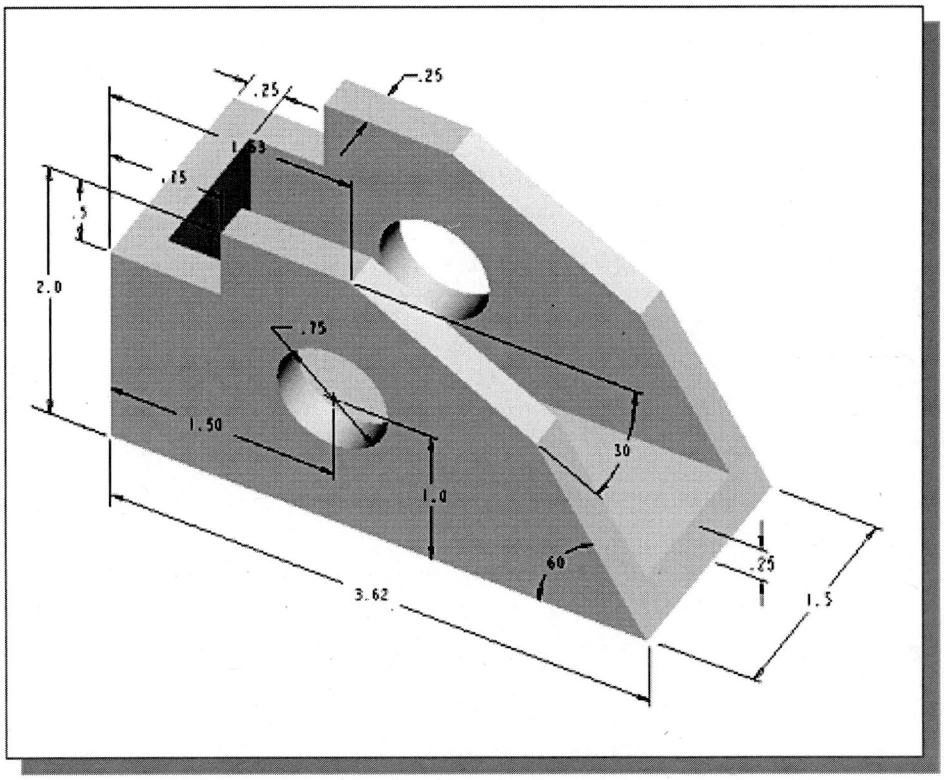

Chapter 3

CSG Concepts and Model History Tree

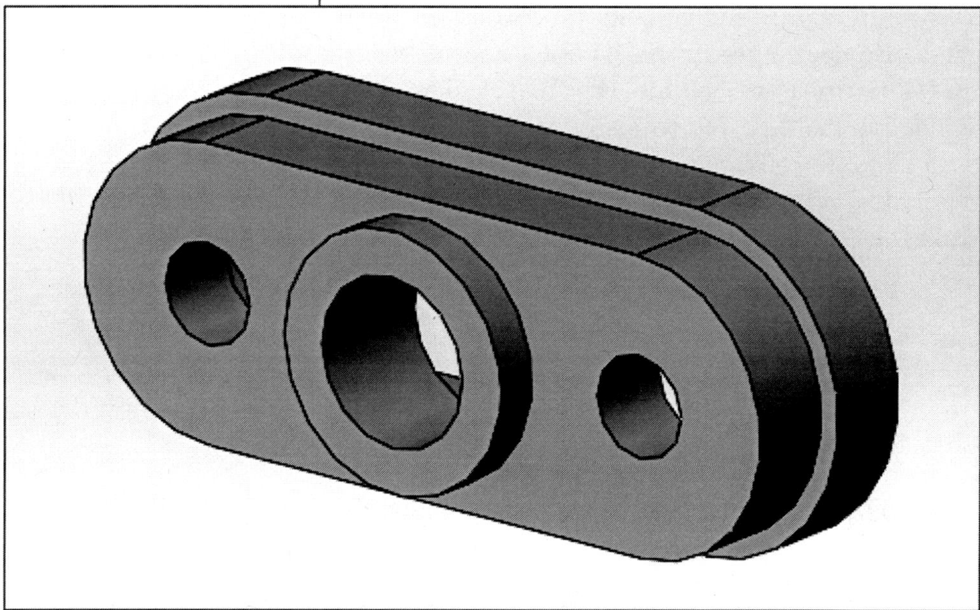

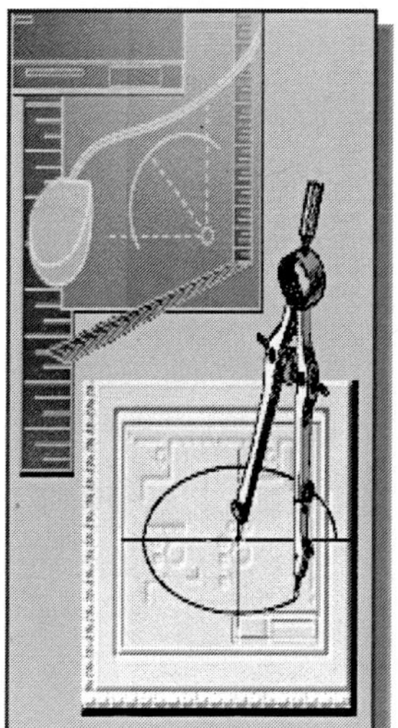

Learning Objectives

- Understand Feature Interactions
- Use the Property Manager to Access the Model Tree
- Modify and Update Feature Dimensions
- Perform History-Based Part Modifications
- Change the Names of Created Features
- Implement Basic Design Changes
- Calculating the Physical Properties of Solid Models

Introduction

In the 1980s, one of the main advancements in **solid modeling** was the development of the **Constructive Solid Geometry** (CSG) method. CSG describes the solid model as combinations of basic three-dimensional shapes (**primitive solids**). The basic primitive solid set typically includes: Rectangular-prism (Block), Cylinder, Cone, Sphere, and Torus (Tube). Two solid objects can be combined into one object in various ways using operations known as **Boolean operations**. There are three basic Boolean operations: **JOIN (Union), CUT (Difference)**, and **INTERSECT**. The *JOIN* operation combines the two volumes included in the different solids into a single solid. The *CUT* operation subtracts the volume of one solid object from the other solid object. The *INTERSECT* operation keeps only the volume common to both solid objects. The CSG method is also known as the **Machinist's Approach**, as the method is parallel to machine shop practices.

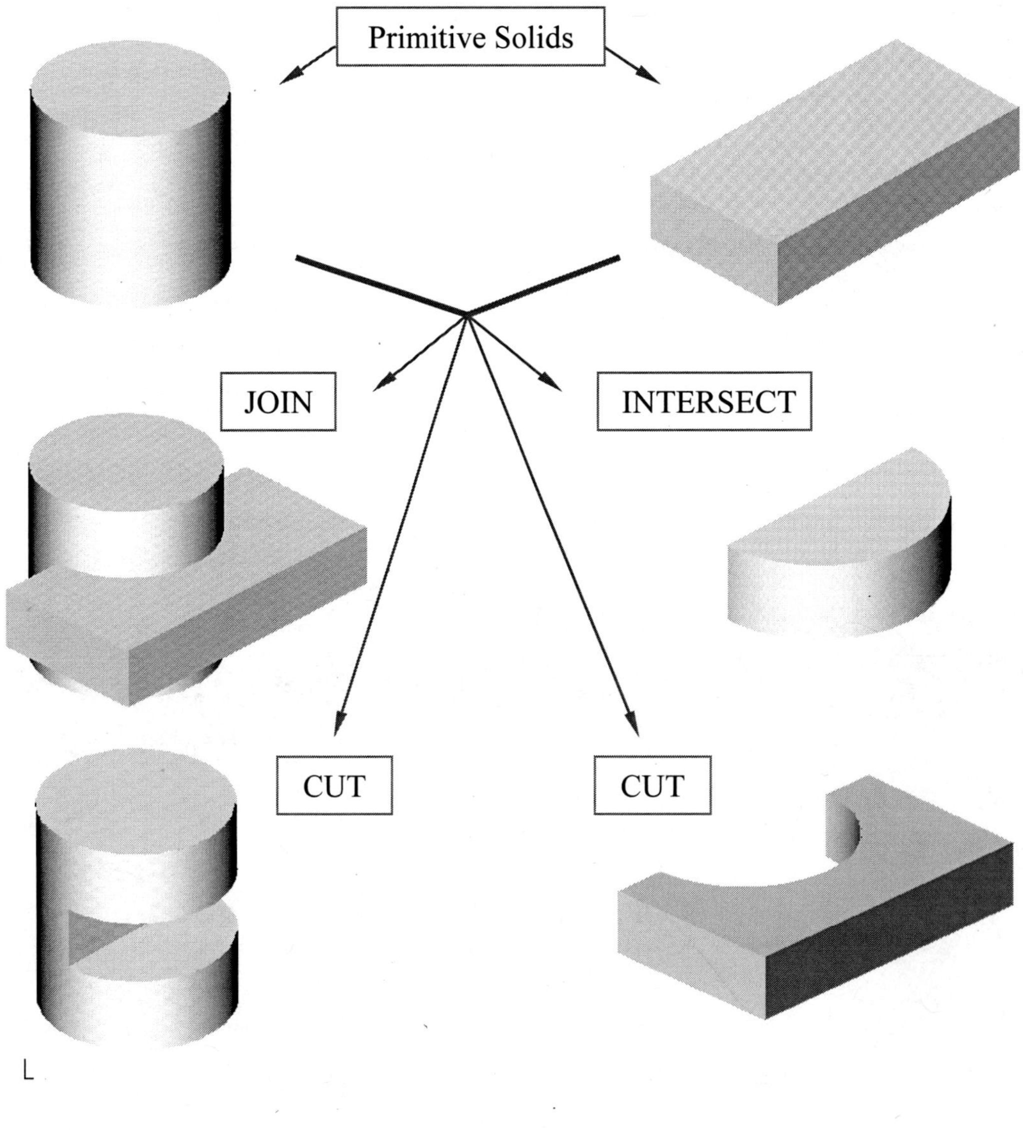

Binary Tree

The CSG is also referred to as the method used to store a solid model in the database. The resulting solid can be easily represented by what is called a **binary tree**. In a binary tree, the terminal branches (leaves) are the various primitives that are linked together to make the final solid object (the root). The binary tree is an effective way to keep track of the *history* of the resulting solid. By keeping track of the history, the solid model can be re-built by re-linking through the binary tree. This provides a convenient way to modify the model. We can make modifications at the appropriate links in the binary tree and re-link the rest of the history tree without building a new model.

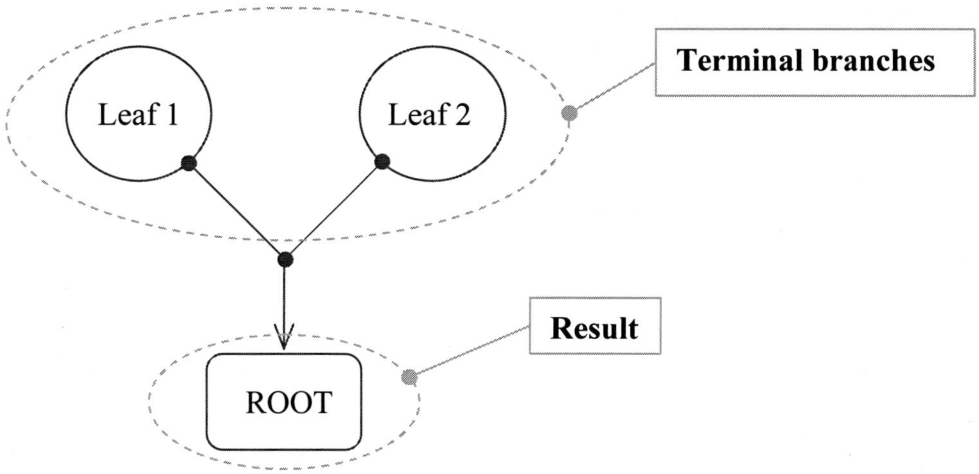

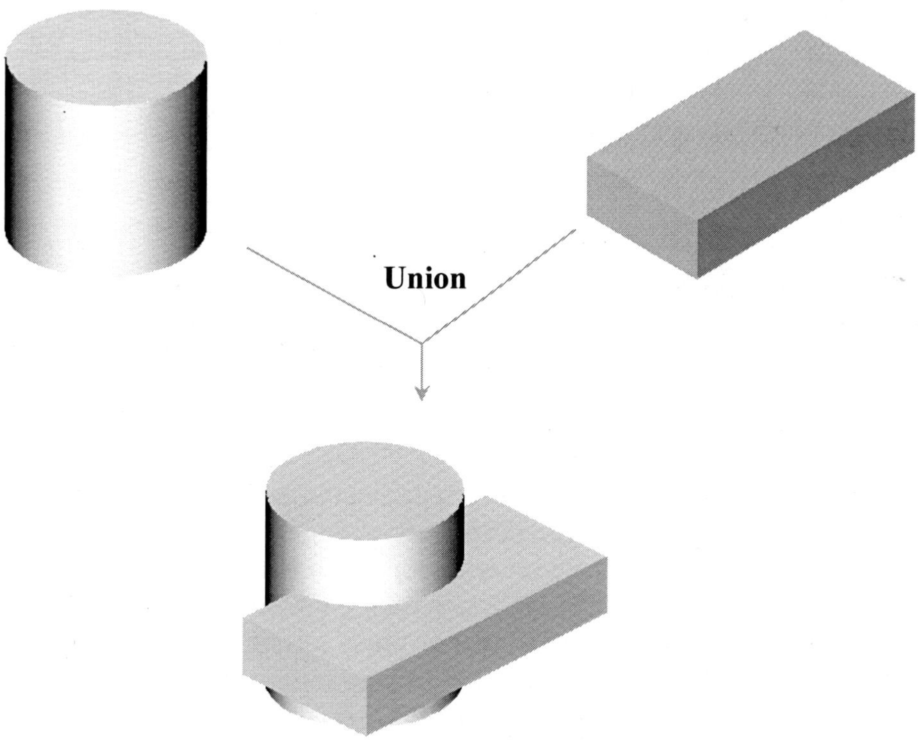

Model History Tree

In *SolidWorks*, the **design intents** are embedded into features in the **history tree**. The structure of the model history tree resembles that of a **CSG binary tree**. A CSG binary tree contains only *Boolean relations*, while the ***SolidWorks* history tree** contains all features, including *Boolean relations*. A history tree is a sequential record of the features used to create the part. This history tree contains the construction steps, plus the rules defining the design intent of each construction operation. In a history tree, each time a new modeling event is created, previously defined features can be used to define information such as size, location, and orientation. It is therefore important to think about your modeling strategy before you start creating anything. It is important, but also difficult, to plan ahead for all possible design changes that might occur. This approach in modeling is a major difference of **FEATURE-BASED CAD SOFTWARE**, such as *SolidWorks*, from previous generation CAD systems.

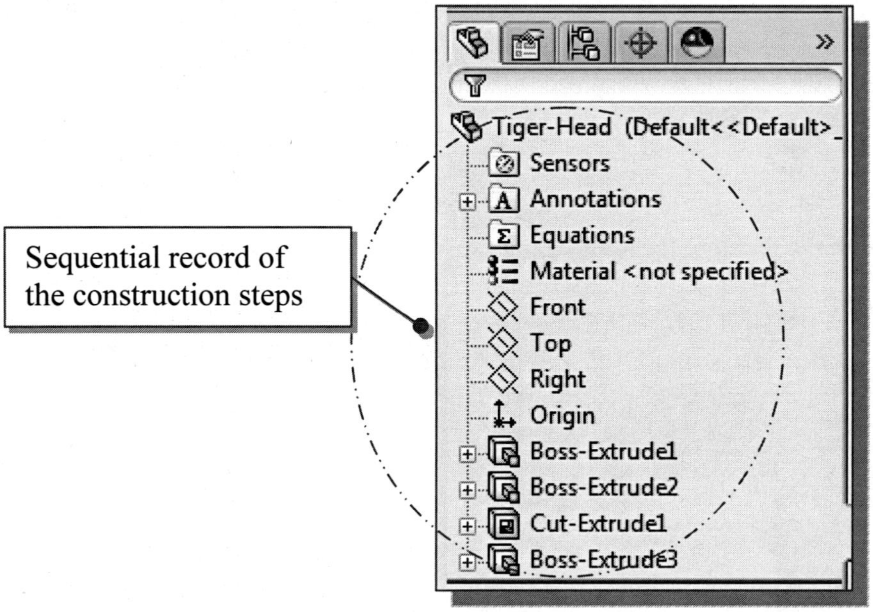

Feature-based parametric modeling is a cumulative process. Every time a new feature is added, a new result is created and the feature is also added to the history tree. The database also includes parameters of features that were used to define them. All of this happens automatically as features are created and manipulated. At this point, it is important to understand that all of this information is retained, and modifications are done based on the same input information.

In *SolidWorks*, the history tree gives information about modeling order and other information about the feature. Part modifications can be accomplished by accessing the features in the history tree. It is therefore important to understand and utilize the feature history tree to modify designs. *SolidWorks* remembers the history of a part, including all the rules that were used to create it, so that changes can be made to any operation that was performed to create the part. In *SolidWorks*, to modify a feature, we access the feature by selecting the feature in the ***Feature Manager*** window.

The *A6-Knee* Part

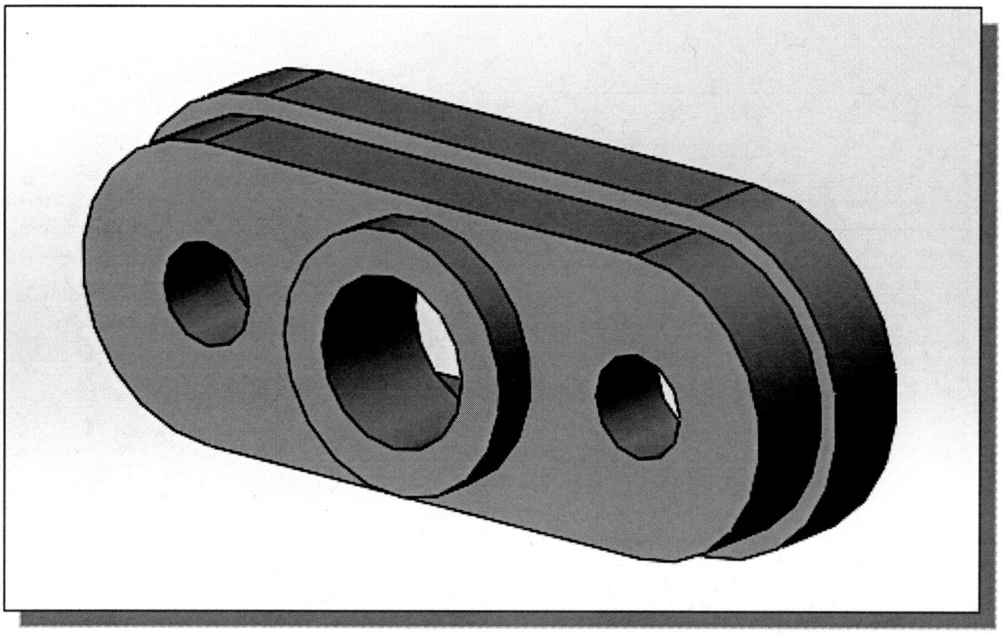

❖ Based on your knowledge of *SolidWorks* so far, how many features would you use to create the design? Which feature would you choose as the **BASE FEATURE**, the first solid feature, of the model? What is your choice in arranging the order of the features? Take a few minutes to consider these questions and do preliminary planning by sketching on a piece of paper. You are also encouraged to create the model on your own prior to following through the tutorial.

Starting *SolidWorks*

1. Select the **SolidWorks** option on the *Start* menu or select the **SolidWorks** icon on the desktop to start *SolidWorks*. The *SolidWorks* main window will appear on the screen.

2. Select the **New** icon on the *Menu Bar* with a single click of the left-mouse-button. The *New SolidWorks Document* dialog box appears.

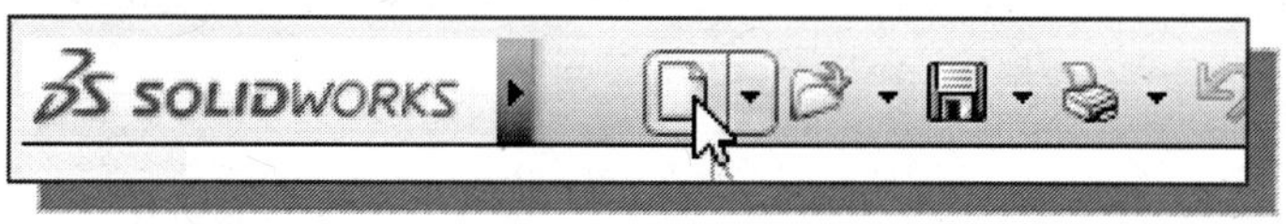

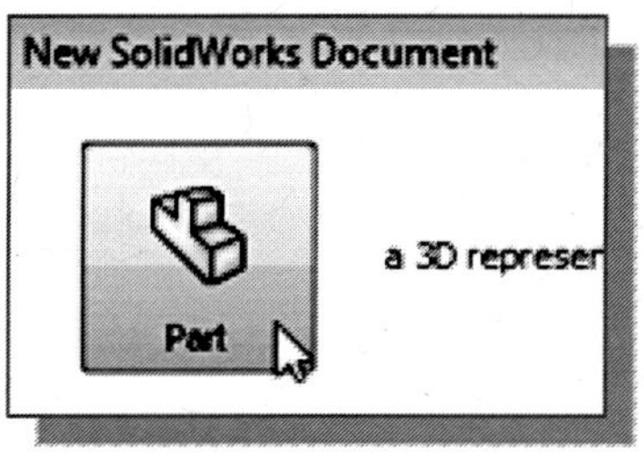

3. Select **Part** by clicking on the first icon in the *New SolidWorks Document* dialog box as shown.

4. Click on the **OK** button to accept the settings.

Modeling Strategy

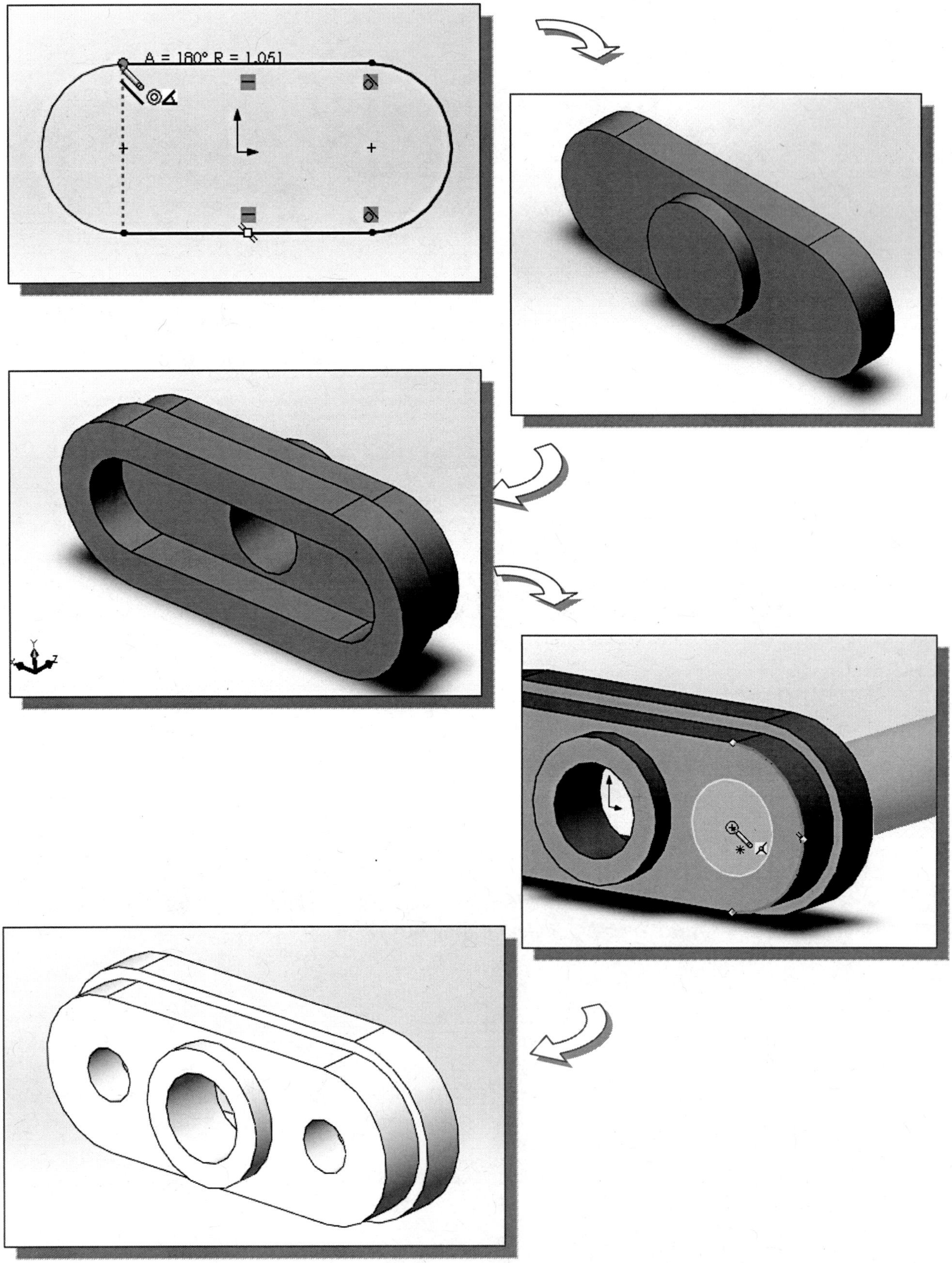

The *SolidWorks Feature Manager*

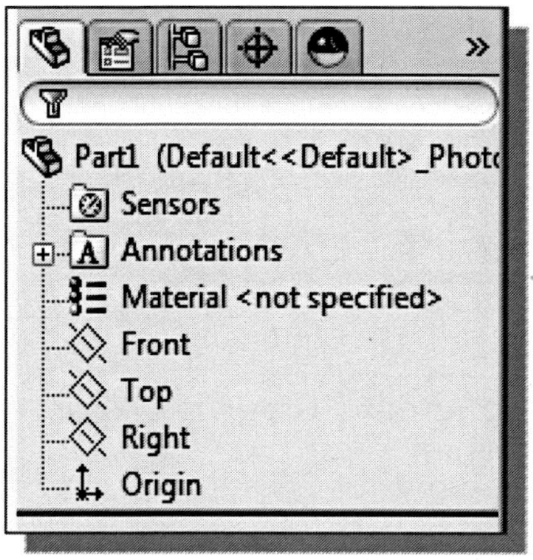

- In the *SolidWorks* screen layout, the ***Feature Manager*** is located to the left of the graphics window. *SolidWorks* can be used for part modeling, assembly modeling, part drawings, and assembly presentation. The *Feature Manager* window provides a visual structure of the features, constraints, and attributes that are used to create the part, assembly, or scene. The *Feature Manager* also provides right-click menu access for tasks associated specifically with the part or feature, and it is the primary focus for executing many of the *SolidWorks* commands.

- The first item displayed in the *Feature Manager* is the name of the part, which is also the file name. By default, the name "Part1" is used when we first start *SolidWorks*. The *Feature Manager* can also be used to modify parts and assemblies by moving, deleting, or renaming items within the hierarchy. Any changes made in the *Feature Manager* directly affect the part or assembly and the results of the modifications are displayed on screen instantly. The *Feature Manager* also reports any problems and conflicts during the modification and updating procedure.

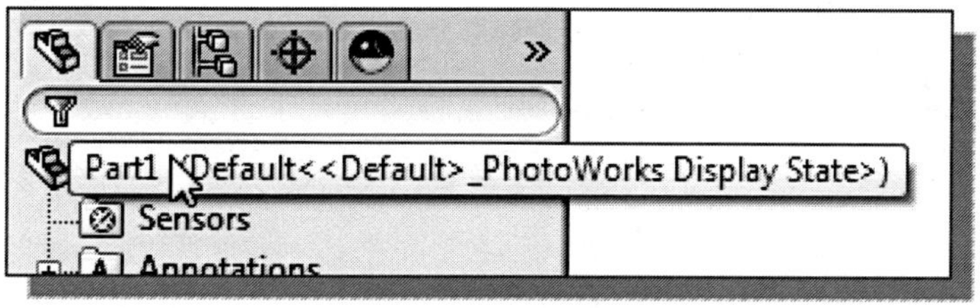

Base Feature

In *parametric modeling*, the first solid feature is called the **base feature**, which usually is the primary shape of the model. Depending upon the design intent, additional features are added to the base feature.

Some of the considerations involved in selecting the base feature are:

- **Design intent** – Determine the functionality of the design; identify the feature that is central to the design.

- **Order of features** – Choose the feature that is the logical base in terms of the order of features in the design.

- **Ease of making modifications** – Select a base feature that is more stable and is less likely to be changed.

Units Setup

1. Select the **Options** icon from the *Menu* toolbar to open the *Options* dialog box.

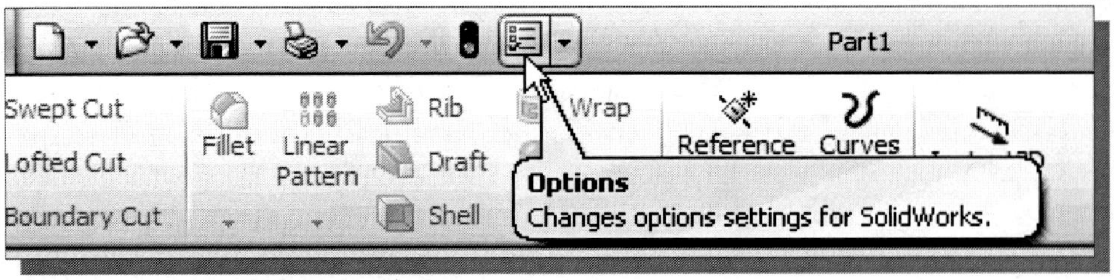

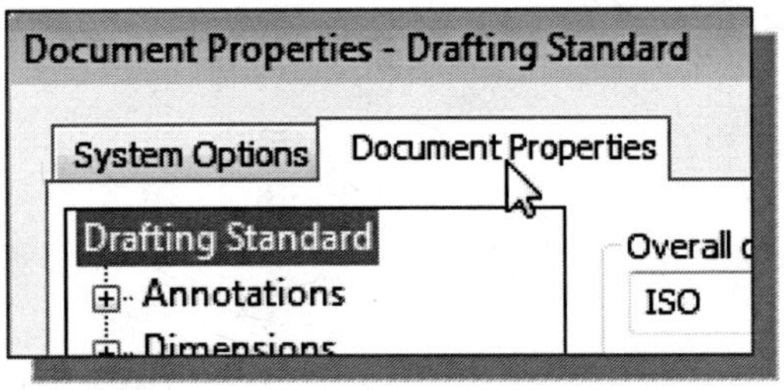

2. Select the **Document Properties** tab as shown in the figure.

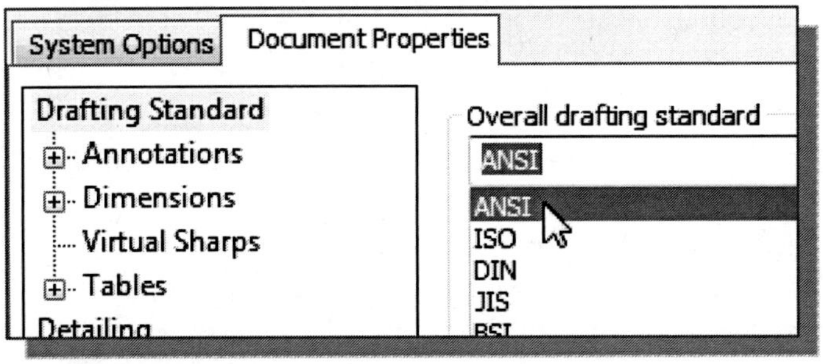

3. Set the *Overall drafting standard* to **ANSI** as shown.

4. Click **Units** as shown in the figure.

5. Select **IPS (inch, pound, second)** under the *Unit system* options.

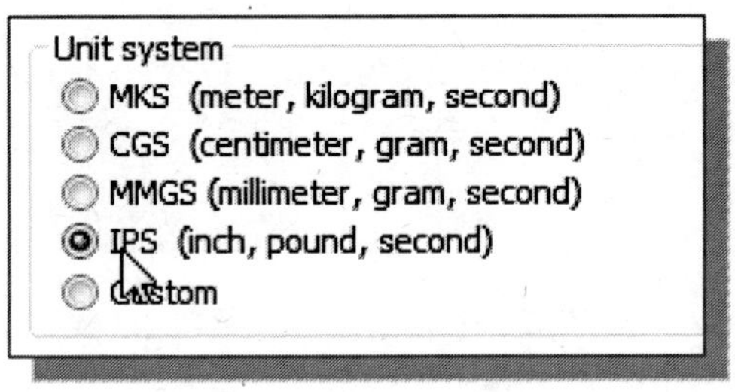

- Note the different options available to set/adjust the display of the selected units set.

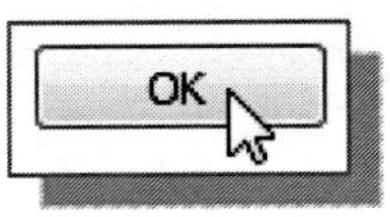

6. Click **OK** in the *Options* dialog box to accept the selected settings.

Create the Base Feature

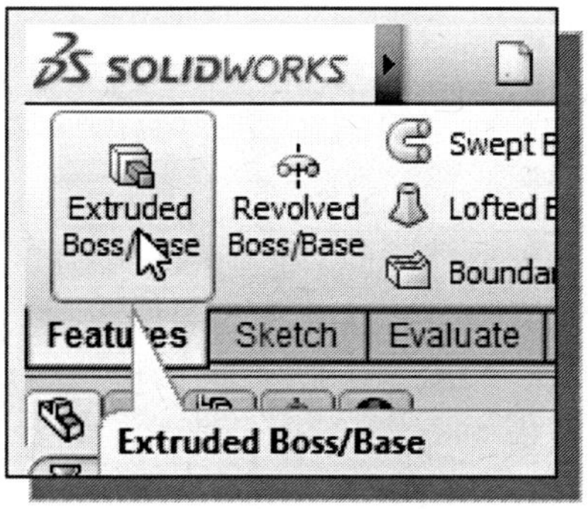

1. In the *Features* toolbar select the **Extruded Boss/ Base** command by clicking once with the left-mouse-button on the icon.

2. Select the Front Plane as the sketch plane for the new sketch.

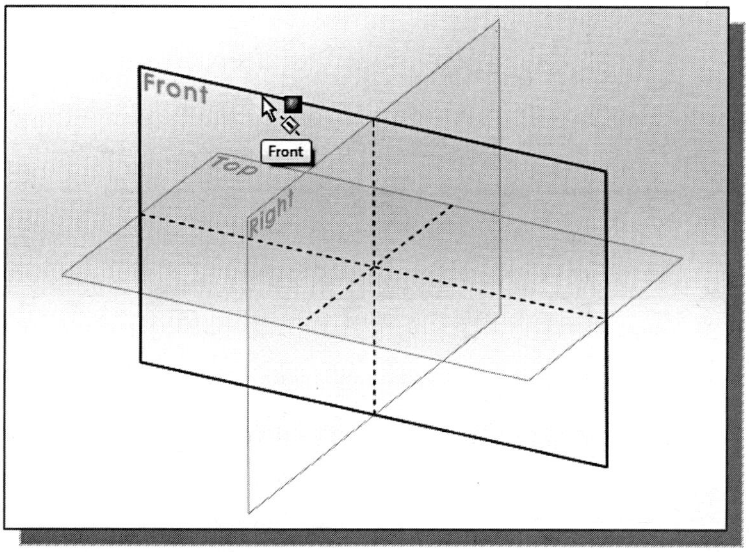

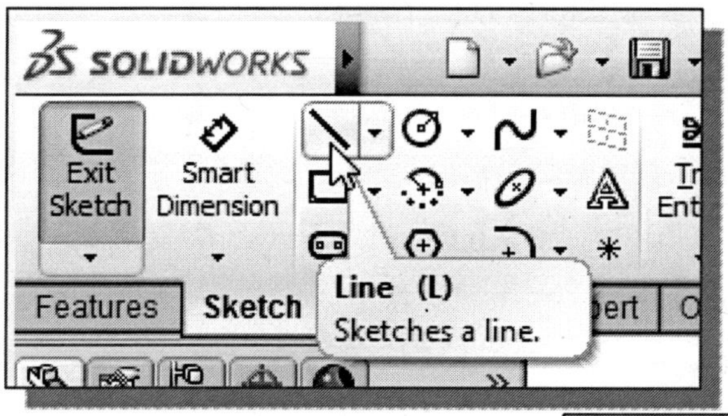

3. Select the **Line** command in the *Sketch* toolbar. The Line command can be used to create line segments and tangent arcs.

4. Create a horizontal line, above the *Origin*, from left to right as shown. Do not exit the Line command yet.

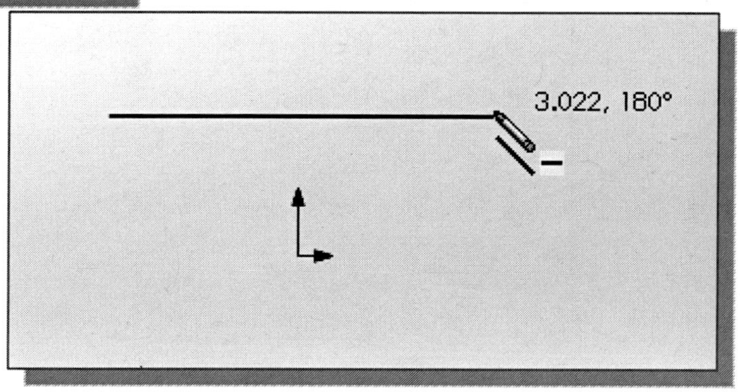

5. Move the cursor on top of the last point of the sketch to activate the **Arc** option. Create an arc on the right and align the other end of the arc as shown.

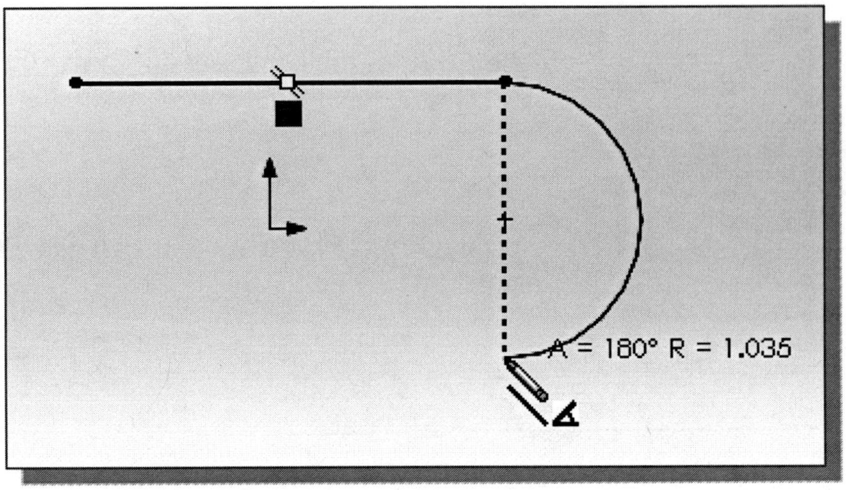

6. Create another horizontal line aligned to the arc as shown.

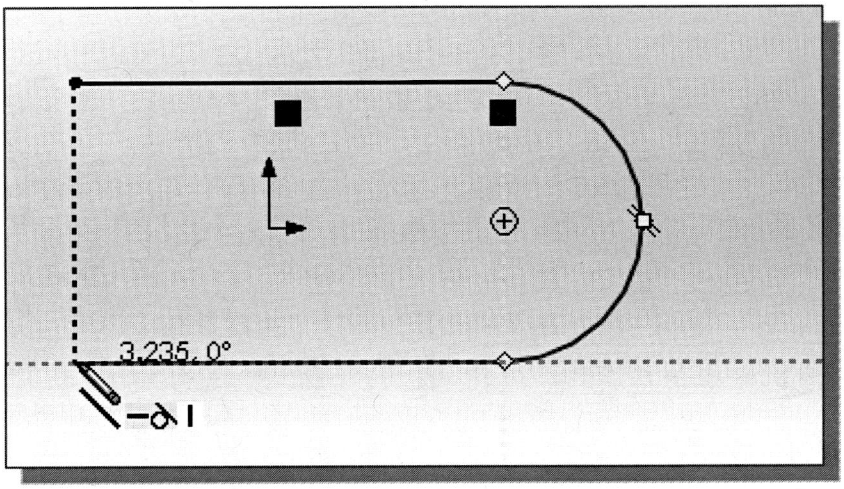

7. Move the cursor on top of the last point of the sketch to activate the **Arc** option. Create another arc on the left to form a closed region as shown.

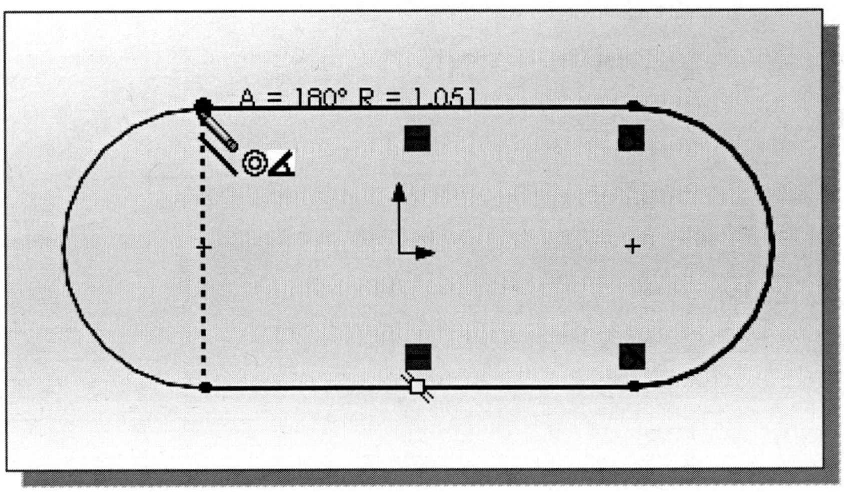

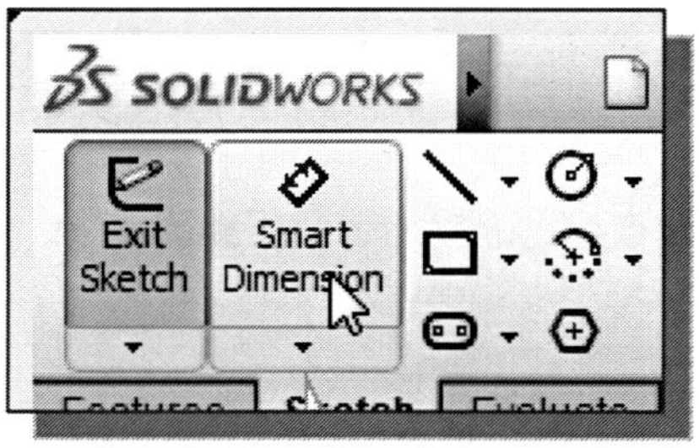

8. Activate the **Smart Dimension** command by clicking once with the left-mouse-button. The **Smart Dimension** command allows us to quickly create and modify dimensions.

9. Select the right arc by left-clicking once on the arc.

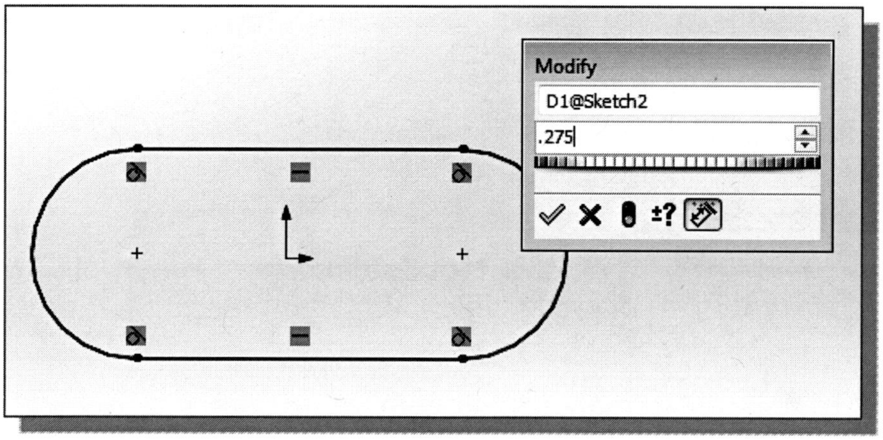

10. Move the graphics cursor to the right of the selected line and left-click to place the dimension. Enter **0.275** to set the radius of the arc.

11. Click on the **OK** button to accept the new dimension.

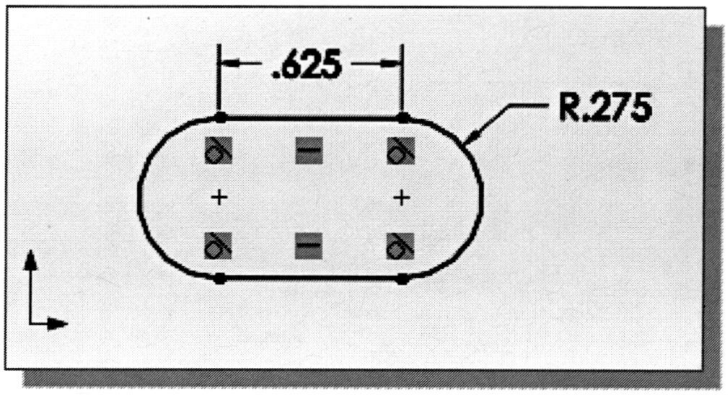

12. On your own, create and modify the center to center distance to **0.625** as shown.

13. Create and modify the *Origin* to center horizontal distance to **0.3125** as shown.

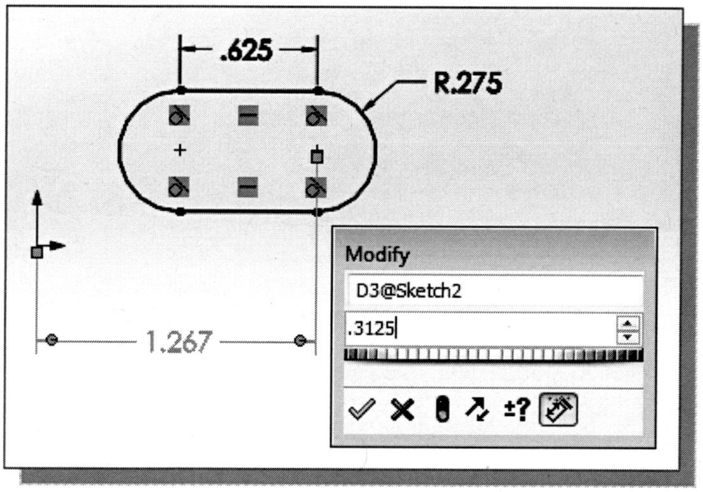

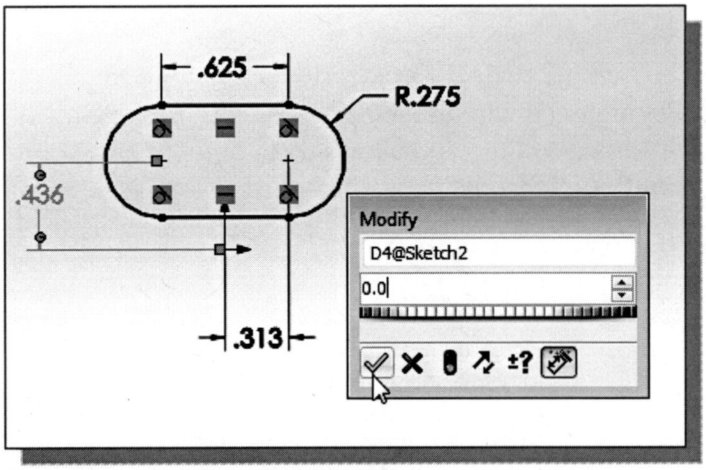

14. Create and modify the *Origin* to center vertical distance to **0.0** as shown.

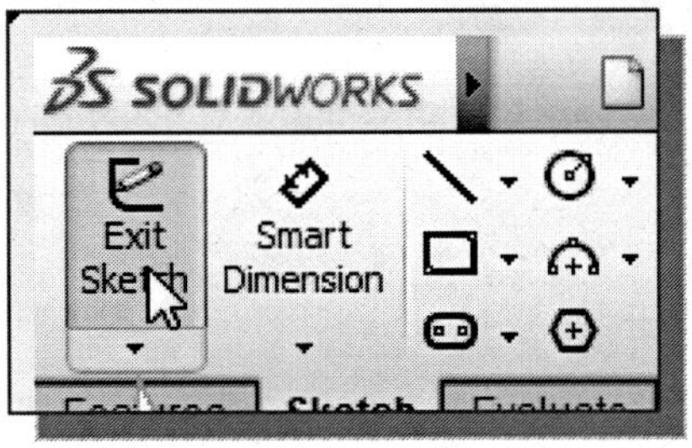

15. Click **Exit Sketch** in the *Sketch* toolbar to end the Sketch mode.

16. In the *Distance* option box, enter **.081** as the total extrusion distance.

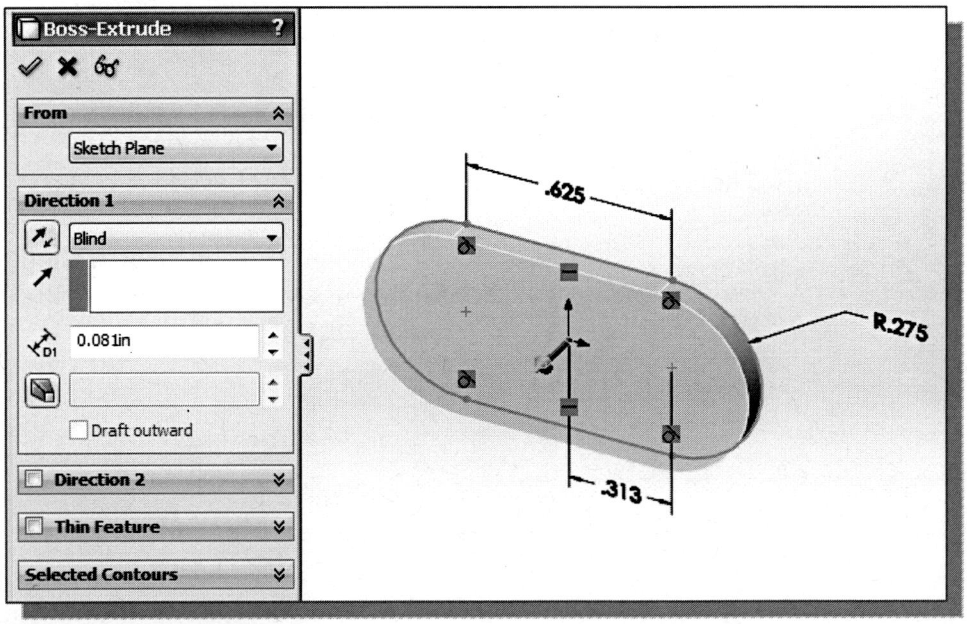

17. Click on the **OK** button to accept the settings and create the base feature.

➢ On your own, use the *Dynamic Viewing* functions to view the 3D model. Also note the extrusion feature is added to the *Model Tree* in the *Feature Manager* area.

Adding the Second Solid Feature

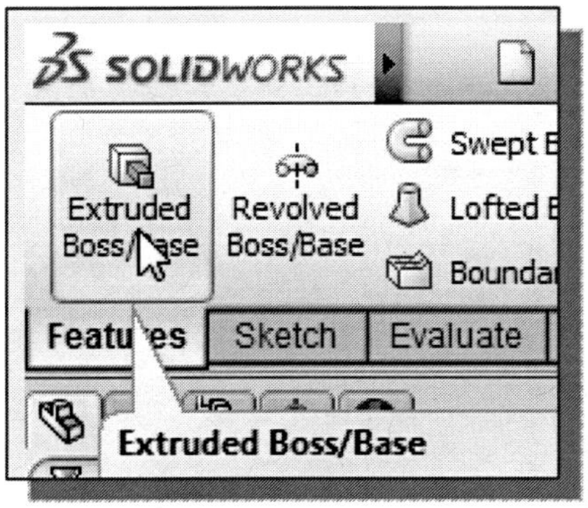

1. In the *Features* toolbar select the **Extruded Boss/ Base** command by clicking once with the left-mouse-button on the icon.

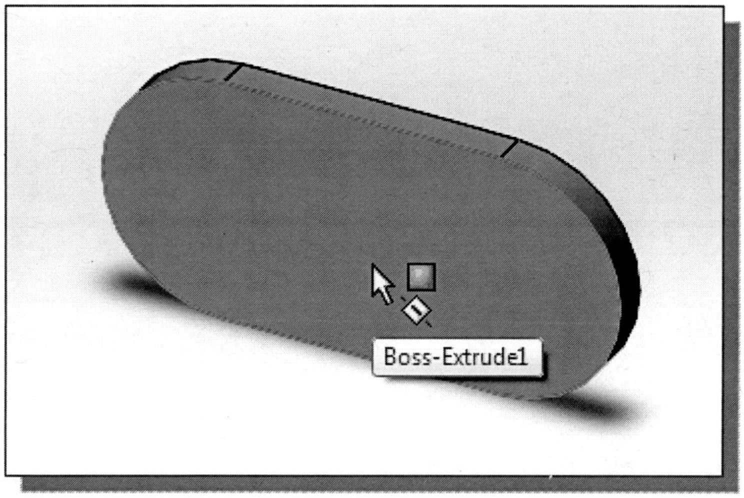

2. Select the **front face** of the model as the sketch plane for the new sketch.

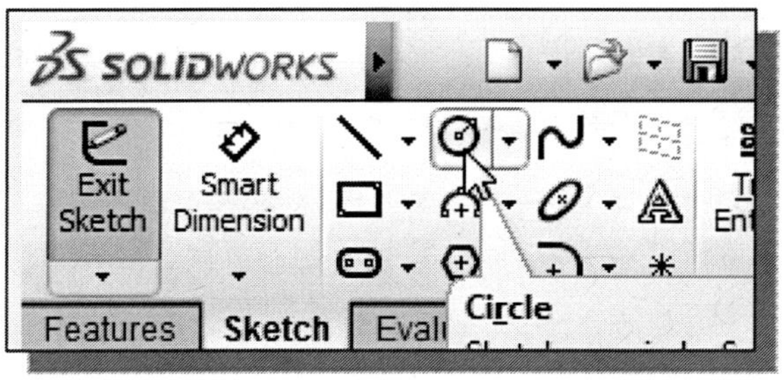

3. Select the **Circle** command by clicking once with the **left-mouse-button** on the icon in the *Sketch* toolbar.

4. Create a circle, with an arbitrary radius, toward the left side as shown.

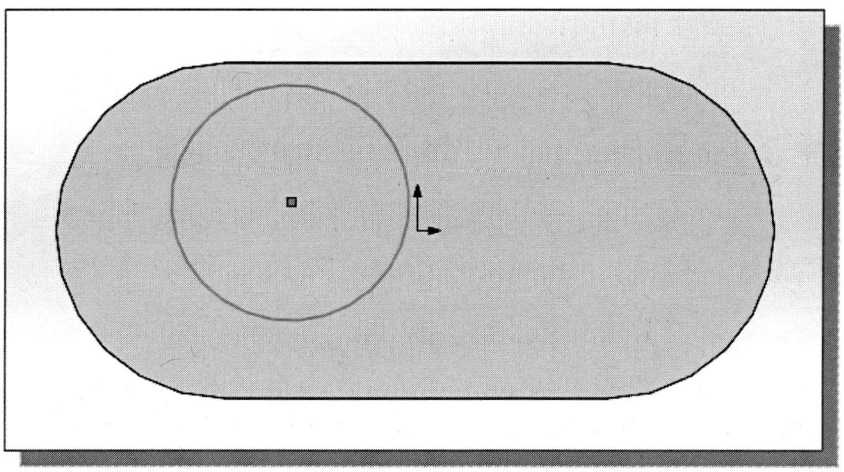

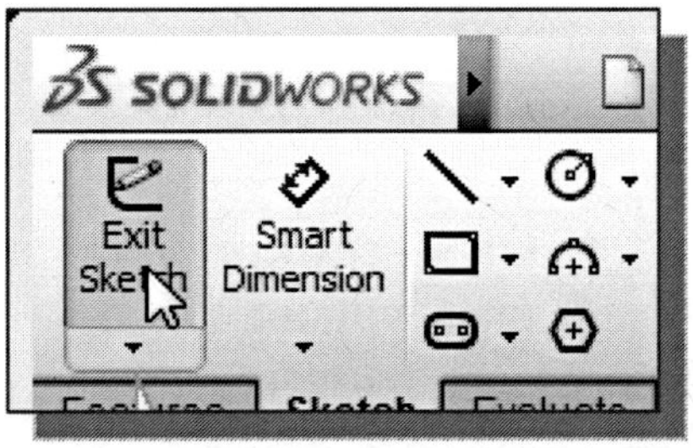

5. Click **Exit Sketch** in the *Sketch* toolbar to end the Sketch mode.

6. In the *Distance* option box, enter **.04** as the extrusion distance.

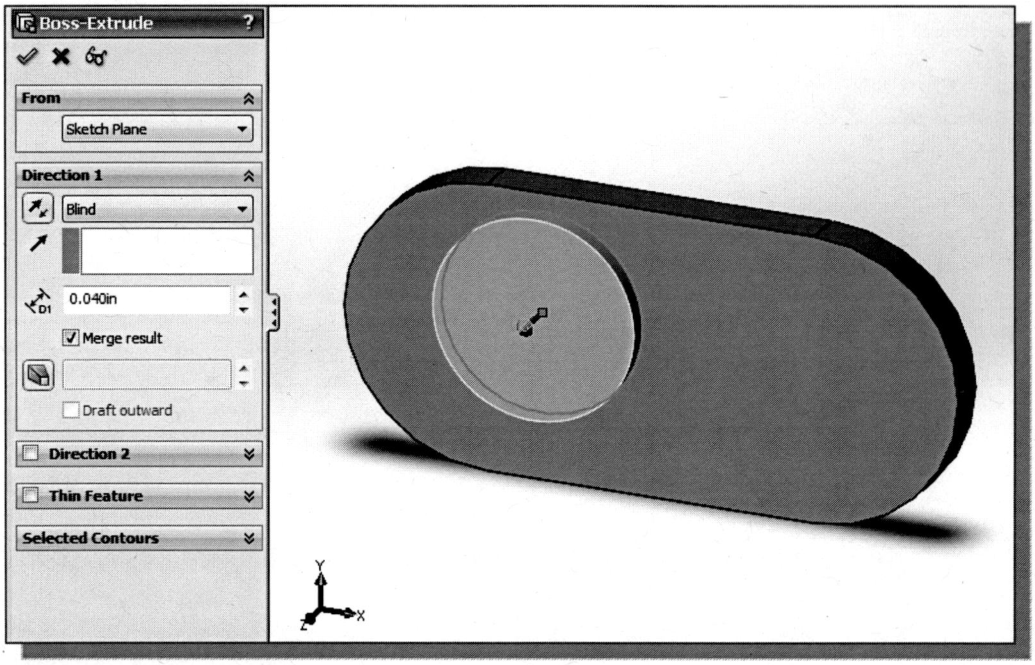

7. Click on the **OK** button to accept the settings and create the base feature.

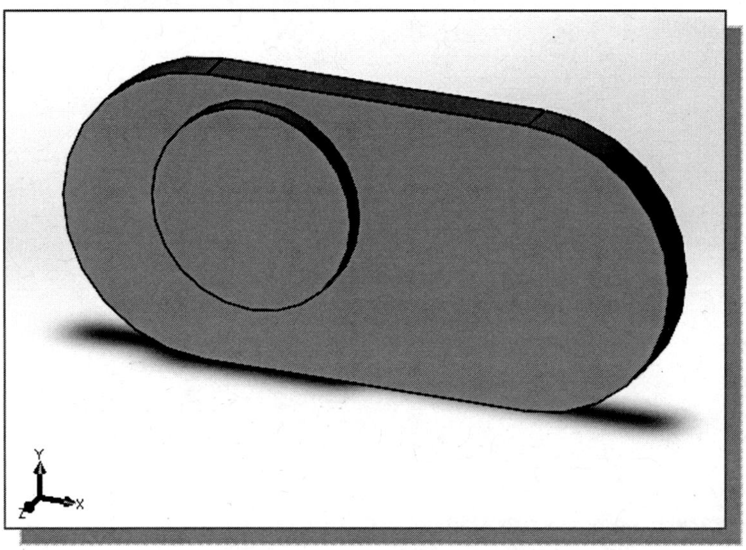

➢ Note that the cylindrical feature is created without adding any dimension to the 2D sketch.

Renaming the Part Features

- Currently, our model contains two extruded features. The feature is highlighted in the display area when we select the feature in the *Feature Manager* window. Each time a new feature is created, that feature is also displayed in the *Model Tree* window. By default, *SolidWorks* will use generic names for part features. However, when we begin to deal with parts with a large number of features, it will be much easier to identify the features using more meaningful names. Two methods can be used to rename the features: 1) **Clicking** twice on the name of the feature and 2) using the **Properties** option. In this example, the use of the first method is illustrated.

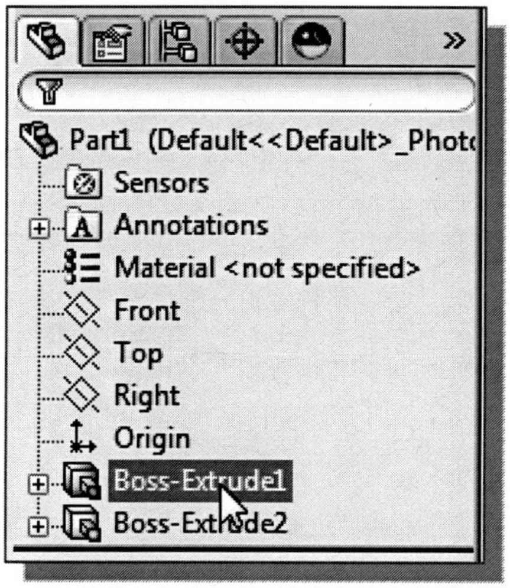

1. Select the first extruded feature in the *Model Feature Manager* area by left-clicking once on the name of the feature, **Boss-Extrude1**. Notice the selected feature is highlighted in the graphics window.

2. Left-mouse-click on the feature name again to enter the *Edit* mode as shown.

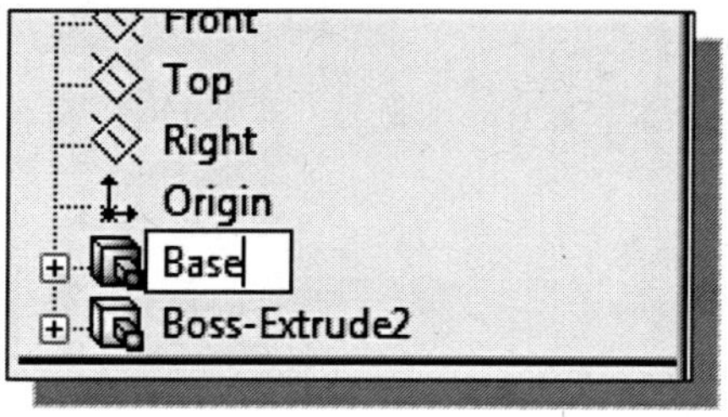

3. Enter **Base** as the new name for the first extruded feature.

4. On your own, rename the second extruded feature to **Center_Cylinder**.

Adjust the Dimensions of the Base Feature

- One of the main advantages of parametric modeling is the ease of performing part modifications at any time in the design process. Part modifications can be done through accessing the features in the history tree. *SolidWorks* remembers the history of a part, including all the rules that were used to create it, so that changes can be made to any operation that was performed to create the part.

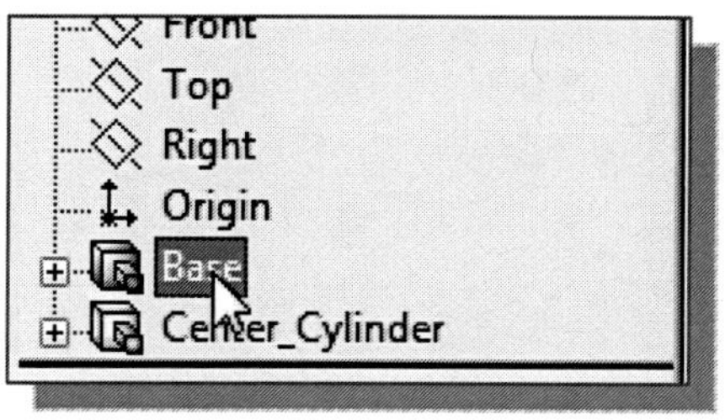

1. Select the first extruded feature, **Base**, in the *Feature Manager* area. Notice the selected feature is also highlighted in the graphics window.

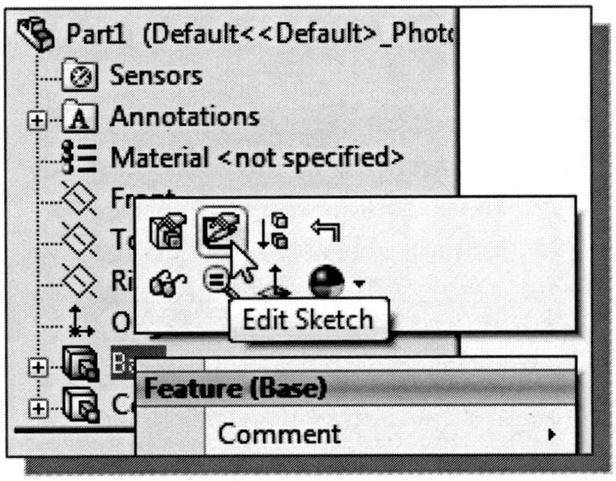

2. Inside the *Feature Manager* area, **right-mouse-click** on the first extruded feature to bring up the option menu and select the **Edit Sketch** option in the pop-up menu.

3. All dimensions used to create the **Base** feature are displayed on the screen. Select the radius of the arc, the **0.275** dimension value, by **double-clicking** on the dimension text as shown below.

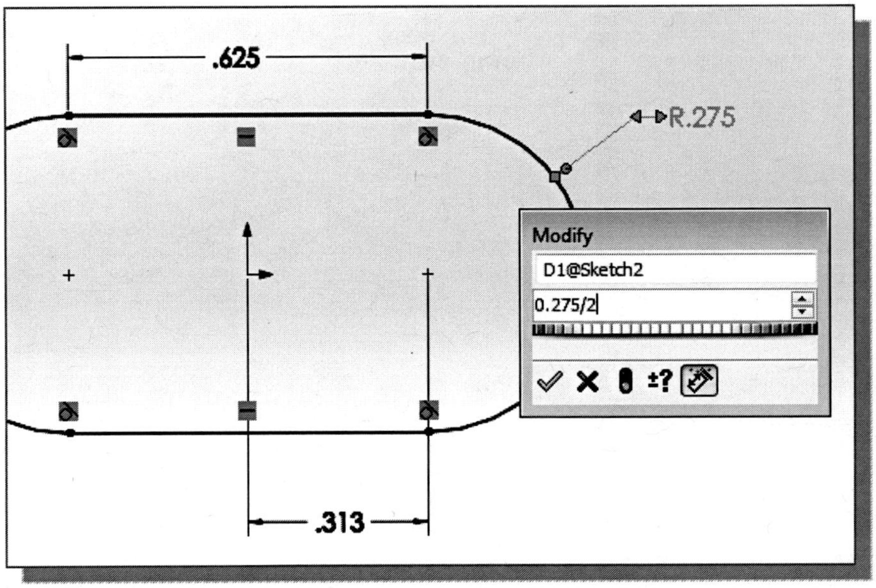

4. Enter **0.275/2** in the *Edit Dimension* window. (Note that *SolidWorks* allows the input of mathematical operations for dimensions.)

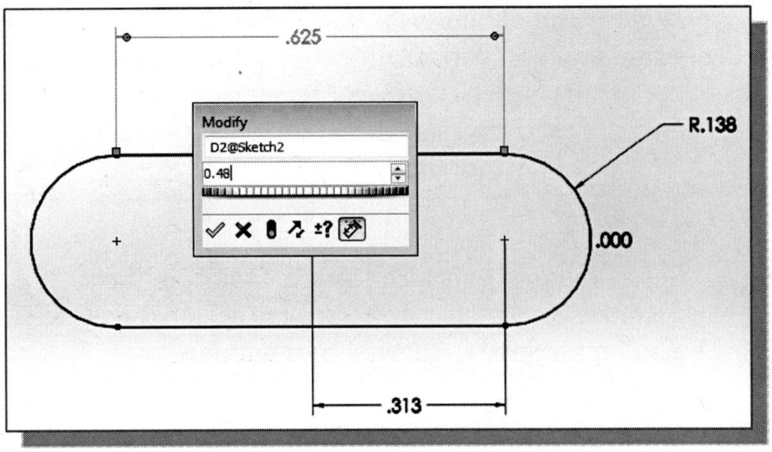

5. On your own, repeat the above steps and modify the *overall length* to **0.48**.

6. On your own, repeat the above steps and modify the *location dimension* to **0.48/2** as shown.

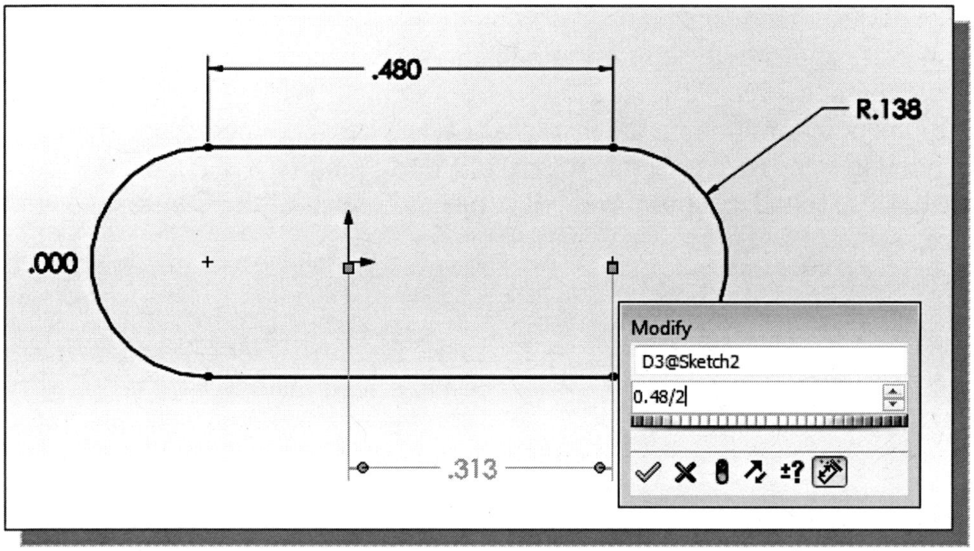

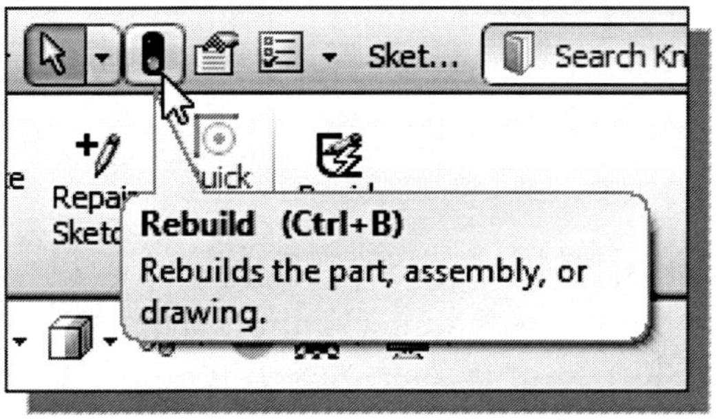

7. Click **Rebuild** in the *Quick Access* toolbar.

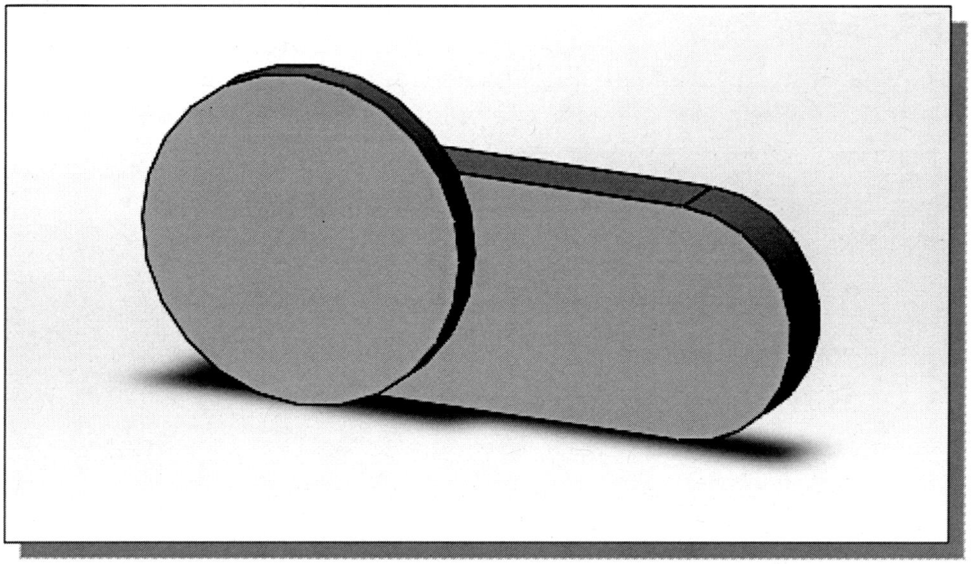

➢ Note that *SolidWorks* updates the model by re-linking all elements used to create the model. Any problems or conflicts that occur will also be displayed during the updating process.

History-Based Part Modifications

- *SolidWorks* uses the *history-based part modification* approach, which enables us to make modifications to the appropriate features and re-link the rest of the history tree without having to reconstruct the model from scratch. We can think of it as going back to the point of defining the original 2D sketches, and modifying some aspects of the modeling steps used to create the part. We can modify any feature we have created. As a second example, we will adjust the sketch of the Center_Cylinder feature.

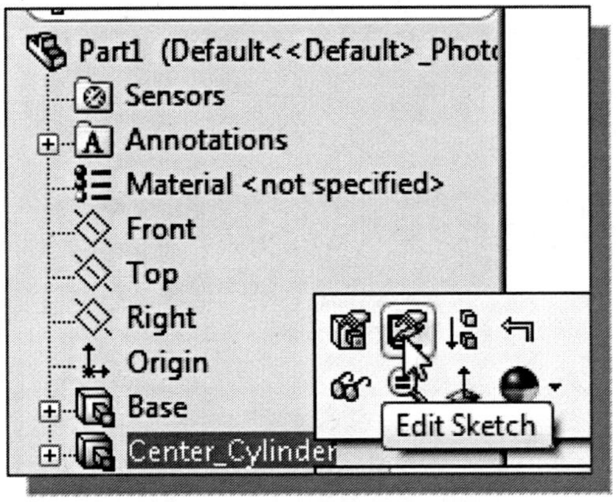

1. In the *Feature Manager* window, select the last extruded feature, **Center_Cylinder**, by left-clicking once on the name of the feature.

2. Select **Edit Sketch** in the pop-up menu. Notice we are returned to the *2D sketch* mode of the **Center_Cylinder** feature.

3. Activate the **Smart Dimension** command by clicking once with the left-mouse-button. The Smart Dimension command allows us to quickly create and modify dimensions.

4. On your own, create and modify the three dimensions, diameter **0.241**, and two location dimensions to align the center to the *Origin* as shown in the figure.

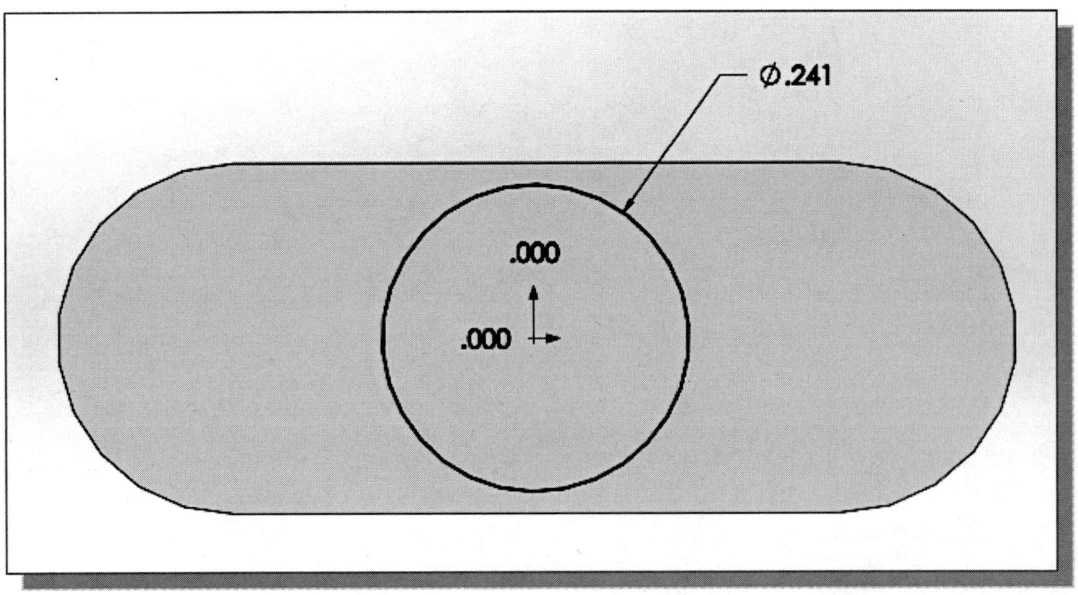

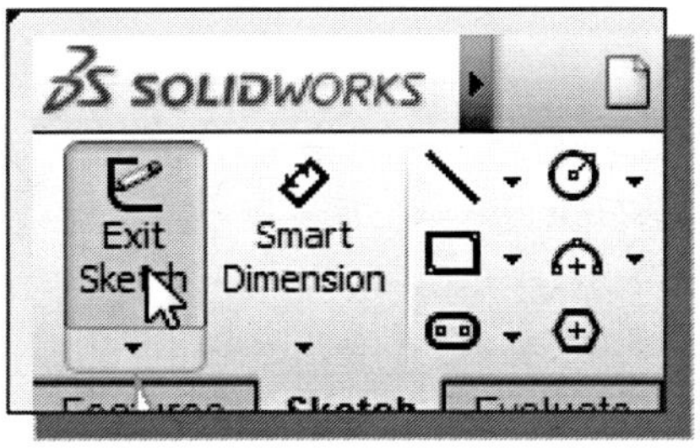

5. Click **Exit Sketch** in the *Sketch* toolbar to end the *Sketch* mode.

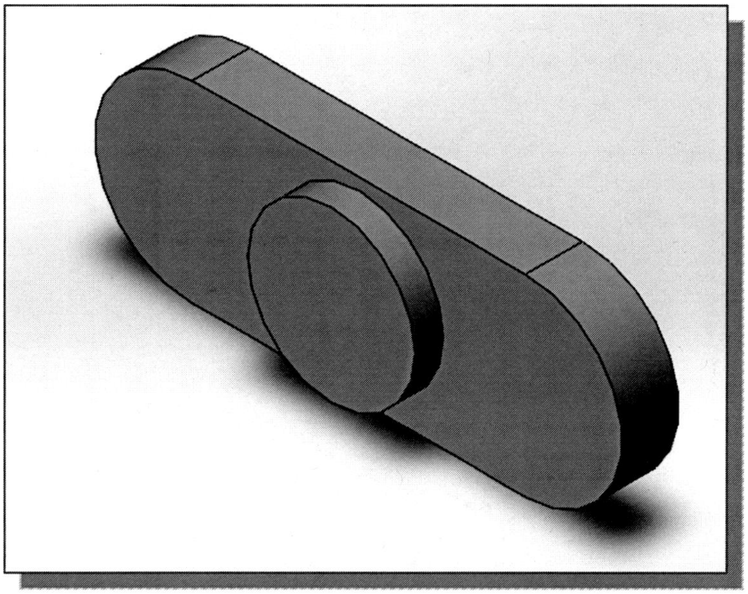

Add a Placed Feature

- In *SolidWorks*, there are two types of geometric features: **placed features** and **sketched features**. The last feature we created is a *sketched feature*, where we created a rough sketch and performed an extrusion operation. We can also create a feature without creating a 2D sketch, which is known a *placed feature*. A *placed feature* is a feature that does not need a sketch and can be created automatically. In parametric modeling, holes, fillets, chamfers, and shells are all placed features.

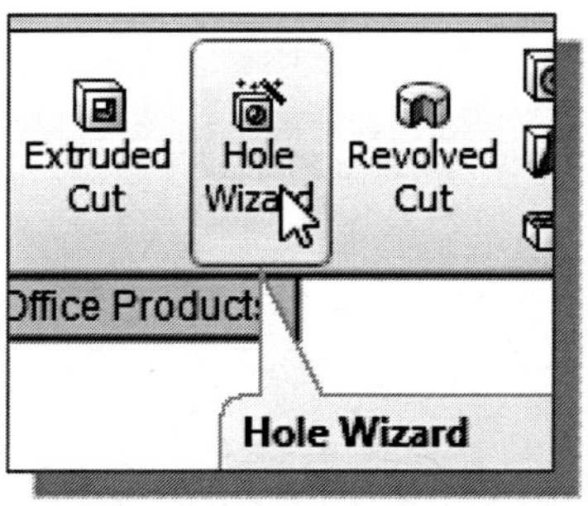

1. In the *Features* toolbar, select the **Hole Wizard** command by clicking the left-mouse-button on the icon.

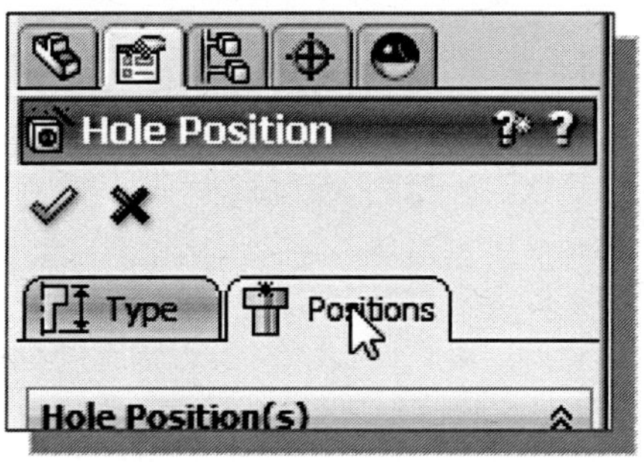

2. In the *Hole Specification Property Manager*, select the **Positions** panel by clicking once with the left-mouse-button on the **Positions** tab as shown. The Positions tab allows you to locate the hole on a planar or non-planar face.

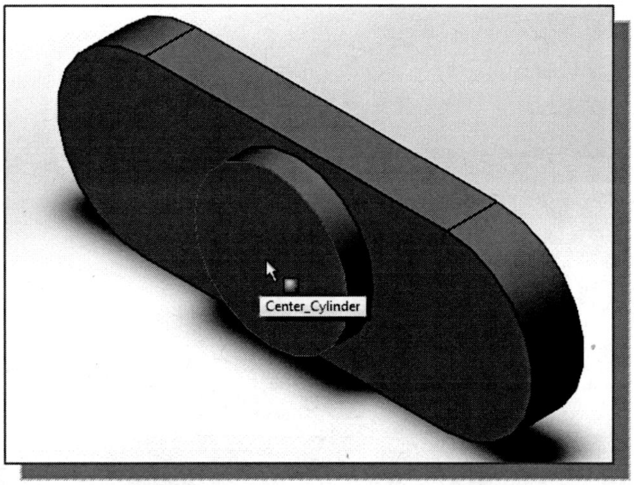

3. Move the cursor over the **front surface** of the cylinder feature. Notice that the surface is highlighted. Click the **left-mouse-button** to select a location inside the surface as the position for the hole.

4. Click on the *Origin* to align the hole feature as **Concentric** as shown.

5. In *Hole Property Manager*, select the **Type** panel by clicking once with the left-mouse-button on the **Type** tab as shown.

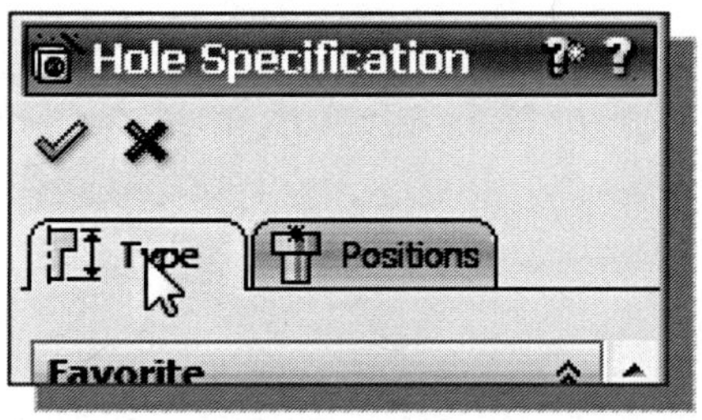

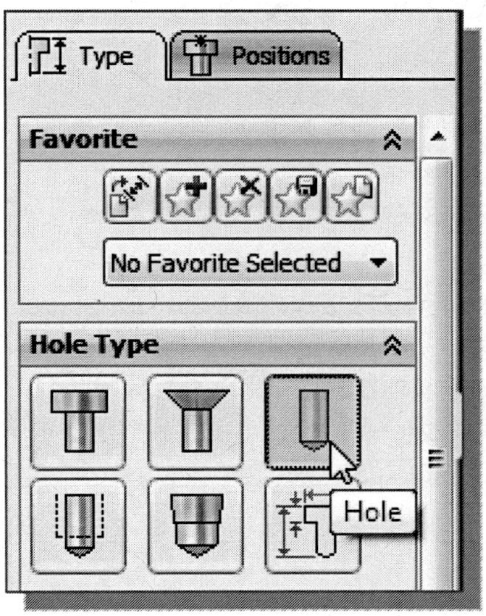

6. Set the *Hole Type* to **Straight Hole** as shown.

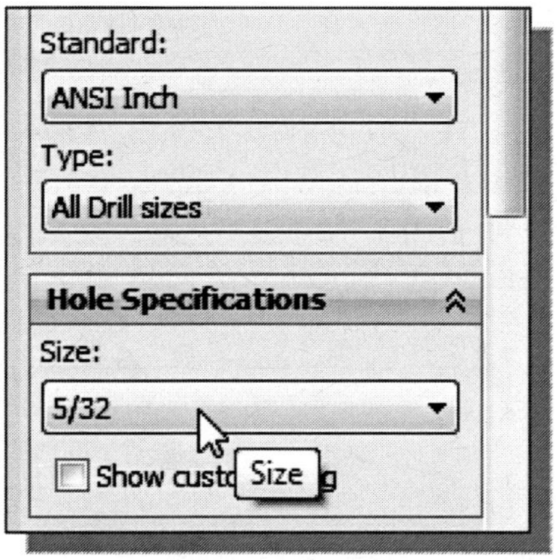

7. Set the *hole diameter* to **5/32** as shown.

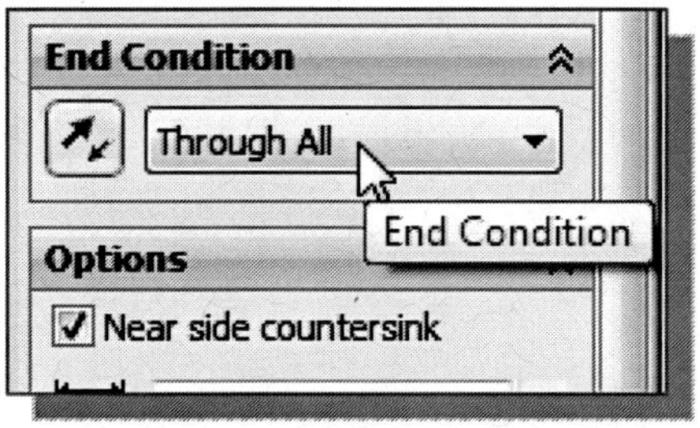

8. Set the *End Condition* to **Through All** as shown.

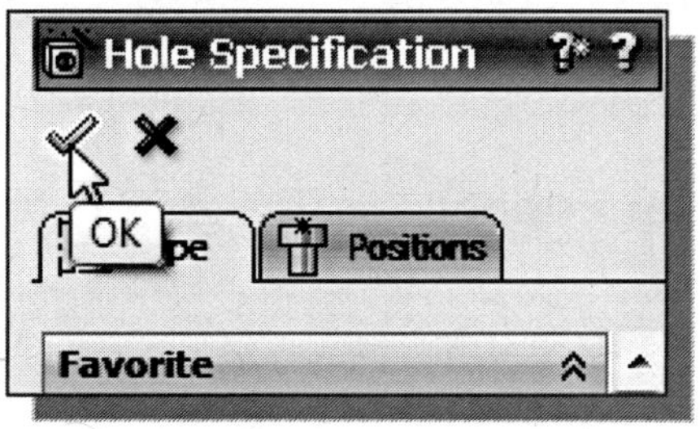

9. Click **OK** to accept the settings and create the *hole* feature.

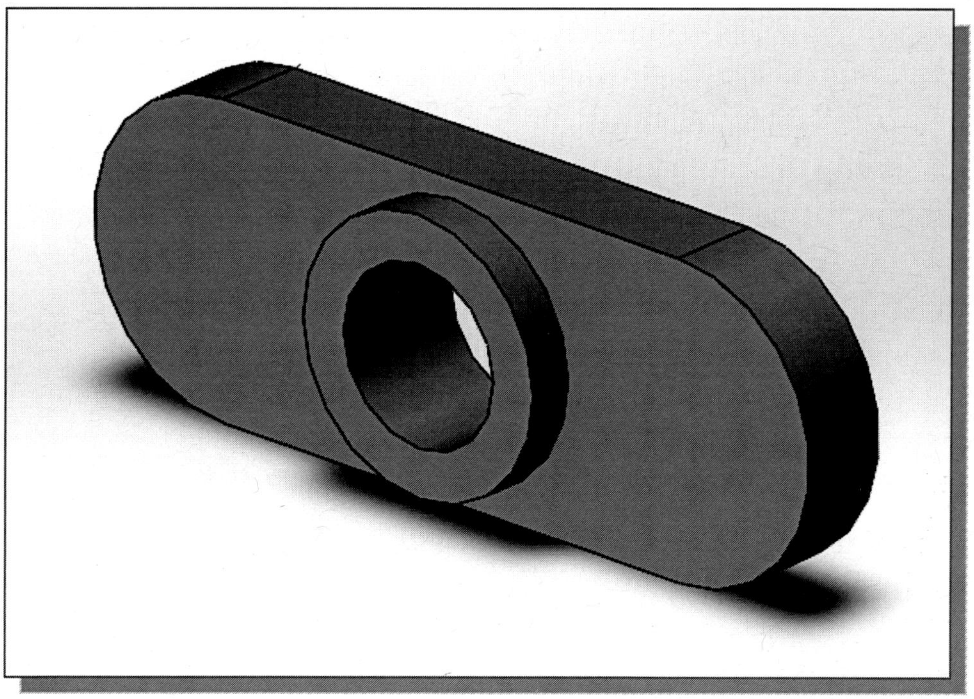

Create an Offset Extrude Feature

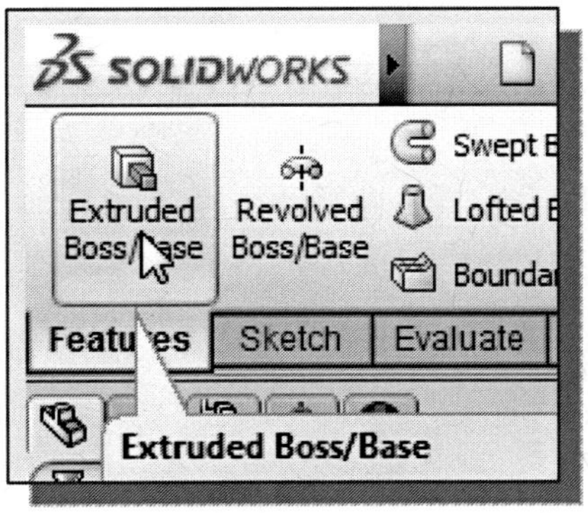

1. In the *Features* toolbar select the **Extruded Boss/ Bass** command by left-clicking once on the icon.

2. Pick the **back face** of the solid as shown.

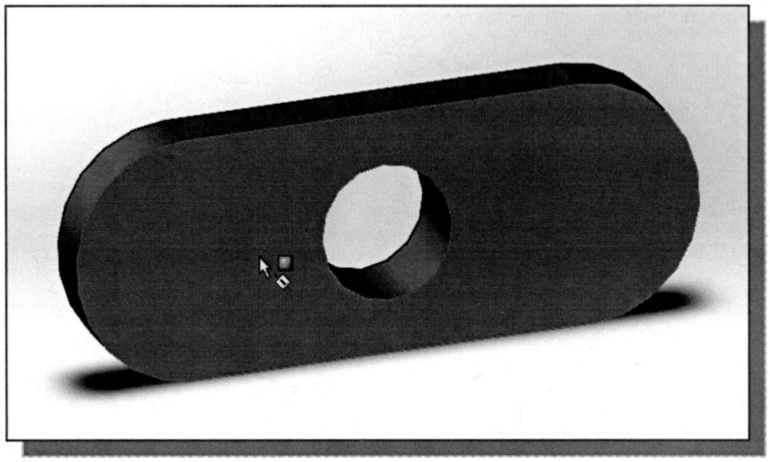

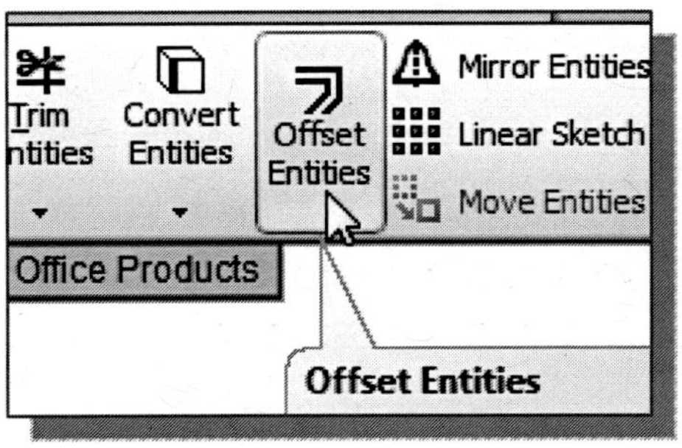

3. Click on the **Offset Entities** icon in the *Sketch* panel.

4. Select the **back face** of the 3D model. *SolidWorks* will automatically select all of the connecting outer edges to form a closed region, and notice an offset copy of the outline is displayed.

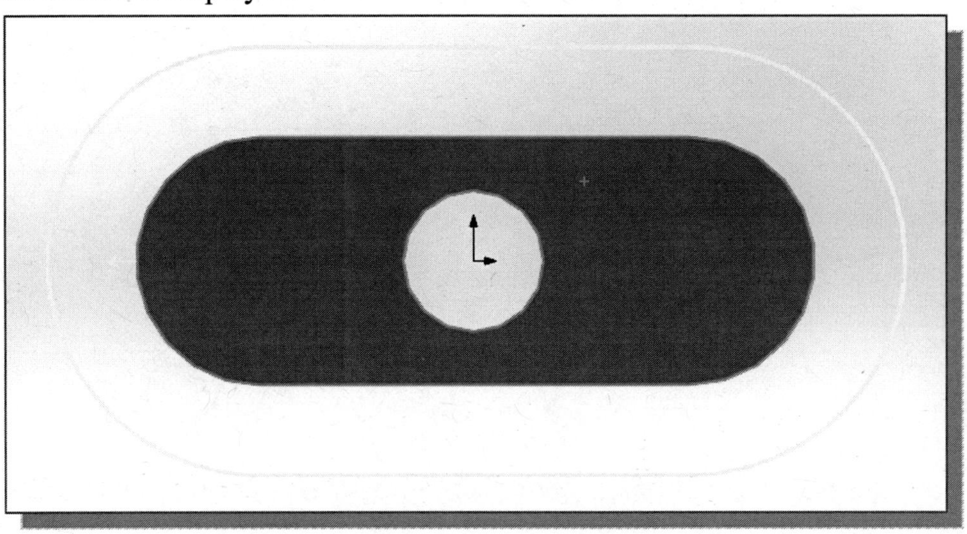

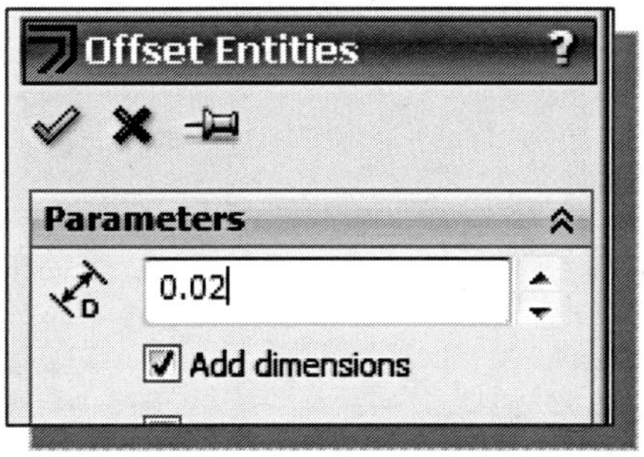

5. Modify the *offset dimension* to **0.02** as shown in the figure.

6. Click **OK** to accept the settings and create the offset entities.

7. On your own, repeat the above steps and create another offset geometry; set the offset dimension to **0.048** as shown. (Use the **Reverse** option to set the direction.)

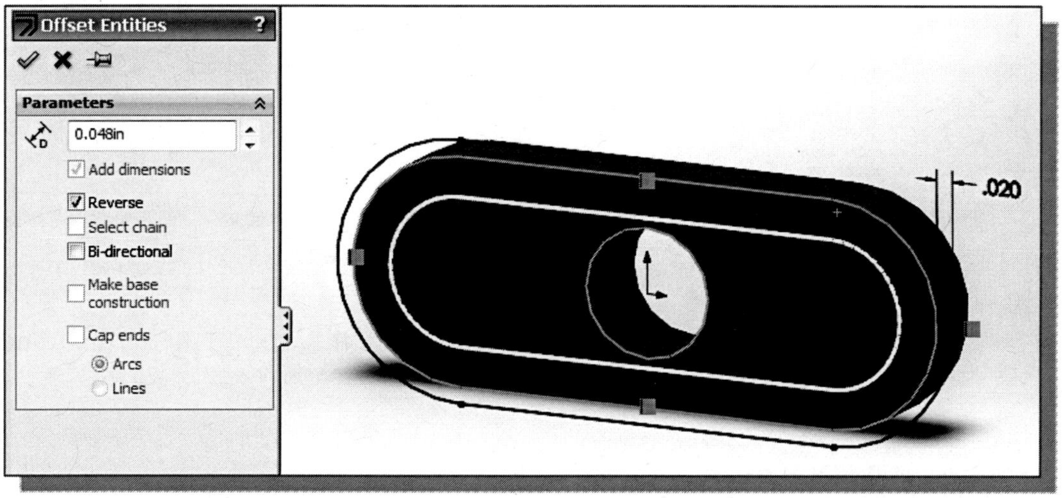

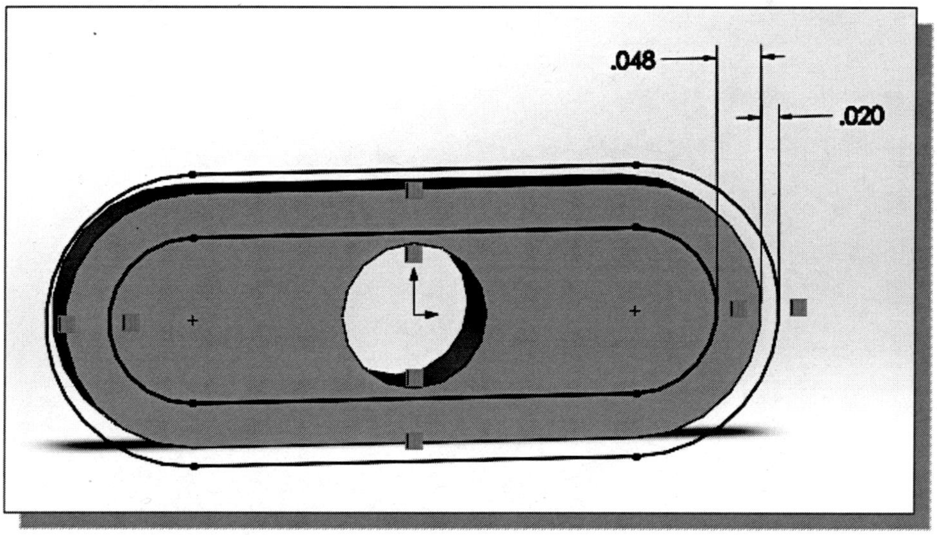

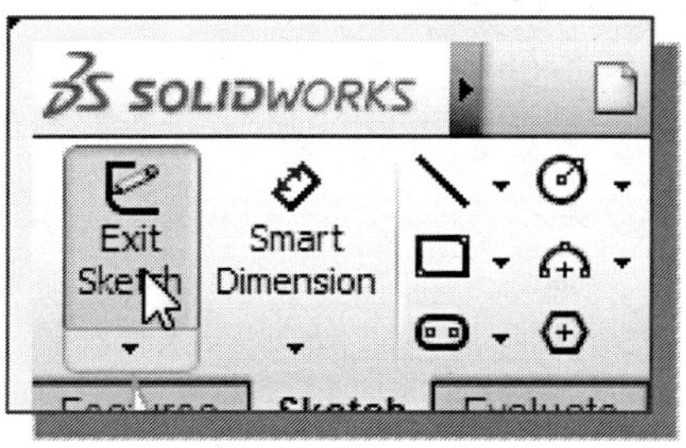

8. Click **Exit Sketch** in the *Sketch* toolbar to end the *Sketch* mode.

➢ Note the two offset dimensions can be used to control the two sets of offset geometry.

9. In the *Distance* option box, enter **.078** as the extrusion distance.

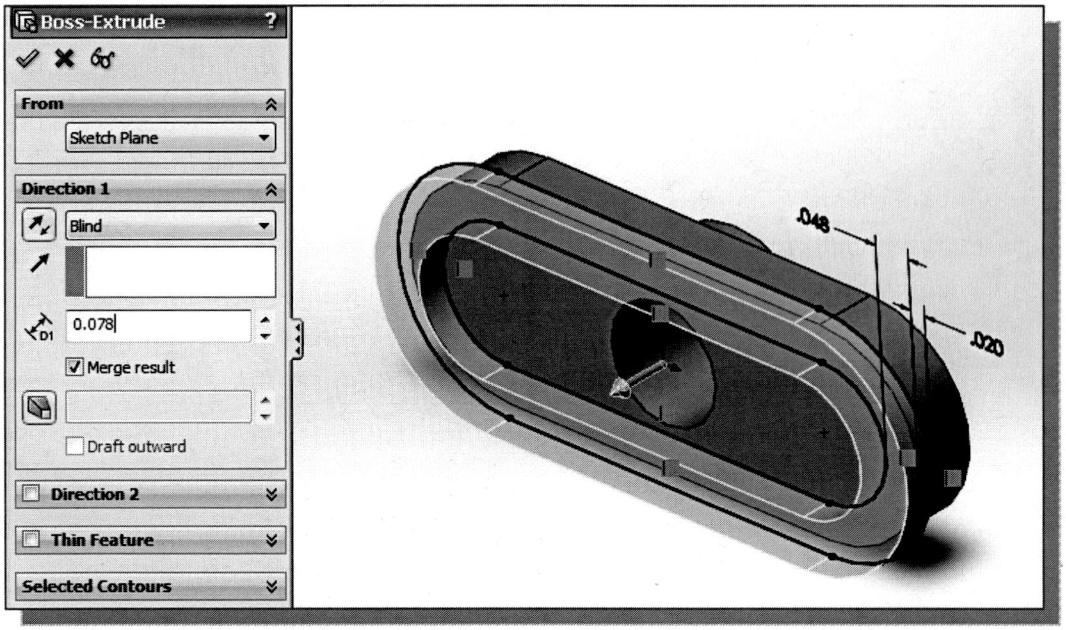

10. Confirm the extrusion direction is toward the back of the base feature as shown.

11. Click on the **OK** button to accept the settings and create the base feature.

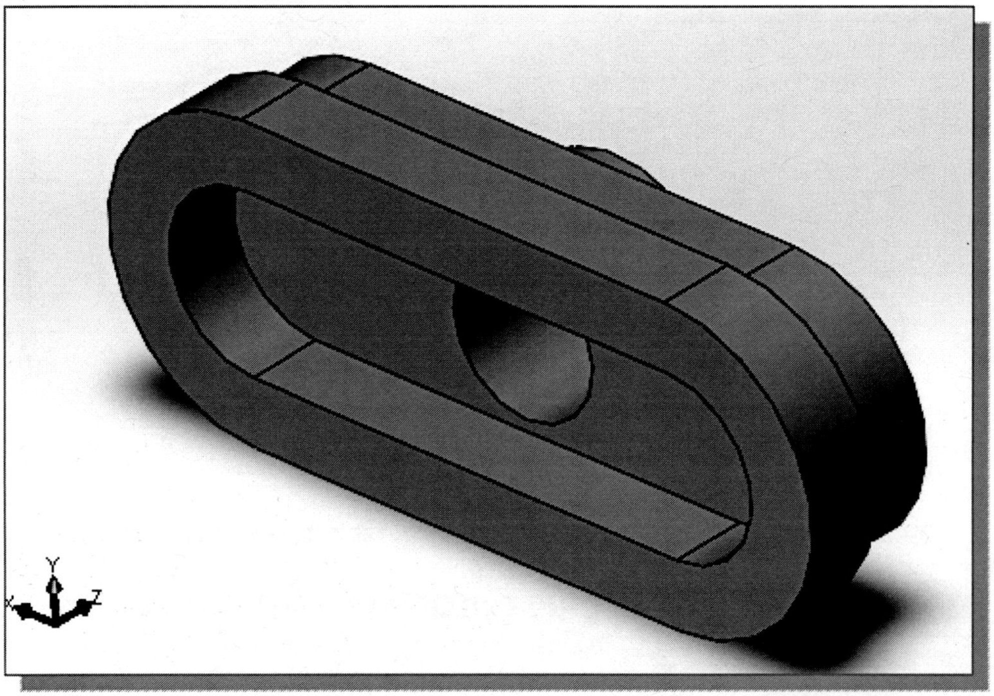

Adding another Hole Feature

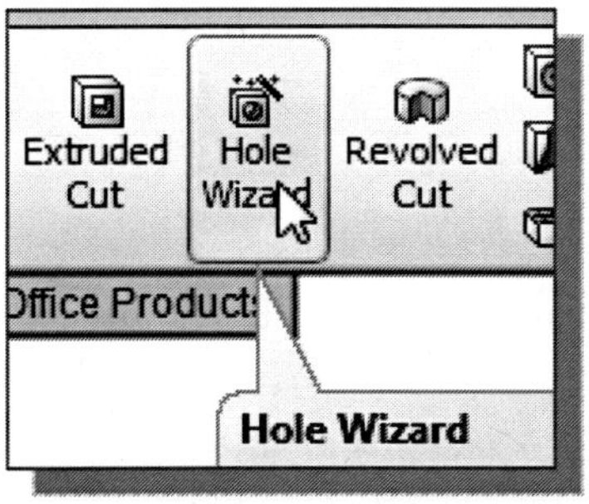

1. In the *Features* toolbar, select the **Hole Wizard** command by clicking the left-mouse-button on the icon.

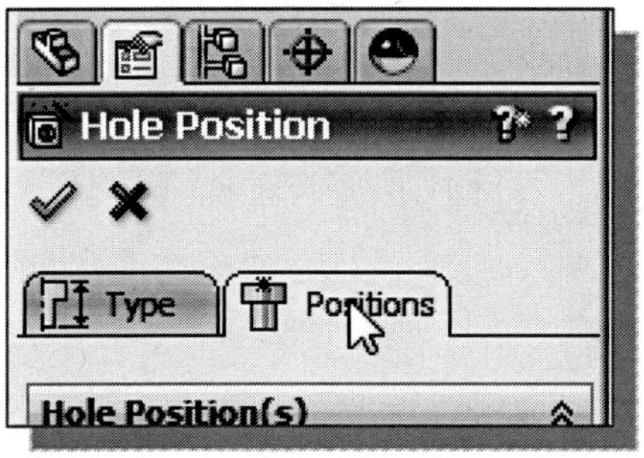

2. In the *Hole Specification Property Manager*, select the **Positions** panel by clicking once with the left-mouse-button on the **Positions** tab as shown. The Positions tab allows you to locate the hole on a planar or non-planar face.

3. Pick the Front Plane of the **Base** feature as the placement plane as shown.

4. Move the cursor on top of the right circular edge and notice the different alignment points are displayed.

5. Click the **center point** to align the *hole* feature.

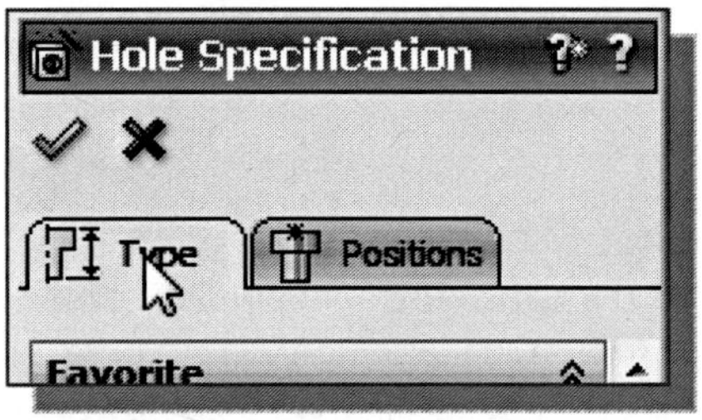

6. In *Hole Property Manager*, select the **Type** panel by clicking once with the left-mouse-button on the **Type** tab as shown.

7. Set the *Hole Type* to **Straight Hole** as shown.

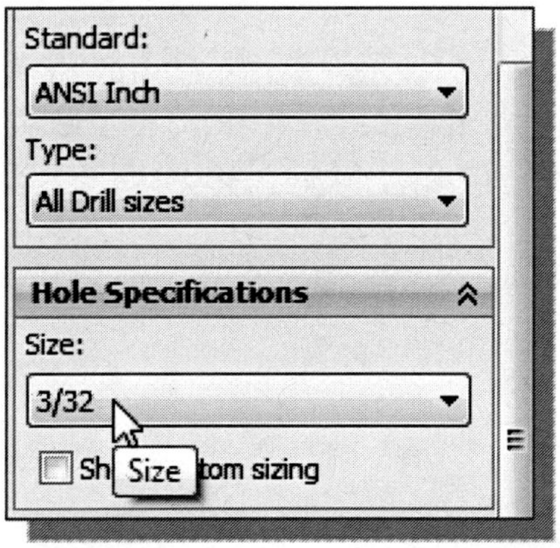

8. Set the *hole diameter* to **3/32** as shown.

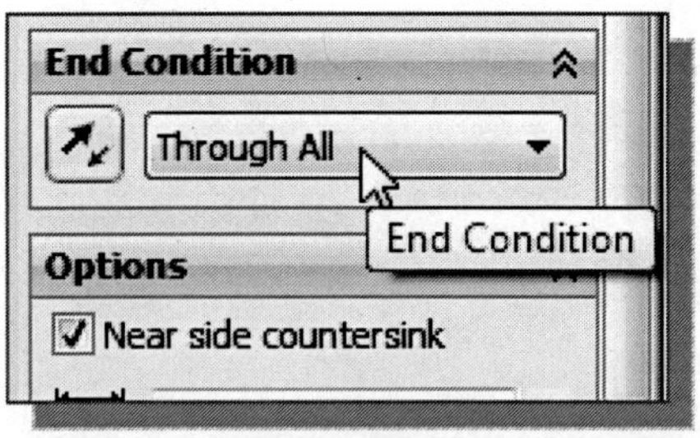

9. Set the *End Condition* to **Through All** as shown.

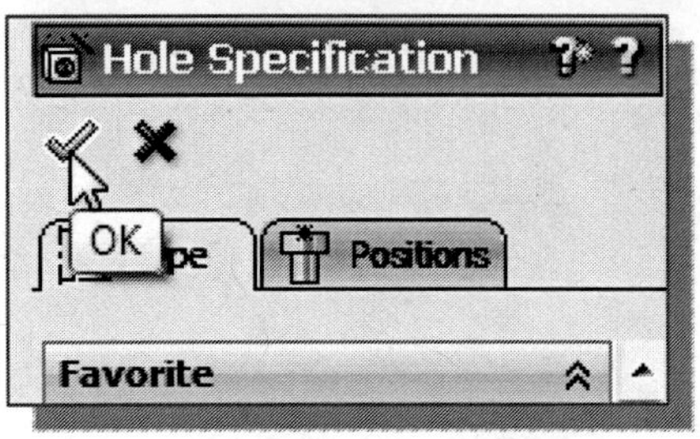

10. Click **OK** to accept the settings and create the *hole* feature.

11. On your own, repeat the above steps and create another *hole* feature on the other side as shown.

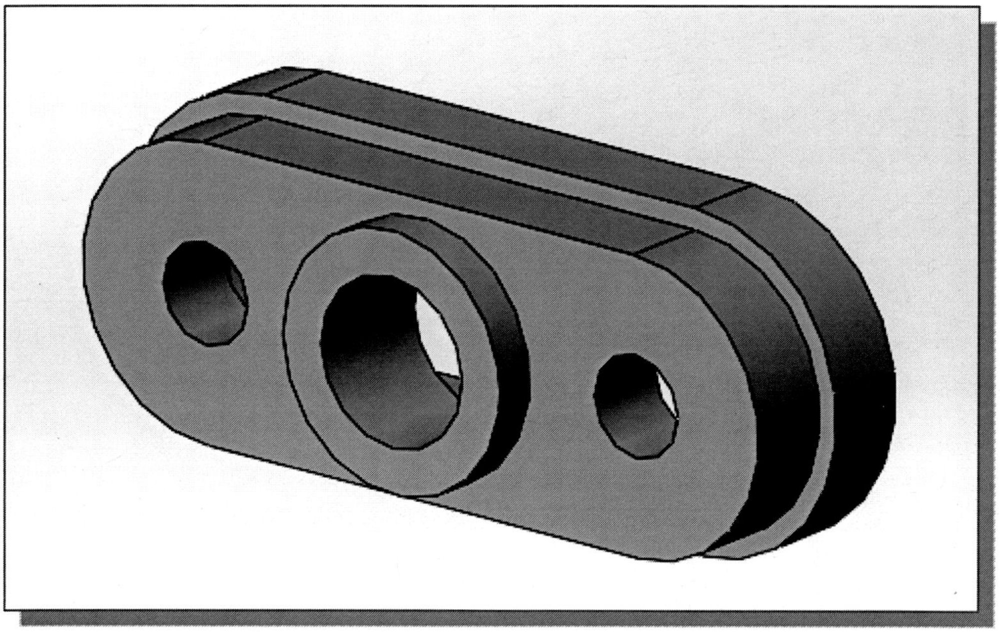

Assigning and Calculating the Associated Physical Properties

❖ *SolidWorks* models have properties called ***iProperties***. The *iProperties* can be used to create reports, and update assembly bills of materials, drawing parts lists, and other information. With *iProperties*, we can also set and calculate physical properties for a part or assembly using the material library. This allows us to examine the physical properties of the model, such as weight or center of gravity.

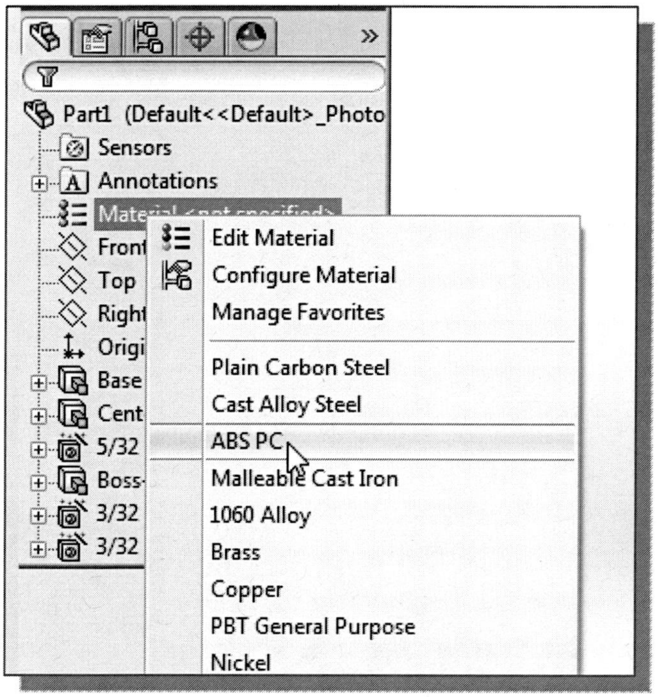

1. In the *Feature Manager*, **right-mouse-click** once on the ***part name*** to bring up the option menu.

2. In the pop-up list, select **ABS PC** (Polycarbonate/Acrylonitrile Butadiene Styrene Plastic) as the **Material** type.

- Note some of the more commonly used materials are listed in the pop-up menu.

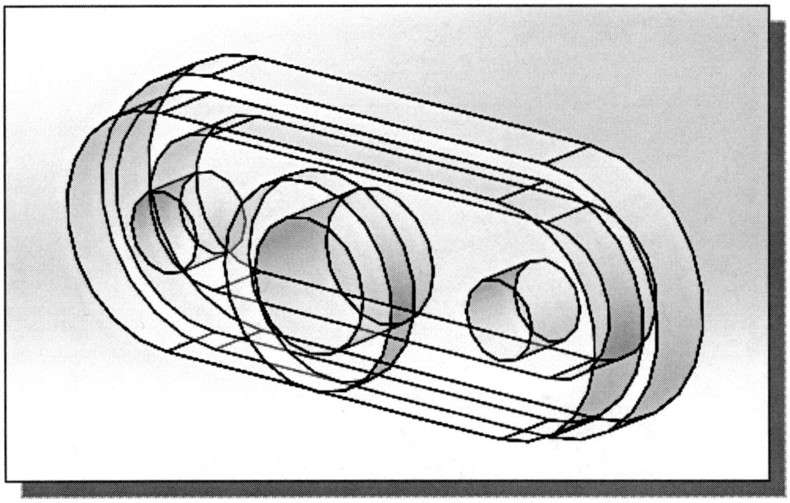

- Notice the display of the model is adjusted based on the assigned material type.

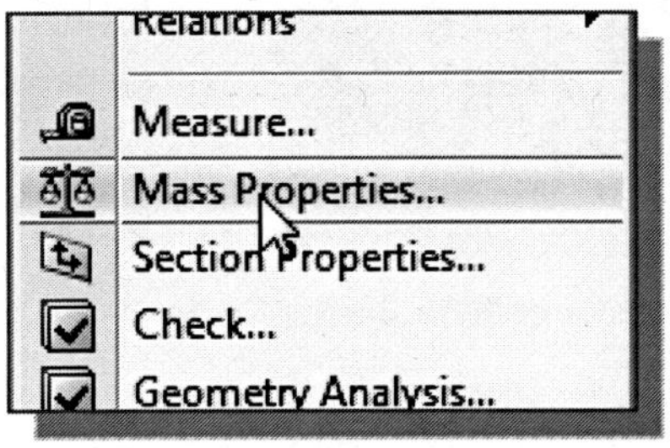

3. Activate the **Mass Properties** command through the **Tools** pull-down menu.

- Note the *Mass Properties* area now has many of the properties information, such as the *Mass*, *Area*, *Volume* and the *Center of Gravity* of the model, based on the assigned material.

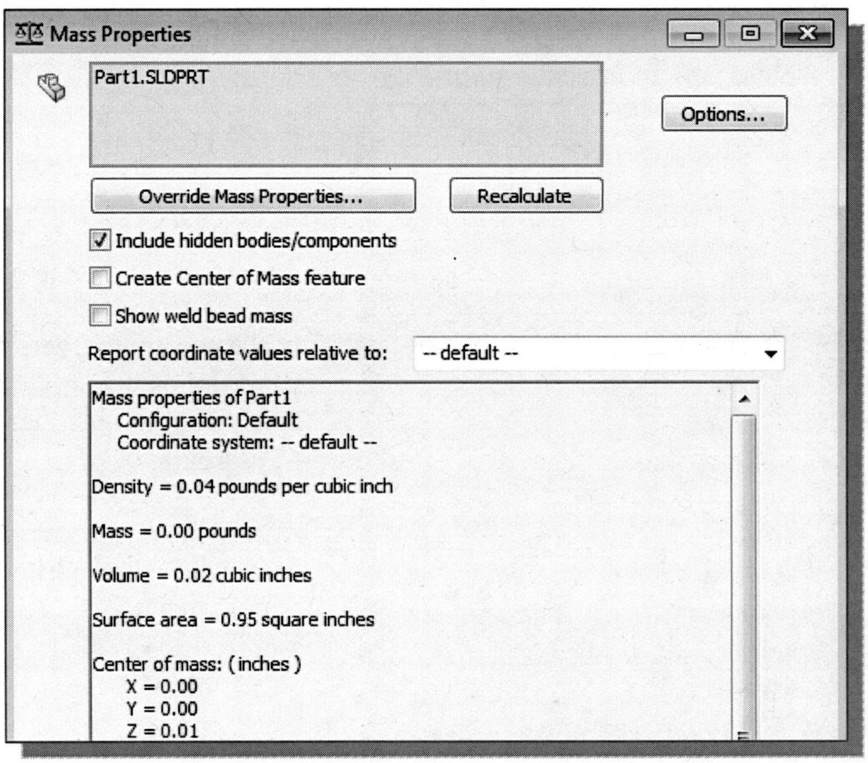

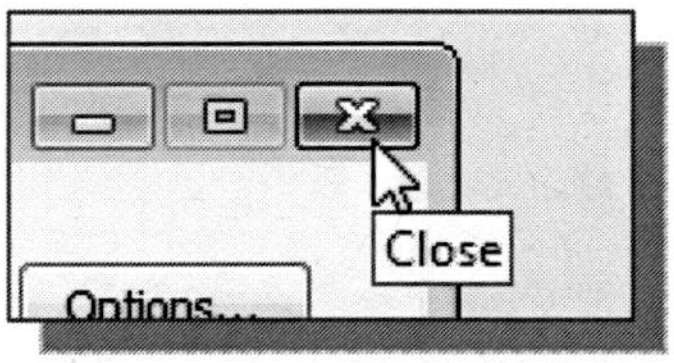

4. Click on the **Close** button to exit the *Mass Properties* dialog box.

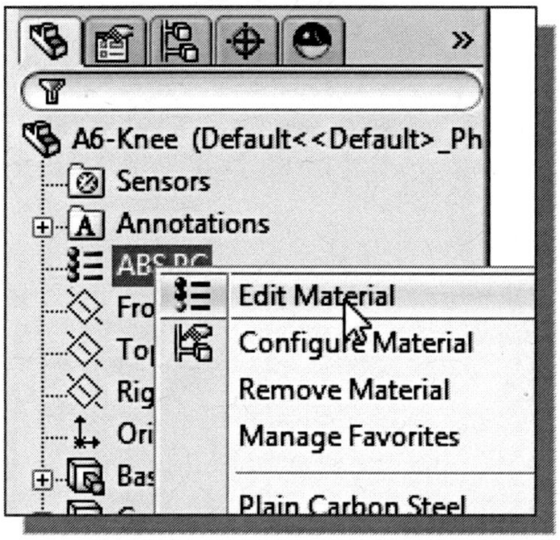

5. In the *Feature Manager*, **right-mouse-click** once on the ***material name***, **ABS PC**, to bring up the option menu; then pick **Edit Material** in the pop-up menu.

❖ Note the *Material Properties* of the selected material is displayed and can be edited. Note that *SolidWorks* provides a library of commonly used materials, as listed to the left panel.

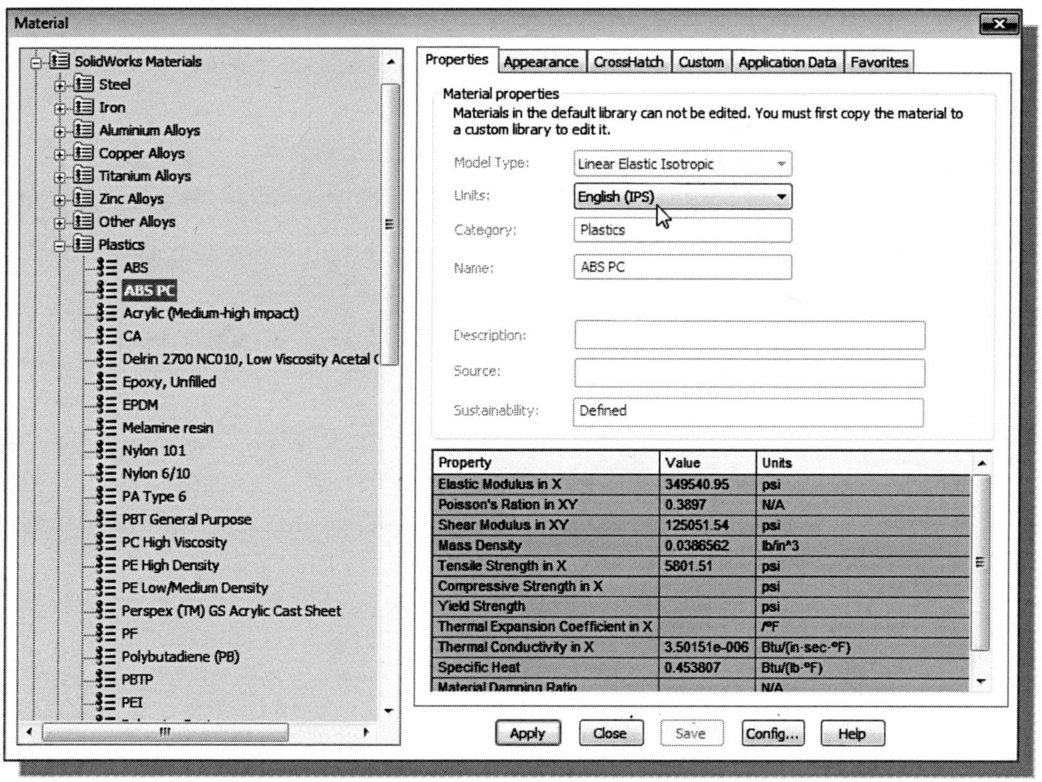

6. On your own, select other types of material as the *Material* type and compare the differences in using the different materials.

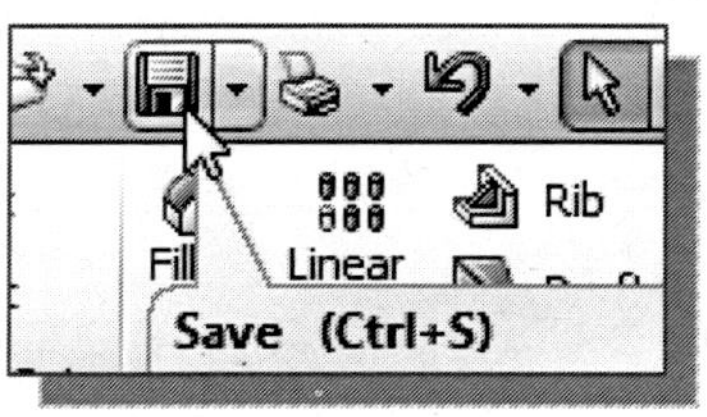

7. On your own, **Save** the model as **A6-Knee** in the *Mechanical Tiger* project folder.

Questions:

1. What are stored in the *SolidWorks History Tree*?

2. When extruding, what is the difference between *Distance* and *Through All*?

3. Describe the *history-based part modification* approach.

4. What determines how a model reacts when other features in the model change?

5. Describe the steps to rename existing features.

6. Describe two methods available in *SolidWorks* to *modify the dimension values* of parametric sketches.

7. Create *History Tree sketches* showing the steps you plan to use to create the two models shown on the following pages:

Ex.3)

Ex.4)

Exercises: (All dimensions are in inches.)

1. **Latch Clip** (thickness: **0.25** inches. Material: **Cast Iron**. Mass and Volume =?)

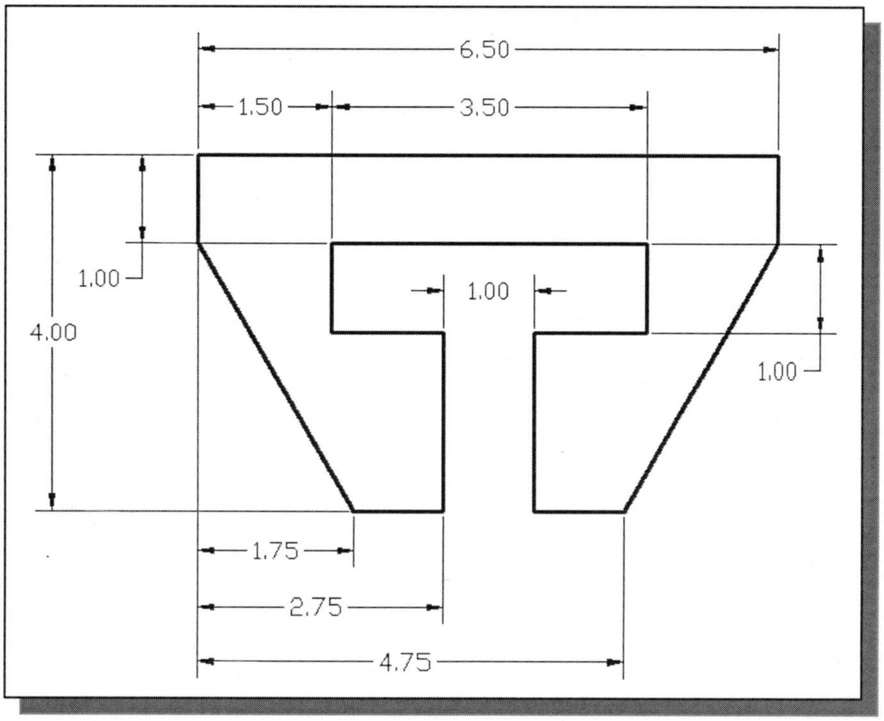

2. **Guide Plate** (thickness: **0.25** inches. Boss height **0.125** inches.)

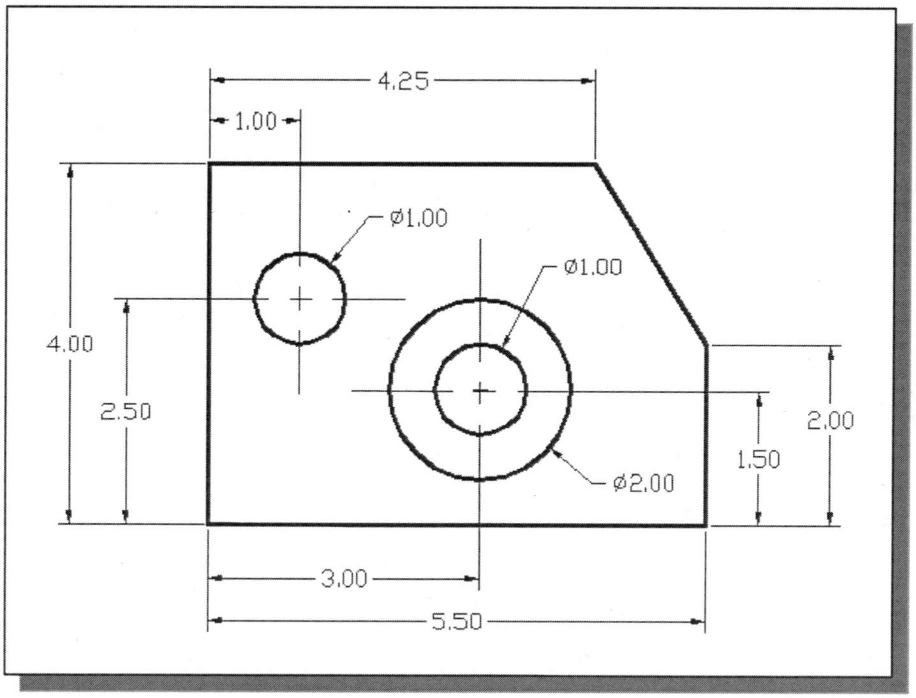

3. **Swivel Yoke** (Material: **Aluminum-6061**. Weight and Volume =?)

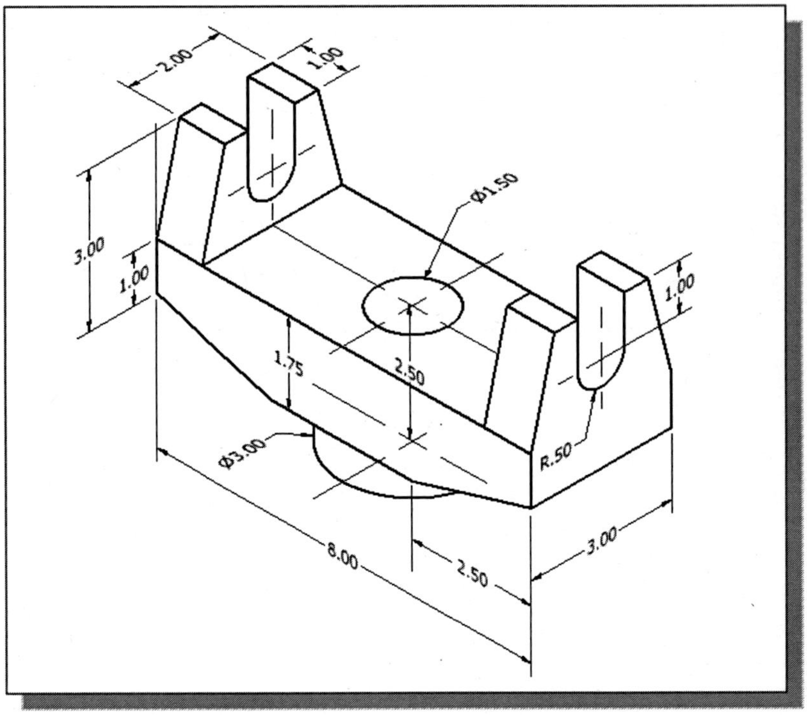

4. **Hanger Jaw**

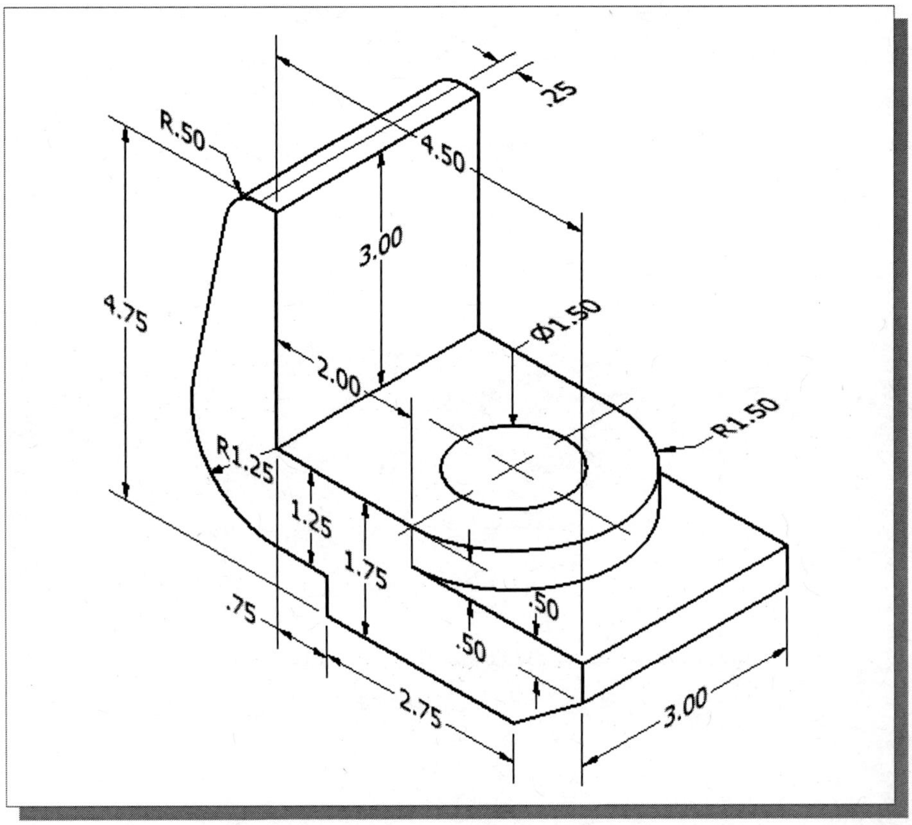

Chapter 4
Parametric Constraints Fundamentals

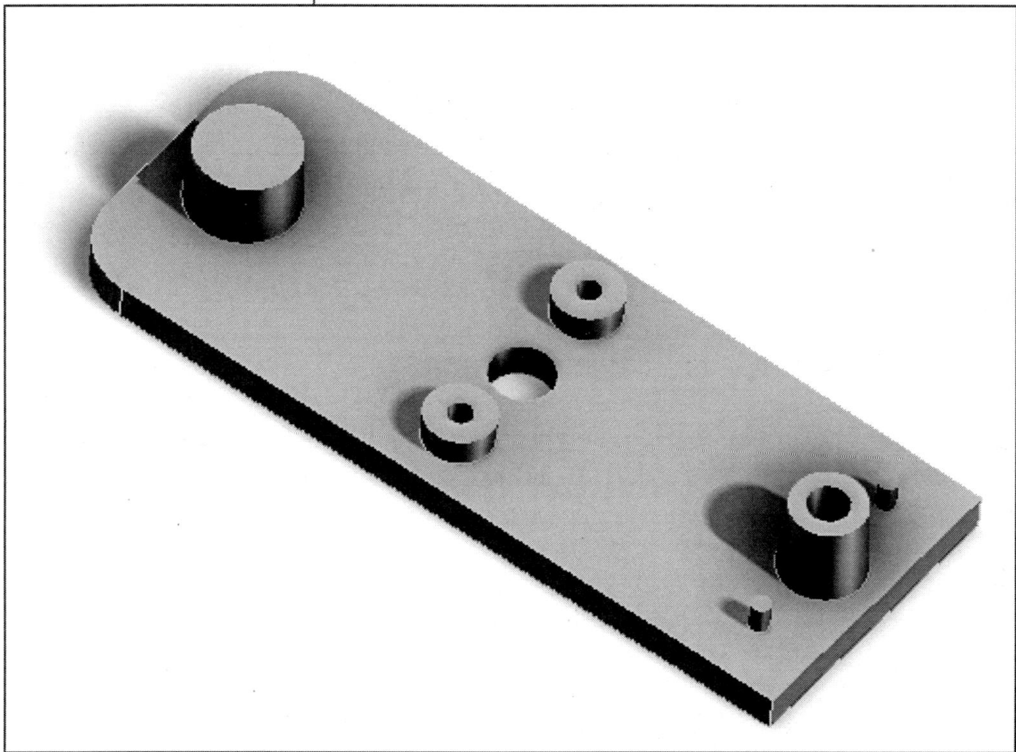

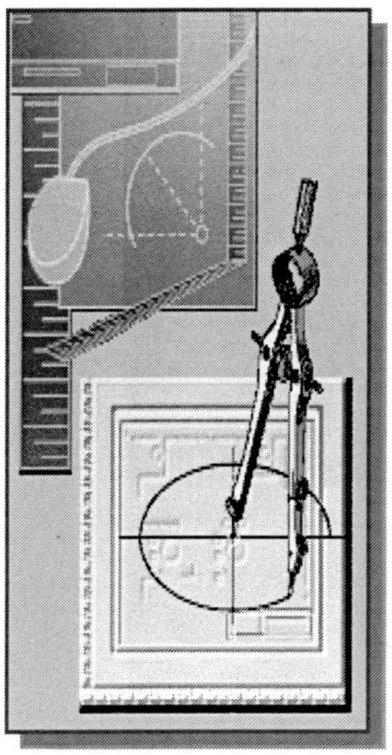

Learning Objectives

- ♦ **Create Parametric Relations**
- ♦ **Use Dimensional Variables**
- ♦ **Display, Add, and Delete Geometric Constraints**
- ♦ **Understand and Apply Different Geometric Constraints**
- ♦ **Display and Modify Parametric Relations**
- ♦ **Create Fully Constrained Sketches**
- ♦ **Create Templates**

DIMENSIONS and RELATIONS

A primary and essential difference between parametric modeling and previous generation computer modeling is that parametric modeling captures the *design intent*. In the previous lessons, we have seen that the design philosophy of "*shape before size*" is implemented through the use of *SolidWorks'* **Smart Dimension** commands. In performing geometric constructions, dimensional values are necessary to describe the **SIZE** and **LOCATION** of constructed geometric entities. Besides using dimensions to define the geometry, we can also apply geometric rules to control geometric entities. More importantly, *SolidWorks* can capture design intent through the use of **geometric constraints, dimensional constraints** and **parametric relations**. **Geometric relations** are geometric restrictions that can be applied to geometric entities; for example, *horizontal*, *parallel*, *perpendicular*, and *tangent* are commonly used *geometric relations* in parametric modeling. For part modeling in *SolidWorks*, relations are applied to *2D sketches*. They can be added automatically as the sketch is created or by using the **Add Relation** command. **Dimensional constraints** are used to describe the SIZE and LOCATION of individual geometric shapes. They are added using the *SolidWorks* **Smart Dimension** command. One should also realize that, depending upon the way the geometric relations and dimensional constraints are applied, the same results can be accomplished by applying different constraints to the geometric entities. In *SolidWorks*, **parametric relations** can be applied using **Equations**. *SolidWorks* **equations** are user-defined mathematical relations between model dimensions, using dimension names as variables. In parametric modeling, features are made of geometric entities with dimensional, geometric, and parametric constraints describing individual design intent. In this lesson, we will discuss the fundamentals of geometric relations and parametric links and equations.

Create a *Simple Triangular Plate* Design

- In parametric modeling, **geometric properties** such as *horizontal*, *parallel*, *perpendicular*, and *tangent* can be applied to geometric entities automatically or manually. By carefully applying proper **geometric relations**, very intelligent models can be created. This concept is illustrated by the following example.

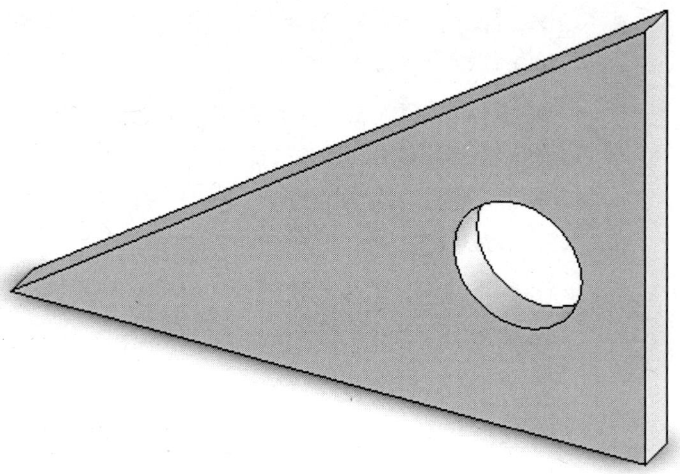

Fully Defined Geometry

In *SolidWorks*, as we create 2D sketches, geometric relations such as *horizontal* and *parallel* are automatically added to the sketched geometry. In most cases, additional relations and dimensions are needed to fully describe the sketched geometry beyond the geometric relations added by the system. Although we can use *SolidWorks* to build partially constrained or totally unconstrained solid models, the models may behave unpredictably as changes are made. In most cases, it is important to consider the design intent, develop a modeling strategy, and add proper constraints to geometric entities. In the following sections, a simple triangle is used to illustrate the different tools that are available in *SolidWorks* to create/modify geometric relations and dimensional constraints.

Starting SolidWorks

1. Select the **SolidWorks** option on the *Start* menu or select the **SolidWorks** icon on the desktop to start *SolidWorks*. The *SolidWorks* main window will appear on the screen.

2. Select the **New** icon with a single click of the left-mouse-button on the *Menu Bar*.

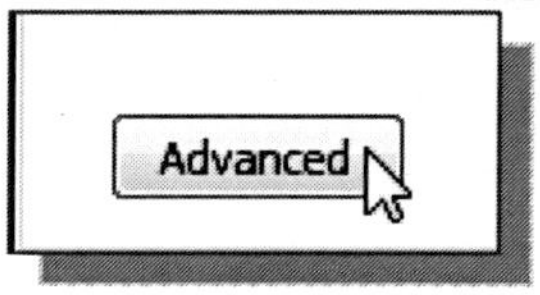

3. The *New SolidWorks Document* dialog box should appear in **Novice** mode. Enter the **Advanced** mode; click once with the left-mouse-button on the **Advanced** icon.

- In Advanced mode, the *New SolidWorks Document* dialog box offers the same three options as in Novice mode. These options allow starting a new document using the default templates for a part, assembly, or drawing. However, the Advanced mode will allow us to start new documents with user-defined templates.

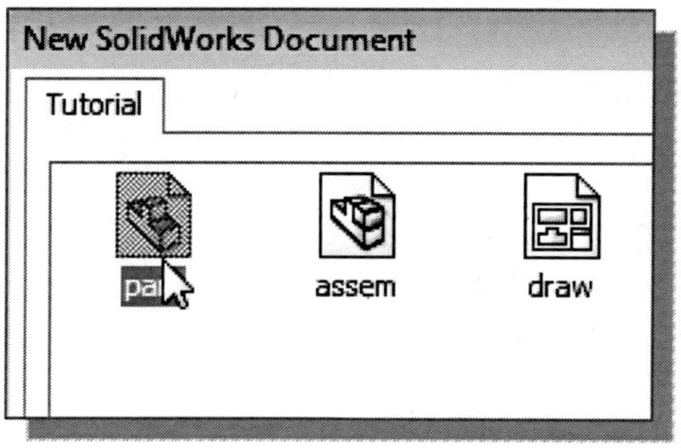

4. Select the **Part** icon with a single click of the left-mouse-button in the *New SolidWorks Document* dialog box.

5. Select **OK** in the *New SolidWorks Document* dialog box to open a new part document

Create a User-Defined Part Template

❖ We will create a part template which includes setting for the use of ANSI standards for dimensions and English (inch, pound, second) units. In the future, using this template will eliminate the need to adjust these document settings each time a new part is started.

1. Select the **Options** icon from the *Menu* toolbar to open the *Options* dialog box.

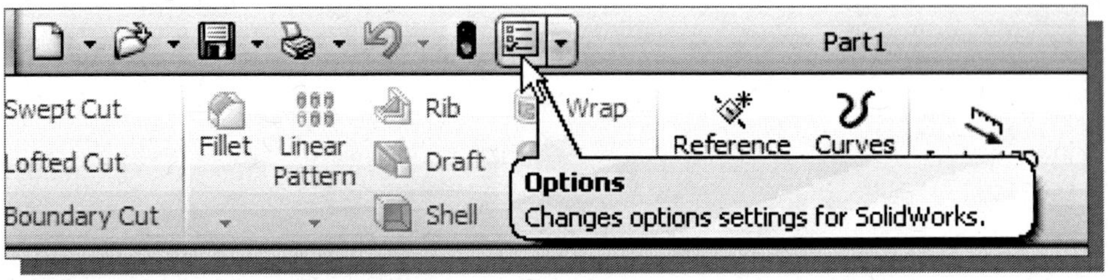

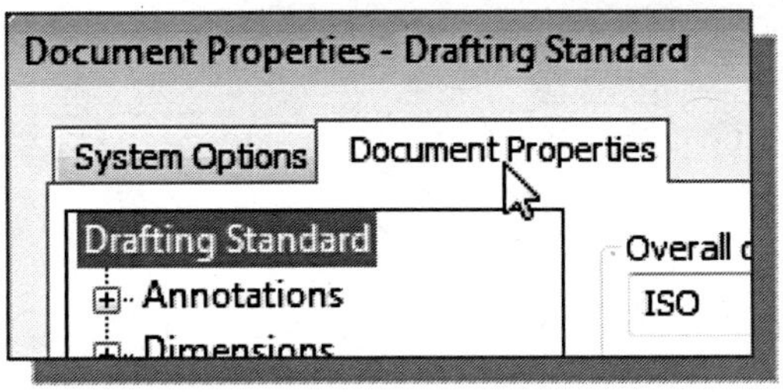

2. Select the **Document Properties** tab as shown in the figure.

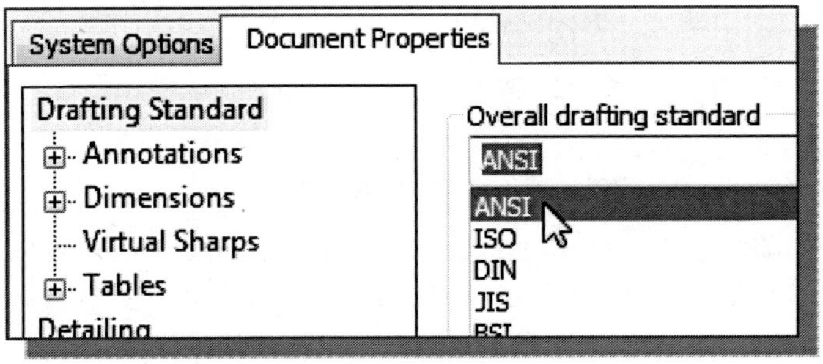

3. Set the *Overall drafting standard* to **ANSI** as shown.

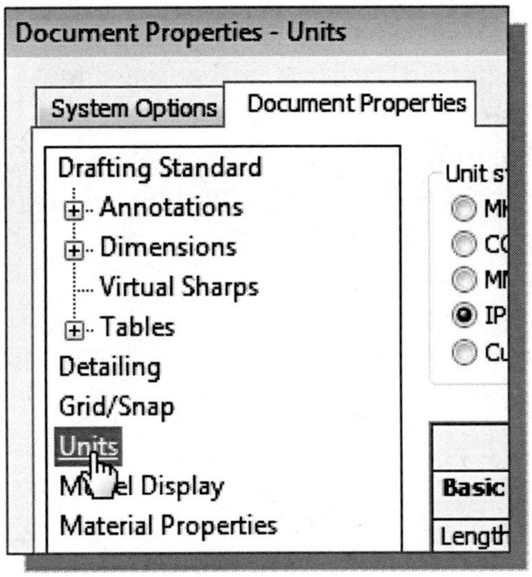

4. Click **Units** as shown in the figure.

5. Select **IPS (inch, pound, second)** under the *Unit system* options.

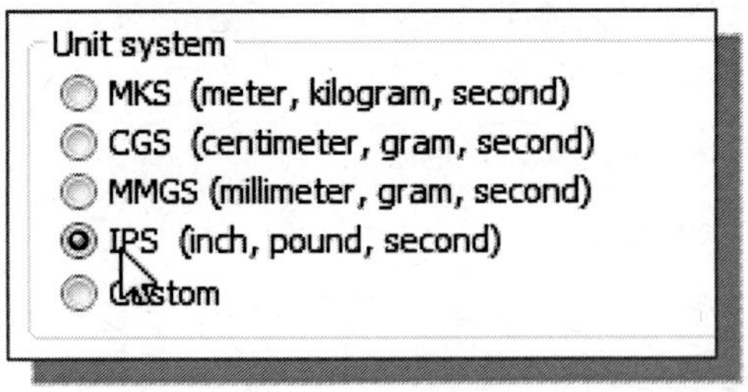

6. On your own, set the length display to 3 digits after the decimal point.

- Note the different options available to set/adjust the display of the selected units set.

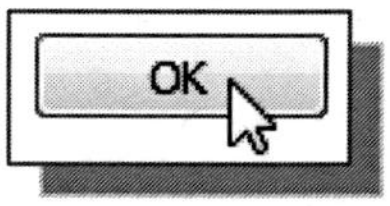

7. Click **OK** in the *Options* dialog box to accept the selected settings.

8. Click the arrow next to the **Save** icon in the *Menu Bar* to reveal the save options and select **Save As**.

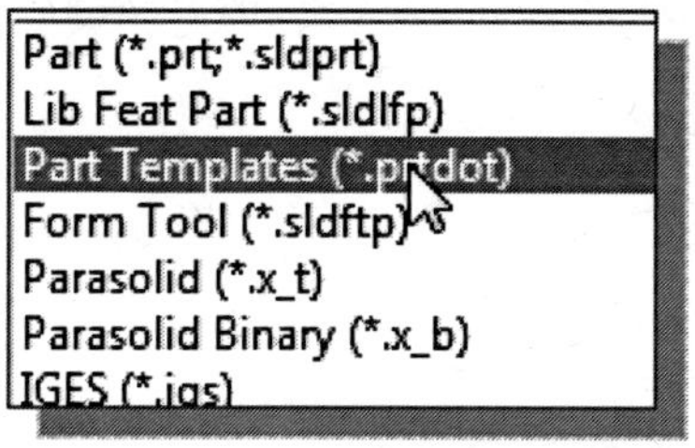

9. Under *Save as type*, select **Part Templates (*.prtdot)**. Notice the browser automatically goes to the default *templates* folder.

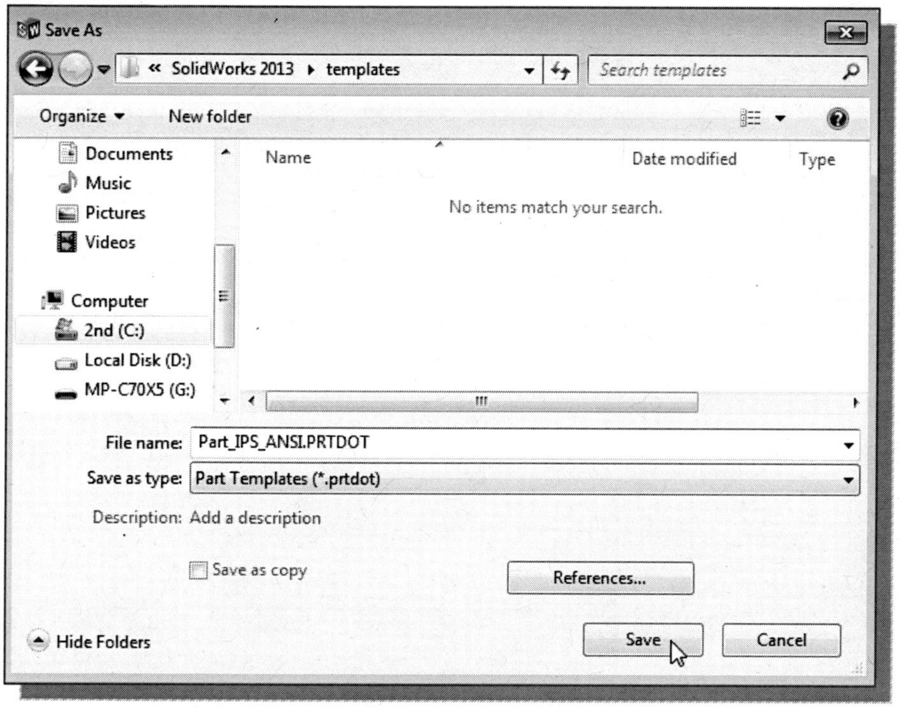

10. Enter the *File name* **Part_IPS_ANSI**.

11. Click **Save** to save the new part template file.

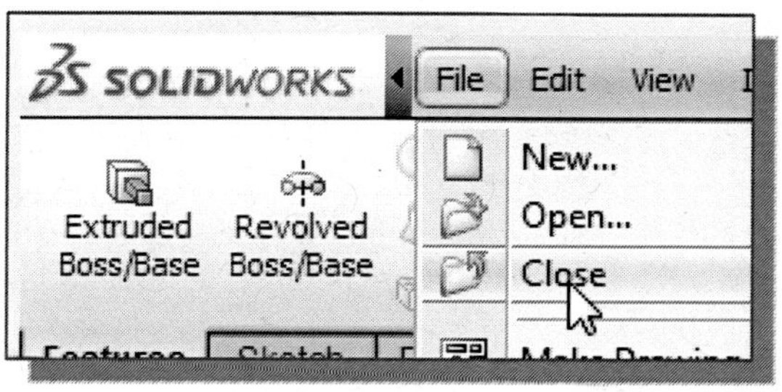

12. Select **Close** in the *File* pull-down menu to close the document. (**NOTE:** You may have to move the mouse over the SolidWorks icon to reveal the pull-down menus.)

Start a New Model using the New Template

1. Select the **New** icon with a single click of the left-mouse-button on the *Menu Bar*.

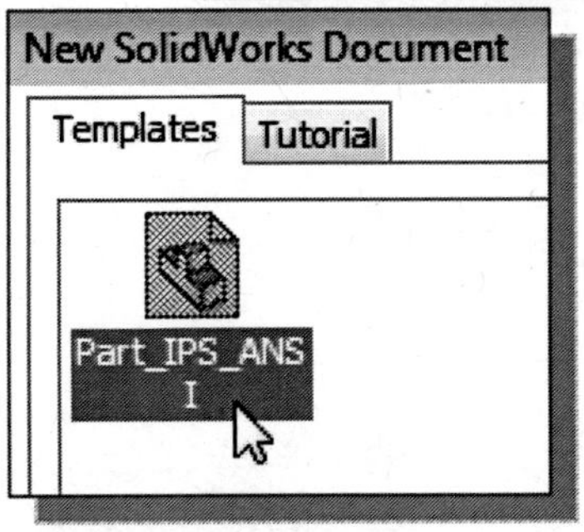

2. Notice the Part_IPS_ANSI template appears in the **Advanced** mode. Select the **Part_IPS_ANSI** template as shown.

3. Click on the **OK** button to open a new document using the Part_IPS_ANSI template. The *Dimensioning Standard* will automatically be ANSI and the units will be set to inch, pound, second as defined in the template.

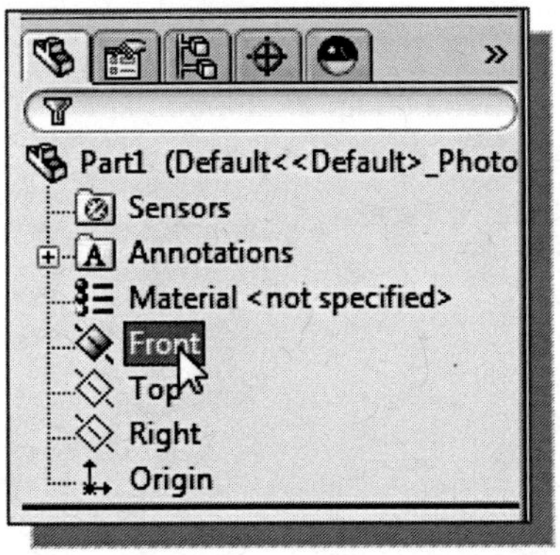

4. In the *Feature Manager Design Tree*, click once with the **left-mouse-button** to pre-select the **Front Plane** as shown.

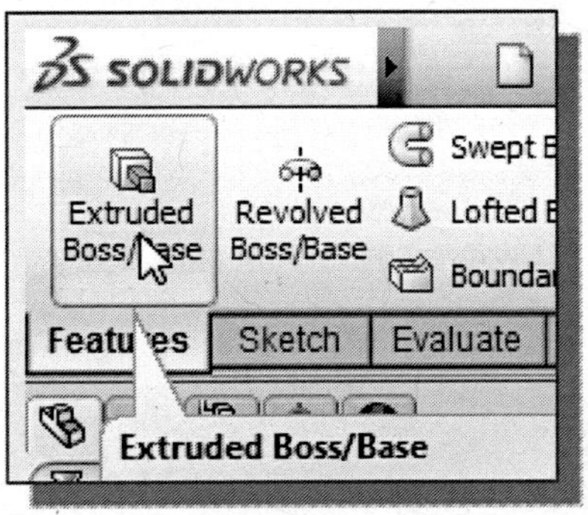

5. In the *Features* toolbar select the **Extruded Boss/ Base** command by clicking once with the left-mouse-button on the icon.

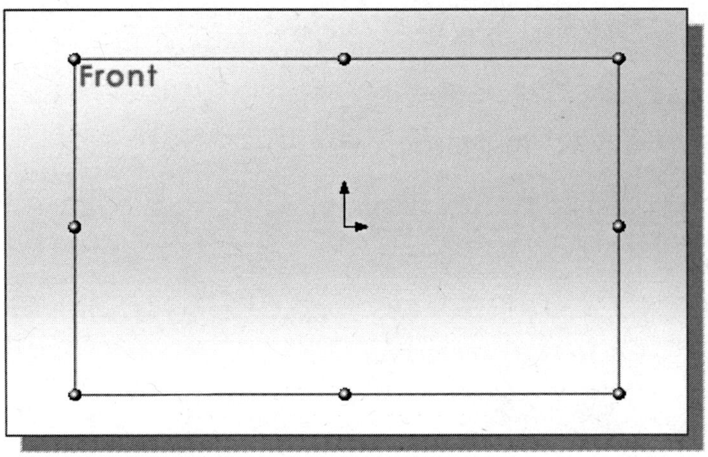

- Note the pre-selection of Front Plane enables the use of the plane as the sketching plane.

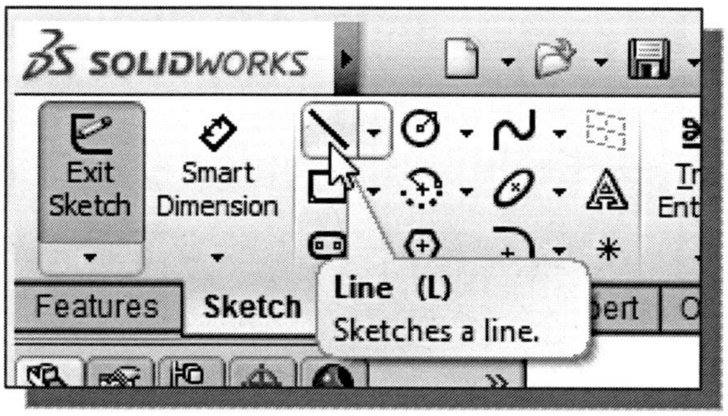

6. Select the **Line** icon on the *Sketch* toolbar by clicking once with the **left-mouse-button.**

7. Create a triangle of arbitrary size positioned near the center of the screen as shown below. (Note that the base of the triangle is horizontal.)

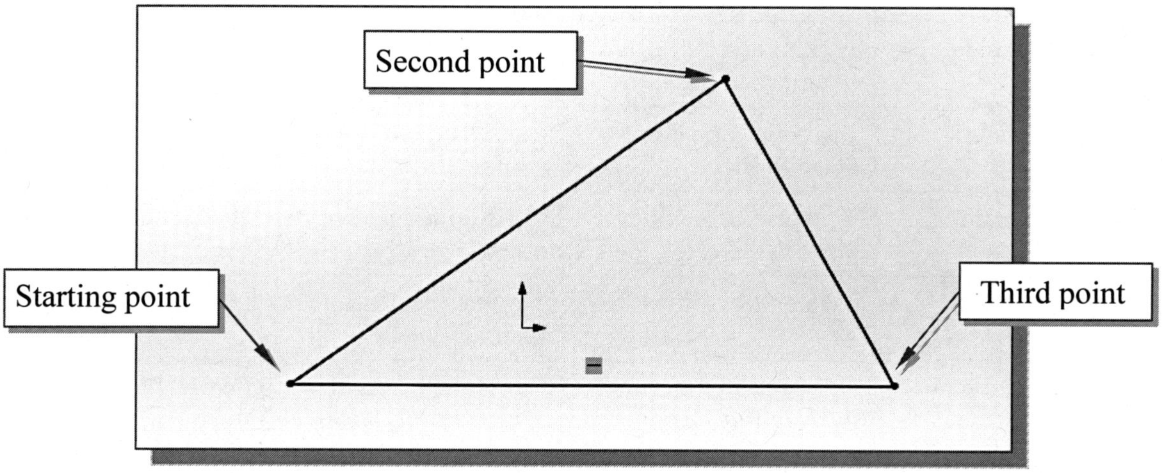

8. Press the **[Esc]** key to exit the Line command.

Display/Hide Applied Geometric Relations

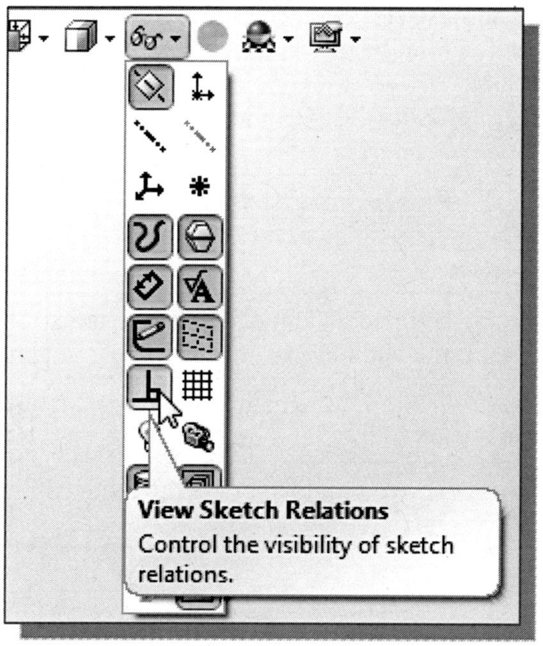

1. Select the **View Sketch Relations** icon under the **Hide/Show Items** icon in the *Heads-up View* toolbar. This allows us to display geometric relations that are already applied to the 2D profile.

2. Click the button again to toggle the visibility of the geometric *Sketch Relations* symbols *ON* and *OFF*.

Applying Geometric Relations/Dimensional Constraints

- *SolidWorks* geometric relations for 2D sketches are summarized below.

Icon	Relation	Entities Selected	Effect
	Perpendicular	Two lines	Causes selected lines to lie at right angles to one another.
	Parallel	Two or more lines	Causes selected lines to lie parallel to one another.
	Tangent	An arc, spline, or ellipse and a line or arc	Constrains two curves to be tangent to one another.
	Coincident	A point and a line, arc, or ellipse	Constrains a point to a curve.
	Midpoint	Two lines or a point and a line	Causes a point to remain at the midpoint of a line.
	Concentric	Two or more arcs, or a point and an arc	Constrains selected items to the same center point.
	Colinear	Two or more lines	Causes selected lines to lie along the same line.
	Horizontal	One or more lines or two or more points	Causes selected items to lie parallel to the X-axis of the sketch coordinate system.
	Vertical	One or more lines or two or more points	Causes selected items to lie parallel to the Y-axis of the sketch coordinate system.
	Equal	Two or more lines or two or more arcs	Constrains selected arcs/circles to the same radius or selected lines to the same length.
	Fix	Any entity	Constrains selected entities to a fixed location relative to the sketch coordinate system. However, endpoints of a fixed line, arc, or elliptical segment are free to move along the underlying fixed curve.
	Symmetric	A centerline and two points, lines, arcs or ellipses	Causes items to remain equidistant from the centerline, on a line perpendicular to the centerline.
	Coradial	Two or more arcs	Causes the selected arcs to share the same center point and radius.
	Intersection	Two lines and one point	Causes the point to remain at the intersection of the two lines.
	Merge Points	Two points (sketch points or endpoints)	Causes the two points to be merged into a single point.

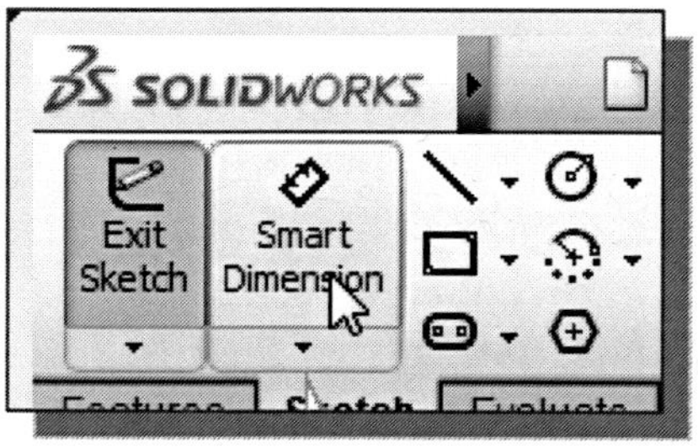

1. Select the **Smart Dimension** command by clicking once with the **left-mouse-button** on the icon in the *Sketch* toolbar.

2. On your own, create the horizontal dimension (your value may be different than what is shown) as shown in the figure below.

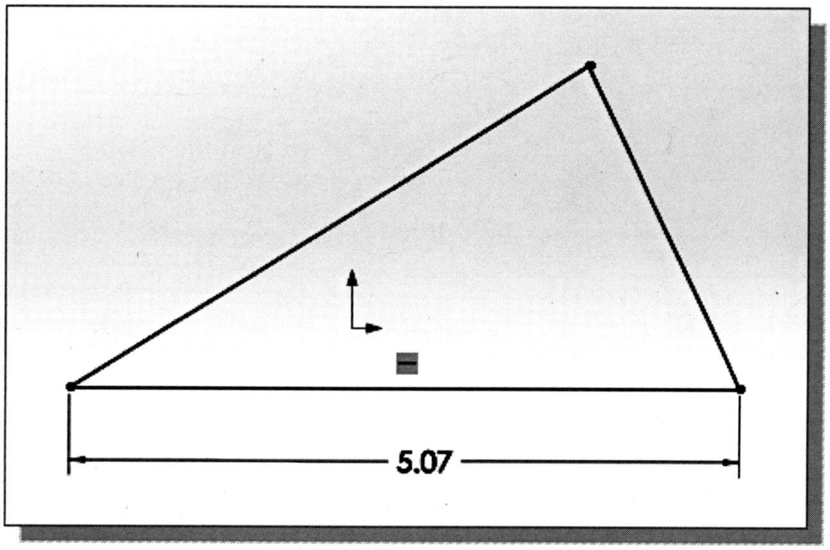

3. Press the [**Esc**] key once to exit the Smart Dimension command.

4. **Left-click** on the arrow below the **Display/ Delete Relations** button on the *Sketch* toolbar to reveal additional sketch relation commands.

5. Select the **Add Relation** command from the pop-up menu.

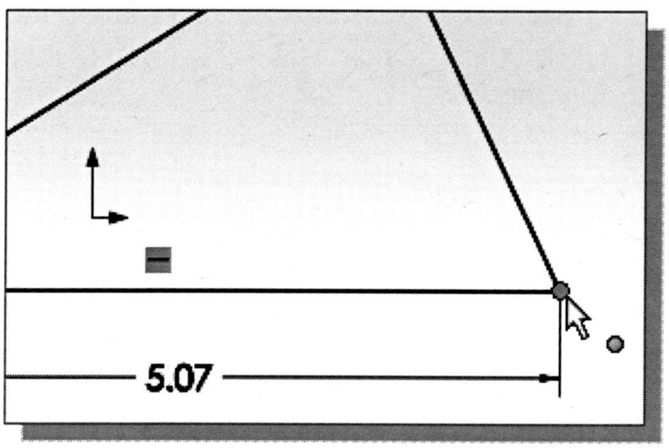

6. Select the lower right corner of the triangle by clicking once with the **left-mouse-button**.

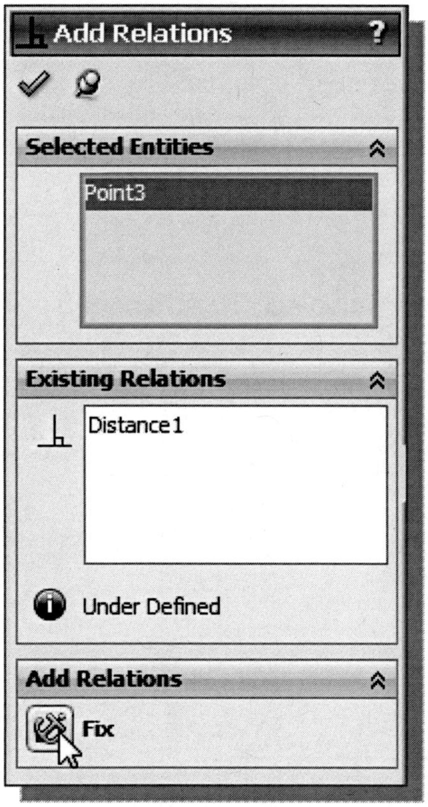

- Look at the *Add Relations Property Manager*. In the *Selected Entities* window '**Point3**' is now displayed. '**Distance1**' appears in the *Existing Relations* window. This refers to the dimension on the horizontal line for which Point3 is an endpoint. In the *Add Relations* menu, the **Fix** relation is displayed. This represents the only relation which can be added for the selected entity.

7. Click once with the left-mouse-button on the **Fix** icon in the *Add Relations Property Manager* as shown. This activates the **Fix** relation.

8. Click the **OK** icon in the *Property Manager*, or hit the [**Esc**] key once, to end the Add Relations command.

9. On your own, turn *ON* the sketch relations visibility to confirm the Fix constraint is properly applied.

- Geometric constraints can be used to control the direction in which changes can occur. For example, in the current design we are adding a horizontal dimension to control the length of the horizontal line. If the length of the line is modified to a greater value, *SolidWorks* will lengthen the line toward the left side. This is due to the fact that the Fix constraint will restrict any horizontal movement of the horizontal line toward the right side.

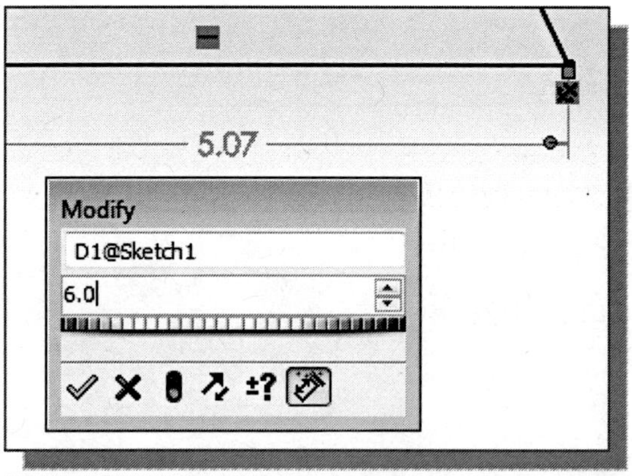

10. Double-click with the left-mouse-button on the dimension text in the graphics area to open the *Modify* dialog box.

11. Enter a value that is greater than the displayed value to observe the effects of the modification. (For example, the dimension value is 5.07; so enter **6.0** in the text box area.) Click the **OK** button in the *Modify* dialog box.

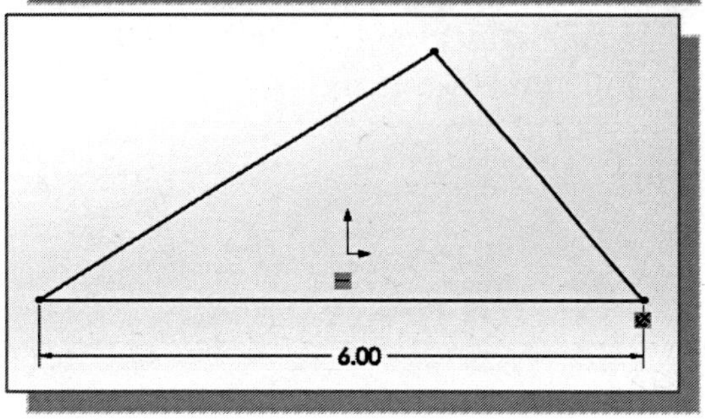

- With the right end fixed, the base of the triangle is lengthened toward the left side. By applying proper constraints, we can control the behavior of the created geometry. The use of the geometric constraints is the key feature of *parametric modeling*.

12. Select the **Add Relation** command from the pop-up menu. Notice the *Add Relations Property Manager* appears. The *Selected Entities* window in the *Add Relations Property Manager* is blank because no entities are selected.

13. Select the inclined line on the right by clicking once with the **left-mouse-button** as shown in the figure.

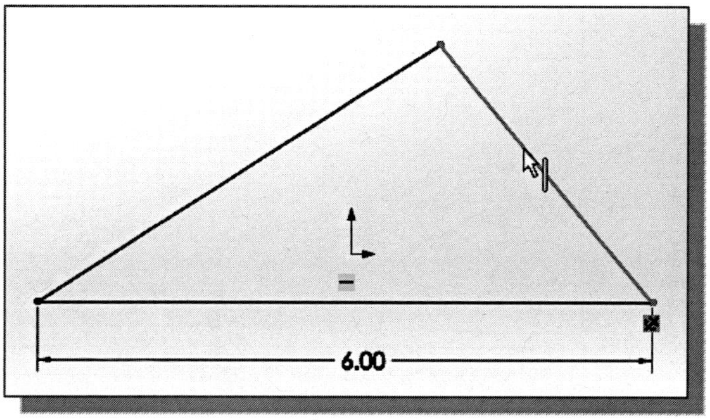

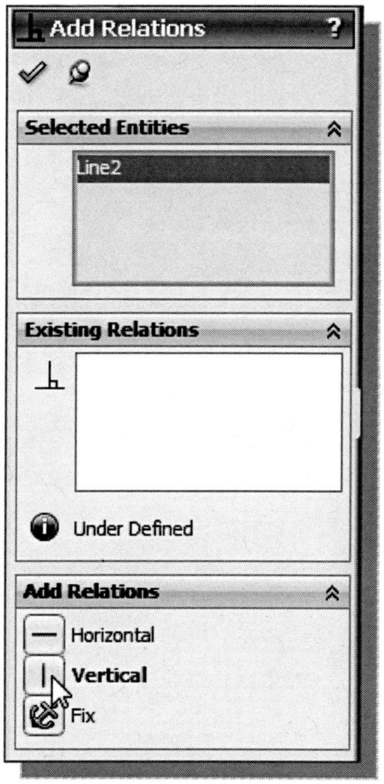

➤ Look at the *Add Relations Property Manager*. In the *Selected Entities* text box '**Line2**' is now displayed. There are no relations in the *Existing Relations* text box. In the *Add Relations* panel, the **Horizontal**, **Vertical**, and **Fix** relations are displayed. These are the relations which can be added for the selected entity.

14. Click once with the left-mouse-button on the **Vertical** icon in the *Add Relations Property Manager* as shown. This activates the **Vertical** relation.

15. Click the **OK** icon in the *Property Manager*, or hit the [**Esc**] key once, to end the Add Relation command.

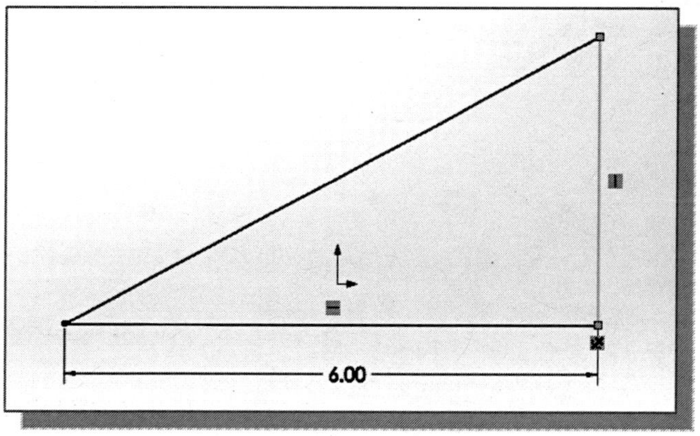

➤ The geometric relations and dimensions are the defining elements for the geometric entities. Which geometric relations or dimensions would you use to fully define the sketched geometry?

Geometric Editing with Drag and Drop

1. Move the cursor on top of the top corner of the triangle.

2. Click and drag the top corner of the triangle and note that the corner can be moved to a new location. Release the mouse button at a new location and notice the corner is adjusted only in an upward or downward direction due to the applied constraints. Note that the two adjacent lines are automatically adjusted to the new location.

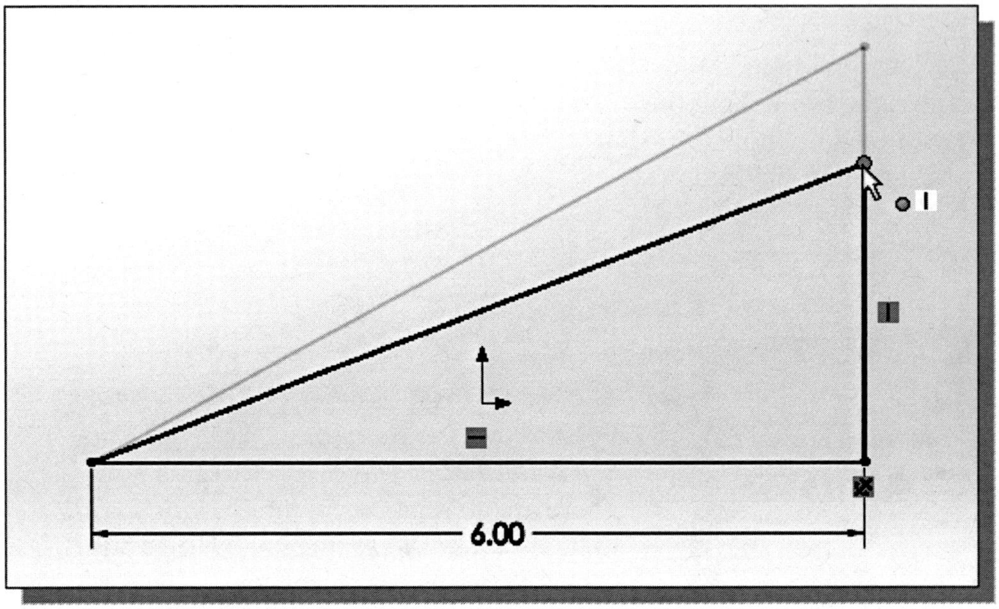

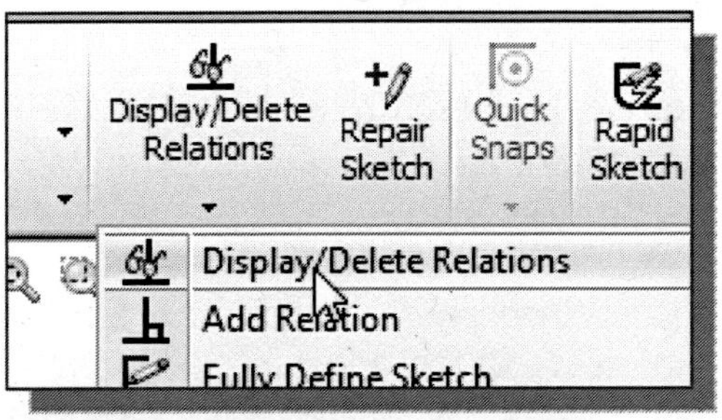

3. Select the **Display/Delete Relations** command from the pop-up menu. Notice the *Display/Delete Relations Property Manager* appears.

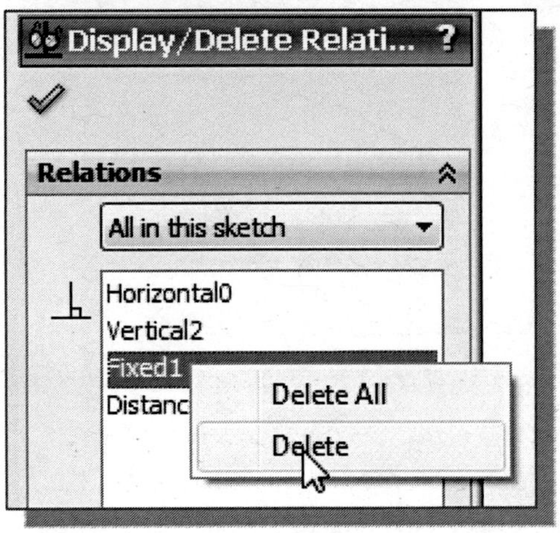

4. In the *Display/Delete Relations Property Manager*, select the **Fixed1** constraint as shown.

5. Right-mouse-click on the **Fixed1** constraint to bring up the option menu.

6. Select **Delete** to remove the constraint.

7. Click the **OK** icon in the *Property Manager*, or hit the [**Esc**] key once, to end the Display/ Delete Relations command.

8. Click and drag the top corner of the triangle and note that the corner can now be moved to a new location. The corner is no longer restricted only in an upward or downward direction. Note that the applied constraints, both dimensional and geometric constraints, are still maintained.

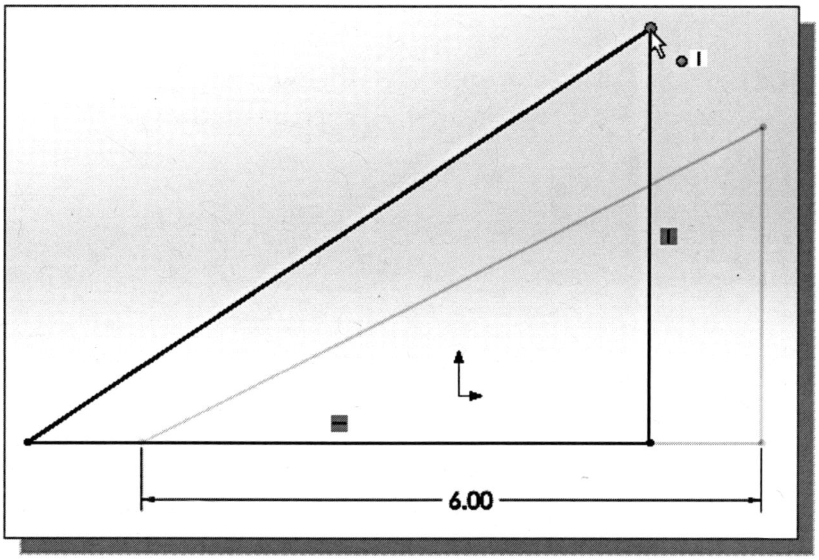

9. On your own, experiment with *dragging and dropping* the sides of the triangle.

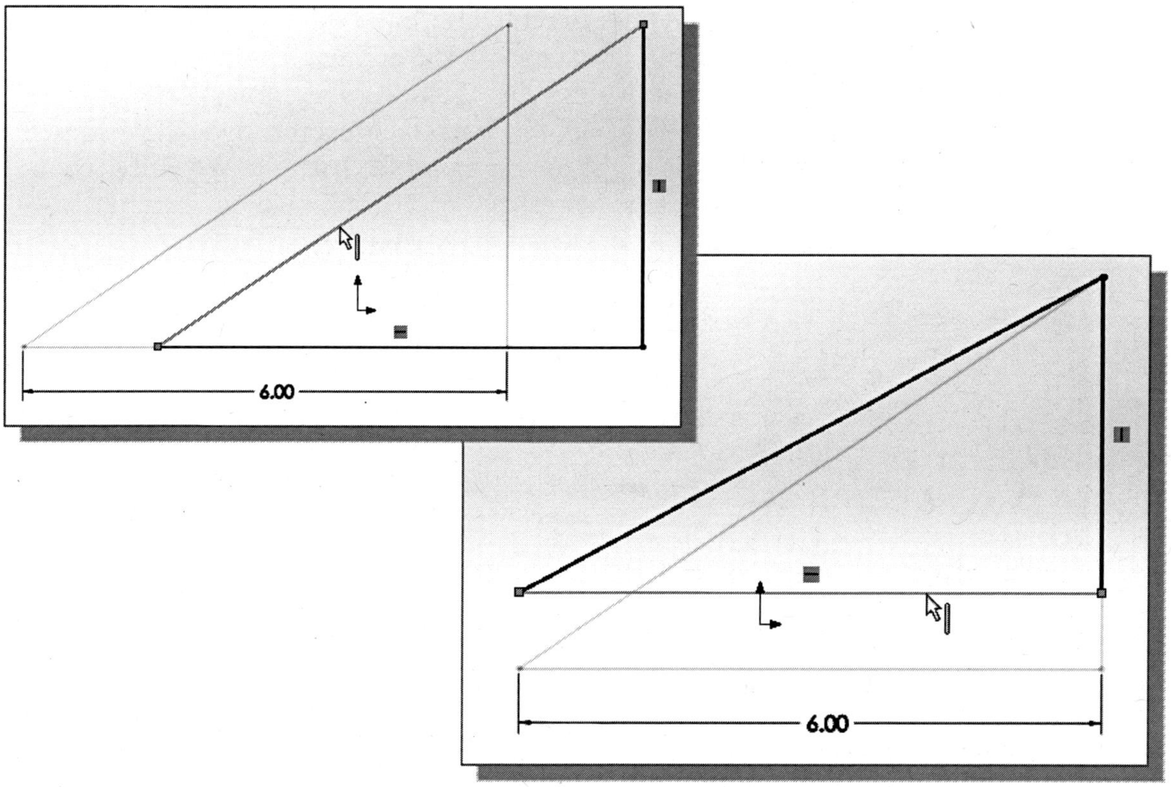

- The ***editing with drag and drop*** approach provides a very flexible way to adjust sketched geometry. Note that it is quite common during the initial conceptual design stage where the forms and shapes of the design are constantly changing.

Create Fully Constrained Sketches

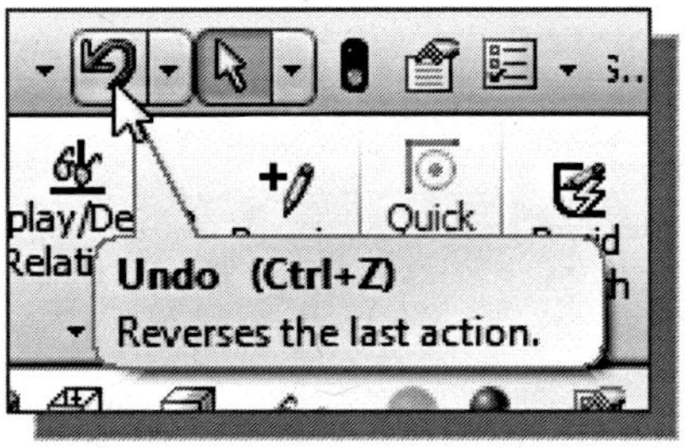

1. Click **Undo** in the *Quick Access* menu to undo the last applied change.

2. Repeat the **Undo** command until the **Fixed1** constraint reappears on the screen.

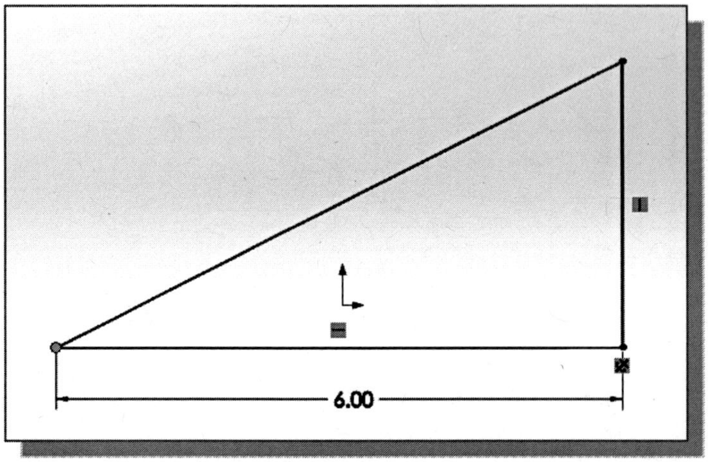

- The Fixed1 geometric relation provides the full description for the location of the lower right corner relative to the 2D virtual space. The applied length dimension, along with the Fixed1 constraint, fully describes the lower left corner of the triangle. However, the **Vertical** relation, along with the **Fix** relation at the lower right corner, does not fully describe the location of the top corner of the triangle. We will need to add additional information, such as the length of the vertical line or an angle dimension to further define the upper corner of the triangle.

3. Select the **Smart Dimension** command by clicking once with the **left-mouse-button** on the icon in the *Sketch* toolbar.

4. Select the **horizontal line**.

5. Select the **inclined line**. Note that selecting two non-parallel lines automatically executes an angle dimension.

6. Select a location for the dimension as shown.

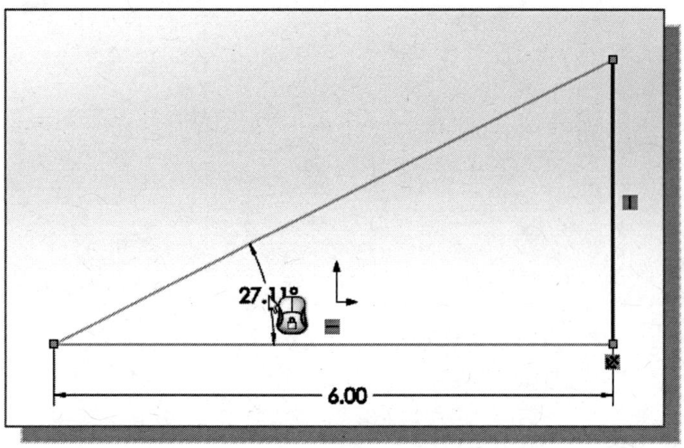

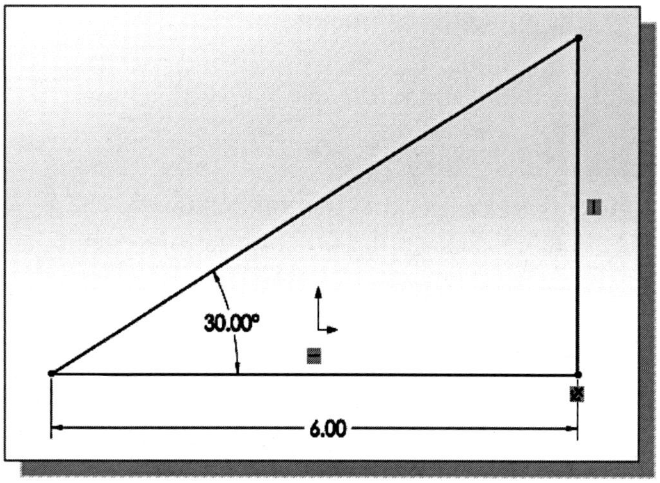

7. Enter **30°** in the *Modify* dialog box and select **OK**.

8. Press the [**Esc**] key once to exit the Smart Dimension command.

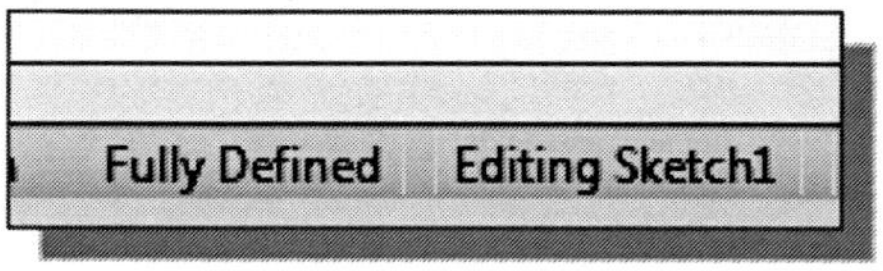

- Note that the sketch is fully defined and **Fully Defined** is displayed in the *Status Bar* at the bottom of the screen.

- Also note that the **color** of all geometry is now **black**. *SolidWorks* uses the following color codes:
    - **Black color** indicates fully defined geometry
    - **Blue color** indicates partially/under defined geometry

❖ In parametric modeling, **geometric relations** and **dimensional constraints** are used to describe the SIZE and LOCATION of individual geometric shapes. **Geometric relations** are **geometric restrictions** that can be applied to geometric entities.

Over-Defining and Driven Dimensions

- We can use *SolidWorks* to build partially defined solid models. In most cases, these types of models may behave unpredictably as changes are made. However, *SolidWorks* will not let us over-define a sketch; additional dimensions can still be added to the sketch, but they are used as references only. These additional dimensions are called ***driven dimensions***. *Driven dimensions* do not constrain the sketch; they only reflect the values of the dimensioned geometry. They are shaded differently (grey by default) to distinguish them from normal (parametric) dimensions. A *driven dimension* can be converted to a normal dimension only if another dimension or geometric relation is removed.

1. Select the **Smart Dimension** command in the *Sketch* toolbar.

2. Select the **vertical line**, the line segment on the right side of the triangle.

3. Pick a location that is to the right side of the triangle to place the vertical dimension text.

4. A *warning* dialog box appears on the screen stating that the dimension we are trying to create will over-define the sketch. Click on the **OK** button to proceed with the creation of a driven dimension.

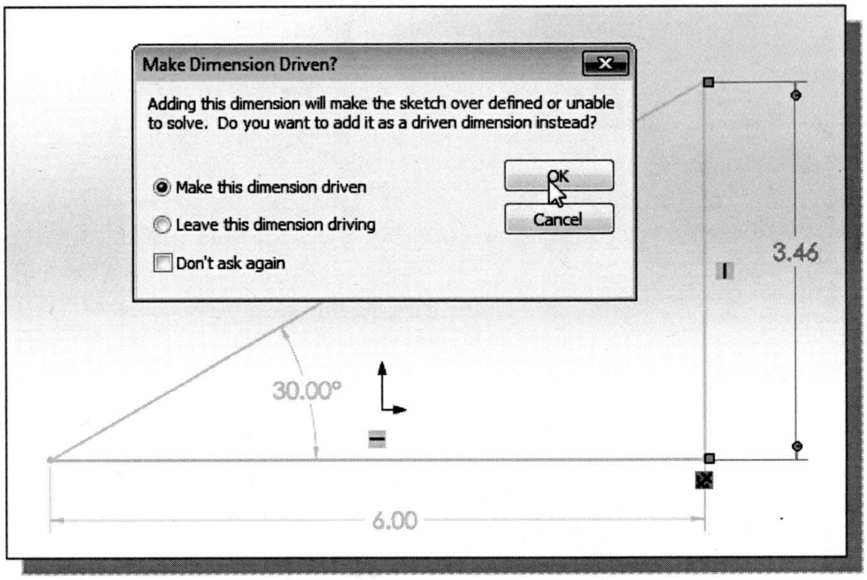

5. Press the [**Esc**] key once to exit the Smart Dimension command.

6. On your own, modify the angle dimension to **35°** and observe the changes to the 2D sketch and the driven dimension.

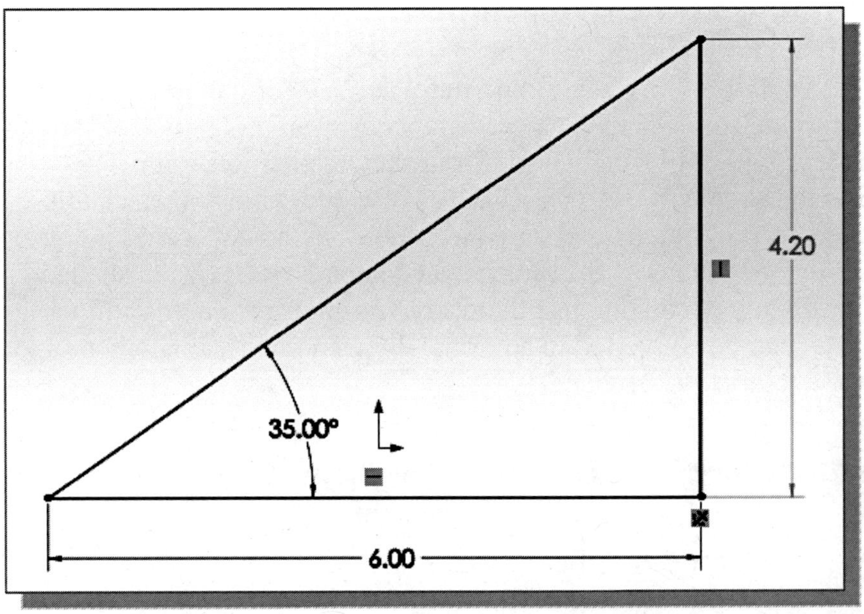

7. Press the [**Esc**] key to ensure that no objects are selected.

Delete the Fix Constraint

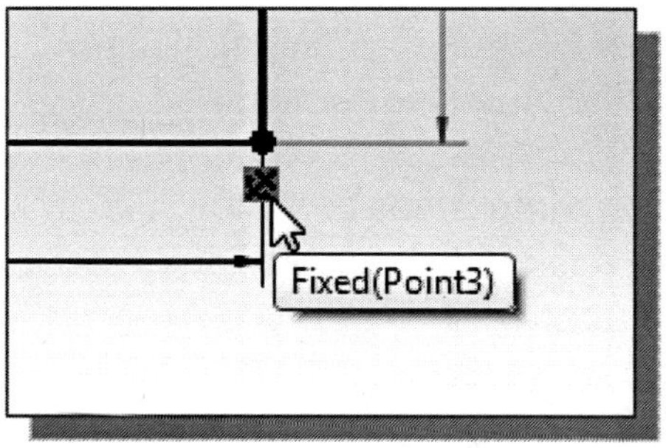

1. Move the cursor on top of the **Fixed constraint** icon and right-mouse-click once to bring up the *option menu.*

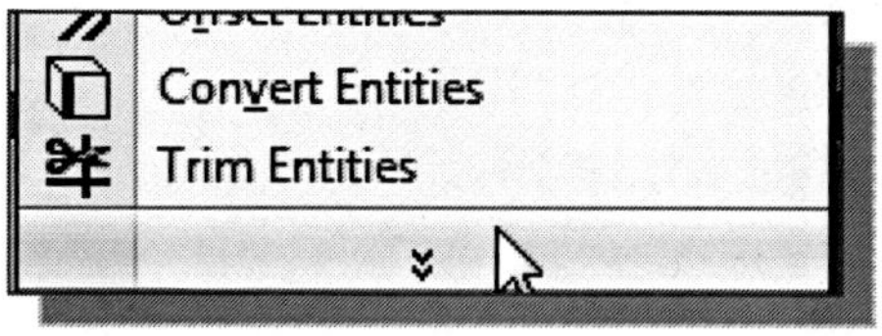

2. Click on the **down arrow** at the bottom of the option list to display additional options.

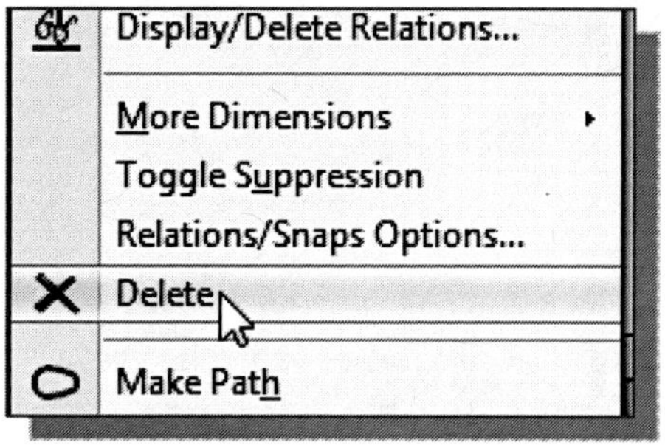

3. Select **Delete** to remove the Fixed constraint that is applied to the lower right corner of the triangle.

4. Drag the top corner of the triangle and note that the entire triangle is free to move in all directions. Drag the corner toward the left and release the mouse button to move the triangle to the new location.

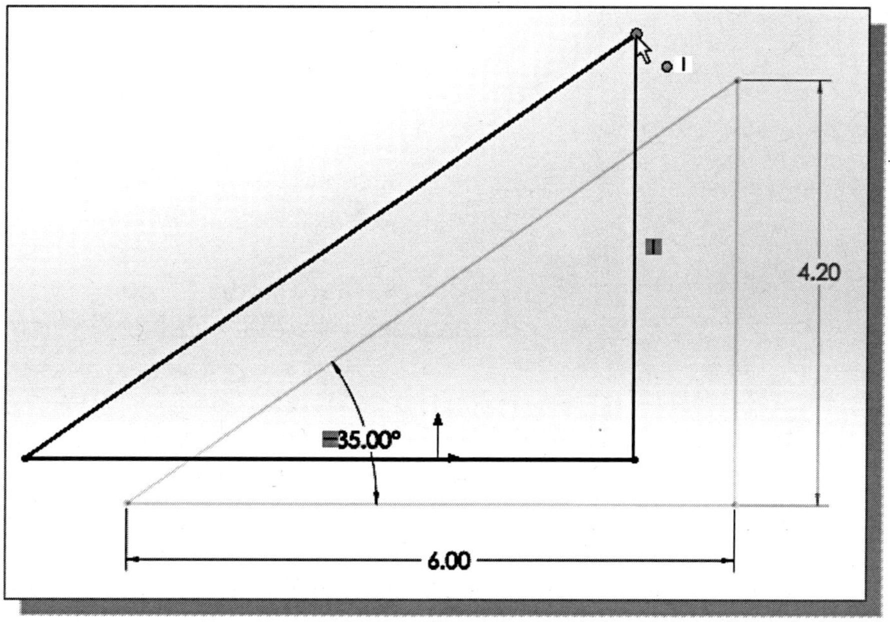

5. On your own, experiment with dragging the other corners and/or the three line segments to new locations on the screen.

Use the Fully Define Sketch Tool

➢ In *SolidWorks*, the **Fully Define Sketch** tool can be used to calculate which dimensions and relations are required to fully define an under defined sketch. Fully defined sketches can be updated more predictably as design changes are implemented. One general procedure for applying dimensions to sketches is to use the **Smart Dimension** command to add the desired dimensions, and then use the **Fully Define Sketch** tool to fully constrain the sketch. It is also important to realize that different dimensions and geometric constraints can be applied to the same sketch to accomplish a fully defined geometry.

1. Select the **Fully Define Sketch** command from the pop-up menu.

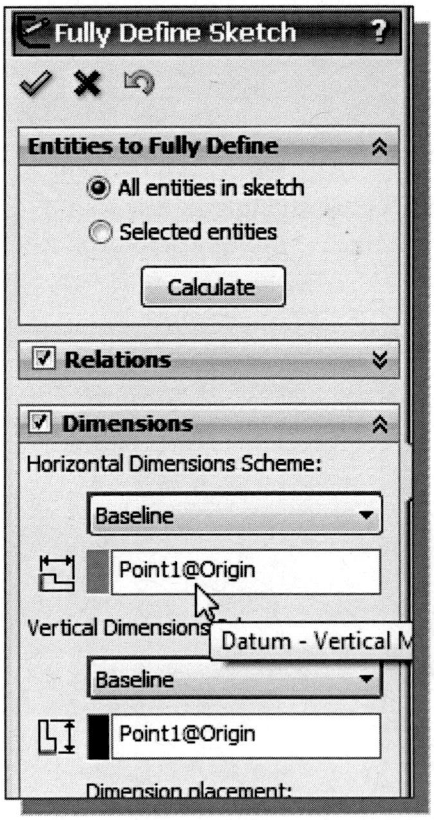

2. The *Fully Define Sketch Property Manager* appears. **If necessary**, click once with the **left-mouse-button** on the arrows to reveal the *Dimensions* option panel as shown.

3. Notice that under the *Horizontal Dimensions Scheme* option, **Baseline** is selected. The *Origin* is selected as the default baseline datum and appears in the datum selection window as **Point1@Origin**.

4. Click once with the **left-mouse-button** in the *Datum* selection text box to select a different datum to serve as the baseline.

5. Select **Calculate** in the *Property Manager* to continue with the Fully Define Sketch command.

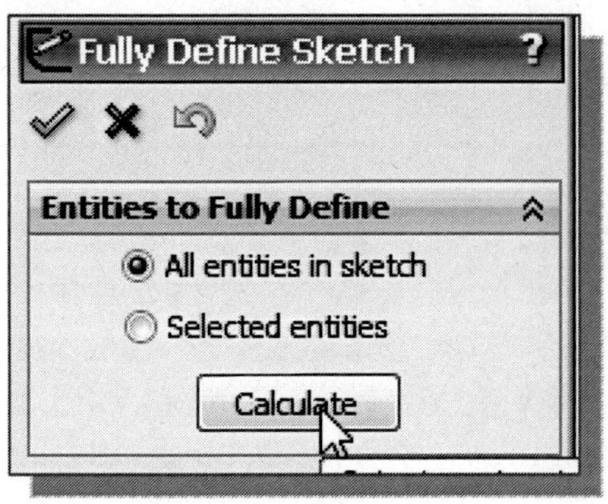

❖ Note that *SolidWorks* automatically determines and applies the two location dimensions of the lower right corner of the triangle, using the *Origin* of the coordinate system as the baseline. Notice that **Fully Defined** is now displayed in the *Status Bar*.

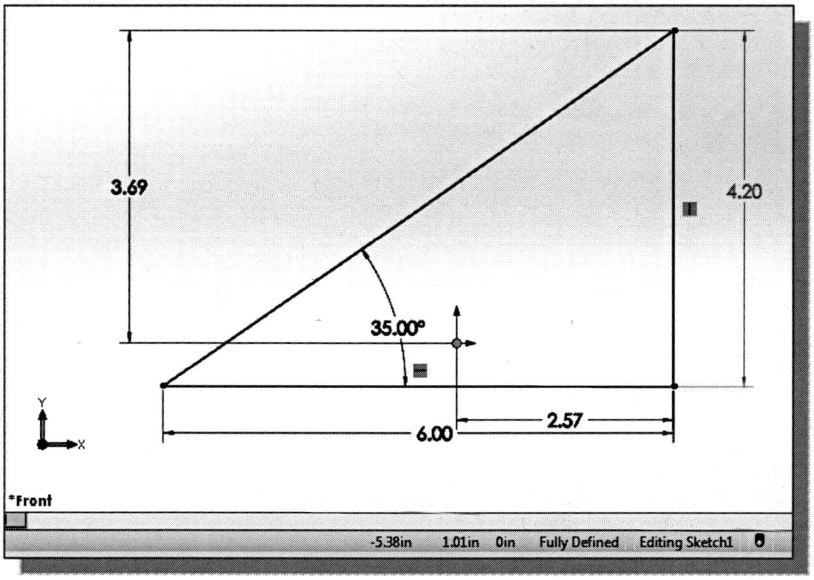

6. Click the **OK** button accept the results and exit the Fully Define Sketch tool.

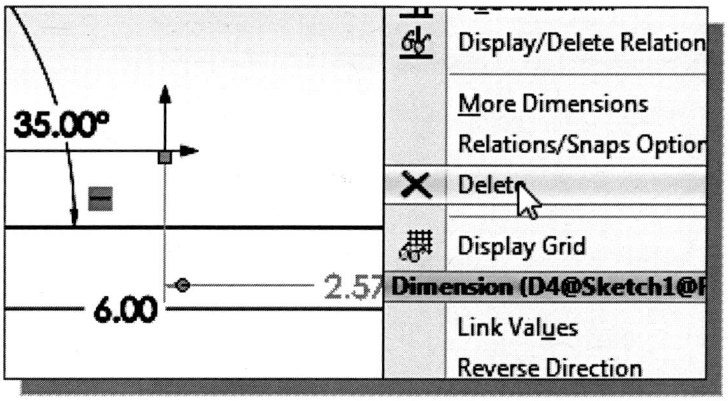

7. On your own, delete the two dimensions created by the Fully Define Sketch tool.

8. Hold down the [**Ctrl**] key and select the ***Origin*** and the **lower right corner** of the triangle as shown.

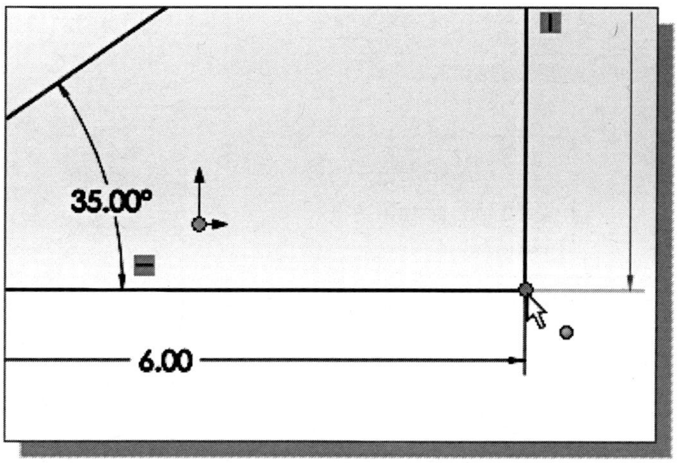

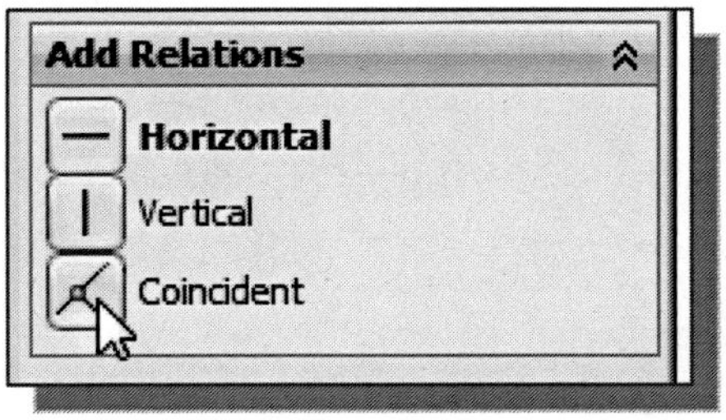

9. Click on the **Coincident** icon to apply the associated constraint to the selected points.

- Note the sketch is again fully constrained with the added constraint.

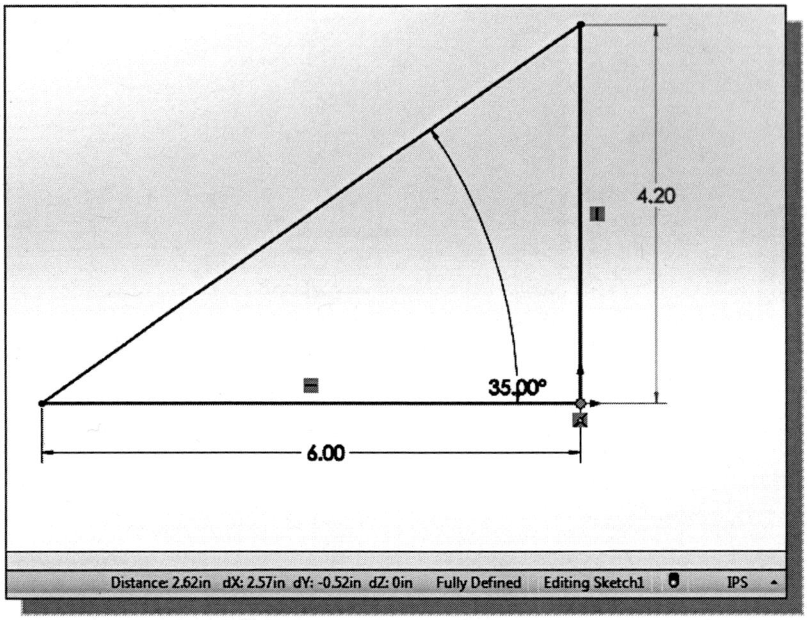

- Different dimensions and geometric constraints can be applied to the same sketch to accomplish a fully defined geometry.

Add Additional Geometry

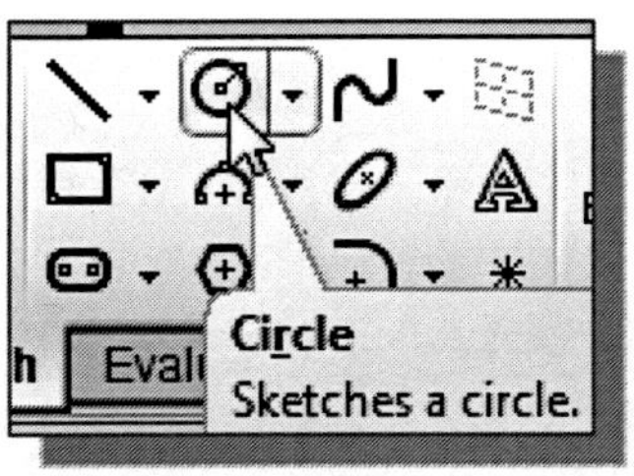

1. Select the **Circle** command by clicking once with the left-mouse-button on the icon in the *Sketch* toolbar.

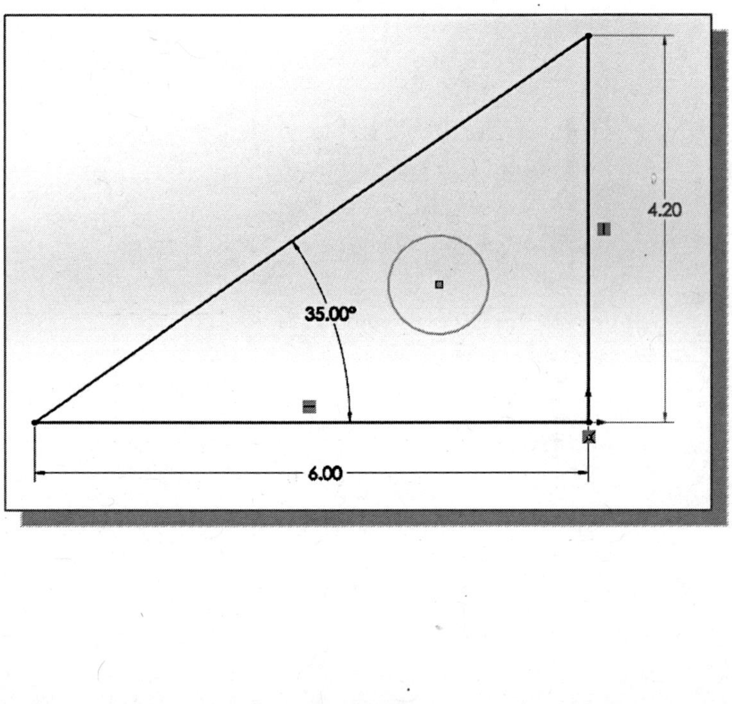

2. On your own, create a circle of arbitrary size inside the triangle as shown.

3. Press the [**Esc**] key to ensure that no objects are selected.

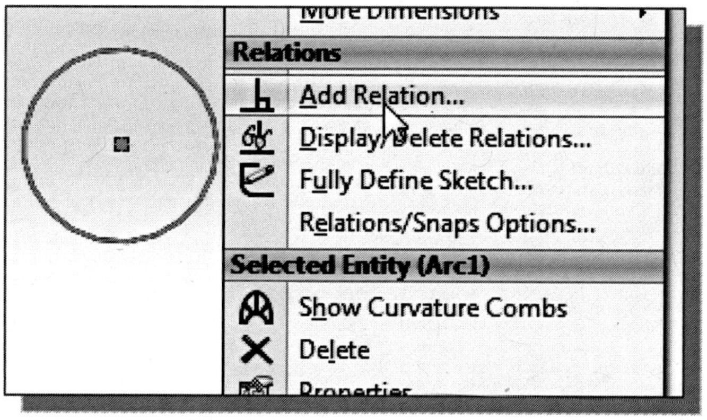

4. Pick the **circle** by right-mouse-clicking once on the geometry.

5. Select **Add Relation** from the pop-up menu as shown.

6. Pick the **inclined line.**

➢ Look at the *Add Relations Property Manager*. In the *Selected Entities* text box **Arc1** and **Line1** are now displayed. There are no relations in the *Existing Relations* window. In the *Add Relations* menu, the **Tangent** and **Fix** relations are displayed. These are the relations which can be added for the selected entities.

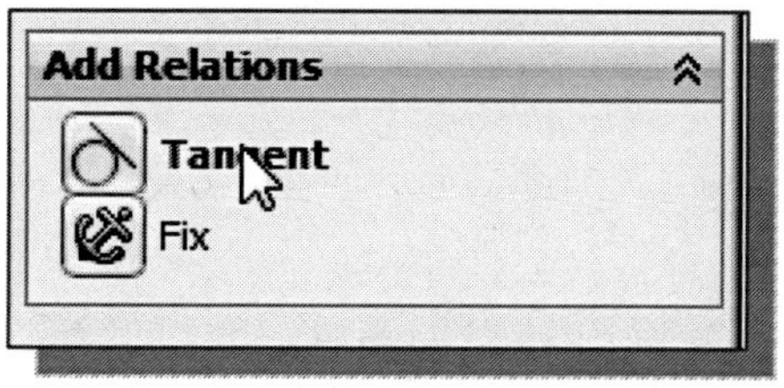

7. Click once with the left-mouse-button on the **Tangent** icon in the *Add Relations Property Manager* as shown. This activates the Tangent relation to the selected entities.

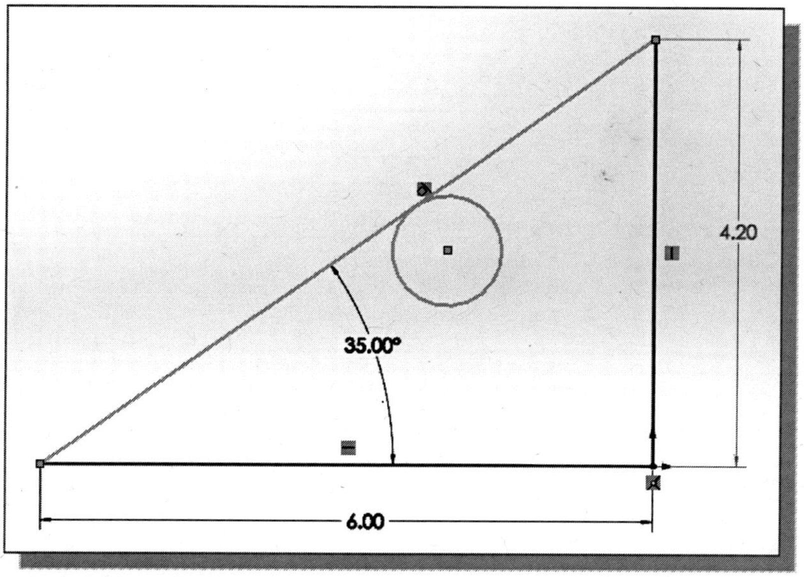

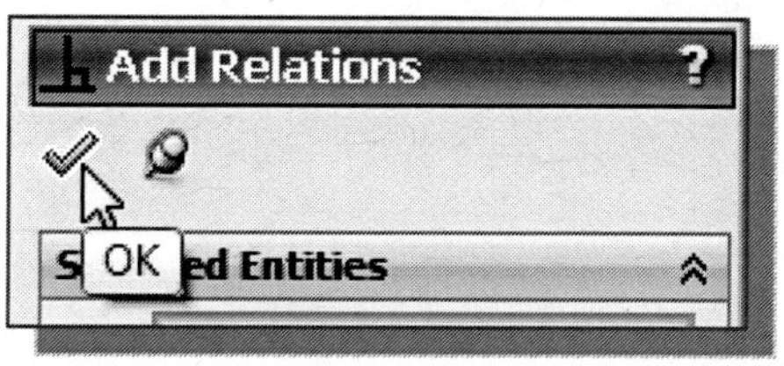

8. Click the **OK** icon in the *Property Manager*, or hit the [**Esc**] key once, to end the Add Relation command.

- Notice that **Under Defined** is displayed in the *Status Bar.* How many more relations or dimensions do you think will be necessary to fully define the circle? Which relations or dimensions would you use to fully define the geometry?

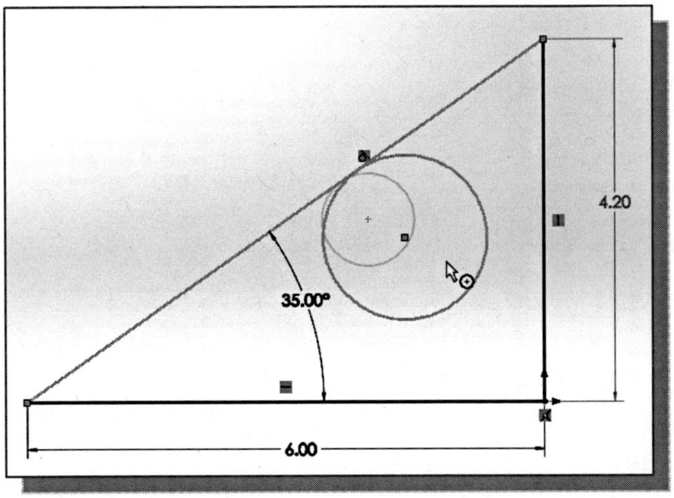

9. Move the cursor on top of the right side of the circle, and then drag the circle toward the right edge of the graphics window. Notice the size of the circle is adjusted while the system maintains the **Tangent** relation.

10. Drag the center of the circle toward the upper right direction. Notice the **Tangent** relation is always maintained by the system.

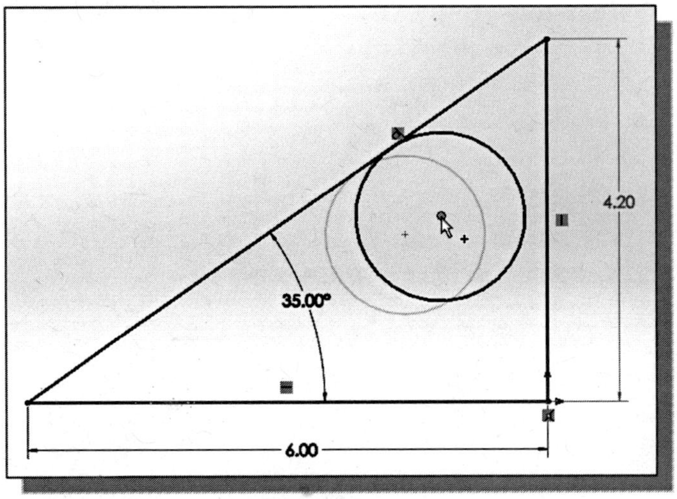

11. Press the [**Esc**] key to ensure that no objects are selected.

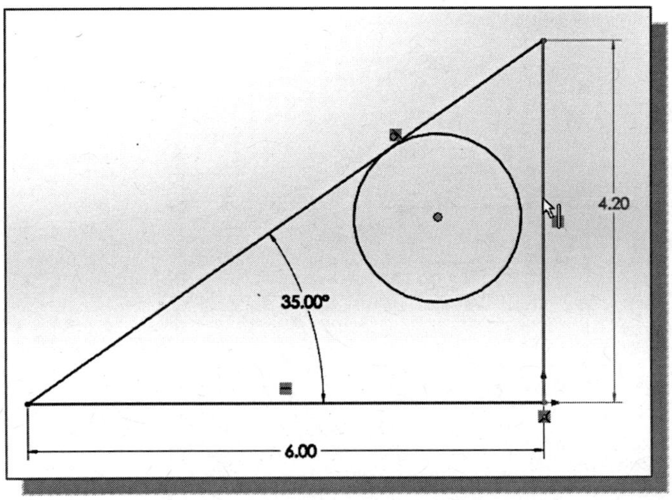

12. Inside the graphics window, click once with the **left-mouse-button** on the **center of the circle** to select the center point.

13. Hold down the [**Ctrl**] key and click once with the **left-mouse-button** on the **vertical line**.

- Holding the [**Ctrl**] key allows selecting the vertical line while maintaining selection of the circle center point. This is a method to select multiple entities. Notice the *Properties Property Manager* for the selected entities is displayed. This provides an alternate way to control the relations for selected properties.

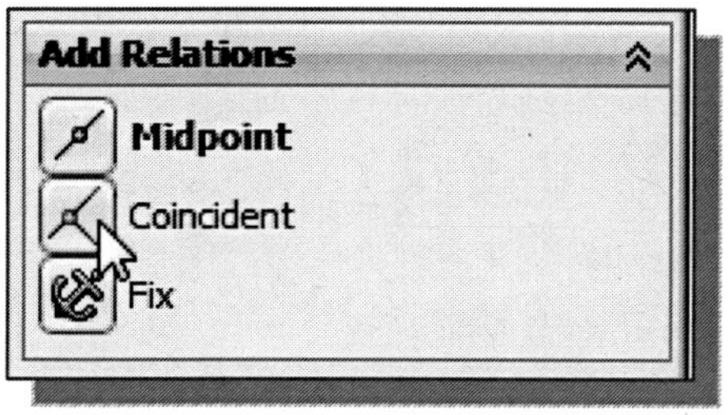

14. Click once with the left-mouse-button on the **Coincident** icon in the *Add Relations* panel in the *Property Manager* as shown. This activates the Coincident relation.

15. Click the **OK** icon in the *Property Manager.*

- Is the circle fully defined? (**HINT:** Drag the circle to see whether it is fully defined.)

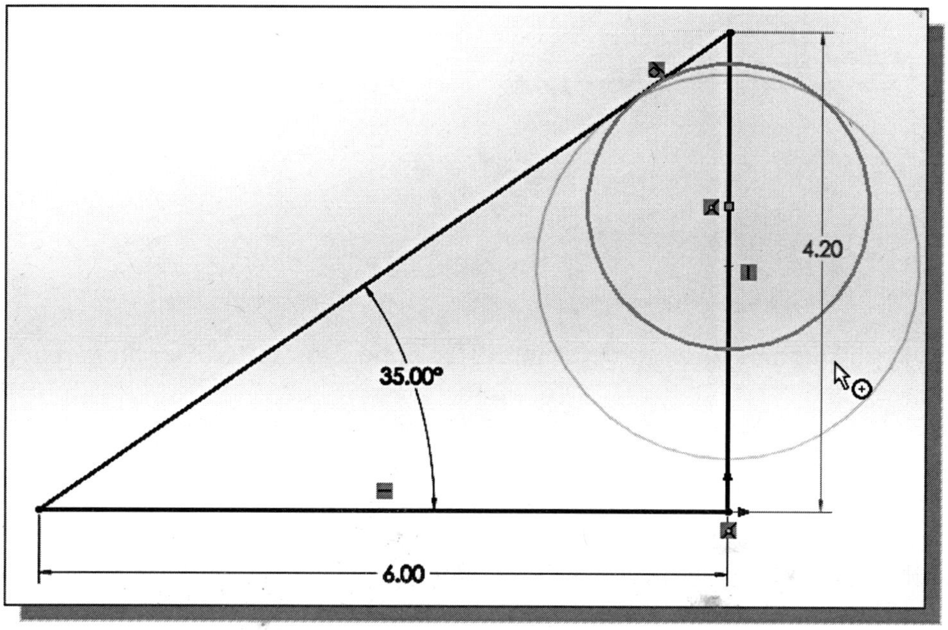

16. On your own, select the circle center point <u>and</u> the vertical line in the graphics area. (Hint: Hold down the [**Ctrl**] key while selecting.)

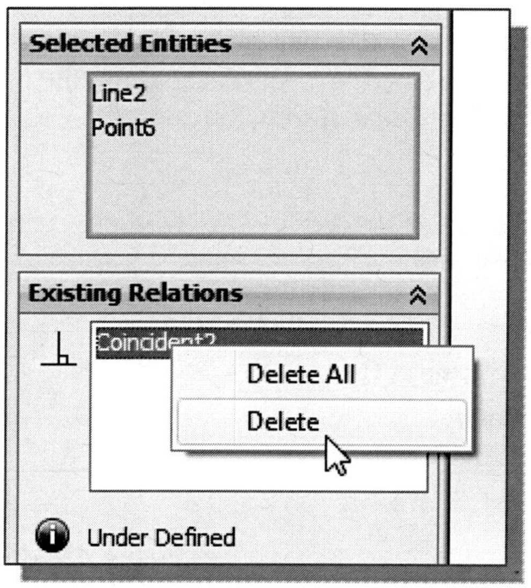

17. In the *Property Manager*, **Coincident2** is listed under *Existing Relations*. Move the cursor over **Coincident2** and click once with the **right-mouse-button.**

18. Select **Delete** in the pop-up menu by clicking once with the **left-mouse-button.**

19. Click the **OK** icon in the *Property Manager.*

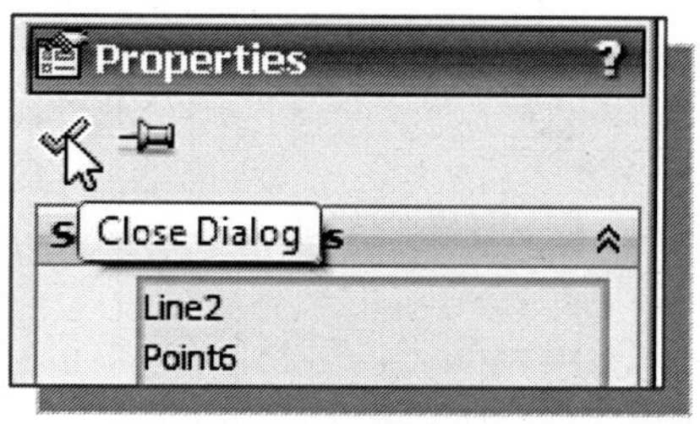

20. On your own, add a **Coincident** relation between the center of the circle and the horizontal line.

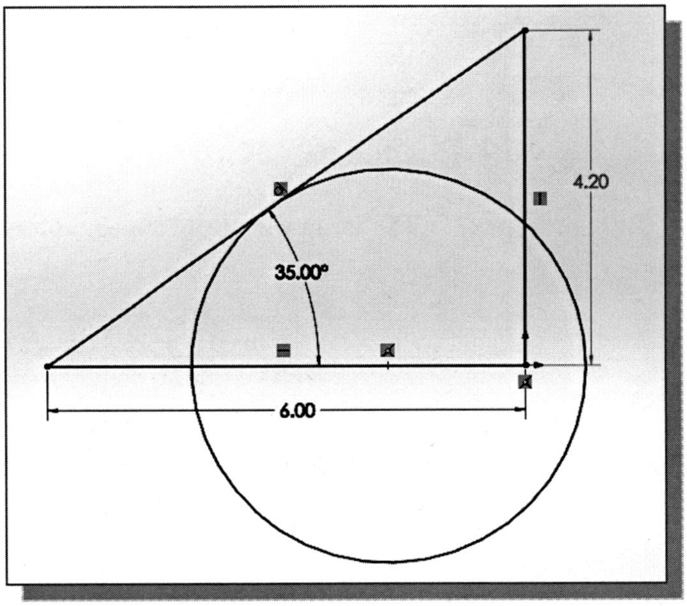

❖ The application of different relations affects the geometry differently. The design intent is maintained in the CAD model's database and thus allows us to create very intelligent CAD models that can be modified/revised fairly easily. On your own, experiment and observe the results of applying different relations to the triangle. For example: (1) adding another **Fix** constraint to the top corner of the triangle; (2) deleting the horizontal dimension and adding another **Fix** relation to the left corner of the triangle; and (3) adding another **Tangent** relation and adding a size dimension to the circle.

Relations Settings

- Select **Options** in the *Menu Bar*. Click on **Relations/Snaps** under the **System Options** tab to display and/or modify the relation settings. On your own, adjust the settings and experiment with the effects on sketching of the different settings.

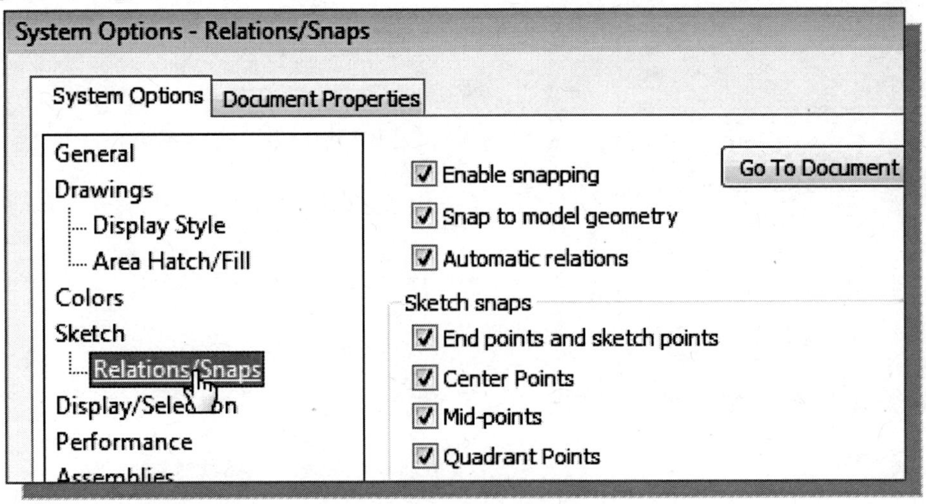

Model the *B3-Leg* Part

1. Select the **New** icon with a single click of the left-mouse-button on the *Menu Bar*.

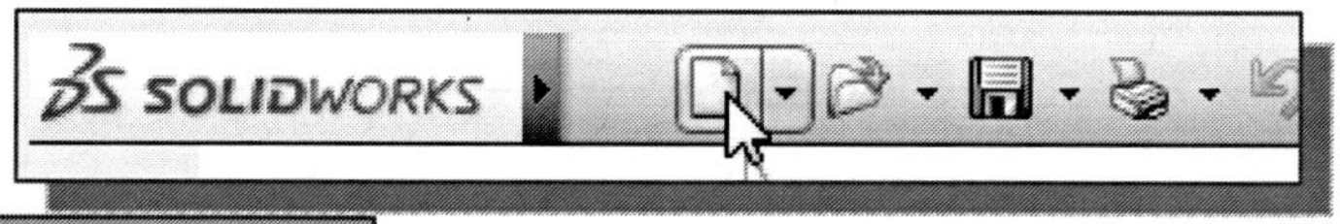

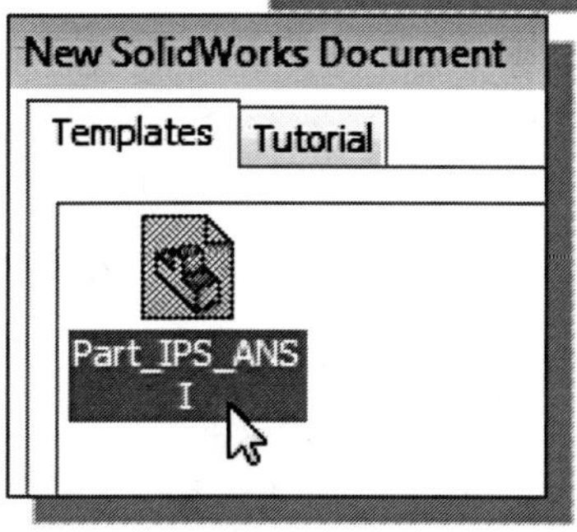

2. Notice the Part_IPS_ANSI template appears in the **Advanced** mode. Select the **Part_IPS_ANSI** template as shown.

3. Click on the **OK** button to open a new document using the Part_IPS_ANSI template. The *Dimensioning Standard* will automatically be ANSI and the units will be set to inch, pound, second as defined in the template.

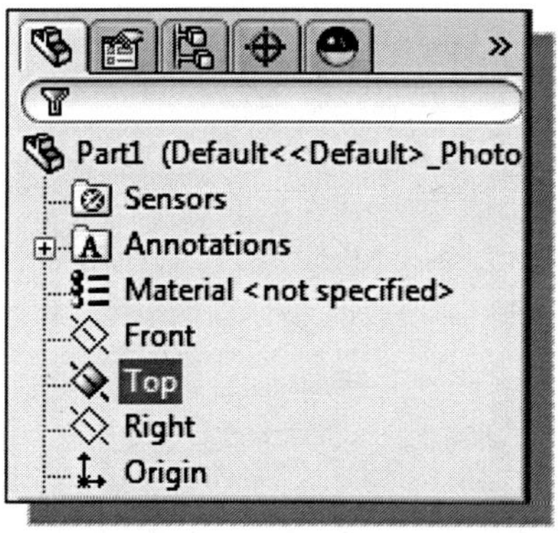

4. In the *Feature Manager Design Tree*, click once with the **left-mouse-button** to pre-select the **Top Plane** as shown.

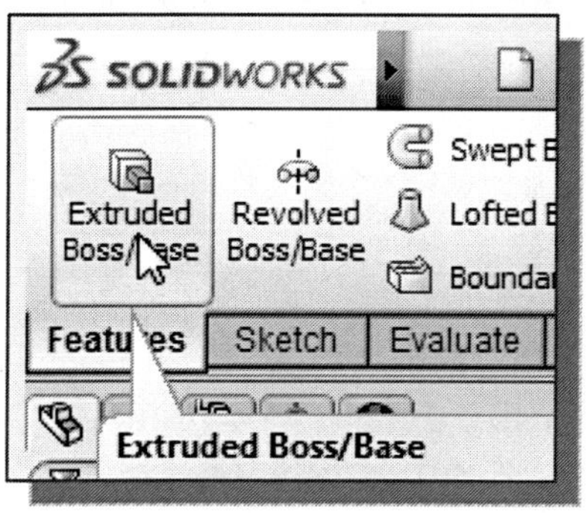

5. In the *Features* toolbar select the **Extruded Boss/ Base** command by clicking once with the left-mouse-button on the icon.

- Note the pre-selection of Top Plane enables the use of the plane as the sketching plane.

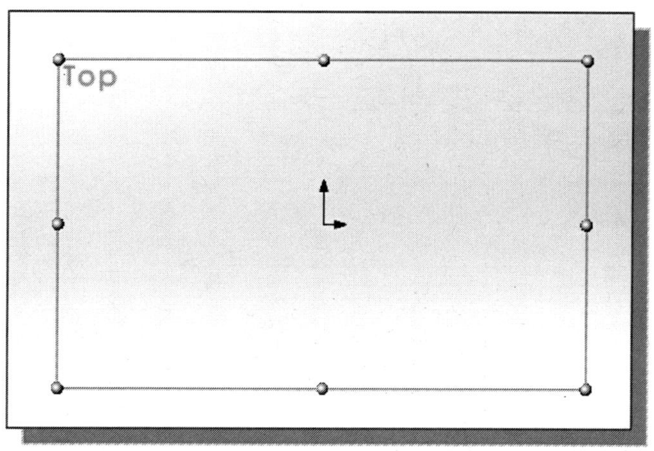

Create the 2D Sketch for the Base Feature

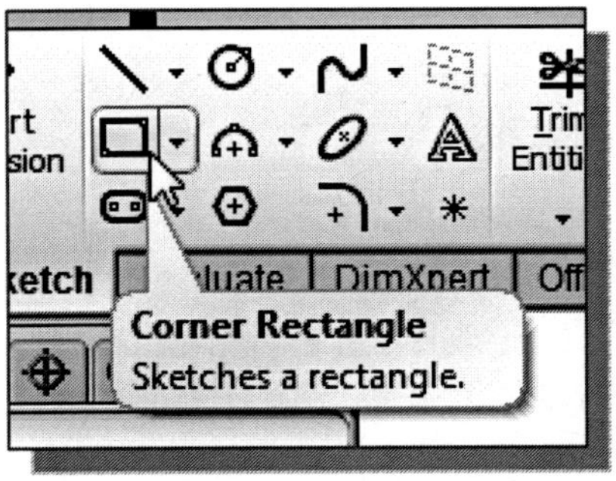

1. Select the **Corner Rectangle** command by clicking once with the **left-mouse-button** on the icon in the *Sketch* toolbar.

2. Create a rectangle of arbitrary size by selecting two locations on the screen as shown below. To demonstrate the effects of parametric equations, we will intentionally position the rectangle away from the *center point* of the coordinate system.

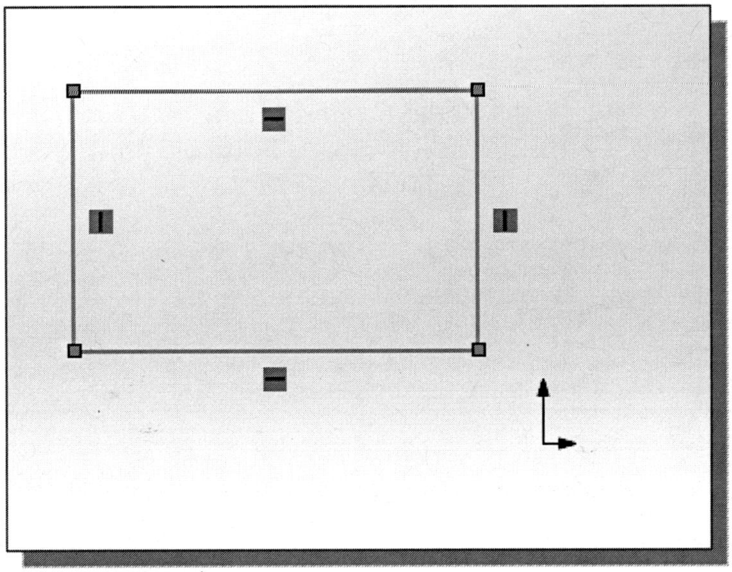

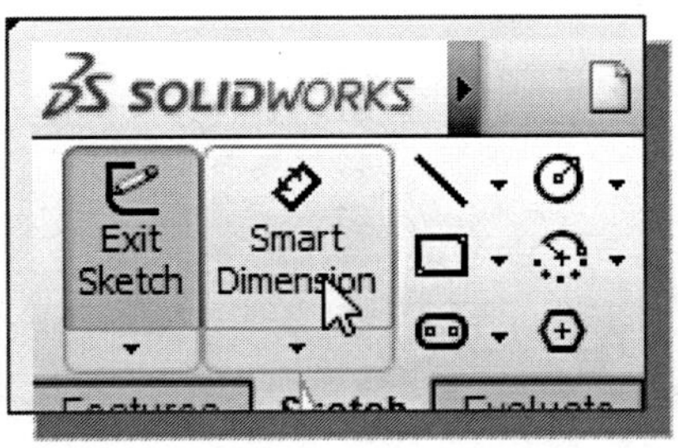

3. On your own, use the **Smart Dimension** command and create the size dimensions of the rectangle as shown in the figure below. Do not exit the Smart Dimension command.

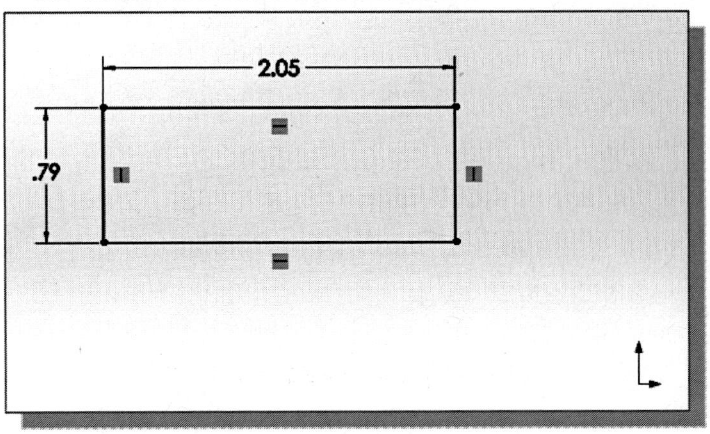

Parametric Relations

Initially in *SolidWorks*, dimension values are used to create different geometric entities. The text created by the **Smart Dimension** command also reflects the actual location and/or size of the entity. Each dimension is also assigned a name that allows the dimension to be used as a control variable. The default format is "Dxx," where the "xx" is a number that *SolidWorks* increments automatically each time a new dimension is added. The full name has the form "Dxx@yyyyy", where the "yyyyy" is the entity in which the dimension is applied. For example "D2@Sketch1" is the full name for the second dimension applied in **Sketch 1**.

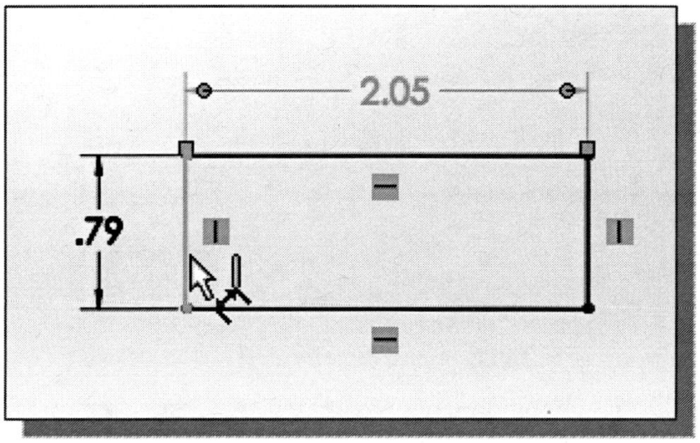

1. Select the left edge of the rectangle as the first item to dimension.

2. Select the *Origin* of the coordinate system as the second item to dimension.

3. Place the location dimension below the rectangle as shown.

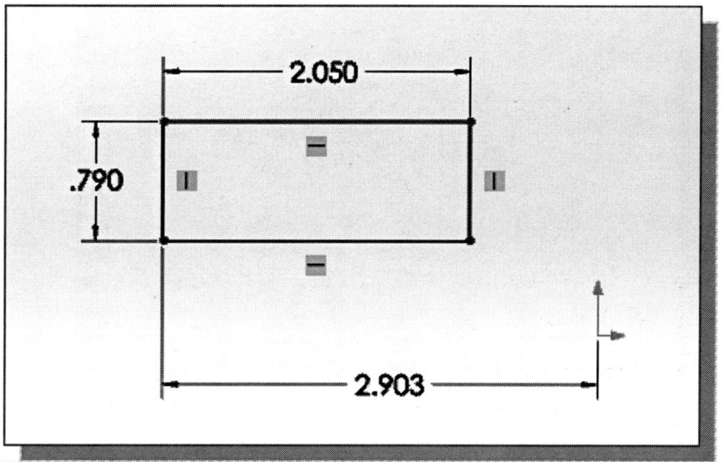

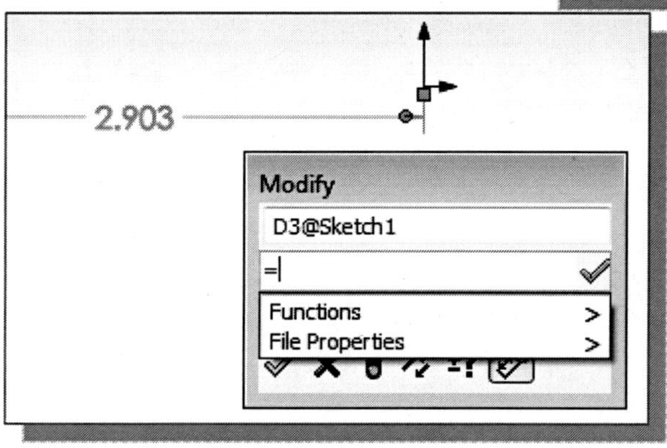

4. In the *Modify* dialog box, note that the dimensional variable name (**D3@Sketch1**) is automatically generated by *SolidWorks*.

5. In the *edit* box, enter **=** (the equal sign) to enter the *Equation* mode to define the dimension.

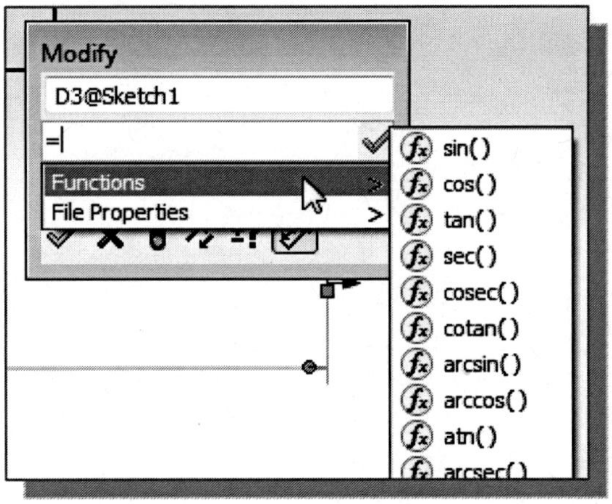

- Note that additional options appeared below the *edit* box as shown.

6. Move the cursor on top of **Functions** to display the available mathematic functions.

- Note the **File Properties** option provides *properties* related to the constructed model.

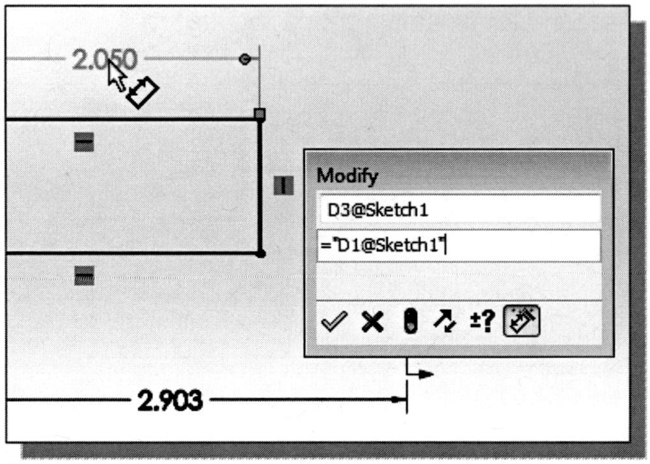

7. Click on the width dimension of the rectangle. Notice the variable name is entered in the *edit dimension* window as shown.

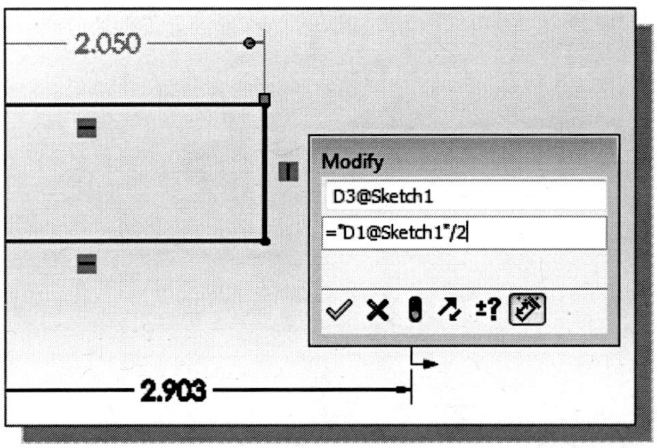

8. In the *edit dimension* window, enter **/2** to set the horizontal location dimension to be one-half of the width of the rectangle.

9. Click on the **check mark** button to close the *edit dimension* window.

❖ Notice, the derived dimension value is displayed with **Σ** in front of the number. The parametric relation we entered is used to control the horizontal location of the rectangle relative to the *Origin*; the horizontal location is now based on the width of the rectangle.

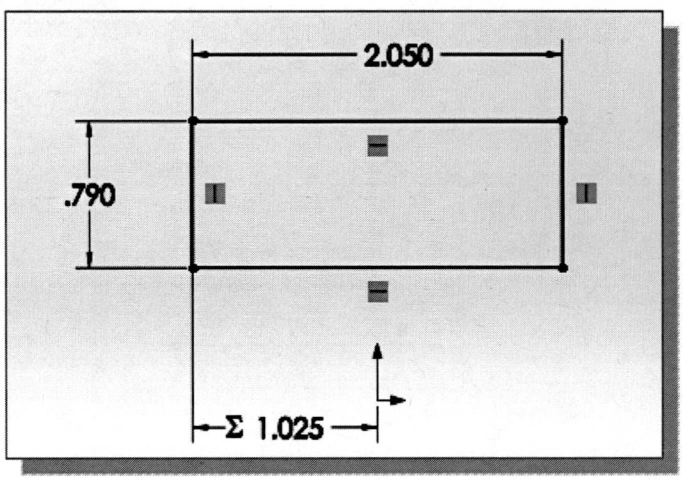

10. Repeat the above steps and create another parametric relation for the vertical location dimension (set the value to equal to one-half of the height of the rectangle.)

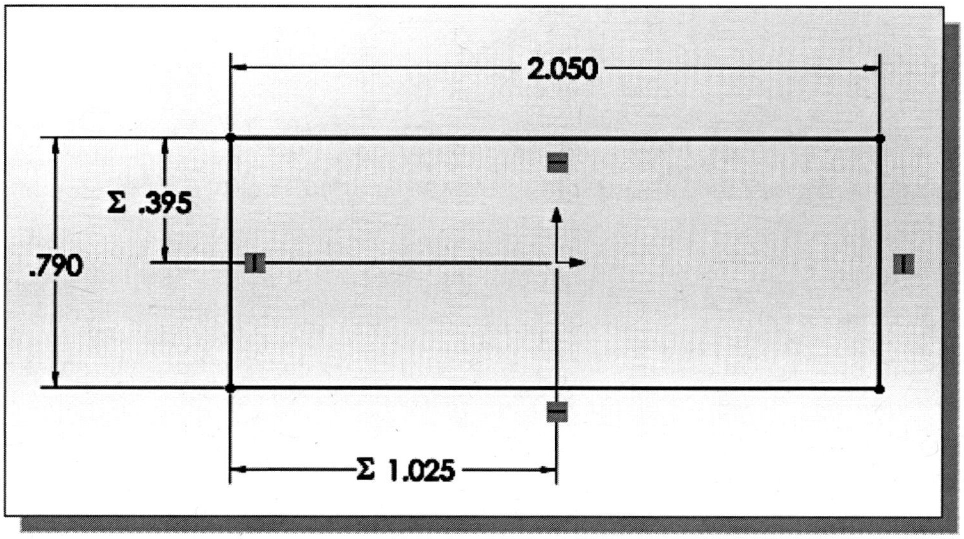

Use the Equations Command

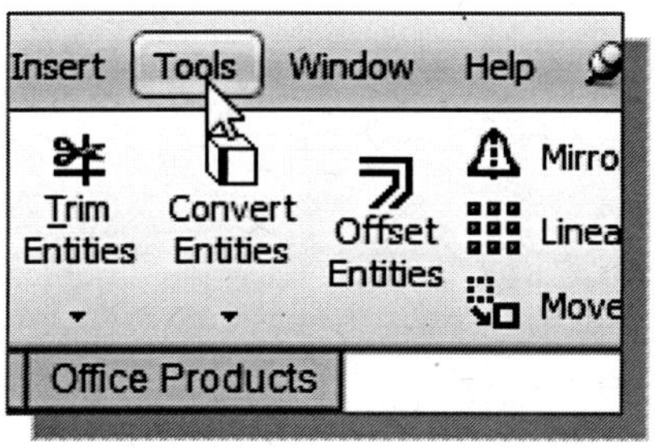

1. Click once with the left-mouse-button on the *Tools* menu and select **Equations** in the pull-down menu as shown.

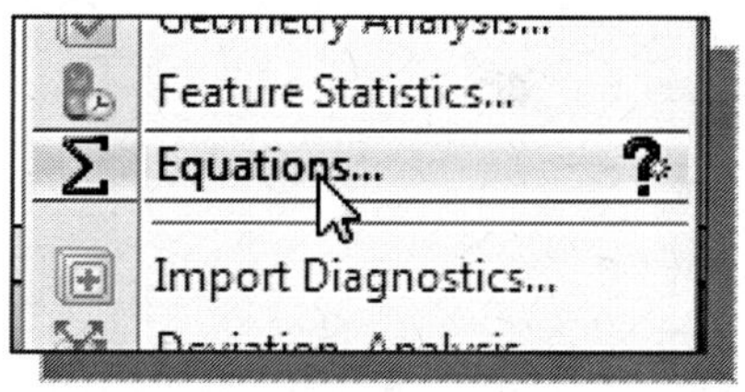

- The Equations command can be used to display all equations used to define the model. We can also edit equations, and create additional design variables and equations.

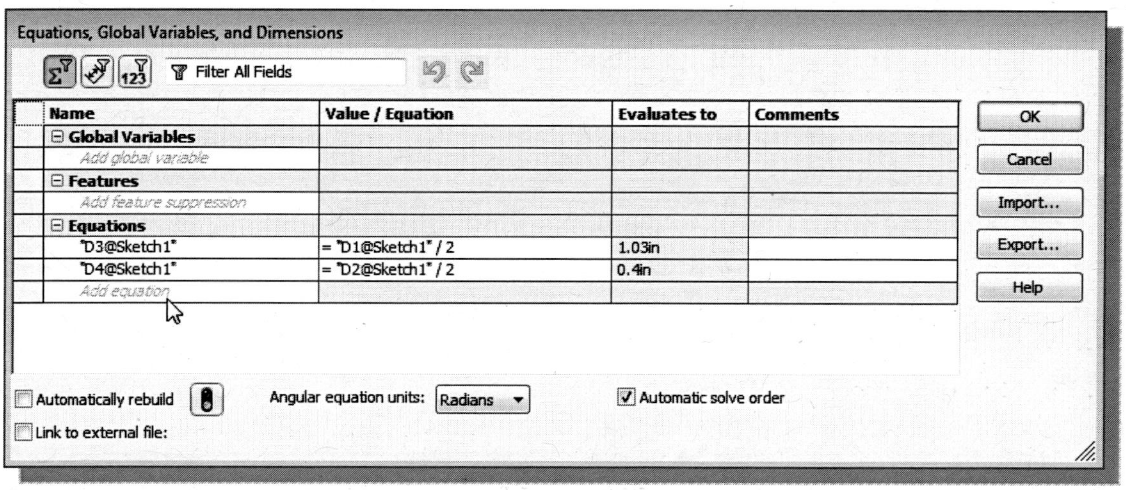

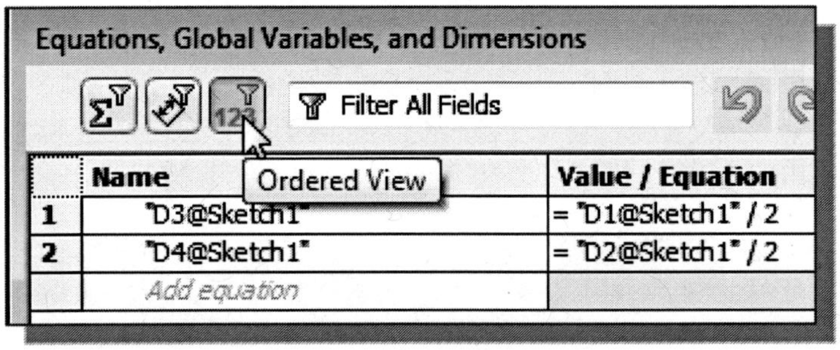

2. On your own, examine the different options available in the *Equations, Global Variables, and Dimensions* dialog box.

- Note that we can modify any of the equations or enter new equations in the dialog box.

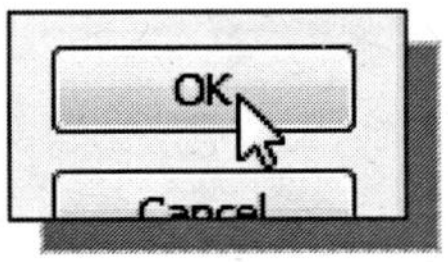

3. Click the **OK** button to exit the *Equations* dialog box.

4. On your own, change the dimensions of the rectangle and observe the changes to the location and size of the rectangle. Reset the values to **2.05 and 0.79** before continuing to the next section.

Complete the Base Feature

1. Select the **Fillet** command by clicking once with the left-mouse-button on the icon in the *Sketch* toolbar.

2. Enter **0.18** as the radius value of the fillet.

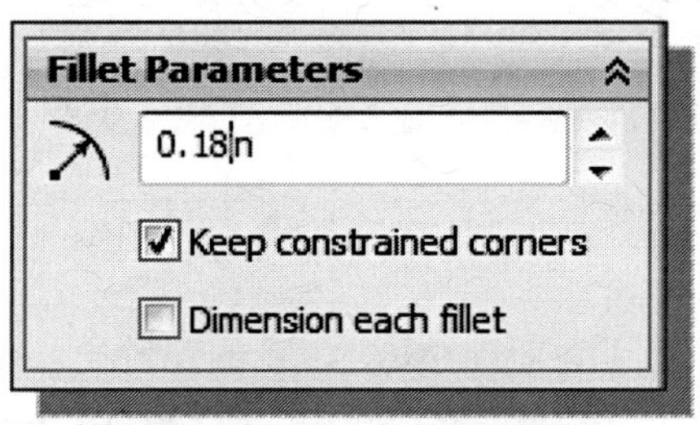

3. Create the two rounded corners toward the left side of the sketched geometry as shown.

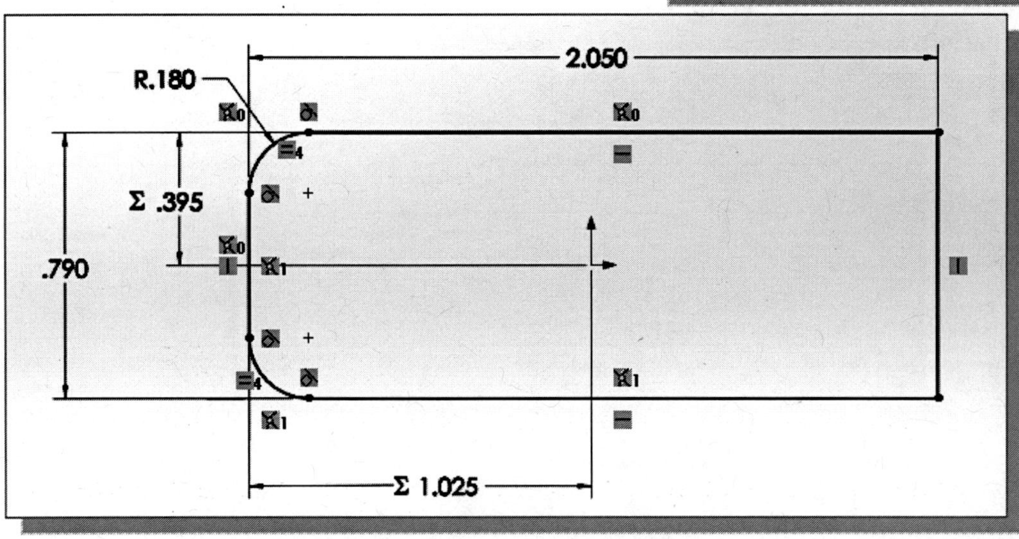

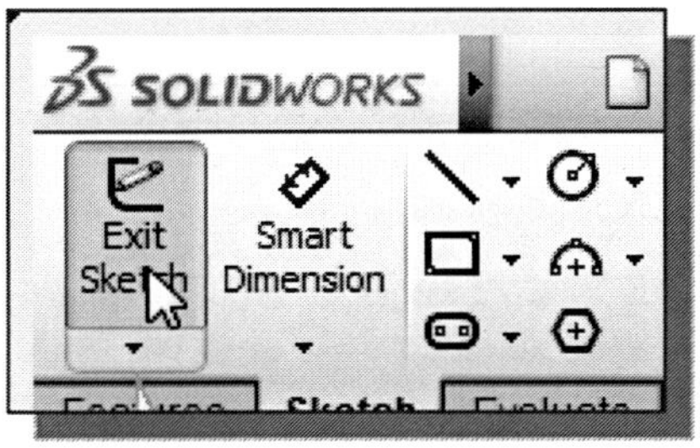

4. Click **Exit Sketch** in the *Sketch* toolbar to end the *Sketch* mode.

5. In the *distance* option box, enter **0.10** as the extrusion distance.

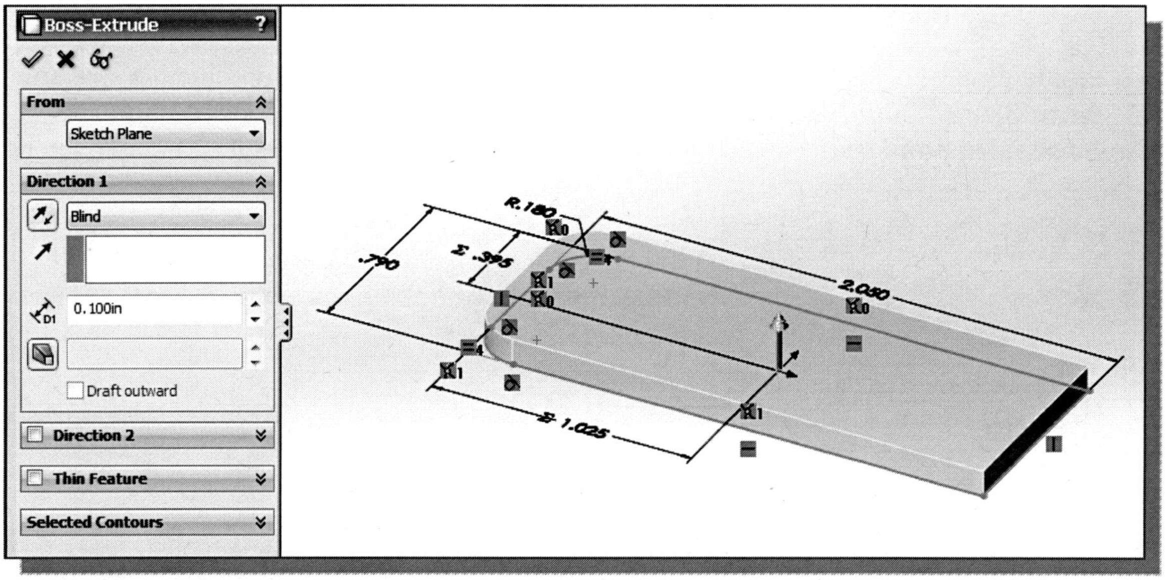

6. Click on the **OK** button to accept the settings and create the base feature.

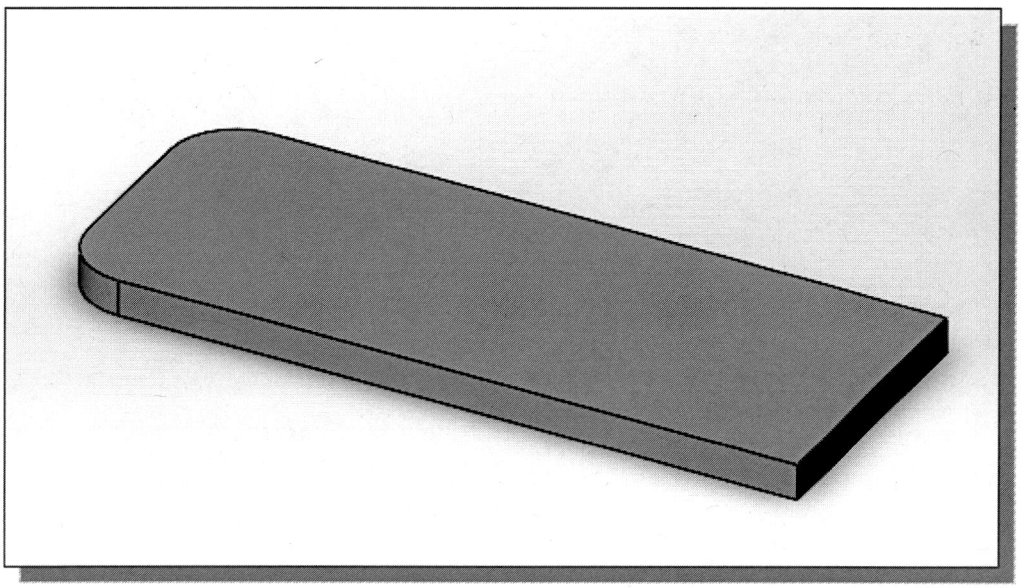

Sketches vs. Profiles

❖ In *SolidWorks*, ***profiles*** are closed regions that are defined from ***sketches***. Profiles are used as cross sections to create solid features. For example, **Extrude**, **Revolve**, **Sweep**, **Loft** and **Coil** operations all require the definition of at least a single profile. The sketches used to define a profile can contain additional geometry since the additional geometry entities are consumed when the feature is created. To create a profile we can create single or multiple closed regions, or we can select existing solid edges to form closed regions. A profile cannot contain self-intersecting geometry; regions selected in a single operation form a single profile. As a general rule, we should dimension and constrain profiles to prevent them from unpredictable size and shape changes. *SolidWorks* does allow us to create under-constrained or non-constrained profiles; the dimensions and/or constraints can be added and edited later.

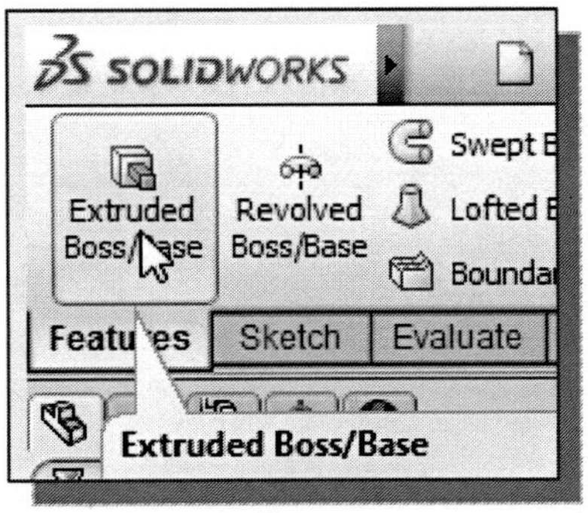

1. In the *Features* toolbar select the **Extruded Boss/ Base** command by clicking once with the left-mouse-button on the icon.

2. Select the **top face** of the model as the sketch plane for the new sketch.

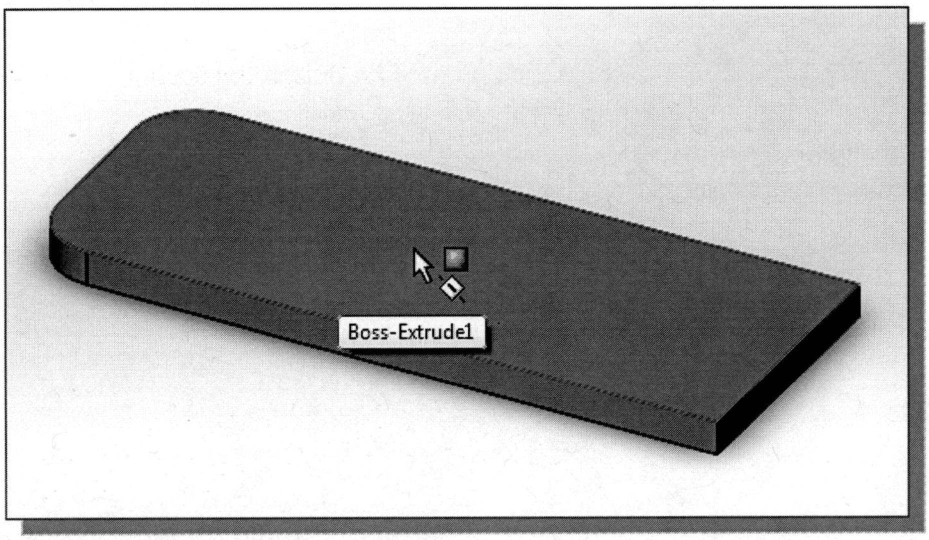

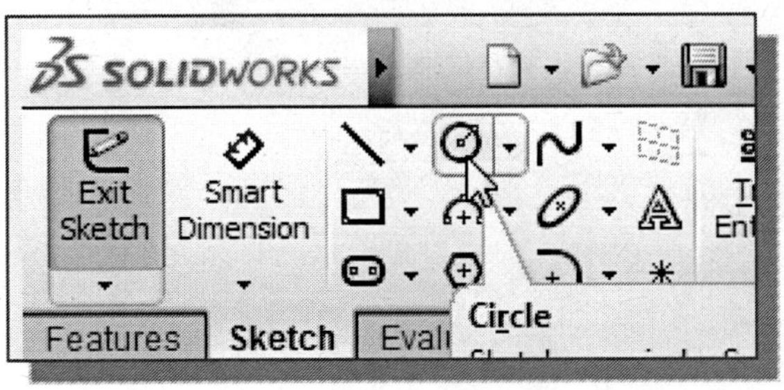

3. Select the **Circle** command by clicking once with the **left-mouse-button** on the icon in the *Sketch* toolbar.

4. On your own, create four circles as shown. If necessary, apply additional constraints to assure the sketch is fully constrained.

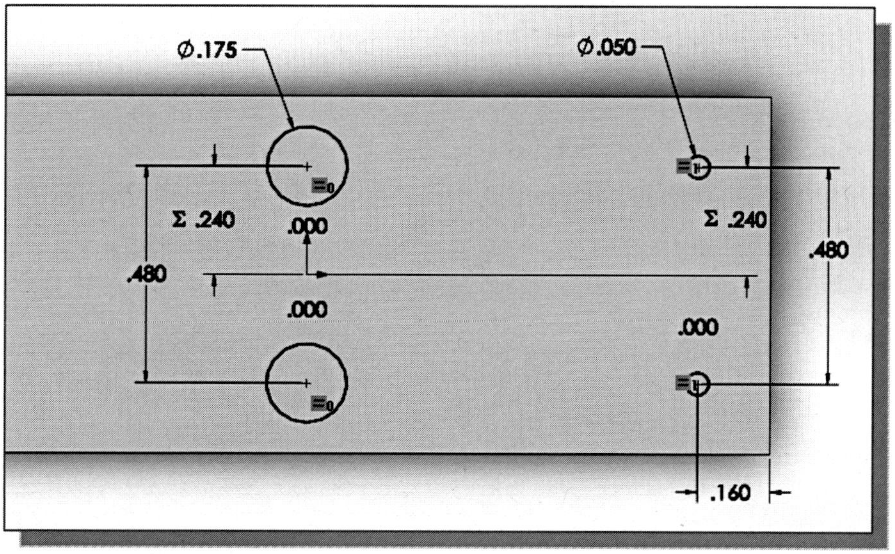

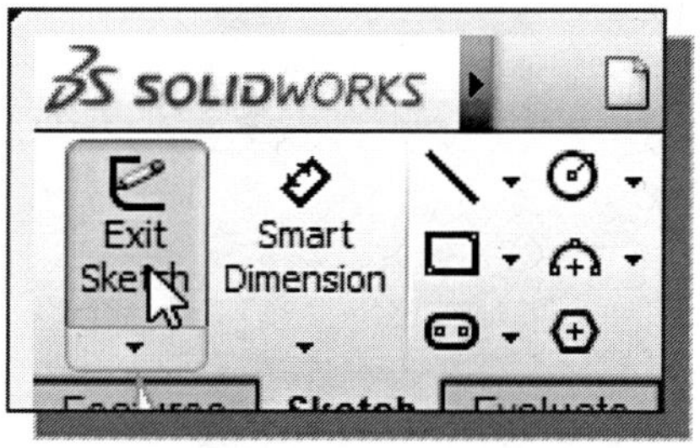

5. Click **Exit Sketch** in the *Sketch* toolbar to end the *Sketch* mode.

6. Set the extrusion distance to **0.08** and also the extrusion direction upward. (**Do not close** the *Boss-Extrude Manager* yet.)

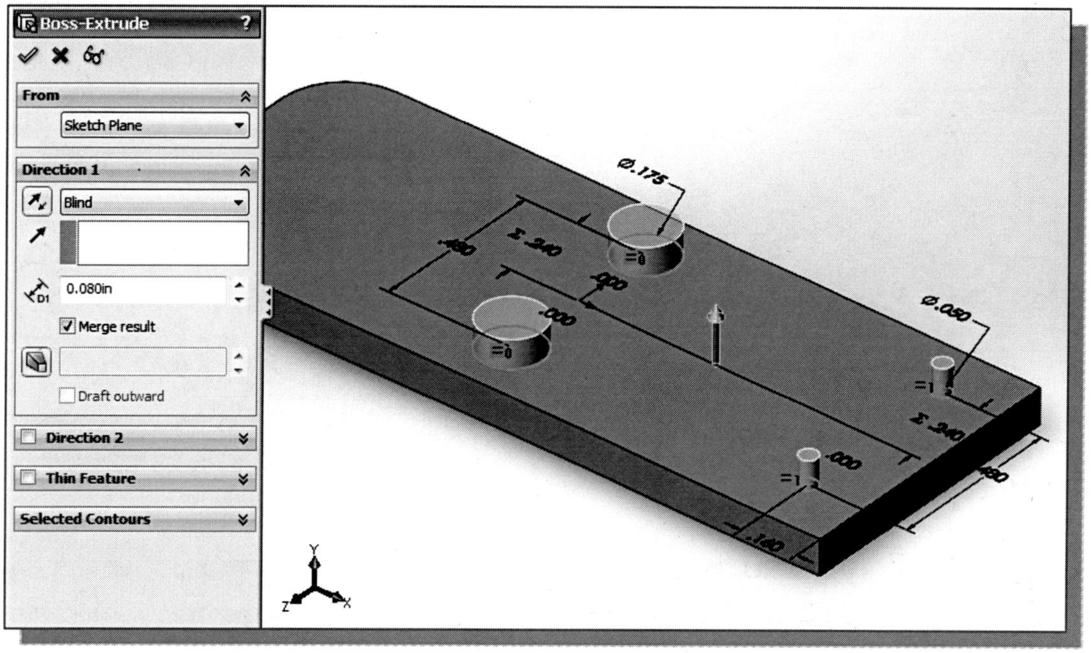

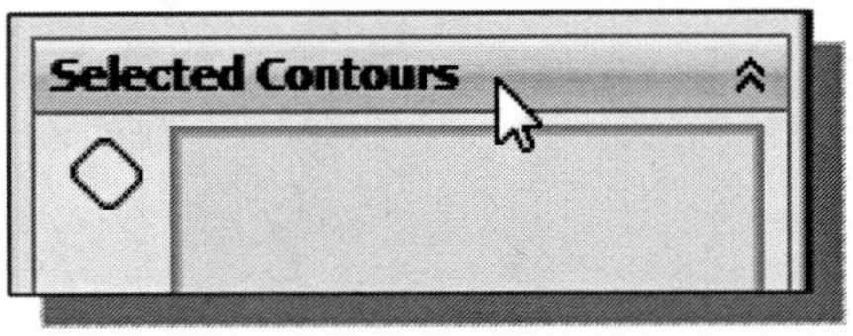

7. Expand the *Selected Contours* option panel by clicking on the title as shown.

8. Select one of the larger circles, by clicking on the circle, as shown. (Use the dynamic **Zoom** option to aid the selection.)

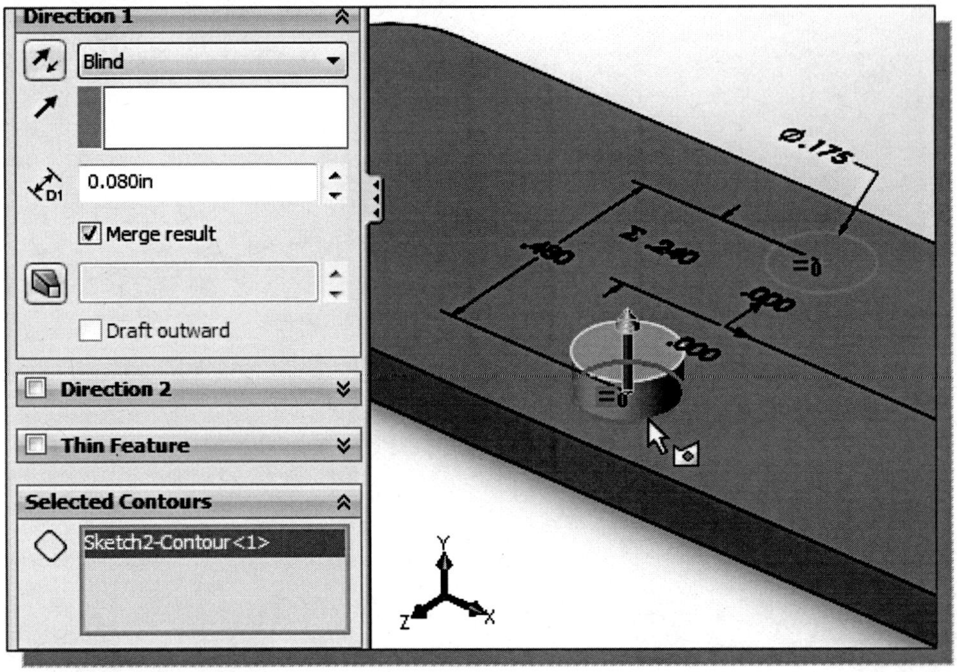

9. Click on the **OK** button to accept the settings and create the extruded feature.

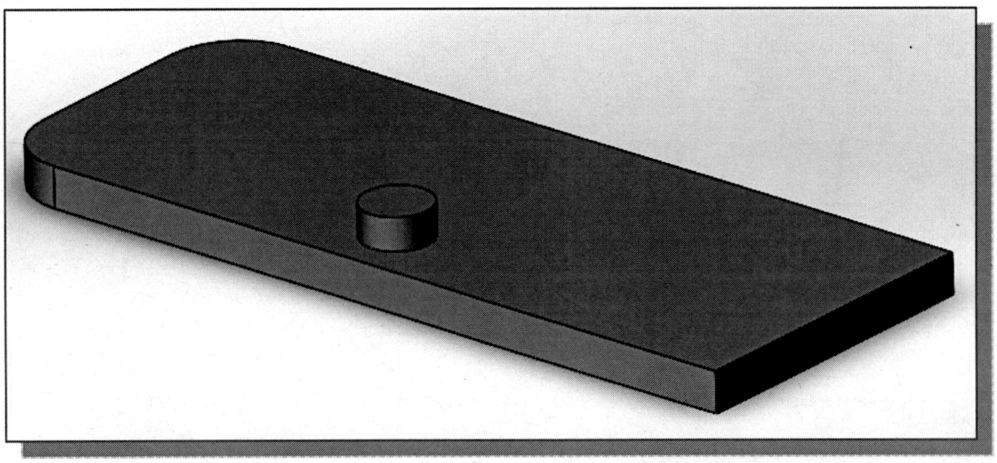

- Note that only the selected region was used to define the profile, which was then used to create the solid feature. Note that the additional geometric entities still exist in the 2D sketch.

Redefine the Profile with Contour Selection

- Engineering designs usually go through many revisions and changes. *SolidWorks* provides an assortment of tools to handle design changes quickly and effectively. We will demonstrate some of the tools available by changing the base feature of the design. The profile used to create the extrusion is selected from the sketched geometry entities. In *SolidWorks*, any profile can be edited and/or redefined at any time. It is this type of functionality in parametric solid modeling software that provides designers with greater flexibility and the ease to experiment with different design considerations.

In the *SolidWorks Property Manager* for features requiring definition of a profile, the ***Selected Contours*** selection window can be used to select sketch contours and model edges, and apply features to them. Contour Selection is a grouping mechanism that allows us to use a partial sketch to create features. It is a tool that helps maintain design intent by reducing the amount of trimming necessary to build the contour. In the previous section, the Boss-Extrude feature was created using a single continuous sketch contour to define the profile. In this section we will demonstrate the utility of the Contour Selection tool to generate a similar profile from a sketch containing self-intersecting geometry and multiple closed regions.

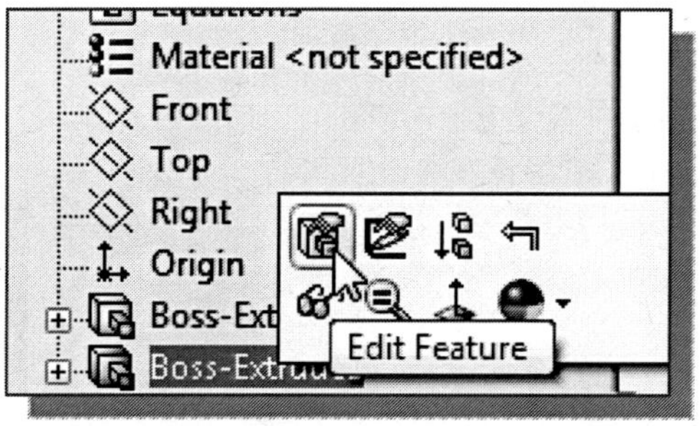

1. In the *Model Tree* area, right-mouse-click on the **Boss-Extrude2** feature to bring up the option menu.

2. Select the **Edit Feature** option as shown.

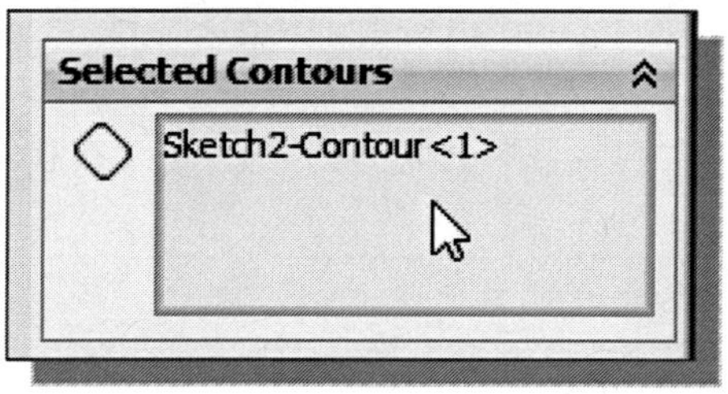

3. Click inside the *Selected Contours* list to activate the Contour Selection option.

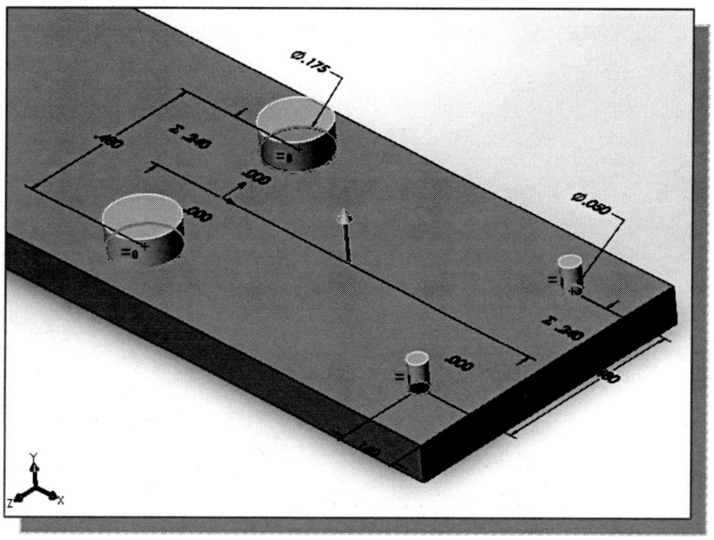

4. Select the other three circles, by clicking on the circles, as shown. (Use the dynamic Zoom option to aid the selection.)

5. Click on the **OK** button to proceed with modifying the solid feature.

Extrusion with the Taper Angle option

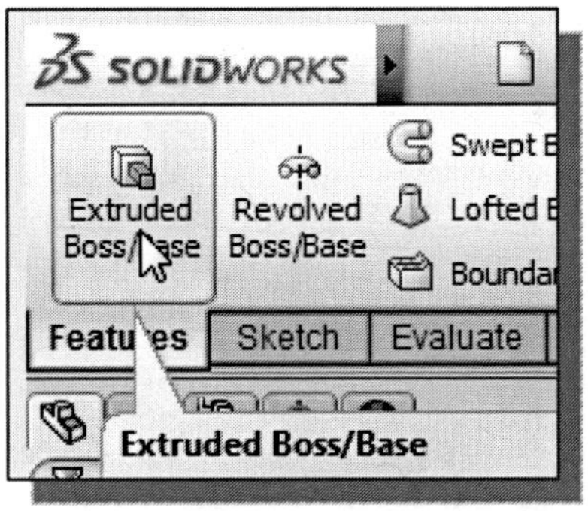

1. In the *Features* toolbar select the **Extruded Boss/ Base** command by clicking once with the left-mouse-button on the icon.

2. Select the **top face** of the model as the sketch plane for the new sketch.

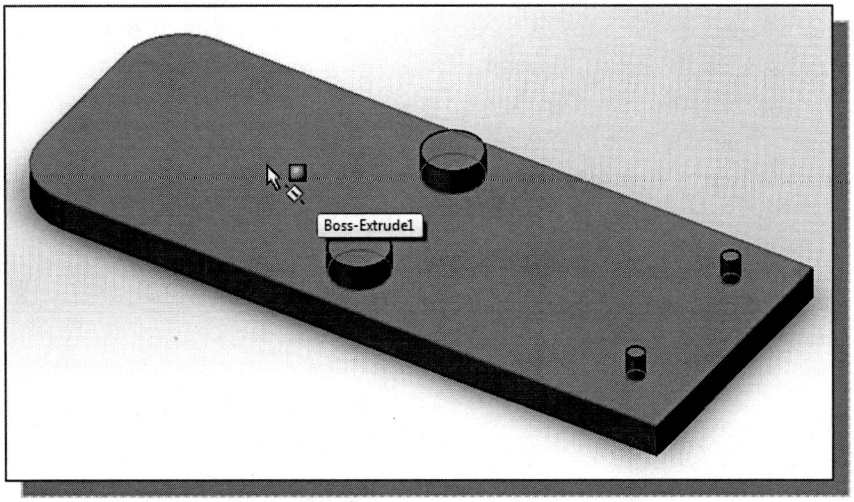

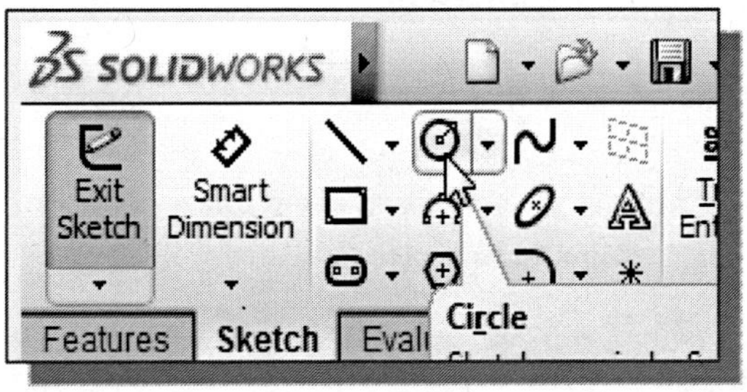

3. Select the **Circle** command by clicking once with the **left-mouse-button** on the icon in the *Sketch* toolbar.

4. On your own, create a circle with the dimensions shown.

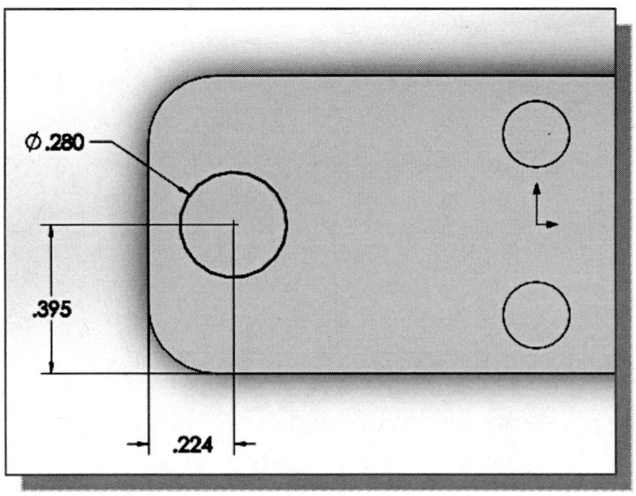

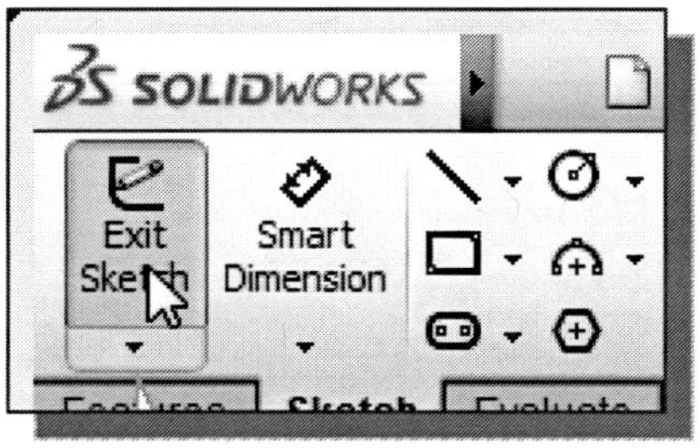

5. Click **Exit Sketch** in the *Sketch* toolbar to end the *Sketch* mode.

6. Set the extrusion distance to **0.18** and also the extrusion direction upward. (**Do not close** the *Boss-Extrude Manager*.)

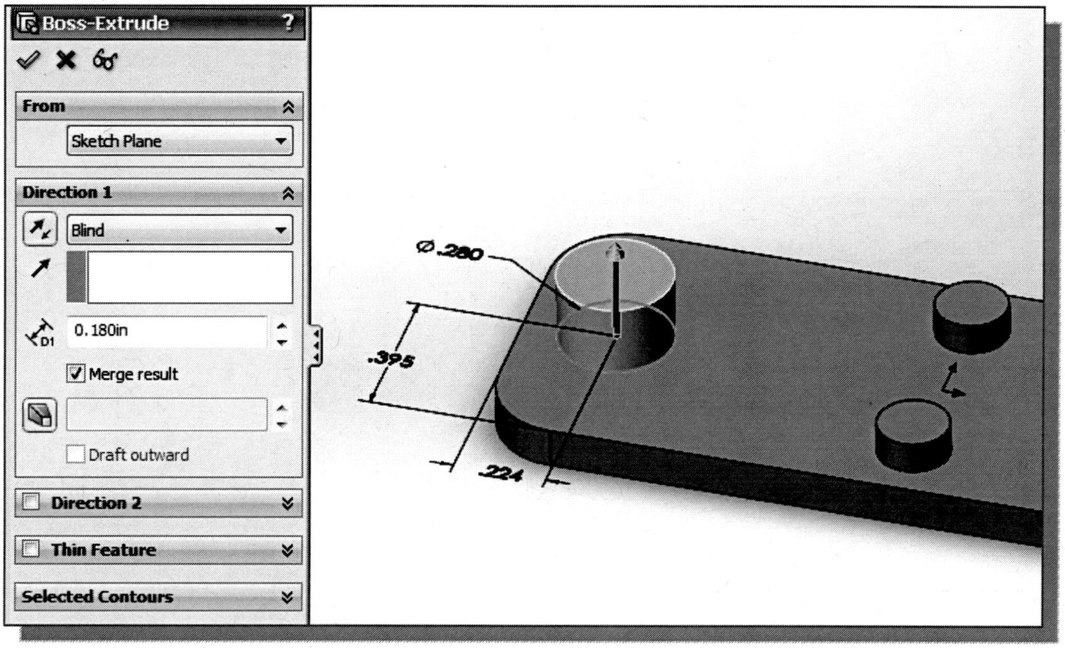

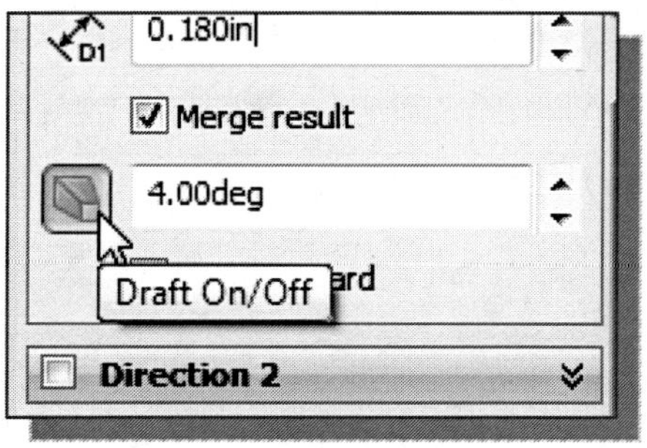

7. Activate the ***draft angle*** option and set the angle to **4.0** degrees as shown.

8. Click on the **OK** button to proceed with creating the solid feature.

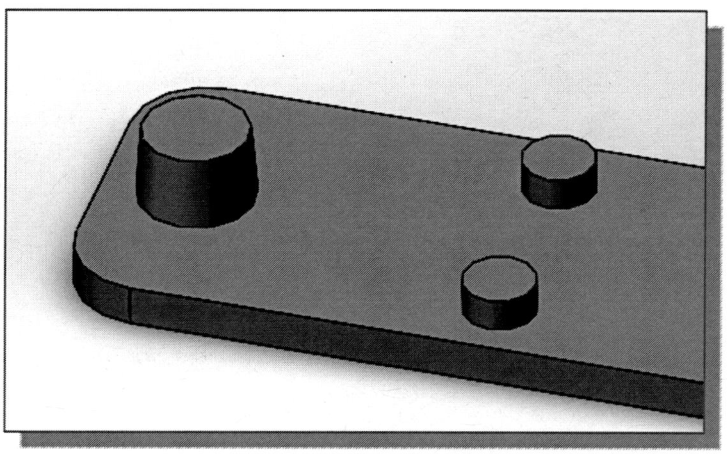

9. On your own, repeat the above steps and create another tapered solid feature as shown: diameter **0.22**, extrusion distance **0.217**, taper angle **4 degrees**.

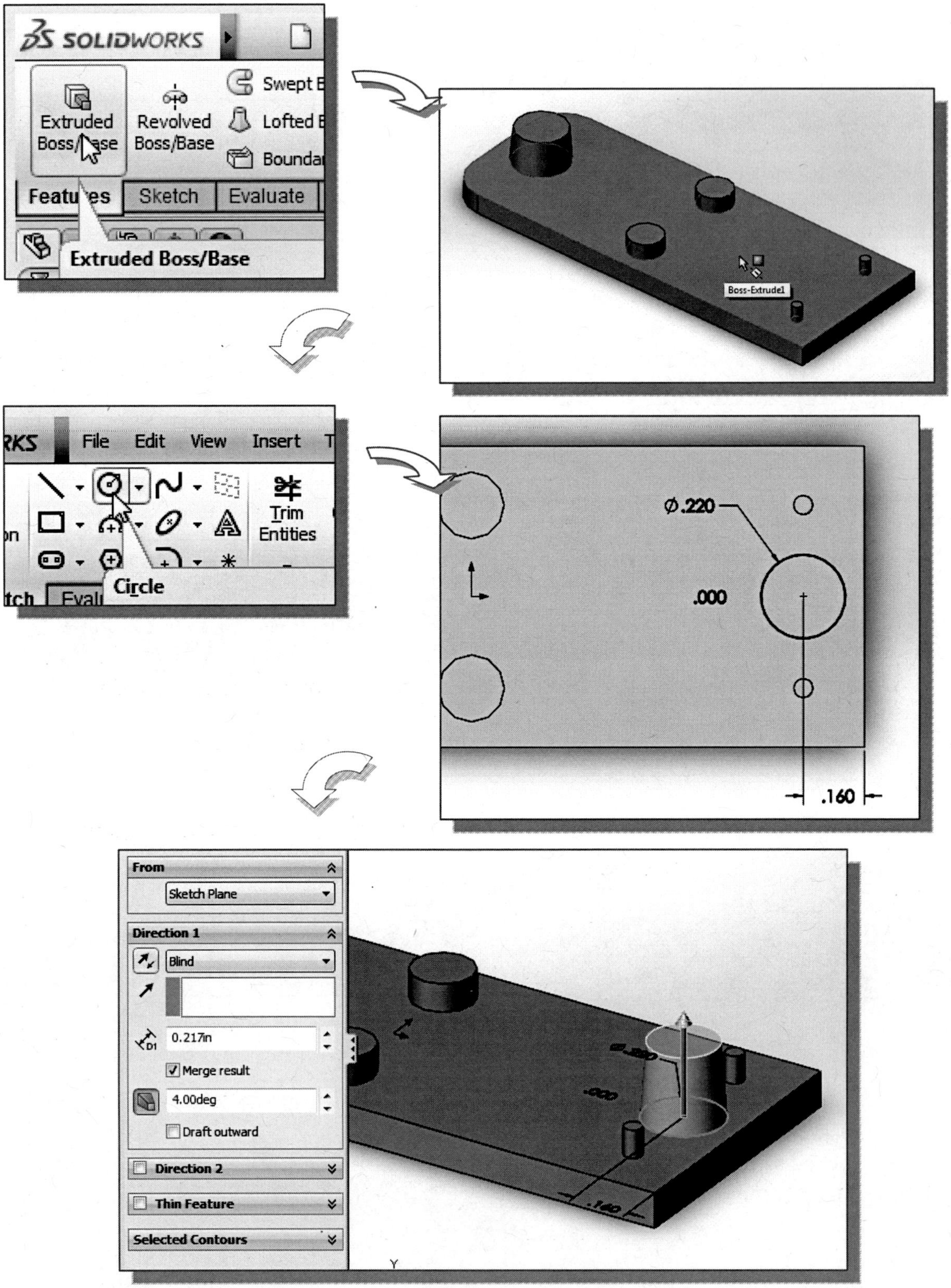

A Profile Containing Multiple Closed Regions

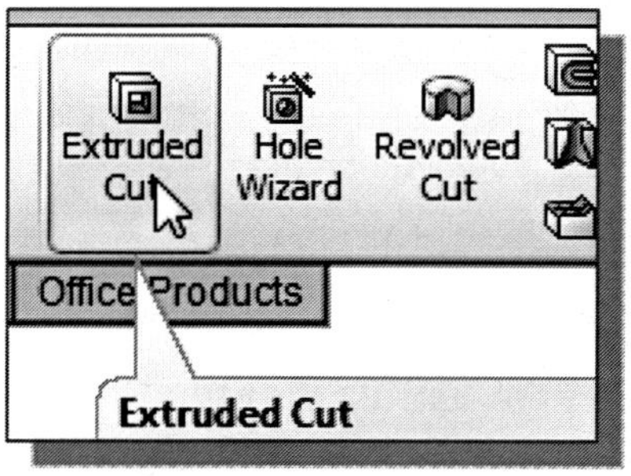

1. In the *Features* toolbar select the **Extruded Cut** command by clicking once with the left-mouse-button on the icon.

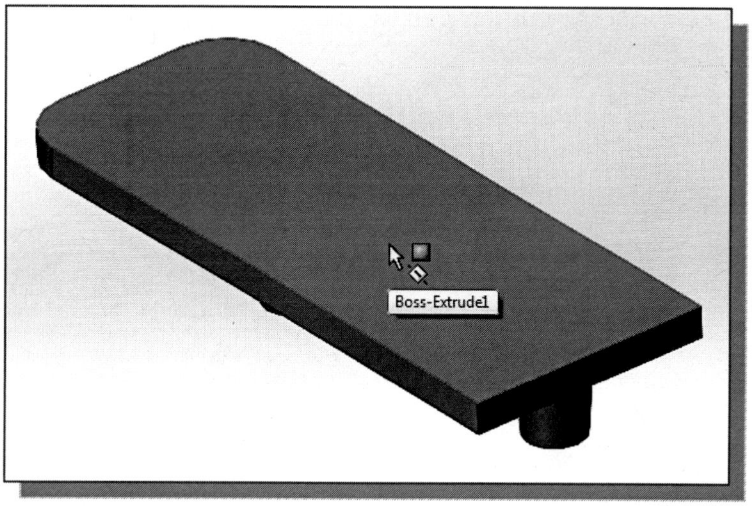

2. Select the **bottom plane of the base feature**, by clicking once with the left-mouse-button, as the sketching plane.

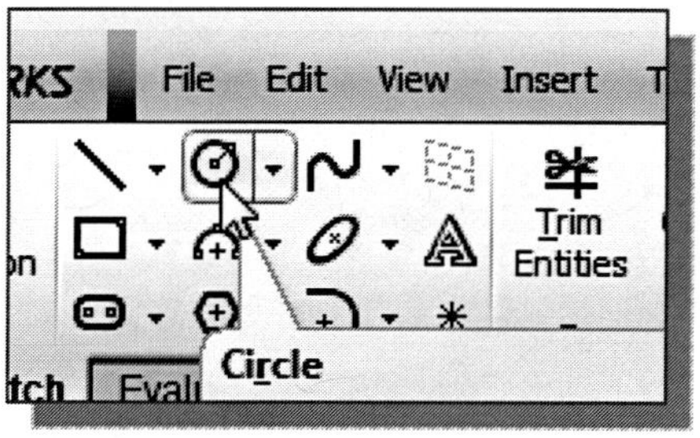

3. Select the **Circle** command by clicking once with the left-mouse-button on the icon in the *Sketch* panel.

4. On your own, create the **five circles** and the associated dimensions as shown.

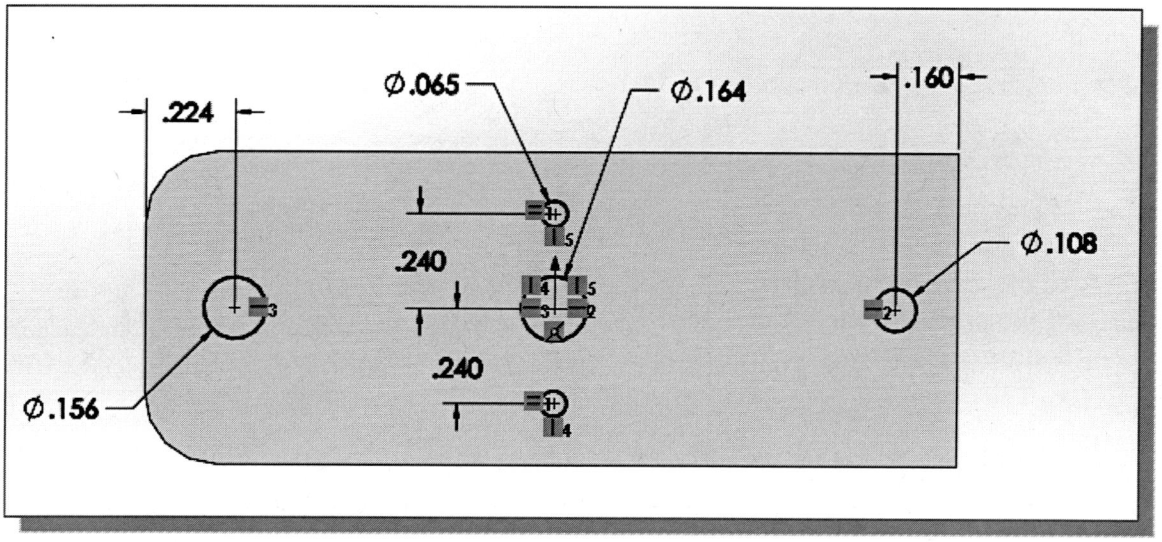

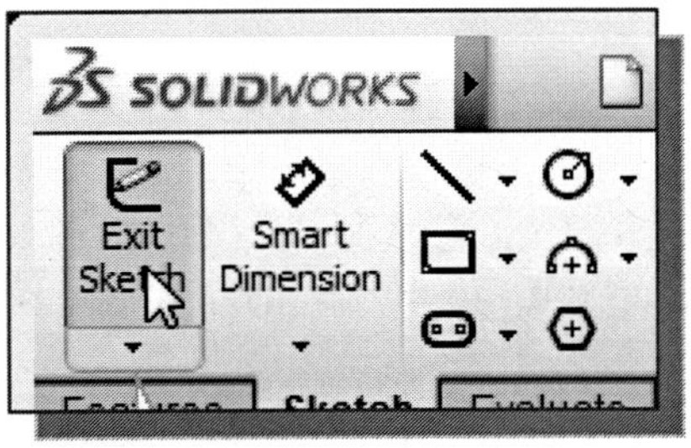

5. Click **Exit Sketch** in the *Sketch* toolbar to end the **Sketch** mode.

6. Set the extrusion distance to **Through All** and confirm the extrusion direction is set to cut through the part.

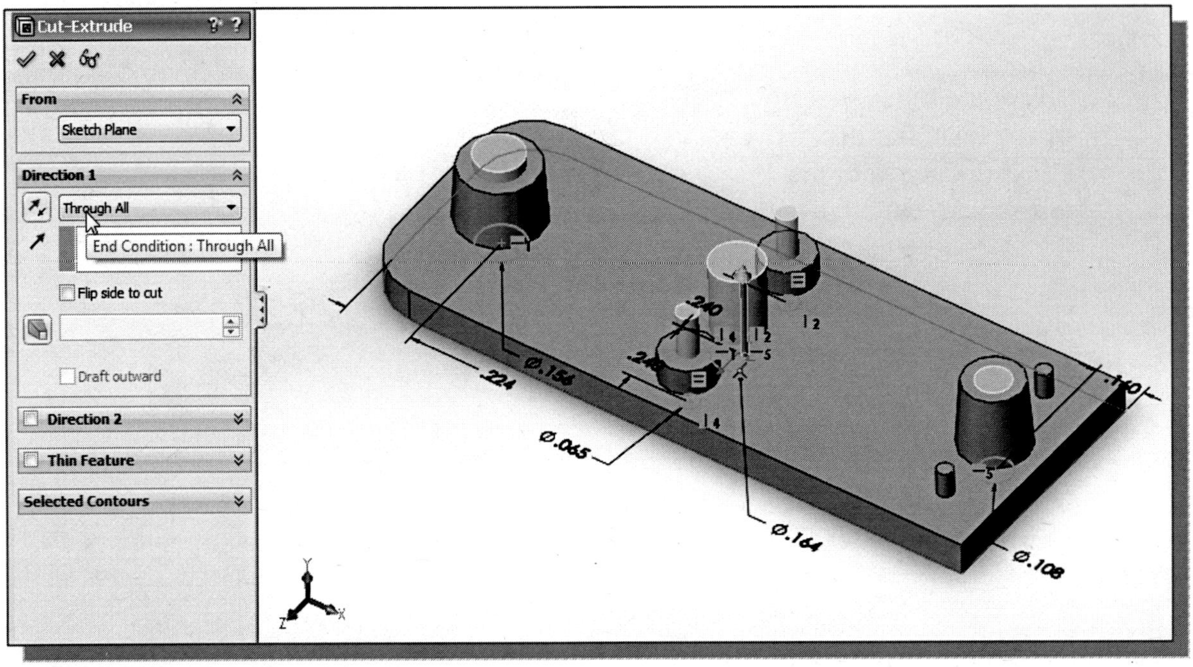

7. Click on the **OK** button to proceed with creating the cut feature.

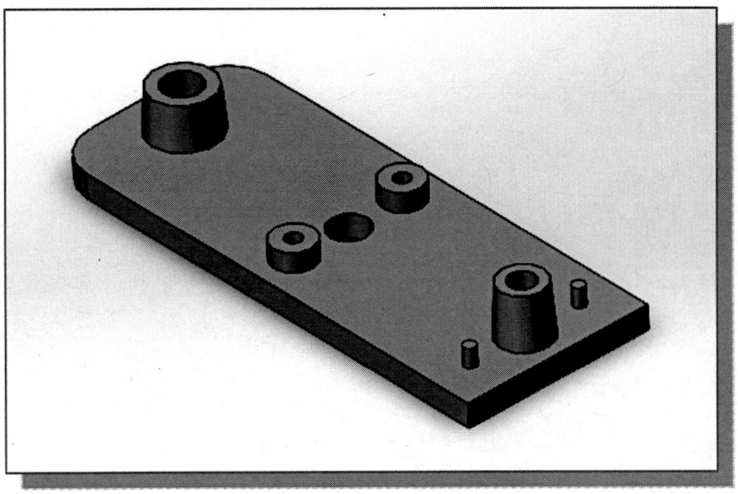

- By default, *SolidWorks* will automatically accept all closed regions as part of the profile of the solid feature.

The Convert Entities Option

- ❖ **Projected geometry** is another type of *reference geometry*. The Convert Entities tool can be used to project geometry from previously defined sketches or features onto the sketch plane. The position of the projected geometry is fixed to the feature from which it was projected. We can use the Convert Entities tool to project geometry from a sketch or feature onto the active sketch plane.

Typical uses of projected geometry include:

- Project a silhouette of a 3D feature onto the sketch plane for use in a 2D profile.
- Project the edges of a surface onto the sketch plane to be reused as a sketch.
- Project a sketch from a feature onto the sketch plane so that the projected sketch can be used to constrain a new sketch.

Add a Feature using existing geometry

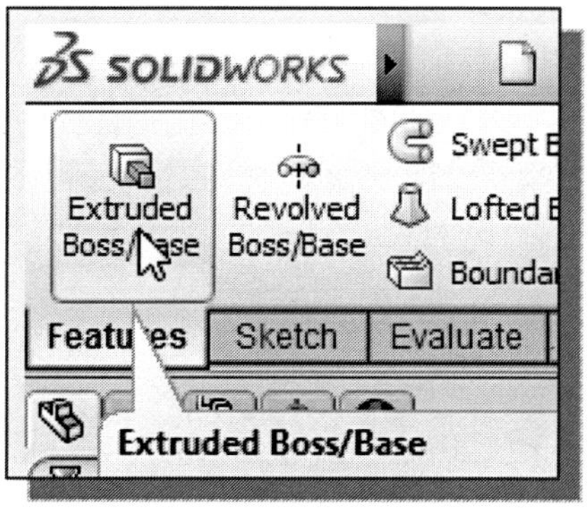

1. In the *Features* toolbar select the **Extruded Boss/ Base** command by clicking once with the left-mouse-button on the icon.

2. Select the **top plane of the left extrude feature**, by clicking once with the left-mouse-button, to align the sketching plane.

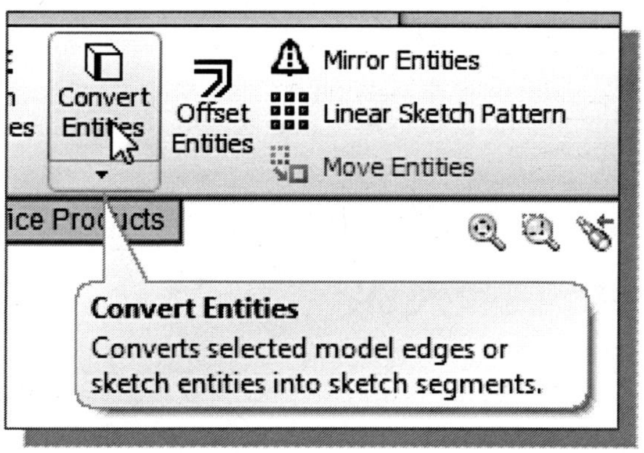

3. Select **Convert Entities** in the *Sketch* toolbar.

- The Convert Entities command can be used to project existing geometry to the sketching plane.

4. Select the inside circle of the extruded feature as shown.

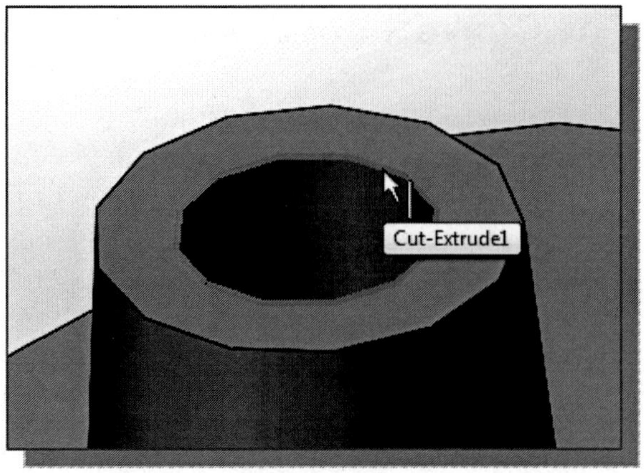

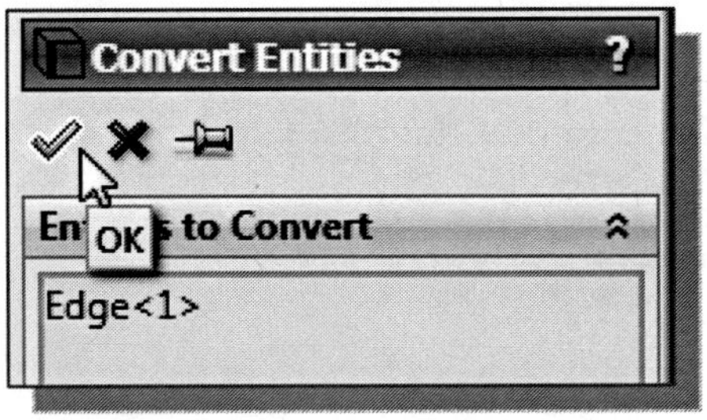

5. Click on the **OK** button to accept the selection and proceed with creating the solid feature.

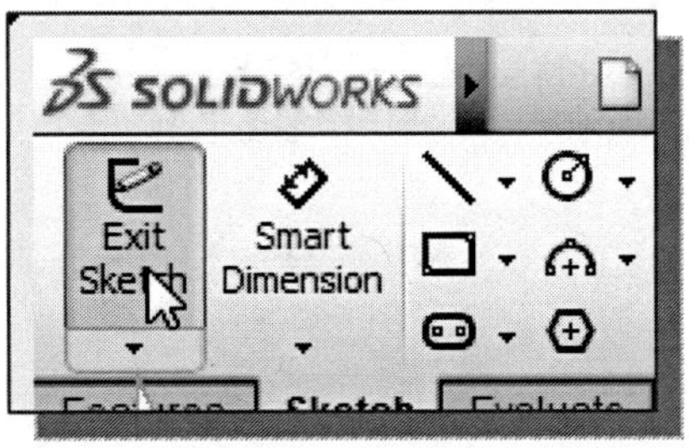

6. Click **Exit Sketch** in the *Sketch* toolbar to end the *Sketch* mode.

7. Set the extrusion distance to **0.08** and set the extrusion direction into the solid model as shown.

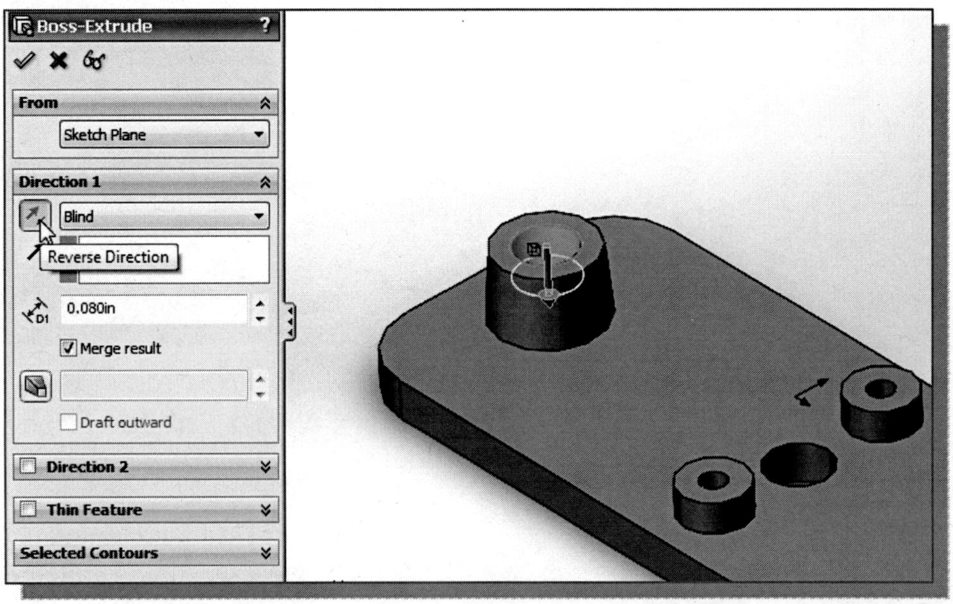

8. Click on the **OK** button to accept the selection and proceed with creating the solid extrusion feature.

Saving the Model File

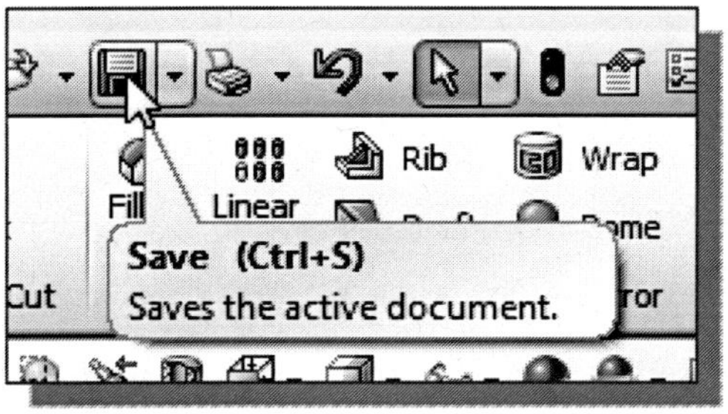

1. Select **Save** in the *Quick Access* toolbar. We can also use the "**Ctrl-S**" combination (press down the "Ctrl" key and hit the "S" key once) to save the part.

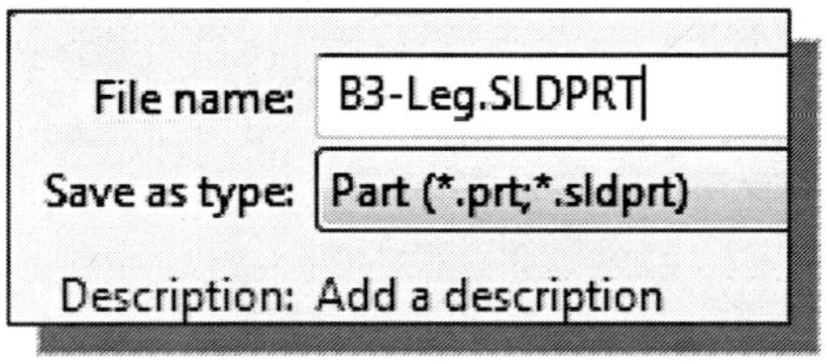

2. In the popup window, enter **B3-Leg** as the name of the file.

3. Click on the **SAVE** button to save the file.

Using the Measure Tools

- Besides using the dimension tools to get geometric information at the 2D level, the measure tools can also be used on 3D models.

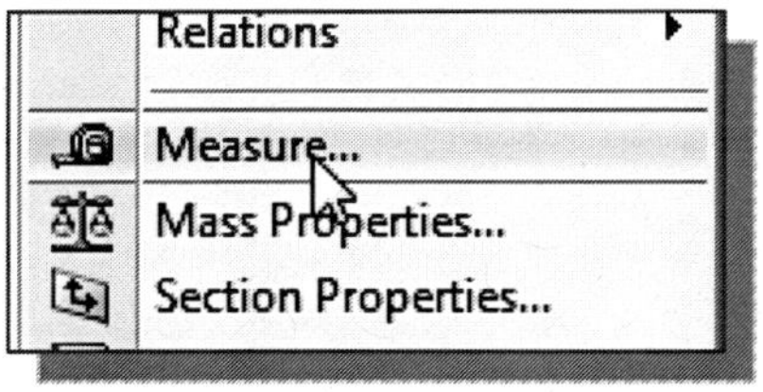

1. In the *Tools* pull-down menu, left-mouse-click once on the **Measure Distance** option as shown.

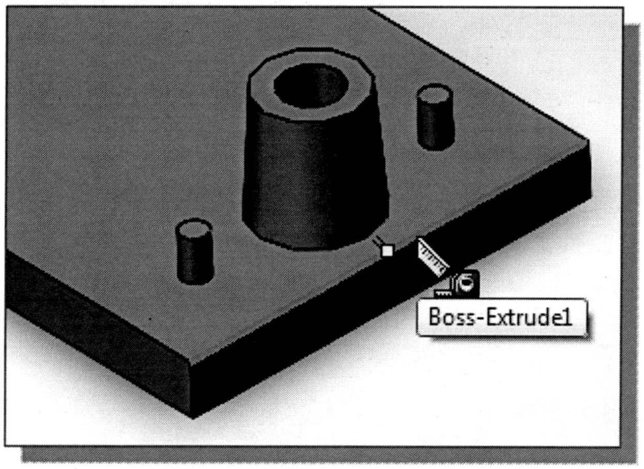

2. Click on the top edge of the rectangular plate as shown.

3. The associated length measurement is displayed next to the selected geometry as shown.

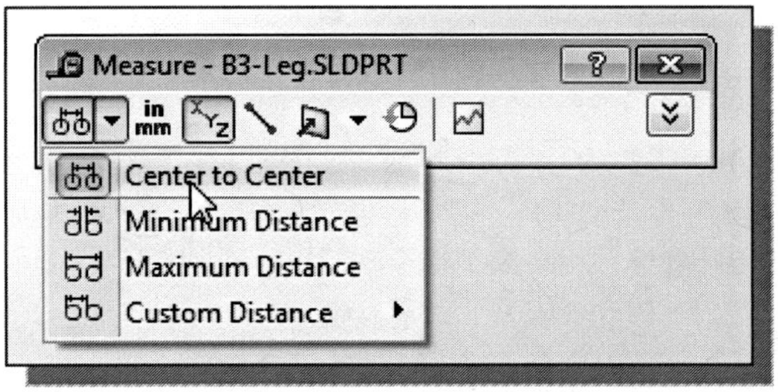

4. Turn off the **Point to Point** option.

5. Select the **Center to Center** option in the *Measure* dialog box.

6. Select one of the circles and note *SolidWorks* displays the distance, including the X, Y, Z increments, from the center point of the circle to the selected edge.

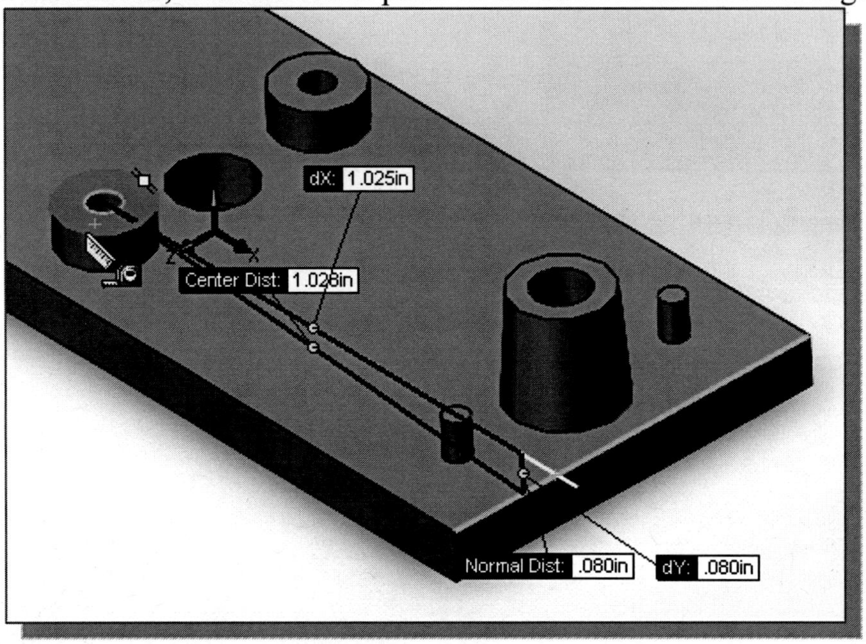

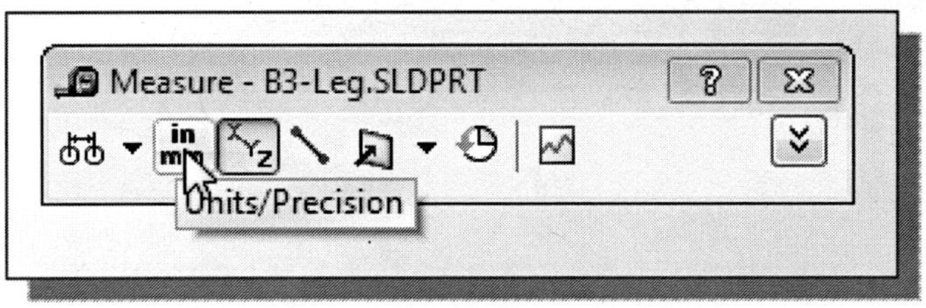

7. Choose **Units/Precision** to display the measurement settings.

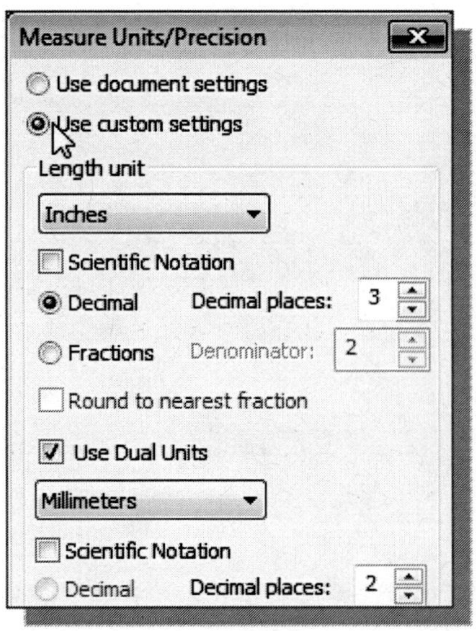

8. In the *Measure Units/Precision* dialog box, choose **Use custom settings**.

9. Switch *ON* the display of **dual dimensions** as shown.

10. Click on the **OK** button to accept the settings.

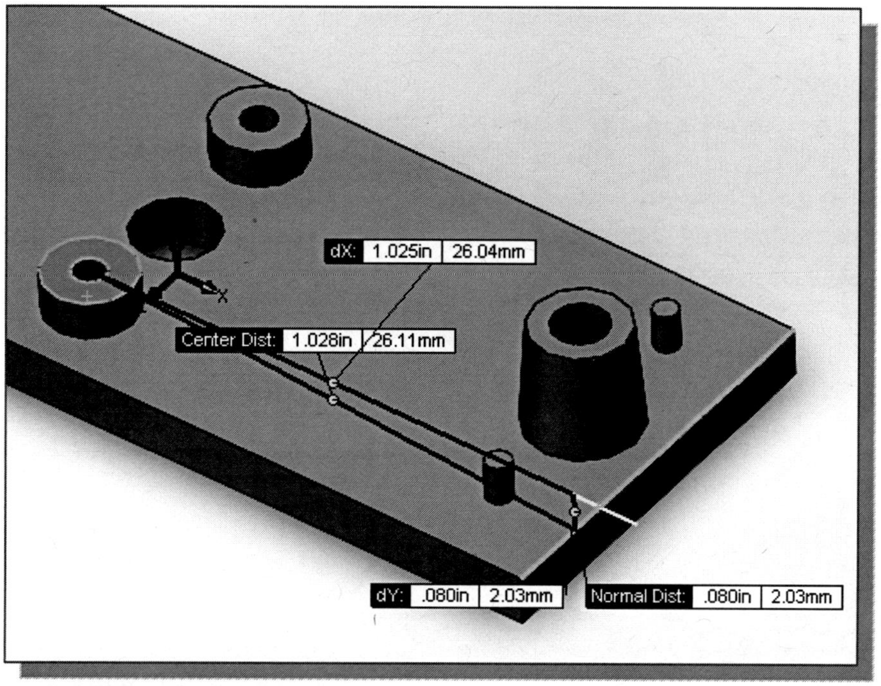

11. Inside the graphics area, click in an empty area to deselect the selected entities.

12. Select the **front vertical surface** as shown.

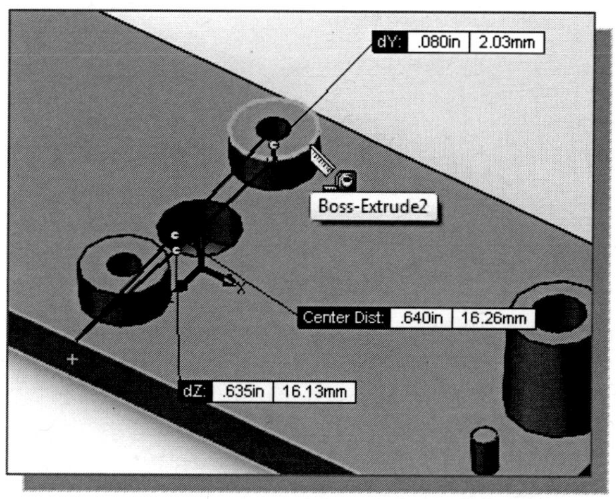

13. Select one of the circles and notice the **perpendicular distance** from the circle center to the surface is displayed. The measurement is based on the selected geometry.

14. On your own, experiment with the different **measure options** available.

Create a Metric Part Template

❖ We will create a metric part template which includes settings for the use of ISO standards for dimensions and Metric (mm, gram, second) units.

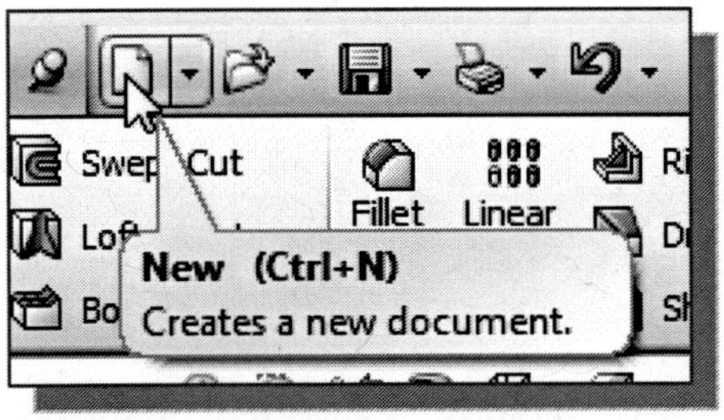

1. Click **New** in the *Quick Access* toolbar as shown.

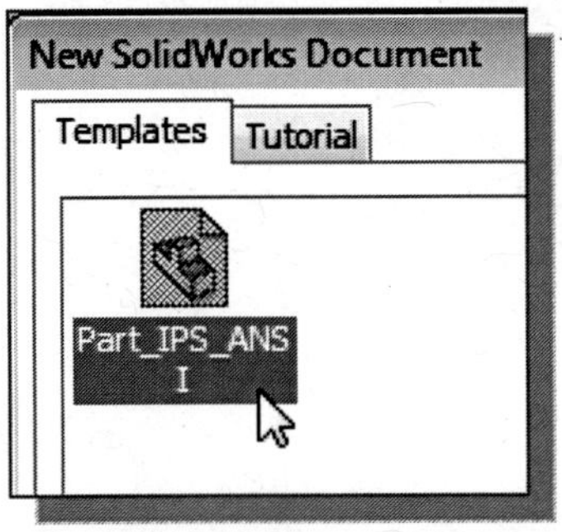

2. Choose the Part_IPS_ANSI template and start a new file.

3. Select the **Options** icon from the *Menu* toolbar to open the *Options* dialog box.

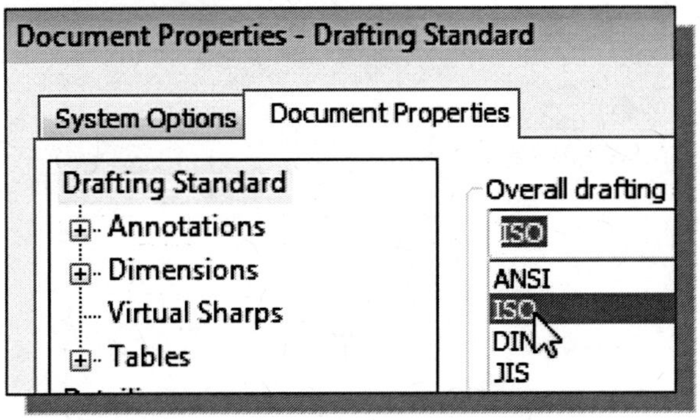

4. Select the **Document Properties** tab as shown in the figure.

5. Set the *Overall drafting standard* to **ISO** as shown.

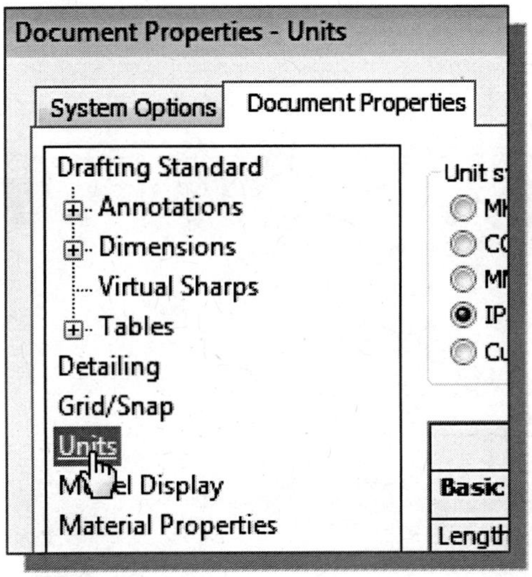

6. Click **Units** as shown in the figure.

7. Select **MMGS (millimeter, gram, second)** under the *Unit system* options.

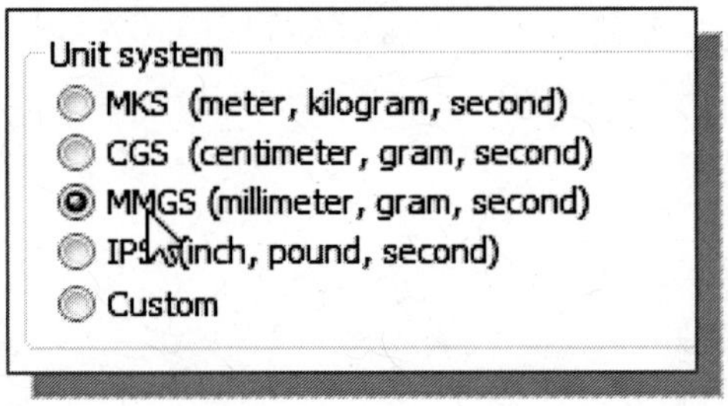

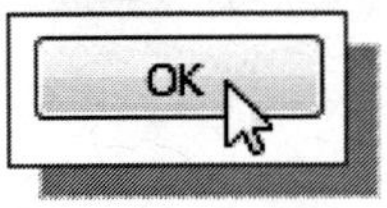

8. Click **OK** in the *Options* dialog box to accept the selected settings.

9. Click the arrow next to the **Save** icon in the *Menu Bar* to reveal the save options and select **Save As**.

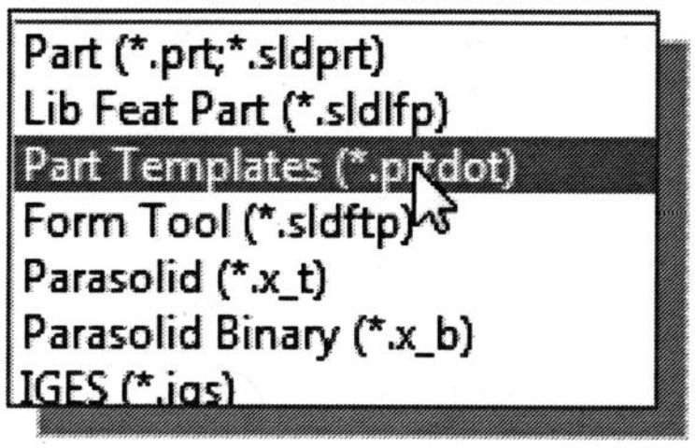

10. Under *Save as type*, select **Part Templates (*.prtdot)**. Notice the browser automatically goes to the default *templates* folder.

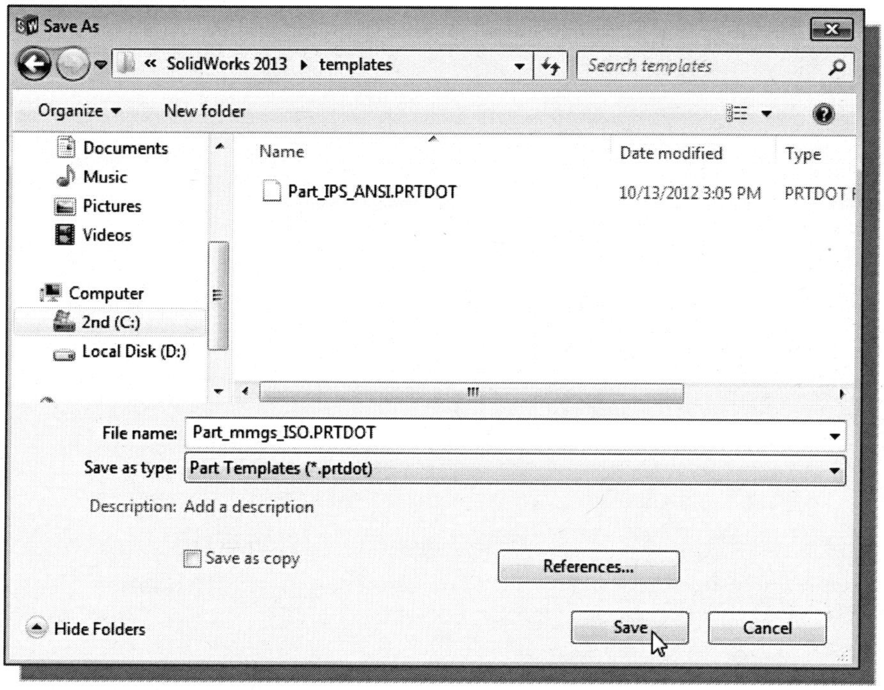

11. Enter the *File name* **Part_mmgs_ISO**.

12. Click **Save** to save the new part template file.

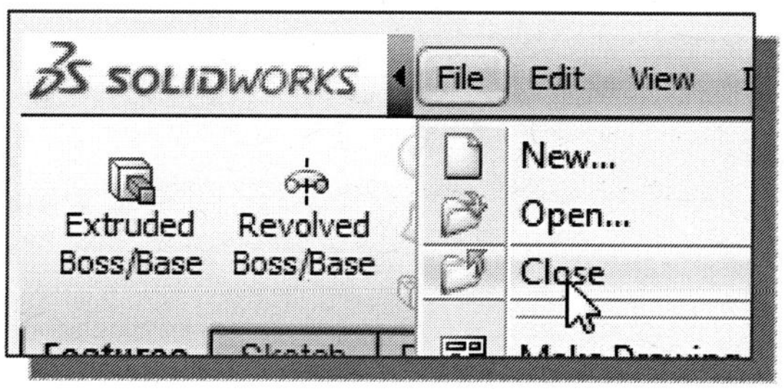

13. Select **Close** in the *File* pull-down menu to close the document. (**NOTE:** You may have to move the mouse over the SolidWorks icon to reveal the pull-down menus.)

The *Boot* Part

1. Select the **New** icon with a single click of the left-mouse-button on the *Menu Bar*.

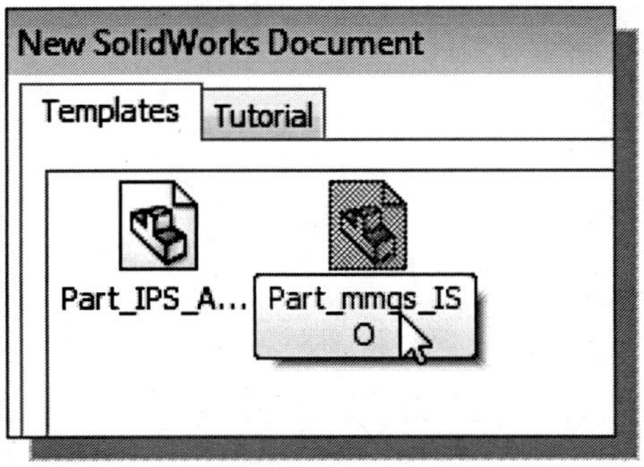

2. Notice the **two** template files which appear in the **Advanced** mode. Select the **Part_mmgs_ISO** template as shown.

3. Click on the **OK** button to open a new document using the selected template. The *Dimensioning Standard* will automatically be ISO and the units will be set as defined in the template.

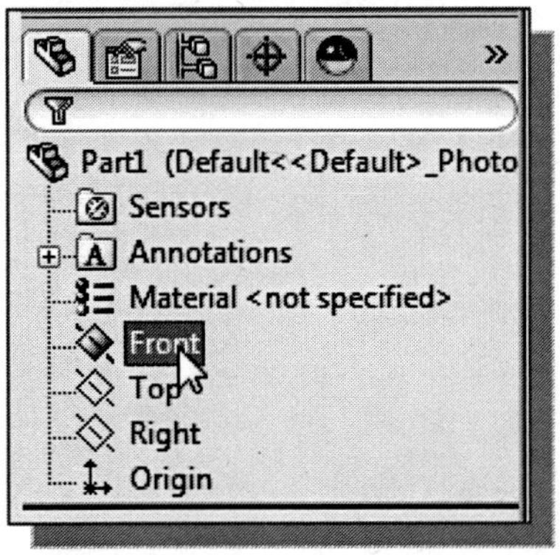

4. In the *Feature Manager Design Tree*, click once with the **left-mouse-button** to select the **Front Plane** as the sketch plane.

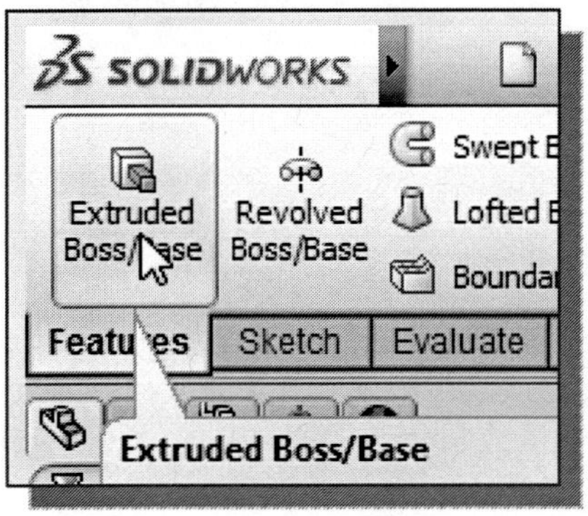

5. In the *Features* toolbar select the **Extruded Boss/ Base** command by clicking once with the left-mouse-button on the icon.

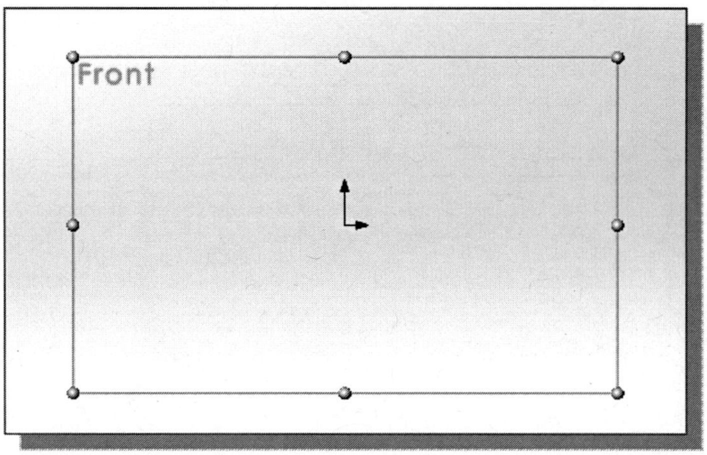

- Note the pre-selection of the Front Plane enables the use of the plane as the sketching plane.

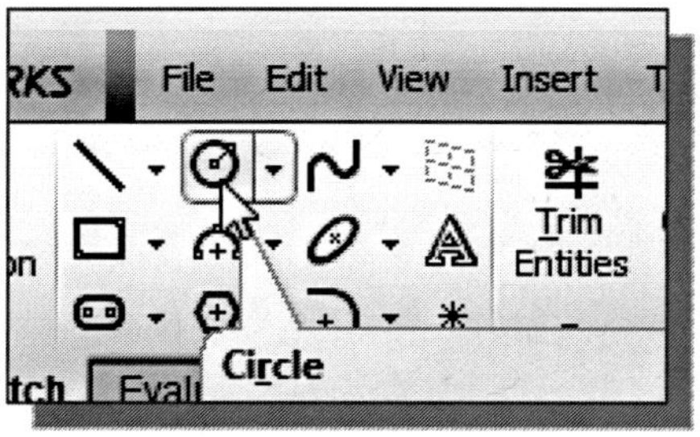

6. Select the **Circle** command by clicking once with the left-mouse-button on the icon in the *Sketch* toolbar.

7. Create **two circles**, with the center points aligned to the *Origin* of the coordinate system as shown.

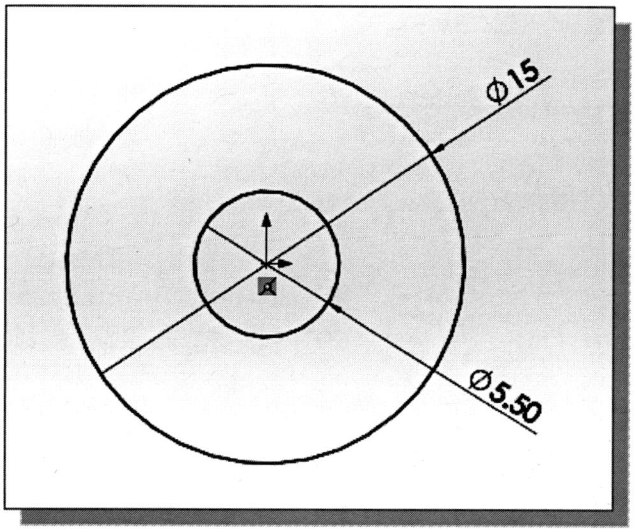

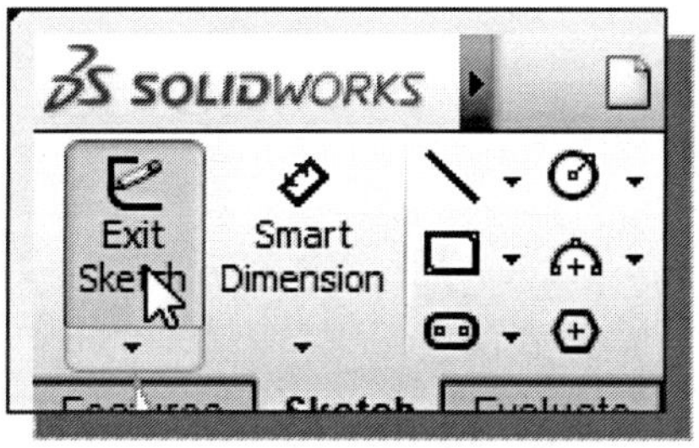

8. Click **Exit Sketch** in the *Sketch* toolbar to end the *Sketch* mode.

9. Set the extrusion distance to **6.0 mm** and set the extrusion direction toward the front side as shown

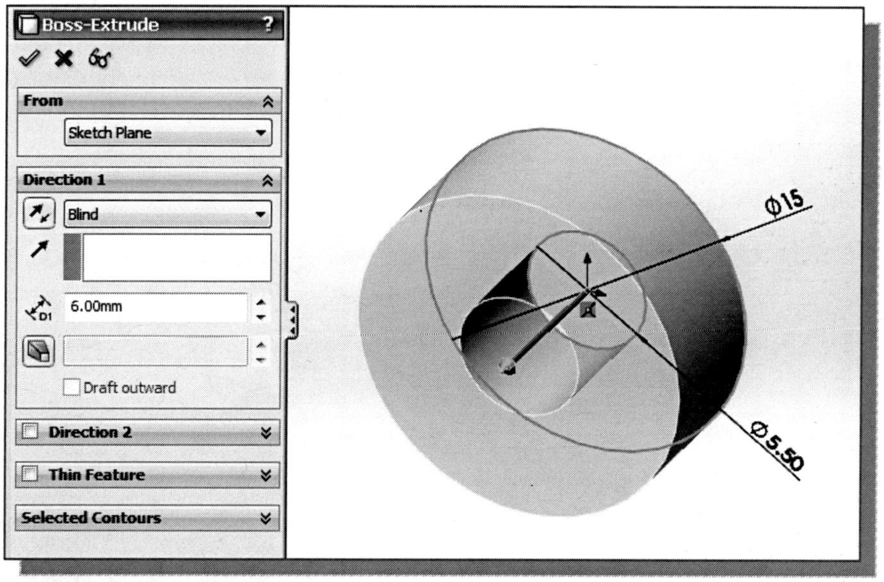

10. Click on the **OK** button to accept the settings and create the solid feature.

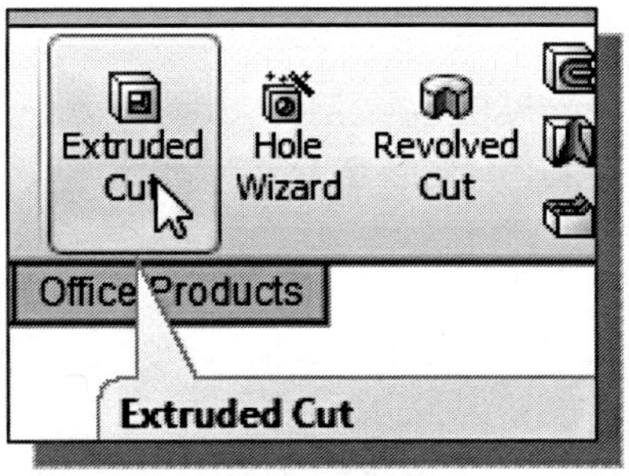

11. In the *Features* toolbar select the **Extruded Cut** command by clicking once with the left-mouse-button on the icon.

12. Select the **front face** of the solid model to align the sketching plane.

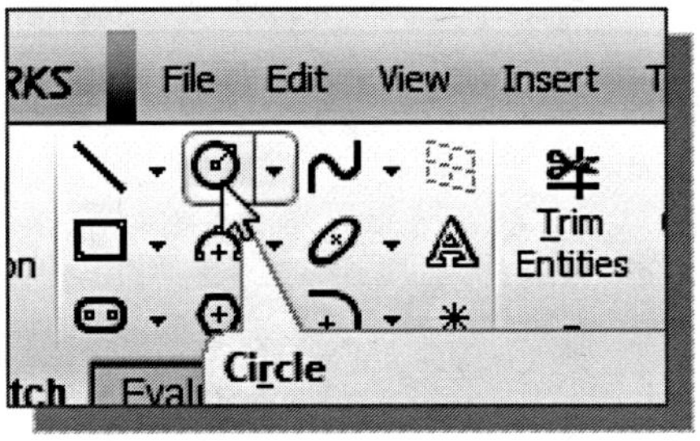

13. Select the **Circle** command by clicking once with the left-mouse-button on the icon in the *Sketch* toolbar.

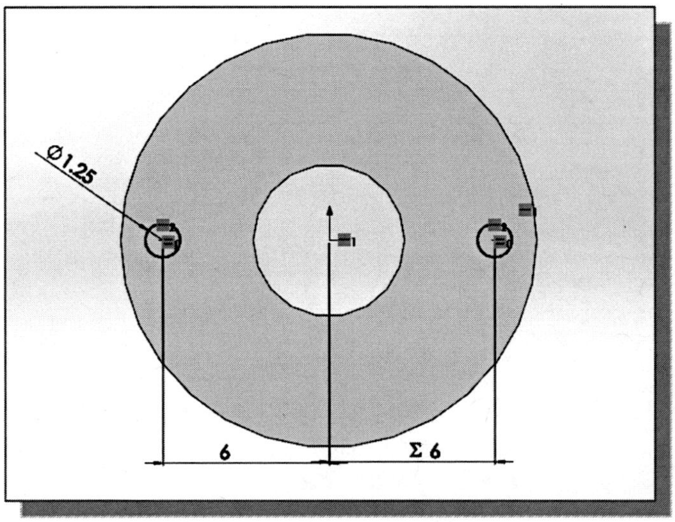

14. Create **two circles**, with the center points aligned horizontally to the *Origin* of the coordinate system as shown.

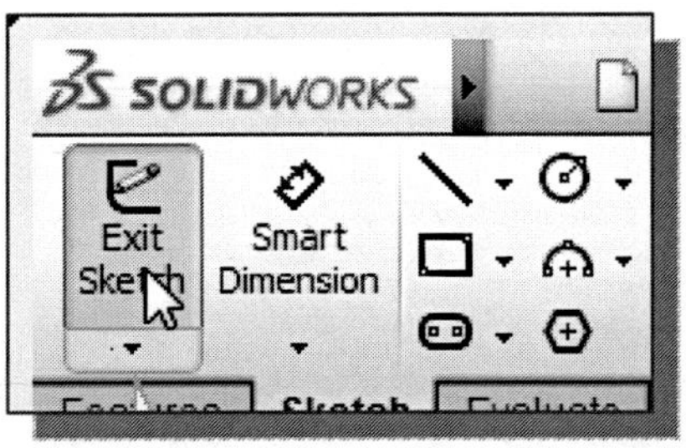

15. Click **Exit Sketch** in the *Sketch* toolbar to end the *Sketch* mode.

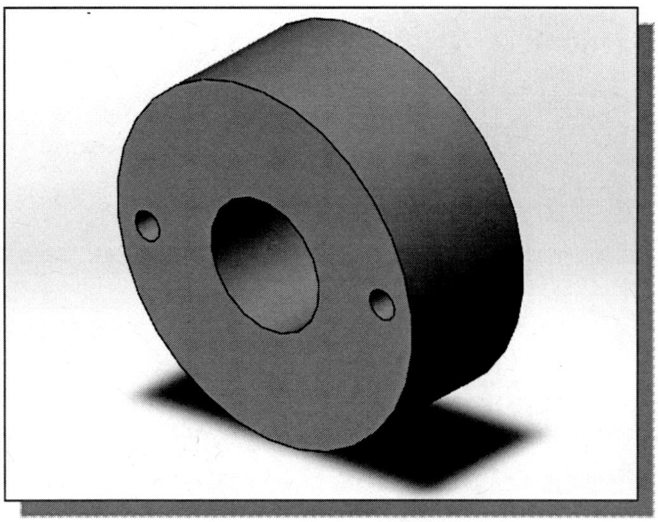

16. On your own, create the cut feature which is **2 mm** deep as shown.

17. Save the model as **Boot.sldprt**.

Questions:

1. What is the difference between *dimensional* constraints and *geometric* constraints?

2. How can we confirm that a sketch is fully constrained?

3. How do we distinguish between derived dimensions and regular dimensions on the screen?

4. Describe the procedure to **Display/Edit** user-defined equations.

5. List and describe three different geometric constraints available in *SolidWorks*.

6. Does *SolidWorks* allow us to build partially constrained or totally unconstrained solid models? What are the advantages and disadvantages of building these types of models?

7. How do we display and examine the existing constraints that are applied to the sketched entities?

8. Describe the advantages of using parametric equations.

9. Can we delete an applied constraint? How?

10. Create the following 2D sketch and measure the associated area and perimeter.

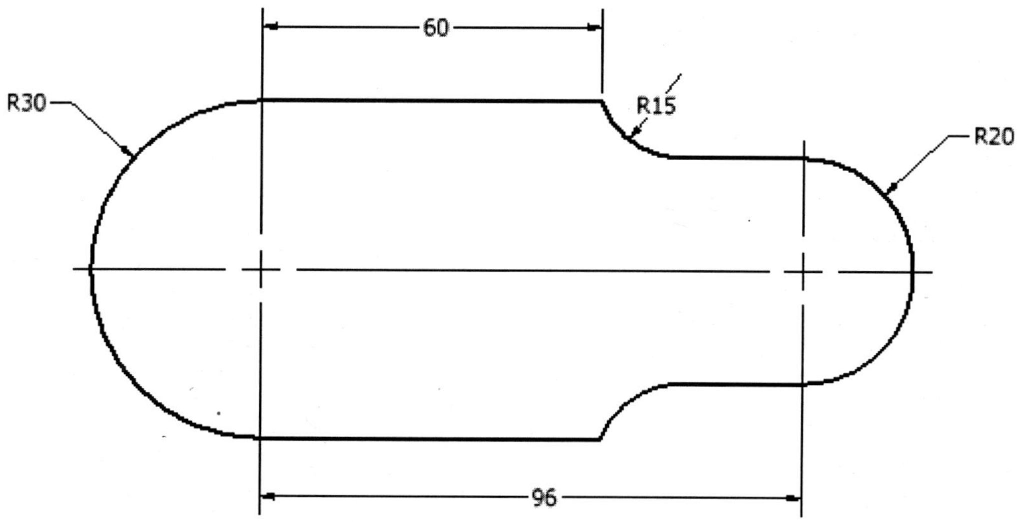

11. Describe the purpose and usage of the **Fully Define Sketch** command.

Exercises:

(Create and establish three parametric relations for each of the following designs.)

1. **Swivel Base** (Dimensions are in millimeters. Base thickness:**10 mm.** Boss: **5 mm.**)

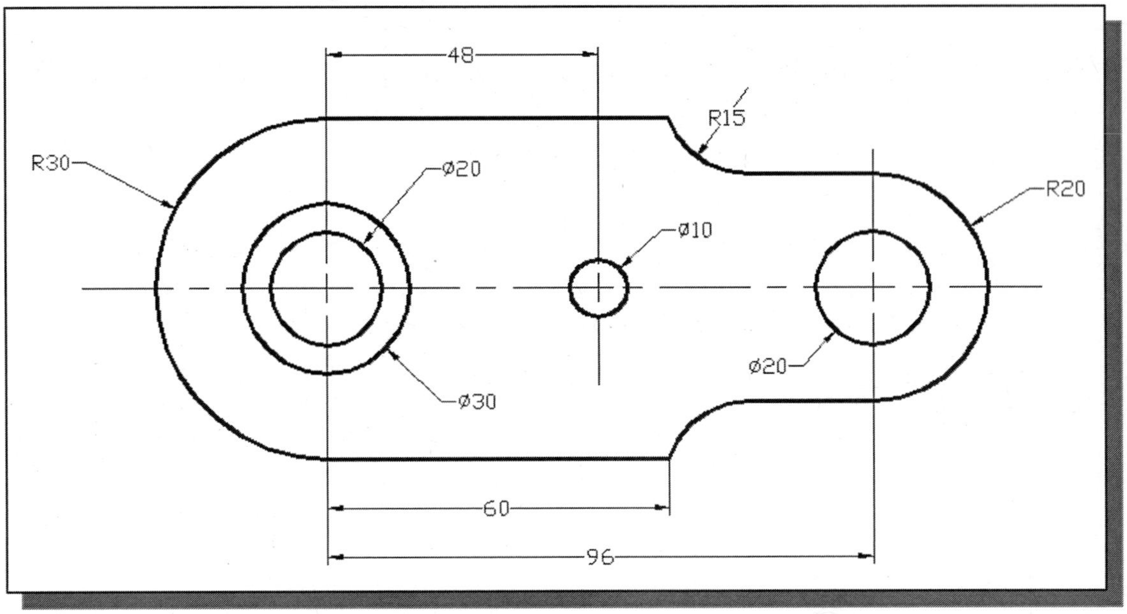

2. **C-Clip** (Dimensions are in inches. Plate thickness: **0.25 inches**.)

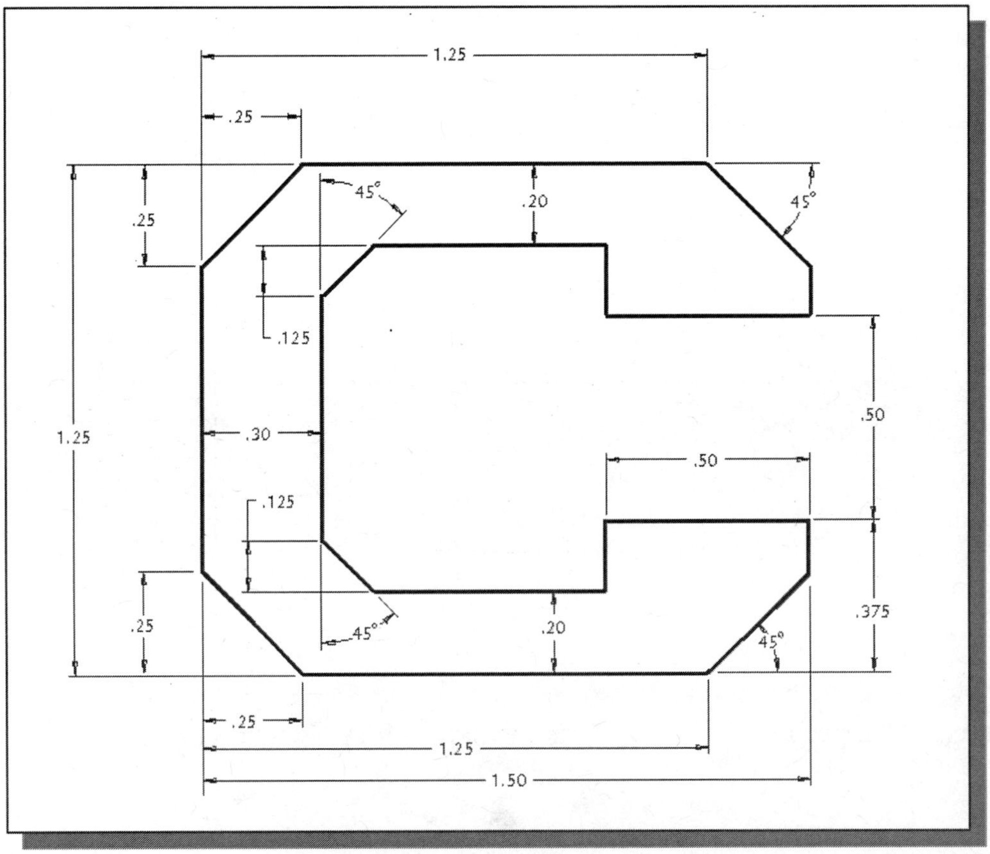

3. **Wedge Block** (Dimensions are in inches)

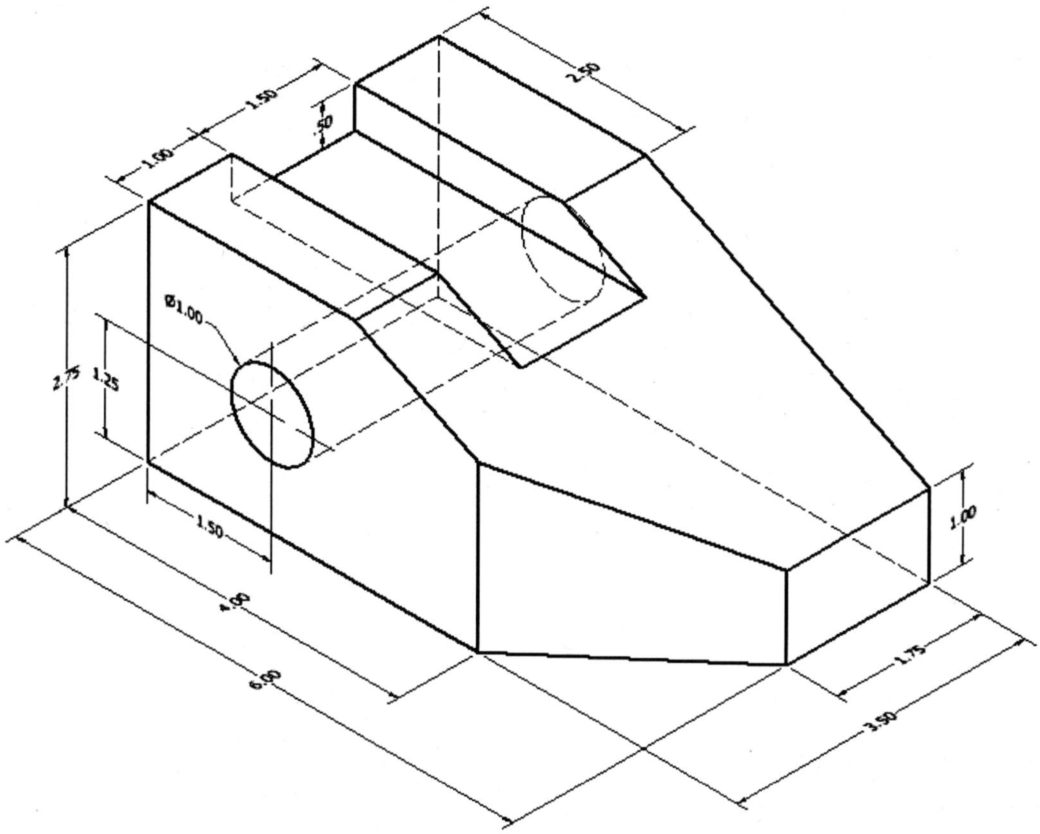

4. **Hinge Guide** (Dimensions are in inches.)

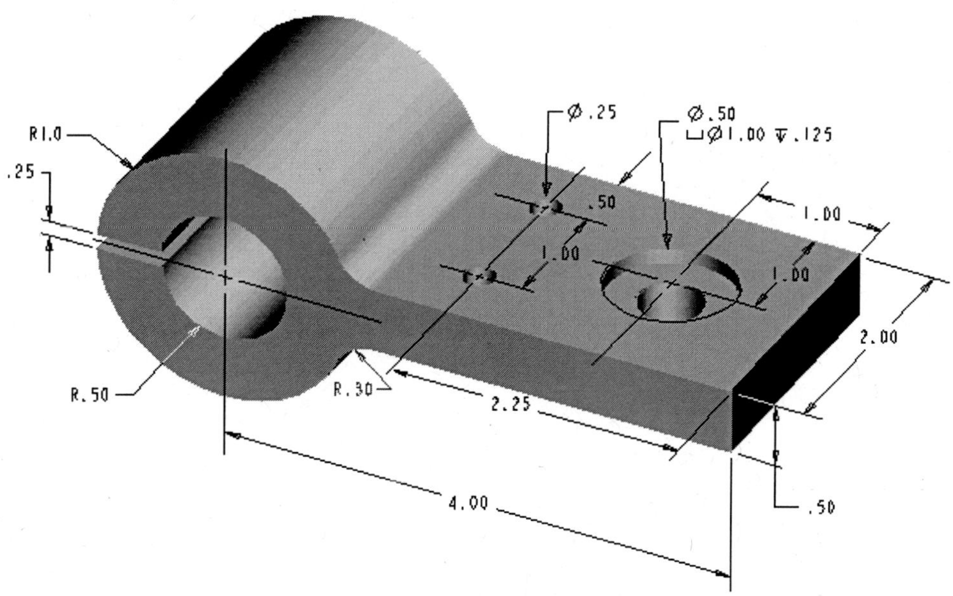

Notes:

Chapter 5
Pictorials and Sketching

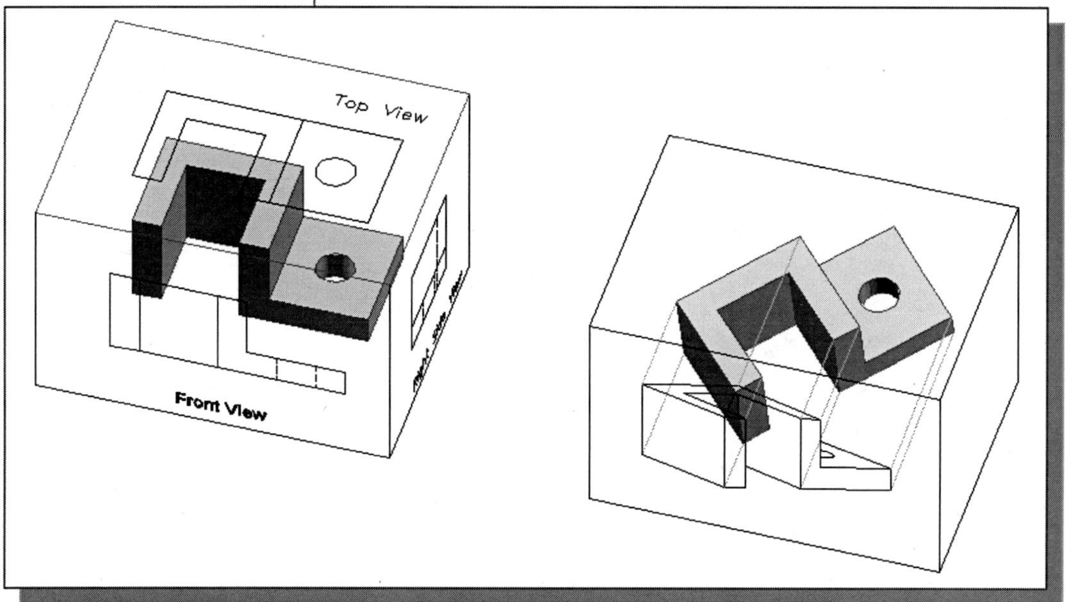

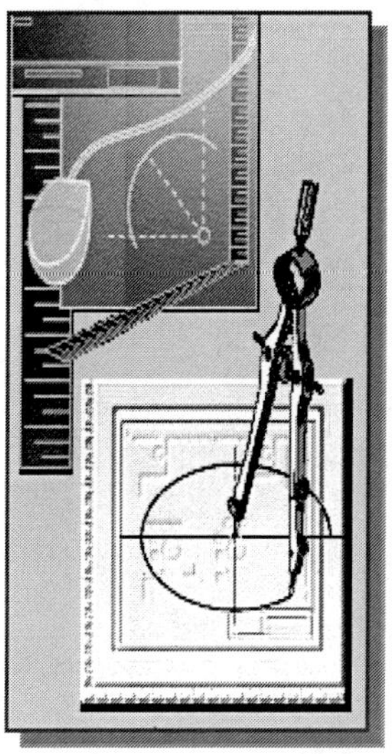

Learning Objectives

- ♦ **Understand the Importance of Freehand Sketching**
- ♦ **Understand the Terminology Used in Pictorial Drawings**
- ♦ **Understand the Basics of the Following Projection Methods: Axnonometric, Oblique and Perspective**
- ♦ **Be Able to Create Freehand 3D Pictorials**

Engineering Drawings, Pictorials and Sketching

One of the best ways to communicate one's ideas is through the use of a picture or a drawing. This is especially true for engineers and designers. Without the ability to communicate well, engineers and designers will not be able to function in a team environment and therefore will have only limited value in the profession.

For many centuries, artists and engineers used drawings to express their ideas and inventions. The two figures below are drawings by da Vinci (1453-1528) illustrating some of his engineering inventions.

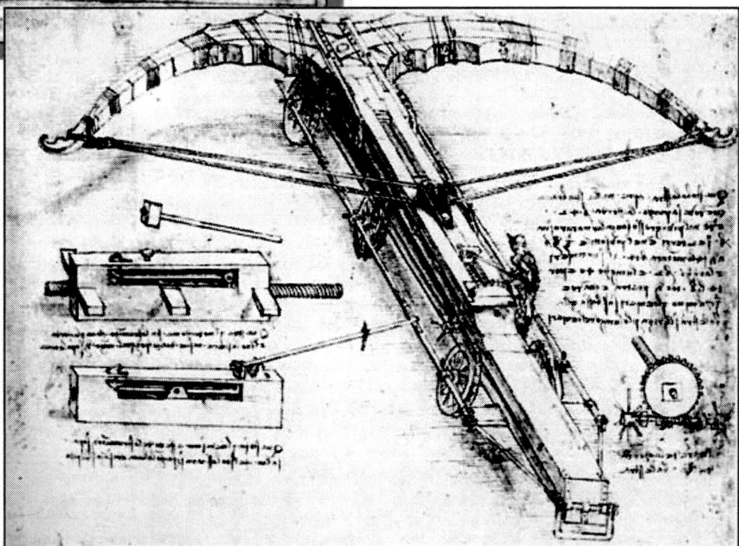

Engineering design is a process to create and transform ideas and concepts into a product definition that meets the desired objective. The engineering design process typically involves three stages: (1) Ideation/conceptual design stage: this is the beginning of an engineering design process, where basic ideas and concepts take shape. (2) Design development stage: the basic ideas are elaborated and further developed. During this stage, prototypes and testing are commonly used to ensure the developed design meets the desired objective. (3) Refine and finalize design stage: This stage of the design process is the last stage of the design process, where the finer details of the design are further refined. Detailed information of the finalized design is documented to assure the design is ready for production.

Two types of drawings are generally associated with the three stages of the engineering process: (1) Freehand Sketches and (2) Detailed Engineering Drawings.

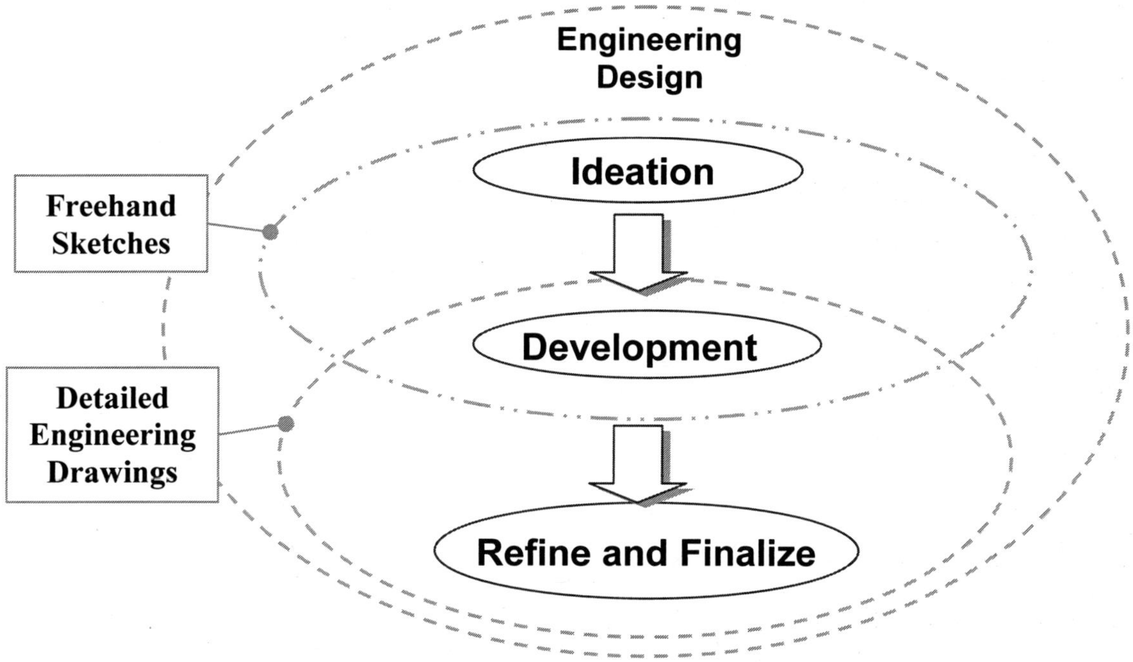

Freehand sketches are generally used in the beginning stages of a design process: (1) to quickly record the designer's ideas and help in formulating different possibilities, (2) to communicate the designer's basic ideas with others, and (3) to develop and elaborate further the designer's ideas/concepts.

During the initial design stage, an engineer will generally picture the ideas in his/her head as three-dimensional images. The ability to think visually, specifically three-dimensional visualization, is one of the most essential skills for an engineer/designer. And freehand sketching is considered as one of the most powerful methods to help develop visualization skills.

Detailed engineering drawings are generally created during the second and third stages of a design process. The detailed engineering drawings are used to help refine and finalize the design and also to document the finalized design for production. Engineering drawings typically require the use of drawing instruments, from compasses to computers, to bring precision to the drawings.

Freehand Sketches and **Detailed Engineering Drawings** are essential communication tools for engineers. By using the established conventions, such as perspective and isometric drawings, engineers/designers are able to quickly convey their design ideas to others.

The ability to sketch ideas is absolutely essential to engineers. The ability to sketch is helpful, not just to communicate with others, but also to work out details in ideas and to identify any potential problems. Freehand sketching requires only simple tools, a pencil and a piece of paper, and can be accomplished almost anywhere and anytime. Creating freehand sketches does not require any artistic ability. Detailed engineering drawing is employed only for those ideas deserving a permanent record.

Freehand sketches and engineering drawings are generally composed of similar information, but there is a tradeoff between the time required to generate a sketch/ drawing versus the level of design detail and accuracy. In industry, freehand sketching is used to quickly document rough ideas and identify general needs for improvement in a team environment.

Besides the 2D views, described in the previous chapter, there are three main divisions commonly used in freehand engineering sketches and detailed engineering drawings: (1) **Axonometric**, with its divisions into **isometric, dimetric** and **trimetric**; (2) **Oblique**; and (3) **Perspective**.

1. **Axonometric projection**: The word *Axonometric* means "to measure along axes." Axonometric projection is a special *orthographic projection* technique used to generate ***pictorials***. **Pictorials** show a 2D image of an object as viewed from a direction that reveals three directions of space. In the figure below, the ***Adjuster*** model is rotated so that a *pictorial* is generated using *orthographic projection* (projection lines perpendicular to the projection plane) as described in Chapter 4. There are three types of axonometric projections: isometric projection, dimetric projection, and trimetric projection. Typically in an axonometric drawing, one axis is drawn vertically.

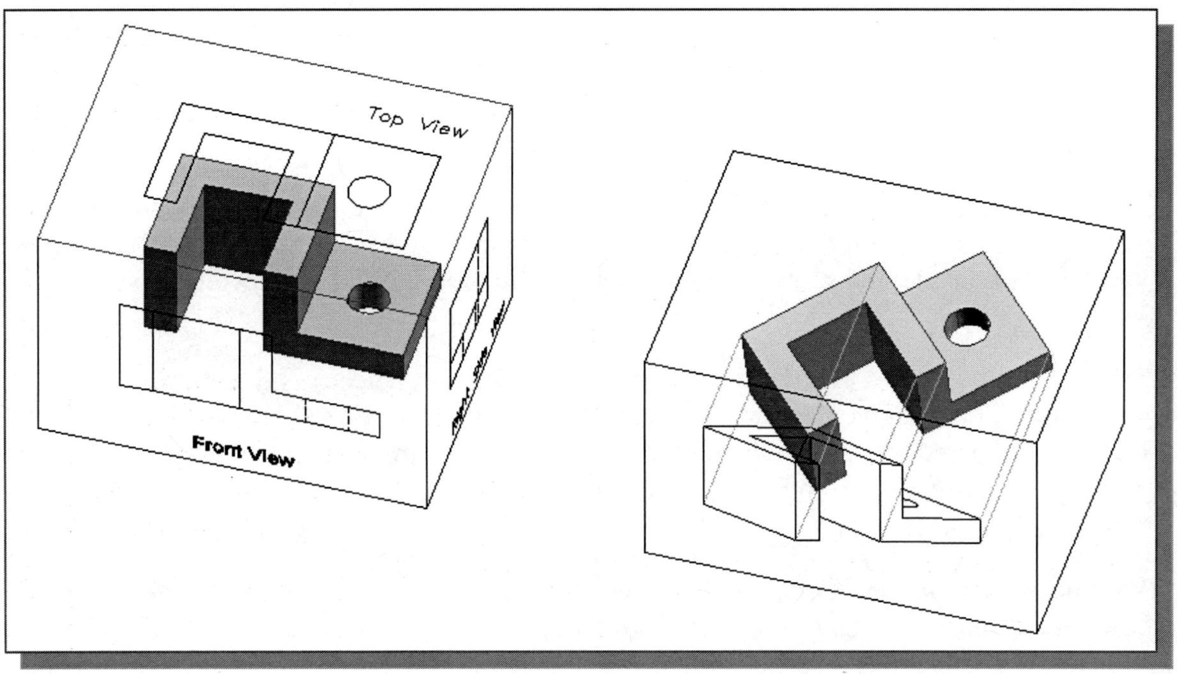

In **isometric projections**, the direction of viewing is such that the three axes of space appear equally foreshortened, and therefore the angles between the axes are equal. In **dimetric projections**, the directions of viewing are such that two of the three axes of space appear equally foreshortened. In **trimetric projections**, the direction of viewing is such that the three axes of space appear unequally foreshortened.

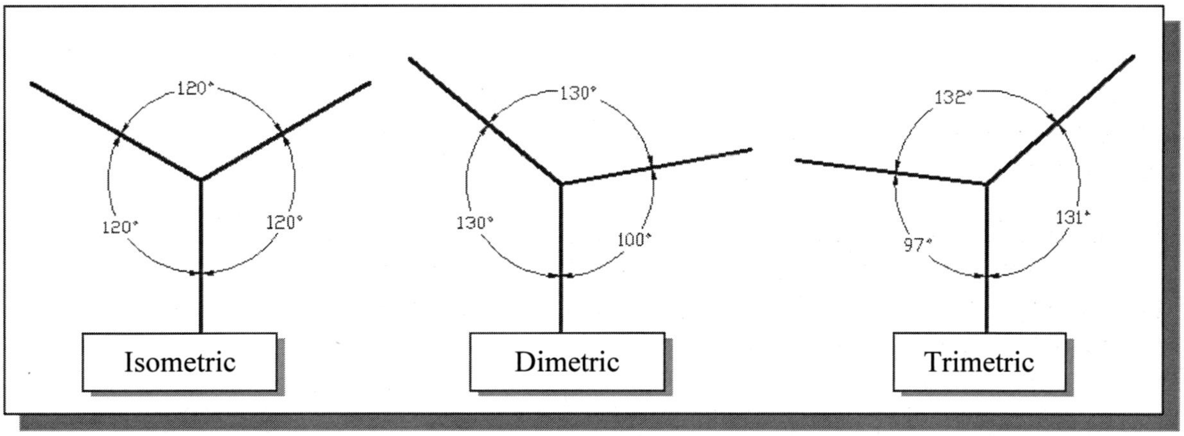

Isometric projection is perhaps the most widely used for pictorials in engineering graphics, mainly because isometric views are the most convenient to draw. Note that the different projection options described here are not particularly critical in freehand sketching as the emphasis is generally placed on the proportions of the design, not the precision measurements. The general procedure for constructing isometric views is illustrated in the following sections.

2. **Oblique Projection** represents a simple technique of keeping the front face of an object parallel to the projection plane and still reveals three directions of space. An **orthographic projection** is a parallel projection in which the projection lines are perpendicular to the plane of projection. An **oblique projection** is one in which the projection lines are other than perpendicular to the plane of projection.

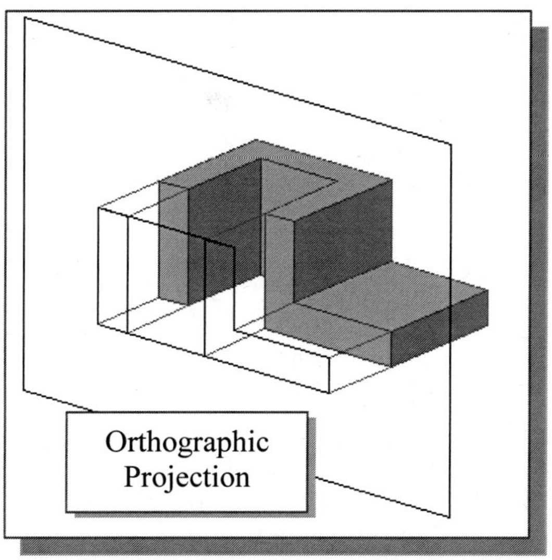

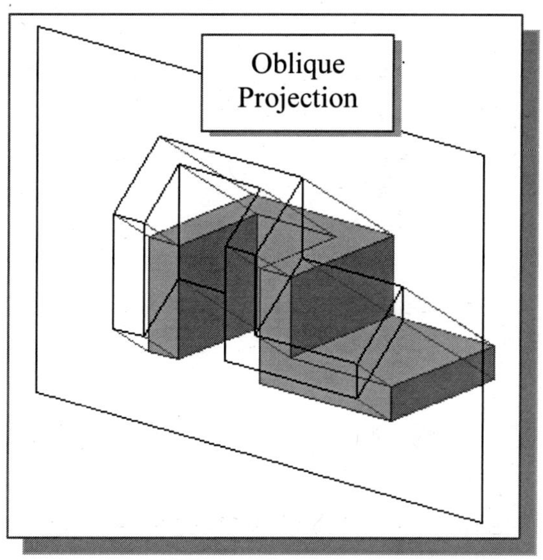

In an oblique drawing, geometry that is parallel to the frontal plane of projection is drawn true size and shape. This is the main advantage of the oblique drawing over the axonometric drawings. The three axes of the oblique sketch are drawn horizontally, vertically, and the 3rd axis can be at any convenient angle (typically between 30 and 60 degrees). The proportional scale along the 3rd axis is typically a scale anywhere between ½ and 1. If the scale is ½, then it is a ***Cabinet*** oblique. If the scale is 1, then it is a ***Cavalier*** oblique.

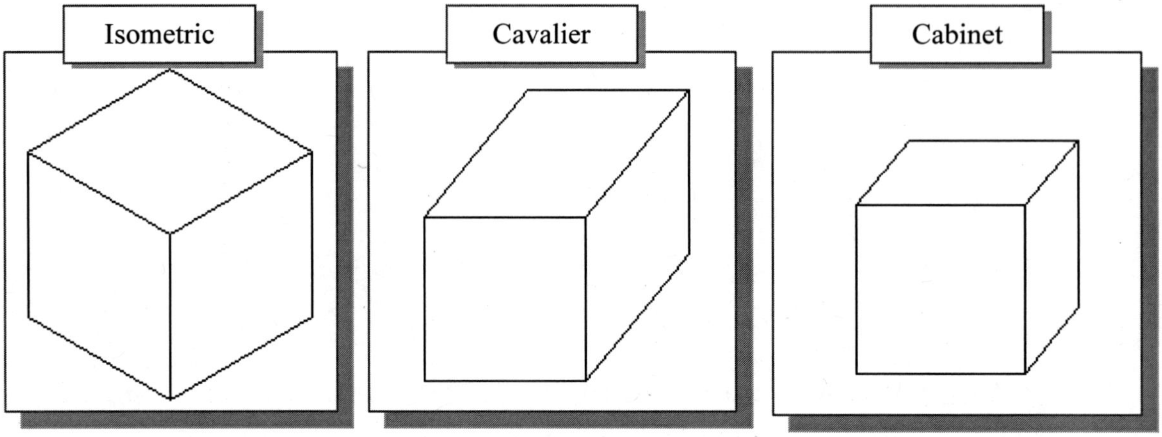

3. **Perspective Projection** adds realism to the three-dimensional pictorial representation. A perspective drawing represents an object as it appears to an observer; objects that are closer to the observer will appear larger to the observer. The key to the perspective projection is that parallel edges converge to a single point, known as the **vanishing point**. If there is just one vanishing point, then it is called a one-point perspective. If two sets of parallel edge lines converge to their respective vanishing points, then it is called a two-point perspective. There is also the case of a three-point perspective in which all three sets of parallel lines converge to their respective vanishing points.

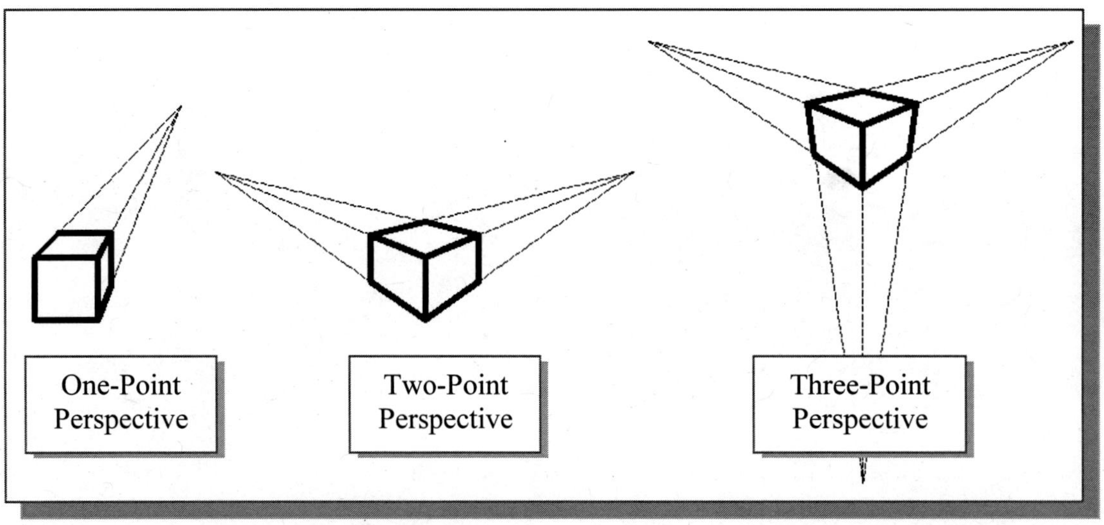

- Although there are specific techniques available to create precise pictorials with known dimensions, in the following sections, the basic concepts and procedures relating to freehand sketching are illustrated.

Isometric Sketching

Isometric drawings are generally done with one axis aligned to the vertical direction. A **regular isometric** is when the viewpoint is looking down on the top of the object, and a **reversed isometric** is when the viewpoint is looking up on the bottom of the object.

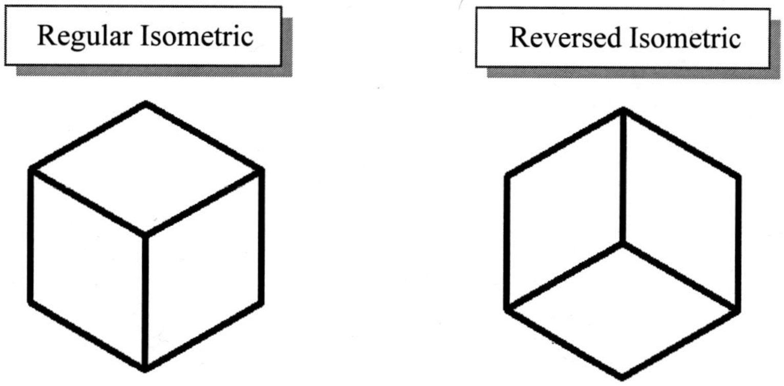

Two commonly used approaches in creating isometric sketches are: (1) the **enclosing box** method and (2) the **adjacent surface** method. The enclosing box method begins with the construction of an isometric box showing the overall size of the object. The visible portions of the individual 2D-views are then constructed on the corresponding sides of the box. Adjustments of the locations of surfaces are then made, by moving the edges, to complete the isometric sketch.

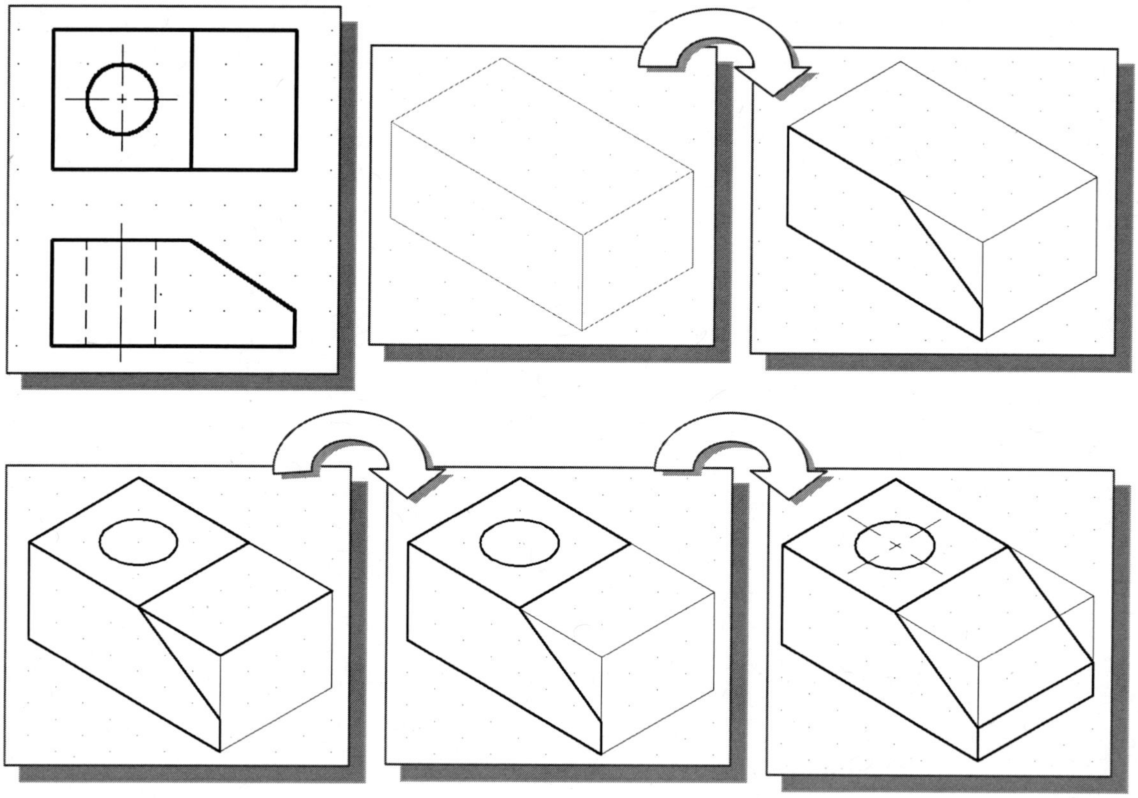

The adjacent surface method begins with one side of the isometric drawing, again with the visible portion of the corresponding 2D-view. The isometric sketch is completed by identifying and adding the adjacent surfaces.

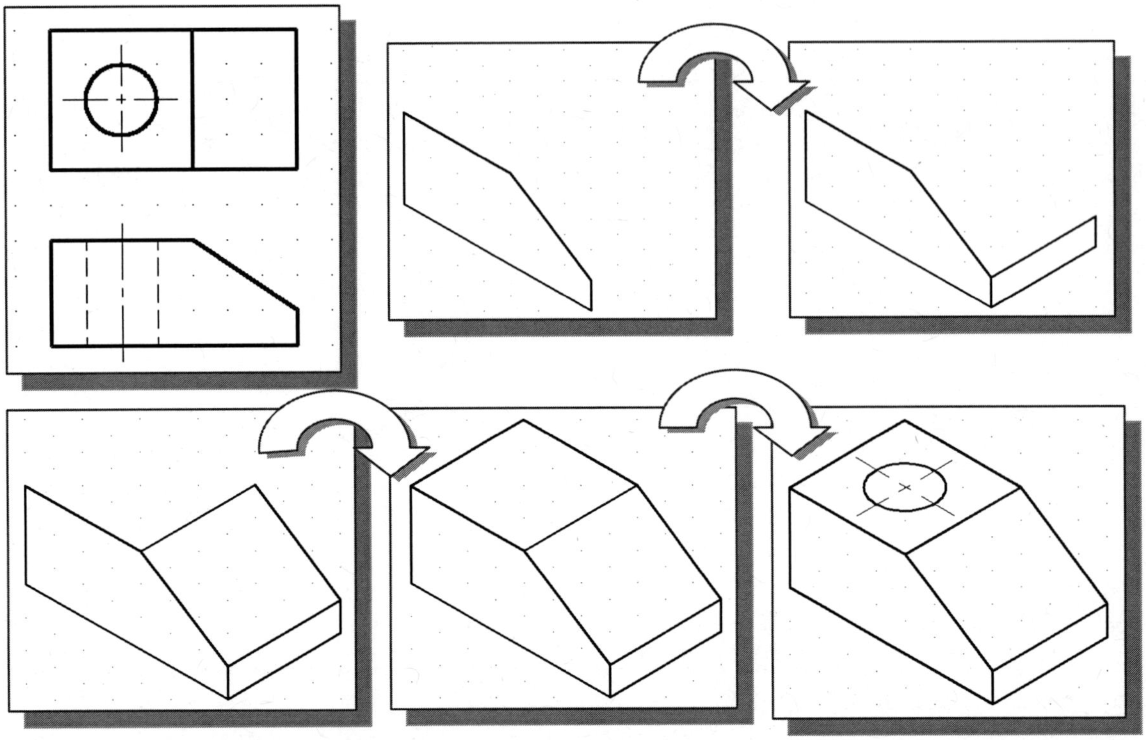

In an isometric drawing, cylindrical or circular shapes appear as ellipses. It can be confusing in drawing the ellipses in an isometric view; one simple rule to remember is the **major axis** of the ellipse is always **perpendicular** to the **center axis** of the cylinder as shown in the figures below.

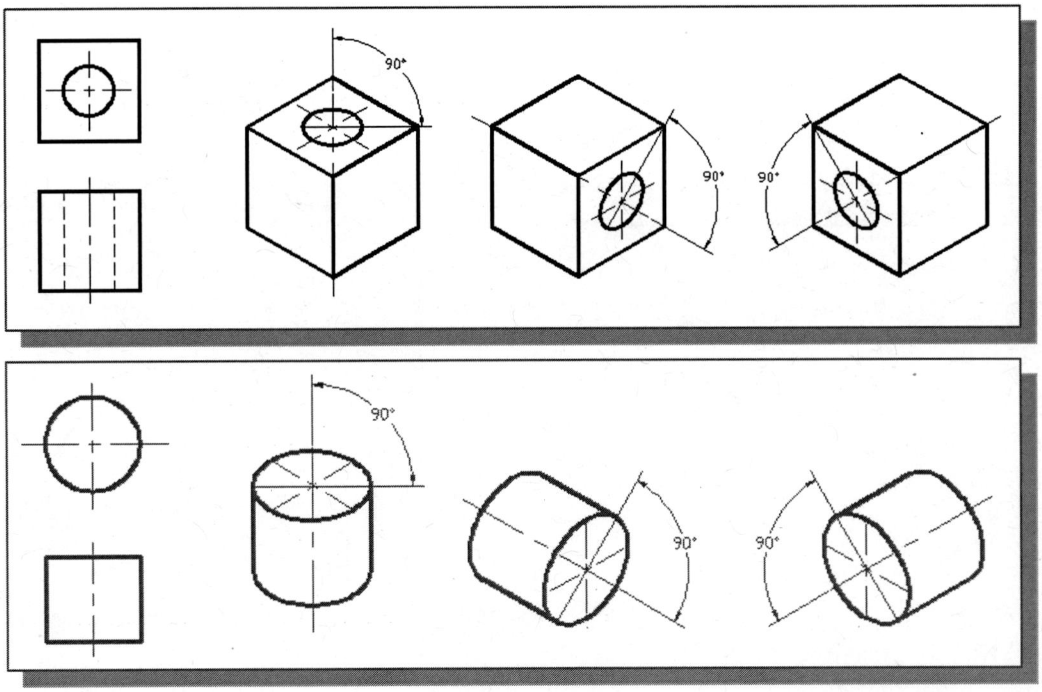

Isometric Sketching Exercises:

Given the Orthographic Top view and Front view, create the isometric view.

1.

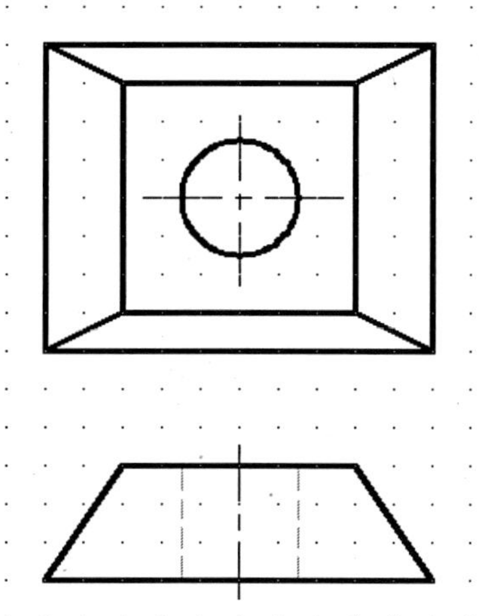

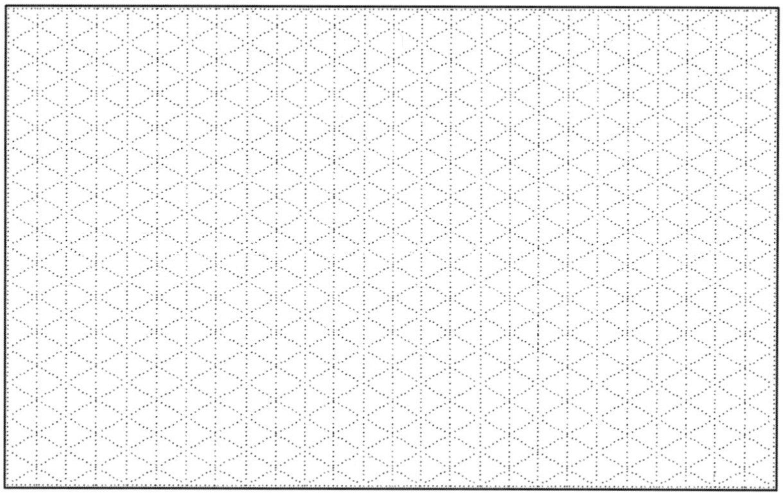

2.

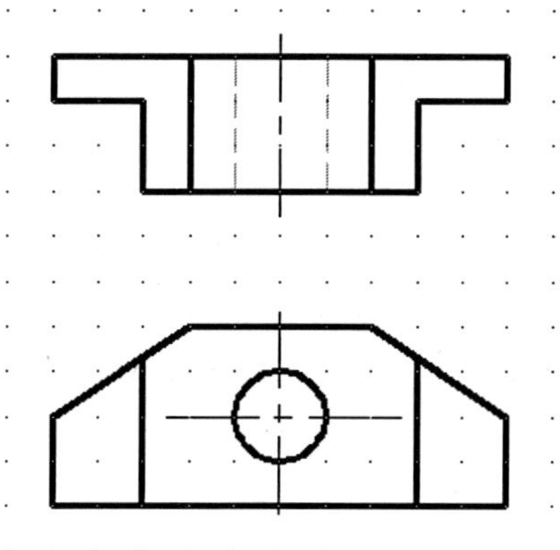

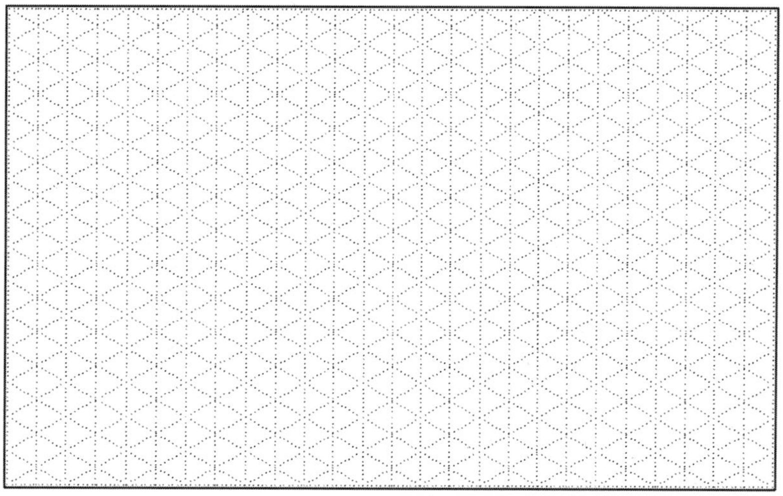

3.

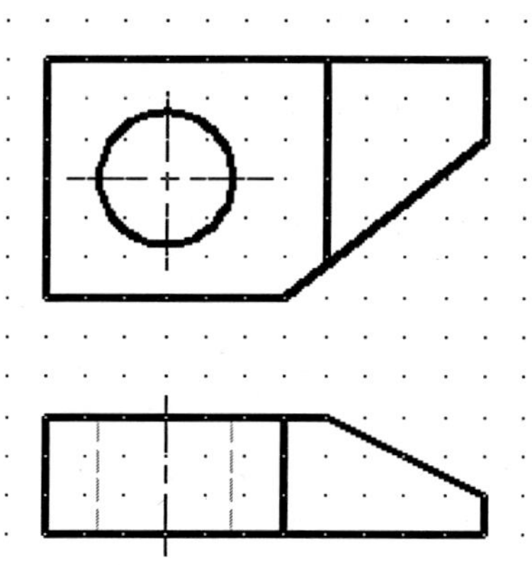

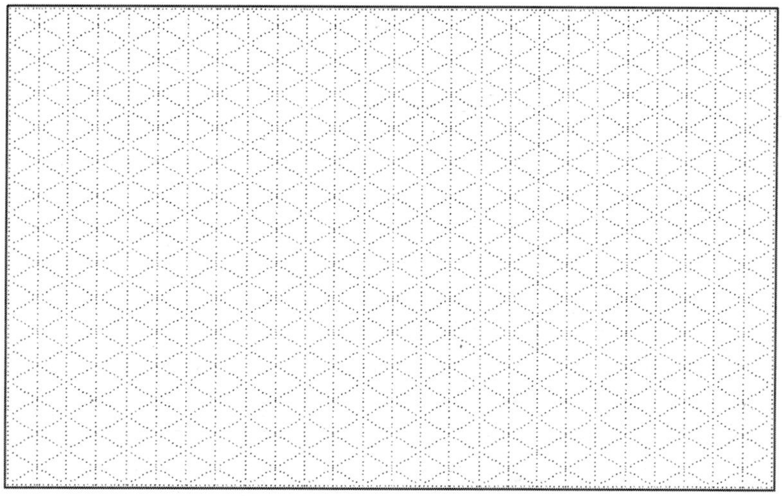

Oblique Sketching

Keeping the geometry that is parallel to the frontal plane true to size and shape is the main advantage of oblique drawings over axonometric drawings. Unlike isometric drawings, circular shapes that are parallel to the frontal view will remain as circles in oblique drawings. Generally speaking, an oblique drawing can be created very quickly by using a 2D view as the starting point. For designs with most of the circular shapes in one direction, an oblique sketch is the ideal choice over the other pictorial methods.

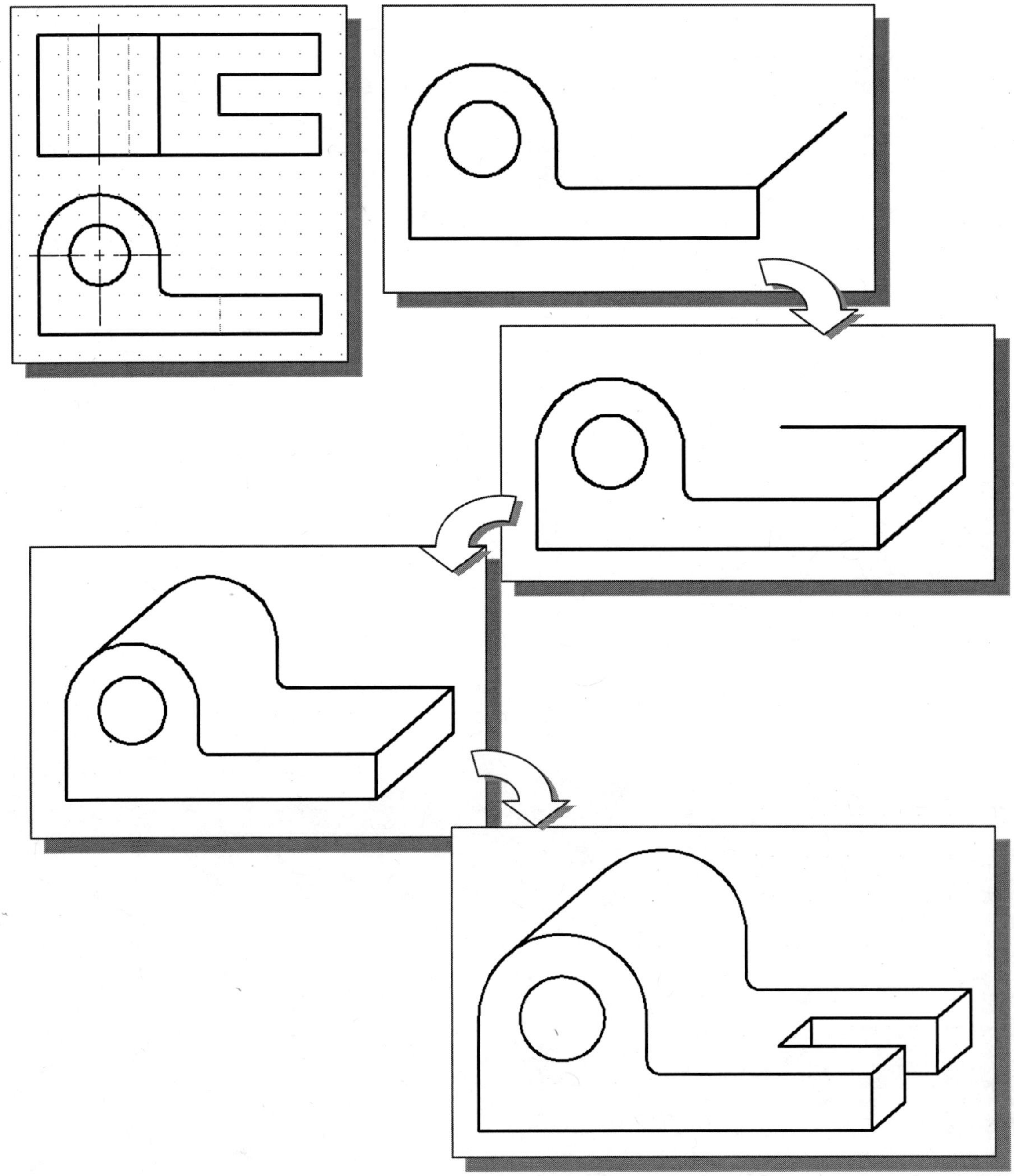

Oblique Sketching Exercises:

Given the Orthographic Top view and Front view, create the oblique view.

1.

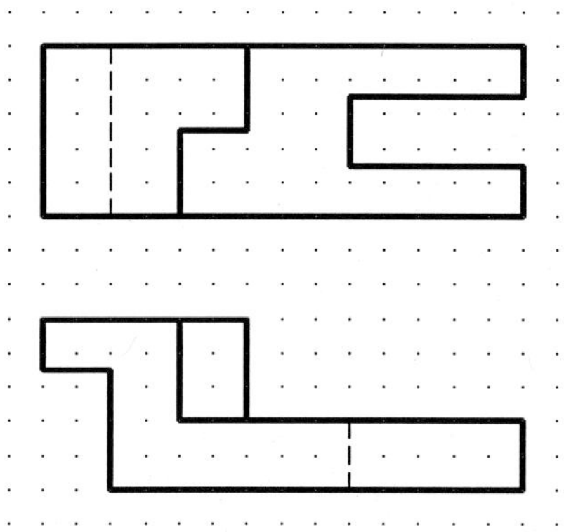

2.

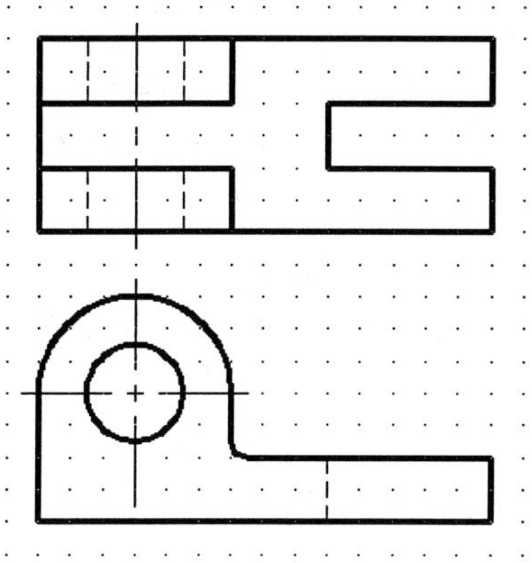

3.

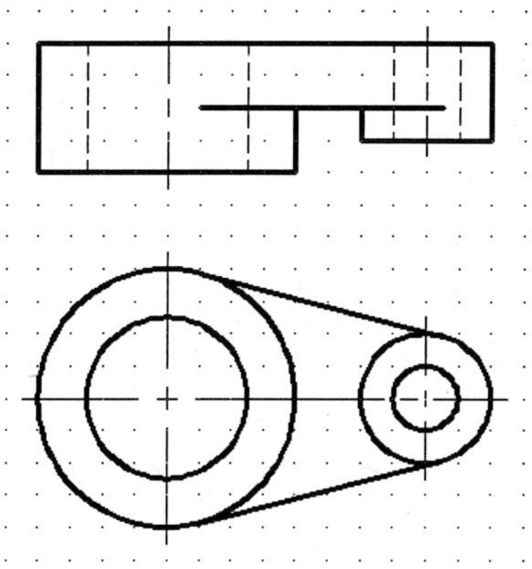

Perspective Sketching

A perspective drawing represents an object as it appears to an observer; objects that are closer to the observer will appear larger to the observer. The key to perspective projection is that parallel edges converge to a single point, known as the **vanishing point**. The vanishing point represents the position where projection lines converge.

The selection of the locations of the vanishing points, which is the first step in creating a perspective sketch, will affect the look of the resulting images.

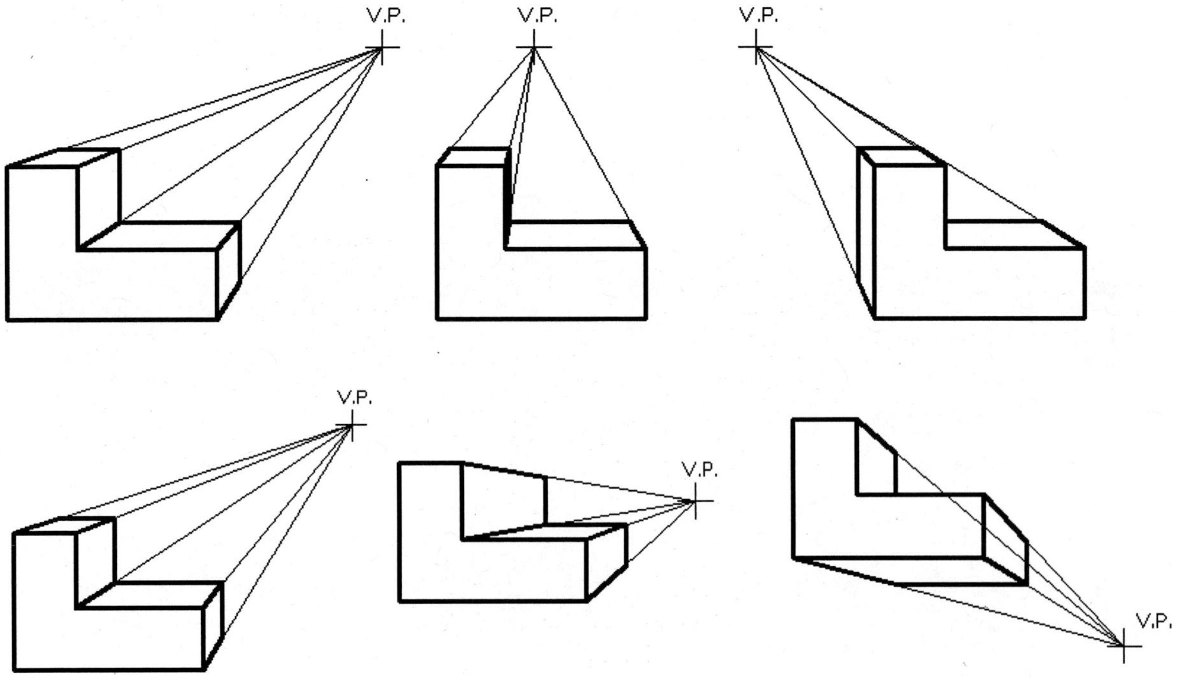

SolidWorks Orthographic vs. Perspective

1. Orthographic View

2. Perspective View

One-point Perspective

One-point perspective is commonly used because of its simplicity. The first step in creating a one-point perspective is to sketch the front face of the object just as in oblique sketching, followed by selecting the position for the vanishing point. For *mechanical* designs, the vanishing point is usually placed above and to the right of the picture. The use of construction lines can be helpful in locating the edges of the object and to complete the sketch.

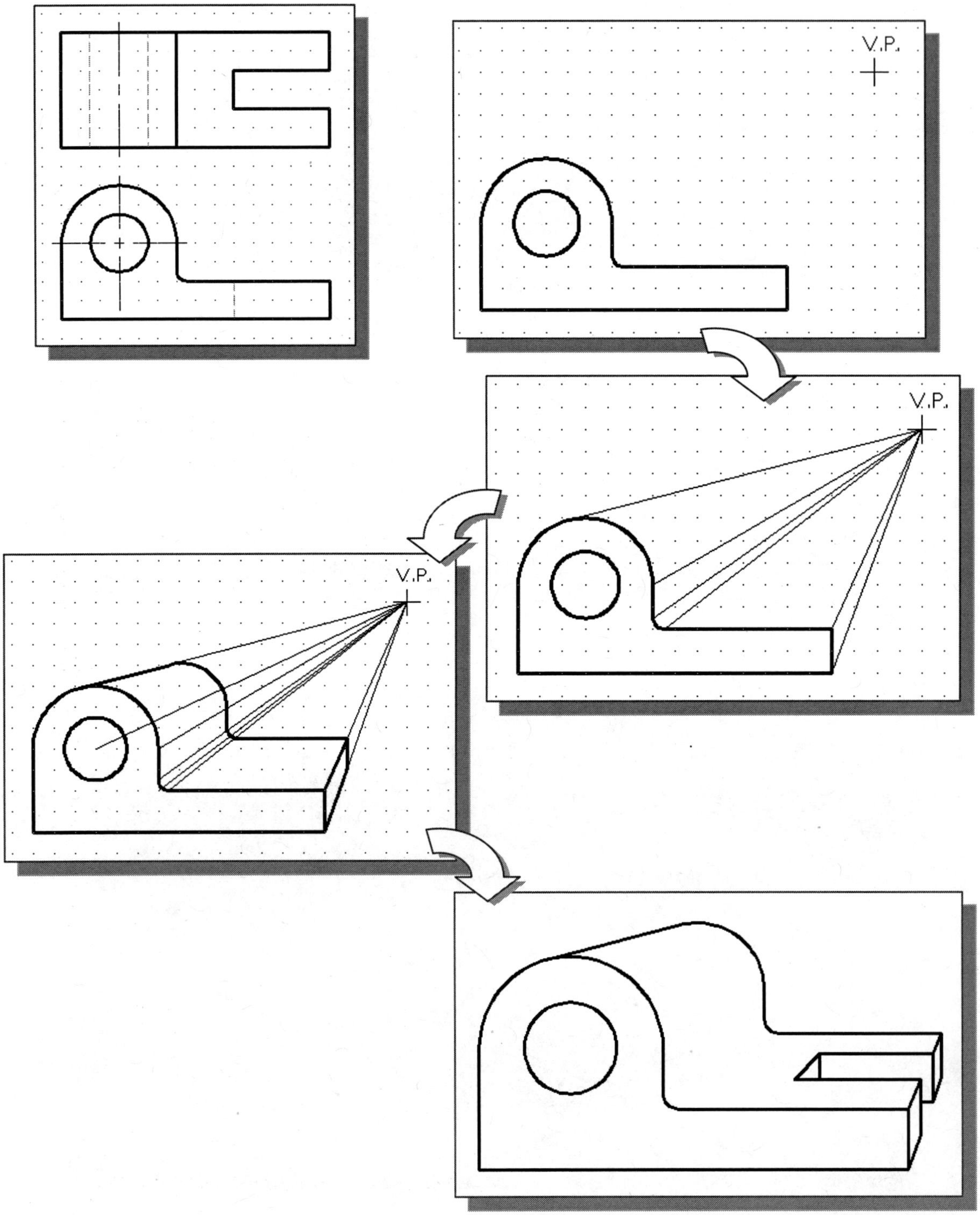

Two-point Perspective

Two-point perspective is perhaps the most popular of all perspective methods. The use of the two vanishing points creates very true-to-life images. The first step in creating a two-point perspective is to select the locations for the two vanishing points, followed by sketching an enclosing box to show the outline of the object. The use of construction lines can be very helpful in locating the edges of the object and to complete the sketch.

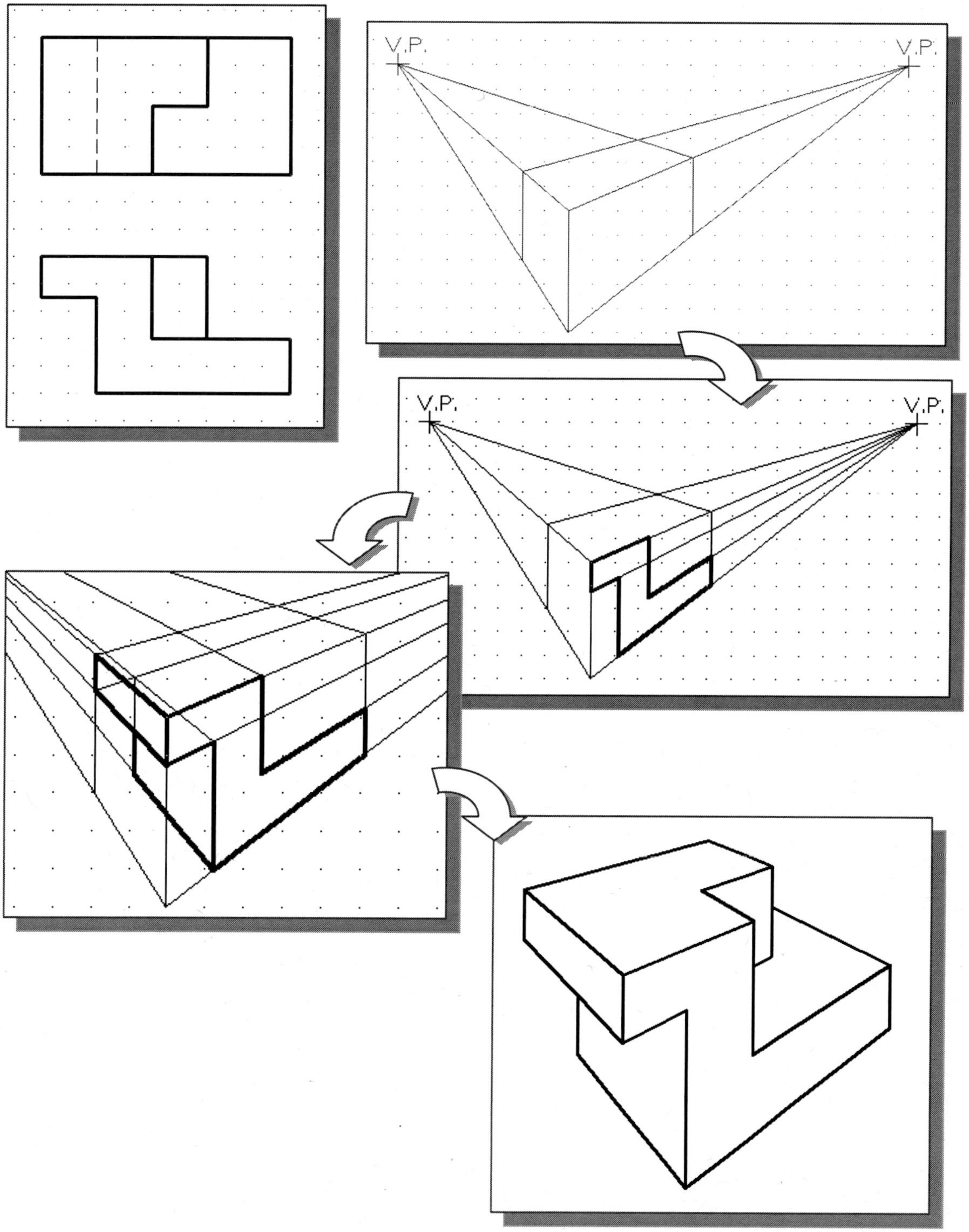

Perspective Sketching Exercises:

Given the Orthographic Top view and Front view, create one-point or two-point perspective views.

1.

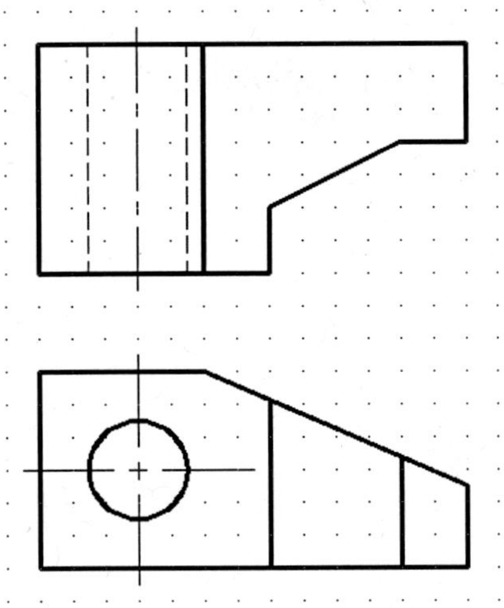

2.

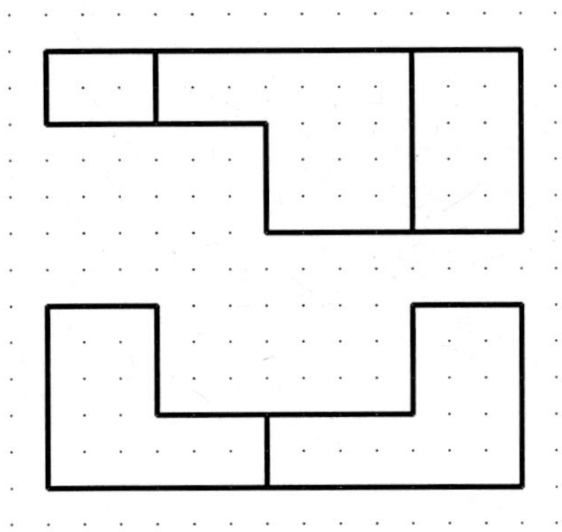

3.

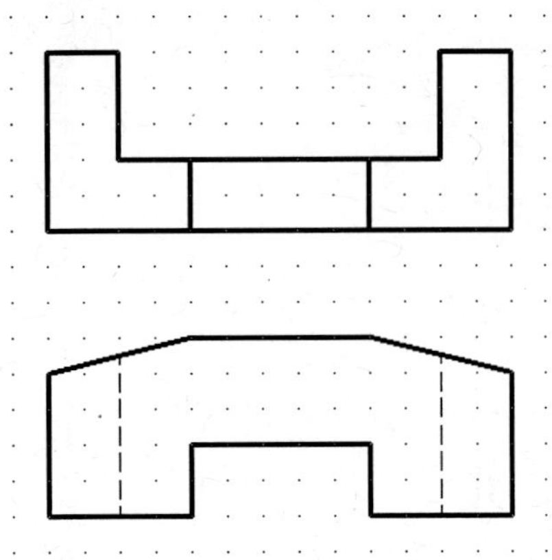

Questions:

1. What are the three types of Axonometric projection?
2. Describe the differences between an Isometric drawing and a Trimetric drawing.
3. What is the main advantage of Oblique projection over Isometric projection?
4. Describe the differences between a one-point perspective and a two-point perspective.
5. Which pictorial methods maintain true size and shape of geometry on the frontal plane?
6. What is a vanishing point in a perspective drawing?
7. What is a Cabinet Oblique?
8. What is the angle between the three axes in an Isometric drawing?
9. In an Axonometric drawing, are the projection lines perpendicular to the projection plane?
10. A cylindrical feature, in a frontal plane, will remain a circle in which pictorial methods?
11. In an Oblique drawing, are the projection lines perpendicular to the projection plane?
12. Create freehand pictorial sketches of:
    - Your desk
    - Your computer
    - One corner of your room
    - The tallest building in your area

Exercises:

1. Given the 2D views, construct the associated isometric views.

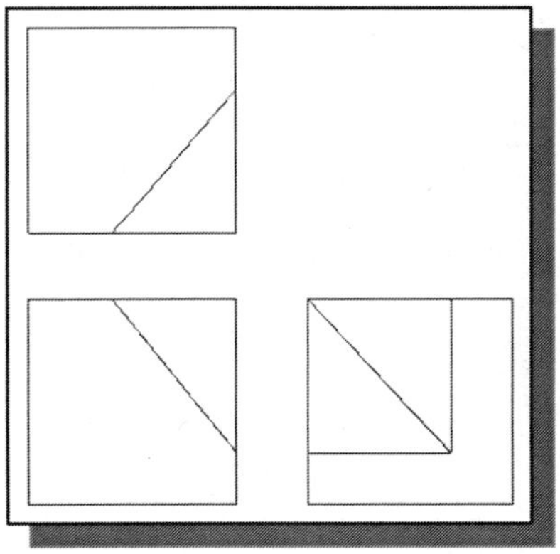

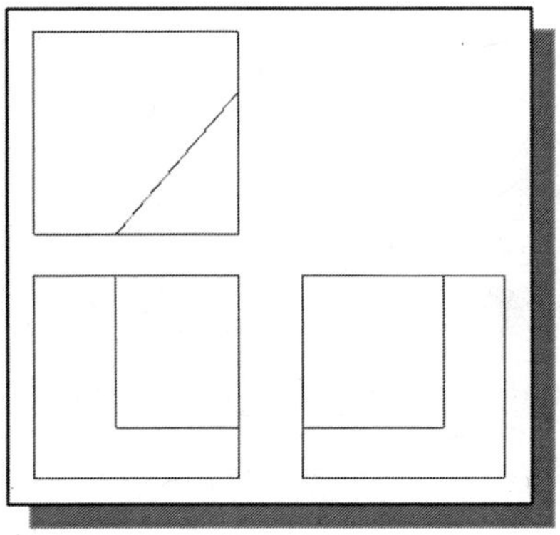

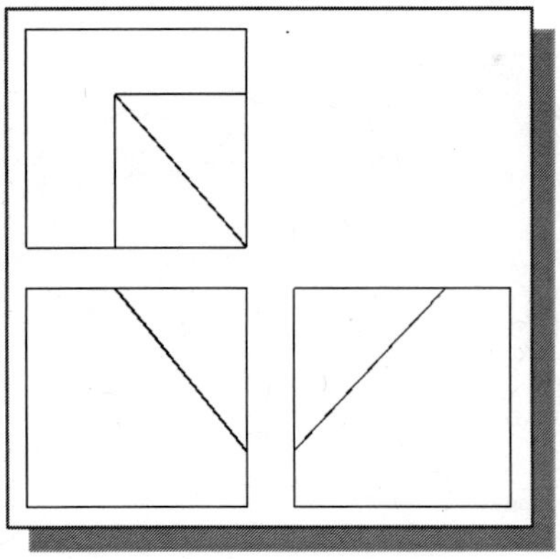

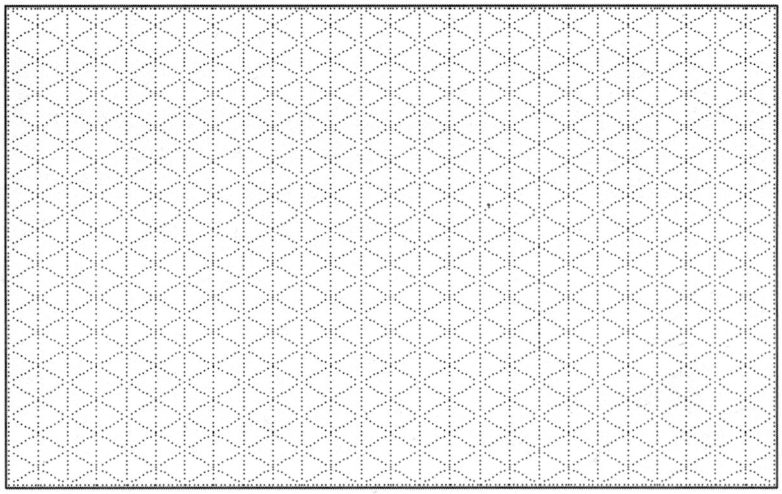

2. Given the 2D views, construct the associated two-point perspective views.

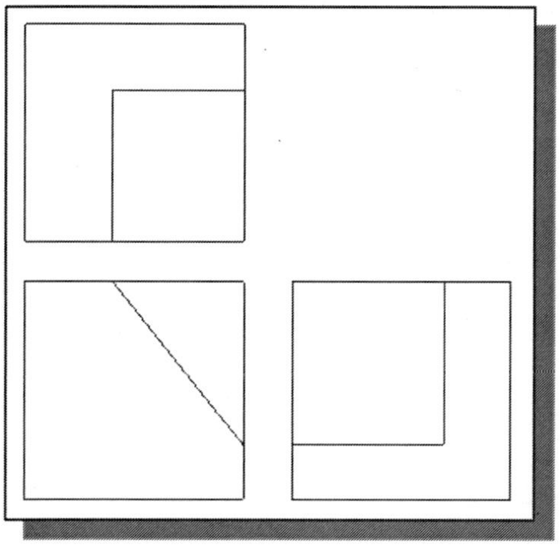

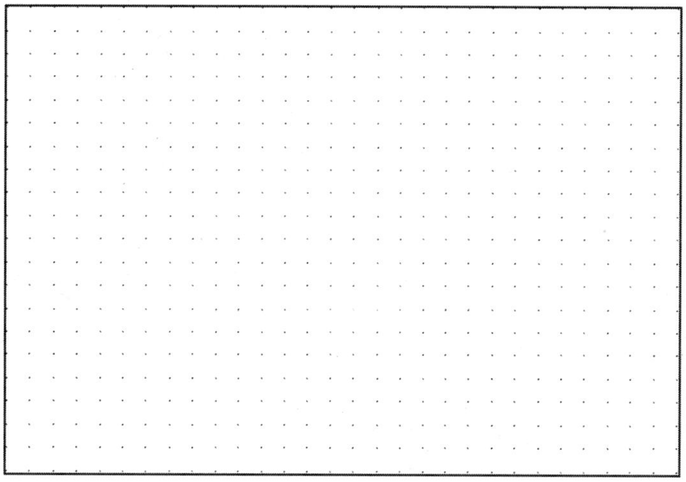

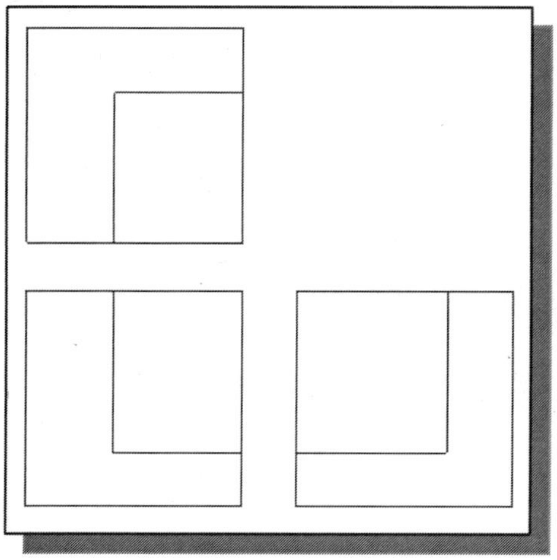

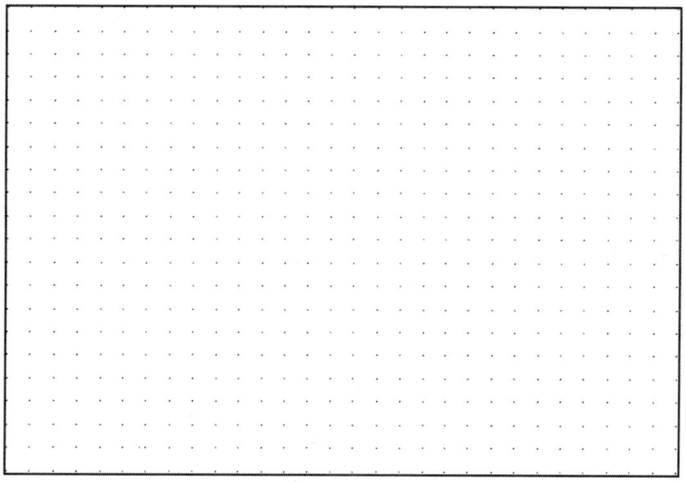

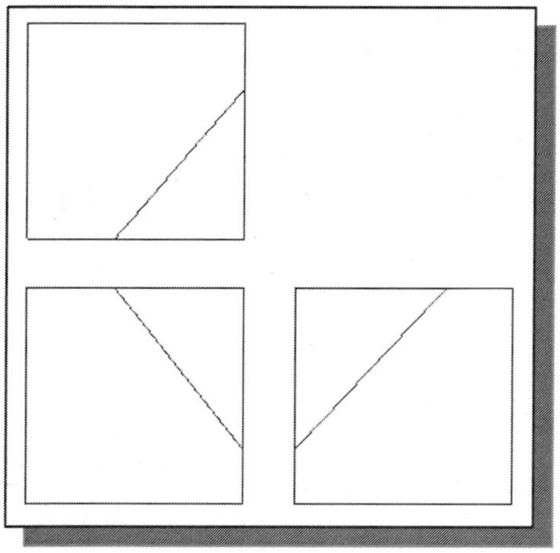

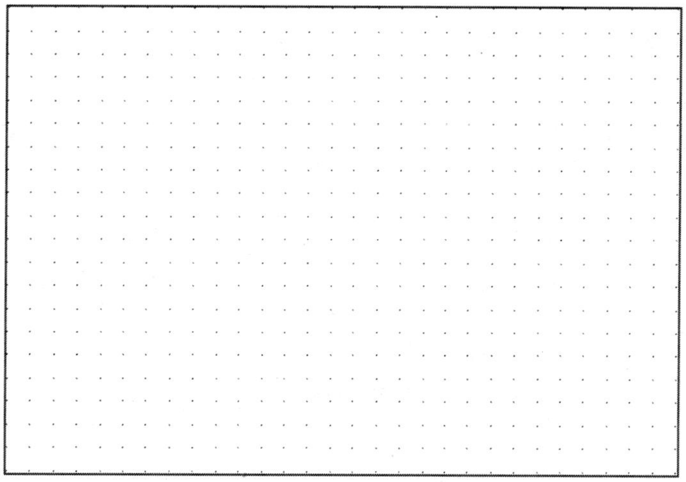

3. Given the 2D views, construct the associated oblique views.

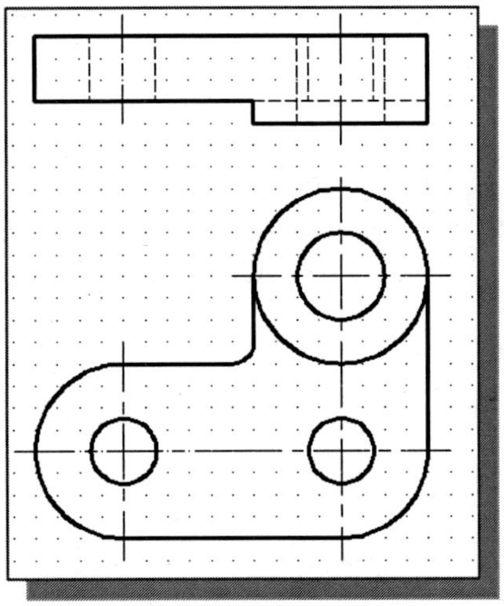

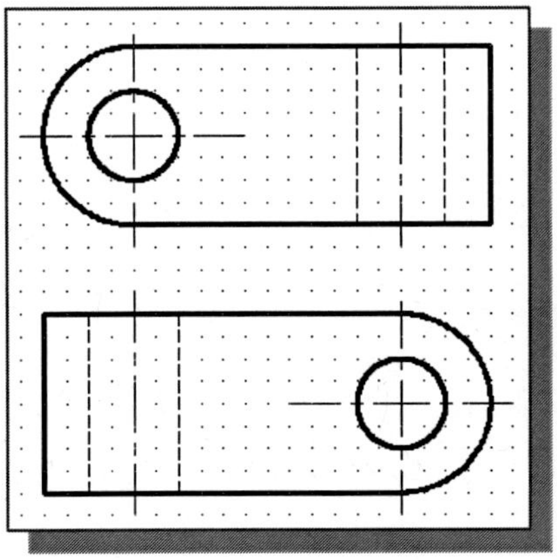

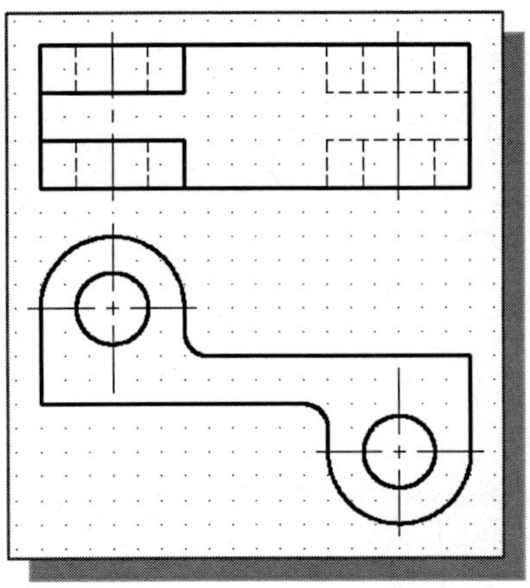

4. Given the 2D views, construct the associated one-point perspective views.

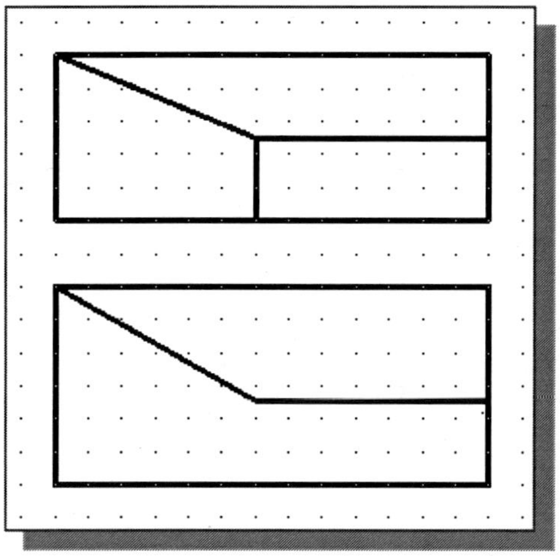

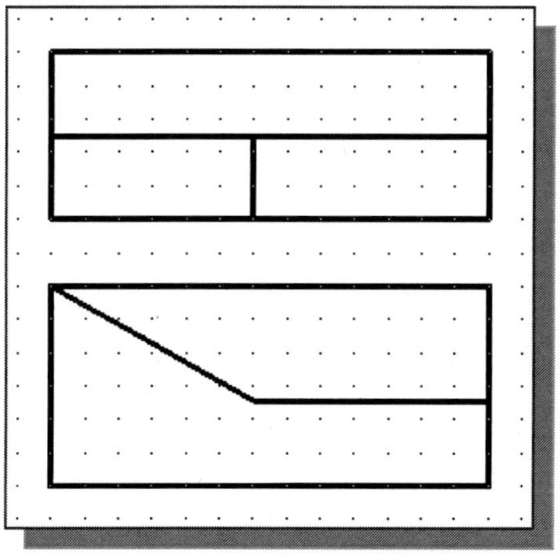

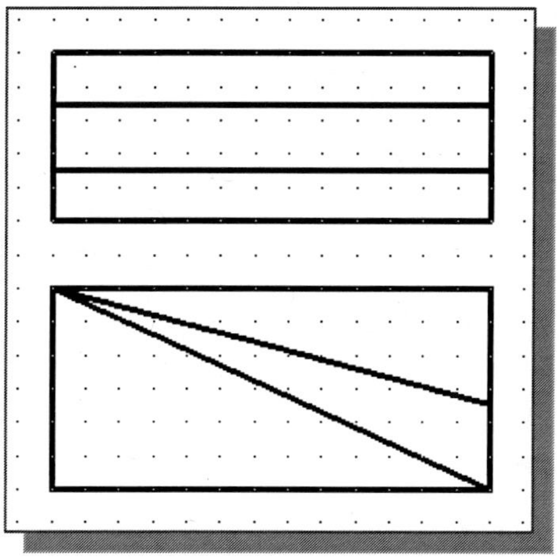

5. Complete the missing views. (Create a pictorial sketch as an aid in reading the views.)

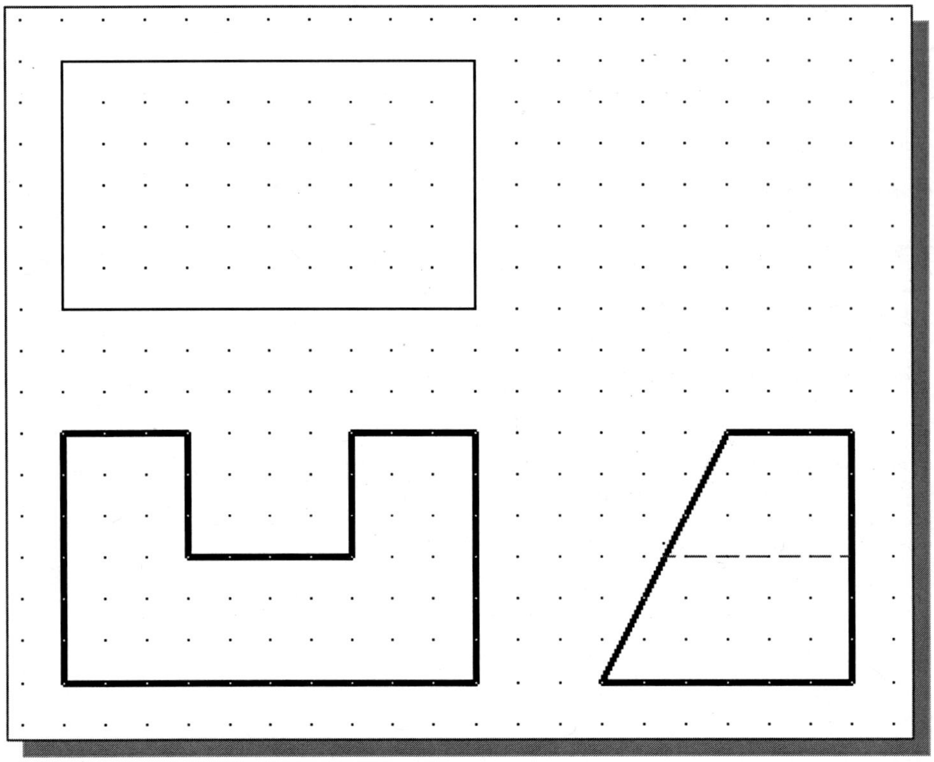

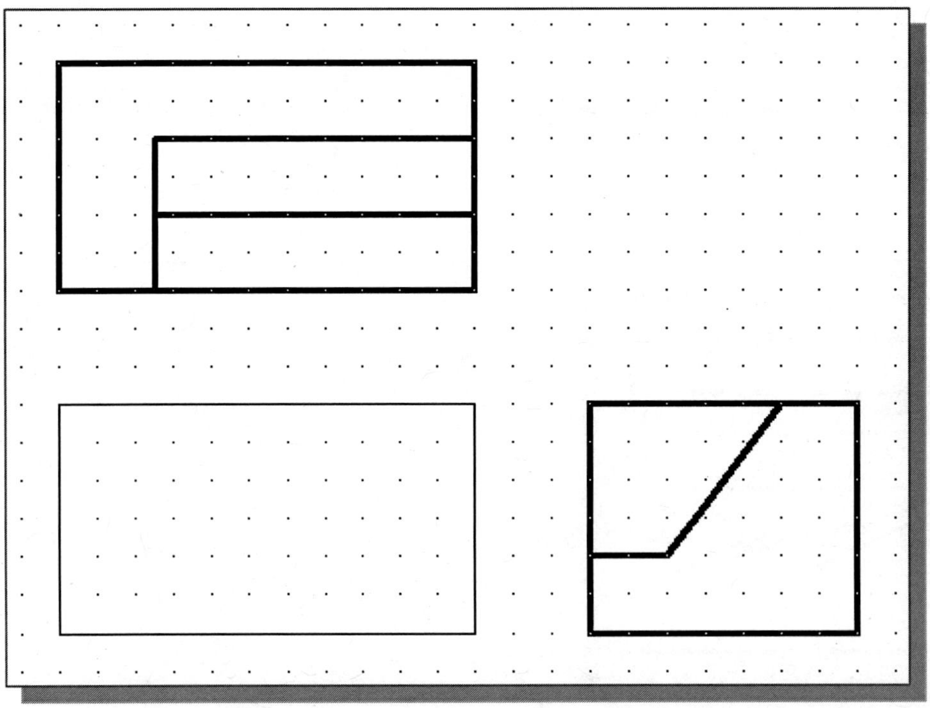

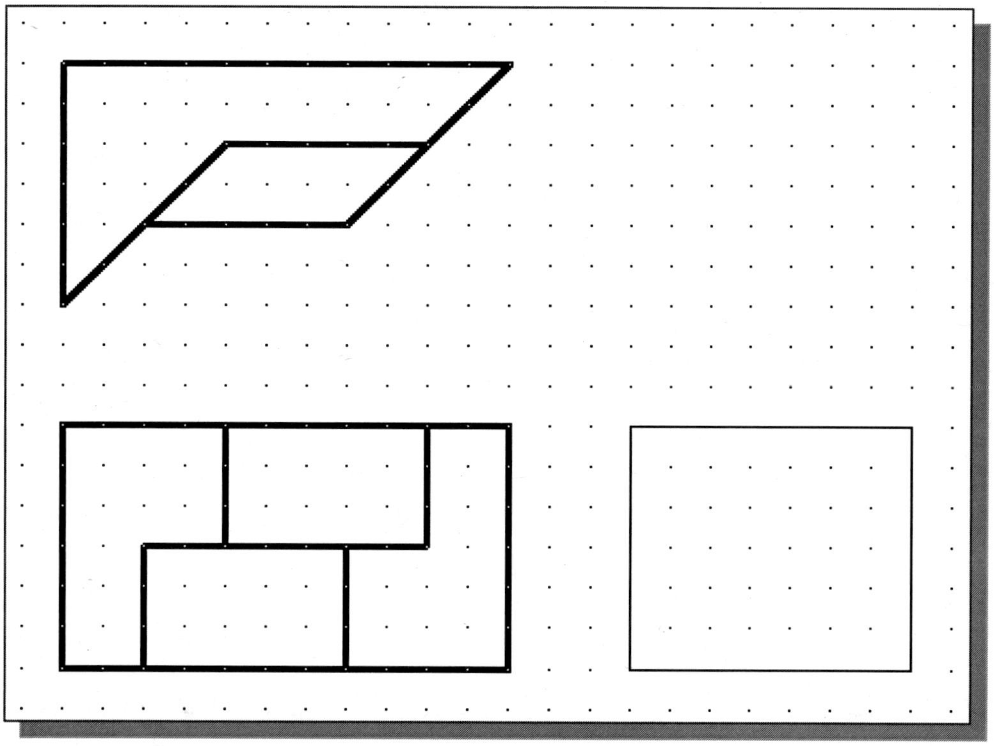

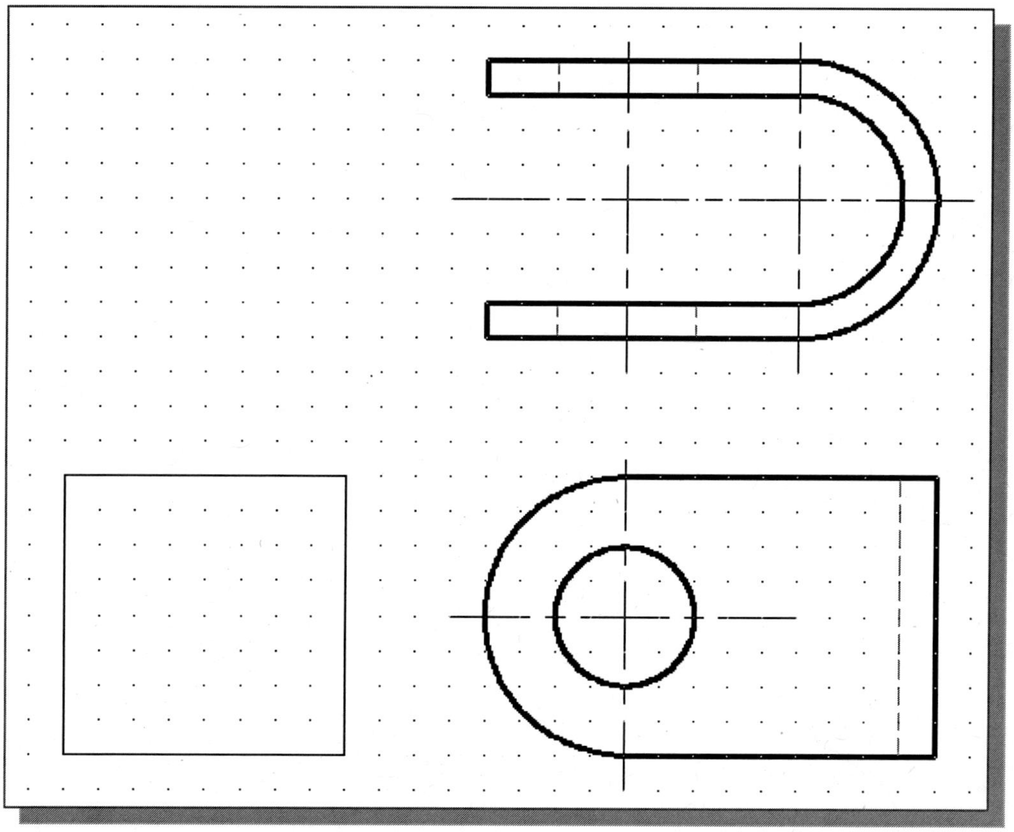

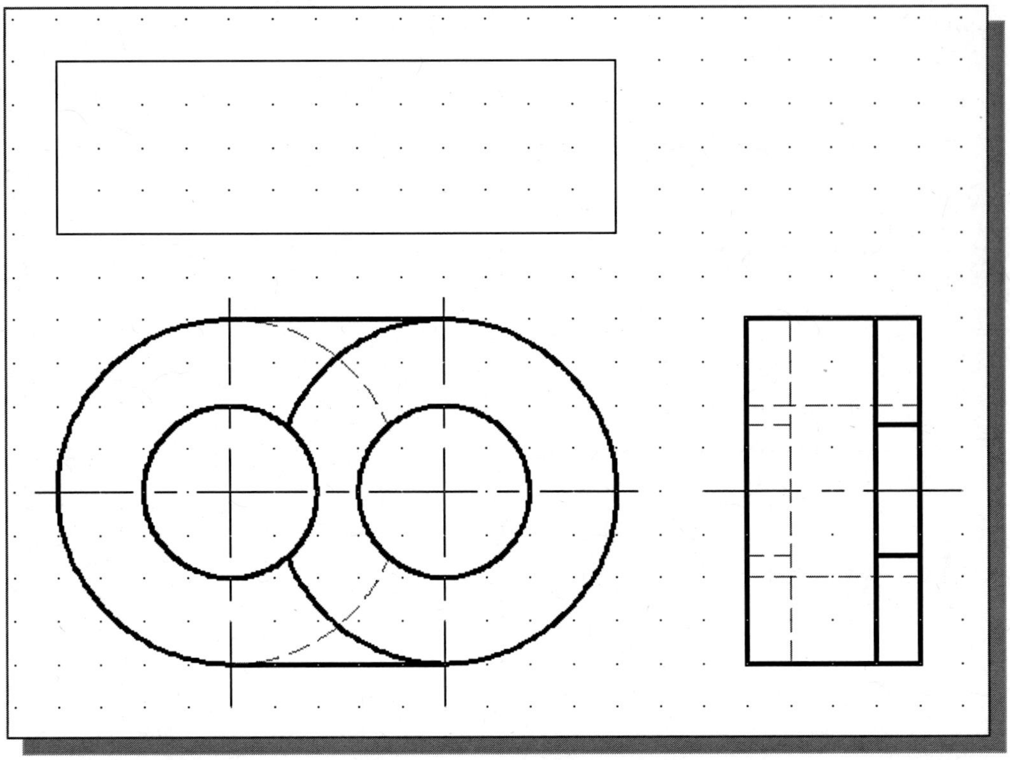

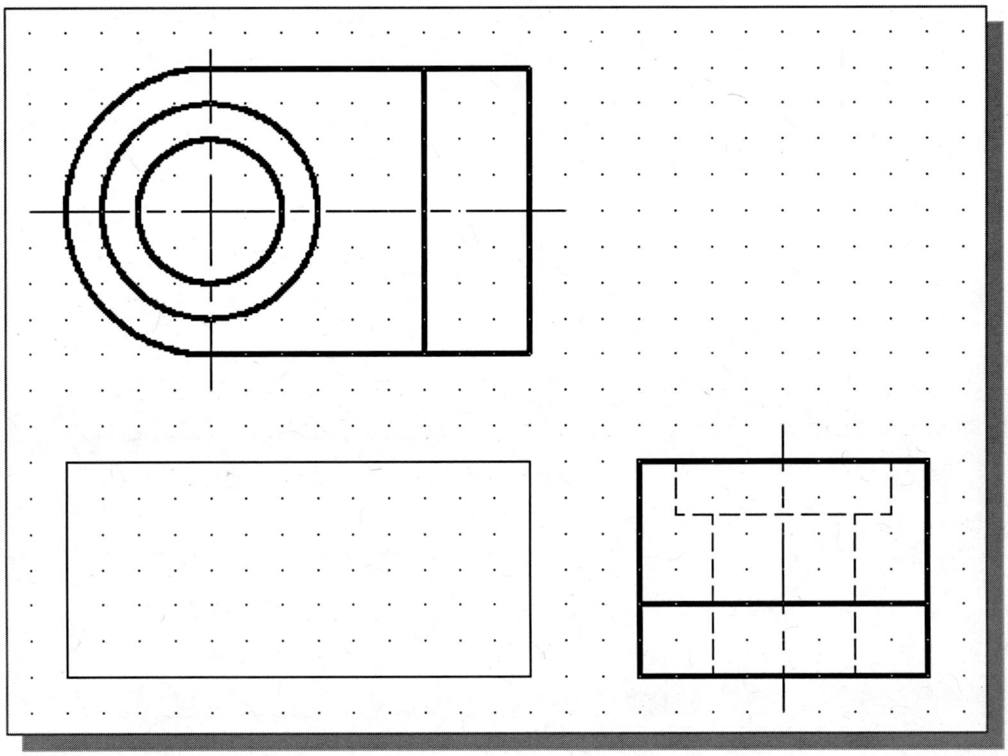

Chapter 6
Symmetrical Features and Part Drawings

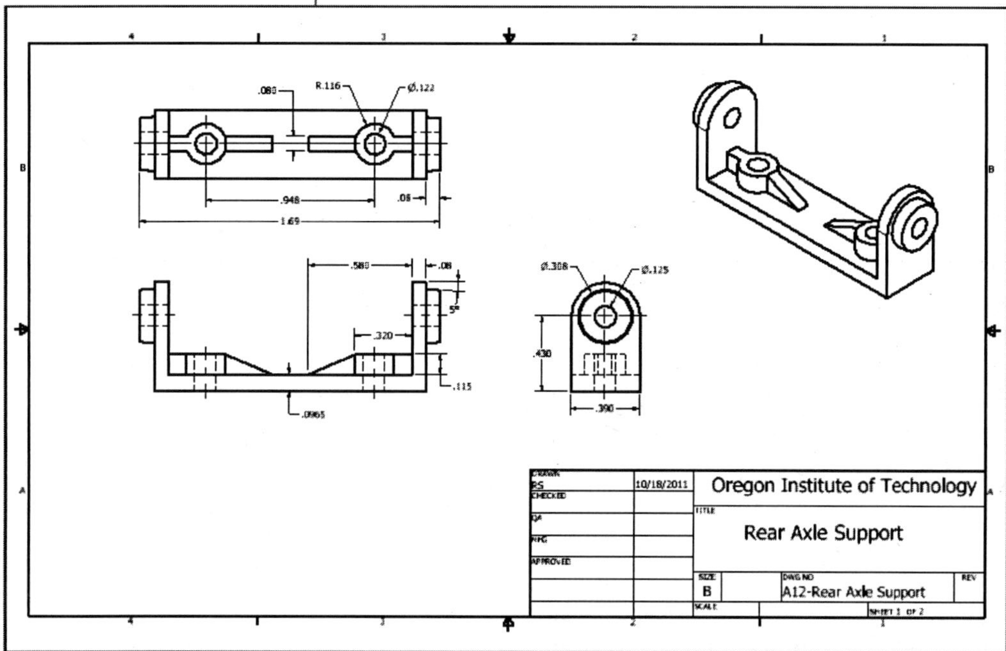

Learning Objectives

- **Create Drawing Layouts from Solid Models**
- **Understand Associative Functionality**
- **Use the Default Borders and Title Block in the Layout Mode**
- **Arrange and Manage 2D Views in Drawing Mode**
- **Display and Hide Feature Dimensions**
- **Create Reference Dimensions**
- **Create 3D Annotations in Isometric Views**

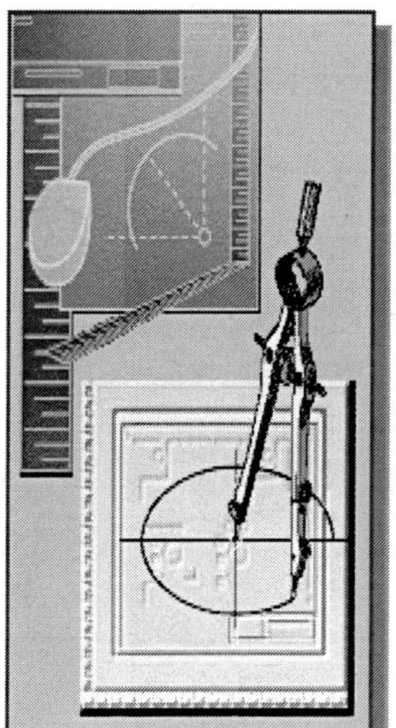

Drawings from Parts and Associative Functionality

In parametric modeling, it is important to identify and determine the features that exist in the design. *Feature-based parametric modeling* enables us to build complex designs by working on smaller and simpler units. This approach simplifies the modeling process and allows us to concentrate on the characteristics of the design. Symmetry is an important characteristic that is often seen in designs. Symmetrical features can be easily accomplished by the assortment of tools that are available in feature-based modeling systems, such as *SolidWorks.*

The modeling technique of extruding two-dimensional sketches along a straight line to form three-dimensional features, as illustrated in the previous chapters, is an effective way to construct solid models. For designs that involve cylindrical shapes, shapes that are symmetrical about an axis, revolving two-dimensional sketches about an axis can form the needed three-dimensional features. In solid modeling, this type of feature is called a ***revolved feature***.

In *SolidWorks*, besides using the **Revolve** command to create revolved features, several options are also available to handle symmetrical features. For example, we can create mirror images of models using the **Mirror Feature** command. We can also use *construction geometry* to assist the construction of more complex features. In this lesson, the construction and modeling techniques of these more advanced options are illustrated.

With the software/hardware improvements in solid modeling, the importance of two-dimensional drawings is decreasing. Drafting is considered one of the downstream applications of using solid models. In many production facilities, solid models are used to generate machine tool paths for *computer numerical control* (CNC) machines. Solid models are also used in *rapid prototyping* to create 3D physical models out of plastic resins, powdered metal, etc. Ideally, the solid model database should be used directly to generate the final product. However, the majority of applications in most production facilities still require the use of two-dimensional drawings. Using the solid model as the starting point for a design, solid modeling tools can easily create all the necessary two-dimensional views. In this sense, solid modeling tools are making the process of creating two-dimensional drawings more efficient and effective.

SolidWorks provides associative functionality in the different *SolidWorks* modes. This functionality allows us to change the design at any level, and the system reflects it at all levels automatically. For example, a solid model can be modified in the *Part Modeling Mode* and the system automatically reflects that change in the *Drawing Mode.* And we can also modify a feature dimension in the *Drawing Mode*, and the system automatically updates the solid model in all modes.

In this lesson, the general procedure of creating multi-view drawings is illustrated. The *A12- Rear Axle Support* part of the *Mechanical Tiger* design is first created, and the associated 2D drawing is then generated from the solid model. The associative functionality between the model and drawing views is also examined.

The *A12- Rear Axle Support* Design

Starting *SolidWorks*

1. Select the **SolidWorks** option on the *Start* menu or select the **SolidWorks** icon on the desktop to start *SolidWorks*. The *SolidWorks* main window will appear on the screen.

2. Select the **New** icon with a single click of the left-mouse-button on the *Menu Bar*.

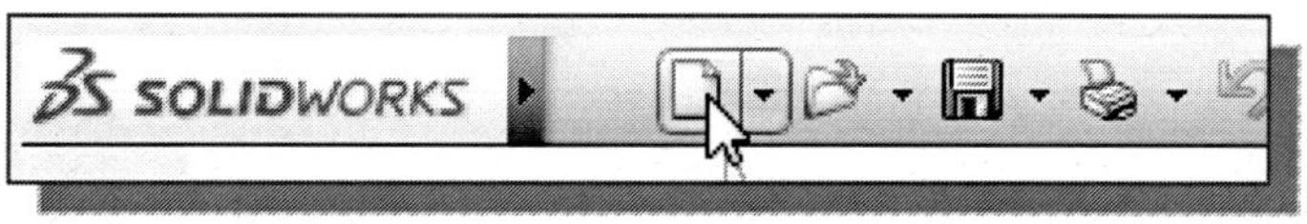

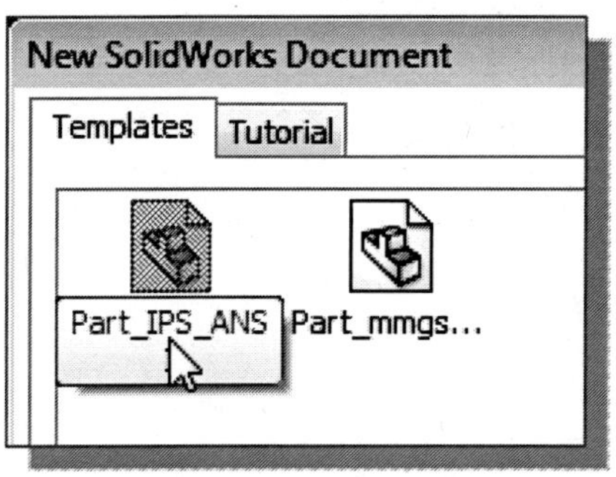

3. Select the **Part_IPS_ANSI** template as shown.

4. Click on the **OK** button to open a new document using the Part_IPS_ANSI template.

- The *Dimensioning Standard* will automatically be ANSI and the units will be set to inch, pound, second as defined in the template.

Modeling Strategy

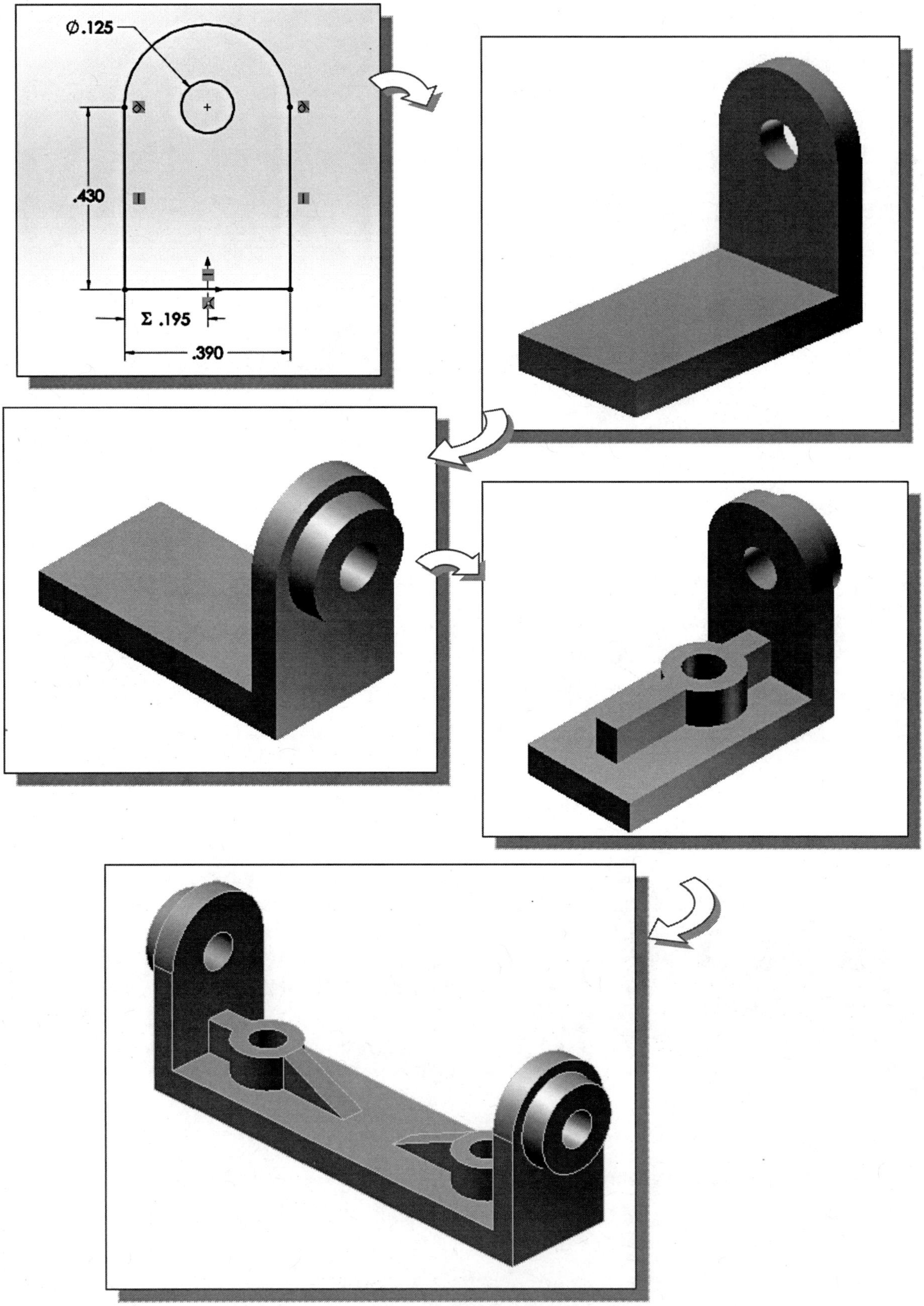

Create the Base Feature

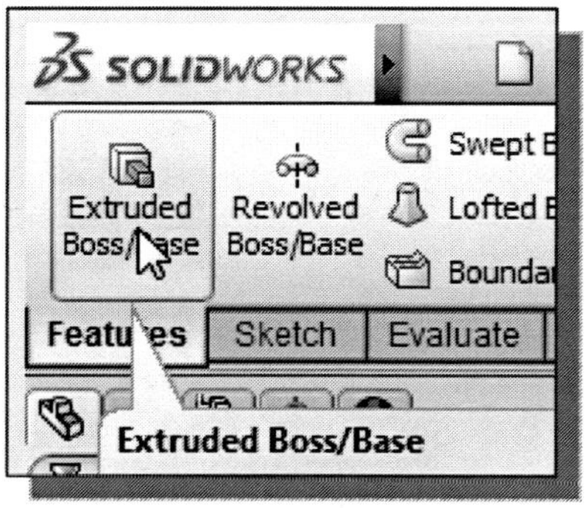

1. In the *Features* toolbar select the **Extruded Boss/ Base** command by clicking once with the left-mouse-button on the icon.

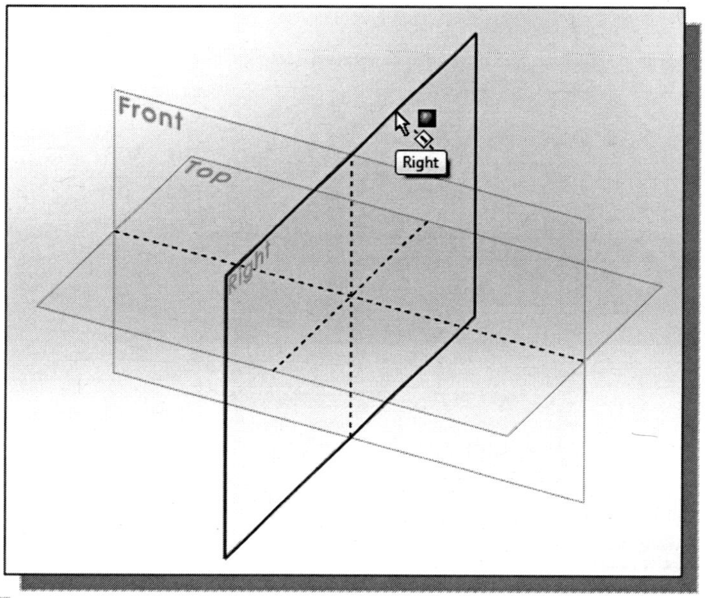

2. Select the **Right Plane** by clicking on any edge of the plane, inside the graphics window, as shown.

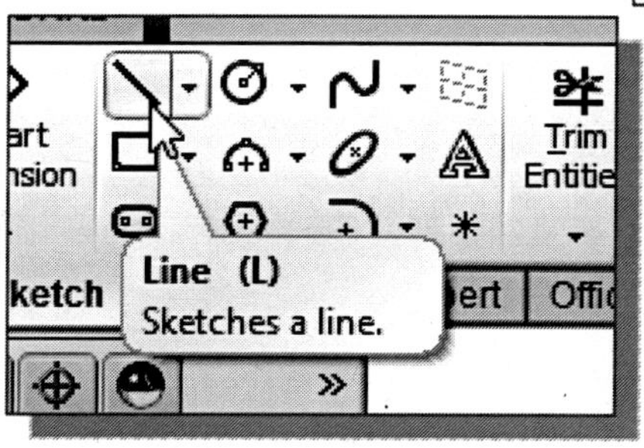

3. Select the **Line** option in the *Sketch* toolbar. A *Help-tip* box appears next to the cursor: "*Sketches a line.*"

4. Create three line segments, lines are either vertical or horizontal, with the two endpoints aligned as shown. Do not exit the Line command.

5. Move the cursor on top of the last endpoint with the left-mouse-button to activate the Arc option.

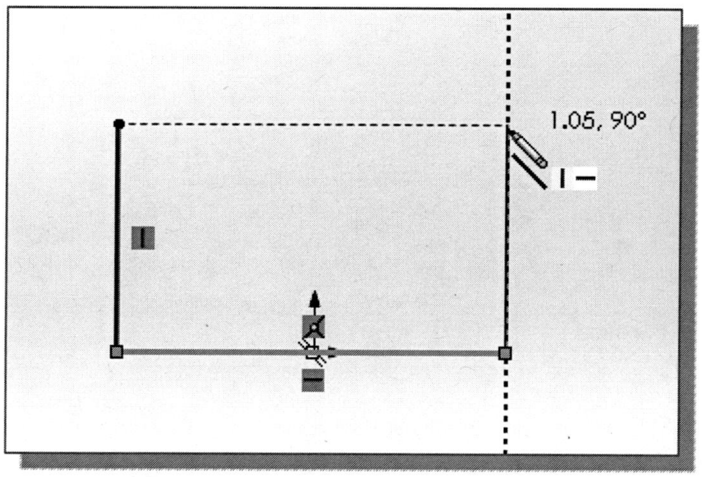

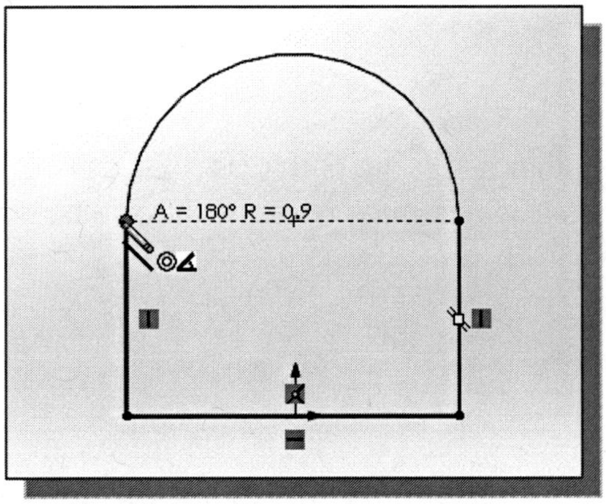

6. Create an arc by clicking on the starting points of the line segments to form a closed region as shown.

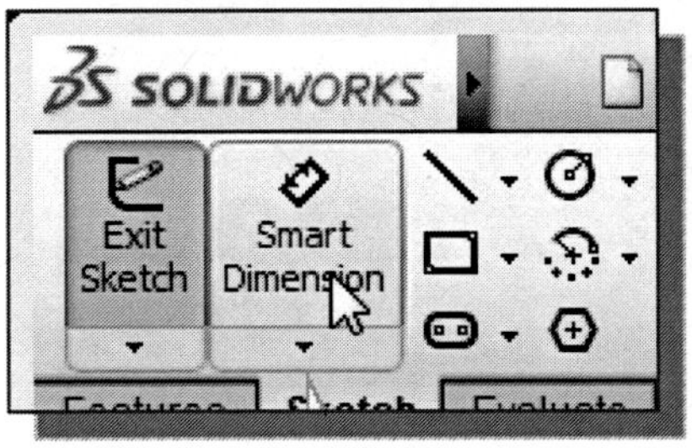

7. On your own, use the **Smart Dimension** command and create the size and location dimensions of the sketch as shown in the figure below.

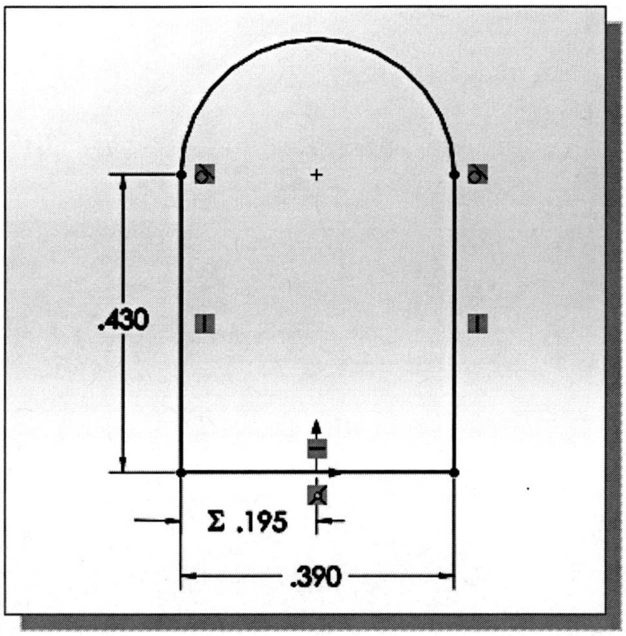

8. On your own, set up a relation to position the sketch aligned to the *Origin* as shown.

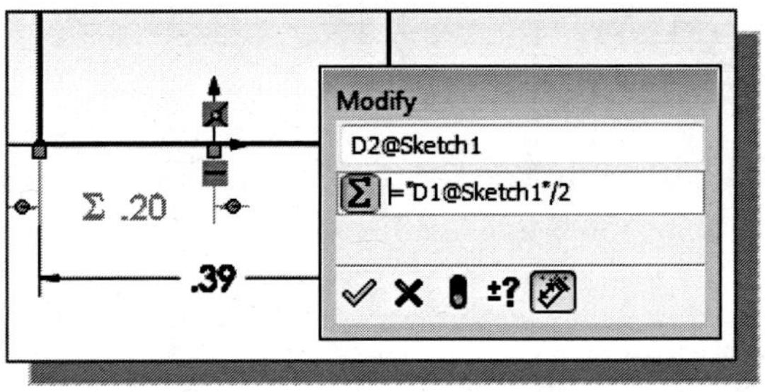

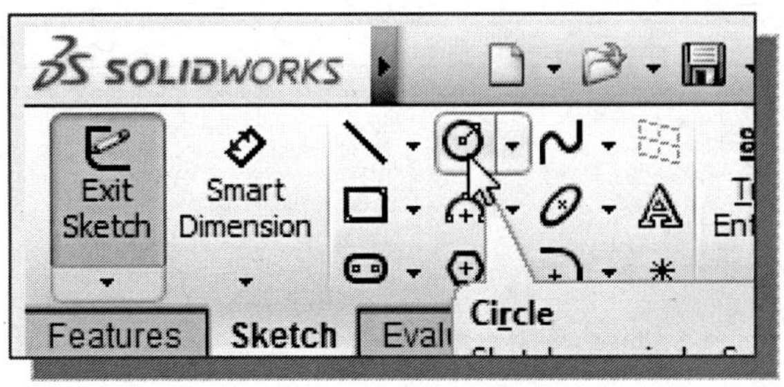

9. Select the **Circle** command by clicking once with the left-mouse-button on the icon in the *Sketch* toolbar.

10. On your own, create a circle aligned to the center of the upper arc as shown.

11. Create and modify the diameter dimension to **0.125** as shown.

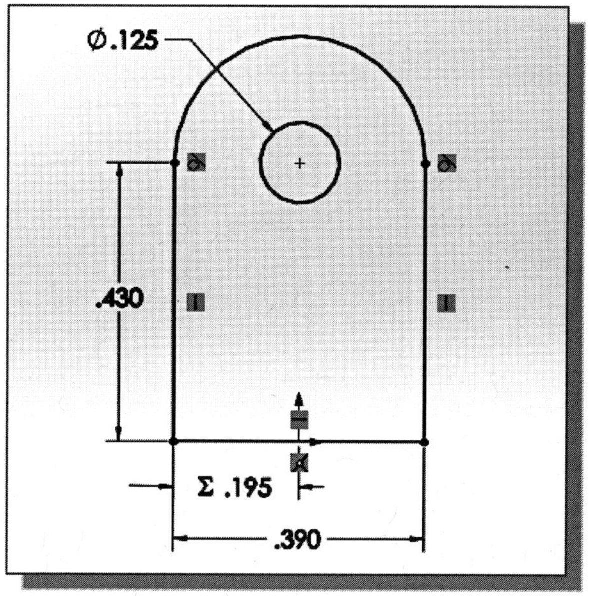

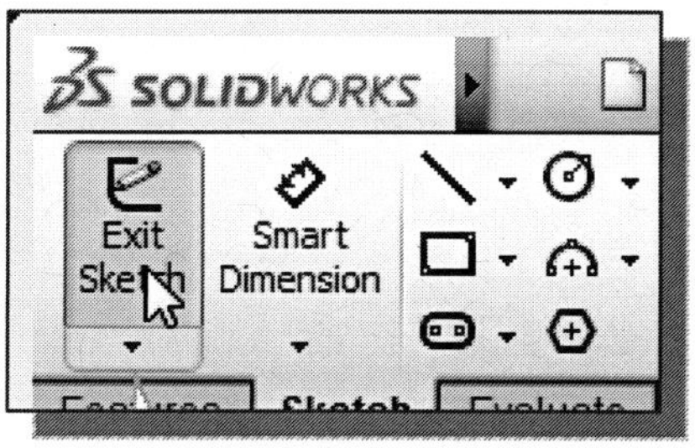

12. Click **Exit Sketch** in the *Sketch* toolbar to end the *Sketch* mode.

13. Set the extrusion distance to **0.764**, and set the extrusion direction toward the right as shown.

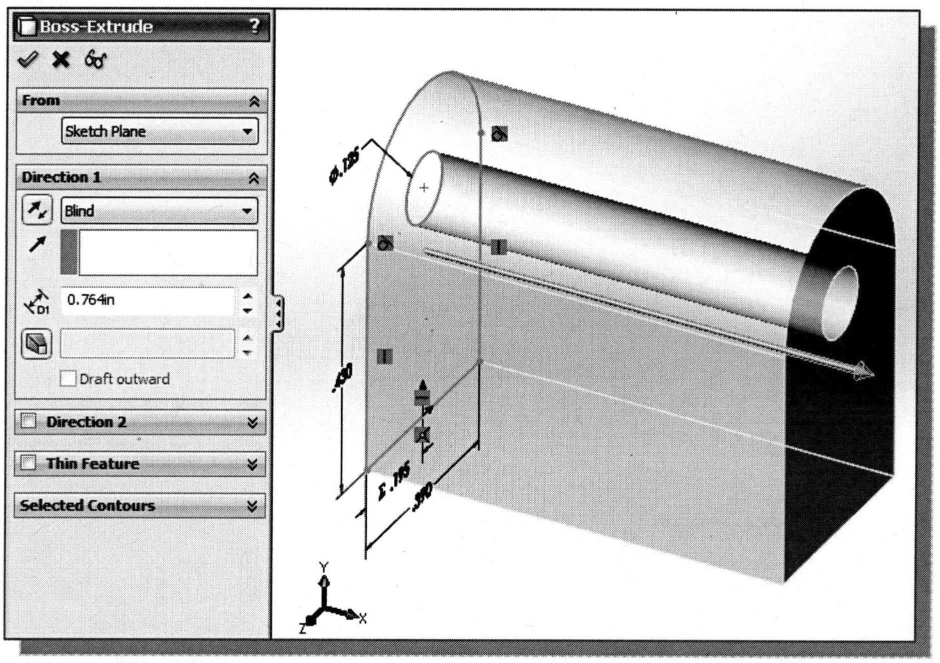

14. Click on the **OK** button to accept the settings and create the solid feature.

Create a Symmetrical Cut Feature

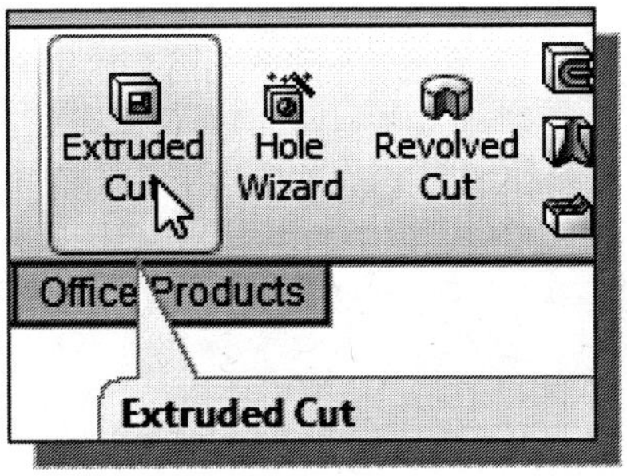

1. In the *Features* toolbar select the **Extruded Cut** command by clicking once with the left-mouse-button on the icon.

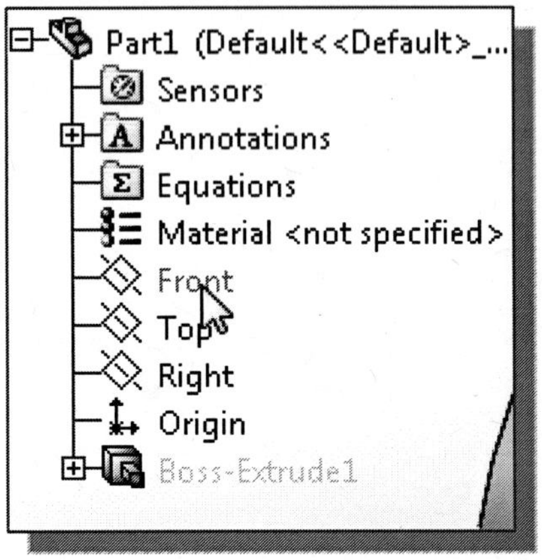

2. Expand the *Model Tree* in the graphics window by clicking the [+] symbol in front of the model name.

3. Select the **Front Plane** by clicking on the *Model Tree* as shown.

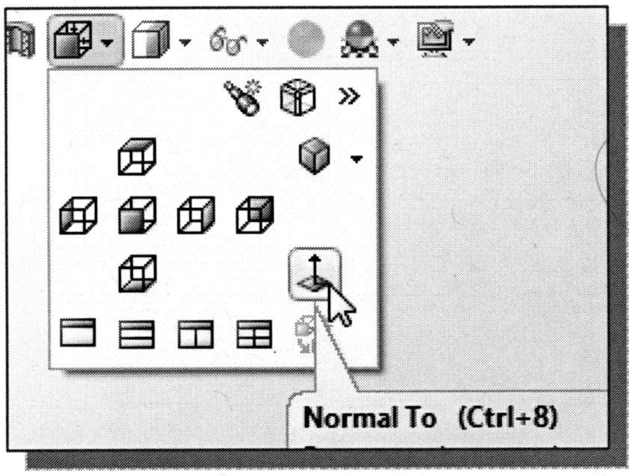

4. Align the view to the screen by using the **Normal To** option as shown.

- Note the view orientation is reset to viewing perpendicular to the sketching plane.

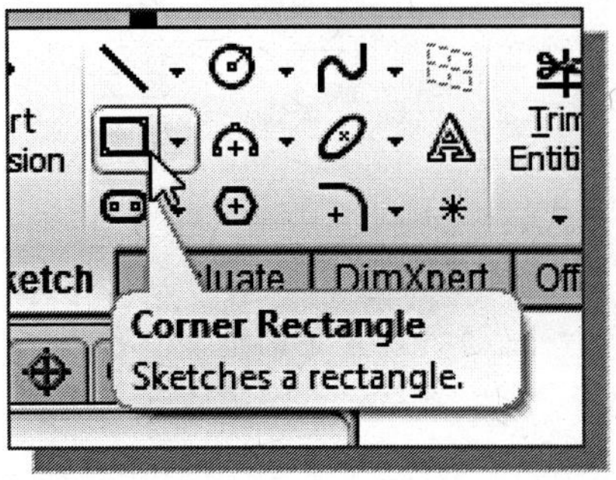

5. Select the **Corner Rectangle** command by clicking once with the **left-mouse-button** on the icon in the *Sketch* toolbar.

6. Create a rectangle with one edge aligned to the vertical Y axis as shown.

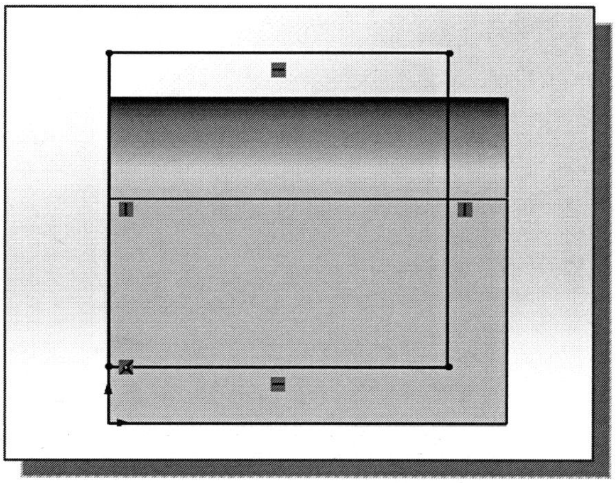

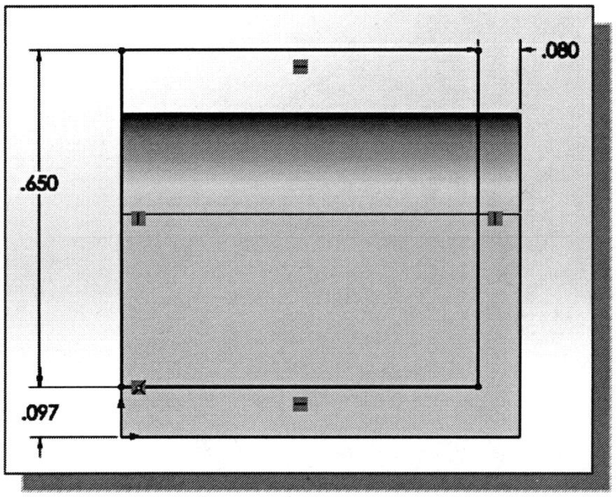

7. Create and modify the three associated dimensions, **0.65**, **0.097**, and **0.08**, as shown.

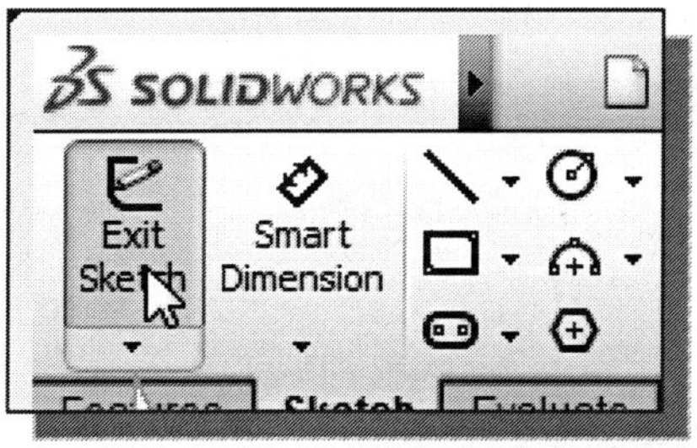

8. Select **Exit Sketch** in the *Sketch* toolbar to exit the 2D *Sketch* module.

9. Set the extrusion extents to **Mid Plane**, and distance to **0.5** as shown in the figure below.

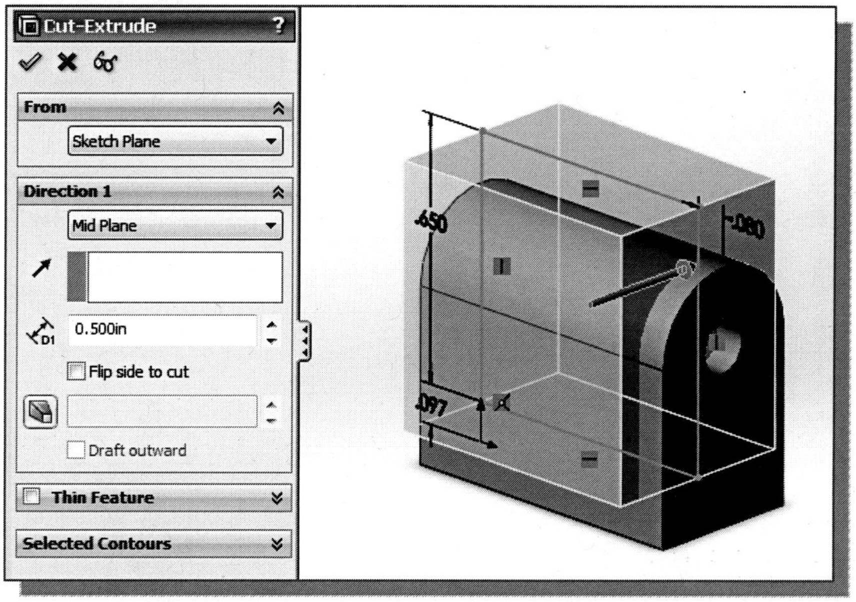

10. Click on the **OK** button to accept the settings and create the cut feature in both directions.

Create a Revolved Feature

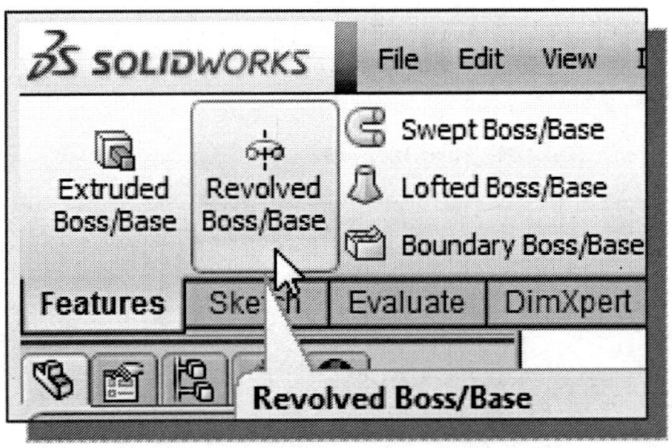

1. In the *Features* toolbar select the **Revolved Boss/Base** command by clicking once with the left-mouse-button on the icon.

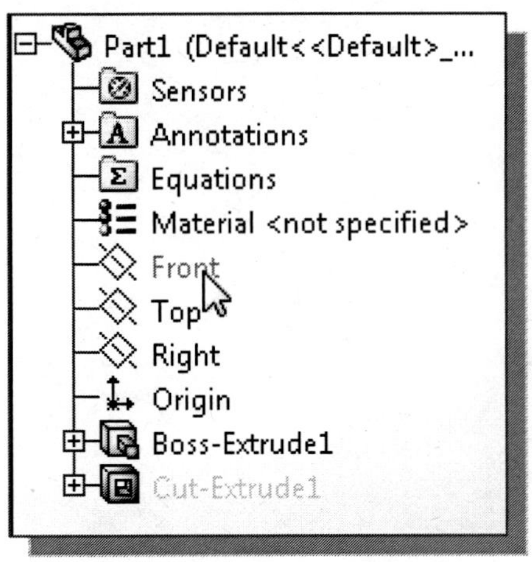

2. Select the **Front Plane** by clicking on the *Model Tree* shown.

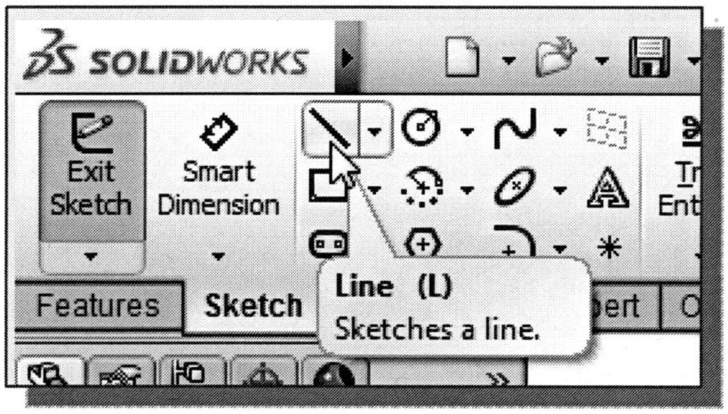

3. Select the **Line** option in the *Sketch* panel.

4. On your own, set the model display to **Hidden Lines Visible**.

5. Create four line segments, with three lines either vertical or horizontal. Note that the lower left corner of the sketch is aligned to the right endpoint of the inside cylindrical surface as shown.

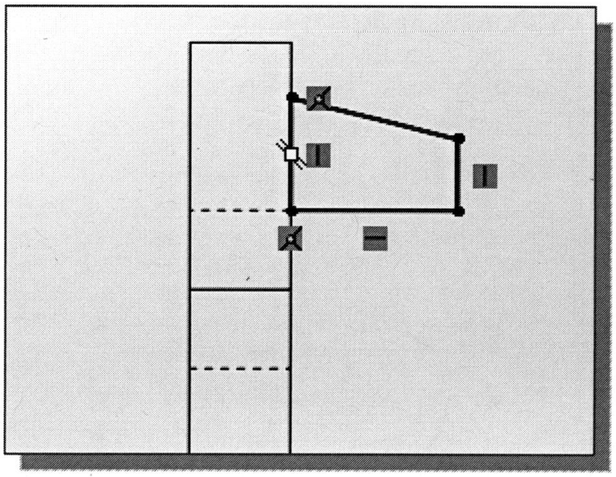

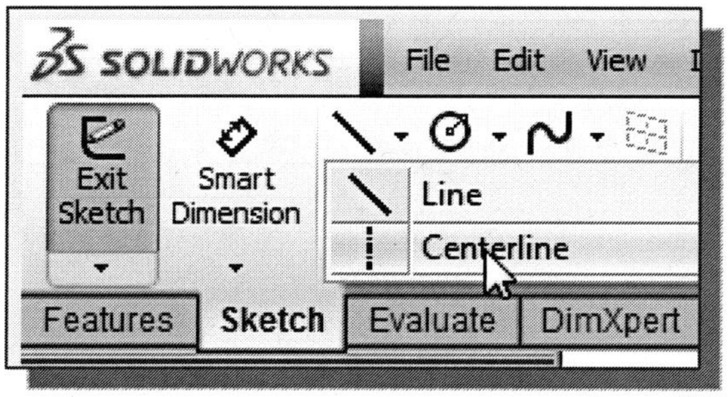

6. Select the **Centerline** option in the *Sketch* panel as shown.

7. Create a horizontal centerline aligned to the center-axis of the cylindrical hole feature.

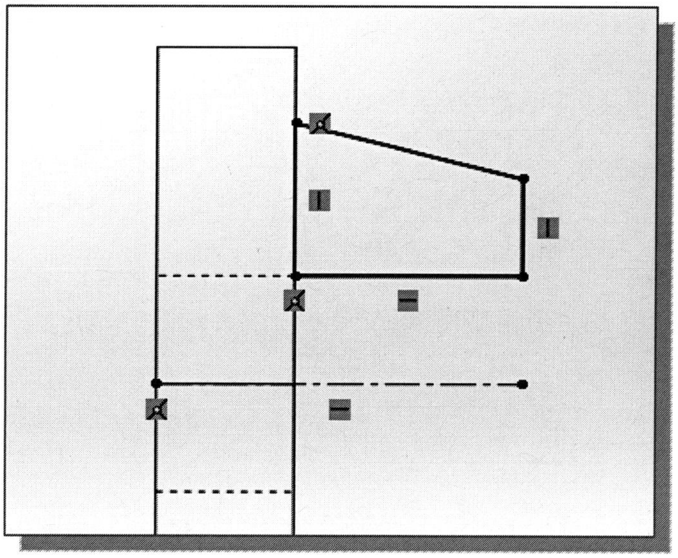

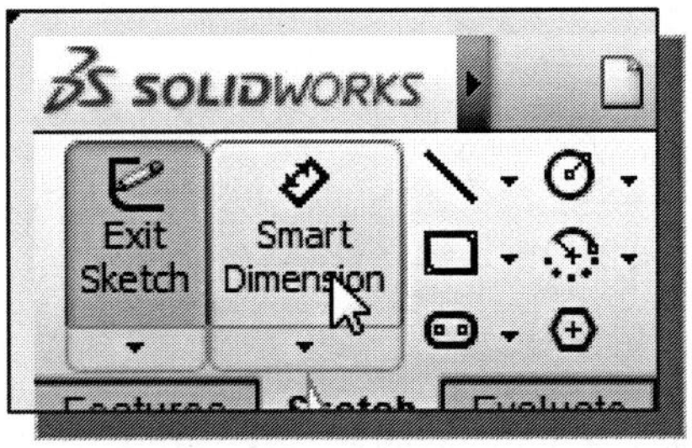

8. Select the **Smart Dimension** command as shown.

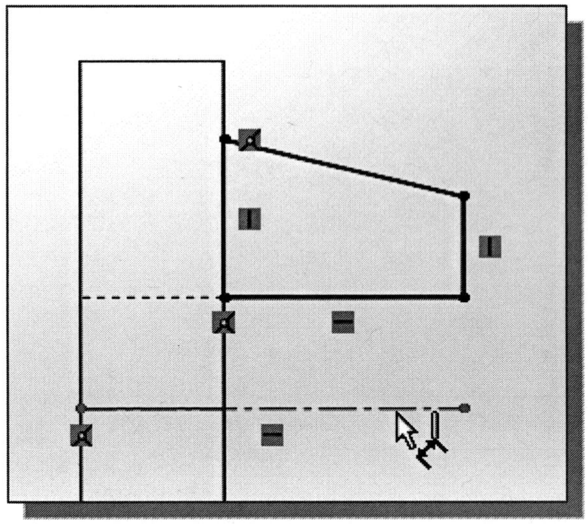

9. Select the **centerline** as the first entity to dimension as shown.

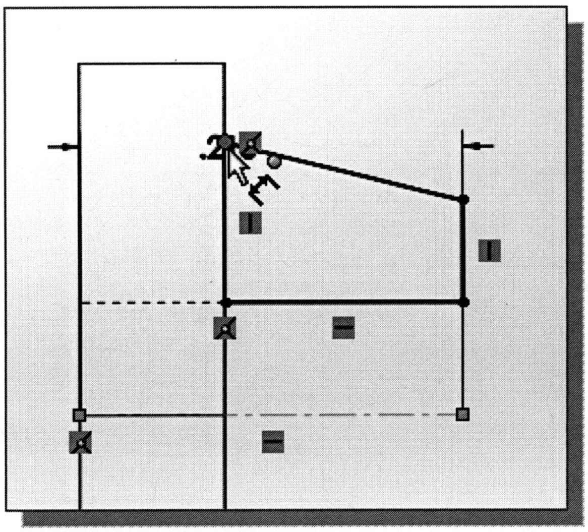

10. Select **top left corner** of the sketch as the second entity to dimension.

11. Place the dimension to the **right** side of the sketch.

12. Enter **0.155** as the radius value as shown.

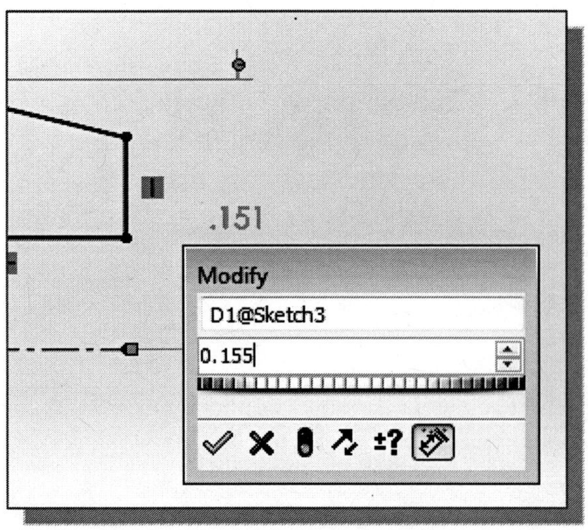

13. Click **OK** to end the Smart Dimension command.

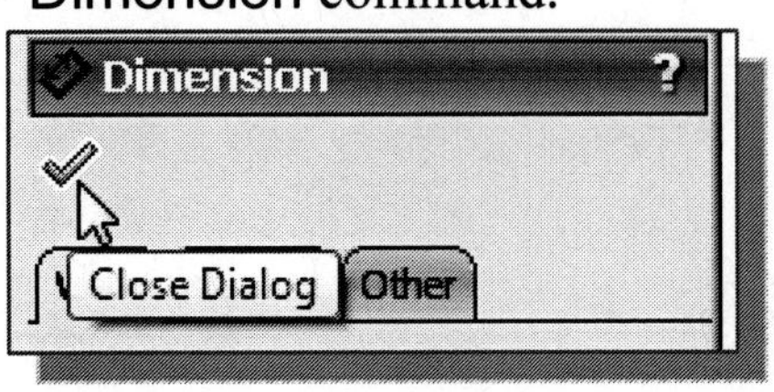

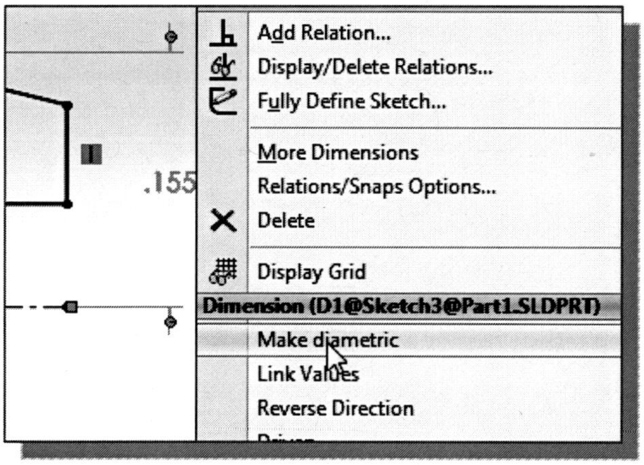

14. Inside the graphics window, right-click once on the dimension to bring up the option menu and select **Make Diametric** as shown.

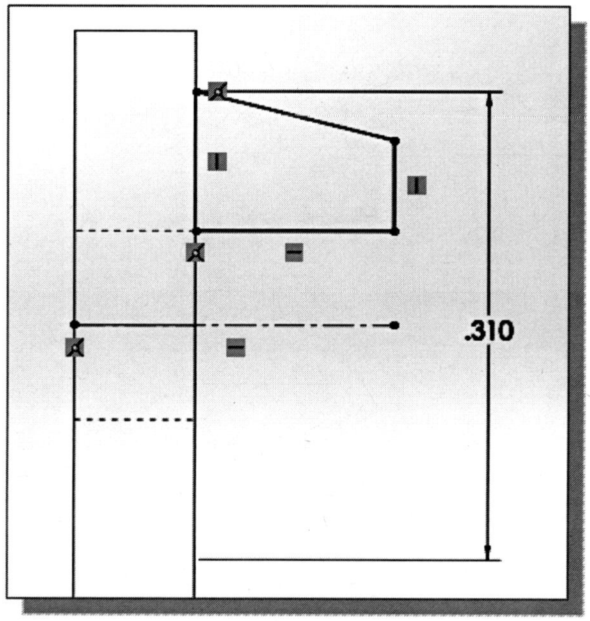

- In *SolidWorks*, a diameter dimension can be created by using a centerline.

15. On your own, create and modify the three dimensions as shown. Note the diameter dimension can also be set in the *Dimension Property Manager* as shown.

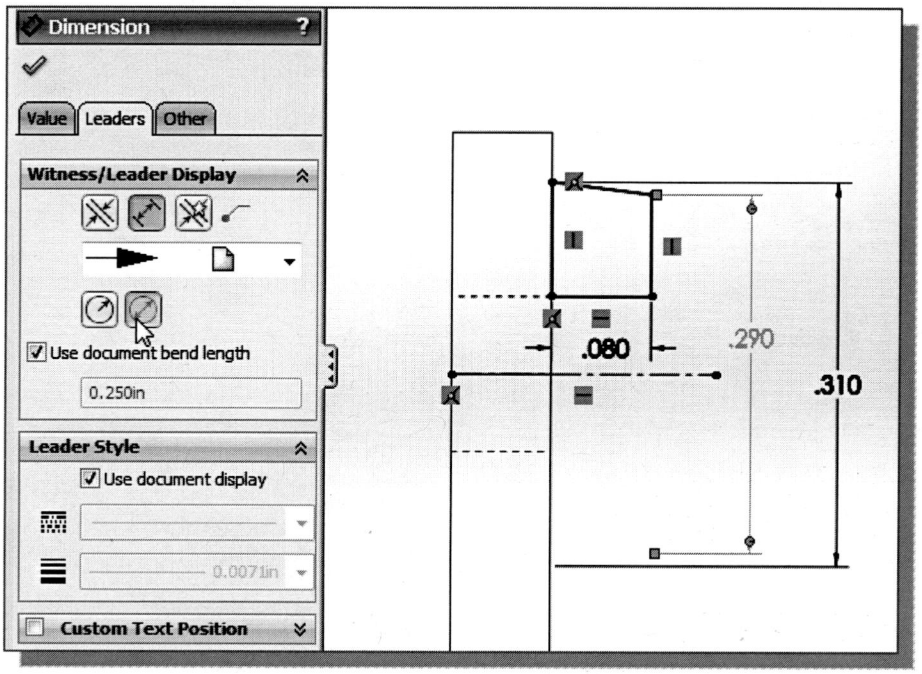

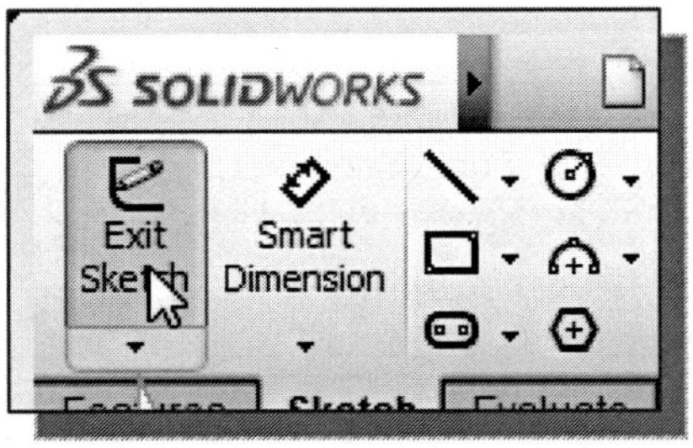

16. Click **Exit Sketch** in the *Sketch* toolbar to end the *Sketch* mode.

17. In the *Revolve Manager*, notice the centerline is automatically used as the center rotation axis of the **Revolve** command.

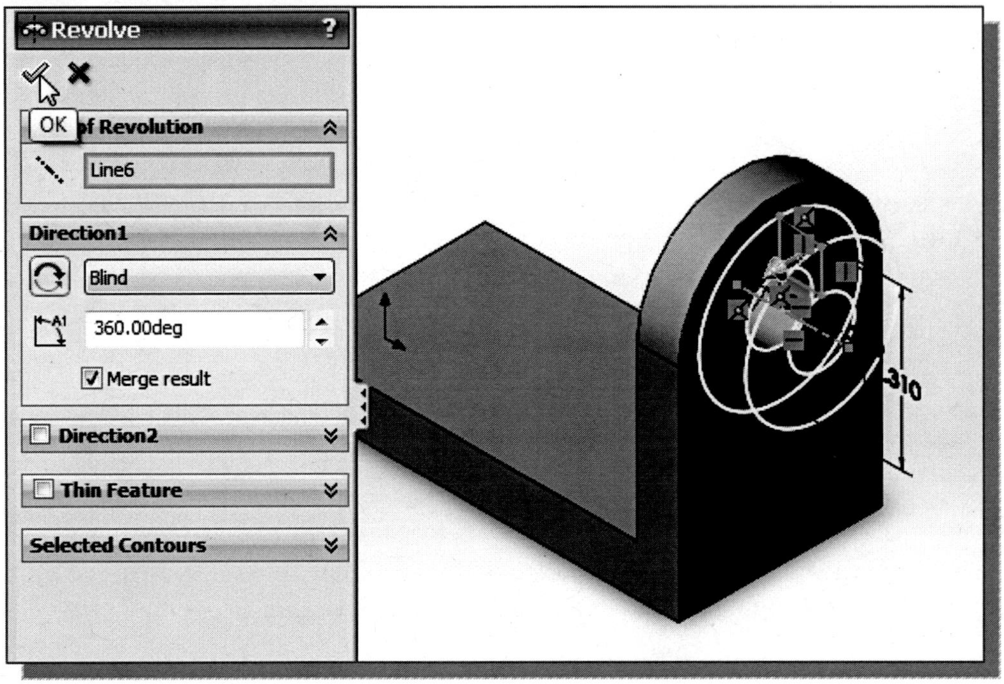

18. Confirm the **Merge result** option is activated and the *revolve angle* option is set to **360 degrees** as shown.

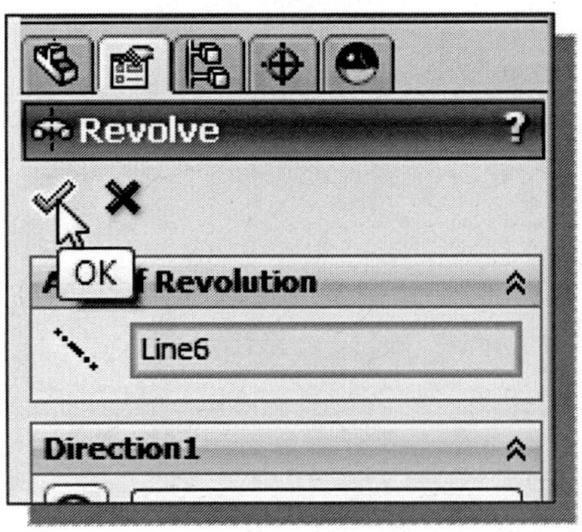

19. Click **OK** to accept the settings and create the revolved feature.

Create another Extrude Feature

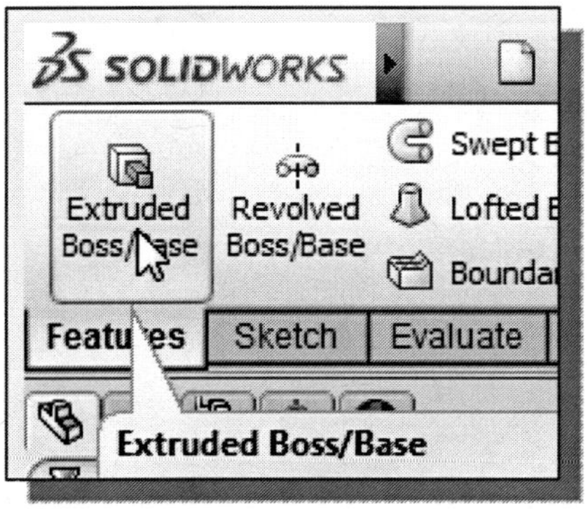

1. In the *Features* toolbar select the **Extruded Boss /Base** command by clicking once with the left-mouse-button on the icon.

2. Select the **Top Plane** of the flat base as shown.

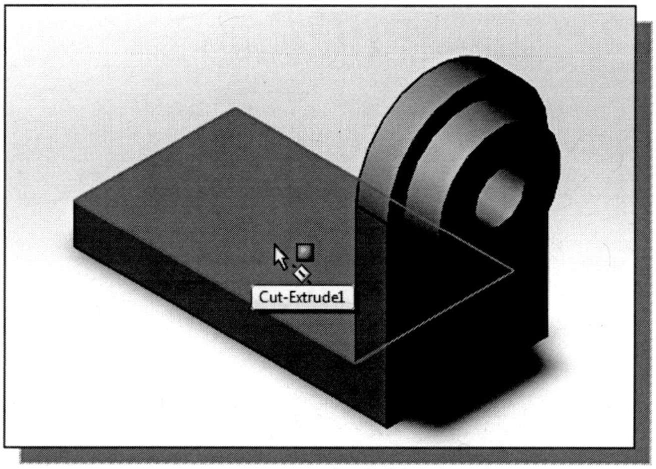

3. On your own, create a rectangle and a circle as shown. (Align the right edge of the rectangle to the adjacent vertical edge.)

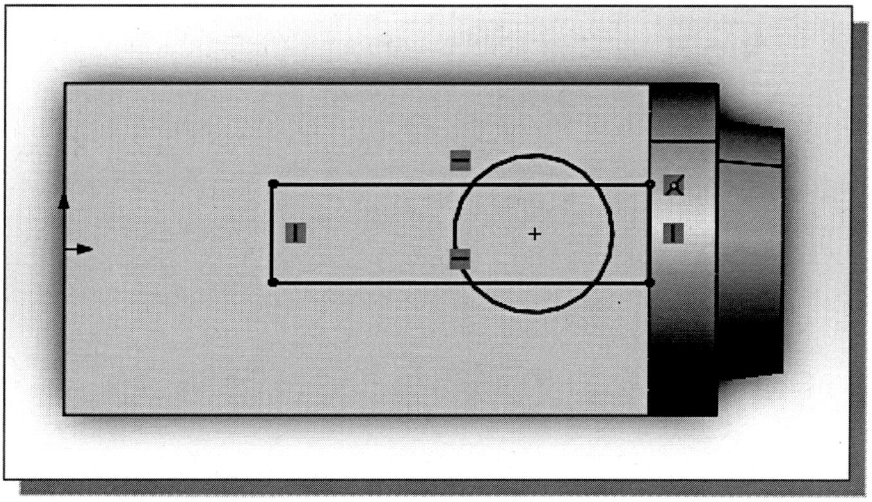

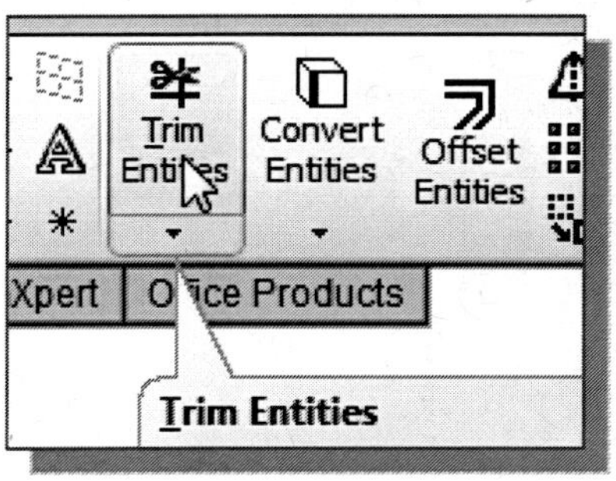

4. In the *Sketch* toolbar, select the **Trim Entities** command by left-mouse-clicking once on the icon.

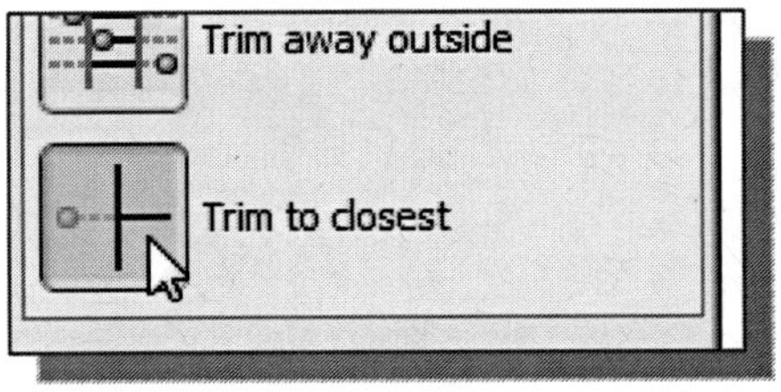

5. In the *Trim Property Manager*, activate the **Trim to closest** option as shown.

6. On your own, trim the geometry so that the sketch contains two horizontal lines and an arc as shown.

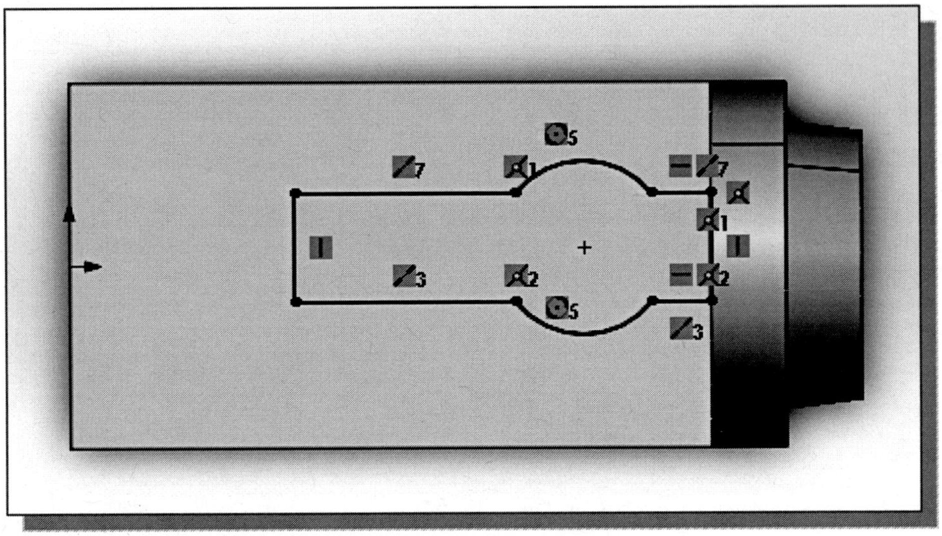

7. On your own, use the **Smart Dimension** command and create the size and location dimensions of the sketch as shown in the figure below.

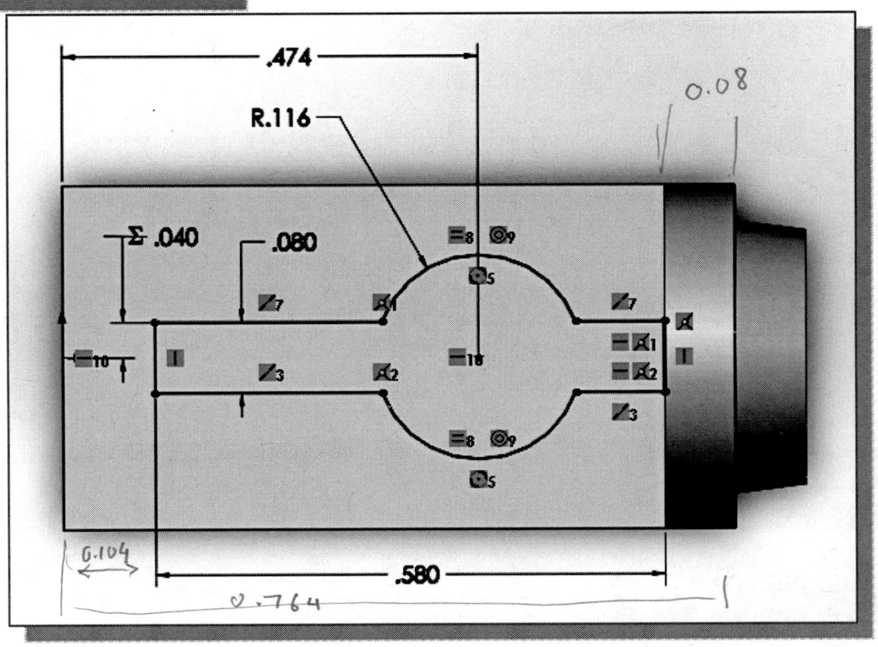

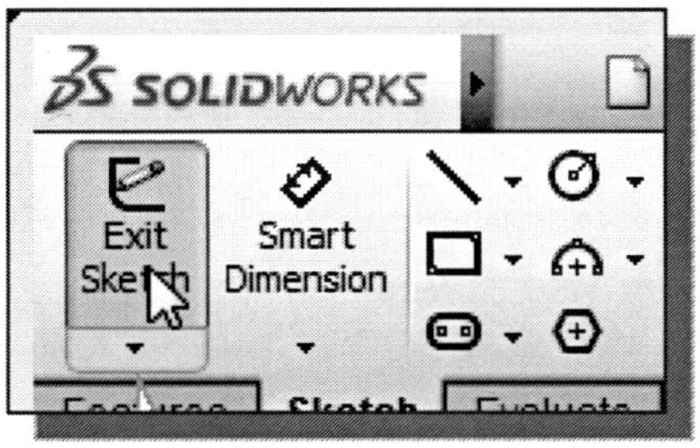

8. Click **Exit Sketch** in the *Sketch* toolbar to end the *Sketch* mode.

9. Set the extrusion distance to **0.115**, and set the extrusion direction upward. Click on the **OK** button to accept the settings and create the solid feature.

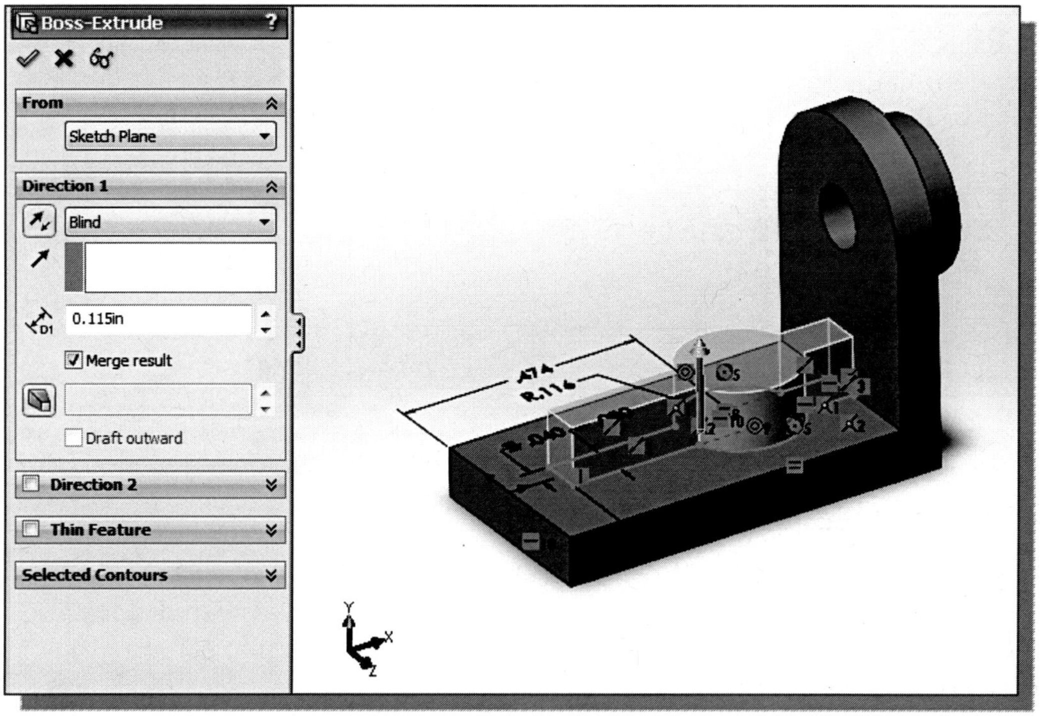

10. On your own, create a concentric hole, diameter **1/8**, as shown.

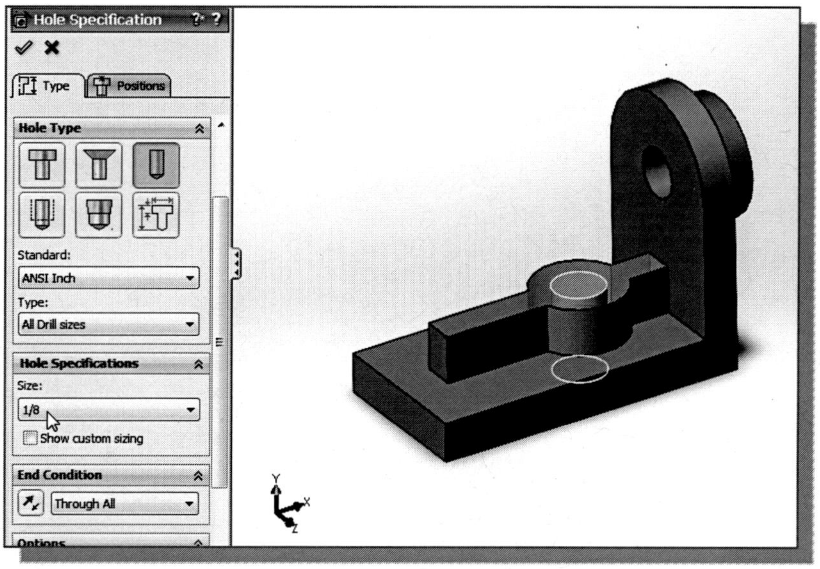

Create a Cut Feature

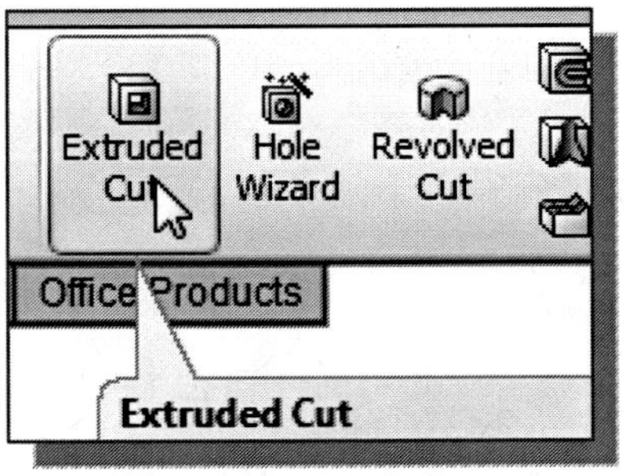

1. In the *Features* toolbar select the **Extruded Cut** command by clicking once with the left-mouse-button on the icon.

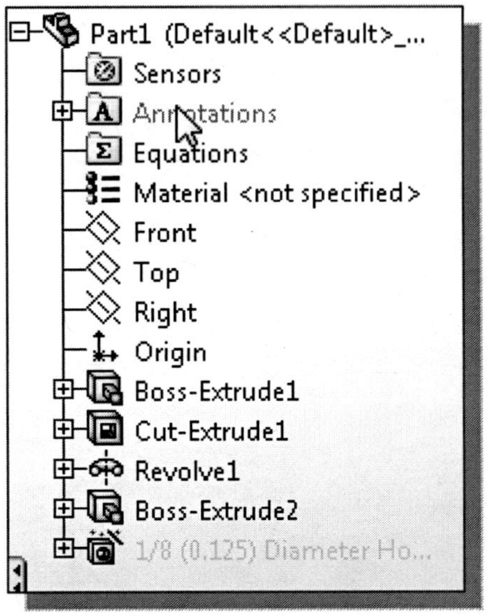

2. Expand the *Model Tree* in the graphics window by clicking the [+] symbol in front of the model name.

3. Select the **Front Plane** by clicking on the *Model Tree* as shown.

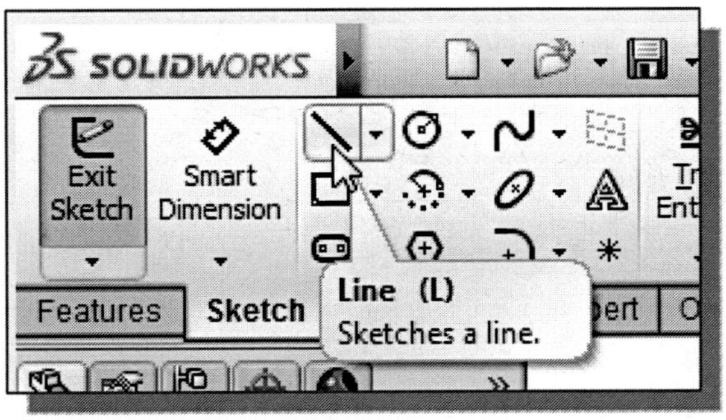

4. Select the **Line** option in the *Sketch* panel.

5. On your own, create a triangle aligned to the left of the last extruded feature, as shown in the figure below.

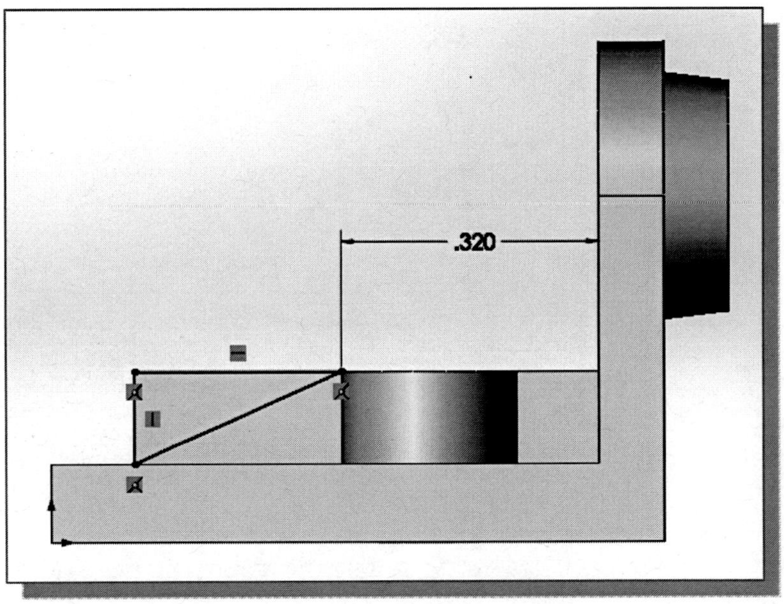

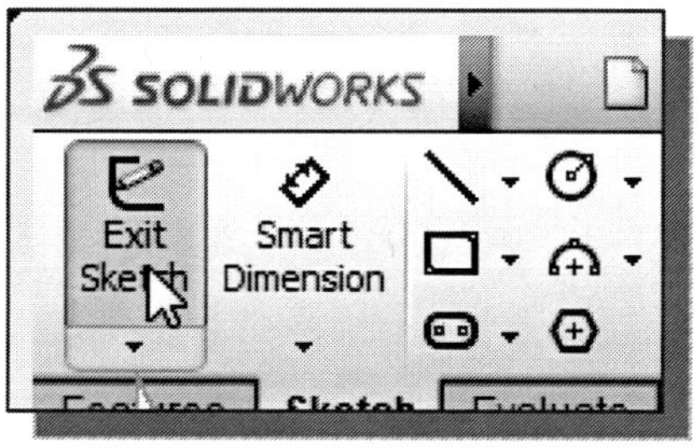

6. Select **Exit Sketch** in the *Sketch* toolbar to leave the *Sketch* mode.

7. Set the extrusion extents to **Mid Plane**, and distance to **0.5** as shown in the figure below.

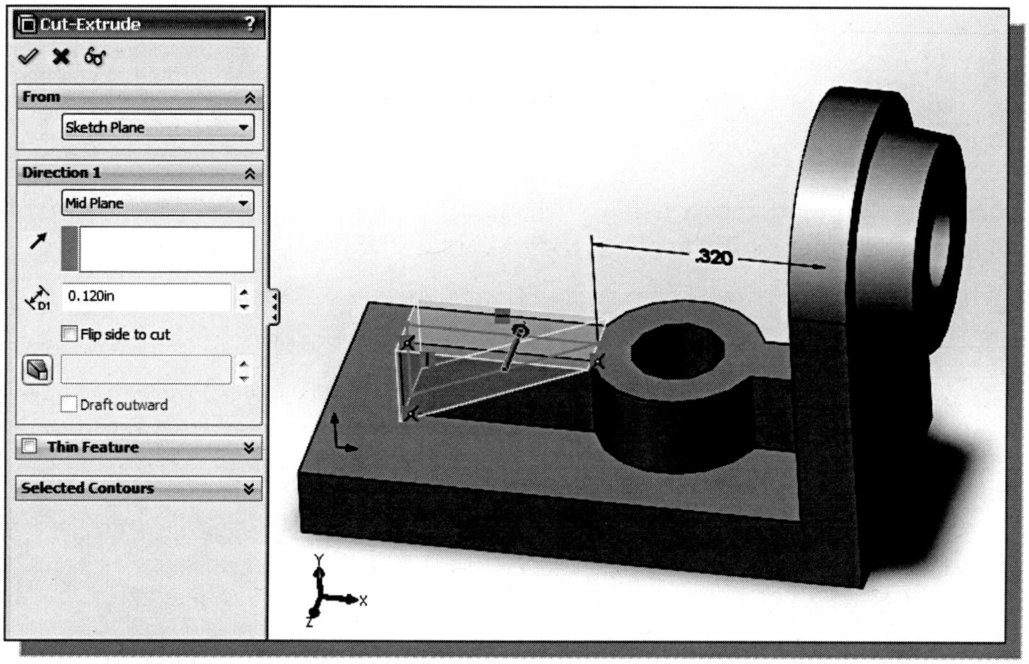

8. Click on the **OK** button to accept the settings and create the cut feature in both directions.

Create a Mirrored Feature

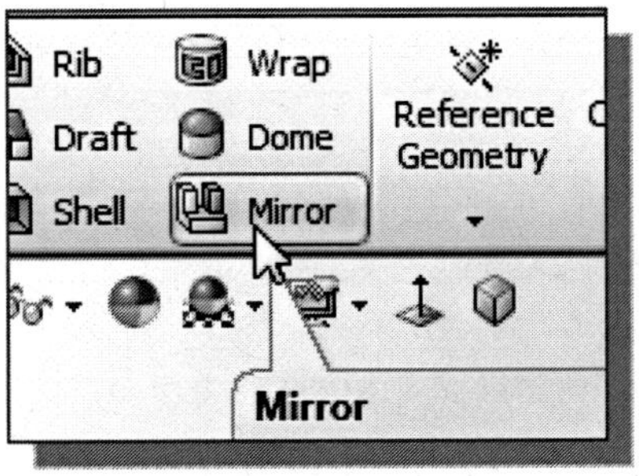

1. In the *Sketch* toolbar select the **Mirror** command by left-clicking once on the icon.

2. Activate the ***Features to Mirror*** list by clicking once in the *Property Manager* as shown.

3. Select **all features** by using a selection window to enclose the solid model.

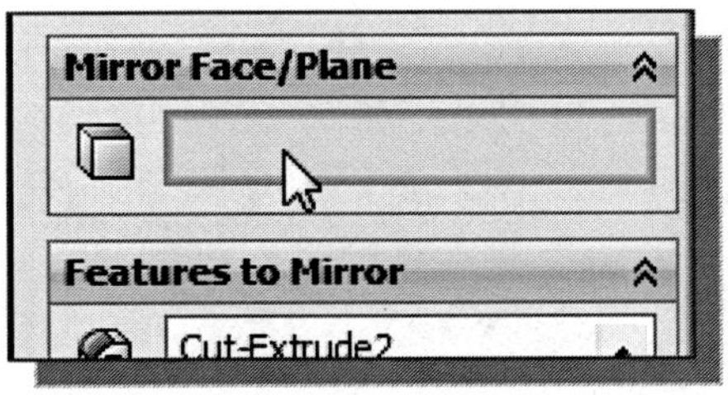

4. Activate the ***Mirror Face/Plane*** option by clicking once in the *Property Manager* as shown

5. Select the left vertical surface to be used as the **Mirror Plane**.

6. Click **OK** to create the mirrored feature as shown.

7. On your own, save the model using ***A12- Rear Axle Support*** as the name of the file.

Drawing Mode – 2D Paper Space

➢ *SolidWorks* allows us to generate 2D engineering drawings from solid models so that we can plot the drawings to any exact scale on paper. An engineering drawing is a tool that can be used to communicate engineering ideas/designs to manufacturing, purchasing, service, and other departments. Until now we have been working in ***model space*** to create our design in ***full size***. We can arrange our design on a two-dimensional sheet of paper so that the plotted hardcopy is exactly what we want. This two-dimensional sheet of paper is known as ***paper space*** in *SolidWorks*. We can place borders and title blocks, objects that are less critical to our design, on *paper space*. In general, each company uses a set of standards for drawing content, based on the type of product and also on established internal processes. The appearance of an engineering drawing varies depending on when, where, and for what purpose it is produced. In *SolidWorks*, creation of 2D engineering drawings from solid models consists of four basic steps: drawing sheet properties, creating/positioning views, annotations, and printing/plotting.

1. Click on the **drop-down arrow** next to the **New File** icon in the *Quick Access* toolbar area to display the available **New File** options.

2. Select **Make Drawing from Part/Assembly** in the list.

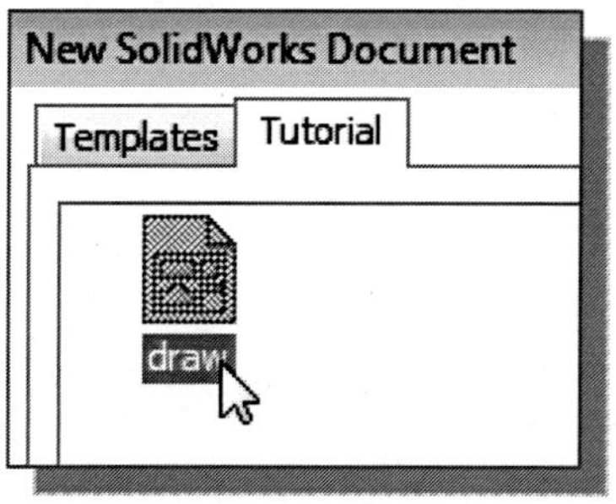

3. In the *New SolidWorks Document* dialog box, select the default **draw** template under the **Tutorial** tab.

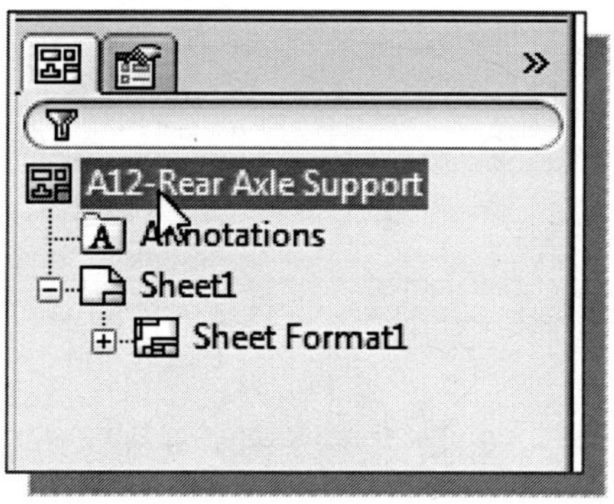

- In the *Feature Manager Design Tree* area, the **drawing icon** is displayed in front of the model name, ***A12- Rear Axle Support***; this indicates that we have switched to ***Drawing*** mode with **Sheet1** being the current drawing sheet.

❖ In the graphics window, *SolidWorks* displays a default drawing sheet that includes a title block. The drawing sheet is placed on the 2D paper space, and the title block also indicates the paper size being used.

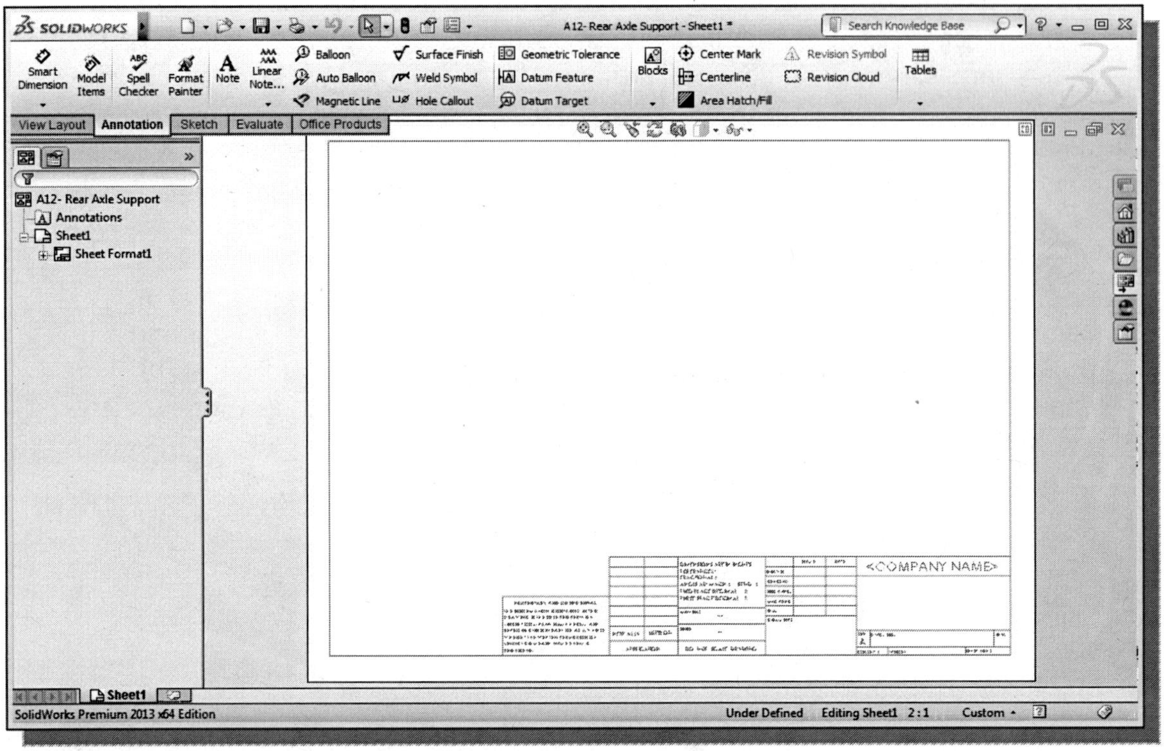

The Drawing Sheet Properties

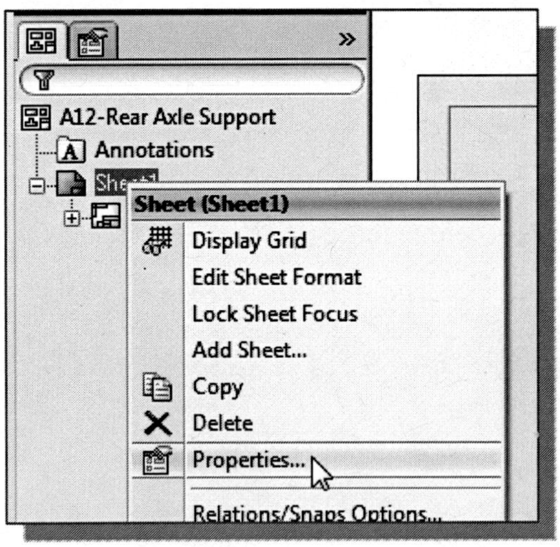

1. In the *Feature Manager Design Tree* area, right-mouse-click on **Sheet1** to bring up the option list.

2. Click **Properties** in the option list as shown.

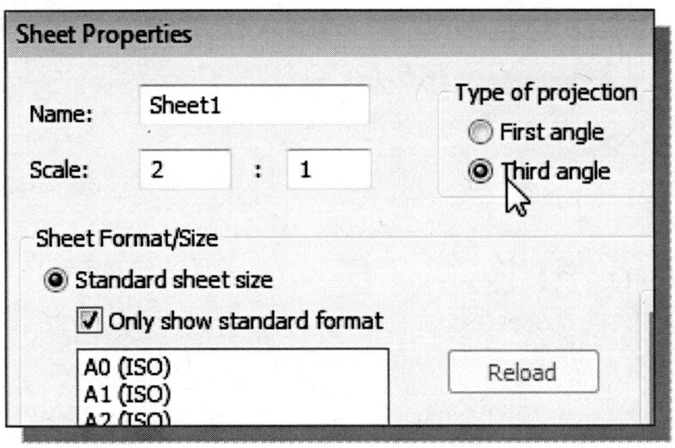

- Confirm the *projection type* is set to **Third Angle** as shown.

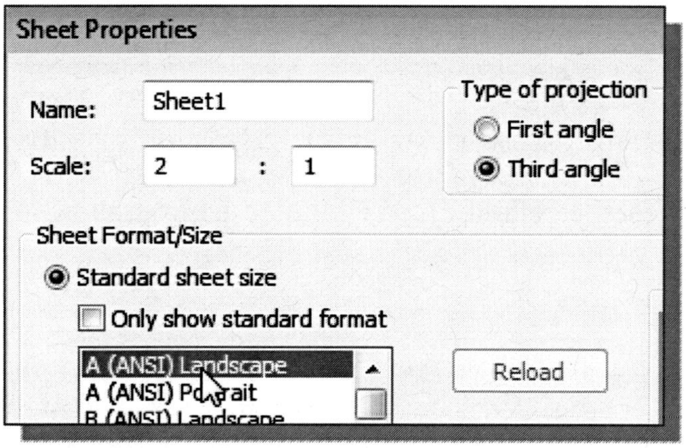

- Note the default *Scale* is set to **2:1**.

3. Turn *OFF* the **Only show standard format** option as shown.

4. Select **A (ANSI) Landscape** in the *Sheet Format/Size* option panel as shown.

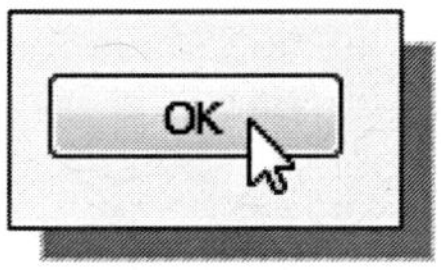

5. Click **OK** to exit the *Drawing Sheet Setup* mode as shown.

6. Select the **Options** icon from the *Menu* toolbar to open the *Options* dialog box.

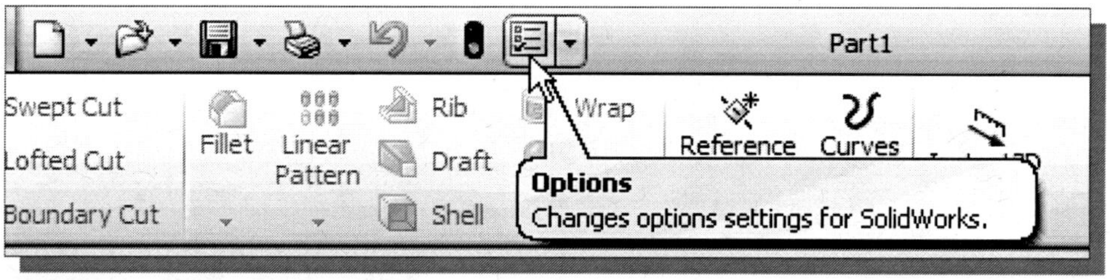

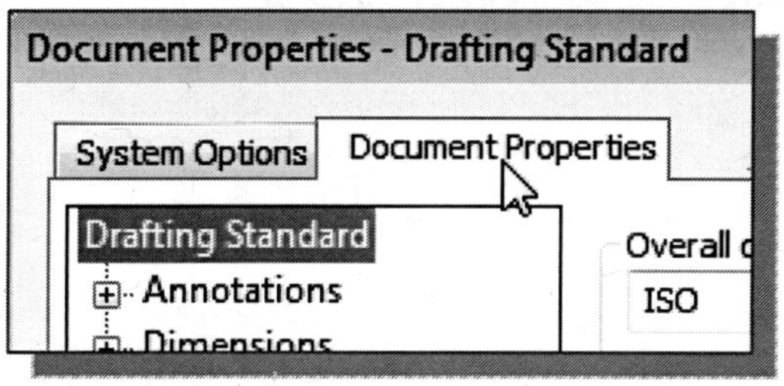

7. Select the **Document Properties** tab as shown in the figure.

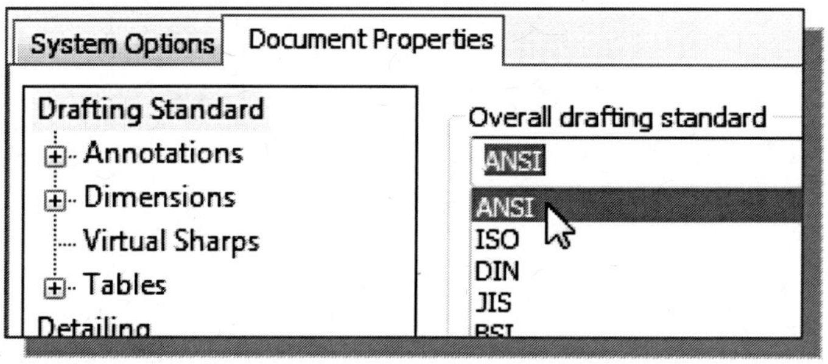

8. Set the *overall drafting standard* to **ANSI** as shown.

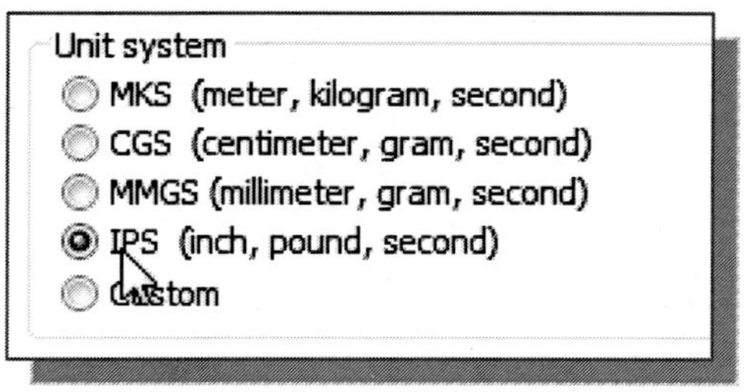

9. Select **IPS (inch, pound, second)** under the *Unit system* options.

10. Click **OK** in the *Options* dialog box to accept the selected settings.

Adding a Base View

❖ In *SolidWorks Drawing* mode, the first drawing view we create is called a **base view**. A *base view* is the primary view in the drawing; other views can be derived from this view. When creating a base view, *SolidWorks* allows us to specify the view to be shown. By default, *SolidWorks* will treat the default Front Plane as the front view of the solid model.

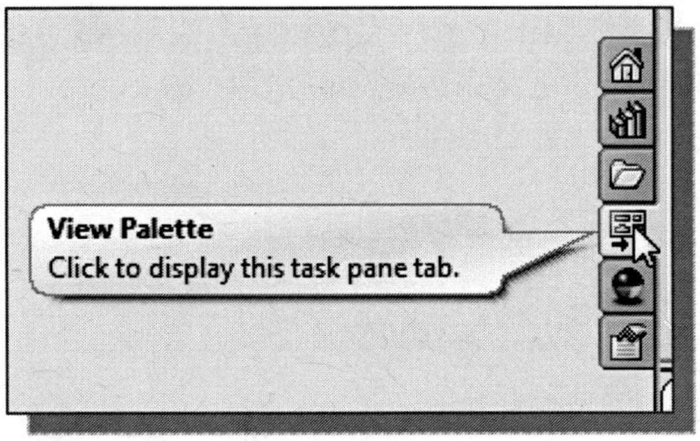

1. In the *task pane*, click on the **View Palette** tab to display the pre-defined 2D standard views that can be placed into the drawing.

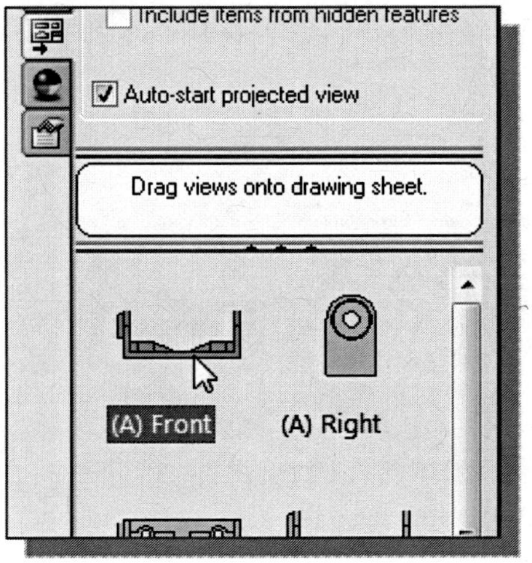

2. Select the **Front** view in the *View Palette* as shown.

3. **Drag and drop** the front view toward the left side of the drawing sheet.

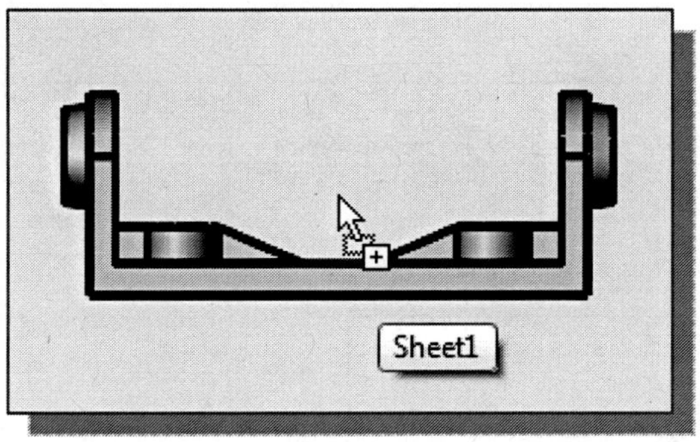

4. Note that the selected view is used as the **Base View**; additional projected views can be created by moving the cursor to the sides as shown.

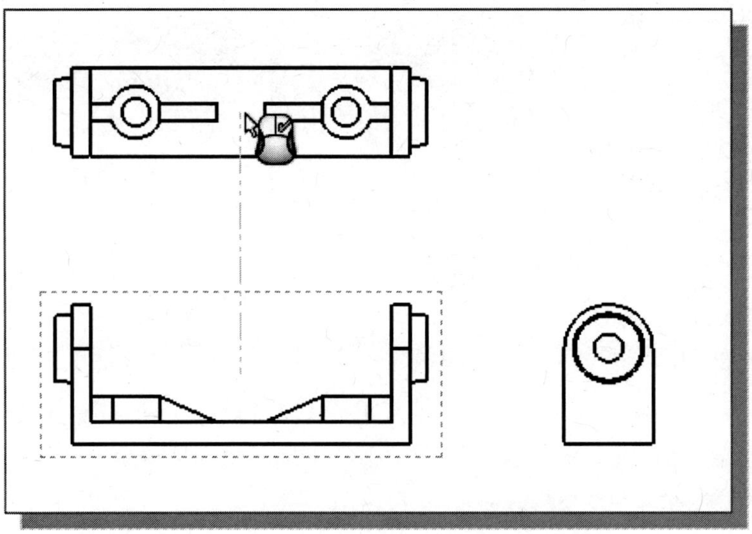

5. On your own, place an **Isometric** view toward the right side of the drawing sheet.

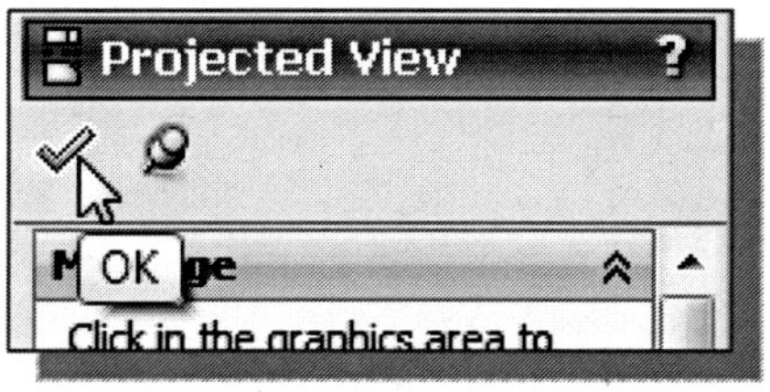

6. Click **OK** in the *Projected View* dialog box to accept the created views.

7. On your own, drag and drop the **Isometric** view toward the right side to rearrange the view.

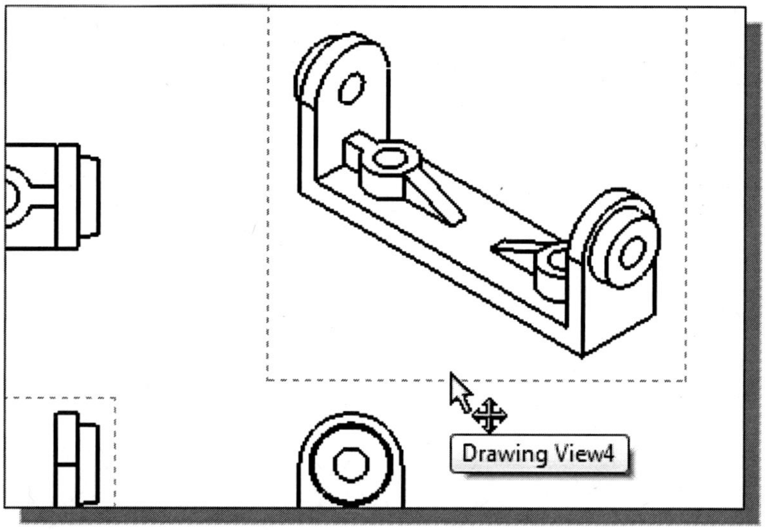

8. Select the **Front** view and set the *Display Style* to **Hidden Lines Visible** as shown. Note all views are updated as the base view is changed.

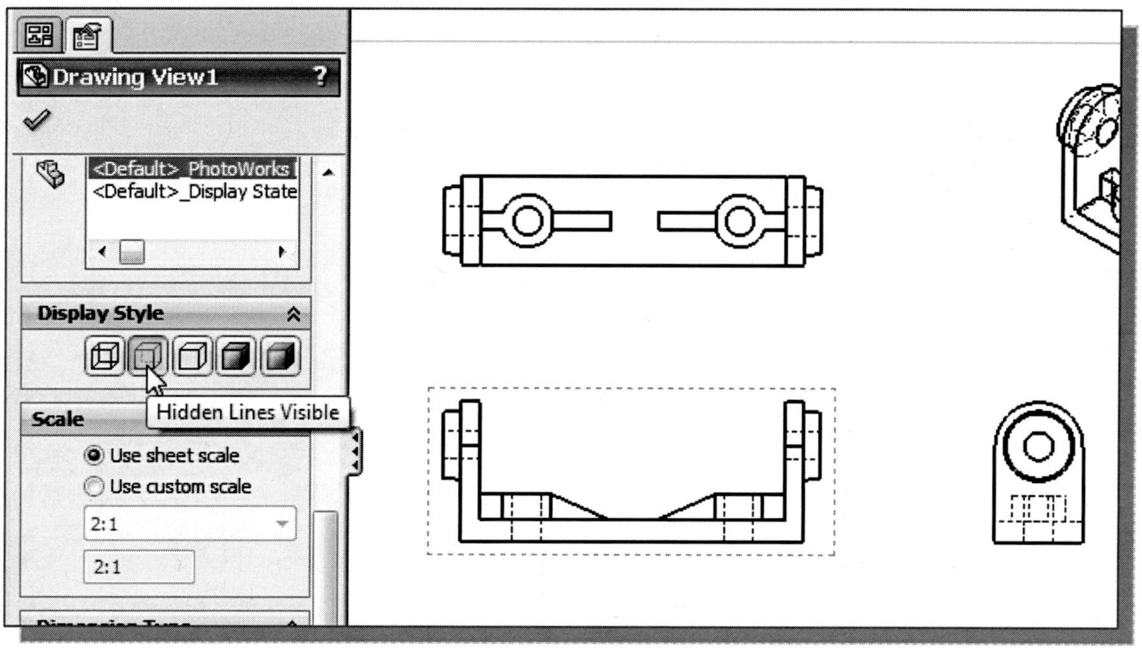

9. Select the **Iso** view and set the *Display Style* to **Hidden Lines Removed** as shown. (Note the change only affects the **Iso** view.)

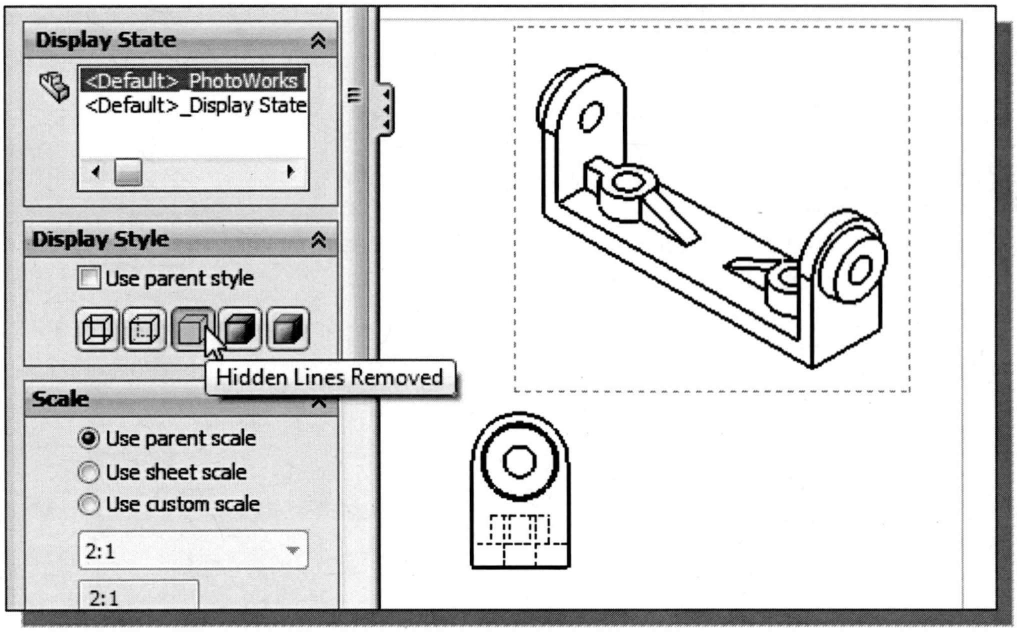

Adding Centerlines

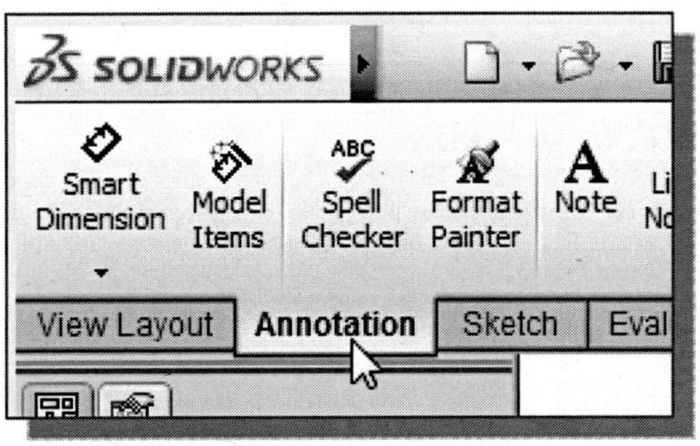

1. Click **Annotation** to switch to the *Annotation* toolbar as shown.

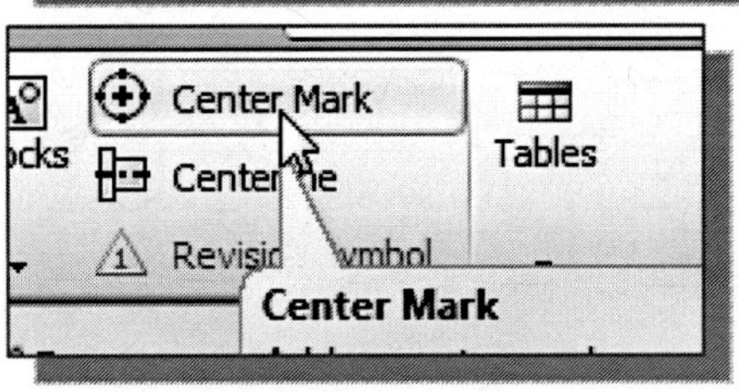

2. In the *Annotation* toolbar, click **Center Mark** to activate the command.

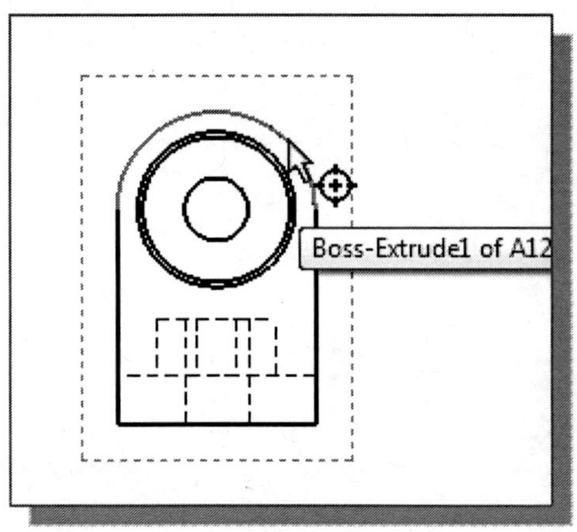

3. Click the **outer arc** in the **right-side view** as shown.

4. On your own, create the three center marks as shown.

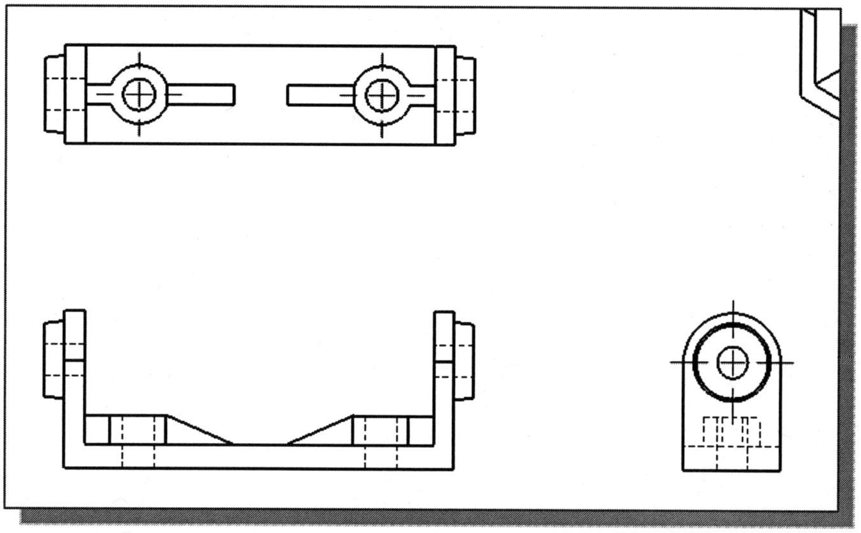

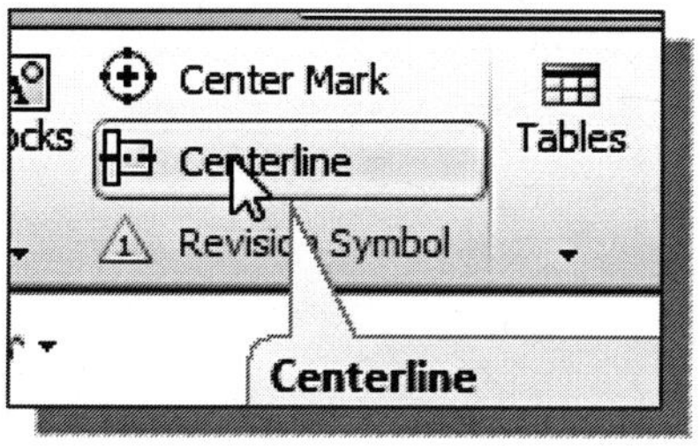

5. In the *Annotation* toolbar, click **Centerline** to activate the command.

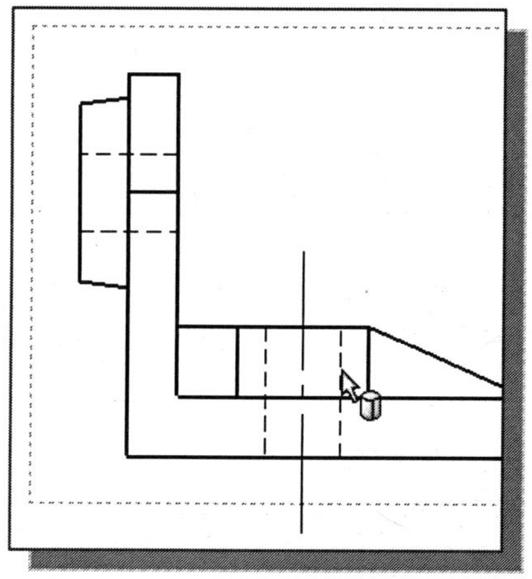

6. In the **Front** view, select the **two vertical hidden lines** to add a vertical centerline aligned to the center axis as shown.

7. On your own, create the additional center lines as shown.

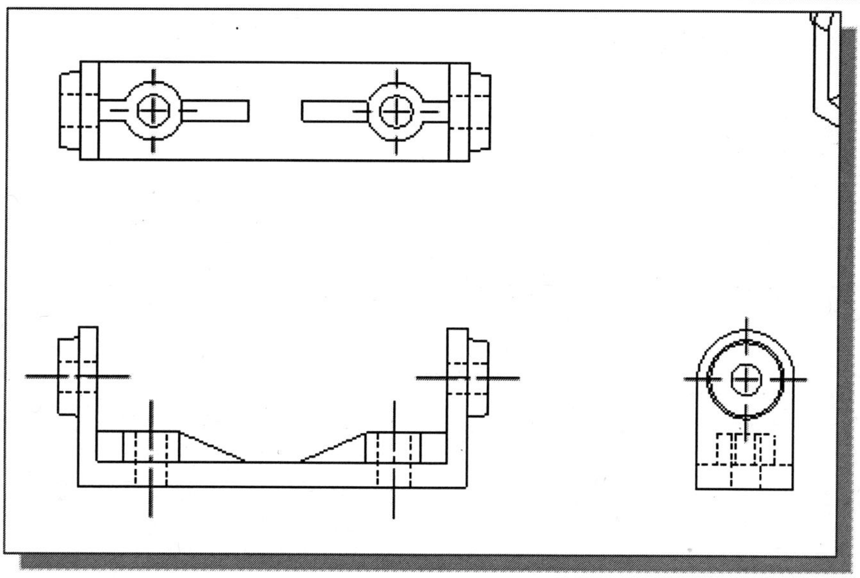

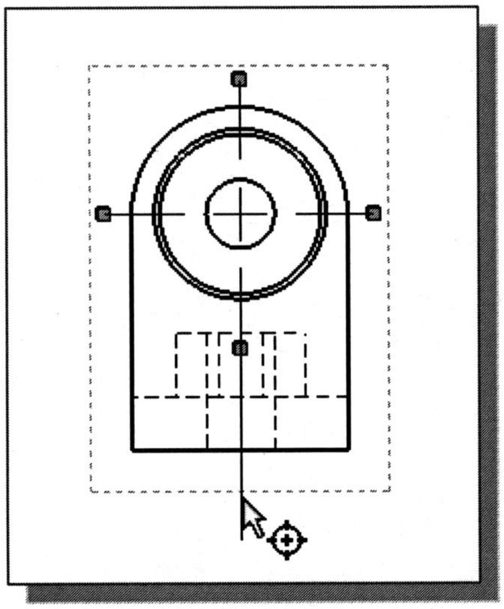

8. Click on the **center mark** in the **right-side view** and note the different **control points** which can be used to adjust the length of center lines.

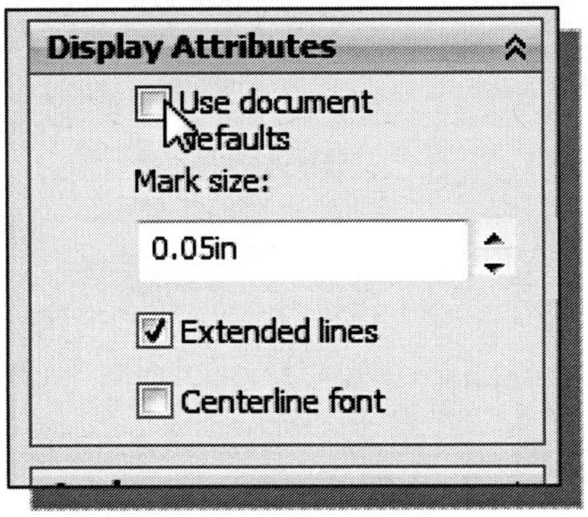

9. In the *Display Attributes* panel, turn *OFF* the **Use document defaults** option and set the *center mark size* to **0.05** as shown.

10. On your own, adjust all of the centerlines/center marks in the views as shown.

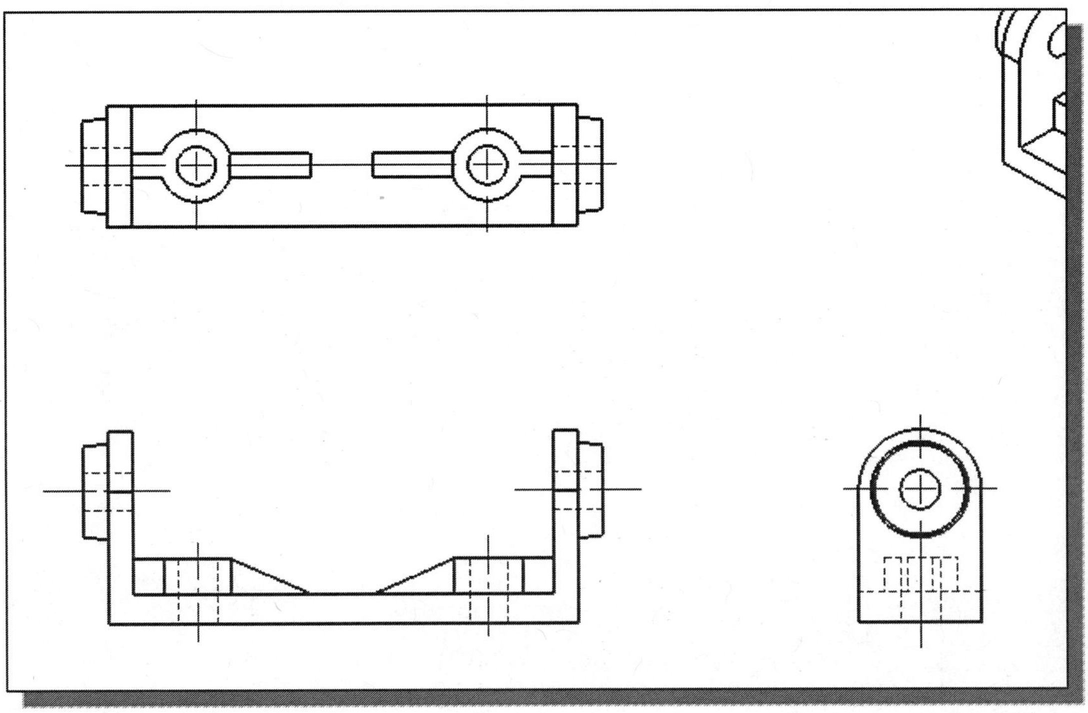

Displaying Feature Dimensions

- By default, feature dimensions are not displayed in 2D views in *SolidWorks*. We can display any of the feature dimensions and place them in any of the created 2D views.

1. Select **Model Items** by left-clicking once in the *Annotation* toolbar.

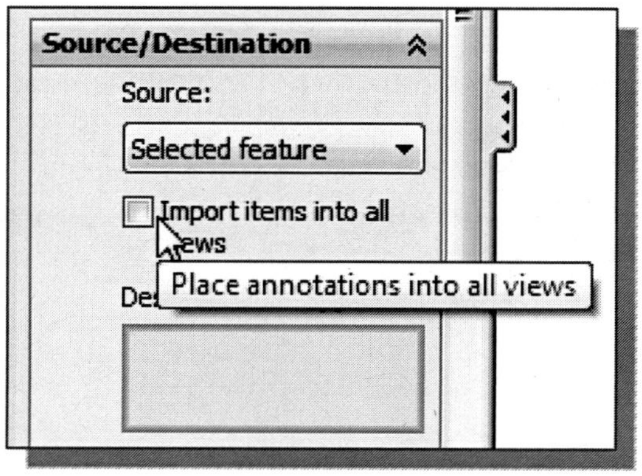

2. In the ***Source/Destination*** option list, set the *Source* to **Selected feature** and turn *OFF* the **Import items into all views** option.

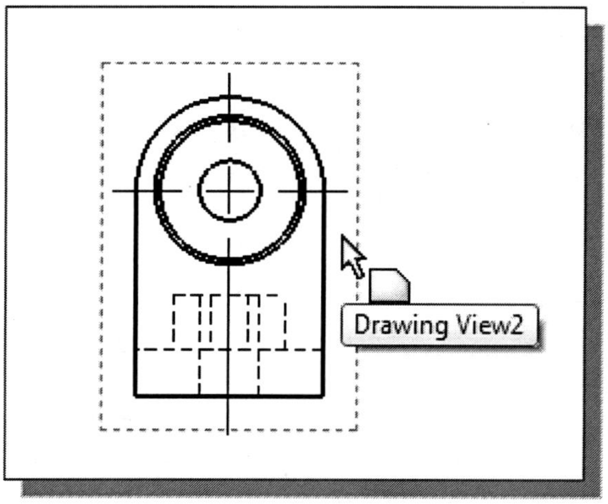

3. Select the right-side view.

4. Inside the right-side view, select the **revolve feature** to display the associated dimensions in the side view as shown. Notice the special note regarding the positioning and hiding the feature dimensions.

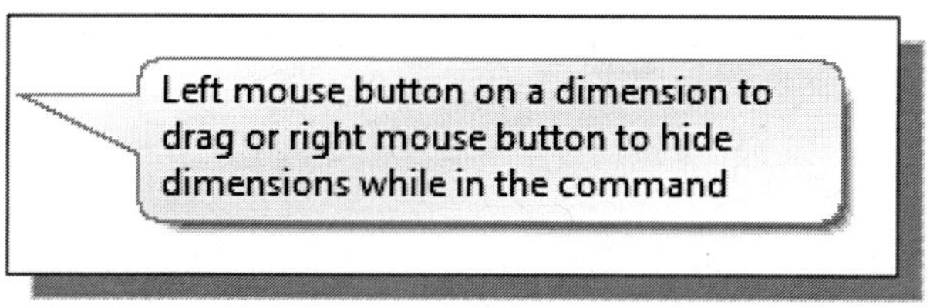

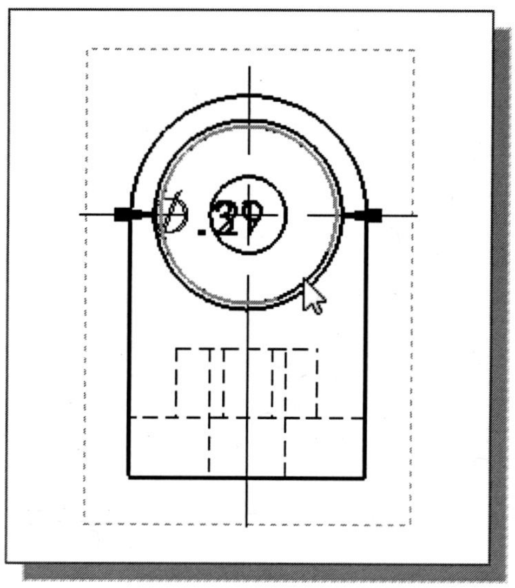

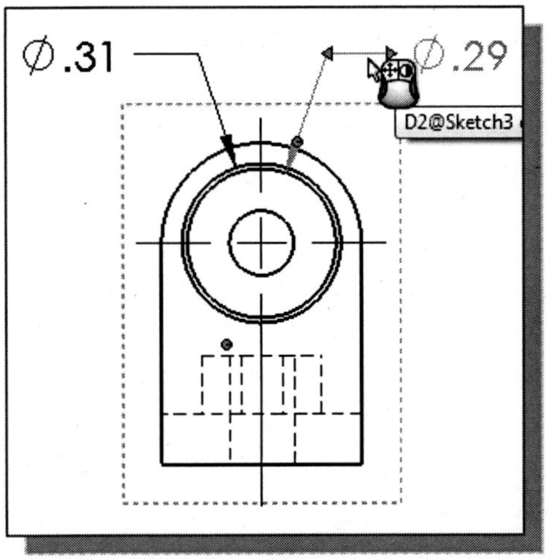

5. Use the left-mouse button to drag and reposition the displayed feature dimensions as shown.

6. Use the right-mouse button on any dimension to hide it. Click again with the right-mouse-button to show the dimension.

7. Select the **base feature** to display the associated dimensions in the side view as shown.

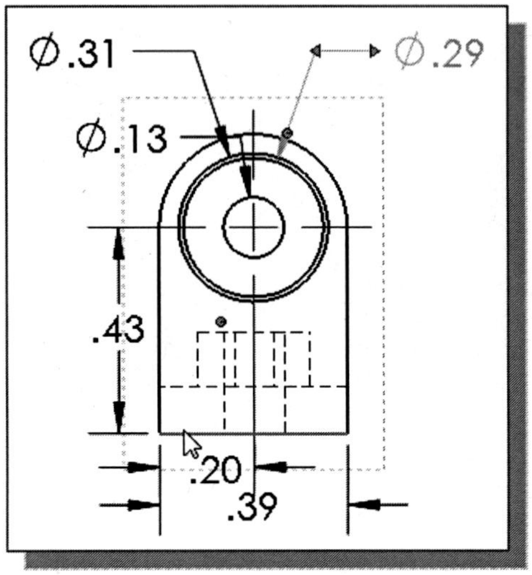

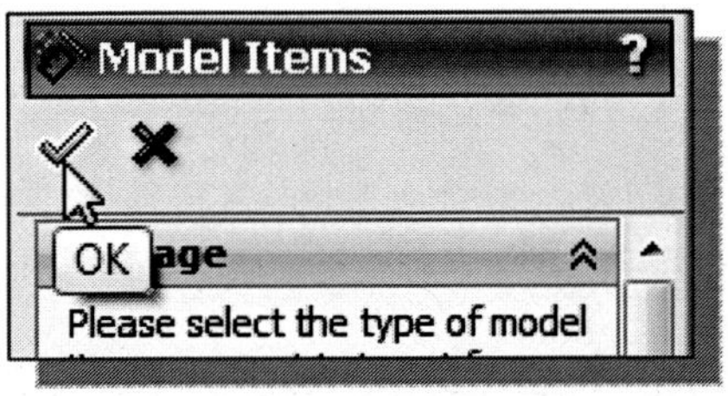

8. Select **Retrieve Dimensions** to display the parametric dimensions used to create the model.

9. Select the **width dimension** in the side view and adjust the dimension display. Also notice the available dimension properties in the *Properties Manager*.

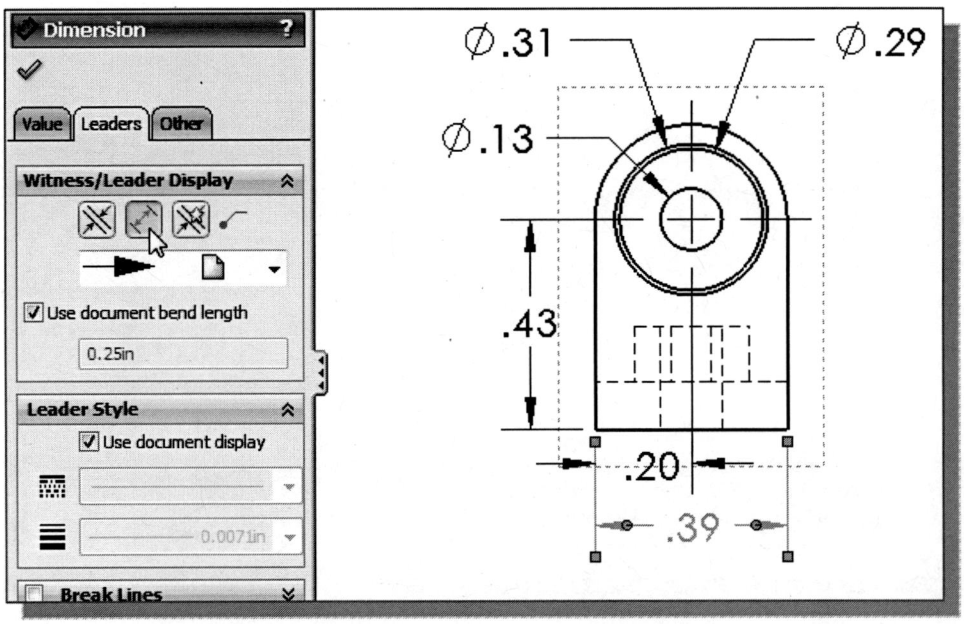

Adding Additional Dimensions – Reference Dimensions

- Besides displaying the **feature dimensions**, dimensions used to create the features, we can also add additional **reference dimensions** in the drawing. *Feature dimensions* are used to control the geometry, whereas *reference dimensions* are controlled by the existing geometry. In the drawing layout, therefore, we can ***add*** or ***delete*** *reference dimensions* but we can only ***hide*** the *feature dimensions.* One should try to use as many *feature dimensions* as possible and add *reference dimensions* only if necessary. It is also more effective to use *feature dimensions* in the drawing layout since they are created when the model was built. Note that additional *Drawing* mode entities, such as lines and arcs, can also be added to drawing views.

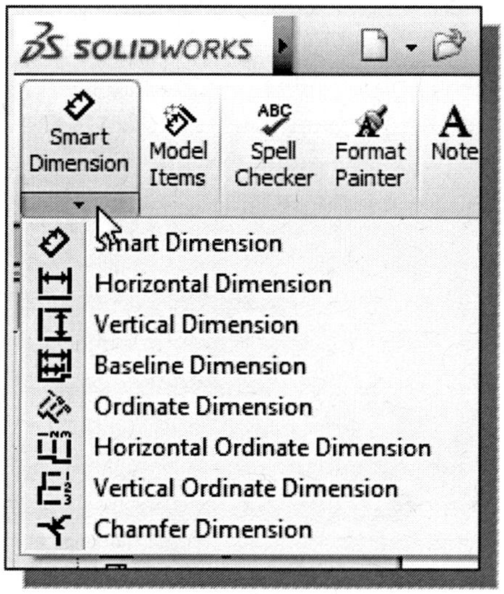

1. Click on the **Smart Dimension** button.

➢ Note the **Smart Dimension** command is similar to the **Smart Dimensioning** command in *3D Modeling* mode. Also note that more specific dimensioning tools are available.

2. In the top view, create the **center to center dimension** as shown.

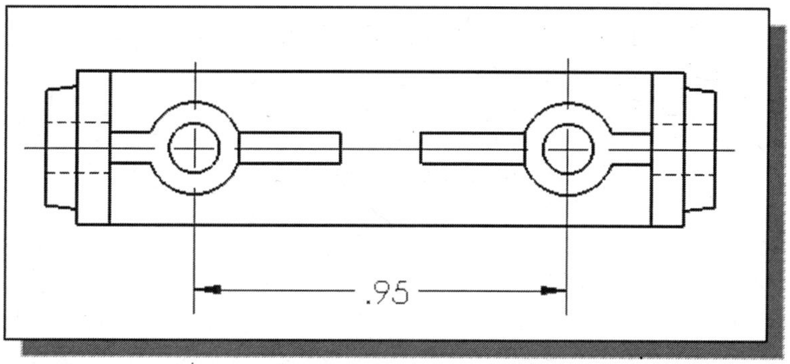

3. On your own, create and position the **overall width dimension** in the **Top** view as shown.

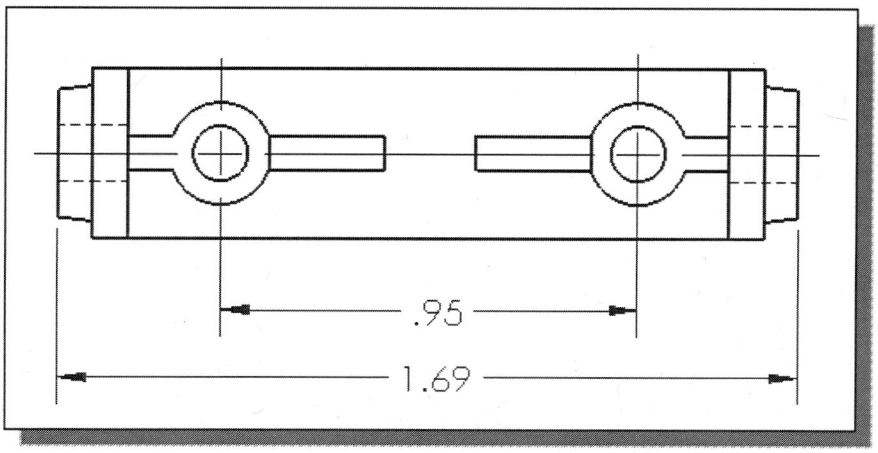

Complete the Drawing Sheet

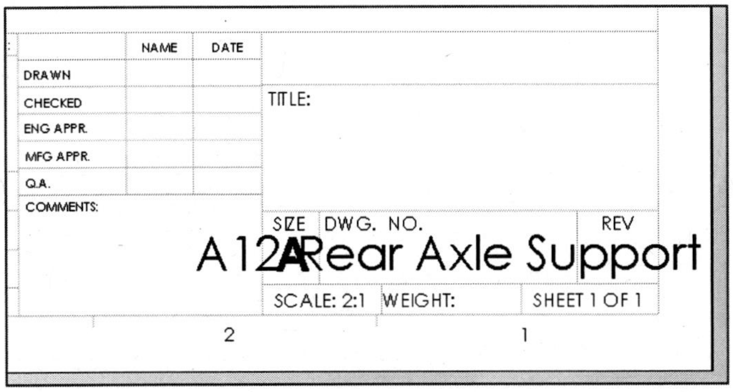

1. On your own, use the **Zoom** and the **Pan** commands to adjust the display as shown; this is so that we can complete the title block.

- Note the model name is displayed under **DWG No**, but the text size needs to be adjusted.

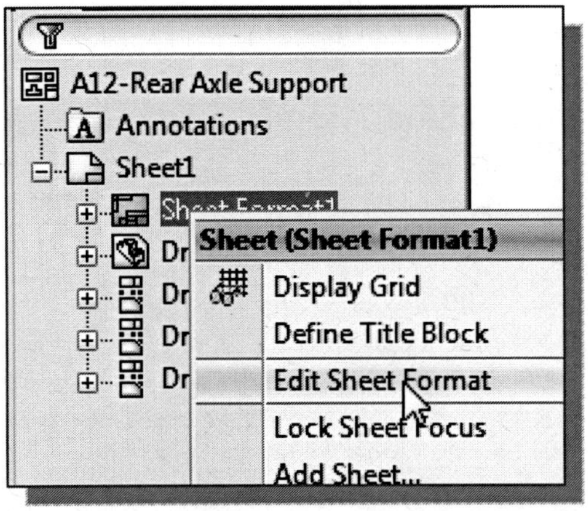

2. In the *Feature Manager Design Tree* area, right-mouse-click on **Sheet Format1** to bring up the option list.

3. Click **Edit Sheet Format** in the option list as shown.

4. Double click on the **model name** to enter the *Edit* mode.

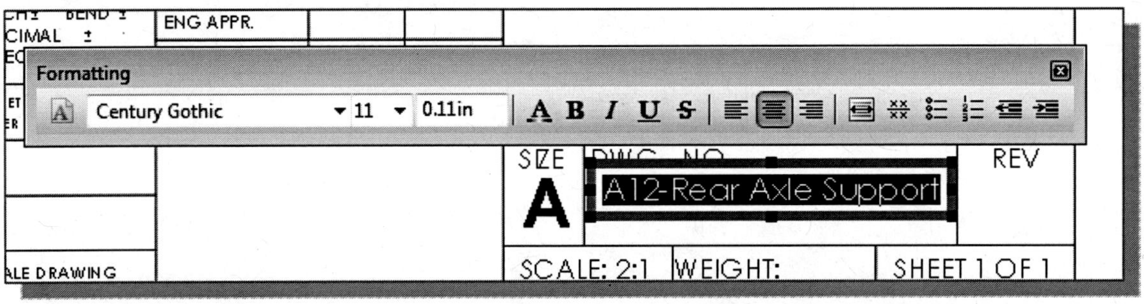

5. Adjust the font size to **11** as shown. Note the different text formatting tools available in the *Formatting* toolbar and in the *PropertiesManager*.

6. Click **Close** to end the **Note** editing tool.

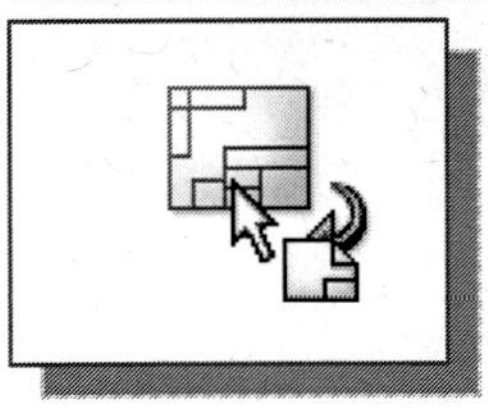

7. At the upper-right corner of the graphics window, click **Exit** to end the **Edit Sheet Format** command as shown.

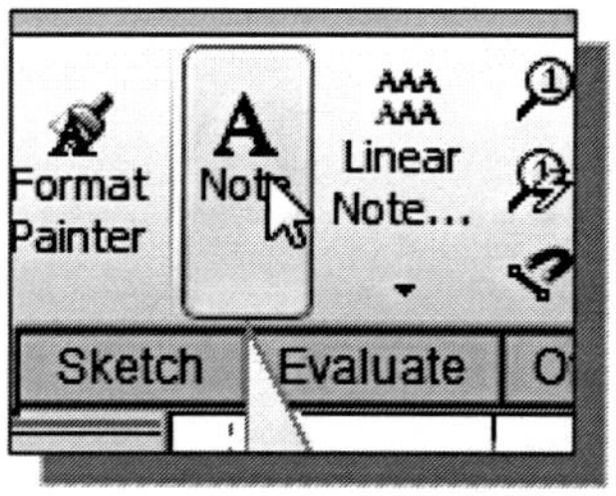

8. In the *Annotation* toolbar, click on the **Note** button.

9. Pick a location that is inside the top block area as the location for the new text to be entered.

10. In the *Formatting* dialog box, enter the name of your organization. Also, note the different settings available.

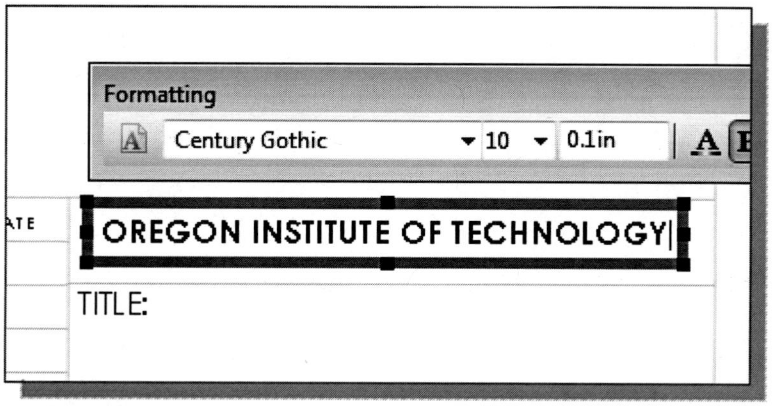

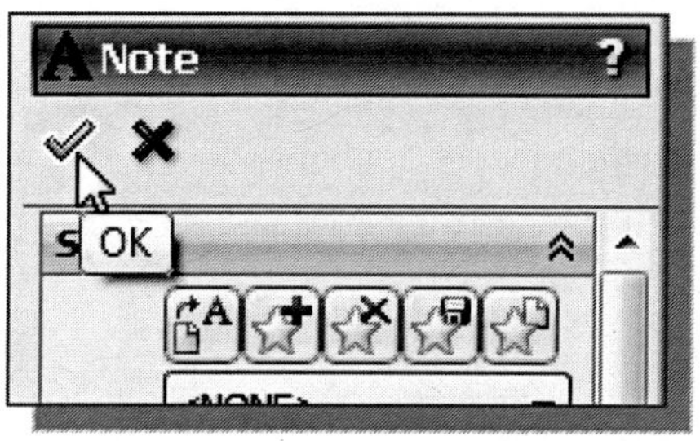

11. Click **OK** to proceed.

12. On your own, repeat the above steps and complete the title block.

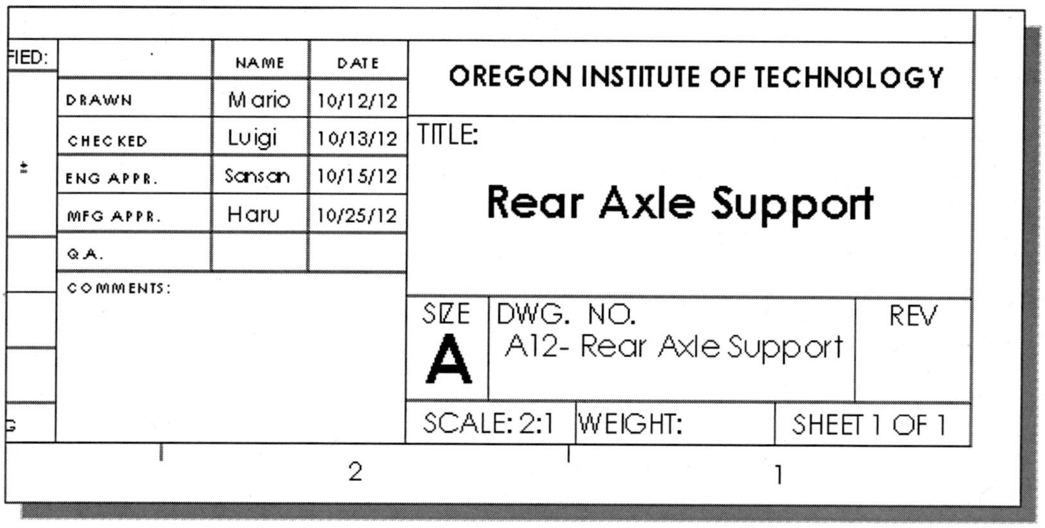

13. On your own, complete the 2D drawing with proper dimensions and notes.

Associative Functionality – Modifying Feature Dimensions

- *SolidWorks's associative functionality* allows us to change the design at any level, and the system reflects the changes at all levels automatically.

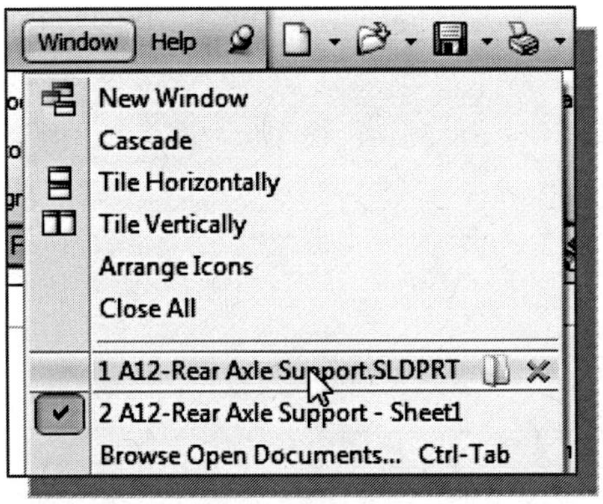

1. In the *Window* pull-down menu, click on the ***A12-Rear Axle Support*** part name to switch to the *Part Modeling* mode.

2. In the *Model Tree* window, right-click once on **base feature** to bring up the option menu.

3. Select **Edit Sketch** in the popup option menu.

4. Double-click on one of the diameter dimensions (**0. 125**) of the hole feature on the base feature as shown in the figure.

5. In the *Modify* dialog box, enter **0.135** as the new diameter dimension.

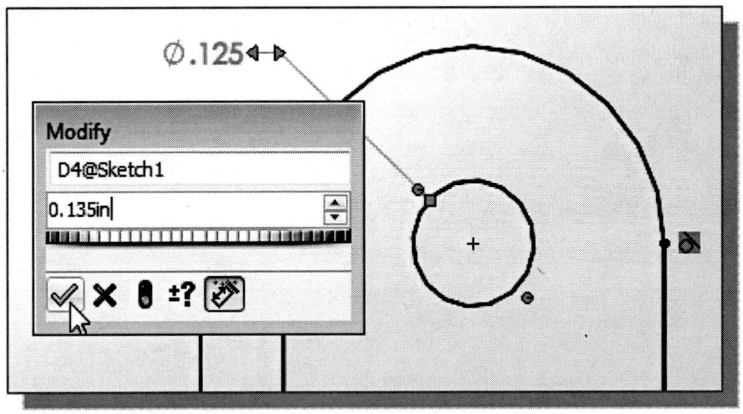

6. Click on the **OK** button to accept the new setting.

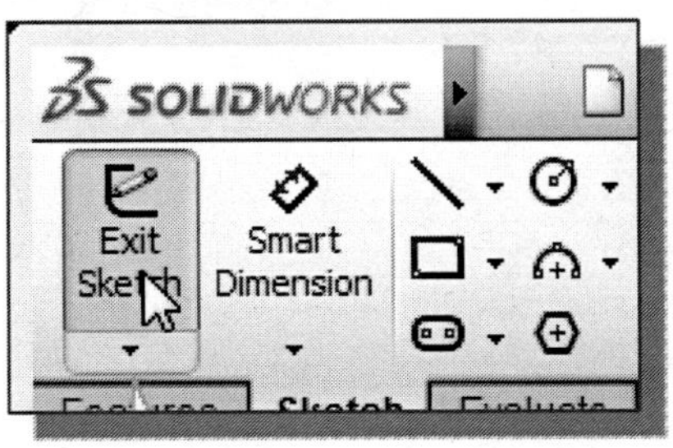

7. Click **Exit Sketch** to end the *Edit Sketch* mode.

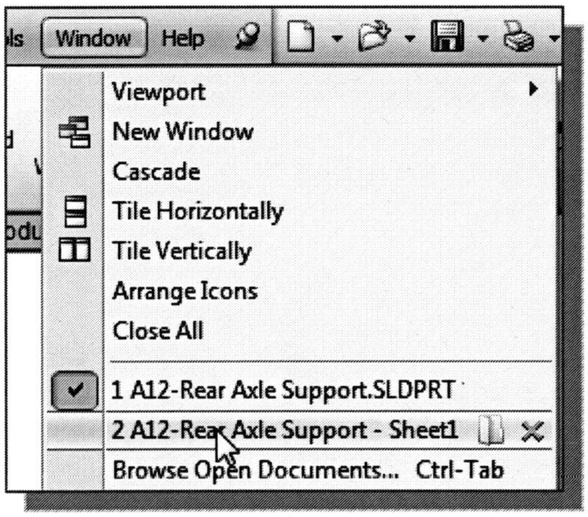

8. In the *Window* pull-down menu, click on the ***A12-Rear Axle Support*** part name to switch to the drawing sheet.

- Note the drawing sheet needs to be updated.

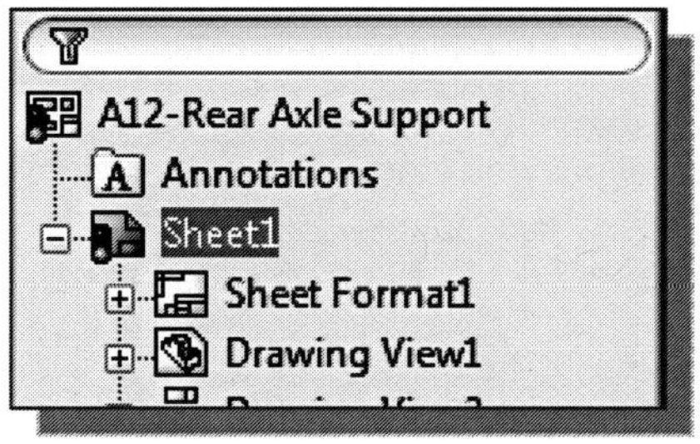

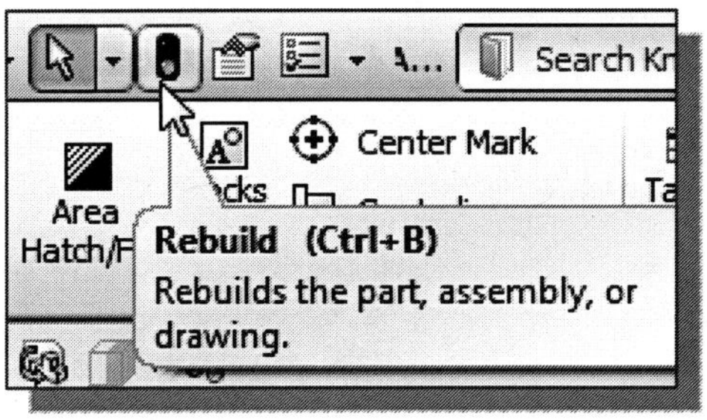

9. Click **Rebuild** to update the drawing.

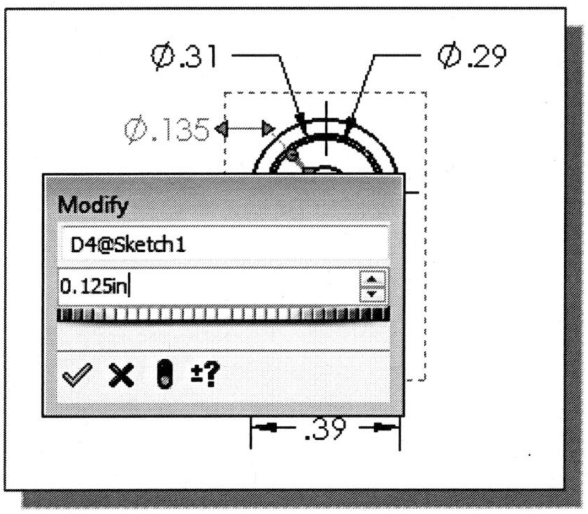

10. Inside the graphics window, double-click the **Ø0.135** dimension in the *side* view to bring up the *Modify* dialog box.

11. Change the dimension to **1.25**.

12. Click on the **check mark** button to accept the setting.

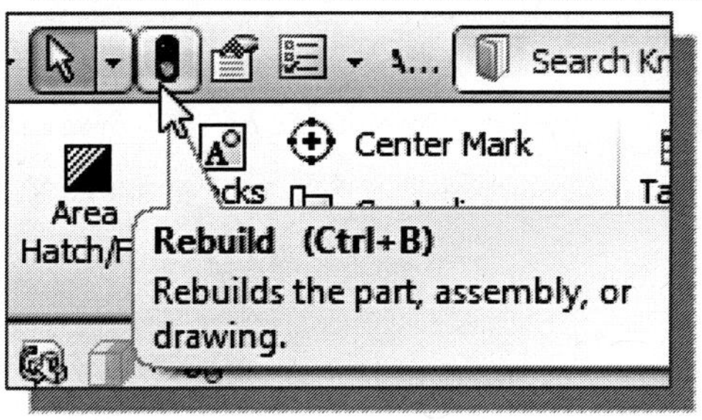

13. Click **Rebuild** to update the drawing and the part.

❖ Note the geometry of the hole feature is updated in all views according to the new value. On your own, switch to the *Part Modeling* mode and confirm the design is updated as well.

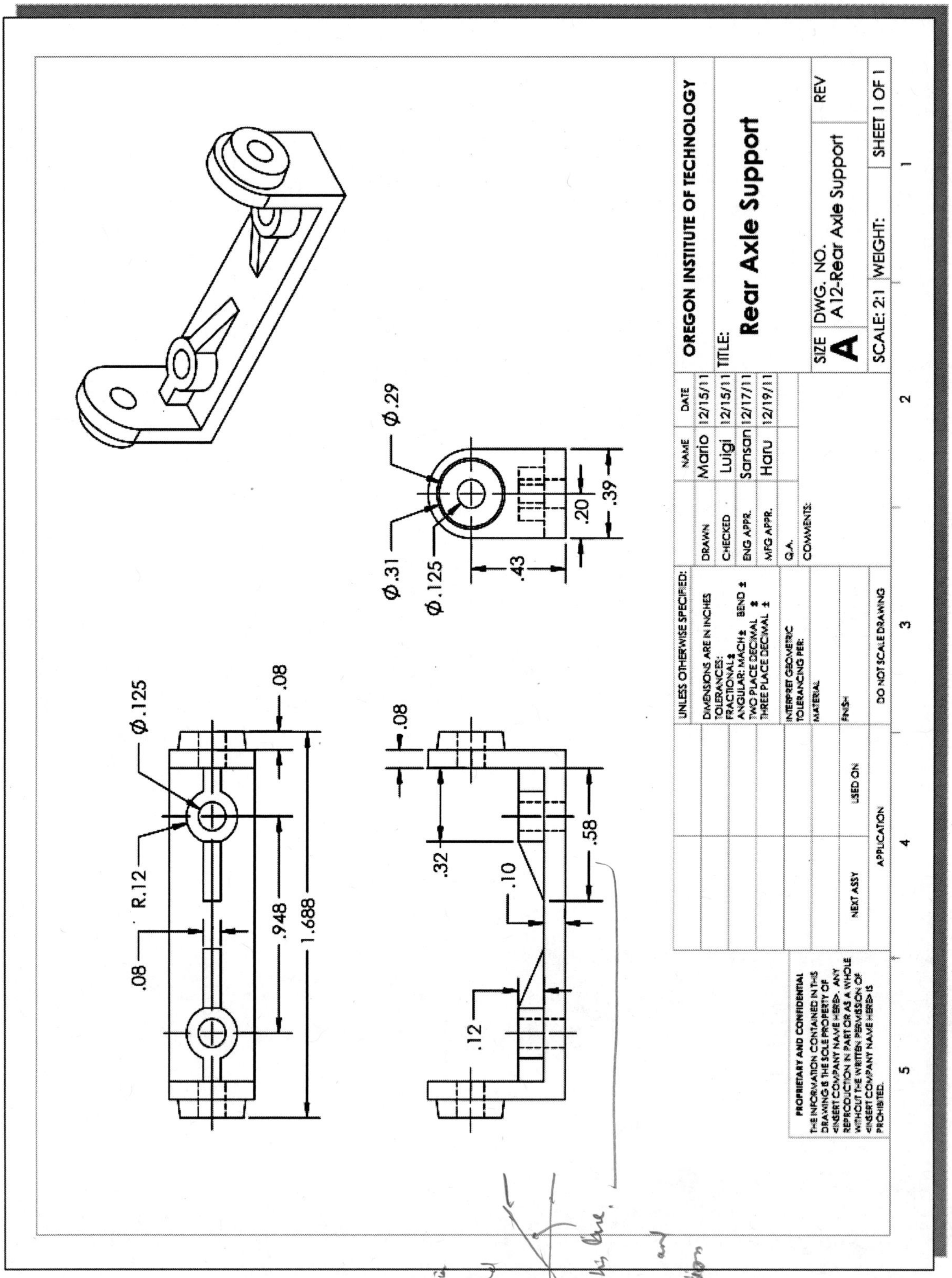
OREGON INSTITUTE OF TECHNOLOGY
TITLE:
Rear Axle Support
SIZE
A
DWG. NO.
A12-Rear Axle Support
REV
SCALE: 2:1
WEIGHT:
SHEET 1 OF 1
NAME
DATE
DRAWN
Mario
12/15/11
CHECKED
Luigi
12/15/11
ENG APPR.
Sansan
12/17/11
MFG APPR.
Haru
12/19/11
Q.A.
COMMENTS:
UNLESS OTHERWISE SPECIFIED:
DIMENSIONS ARE IN INCHES
TOLERANCES:
FRACTIONAL ±
ANGULAR: MACH ± BEND ±
TWO PLACE DECIMAL ±
THREE PLACE DECIMAL ±
INTERPRET GEOMETRIC TOLERANCING PER:
MATERIAL
FINISH
DO NOT SCALE DRAWING
NEXT ASSY
USED ON
APPLICATION
PROPRIETARY AND CONFIDENTIAL
THE INFORMATION CONTAINED IN THIS DRAWING IS THE SOLE PROPERTY OF <INSERT COMPANY NAME HERE>. ANY REPRODUCTION IN PART OR AS A WHOLE WITHOUT THE WRITTEN PERMISSION OF <INSERT COMPANY NAME HERE> IS PROHIBITED.
Ø.125
R.12
.08
.948
1.688
.08
.32
.10
.58
.12
.08
Ø.31
Ø.125
Ø.29
.43
.20
.39
1
2
3
4
5

To add this dimension Go to sketch add a point and make it coincident with this line. Go to Annotation and add dimension

Questions:

1. What does *SolidWorks*'s *associative functionality* allow us to do?

2. How do we move a view on the *drawing sheet*?

3. Why is it important to identify symmetrical features in designs?

4. How do we display feature/model dimensions in the *Drawing* mode?

5. What is the difference between a *feature dimension* and a *reference dimension*?

6. How do we reposition dimensions?

7. What is a *base view*?

8. Can we delete a drawing view? How?

9. Can we adjust the length of centerlines in the *Drafting* mode of *SolidWorks*? How?

Exercises:

1. **Slide Mount** (Dimensions are in inches.)

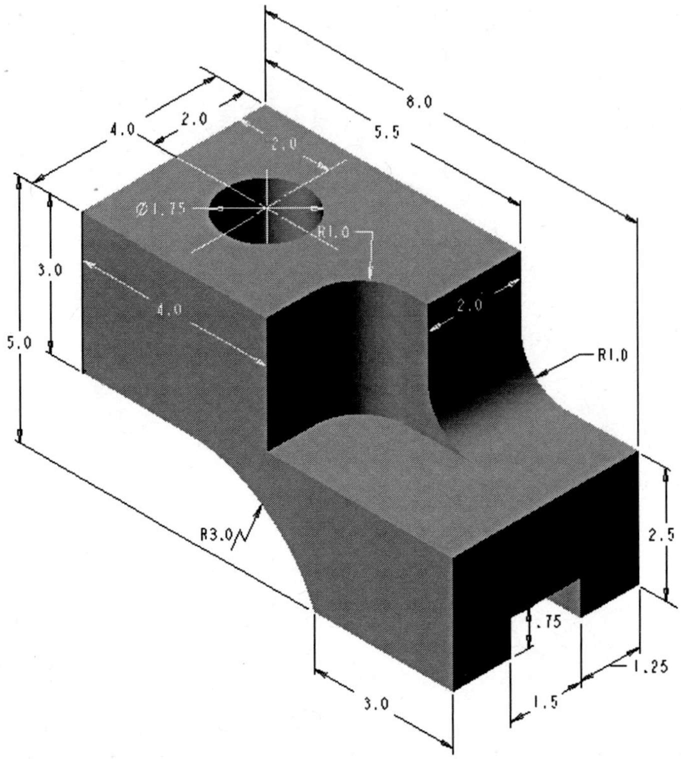

2. **Corner Stop** (Dimensions are in inches.)

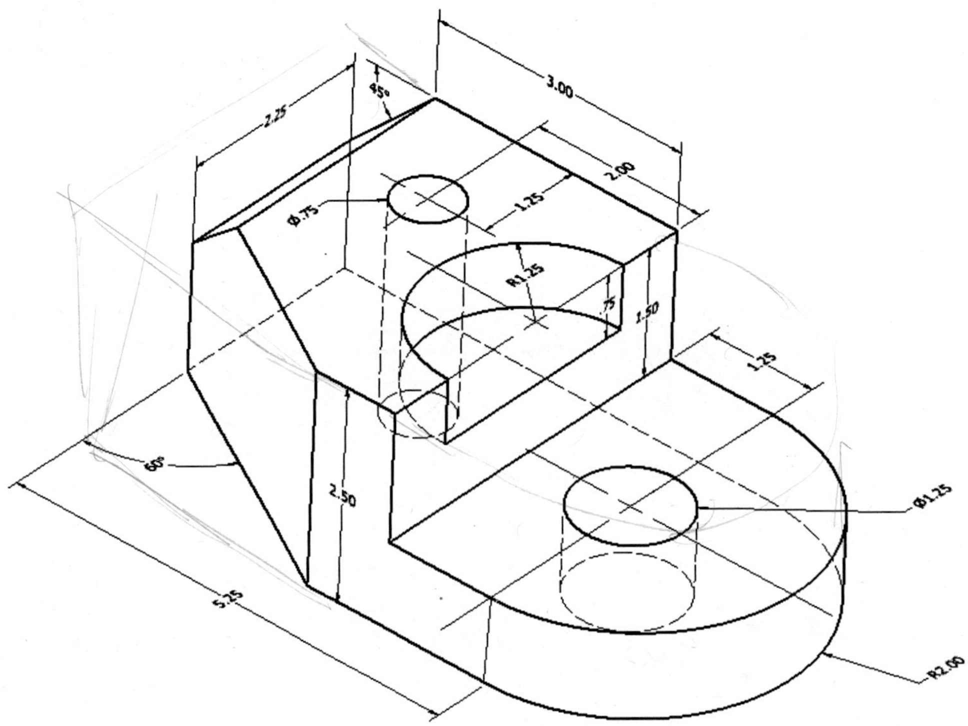

3. **Ratchet Plate** (thickness: **0.125 inch**)

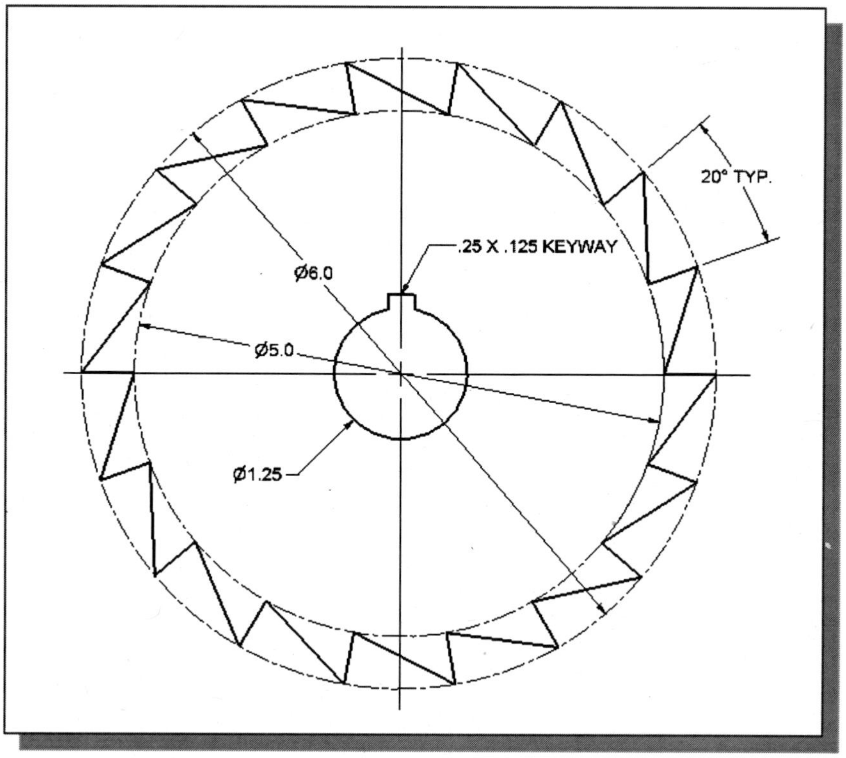

4. **Angle Support** (Dimensions are in inches)

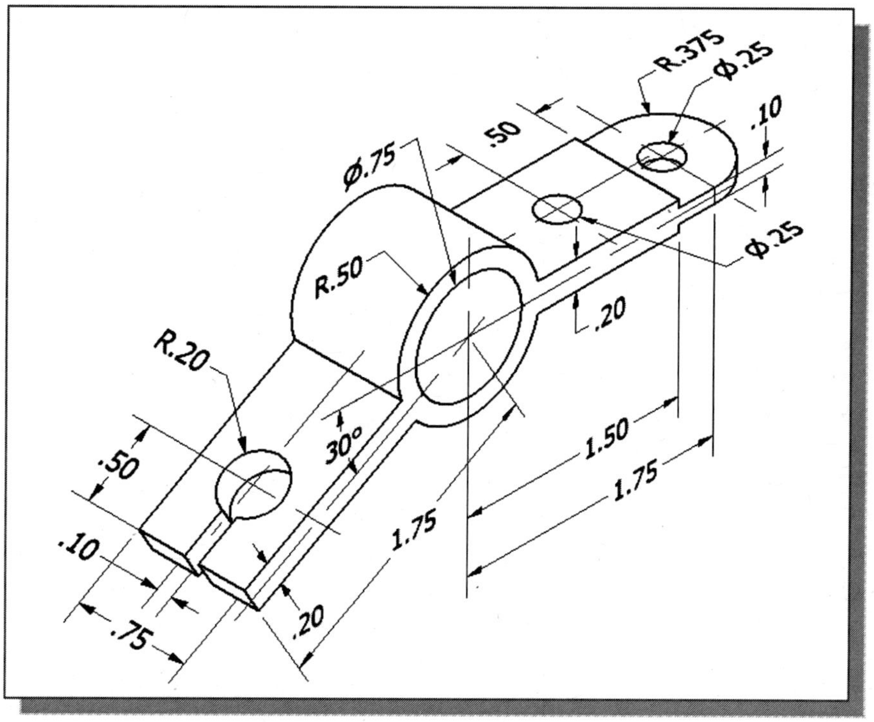

Notes:

Chapter 7
Datum Features in Designs

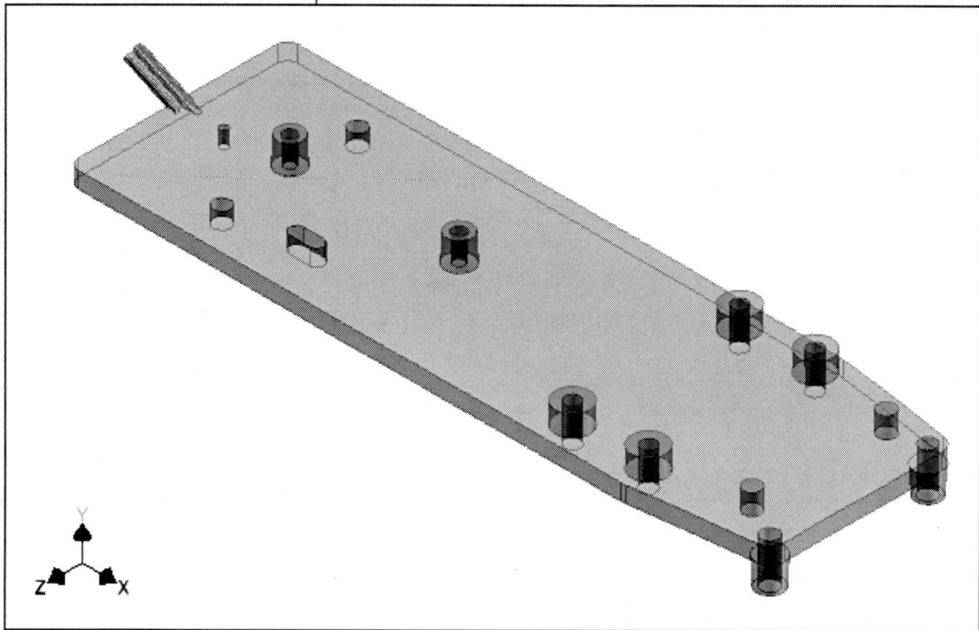

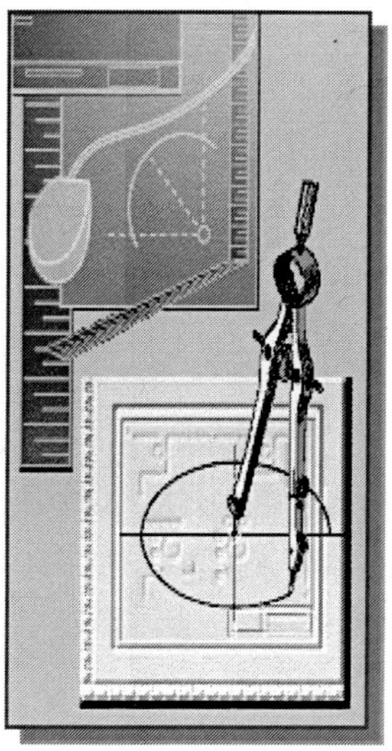

Learning Objectives

- ♦ Understand the Concepts and the Use of Reference Geometry
- ♦ Using the Different Options to Create Reference Geometry
- ♦ Create Revolved Features
- ♦ Create Tapered Features
- ♦ Adjust the Color of the Models

Reference Features

Feature-based parametric modeling is a cumulative process. The relationships that we define between features determine how a feature reacts when other features are changed. Because of this interaction, certain features must, by necessity, precede others. A new feature can use previously defined features to define information such as size, shape, location and orientation. *SolidWorks* provides several tools to automate this process. ***Reference Features*** can be thought of as user-definable datum features, which can be updated with the part geometry. We can create datum planes, axes, or points that do not already exist. Reference features can also be used to align features or to orient parts in an assembly. In this chapter, the use of **reference features** to create new datum planes, surfaces that do not already exist, is illustrated. By creating *parametric reference features*, the established feature interactions in the CAD database assure the capturing of the design intent. Note the use of the default datum planes, which are aligned to the *Origin* of the coordinate system, can assist the construction of the more complex geometric features.

The *B2-Chassis* Part

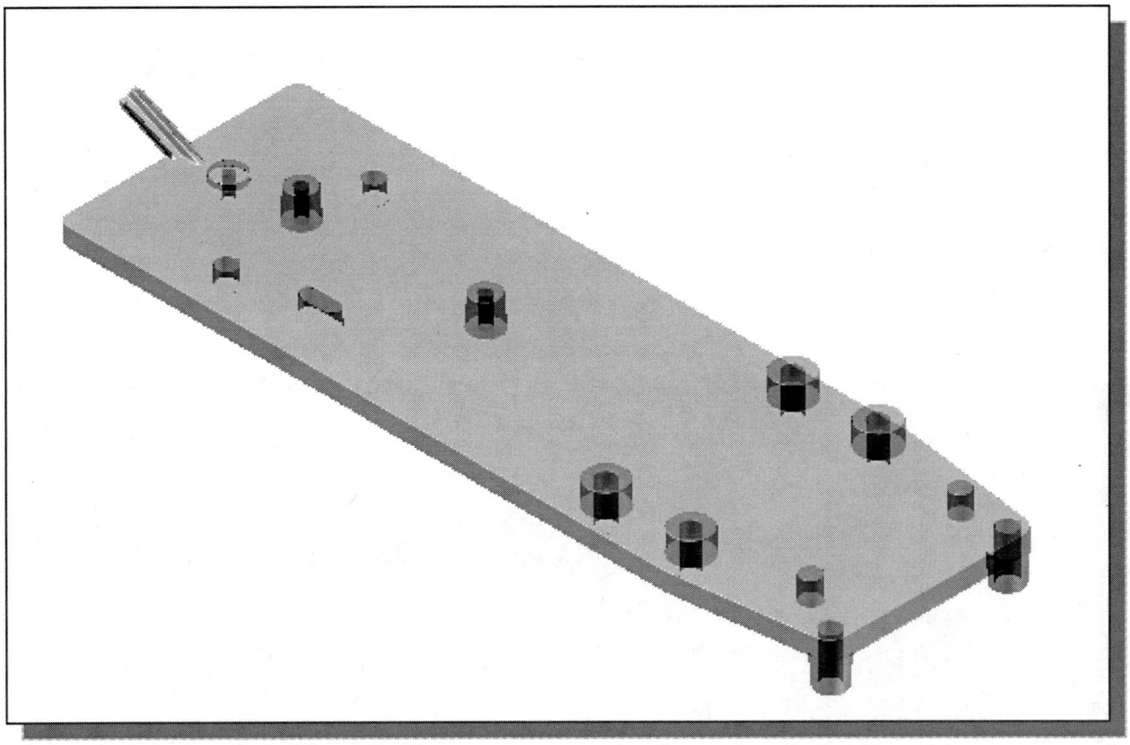

- Based on your knowledge of *SolidWorks* so far, how many features would you use to create the model? What are the more difficult features involved in the design? Which feature would you choose as the **base feature**? What is your choice for arranging the order of the features?

Modeling Strategy

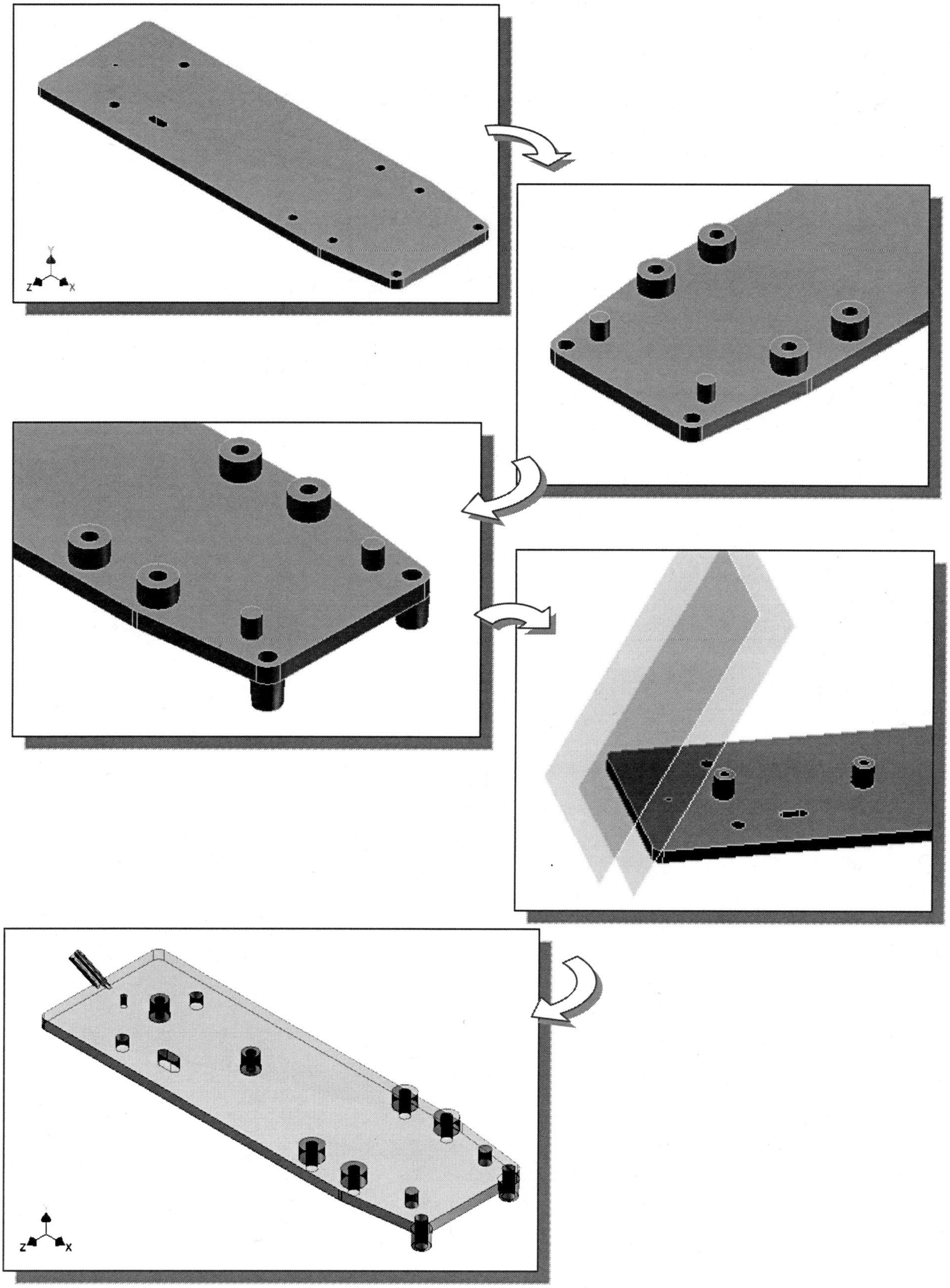

Starting *SolidWorks*

1. Select the **SolidWorks** option on the *Start* menu or select the **SolidWorks** icon on the desktop to start *SolidWorks*. The *SolidWorks* main window will appear on the screen.

2. Select the **New** icon with a single click of the left-mouse-button on the *Menu Bar*.

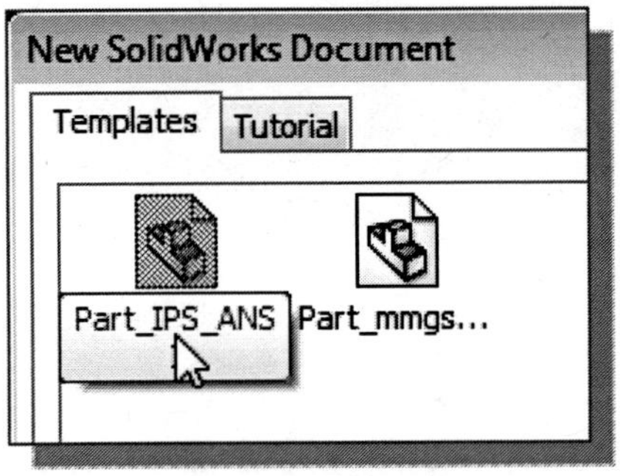

3. Select the **Part_IPS_ANSI** template as shown.

4. Click on the **OK** button to open a new document using the Part_IPS_ANSI template.

5. Select the **Options** icon from the *Menu* toolbar to open the *Options* dialog box.

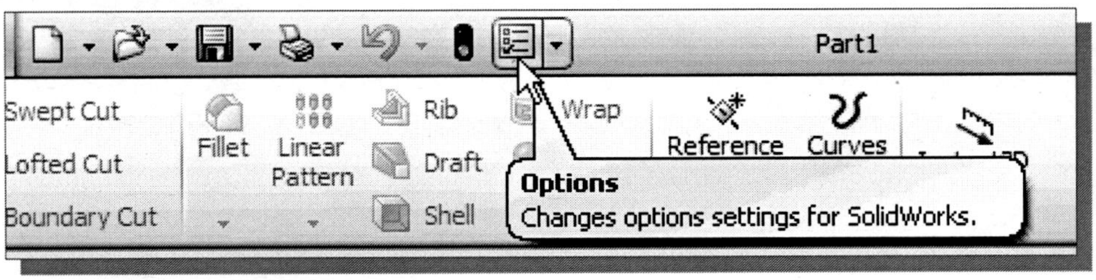

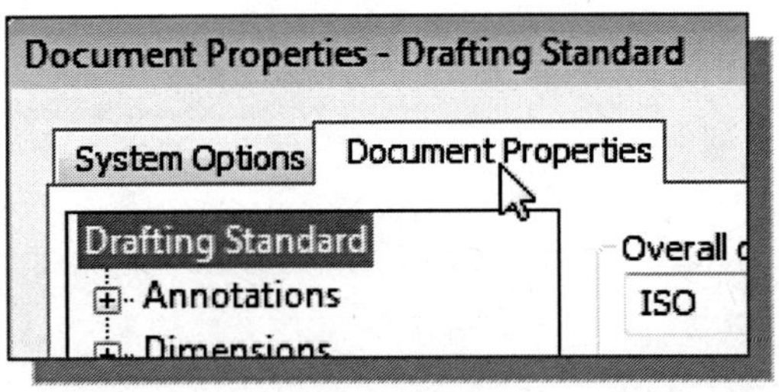

6. Select the **Document Properties** tab as shown in the figure.

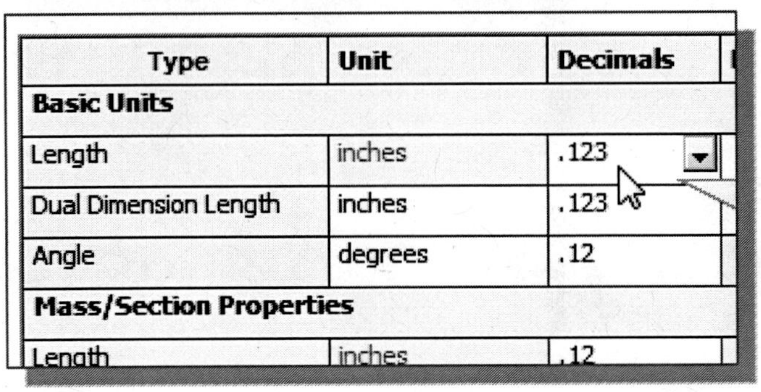

7. On your own, set the length units to display **three digits** after decimal point as shown.

- Note that after changing the number of display digits, the drafting standard is now changed to *Modified-ANSI*.

Create the Base Feature

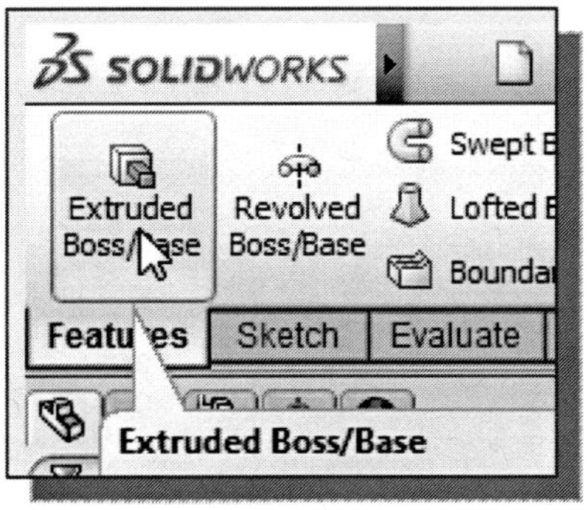

1. In the *Features* toolbar select the **Extruded Boss/Base** command by clicking once with the left-mouse-button on the icon.

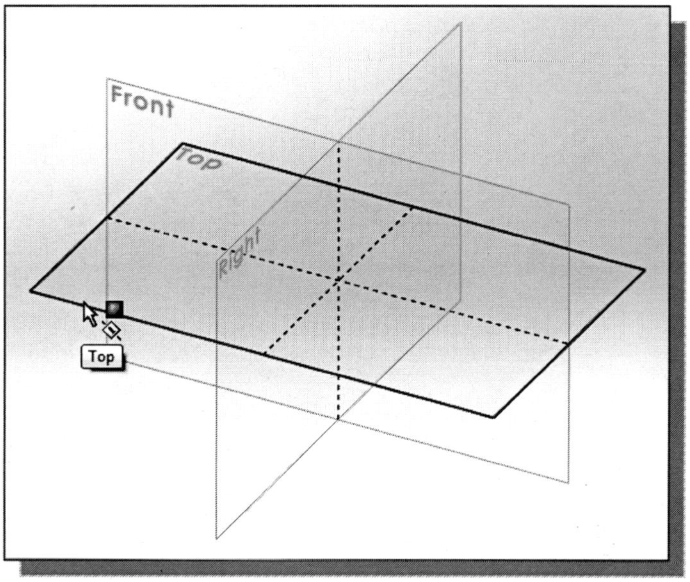

2. Select the **Top Plane** by clicking on any edge of the plane, inside the graphics window, as shown.

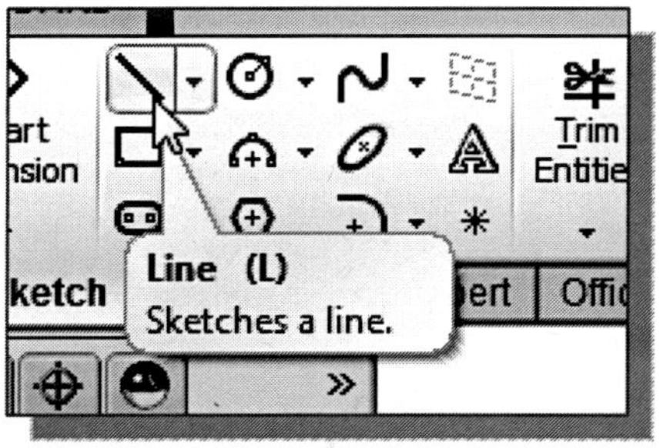

3. Select the **Line** option in the *Sketch* panel. A *Help-tip* box appears next to the cursor: "*Sketches a line.*"

4. Create the closed region sketch, with the center of the sketch aligned to the *Origin*, as shown. Note the three sets of rounded corners.

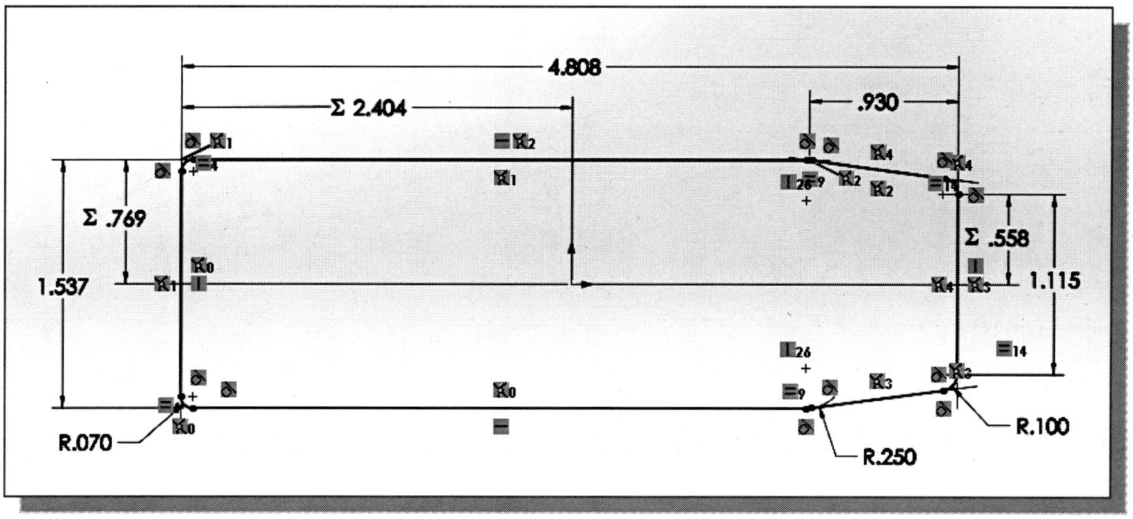

5. On your own, create six circles of the same diameter; the four circle-centers on the left are aligned both horizontally and vertically as shown. Also create and modify the associated dimensions as shown in the figure.

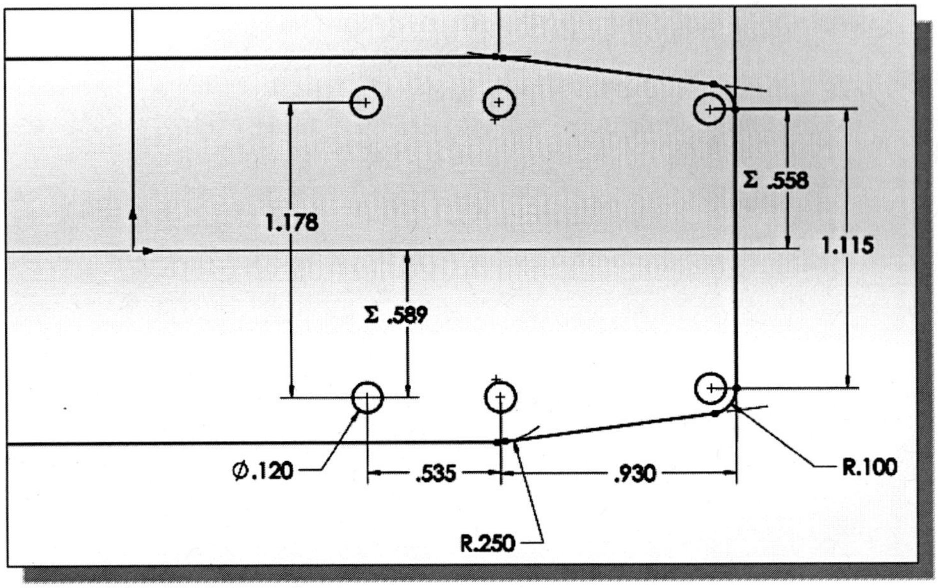

6. On your own, create the four closed regions on the left as shown.

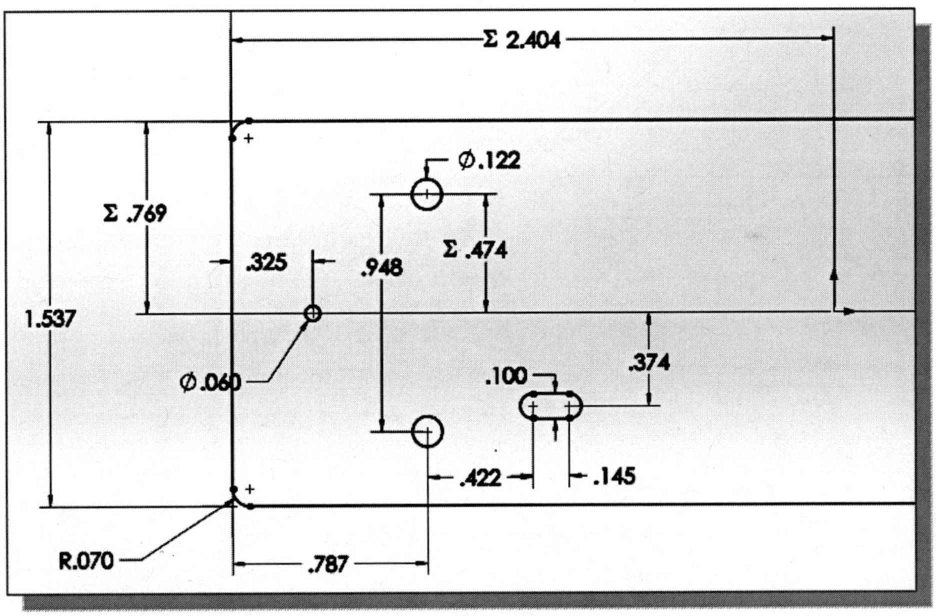

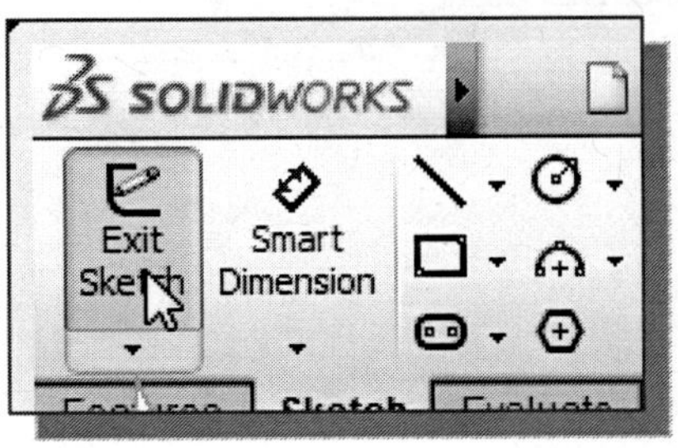

7. Click **Exit Sketch** in the *Sketch* toolbar to end the *Sketch* mode.

8. In the *Boss-Extrude Property Manager*, enter **0.118** as the extrusion distance.

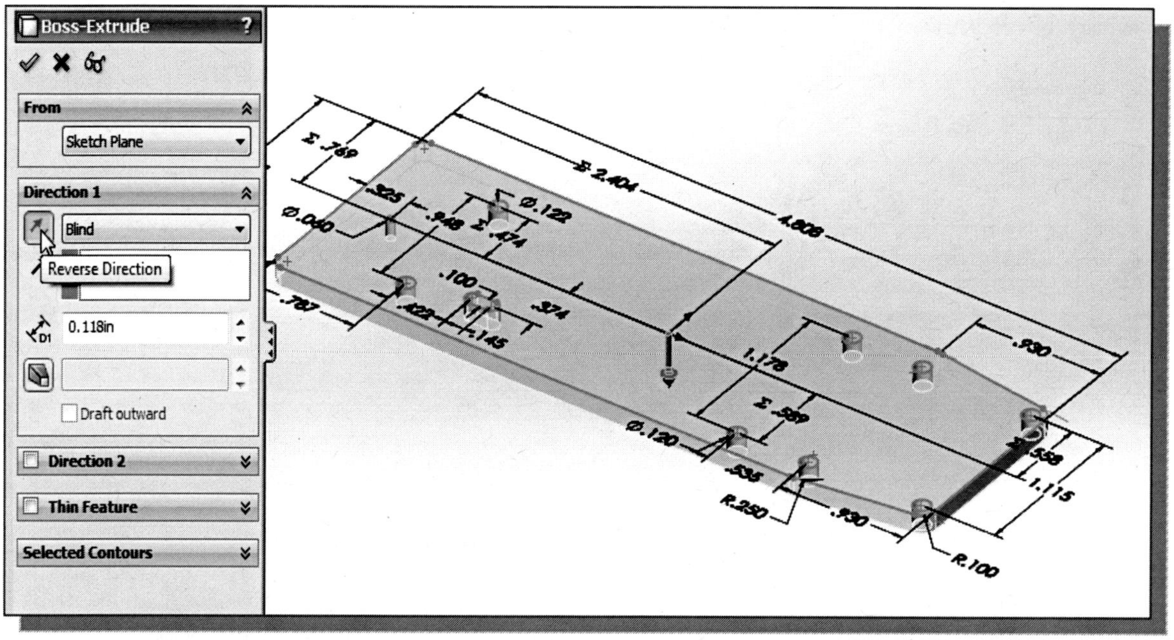

9. Click once on the **Reverse Direction** button to set the extrusion direction to downward as shown.

10. Click on the **OK** button to proceed with creating the feature.

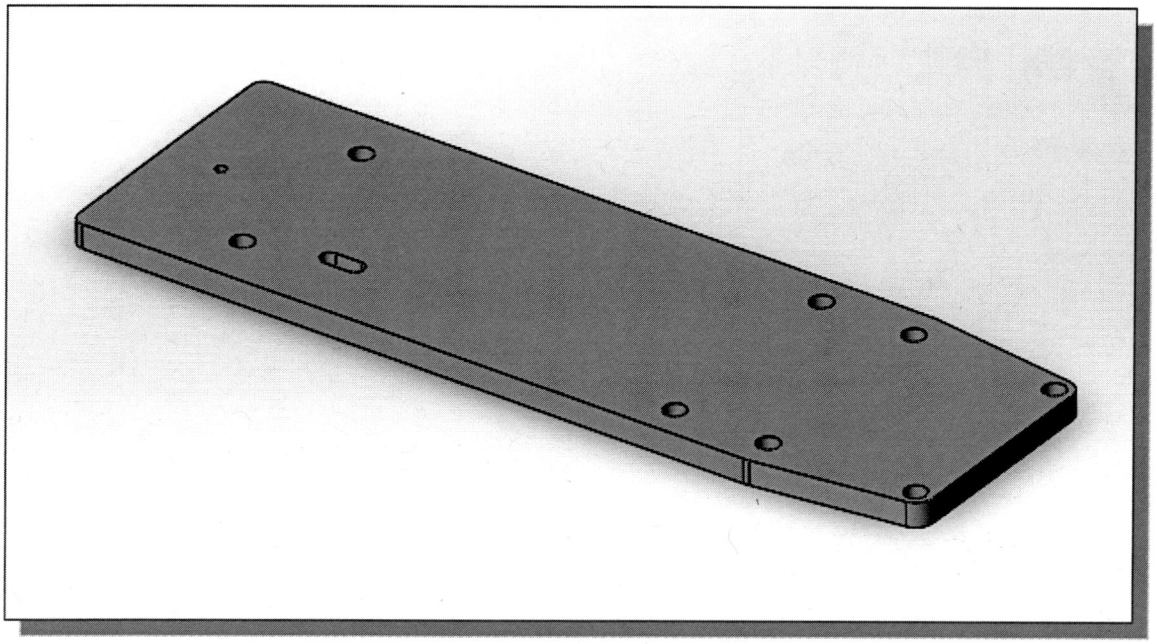

Create the Second Extruded Feature

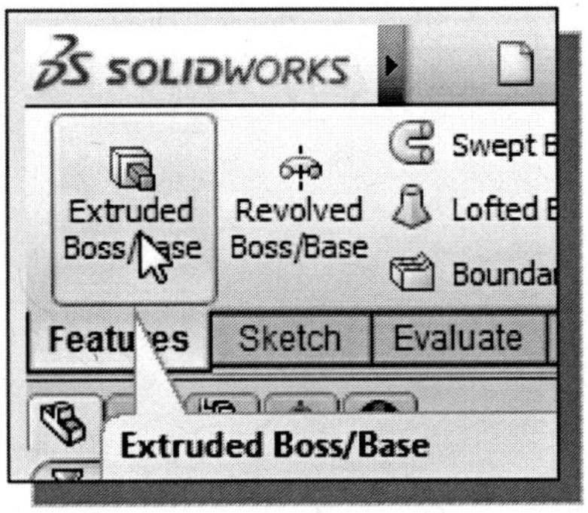

1. In the *Features* toolbar select the **Extruded Boss/ Base** command by clicking once with the left-mouse-button on the icon.

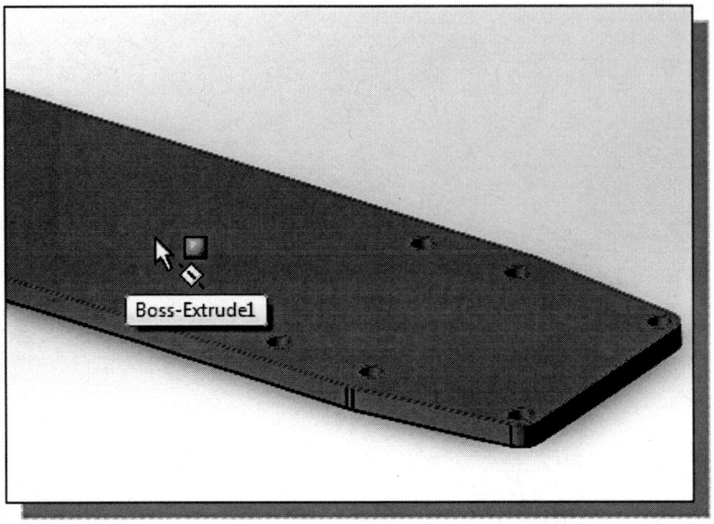

2. Select the **top surface** as the sketching plane as shown.

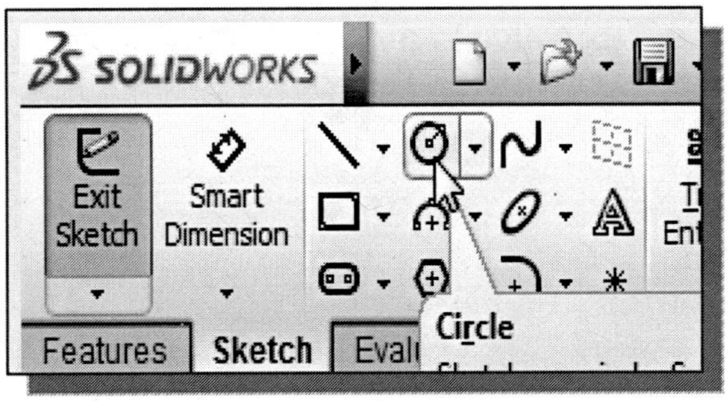

3. Select the **Center** command by clicking once with the left-mouse-button on the icon in the *Sketch* toolbar.

4. On your own, create six circles, as shown in the figure below. The centers of the four circles on the left are aligned to the existing holes.

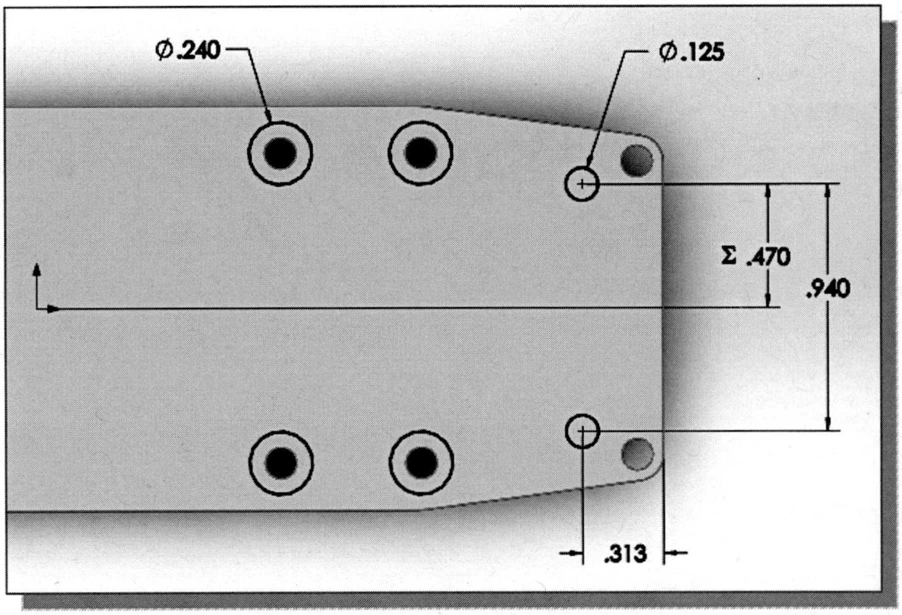

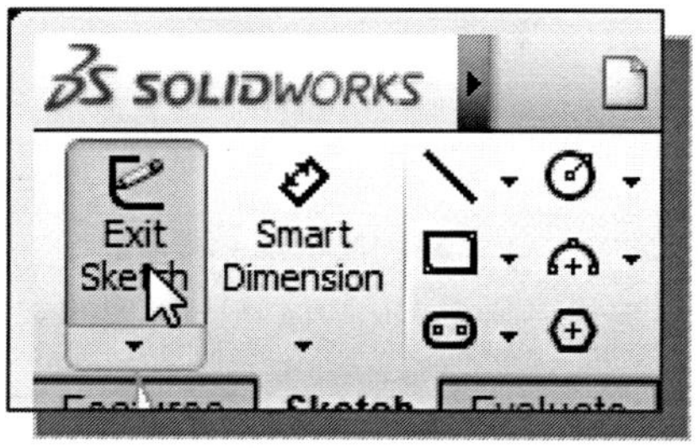

5. Click **Exit Sketch** in the *Sketch* toolbar to end the *Sketch* mode.

6. On your own, use the **Contour** option and select the **six regions** of the 2D sketch as shown.

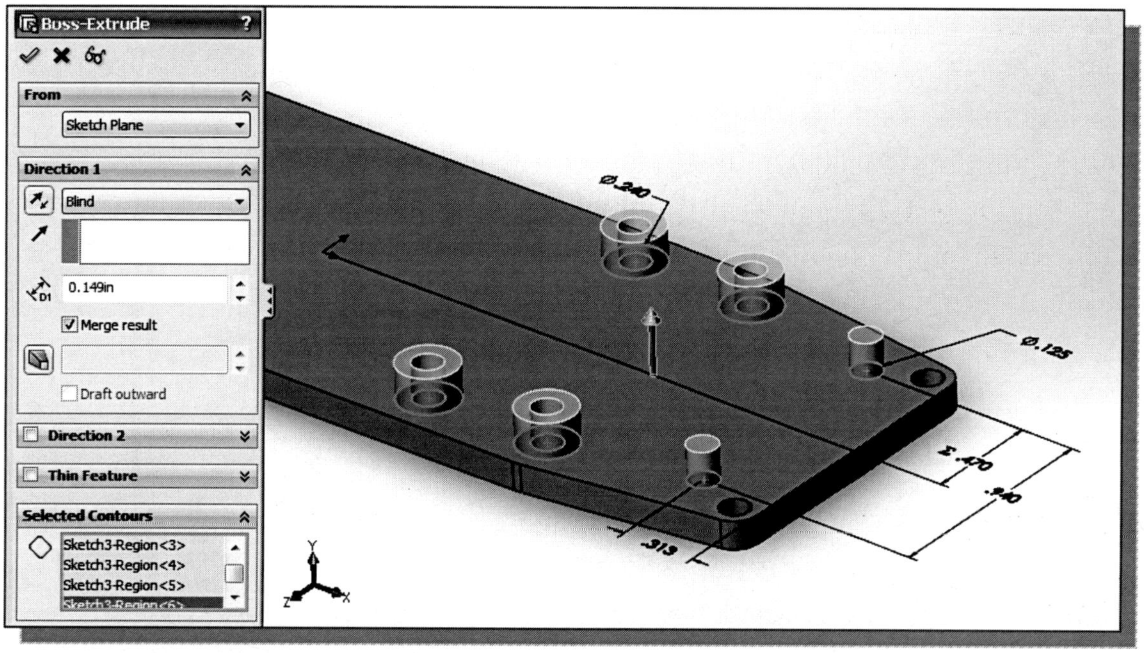

7. In the *Extrude* popup window, enter **0.149** as the extrusion distance.

8. Click on the **OK** button to proceed with creating the features.

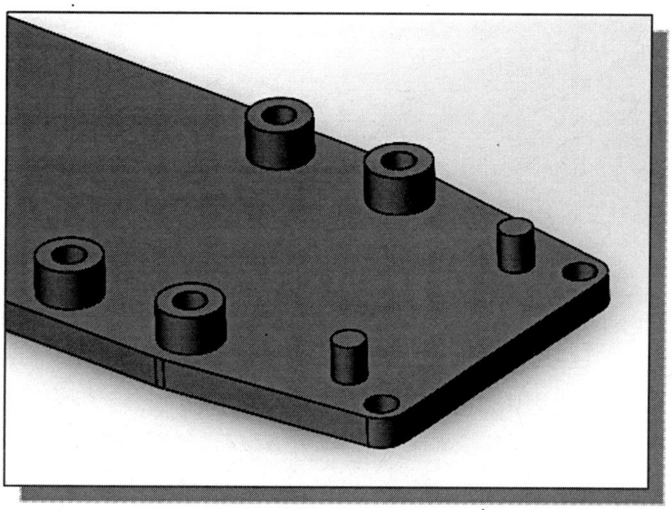

Create a Tapered Extruded Feature

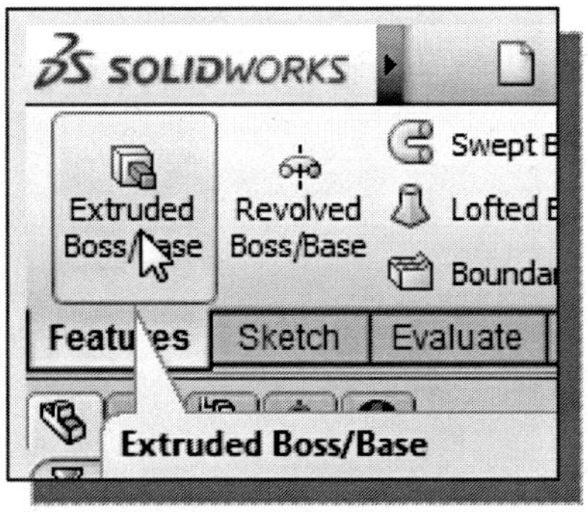

1. In the *Features* toolbar select the **Extruded Boss/ Base** command by clicking once with the left-mouse-button on the icon.

2. Select the **top surface** as the sketching plane.

3. On your own, create four circles with the dimensions as shown in the figure.

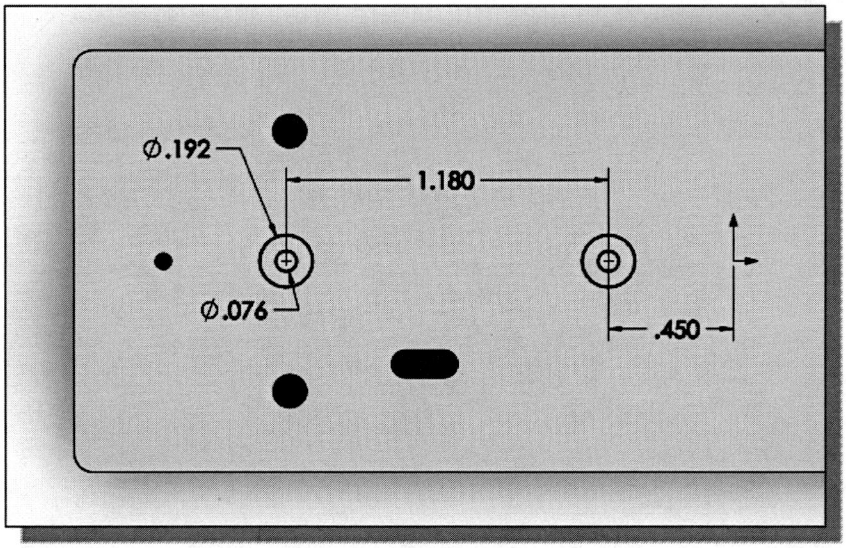

4. Create an extruded feature, with extrusion *distance* set to **0.20** and *taper angle* set to **2.5** degrees.

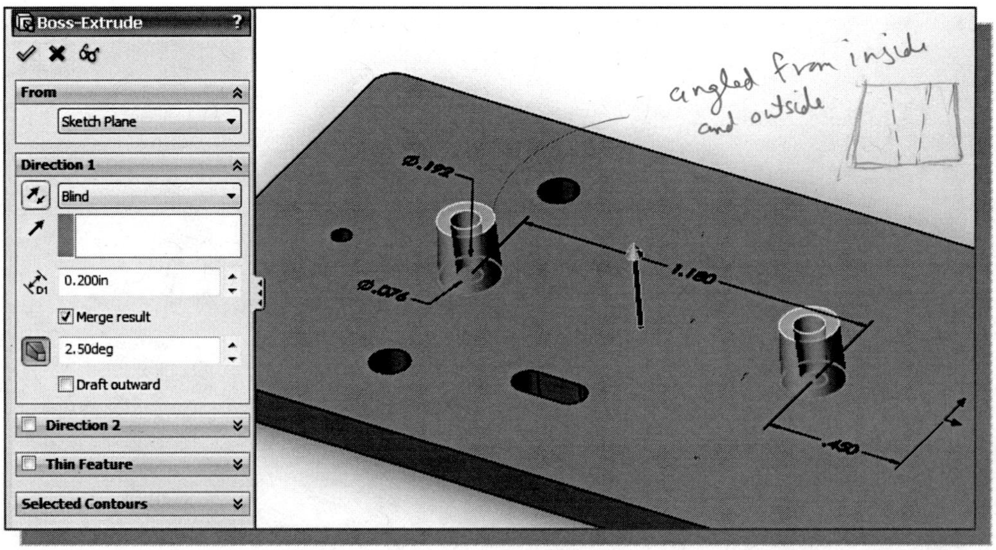

5. Click on the **OK** button to proceed with creating the feature.

Create an Offset Reference Plane

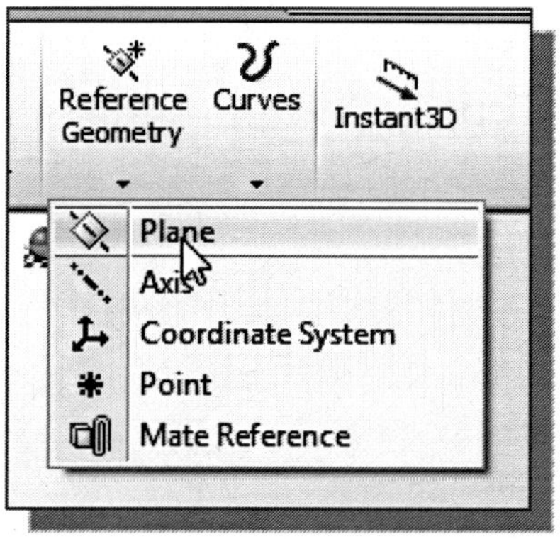

1. In the *Features* toolbar, select the **Reference plane** command by left-clicking the icon.

- Note that other types of *reference features* are available.

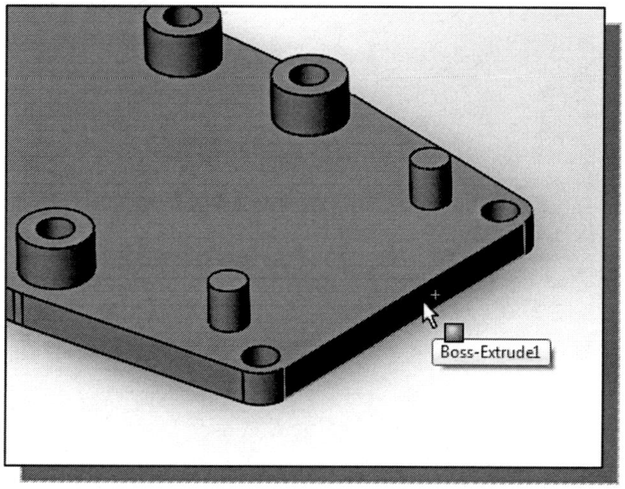

2. Inside the graphics window, select the **right vertical plane** of the base feature as the reference of the new reference plane.

3. Click **Flip** to switch the offset direction, and set the distance to **0.1** inch as shown.

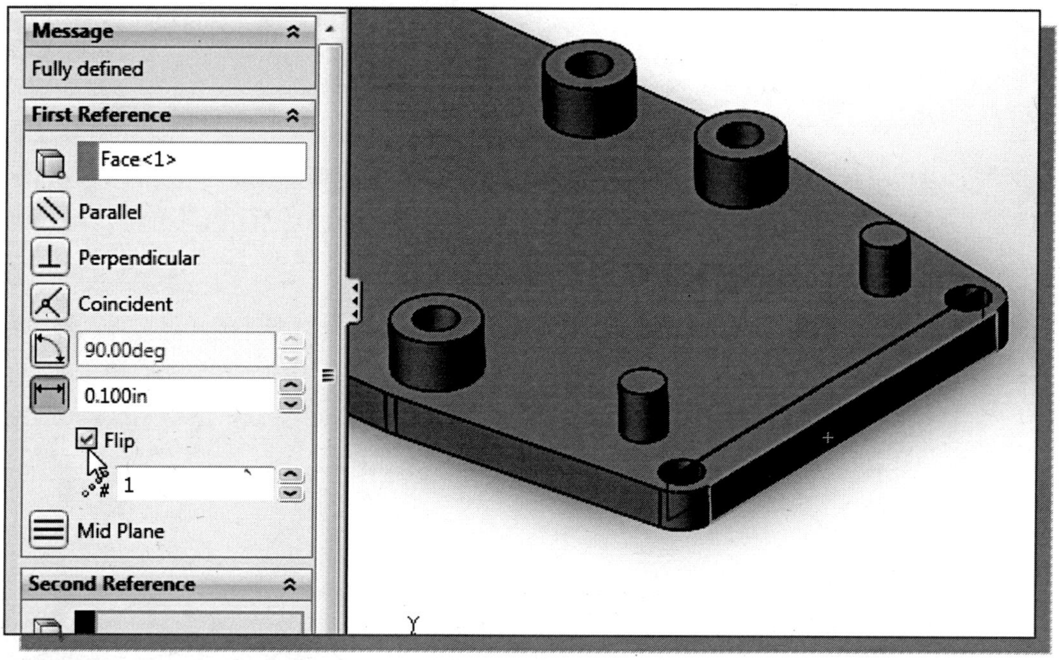

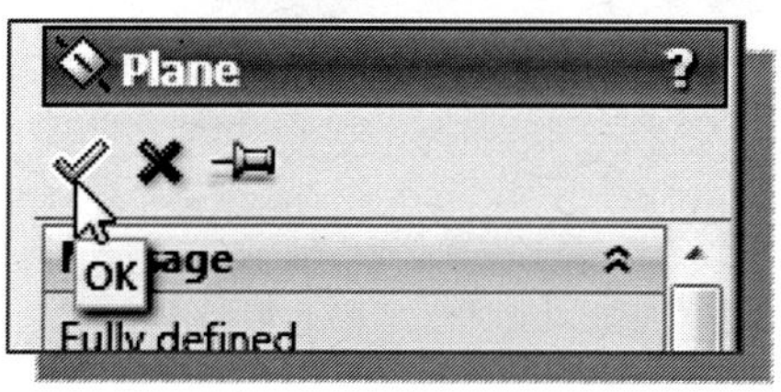

4. Click **OK** to create an offset plane that passes through the centers of the two small holes.

Create a Revolved Feature

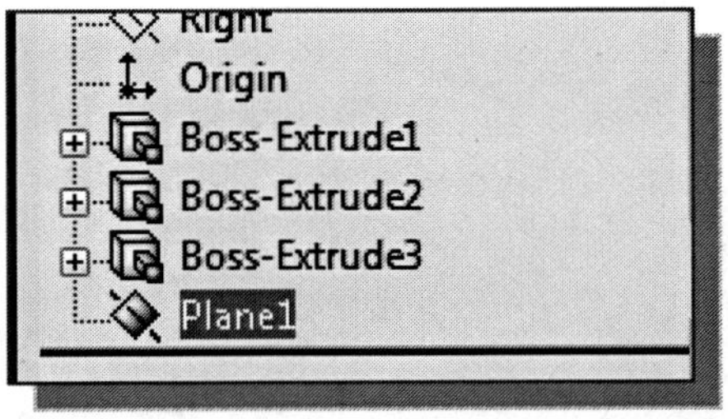

1. In the *FeatureManager Model Tree* area, confirm the new reference plane, Plane1, is pre-selected as shown.

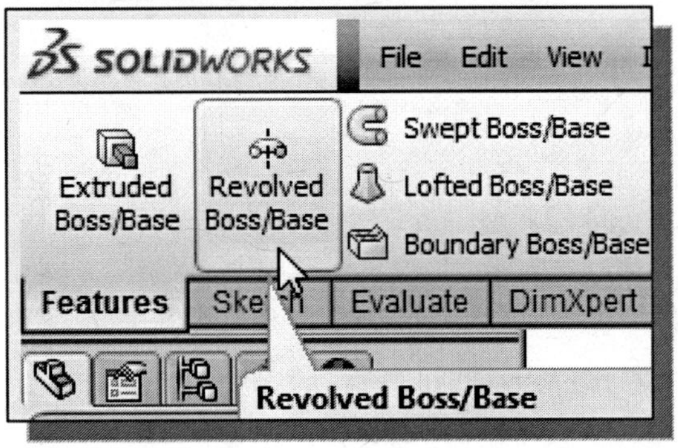

2. In the *Features* toolbar select the **Revolved Boss/Base** command by clicking once with the left-mouse-button on the icon.

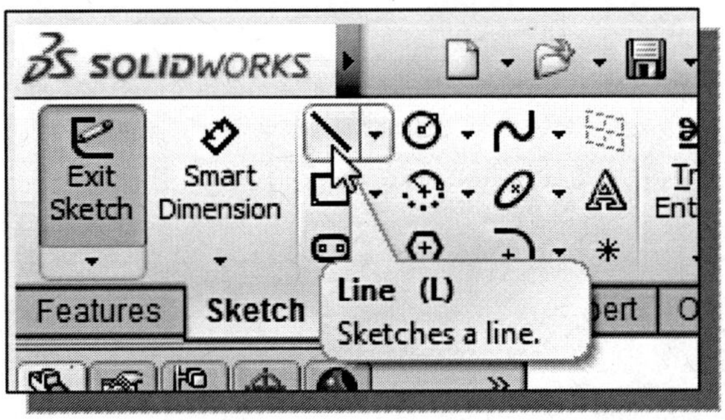

3. Select the **Line** command by clicking once with the left-mouse-button on the icon in the *Sketch* toolbar.

4. Create the closed region sketch, with the upper right corner aligned to the projected left edge of the cylindrical feature as shown. (Hint: Switch to the Hidden Lines visible display option.)

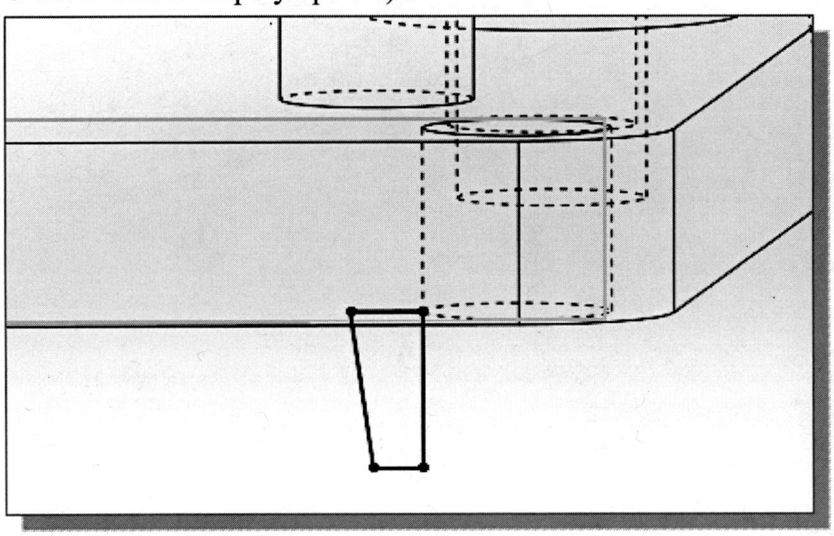

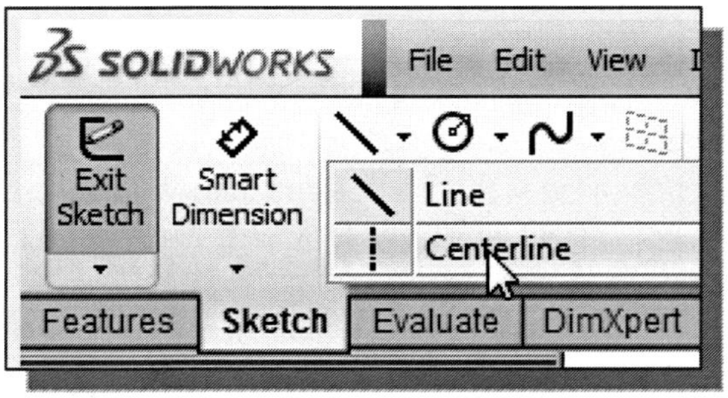

5. Select the **Centerline** option in the *Sketch* panel as shown.

6. Create a vertical centerline aligned to the center axis of the hole feature.

7. On your own, create the four dimensions as shown in the figure.

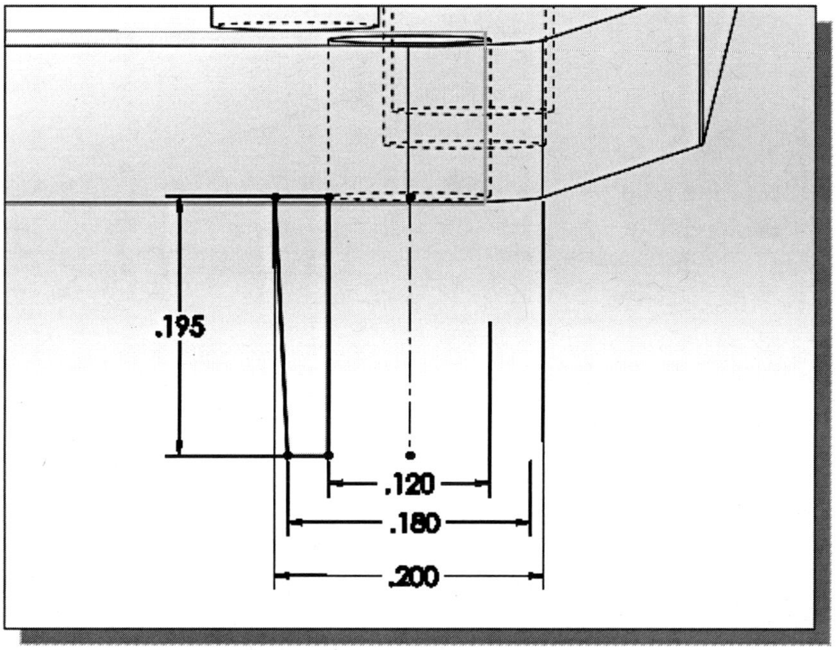

8. On your own, complete the **Revolve** feature as shown.

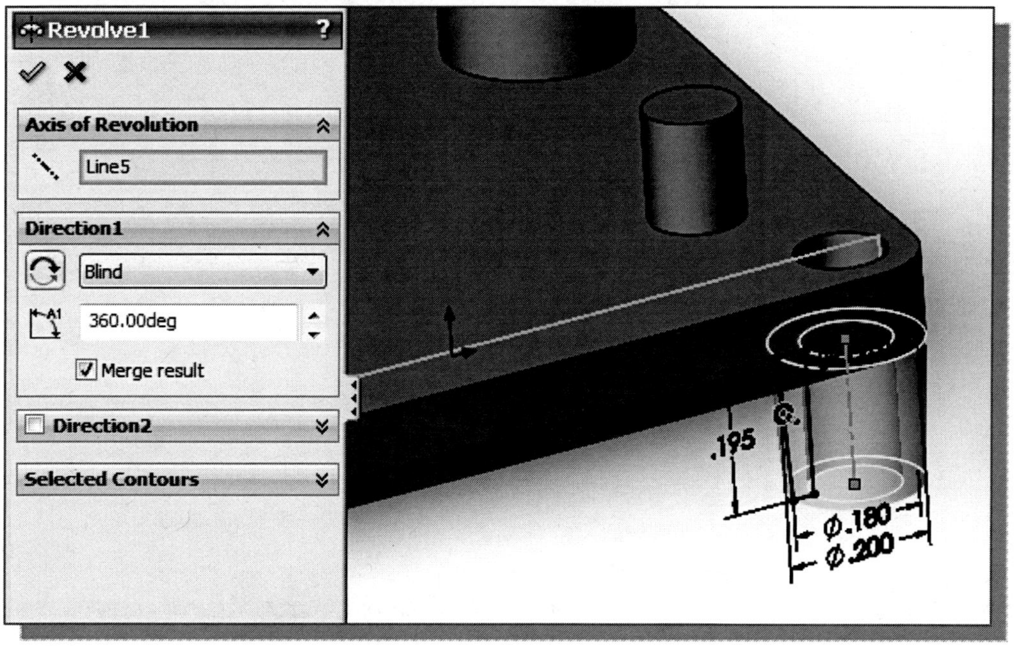

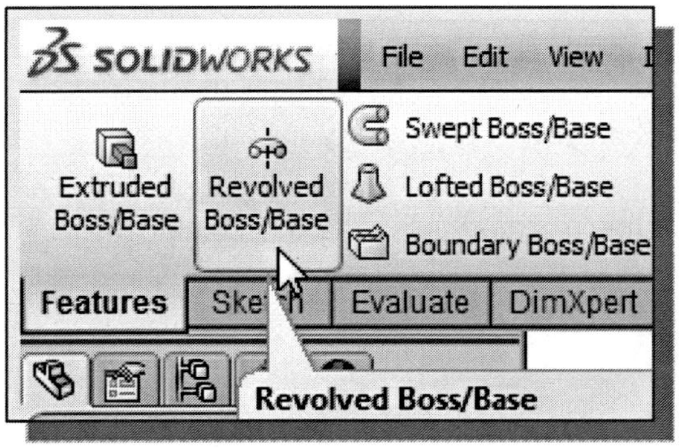

9. In the *Features* toolbar select the **Revolved Boss/Base** command by clicking once with the left-mouse-button on the icon.

10. Select the reference Plane1 to align the sketching plane.

11. On your own, create a center line through the center axis of the hole feature. Also create a closed region, with the upper left corner aligned to the projected edge, as shown.

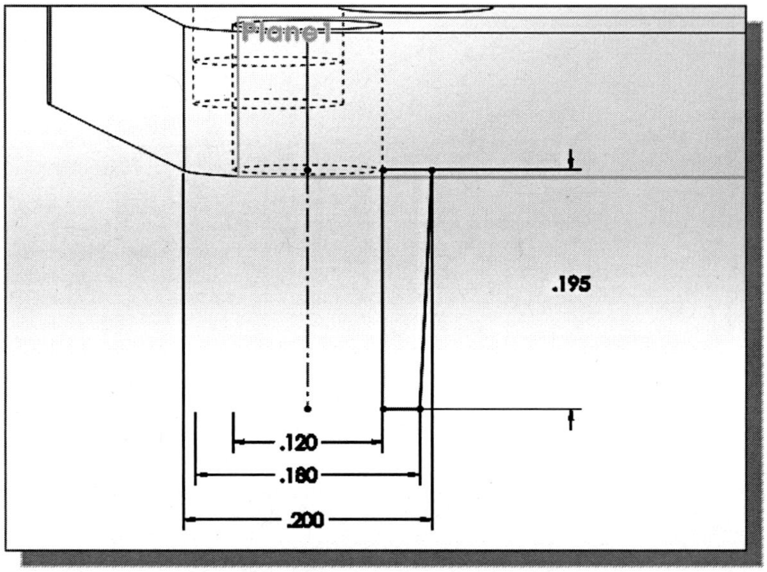

12. On your own, create another revolved feature as shown.

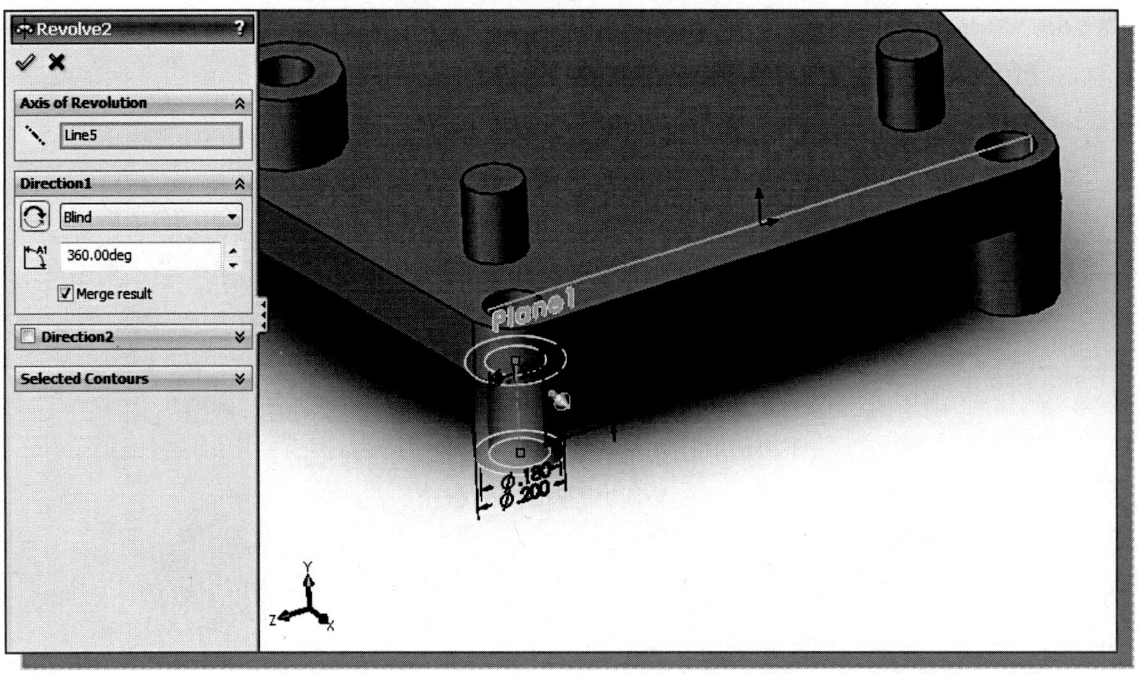

use mirror with Front as mirror plan

Create an Angled Reference Plane

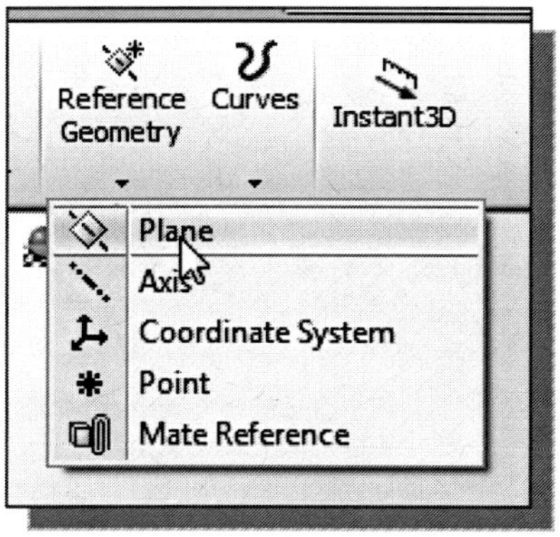

1. In the *Features* toolbar, select the **Reference Plane** command by left-clicking the icon.

➢ For an *angled reference plane*, *SolidWorks* expects us to select a line and a plane to be used as references for the new reference plane.

2. Inside the graphics window, select the **left vertical plane** of the base feature as the first reference.

3. Select the **top edge** as the second reference for the new reference plane.

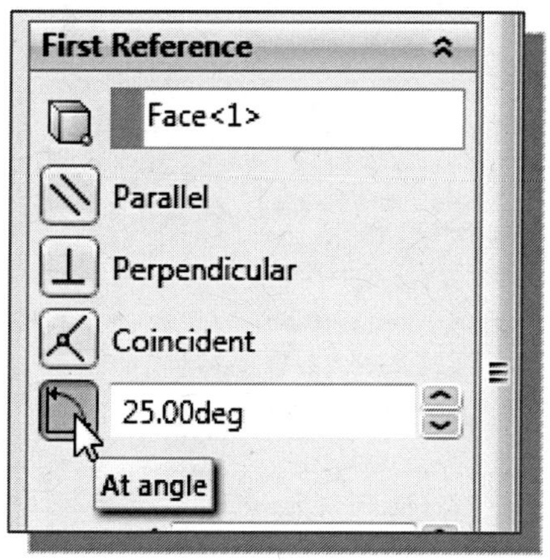

4. In the *First Reference* option list, select the **At Angle** option by left-clicking on the icon.

5. In the *At Angle* option box, enter **25** degrees as the rotation angle for the new angled reference plane.

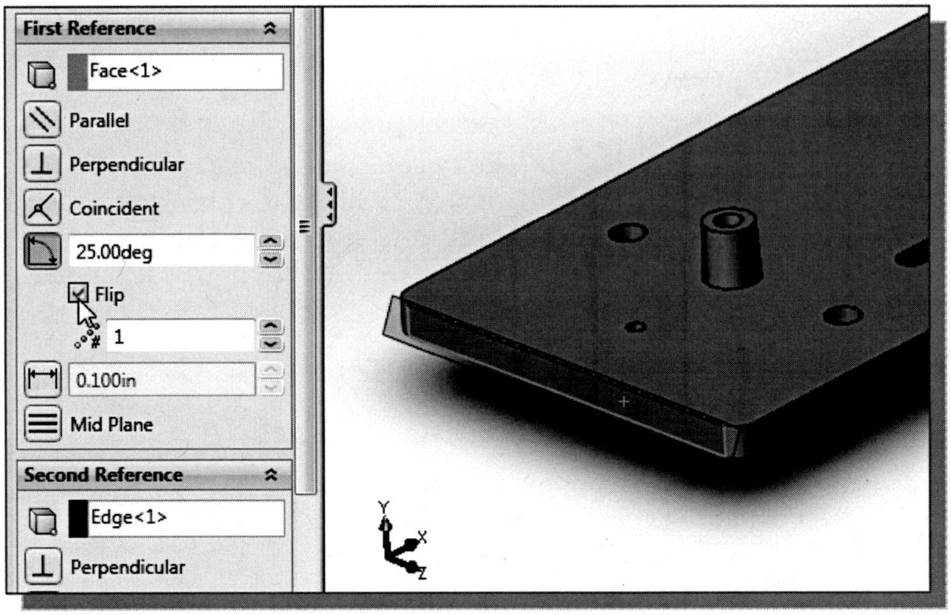

6. Click on the **Flip** option to set the direction of angle as shown.

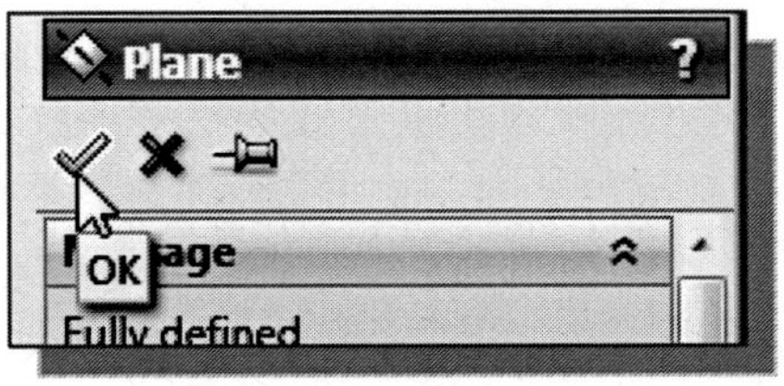

7. Click on the **check mark** button to accept the settings.

Create another Offset Reference plane

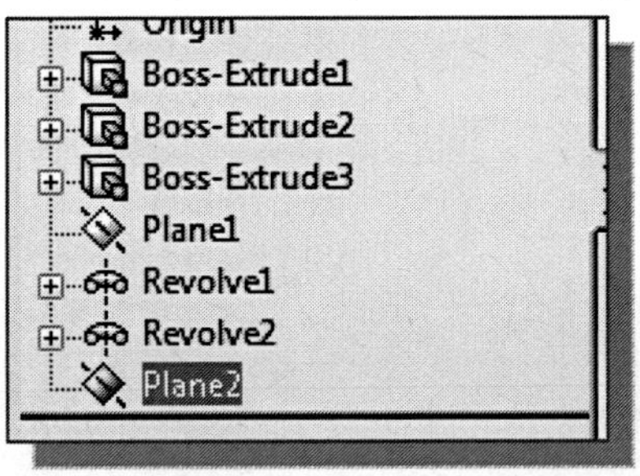

1. In the *FeatureManager Model Tree* area, confirm the new reference plane, **Plane2**, is pre-selected as shown.

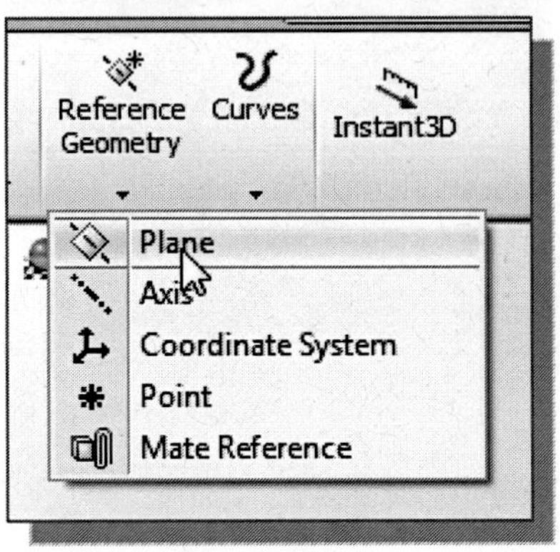

2. In the *Features* toolbar, select the **Reference Plane** command by left-clicking the icon.

3. In the *Offset* edit box, enter **0.34** as the offset distance as shown.

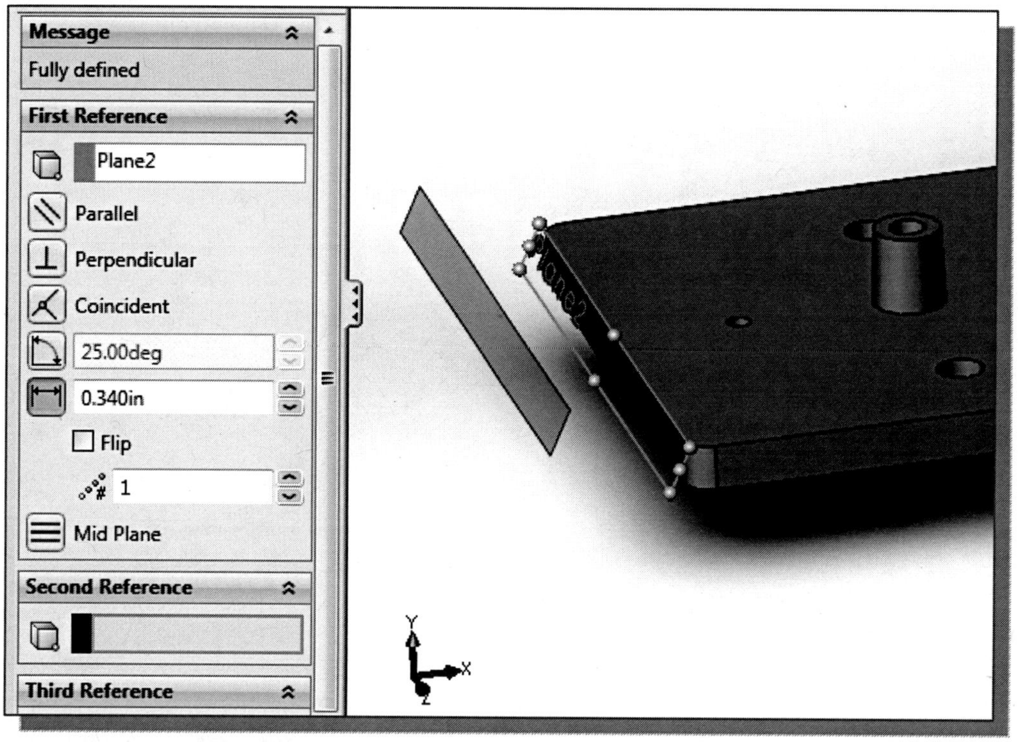

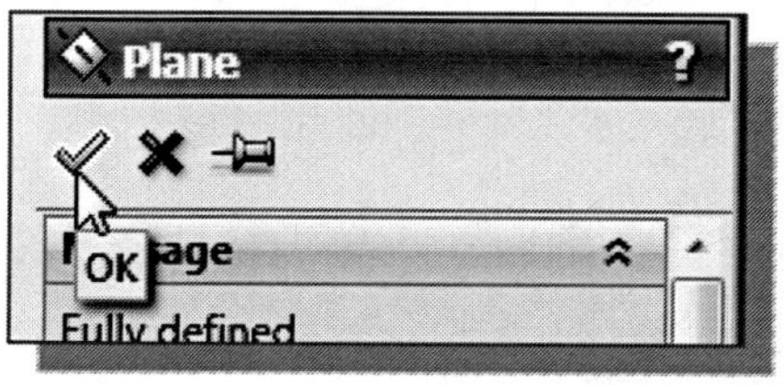

4. Click on the check mark button to accept the settings.

➢ Note that all three reference planes, **Plane1**, **Plane2** and **Plane3**, are listed as features in the *Model History Tree*. The reference planes are created to allow the construction of more complex solid features.

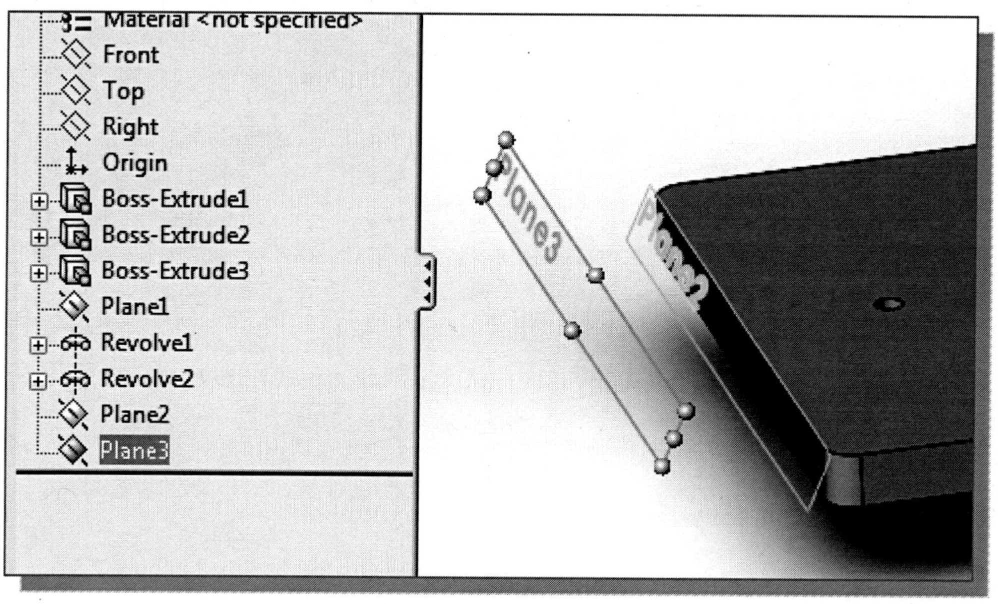

Create an Extruded Feature with Reference Plane 3

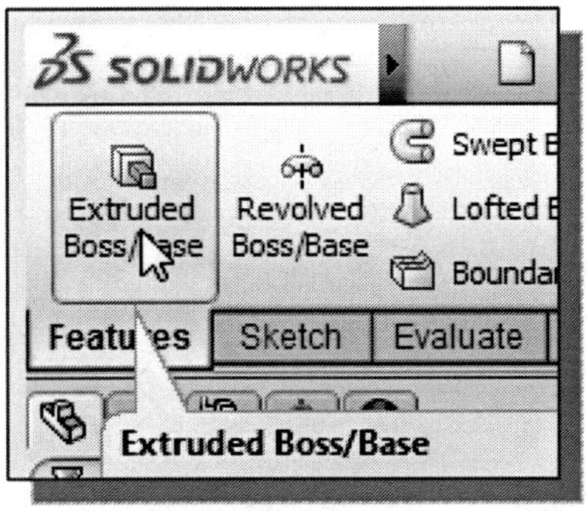

1. In the *Features* toolbar select the **Extruded Boss/ Base** command by left-clicking once on the icon.

2. Pick reference **Plane3** by clicking the reference plane inside the graphics window as shown.

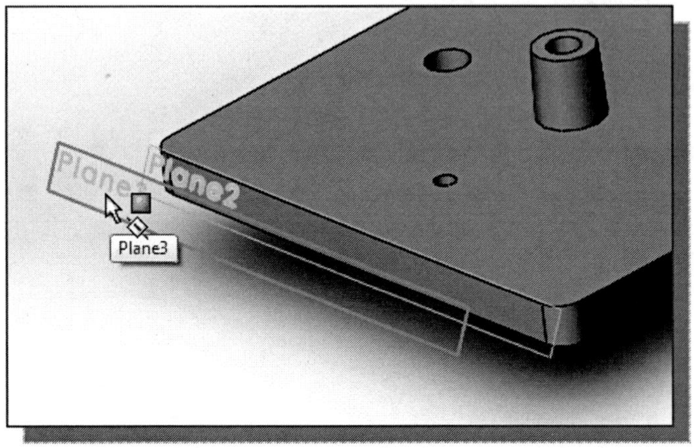

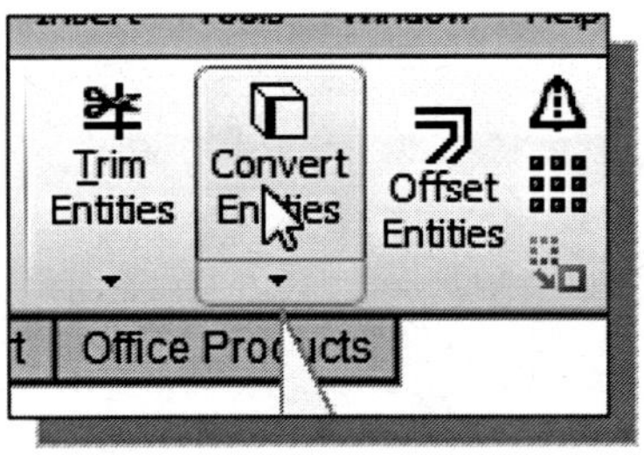

3. Select **Convert Entities** in the *Sketch* toolbar.

4. Select the **top edge** of the base feature as shown.

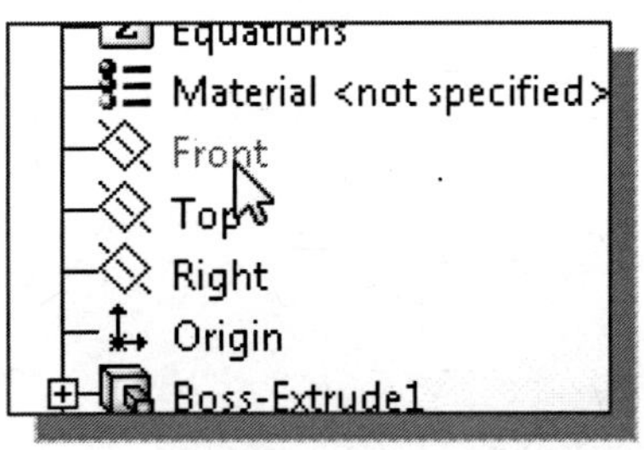

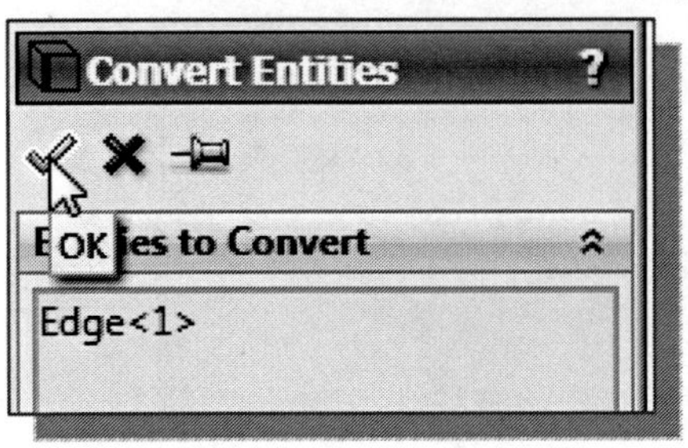

5. Click on the check mark button to accept the settings.

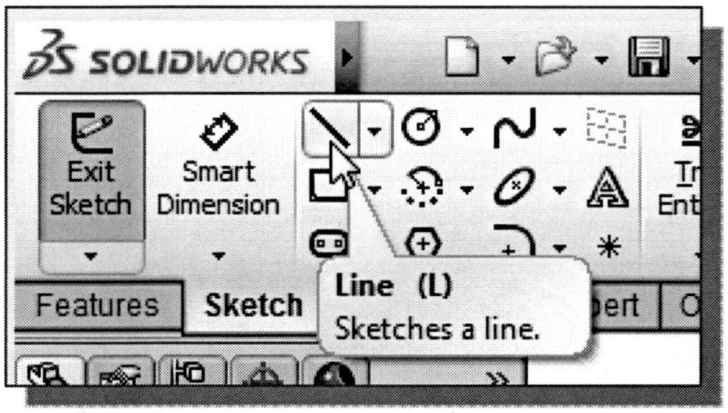

6. In the *Sketch* toolbar, click on the **Line** icon with the left-mouse-button to activate the Line command.

7. Create a rough sketch using the projected edge roughly at the center as shown in the figure. (Note that all edges are either horizontal or vertical.)

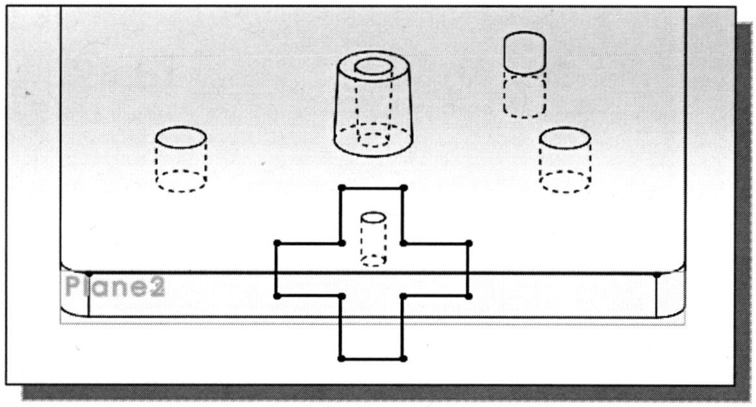

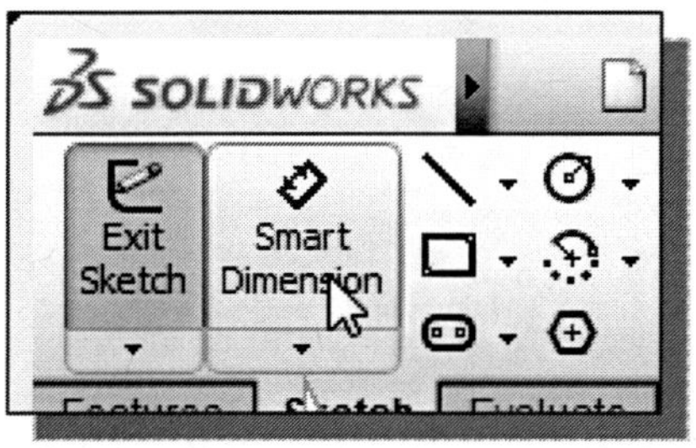

8. Left-click once on the **Smart Dimension** icon to activate the Smart Dimension command.

9. On your own, create additional constraints and dimensions as shown; note that the sketch is symmetrical vertically and horizontally.

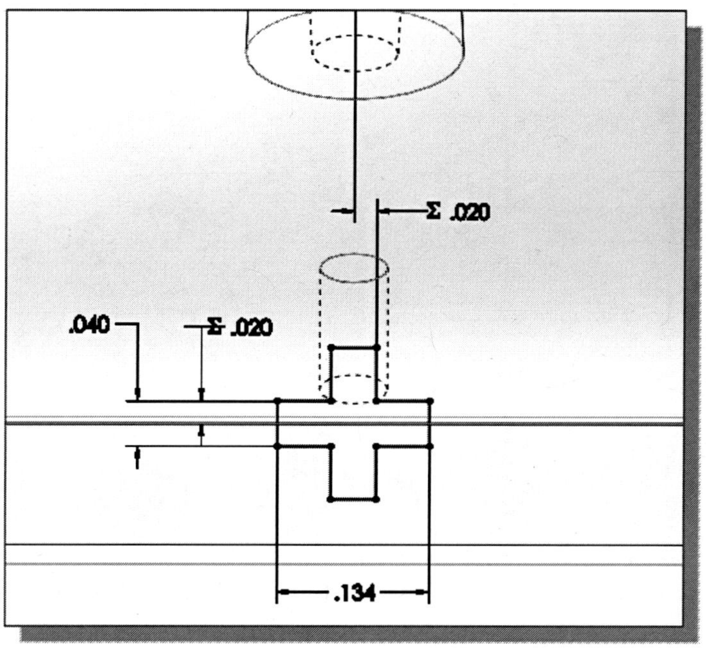

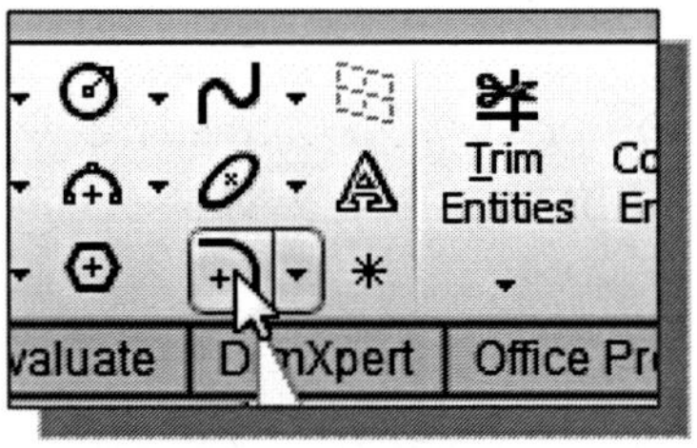

10. Select the **Fillet** option in the *Sketch* toolbar as shown.

11. On your own, add the rounded corners, radius **0.008**, to the sketch as shown.

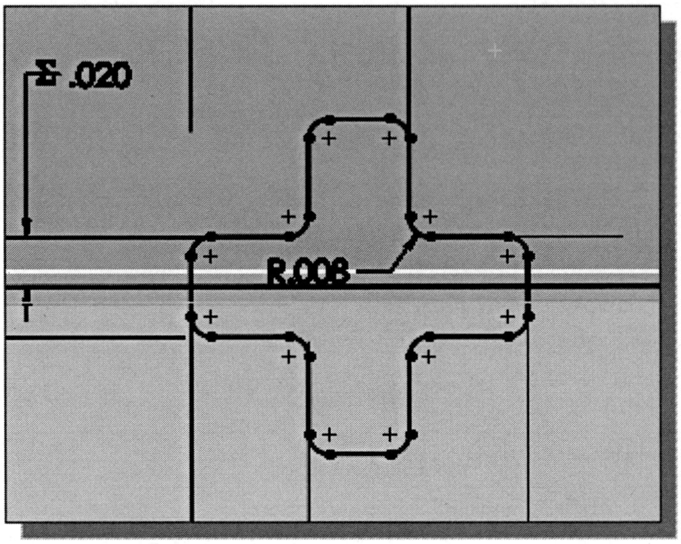

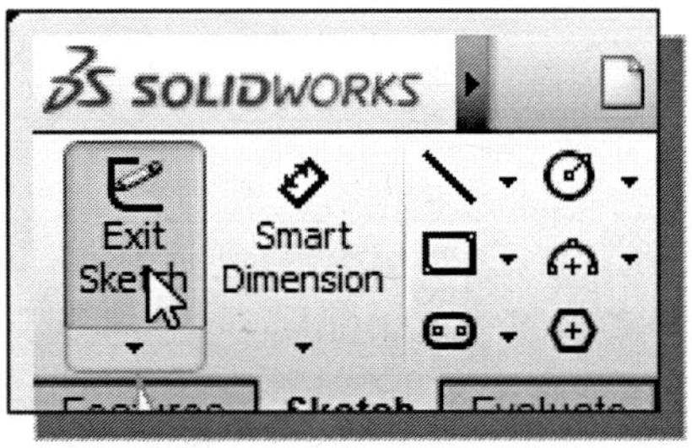

12. Select **Exit Sketch** in the *Sketch* toolbar to exit the *Sketch* mode.

13. Activate the **Contour** option and select the **two closed regions** defined by the 2D sketch.

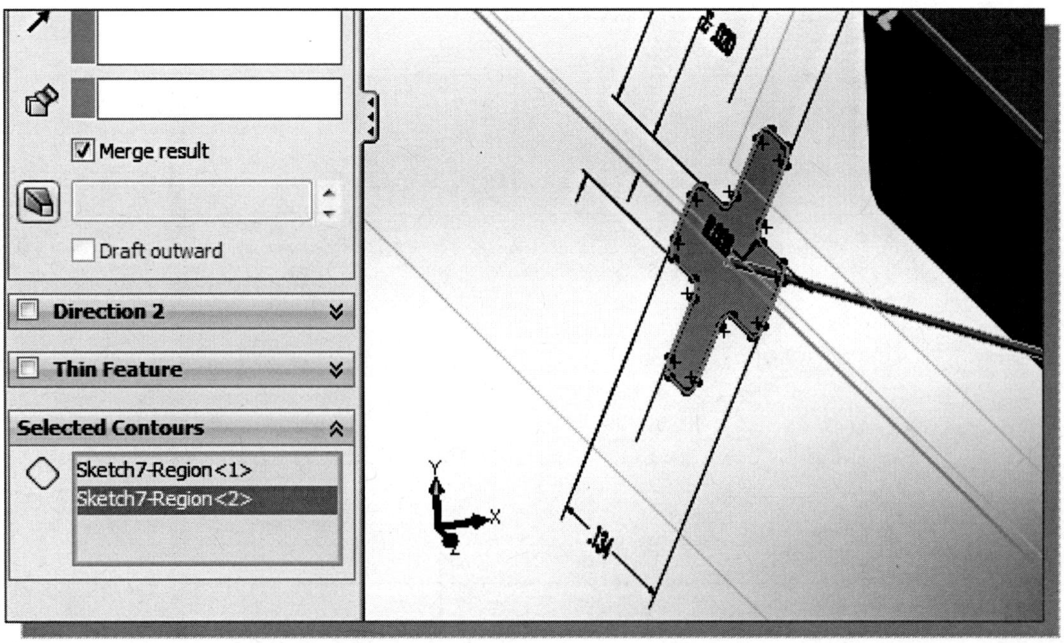

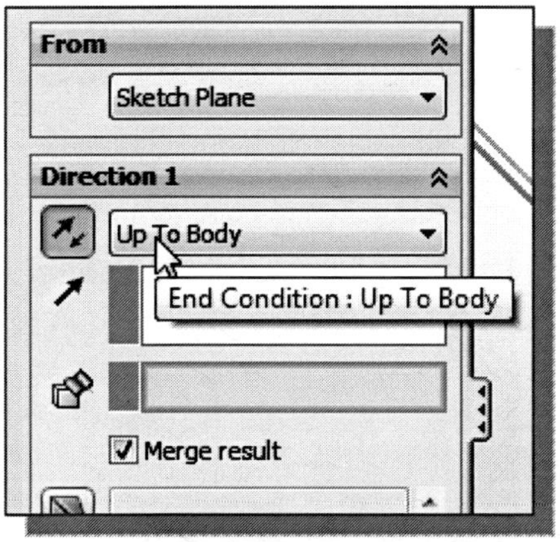

14. In the *PropertiesManager*, set the extrude option to **Up To Body** and set the extrusion direction as shown.

15. Click on the solid model to set the extrusion termination option as shown.

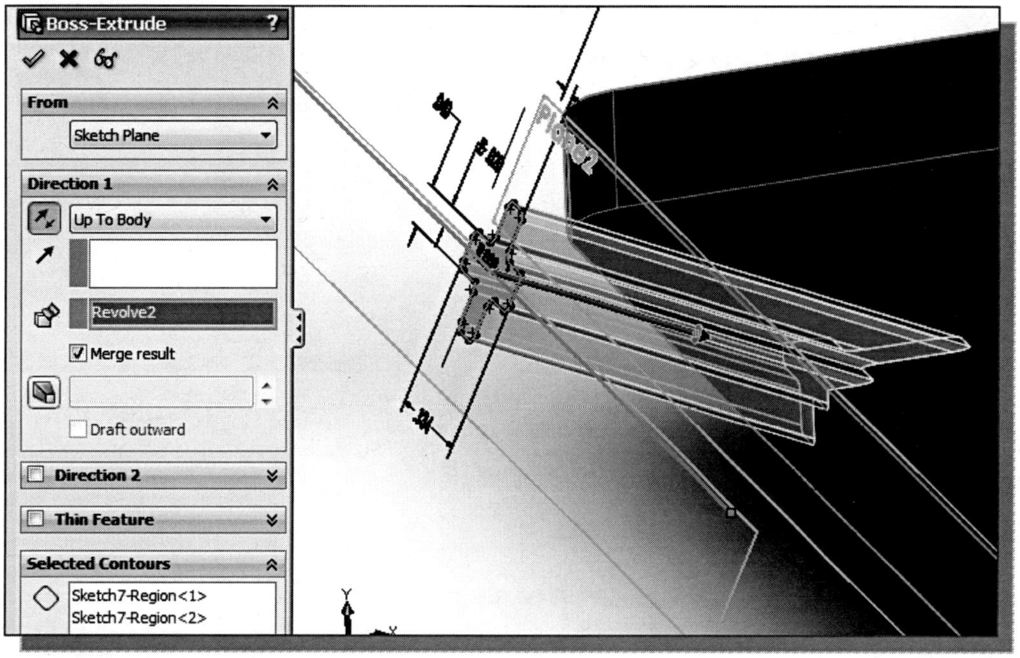

16. Click on the **OK** button to accept the settings and create the solid feature.

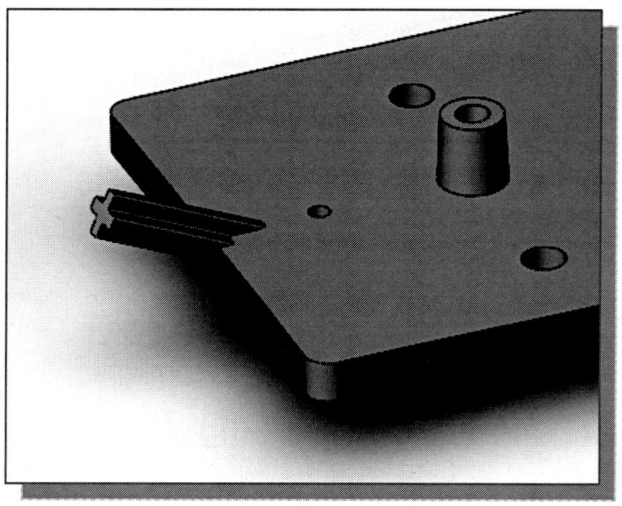

17. On your own, save the model using filename **B2-Chassis**.

Change the Appearance of the Solid Model

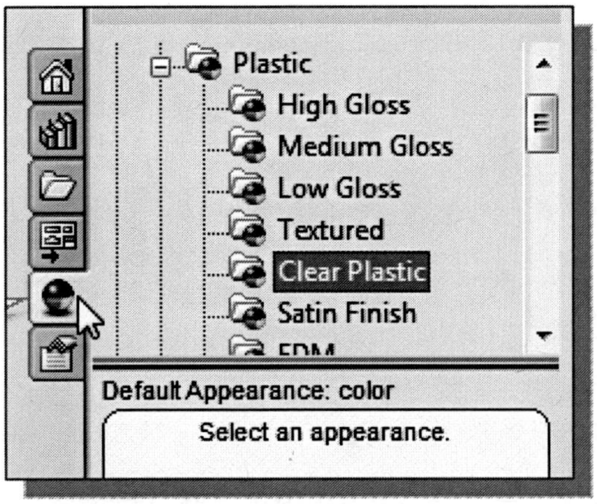

1. Click on the **Display** tab in the *task pane* and choose **Clear Plastic** as shown.

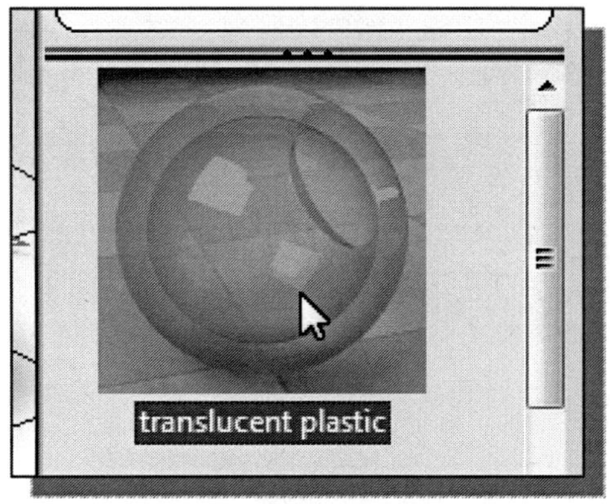

2. Select **translucent plastic** as shown.

3. Drag the appearance to the model in the graphics area.

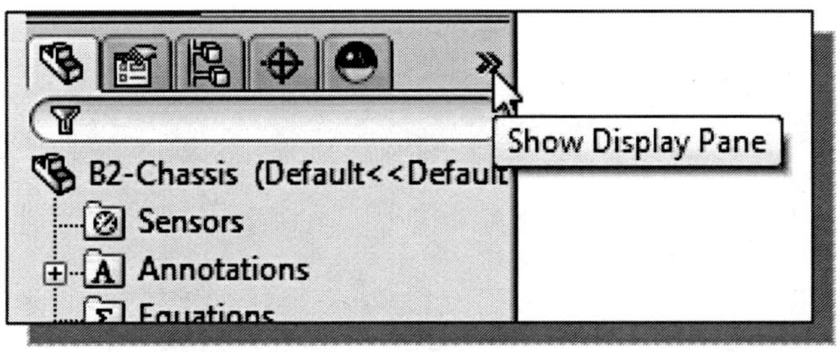

4. Expand the **Display Pane** by clicking on the arrow in the title area as shown.

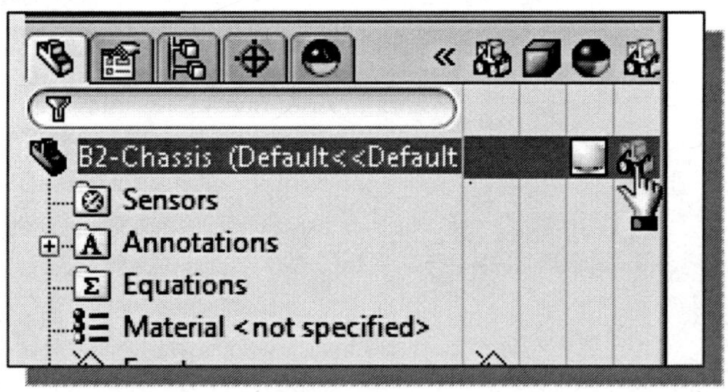

5. Click on the **Show Transparency** icon to adjust the display transparency.

- Note the icon acts as a toggle switch.

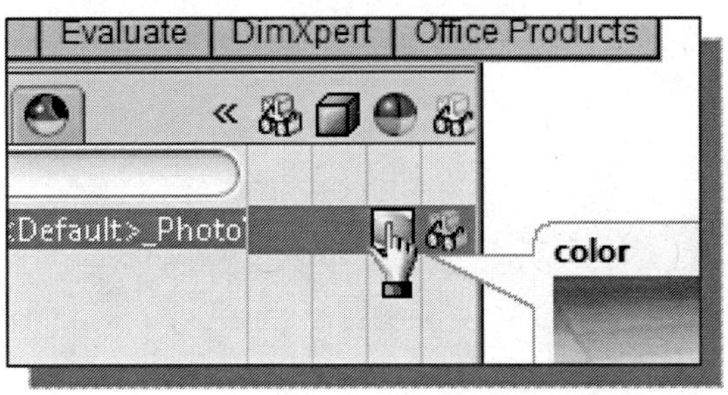

6. Click on the **Color** icon to show the available options.

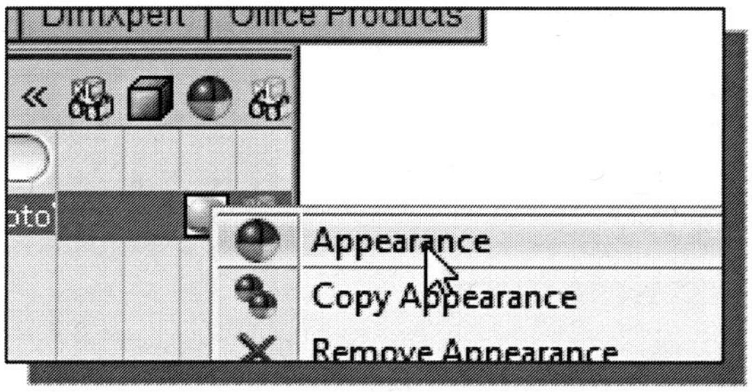

7. Choose **Appearance** in the available option list as shown.

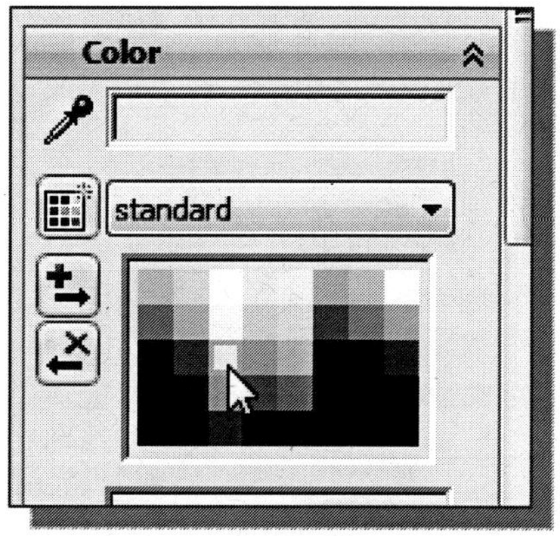

8. In the *Color* option panel, set the color to **yellow**.

9. Click **OK** to accept the settings.

10. On your own, activate the **Show Transparency** option.

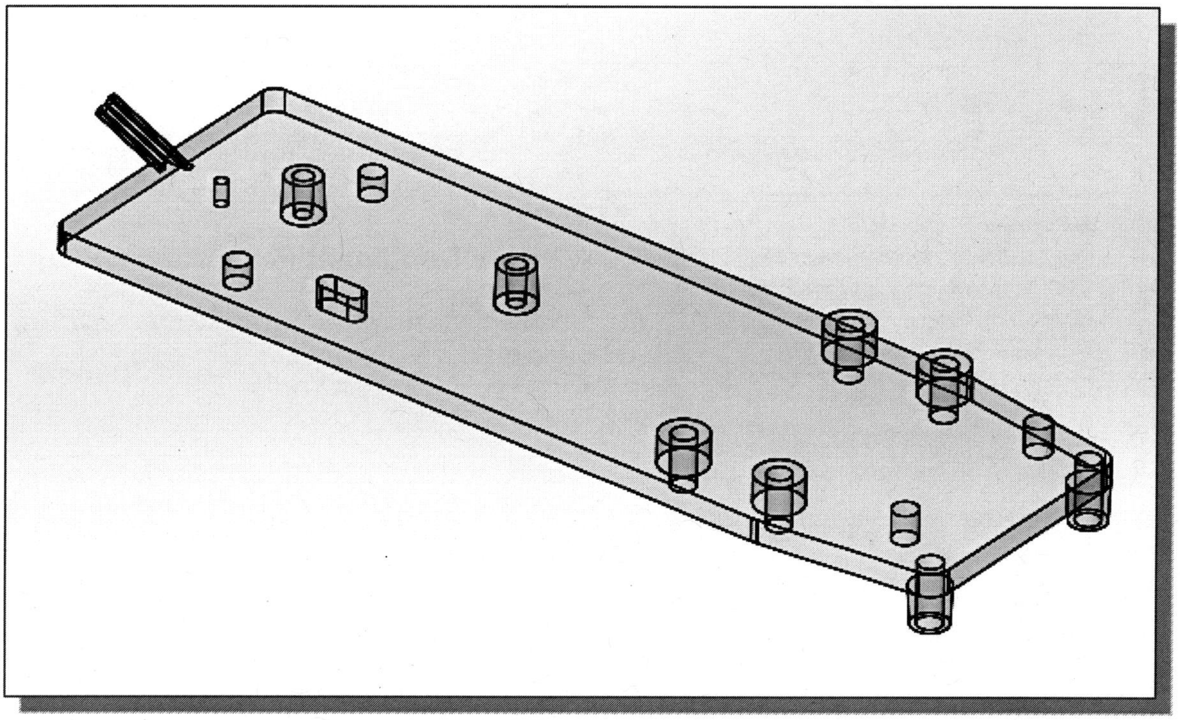

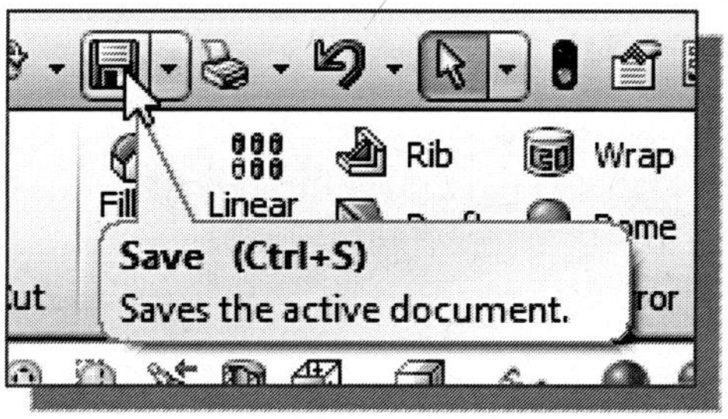

11. In the *Quick Access* toolbar, click the **Save** button to save the model.

Create another Metric Template

1. Select the **New** icon with a single click of the left-mouse-button on the *Menu Bar*.

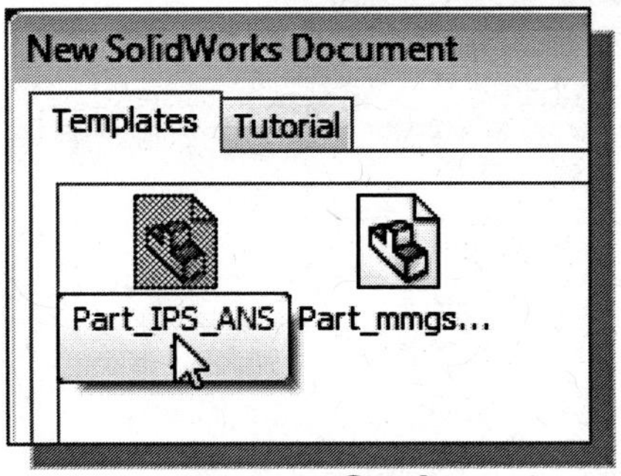

2. Select the **Part_IPS_ANSI** template as shown.

3. Click on the **OK** button to open a new document using the Part_IPS_ANSI template.

4. Select the **Options** icon from the *Menu* toolbar to open the *Options* dialog box.

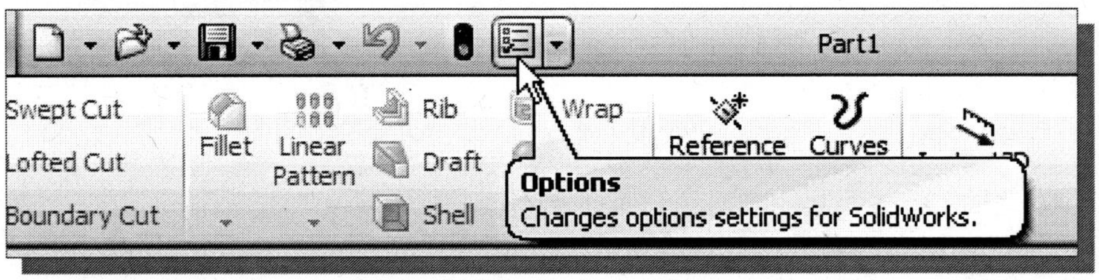

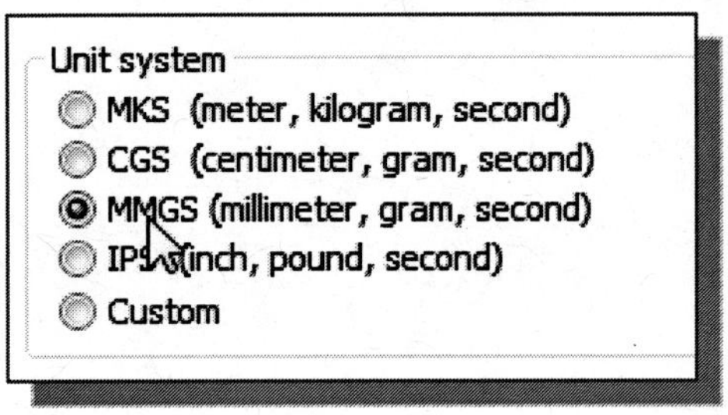

5. Select the **Document Properties** tab.

6. Set the *Units* to **MMGS (millimeter, gram, second)** as shown.

7. Click the arrow next to the **Save** icon in the *Menu Bar* to reveal the save options and select **Save As**.

8. Under *Save as type*, select **Part Templates (*.prtdot)**. Notice the browser automatically goes to the default *templates* folder.

9. Save the template using the *File name* **Part_mmgs_ANSI**, and close the file.

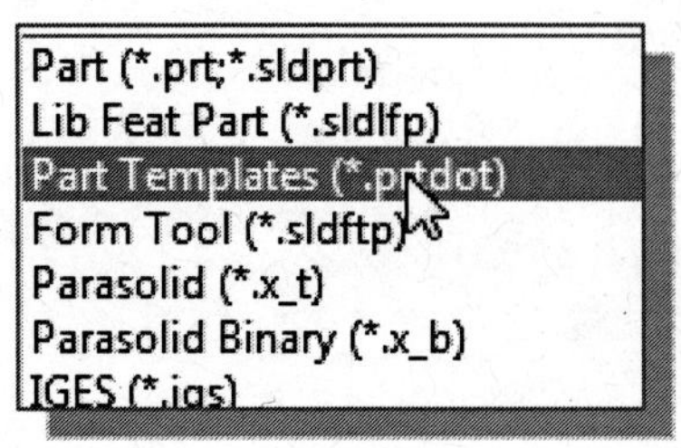

The *Crank-Right* Part

1. Select the **New** icon with a single click of the left-mouse-button on the *Menu Bar*.

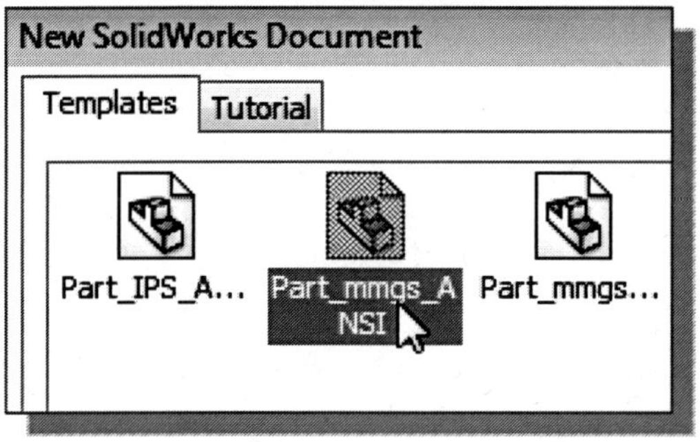

2. Notice the **three template files** appear in the **Advanced** mode. Select the **Part_mmgs_ANSI** template as shown.

3. Click on the **OK** button to open a new document using the selected template.

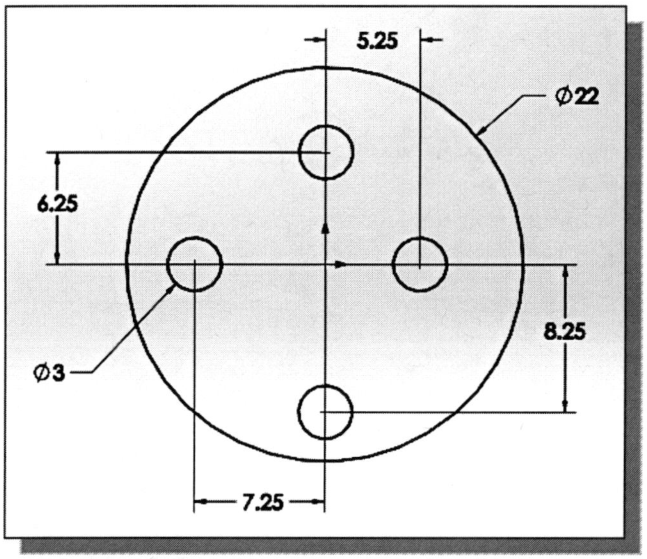

4. Create the base extrude feature, **2mm**, starting on one of the datum planes.

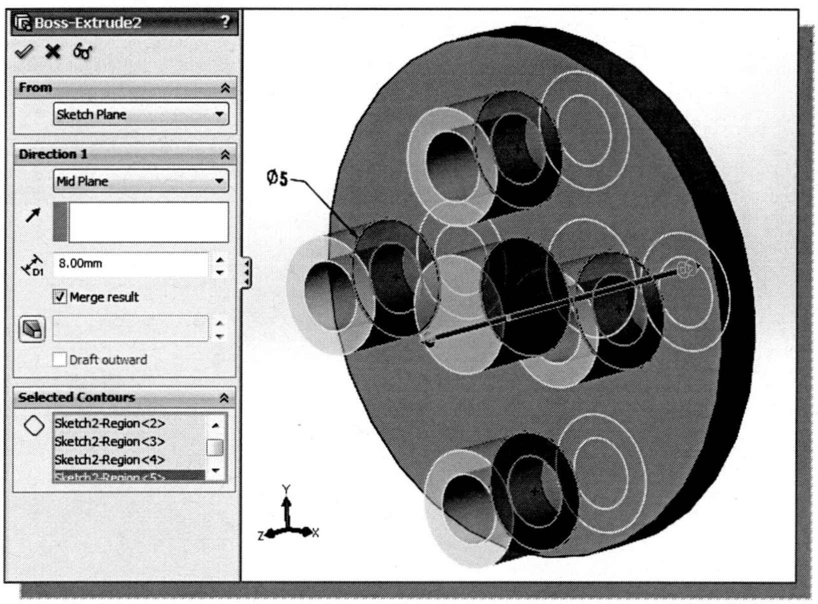

5. Create five diameter **5.0 mm** circles, coinciding with the five existing center points, and extrude **8 mm** using the **Mid Plane** option.

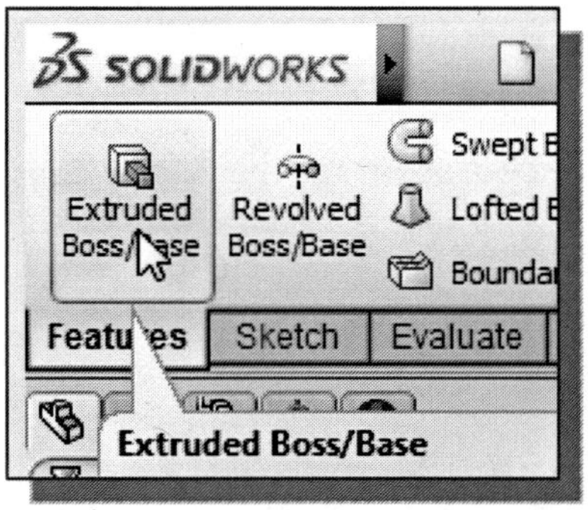

6. In the *Features* toolbar select the **Extruded Boss/ Base** command by clicking once with the left-mouse-button on the icon.

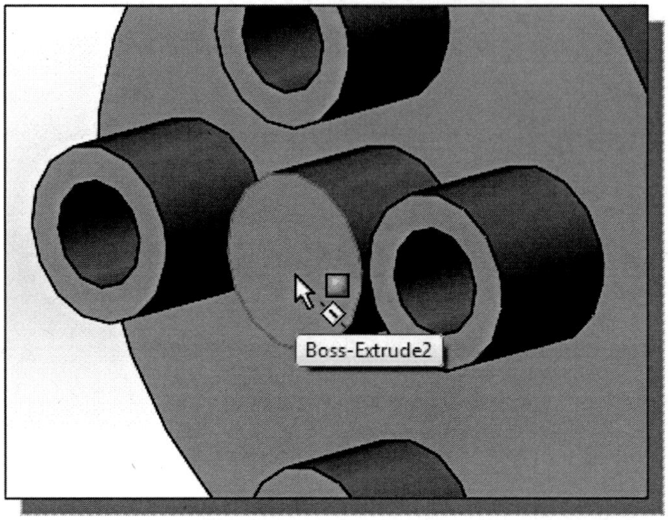

7. Select the **front face** of the center cylinder by clicking on the plane as shown.

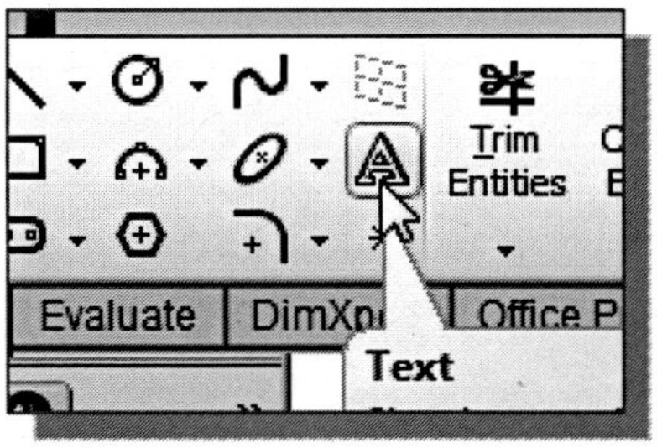

8. On the center cylinder, use the **Text** command and create the letter **R**.

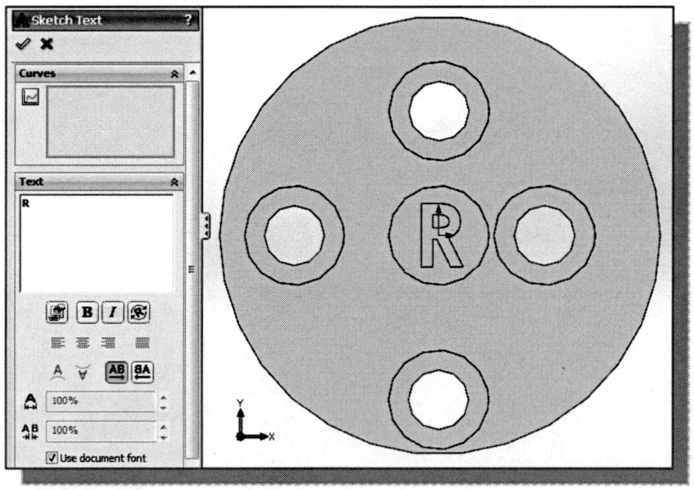

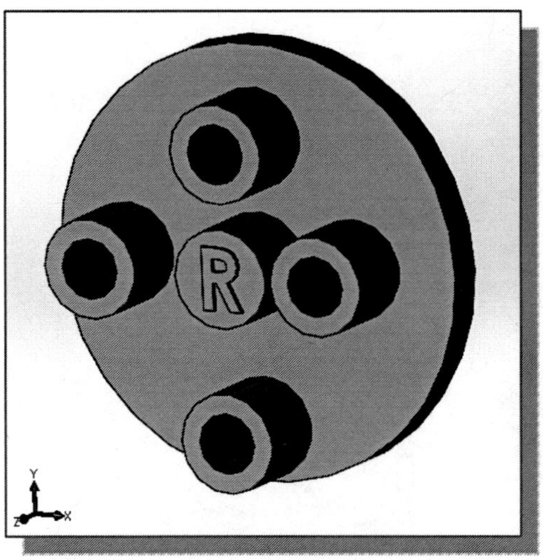

9. Create the **0.2 mm** extruded feature as shown.

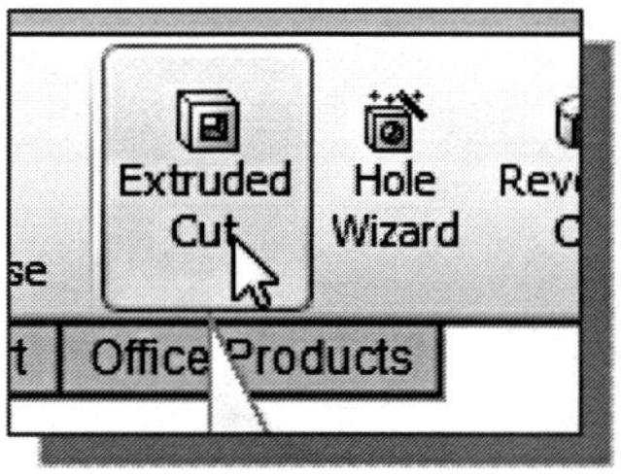

10. In the *Features* toolbar select the **Extruded Cut** command by clicking once with the left-mouse-button on the icon.

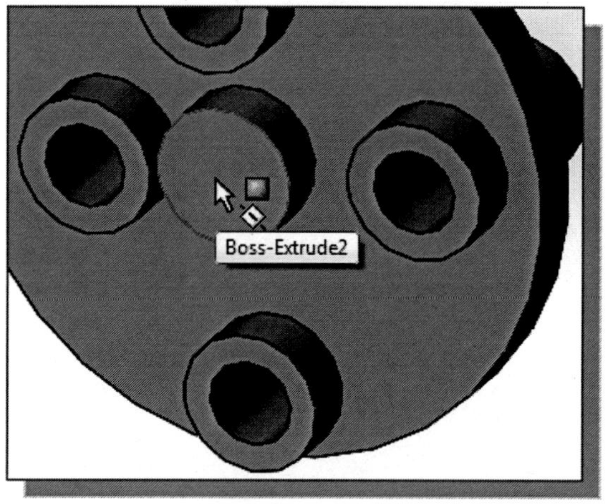

11. Select the **back face** of the center cylinder by clicking on the surface as shown.

12. Create a hexagonal cut feature, flat to flat distance **2.5 mm**, depth **4 mm** as shown.

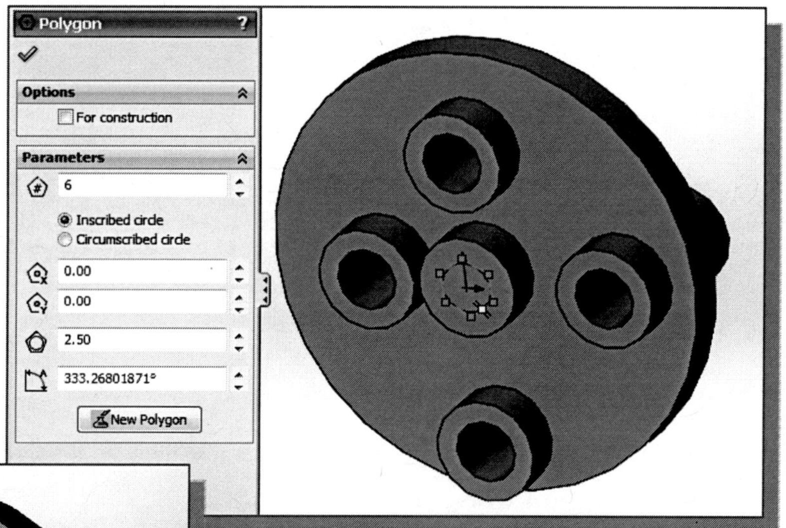

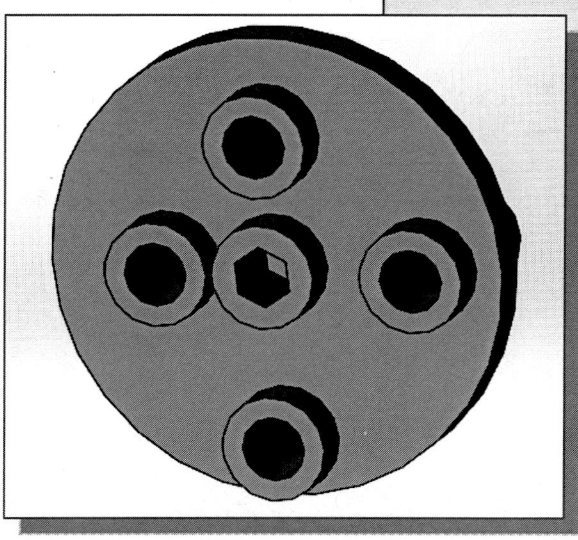

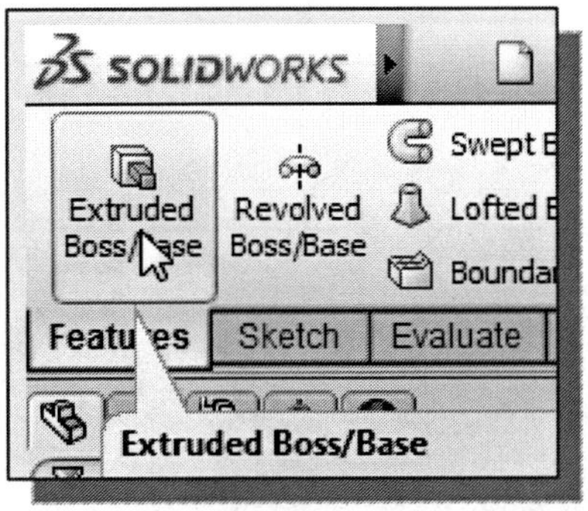

13. In the *Features* toolbar select the **Extruded Boss/ Base** command by clicking once with the left-mouse-button on the icon.

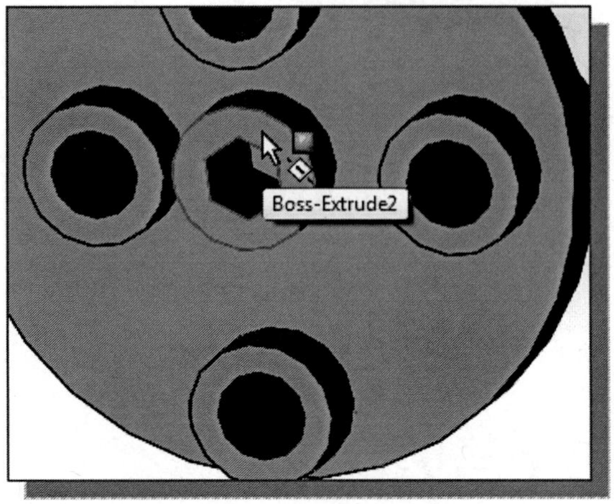

14. Select the **back face** of the center cylinder by clicking on the surface as shown.

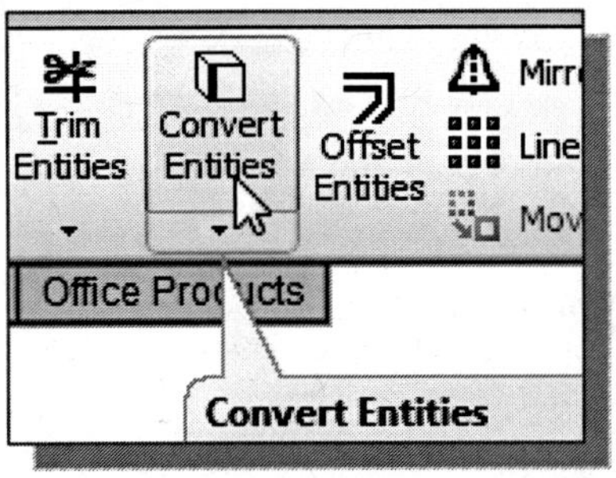

15. Select **Convert Entities** in the *Sketch* toolbar and project the hexagon and circle.

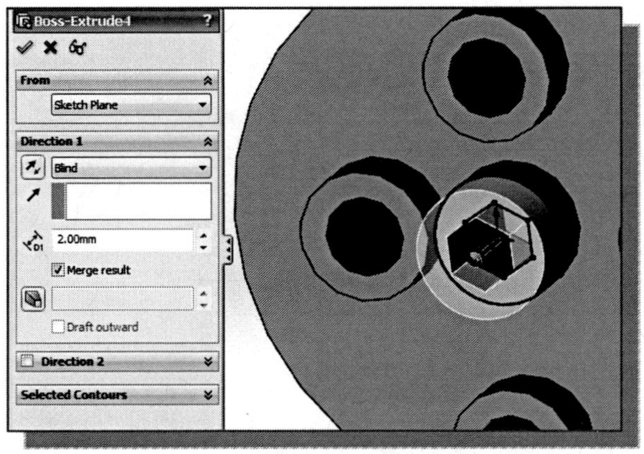

16. On your own, extend the center cylindrical feature by **2 mm**.

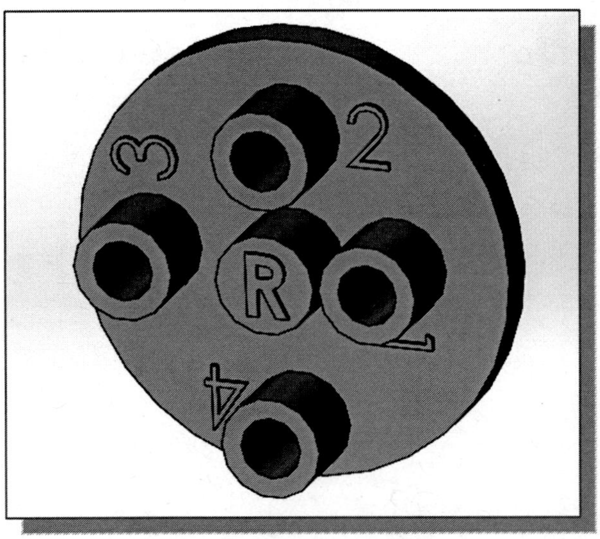

17. Create the extruded labels next to the holes.

18. Save the model using filename **A9-Crank-Right**.

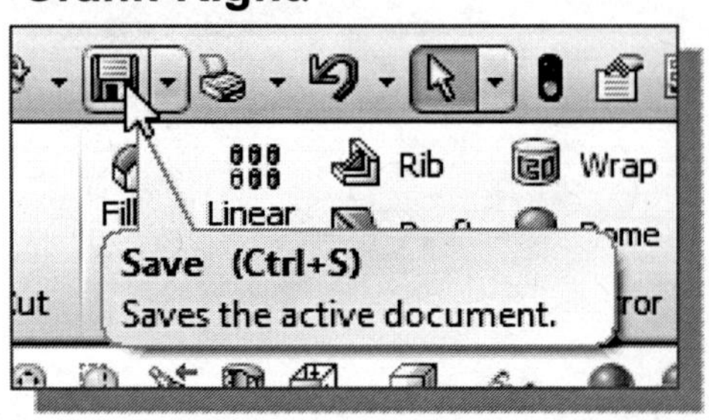

The *A10-Crank Left* Part

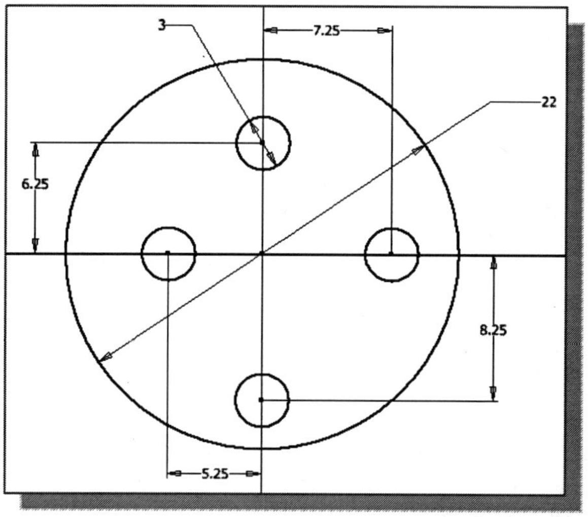

1. Start a new **Metric (mm)** model using the **Part_mmgs_ANSI** template.

2. Create the base extruded **2 mm** feature, starting on one of the datum planes.

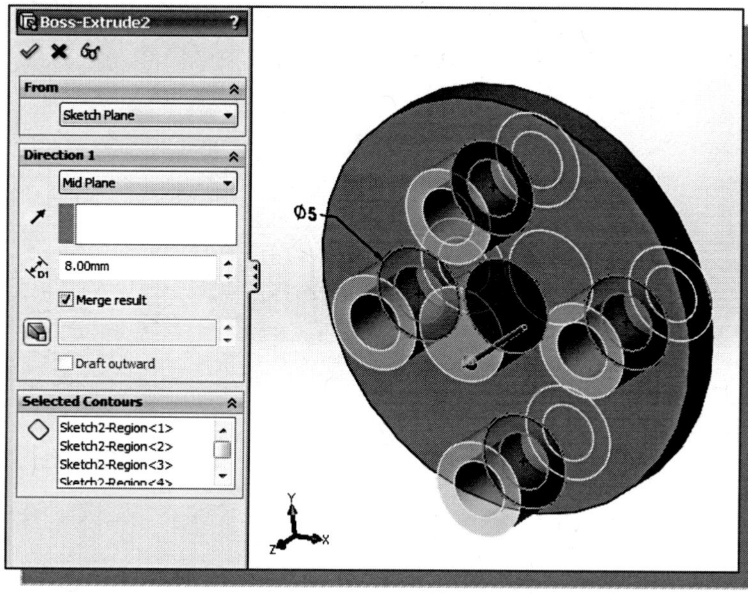

3. Create five diameter **5.0 mm** circles, coinciding with the five existing center points, and extrude **8 mm** using the **Mid Plane** option.

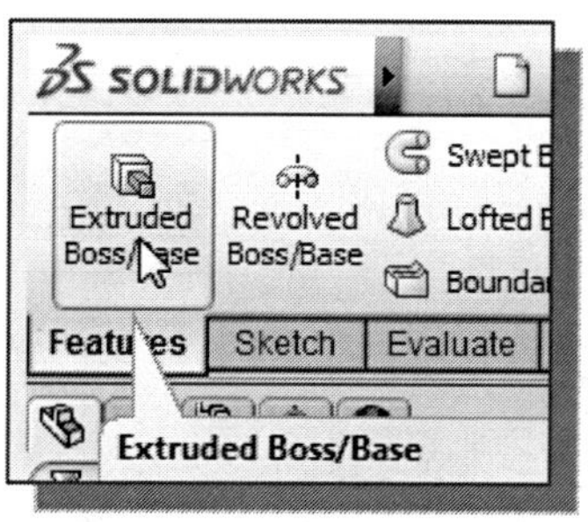

4. On the center cylinder, use the **Text** and **Extrude** commands to create the letter **L** extruded feature, depth **0.2 mm**.

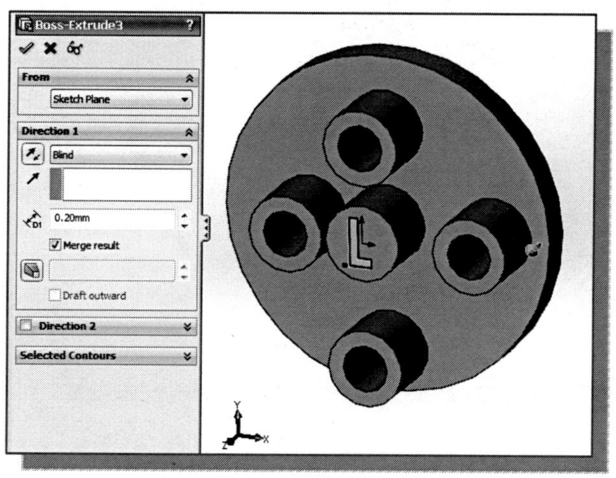

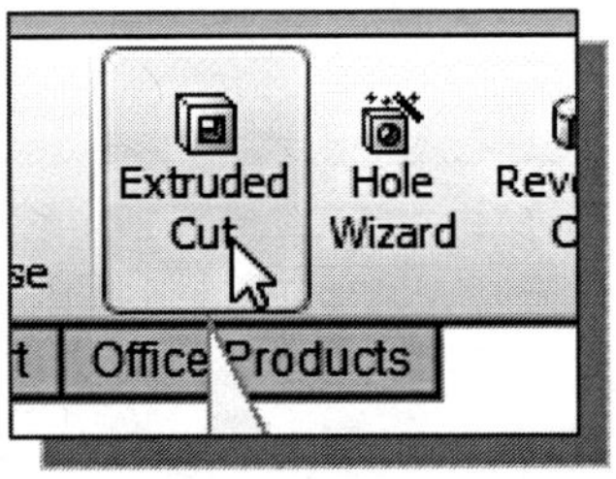

5. Create a hexagonal cut feature on the back side, flat to flat distance **2.5 mm, 4 mm** depth as shown.

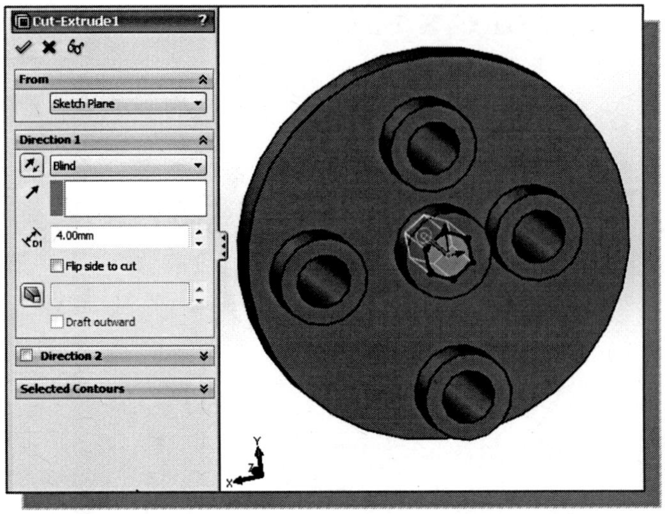

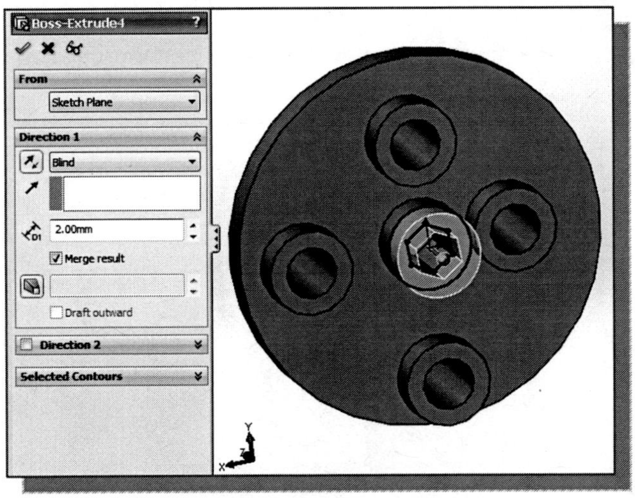

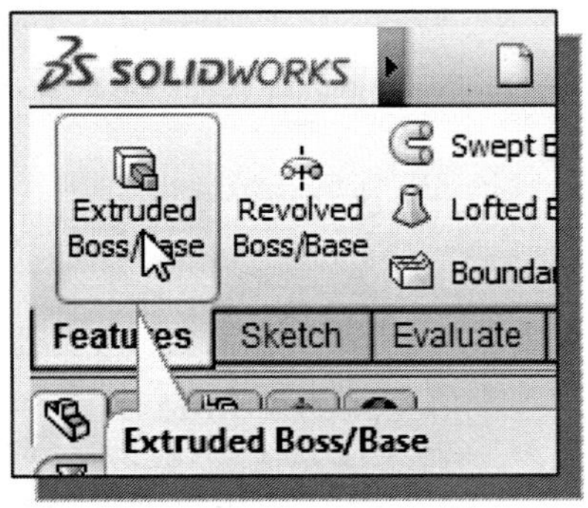

6. Extend the center cylindrical feature by **2 mm**.

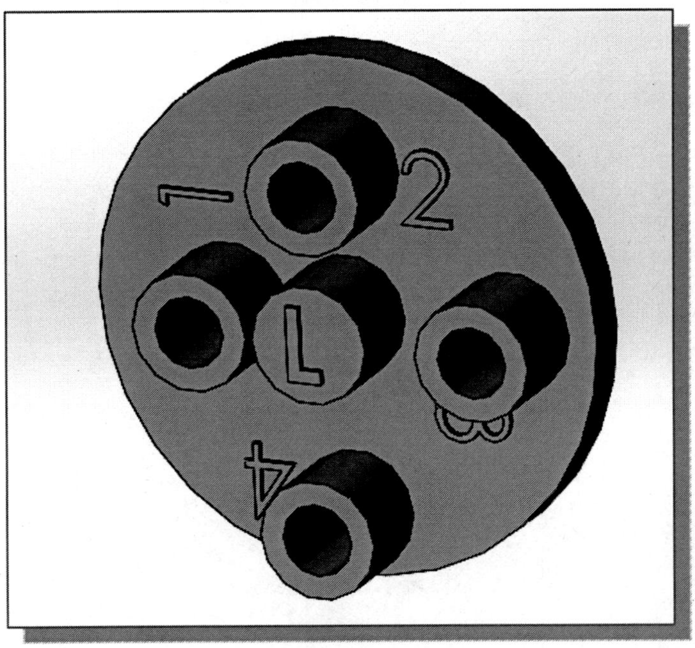

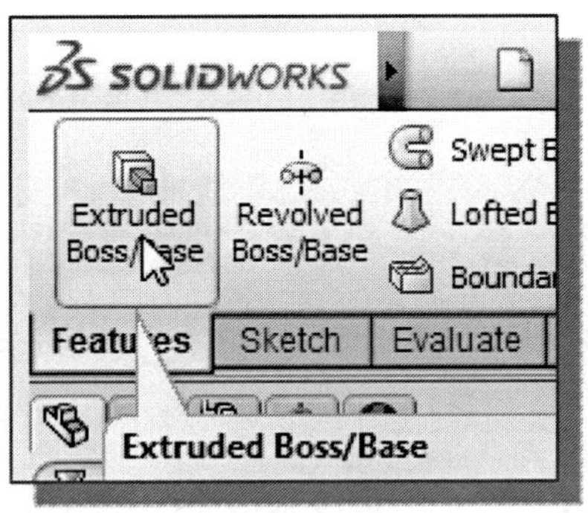

7. Create the extruded labels next to the holes.

8. Save the model using filename **A10-Crank-Left**.

The *Motor*

1. Start a new **Metric (mm)** model using the **Part_mmgs_ANSI** template.

2. Create the following 2D sketch on the **Front** datum plane.

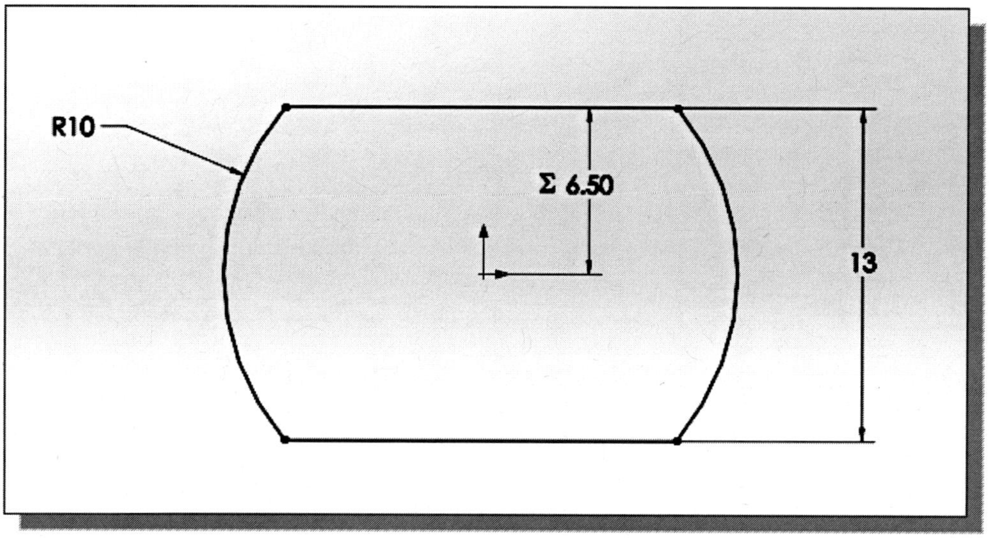

3. Create the base extruded feature, **Mid Plane**, depth **25 mm**, as shown.

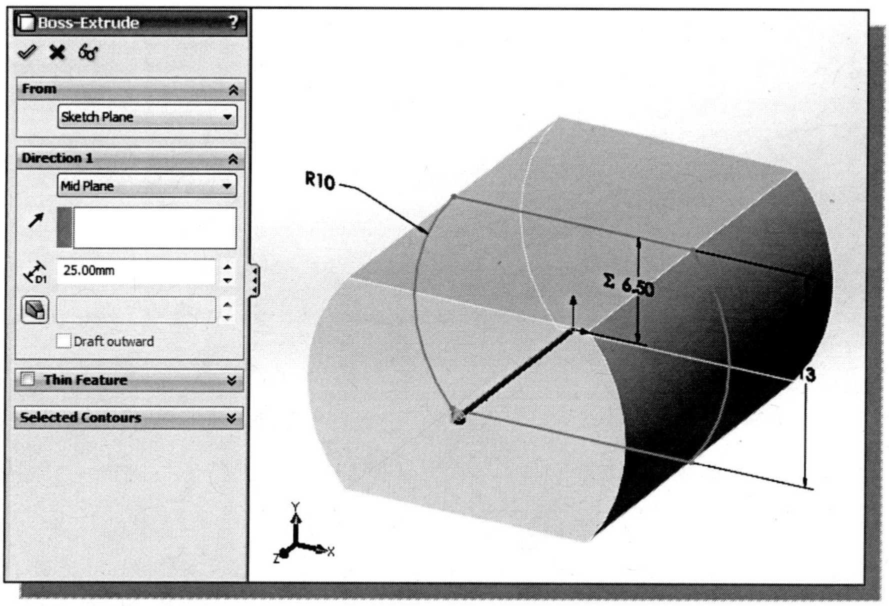

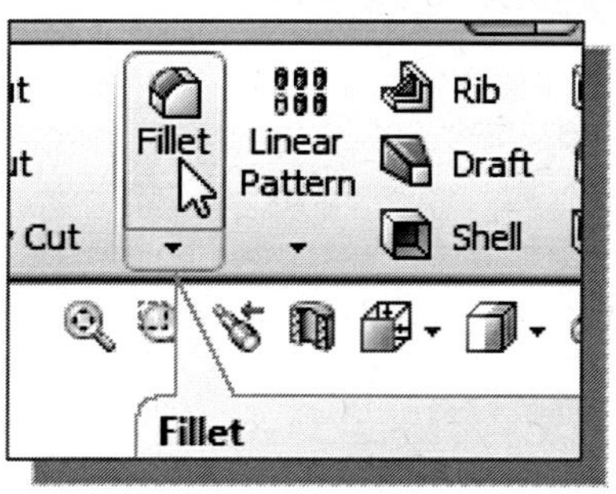

4. In the *Sketch* toolbar, select the **Fillet** command by clicking the left-mouse-button on the icon.

5. Enter **2.5 mm** as the radius value, and select the **four arcs** to set the fillets as shown.

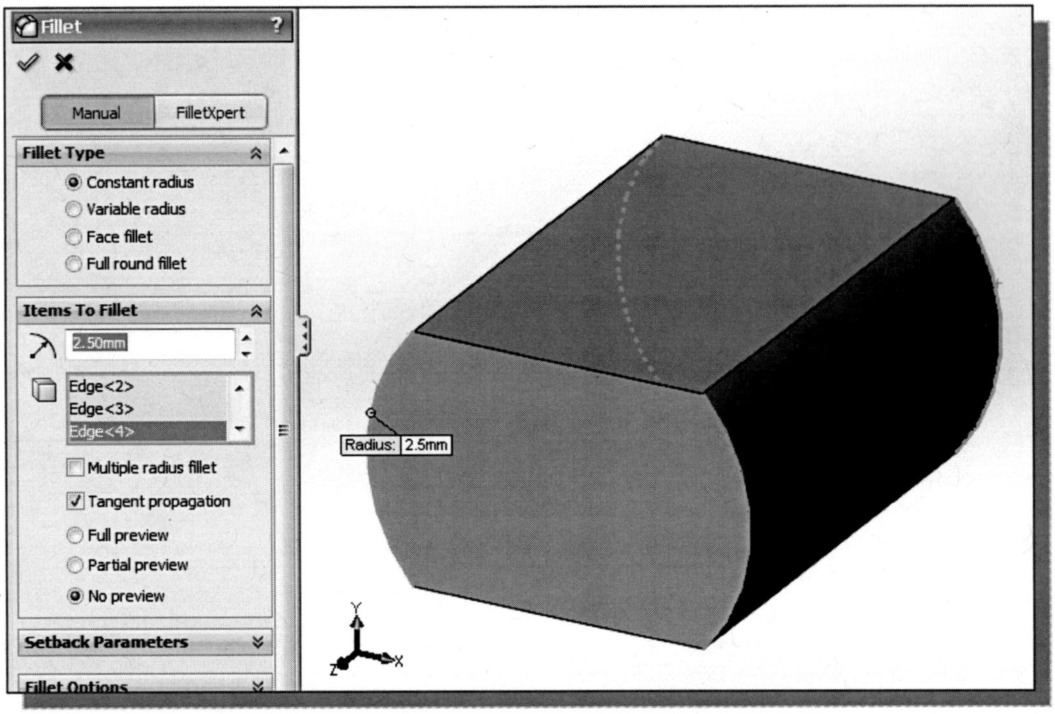

6. On your own, create another fillet feature, radius **0.6 mm**, on the top and bottom surfaces of the model as shown.

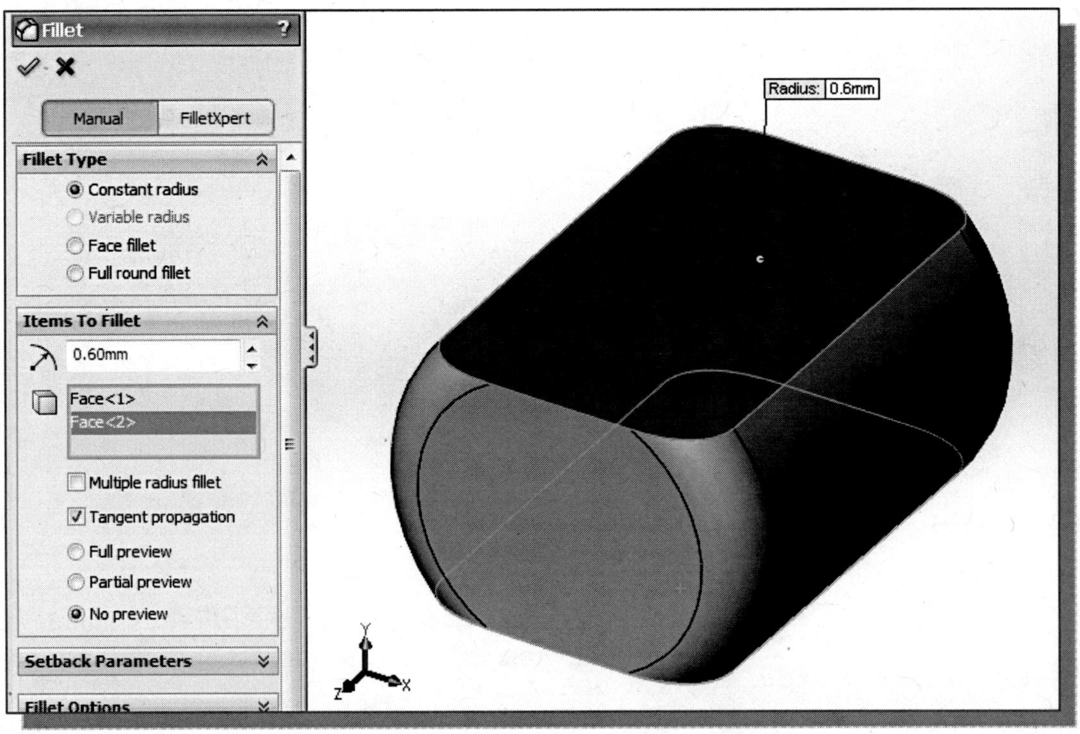

7. Create a circular extruded feature, diameter **6 mm** and depth **1.5 mm** as shown.

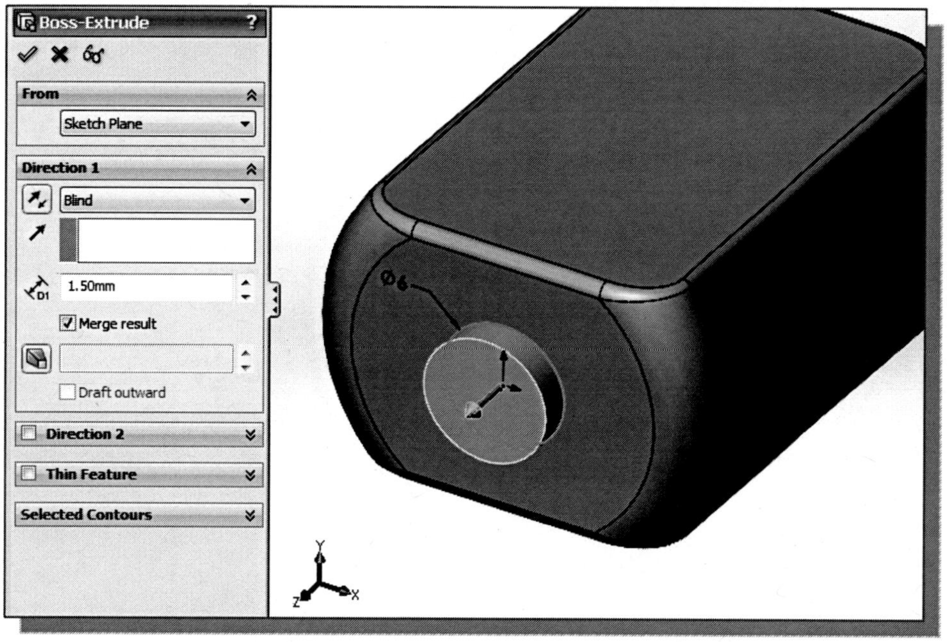

8. On your own, create the shaft portion of the **Motor**; the diameter is **2 mm** and the depth is **7.5** mm as shown.

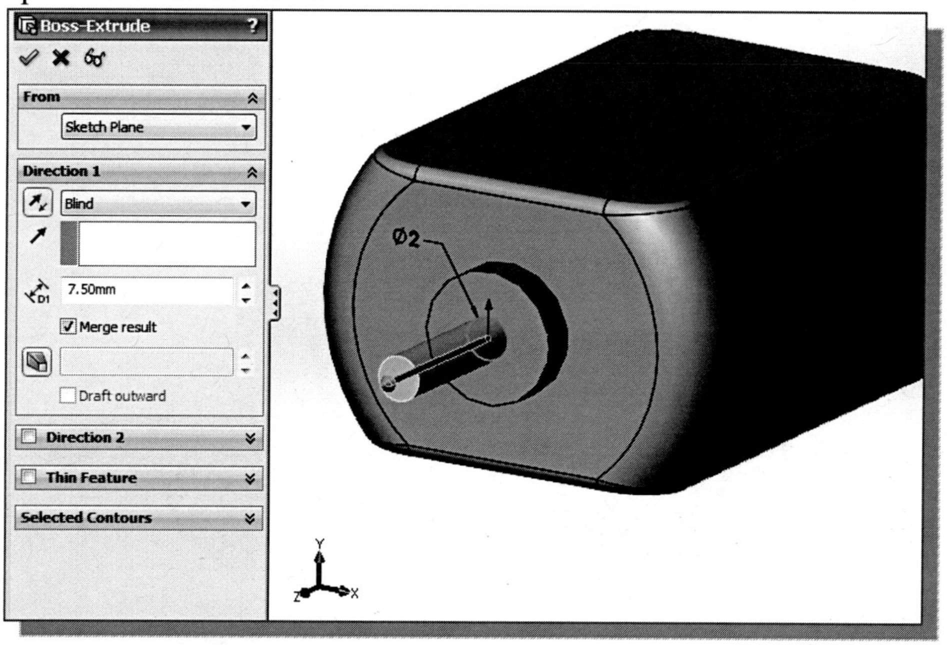

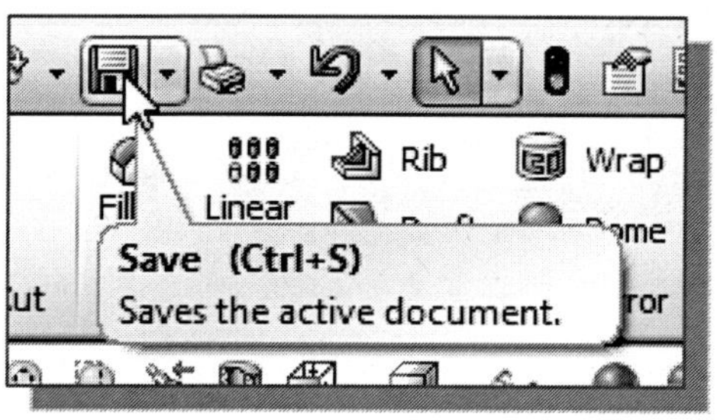

9. In the *Quick Access* menu, select **Save** to save the current model to disk.

10. On your own, save the model using filename **Motor**.

The *A1-Axle End Cap* Part

1. Start a new **Metric (mm)** model using the **Part_mmgs_ANSI** template.

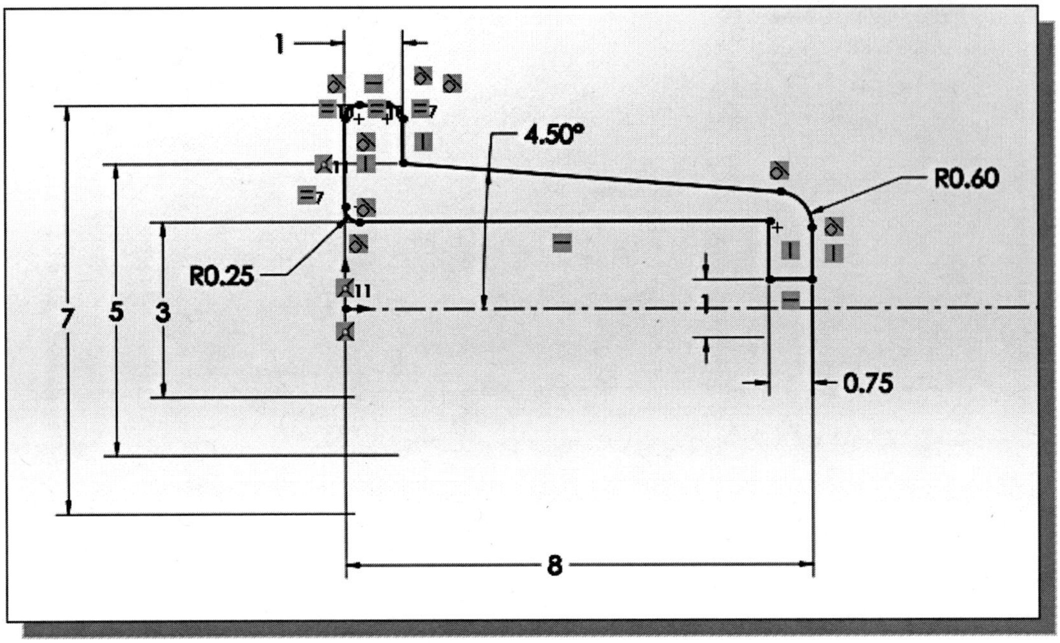

2. Create the base **revolved 360 degrees** feature, starting on the **Top** datum plane.

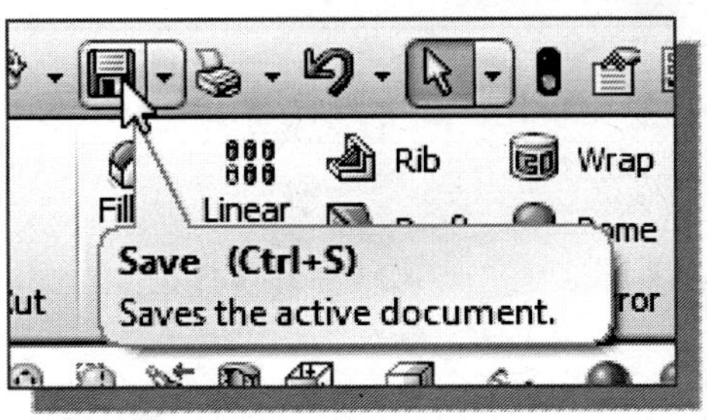

3. Save the model using filename **A1-Axle-EndCap**.

The *Hex Shaft Collar* Part

1. Start a new **Metric (mm)** model using the **Part_mmgs_ANSI** template.

2. Create a new **Extruded Feature** on the **Right** datum plane.

3. Use the **Polygon** command and create two six-sided hexagons, with the centers aligned to the *Origin*, as shown.

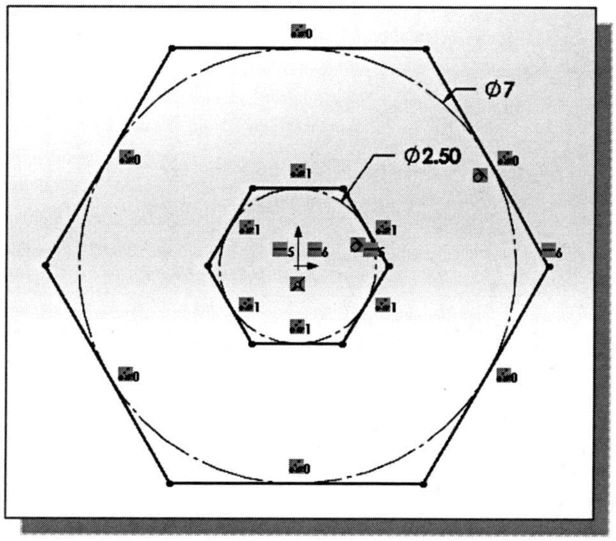

4. On your own, extrude **5 mm** using the **Mid Plane** option.

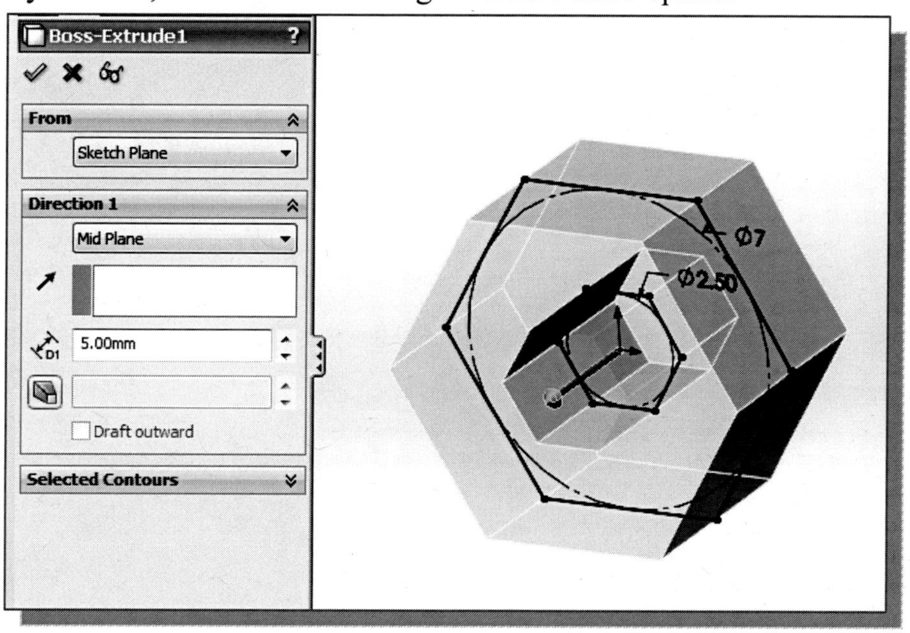

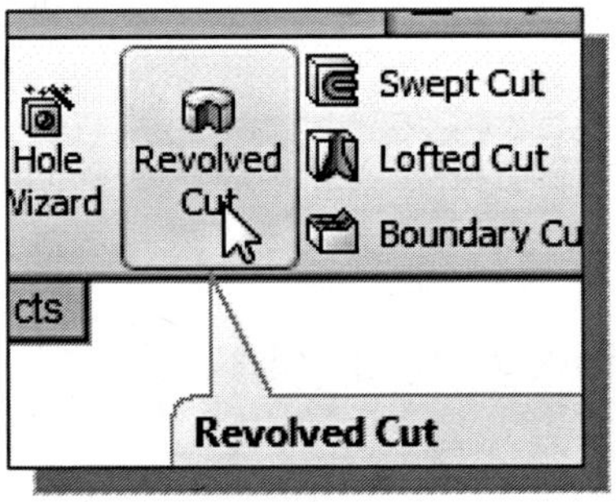

5. In the *Features* toolbar select the **Revolved Cut** command by clicking once with the left-mouse-button on the icon.

6. Pick the **Front** datum plane to align the *sketching plane*.

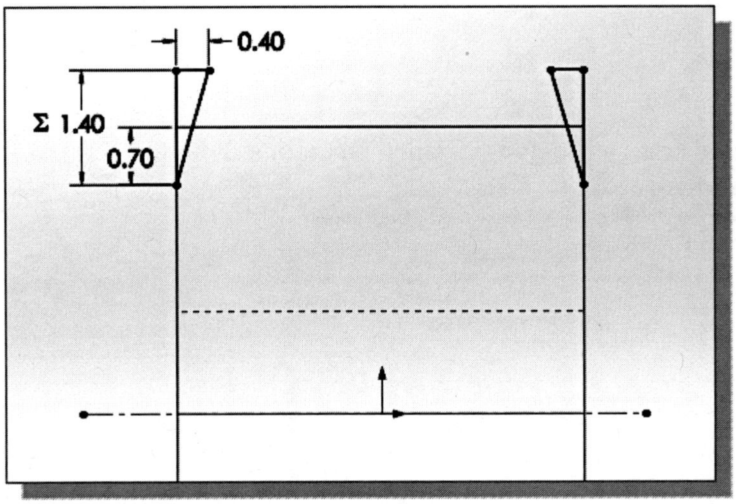

7. Create two same-sized triangles aligned to the **top edge** and the **adjacent edges** using the three dimensions as shown.

8. Create a **centerline** aligned to the *Origin* of the coordinate system.

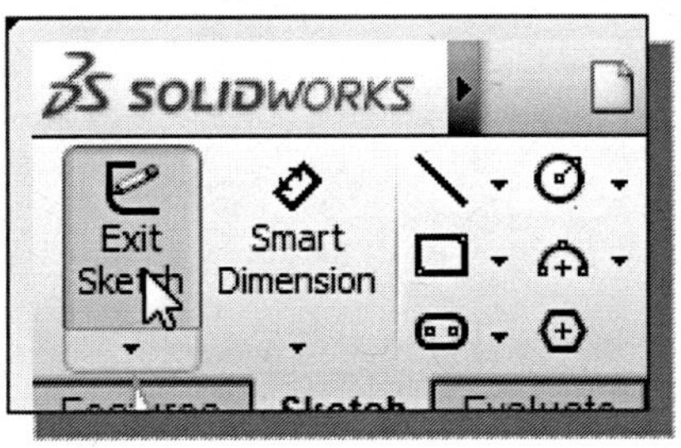

9. Select **Exit Sketch** in the *Sketch* toolbar to exit *Sketch* mode.

10. Create the revolved cut feature by selecting the two triangular regions as shown.

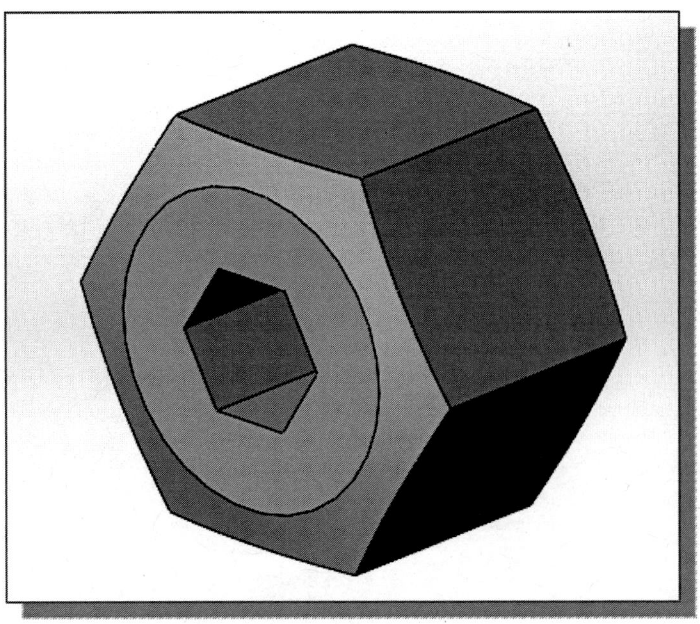

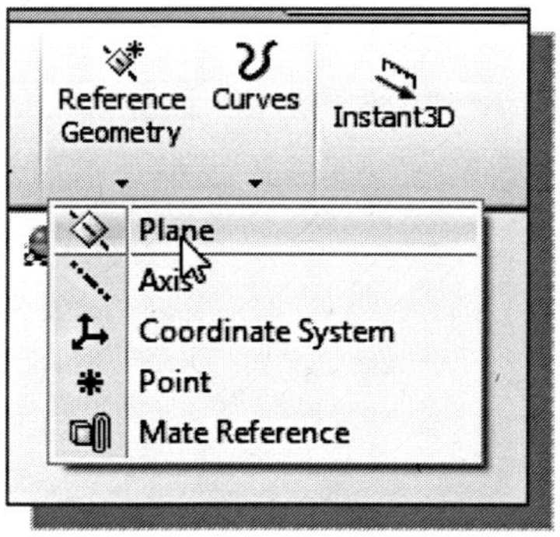

11. Use the **Reference Plane** command and create an **Offset** reference plane feature that is **17.86 mm** away from the front face of the base feature.

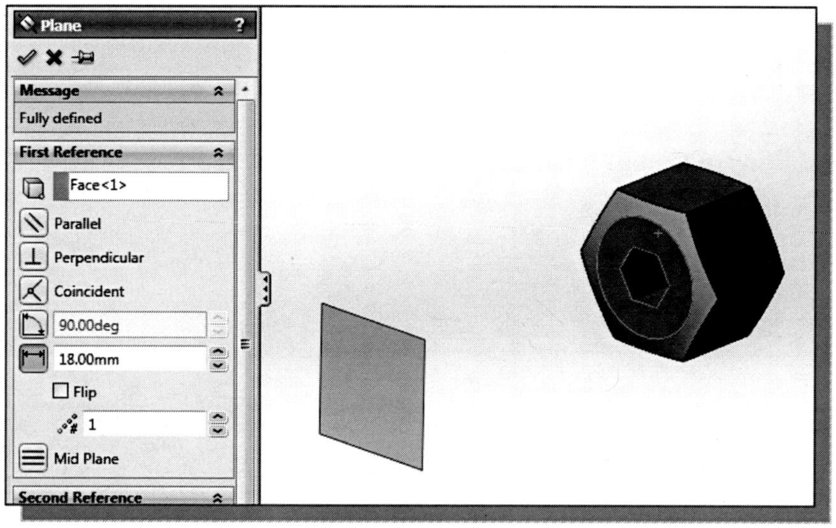

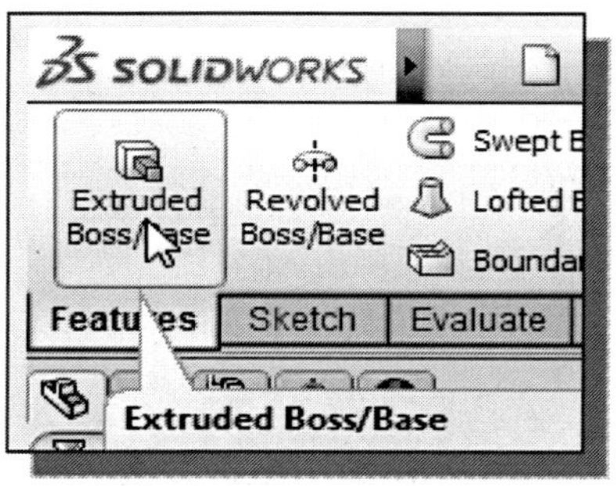

12. In the *Features* toolbar select the **Extruded Boss/ Base** command by clicking once with the left-mouse-button on the icon.

13. Select the new **reference plane** to align the sketching plane.

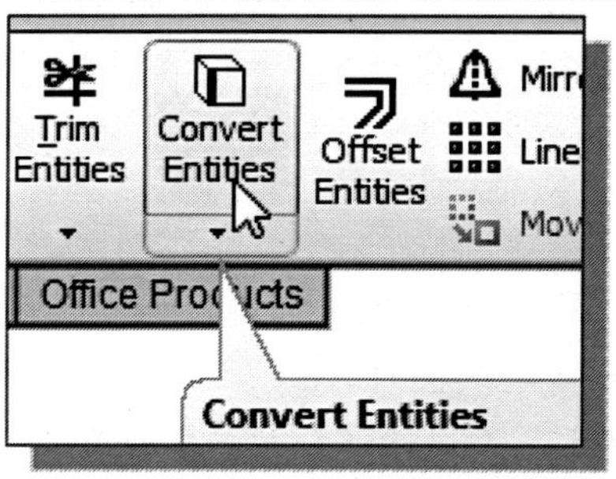

14. Select **Convert Entities** in the *Sketch* toolbar and project **six edges of the inside hexagon** onto the sketch plane as shown.

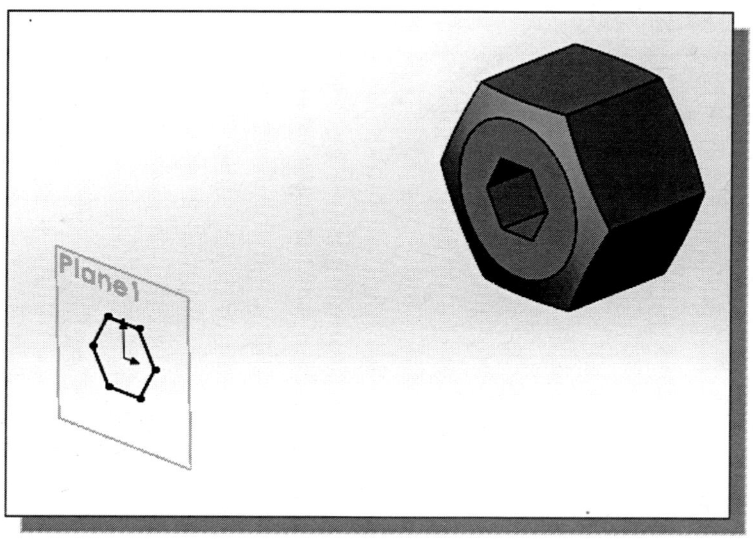

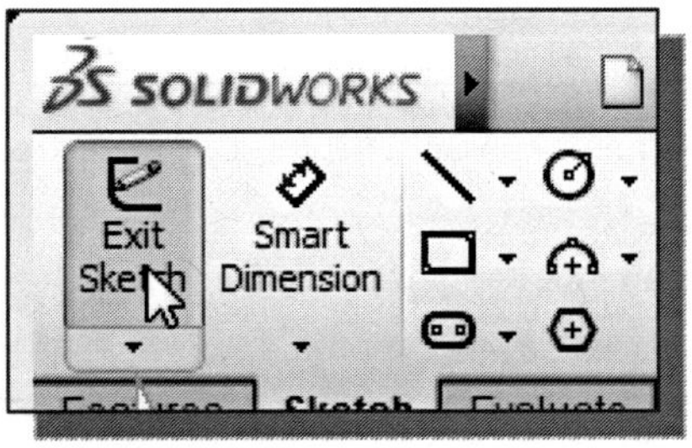

15. Select **Exit Sketch** in the *Sketch* toolbar to exit *Sketch* mode.

16. Set the extrude distance to **49.5mm** and create the feature as shown.

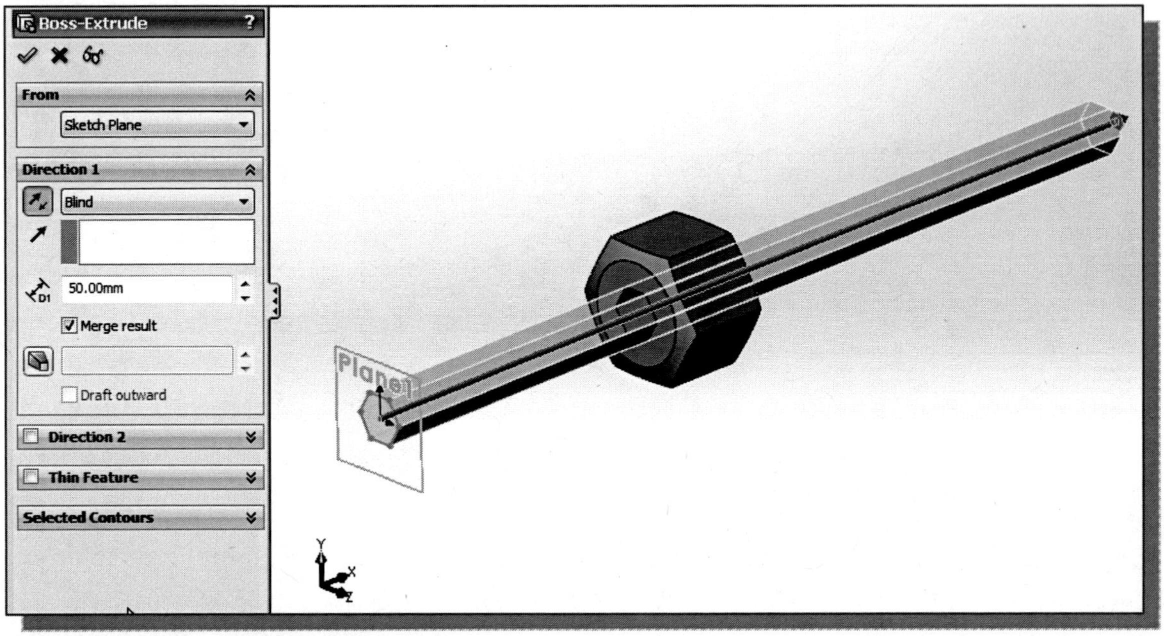

17. Click on the **OK** button to accept the settings and create the solid feature.

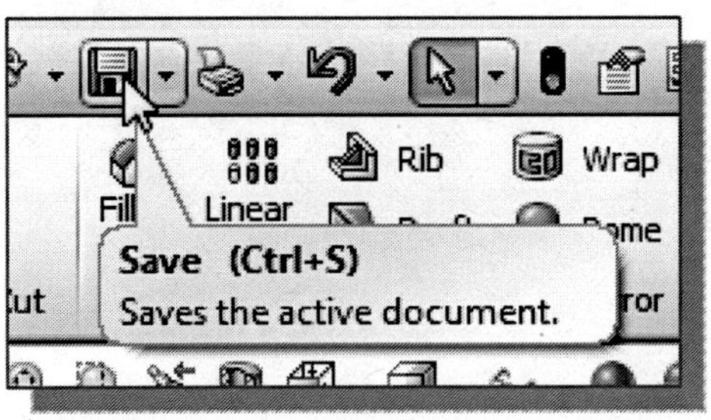

18. In the *Quick Access* menu, select **Save** to save the current model to disk.

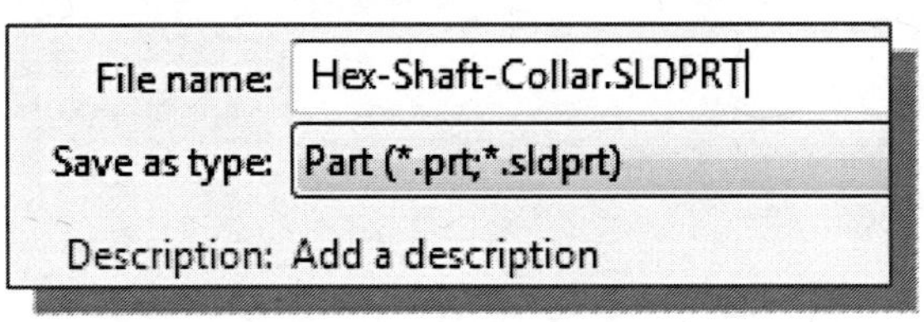

19. On your own, save the model using the filename **Hex-Shaft-Collar**.

The *A8-Rod Pin* Part

1. Start a new **Metric (mm)** model using the **Part_mmgs_ANSI** template.

2. Create the base **revolved 360 degrees** feature, starting on one of the datum planes.

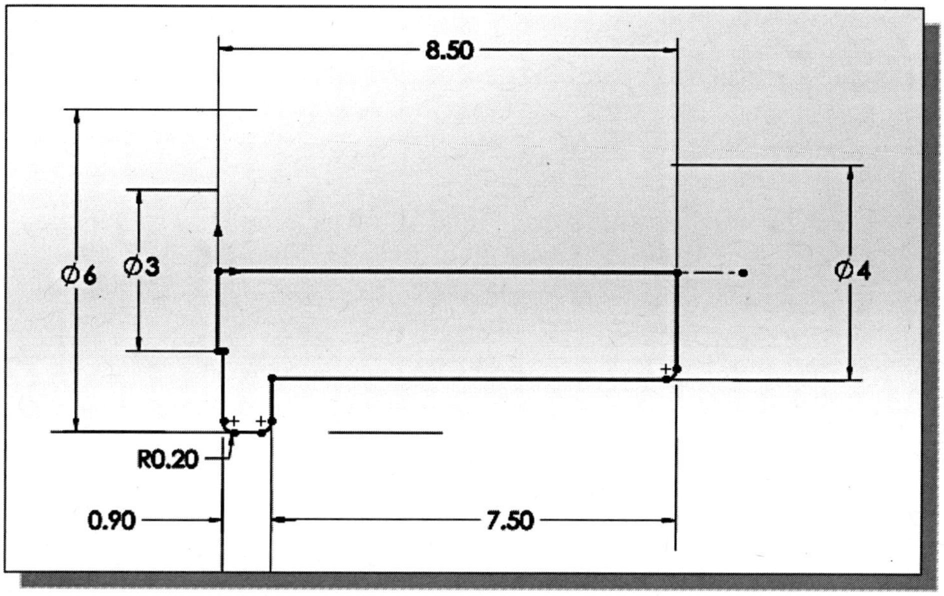

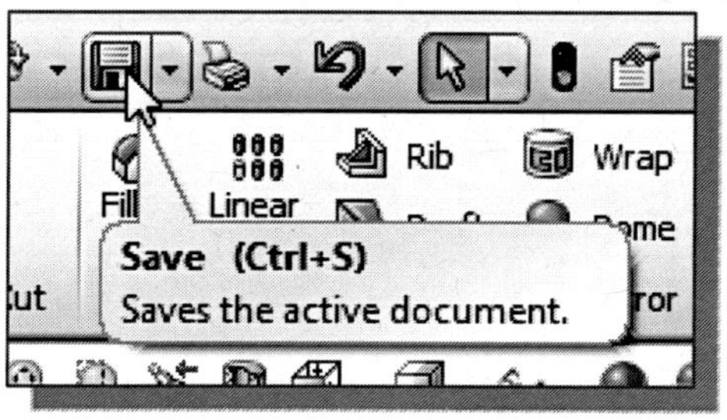

3. Save the model using the filename **A8-RodPin**.

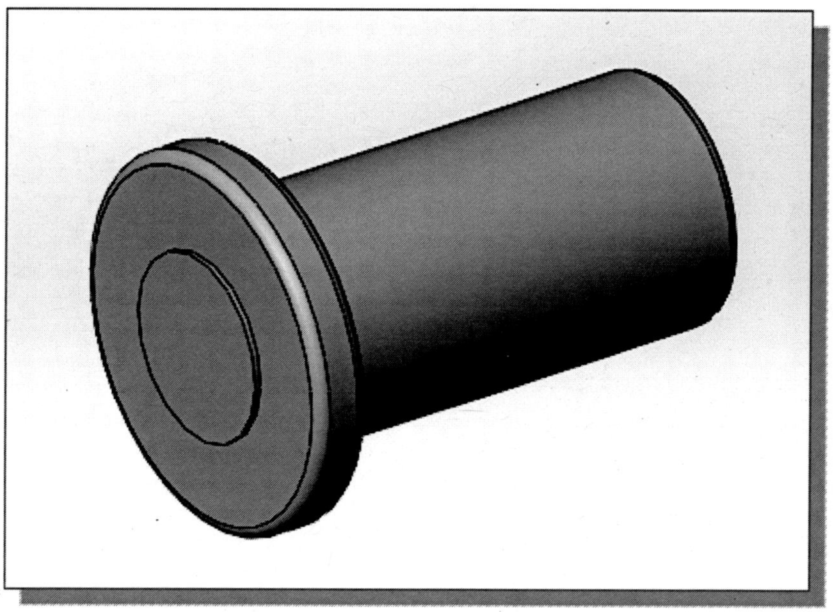

Questions:

1. What are the different types of *reference features* available in *SolidWorks*?
2. Why are *reference features* important in parametric modeling?
3. Can we create auxiliary views in 2D drawings?
4. Can we create a profile with extra 2D geometry entities in *SolidWorks*?
5. How do we access *SolidWorks's* **Edit Sketch** option?
6. What does the **Convert Entities** command allow us to do in *Sketch* mode?
7. What are the required elements to create a *revolved feature*?
8. How do we align the *sketch plane* of a selected entity to the screen?

Exercises:

1. **Rod Slide** (Dimensions are in inches.)

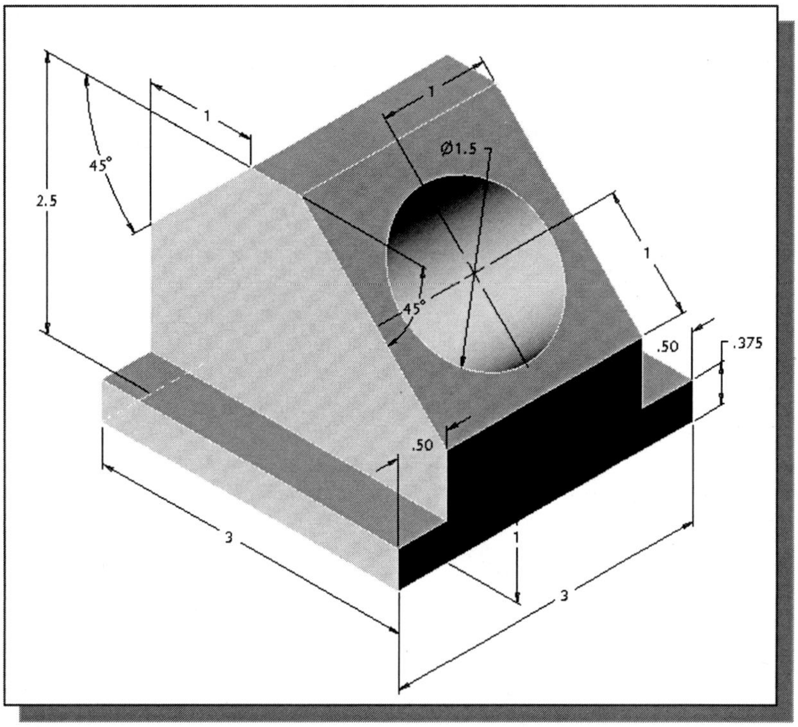

2. **Angle Support** (Dimensions are in millimeters.)

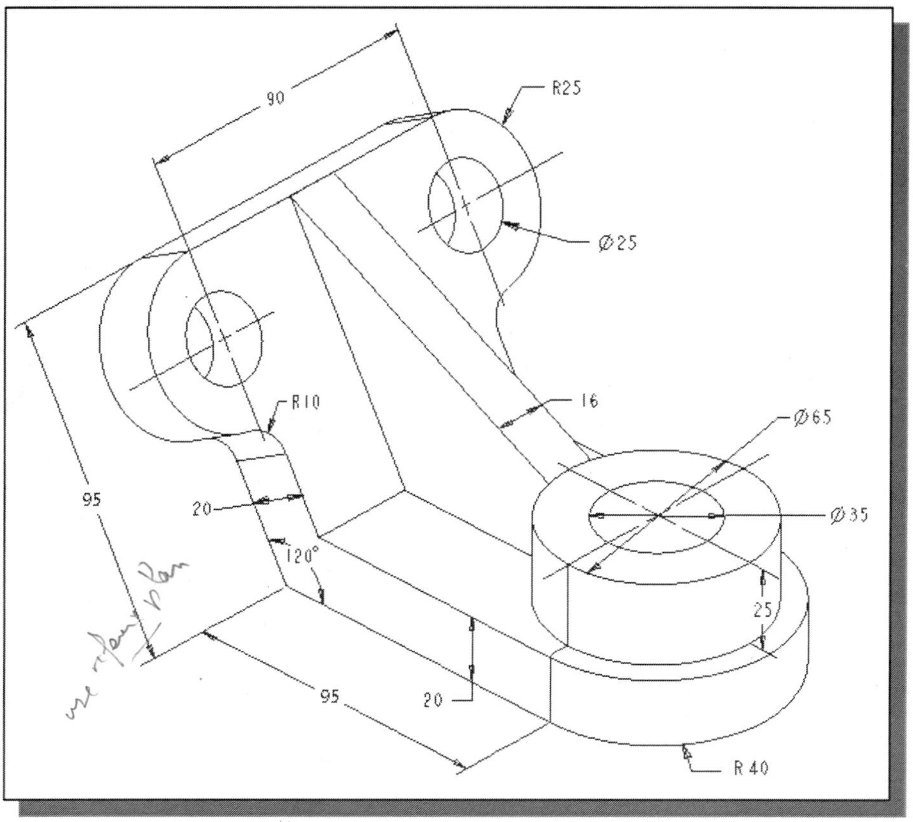

3. **Anchor Base** (Dimensions are in inches)

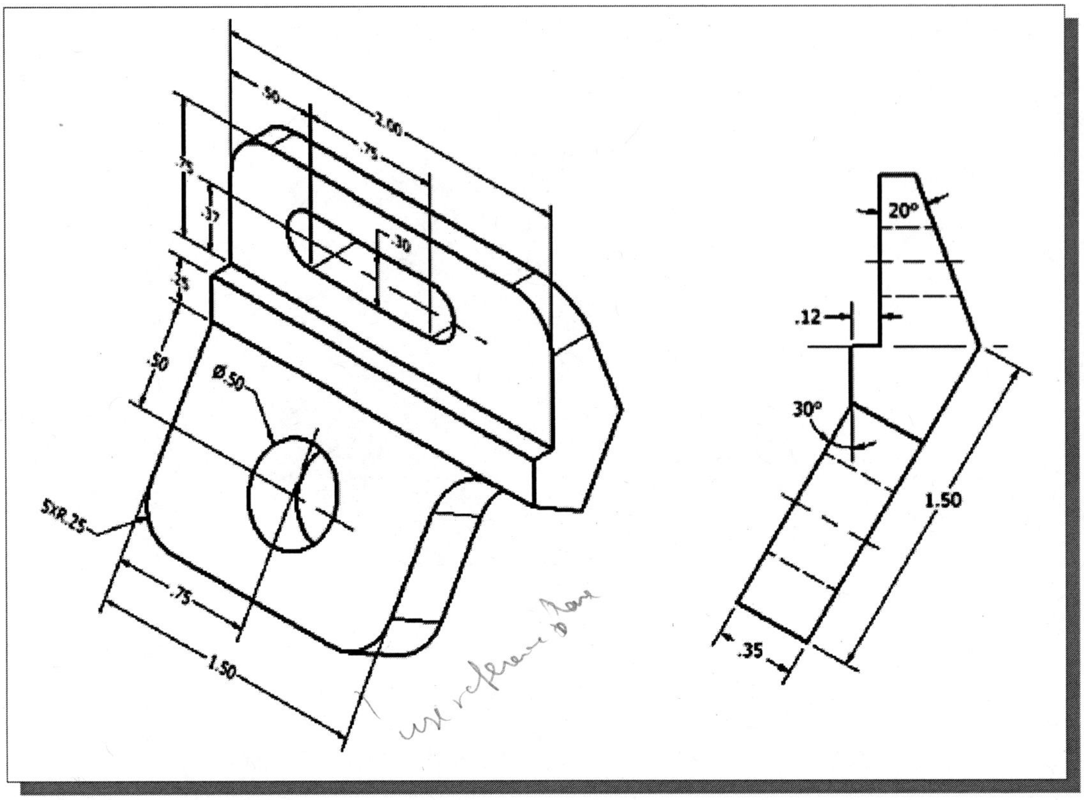

4. **Bevel Washer** (Dimensions are in inches)

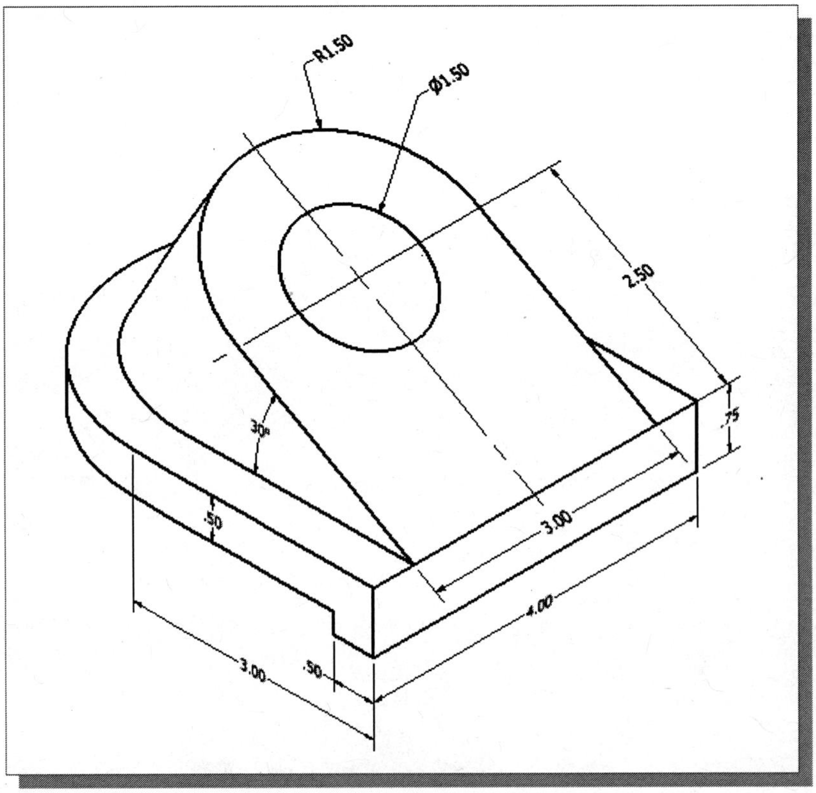

Chapter 8
Gears and SolidWorks Design Library

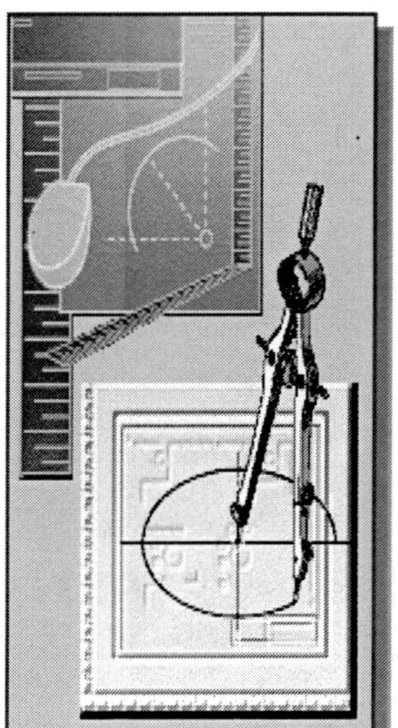

Learning Objectives

- ♦ **Understand the Gear Nomenclature**
- ♦ **Understand the Basic Usage of SolidWorks Design Library**
- ♦ **Use the SolidWorks Design Toolbox**
- ♦ **Use the Spur Gear Toolbox**
- ♦ **Export and Reuse the Tooth Profile**

Introduction to Gears

- A **gear** is a rotating machine part having cut *teeth*, which *mesh* with another toothed part in order to transmit mechanical motion and power. Two or more gears working in tandem are called a *gear train* and can produce a mechanical advantage through a designed gear ratio. Gears are very versatile machine elements; they range in size and use from tiny gears in watches to large driving gears in punch presses. Geared devices can be used to change the speed, torque, and direction of a power source. The most common situation is for a gear to mesh with another gear having parallel shaft axes; however a gear can also mesh with another toothed part in a way to producing motion in a nonparallel axis direction. The more commonly used types of gears include the **Spur Gear**, the **Bevel Gear**, the **Helical Gear**, the **Worm Gear** and the **Rack and Pinion**.

Spur Gear

Bevel Gear

Worm Gear

Helix Gear

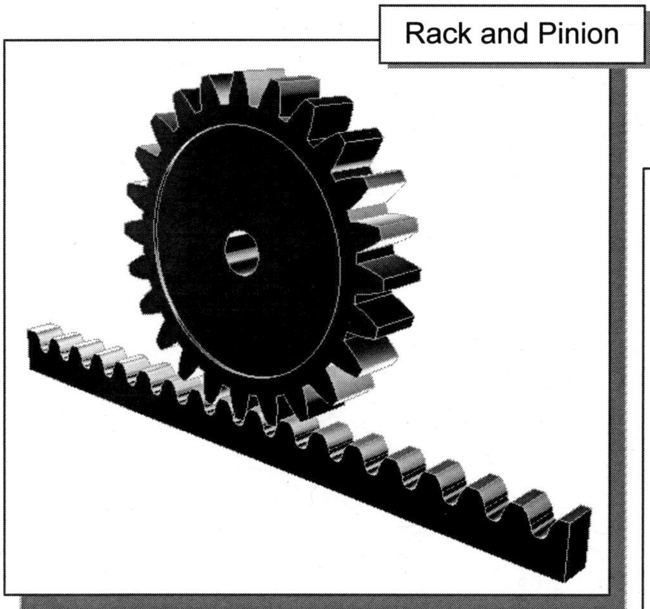

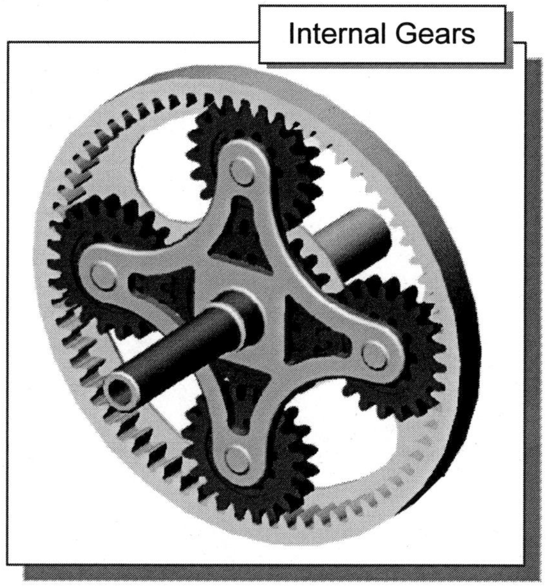

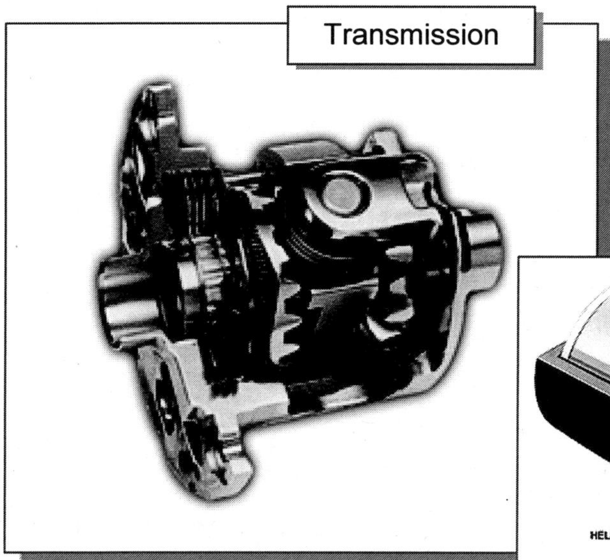

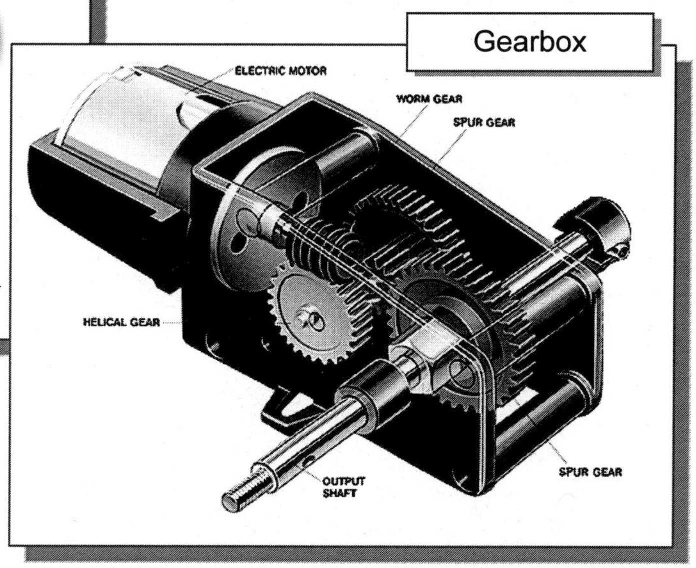

Two or more gears working in tandem are called a ***gear train*** and can produce a mechanical advantage through a designed gear ratio. For gears to function properly, they must fulfill the following basic requirements: (1) Transmit motion smoothly and efficiently; (2) Maintain fixed angular relationships between members; (3) Must be interchangeable with other gears having the same tooth size.

Spur Gear Nomenclatures

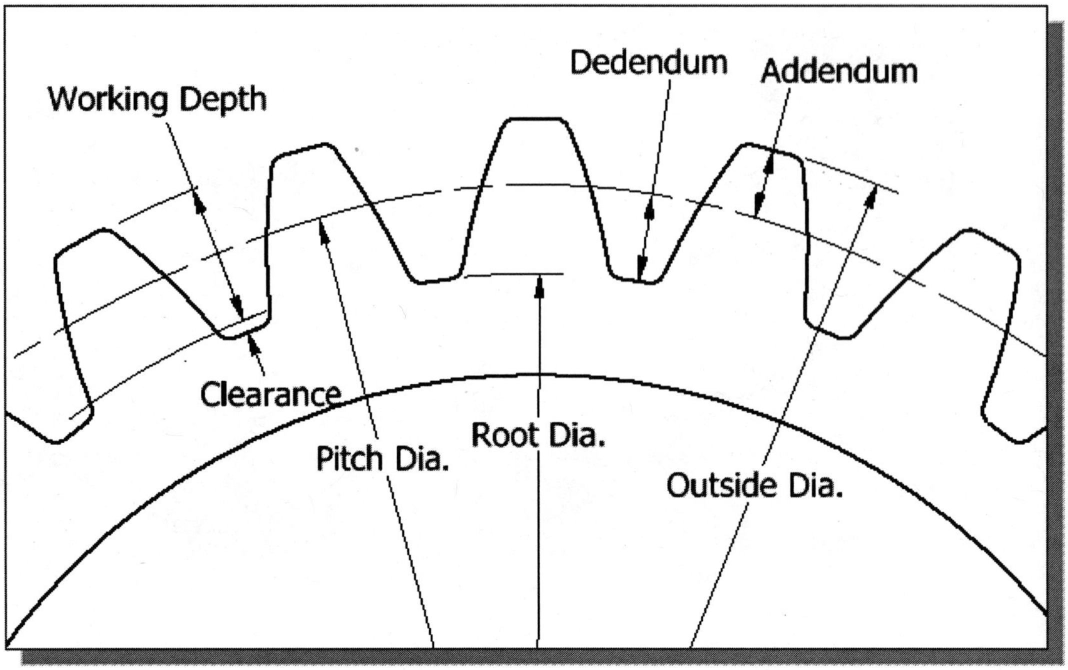

Outside diameter (Addendum diameter)
Diameter of gear blank, measured prior to cutting the teeth.

Root diameter
Diameter of the gear, measured across the bottom of the teeth.

Pitch diameter
Diameter of the pitch circle; the standard pitch diameter is a basic dimension at which the thread tooth and the thread space are equal. The circular tooth thickness, pressure angle and helix angles are all defined at the pitch circle.

Addendum
The top portion of the gear tooth; it is measured from the pitch circle to the outermost point of the tooth.

Dedendum
The bottom portion of the gear tooth; it is measured from the root circle to the pitch circle.

Clearance
Distance between the root circle of a gear and the addendum circle of its mate.

Working depth
Depth of engagement of two gears, that is, the sum of their operating addendums.

Whole depth
The distance from the top of the tooth to the root; it is equal to addendum plus dedendum or to working depth plus clearance.

Circular Pitch

Circular pitch is the distance measured along the pitch circle, from a point on one tooth to the corresponding point on the adjacent tooth.

Circular Pitch = Pitch diameter / No. of teeth

Pitch, Diametral Pitch

Diametral pitch of a gear is an expression of tooth size. It is the ***number of teeth per inch of pitch diameter***. Thus, a gear with a 2-in. pitch diameter and 40 teeth is a 20-pitch gear. Any two gears having the same pitch will operate together, provided they are based on the same gear system.

Diametral Pitch = No. of teeth / Pitch diameter = 40/2 = 20-Pitch

Module

A scaling factor used in **metric** gears with units in millimeters whose effect is to enlarge the gear tooth size as the module increases and reduce the size as the module decreases.

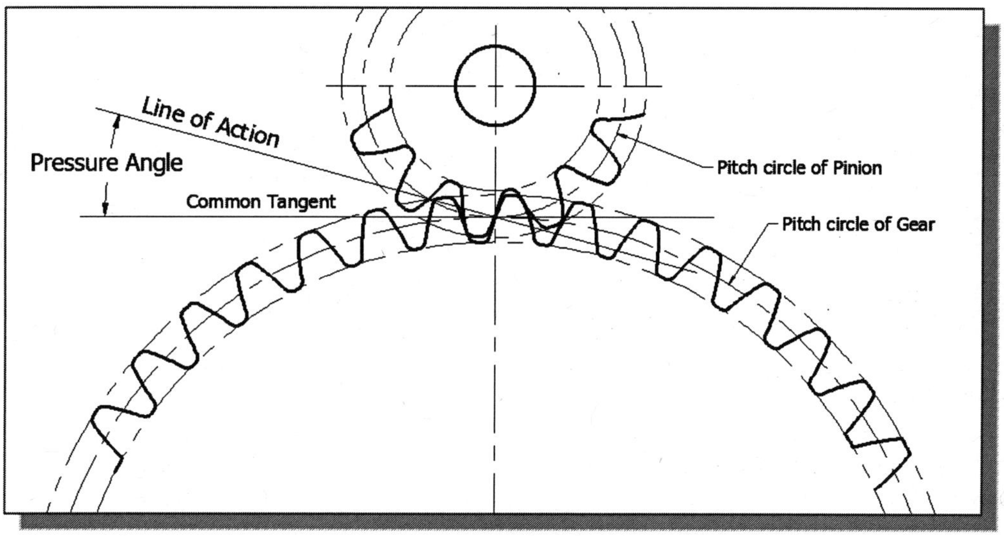

Gear: The larger of two interacting gears or a gear on its own.

Pinion: The smaller of two interacting gears.

Pitch point: Point where the line of action crosses a line joining the two gear axes.

Line of action, pressure line

Line of action is the line along which the force between two meshing gear teeth is directed. In general, the line of action changes from moment to moment during the period of engagement of a pair of teeth. For involute gears, however, the tooth-to-tooth force is always directed along the same line.

Pressure angle

The angle formed between the direction of the teeth exerting force on each other, and the common tangent line of the two pitch circles of the two gears. For involute gears, the teeth always exert force along the line of action, which, for involute gears, is a straight line; and thus, for involute gears, the pressure angle is constant.

Basic Involute Tooth Profile

- For gears to transmit uniform motion from one gear to another, the tooth profiles must have the proper form. There are a number of mathematical curves that can fulfill the requirements of the tooth contact, but the most commonly employed is the ***Involute curve***. The *Involute curve* forms the basis upon which several forms of American Standard gear teeth are based.

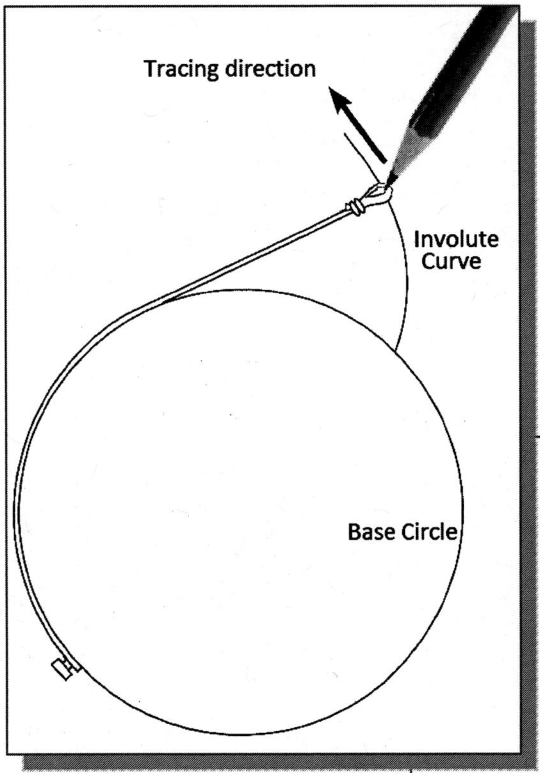

- The *Involute curve* can be generated by unwrapping of the circumference of a base circle. The tangency from the pencil to the base circle is always maintained.

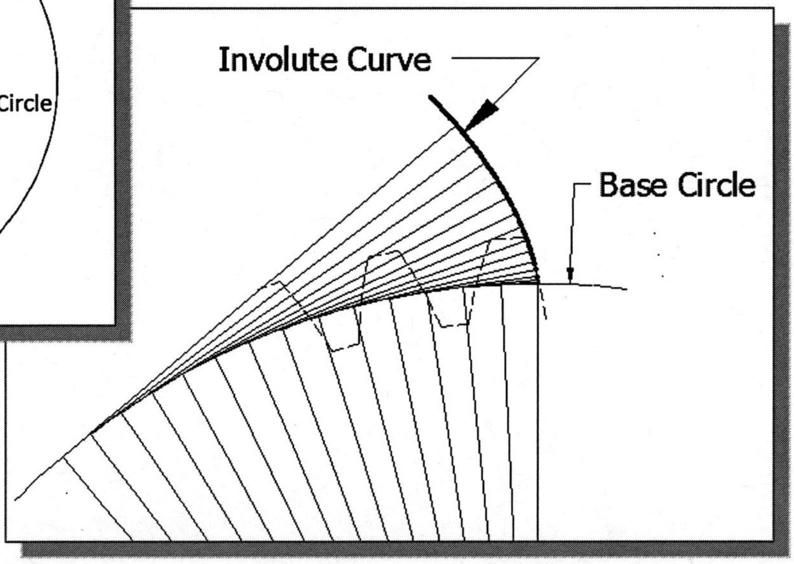

Note that several mathematic equations are available to generate an *Involute curve*.

The basic set of **Parametric Cartesian equations** of an ***Involute curve*** is:

$$x = a(\cos(t) + t\sin(t))$$
$$y = a(\sin(t) - t\cos(t))$$

This set of equations use the radius of the circle a and the angular parameter t to generate the *Involute curve*.

Gear Ratio

A ***gear train*** is two or more gears working in tandem for the purpose of transmitting motion from one axis to another. A gear train is called an **ordinary gear train** if all the rotating shafts are mounted on a common stationary frame. A **simple ordinary train** is seen to be one in which there is only one gear for each axis. A **compound ordinary train** is seen to be one in which two or more gears may rotate about a single axis.

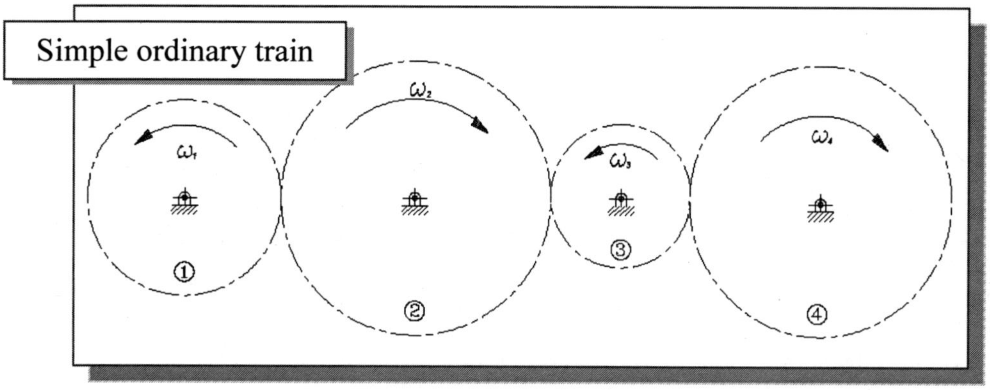

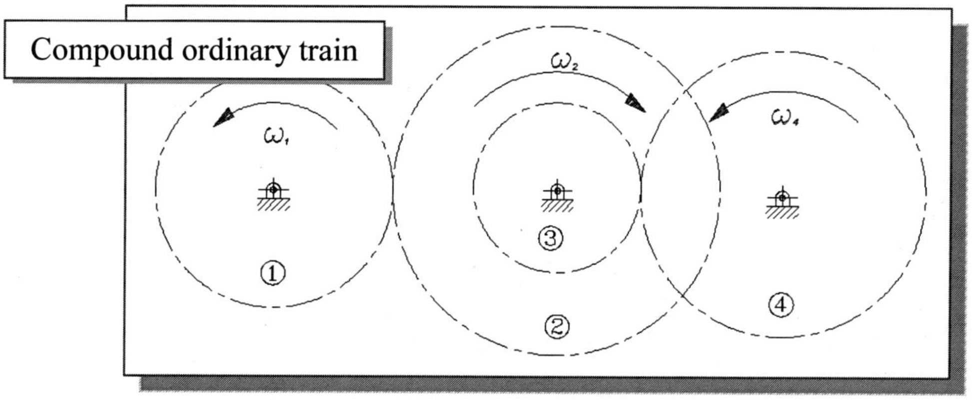

The **gear ratio** of a *gear train* is the ratio of the angular velocity of the input gear to the angular velocity of the output gear, also known as the *speed ratio* of the gear train. The **speed ratio** of a pair of gears is the inverse proportion of the diameters of their pitch circle. The gear ratio can also be computed directly from the numbers of teeth of the various gears that engage to form the gear train. For two meshing gears, the gear ratio is calculated as:

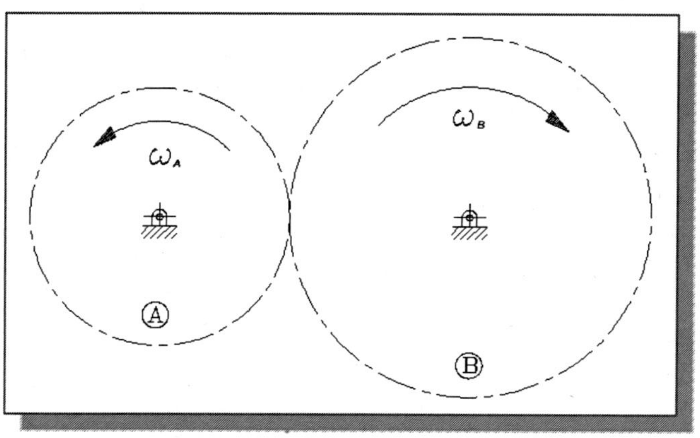

$$\text{Gear Ratio} = \frac{\omega_A}{\omega_B} = \frac{N_B}{N_A}$$

(1) Consider the *simple ordinary gear train* in the figure below; the gear train contains three pairs of meshing gears. (Note that Gear 2 and Gear 3 are *idler gears*. An intermediate gear which does not drive a shaft to perform any work is called an *idler gear.*)

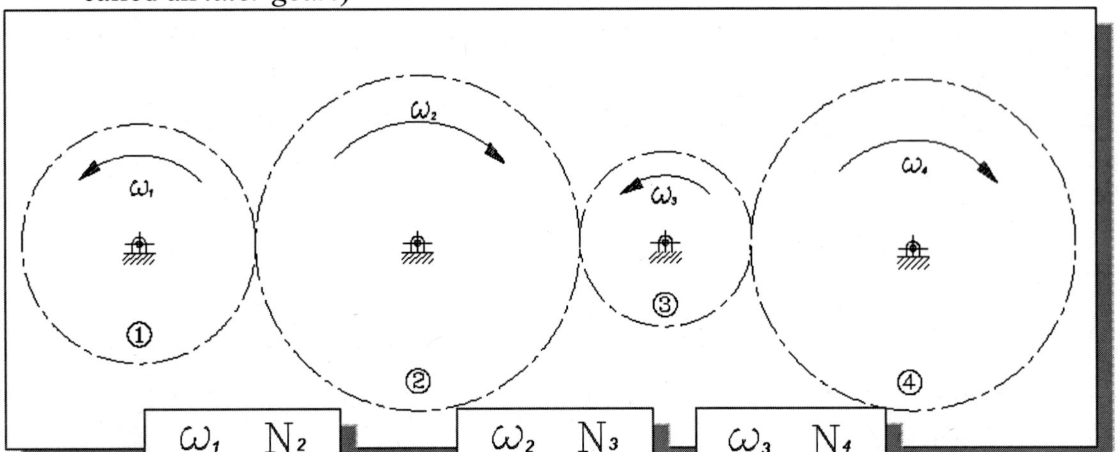

$$\frac{\omega_1}{\omega_2} = \frac{N_2}{N_1} \qquad \frac{\omega_2}{\omega_3} = \frac{N_3}{N_2} \qquad \frac{\omega_3}{\omega_4} = \frac{N_4}{N_3}$$

$$\frac{\omega_1}{\omega_4} = \frac{N_2\,N_3\,N_4}{N_1\,N_2\,N_3} = \frac{N_4}{N_1}$$

(2) Consider the *compound ordinary gear train* in the figure below; the gear train contains two pairs of meshing gears. (Note that Gear 3 moves with Gear 2 and therefore has the same speed as Gear 2.)

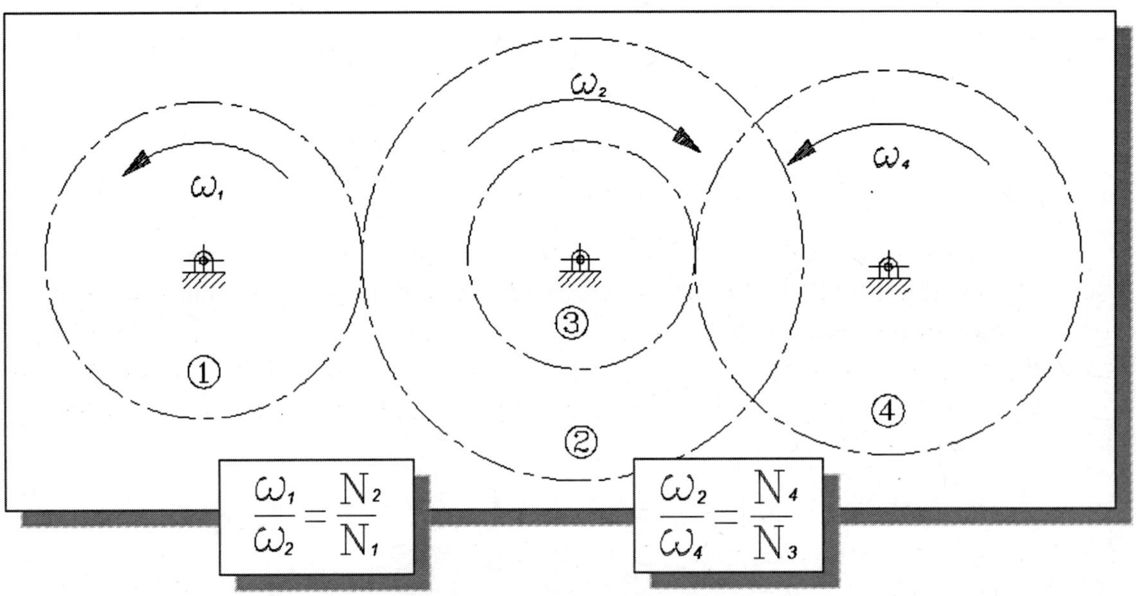

$$\frac{\omega_1}{\omega_2} = \frac{N_2}{N_1} \qquad \frac{\omega_2}{\omega_4} = \frac{N_4}{N_3}$$

$$\frac{\omega_1}{\omega_4} = \frac{N_2\,N_4}{N_1\,N_3}$$

SolidWorks Gear Toolbox

In this lesson, we will examine some of the procedures that are available in *SolidWorks* to create a **spur gear** and also to reuse existing 2D data to create 3D parts. In *SolidWorks*, several design tools are included, such as *SolidWorks Toolbox*, to aid the creation of designs.

In *SolidWorks*, we have the option of using the standard parts library through what is known as the ***Design Toolbox***. The *Design Toolbox* consists of multiple libraries of standard parts that have been created based on industry standards. Significant amounts of time can be saved by using these parts. Note that we can also create and publish our libraries so that others can reuse our parts.

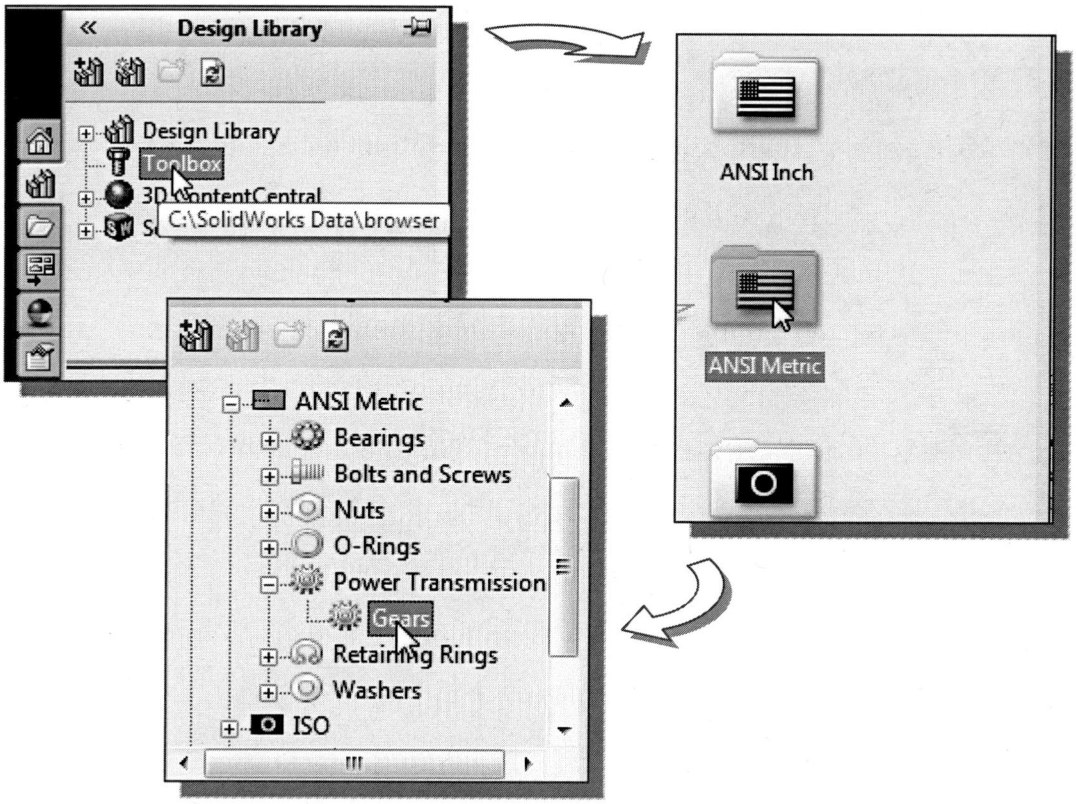

Besides using the standard part libraries through the ***Design Toolbox***, other types of design components can also be created through the *SolidWorks* ***Design Library***. A variety of design components can be generated through the different tools available in the *Design Library Panel*. Note that the ***Design Library*** can be accessed through the **Task Pane** or the **Assembly Modeling** module.

In this chapter, the procedures of accessing the *Gear Toolbox* are illustrated. For the *Mechanical Tiger* design, custom spur gear parts will be created from the *Design Toolbox*. Note that the nylon gears in the *Mechanical Tiger* design are specifically designed for the *Tamiya* kits, and therefore the tooth profiles do not match with the gears generated in *SolidWorks*. Also, note the parts in the *Mechanical Tiger* design are using the metric system.

Starting *SolidWorks*

1. Select the **SolidWorks** option on the *Start* menu or select the **SolidWorks** icon on the desktop to start *SolidWorks*. The *SolidWorks* main window will appear on the screen.

Open the SolidWorks Design Library

1. In the *task pane* select the **Design Library** command by left-mouse-clicking the icon.

2. Select the **Toolbox** category in the *Design Library* panel as shown.

3. Click **Add in now** under the *Toolbox* panel if necessary.

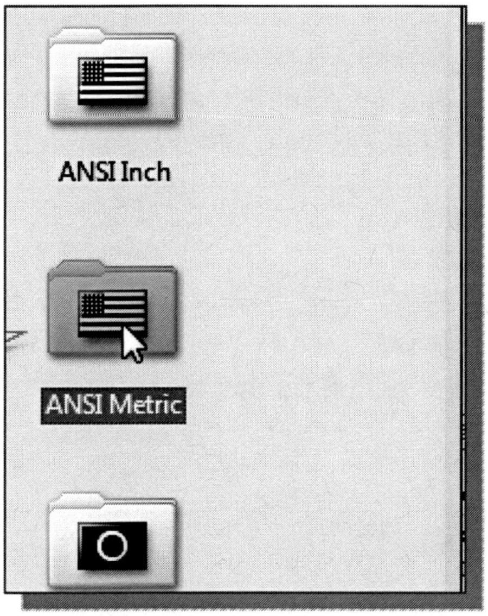

4. Select **ANSI Metric** to view the standard parts under this category as shown in the figure.

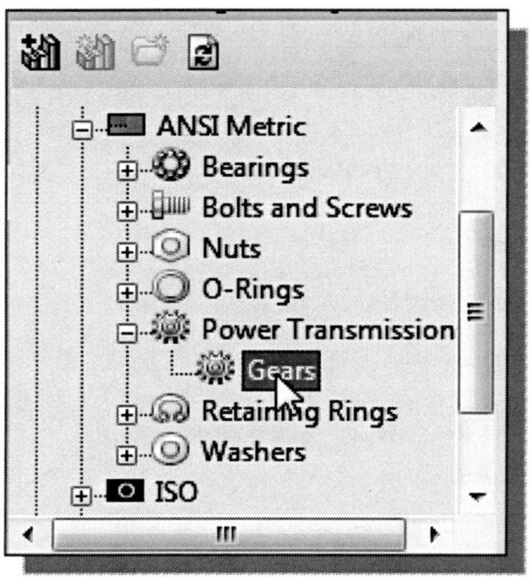

5. Click **Gears** to enter the selection dialog box.

6. **Right-mouse-click** once on the **Spur Gear** icon to open the option menu.

7. Select **Create Part** as shown.

The *SolidWorks* Spur Gear Toolbox

- In this section, we will illustrate the procedures to configure and create gears with the *Spur Gear* toolbox. Note that the nylon gears in the *Tamiya Tiger* kit are specifically designed for the *Tamiya* kits, and therefore the tooth profiles do not match with the standard gear profiles generated using the *SolidWorks Gear Toolbox.*

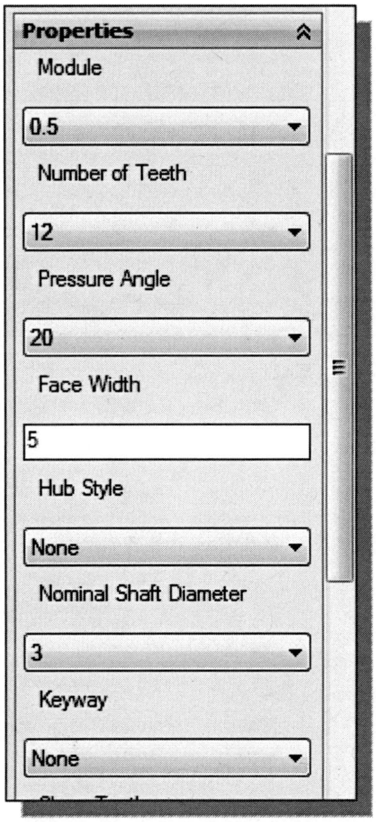

1. In the *Properties Manager* panel, set the ***Module*** to **0.5**.

2. Set the ***Number of Teeth*** to **12**.

3. Enter **5** in the ***Face Width*** edit box.

4. Set the ***Hub Style*** to **None** as shown.

5. Set the ***Nominal Shaft Diameter*** to **3**.

6. Set the ***Keyway*** option to **None**.

7. Click **OK** to accept the configuration settings and generate the gear part.

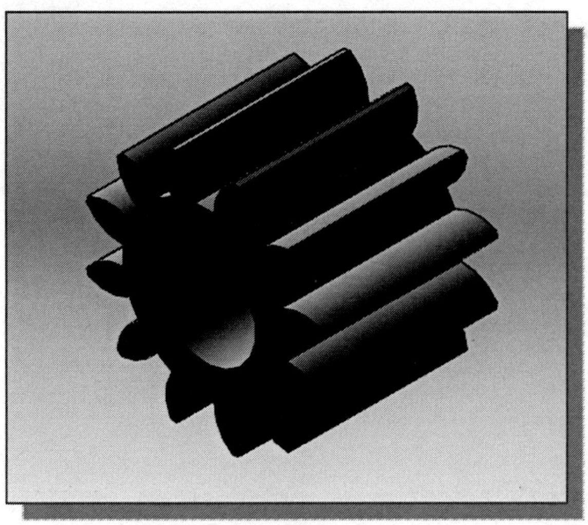

- Note the specified gear part is created. The part is saved under the default *SolidWorks* data folder.

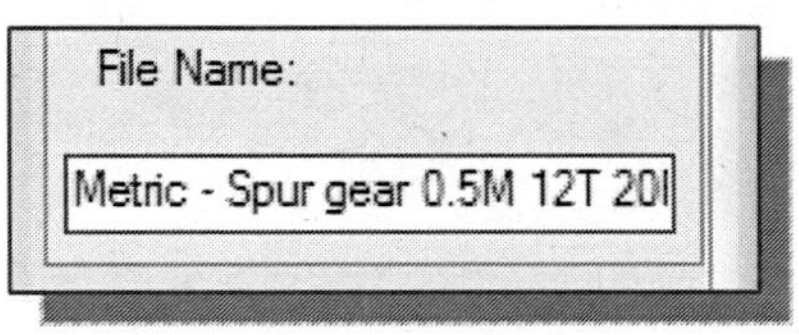

Create a 42 Teeth Spur Gear

- We will generate a second gear using the SolidWorks *Gear toolbox*.

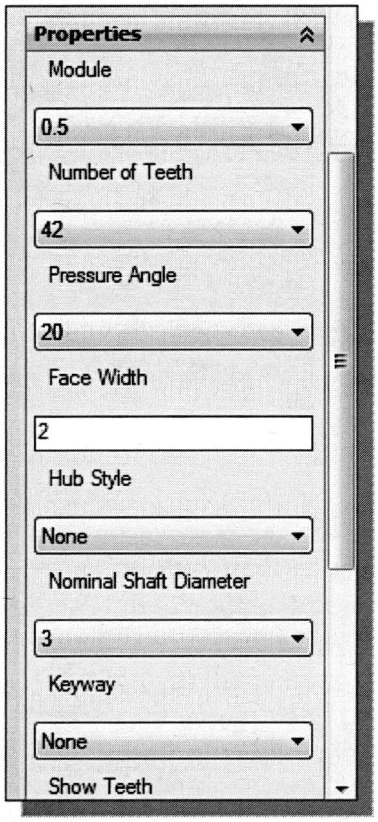

1. In the *Properties Manager* panel, set the ***Module*** to **0.5**.
2. Set the ***Number of Teeth*** to **42**.
3. Enter **2** in the ***Face Width*** edit box.
4. Set the ***Hub Style*** to **None** as shown.
5. Set the ***Nominal Shaft Diameter*** to **3**.
6. Set the ***Keyway*** option to **None**.

7. Click **OK** to accept the configuration settings and generate the gear part.

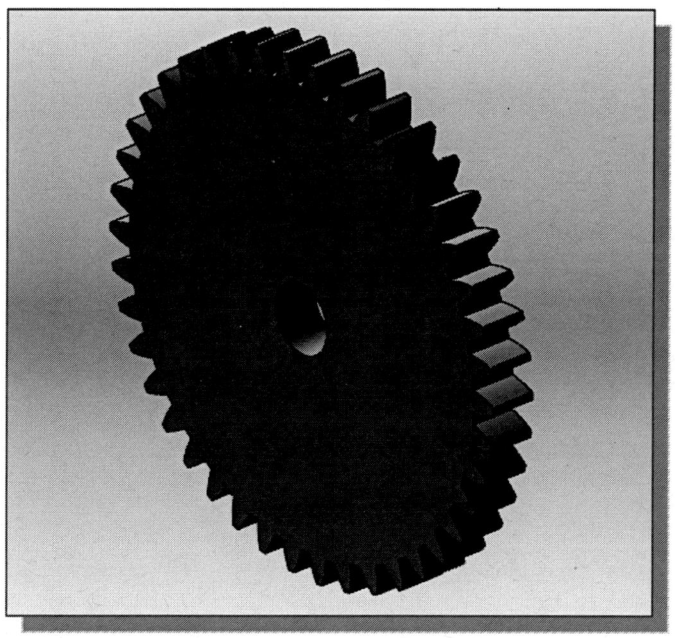

- Note the creation of true gear tooth profiles can be very time consuming by traditional methods. The created gears can also be edited and modified just as a regular *SolidWorks* part. In the next sections, we will modify these two gears to create the parts needed for the *Tamiya Tiger* kit.

Modify the Generated 42T Gear

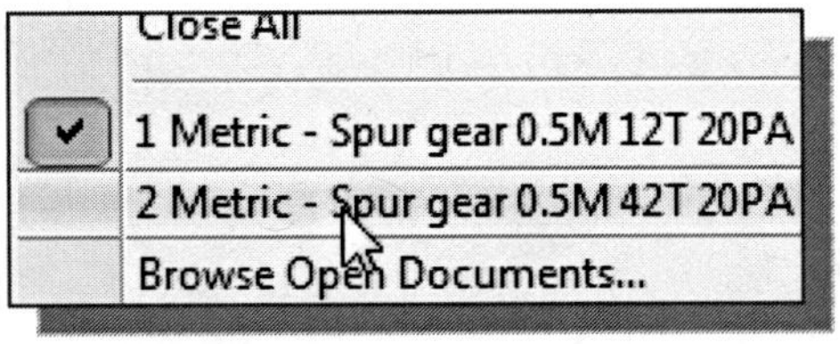

1. Through the *Window* pull-down menu, switch to the **42T Gear** model as shown.

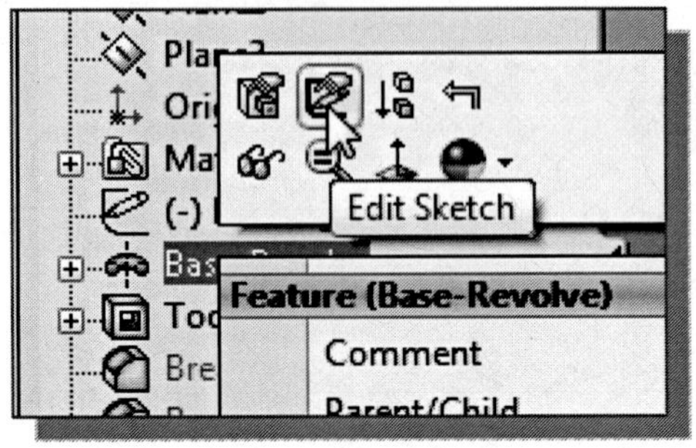

2. Inside the *Model History Tree*, right-click once on **Base-Revolve** to bring up the option menu.

3. In the option menu, choose **Edit Sketch** to open the selected feature.

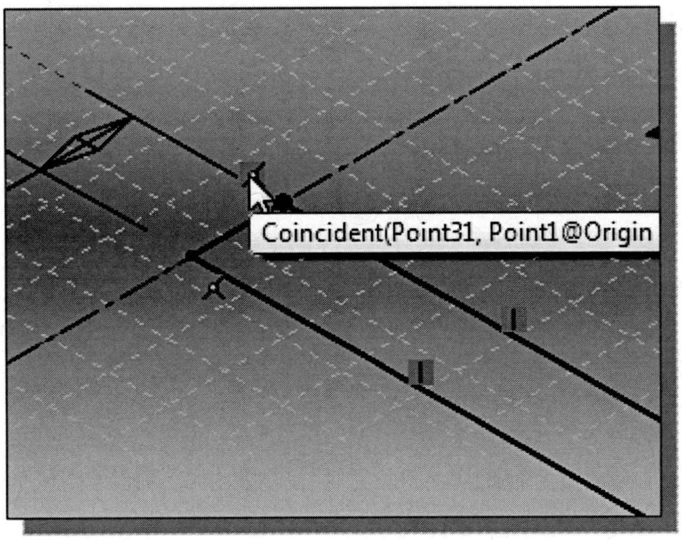

4. Select the **Coincident** constraint applied to the *Origin* and the *corner point*. (Note there is another Coincident constraint aligning the corner point to the center line.)

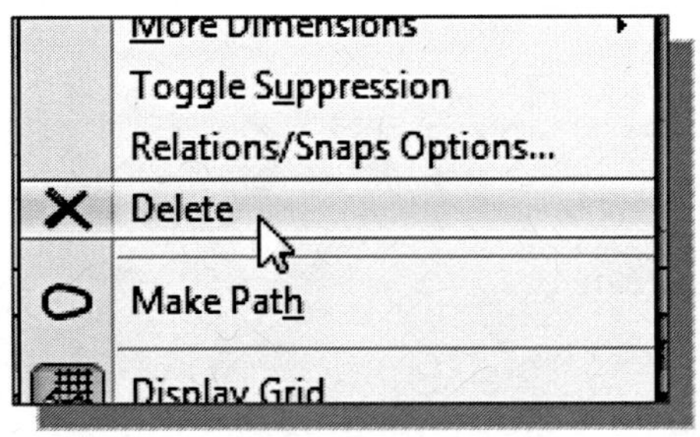

5. Inside the graphics window, right-click once to bring up the option menu and select **Delete** to remove the applied constraint.

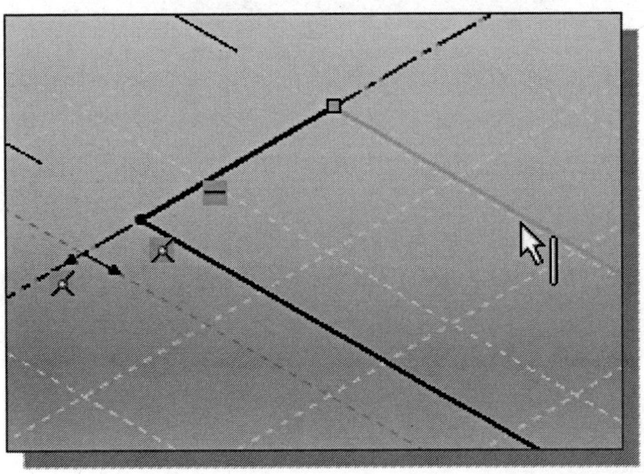

6. On your own, drag the sketch to the right side, so that the corner is not aligned to the origin.

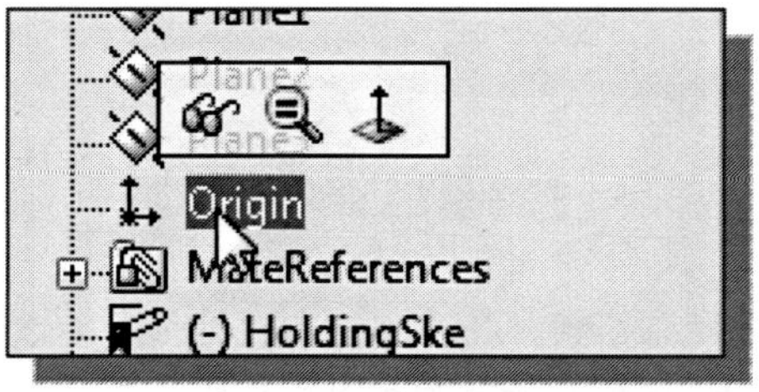

7. On your own, switch ***ON*** the display of the model **Origin** as shown.

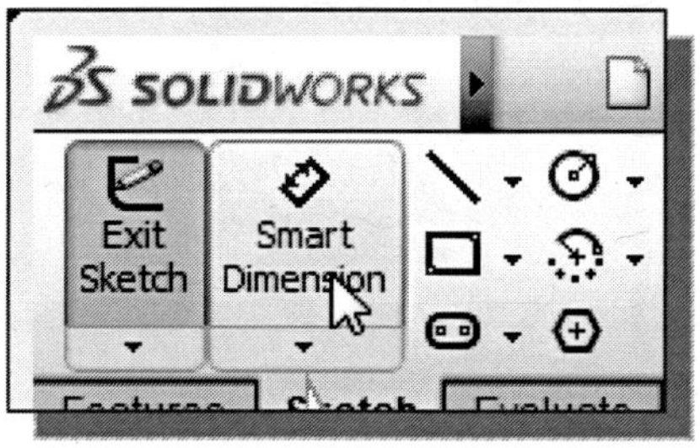

8. Activate the **Smart Dimension** command by clicking on the associated icon as shown.

9. Create the location dimension referencing the width dimension as shown.

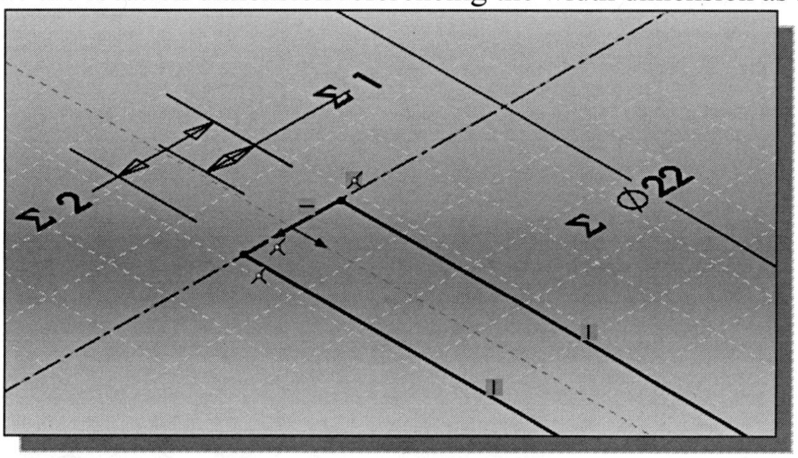

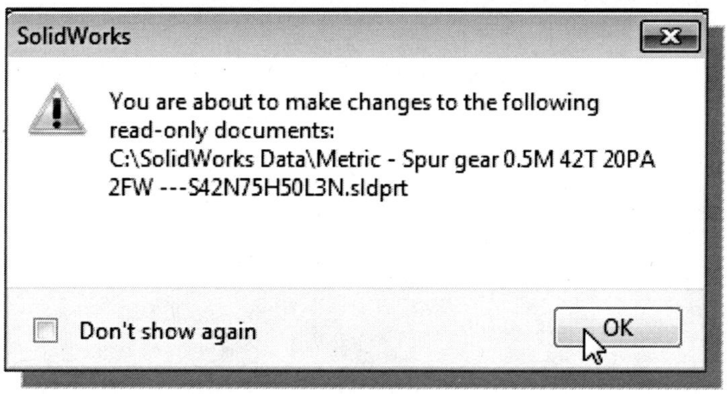

10. Note the generated gear part is automatically saved as read-only in the default *SolidWorks* data folder. Click **OK** to close the message window.

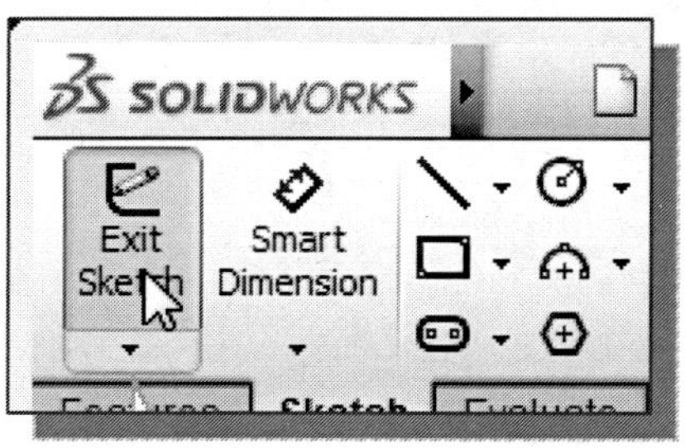

11. In the *Sketch* toolbar, click **Exit Sketch** to end the *Edit Sketch* mode.

- Note the gear has been modified, but more editing is needed.

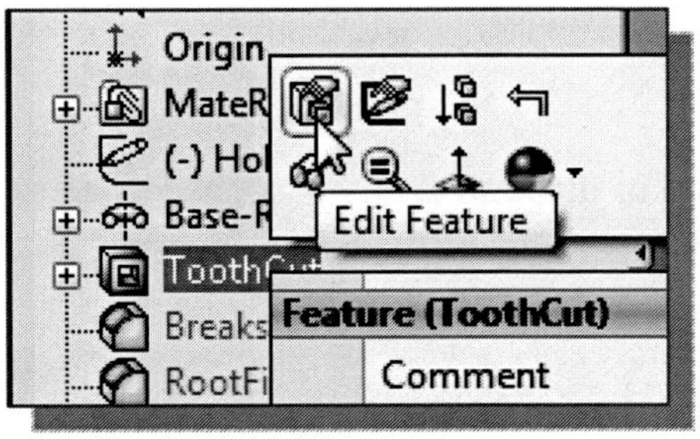

12. Inside the *Model History Tree*, right-click once on **ToothCut** to bring up the option menu.

13. In the option menu, choose **Edit Feature** to open the selected feature.

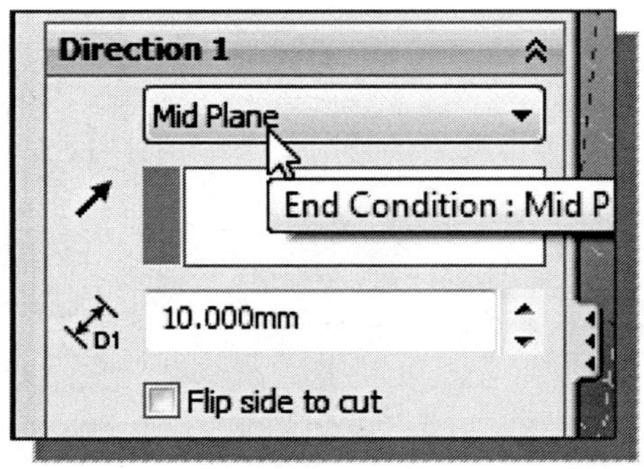

14. In the *Properties Manager*, set the extrusion direction to **Mid Plane** as shown.

15. Confirm the *depth* value is set to **10 mm** as shown.

16. In the *ToothCut* window, select **OK** as shown.

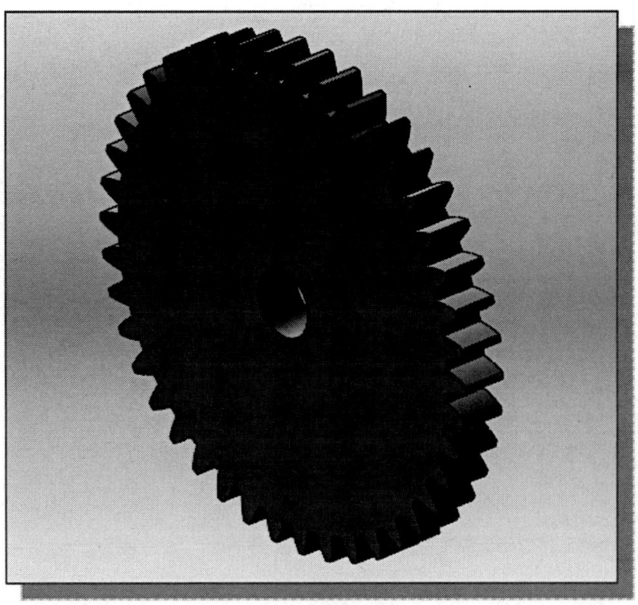

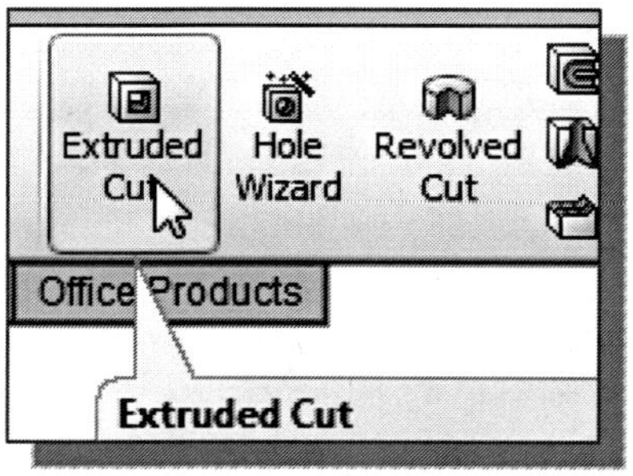

17. In the *Features* toolbar select the **Extruded Cut** command by clicking once with the left-mouse-button on the icon.

18. Select the **front surface** of the gear by clicking once with the left-mouse-button.

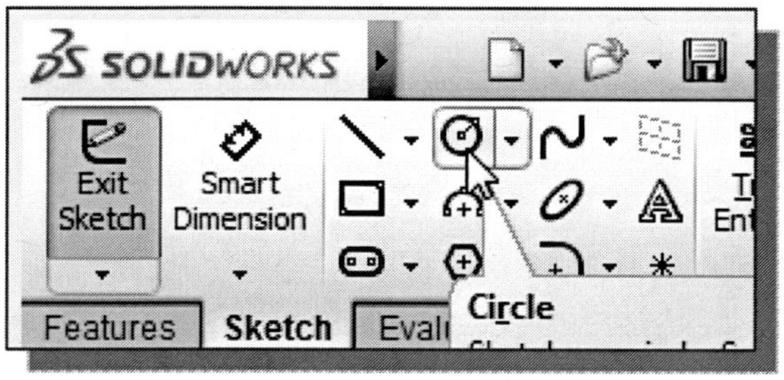

19. Select the **Circle** command by clicking once with the left-mouse-button on the icon in the *Sketch* toolbar.

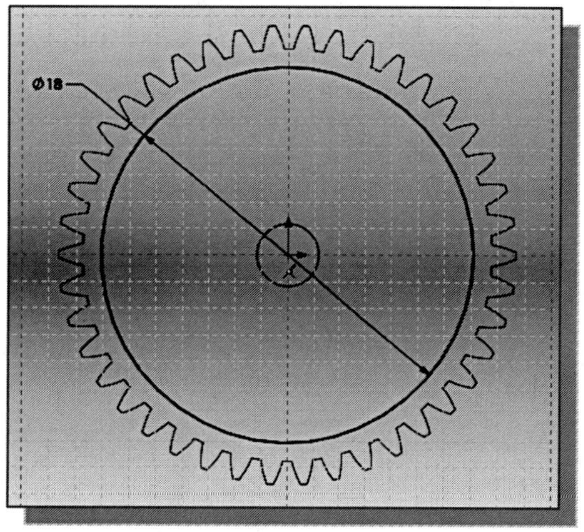

20. On your own, create a circle and the associated dimension, diameter of **18 mm**, as shown in figure.

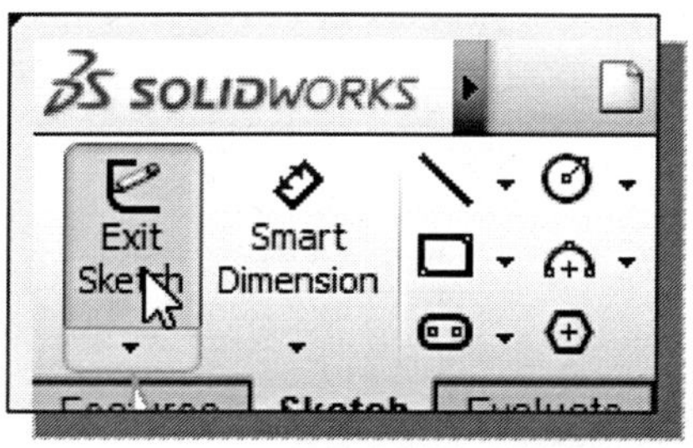

21. In the *Sketch* toolbar, click **Exit Sketch** to end the *Edit Sketch* mode.

22. On your own, set the extrude value to **0.25mm** and create the *Cut* feature as shown.

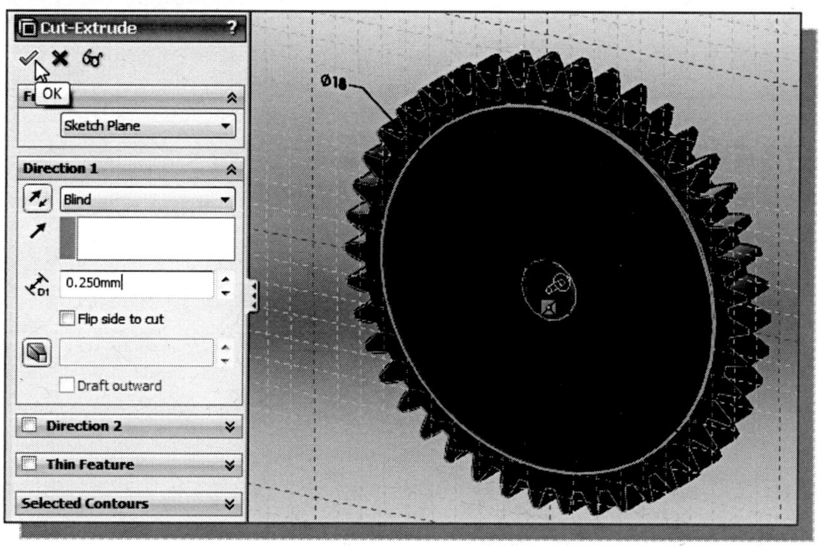

Create a Mirrored Feature

❖ The **Mirror** command can be used to create duplicates of existing features, with respect to a mirror image plane.

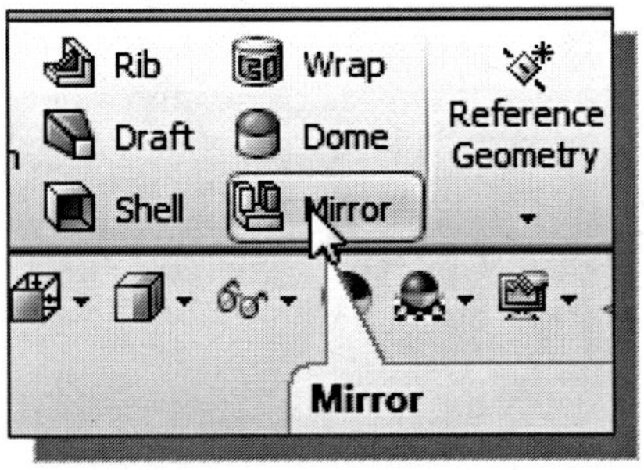

1. In the *Features* toolbar, select the **Mirror** command as shown.

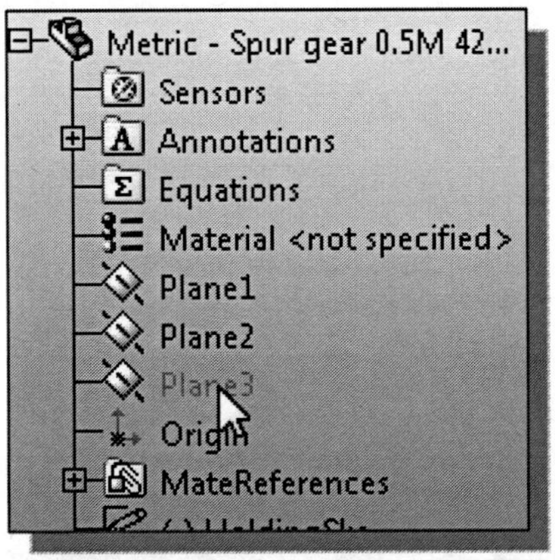

2. In the *Model History Tree*, select **Plane3** as the mirror image plane as shown.

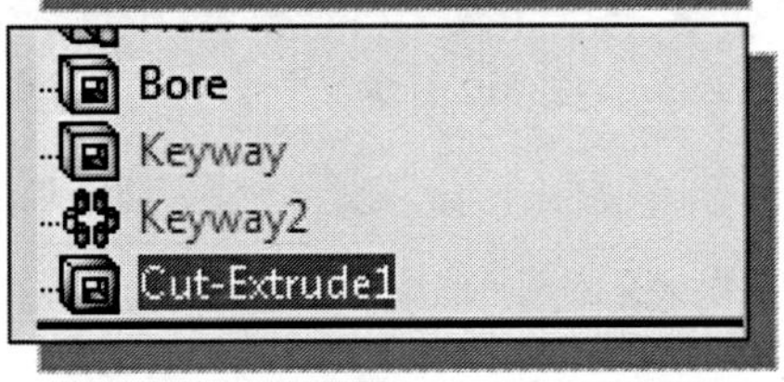

3. Select the **Cut-Extrude1** feature we just created in the *Model Tree.*

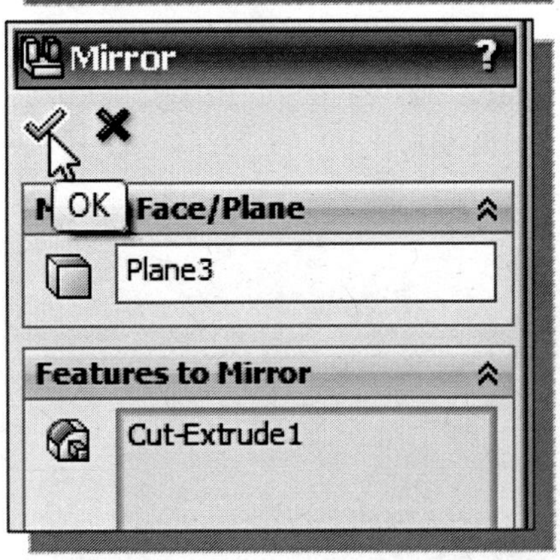

4. Click **OK** to create the *mirrored* feature.

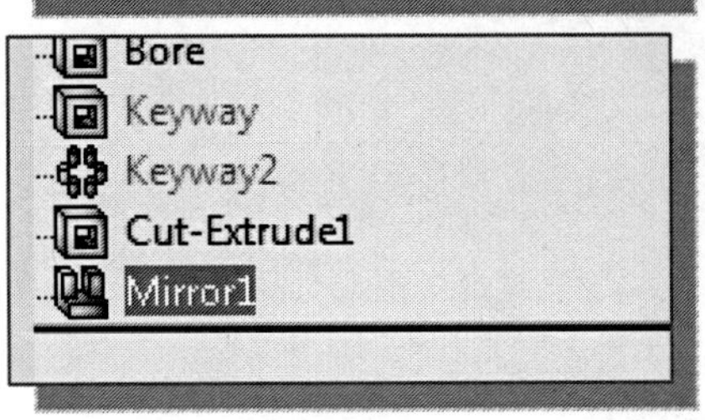

- Note the mirrored feature is created and it is listed in the *Model History Tree.*

Importing the Profile of the Pinion Gear

- For the next feature, we will import the profile of the gear teeth of the pinion gear from the generated gear assembly.

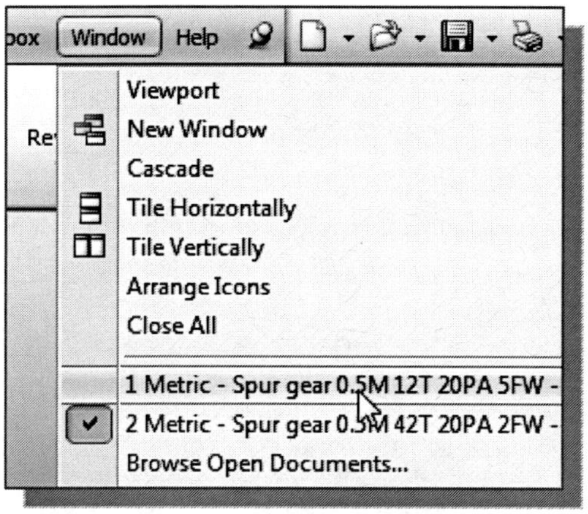

1. In the *Window* pull-down menu, switch to the other gear file by selecting the **0.5M 12T** file as shown.

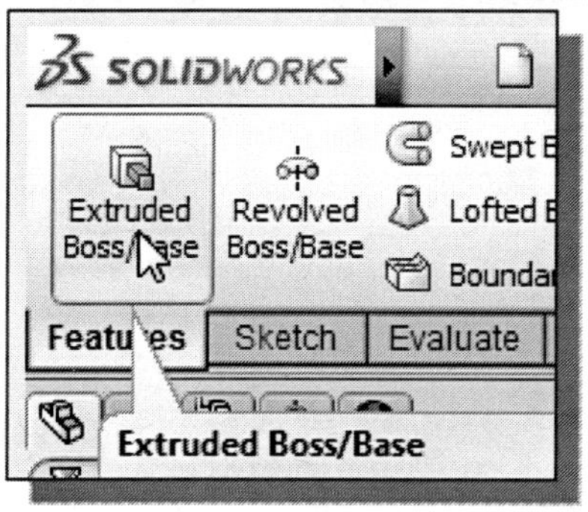

2. In the *Features* toolbar, select the **Extruded Boss/Base** command by left-clicking once on the icon.

3. Select the **front plane** of the pinion gear as the sketching plane.

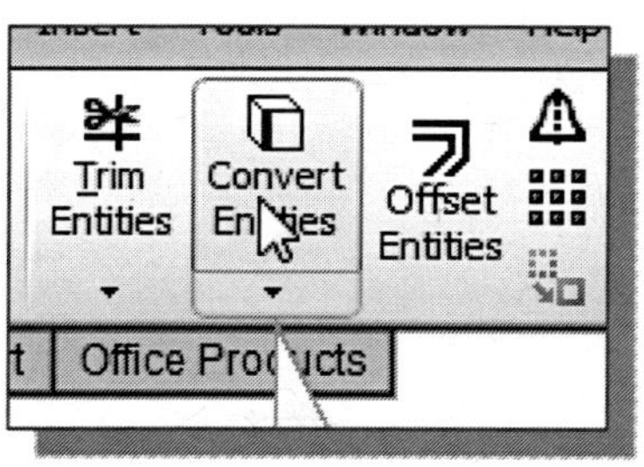

4. Select **Convert Entities** in the *Sketch* toolbar.

5. In the graphics window, use the left-mouse-button and select one set of the tooth profiles as shown.

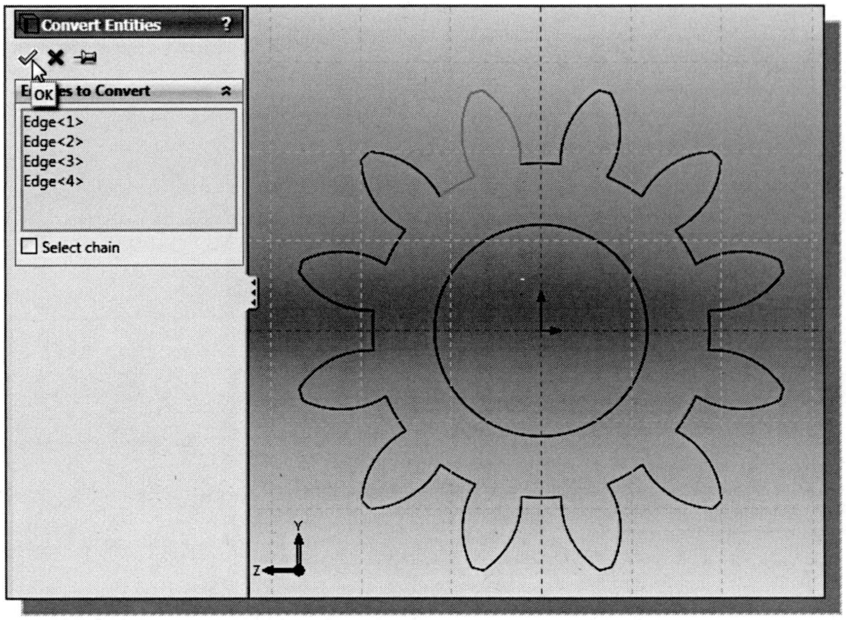

6. Click on the **check mark** button to accept the settings.

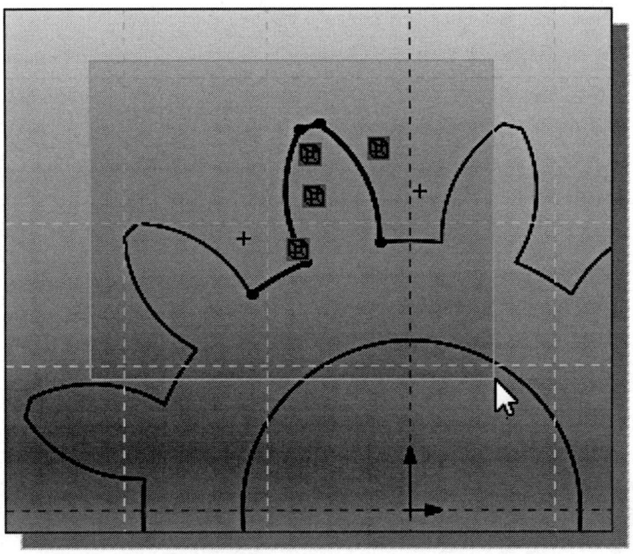

7. Inside the graphics window, use a **selection window** to select the projected entities as shown.

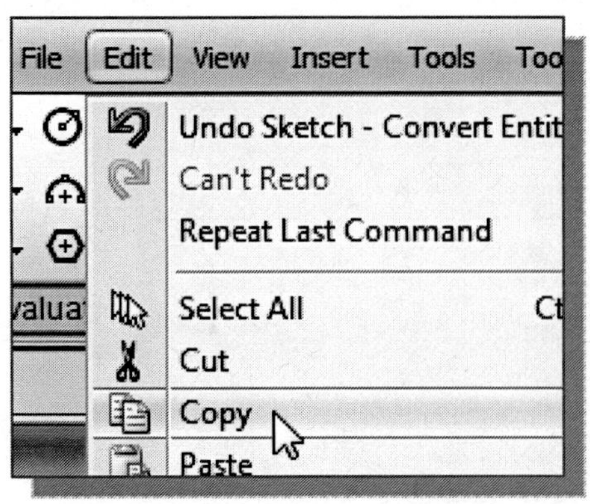

8. Select **Copy** in the *Edit* pull-down menu as shown. Note that we are using the copy function of the *operating system clipboard.*

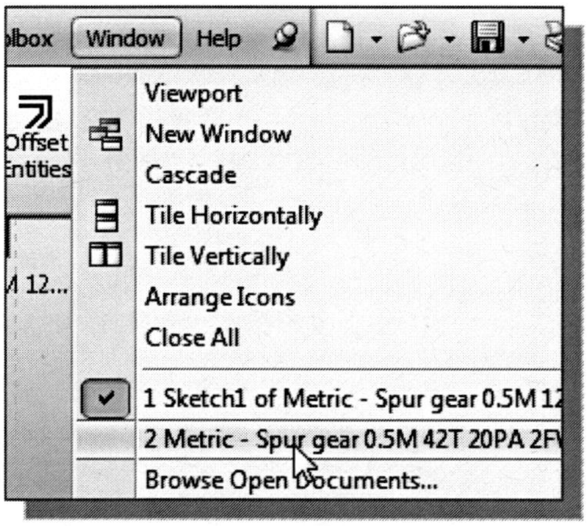

9. In the *Window* pull-down menu, switch to the other gear file by selecting the **0.5M 42T** file as shown.

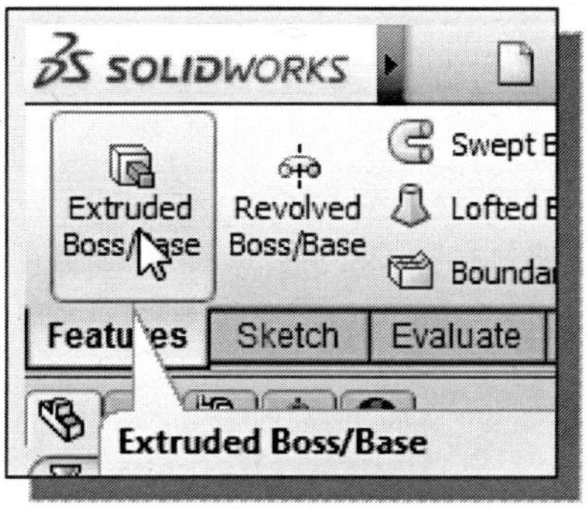

10. In the *Features* toolbar, select the **Extruded Boss/ Base** command by left-clicking once on the icon.

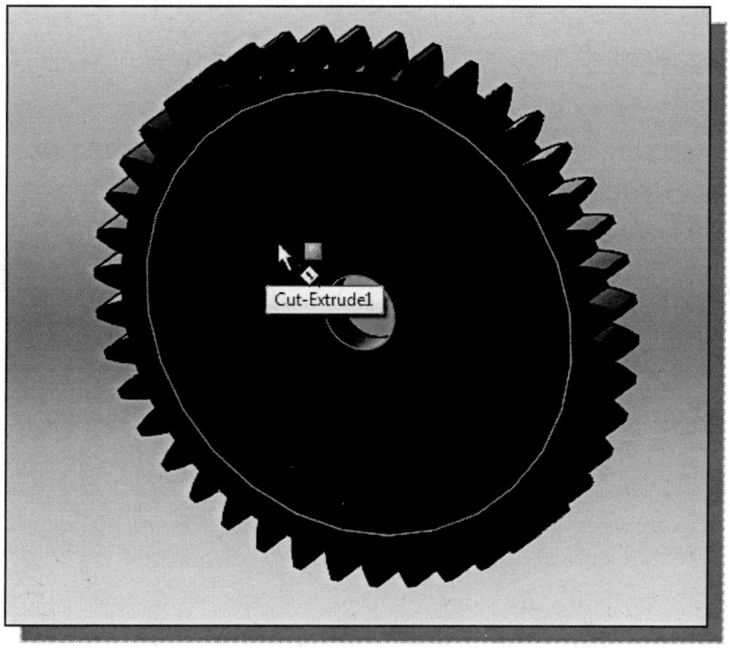

11. Select the **front face** of the **42T** gear to align the sketching plane.

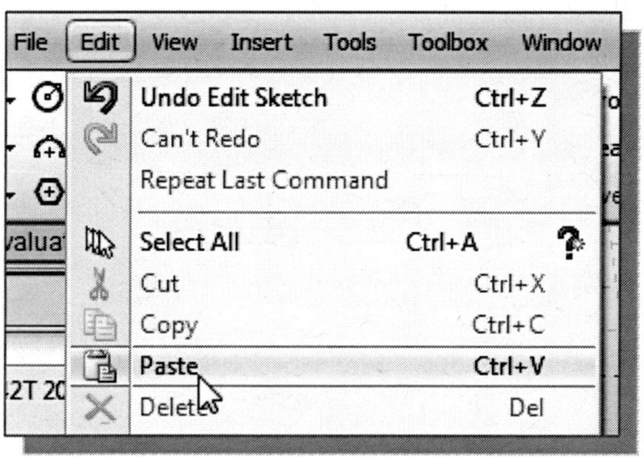

12. In the *Edit* pull-down menu, select the **Paste** command by left-clicking once on the icon as shown.

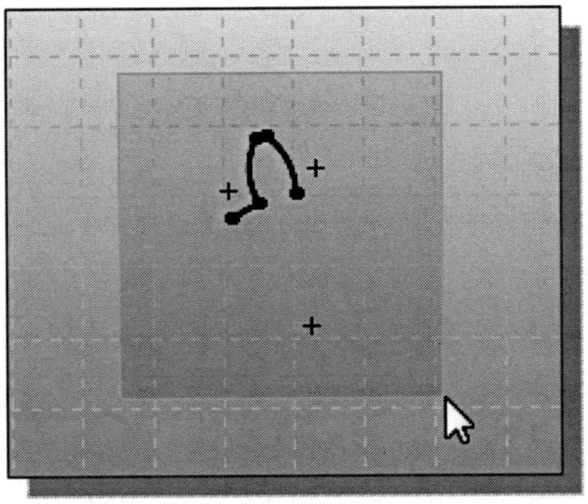

13. Inside the graphics window, use a **selection window** to select the projected entities as shown.

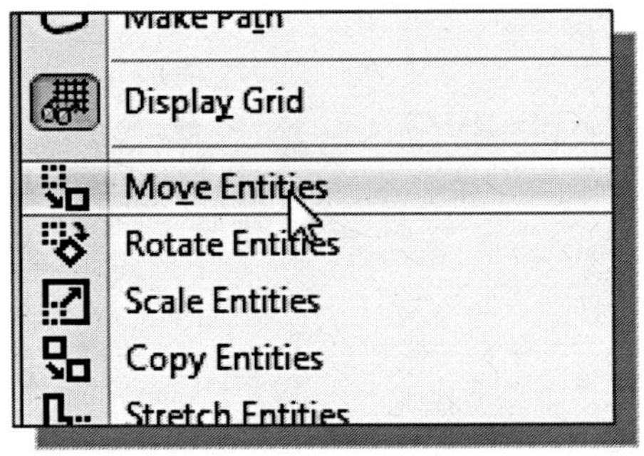

14. Inside the graphics window, right-click once to bring up the option menu and select **Move Entities** as shown.

15. On your own, reposition the selected entities using **drag & drop** to align the center point to the *Origin* as shown.

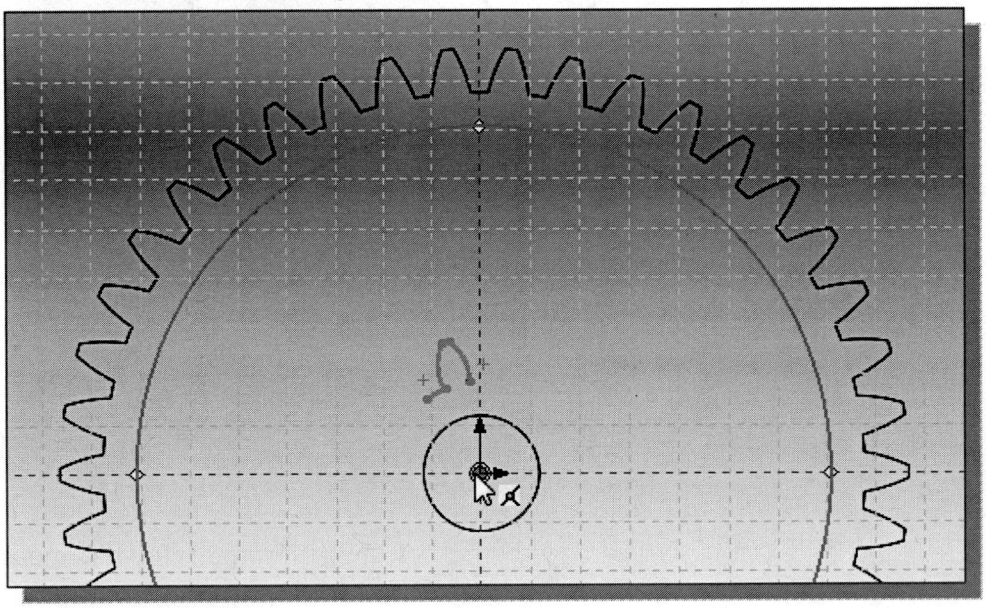

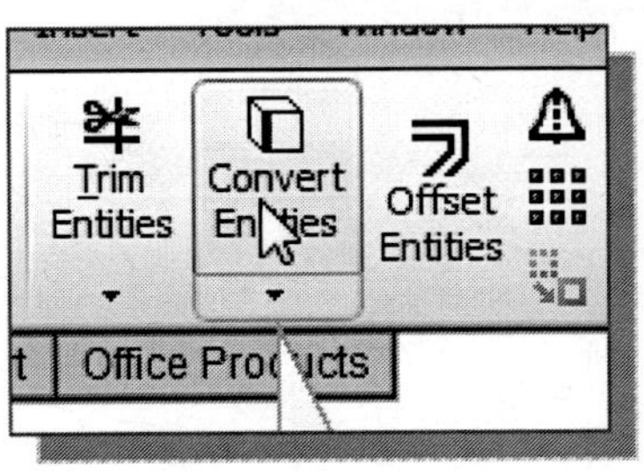

16. Select **Convert Entities** in the *Sketch* toolbar.

17. Select the **inside circle** to project the geometry to the sketching plane.

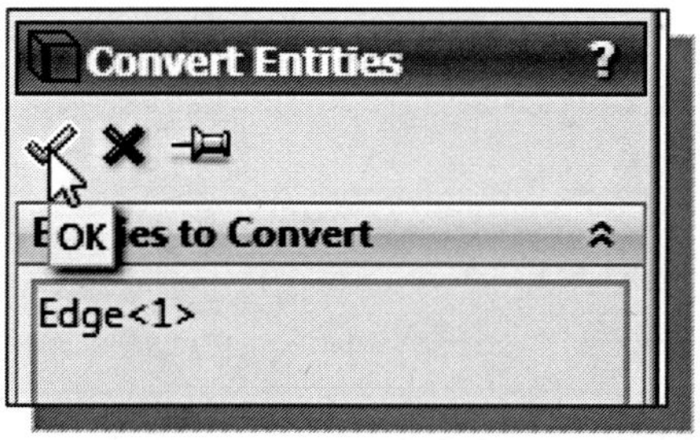

18. Click on the **check mark** button to accept the settings.

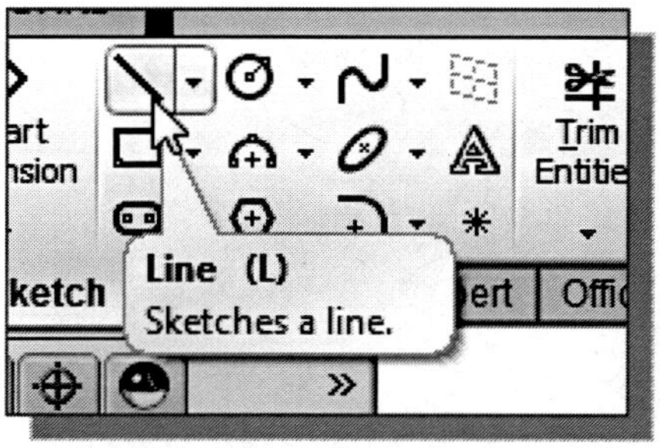

19. Select the **Line** option in the *Sketch* panel. A *Help-tip* box appears next to the cursor: "*Sketches a line.*"

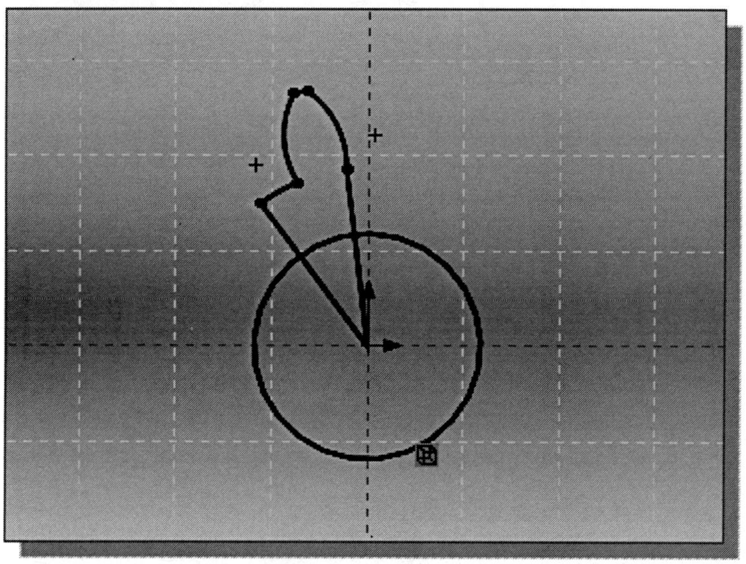

20. Create **two line segments** to form the closed region aligned to the *Origin* as shown.

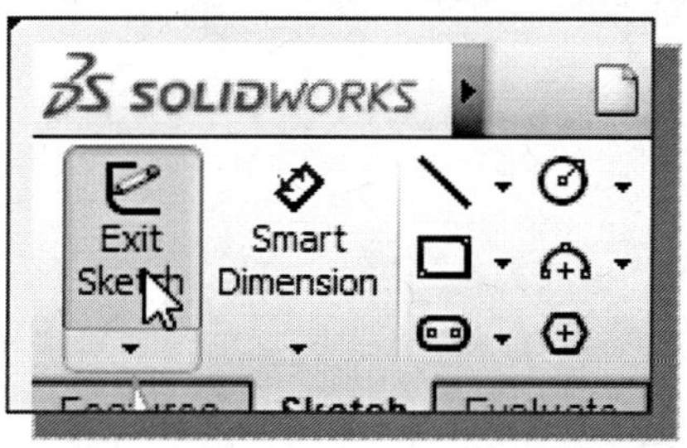

21. Click **Exit Sketch** in the *Sketch* toolbar to end the *Sketch* mode.

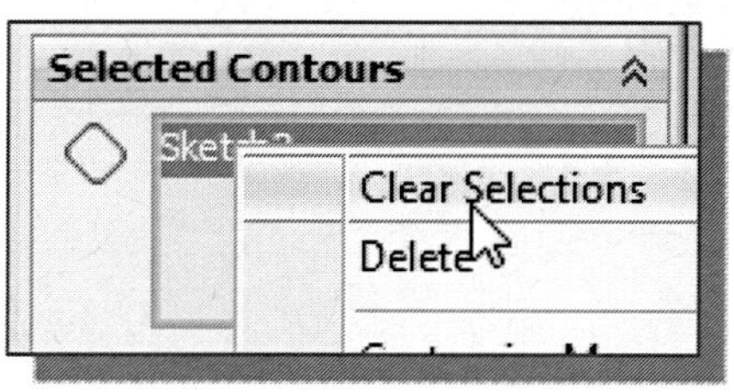

22. In the **Selected Contours** list, remove any pre-selected item through the right-mouse-click.

23. Select the **tooth region** as shown in the figure below.

24. Set the extrude distance to **4.75 mm** and create the feature as shown.

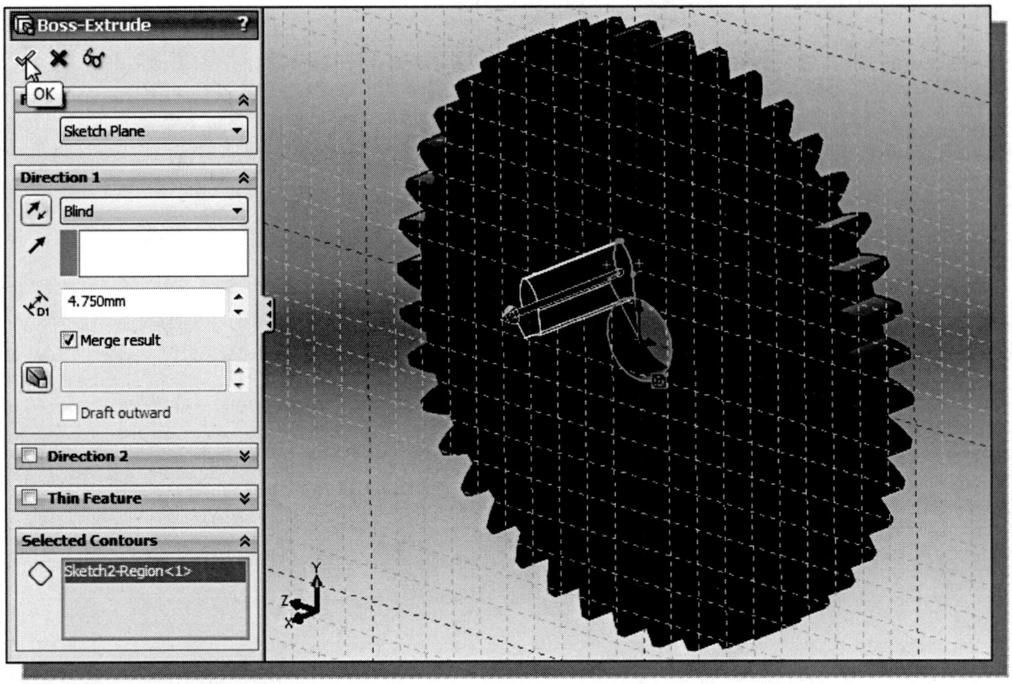

25. Click on the **check mark** button to accept the settings and create the feature.

Complete the *G2-Spur Gear* Part

❖ Next we will complete the small pinion gear by using the **Circular Pattern** command.

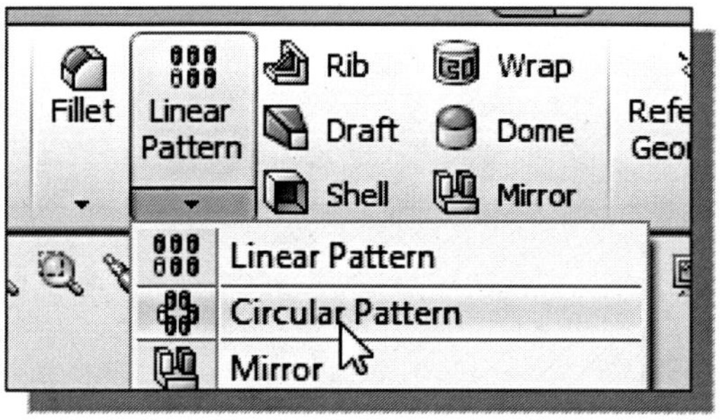

1. In the *Features* toolbar, select the **Circular Pattern** command by clicking the left-mouse-button on the icon.

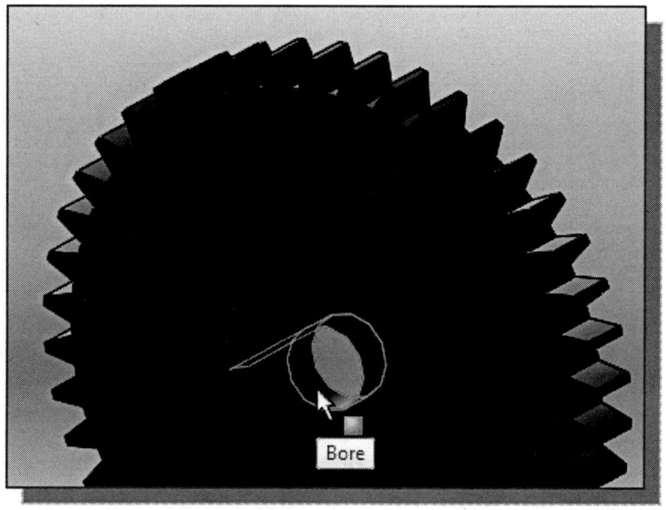

2. On your own, select the center **cylindrical surface** to set the *axis of rotation*.

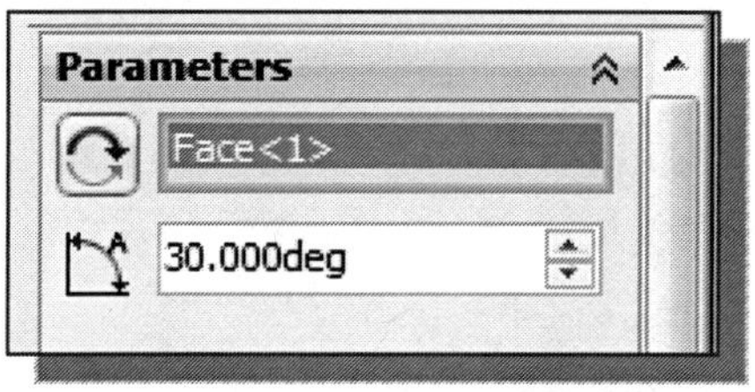

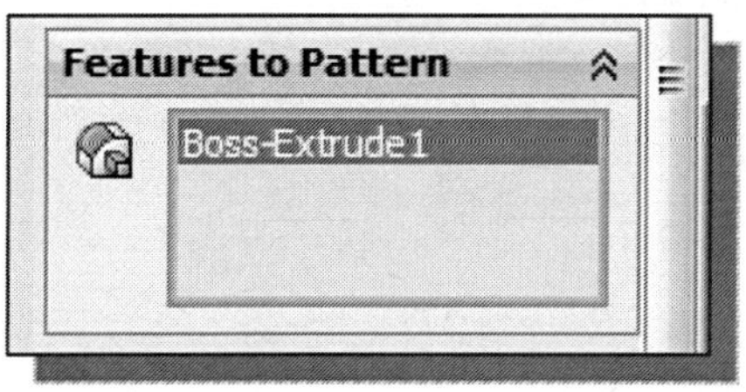

3. Select the **Boss-Extrude1** feature we just created as the feature to be patterned as shown

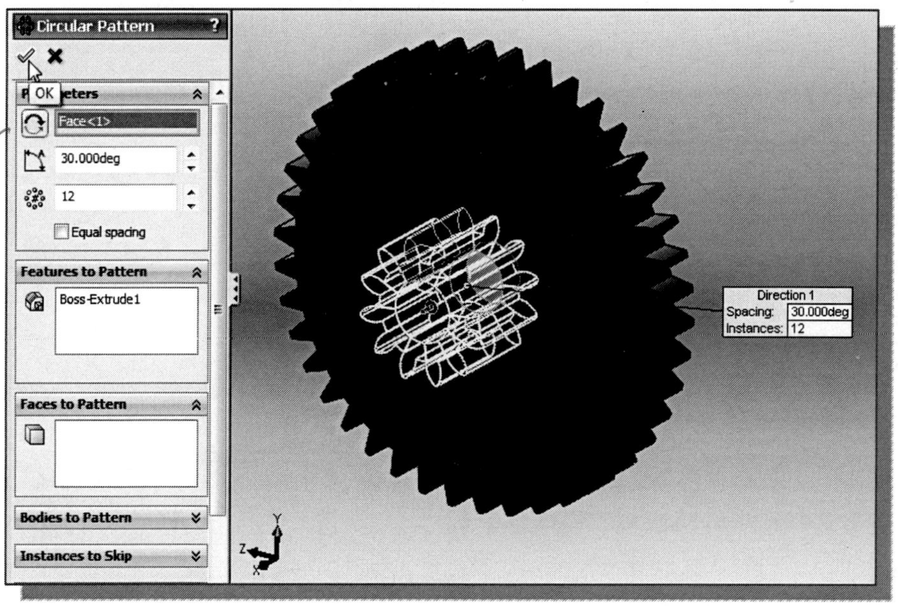

4. *Uncheck* the **Equal Spacing** option.

5. Set the *spacing angle* to **30** degrees and the *number of instances* to **12** as shown.

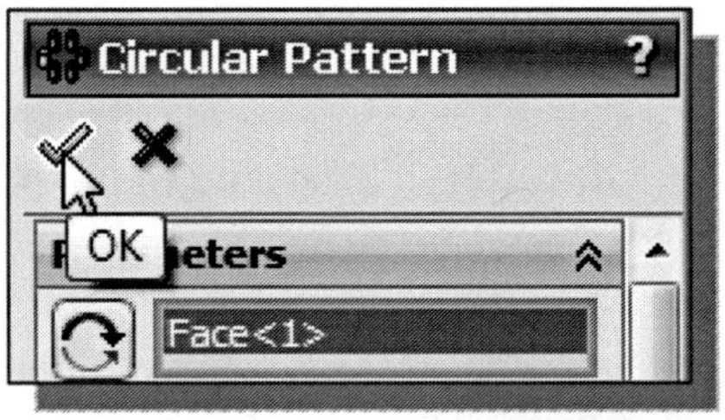

6. Click on the **check mark** button to accept the settings and create the feature.

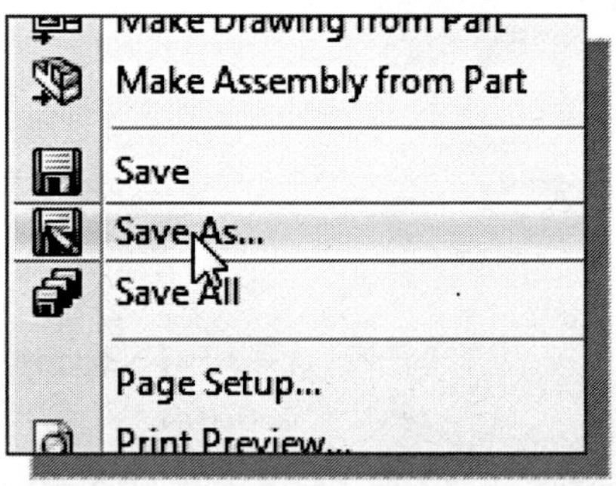

7. Select the **Save As** command in the *File* pull-down menu.

8. On your own, save the current model as a new part using **G2-Spur Gear** as the part file name.

Create the *G3-Spur Gear* Part

❖ Next we will modify the current **G2-Spur Gear** part to create the *G3-Spur Gear* part.

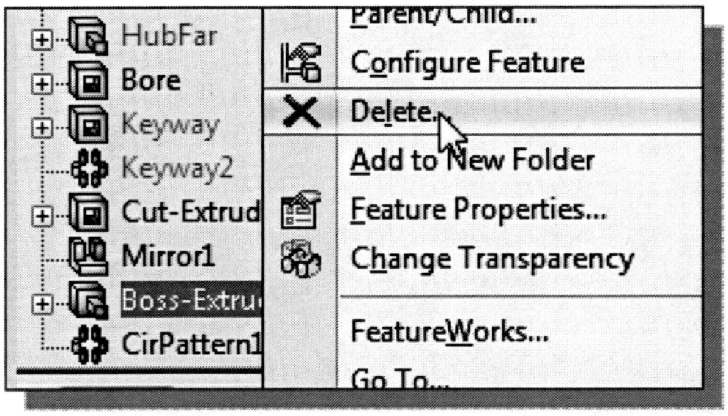

1. Inside the *browser* window, right-mouse-click on **Boss-Extrude1** to bring up the option menu as shown.

2. In the option menu, select **Delete** to remove the extrusion feature as shown.

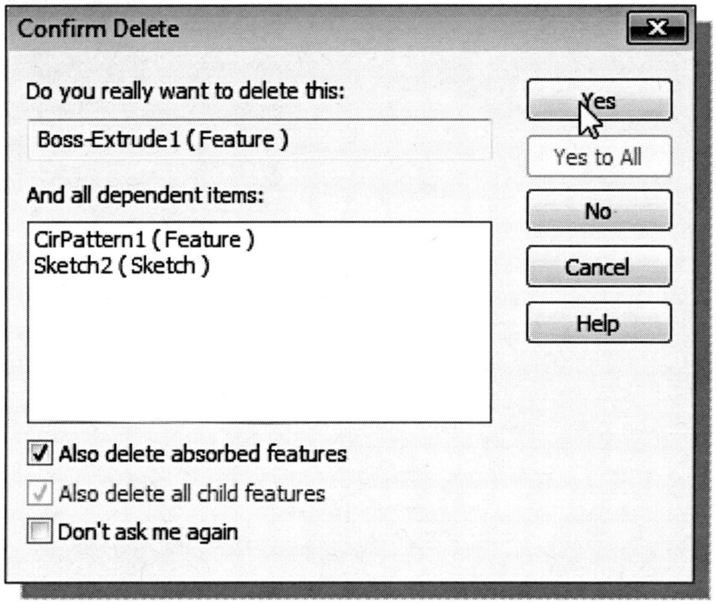

- Inside the *Confirm Delete* dialog box, note the **circular pattern** is listed as the dependent item that will be deleted.

3. Switch ***ON*** the **Also delete absorbed features** option. This will delete the associated sketch.

4. Click **Yes** to accept the settings and delete the selected features.

- Note the smaller gear has been removed from the model.

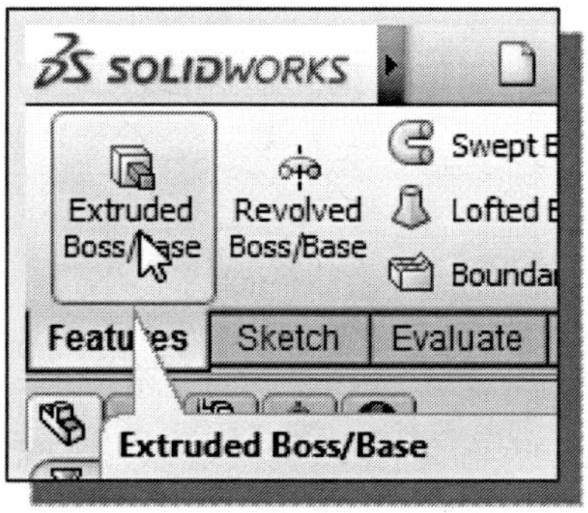

5. In the *Features* toolbar, select the **Extruded Boss/ Base** command by left-clicking once on the icon.

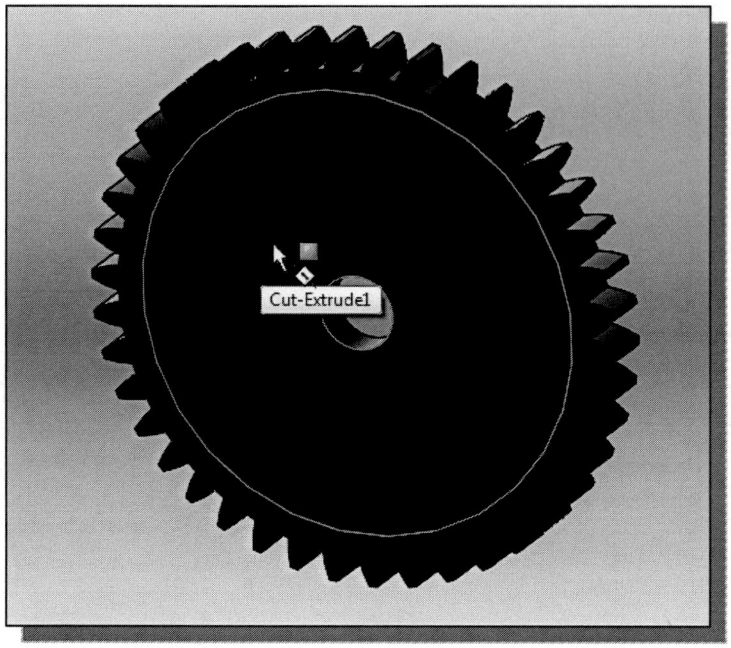

6. Select the **front face** of the gear to align the sketching plane.

7. In the *Sketch* toolbar panel, select the **Polygon** command by left-mouse-clicking once on the icon.

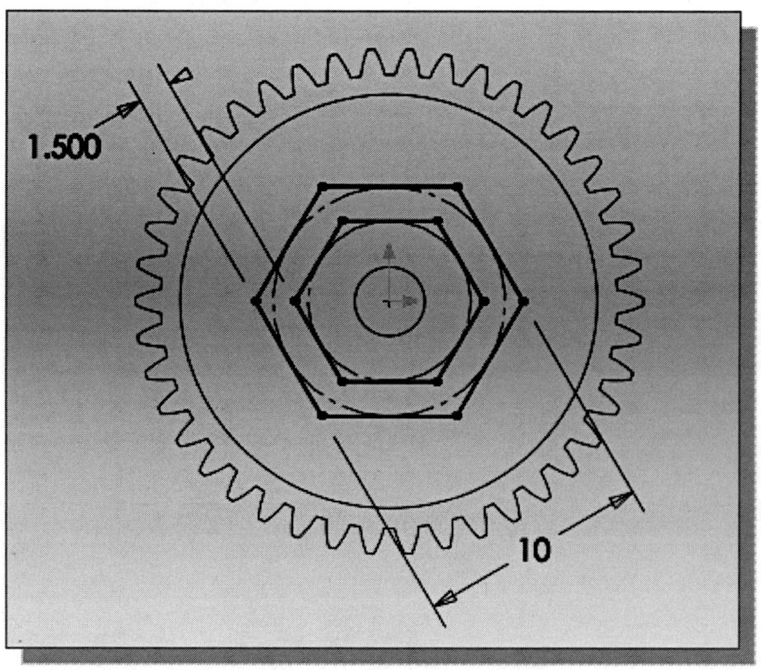

8. Create two polygons aligned to the center point of the gear as shown.

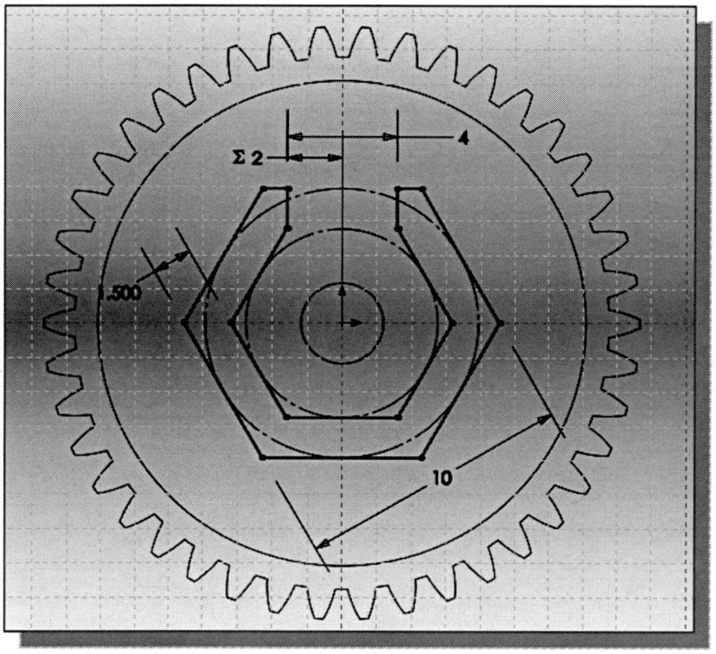

9. On your own, modify and complete the sketch as shown in the figure.

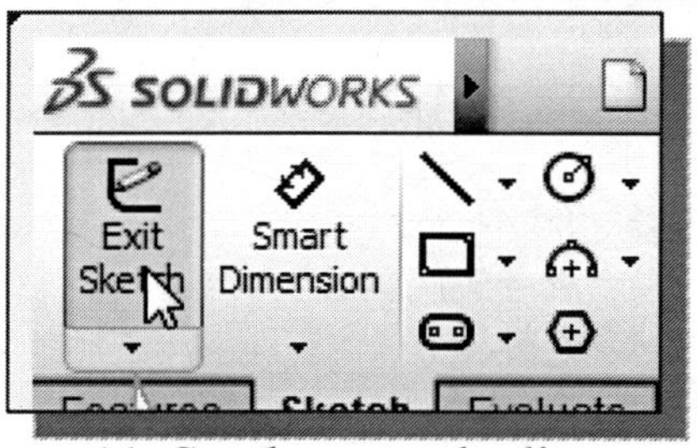

10. Click **Exit Sketch** in the *Sketch* toolbar to end the *Sketch* mode.

11. Set the extrude distance to **2.75 mm** as shown.

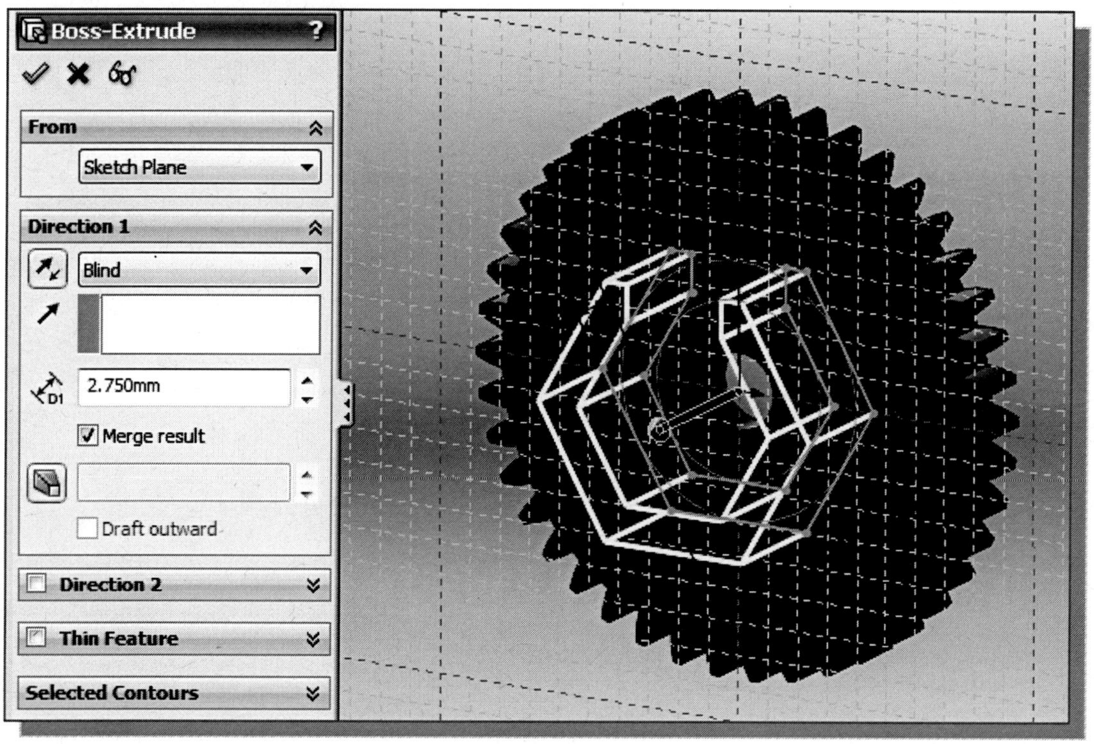

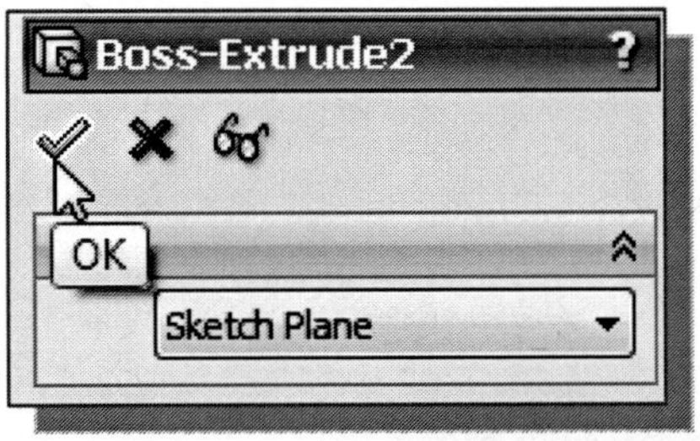

12. Click on the **check mark** button to accept the settings and create the feature.

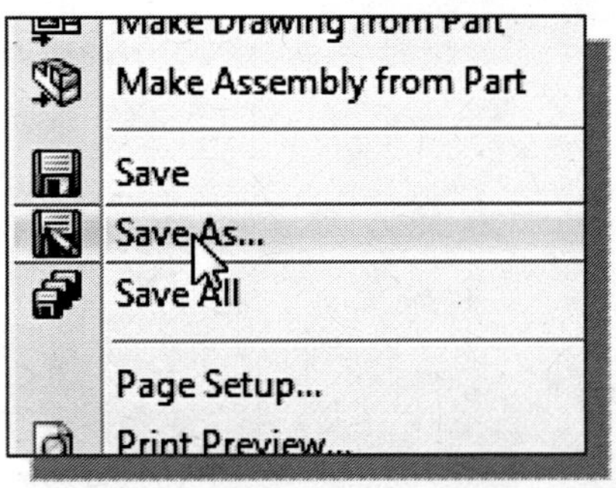

13. Select the **Save As** command in the *File* pull-down menu.

14. On your own, save the current model as a new part using **G3-Spur Gear** as the part file name.

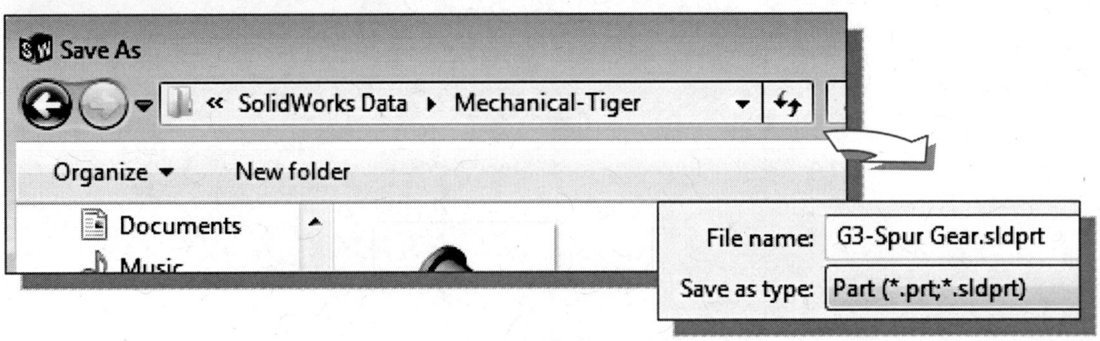

Create the G0-Pinion Part

❖ The **G0-Pinion Gear** of the *Mechanical Tiger* kit is a non-standard eight teeth pinion gear. Instead of doing the tedious task of creating the non-standard gear, we will replace the gear by using the *SolidWorks Gear Toolbox* to generate a ten teeth ANSI metric gear.

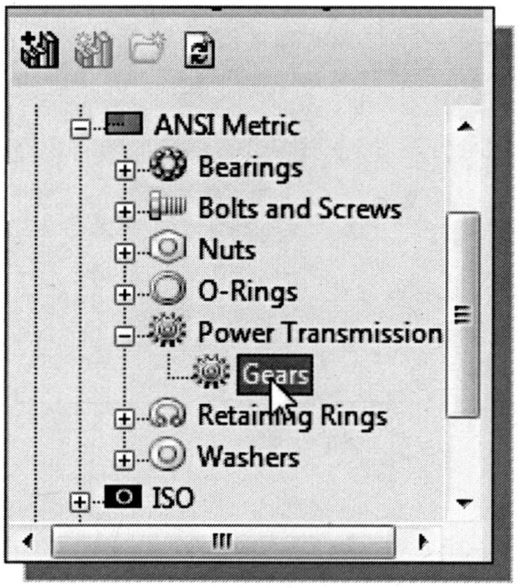

1. Click **ANSI Metric Gears** in the *Design Library task pane* as shown.

2. **Right-mouse-click** once on the **Spur Gear** icon to open the option menu.

3. Select **Create Part** as shown.

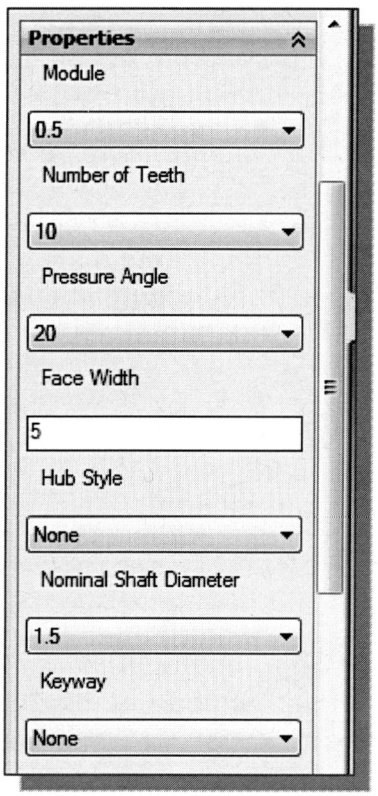

4. In the *Properties Manager* panel, set the *Module* to **0.5.**

5. Set the *Number of Teeth* to **10**.

6. Enter **5** in the *Face Width* edit box.

7. Set the *Hub Style* to **None** as shown.

8. Set the *Nominal Shaft Diameter* to **1.5**.

9. Set the *Keyway* option to **None**.

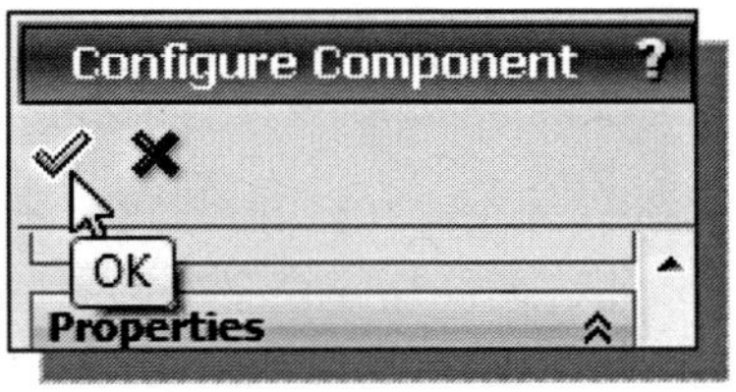

10. Click **OK** to accept the configuration settings and generate the gear part.

11. Switch to the **10T Gear** model as shown.

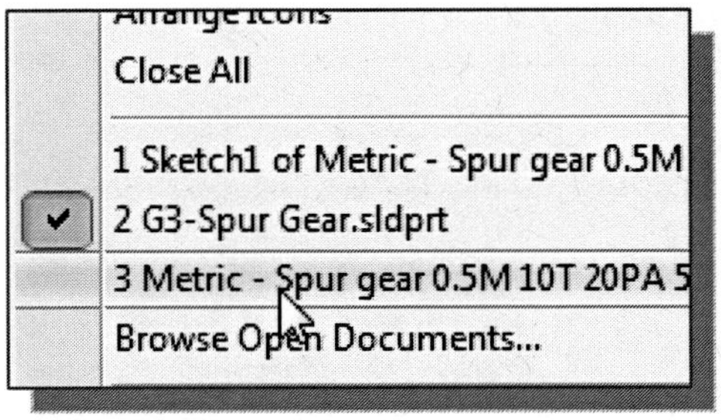

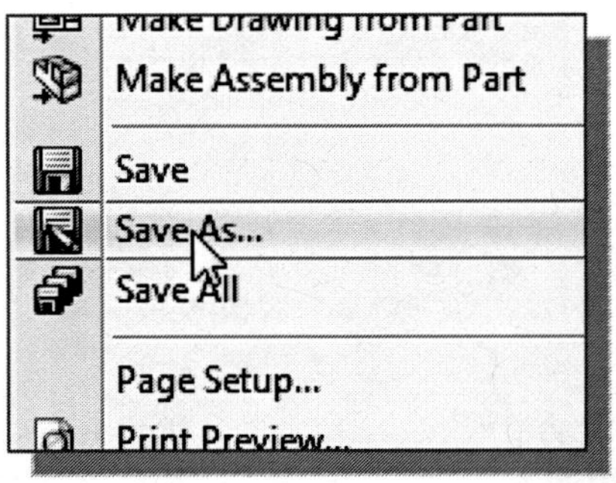

12. Select the **Save As** command in the *File* pull-down menu.

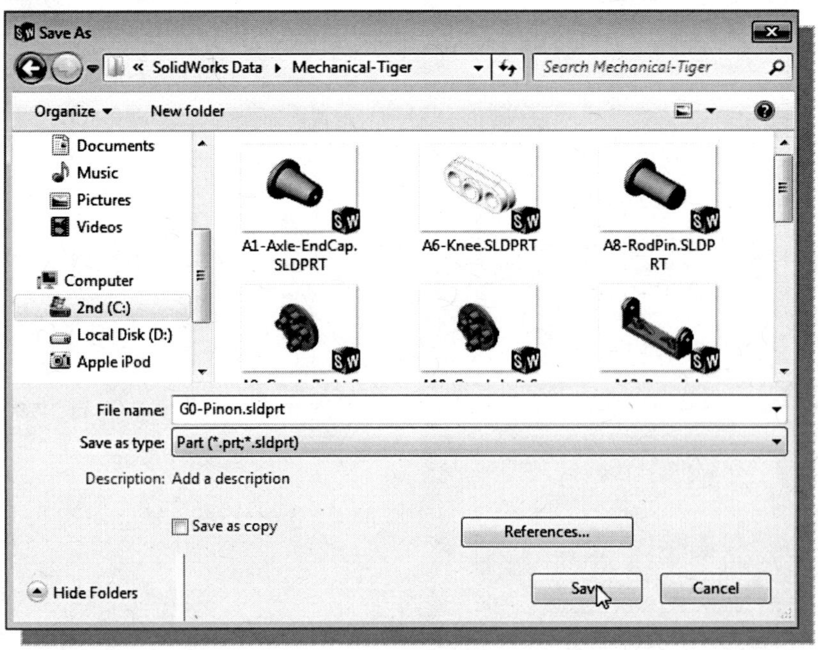

13. On your own, save the current model as a new part using **G0-Pinon** as the part file name.

Start a New Part File

❖ The last gear we need for the *Tamiya Tiger* kit is a non-standard compound gear. We will create this gear using several options, with a portion of it using the **Revolve** and **Pattern** commands.

1. Select the **New** icon with a single click of the left-mouse-button on the *Menu Bar*.

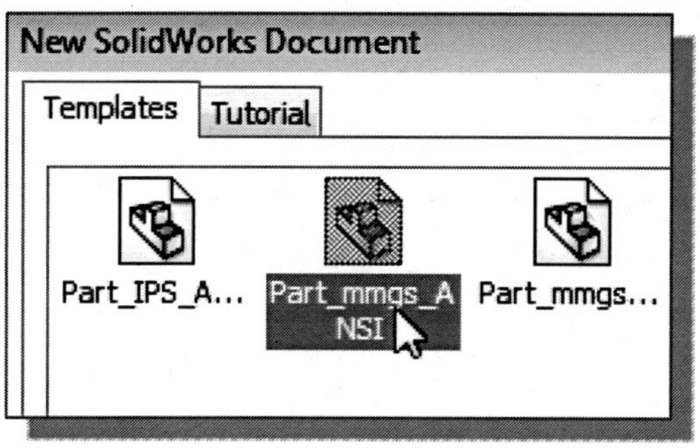

2. Notice the **three** template files appear in the **Advanced** mode. Select the **Part_mmgs_ANSI** template as shown.

3. Click on the **OK** button to open a new document using the selected template.

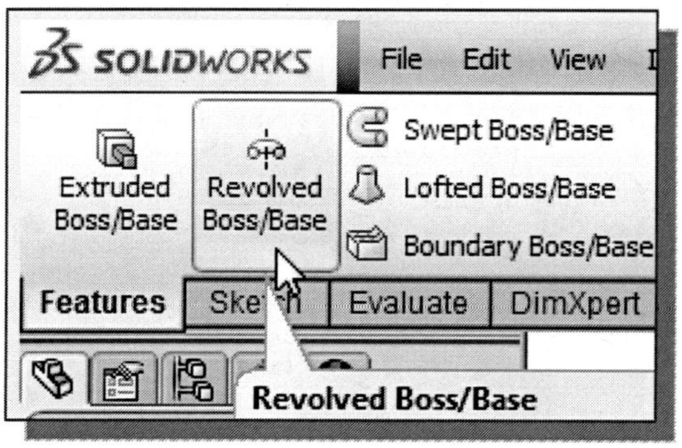

4. In the *Features* toolbar select the **Revolved Boss/Base** command by clicking once with the left-mouse-button on the icon.

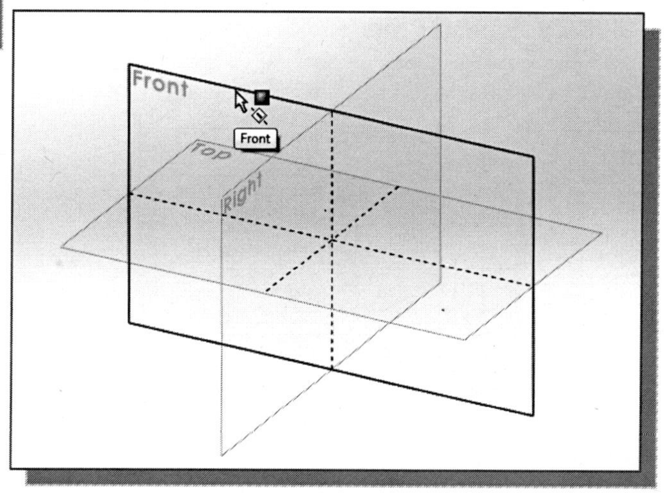

5. Inside the graphics window, select the **Front Plane** as the sketching plane as shown.

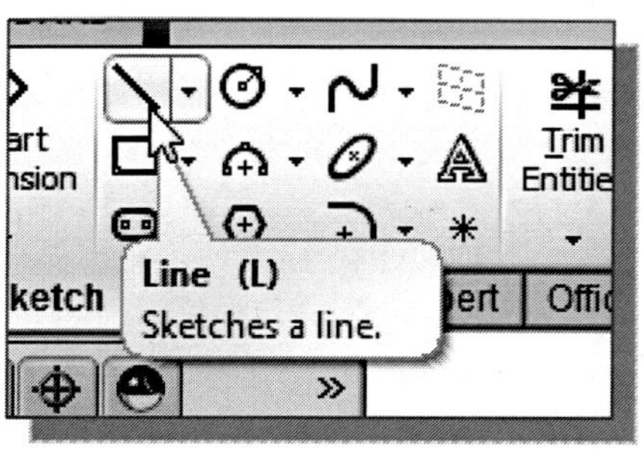

6. Select the **Line** option in the *Sketch* panel. A *Help-tip* box appears next to the cursor: "*Sketches a line.*"

7. Create a **closed region** sketch to the right side of the center point; also create a vertical centerline aligned to the center point of the coordinate system as shown.

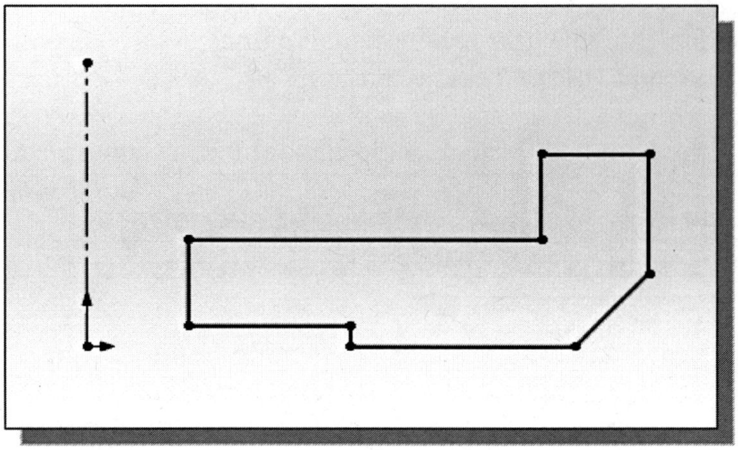

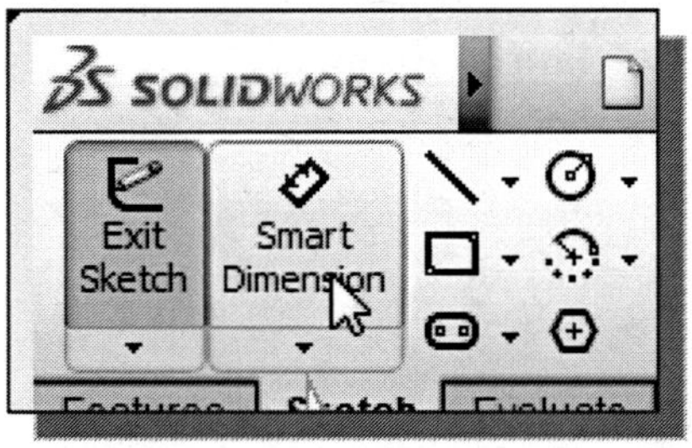

8. Select the **Smart Dimension** command in the *Sketch* toolbar panel.

9. Pick the **center line** as the first entity to dimension as shown in the figure.

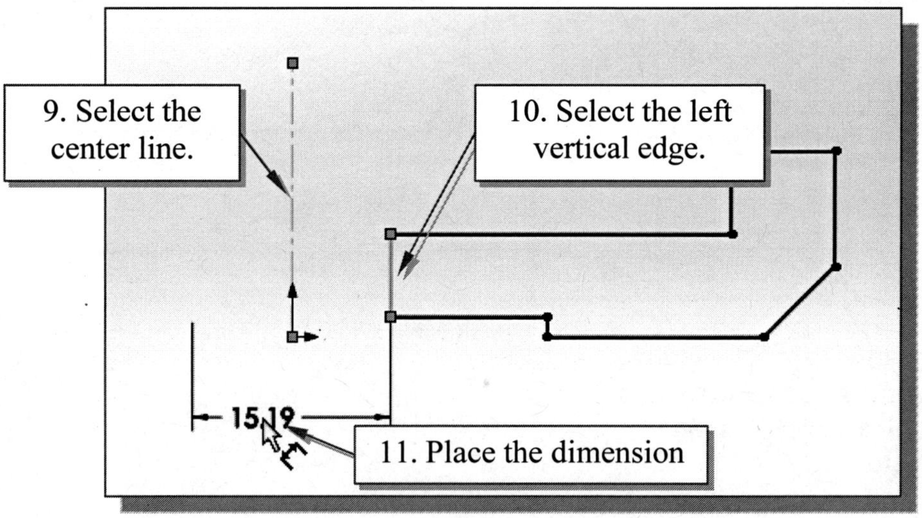

10. Select the **left vertical line** as the second object to dimension.

11. Place the dimension text toward the left side of the centerline to create a **diameter dimension.**

- **To create a dimension that will account for the symmetrical nature of the design, pick the axis of symmetry, pick the entity, and then place the dimension to the other side of the centerline. (The Diameter Dimension option is also available through the right-mouse-click option menu.)**

12. On your own, create the dimensions as shown in the figure below.

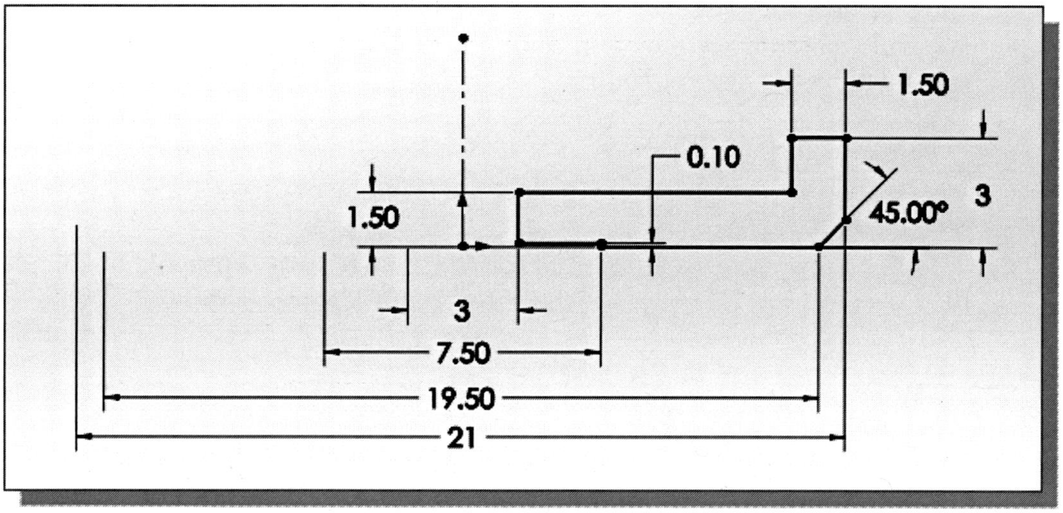

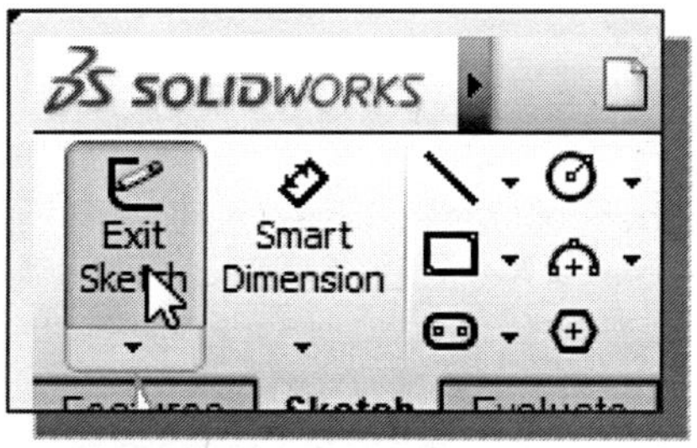

13. Click **Exit Sketch** in the *Sketch* toolbar to end the *Sketch* mode.

14. Confirm the revolve angle is set to **360** degrees. Note the profile and the center axis are automatically selected for the revolved feature.

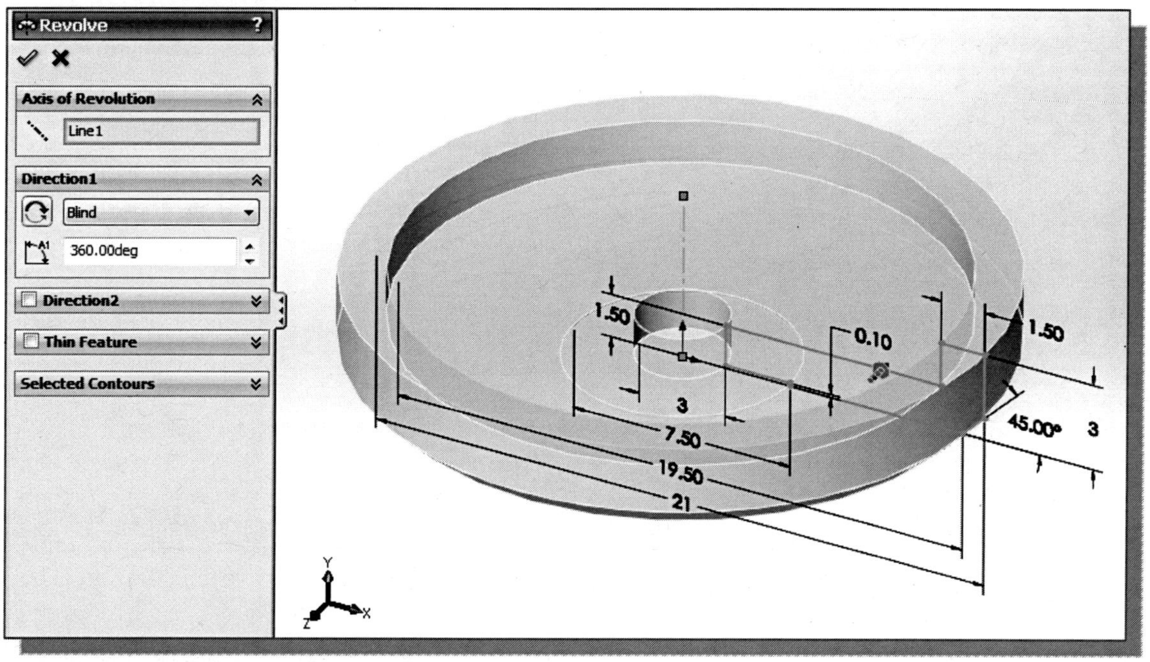

15. Click **OK** to accept the selection and create a revolved feature.

Export/Import the Generated Gear Profile

- We will create the *teeth* by importing the tooth profile from the **G3-Spur Gear** generated by the *Design Toolbox*.

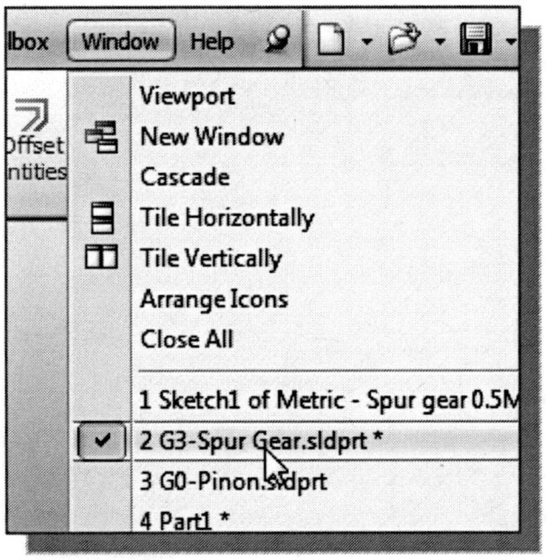

1. Select the *Window* pull-down menu as shown.

2. Switch to the **G3-Spur Gear** file by clicking on the associated filename as shown.

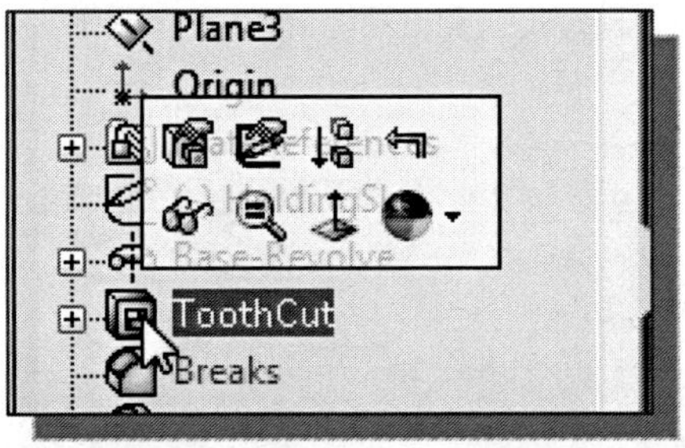

3. Inside the *Model History Tree*, left-mouse-click on **ToothCut** to bring up the option menu as shown.

4. In the option menu, select **Edit Sketch**.

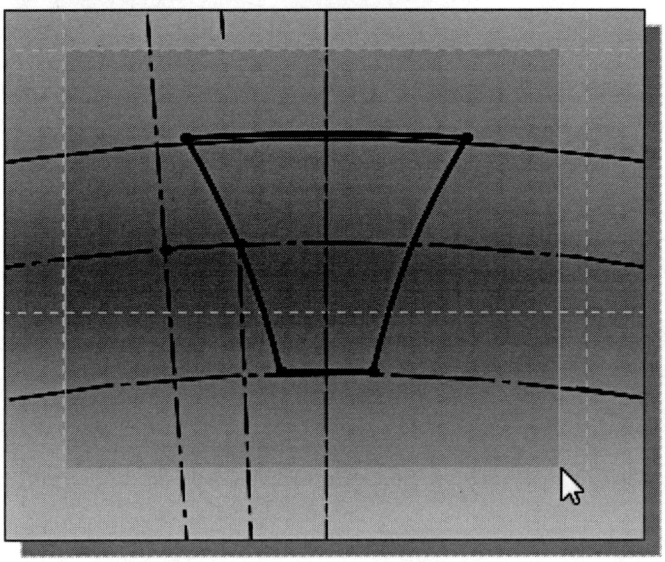

5. Inside the graphics window, use a **selection window** to select the **ToothCut** sketch as shown.

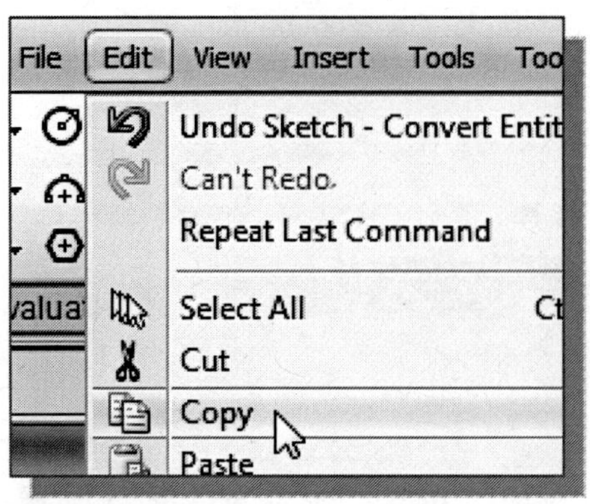

6. Select **Copy** in the *Edit* pull-down menu as shown. Note that we are using the copy function of the *operating system clipboard.*

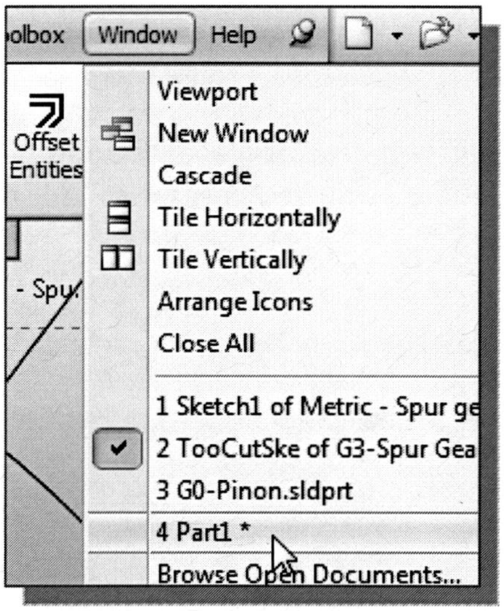

7. Select the *Window* pull-down menu as shown.

8. Switch to the **G3-Spur Gear** file by clicking on the associated filename as shown.

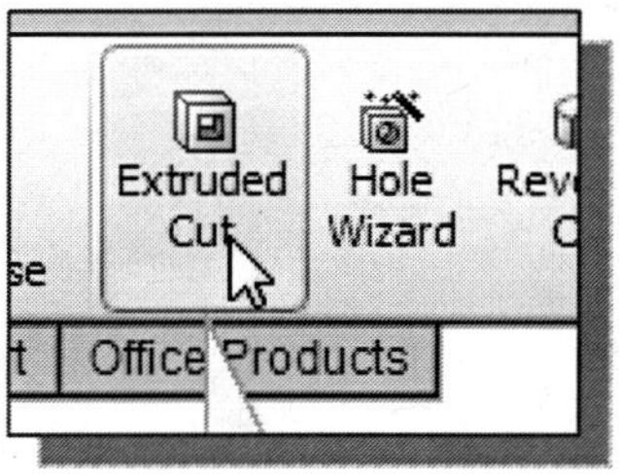

9. In the *Features* toolbar, select the **Extruded Cut** command by left-clicking once on the icon.

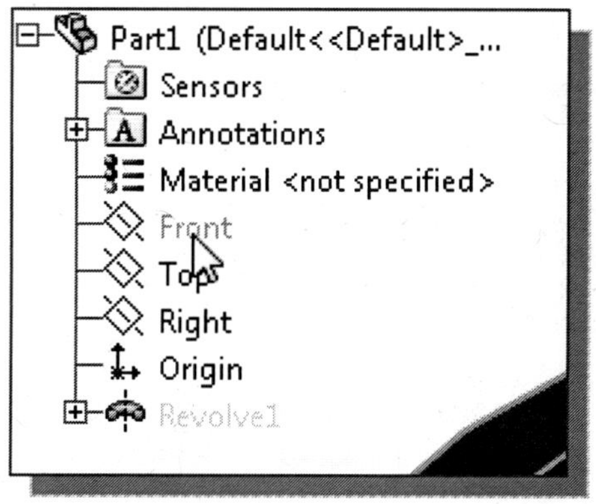

10. Select the **Front datum plane** to align the sketching plane.

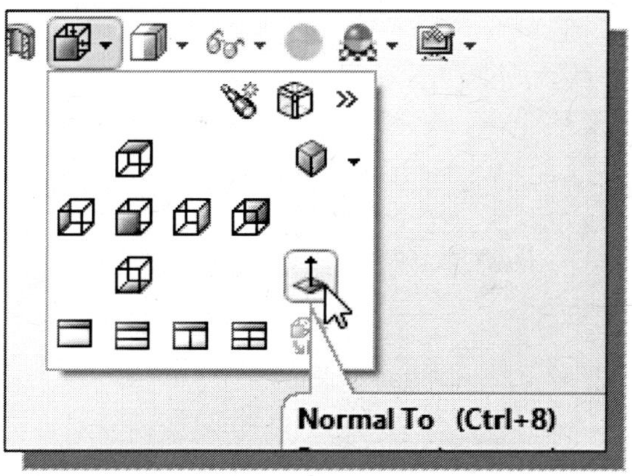

11. Align the sketching plane to the screen by using the **Normal To** option as shown.

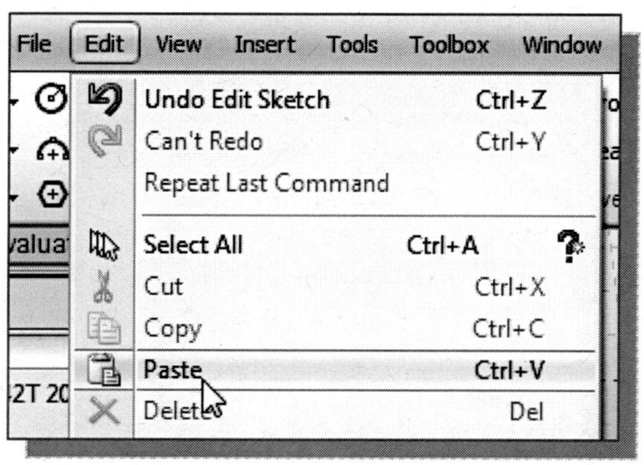

12. In the *Edit* pull-down menu, select the **Paste** command by left-clicking once on the icon as shown.

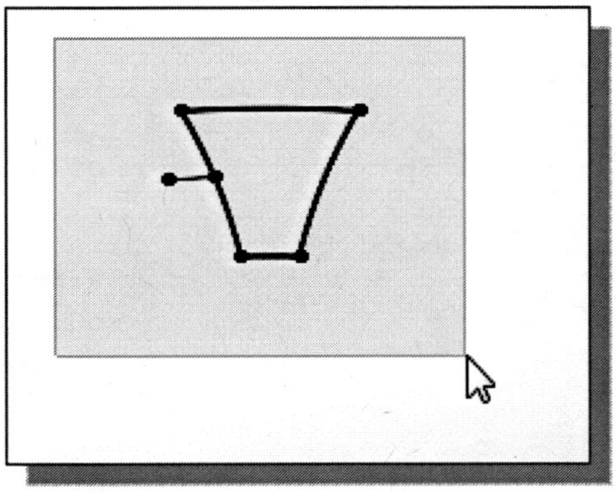

13. Inside the graphics window, use a **selection window** to select the projected entities as shown.

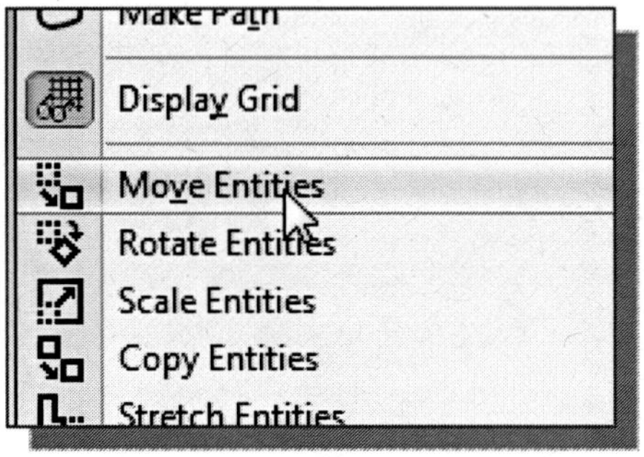

14. Inside the graphics window, right-click once to bring up the option menu and select **Move Entities** as shown.

15. On your own, reposition the selected entities using **drag & drop** as shown.

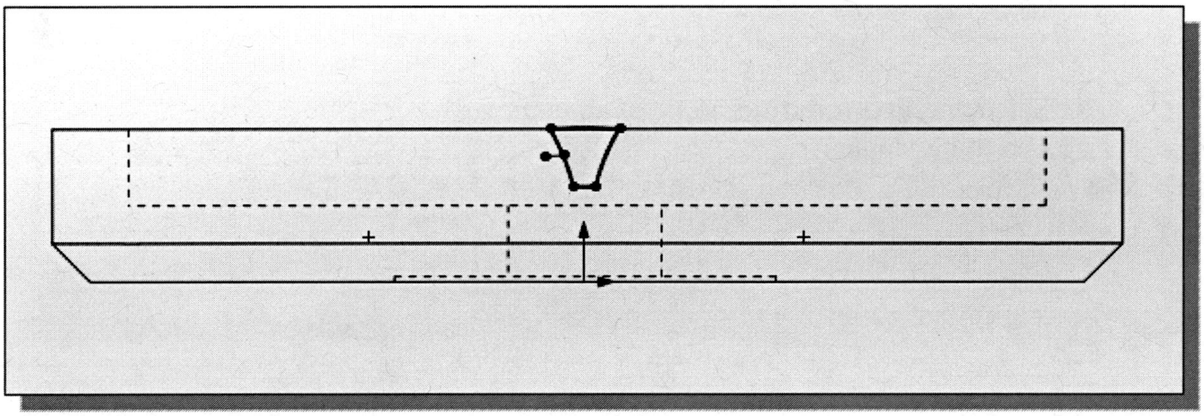

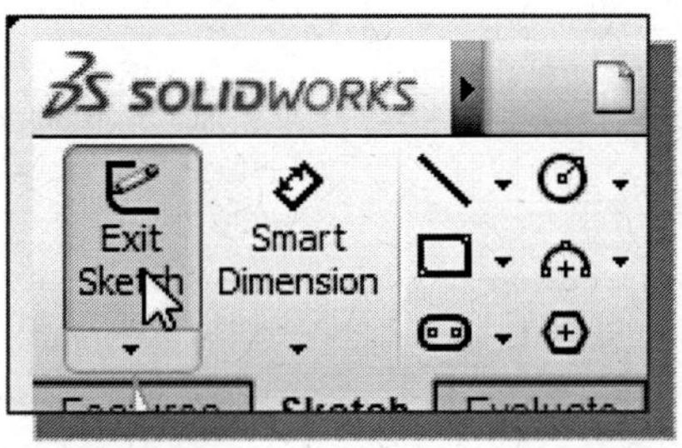

16. Click **Exit Sketch** to exit the *Edit Sketch* mode as shown.

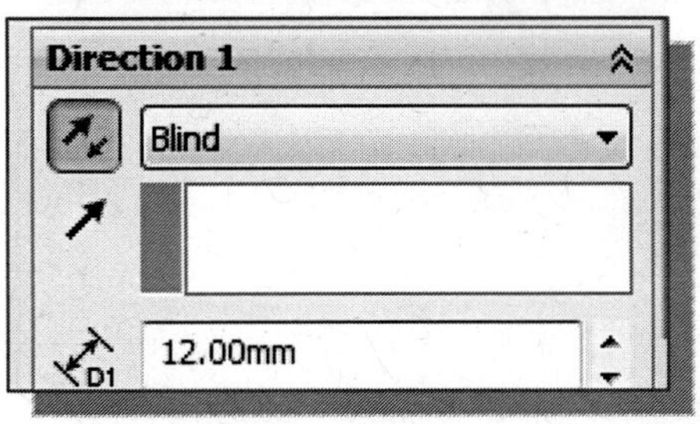

17. On your own, reverse the *extrusion direction* and set the *end condition* to **12** and create the cut feature.

Create a Circular pattern

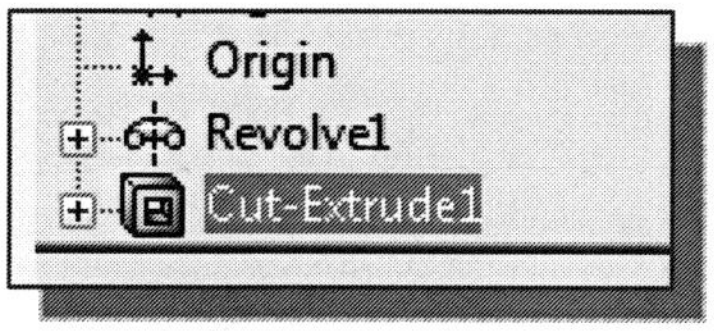

1. Confirm the **Cut-Extrude1** feature is *pre-selected* as shown.

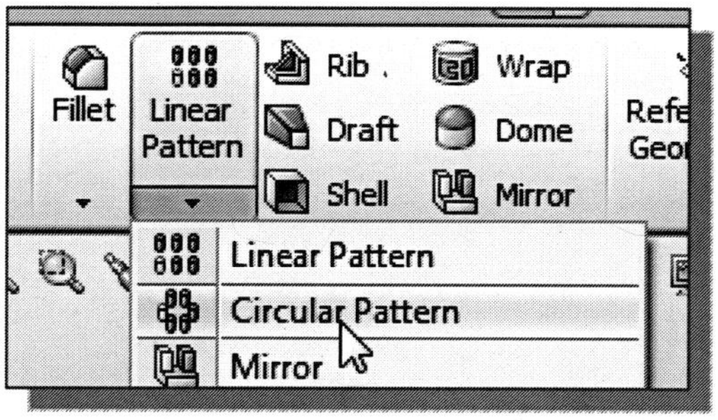

2. In the *Features* toolbar, select the **Circular Pattern** command by clicking the left-mouse-button on the icon.

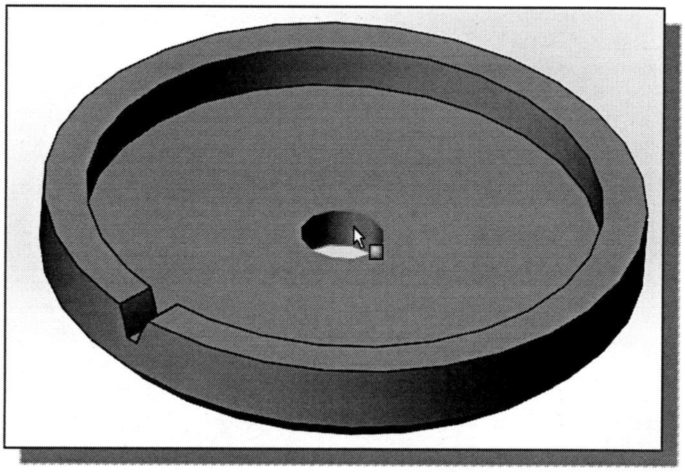

3. Select the center **cylindrical surface** to set the *axis of rotation.*

4. Switch *ON* the **Equal Spacing** option and set the *number of instances* to **40** as shown.

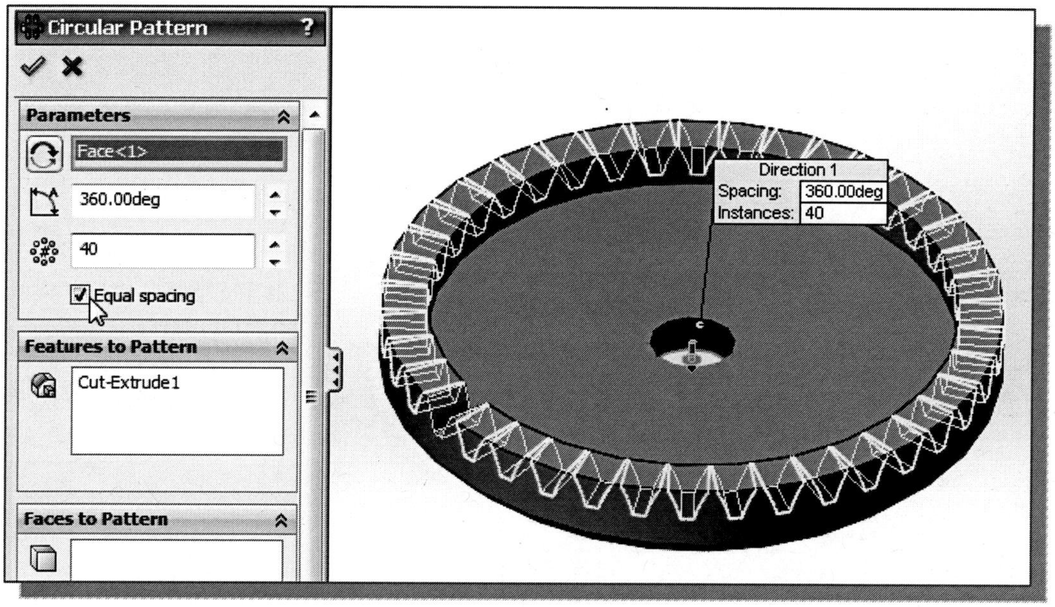

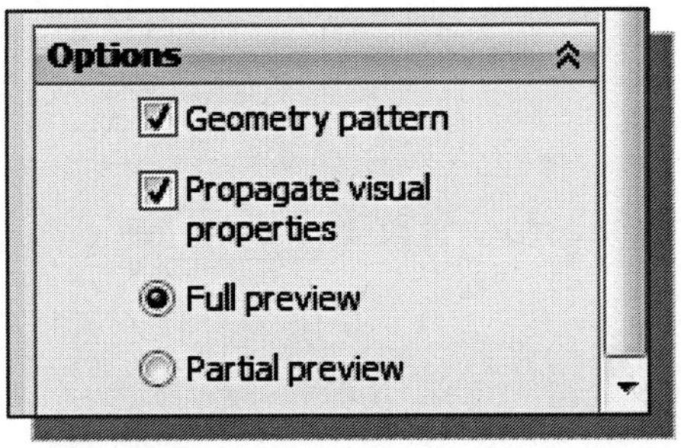

5. In the *Options* panel, switch *ON* the **Geometry pattern** and the **Full preview** options as shown.

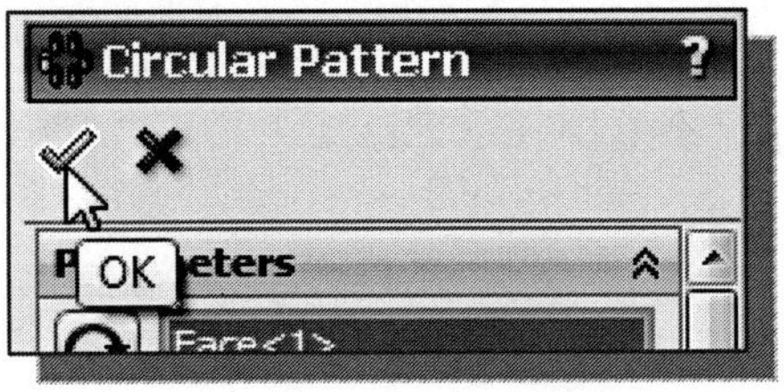

6. Click on the **OK** button to accept the settings and create the pattern feature.

7. On your own, **Save** the current model using the filename ***G1-Spur Gear***.

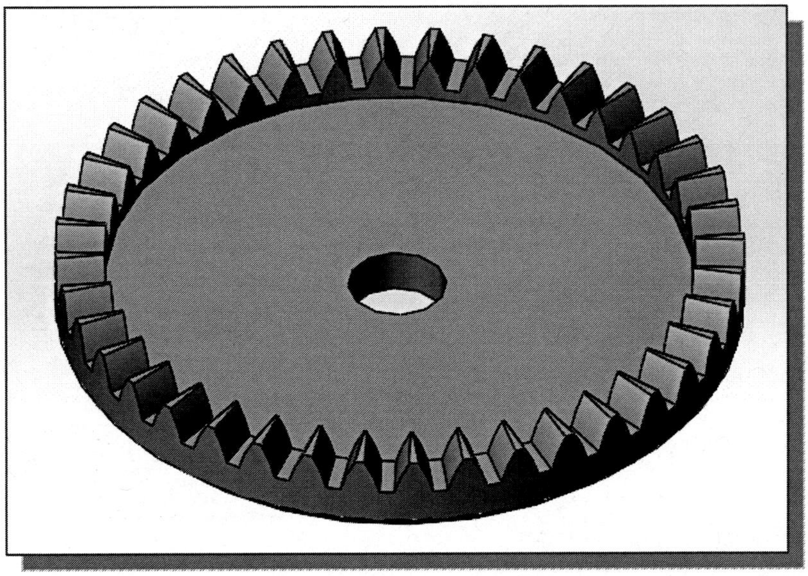

- The **Circular Pattern** command can be used to quickly create duplicates about a center axis of rotation.

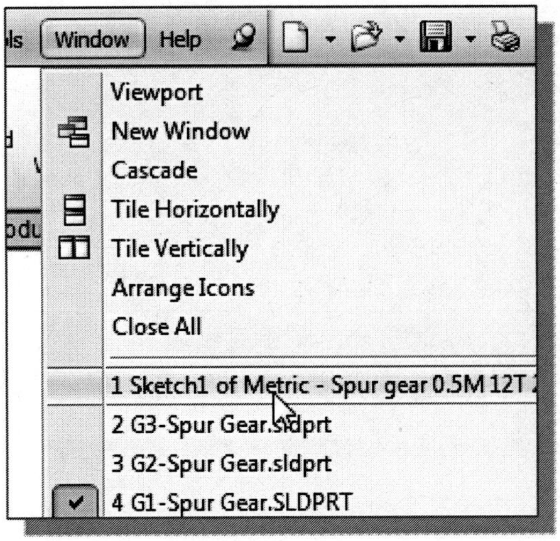

- For the compound gear portion, we will import the **12T** gear profile generated from the *SolidWorks Design Toolbox.*

8. In the *Window* pull-down menu, switch to the other gear file by selecting the generated **0.5M12T** file as shown.

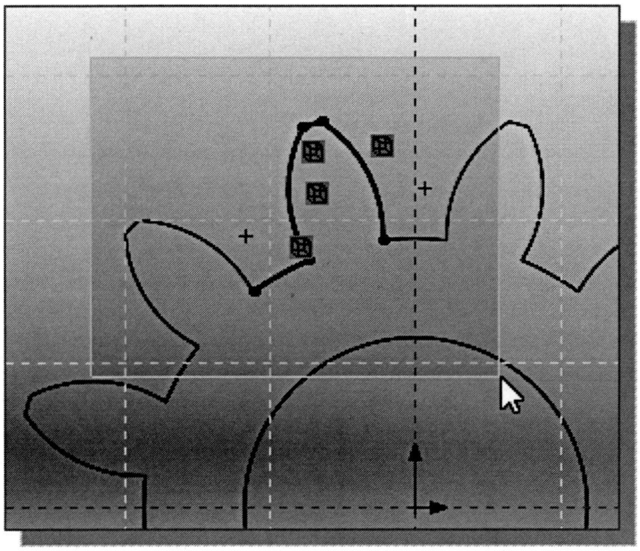

9. Inside the graphics window, use a **selection window** to select the projected entities as shown.

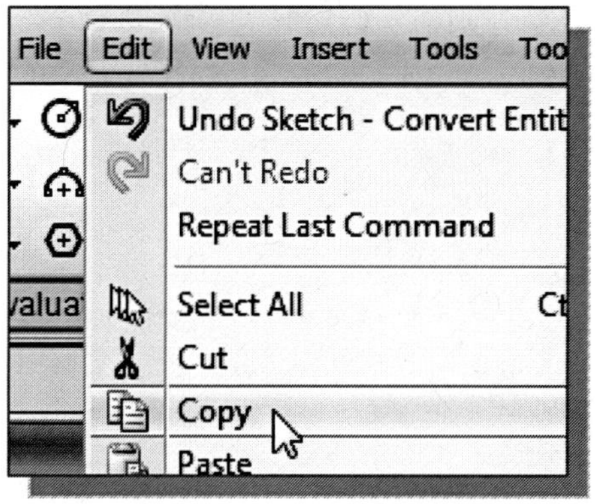

10. Select **Copy** in the *Edit* pull-down menu as shown. Note that we are using the copy function of the *operating system clipboard.*

11. In the *Window* pull-down menu, switch to the other gear file by selecting the generated **G1-Spur Gear** file as shown.

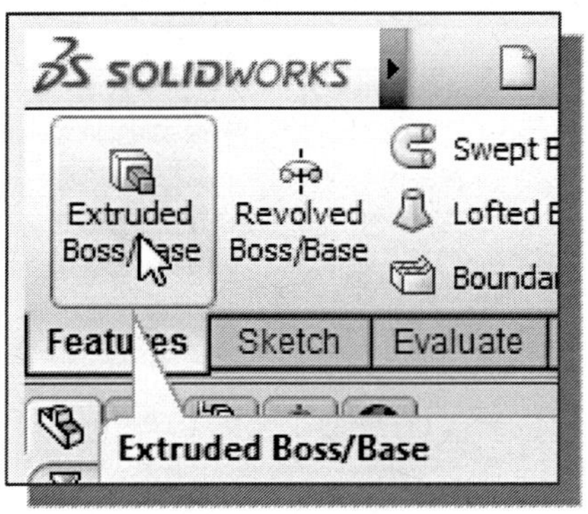

12. In the *Features* toolbar, select the **Extruded Boss/ Base** command by left-clicking once on the icon.

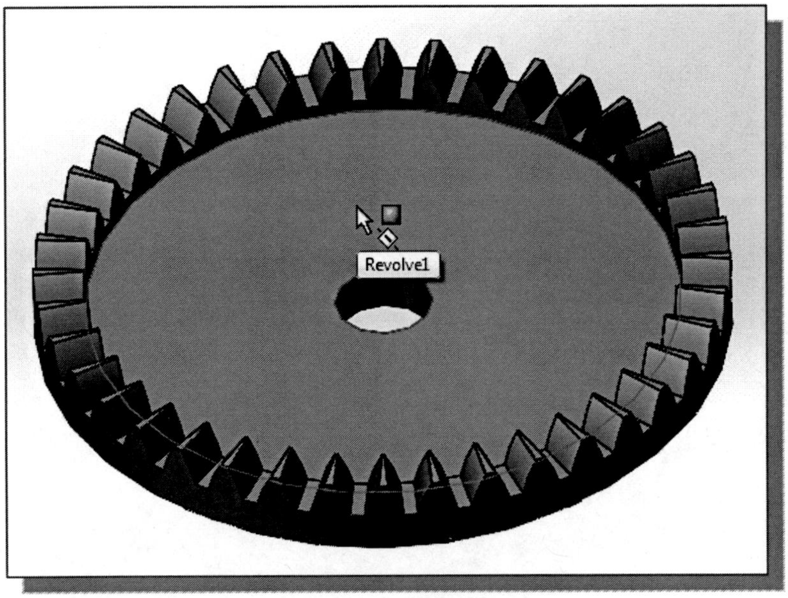

13. Select the **top face** of the **G1-Spur** gear to align the sketching plane as shown.

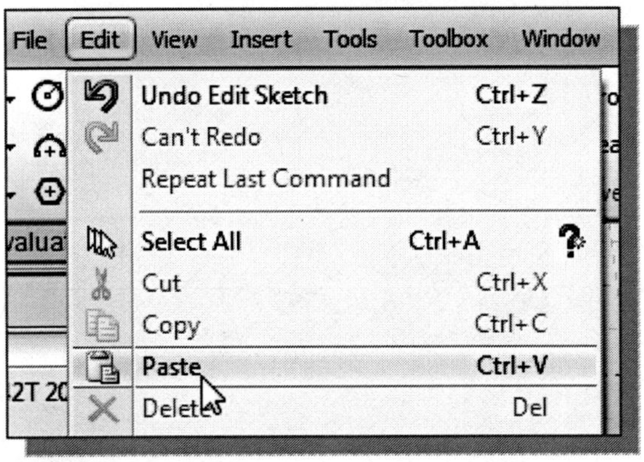

14. In the *Edit* pull-down menu, select the **Paste** command by left-clicking once on the icon as shown.

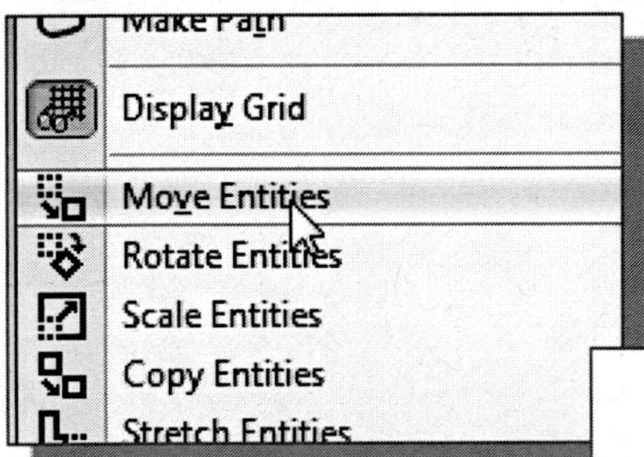

15. On your own, reposition the pasted entities to be aligned to the *Origin* as shown.

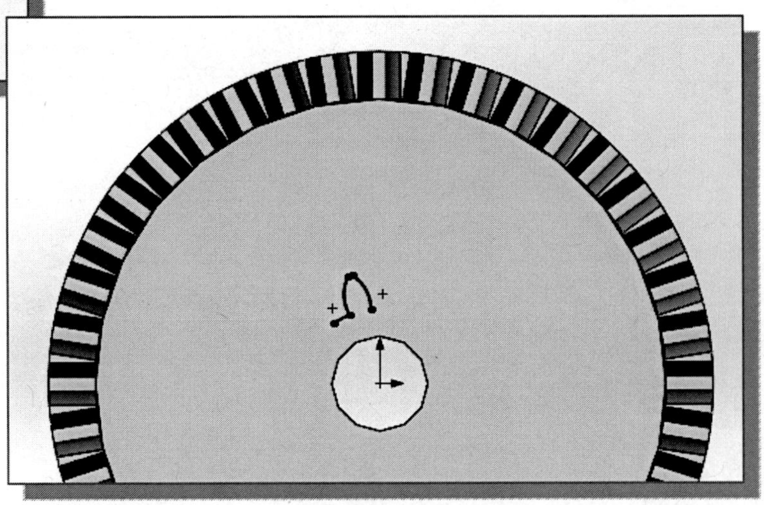

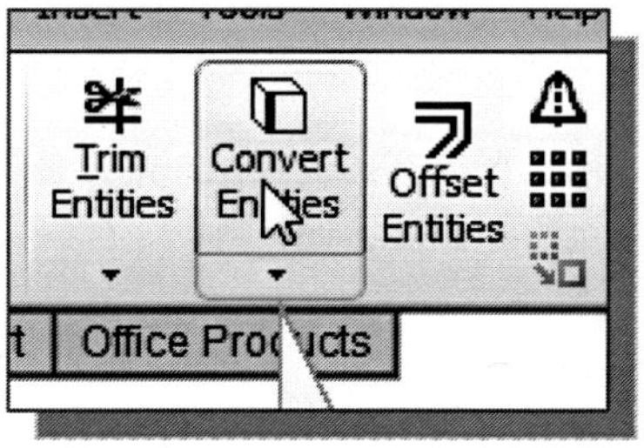

16. Select **Convert Entities** in the *Sketch* toolbar.

17. Select the **inside circle** to project the geometry to the sketching plane.

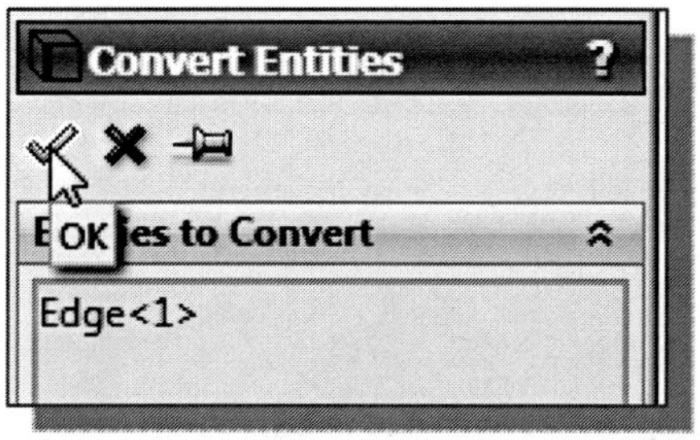

18. Click on the **check mark** button to accept the settings.

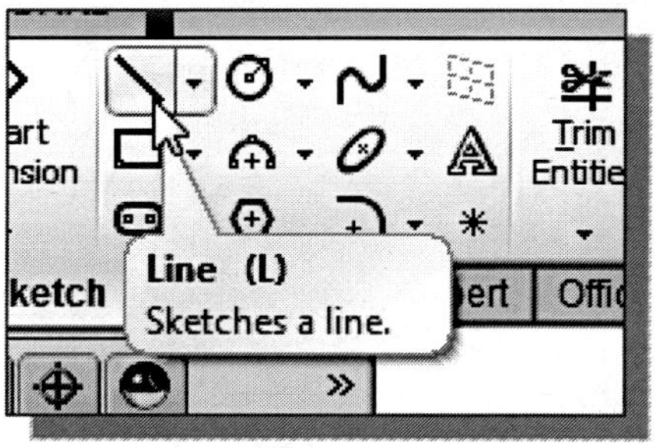

19. Select the **Line** option in the *Sketch* panel. A *Help-tip* box appears next to the cursor: "*Sketches a line.*"

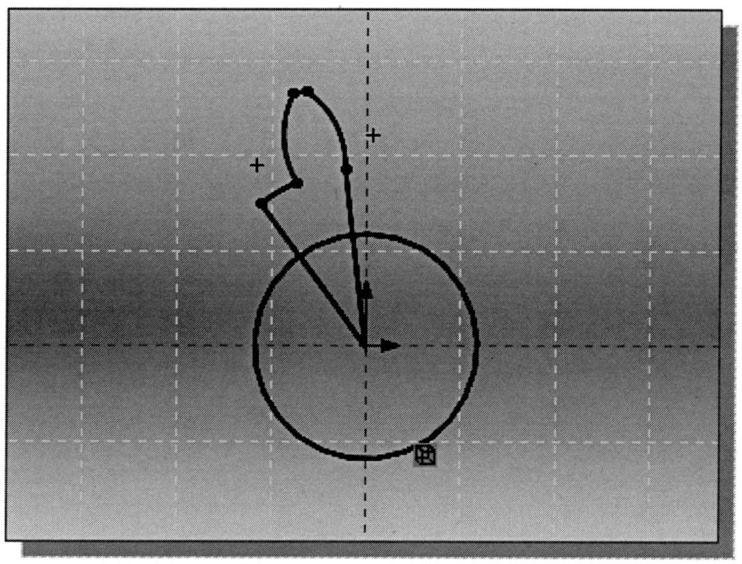

20. Create **two line segments** to form the closed region aligned to the *Origin* as shown.

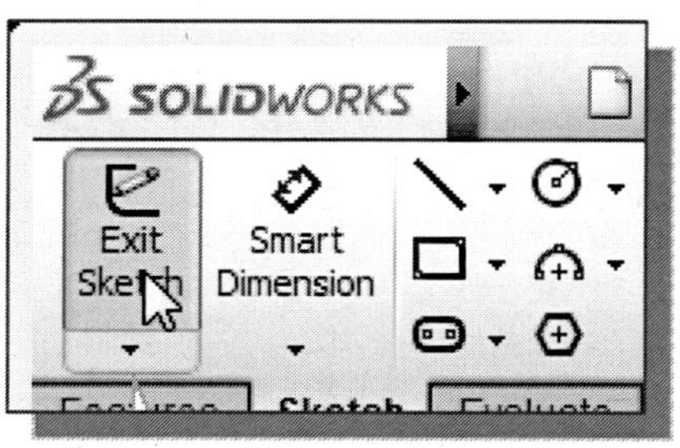

21. Click **Exit Sketch** in the *Sketch* toolbar to end the *Sketch* mode.

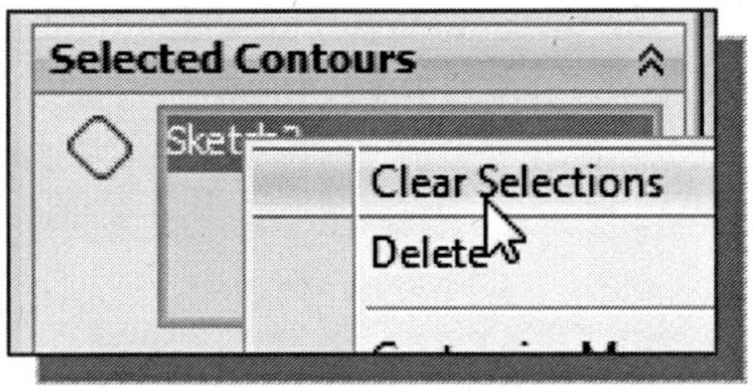

22. In the **Selected Contours** list, remove any pre-selected item through the right-mouse-click.

23. Select the **tooth region** as shown in the figure below.

24. Set the extrude distance to **6.5 mm** and create the feature as shown.

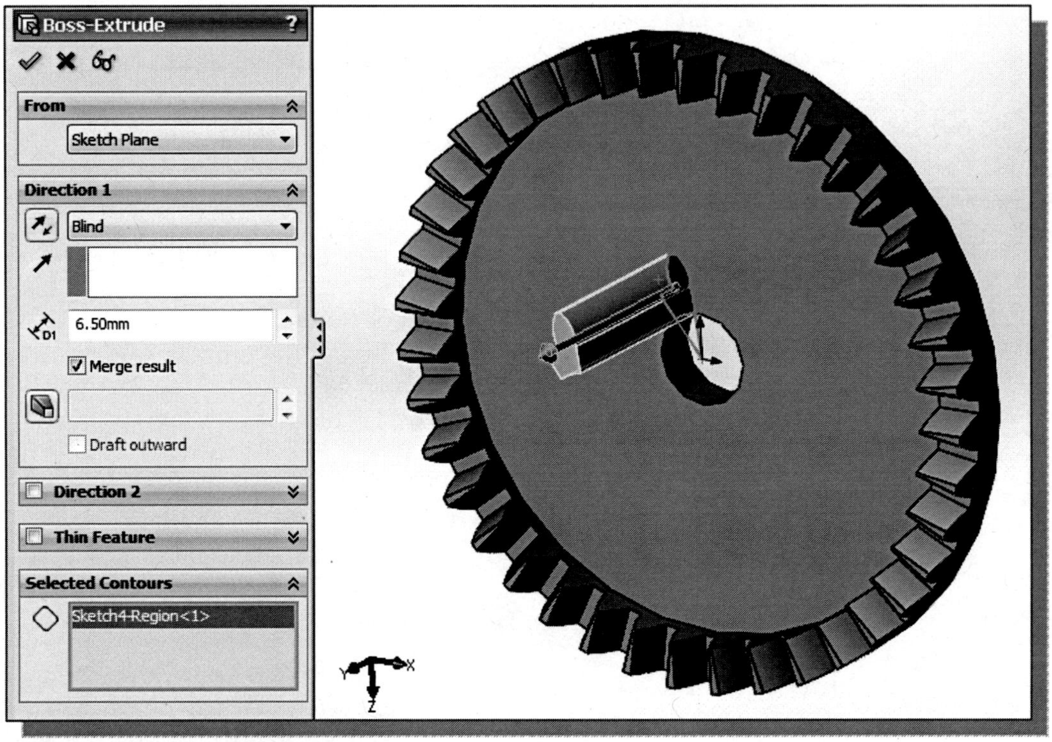

25. Click on the **check mark** button to accept the settings and create the feature.

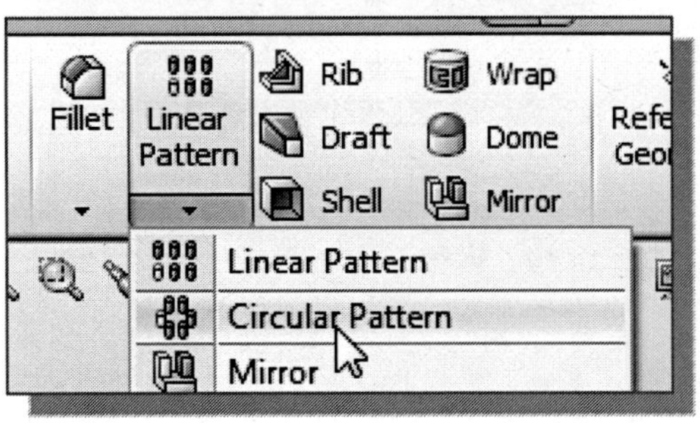

26. In the *Features* toolbar, select the **Circular Pattern** command by clicking the left-mouse-button on the icon

27. On your own, create the circular pattern by setting the *Equal spacing angle* to **360** degrees and the *number of instances* to **12**. (Uncheck the **Geometry Pattern** option.)

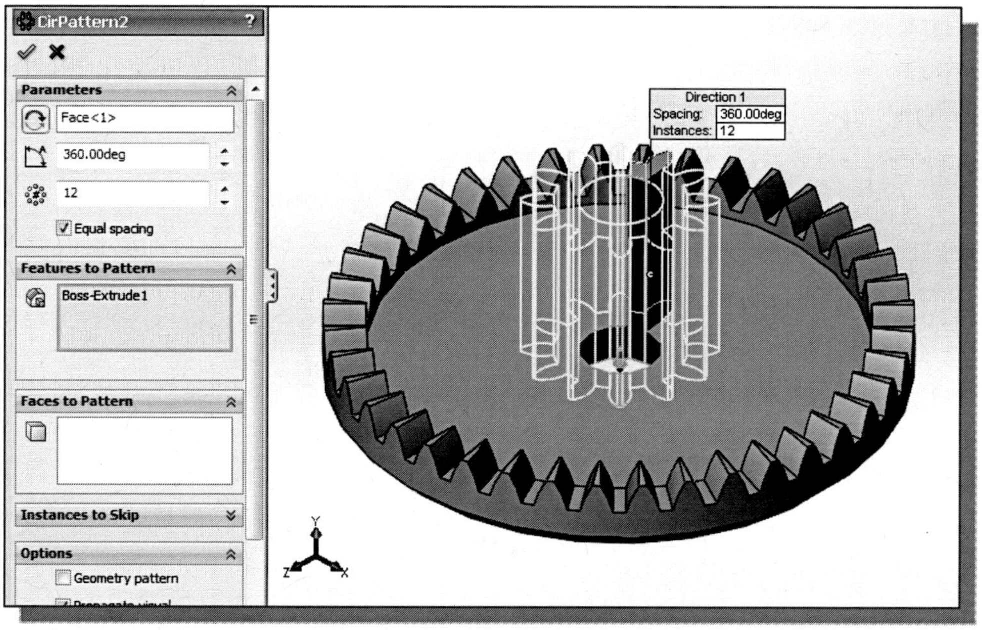

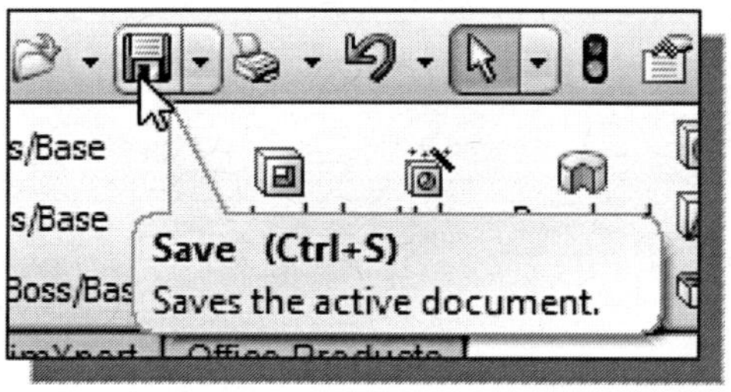

28. Click **Save** to save the current model.

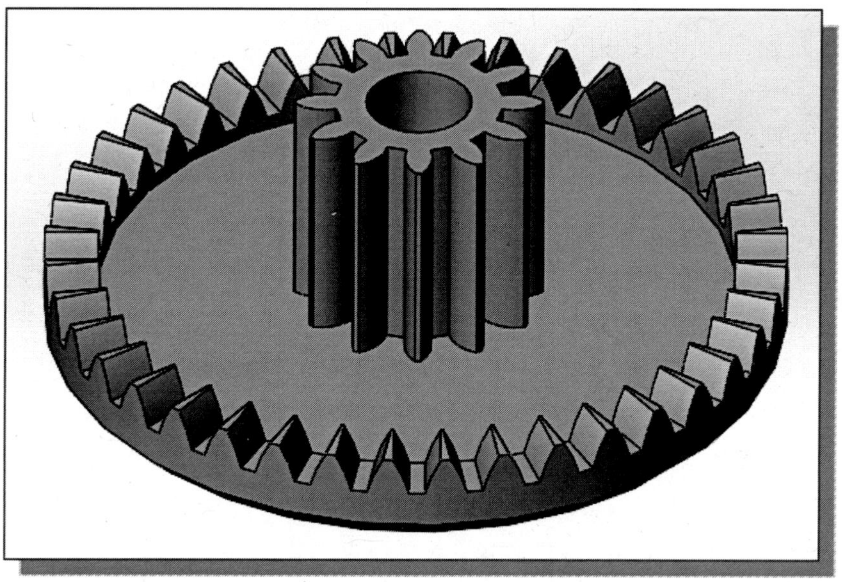

- Note that all of the required gears for the *Tamiya Tiger* kit have been created.

Questions:

1. List three types of commonly used gears.

2. What is the difference between ***pitch diameter*** and ***outside diameter*** on a spur gear?

3. How do we access the ***SolidWorks Spur Gear Generator***?

4. What is the definition of ***gear ratio*** in a *gear train*?

5. What is included in the ***SolidWorks Design Library***?

6. Why is it important to identify symmetrical features in designs?

7. When and why should we use the ***Pattern*** option?

8. How do we create a ***linear diameter dimension*** for a revolved feature?

9. Can we export and reuse the ***tooth profile*** of a *spur gear*?

Exercises:

1. **Shaft Support** (Dimensions are in inches.)

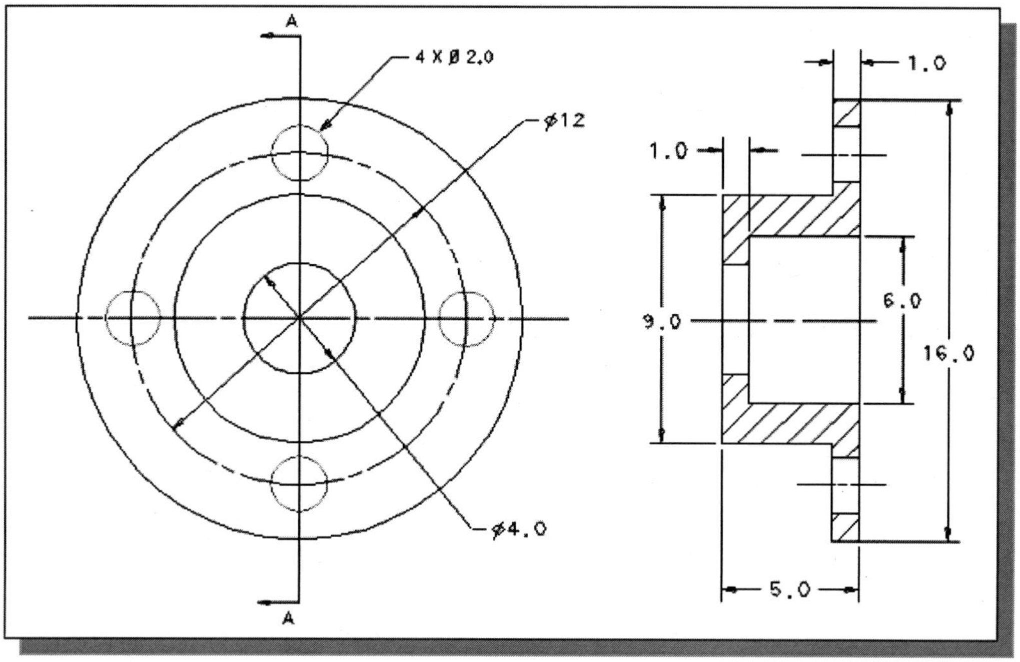

2. **Guide Base** (Dimensions are in mm.)

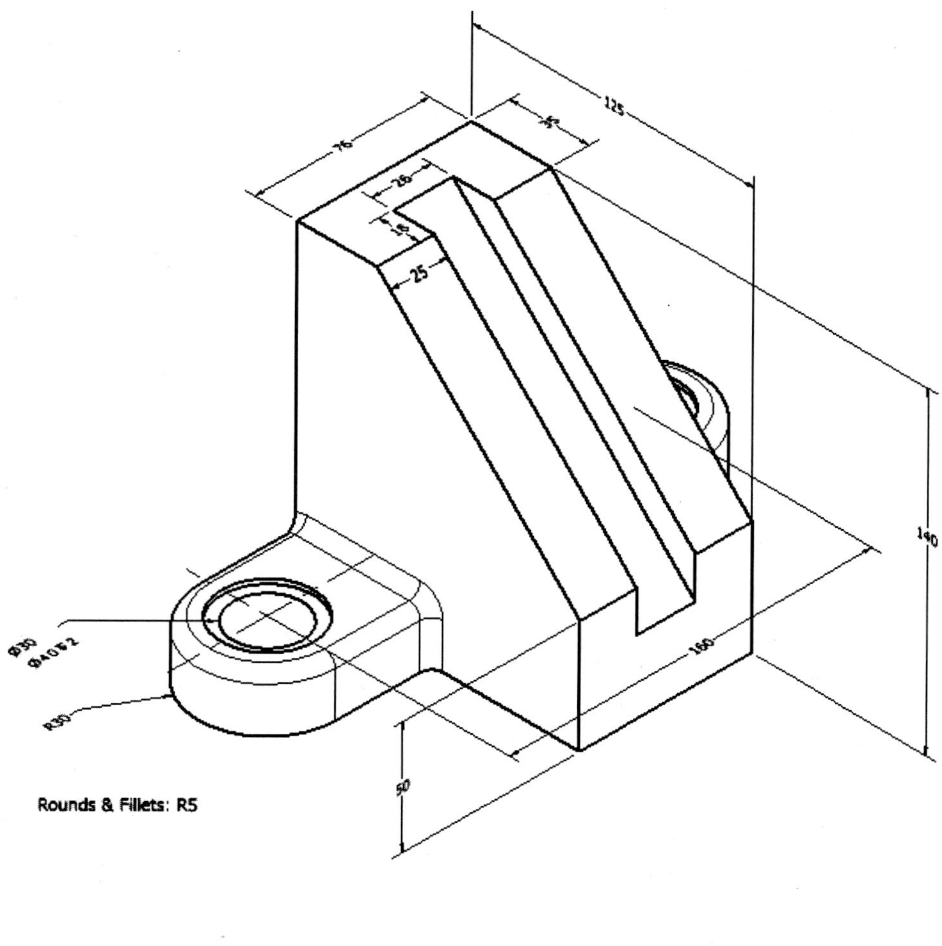

3. **Geneva Wheel** (Dimensions are in inches.)

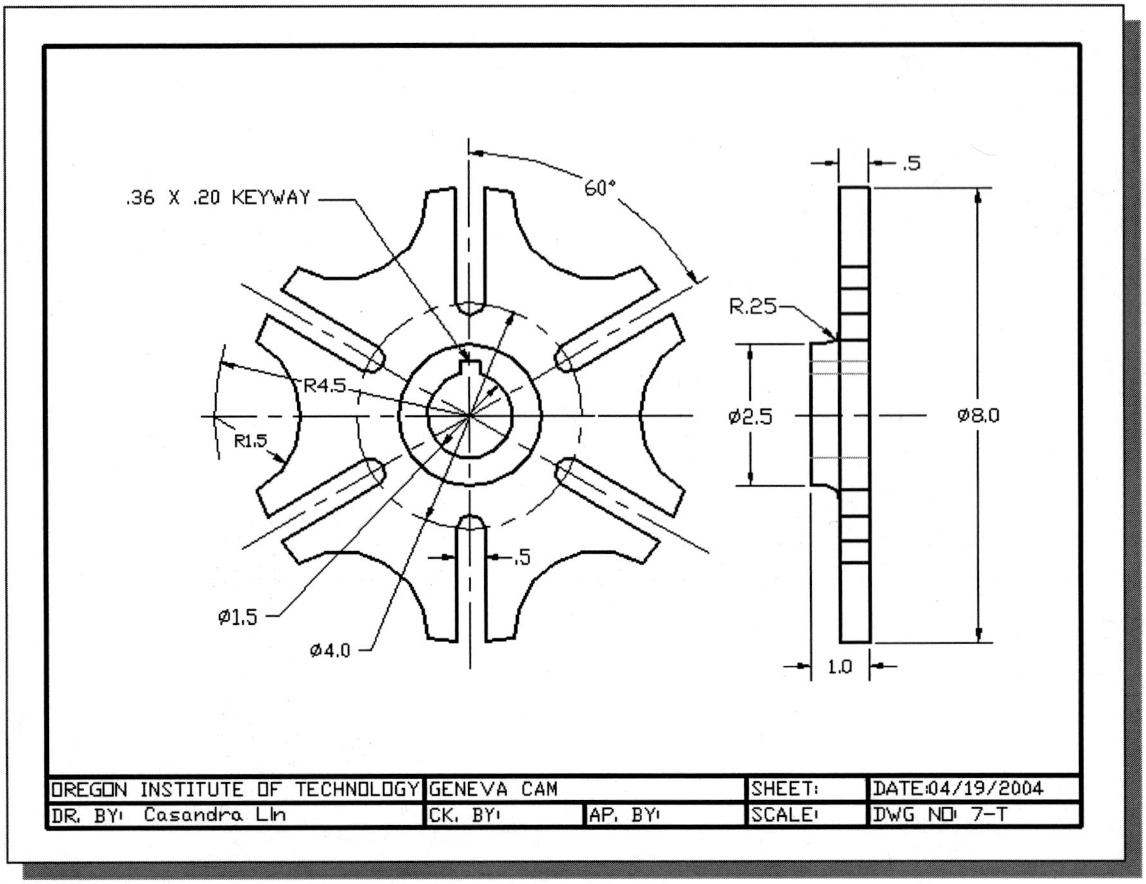

4. **Support Mount** (Dimensions are in inches.)

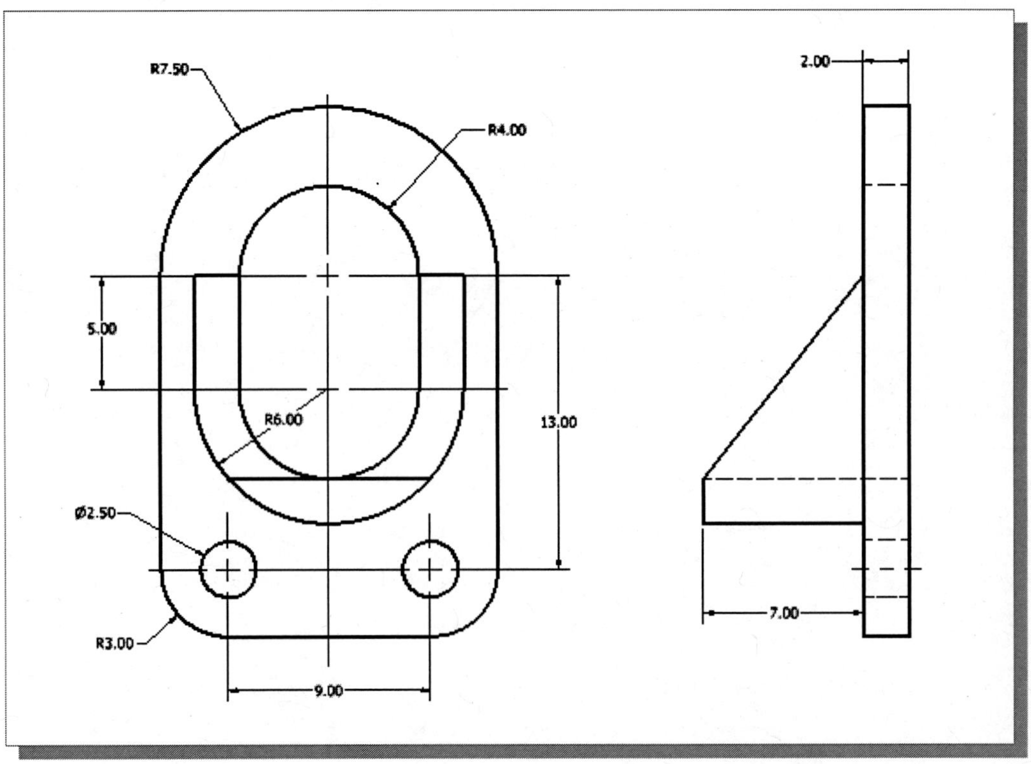

Chapter 9
Advanced 3D Construction Tools

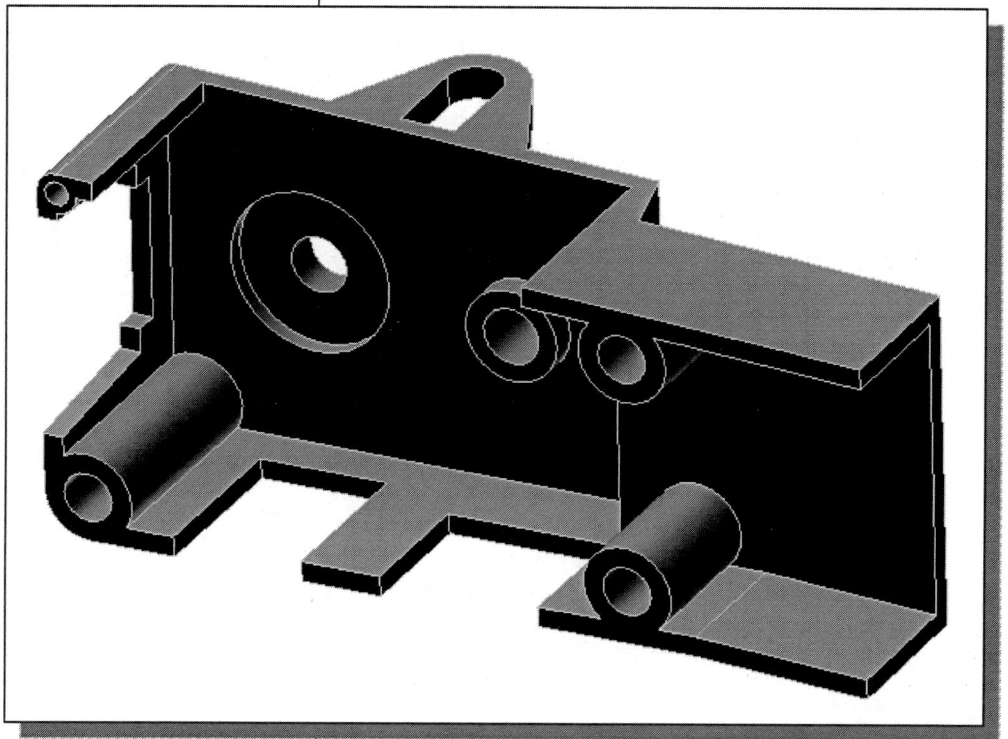

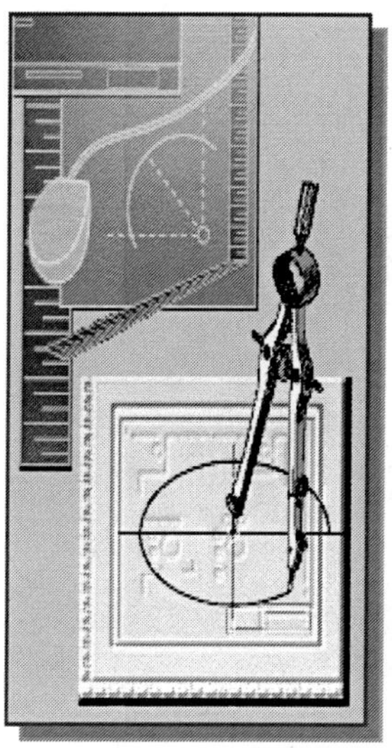

Learning Objectives

- ♦ **Understand the Concepts Behind the Different 3D Construction Tools**
- ♦ **Set up Multiple Work Planes**
- ♦ **Create Swept Features**
- ♦ **Use the Shell Command**
- ♦ **Create 3D Rounds & Fillets**

Introduction

SolidWorks provides an assortment of three-dimensional construction tools to make the creation of solid models easier and more efficient. As demonstrated in the previous lessons, **extruded** features and **revolved** features are the two most common methods used to create 3D models. In this next example, we will examine the procedures for using the **Sweep** command, the **Mirror Feature** command, and the **Shell** command. These types of features are common characteristics of molded parts.

The **Sweep** option is defined as moving a cross-section through a path in space to form a three-dimensional object. To define a sweep in *SolidWorks*, we define two sections: the trajectory and the cross-section.

The **Mirror** command allows us to create mirror images of features. A reference plane, such as a datum plane or an existing surface, is required to use the command. We can create a mirrored feature while maintaining the original parametric definitions, which can be quite useful in creating symmetrical features. For example, we can create one quadrant of a feature, and then mirror it twice to create a solid with four identical quadrants.

The **Shell** option is defined as hollowing out the inside of a solid, leaving a shell of specified wall thickness.

A Thin-Walled Design: *Battery Case*

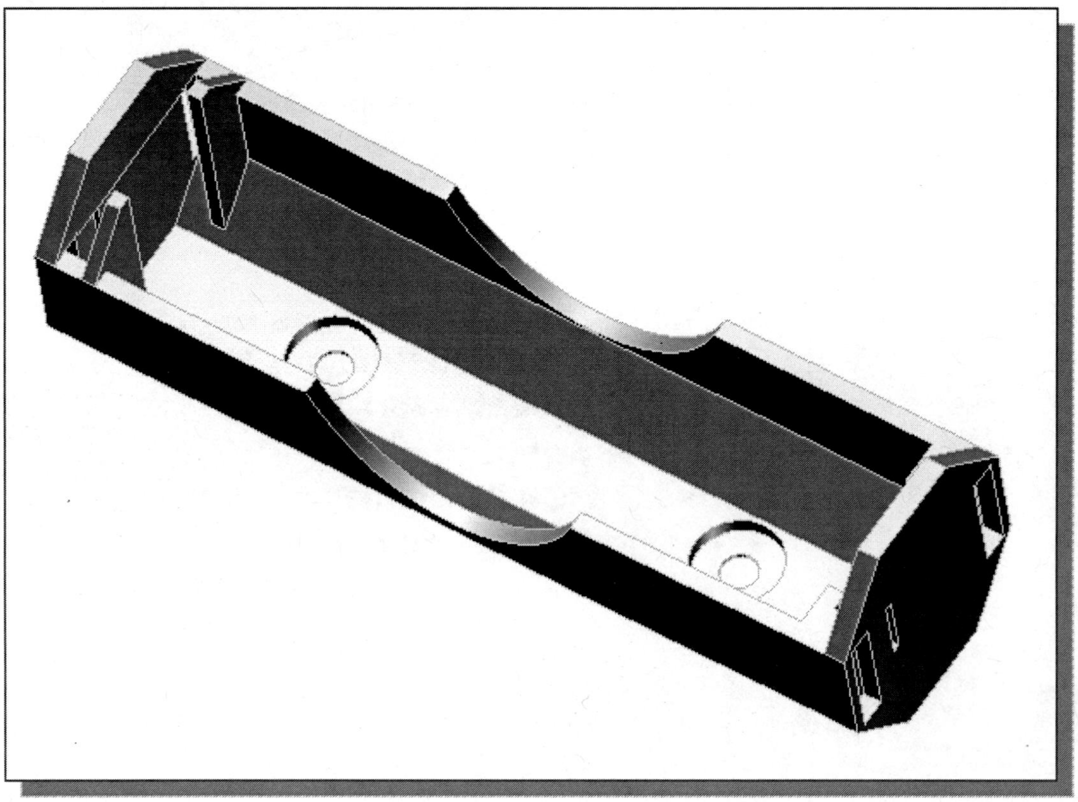

Modeling Strategy

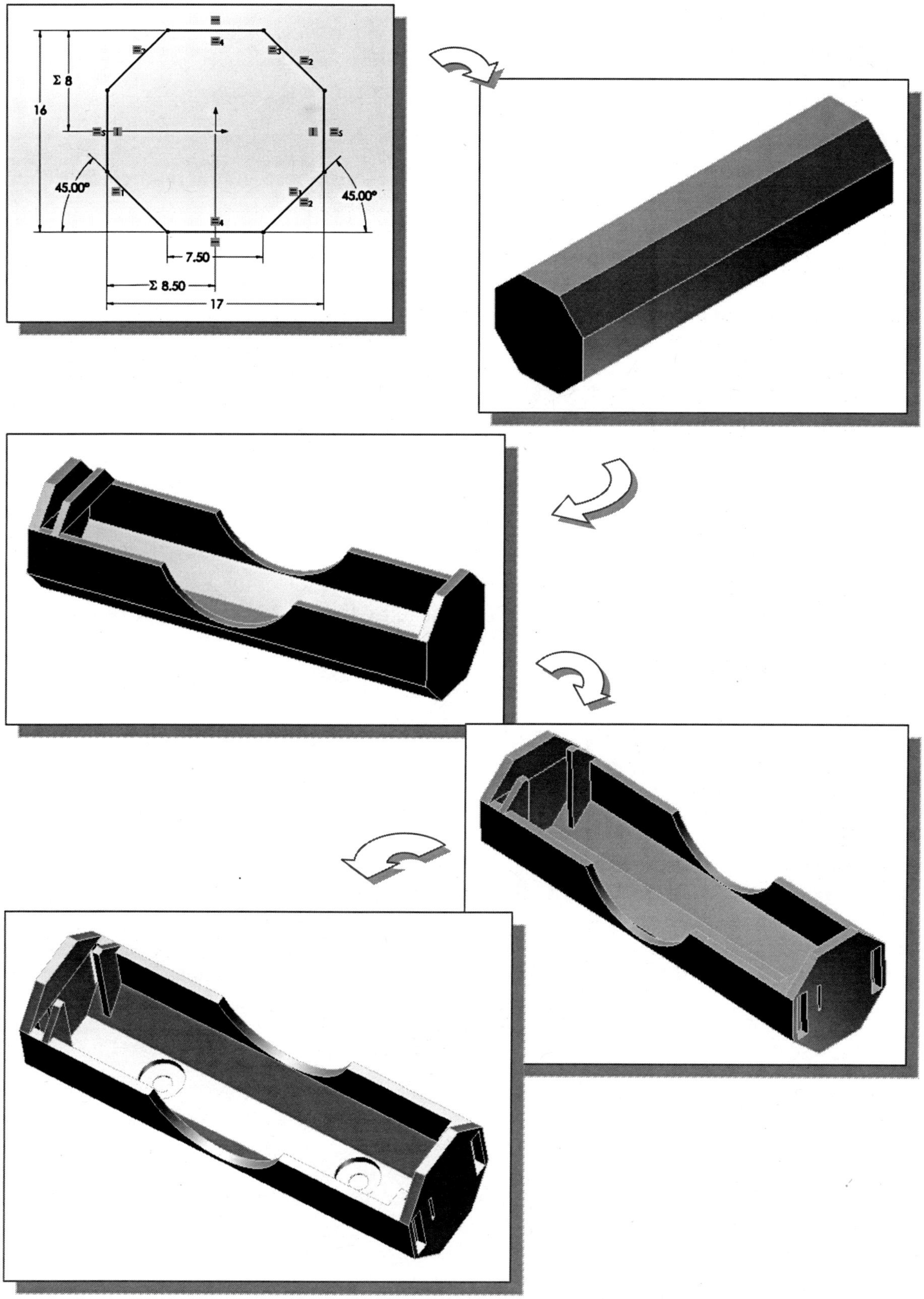

Starting *SolidWorks*

1. Select the **SolidWorks** option on the *Start* menu or select the **SolidWorks** icon on the desktop to start *SolidWorks*. The *SolidWorks* main window will appear on the screen.

2. Select the **New** icon with a single click of the left-mouse-button on the *Menu Bar*.

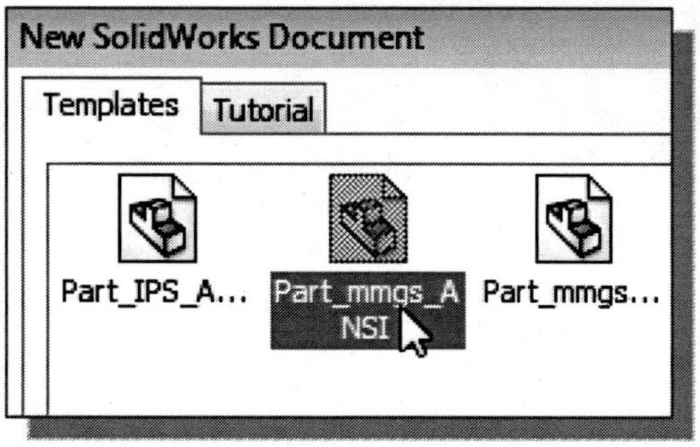

3. Notice the three template files appear in the **Advanced** mode. Select the **Part_mmgs_ANSI** template as shown.

4. Click on the **OK** button to open a new document using the selected template.

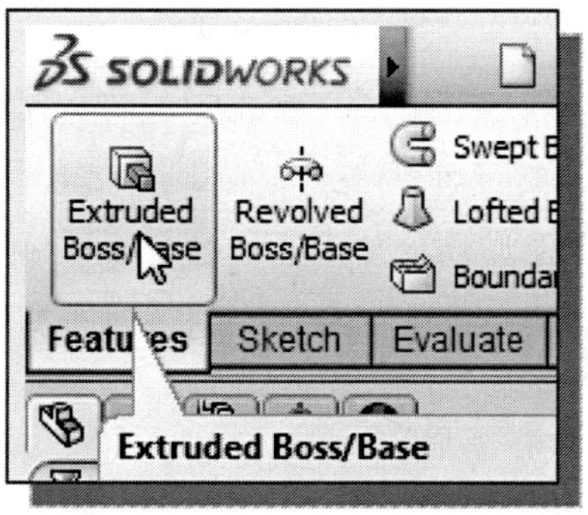

5. In the *Features* toolbar, select the **Extruded Boss/ Base** command by left-clicking once on the icon.

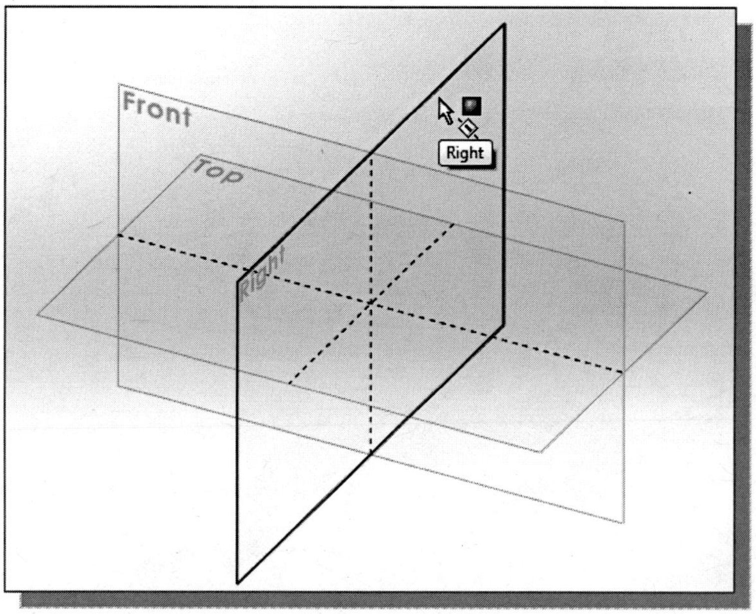

6. Inside the graphics window, select the **Right Plane** as the sketching plane as shown

Create the Base Feature

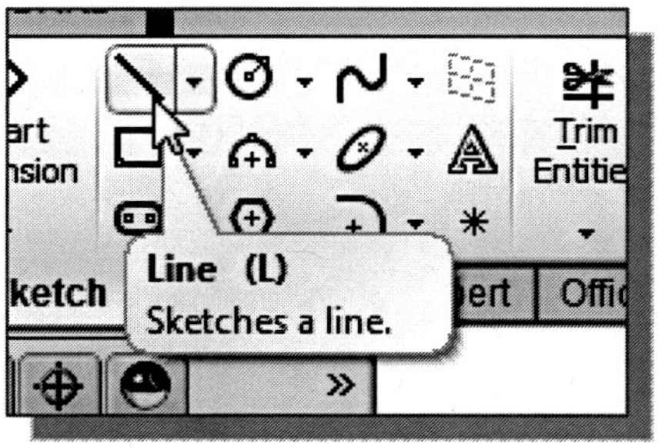

1. Select the **Line** option in the *Sketch* panel. A *Help-tip* box appears next to the cursor: "*Sketches a line.*"

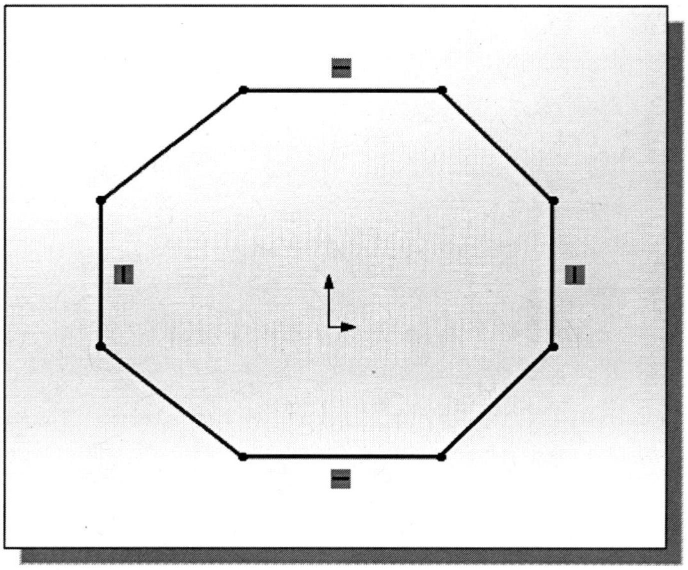

2. Create eight connected line segments of arbitrary size, with the center near the *Origin* as shown.

- Note the required eight-sided shape for the battery case is not a standard **octagon**.

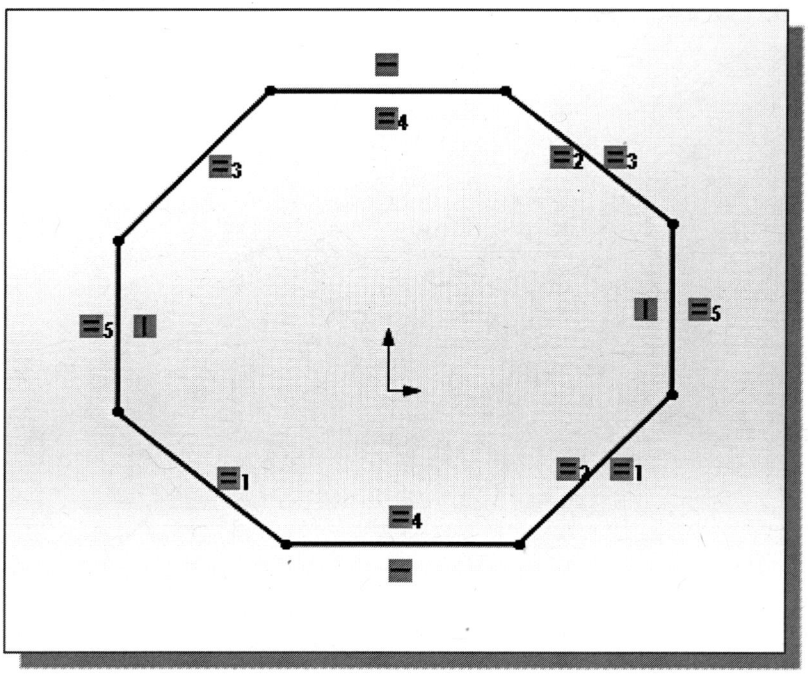

3. On your own, set the **four inclined lines** equal length.

4. Set the **two horizontal lines** equal length.

5. Set the **two vertical lines** equal length.

6. On your own, create and modify the **six dimensions** and center the sketch as shown.

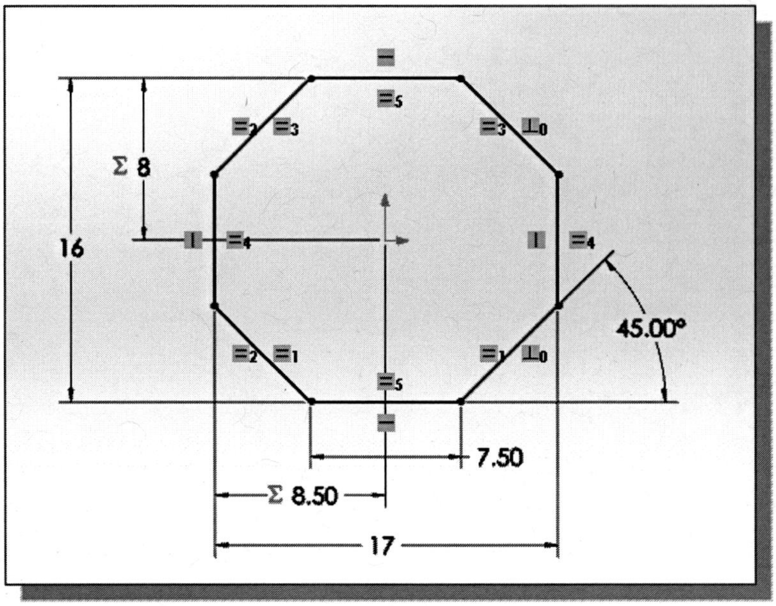

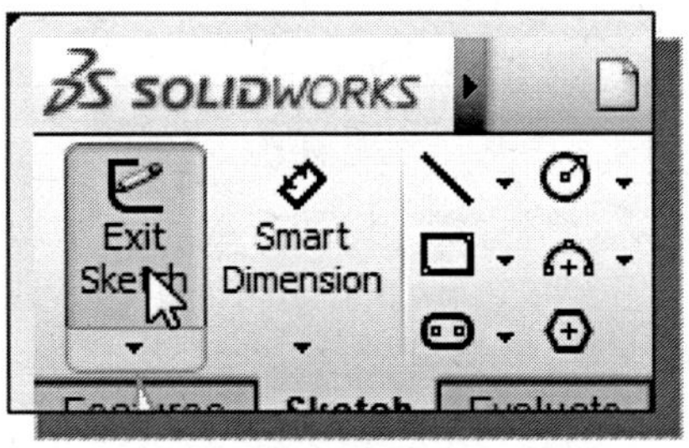

7. Click **Exit Sketch** in the *Sketch* toolbar to end the *Sketch* mode.

8. In the *Extrude Property Manager*, set the extrude direction option to **Mid Plane** and enter **60 mm** as the extrusion distance.

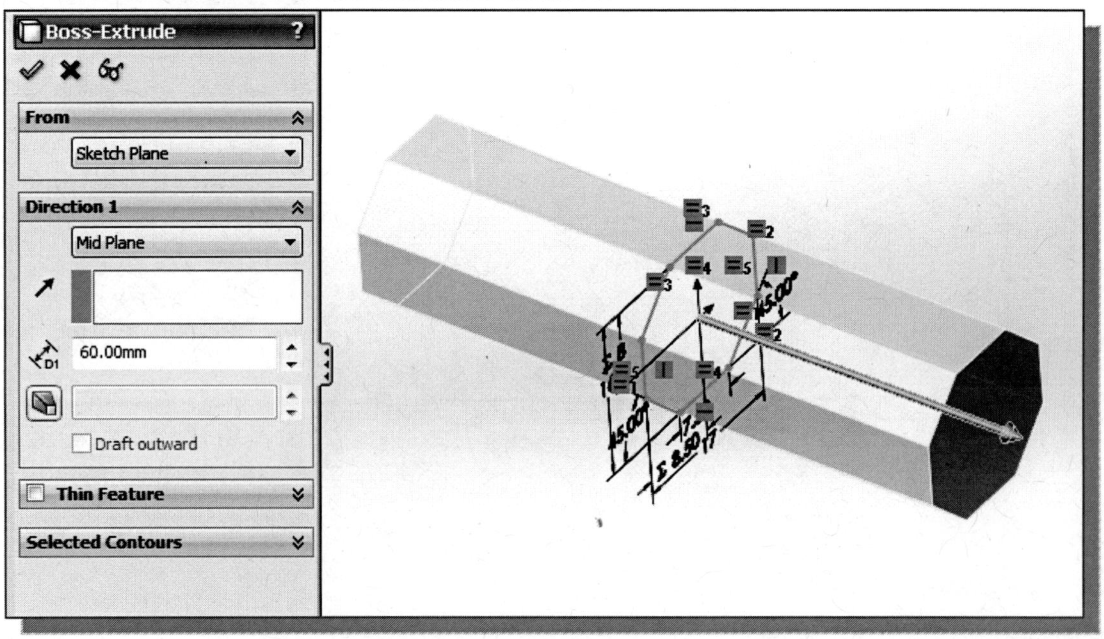

9. Click on the **OK** button to proceed with creating the feature.

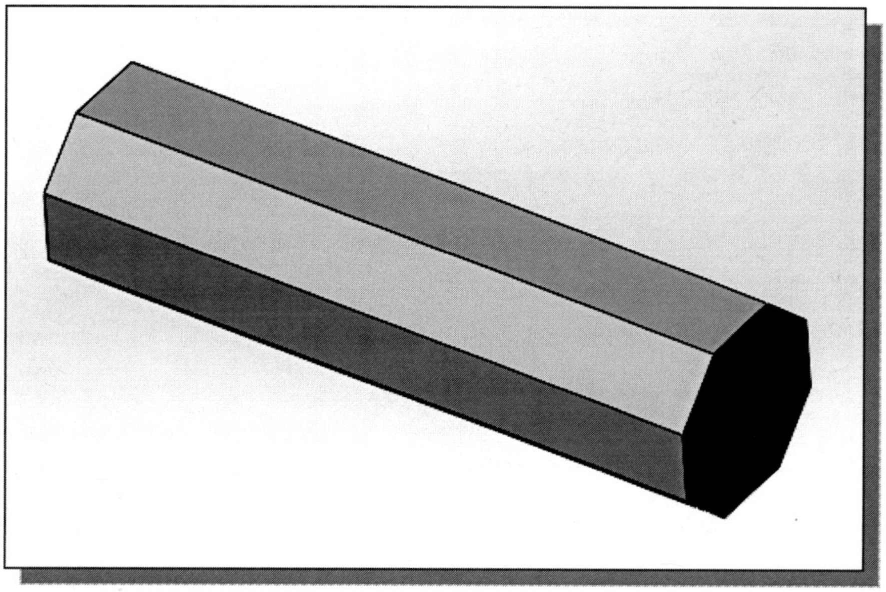

Create a Cut Feature

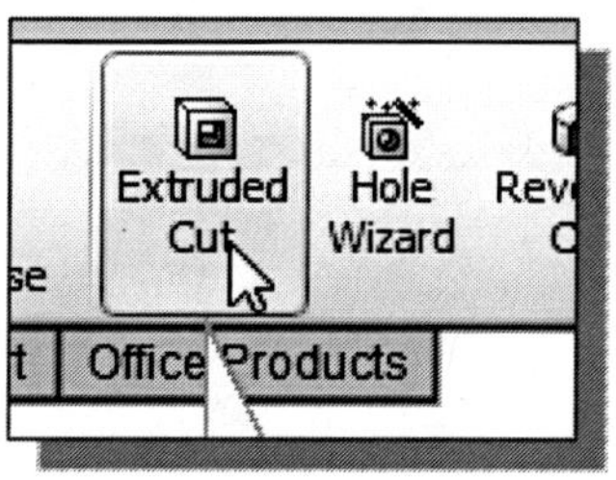

1. In the *Features* toolbar, select the **Extruded Cut** command by left-clicking once on the icon.

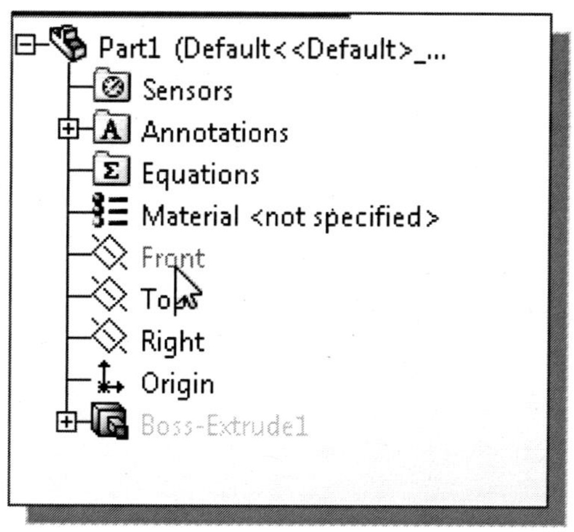

2. Select the **Front datum plane** to align the sketching plane.

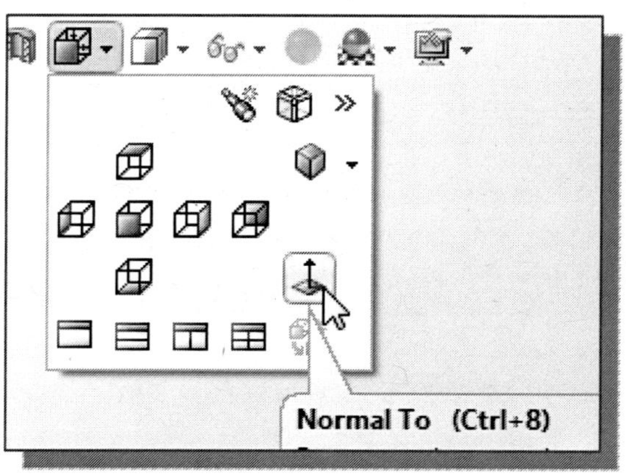

3. Align the sketching plane to the screen by using the **Normal To** option as shown.

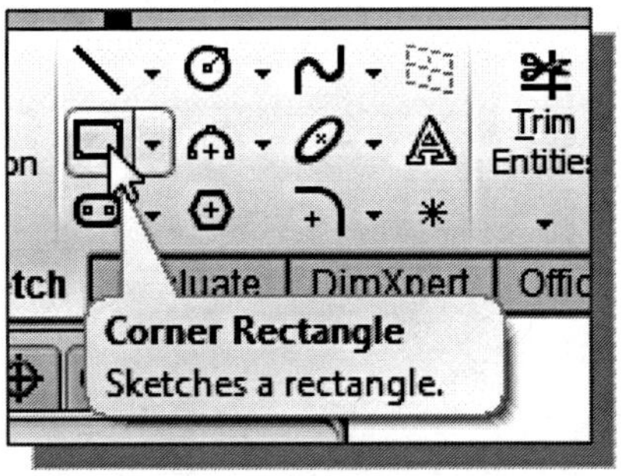

4. Click on the **Rectangle** icon in the *Sketch* panel.

5. Create a rectangle aligned to the top two horizontal lines as shown.

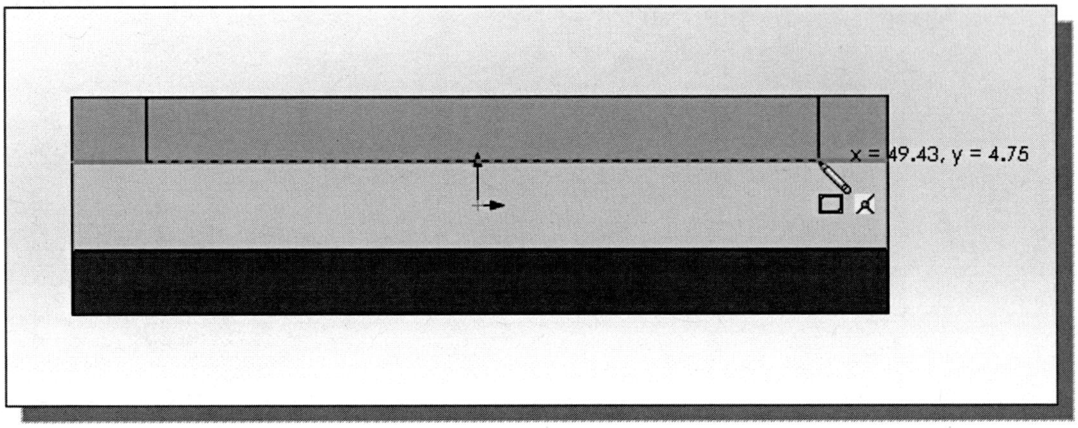

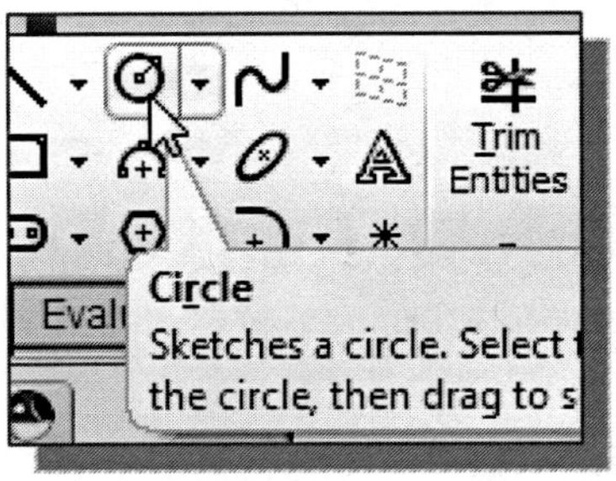

6. Select the **Circle** command by clicking once with the left-mouse-button on the icon in the *Sketch* toolbar.

7. On your own, create a circle with the center aligned to the top horizontal line as shown.

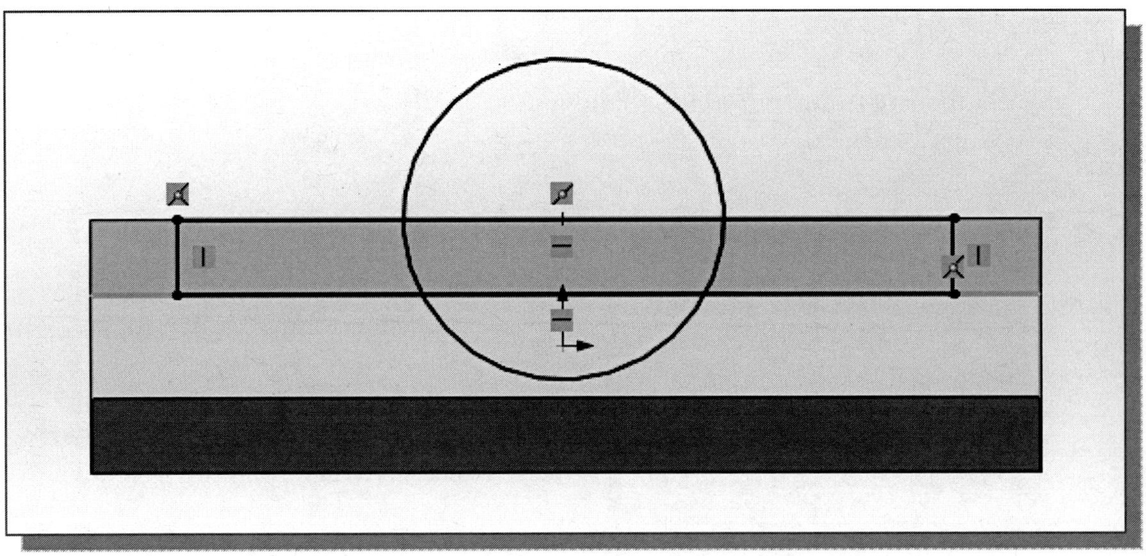

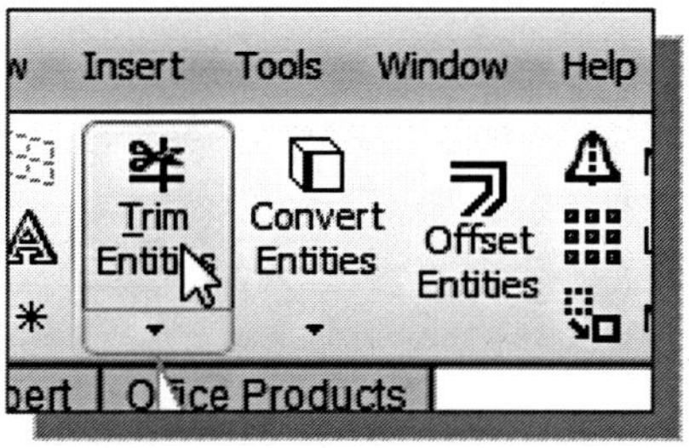

8. On your own, use the **Trim** command and modify the sketch as shown in the figure below.

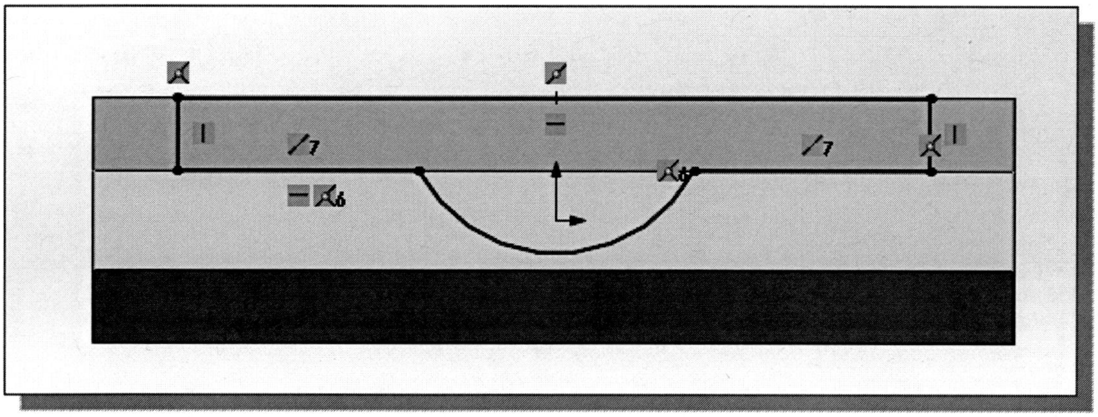

9. On your own, use the **Line** command and also modify the sketch as shown in the figure below.

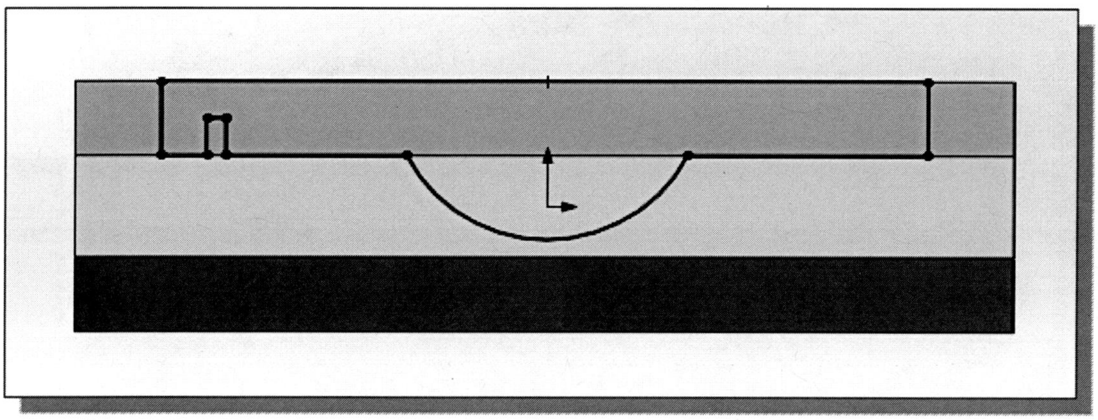

10. On your own, create and modify the dimensions as shown.

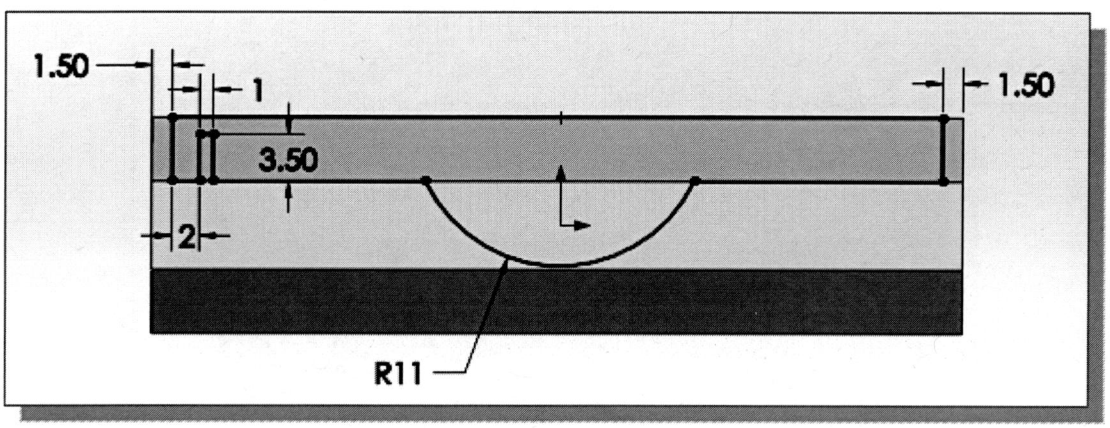

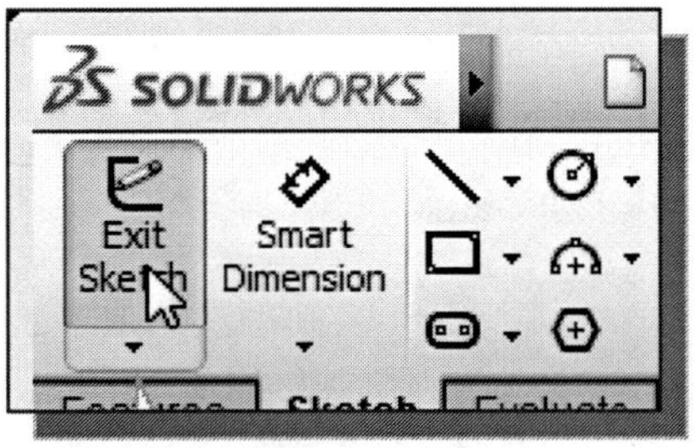

11. Click **Exit Sketch** to exit the *Edit Sketch* mode as shown.

12. In the *Extrude Property Manager*, set the extrude option to **Mid Plane** and enter **20mm** as the extrusion distance.

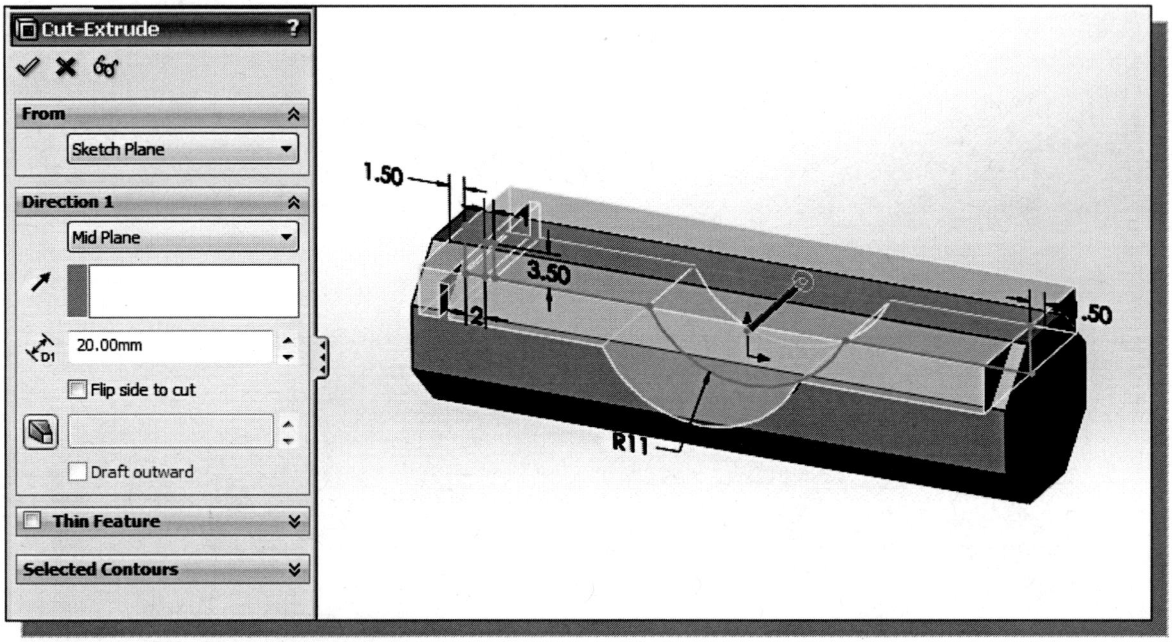

13. Click **OK** to create the extruded feature.

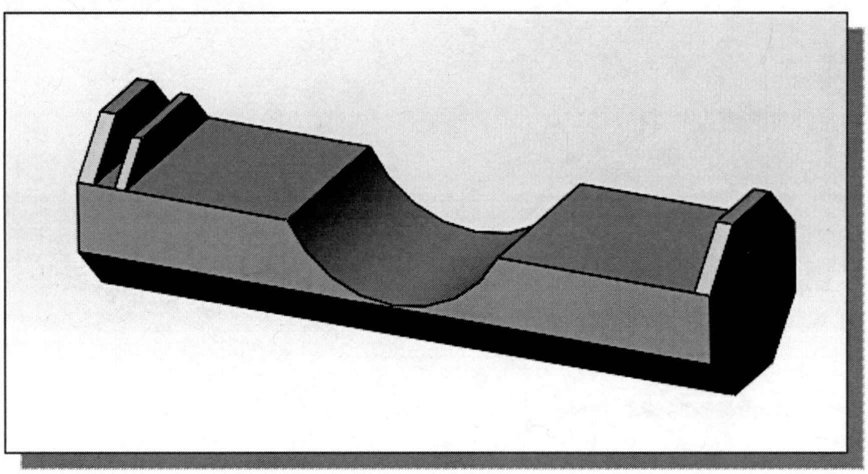

Create a Shell Feature

- The **Shell** command can be used to hollow out the inside of a solid, leaving a shell of specified wall thickness.

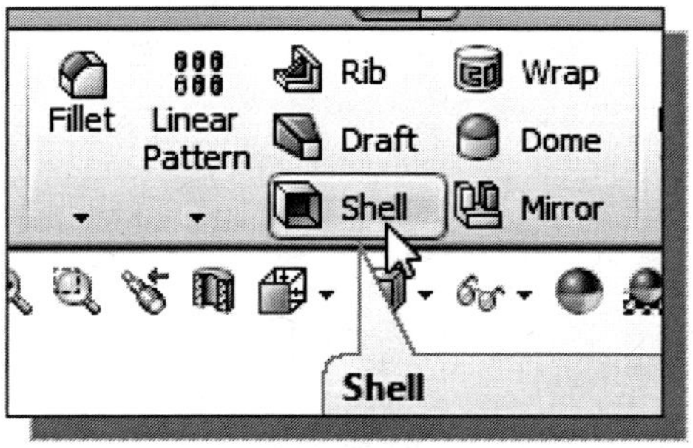

1. In the *Features* toolbar, select the **Shell** command by left-clicking once on the icon.

2. In the *Shell Property Manager*, the **Remove Faces** option is activated. Select the four faces as shown below.

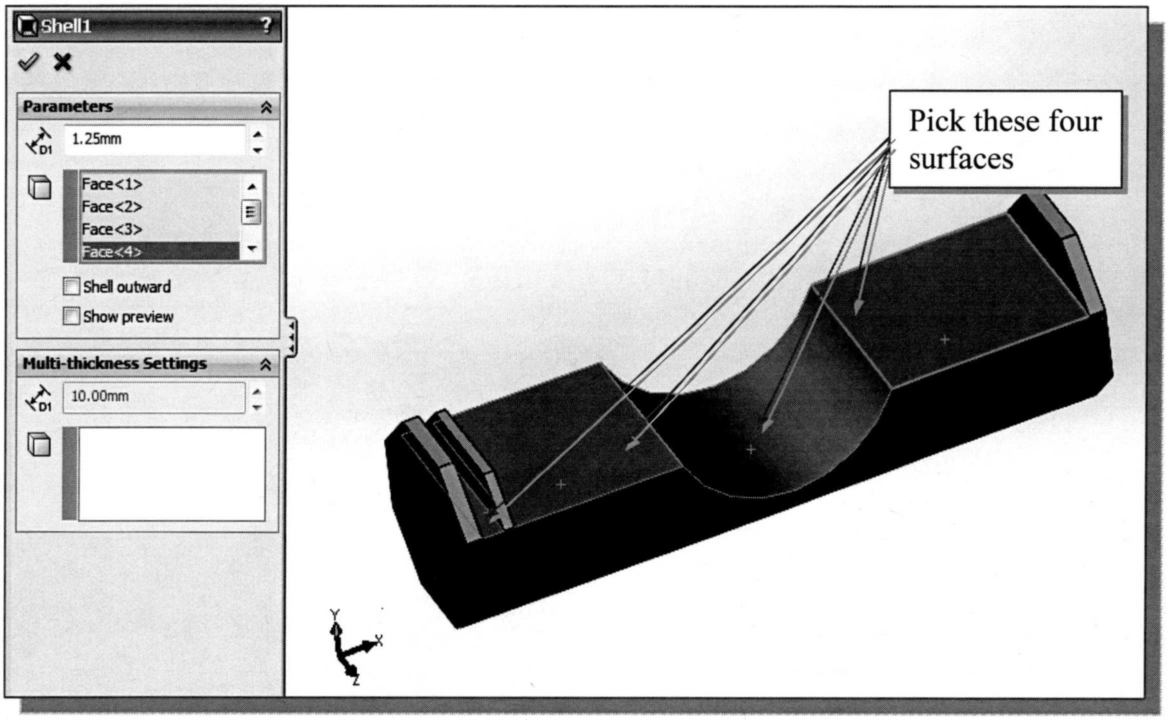

3. In the *Shell Property Manager*, set the option to **Inside** with a value of **1.25mm** as shown.

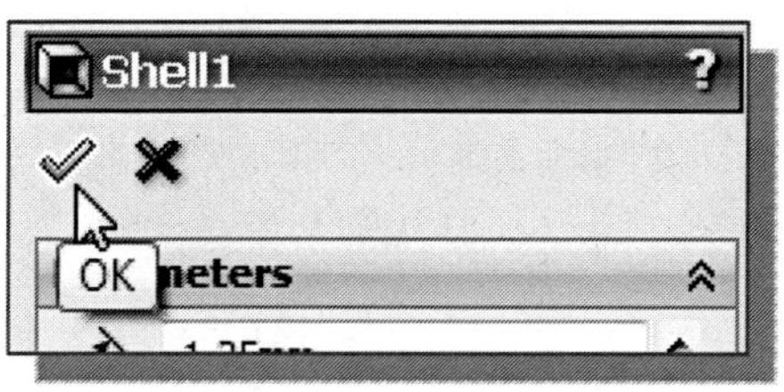

4. In the *Shell Property Manager*, click on the **OK** button to accept the settings and create the shell feature.

- Note the **Shell** command hollowed out the inside of the solid model.

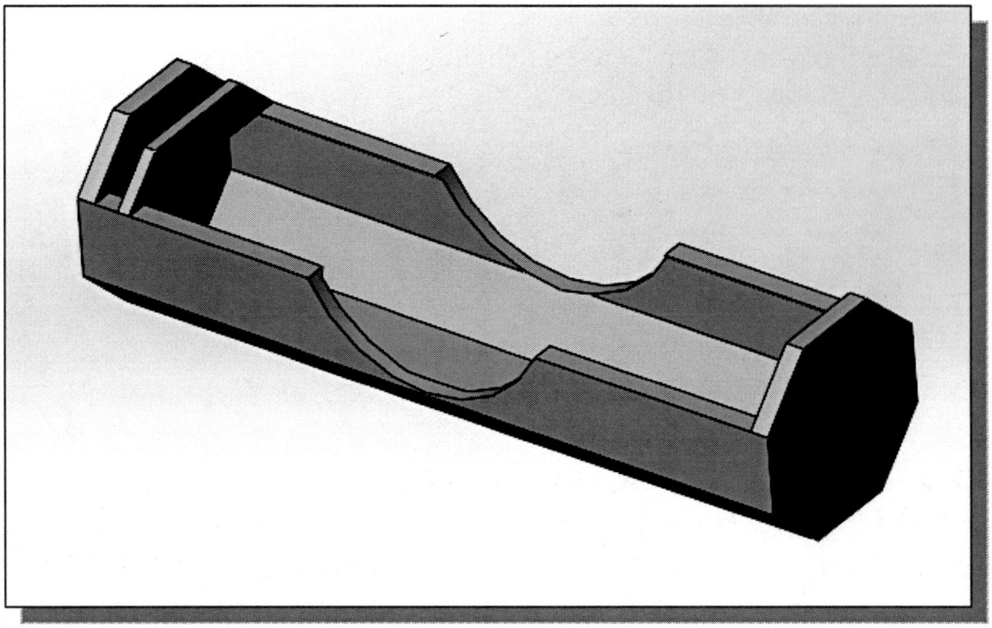

Create a Cut Feature

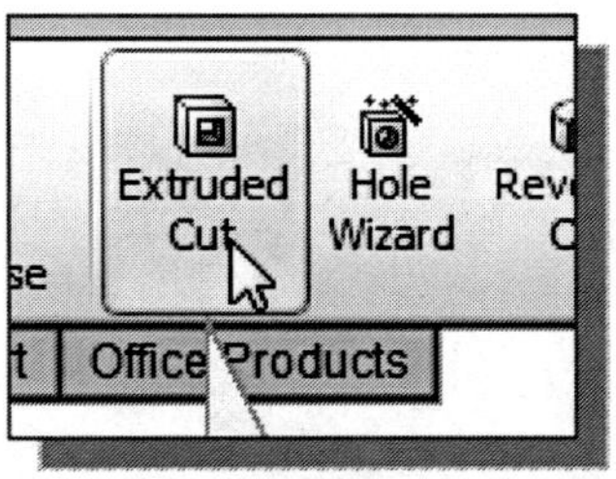

1. In the *Features* toolbar, select the **Extruded Cut** command by left-clicking once on the icon.

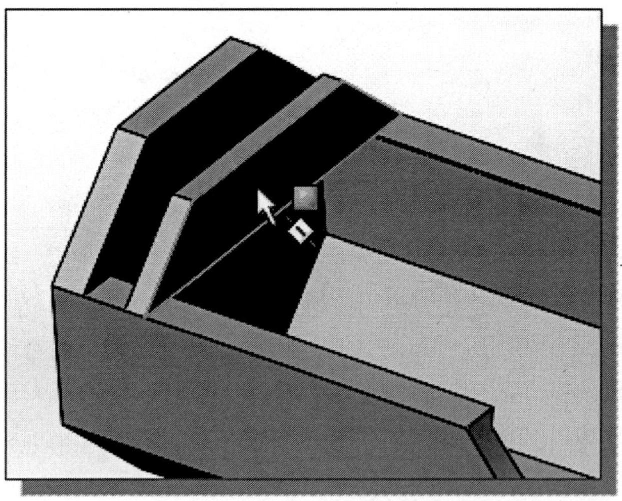

2. Select the **inside vertical face** to align the sketching plane.

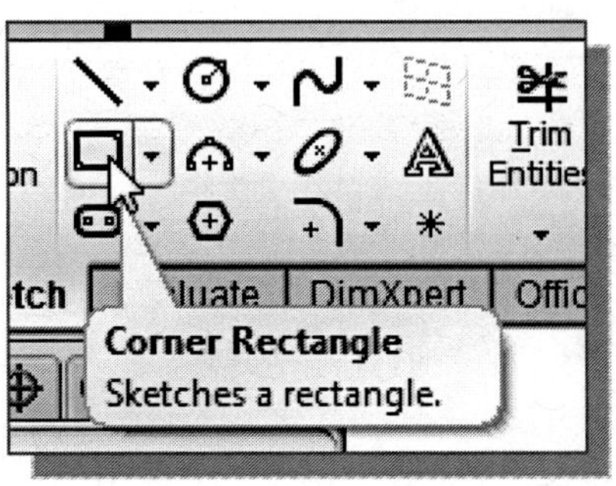

3. Select the **Corner Rectangle** command by clicking once with the left-mouse-button on the icon.

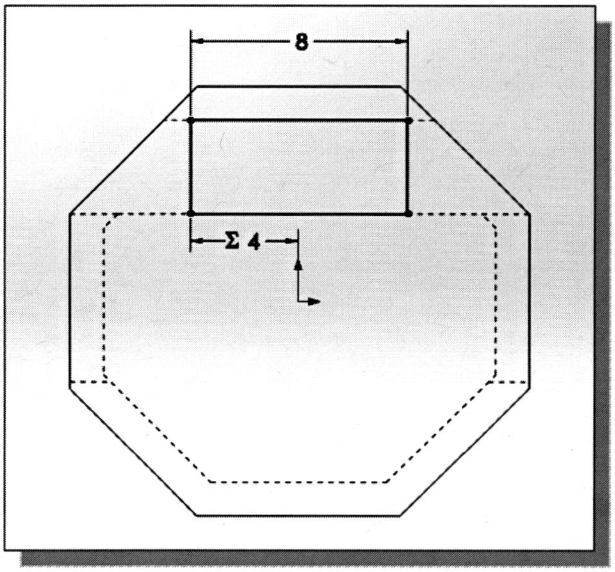

4. Create a rectangle, aligned to the top and bottom edges of the sketching plane, and modify the dimensions as shown

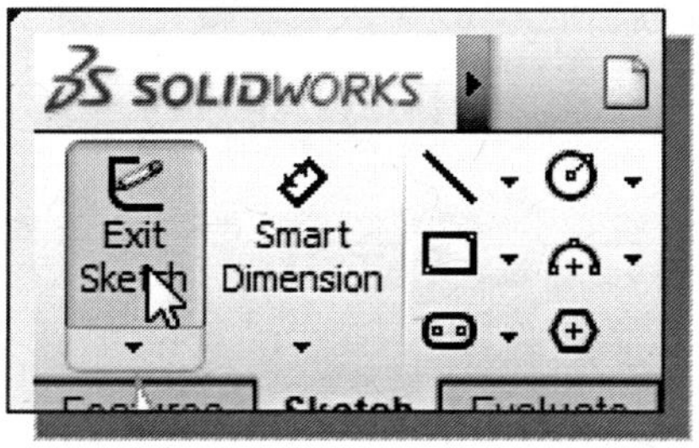

5. Click **Exit Sketch** to exit the *Edit Sketch* mode as shown.

6. In the *Extrude Property Manager*, set the extrude option to **Up To Next**.

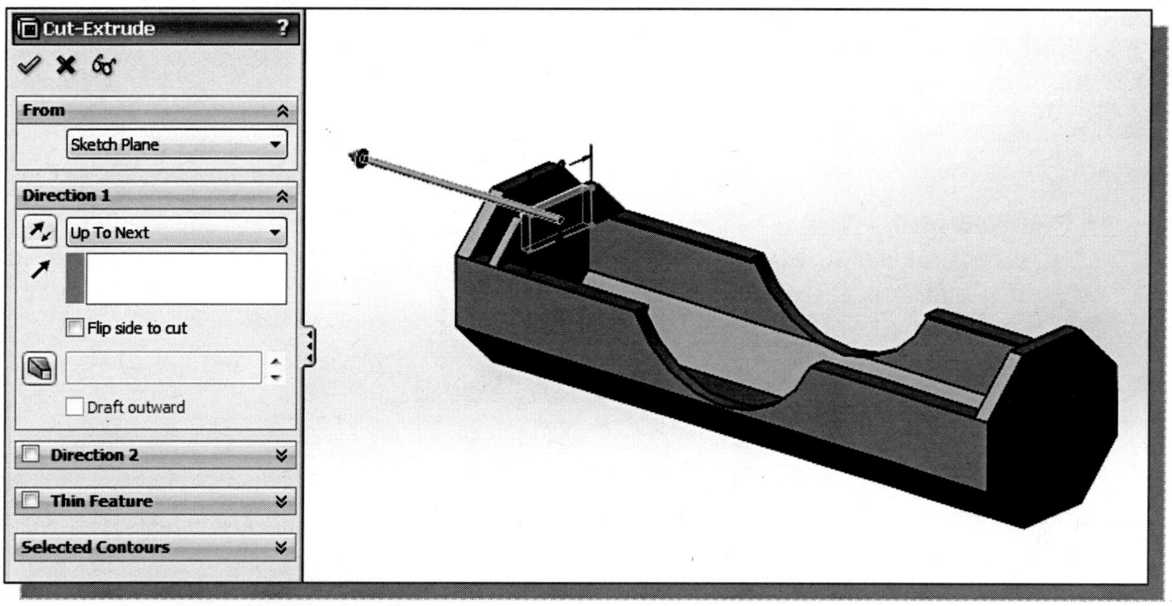

7. Click **OK** to create the extruded feature.

Create another Extruded Feature

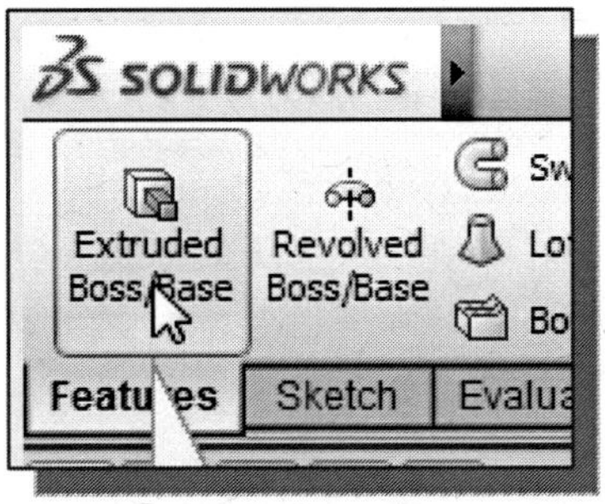

1. In the *Features* toolbar, select the **Extruded Boss/Base** command by left-clicking once on the icon.

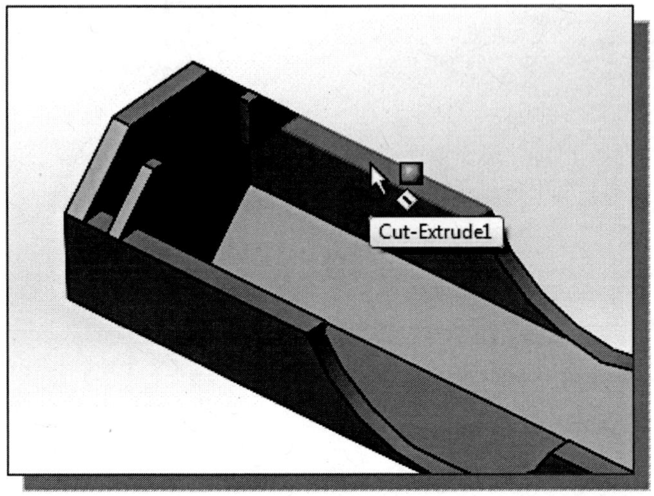

2. Select the **top face** of the solid model to align the sketching plane.

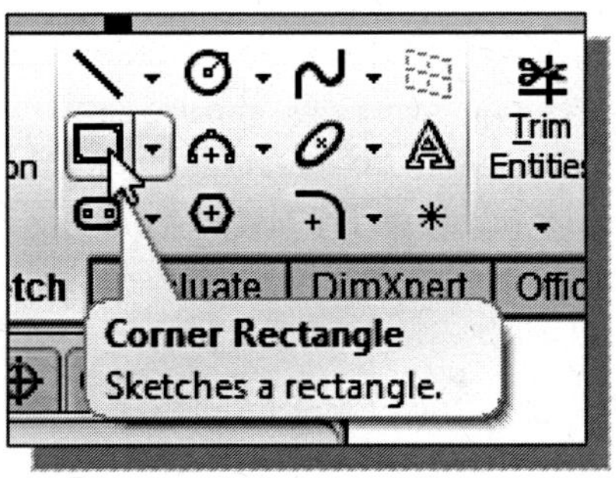

3. Select the **Corner Rectangle** command by clicking once with the left-mouse-button on the icon.

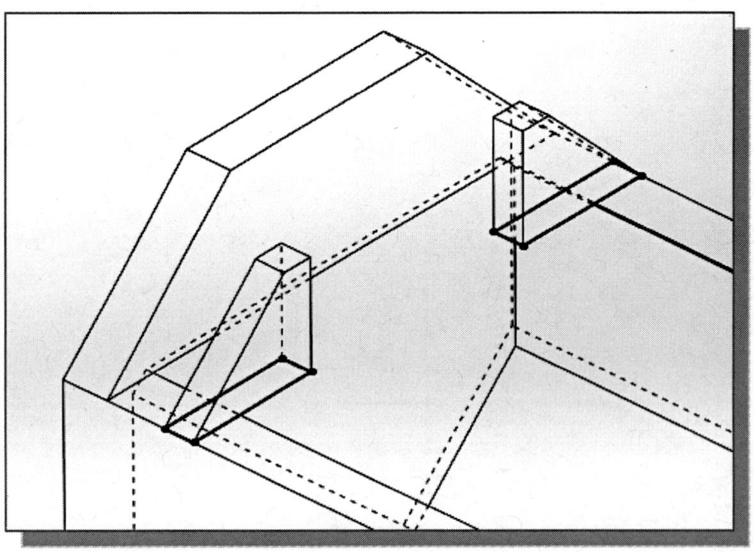

4. On your own, create **two rectangles** aligned to the bottom of the two extruded portions as shown.

- Note the two rectangles are fully constrained as shown near the bottom of the window.

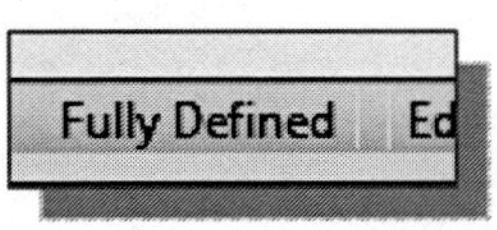

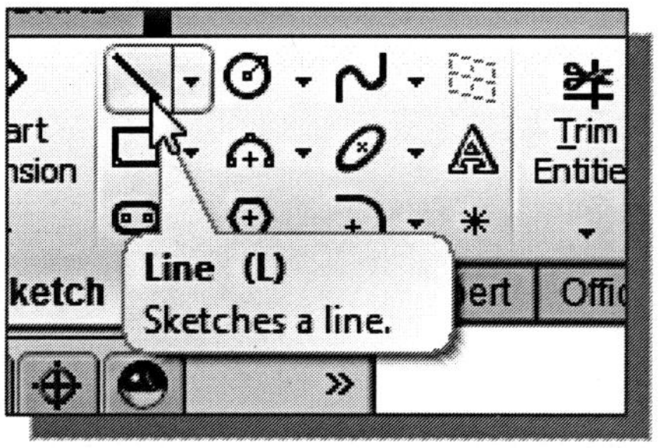

5. Select the **Line** option in the *Sketch* panel. A *Help-tip* box appears next to the cursor: "*Sketches a line.*"

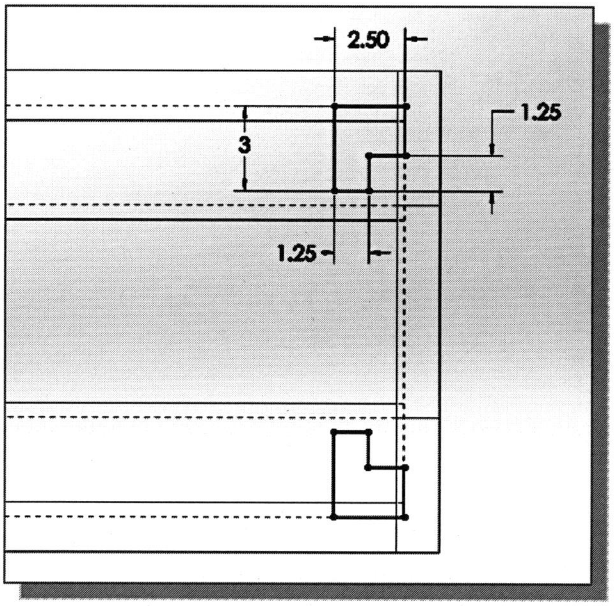

6. Create the two sets of six connected line segments, with the corners aligned to the inside corners as shown.

7. On your own, create and modify the **four dimensions** as shown.

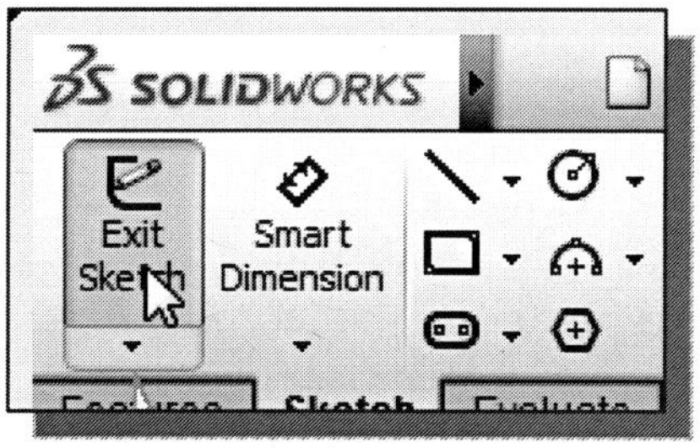

8. Click **Exit Sketch** in the *Sketch* toolbar to end the *Sketch* mode.

9. In the *Extrude Property Manager*, flip the extrusion direction and set the extrude option to **Up To Next**.

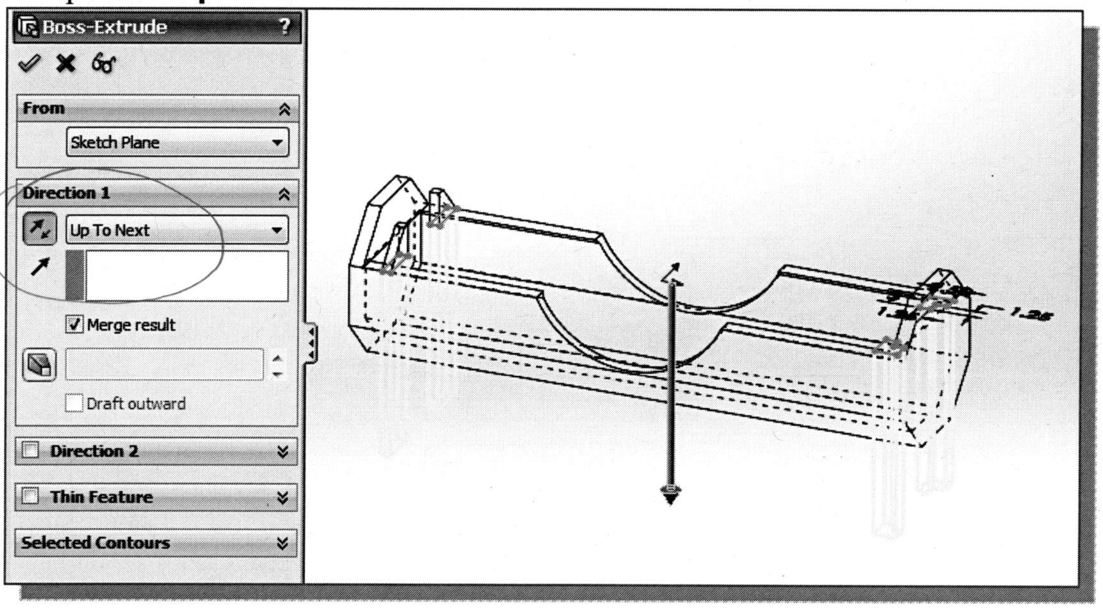

10. In the *Extrude Property Manager*, click on the **OK** button to proceed with creating the cut feature.

Create another Cut Feature

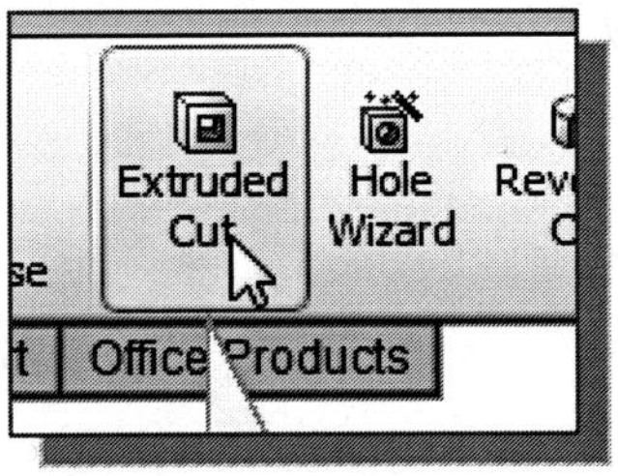

1. In the *Features* toolbar, select the **Extruded Cut** command by left-clicking once on the icon.

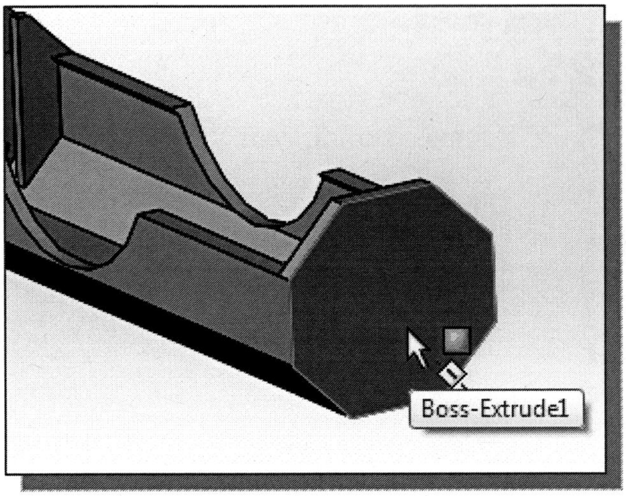

2. Select the **right-end vertical face** to align the sketching plane.

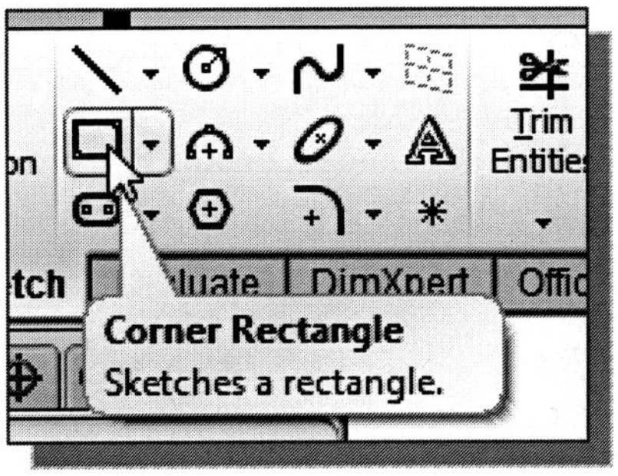

3. Select the **Corner Rectangle** command by clicking once with the left-mouse-button on the icon.

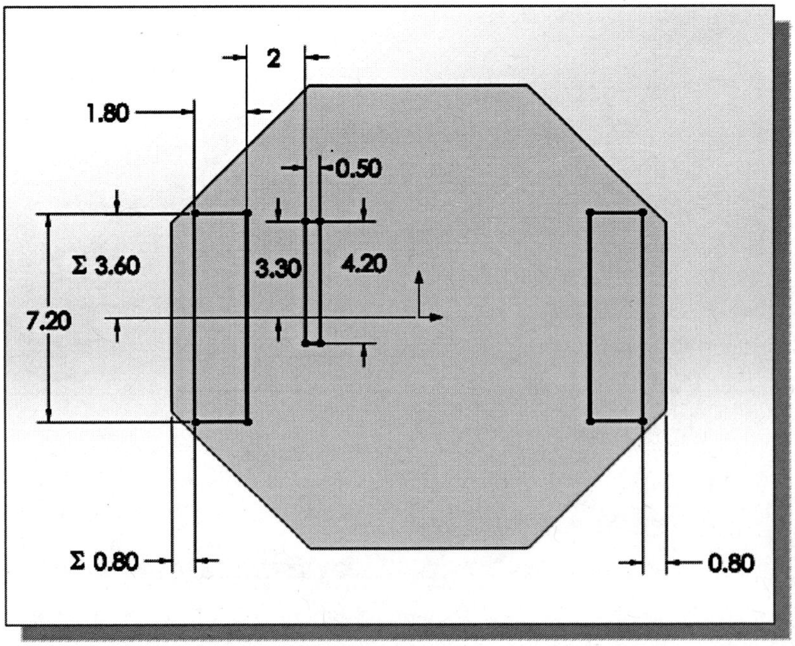

4. On your own, create three rectangles aligned to the center point as shown. Note the larger rectangles are of the same size.

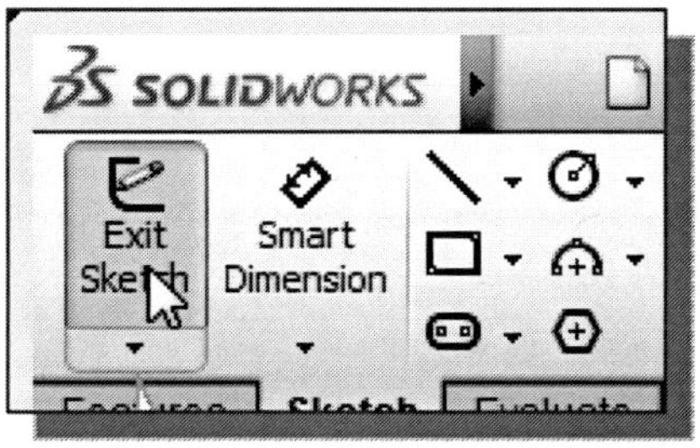

5. Click **Exit Sketch** to exit the *Edit Sketch* mode as shown.

6. In the *Extrude Property Manager*, set the extents distance to **1.5mm** as shown.

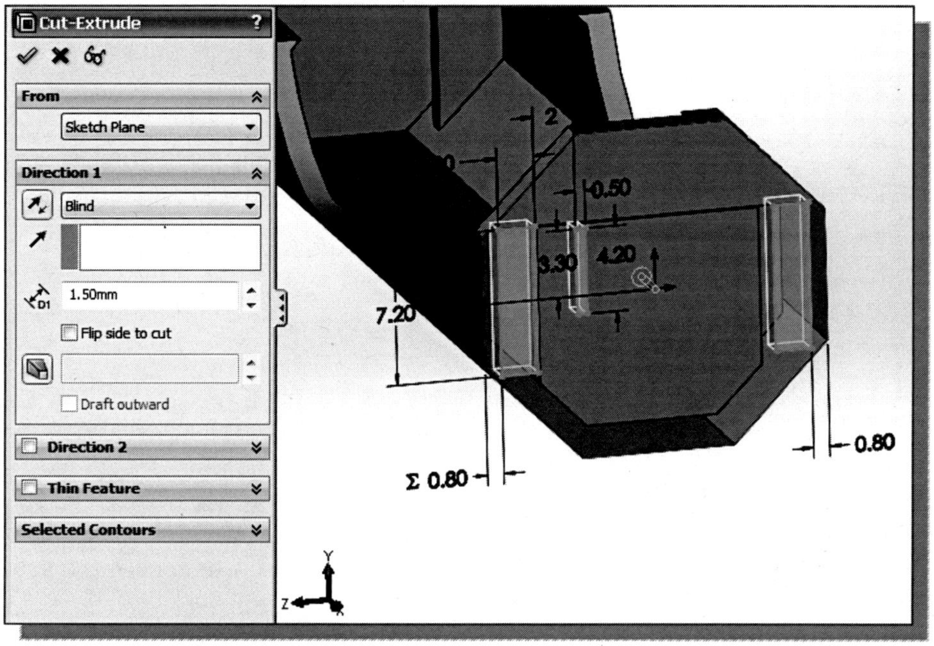

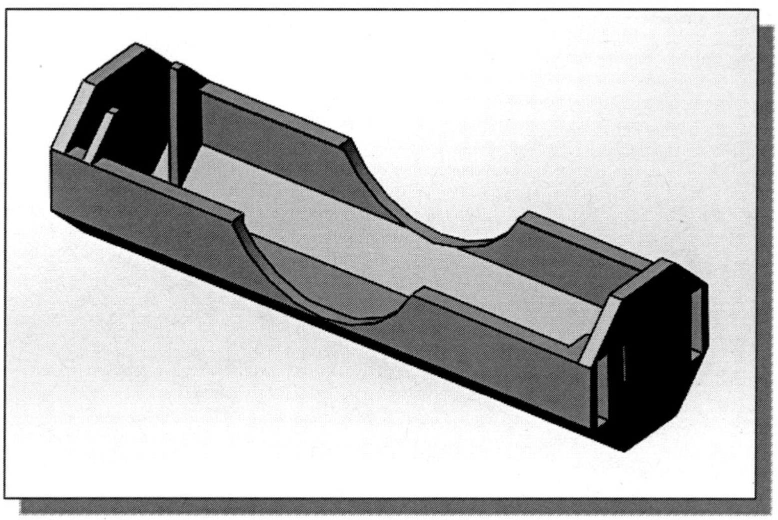

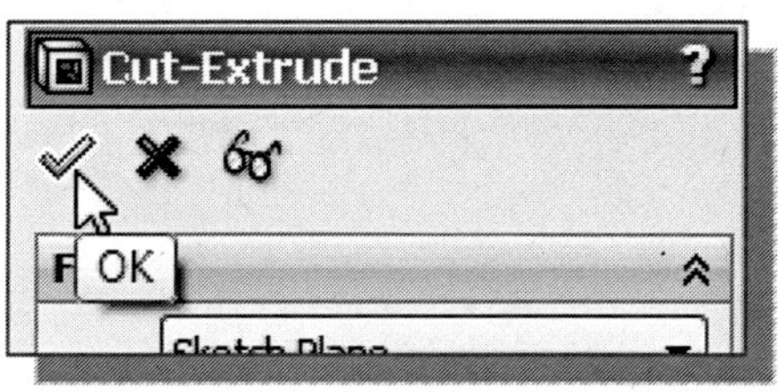

7. In the *Extrude Property Manager*, click on the **OK** button to proceed with creating the cut feature.

Mirror the Last Feature

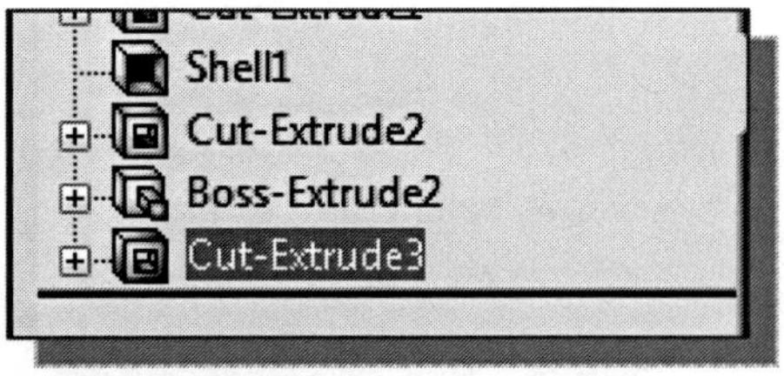

1. Confirm the last **Cut-Extrude** feature we just created is *pre-selected.*

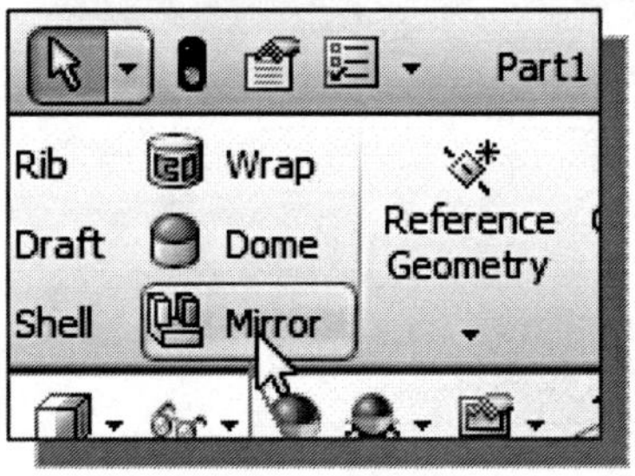

2. In the *Features* toolbar, select the **Mirror Feature** command by releasing the left-mouse-button on the icon.

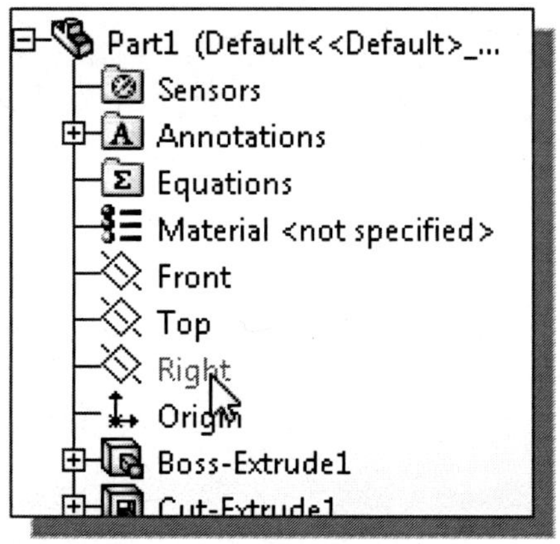

3. In the *Model History Tree*, select the **Right Plane** as the mirror image plane as shown.

4. Click on the **OK** button to accept the settings and create a mirrored feature.

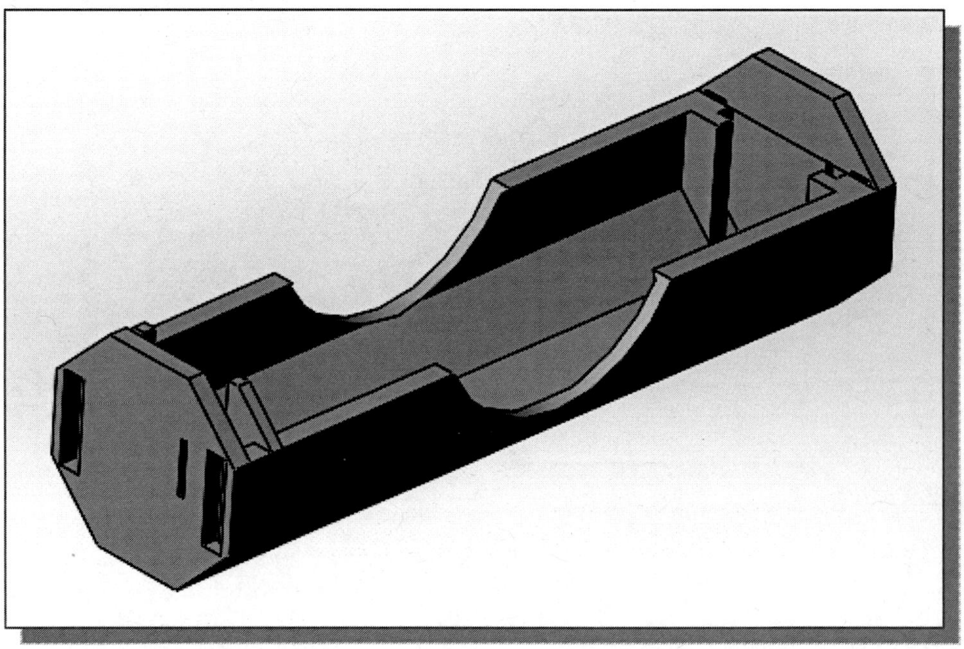

Create another Cut Feature

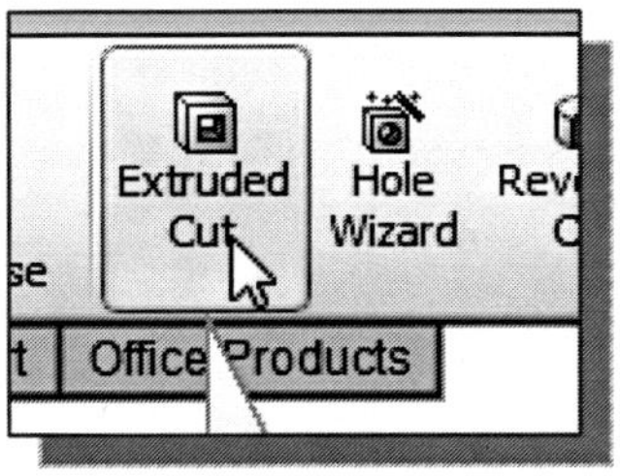

1. In the *Features* toolbar, select the **Extruded Cut** command by left-clicking once on the icon.

2. Select the **inside horizontal face** to align the sketching plane.

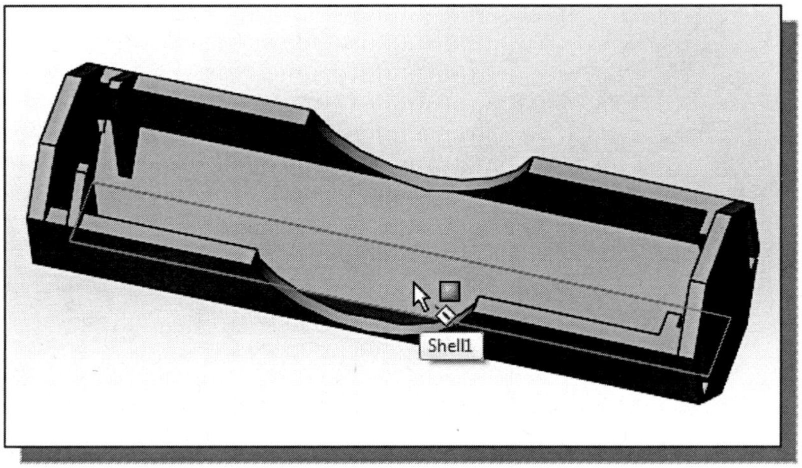

3. On your own, create two circles aligned to the center point as shown.

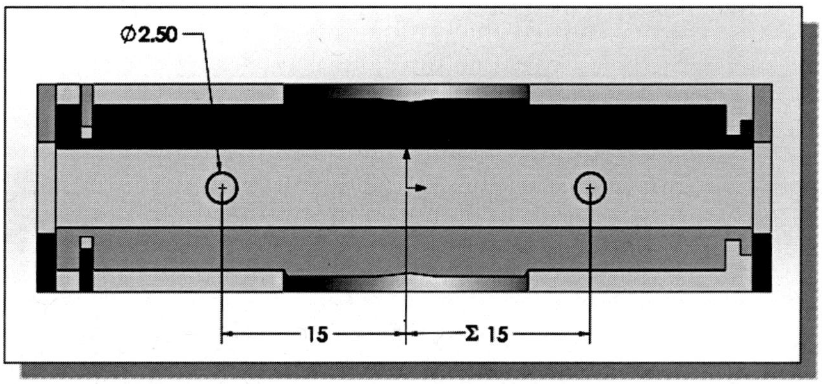

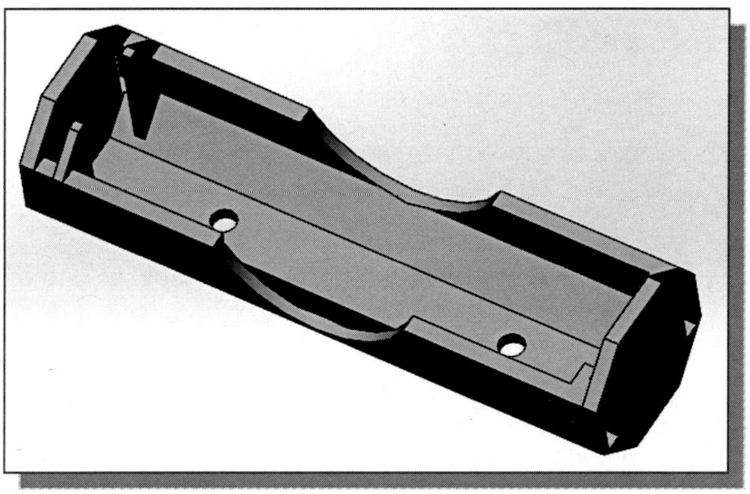

4. On your own, complete the cut feature using the **Thru All** option.

Complete the Model

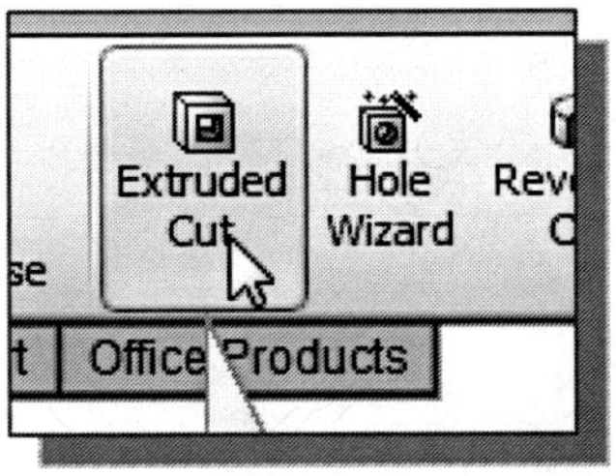

1. In the *Features* toolbar, select the **Extruded Cut** command by left-clicking once on the icon.

2. Select the **inside horizontal face** to align the sketching plane.

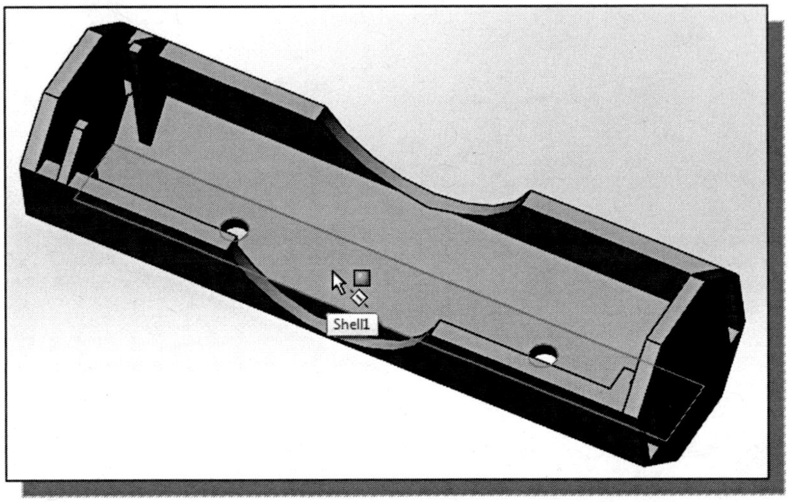

3. On your own, create two circles, diameter **6 mm**, aligned to the two holes as shown.

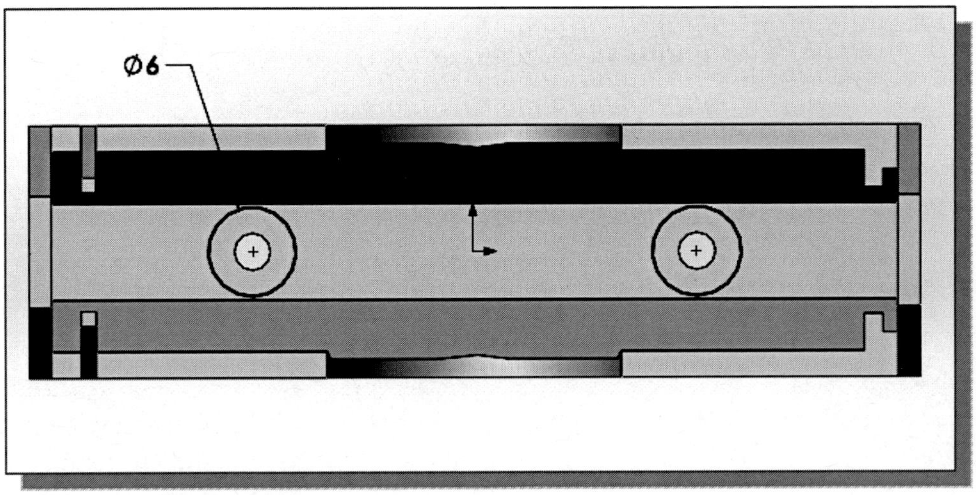

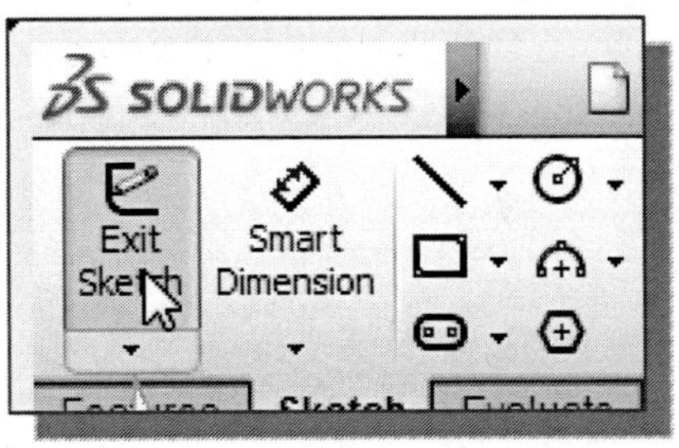

4. Click **Exit Sketch** in the *Sketch* toolbar to end the *Sketch* mode.

5. In the *Extrude* dialog box, set the extents distance to **1mm** as shown.

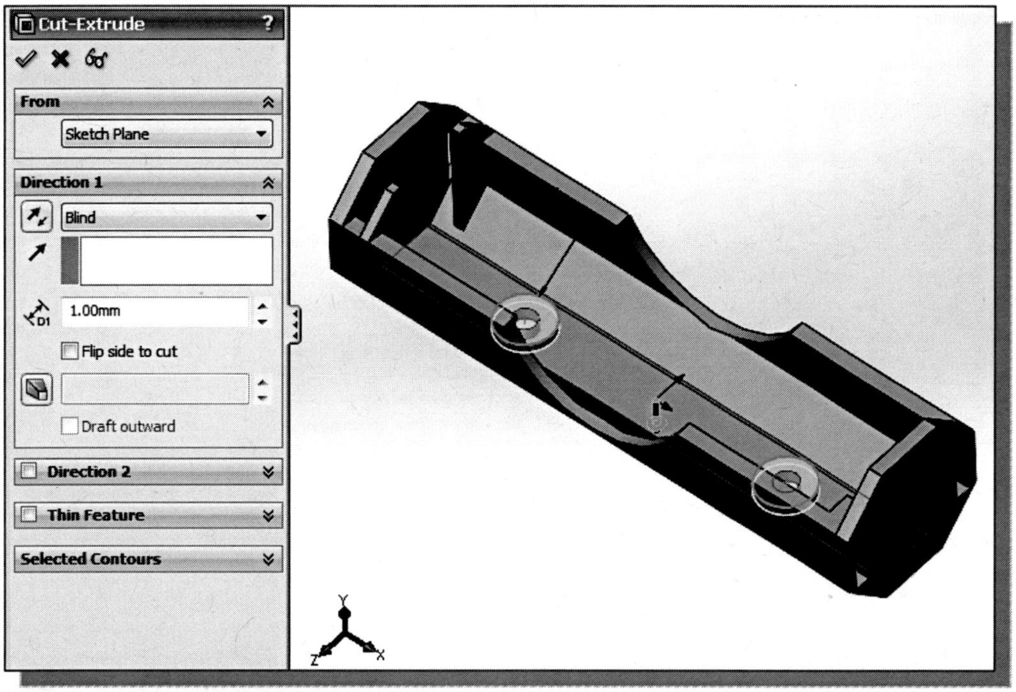

6. In the *Extrude* dialog box, click on the **OK** button to proceed with creating the cut feature.

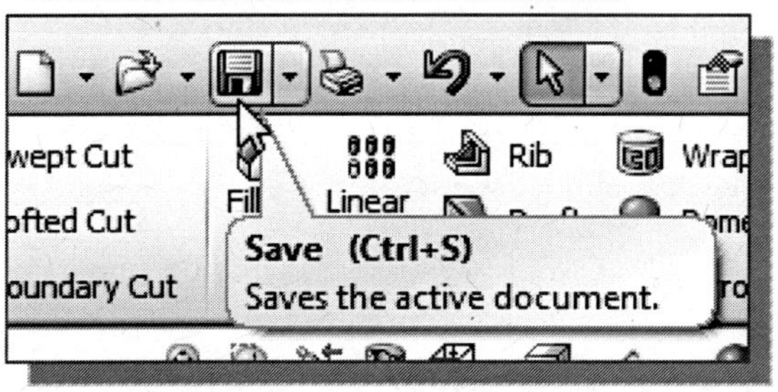

7. Select **Save** in the *Quick Access* toolbar, or you can also use the "**Ctrl-S**" combination (hold down the "Ctrl" key and hit the "S" key once) to save the part.

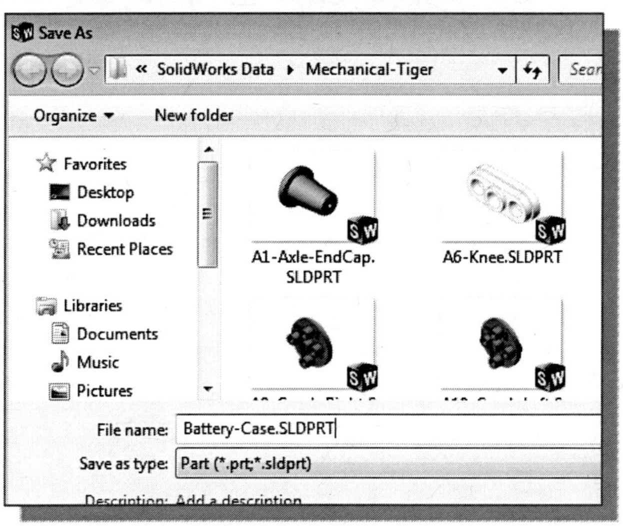

8. Confirm the folder is set to the *Tiger* kit folder, ***Mechanical-Tiger***, as shown.

9. On your own, save the model using **Battery-Case** as the file name.

A Thin-Wire Design: *Linkage Rod*

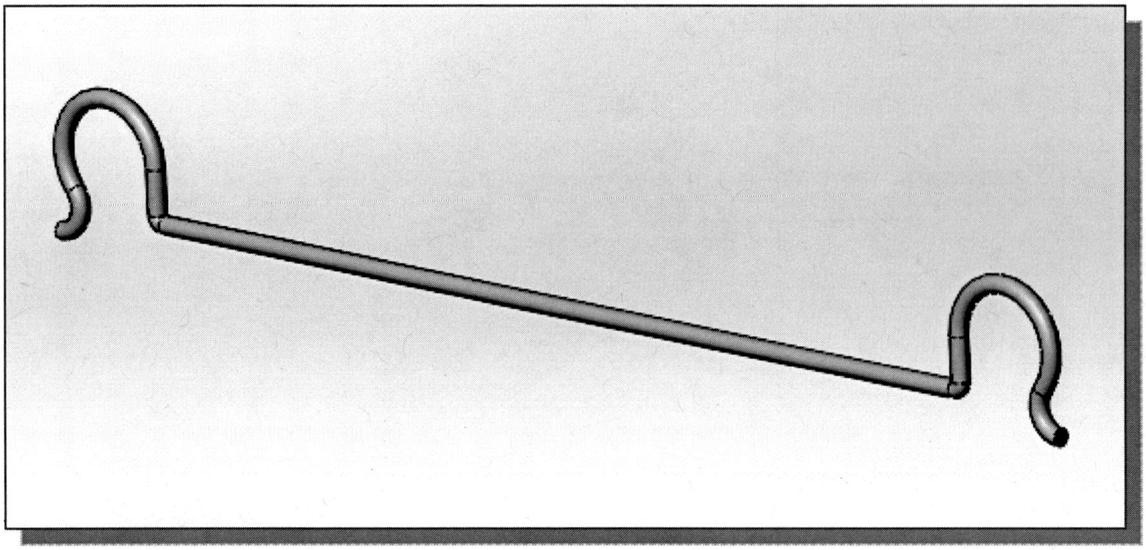

The Sweep Operation

❖ The **Sweep** operation is defined as moving a planar section through a planar (2D) or 3D path in space to form a three-dimensional solid object. The path can be an open curve or a closed loop, but must be on an intersecting plane with the profile. The **Extrusion** operation, which we have used in the previous lessons, is a specific type of sweep. The **Extrusion** operation is also known as a ***linear sweep*** operation, in which the sweep control path is always a line perpendicular to the two-dimensional section. Linear sweeps of unchanging shape result in what are generally called ***prismatic solids*** which means solids with a constant cross-section from end to end. In *SolidWorks*, we create a ***swept feature*** by defining a path and then a 2D sketch of a cross section. The sketched profile is then swept along the planar path. The Sweep operation is used for objects that have uniform shapes along a trajectory.

Start a New Model

1. Select the **New** icon with a single click of the left-mouse-button on the *Menu Bar*.

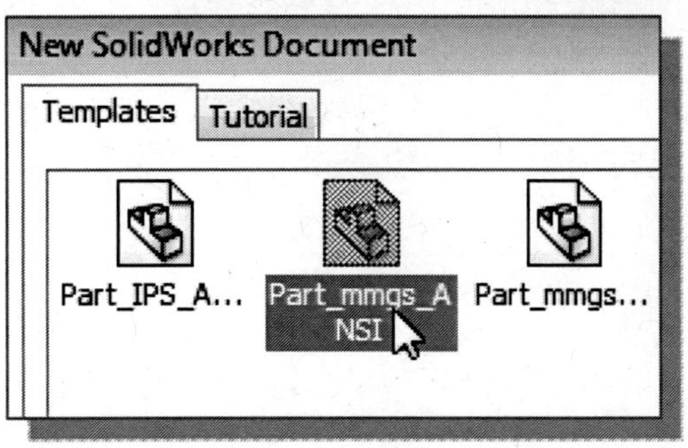

2. Notice the three template files appear in the **Advanced** mode. Select the **Part_mmgs_ANSI** template as shown.

3. Click on the **OK** button to open a new document using the selected template.

♦ Define a Sweep Path

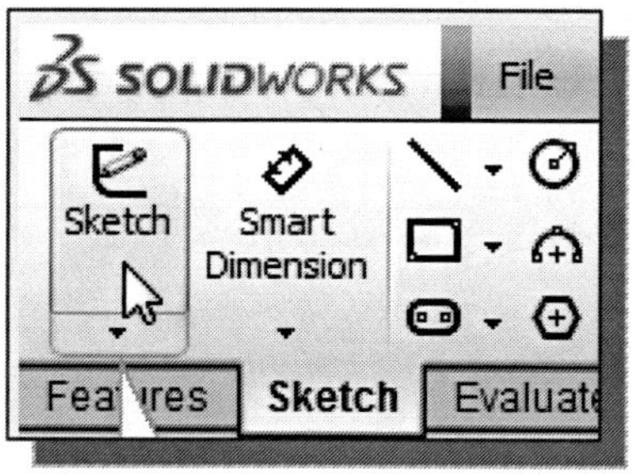

1. In the *Sketch* toolbar select the **Sketch** command by left-clicking once on the icon.

2. Inside the graphics window, select the **Front Plane** as the sketching plane as shown.

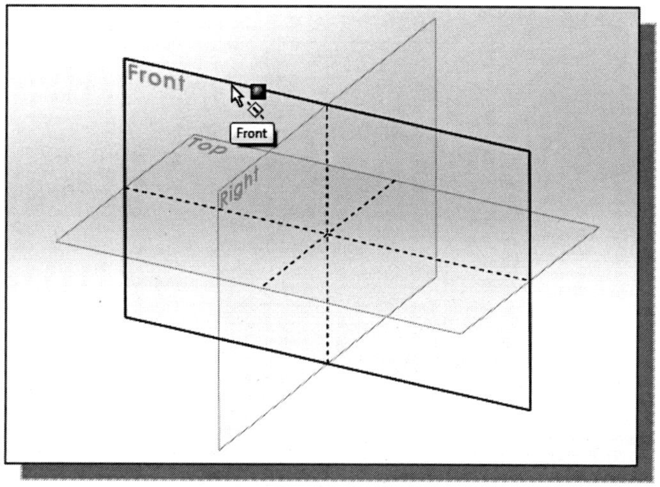

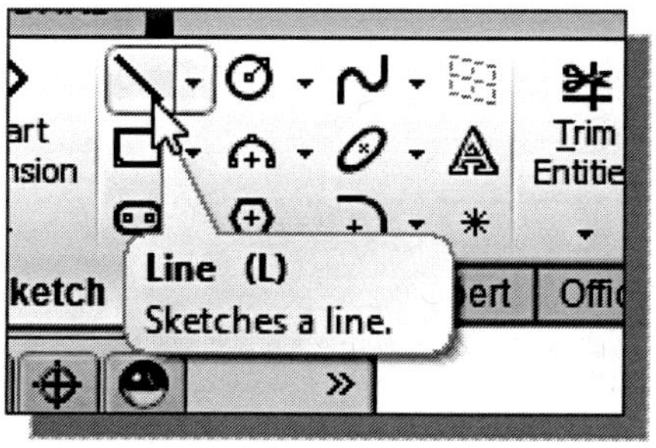

3. Select the **Line** option in the *Sketch* panel. A *Help-tip* box appears next to the cursor: "*Sketches a line.*"

4. On your own, create the **sweep path** with two line segments and 3 arcs as shown. Note the right endpoint of the horizontal line is aligned to the *Origin* of the coordinate system. Also, the center of the left arc is also aligned horizontally to the *Origin.*

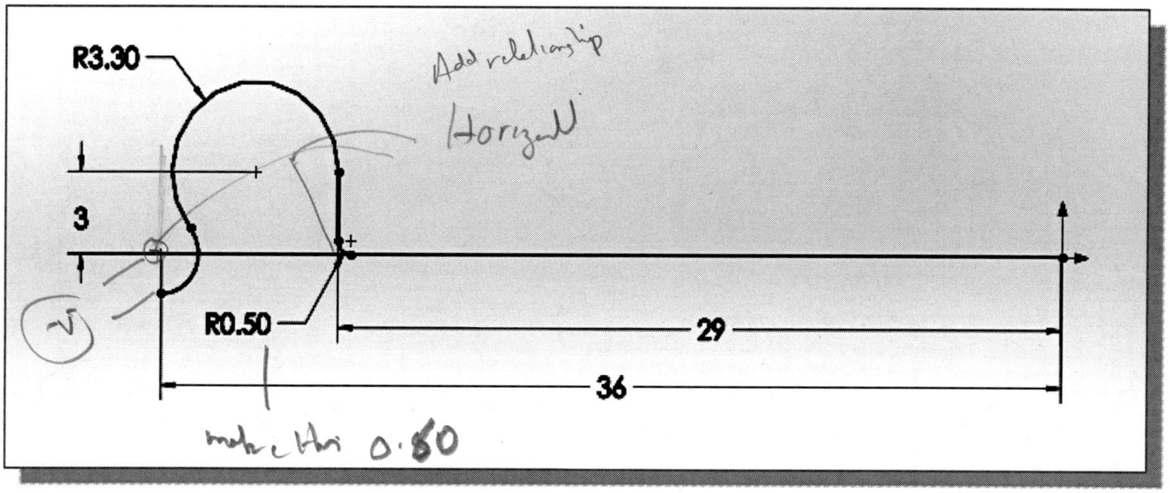

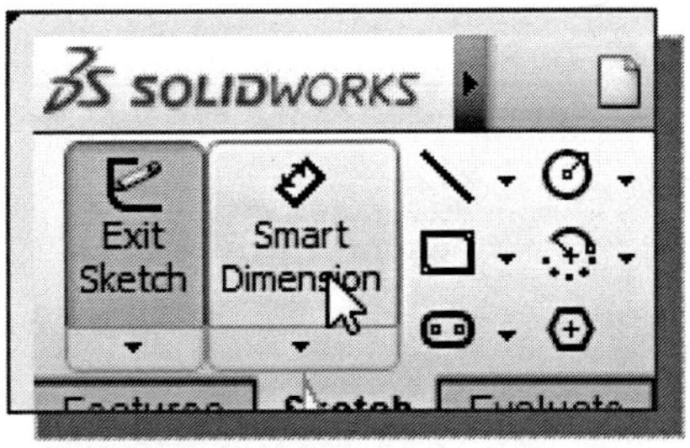

5. On your own, use the **Smart Dimension** command to create the necessary dimensions.

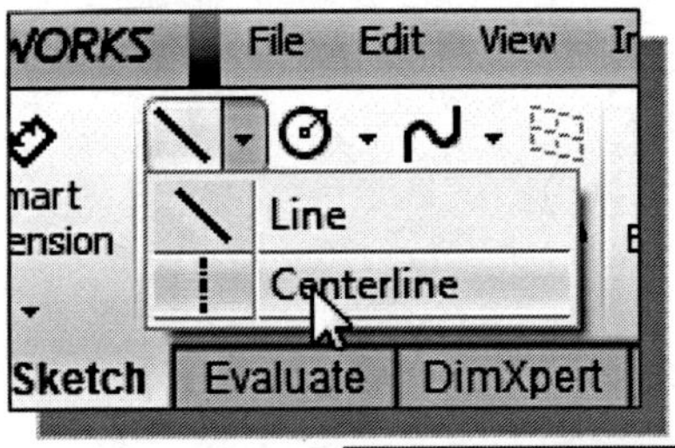

6. Select the **Centerline** option in the *Sketch* panel.

7. On your own, create a vertical centerline aligned to the *Origin* as shown.

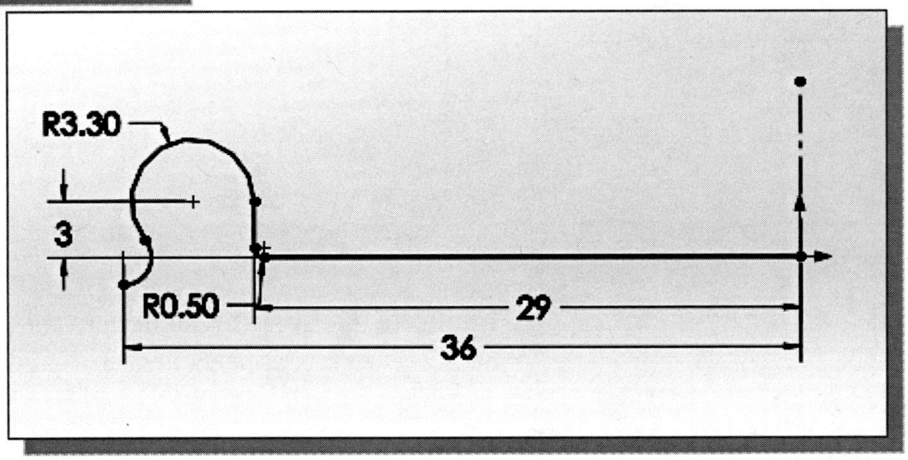

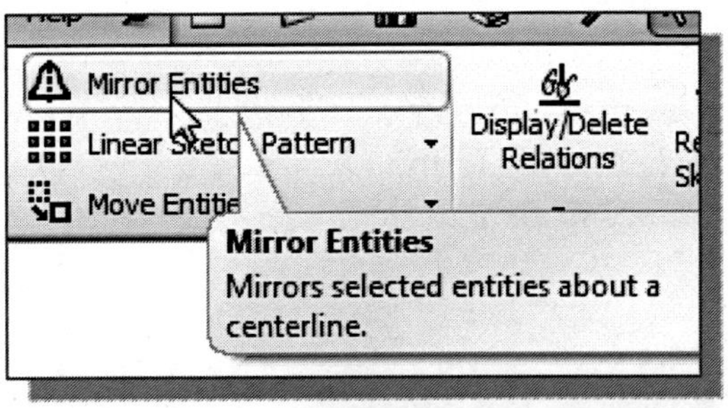

8. Select the **Mirror Entities** command in the *Sketch* panel.

9. Select the **center point** of the larger arc as the *entity to mirror*; also select the **centerline** as the *mirror reference line.*

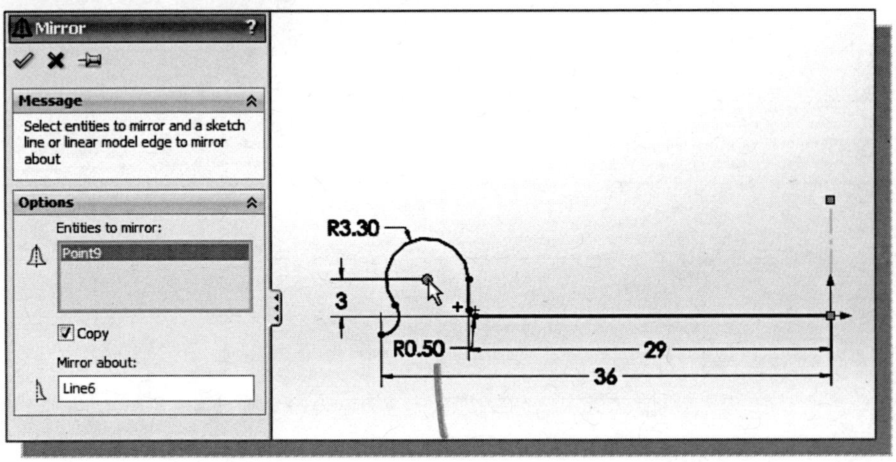

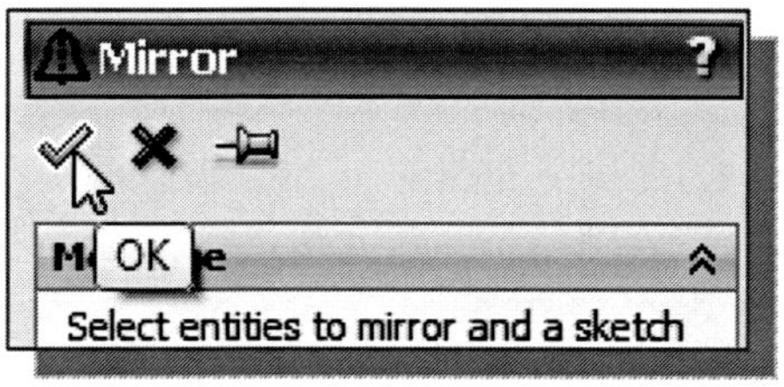

10. In the *Property Manager*, click **OK** to accept the settings and create the mirror entity.

- Note the mirrored point will be used in the assembly model.

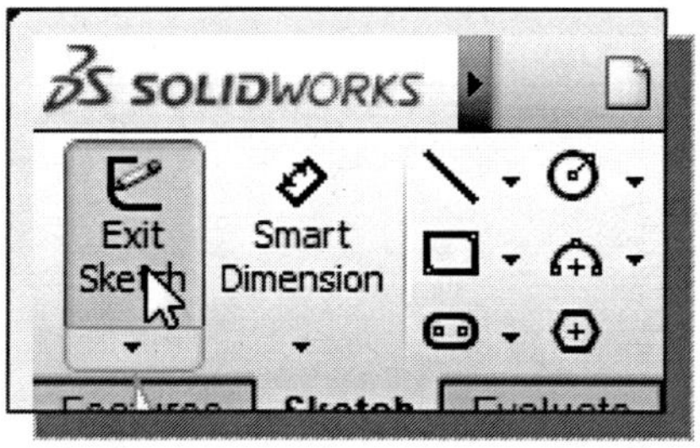

11. Click **Exit Sketch** in the *Sketch* toolbar to end the *Sketch* mode.

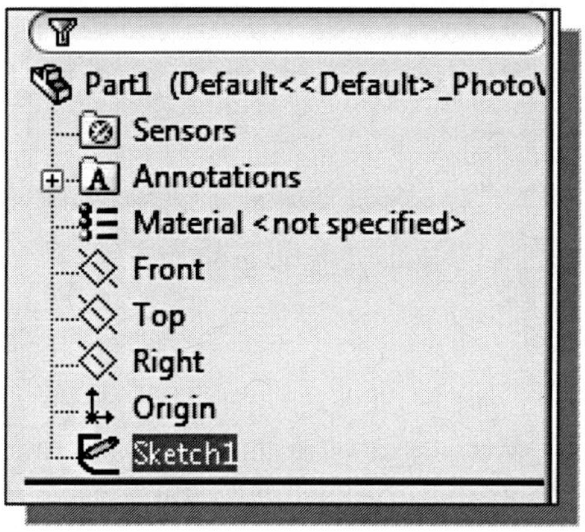

- Notice in the browser window, the sweep path is defined as the first 2D sketch.

♦ **Define the Sweep Section**

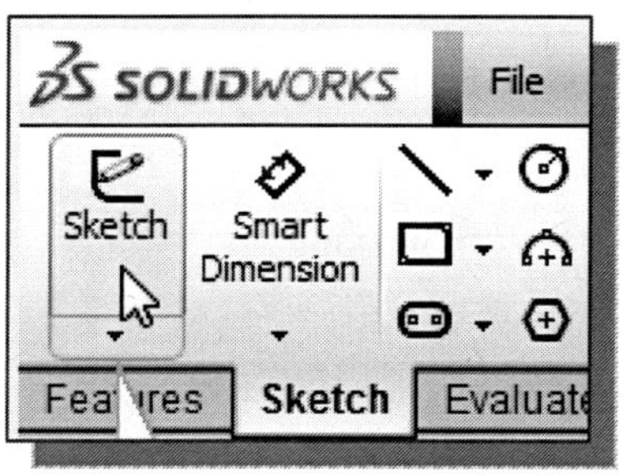

1. In the *Sketch* toolbar select the **Sketch** command by left-clicking once on the icon.

2. Inside the graphics window, select the **Right Plane** as the sketching plane as shown.

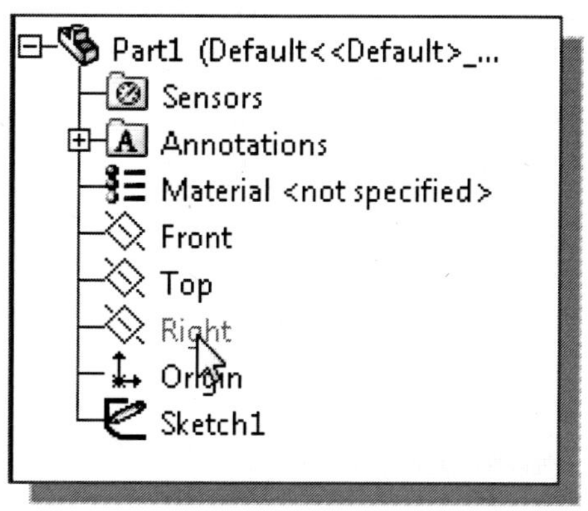

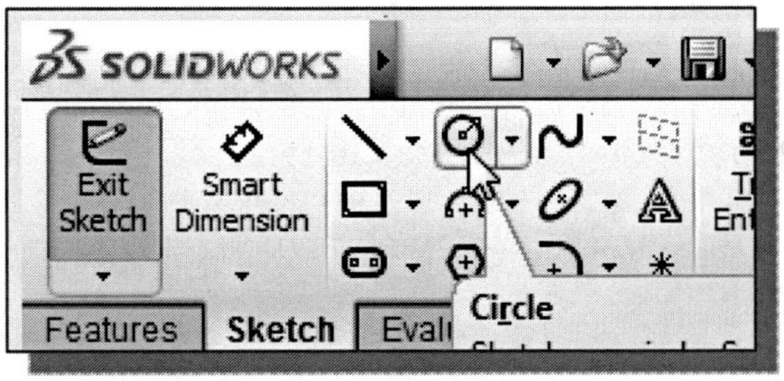

3. Select the **Circle** command by clicking once with the left-mouse-button on the icon in the *Sketch* panel.

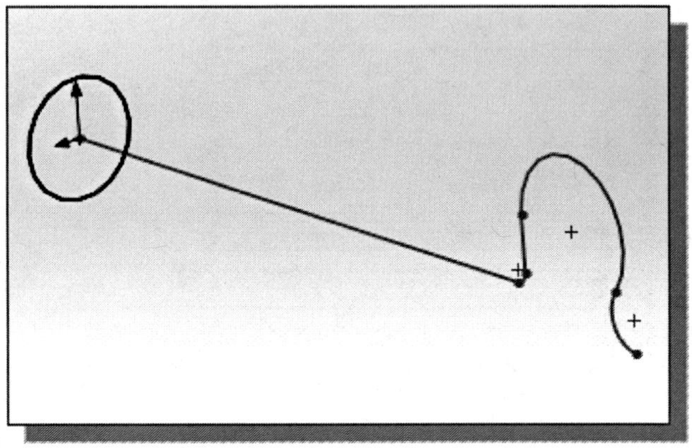

4. Create a circle that is aligned to the *Origin* of the coordinate system as shown.

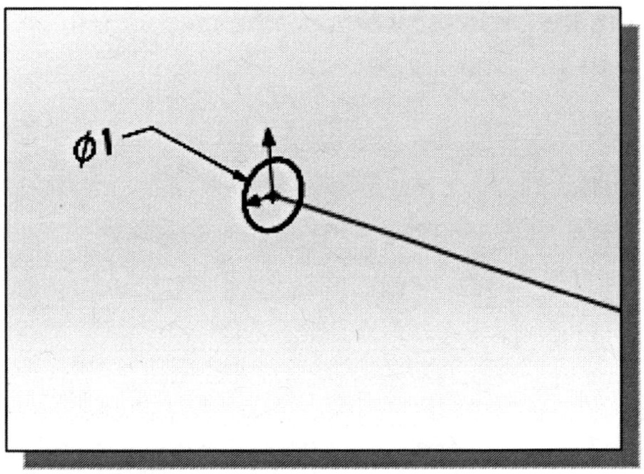

5. On your own, create the size dimension, **1mm**, to adjust the circle as shown.

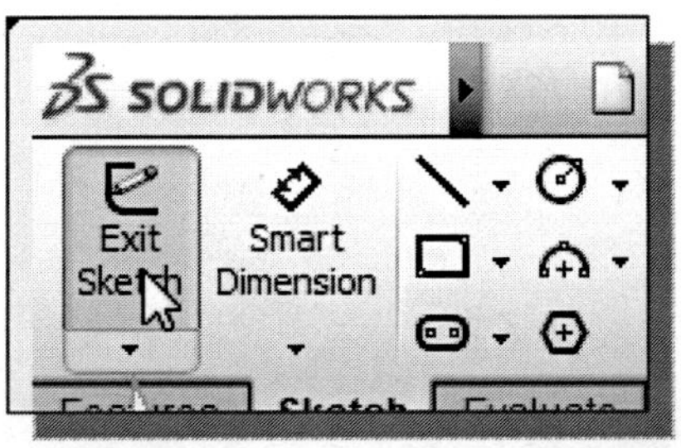

6. In the *Sketch* toolbar, click once with the left-mouse-button on **Exit Sketch** to end the *Sketch* option.

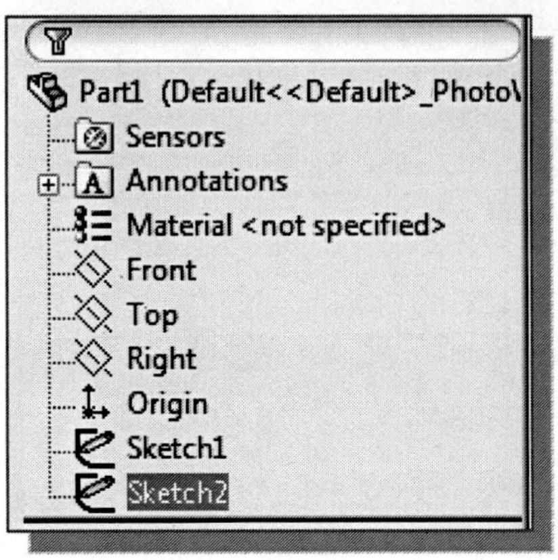

- The created 2D sketch will be used as the sweep section of the feature.

♦ Completing the Swept Feature

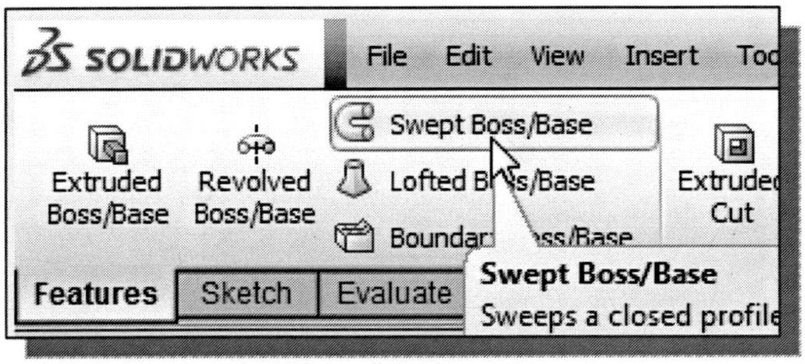

1. In the *Features* toolbar, select the **Swept Boss/Base** command by left-clicking once on the icon.

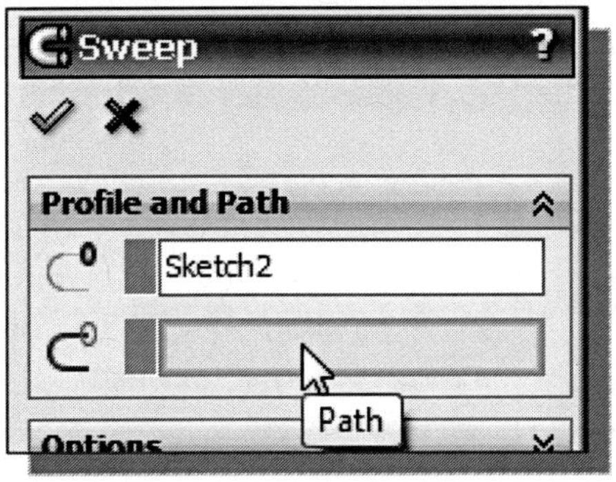

2. Notice the circle, Sketch2, is automatically selected to be used as the sweep section. (Note the *sweep section* must be a closed region.)

3. Click in the **Path** selection box to activate the selection as shown.

4. Click on the open curve, Sketch1, we created as the sweep path as shown in the figure.

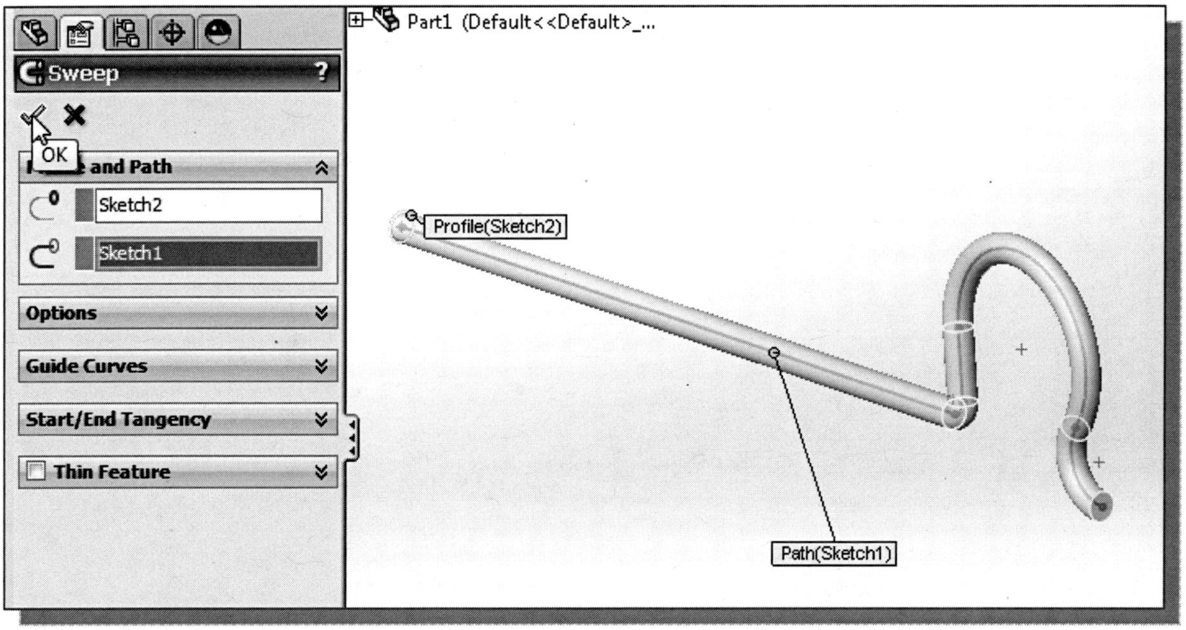

5. Click the **OK** button to accept the settings and create the swept feature.

Create a Mirrored Feature

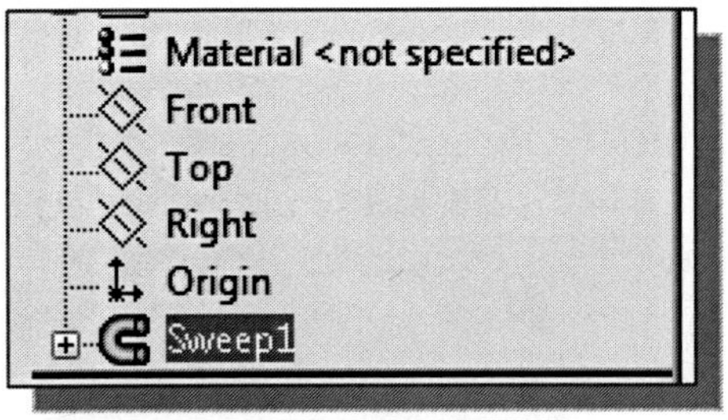

1. Confirm the last **Sweep1** feature we just created is *pre-selected.*

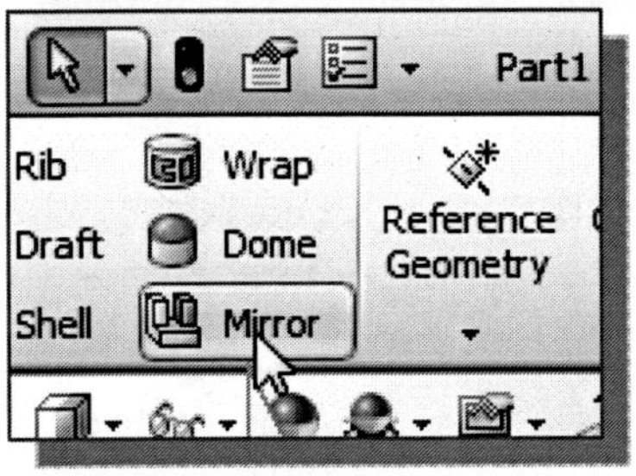

2. In the *Features* toolbar, select the **Mirror Feature** command by releasing the left-mouse-button on the icon.

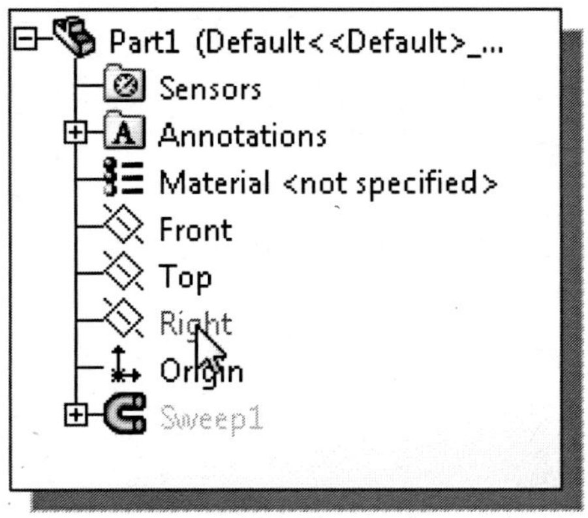

3. In the *Model History Tree*, select the **Right Plane** as the mirror image plane as shown.

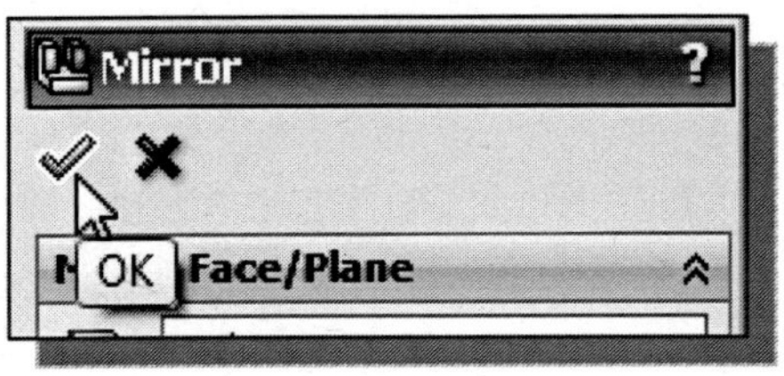

4. Click on the **OK** button to accept the settings and create a mirrored feature.

5. On your own, save the model as **Linkage-Rod**.

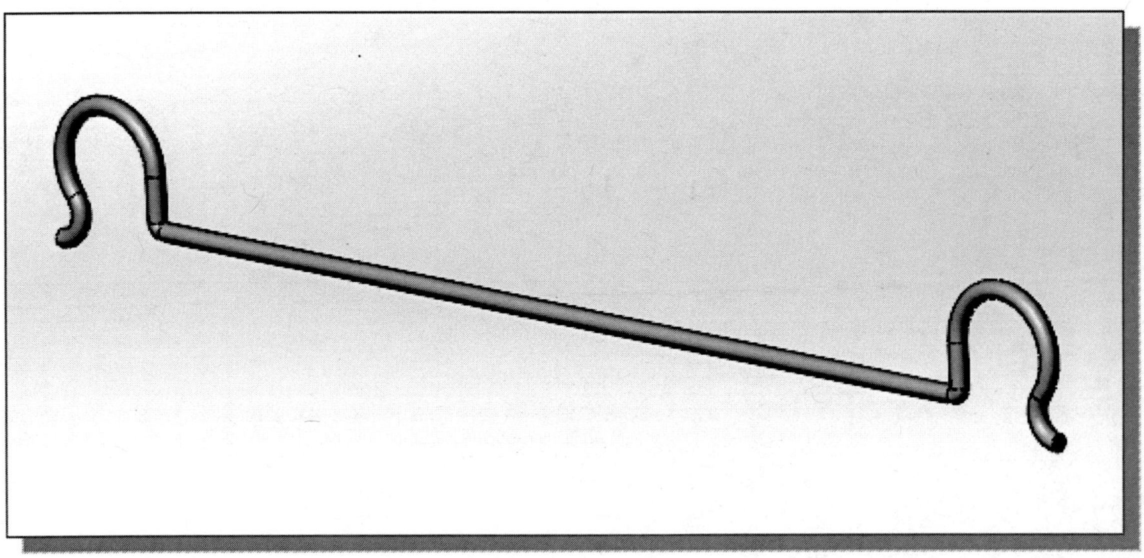

The *Gear Box Right* Part

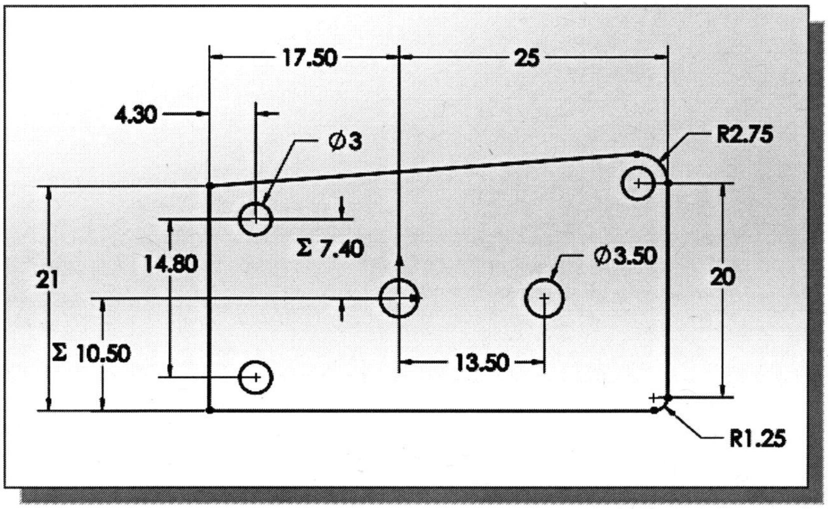

1. Start a new Metric (mm) model using the **Part_mmgs_ANSI** template.

2. Create the base extrude feature, **9.2mm**, starting on one of the datum planes.

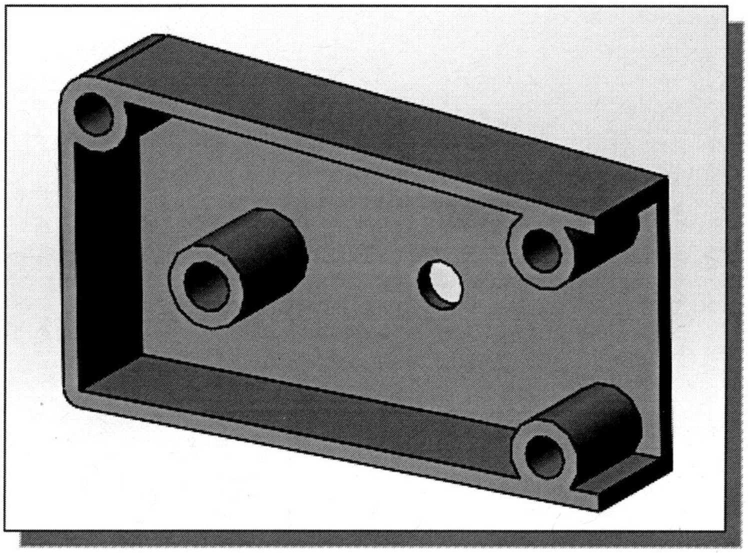

3. Use the **Shell** command, with shell thickness **1.25 mm**, and remove the back face and the shorter side face as shown.

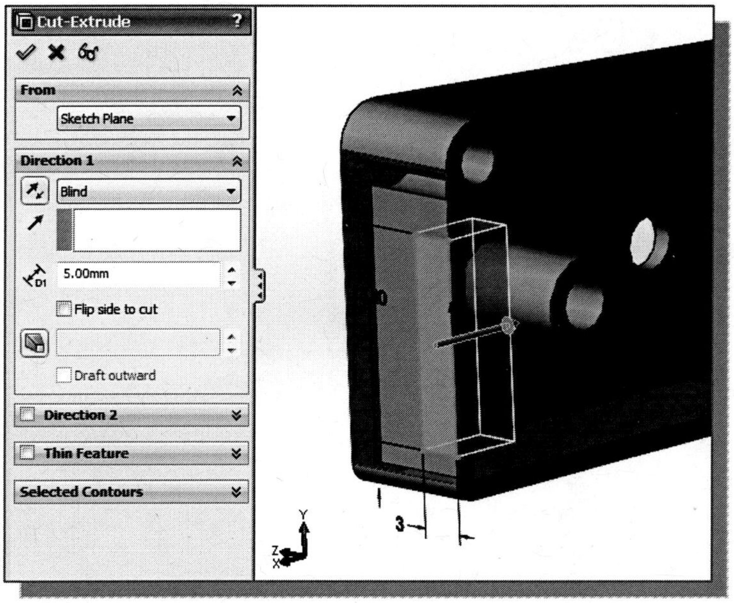

4. Create a cut feature, **13.8x3.0 mm**, as shown.

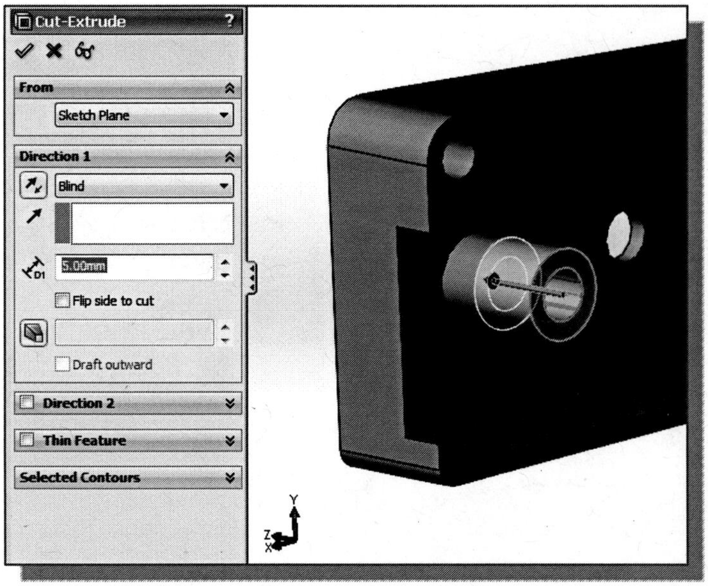

5. Shorten the center support by **5 mm**.

6. Create an undercut feature, diameter **10 mm** and depth **0.5 mm**, as shown.

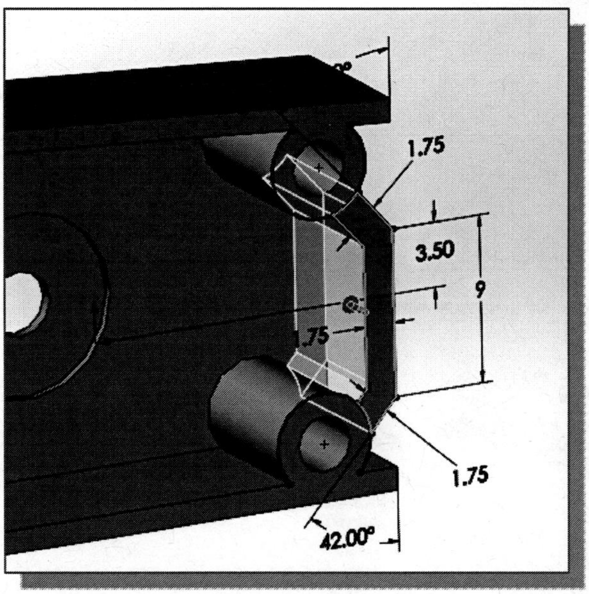

7. Create the additional support wall as shown.

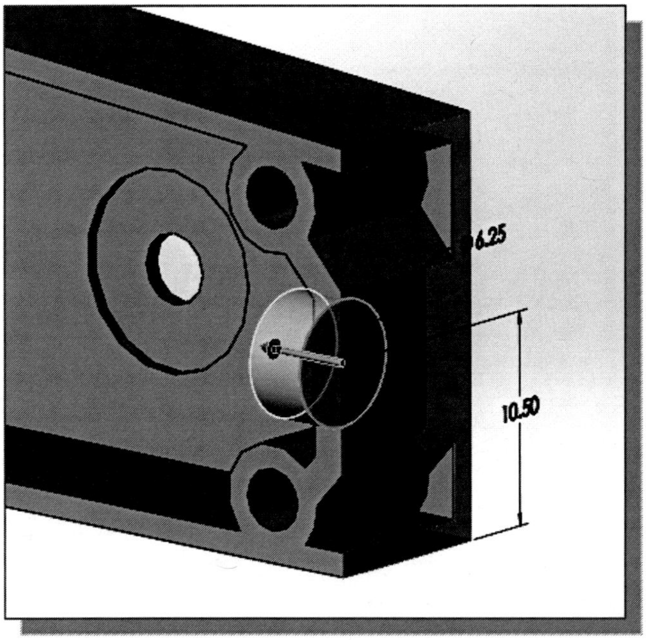

8. Create a cut feature, diameter **6.25 mm** and depth **3 mm**, as shown.

9. Create another cut feature **27 mm** long, as shown.

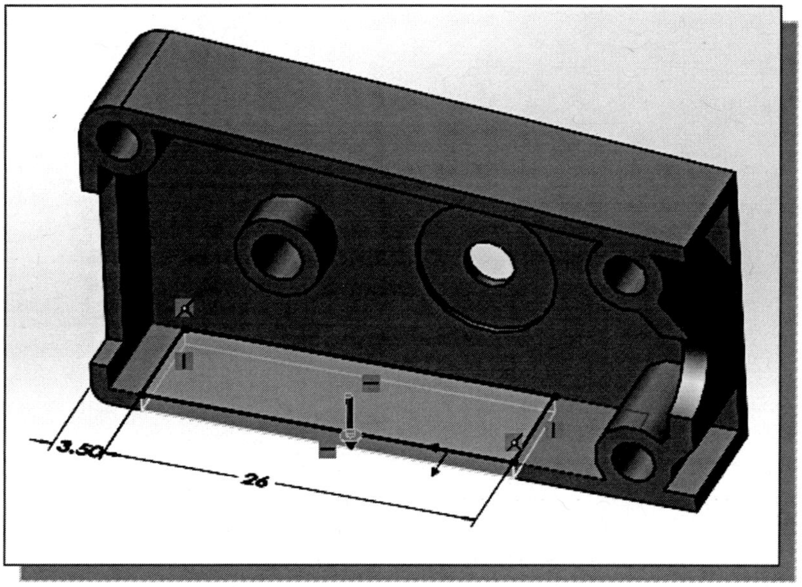

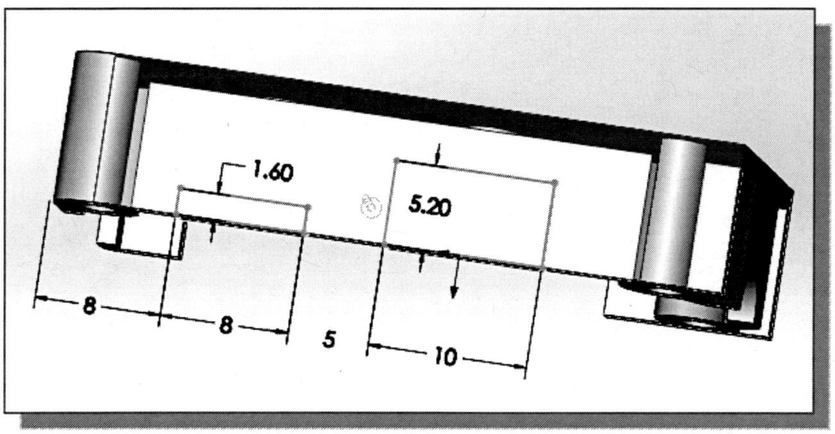

10. Create another cut feature on the opposite side of the model.

11. Create another circular extruded feature, diameter **7.5 mm** and depth **2 mm**, as shown.

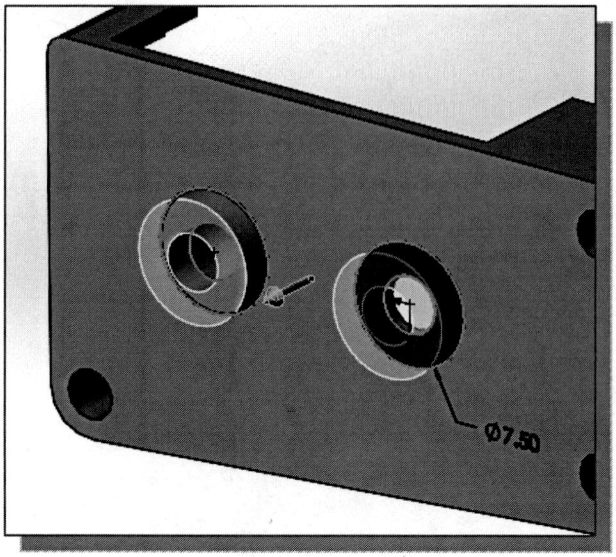

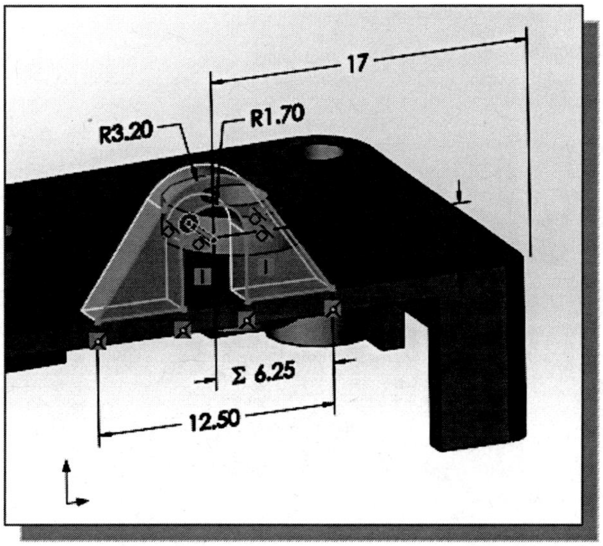

12. Add the side feature, depth **2mm**, on the side surface as shown.

13. On the rounded corner, add another circular extruded feature, diameter **1.5 mm** and depth **11 mm**, as shown.

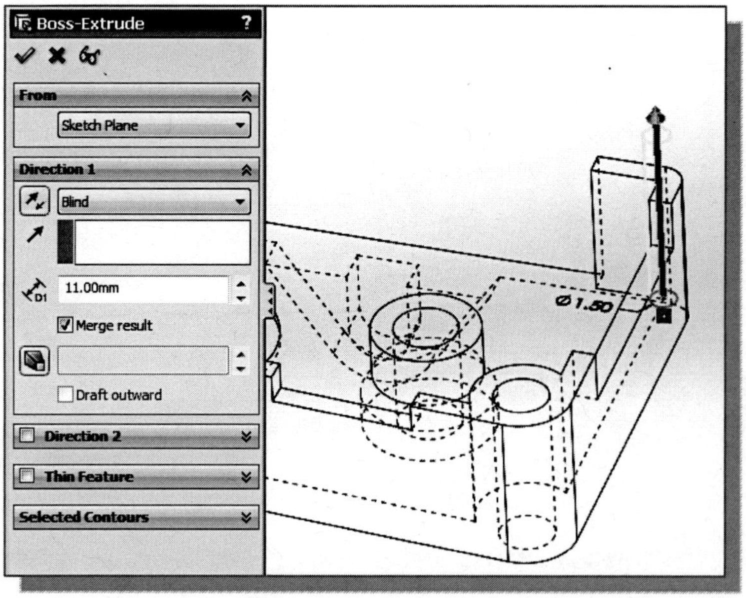

14. Create the last symmetric feature, width **11.5mm**, with the sketch aligned to the center datum plane.

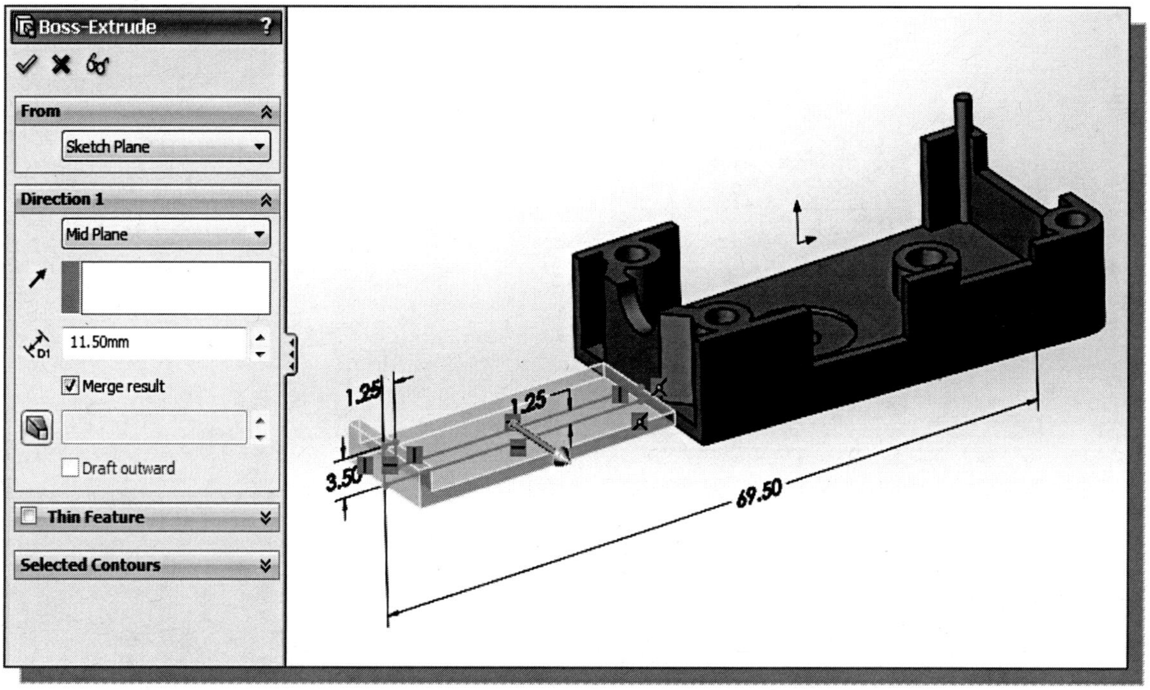

15. Save the model as ***GearBox-Right***.

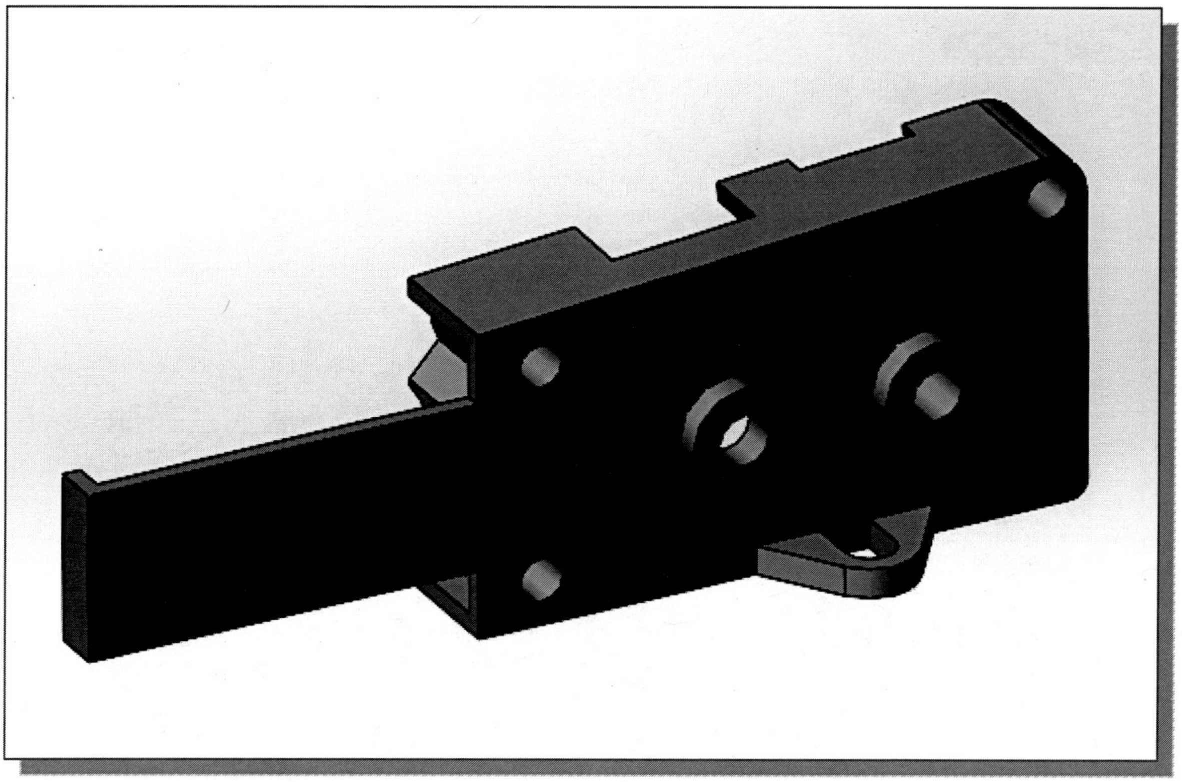

The *Gear Box Left* Part

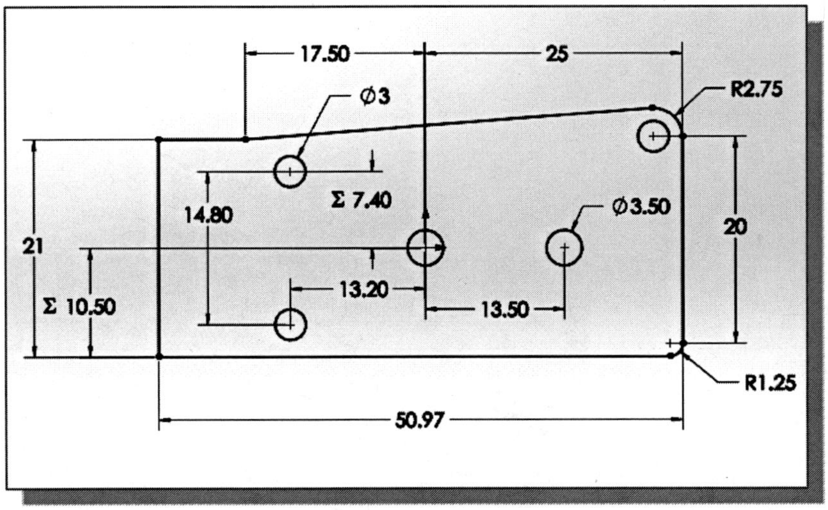

1. Start a new **Metric (mm)** model.

2. Create the base extruded feature, depth **14.0 mm**, starting on one of the datum planes.

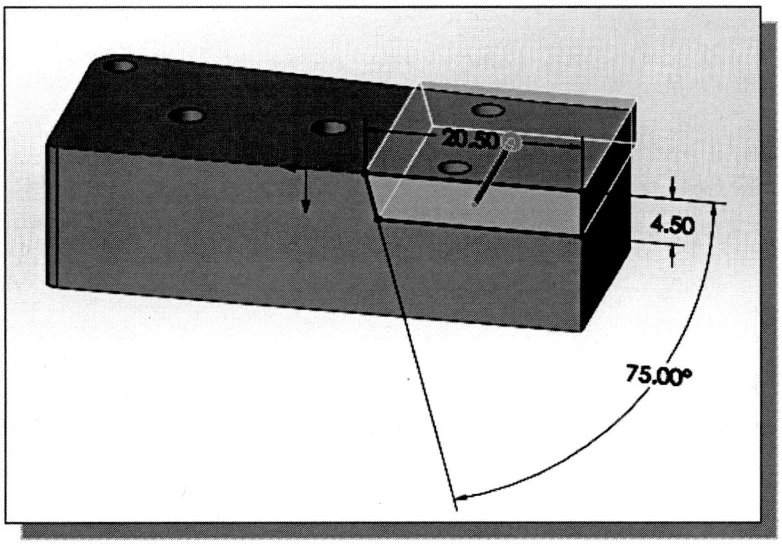

3. Create a cut feature, **20.5 mm x 4.5 mm** and **75 degrees**.

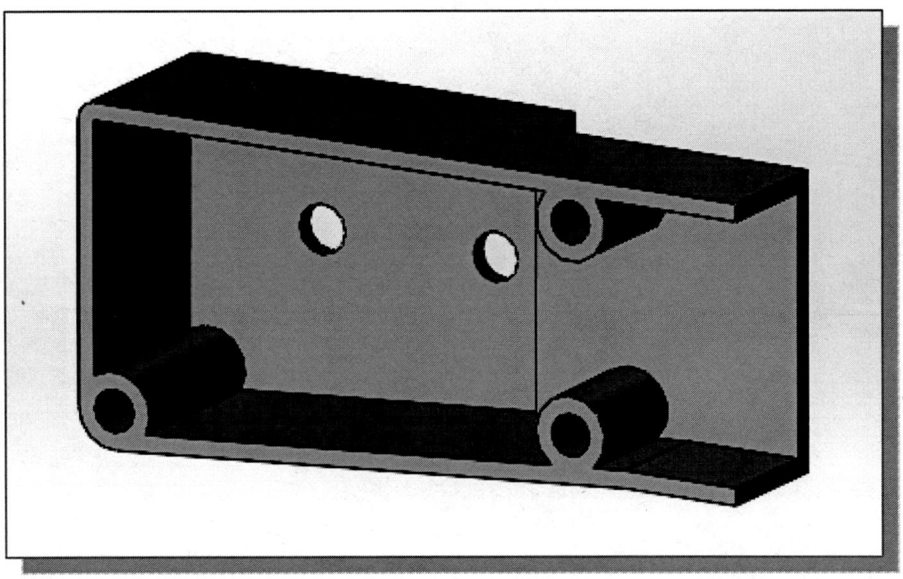

4. Use the **Shell** command, with shell thickness **1.25 mm**, and remove the back face and the shorter side face as shown.

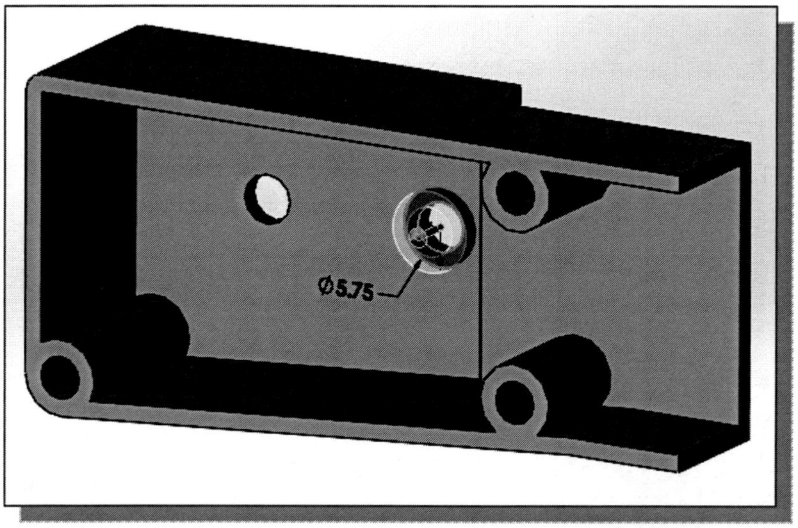

5. Create a boss/base extrude feature, diameter **5.75 mm** and depth **1.5 mm**, as shown.

6. Create a cut feature on the side surface with the dimensions as shown.

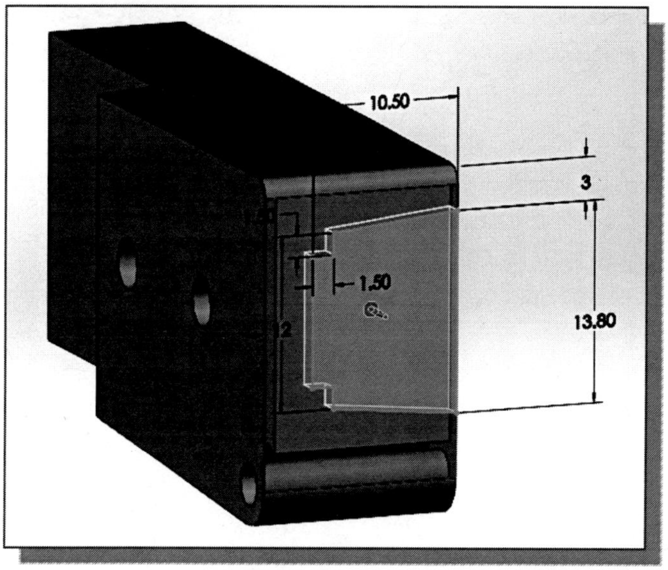

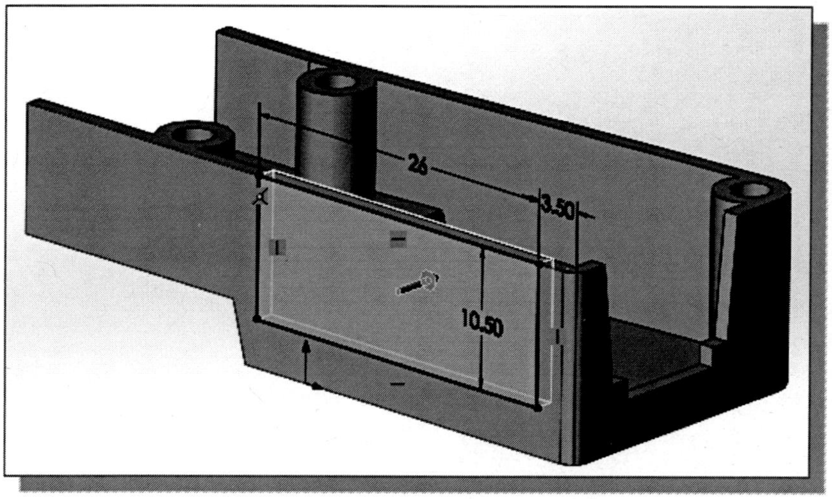

7. Create another cut feature on the adjacent surface as shown.

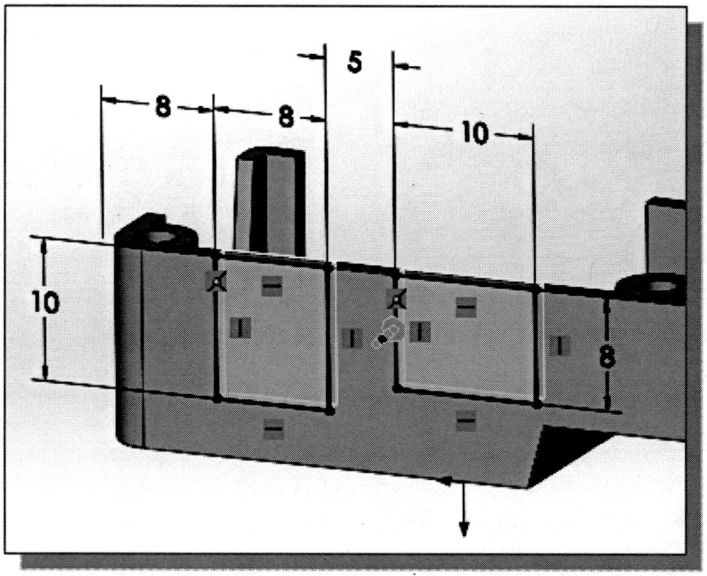

8. Create another cut feature on the opposite surface as shown.

9. Create another circular extruded feature, diameter **7.5 mm** and depth **2 mm**, as shown.

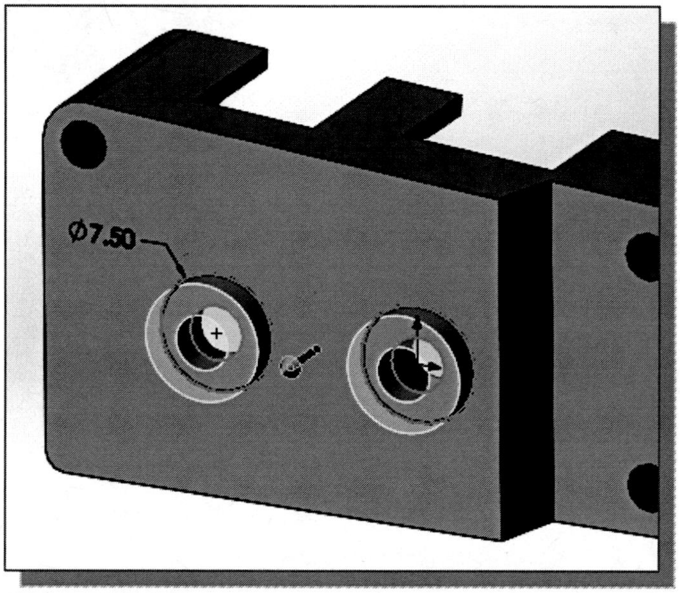

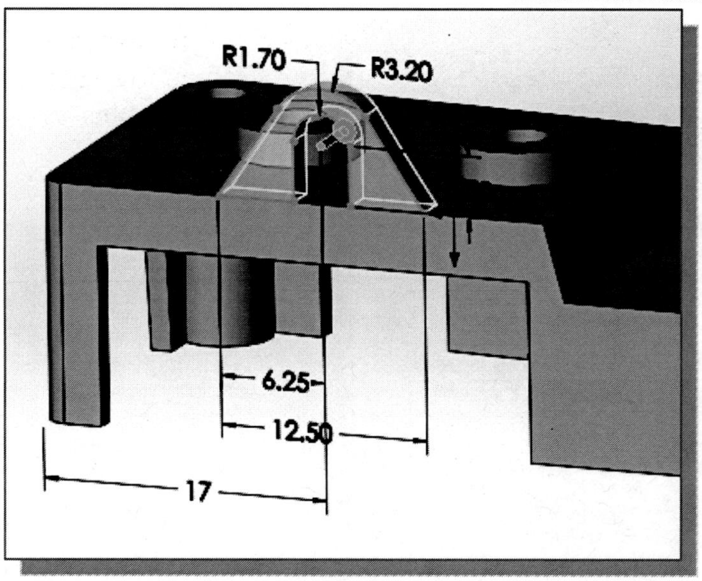

10. Add the side feature, **depth 2mm**, on the top surface as shown.

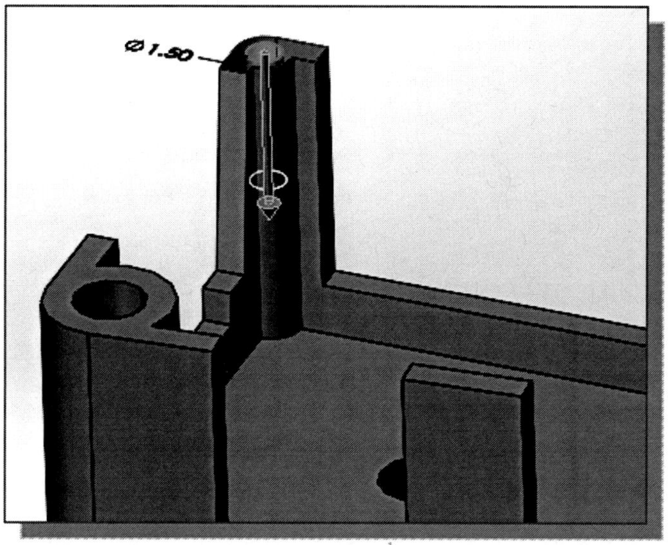

11. Create additional features at the rounded corner, first a cylindrical extruded (**2mm**) feature and then a cut feature for the **1.5 mm** hole, depth **6 mm**, as shown.

12. Create an undercut feature, diameter **10 mm** and depth **1 mm**, as shown.

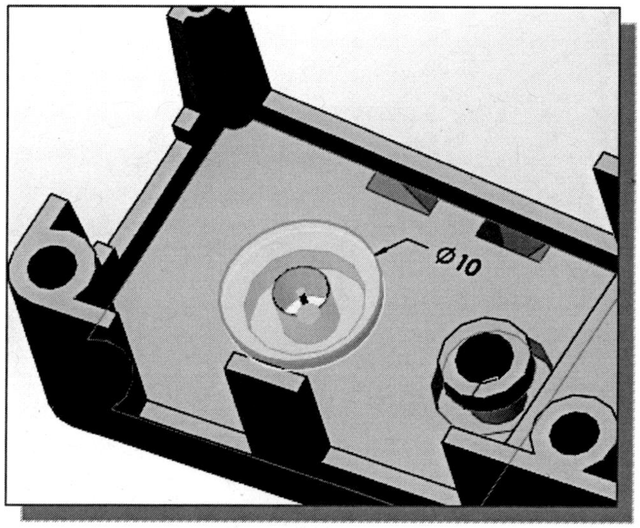

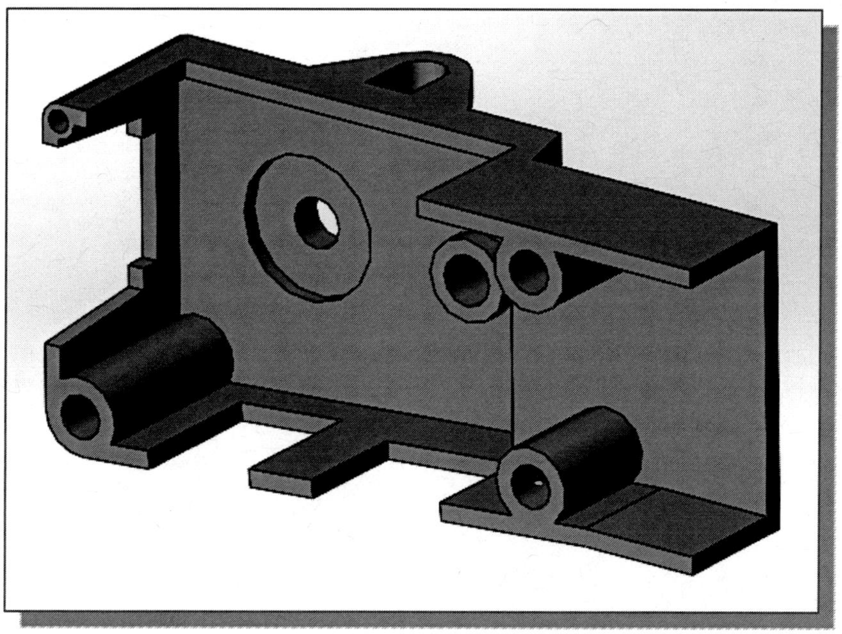

13. On your own, save the model using the filename: ***GearBox-Left***.

Questions:

1. Keeping the *History Tree* in mind, what is the difference between *cut with a pattern* and *cut each one individually*?

2. What is the difference between **Sweep** and **Extrude**?

3. What are the advantages and disadvantages of creating fillets using the **3D Fillets** command and creating fillets in the 2D profiles?

4. Describe the steps used to create the *Shell* feature in the lesson.

5. How do we modify the *Shell* parameters after the model is built?

6. Describe the elements required in creating a *Swept* feature.

7. Create sketches showing the steps you plan to use to create the model shown on the next page:

Exercises:

1. **Motor Housing** (Dimensions are in inches.)

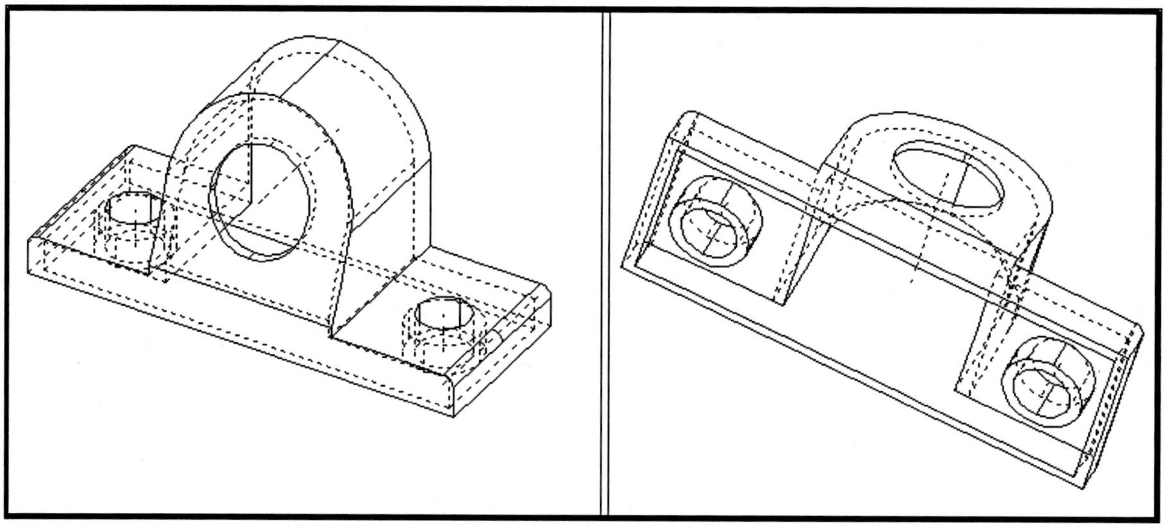

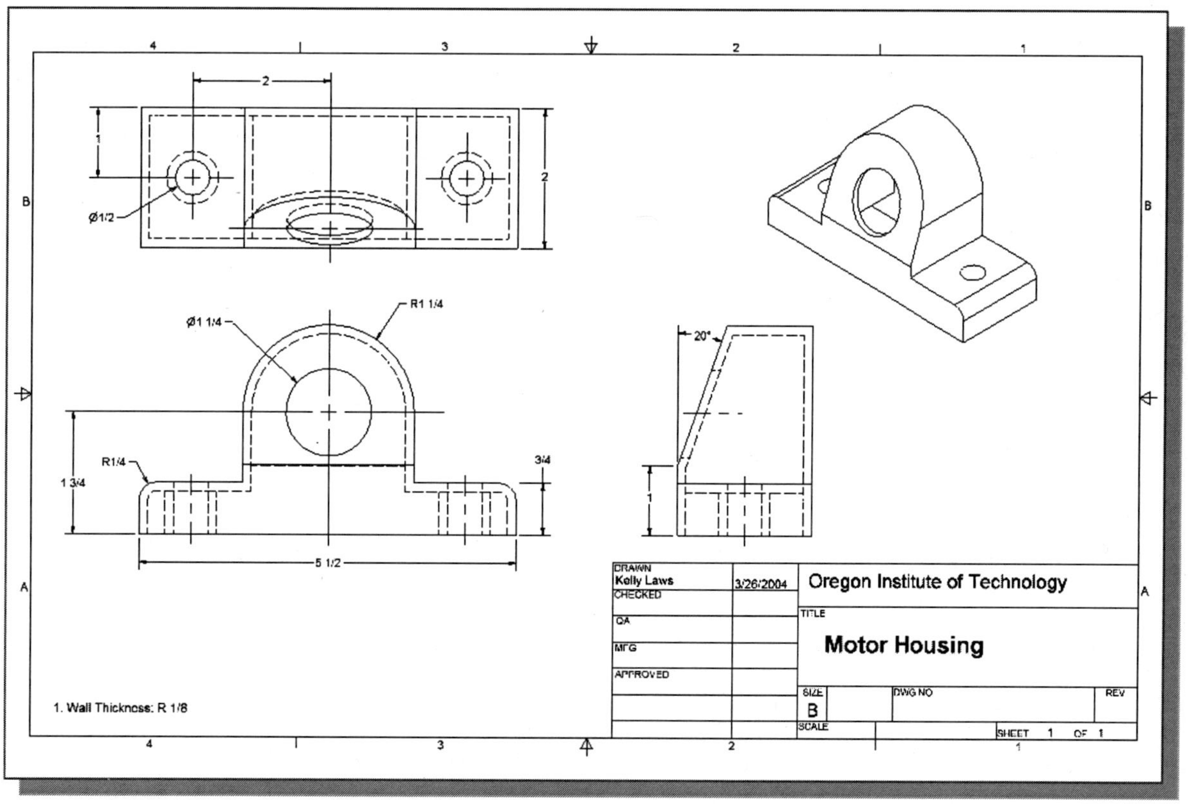

2. **Switch Base** (Dimensions are in inches.)

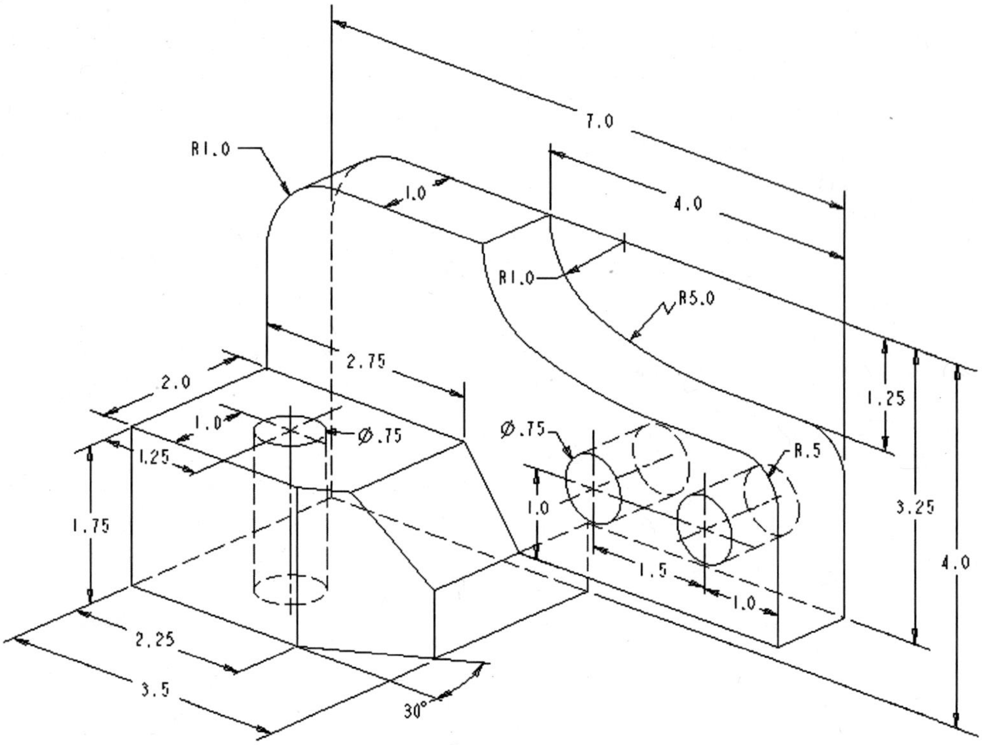

3. **Piston Cap** (Dimensions are in inches)

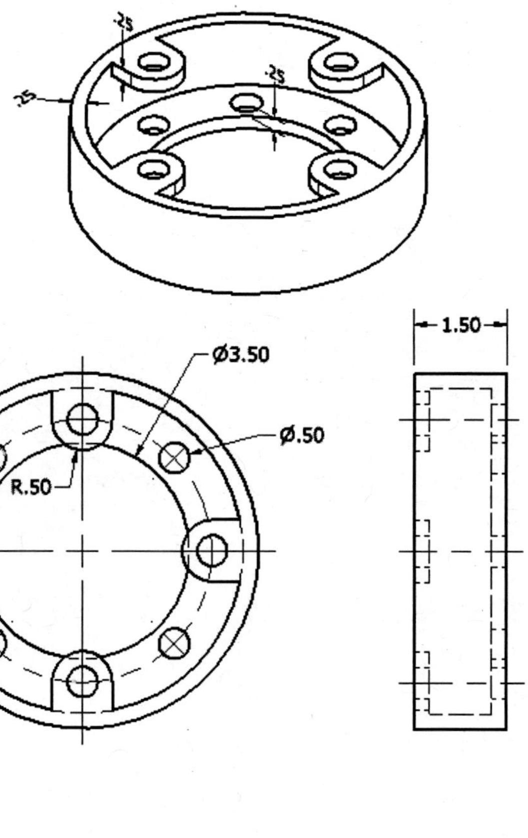

Chapter 10
Planar Linkage Analysis using GeoGebra

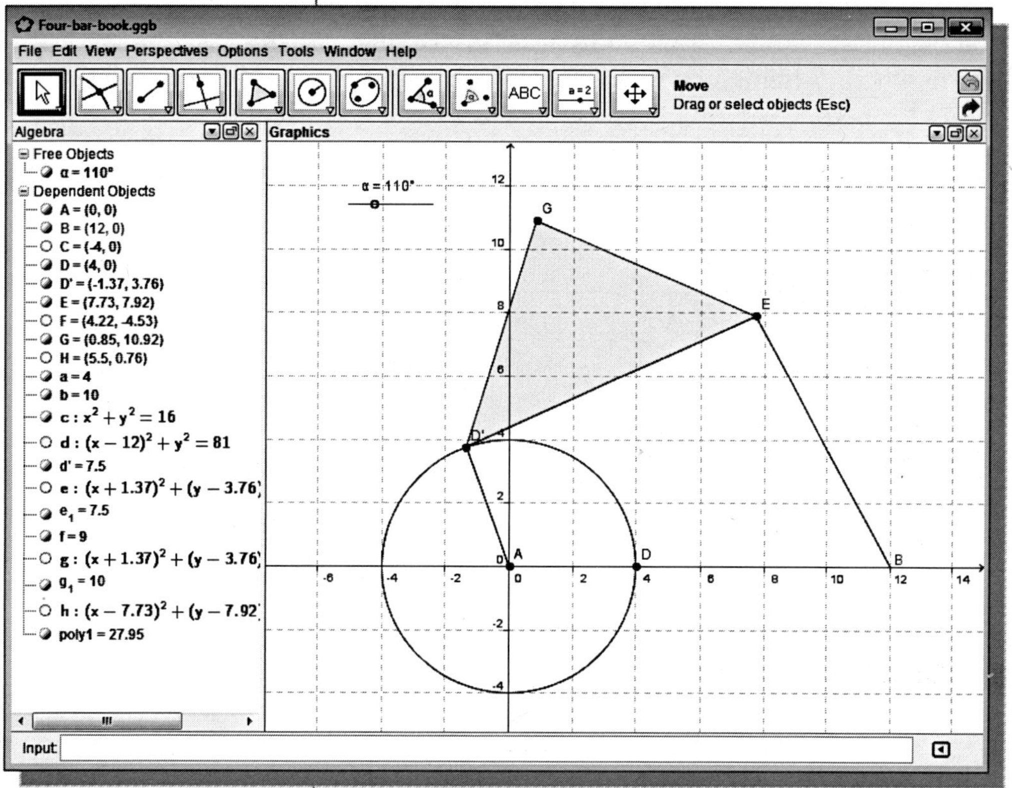

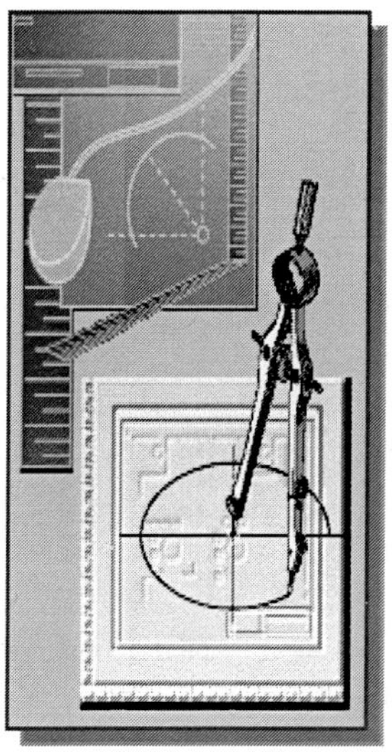

Learning Objectives

- **Understand the Basic Types of Planar Four-Bar Linkages**
- **Learn the Basic Geometric tools available in GeoGebra**
- **Use GeoGebra to Construct Planar Four-Bar Linkages**
- **Use GeoGebra to Create Animations of Four-Bar Linkages**

Introduction to Four-Bar Linkages

A machine is a system or device consisting of fixed and moving parts that modifies mechanical energy to do work. Assemblies within a machine that control movement are often called **mechanisms**. A ***mechanism*** is a group of links connected together for the purpose of transmitting forces or motions. A **four-bar linkage** or **four-bar mechanism** is the simplest movable mechanism commonly used in machines. A ***four-bar linkage*** consists of four rigid bodies (called *bars* or *links*) with one link fixed. The four links are each attached to two others by single joints (pivots) to form a closed loop. The fixed link is referred to as the **frame**; one of the rotating links is called the **driver** or **crank**; the other rotating link is called the **follower** or **rocker**; and the floating link is called the **connecting rod** or **coupler**. Some of the more commonly used four-bar linkages are listed below.

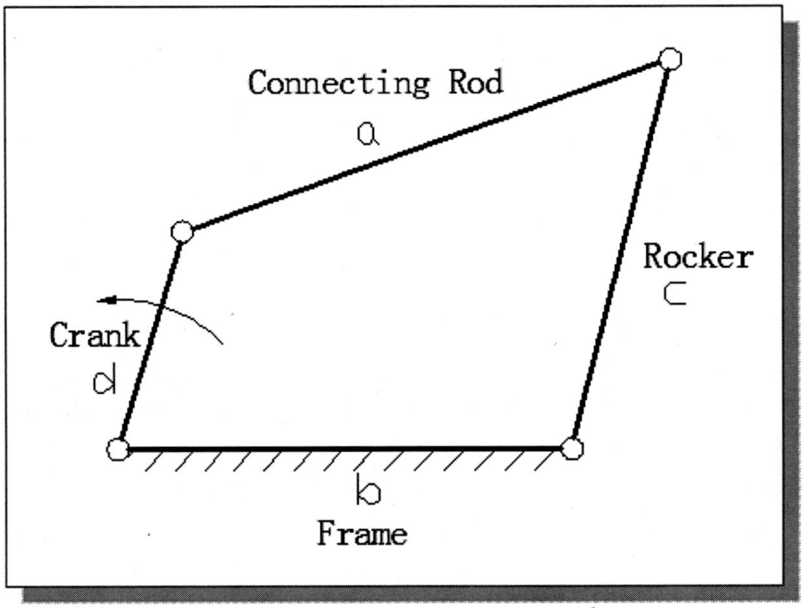

- Depending upon the arrangement and lengths of the links, different types of motions can be generated. Different mechanisms can also be formed by fixing different links of the same chain.

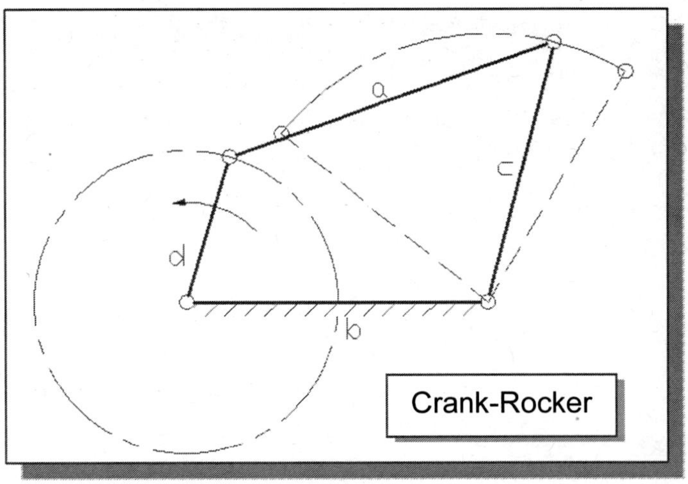

➢ The **Crank-Rocker** mechanism is a four-bar linkage in which the shorter link makes a complete revolution and the opposite link rocks (oscillates) back and forth.

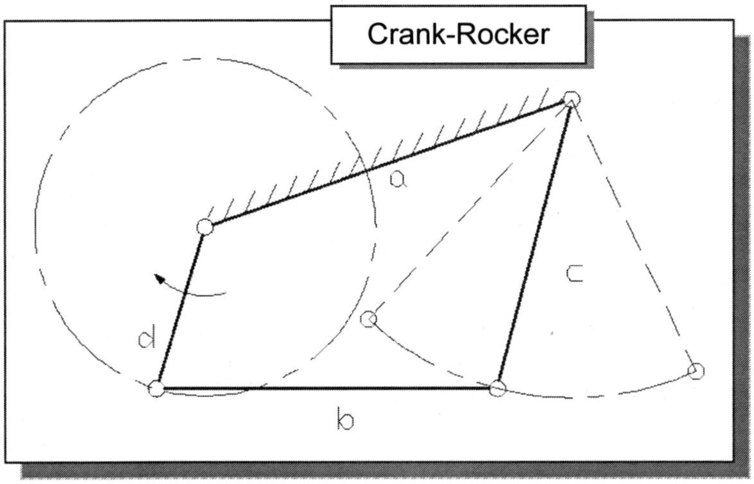

- Note that by fixing the opposite link of the same mechanism, another **Crank-Rocker** mechanism is formed.

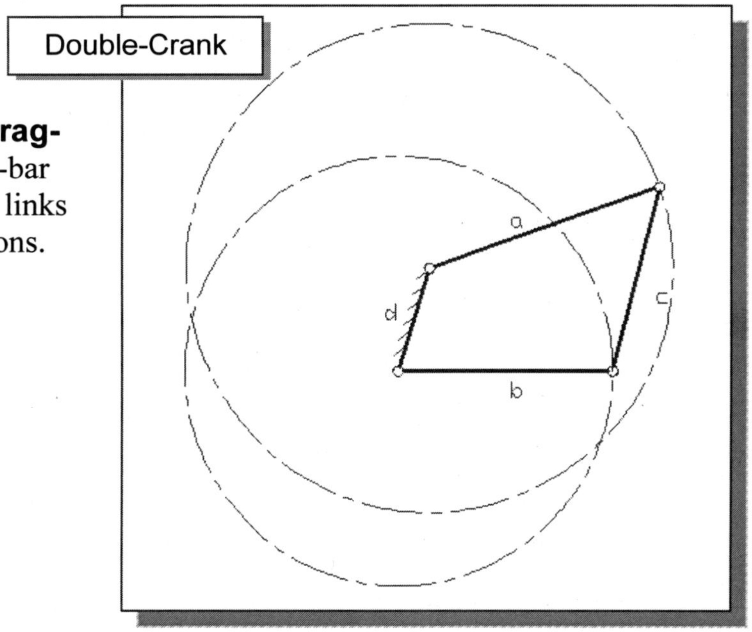

- The **Double-Crank** or **Drag-Link** mechanism is a four-bar linkage with two opposite links making complete revolutions.

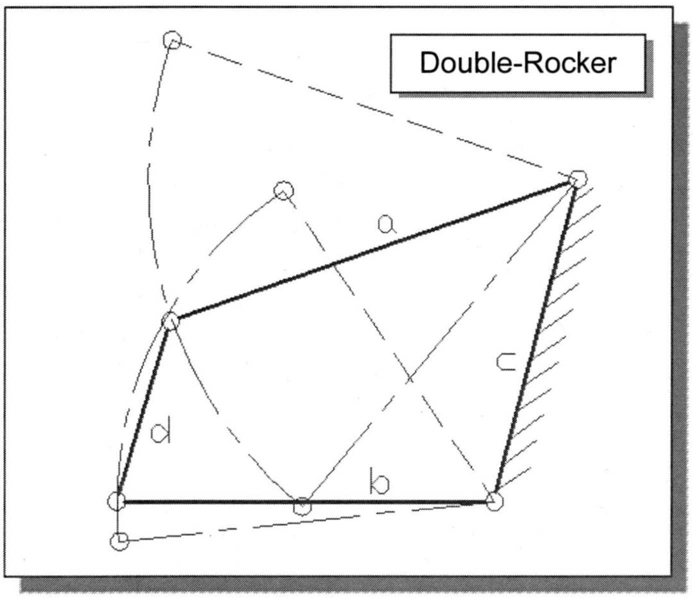

- The **Double-Rocker** mechanism is a four-bar linkage in which the crank and follower rock (oscillate) back and forth; none of the links can make full revolution.

- Note the four different mechanisms above are formed by fixing different links of the same links.

➤ The **Slider-Crank** mechanism is a special case of the four-bar linkage. As the follower link of a *crank-rocker* linkage gets longer, the path of the pin joint between the connecting rod and the follower approaches a straight line. Slider-Crank is a mechanism for converting the linear motion of a slider into rotational motion or vice-versa.

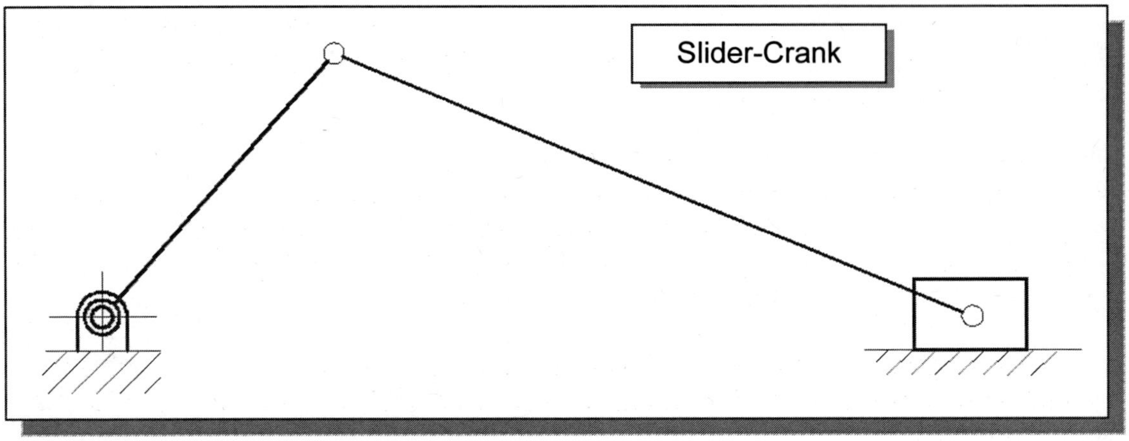

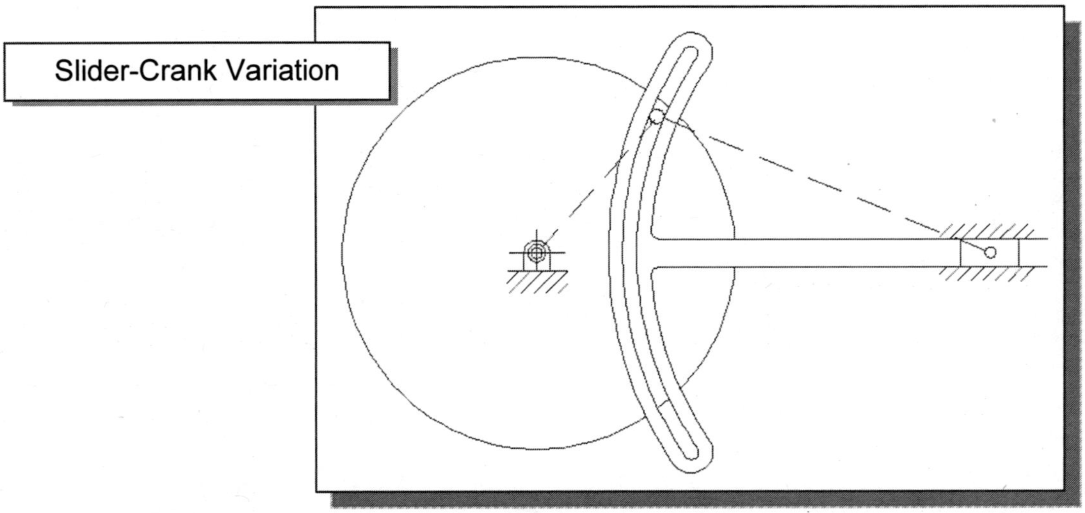

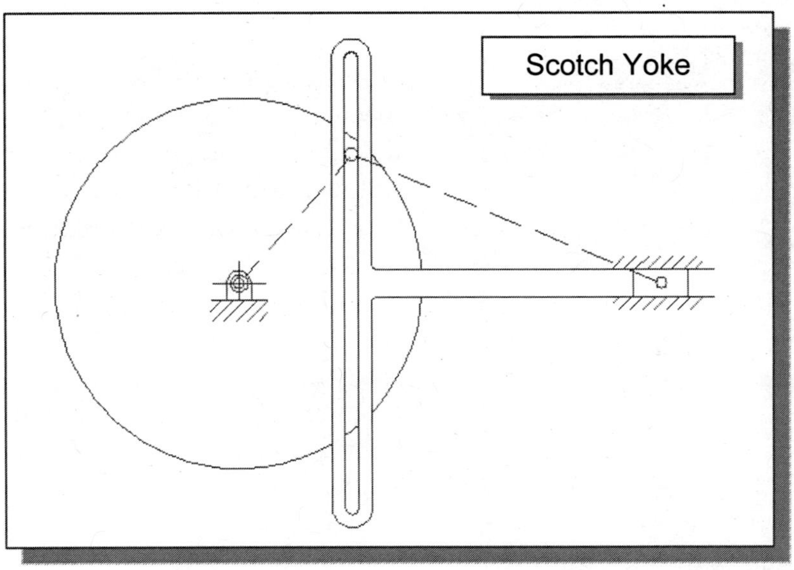

➤ The **Scotch Yoke** is most commonly used in reciprocating piston pumps and in control valve actuators in high pressure oil and gas pipelines.

Introduction to GeoGebra

GeoGebra is an award winning **interactive dynamic geometry software** that joins geometry, algebra and calculus. ***Interactive dynamic geometry software*** is a type of computer program that allows the creation and then manipulation of geometric constructions. In most *interactive geometry software*, constructions can be made with points, vectors, segments, lines, polygons, conic sections, inequalities, implicit polynomials and functions.

The development of *GeoGebra* was started by Prof. **Markus Hohenwarter** for mathematic education. Prof. Markus Hohenwarter started the project in 2001 at the *University of Salzburg*, continuing it at *Florida Atlantic University* (2006–2008), *Florida State University* (2008–2009), and now at the *University of Linz*, together with the help of open-source developers and translators all over the world.

In *GeoGebra*, geometric entities can be entered and modified directly on screen, or through the *Input Bar*. *GeoGebra* has the ability to use variables for numbers, vectors and points; derivatives and integrals of functions can also be evaluated.

The main webpage of *GeoGebra* is at http://www.geogebra.org/cms/en

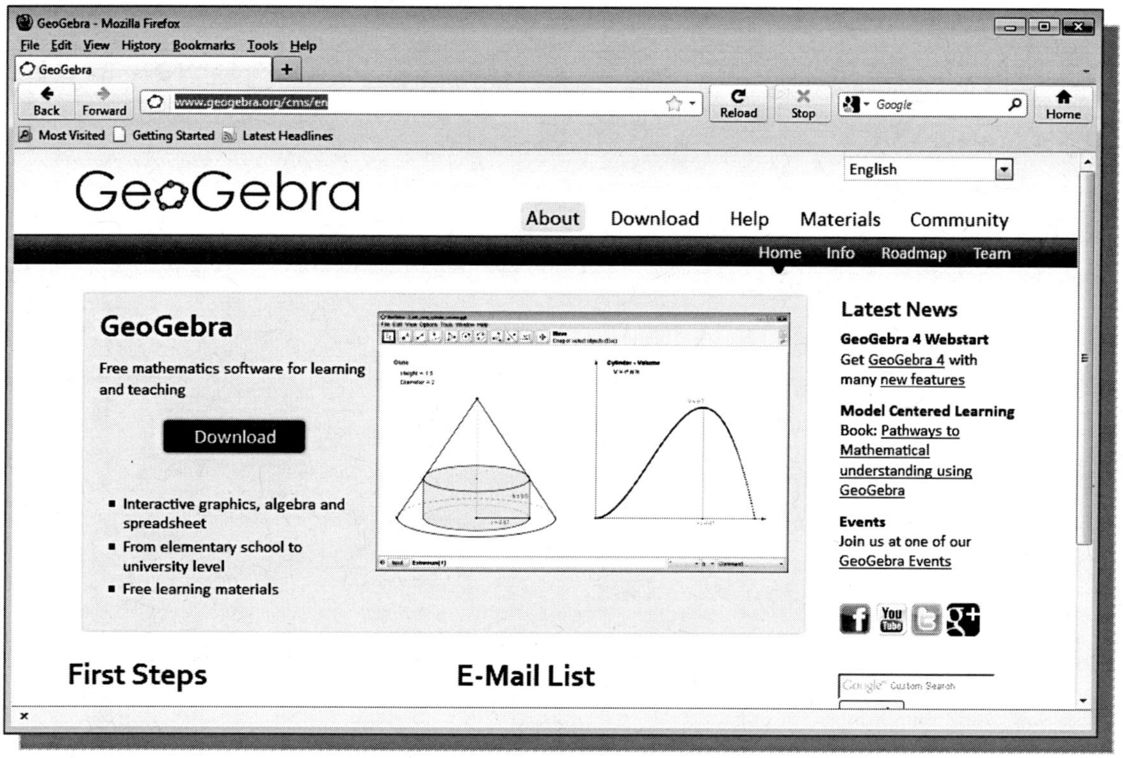

- *GeoGebra* is an open source free software, written in Java and thus available for multiple platforms, including *Windows*, *Mac* and *Linux* systems.

- Two versions of *GeoGebra* are available for download. *GeoGebra* is the full version and *GeoGebraPrim* has the same capabilities as the full version but uses a more simplified user interface. Files created in *GeoGebra* can be loaded in *GeoGebraPrim* and vice versa.

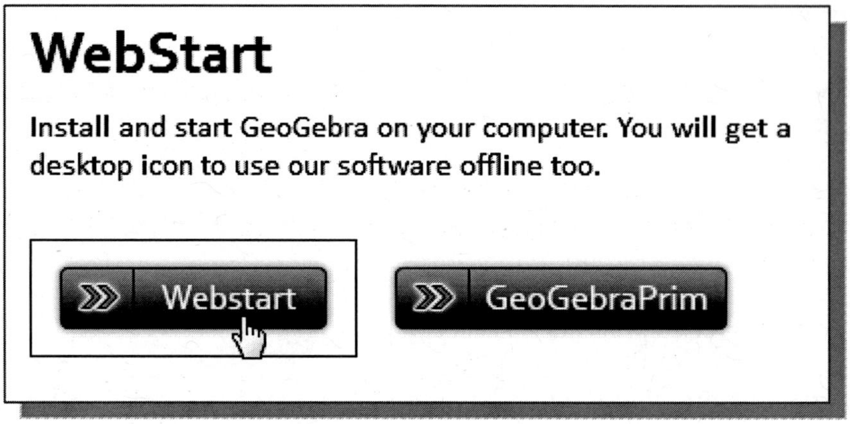

- Note the installation of the ***Java Platform*** is required as *GeoGebra* is written in Java.

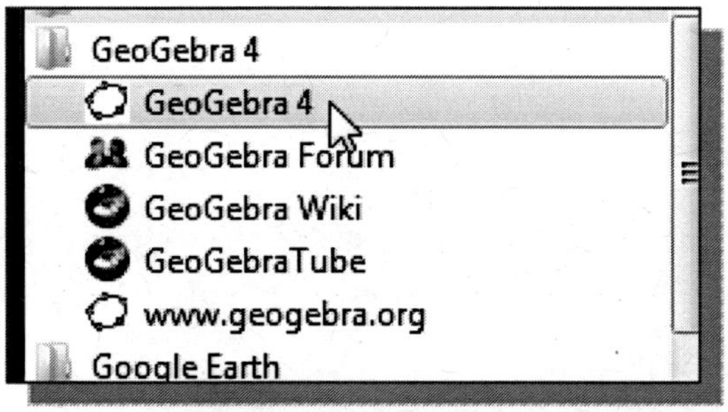

- For most versions of *GeoGebra*, the installed program can be accessed through the *Start* menu or the **GeoGebra** icon on the desktop.

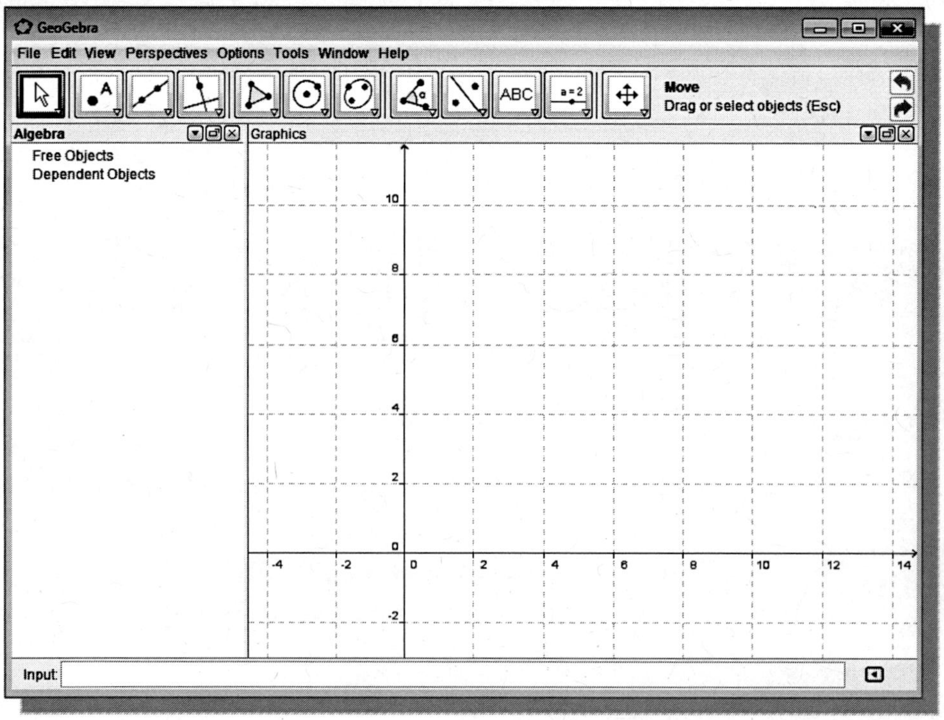

1. Select the **GeoGebra** option on the *Start* menu or select the **GeoGebra** icon on the desktop to start *GeoGebra*. The *GeoGebra* main window will appear on the screen.

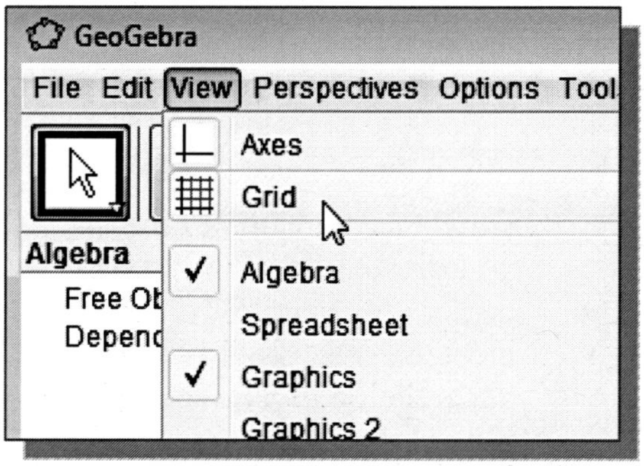

2. In the **View** pull-down menu, switch on the **Grid** display by clicking on the icon with the left-mouse-button as shown.

- The *GeoGebra* screen layout contains the ***pull-down*** menus, the ***Standard*** toolbar, the ***Algebra*** area, the ***graphics*** area, and the ***Input Bar*** at the bottom of the screen.

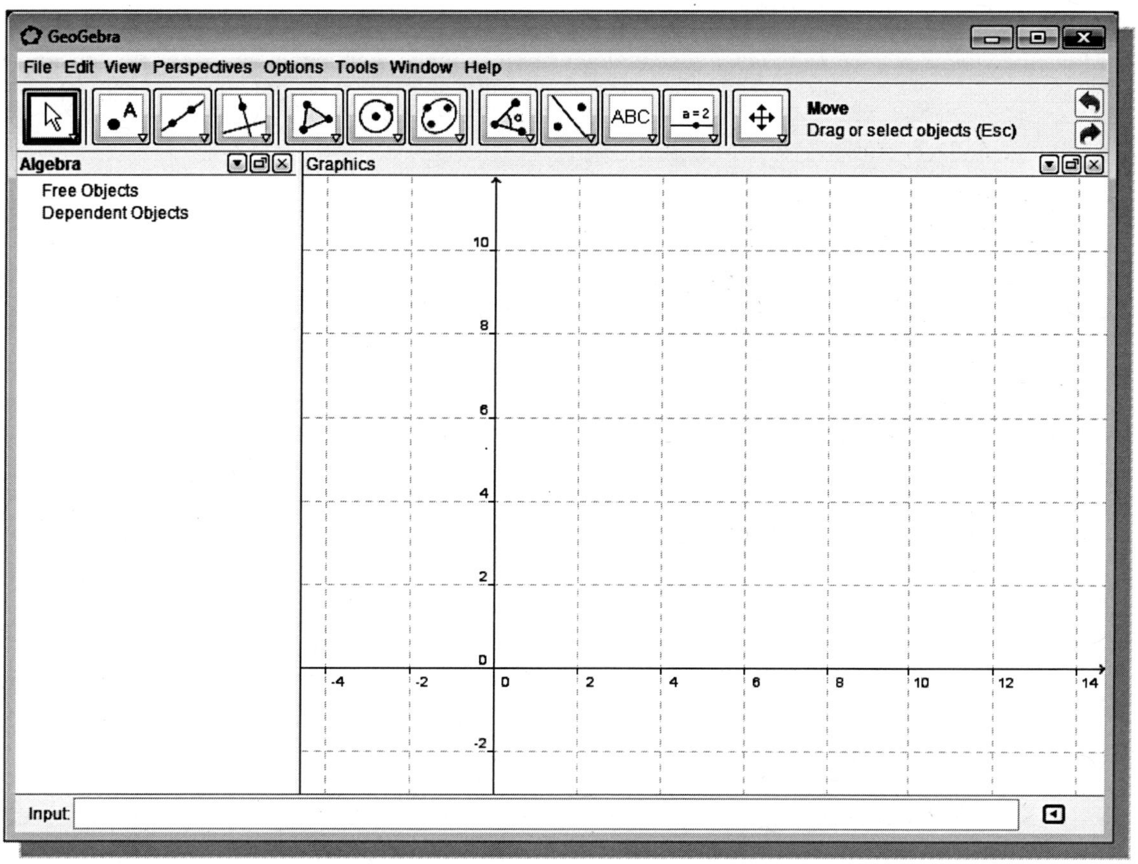

3. On your own, adjust the display of the *GeoGebra* main screen so that the *Algebra* area and the *Input Bar* are available as shown.

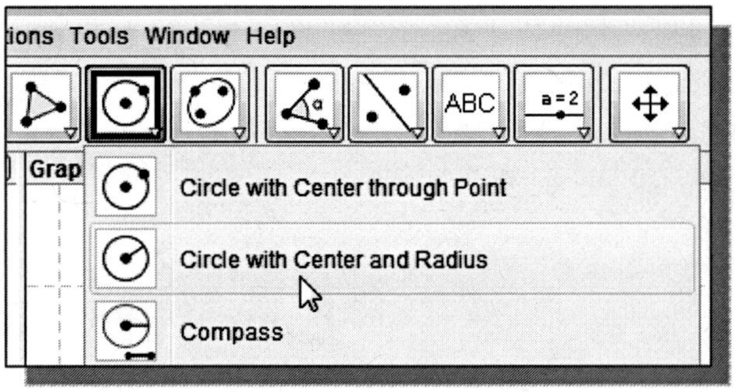

4. Select the **Circle with Center and Radius** icon in the *Standard* toolbar area.

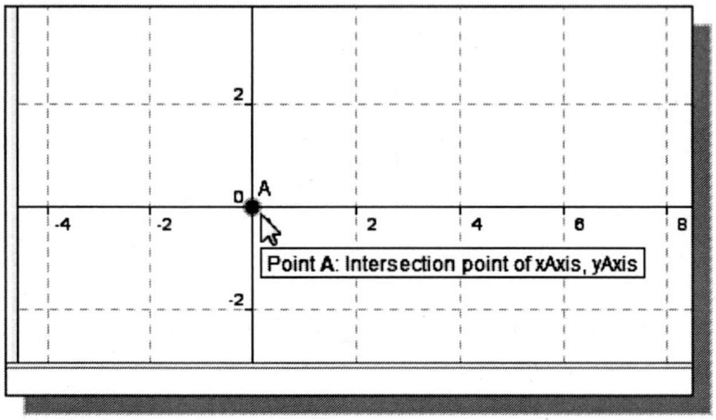

5. Click on the *Origin* of the coordinate system to place the center of the circle. Note the created center point is also added in the *Algebra* area that is toward the left.

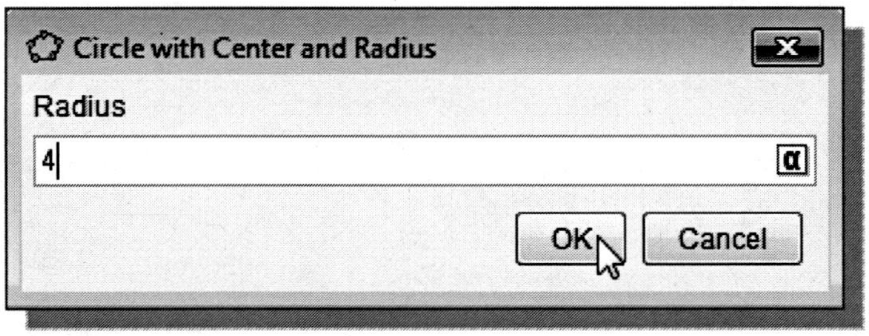

6. In the *Radius* input box, enter **4** to create a circle with a radius of **4 units** in size.

7. Pick **OK** to accept the selected settings.

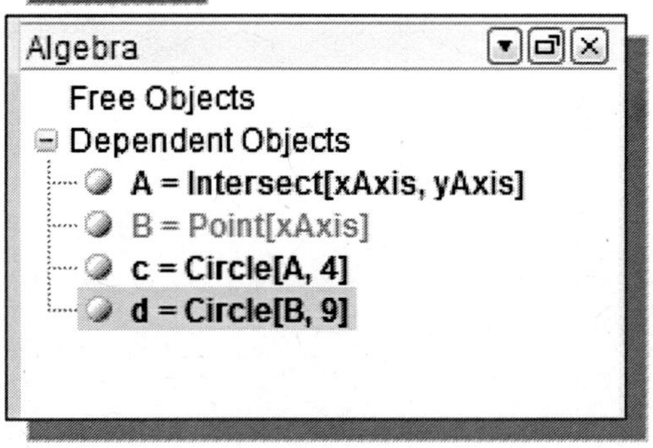

8. On your own, create another circle at coordinates (**12,0**) and radius **9 units** as shown.

9. Use the **mouse wheel** to **Zoom/Pan** and adjust the current display.

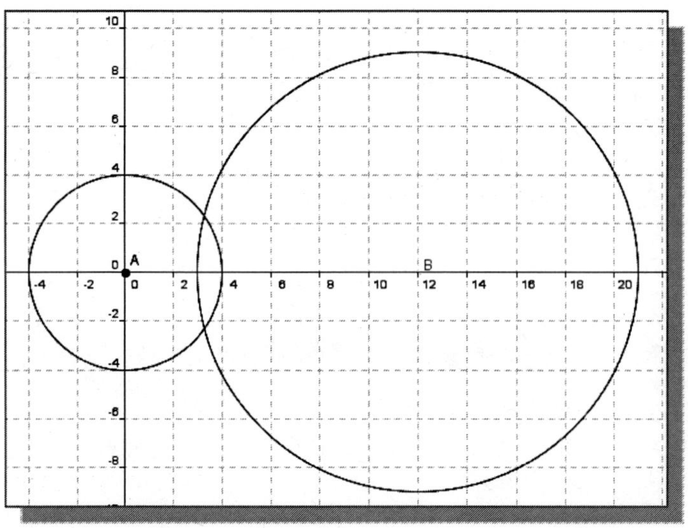

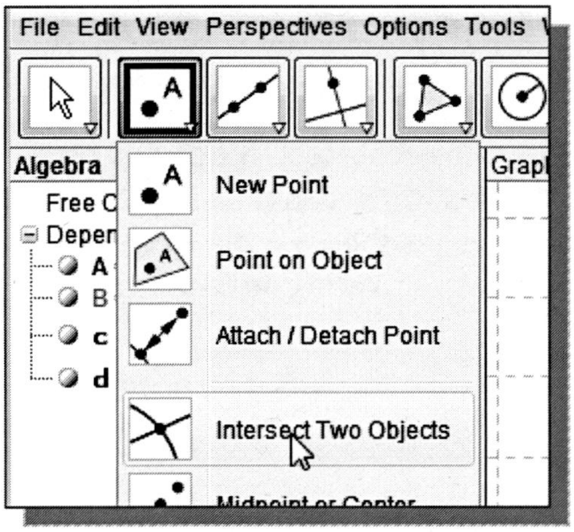

10. Activate the **Intersect Two Objects** command by clicking on the icon as shown. This will create points at the intersections of two selected objects.

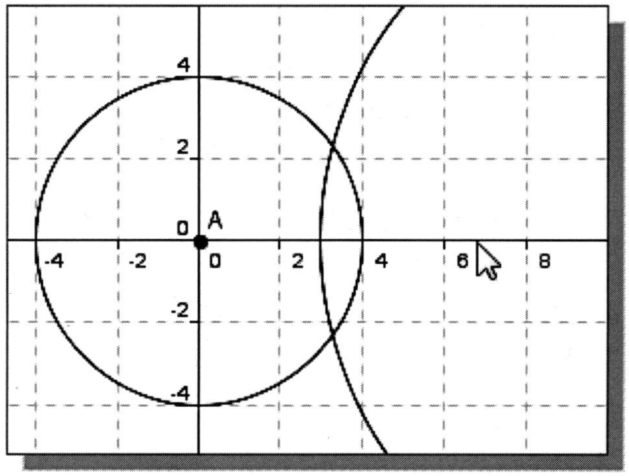

11. Select the **X Axis** as the first entity to define the intersection points.

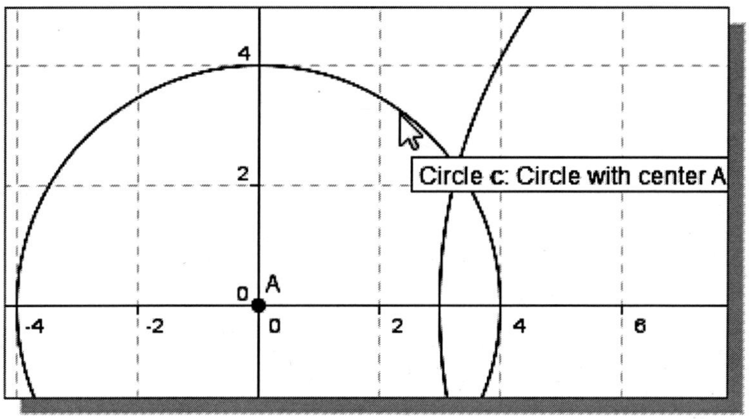

12. Select the **smaller circle** as the second entity to define the intersection points.

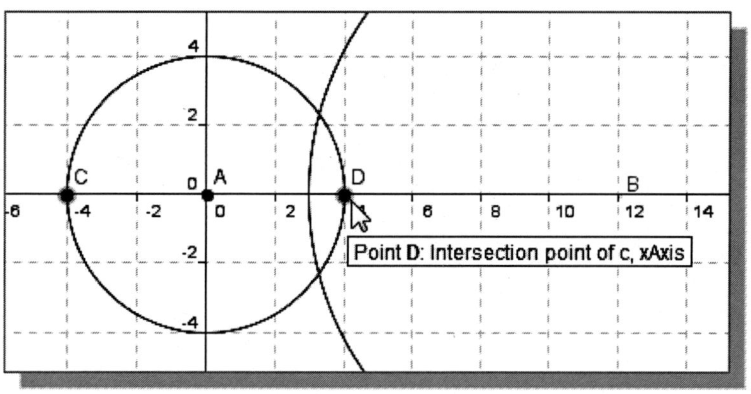

- Note two intersection points are created, **Point C** and **Point D**.

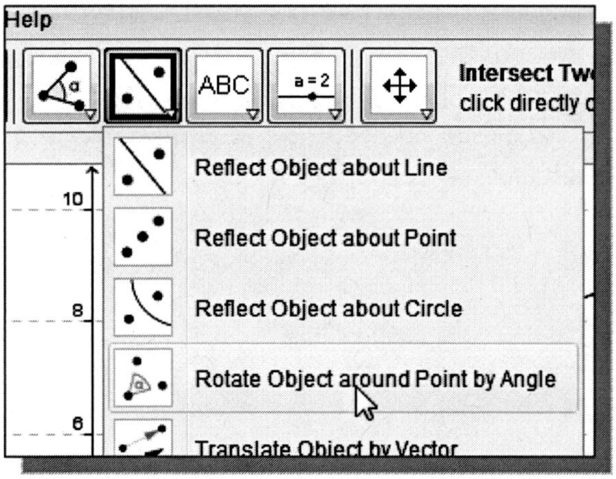

13. Activate the **Rotate Object around Point by Angle** command by clicking on the icon as shown. This will create a new point by rotating an existing point.

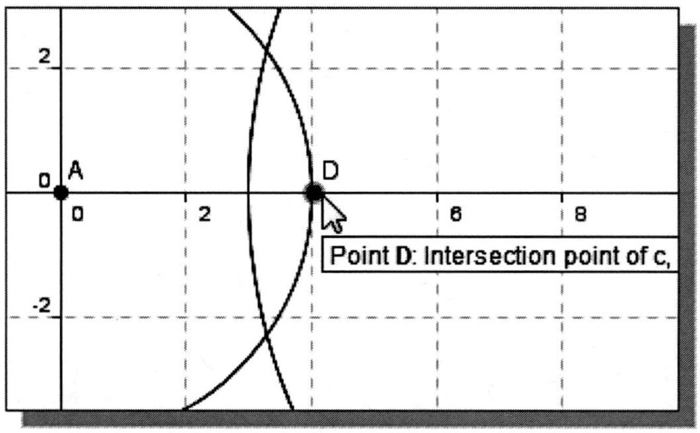

14. Select **Point D** as the object to be rotated.

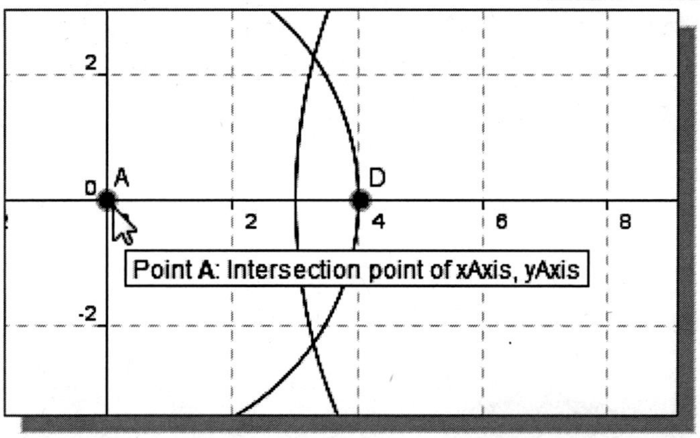

15. Select **Point A** as the reference axis of rotation.

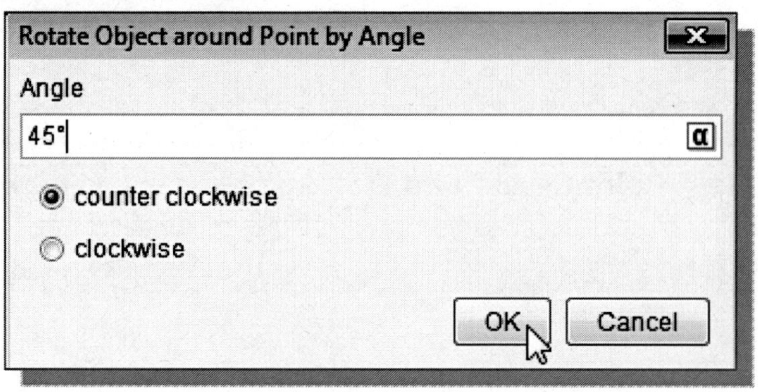

16. In the *Angle* input box, enter **45** as the angle of rotation.

17. Click **OK** to accept the setting and create the new point.

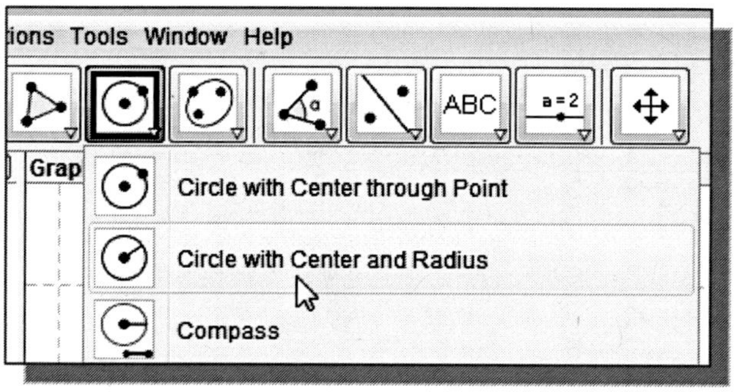

18. Select the **Circle with Center and Radius** icon in the *Standard* toolbar area.

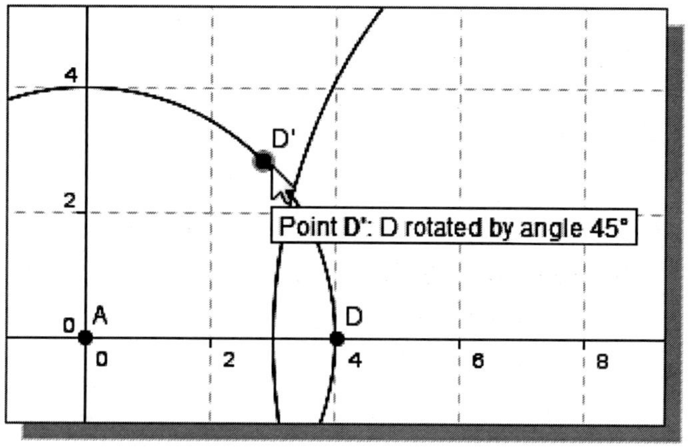

19. Select **Point D'** as the center of the new circle. Note the created center point is also added in the *Algebra* area that is toward the left.

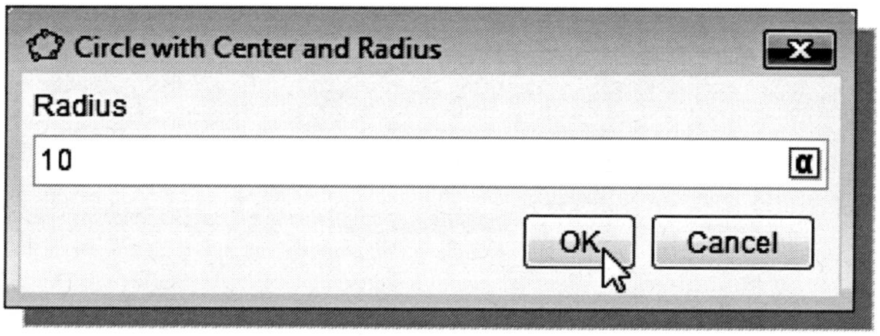

20. In the *Radius* input box, enter **10** to create a circle with a radius of **10 units** in size.

21. Click **OK** to accept the selected settings.

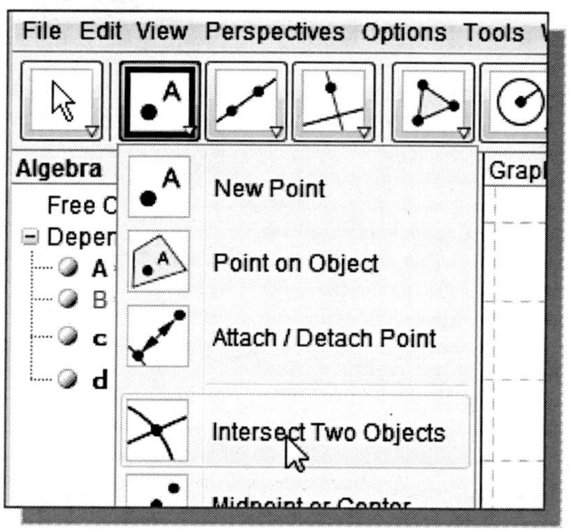

22. Activate the **Intersect Two Objects** command by clicking on the icon as shown. This will create points at the intersections of two selected objects.

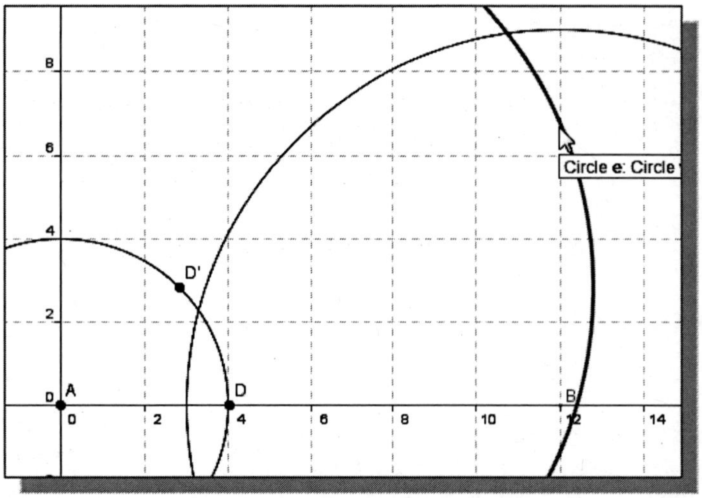

23. Select **Circle e** as the first entity to define the intersection points.

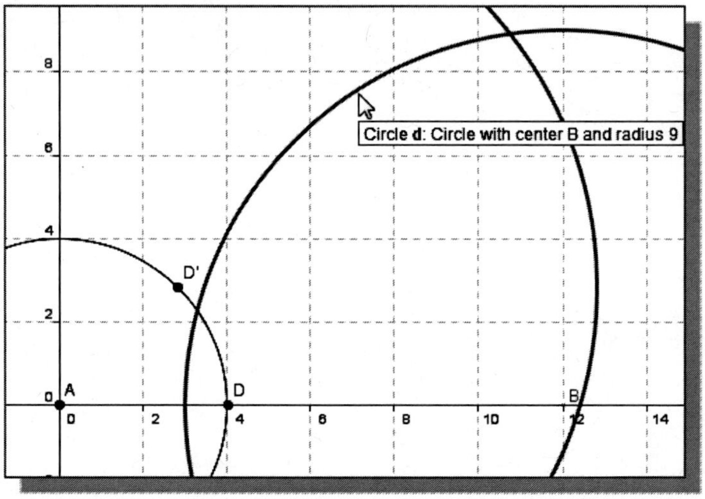

24. Select **Circle d** as the second entity to define the intersection points.

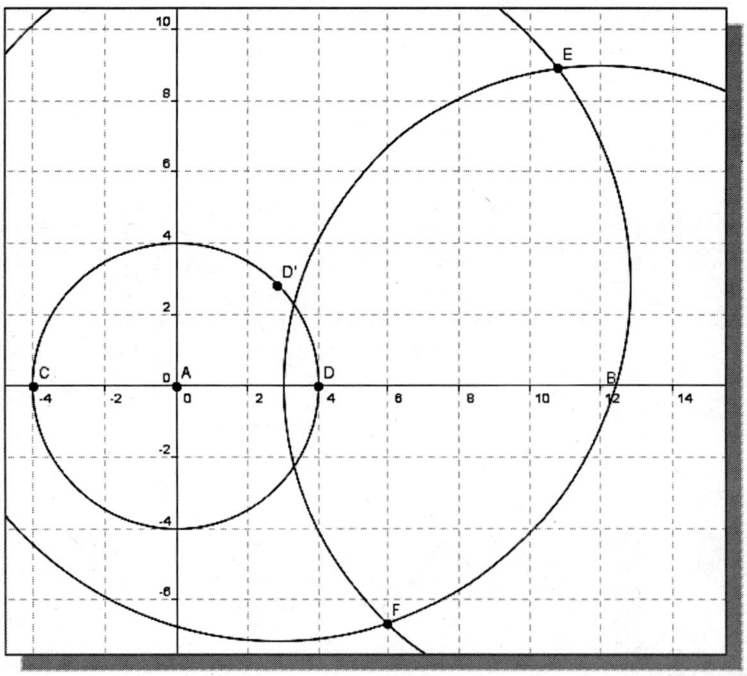

- Note two intersection points are created, **Point E** and **Point F**.

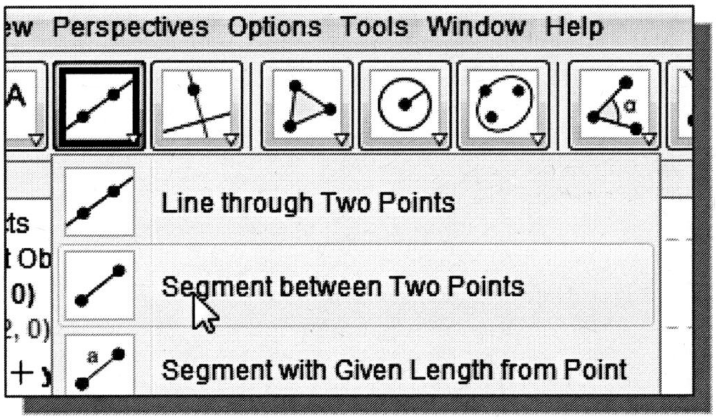

25. Activate the **Segment between Two Points** command by clicking on the icon as shown. This will create a line by selecting two endpoints.

26. Click on **Point A** to place the first point of the line.

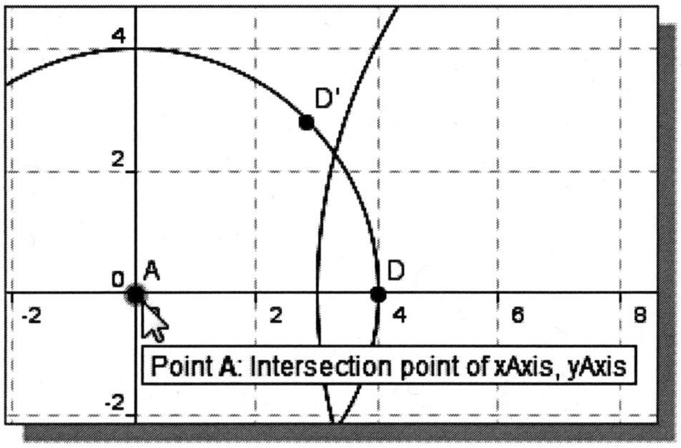

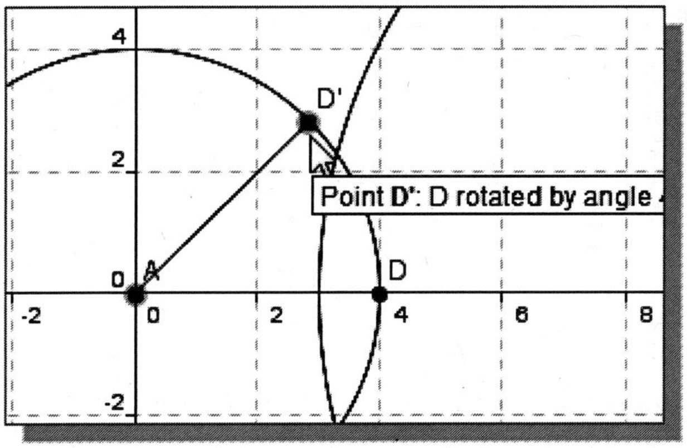

27. Click on **Point D'** to create a line as shown.

28. On your own, create two additional line segments, **Line DE** and **Line EB** as shown.

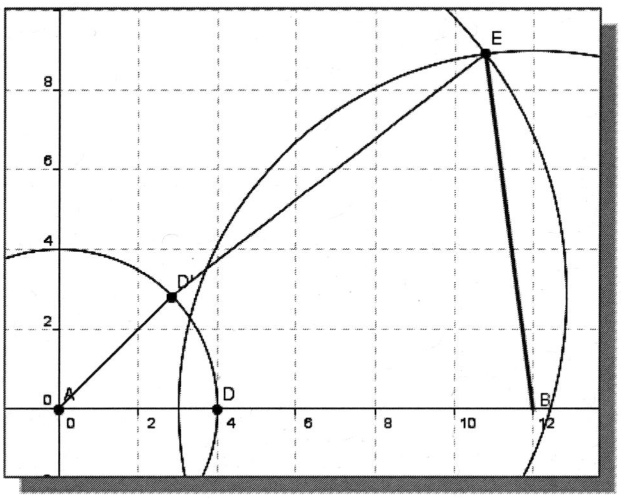

Turn off the Display of Objects

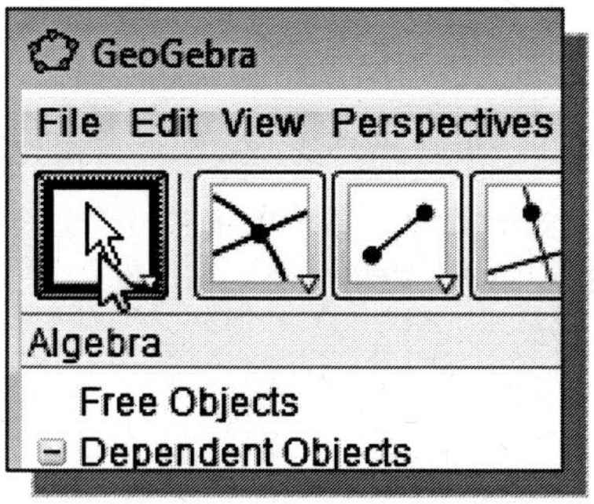

1. In the *Standard* toolbar area, click on the **Move** icon to activate the command.

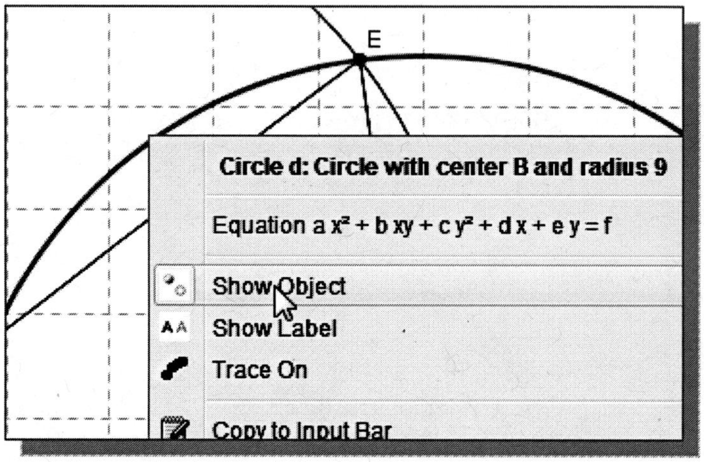

2. Select **Circle d**, the circle on the right, as shown.

3. Inside the graphics area, right-mouse-click once to bring up the option menu.

4. Click the **Show Object** icon to turn *OFF* the display of the selected circle.

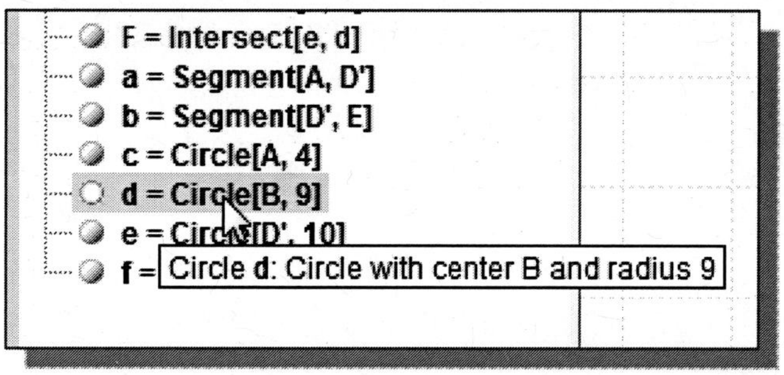

- Note the corresponding circle, **Circle d**, is also highlighted in the ***Algebra*** area. The unfilled icon indicates the display of the object has been turned *OFF*.

5. Inside the ***Algebra*** area, click once with the right-mouse-button on **Circle e** to display the option menu. Click on **Show Object** to toggle *OFF* the display of the circle.

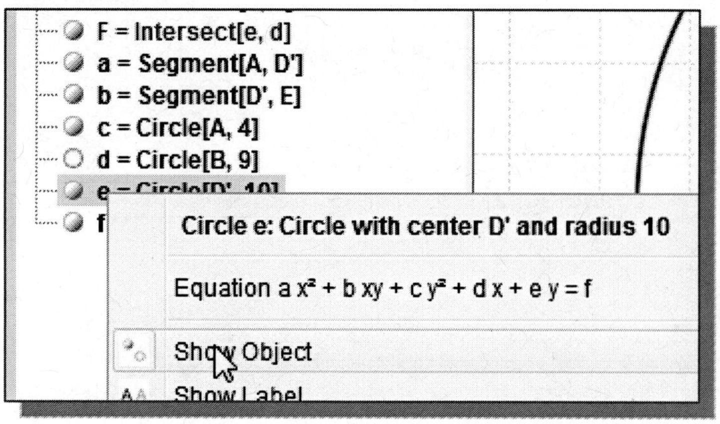

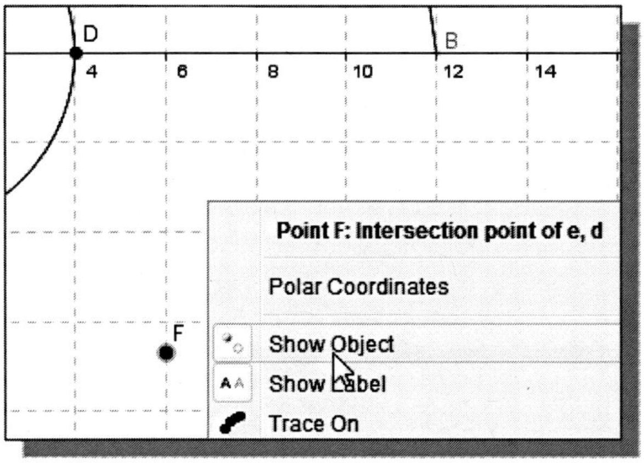

6. Select **Point F**, the point below the line segments, as shown.

7. On your own, turn *OFF* the display of the object through the right-click option menu as shown.

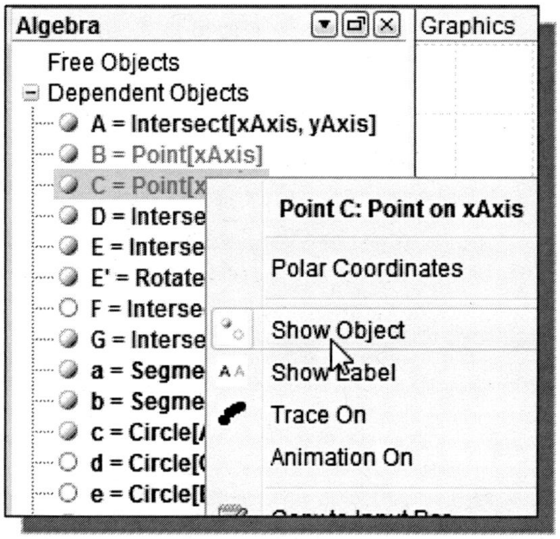

8. In the ***Algebra*** area, click once with the right-mouse-button on **Point C** to display the option menu. Click on **Show Object** to toggle *OFF* the display of the selected item.

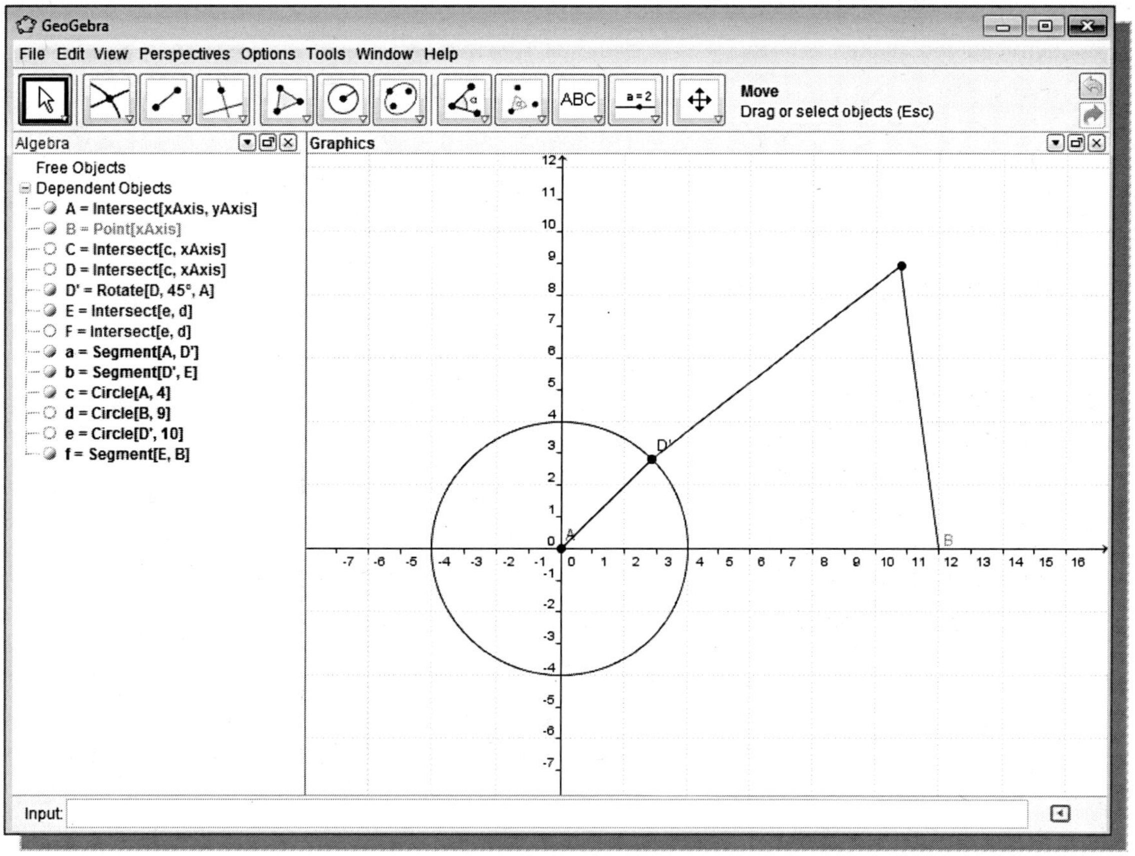

Adding a Slider Control

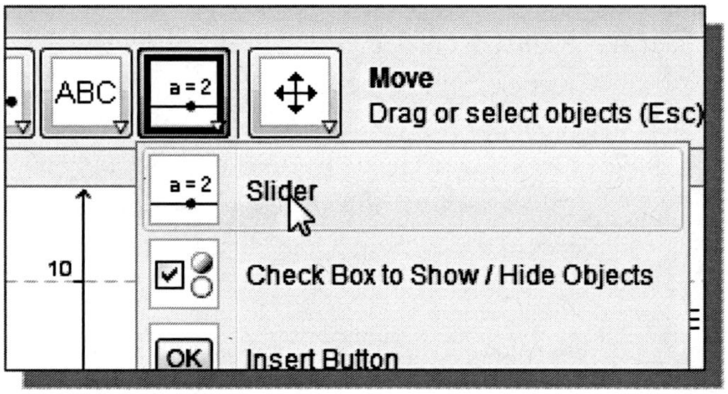

1. In the *Standard* toolbar select the **Slider** command by left-clicking once on the icon.

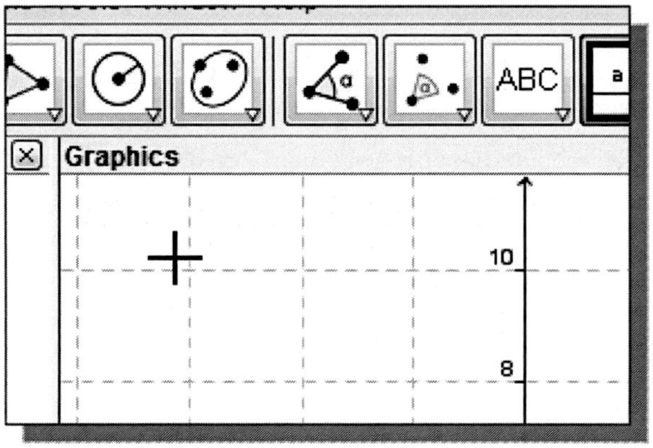

2. In the graphics area, select a location near the **upper left corner** to place the **Slider Control** as shown.

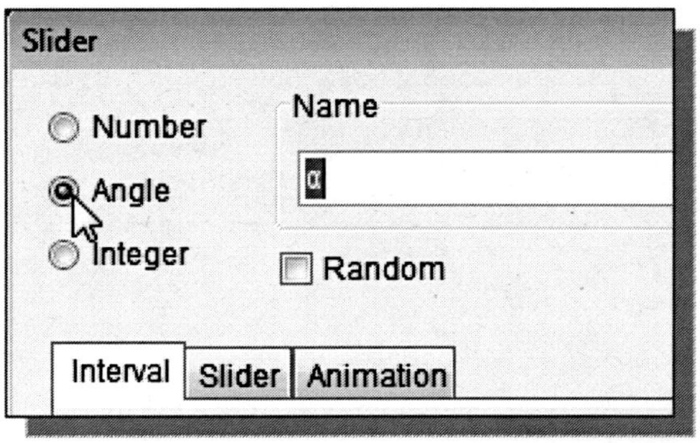

3. Set the *Slider* option to **Angle** as shown. Note the angle name is automatically set to **α**.

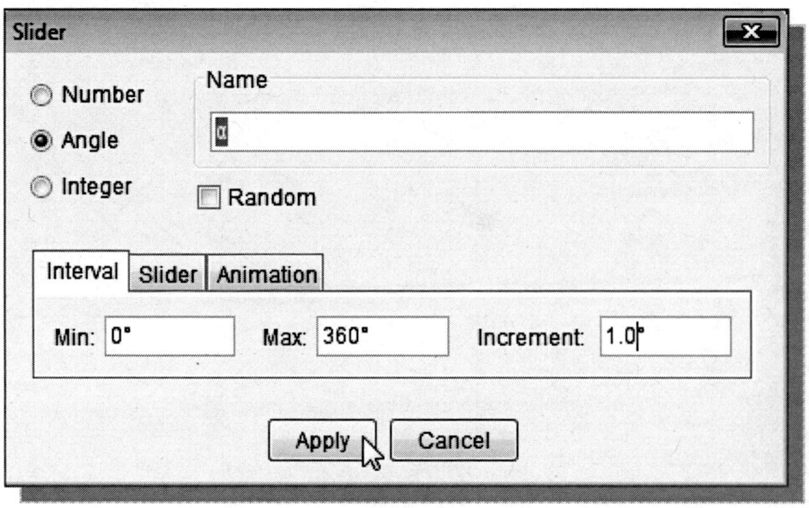

4. Set the **Interval** settings to the three values, **0**, **360** and **1.0**, as shown.

5. Click **Apply** to accept the selected settings

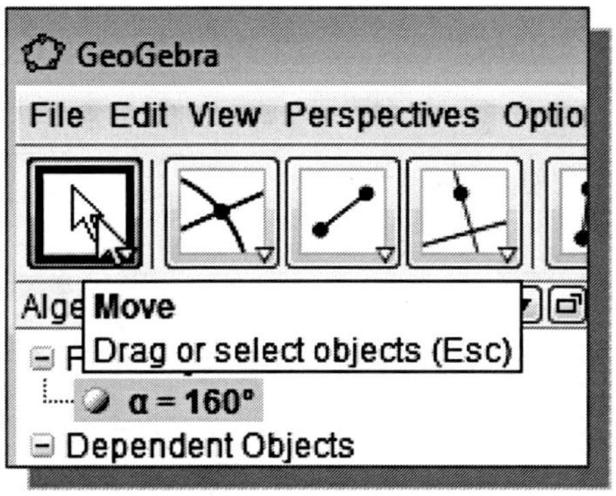

6. In the *Standard* toolbar area, click on the **Move** icon to activate the command.

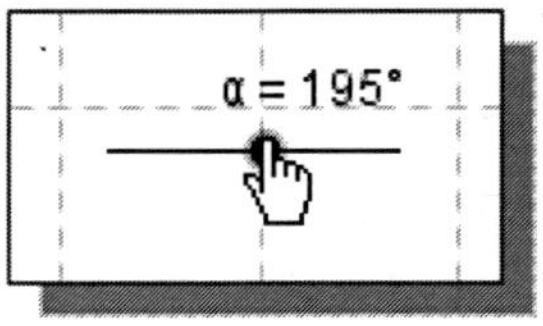

7. Drag the **handle** of the **Slider Control**, and notice **Angle α** is adjusted.

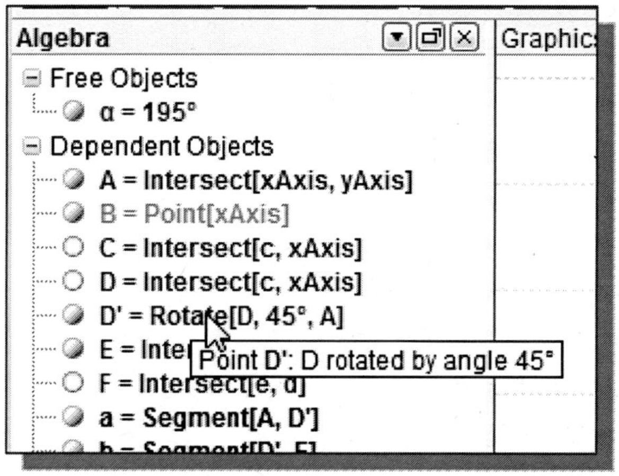

8. In the ***Algebra*** area, double click with the left-mouse-button on **Point D'** to enter the **Object Redefine** mode.

9. Modify the **angle variable**, the second variable in the edit box, to **α** as shown.

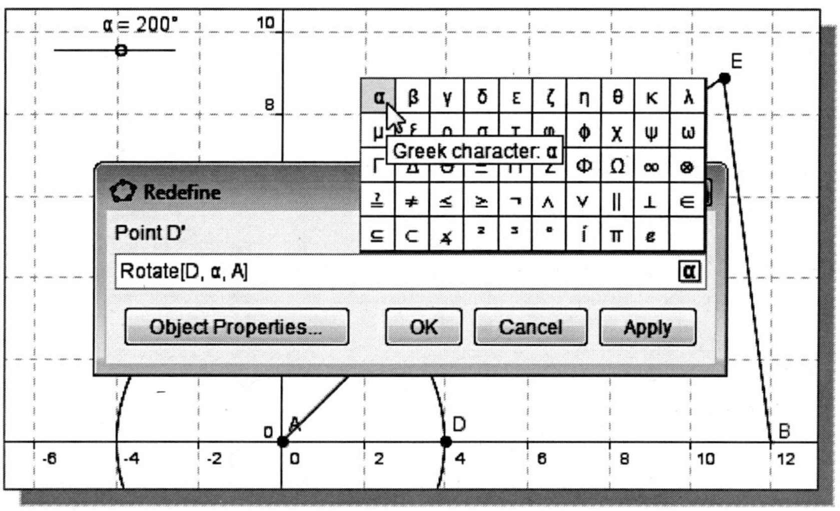

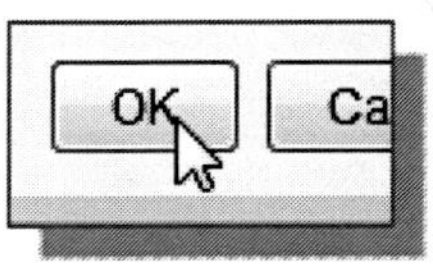

10. Click **OK** to accept the setting and exit the Redefine command.

11. Drag the **handle** of the **Slider Control**, and notice the positions of the links of the four-bar linkage are adjusted accordingly.

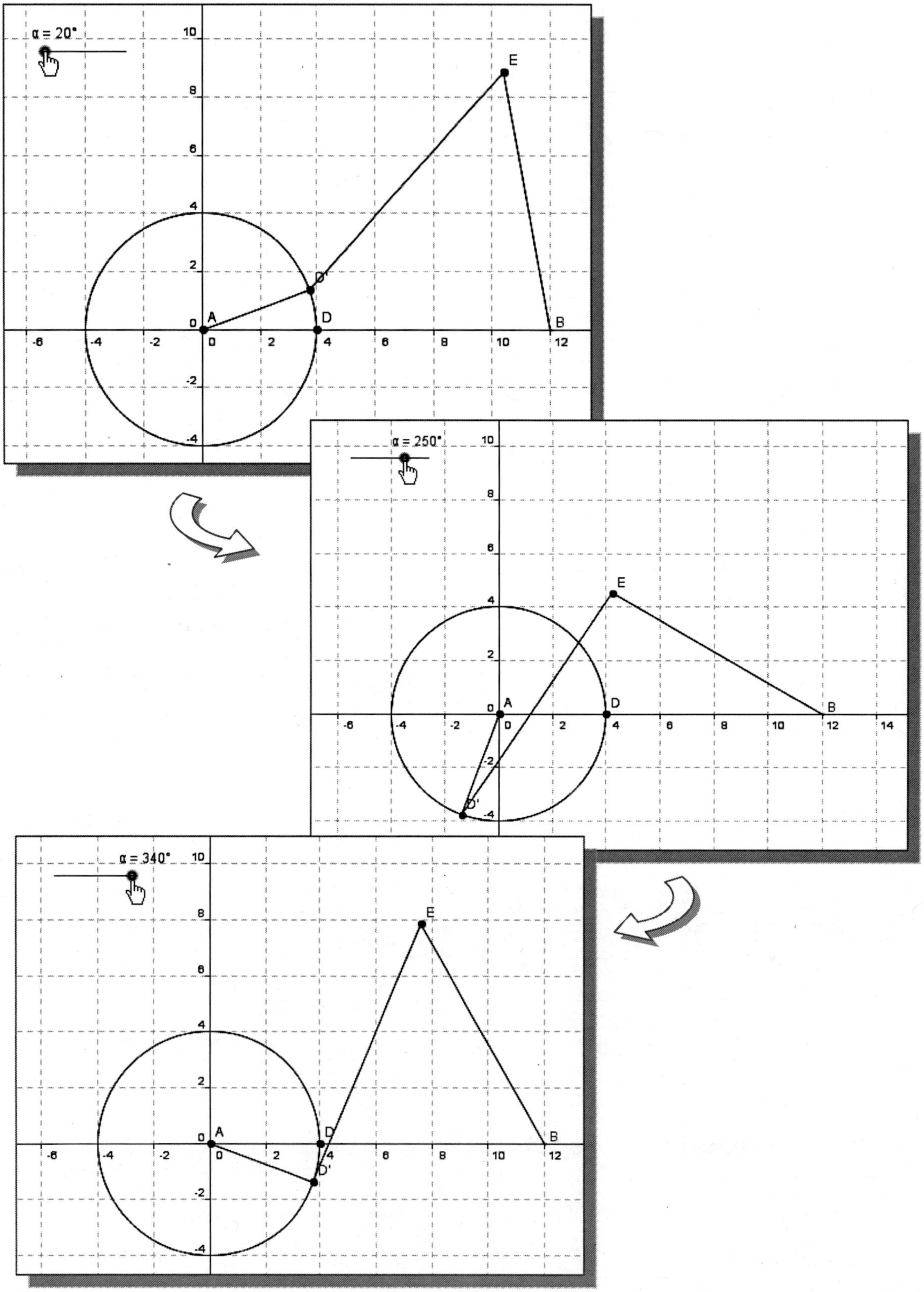

Using the Animate option

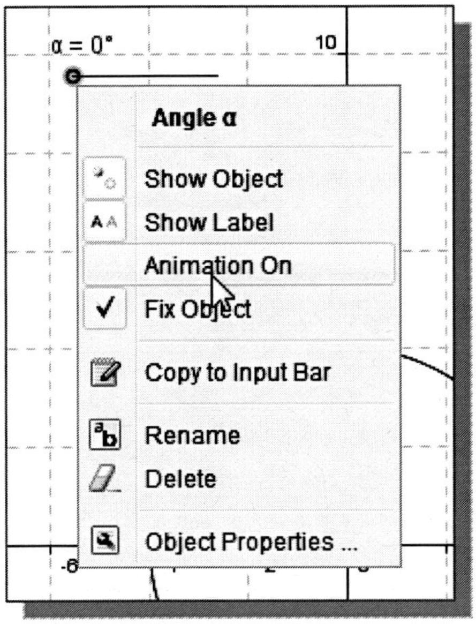

1. Inside the graphics area, click once with the right-mouse-button on **Slider Control** to display the option menu. Click on **Animation On** to toggle *ON* the animation of the Slider Control.

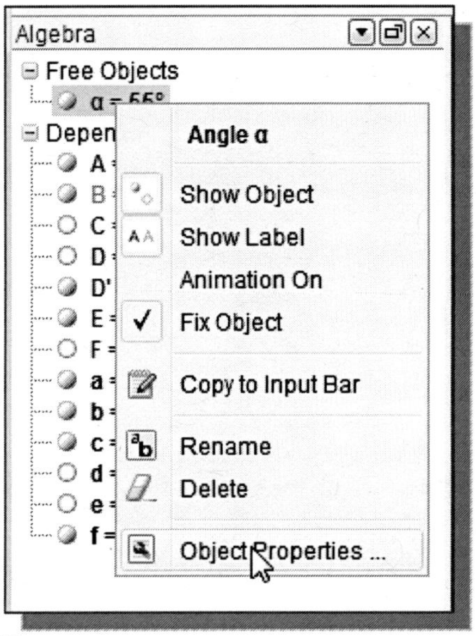

2. Inside the ***Algebra*** area, click once with the right-mouse-button on **Angle** to display the option menu. Click on **Object Properties** to activate the command.

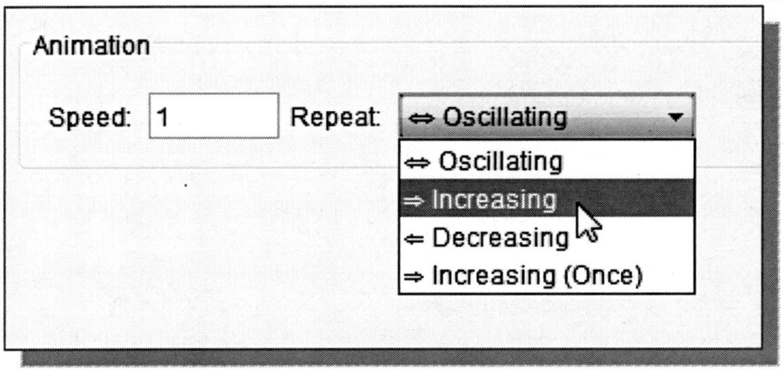

3. Set the animation repeat option to **Increasing** as shown.

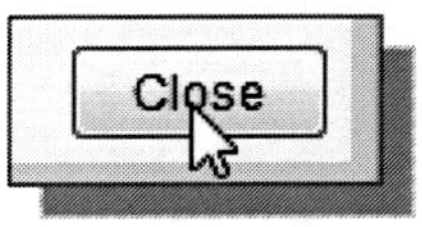

4. Click **Close** to accept the setting and exit the *object properties* command.

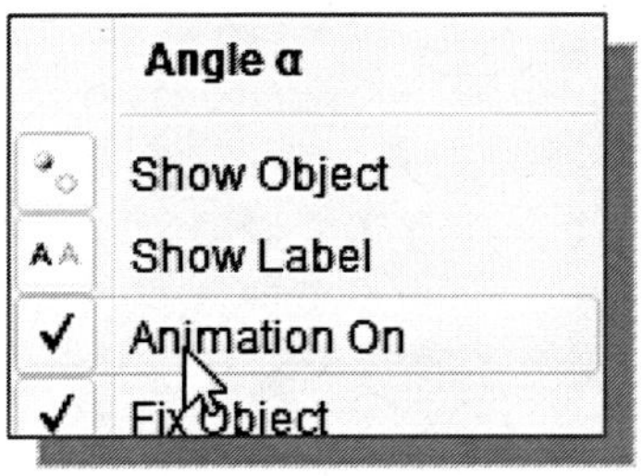

5. On your own, examine the animation of the four-bar linkage; turn ***OFF*** the animation option before proceeding to the next section.

Tracking the Path of a point on the Coupler

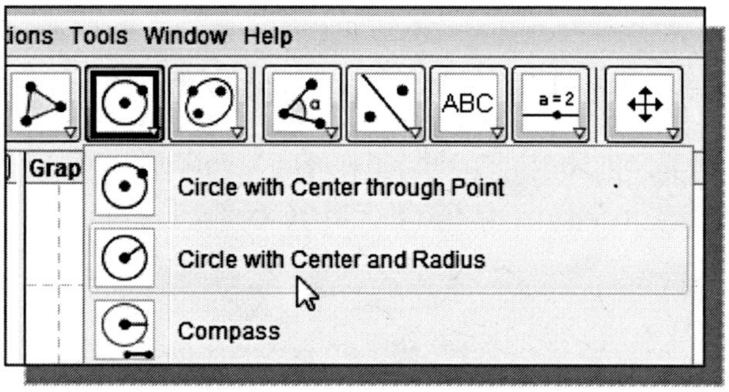

1. Select the **Circle with Center and Radius** icon in the *Standard* toolbar area.

2. Select **Point D'** as the center of the new circle.

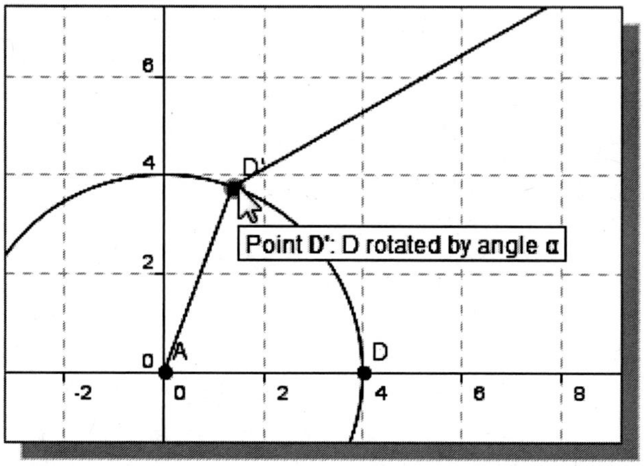

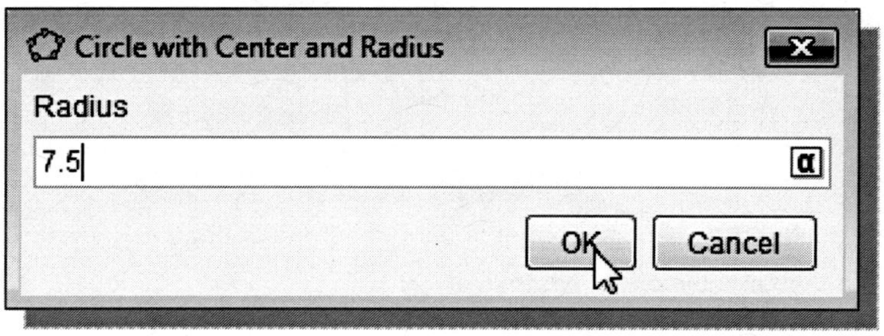

3. In the *Radius* input box, enter **7.5** as the radius.

4. Click on the **OK** button to accept the settings and create the circle.

5. On your own, create another **radius 7.5 circle** centered at **Point E** as shown.

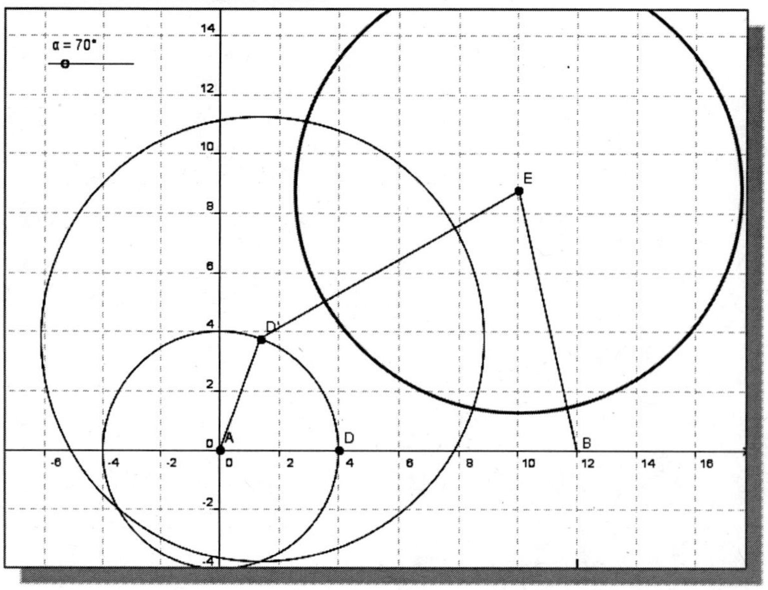

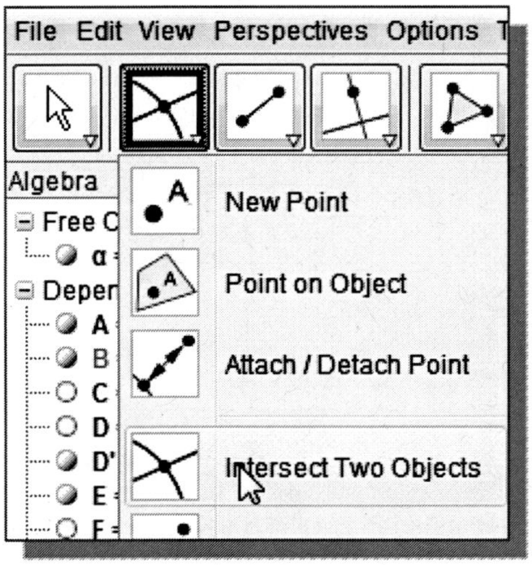

6. Activate the **Intersect Two Objects** command by clicking on the icon as shown. This will create points at the intersections of two selected objects.

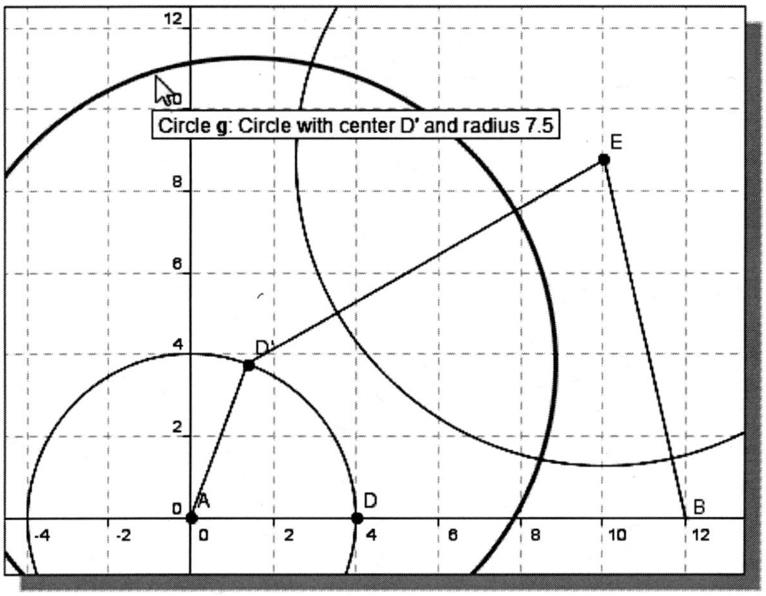

7. Select **Circle g** as the first entity to define the intersection points.

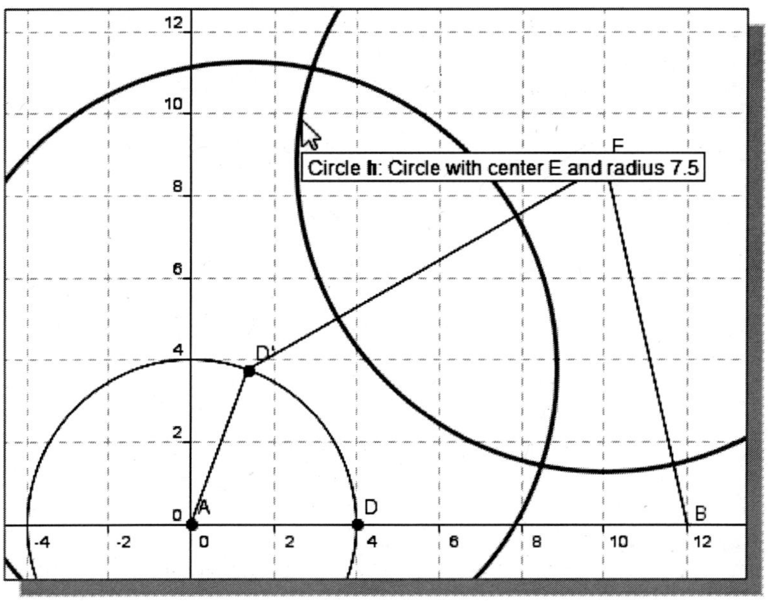

8. Select **Circle h** as the second entity to define the intersection points.

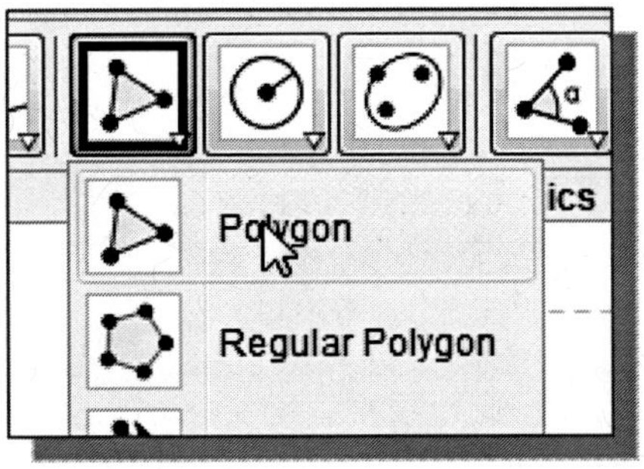

9. Activate the **Polygon** command by clicking on the icon as shown. This will create a polygon by defining the corner points of a polygon.

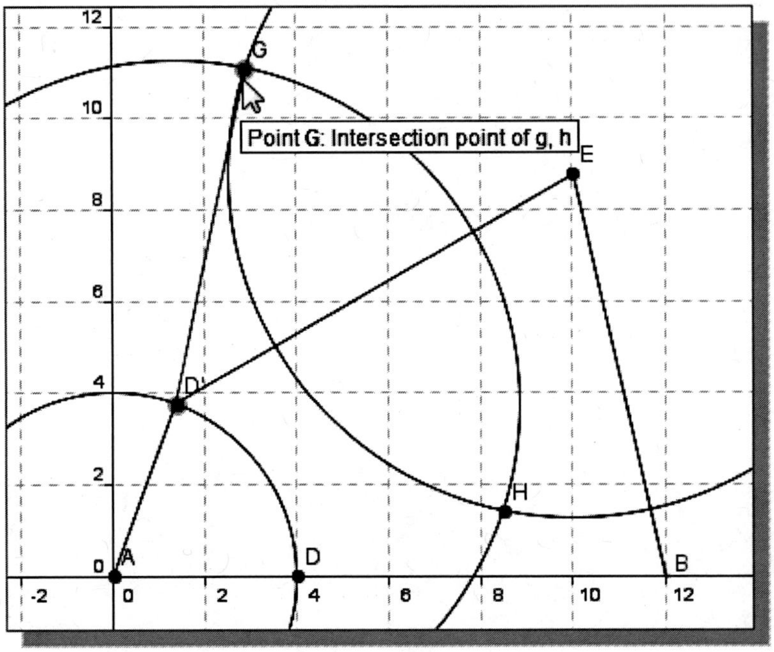

10. Select **Point D'** as the first corner of the polygon.

11. Select **Point G** as the second corner of the polygon.

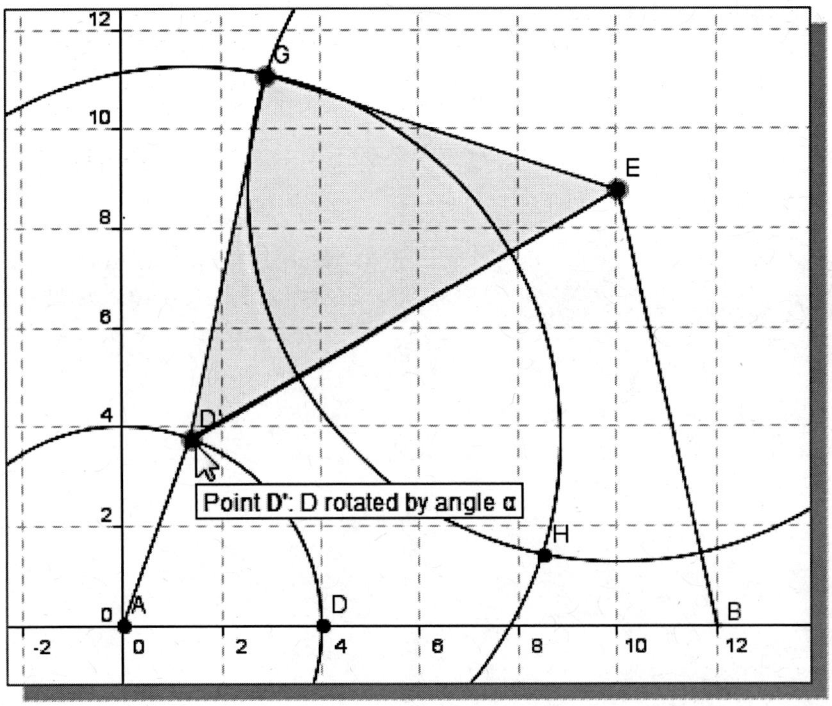

12. Select **Point E** as the third corner of the polygon.

13. Select **Point D'** again to form a triangle.

14. On your own, turn *OFF* the display of **Point H, Circle g** and **Circle h**.

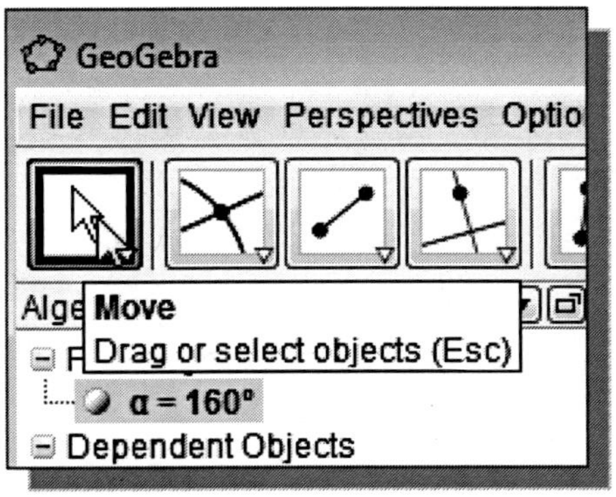

15. In the *Standard* toolbar area, click on the **Move** icon to activate the command.

16. In the graphics area, select **Point G** as shown.

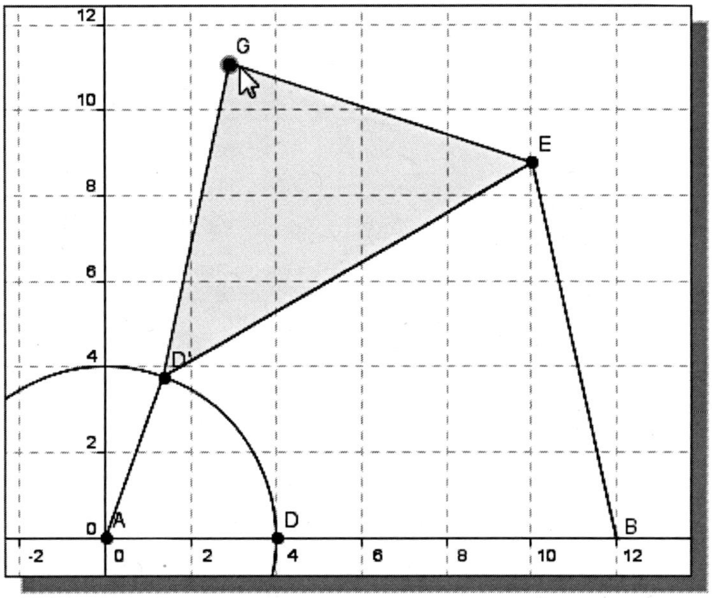

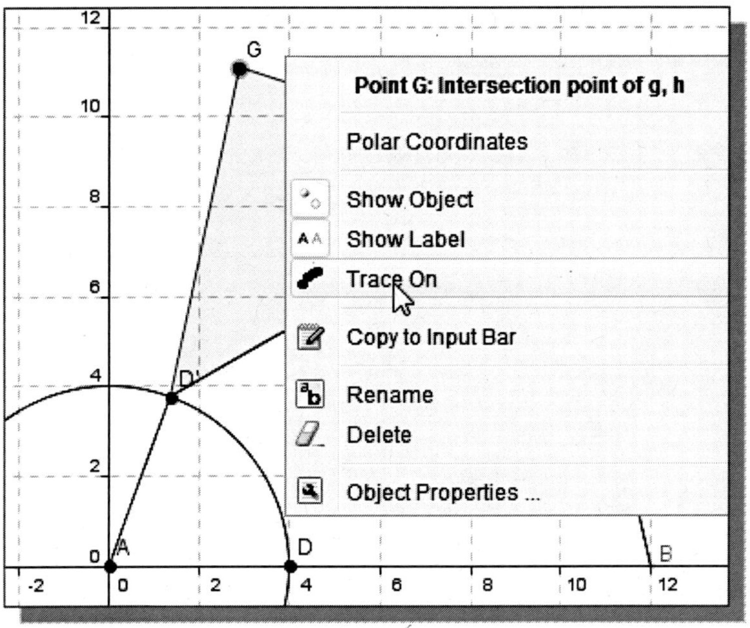

17. Inside the graphics area, click once with the right-mouse-button to display the option menu. Click on **Trace On** to activate the command.

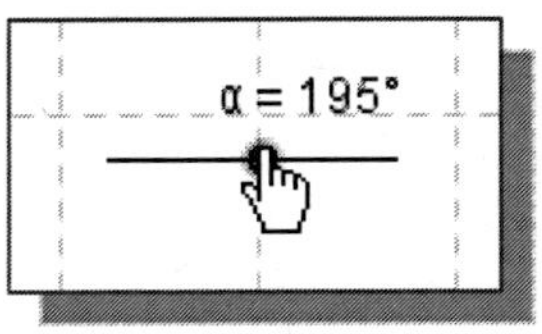

18. Drag the **handle** of the **Slider Control**, and notice **Angle α** is adjusted.

- The locus of point G, also known as a **coupler curve**, is generated as **Angle α** is adjusted. Note that by varying the lengths of the links in the mechanism, different coupler curves can be generated. The *interactive dynamic geometry* software can be used to aid linkage design and analysis.

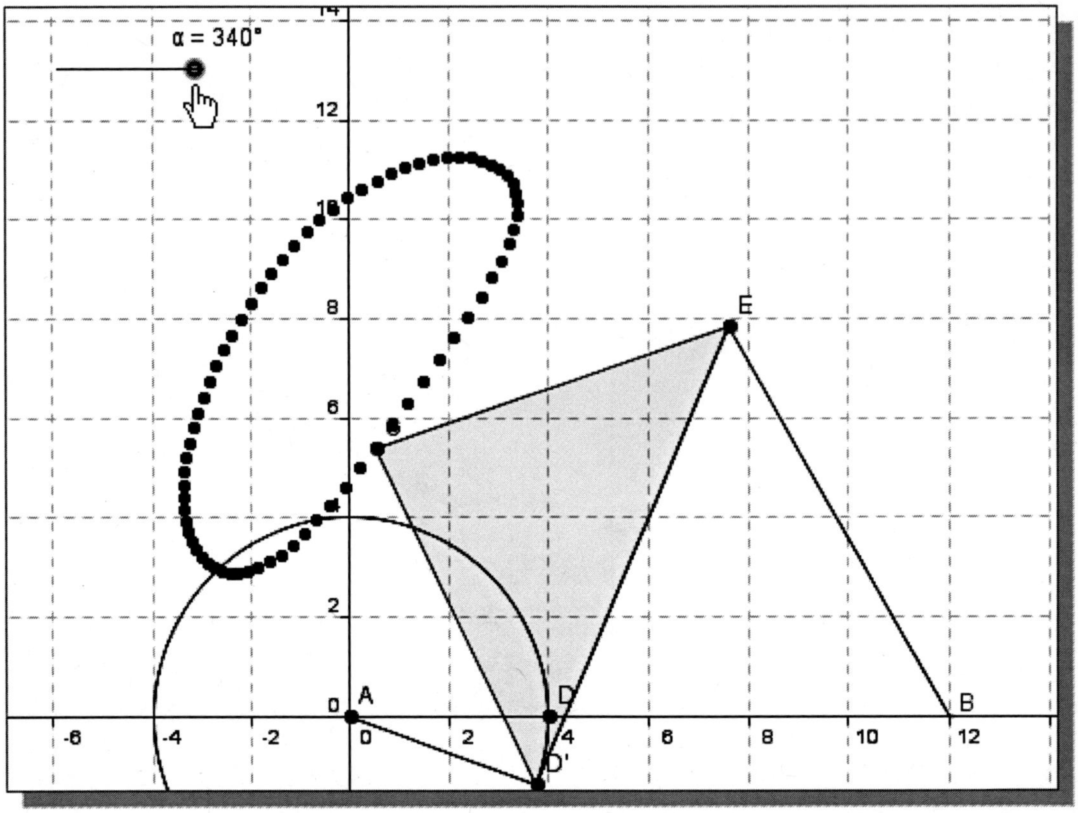

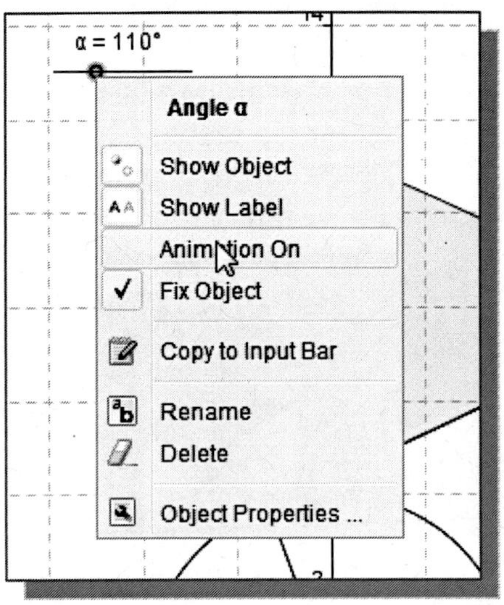

- Note that the **Animation On** command can also be used to generate the coupler curve.

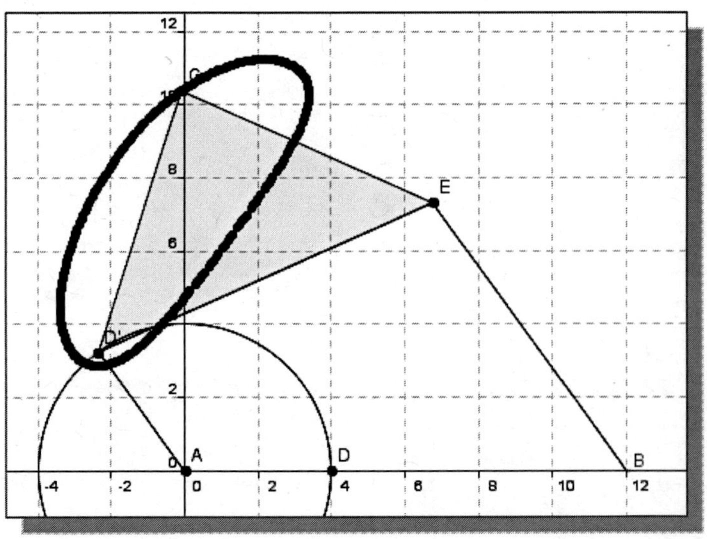

Exercises:

1. **Crank-Slider Mechanism**

AB = 2.5, BC = 5

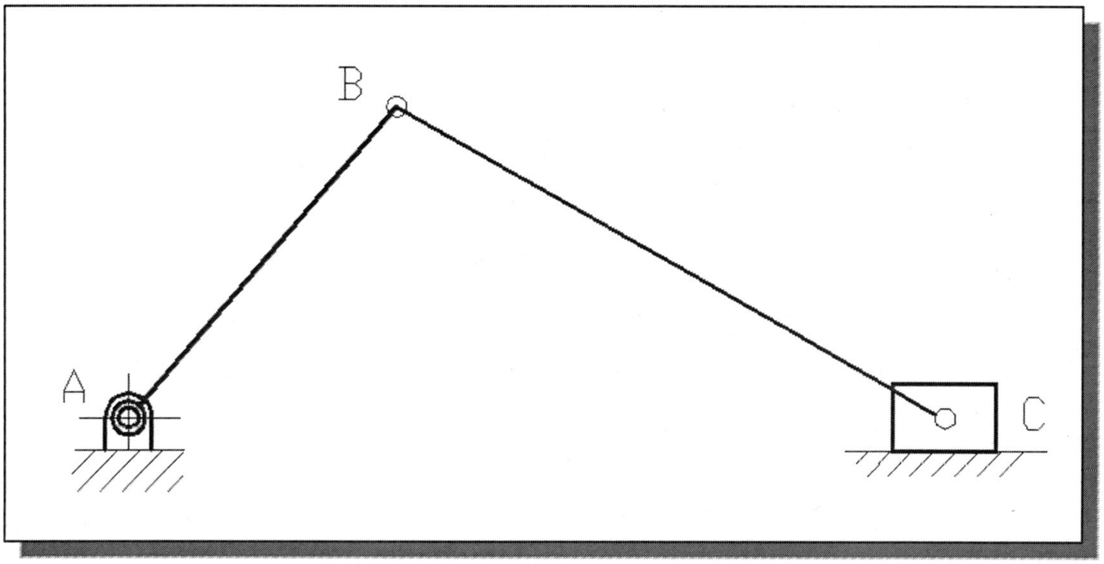

2. **Watt Straight Line Mechanism**

AD''=BE, ED''=1/2 AD'', AB = 2 BE, G is at the midpoint of ED''.
A and B are fixed points.

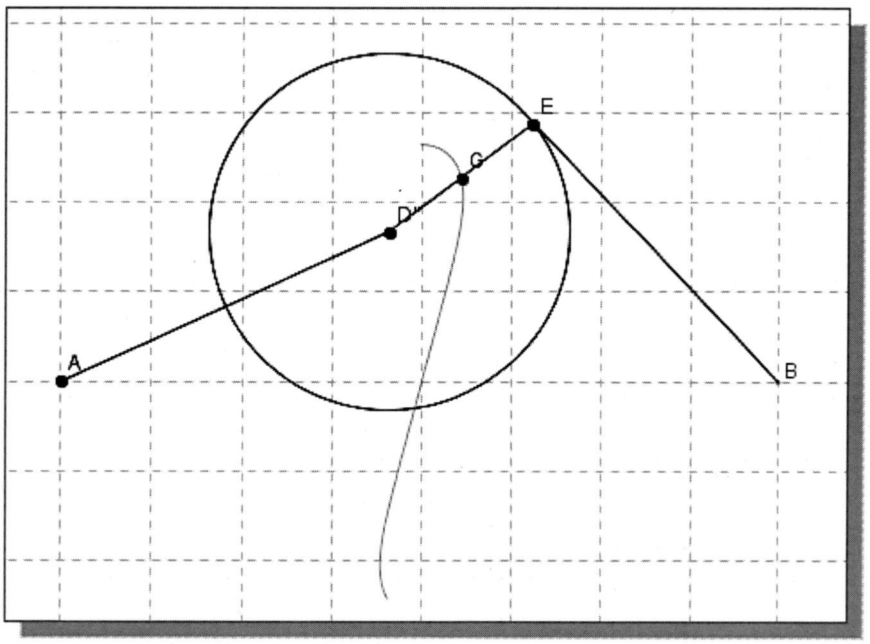

3. **Hoekens Straight Line Mechanism**

BE = EC' = EH = 2.5 AC', AB = 2 AC'
A and B are fixed points and Link C'-E-H is a rigid link.

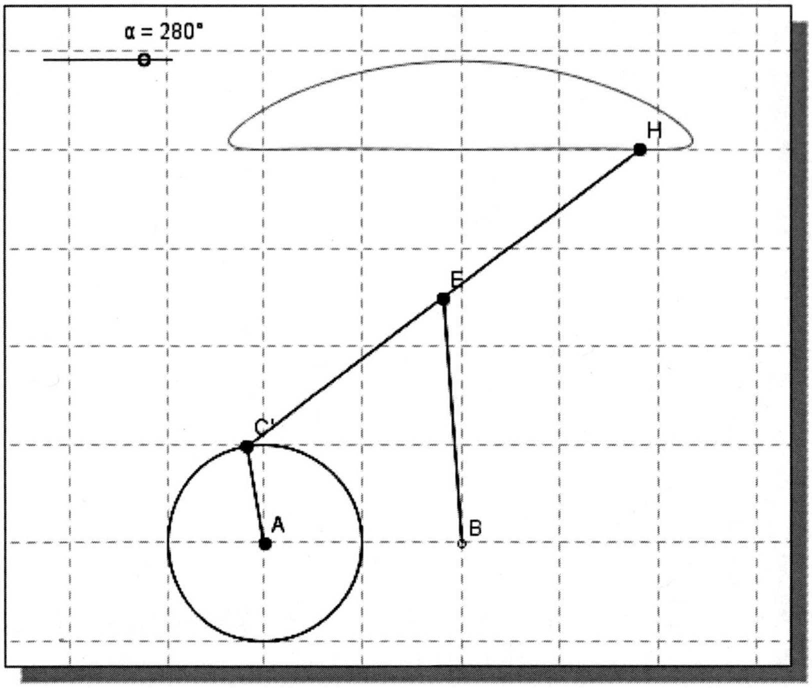

Lesson 11
Design Makes the Difference

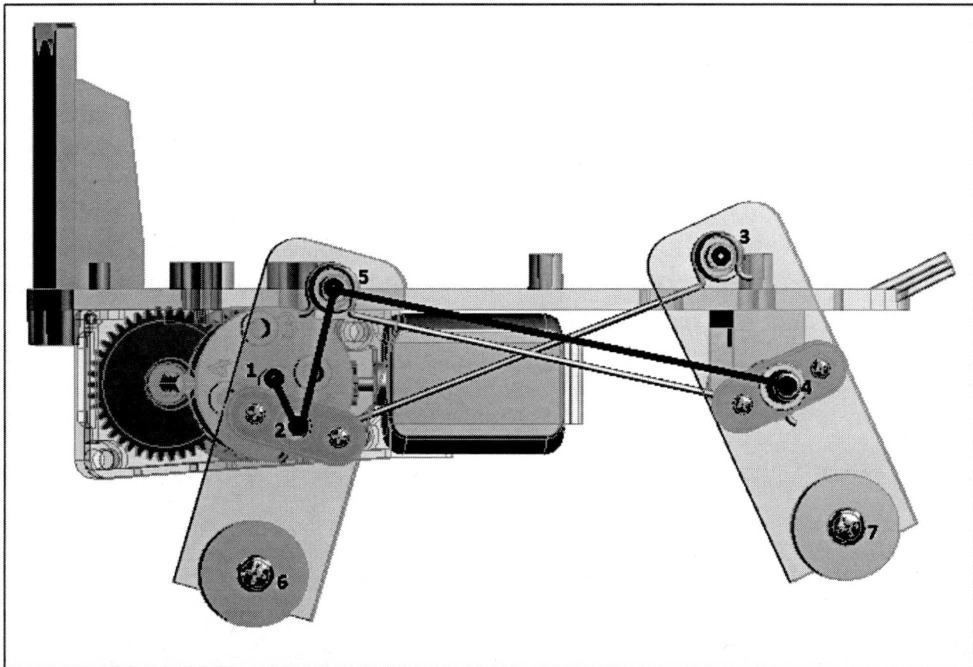

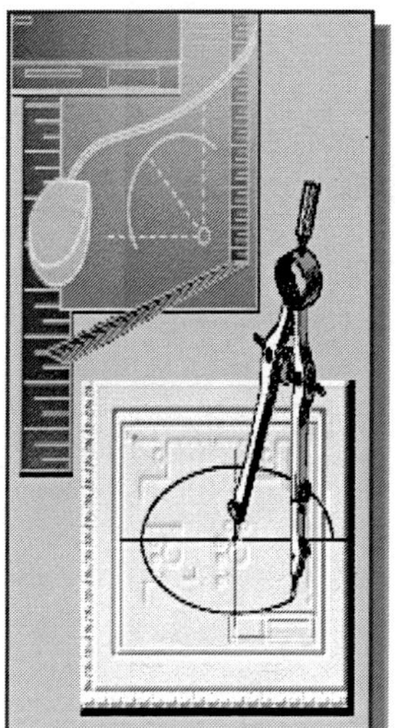

Learning Objectives

- Identify the Compound Mechanism used in the Mechanical Tiger
- Create and Construct the Leg Linkage using GeoGebra
- Generate the Foot Path of the Mechanical Tiger Design
- Examine the Jansen Mechanism and the Klann Mechanism.

Engineering Analysis – How does this work?

Have you ever wondered how a certain machine worked and how the machine can work better? Possessing this type of engineering curiosity may indicate you are an engineer at heart. The modeling of the *Mechanical Tiger* design in the previous chapters simply provides a starting point for further studying of **engineering design**. Engineering design is the ability to create and transform ideas and concepts into a product definition that meets the desired objective. Engineering design also involves activities, such as dissecting and analyzing, to identify the advantages and/or disadvantages of different designs. In the last two decades, Computer Aided Engineering has greatly enhanced engineers' abilities to perform *Engineering Analyses*.

Prior to creating the *Mechanical Tiger* assembly models in the *SolidWorks* 3D environment, let us examine the leg linkage used. The *Mechanical Tiger* is a relatively simple *Walking Robot* design. More complex linkage designs are typically used for larger scale walking robots; two such mechanisms are the ***Jansen Mechanism*** and ***Klann Mechanism***.

Theo Jansen is a Dutch artist and an engineer. He builds large artworks which resemble skeletons of animals that are able to walk using *wind power*. His animated artworks, also known as ***kinetic sculptures***, are a fusion of art and engineering. One of Theo Jansen's most inspirational quotes is: ***"The walls between art and engineering exist only in our minds."*** In the recent year, Theo Jansen has also incorporated artificial intelligence into his creations, so that the *kinetic sculptures* can avoid the ocean by changing course, or anchor themselves when strong wind is detected. His works were first revealed to the public in 2006, after he had worked on them for 16 years. His *kinetic sculptures* are relatively light-weight, with a fairly well-balanced mechanism assembly; and not much power is needed to drive them. The main eight-bar linkage, known as the ***Jansen Mechanism***, was developed by Theo Jansen himself. The mechanism development was done through the use of computers using a genetic algorithm.

The ***Walking Beast***, built by *Moltensteelman*, is a mechanical creature that walks on eight legs. The creature weighs approximately 6 1/2 tons (13,000 lbs), and stands 11′ tall, 8′ 4″ wide and 24′ long. It has a step height of 41 inches and a stride of 5 feet. The machine is powered by a 454 cubic inch Chevy V-8 engine connected to a modified TH400 transmission and two Klune reduction gear boxes coupled to a modified Rockwell 2 1/2 ton military differential that supplies power to the crank shafts of the legs. The leg linkage used is a six-bar mechanism designed by ***Joe Klann***. The *Klann Mechanism* was developed in 1994 as an expansion of *Burmester* curves, which are used to develop four-bar double-rocker linkages. Since the shape of the *Klann Mechanism* resembles the leg of a spider, many of the walking robots built using this mechanism are known as the **mechanical spiders**.

In this chapter, we will first examine the leg mechanism of the *Mechanical Tiger.* We will also examine the ***Jansen Mechanism*** and ***Klann Mechanism***. It should be noted that a majority of the mechanisms used in mechanical design are 2D planar mechanisms. In most cases, it is more practical to perform 2D analyses prior to the more time consuming 3D analyses.

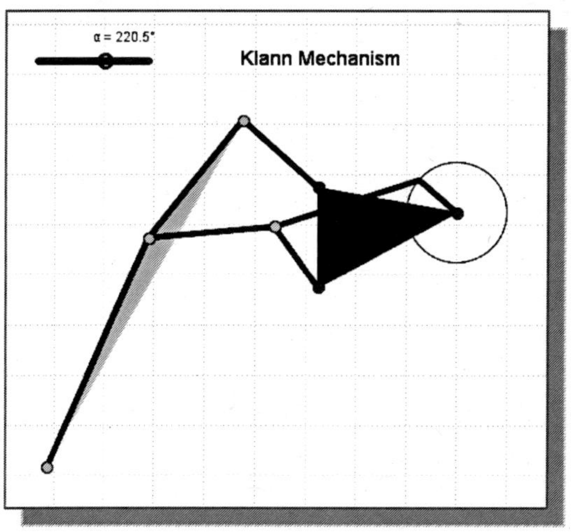

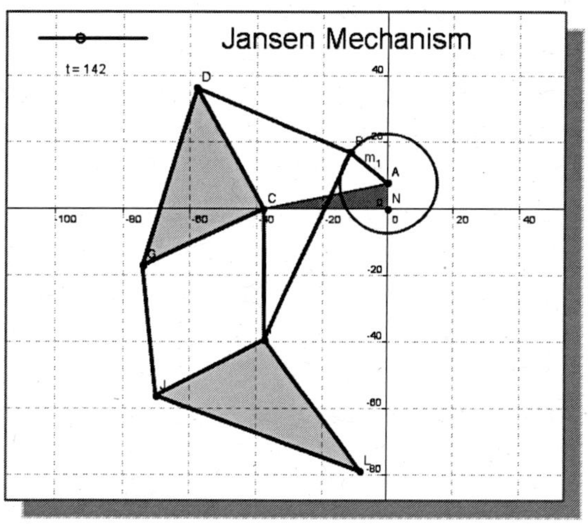

Identify the Six-bar Linkage of the *Mechanical Tiger*

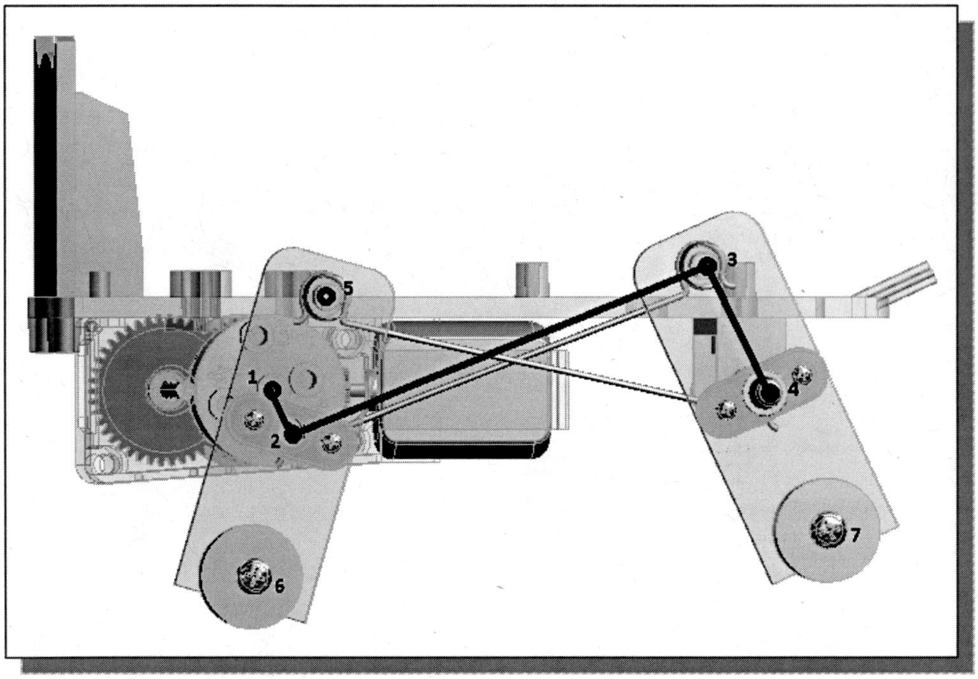

The leg linkage of the *Mechanical Tiger* has six-links and the design consists of a compound mechanism, two combined four-bar mechanisms. The first four-bar mechanism is formed by Points 1-2-3-4, where link 1-2 (from Point 1 to Point 2) is on the rotating A9-crank part; Point 1 is aligned to the axis of the rotating shaft. Point 2 is a moving point on the Crank part. Link 1-2 is therefore the **crank**, or **driver** link. Point 4 is aligned to the rear axle. Since Point 1 and Point 4 are fixed to the chassis, link 1-4 is a fixed link, also known as the **frame**. Link 3-4 is the **follower** link, which rocks back and forth about Point 4. Link 2-3 is the connecting rod. These four links form a four-bar ***Crank-Rocker*** mechanism, as discussed in the previous chapter.

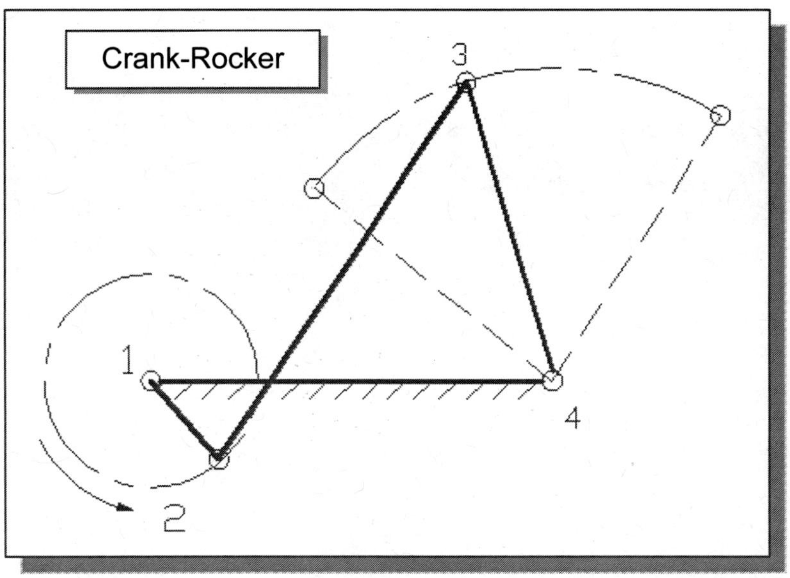

Length of the links used by the *Mechanical Tiger* design:

Link 1-2: **5.25 mm**
Link 2-3: **64.9 mm**
Link 3-4: **20.5 mm**
Link 1-4: **70.5 mm**
Link 3-7: **42.2 mm**

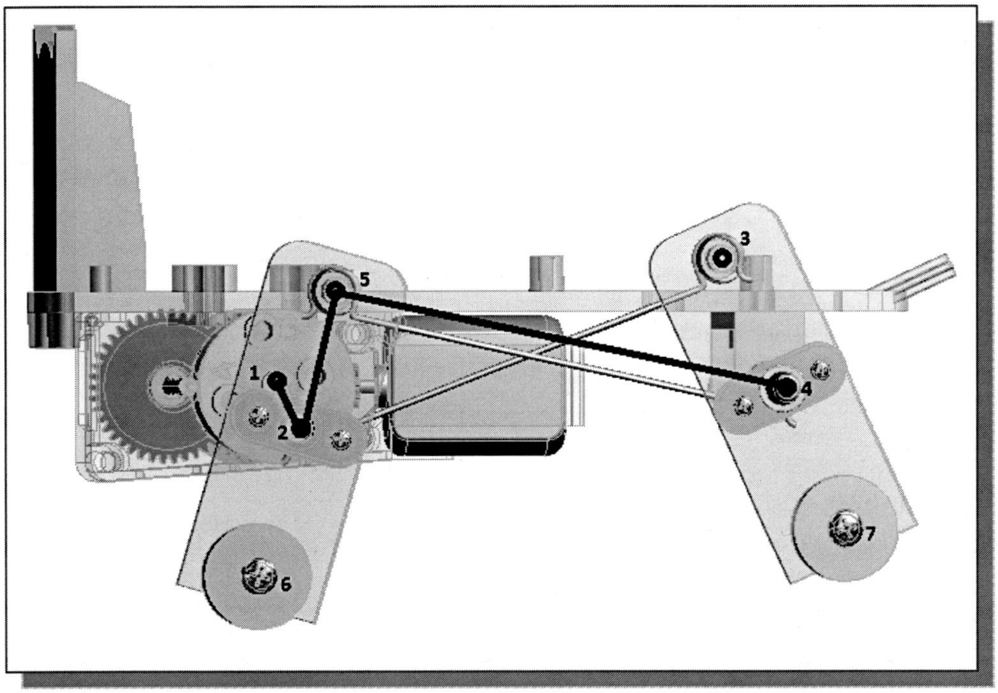

The second four-bar mechanism is formed by Points 1-2-5-4, where link 1-2 is still the **crank**, or **driver**. Both Point 1 and Point 4 are aligned to the front and rear axles; link 1-4 is the **frame**. Link 5-4 is the **follower** link, which rocks back and forth about Point 4. Link 2-5 is the **connecting rod**. These four links also form a four-bar ***Crank-Rocker*** mechanism, similar to the first four-bar mechanism. Note that by using the same driver and frame for both mechanisms, the front legs and back legs are synchronized. The two sets of connecting rod and follower are generating the necessary rocking motion for the walking motion. For the feet locations of the design, Points 6 and 7, they are driven by the rocker link 3-4 in the first mechanism and the connecting rod 2-5 of the second mechanism. Point 7 is part of the link 3-4 and Point 6 is part of the link 2-5. The combination of the two sets of four-bar mechanisms is well designed to generate the walking motion. By cleverly attaching the second set of linkages on the other side, all four legs are synchronized to generate the desired motion.

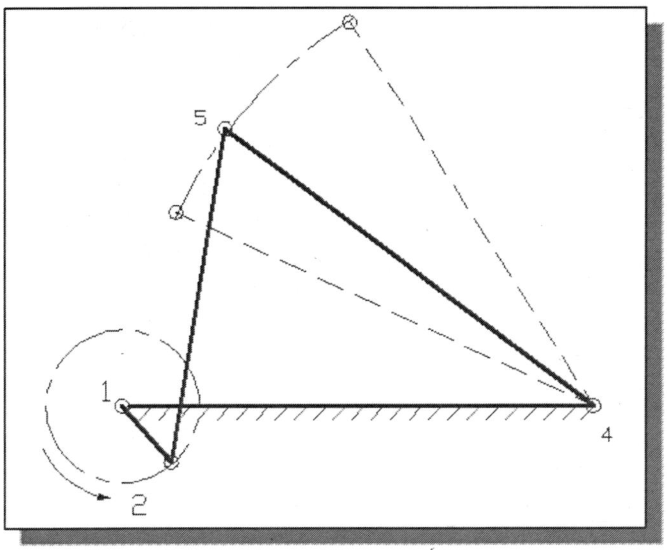

Length of the links used by the *Mechanical Tiger* design:
Link 1-2: **5.25 mm**
Link 2-5: **64.9 mm**
Link 4-5: **20.5 mm**
Link 1-4: **70.5 mm**
Link 5-6: **42.2 mm**

Starting *GeoGebra*

1. Select the **GeoGebra** option on the *Start* menu or select the **GeoGebra** icon on the desktop to start *the software*. The *GeoGebra* main window will appear on the screen.

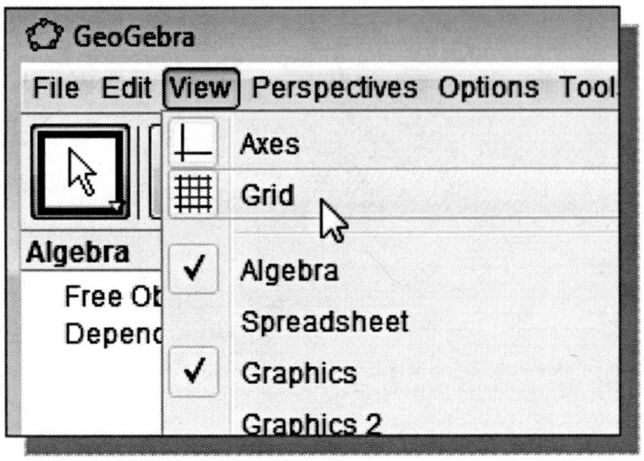

2. In the **View** pull-down menu, switch on the **Grid** display by clicking on the icon with the left-mouse-button as shown.

3. On your own, adjust the display of the *GeoGebra* main screen so that the *Algebra* area and the *Input Bar* are available as shown.

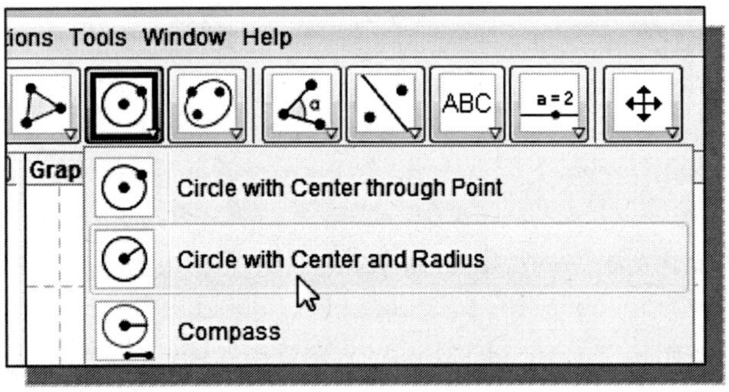

4. Select the **Circle with Center and Radius** icon in the *Standard* toolbar area.

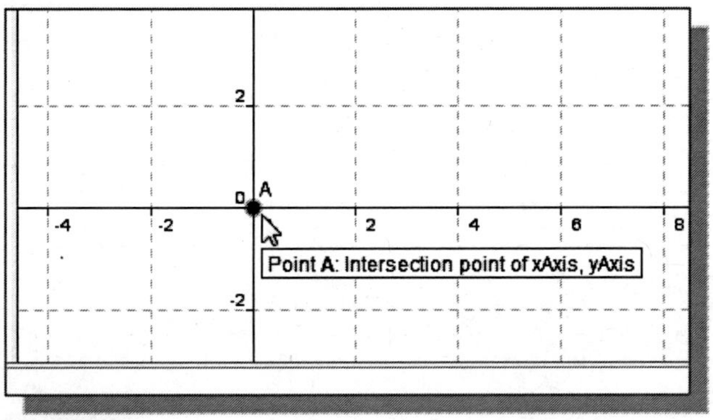

5. Click on the *Origin* of the coordinate system to place the center of the circle. Note the created center point is also added in the *Algebra* area that is toward the left.

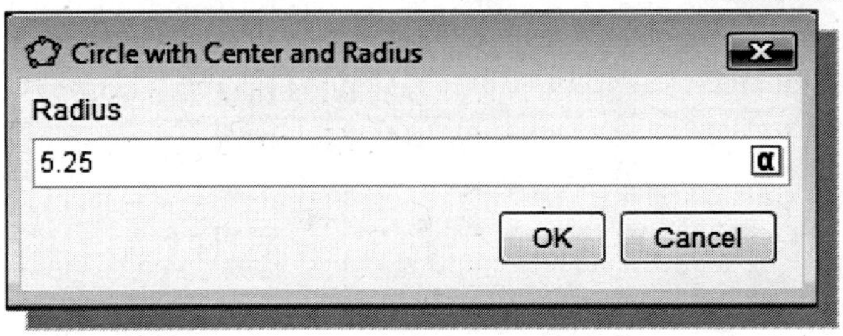

6. In the *Radius* input box, enter **5.25** to create a circle with a radius of **5.25 mm** in size.

7. Pick **OK** to accept the selected settings.

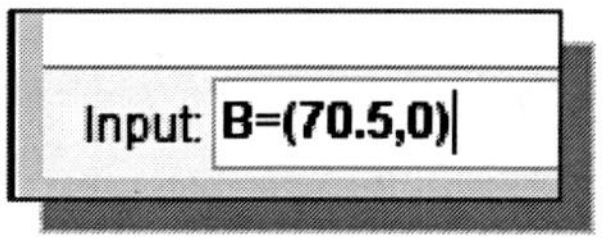

8. In the *Input bar* area, enter **B = (70.5,0)** to create Point B at the specified coordinates.

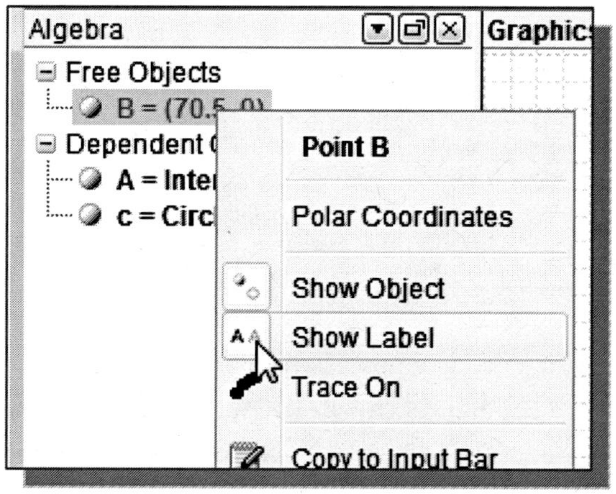

9. In the *Algebra* area, right-mouse-click once on Point B and switch *ON* the display of the label as shown.

10. On your own, use the mouse-wheel to adjust the display of the graphics area so that Point B is visible.

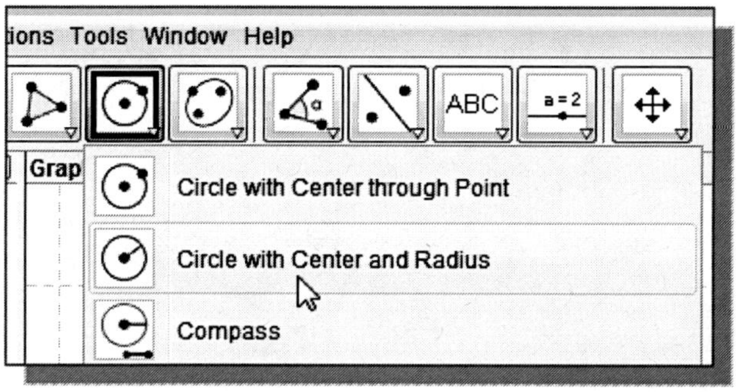

11. Select the **Circle with Center and Radius** icon in the *Standard* toolbar area.

12. Click on **Point B** to place the center of the circle.

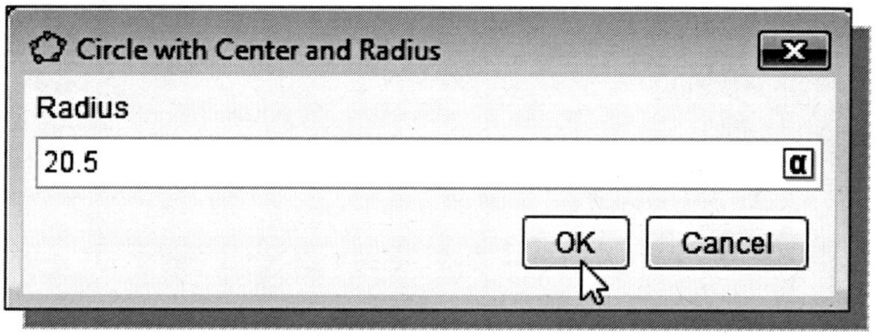

13. In the *Radius* input box, enter **20.5** to create a circle with a radius of **20.5 mm** in size.

14. Pick **OK** to accept the selected settings.

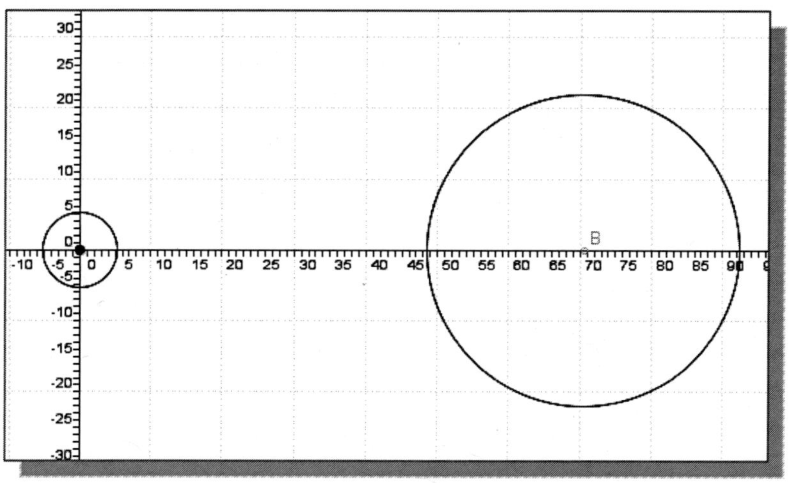

15. Use the **mouse wheel** to Zoom/Pan and adjust the current display.

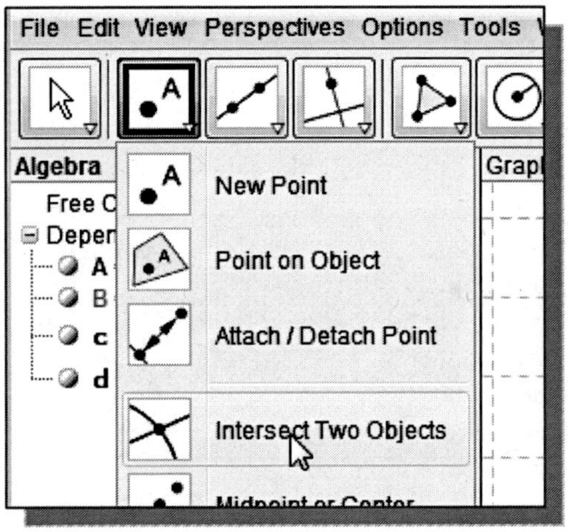

16. Activate the **Intersect Two Objects** command by clicking on the icon as shown. This will create points at the intersections of two selected objects.

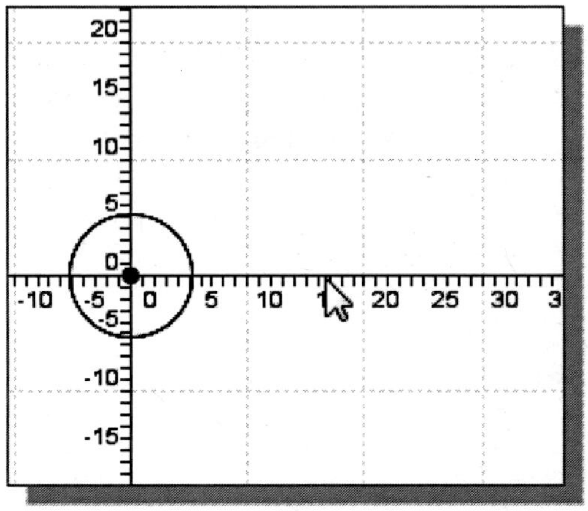

17. Select the **X-Axis** as the first entity to define the intersection points.

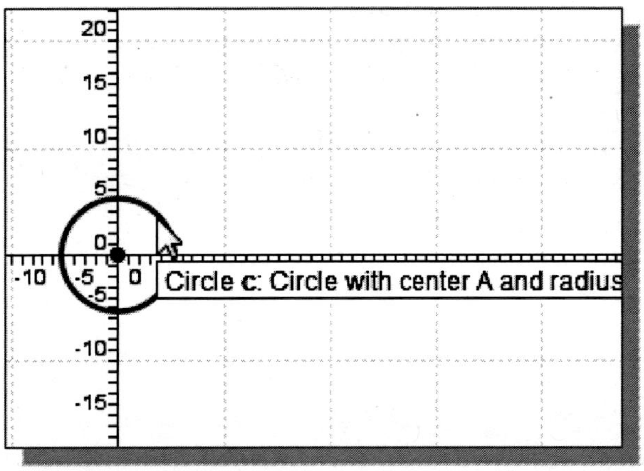

18. Select the **smaller circle** as the second entity to define the intersection points.

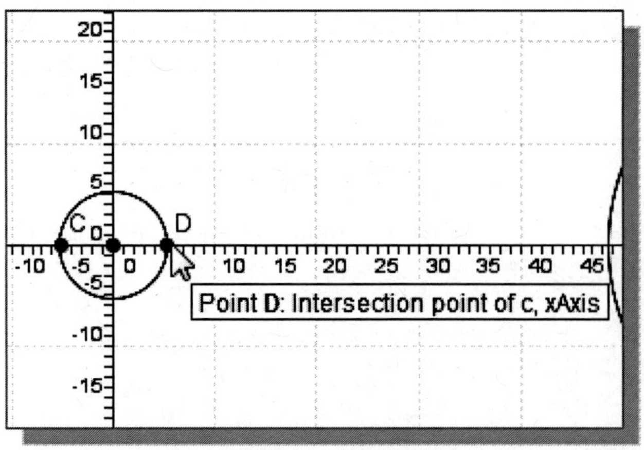

- Note two intersection points are created, **Point C** and **Point D**.

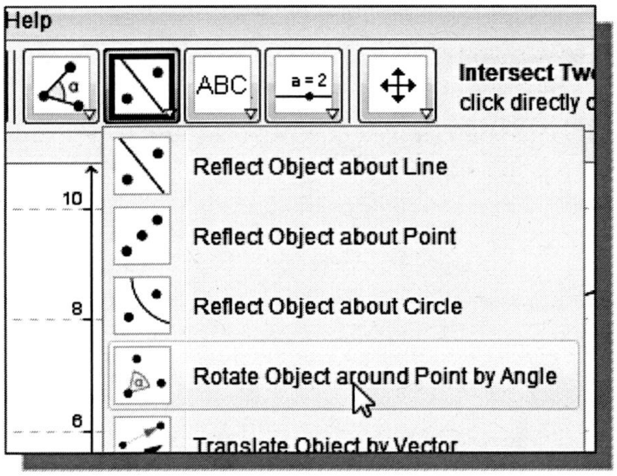

19. Activate the **Rotate Object around Point by Angle** command by clicking on the icon as shown. This will create a new point by rotating an existing point.

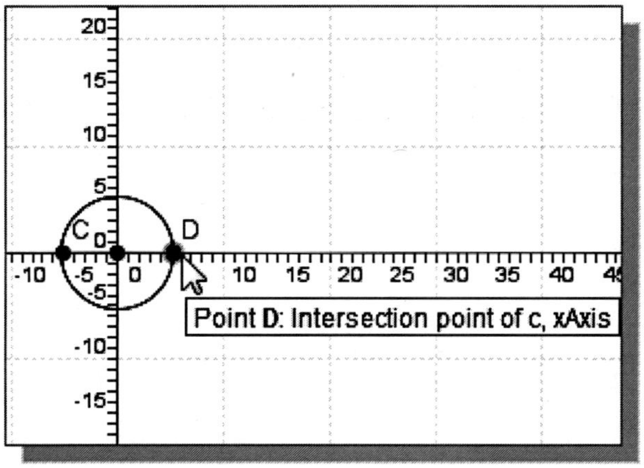

20. Select **Point D** as the object to be rotated.

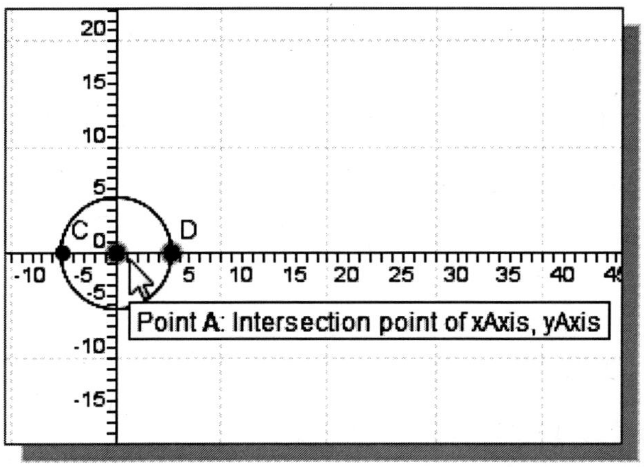

21. Select **Point A** as the reference axis of rotation.

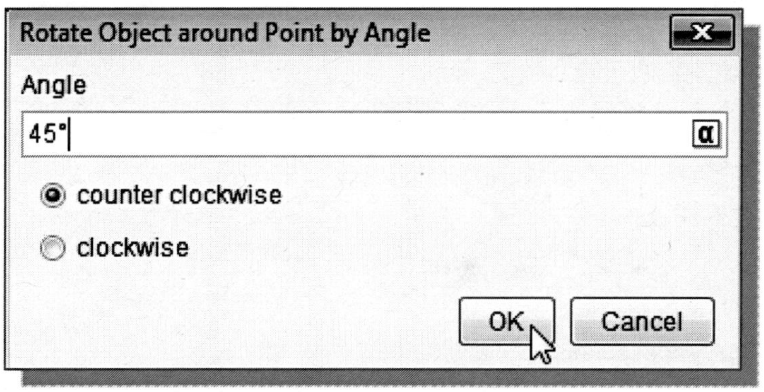

22. In the *Angle* input box, enter **45** as the angle of rotation.

23. Click **OK** to accept the setting and create the new point.

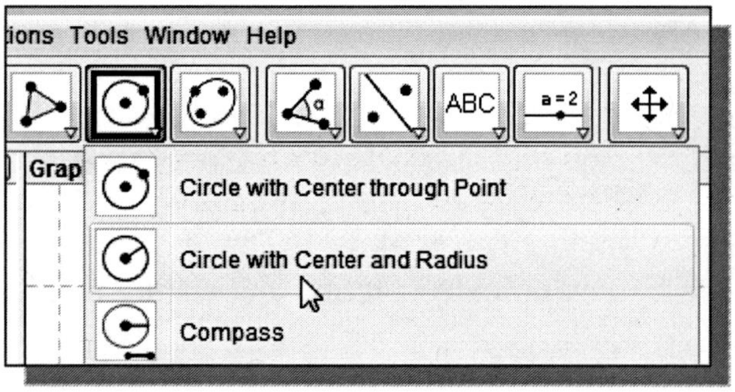

24. Select the **Circle with Center and Radius** icon, in the *Standard toolbar* area.

25. Select **Point D'** as the center of the new circle. Note the created center point is also added in the *Algebra* area that is toward the left.

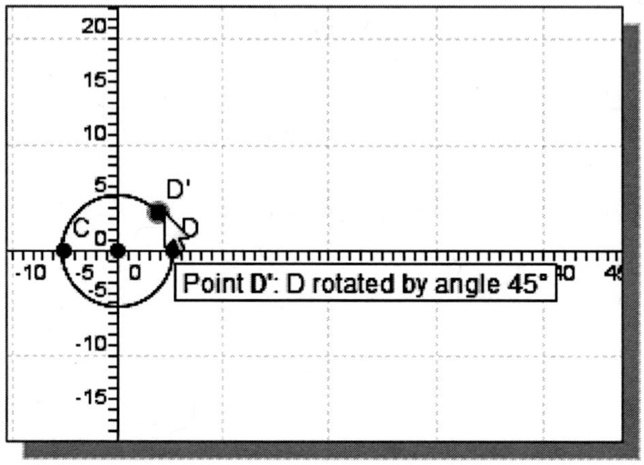

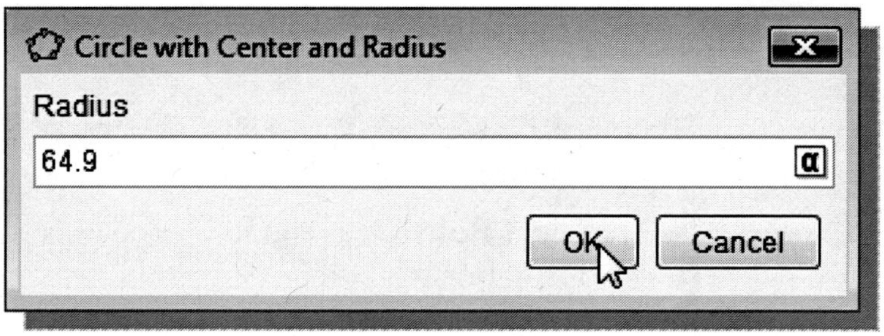

26. In the *Radius* input box, enter **64.9** to create a circle with a radius of **64.9 mm** in size.

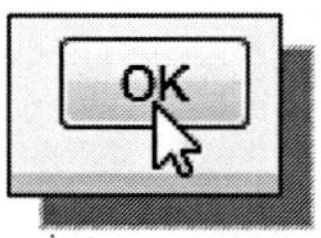

27. Click **OK** to accept the selected settings.

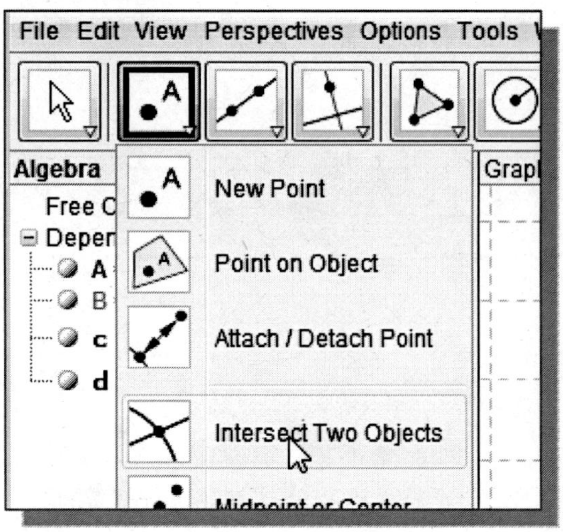

28. Activate the **Intersect Two Objects** command by clicking on the icon as shown. This will create points at the intersections of two selected objects.

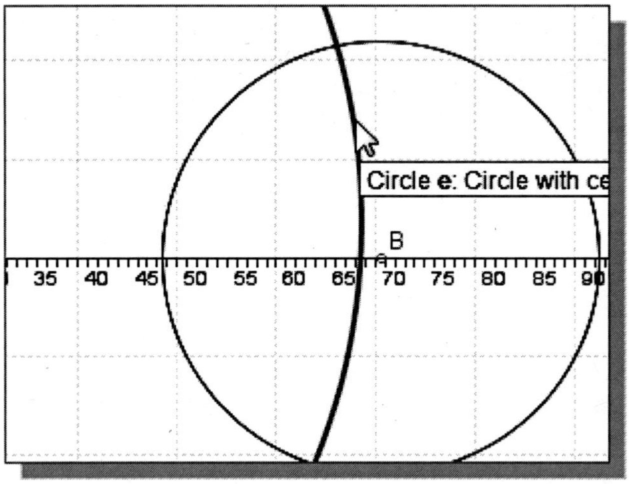

29. Select **Circle e** as the first entity to define the intersection points.

30. Select **Circle d** as the second entity to define the intersection points.

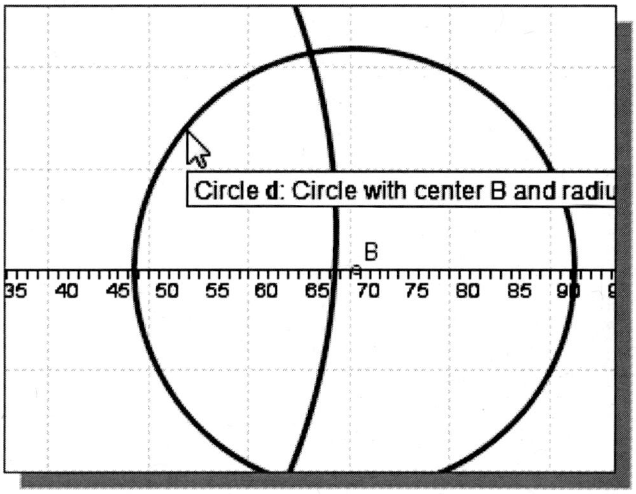

- Note two intersection points are created, **Point E** and **Point F**.

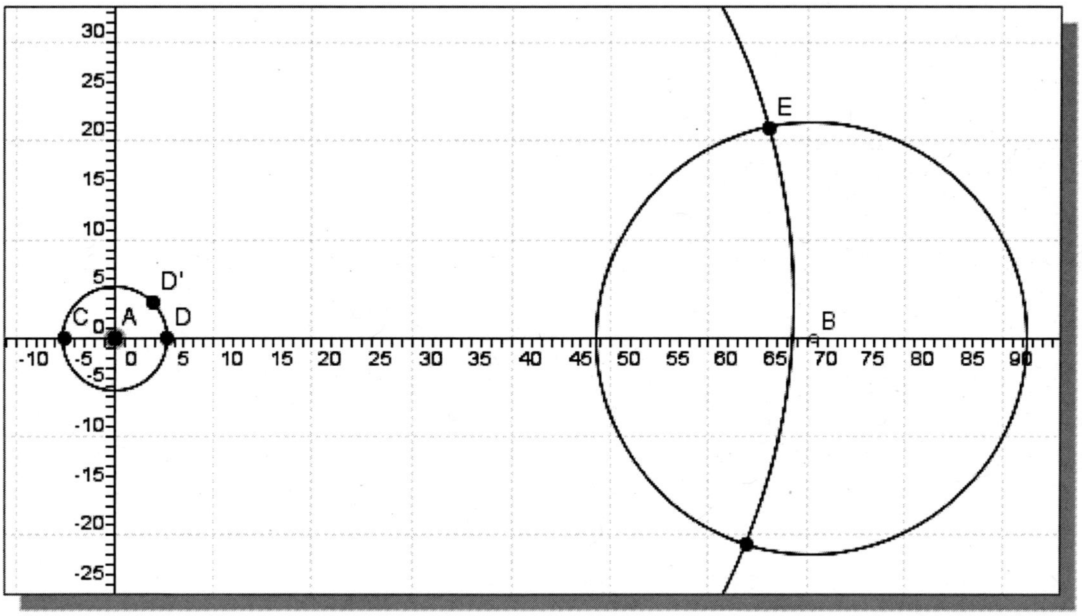

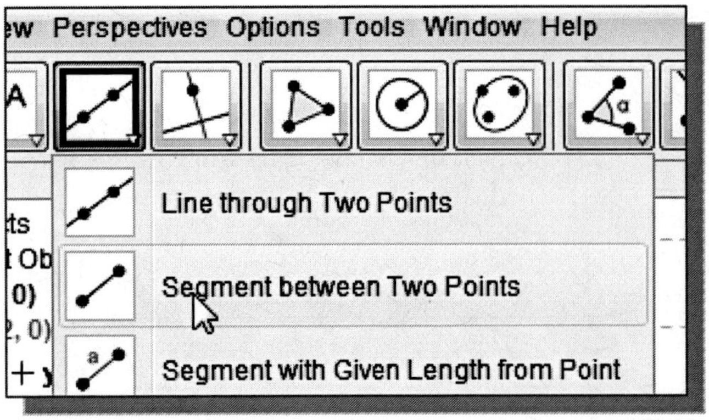

31. Activate the **Segment between Two Points** command by clicking on the icon as shown. This will create a line by selecting two endpoints.

32. Click on **Point A** to place the first point of the line.

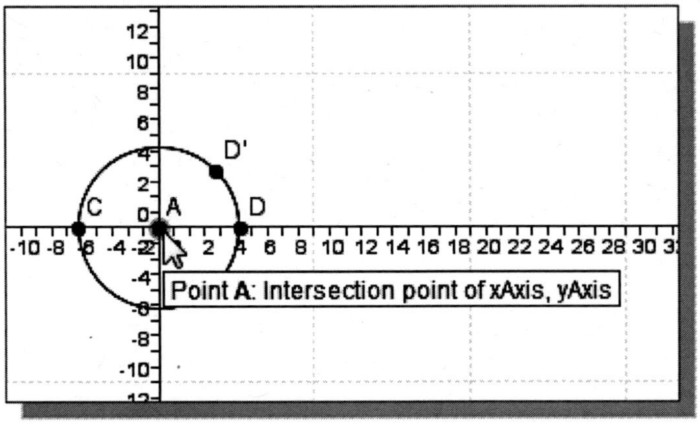

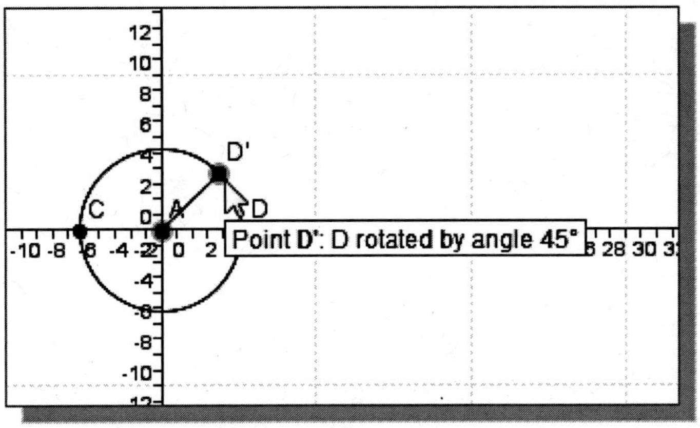

33. Click on **Point D'** to create a line as shown.

34. On your own, create two additional line segments, **line DE** and **line EB** as shown.

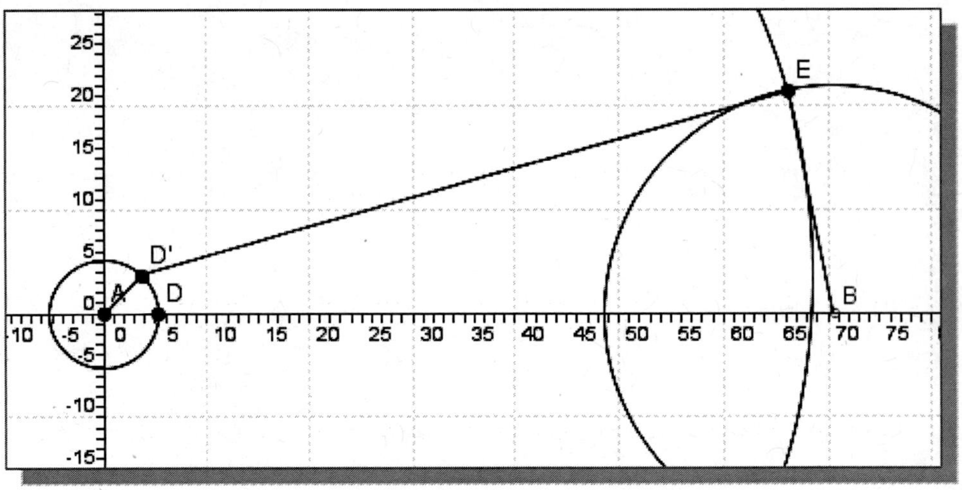

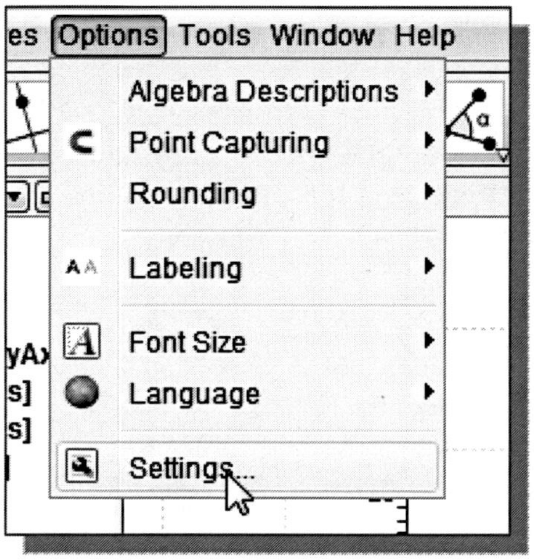

35. In the pull-down menu, select **Options → Settings** to access the *Settings* dialog box.

36. Click on the **Graphics** icon and select the **Grid** tab.

37. On your own, adjust the settings of the **Grid** display as shown.

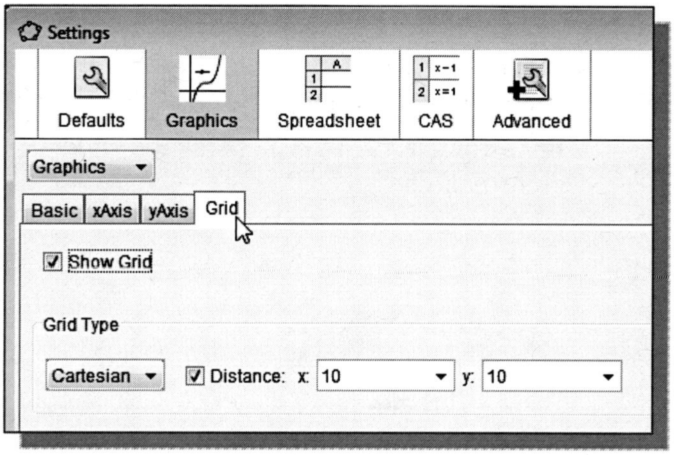

38. Click **Save Settings** to store the adjusted settings.

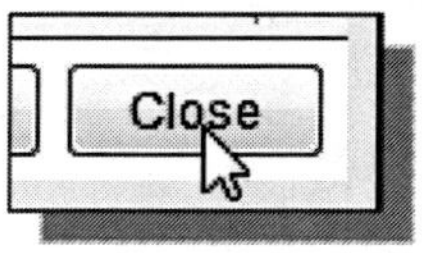

39. Click **Close** to exit the ***Settings*** dialog box.

40. On your own, hide the extra geometry so that the display is as shown in the figure.

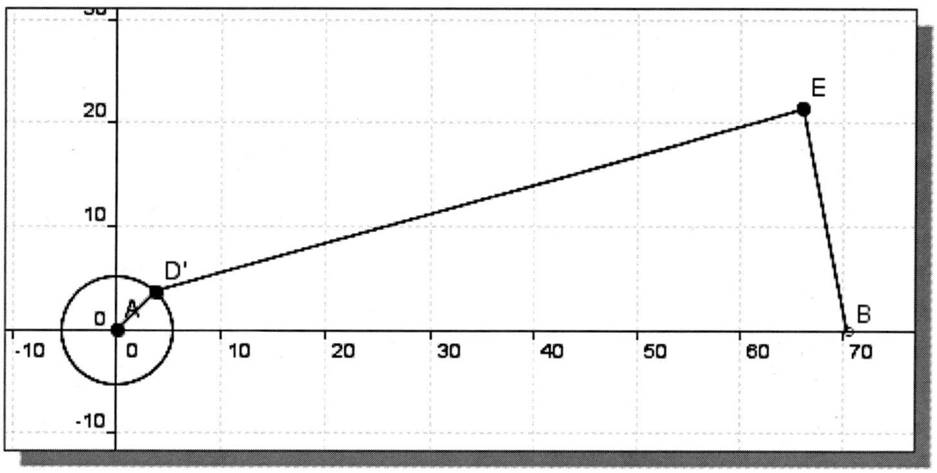

Create a Slider Control

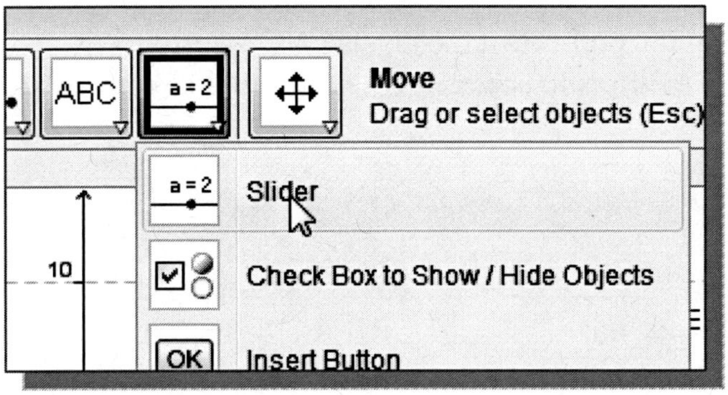

1. Activate the **Slider** command by clicking on the icon as shown.

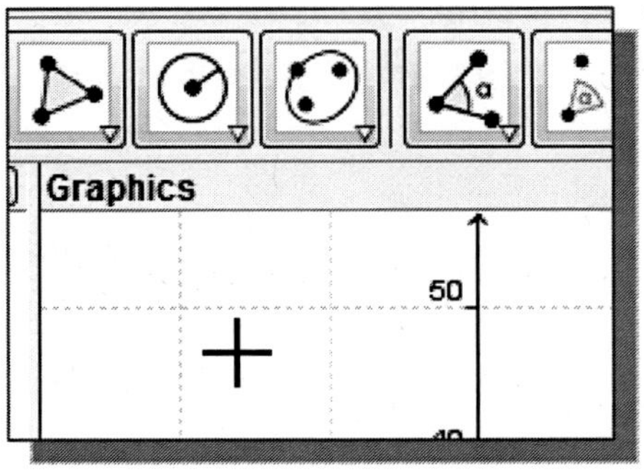

2. In the graphics area, select a location near the **upper left corner** to place the slider control as shown.

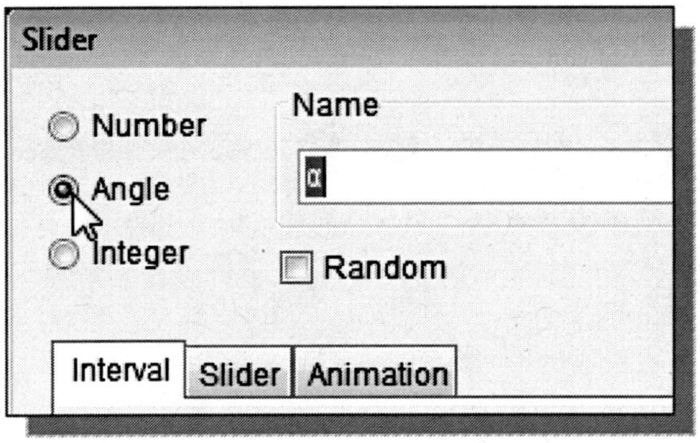

3. Set the slider option to **Angle** as shown. Note the angle name is automatically set to **α** when the angle option is selected.

4. Set the **Interval** settings to the three values, **0**, **360** and **1.0**, as shown.

5. Click **Apply** to accept the selected settings

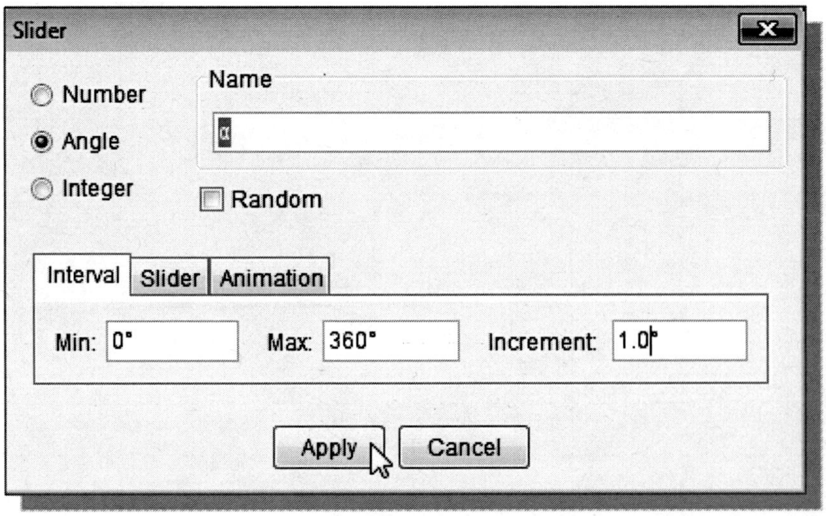

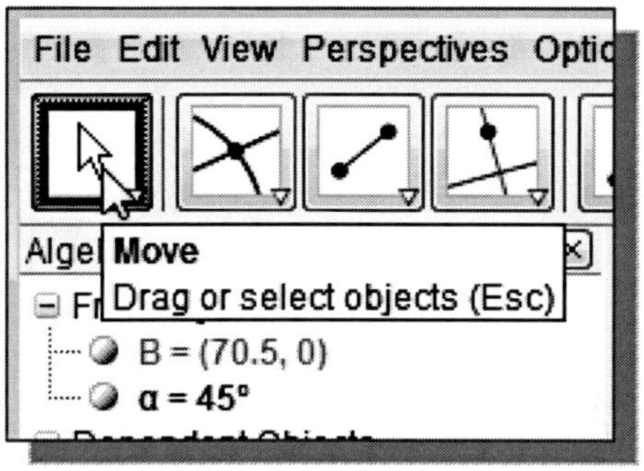

6. In the *Standard* toolbar area, click on the **Move** icon to activate the command.

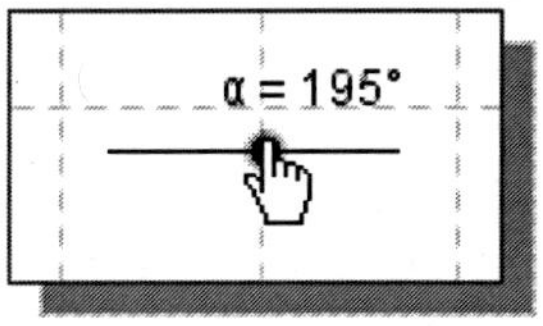

7. Drag the **handle** of the slider control, and notice **Angle α** is adjusted.

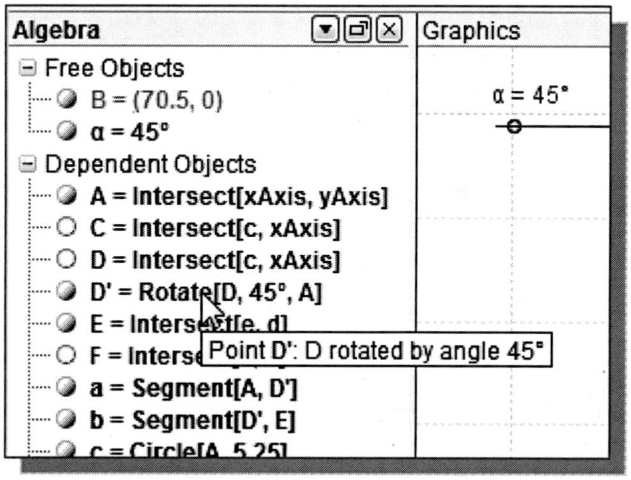

8. In the *Algebra* area, double click with the left-mouse-button on **Point D'** to enter the **Object Redefine** mode.

9. Modify the **angle variable**, the second variable in the edit box, to **α** as shown.

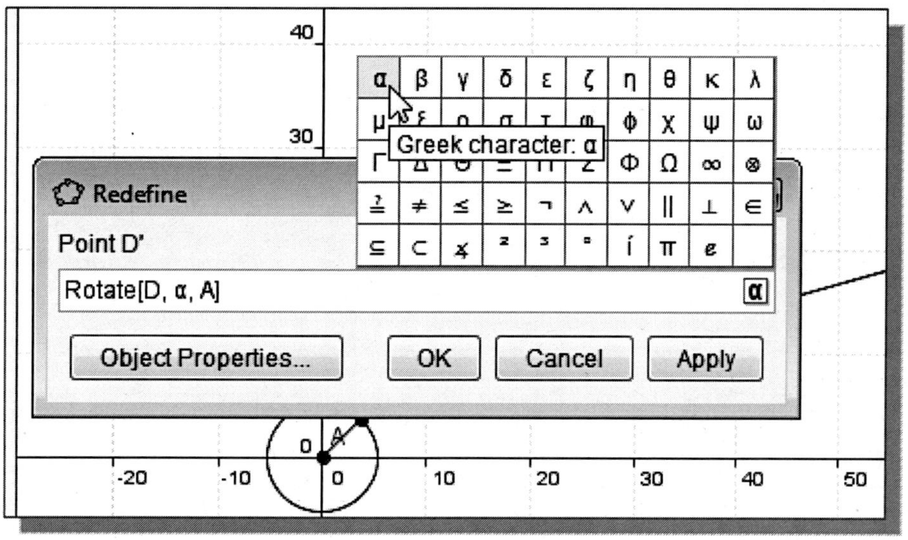

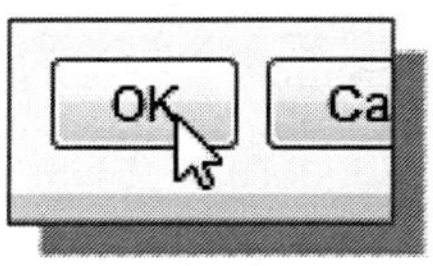

10. Click **OK** to accept the setting and exit the Redefine command.

Create the Second Four-bar Mechanism

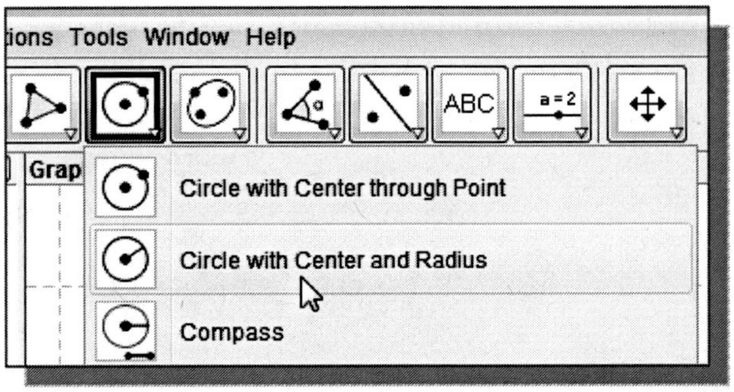

1. Select the **Circle with Center and Radius** icon, in the *Standard* toolbar area.

2. Click on **Point B** to place the center of the circle.

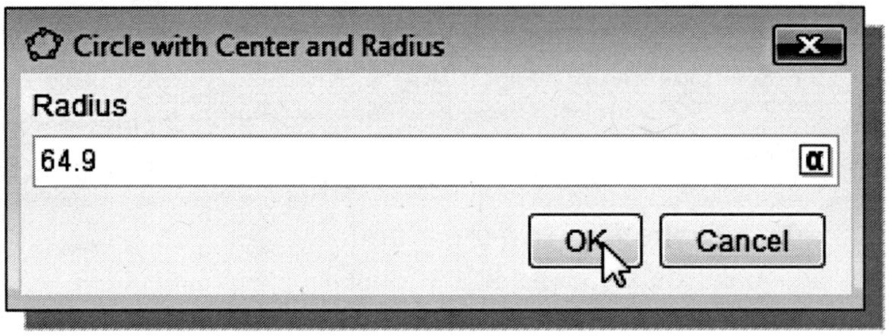

3. In the *Radius* input box, enter **64.9** to create a circle with a radius of **64.9 mm** in size.

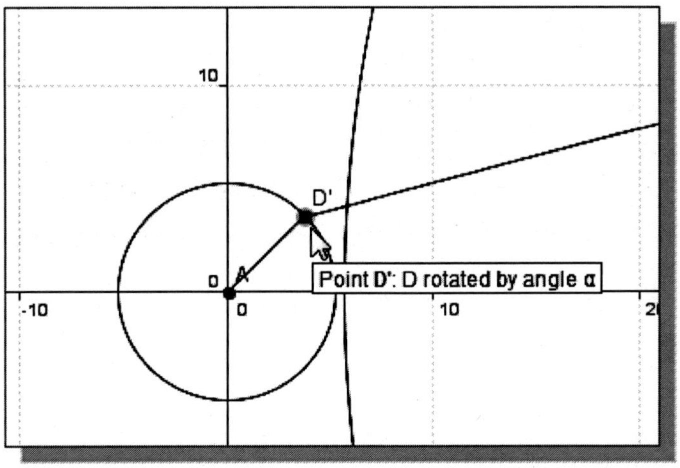

4. Next, click on **Point D'** to place the center of the circle.

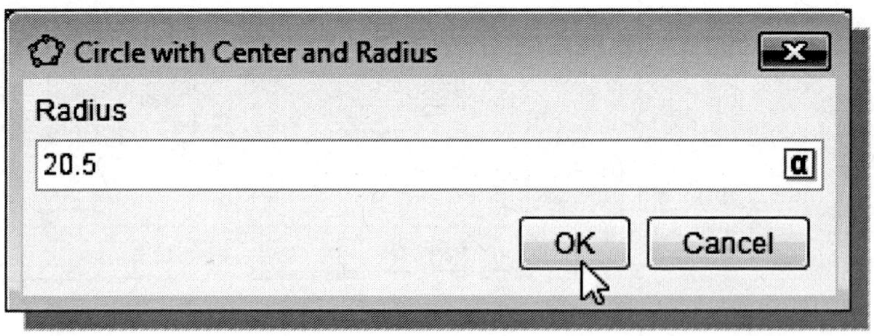

5. In the *Radius* input box, enter **20.5** to create a circle with a radius of **20.5 mm** in size.

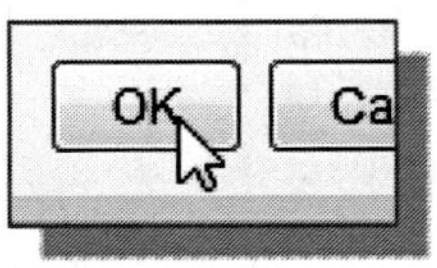

6. Click **OK** to accept the setting and exit the Circle with Center and Radius command.

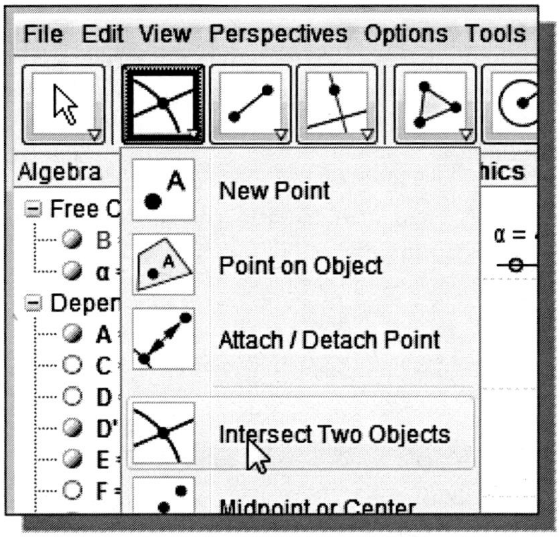

7. Activate the **Intersect Two Objects** command by clicking on the icon as shown.

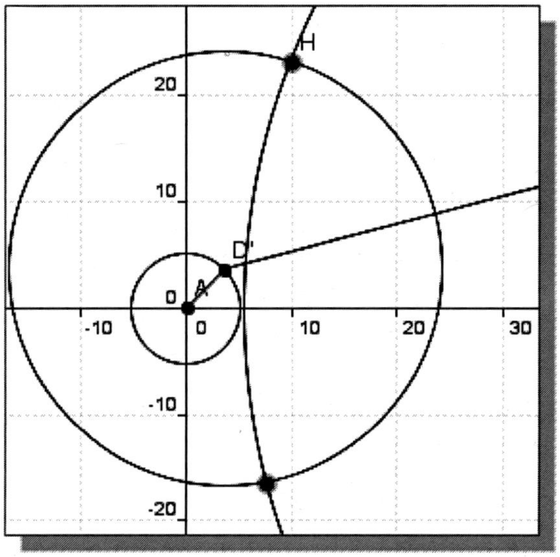

8. Select the two circles we just created to define the intersection points.

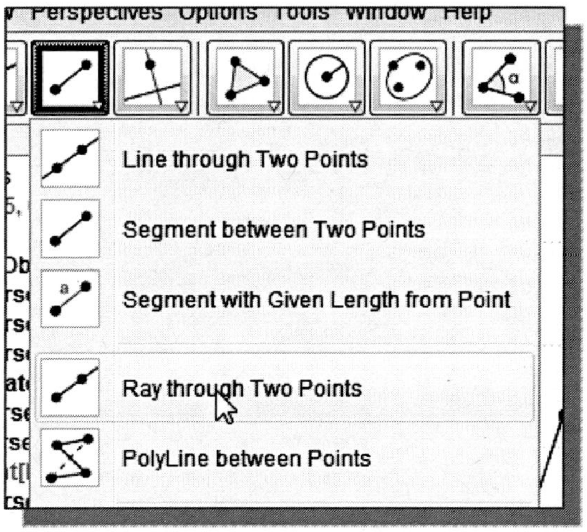

9. Activate the **Ray through Two Points** command by clicking on the icon as shown. This command will create a ray of line through two selected points.

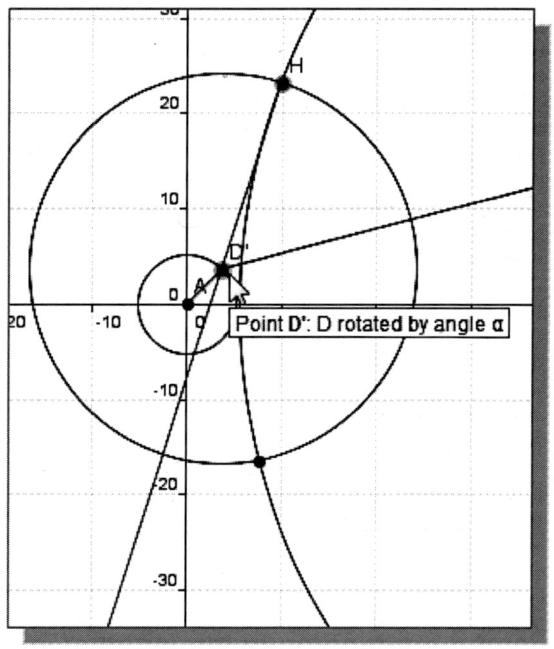

10. Create a ray by selecting **Point H** first and then pick **Point D'** as shown.

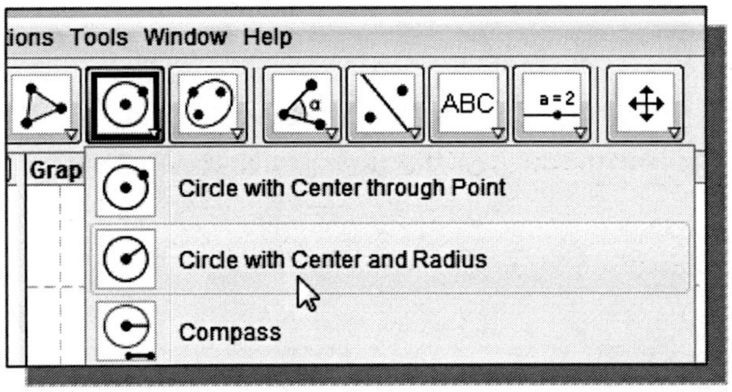

11. Select the **Circle with Center and Radius** icon in the *Standard* toolbar area.

12. Click on **Point H** to place the center of the circle.

13. In the *Radius* input box, enter **42.2** to create a circle with a radius of **42.2 mm** in size.

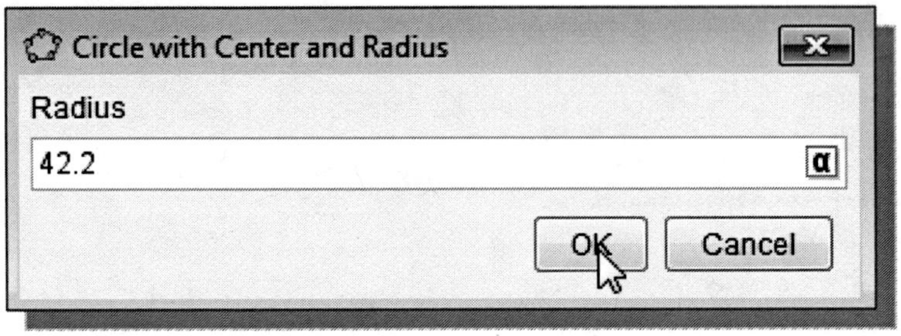

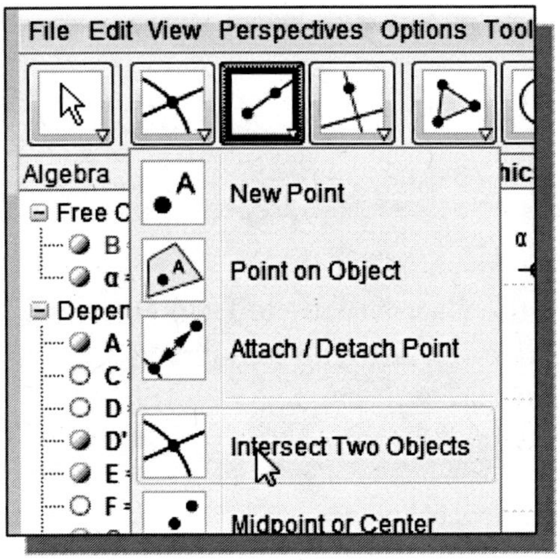

14. Activate the **Intersect Two Objects** command by clicking on the icon as shown. This will create points at the intersections of two selected objects.

15. Select the **Ray** and **Circle k** to find the intersection **Point M** as shown.

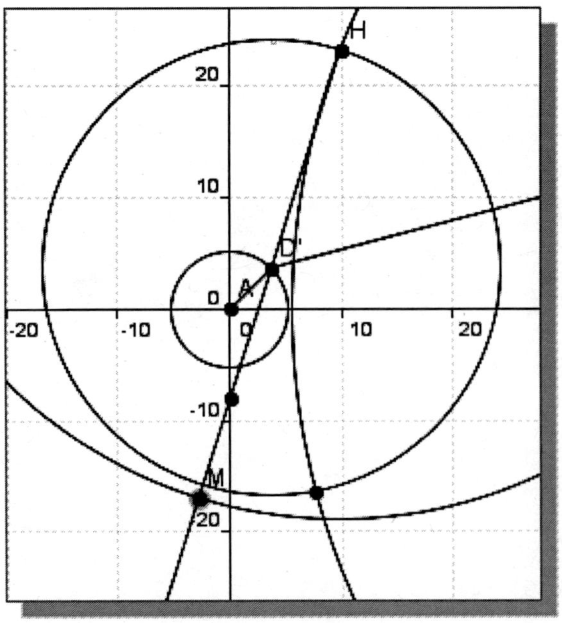

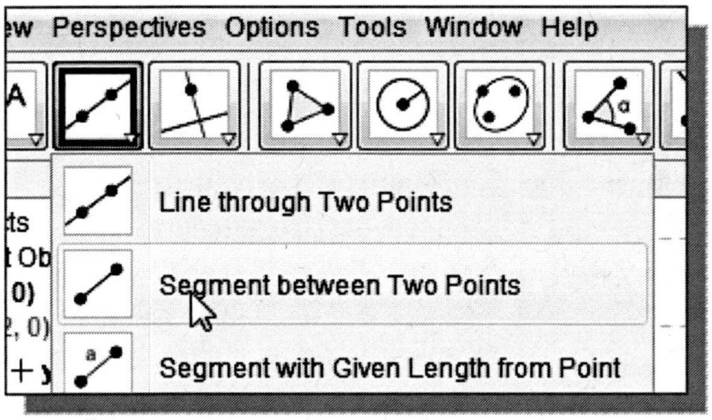

16. Activate the **Segment between Two Points** command by clicking on the icon as shown.

17. On your own, create **line KH** and **line BH** as shown.

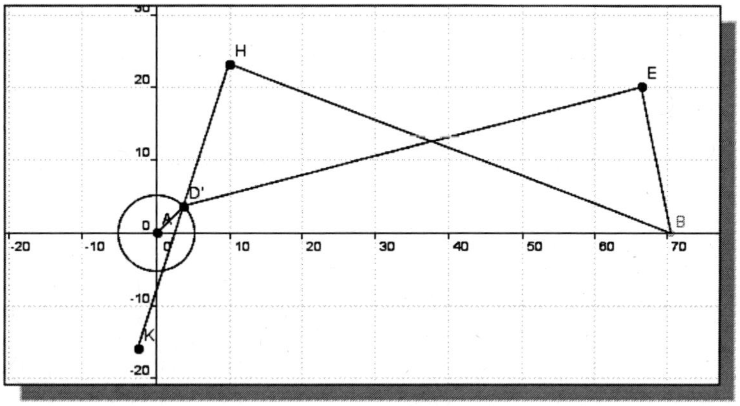

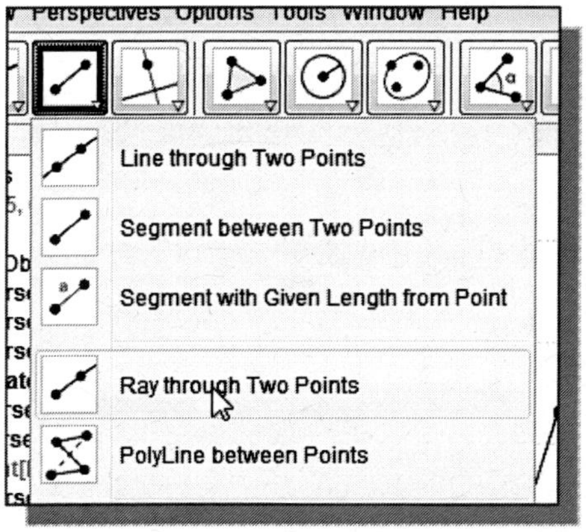

18. On your own, repeat the above steps and create a **Ray** through **Point E** and **Point B**.

19. Also create a circle with center point aligned to **Point E** and a radius of **42.2 mm**.

20. Locate the intersection between the *ray* and the *circle*.

21. On your own, complete the geometry construction as shown.

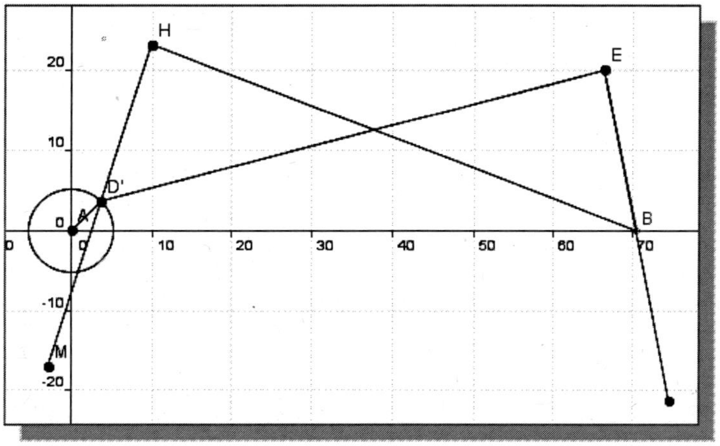

Using the Animate Option

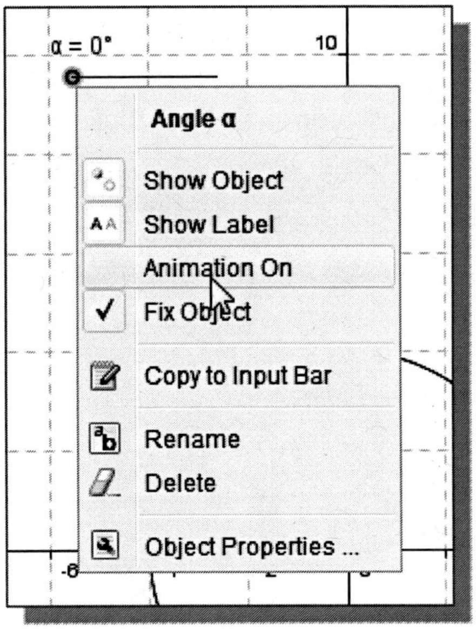

1. Inside the graphics area, click once with the right-mouse-button on the **Slider Control** to display the option menu. Click on **Animation On** to toggle *ON* the animation of the Slider Control.

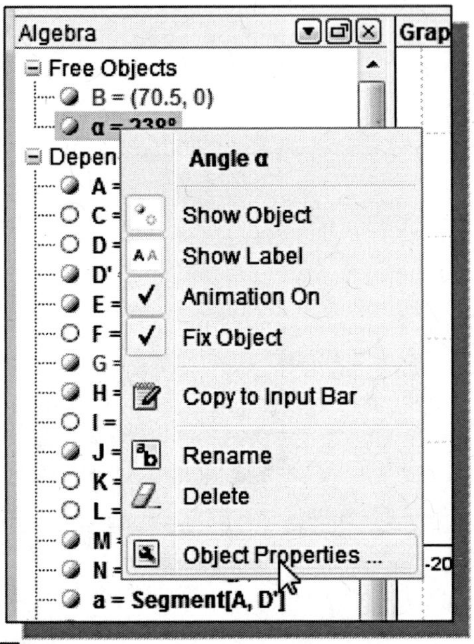

2. Inside the *Algebra* area, click once with the right-mouse-button on **Angle α** to display the option menu. Click on **Object Properties** to activate the command.

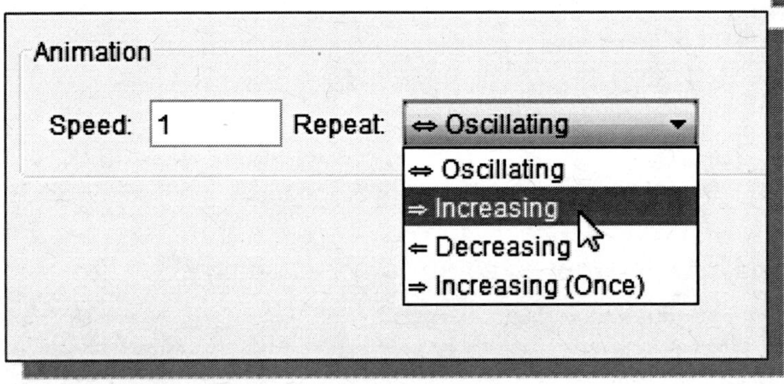

3. Set the *Animation Repeat* option to **Increasing** as shown.

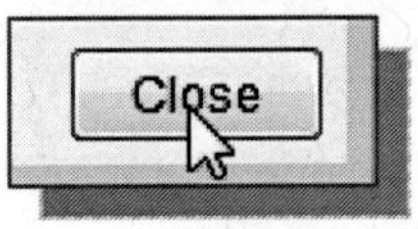

4. Click **Close** to accept the setting and exit the Object Properties command.

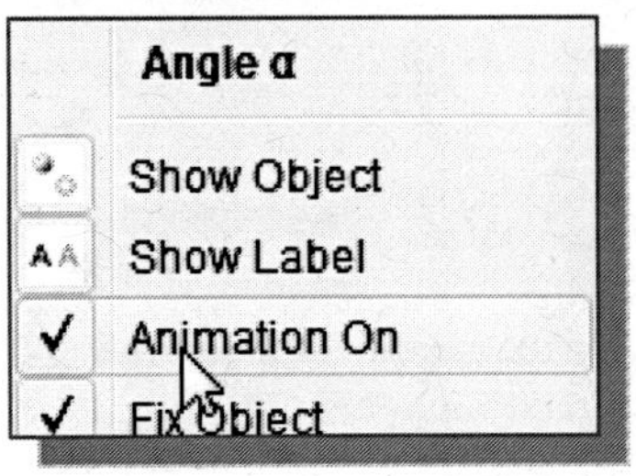

5. On your own, examine the animation of the four-bar linkage; turn *OFF* the *Animation* option before proceeding to the next section.

Tracking the Paths of the Feet

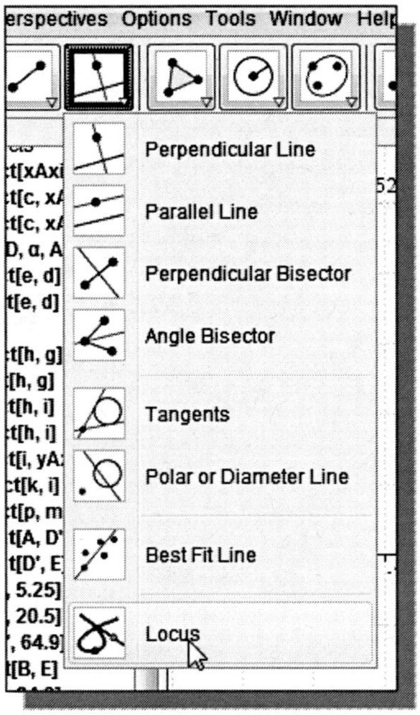

1. Select the **Locus** command in the *Standard* toolbar area.

2. Select the point representing the front foot, **Point M**, as shown.

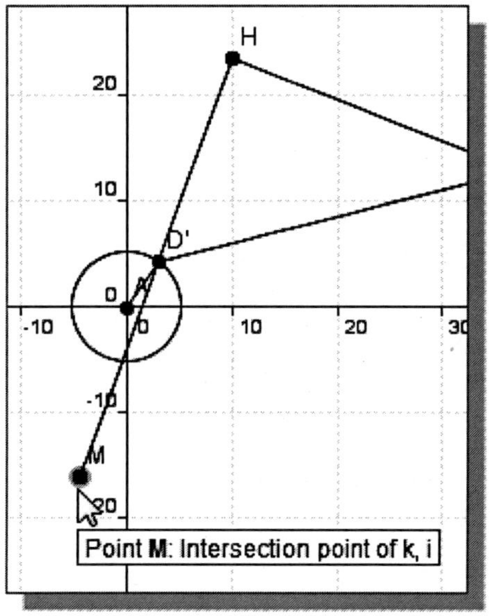

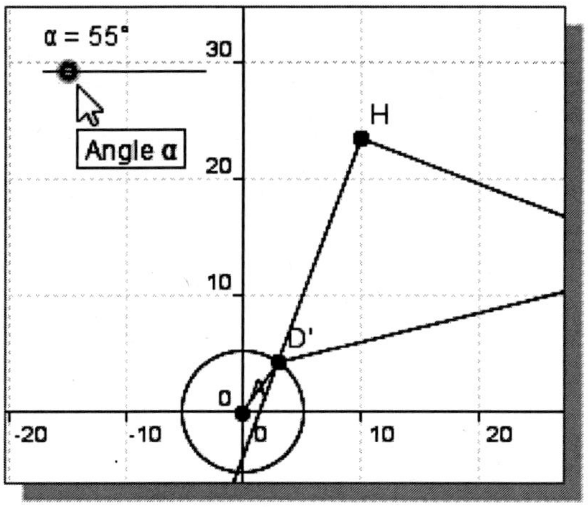

3. Next select the **Slider** as the increment source.

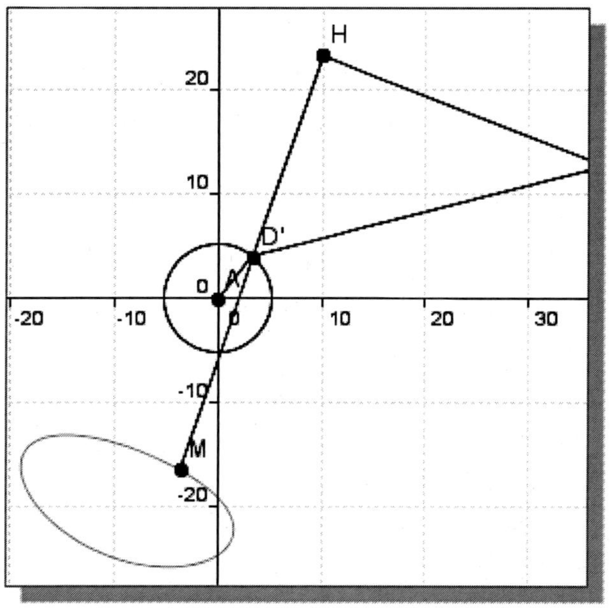

- The displayed locus indicates the foot of the front leg lifts up more than 10 mm and the contact to the ground is a curved path. The soft boots of the *Mechanical Tiger* are therefore necessary to make the walking action more effective.

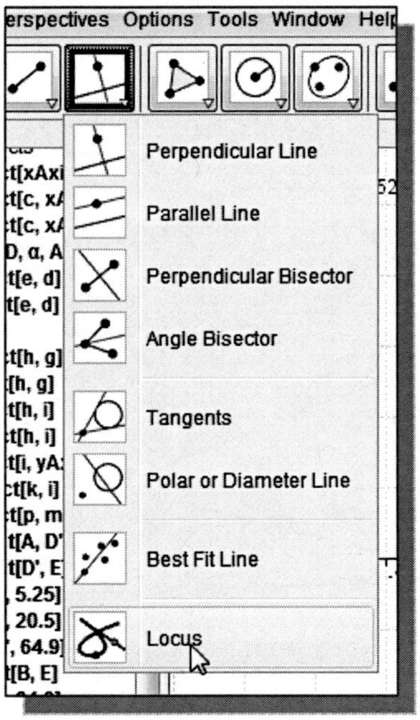

4. On your own, use the **Locus** command and display the path of the rear foot.

   - Note the rear foot does not lift up; the path is an arc. The rear leg only swings back and forth.

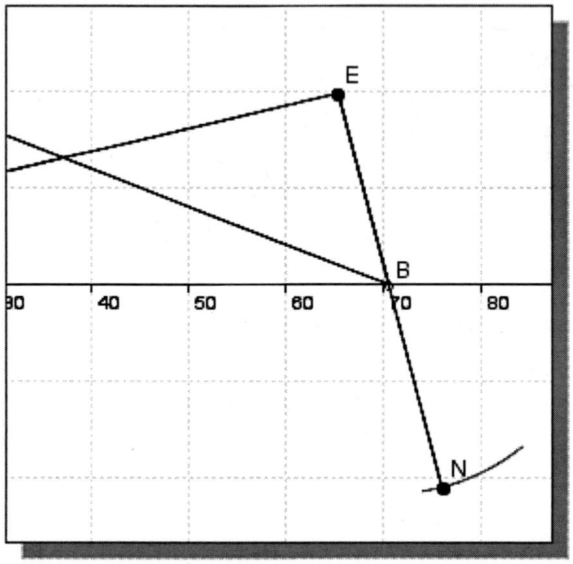

5. On your own, show the loci of the top joints of the legs; also turn *ON* the *Animation* option to observe the behavior of the six-bar linkage.

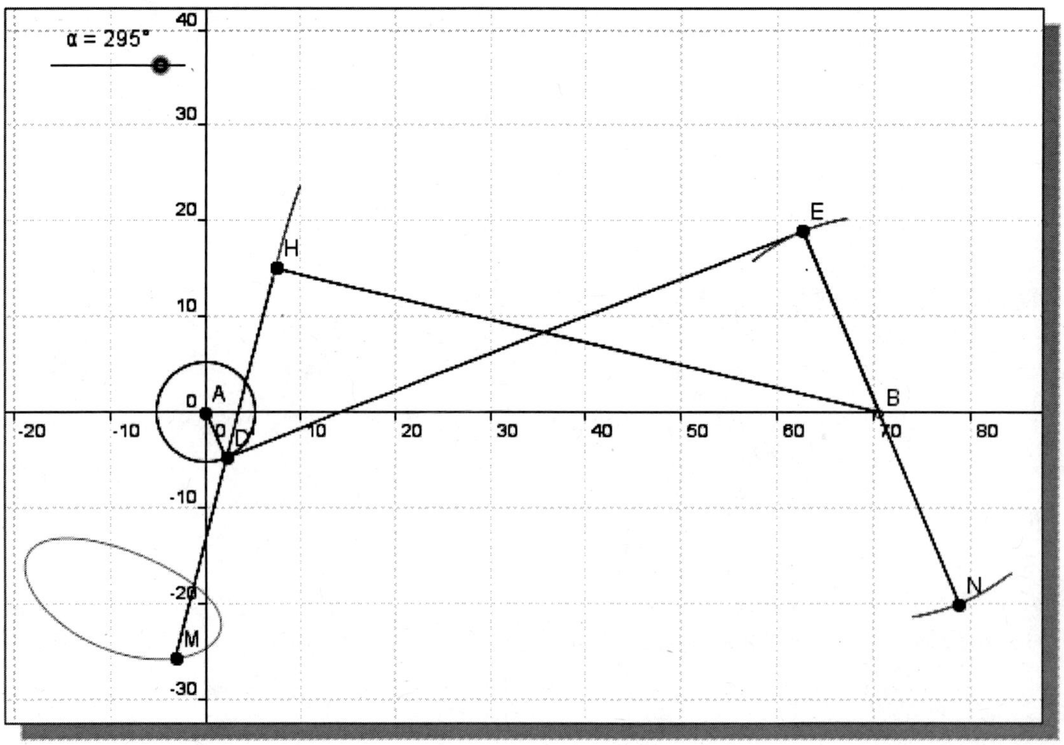

Adjusting the Crank Length

- Mounting the front leg to the different holes on the crank will result in different stride length and lift distance.

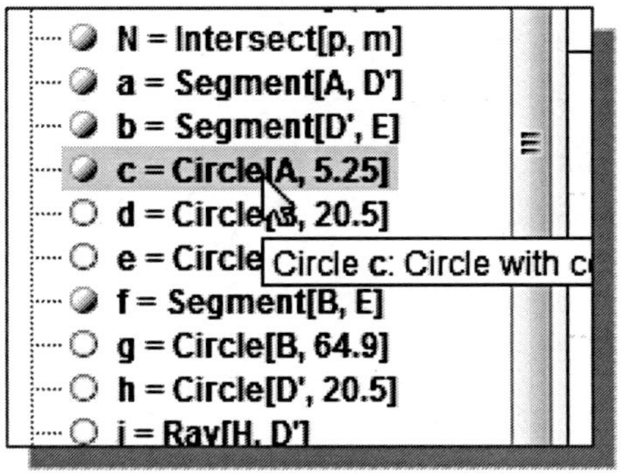

1. In the *Algebra* area, double click with the left-mouse-button on **Circle c** to enter the **Object Redefine** mode.

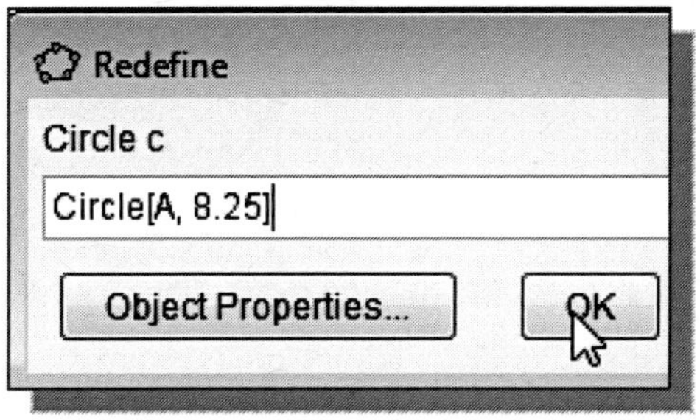

2. Enter **8.25** as the new radius value.

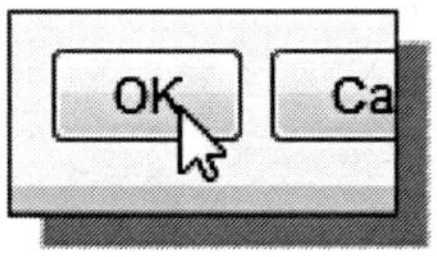

3. Click **OK** to accept the setting and exit the **Redefine** command.

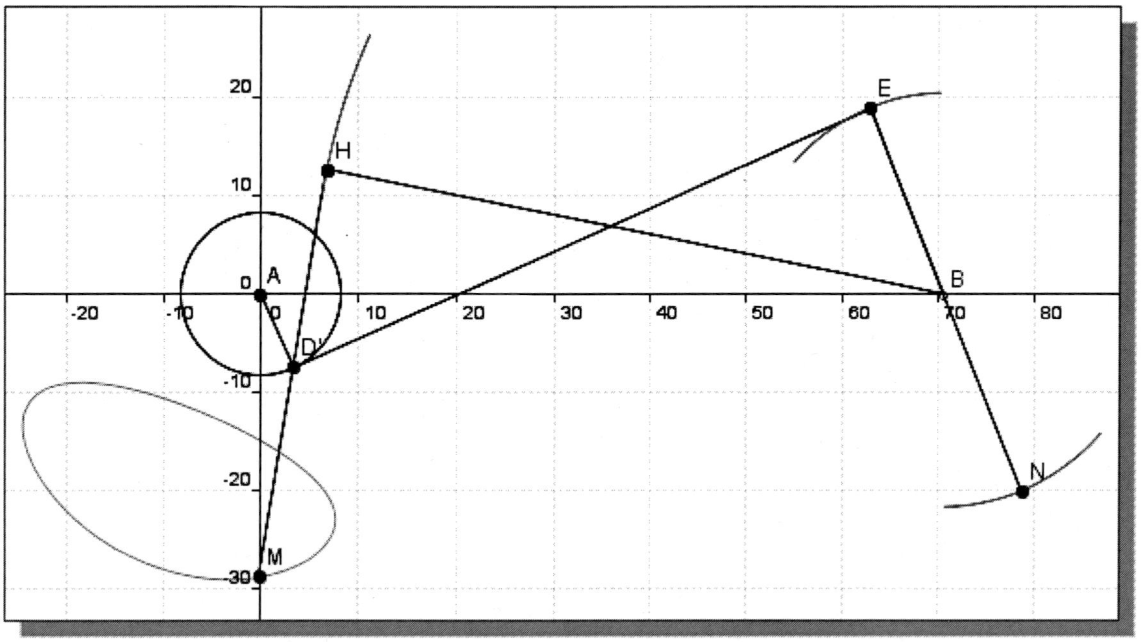

- Note the locus of the front foot has been updated; both the height and length have almost doubled in size.

The Jansen Mechanism

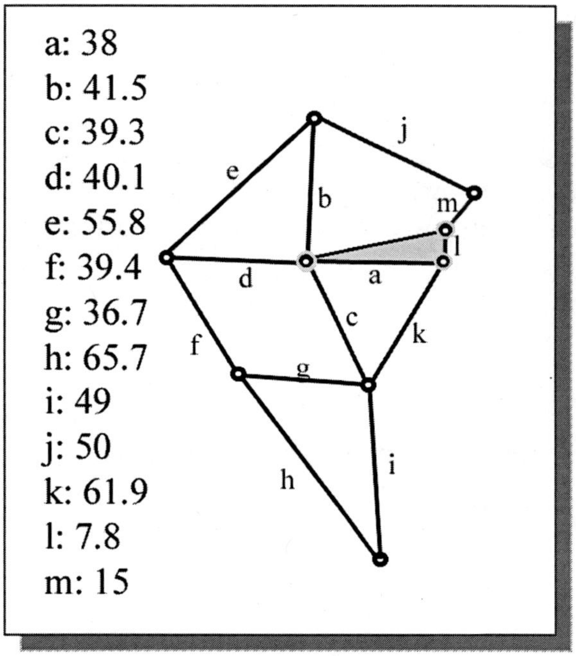

The ***Jansen Mechanism*** is an eight-bar linkage; the dimensions of the mechanism are as shown in the figure. Note that the shaded triangle represents the **Frame**, and **m** is the **Crank**.

- The locus of the foot shows the design grants very straight contact path to the ground and also has good lift height.

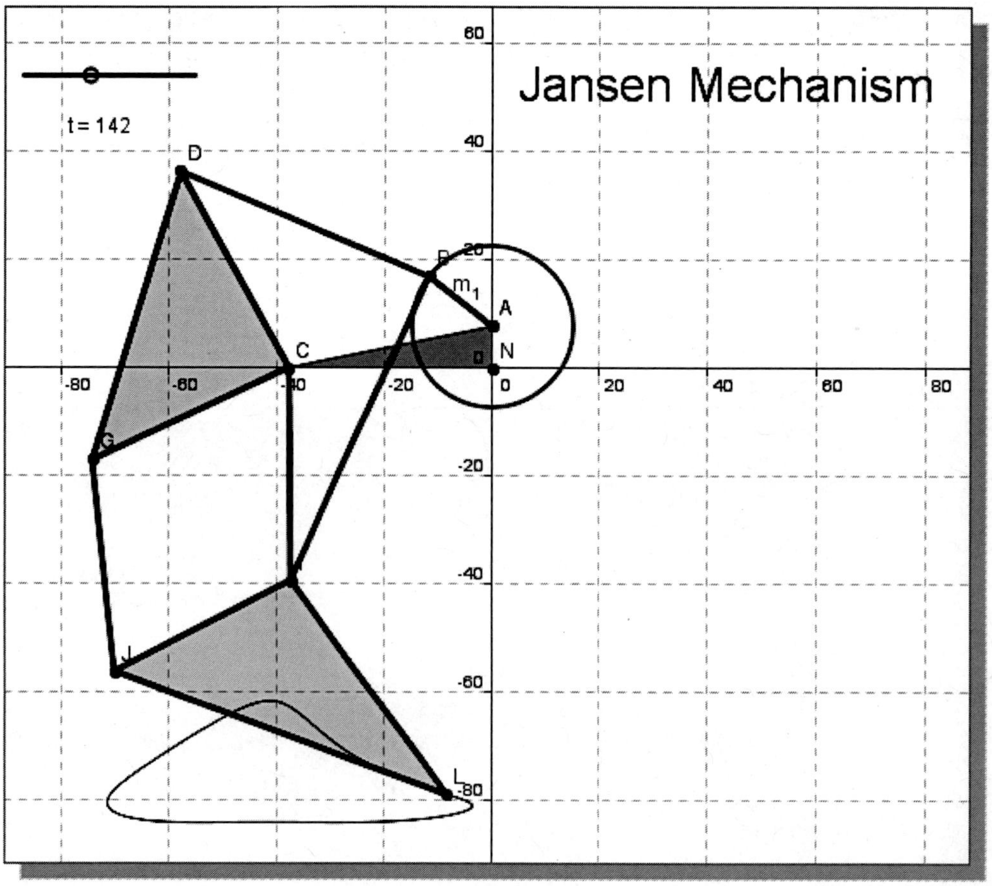

The Klann Mechanism

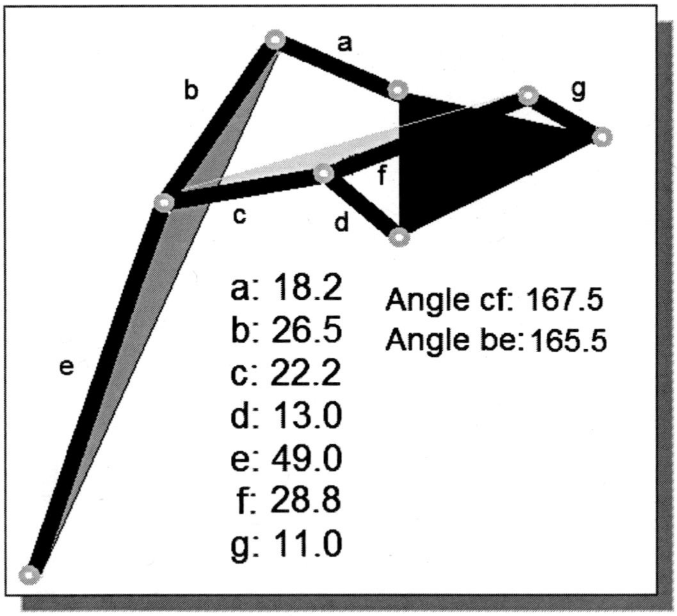

The ***Klann Mechanism*** is a six-bar linkage; the dimensions of the mechanism are as shown in the figure. Note that the dark shaded triangle represents the **Frame**, the light shaded triangles indicate the two rigid links, and **g** is the **Crank**.

- The locus of the foot shows the design also grants relatively straight contact path to the ground and good height of the foot lift.

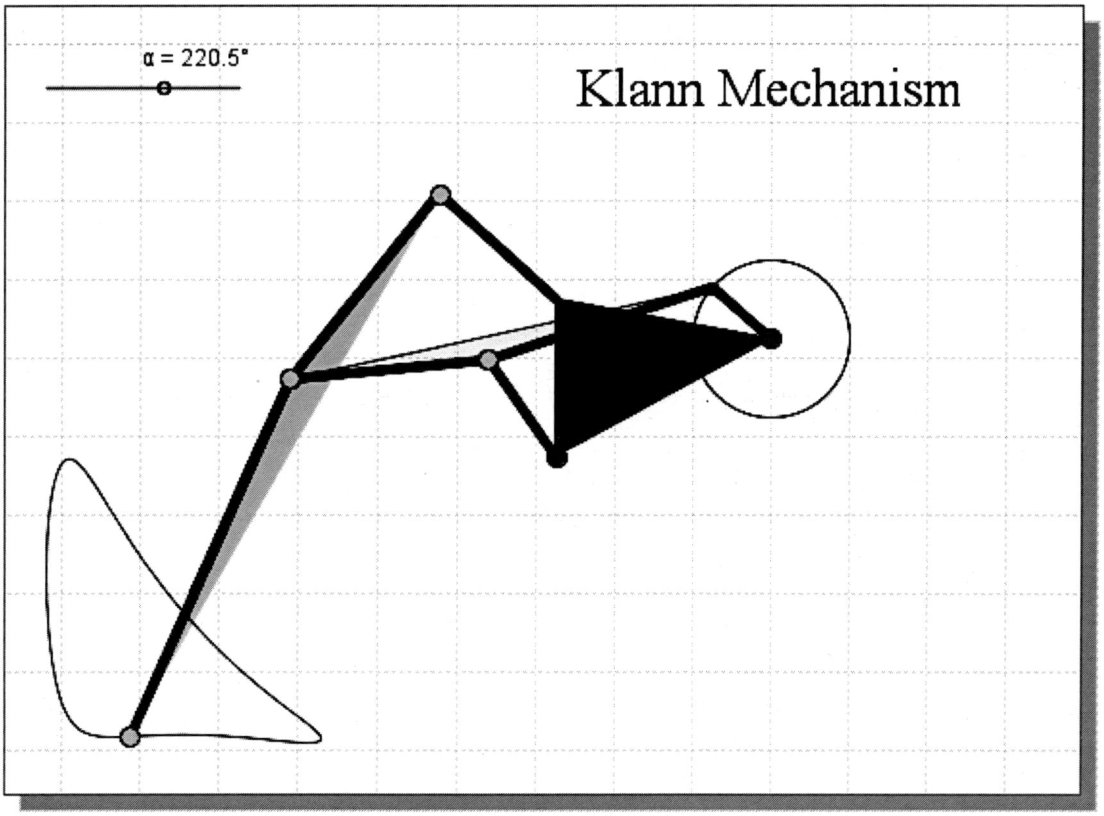

- Adding a second leg on the other side of the two mechanisms will show both of the configurations provide good walking motions.

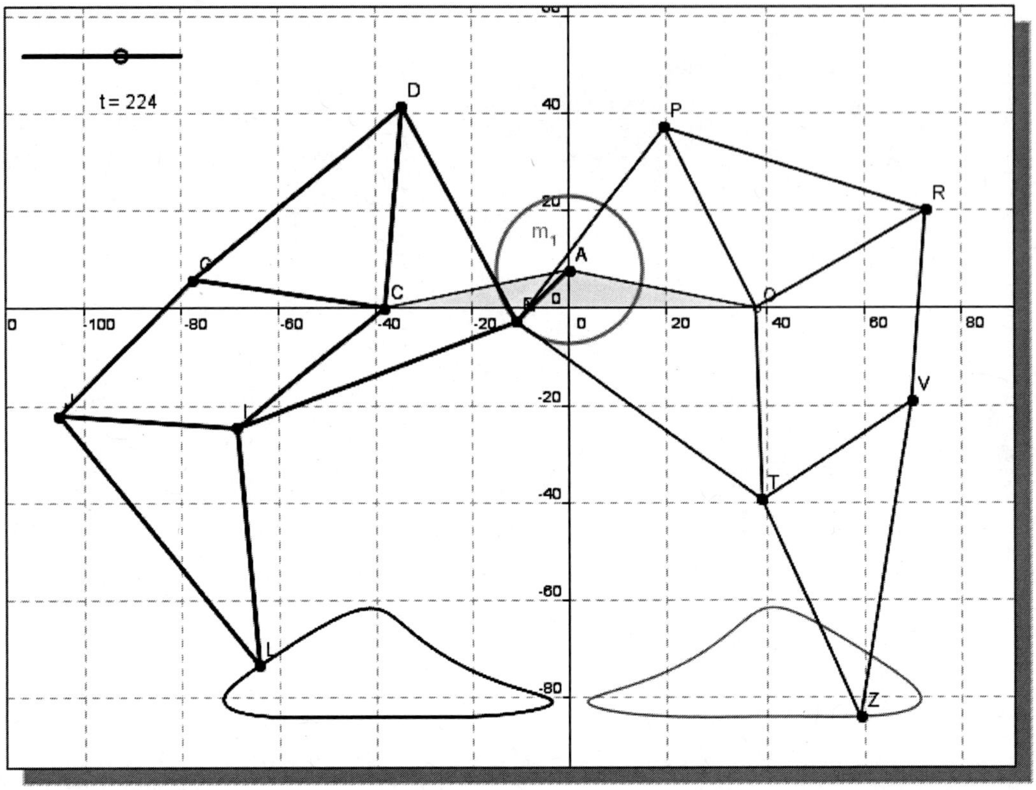

- Multiple copies of the same mechanism can provide better sychroization of the leg motions, also the center of gravity will always be at the center of the design.

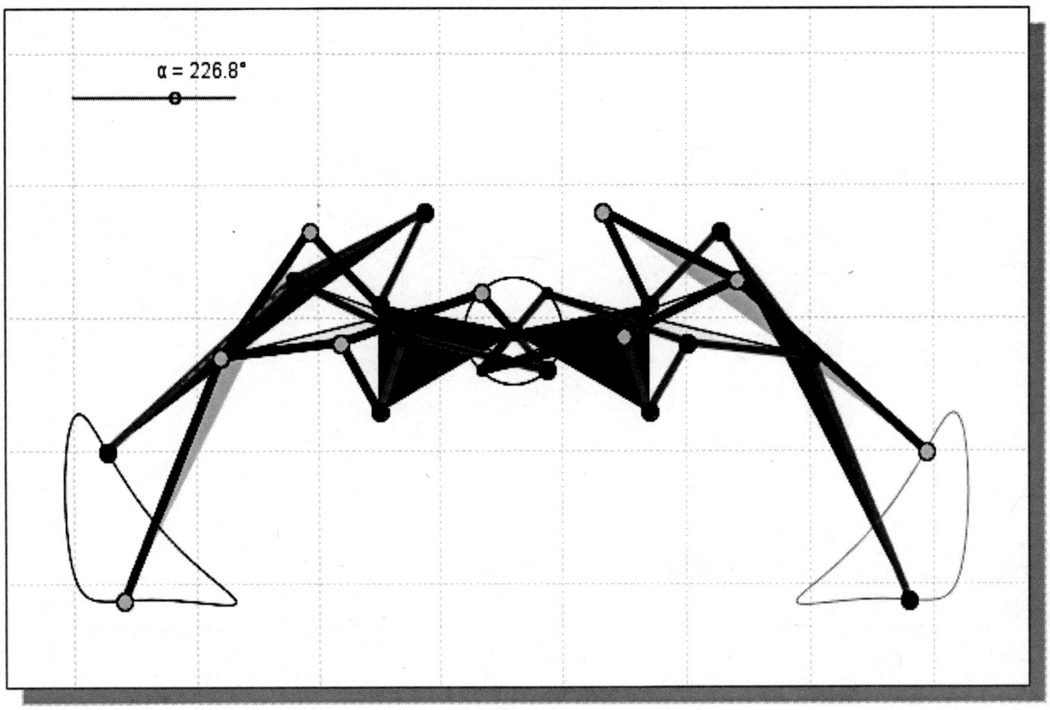

Exercises: (Design the following Planar Mechanisms with *GeoGebra*)

1. **Peaucellier Straight Line Mechanism**

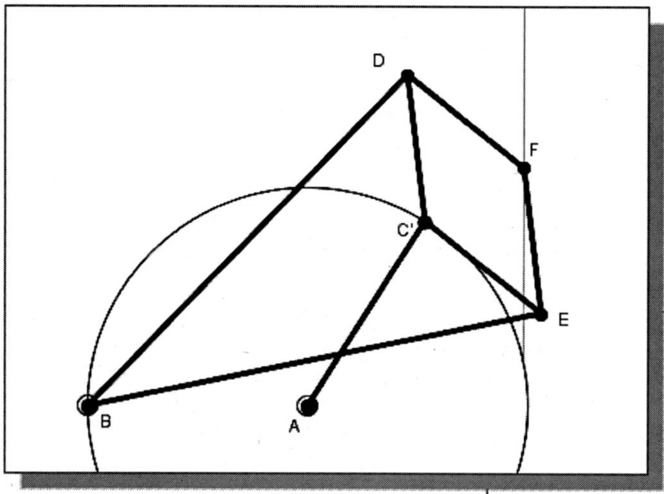

C'D = C'E = DF = EF

BD = BE

AC' = AB

A and B are fixed points.

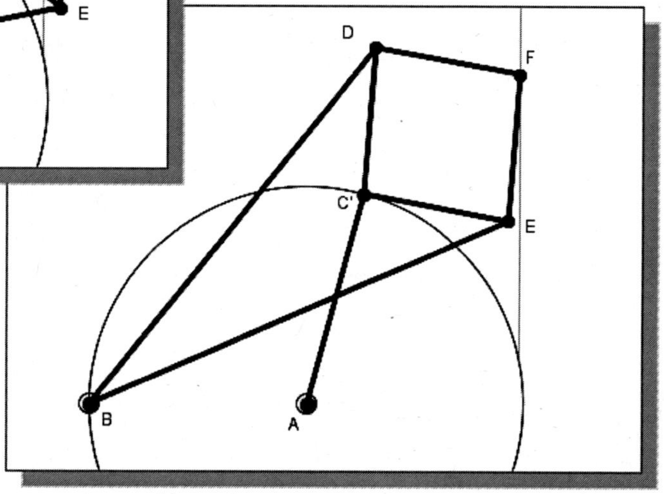

2. **Compound Mechanism**

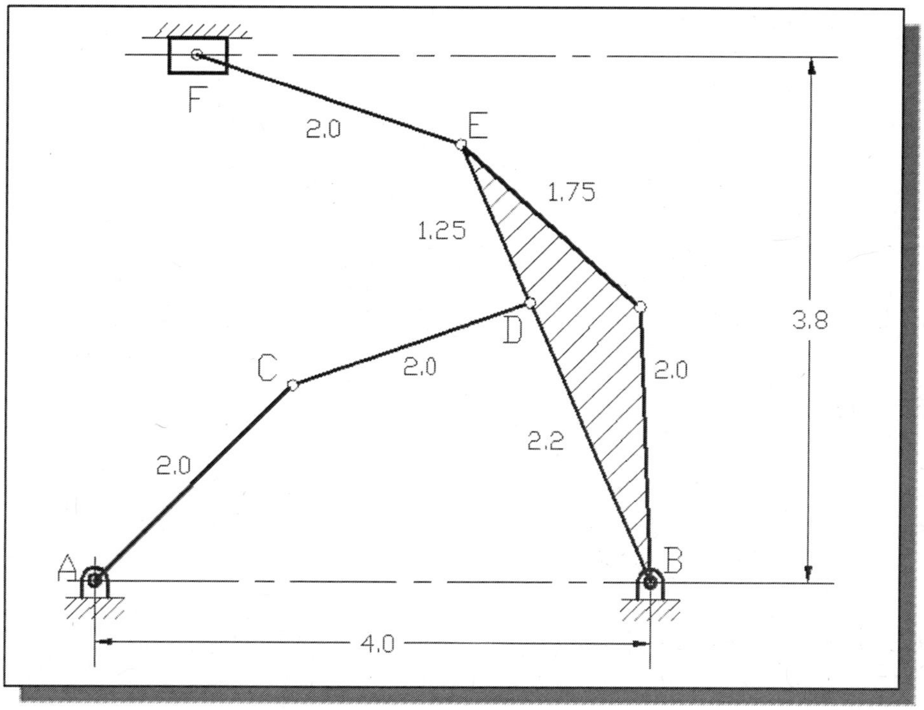

3. **Oscillating Sprinkler Mechanism**

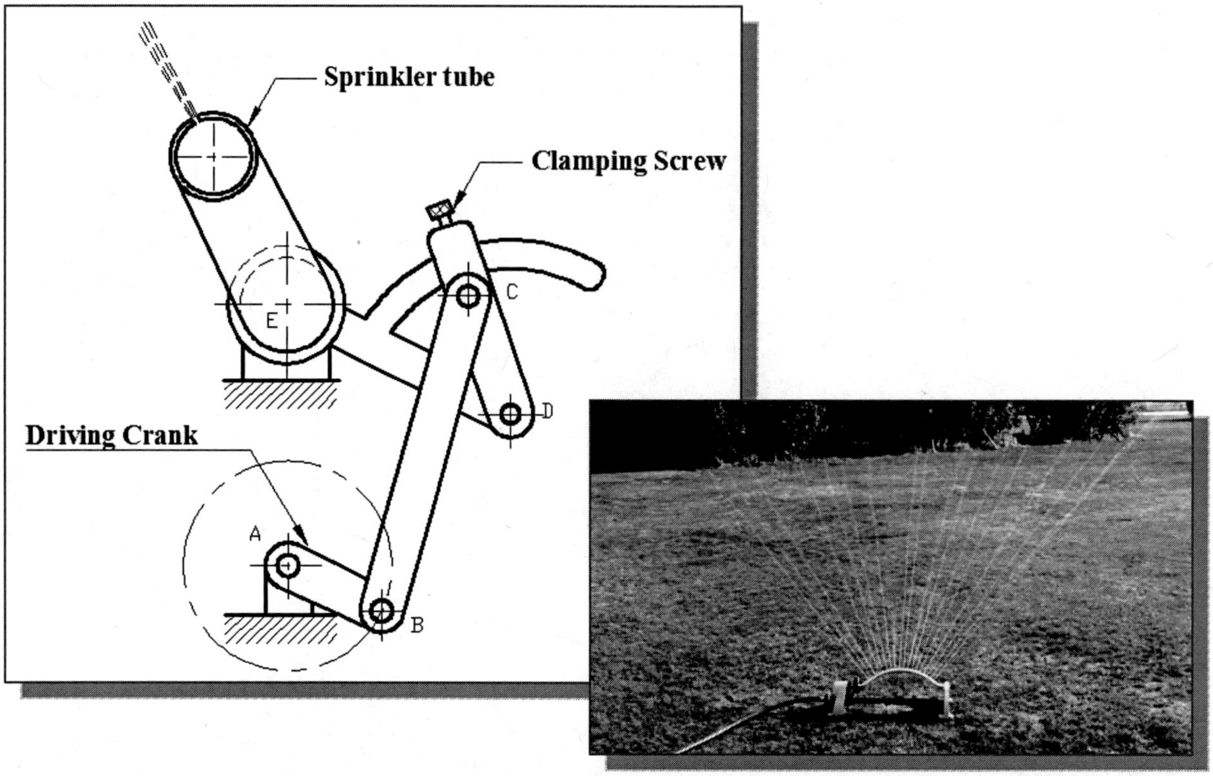

4. **Compound Mechanism (Point C slides on rigid Link BD)**

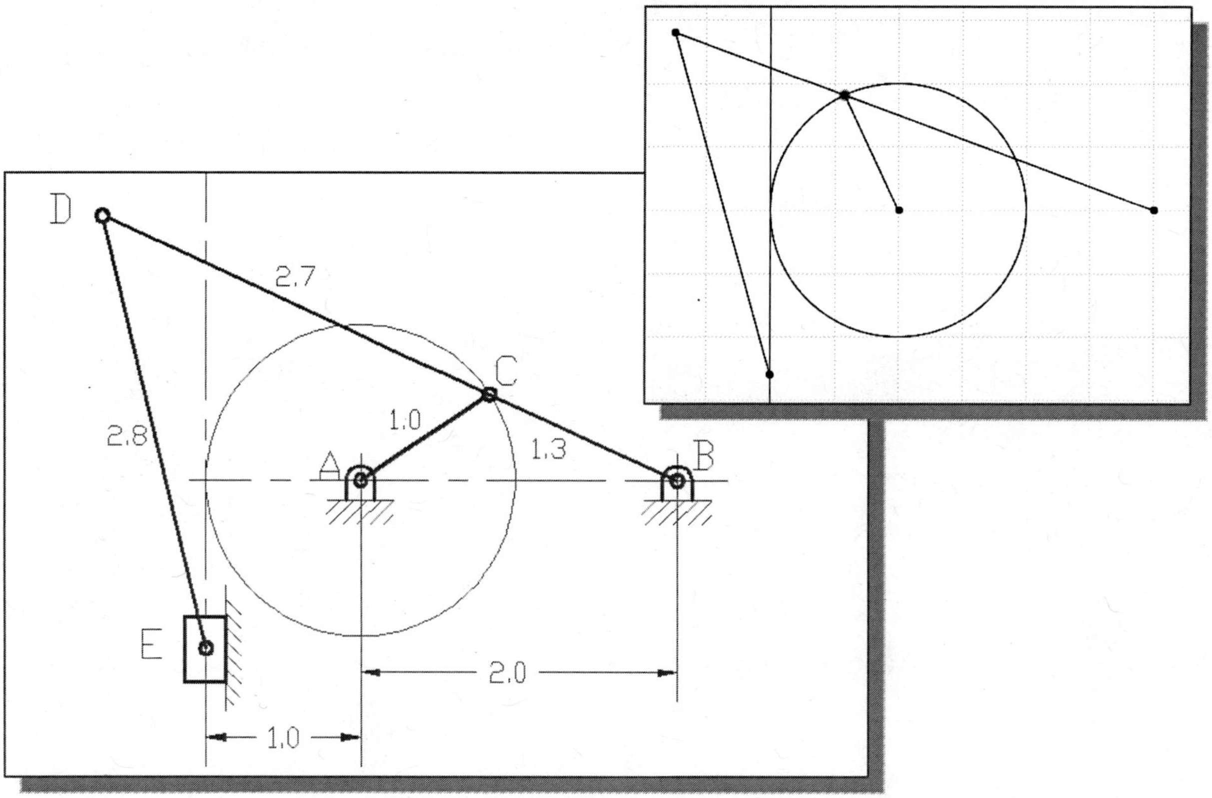

Chapter 12
Assembly Modeling and Motion Analysis

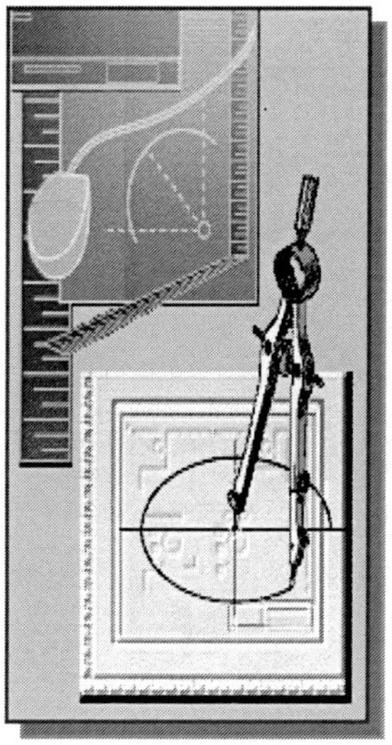

Learning Objectives

- Understand the Assembly Modeling Methodology
- Understand and Utilize Assembly relations
- Be able to use the mechanical Mates
- Utilize the SolidWorks Motion Analysis Option
- Record Animation Movies

Introduction

In the previous lessons, we have gone over the fundamentals of creating basic parts and drawings. In this lesson, we will examine the assembly modeling functionality of *SolidWorks*. We will start with a demonstration on how to create and modify assembly models. The main task in creating an assembly is establishing the assembly relationships between parts. To assemble parts into an assembly, we will need to consider the assembly relationships between parts. It is a good practice to assemble parts based on the way they would be assembled in the actual manufacturing process. We should also consider breaking down the assembly into smaller subassemblies, which helps the management of parts. In *SolidWorks*, a subassembly is treated the same way as a single part during assembling. Many parallels exist between assembly modeling and part modeling in parametric modeling software such as *SolidWorks*.

SolidWorks provides full associative functionality in all design modules, including assemblies. When we change a part model, *SolidWorks* will automatically reflect the changes in all assemblies that use the part. We can also modify a part in an assembly. **Bi-directional full associative functionality** is the main feature of parametric solid modeling software that allows us to increase productivity by reducing design cycle time.

Motion analysis can also be performed to visually confirm the proper assembly of the designs, also to check for any interference between mating parts and any other potential problems. In *SolidWorks*, several options are available to perform motion analysis, for example, the **Dynamic Simulation** module, the **SolidWorks Studio** module and the **Drive Constraint** tool. The Dynamic Simulation module can be used to perform a fairly in-depth motion analysis, while the Drive Constraint tool provides a relatively simple motion analysis that can be done in a matter of seconds.

In this chapter, the concepts and procedures of creating assemblies and using the *Design Library* for standard parts are illustrated. The procedure for basic motion analysis of the *Mechanical Tiger* assembly is also illustrated using the Drive Constraint tool.

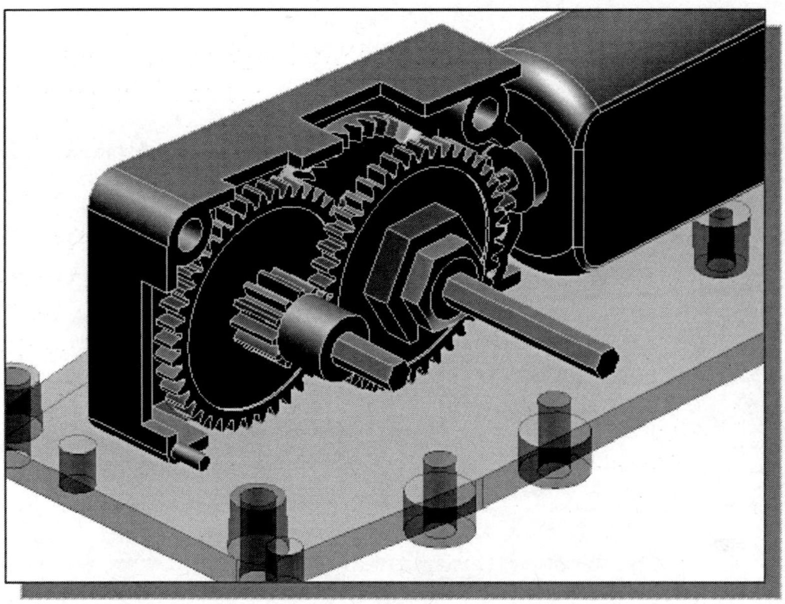

Assembly Modeling Methodology

The *SolidWorks Assembly Modeler* provides tools and functions that allow us to create 3D parametric assembly models. An assembly model is a 3D model with any combination of multiple part models. *Parametric assembly relations* can be used to control relationships between parts in an assembly model.

SolidWorks can work with any of the assembly modeling methodologies:

The Bottom Up Approach

The first step in the *bottom up* assembly modeling approach is to create the individual parts. The parts are then pulled together into an assembly. This approach is typically used for smaller projects with very few team members.

The Top Down Approach

The first step in the *top down* assembly modeling approach is to create the assembly model of the project. Initially, individual parts are represented by names or symbols. The details of the individual parts are added as the project gets further along. This approach is typically used for larger projects or during the conceptual design stage. Members of the project team can then concentrate on the particular section of the project to which he/she is assigned.

The Middle Out Approach

The *middle out* assembly modeling approach is a mixture of the bottom-up and top-down methods. This type of assembly model is usually constructed with most of the parts already created, and additional parts are designed and created using the assembly for construction information. Some requirements are known and some standard components are used, but new designs must also be produced to meet specific objectives. This combined strategy is a very flexible approach for creating assembly models.

The different assembly modeling approaches described above can be used as guidelines to manage design projects. Keep in mind that we can start modeling our assembly using one approach and then switch to a different approach without any problems.

In this lesson, the *bottom up* assembly modeling approach is illustrated. All of the parts (components) required to form the assembly are created first. *SolidWorks's* assembly modeling tools allow us to create complex assemblies by using components that are created in part files or are placed in assembly files. A component can be a subassembly or a single part, where features and parts can be modified at any time. The sketches and profiles used to build part features can be fully or partially constrained. Partially constrained features may be adaptive, which means the size or shape of the associated parts are adjusted in an assembly when the parts are constrained to other parts. The basic concept and procedure of using the adaptive assembly approach is demonstrated in the tutorial.

The *Mechanical Tiger* Assembly

Additional Parts

- Five additional parts are also required for the assembly: (1) ***Hex Shaft***, (2) ***Short Spacer***, (3) ***M1-Spacer***, (4) ***A3-Spacer*** and (5) **Shaft-3x80.** On your own, create the four parts as shown below; save the models as separate part files as shown.

(1) ***Hex Shaft (Flat to Flat 2.5mm x 27mm, Hex-Shaft.sldprt)***

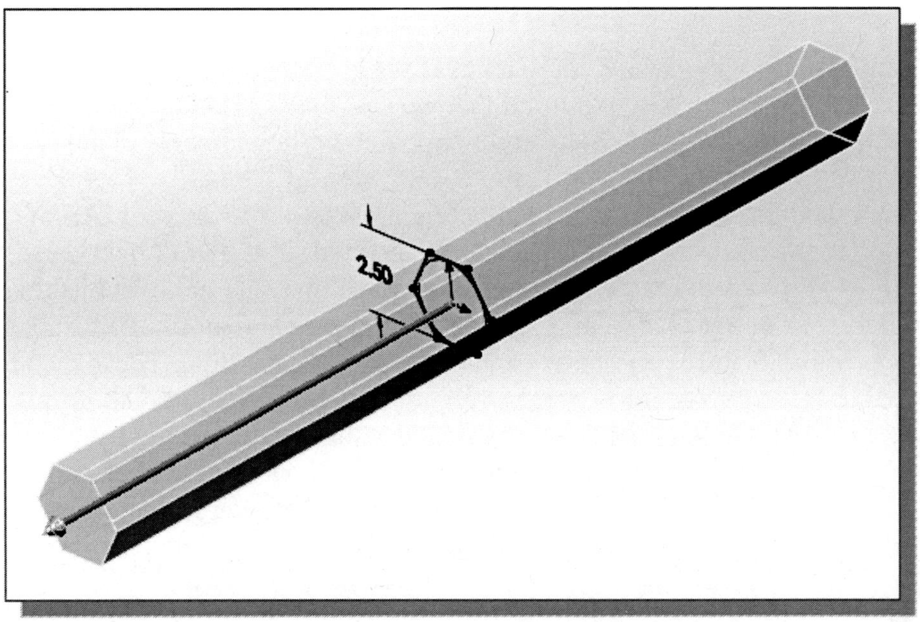

(2) ***Short Spacer (5.5mm x 3mm x 3.2mm, Spacer-Short.sldprt)***

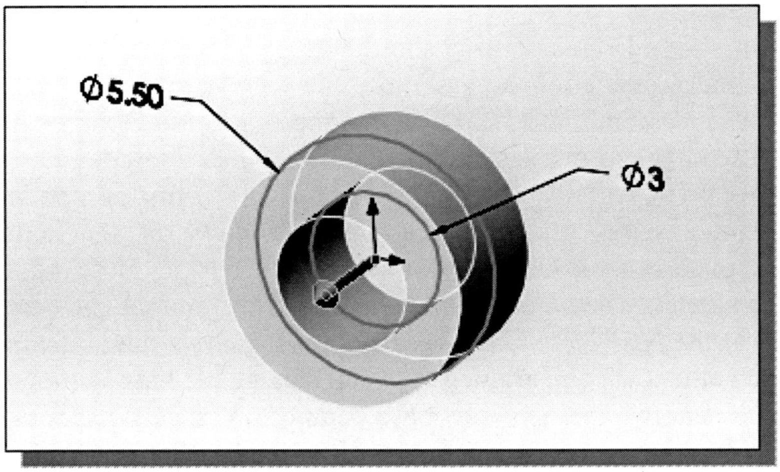

(3) ***M1-Spacer*** **(*6mm x 3mm x 5mm, M1-Spacer.sldprt*)**

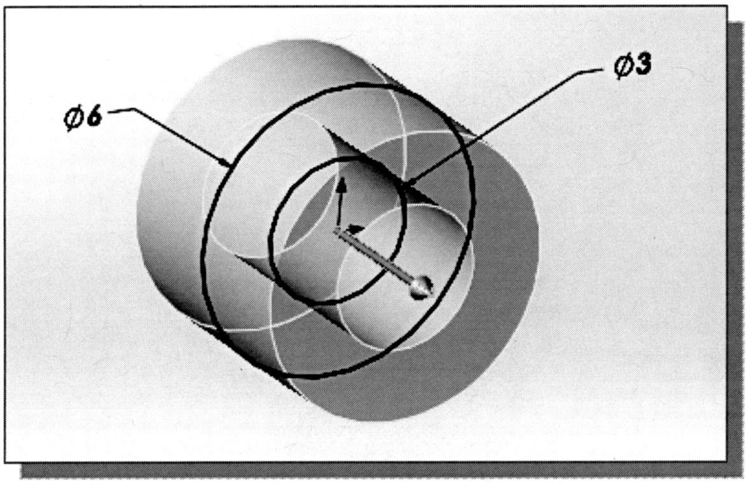

(4) ***A3-Spacer (6mm x 3mm x 7.5 mm, A3-Spacer.sldprt)***

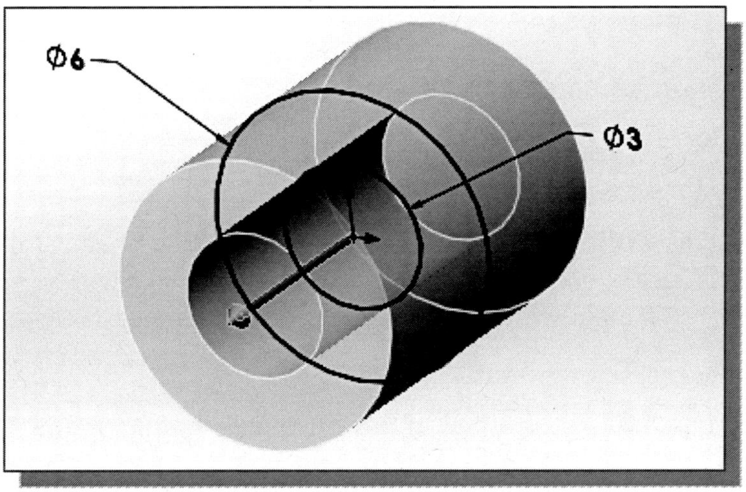

(5) ***Shaft-3x80*** **(Diameter 3mm X 80mm length, Shaft-3x80.sldprt)**
(Note: No image is provided for this simple part.)

Creating the Leg Subassembly

- The first component placed in an assembly should be a fundamental part or subassembly. The first component in an assembly file sets the orientation of all subsequent parts and subassemblies. The *Origin* of the first component is aligned to the *Origin* of the assembly coordinates and the part is grounded (all degrees of freedom are removed). The rest of the assembly is built on the first component, the ***base component***. In most cases, this *base component* should be one that is **not likely to be removed** and **preferably a non-moving part** in the design. Note that there is no distinction in an assembly between components; the first component we place is usually considered as the *base component* because it is usually a fundamental component to which others are constrained. We can change the base component to a different base component by placing a new base component, specifying it as grounded, and then re-constraining any components placed earlier, including the first component. For our project, we will use the ***B3-Leg*** as the base component in the assembly.

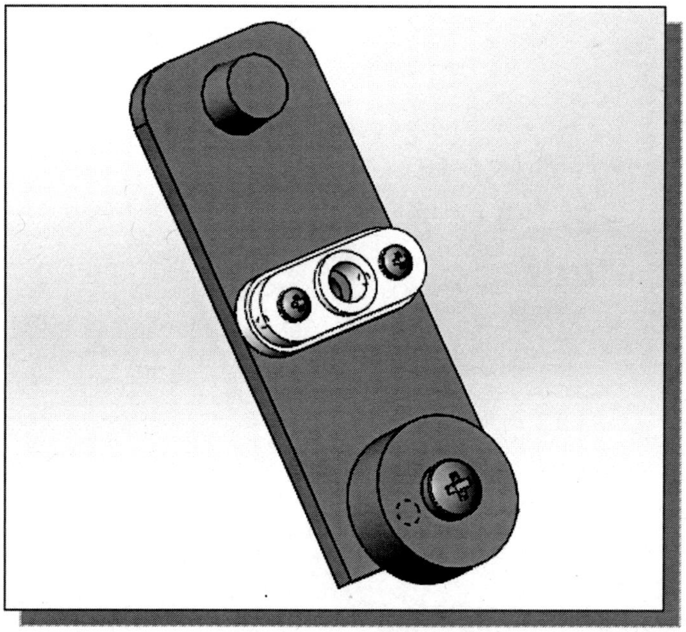

Starting *SolidWorks*

1. Select the **SolidWorks** option on the *Start* menu or select the **SolidWorks** icon on the desktop to start *SolidWorks*. The *SolidWorks* main window will appear on the screen.

2. Select the **New** icon with a single click of the left-mouse-button on the *Menu Bar*.

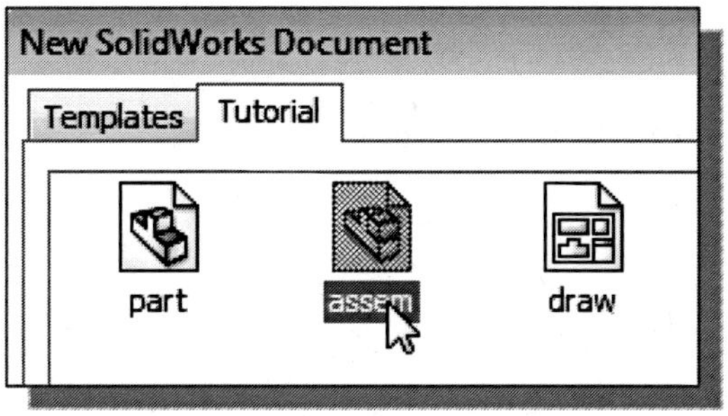

3. Select the **assem** template under the **Tutorial** tab as shown.

4. Click on the **OK** button to open a new assembly model.

❖ *SolidWorks* opens an assembly file, and automatically opens the *Begin Assembly Property Manager*. The message "*Select a part or assembly to insert ...*" appears in the *Property Manager*. *SolidWorks* expects you to insert the first component. We will first set the document properties before placing the components in the assembly.

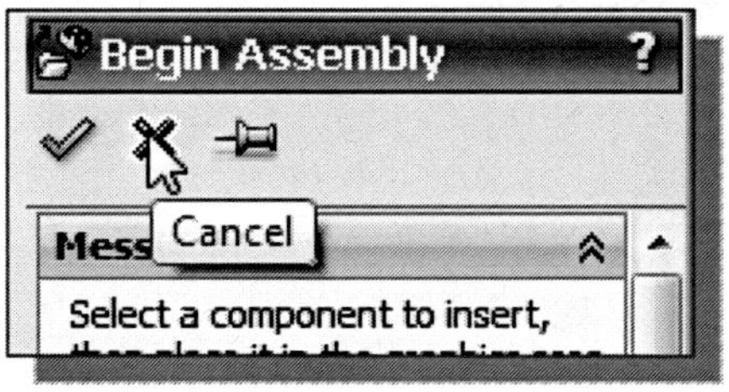

5. Cancel the **Begin Assembly** command by clicking once with the left-mouse-button on the **Cancel** icon in the *Property Manager* as shown.

Document Properties

1. Select the **Options** icon from the *Menu Bar* to open the *Options* dialog box.

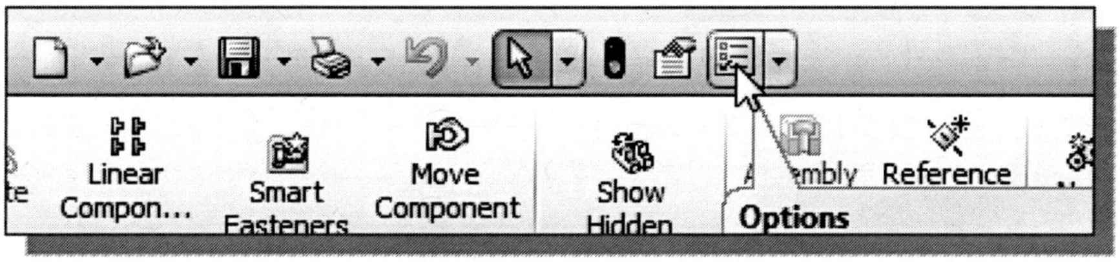

2. Select the **Document Properties** tab.

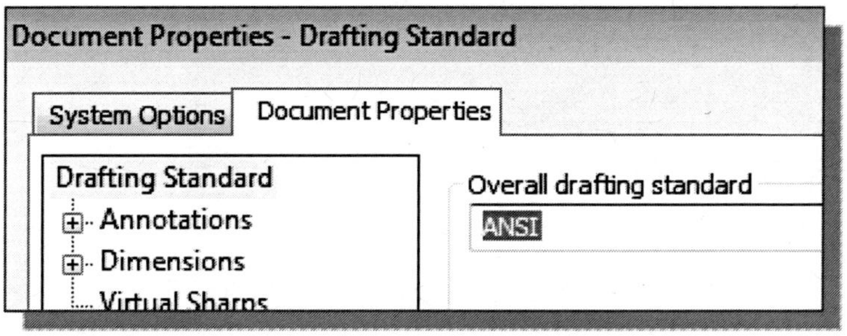

3. Select **ANSI** in the pull-down selection window under the *Overall drafting standard* panel as shown.

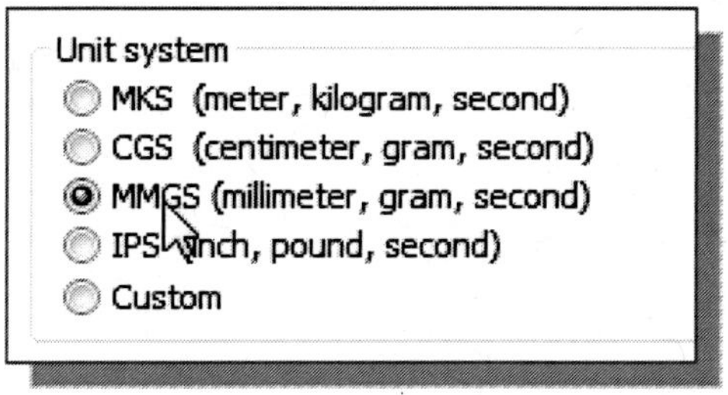

4. On your own, set the *Unit system* to **MMGS** as shown in the figure.

5. Click **OK** to accept the settings.

Place the First Component

- The first component inserted in an assembly should be a fundamental part or subassembly. The first component in an assembly file sets the orientation of all subsequent parts and subassemblies. The *Origin* of the first component is aligned to the *Origin* of the assembly coordinates and the part is grounded (all degrees of freedom are removed). The rest of the assembly is built on the first component, the ***base component***. In most cases, this *base component* should be one that is **not likely to be removed** and **preferably a non-moving part** in the design. Note that there is no distinction in an assembly between components; the first component we place is usually considered as the *base fixed component* because it is usually a fundamental component to which others are constrained. We can change the base component if desired. For our project, we will use the ***Leg*** part as the base component in the subassembly.

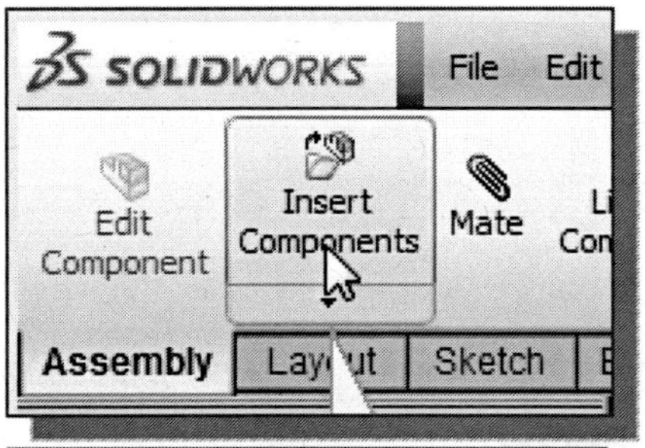

1. In the *Assembly* toolbar panel, select the **Insert Components** command by left-mouse-clicking the icon.

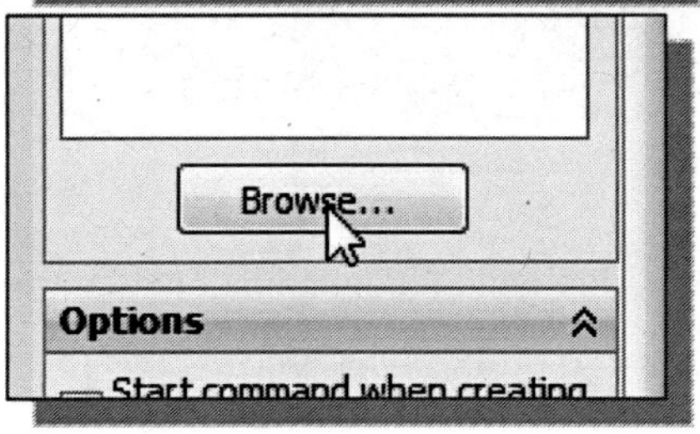

2. Click **Browse** in the *Property Manager* as shown.

3. Select the ***B3-Leg*** (part file: ***B3-Leg.sldprt***) in the list window.

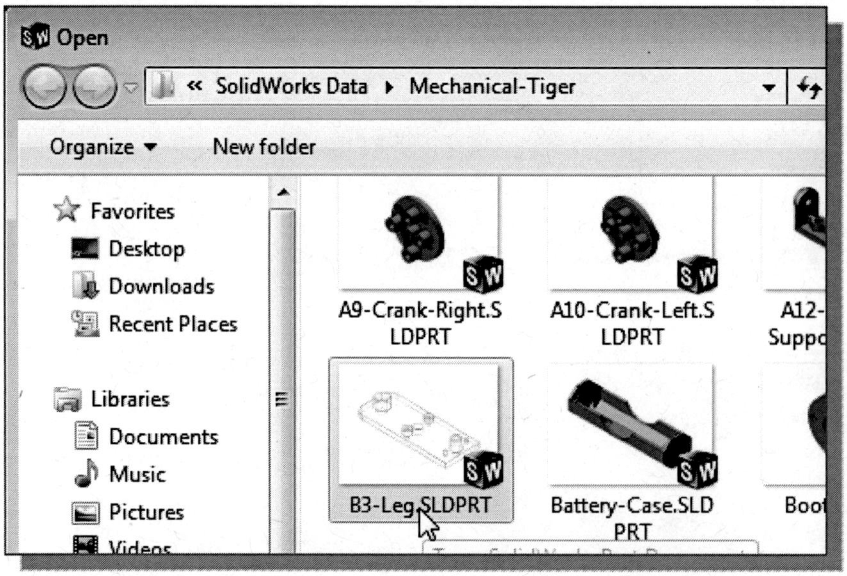

4. Click on the **Open** button to retrieve the model.

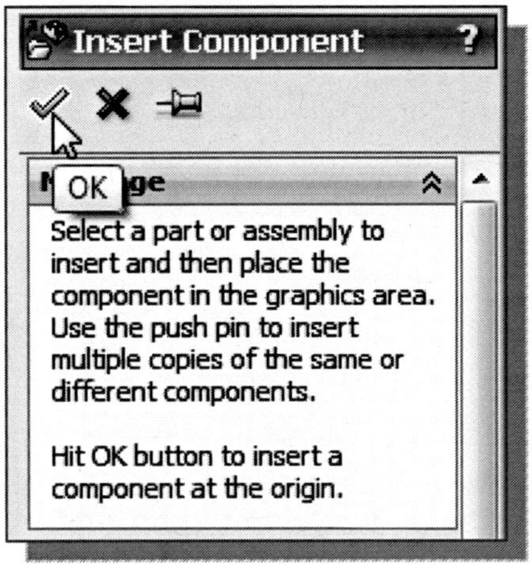

5. Note that we can place the component anywhere or click **OK** to align the component *Origin* to the *Origin* of the assembly model. Click **OK** to place the *B3-Leg* part.

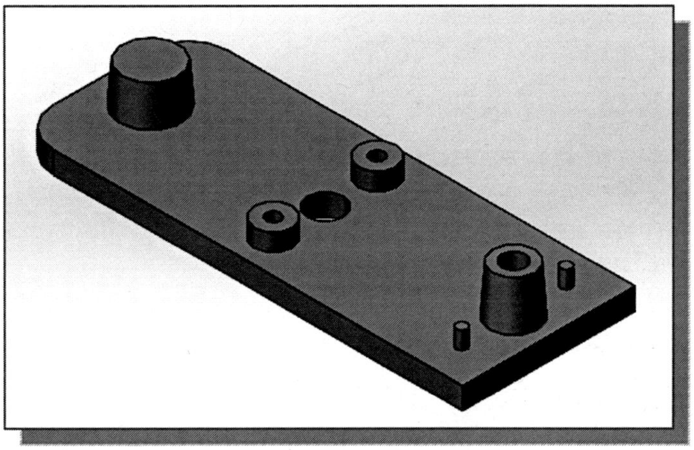

Place the Second Component

➢ We will retrieve the *Knee* part as the second component of the assembly model.

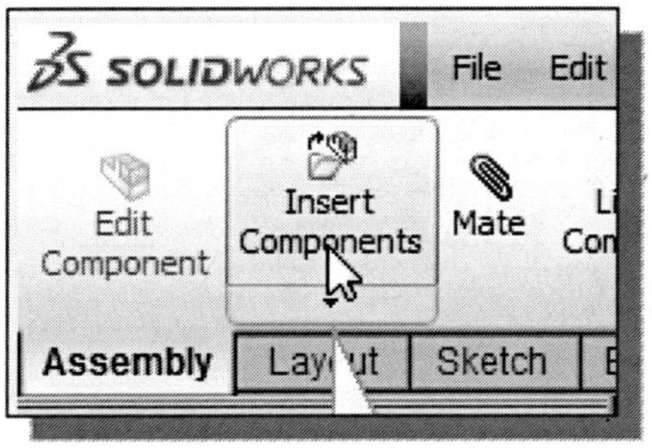

1. In the *Assembly* toolbar panel, select the **Insert Components** command by left-mouse-clicking the icon.

2. On your own, select the ***Knee*** design (part file: ***A6-Knee.sldprt***) in the list window.

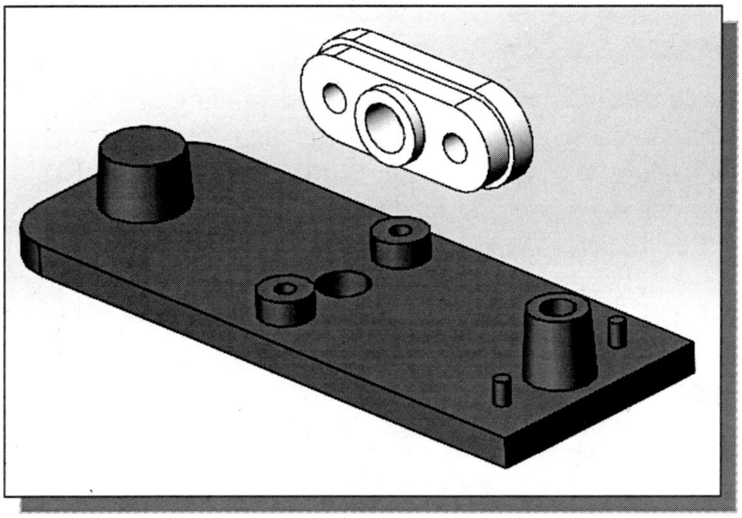

3. Place the *A6-Knee* part toward the upper right side of the base component, as shown in the figure.

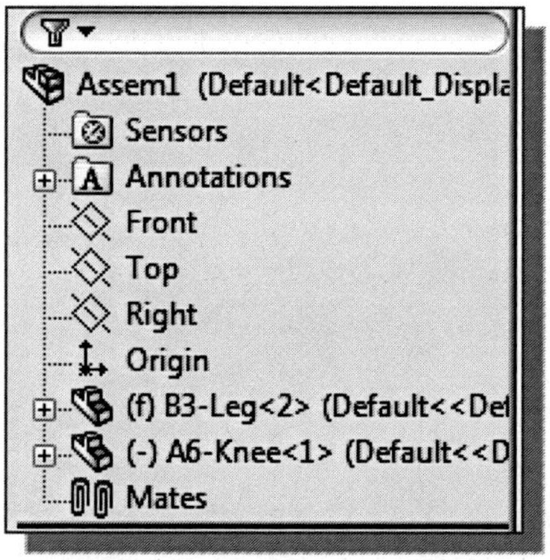

- Inside the *Model History* area, the retrieved parts are listed in their corresponding order. The **(f)** in front of the B3-Leg filename signifies the part is grounded and all ***six degrees of freedom*** are restricted. The number behind the filename is used to identify the number of copies of the same component in the assembly model.

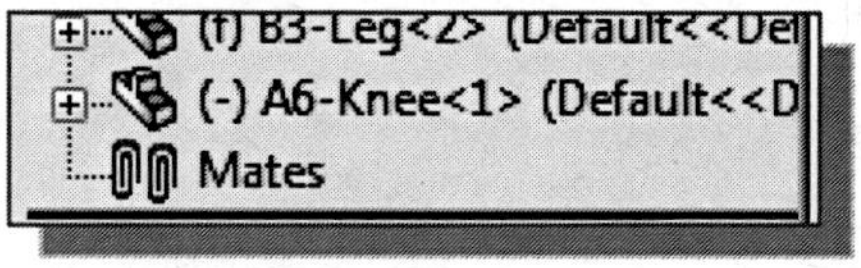

- The **Mates** item listed in the *Model History* area will include all of the applied ***assembly relations***.

Degrees of Freedom and Assembly Relations

- Each component in an assembly has six **degrees of freedom** (**DOF**), or ways in which rigid 3D bodies can move: movement along the X, Y, and Z axes (translational freedom), plus rotation around the X, Y, and Z axes (rotational freedom). *Translational DOF*s allow the part to move in the direction of the specified vector. *Rotational DOF*s allow the part to turn about the specified axis.

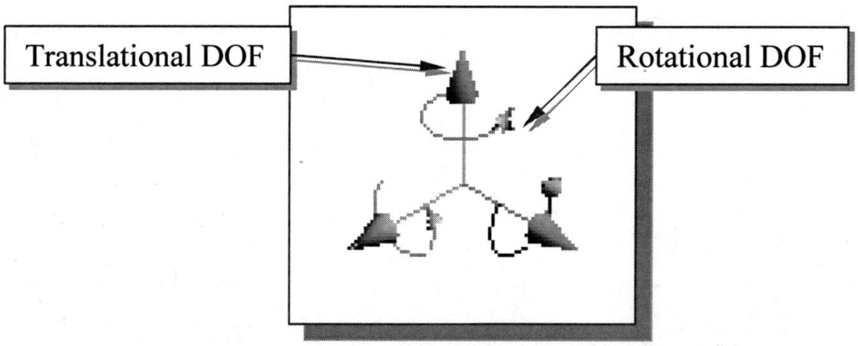

➢ It is usually a good idea to fully constrain components so that their behavior is predictable as changes are made to the assembly. Leaving some degrees of freedom open can sometimes help retain design flexibility. As a general rule, we should use only enough assembly mate relations to ensure predictable assembly behavior and avoid unnecessary complexity. For the leg subassembly, we want to constrain all parts, as there are no moving parts in the assembly. However, for the main assembly of the *Mechanical Tiger* design, the proper assembly of all of the moving parts is critical; this is to assure the simulation of the design can be achieved. In *SolidWorks*, the *assembly relations* are called ***assembly mates***.

Assembly Mates

- We are now ready to assemble the components together. We will start by placing assembly relations on the ***Leg*** and the ***Knee*** using *SolidWorks* ***assembly mates***. Mates create geometric relationships between assembly components. Mates define the allowable directions of linear or rotational motion of the components, limiting the degrees of freedom. A component can be moved within its degrees of freedom, visualizing the assembly's behavior.

  To assemble components into an assembly, we need to establish the assembly relationships between components. It is a good practice to assemble components the way they would be assembled in the actual manufacturing process. **Assembly mates** create a parent/child relationship that allows us to capture the design intent of the assembly. Because the component that we are placing actually becomes a child to the already assembled components, we must use caution when choosing mate types and references to make sure they reflect the intent.

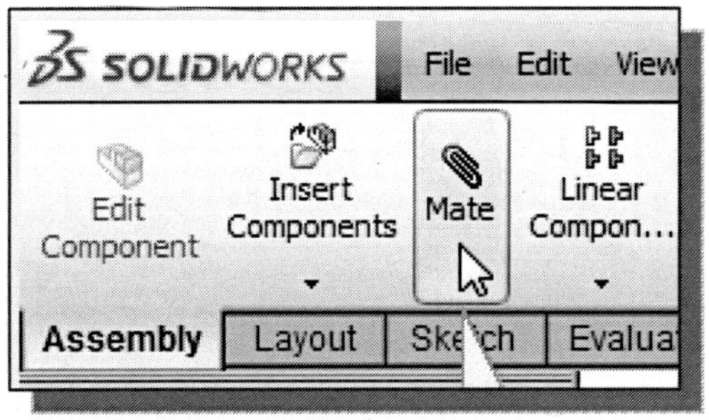

1. In the *Assembly* toolbar, select the **Mate** command by left-mouse-clicking once on the icon.

- The *Mate Property Manager* appears on the screen.

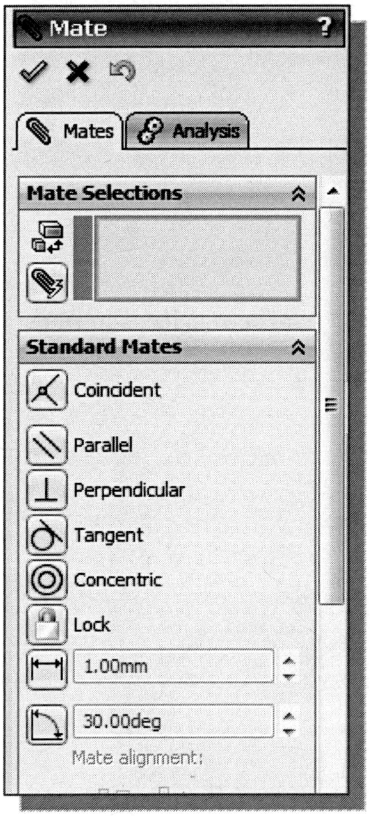

- Assembly models are created by applying proper *assembly relations* to the individual components. The Mate relations are used to restrict the movement between parts. Mate relations eliminate rigid body degrees of freedom (**DOF**). A 3D part has *six degrees of freedom* since the part can rotate and translate relative to the three coordinate axes. Each time we add a Mate relation between two parts, one or more DOF is eliminated. The movement of a fully constrained part is restricted in all directions.

- Seven basic types of assembly mates, called Standard Mates, are available in *SolidWorks*: Coincident, Parallel, Perpendicular, Tangent, Concentric, Distance, and Angle. Each type of mate removes different combinations of rigid body degrees of freedom. Note that it is possible to apply different constraints and achieve the same results.

- **Mechanical Mates** includes mates for mechanical devices, such as Cam and Gear.

The **Standard Mates** are described below:

- **Coincident** – positions selected faces, edges, and planes (in combination with each other or combined with a single vertex) so they share the same infinite line. Positions two vertices so they touch.

- **Parallel** – places the selected items so they lie in the same direction and remain a constant distance apart from each other.

- **Perpendicular** – places the selected items at a 90 degree angle to each other.

- **Tangent** – places the selected items in a tangent mate (at least one selection must be a cylindrical, conical, or spherical face).

- **Concentric** – places the selections so that they share the same center point.

- **Lock** – remove all six degrees of freedom.

- **Distance** – places the selected items with the specified distance between them.

- **Angle** – places the selected items at the specified angle to each other.

Apply the First Assembly Mate

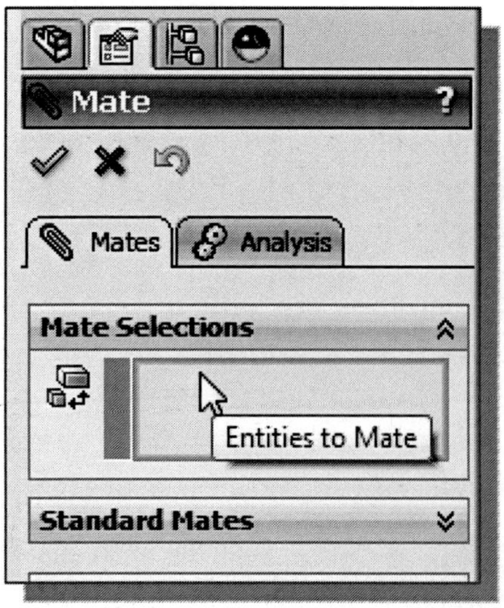

1. Note that the *Mate Selections* panel in the *Mate Property Manager* is highlighted.

2. Select the **top horizontal surface** of the flat plate of the *B3-Leg* part as the first selection for the Mate command.

3. On your own, dynamically rotate the displayed model to view the bottom of the ***Knee*** part, as shown in the figure.

4. Click on the bottom face of the ***Knee*** part as the second part selection to apply the constraint.

5. Confirm the *mate type* is set to **Coincident** and click on the **OK** button to accept the selection and apply the Coincident mate.

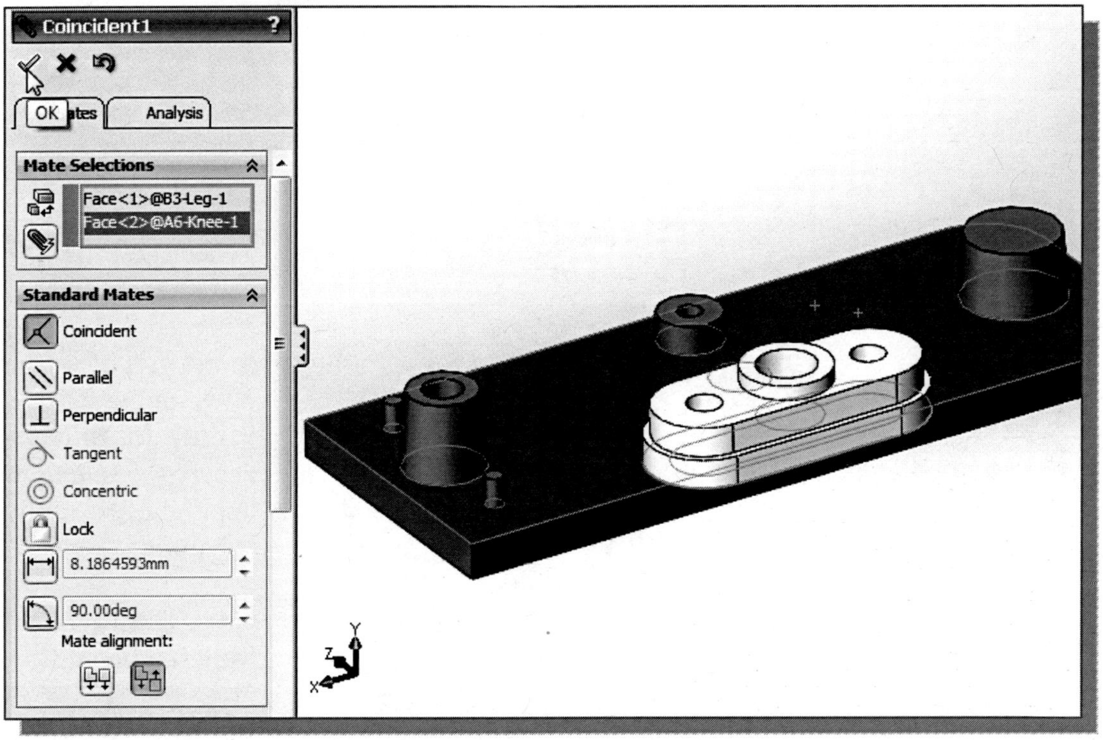

❖ The applied Coincident mate constraint removes one degree of linear translation and two degrees of angular rotation between the selected planar surfaces. The ***A6-Knee*** part can still move along two axes and rotate about the third axis.

Apply a Second Assembly Mate

❖ The **Concentric** constraint can be used to align axes of cylindrical features.

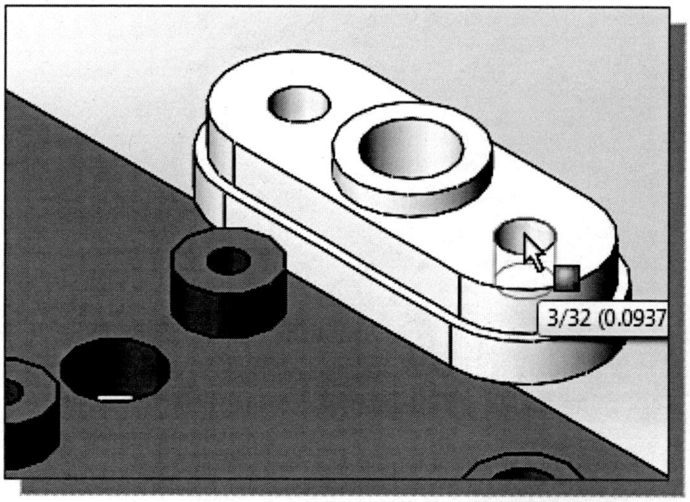

1. Move the cursor near the cylindrical surface of the right hole of the ***Knee*** part. Select the cylindrical surface when it is highlighted as shown. (Hint: Use the dynamic **Zoom** option to assist the selection.)

2. Move the cursor near the cylindrical surface of the small hole on the ***B3-Leg*** part. Select the surface when it is highlighted as shown.

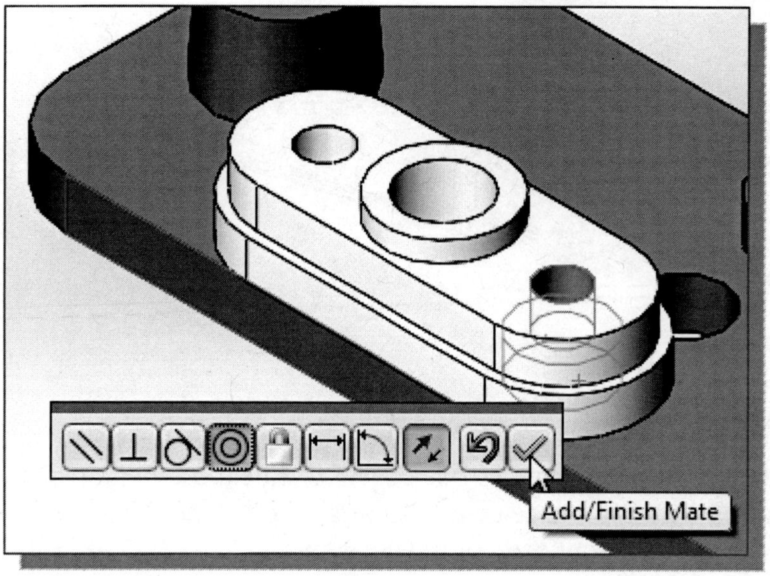

3. In the graphics window, click on the **Add/ Finish Mate** button to accept the selection and apply the assembly constraint.

4. Click **Close** to exit the Mate command.

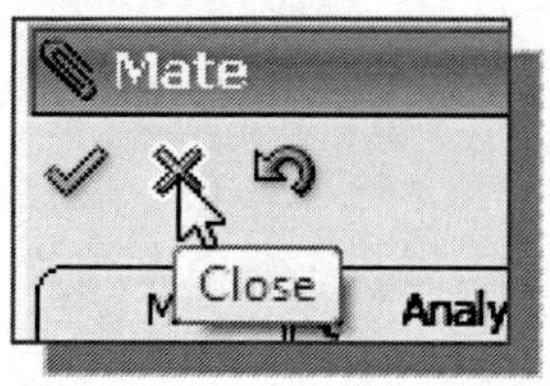

Constrained Move

❖ To see how well a component is constrained, we can perform a ***constrained move***. A constrained move is done by dragging the component in the graphics window with the left-mouse-button. A constrained move will honor previously applied assembly relations. That is, the selected component and parts constrained to the component move together in their constrained positions. A grounded component remains grounded during the move.

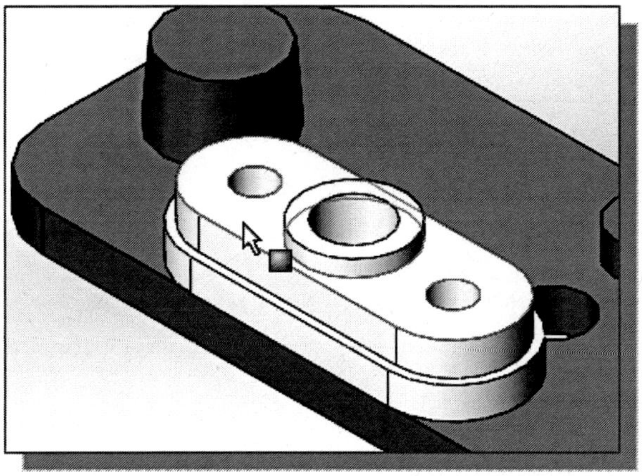

1. Inside the graphics window, move the cursor on top of the larger horizontal surface of the *Knee* part as shown in the figure.

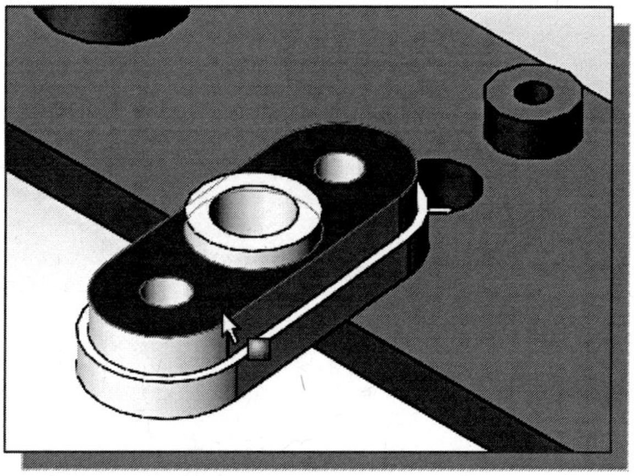

2. Press and hold down the left-mouse-button and drag the *A6-Knee* part toward the front side.

❖ The *A6-Knee* part can still rotate about the displayed axis, while the applied constraints are maintained.

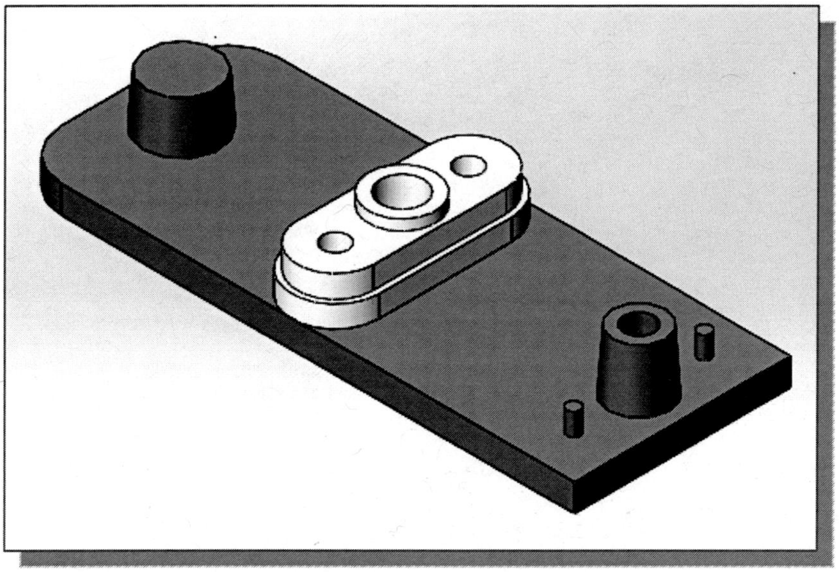

3. On your own, apply another **Mate** constraint to align the *A6-Knee* part as shown.

❖ Note the parts in the assembly are fully constrained.

Place the Third Component

➢ We will retrieve the *A8-Rod Pin* part as the third component of the assembly model.

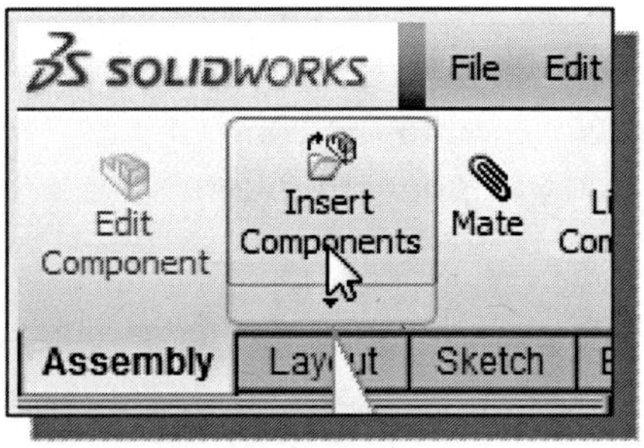

1. In the *Assembly* toolbar, select the **Insert Components** command by left-mouse-clicking the icon.

2. Click **Browse** in the *Property Manager*.

3. Select the ***A8-Rod Pin*** design in the list window. Click on the **Open** button to retrieve the model.

4. Place the *A8-Rod Pin* part toward the upper right corner of the graphics window, as shown in the figure.

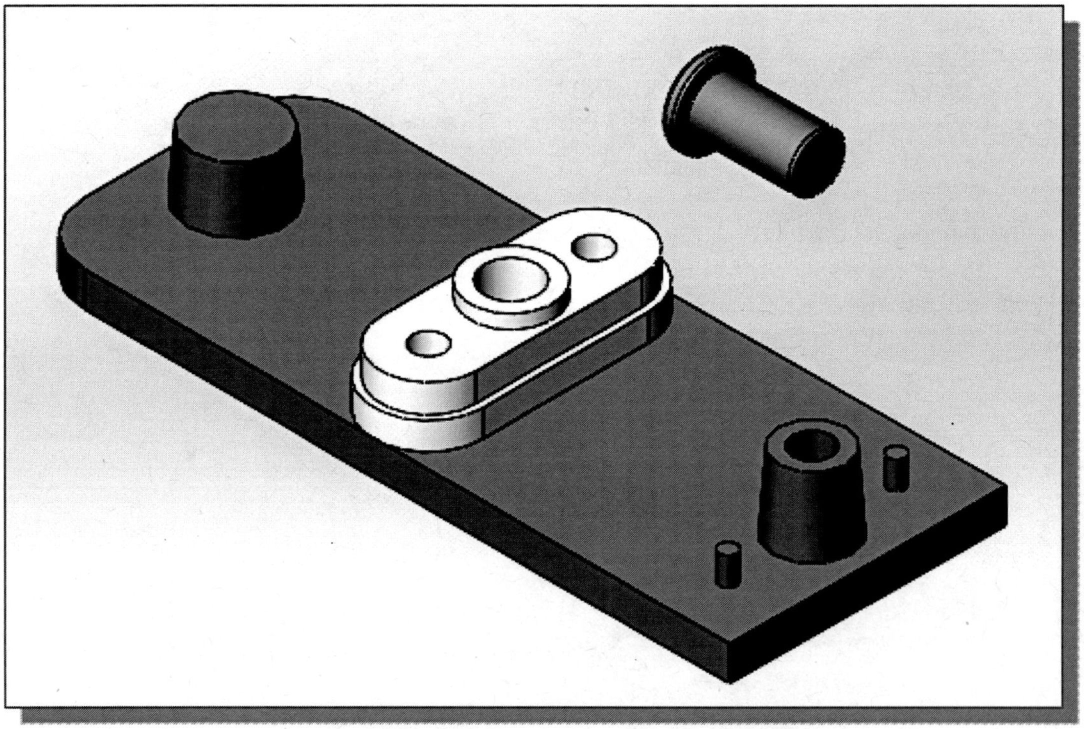

❖ Notice the *A8-Rod Pin* part was created using the Metric (mm) units set, while the *Leg* part was created using the English (inch) units set. Models created in *SolidWorks* can be using different units, for both size and location definitions. Any adjustments to dimensions can also be done using any units.

Apply a Coincident Mate

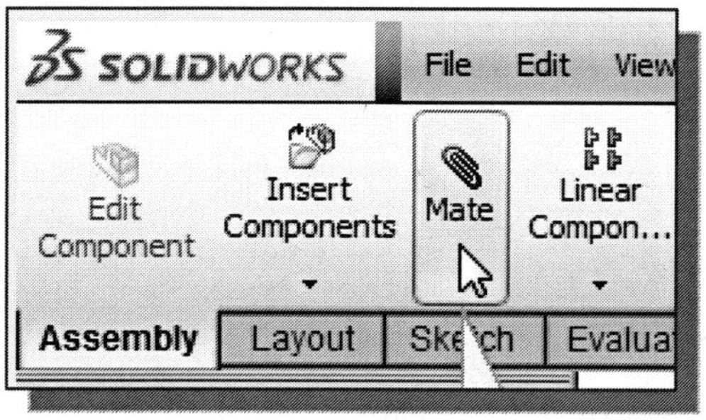

1. In the *Assembly* panel, select the **Mate** command by left-mouse-clicking once on the icon.

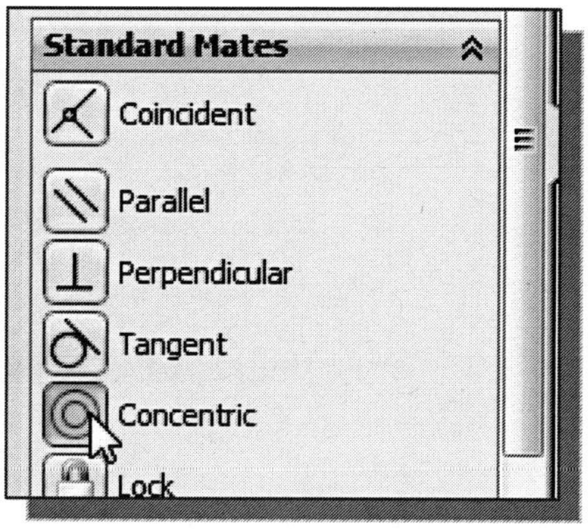

2. In the *Standard Mates* option list, switch to the **Concentric** mate constraint.

3. Select the end circle of the ***A8-Rod Pin*** part as the first object to apply the **Concentric** constraint, as shown in the figure.

4. Use the quick-key combination and dynamically rotate the display to view the bottom side of the ***Leg*** part; select the top cylindrical surface as shown.

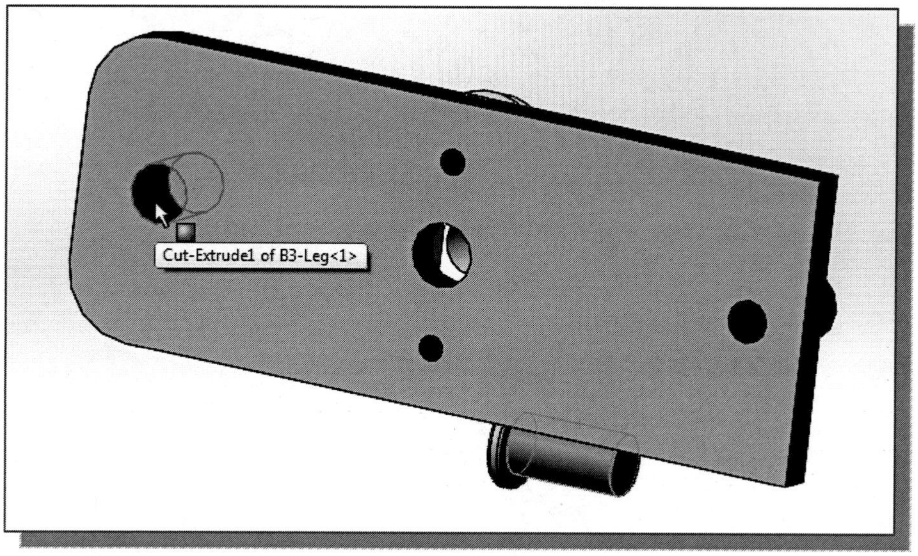

5. Select the inside circle of the top cylindrical surface of the *B3-Leg* part as the second surface to apply the **Concentric** constraint, as shown in the figure.

6. Click on the **Add/Finish Mate** button to accept the settings.

7. On your own, apply a **Coincident** mate to the end surface of the *A8-Rod Pin* part

➢ Note that one rotational degree of freedom remains open; the *A8-Rod Pin* part can still freely rotate about its center axis.

Apply an Anti-Aligned Mate

- Besides selecting the surfaces of solid models to apply constraints, we can also select the established datum planes to apply the assembly relations. This is an additional advantage of using the *BORN* technique in creating part models. For the *A8-Rod Pin* part, we will apply another **Mate** constraint to two of the datum planes and eliminate the last rotational DOF.

1. On your own, inside the graphics window expands the *Model Tree* of the *B3-Leg* part.

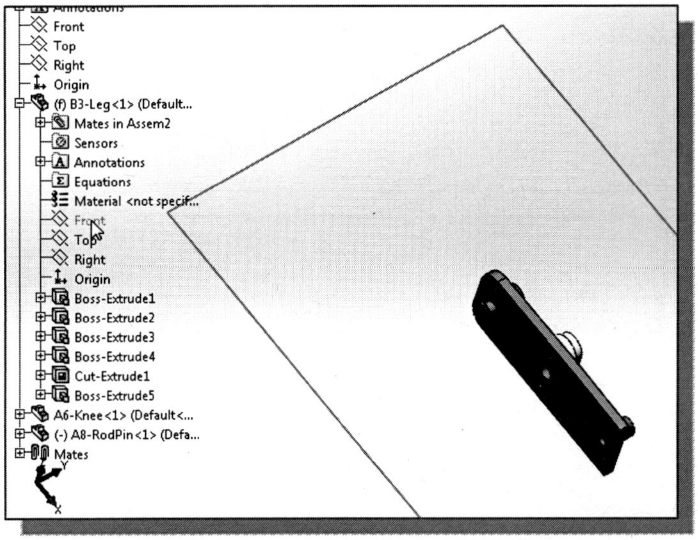

2. Select the **datum plane** of the *B3-Leg* part aligned in the length direction as the first part for the **Coincident** mate command.

3. Select the corresponding **datum plane** of the *A8-Rod Pin* part as the second part for the **Coincident** command.

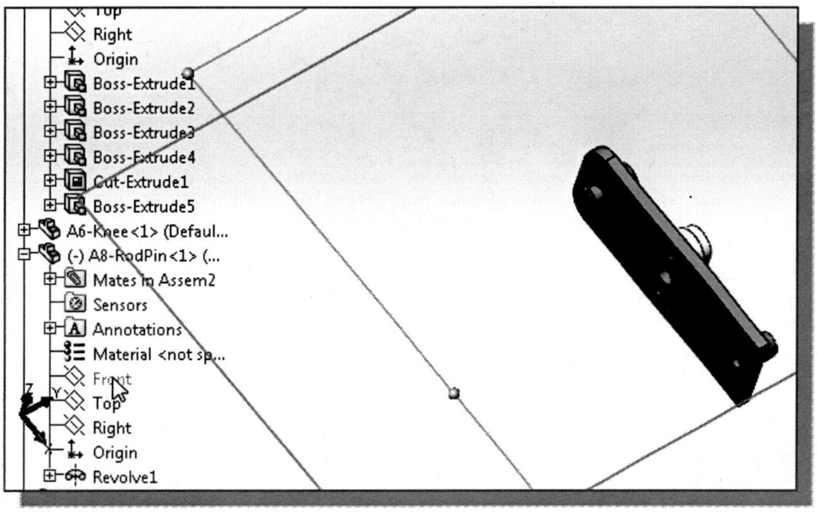

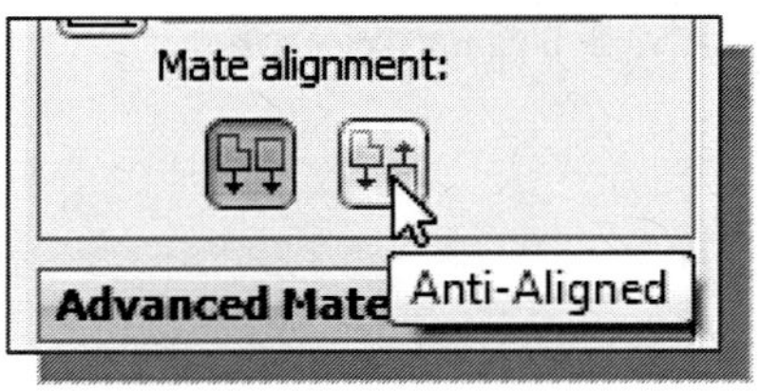

- ❖ Note that the **Anti-Aligned Coincident** constraint makes two planes coplanar with their faces facing each other.

4. In the *Mate Property Manager*, click on the **OK** button to accept the settings.

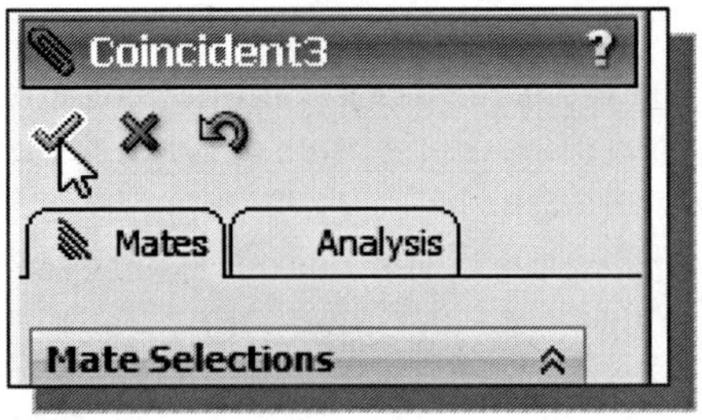

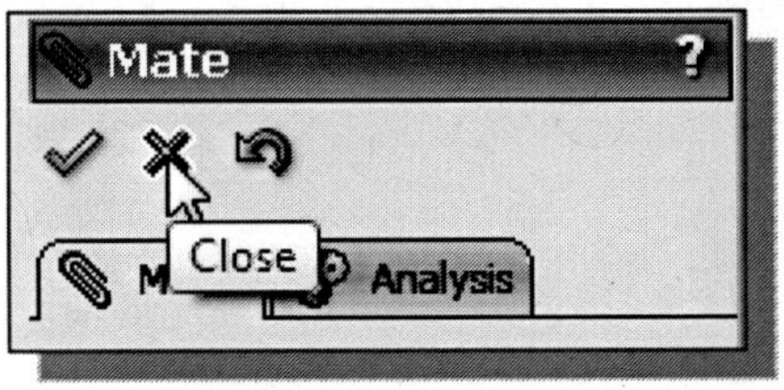

5. In the *Property Manager*, click on the **Cancel** button to exit the **Mate** command.

❖ Note all of the parts in the assembly are now all fully constrained.

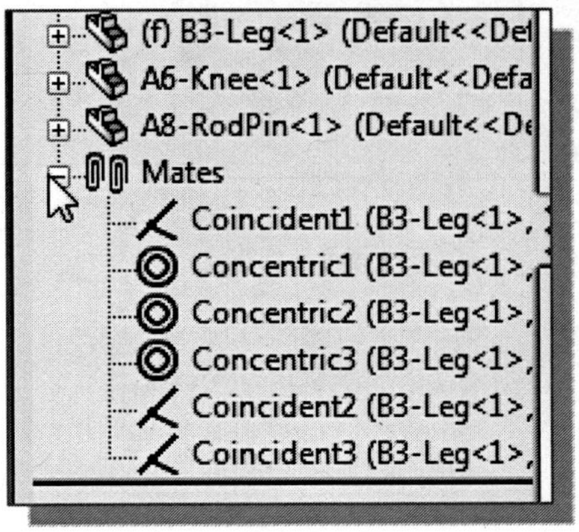

- Note the applied assembly mate constraints are also listed in the property manager. The *Model History Tree* for an assembly model behaves very similarly to a regular parametric part; all modifications can be performed throughout the *Model History Tree.*

Edit Parts in the Assembly Mode

❖ We will next place a copy of the *Boot* part in the assembly model. We will also illustrate the procedure to edit parts in the *Assembly* mode.

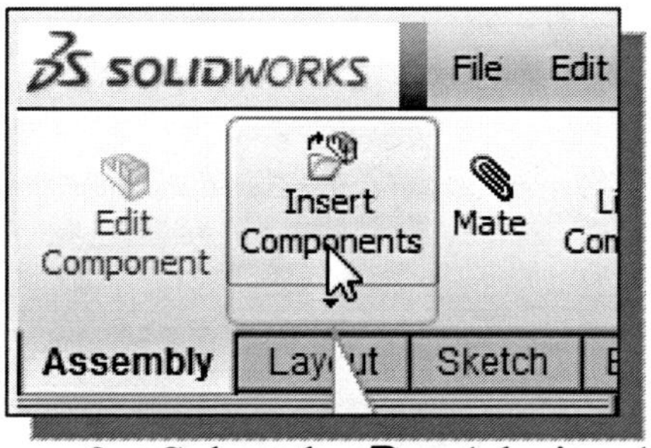

1. In the *Assembly* toolbar, select the **Insert Components** command by left-mouse-clicking once on the icon.

2. Click **Browse** in the *Property Manager*.

3. Select the ***Boot*** design (part file: ***Boot.sldprt***) in the list window. Click on the **Open** button to retrieve the model.

4. Place a copy of the ***Boot*** part on one side of the *A8-Rod Pin* by clicking once on the screen as shown in the figure.

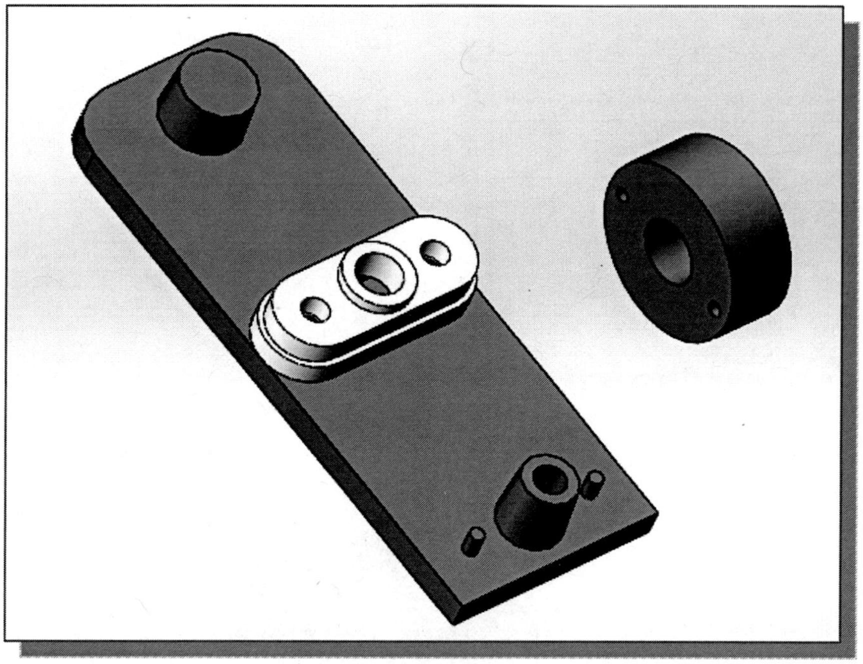

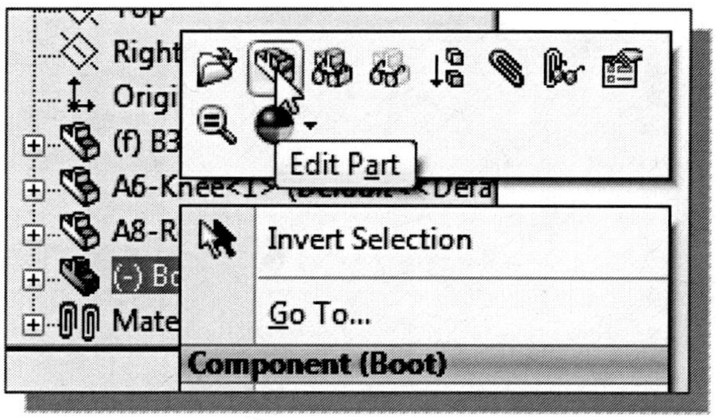

➢ Note that the *Boot* part was created using the metric units, while the other parts were done in inches. Let's adjust some of the key dimensions so that they can be assembled.

5. Inside the *Property Manager*, right-mouse-click once on top of the *Boot* part to bring up the option menu and select **Edit Part** to start the *Edit Part* mode.

6. Click **Save and Continue** to proceed with saving the model.

7. On your own, save the model using the filename **Knee-Leg-SubAssembly**.

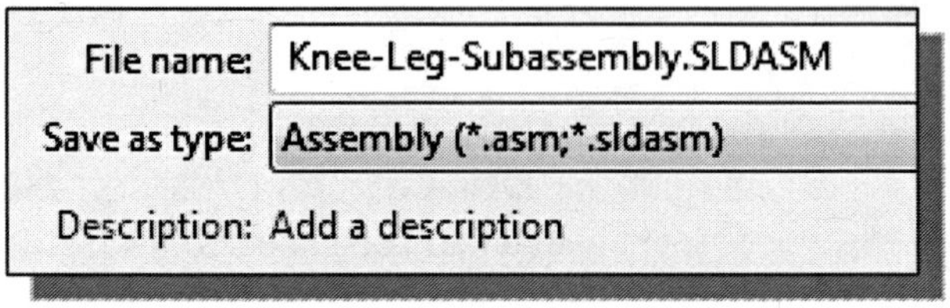

8. Click **OK** to proceed with editing the part.

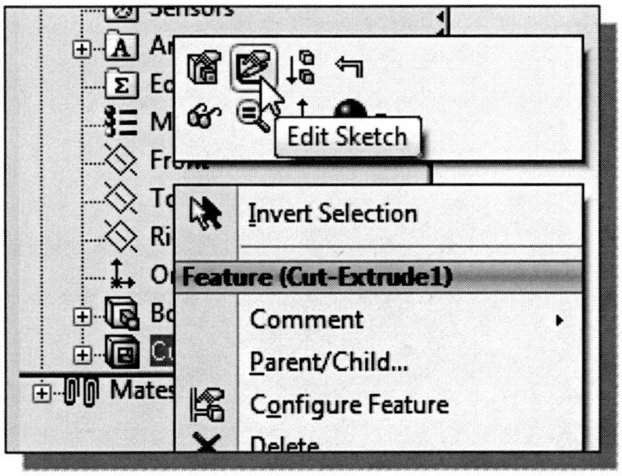

9. Inside the *Property Manager*, right-mouse-click once on top of the last feature of the *Boot* part to bring up the option menu and select **Edit Sketch**.

10. Note the dimensions, **6 mm** and **diameter 1.25 mm**, associated to the cut feature of the *Boot* part.

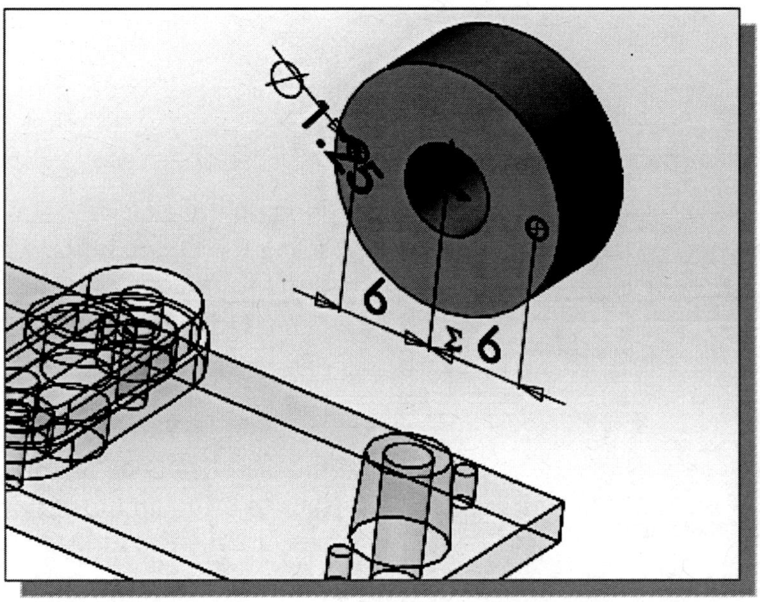

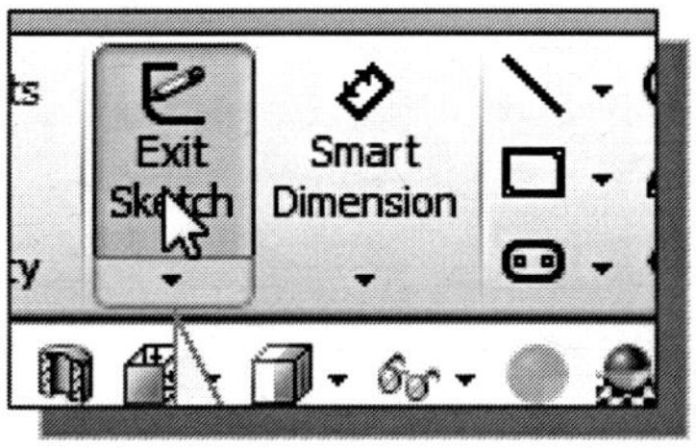

11. In the *Sketch* toolbar panel, click once on the **Exit Sketch** icon and exit the *Edit Sketch* mode.

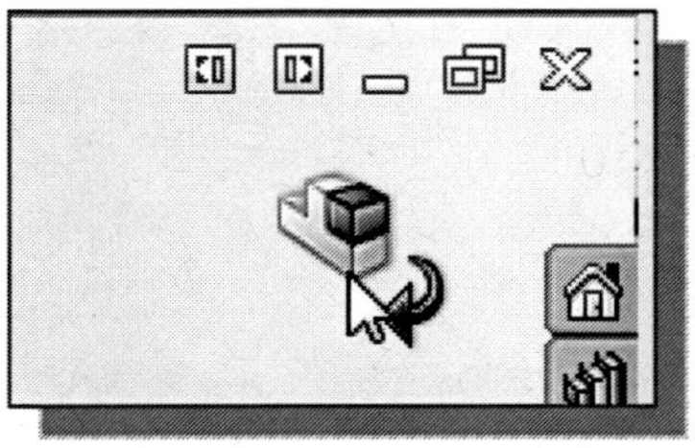

12. In the graphics window, click once on the **Exit Part** icon and exit the *Edit Part* mode.

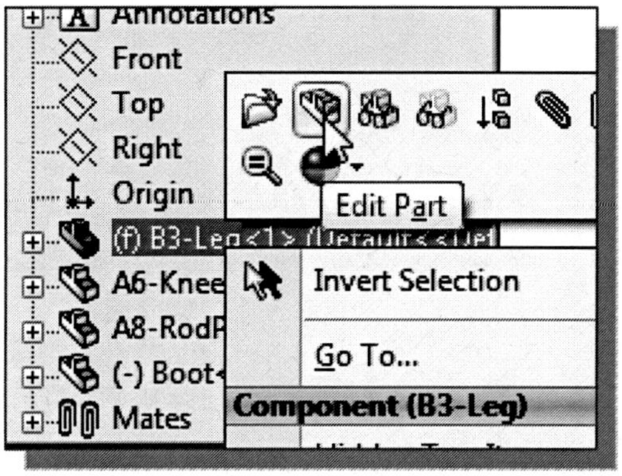

13. Inside the *Property Manager*, right-mouse-click once on top of the *B3-Leg* part to bring up the option menu and select **Edit Part** to start the *Edit Part* mode.

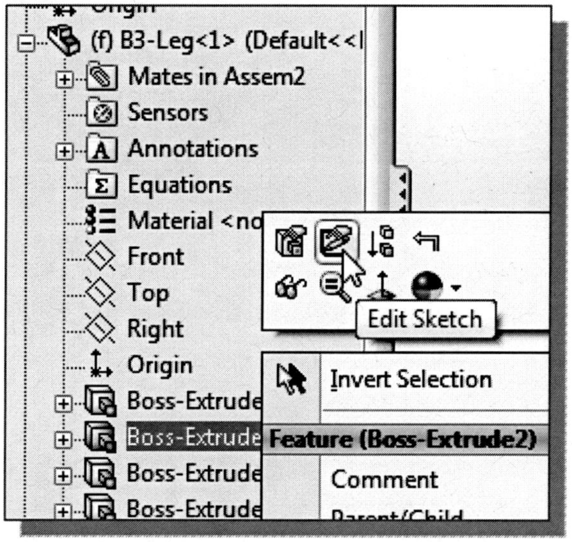

14. Inside the *Property Manager*, right-mouse-click once on top of the **Extrude2** feature of the *B3-Leg* part to bring up the option menu and select **Show dimensions**.

15. Double-click on the **0.480 inch** dimension and enter **12 mm** in the *Modify Dimension* box as shown.

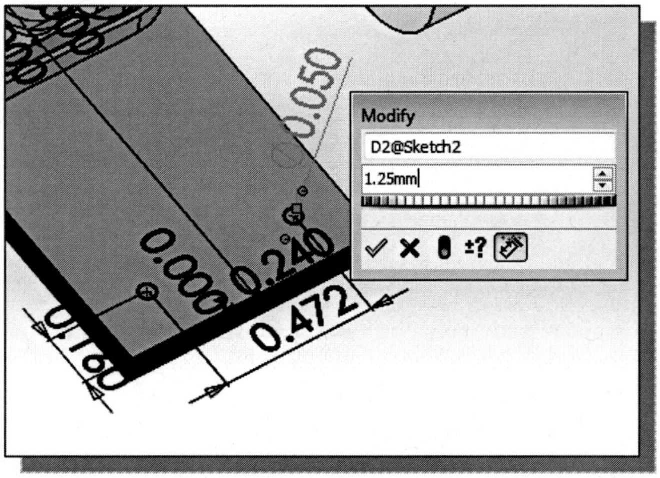

16. Double-click on the **diameter 0.05 inch** dimension and enter **1.25 mm** in the *Modify Dimension* box as shown.

17. Note the adjusted dimensions are displayed in **inches**, the part units set that was established through the *Options* menu.

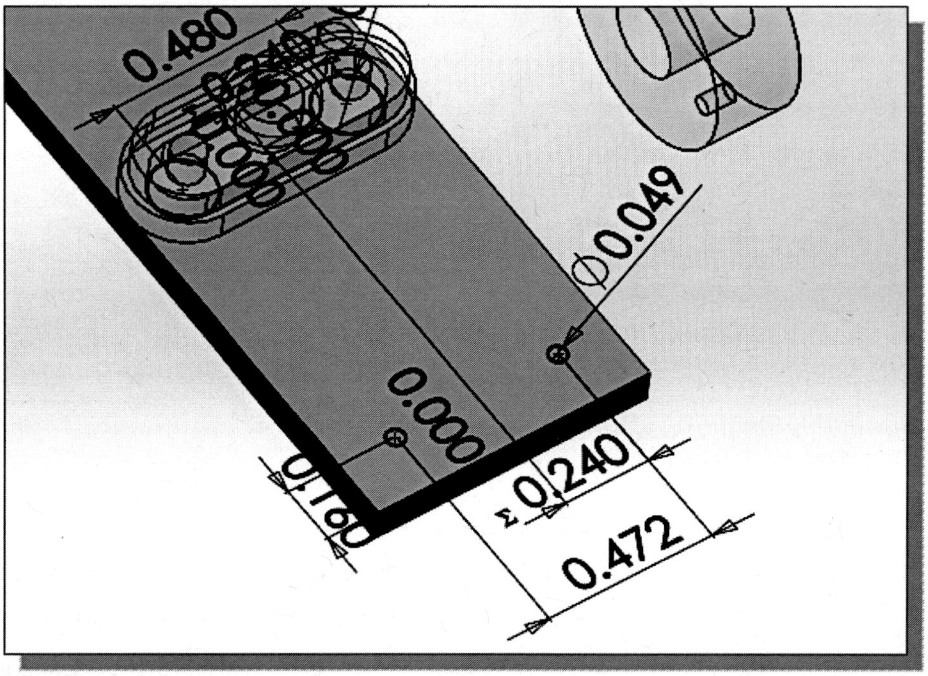

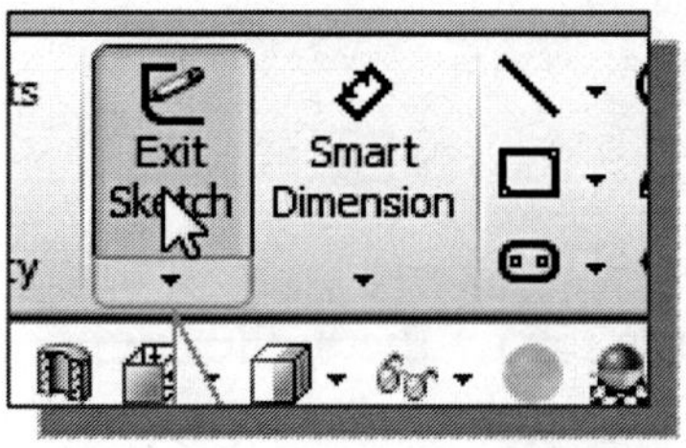

18. In the *Sketch* toolbar panel, click once on the **Exit Sketch** icon and exit the *Edit Sketch* mode.

19. In the graphics window, click once on the **Exit Part** icon and exit the *Edit Part* mode.

- Note the *B3-Leg* part has been updated through the *Assembly* mode; *parametric modeling* allows parts to be modified at all levels.

Assemble the Boot part

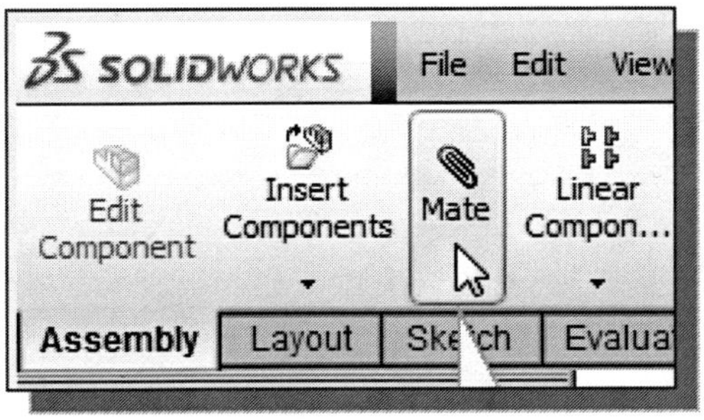

1. In the *Assembly* panel, select the **Mate** command by left-mouse-clicking once on the icon.

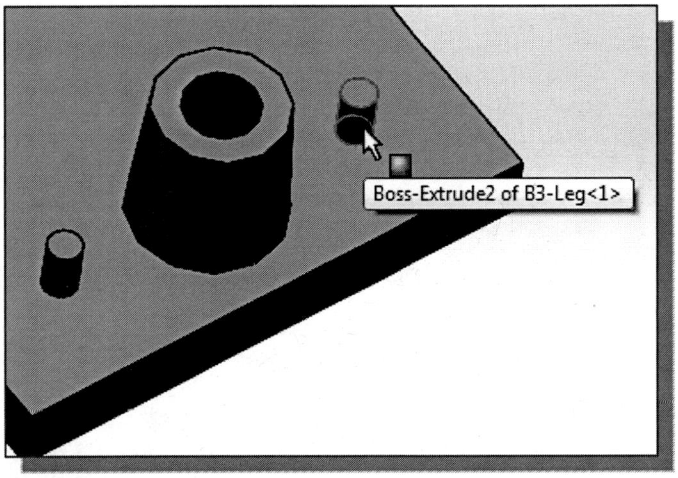

2. Select one of the small **cylindrical surfaces** of the *B3-Leg* part as the first object to apply the constraint, as shown in the figure.

3. Select one of the small **cylindrical surfaces** of the *Boot* part as the second object to apply the constraint as shown.

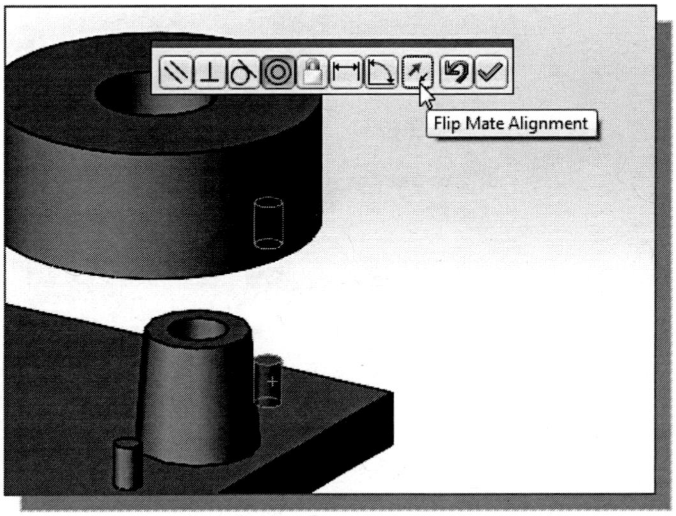

4. Confirm the alignment of the two parts is as shown. Use the **Flip Alignment** button to change the alignment direction if necessary.

5. In the *Mate Property Manager*, click on the **OK** button to accept the settings.

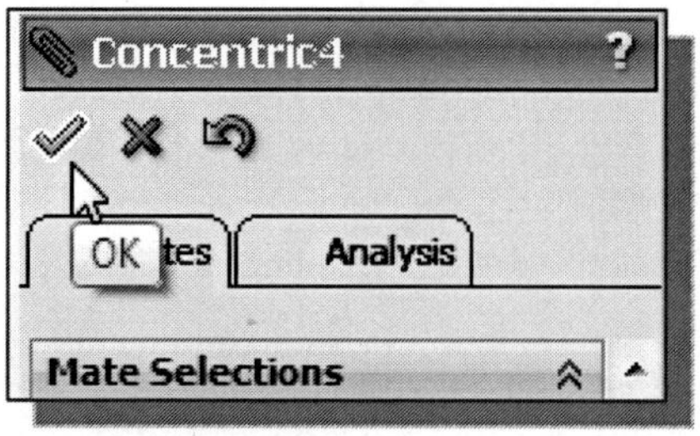

6. On your own, apply another **Mate** constraint to the two flat surfaces as shown.

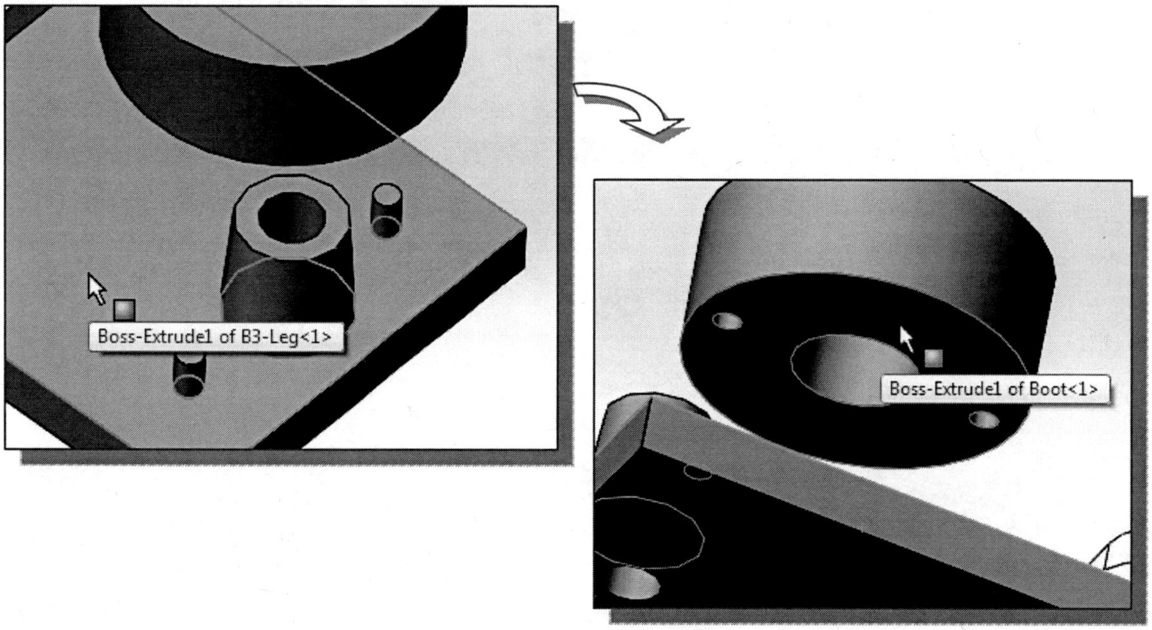

7. On your own, fully constrain the *Boot* part by using a **Concentric** constraint to align the two associated ***center axes*** as shown.

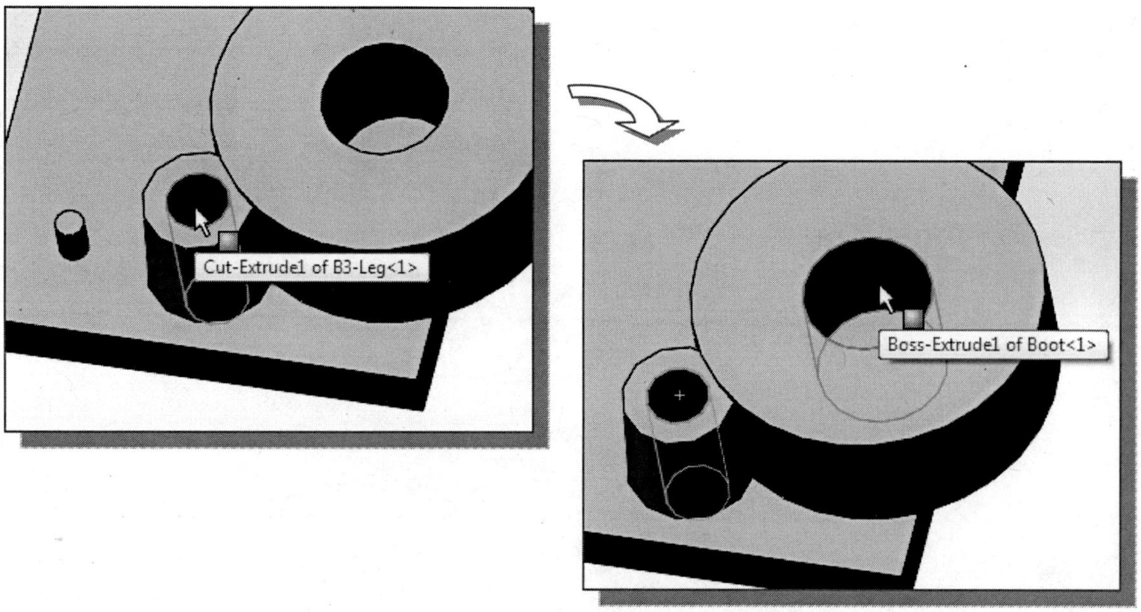

Use the Design Library and Assemble Two Screws

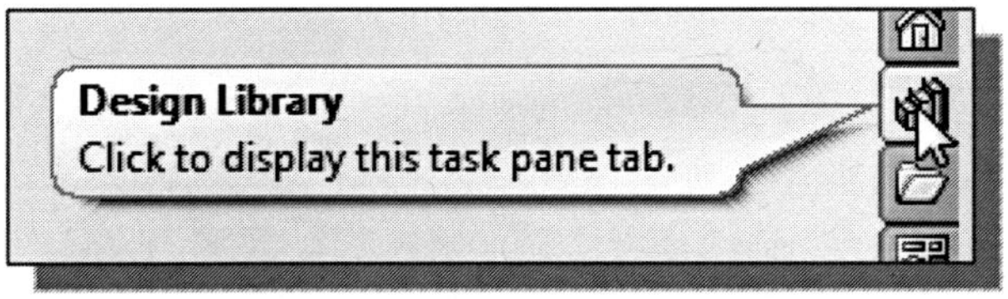

1. In the *task pane*, select the **Design Library** command by left-mouse-clicking the associated tab.

2. Select the **Toolbox** category and then **JIS → Bolts and Screws → Cross Recessed Head Screws** as shown.

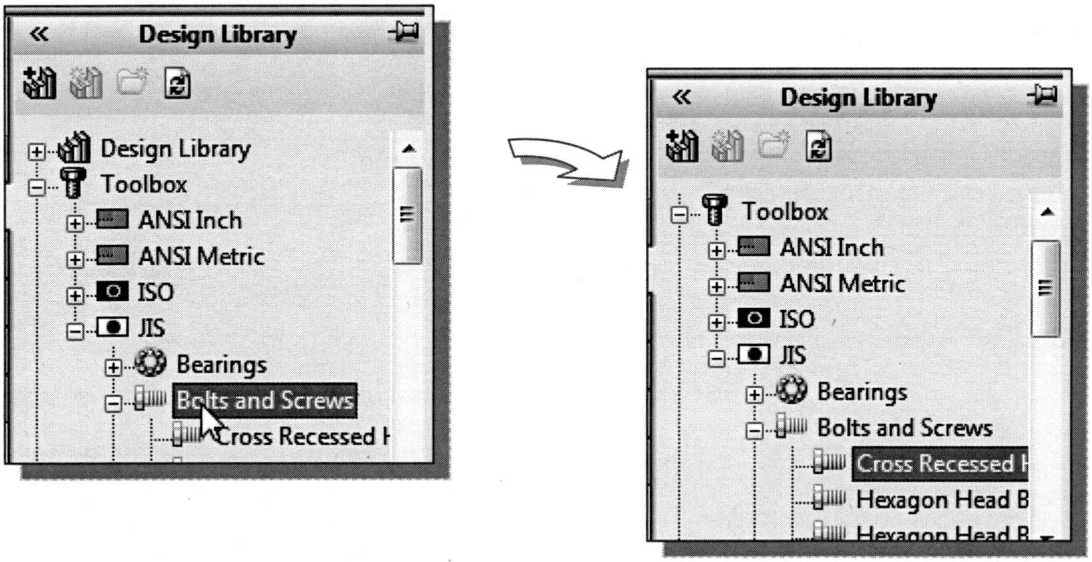

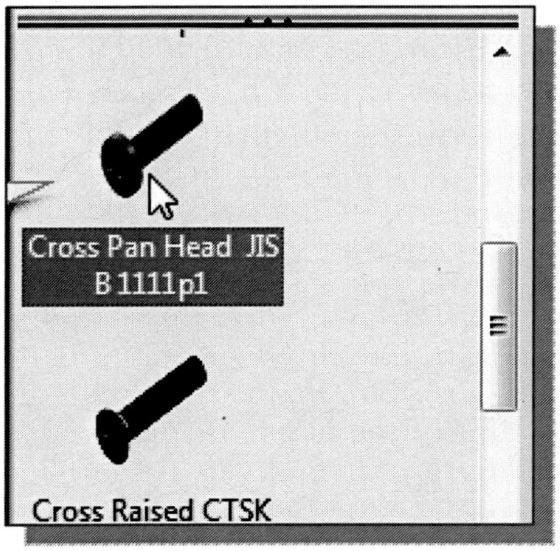

3. Select ***Cross Pan Head JIS B 1111p1*** as shown in the figure.

4. On your own, **drag** the selected file into the graphics window.

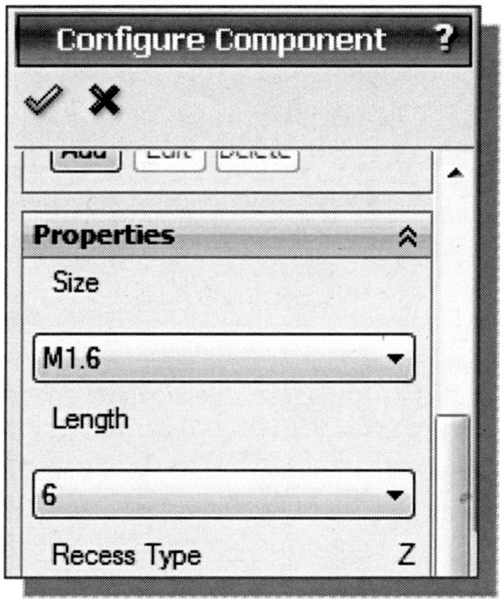

5. In the *Property Manager*, set the thread type to **M1.6** and the nominal length to **6** mm.

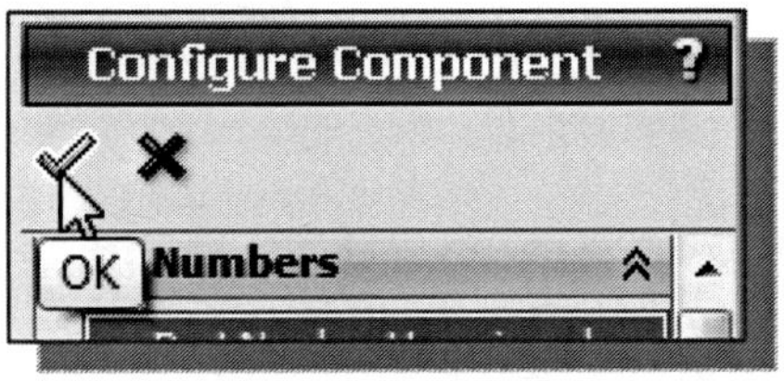

6. Click **OK** to accept the configuration of the screw.

7. On your own, place two copies of the ***M1.6x6 Screw*** part on both sides of the *B3-Leg.*

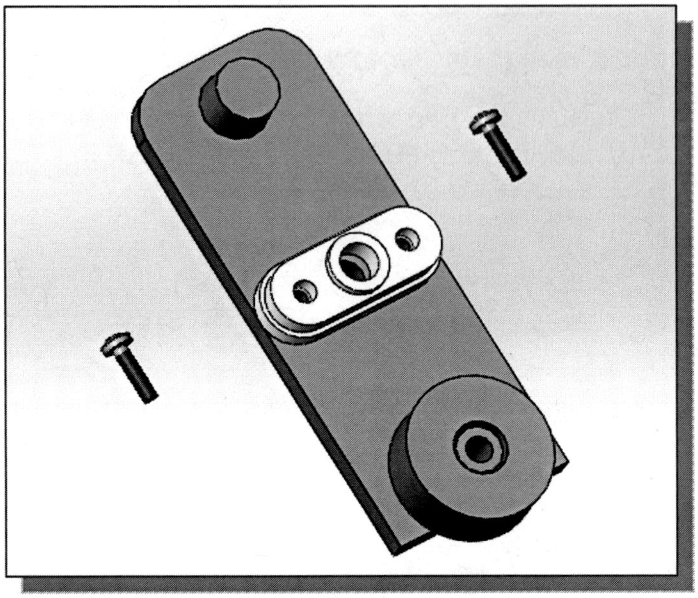

❖ Note that each *Recessed Screw* has six degrees of freedom. Both parts are referencing the same external part file, but each can be constrained independently.

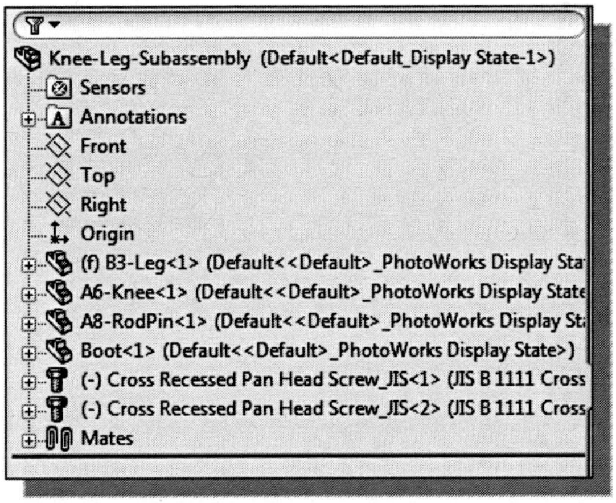

- Inside the *Property Manager*, the retrieved parts are listed in the order they were placed. The number behind the part name is used to identify the number of copies of the same part in the assembly model. Move the cursor to the last part name and notice the corresponding part is highlighted in the graphics window.

8. On your own, place a copy of the ***M3x8* Cross Pan Head JIS B 1111p1** and apply the necessary constraints to assemble the three screws as shown.

9. In the *Quick Access* menu, select **Save** and save the model as the ***Knee-Leg-SubAssembly***.

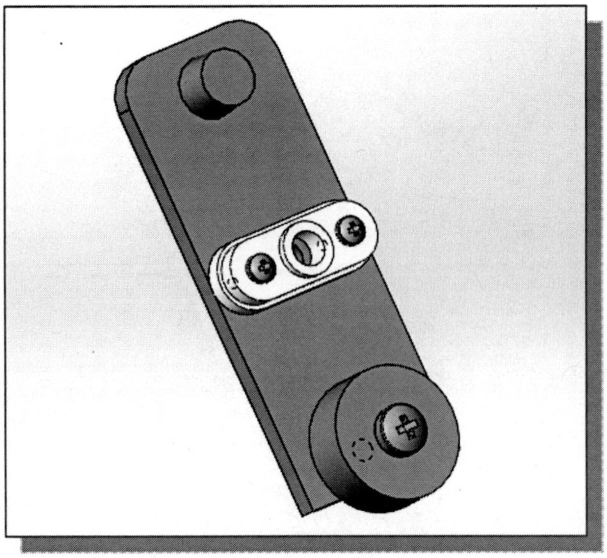

Start the *Main Assembly*

1. Select the **New File** icon with a single click of the left-mouse-button in the *Quick Access* toolbar as shown.

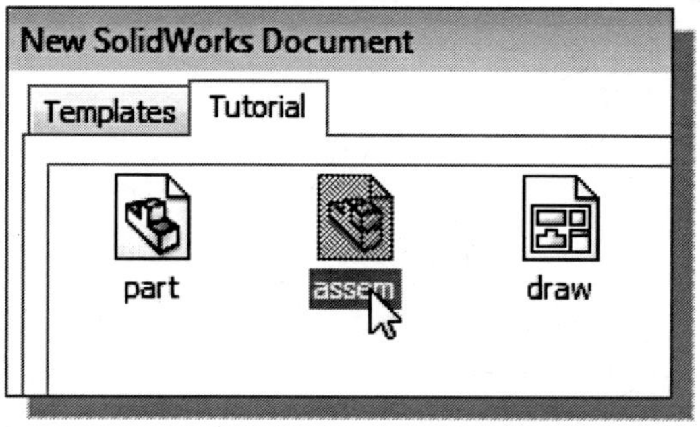

2. Select the **assem** template under the **Tutorial** tab as shown.

3. Click on the **OK** button to start a new assembly model.

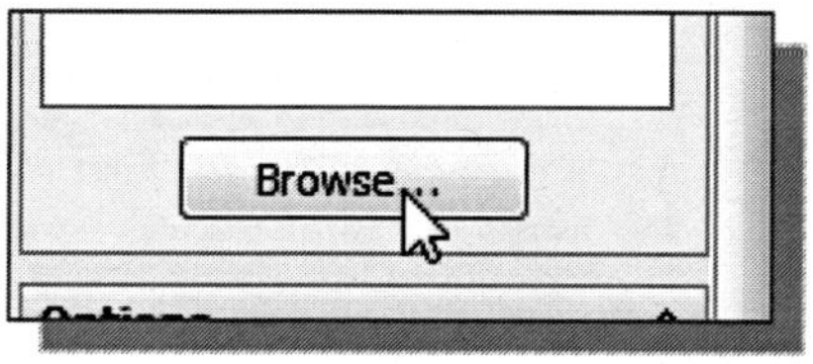

4. Click **Browse** in the *Property Manager*.

5. Select the ***Chassis*** (part file: ***B2-Chassis.sldprt***) in the list window.

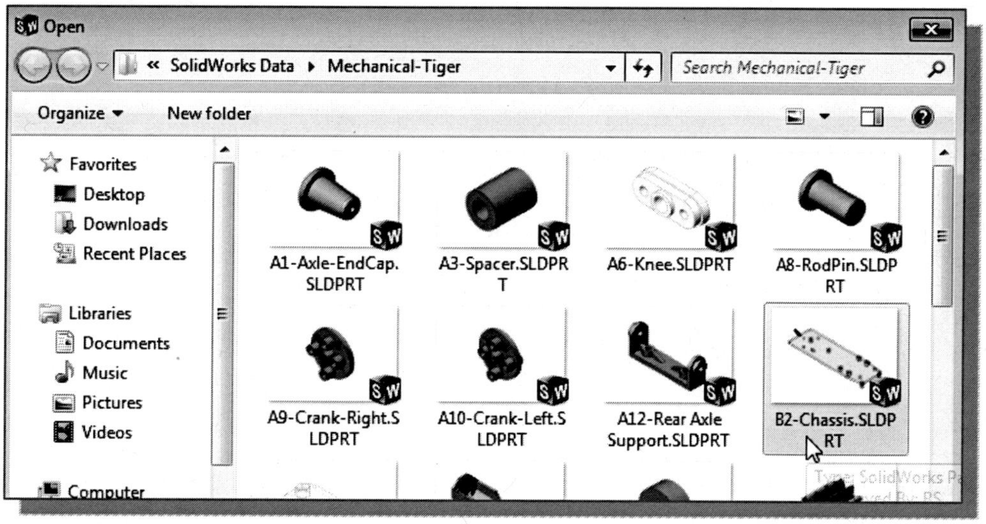

6. Click on the **Open** button to retrieve the model.

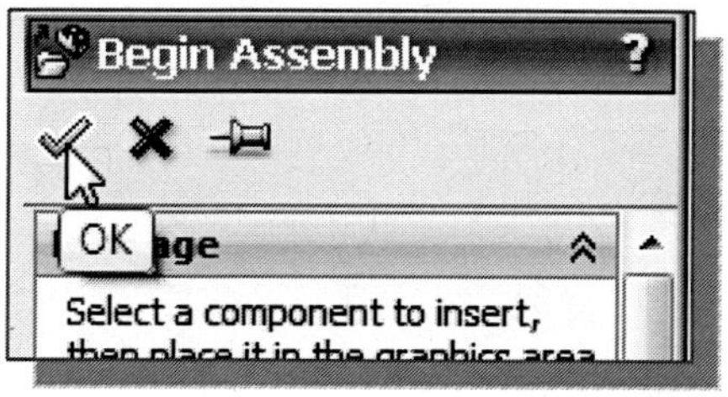

7. Note that we can place the component anywhere or click **OK** to align the component *Origin* to the *Origin* of the assembly model. Click **OK** to place the ***Chassis*** part.

8. Select the **Options** icon from the *Menu Bar* to open the *Options* dialog box.

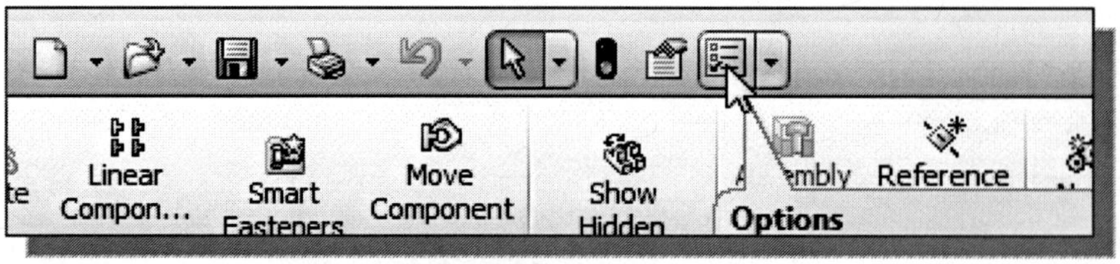

9. Select the **Document Properties** tab.

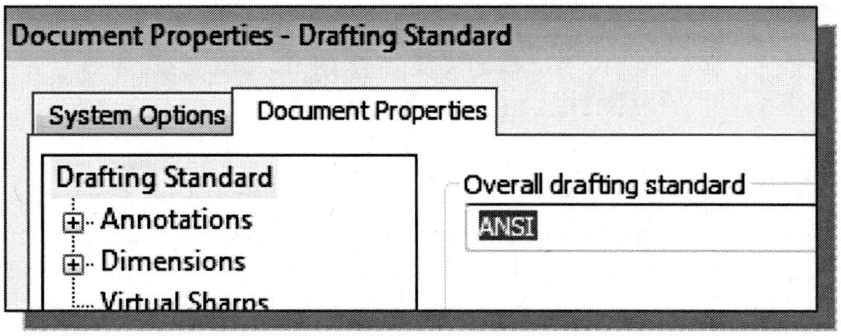

10. Select **ANSI** in the pull-down selection window under the *Overall drafting standard* panel as shown.

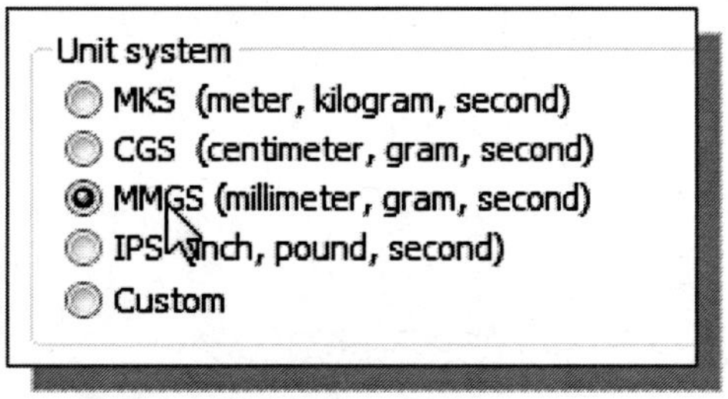

11. On your own, set the *Unit system* to **MMGS** as shown in the figure.

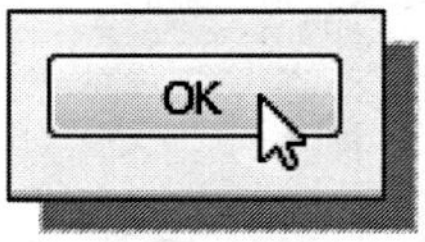

12. Click **OK** to accept the settings.

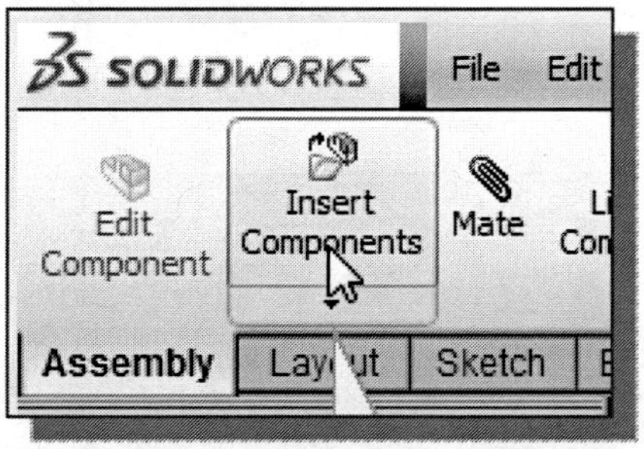

13. In the *Assembly* toolbar, select the **Insert Components** command by left-mouse-clicking once on the icon.

14. In the *Property Manager*, click **Browse** in the *Part/Assembly to Insert* panel.

15. Select the ***Rear Axle Support*** (part file: ***A12-Rear Axle Support.sldprt***) in the list window.

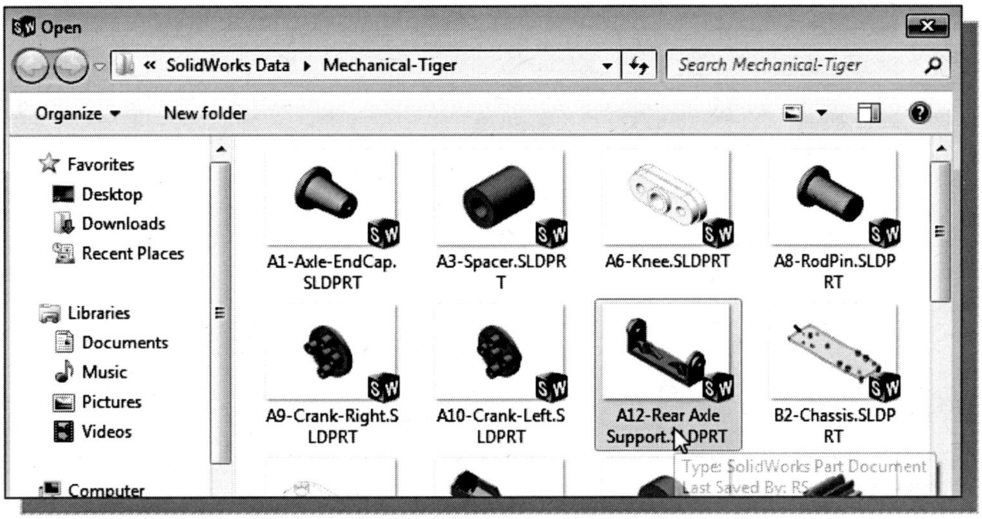

16. Place a copy of the selected part on the screen next to the *Chassis*.

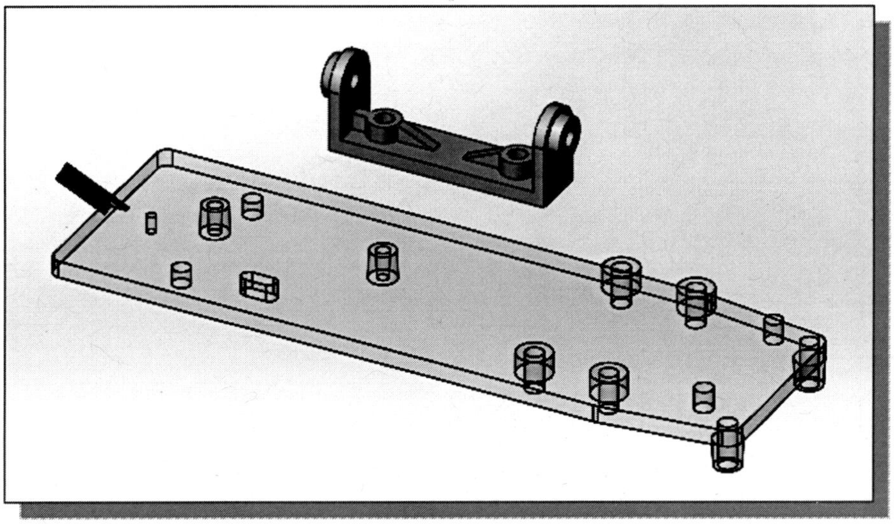

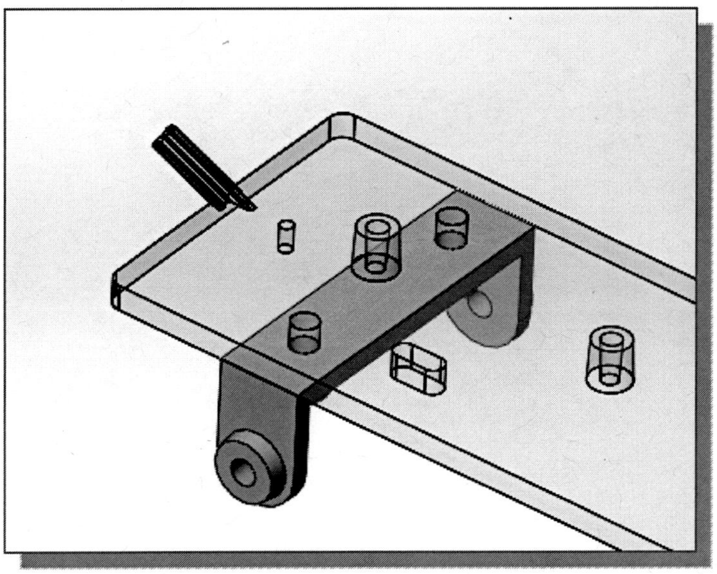

17. On your own, apply three constraints to assemble the *Rear Axle Support* to the bottom of the *Chassis* as shown.

Assemble the Gear Box Right Part

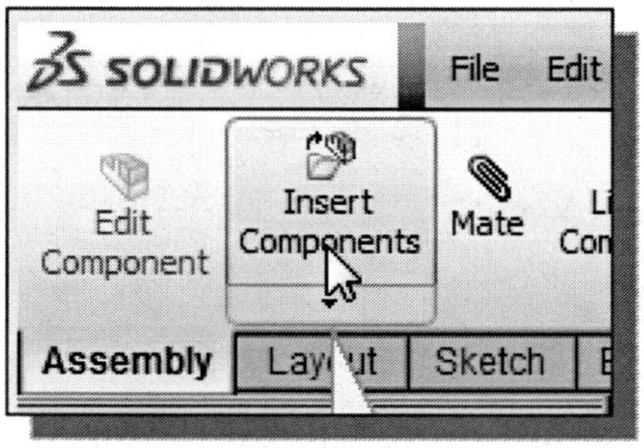

1. In the *Assembly* toolbar, select the **Insert Components** command by left-mouse-clicking the icon.

2. Click **Browse** in the *Property Manager.*

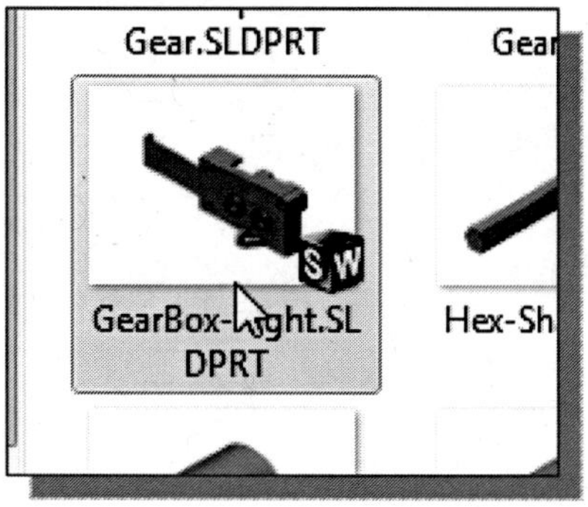

3. Select the ***GearBox-Right*** part in the list window.

4. Click on the **Open** button to retrieve the model.

5. Place a copy of the selected part on the screen next to the *Chassis*.

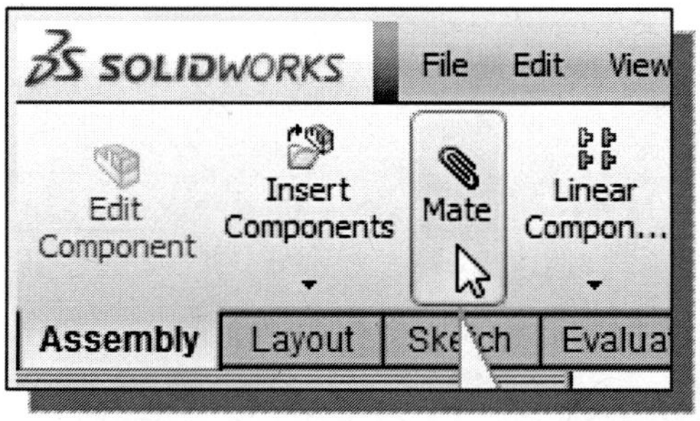

6. In the *Assembly* panel, select the **Mate** command by left-mouse-clicking once on the icon.

7. On your own, apply a **Coincident** constraint to assemble the top side of the *GearBox-Right* part to the **bottom** of the *Chassis*.

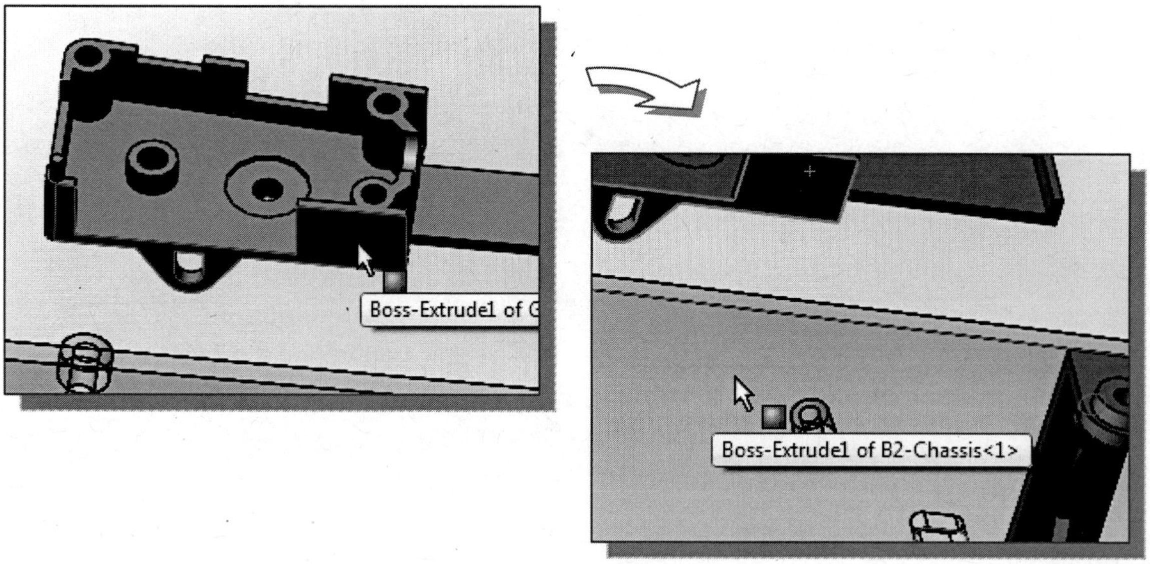

8. On your own, apply another **Mate** constraint to assemble the circular surface to the cylindrical surface of the *Chassis* as shown. (Note the figures below are viewing the bottom of the *Chassis*.)

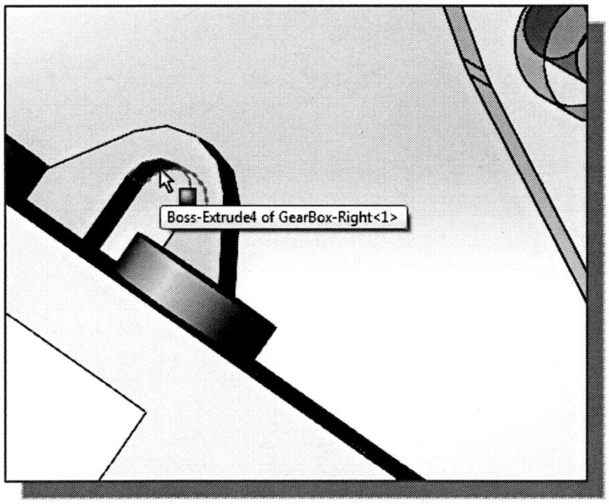

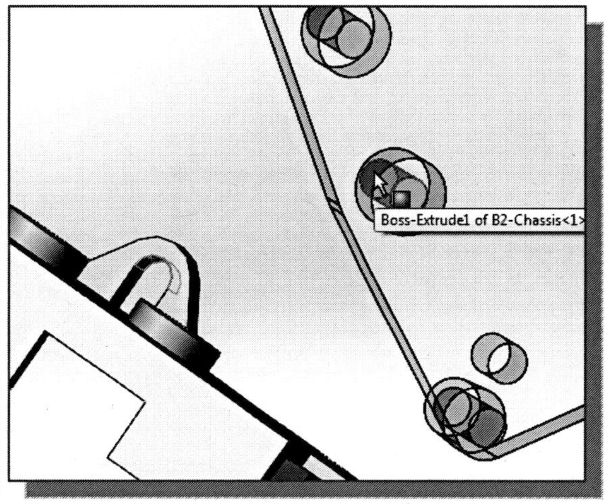

9. On your own, use the constrained move option and adjust the orientation of the *GearBox-Right* part roughly parallel to the *Chassis* part as shown.

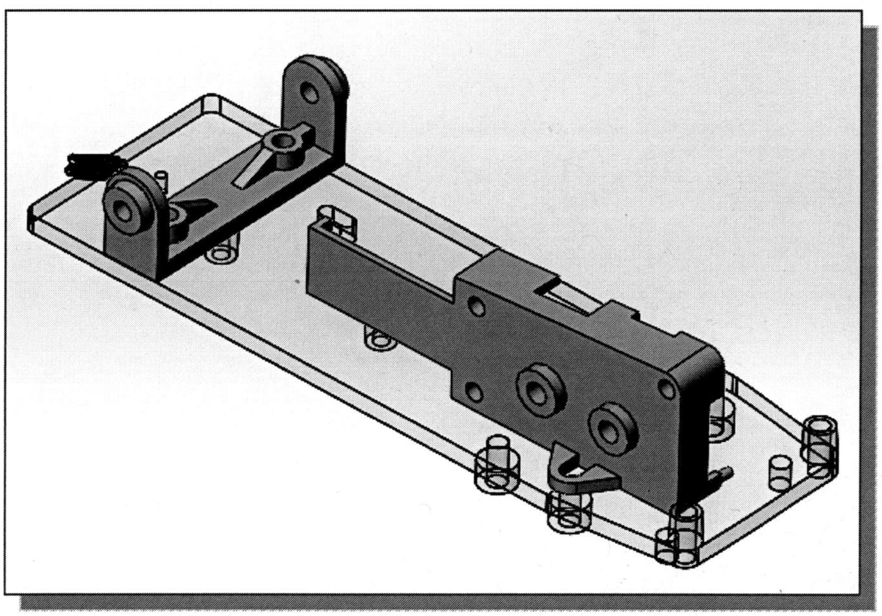

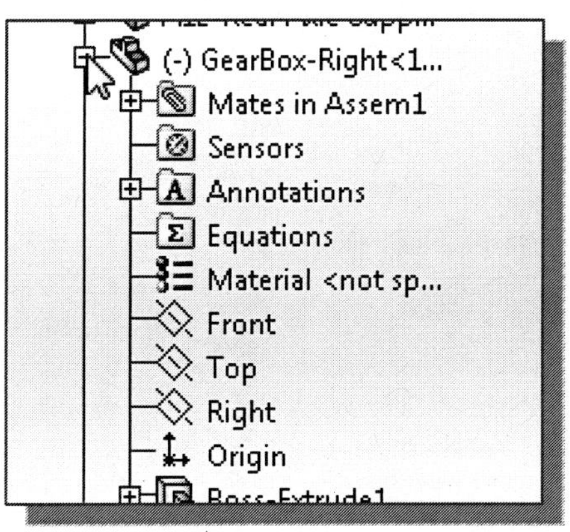

10. In the graphics window, expand the *Model Tree* of the *GearBox-Right* part as shown.

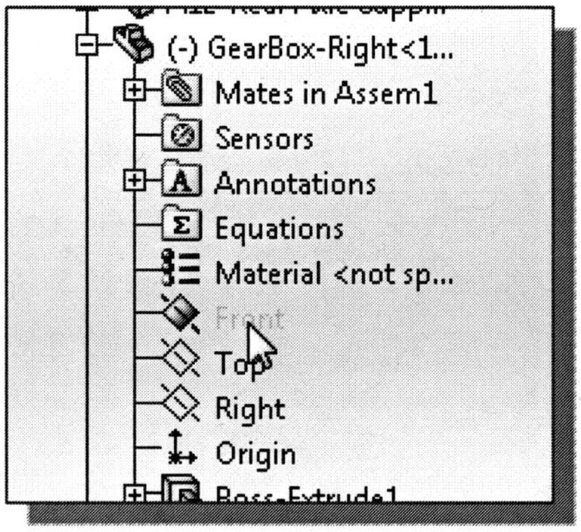

11. In the *Model Tree*, select the **Front Plane** of the *GearBox-Right* part as shown.

12. In the *Model Tree*, select the **Front Plane** of the *Chassis* part as shown

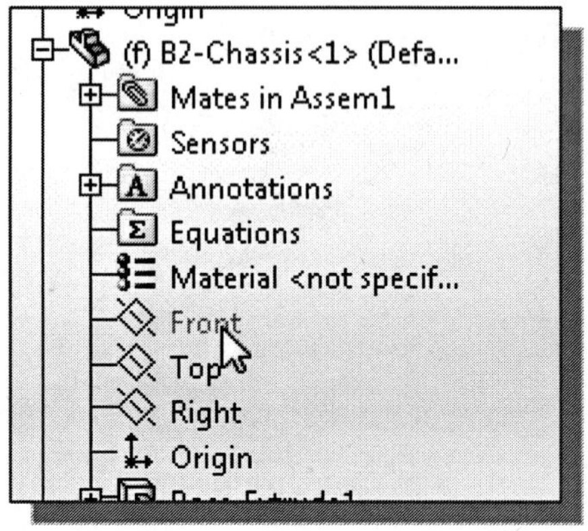

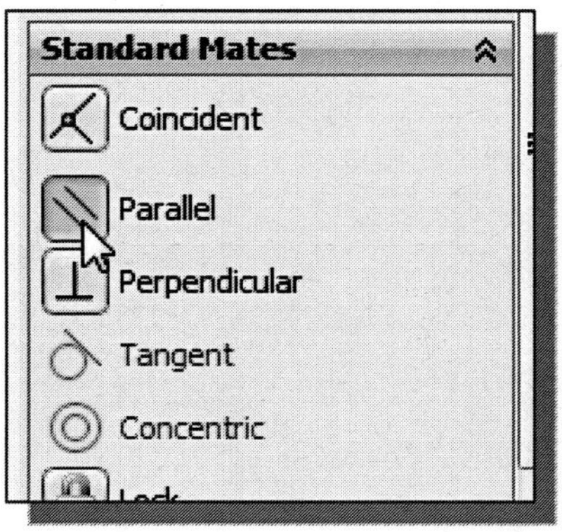

13. In the *Property Manager,* activate the **Parallel** constraint to assemble the corresponding reference planes as shown.

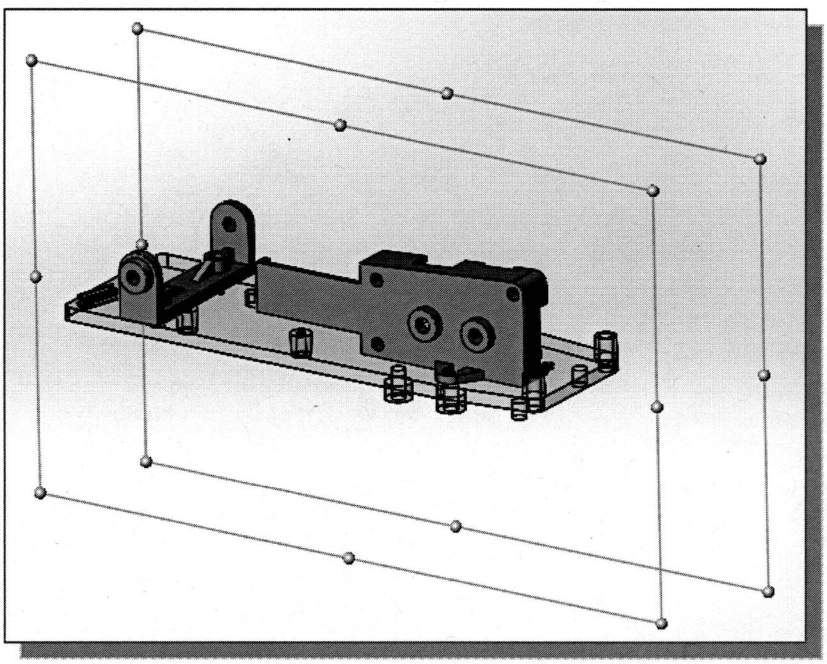

Assemble the Motor and the Pinion Gear

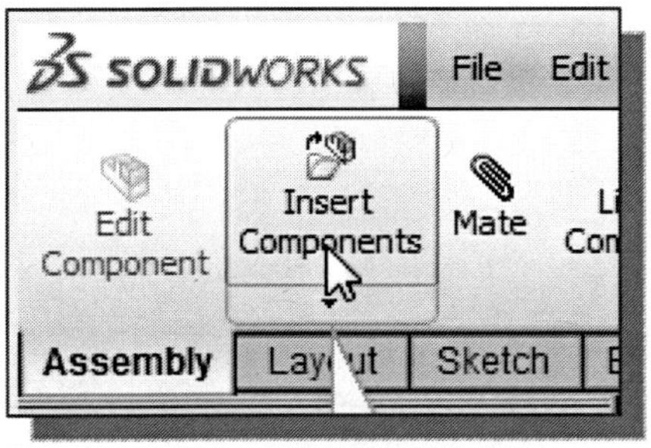

1. In the *Assembly* toolbar, select the **Insert Components** command by left-mouse-clicking the icon.

2. Click **Browse** in the *Property Manager.*

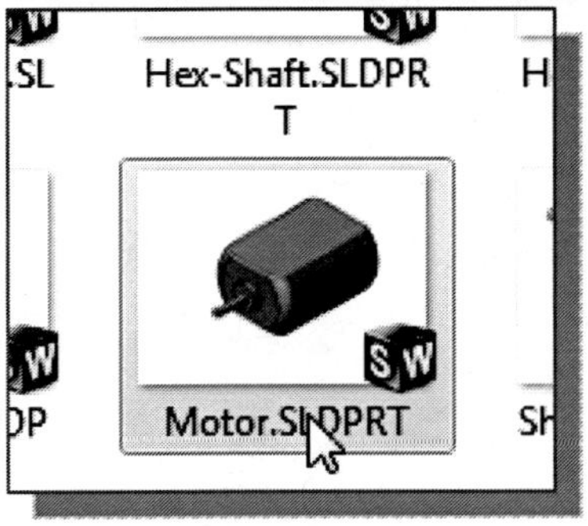

3. Select the ***Motor*** part in the list window.

4. On your own, place a copy of the selected part on the screen next to the *Chassis*.

5. On your own, apply a **Coincident** constraint to align the *Motor* part to the *GearBox-Right* part as shown.

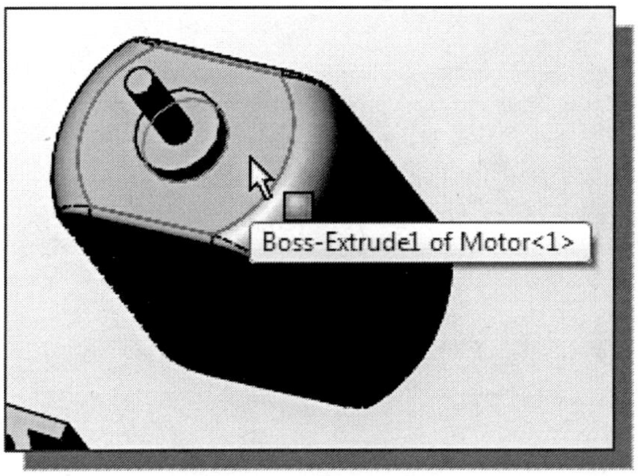

6. On your own, apply another **Concentric** constraint to align the center axes of the *Motor* part and the *GearBox-Right* part as shown.

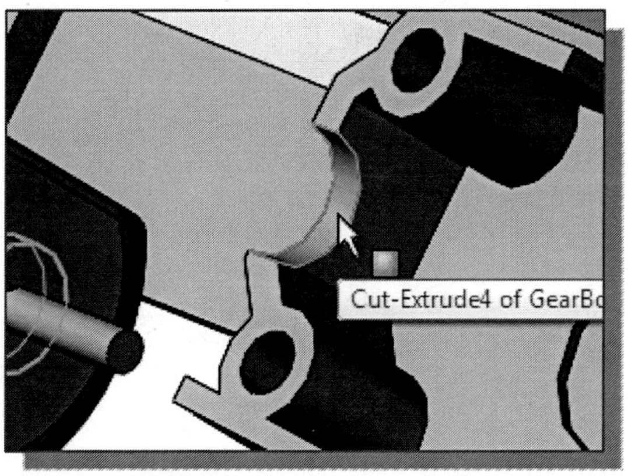

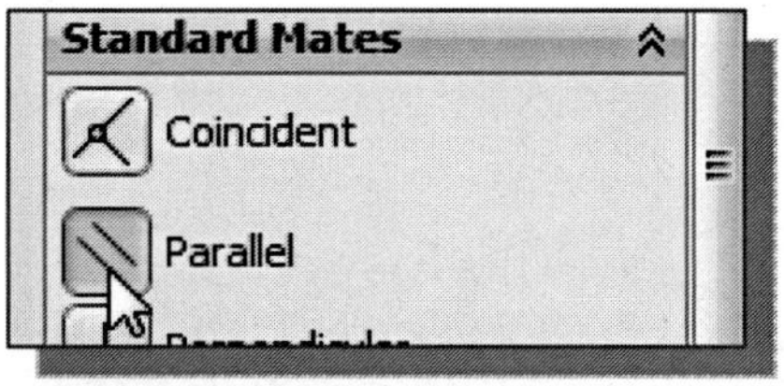

7. On your own, apply a **Parallel** constraint to align the ***Motor*** part to the ***GearBox-Right*** part as shown.

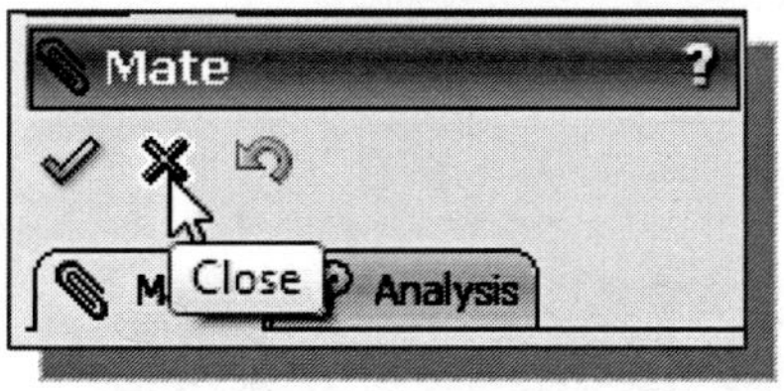

8. Click **Close** to end the **Mate** command.

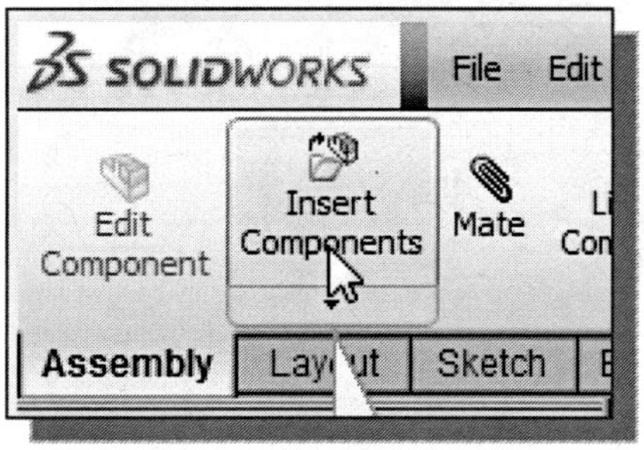

9. In the *Assembly* toolbar, select the **Insert Components** command by left-mouse-clicking the icon.

10. Click **Browse** in the *Property Manager.*

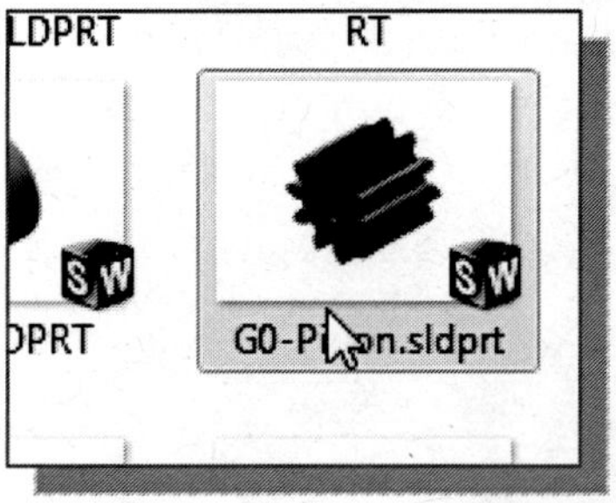

11. Select the ***G0-Pinion*** part in the list window.

12. On your own, place a copy of the selected part on the screen next to the ***Chassis***.

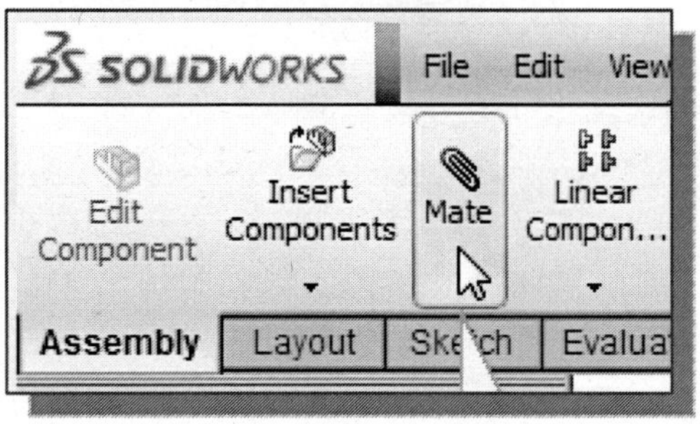

13. In the *Assembly* panel, select the **Mate** command by left-mouse-clicking once on the icon.

14. On your own, apply a **Coincident** constraint to align the *G0-Pinion* part to the *Motor* part as shown.

15. On your own, apply a **Concentric** constraint to align the *G0-Pinion* part to the *Motor* part as shown.

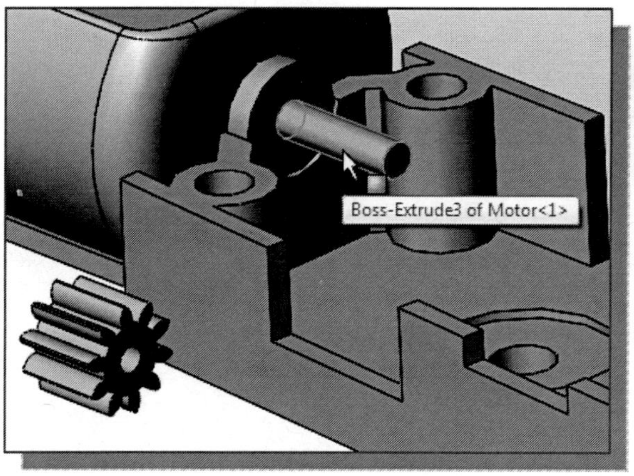

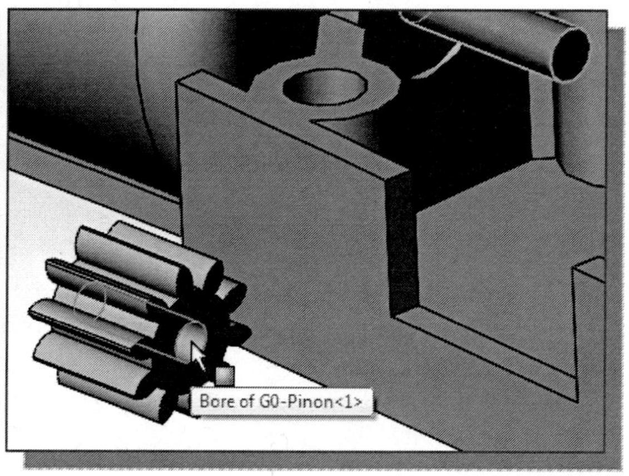

Assemble the G1 Gear

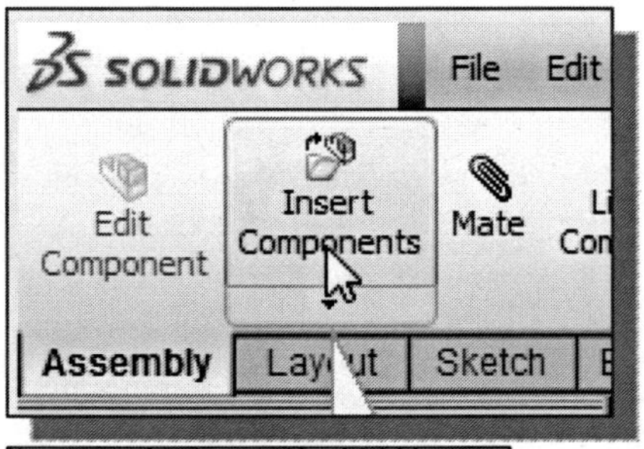

1. In the *Assembly* toolbar, select the **Insert Components** command by left-mouse-clicking the icon.

2. Click **Browse** in the *Property Manager.*

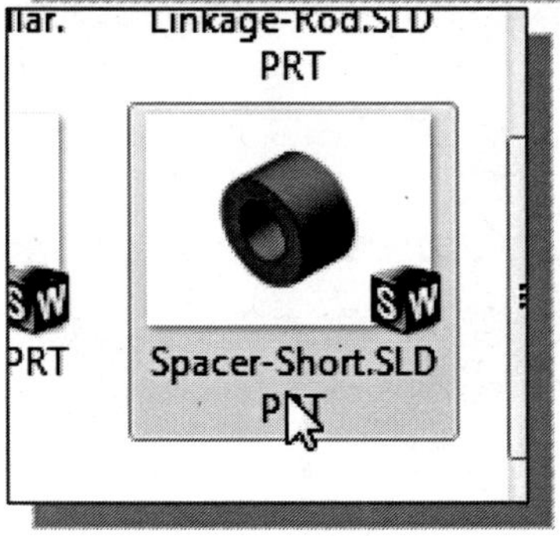

3. Select the ***Spacer-Short*** part in the list window.

4. On your own, place a copy of the selected part on the screen next to the *GearBox*.

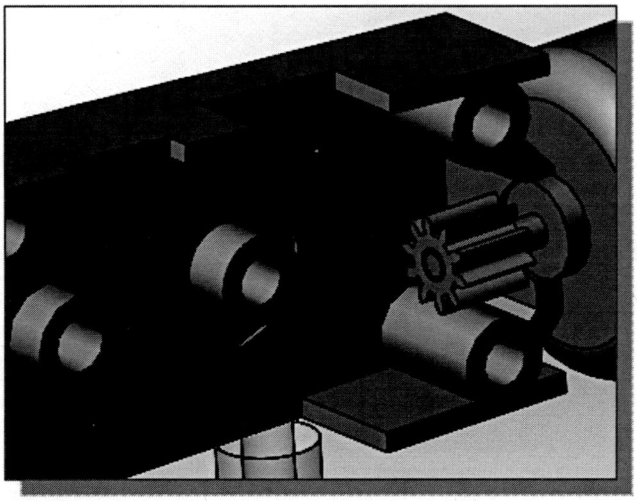

5. On your own, apply three constraints to assemble the ***Spacer-Short*** as shown. (Hint: Apply a **Parallel** constraint on one of the datum planes.)

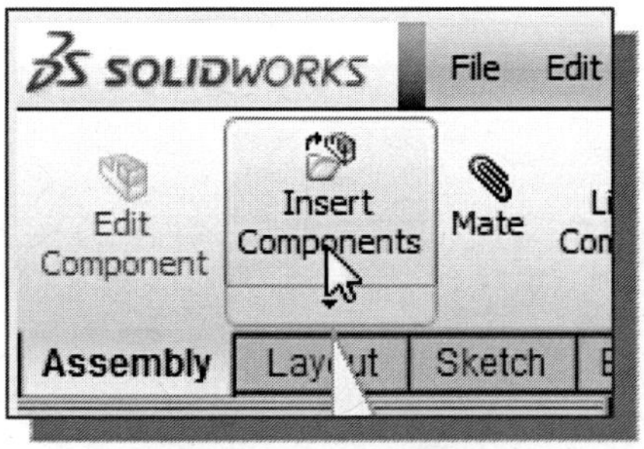

6. In the *Assembly* toolbar, select the **Insert Components** command by left-mouse-clicking the icon.

7. Click **Browse** in the *Property Manager.*

8. Select the ***G1-Spur Gear*** part in the list window.

9. On your own, place a copy of the selected part on the screen next to the *GearBox*.

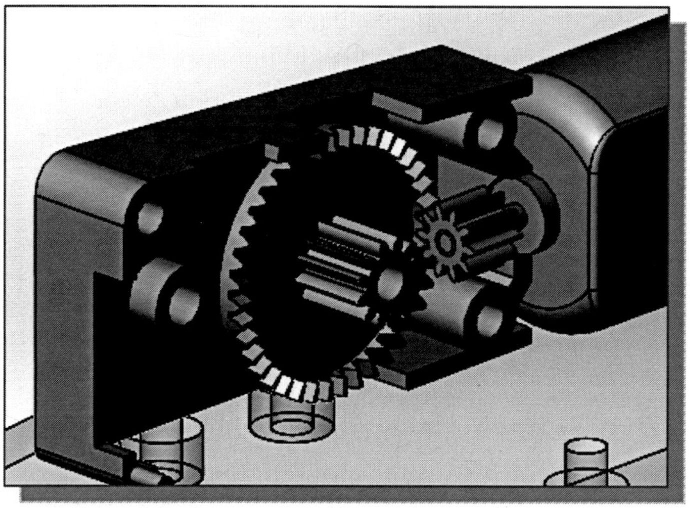

10. On your own, apply a **Coincident** constraint and a **Concentric** constraint to assemble the *G1-Spur Gear* part next to the *Spacer-Short* part as shown.

11. Use the **constrained move** option on the *Spur Gear* to adjust the mesh between the two gears.

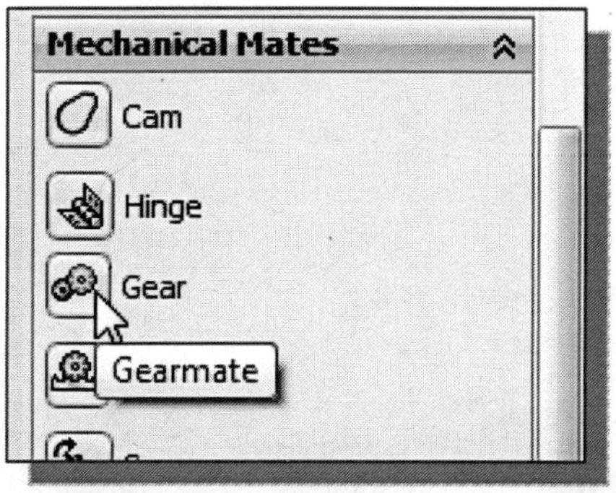

12. In the *Property Manager*, expand the ***Mechanical Mates*** panel.

13. Activate the **Gear** icon to apply a **Gearmate**.

14. Select one of the cylindrical surfaces of the *Pinion* gear as the first gear as shown.

15. In the *info-box*, enter **10** as the number of teeth for the pinion.

16. Select the outer surface of the ***G1-Spur Gear*** as the second gear as shown.

17. In the *info-box*, enter **40** as the number of teeth for the ***G1-Spur Gear.***

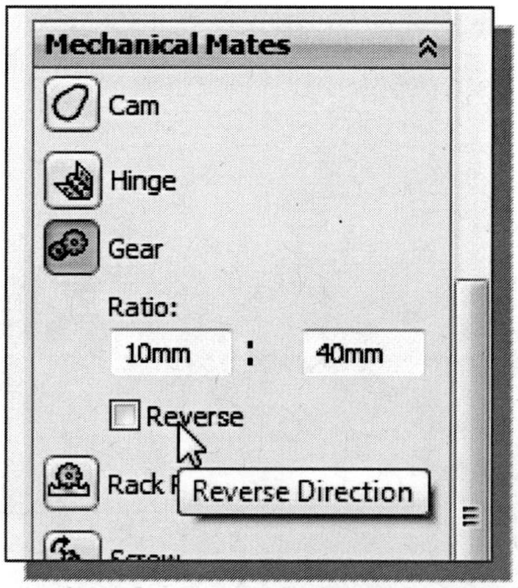

18. In the *Mechanical Mates* panel, activate the **Reverse Direction** option as shown.

19. On your own, **drag** the *Pinion* gear in the assembly and confirm the *G1-Spur Gear* is moving in the correct direction.

- Note the **Reverse Direction** button is also available to switch the rotation direction of the gear pair.

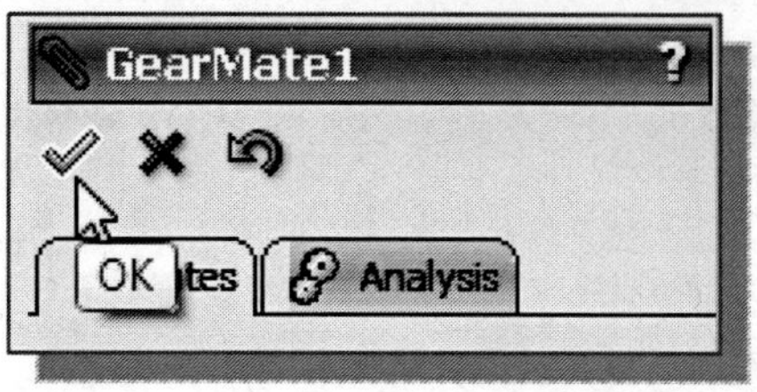

20. Click **OK** to accept the settings.

21. Click **Close** to end the Mate command.

SolidWorks Motion Study

- The *SolidWorks* **Motion Study** tool allows us to perform basic motion analysis by creating simulations of assemblies with moving parts.

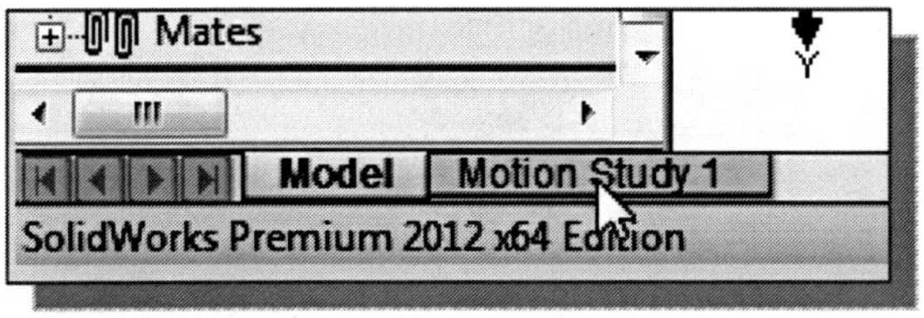

1. Select the **Motion Study** tab at the bottom of the *SolidWorks* window.

❖ The *SolidWorks Motion Manager* appears. The *Motion Manager* is a timeline-based interface with motion study tools located on the *Motion Study* toolbar.

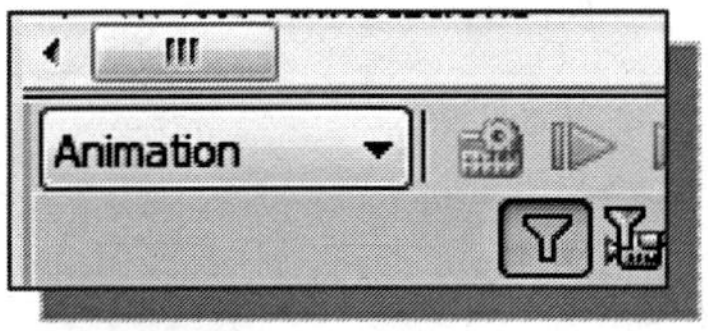

- The **Animation** option in the *Type of Study* list allows us to create animation binding by the applied constraints.

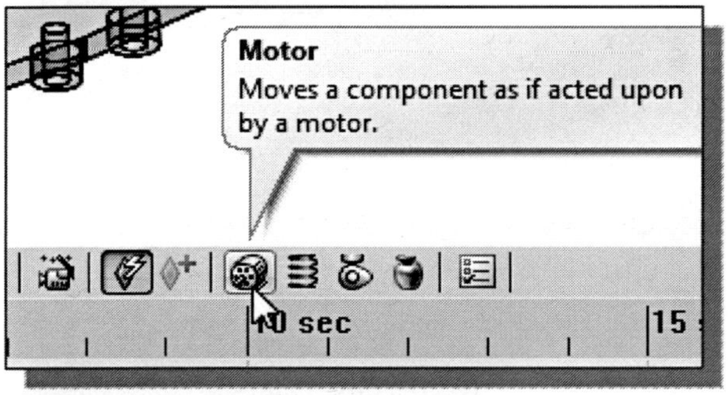

2. Move the cursor over the **Motor** command on the *Motion Manager* toolbar and click once with the left mouse button to create a motor to drive the motion for the study.

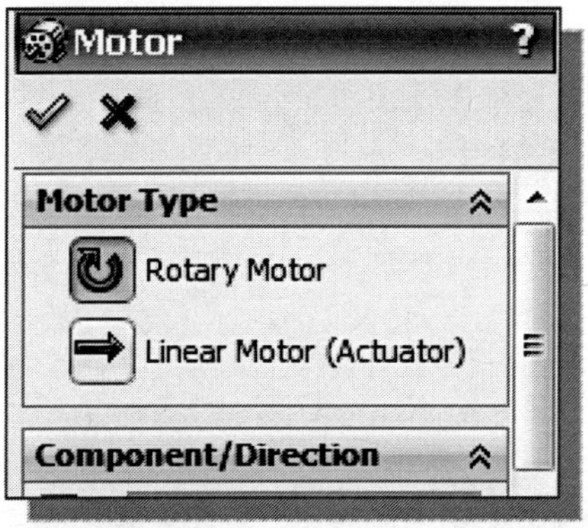

3. In the *Motor Property Manager*, select **Rotary Motor** as the *Motor Type*; note the linear motor option is also available to produce straight-line motion.

4. Select one of the cylindrical surfaces of the *Pinion* gear to attach the *Motor.* Note the center axis of the *Pinion* gear is used for the generation of the rotary motion.

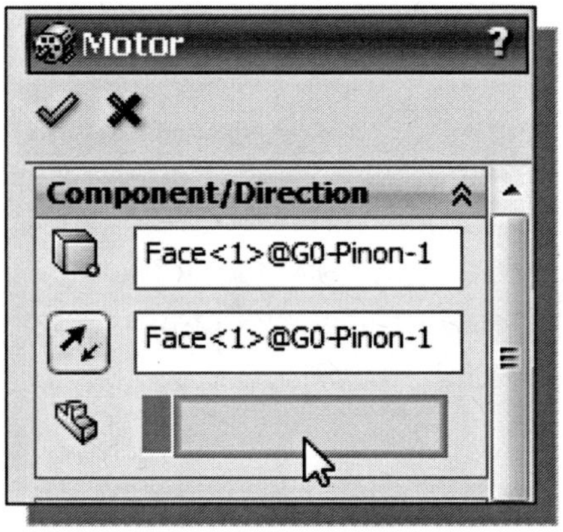

5. Activate the selection of a **reference component** by clicking once in the **Component to move relative to** box as shown.

6. Select the *Motor* as the reference component by clicking on one of the surfaces of the *Motor* model as shown.

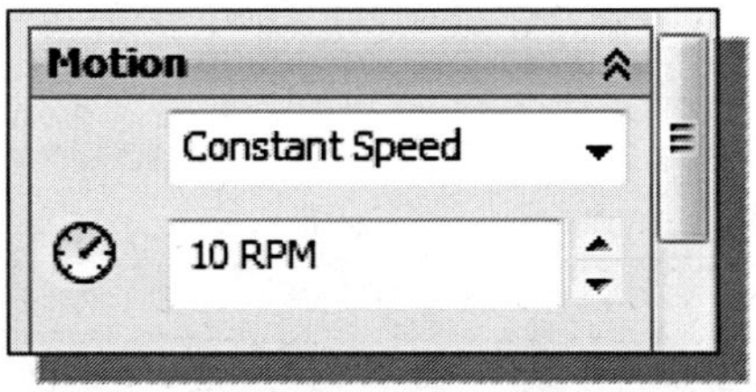

7. Select the **Constant Speed** option on the *Motion* panel and enter **10 RPM** for the speed.

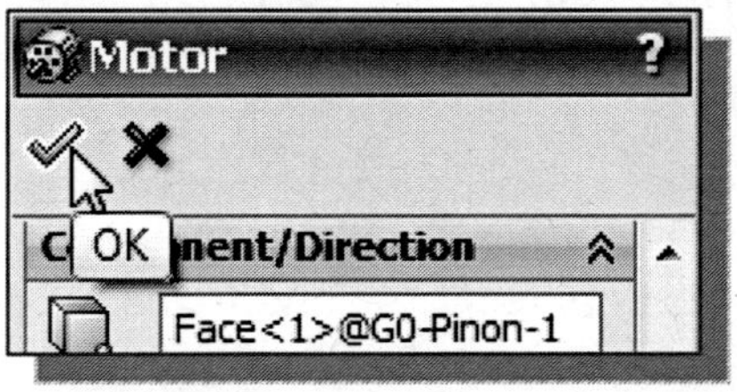

8. Click **OK** in the *Property Manager* to accept the settings and create the *Motor*.

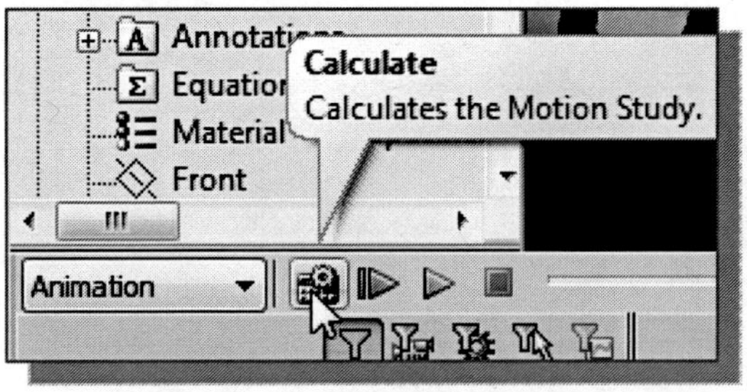

9. Move the cursor over the **Calculate** command on the *Motion Manager* toolbar and click once with the left-mouse-button to calculate the *Motion Study*.

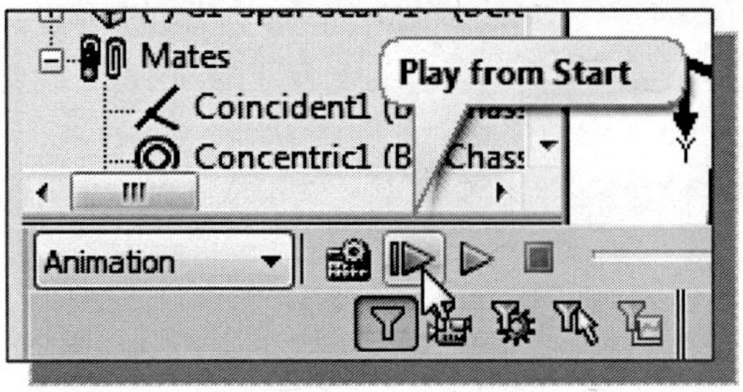

➢ Once it has been calculated, the *Motion Study* can be viewed using the **Play from Start**, **Play** and **Stop** buttons on the *Motion Manager* toolbar

10. On your own, experiment with the **Play from Start**, **Play** and **Stop** tools.

Assemble the G2 Gear

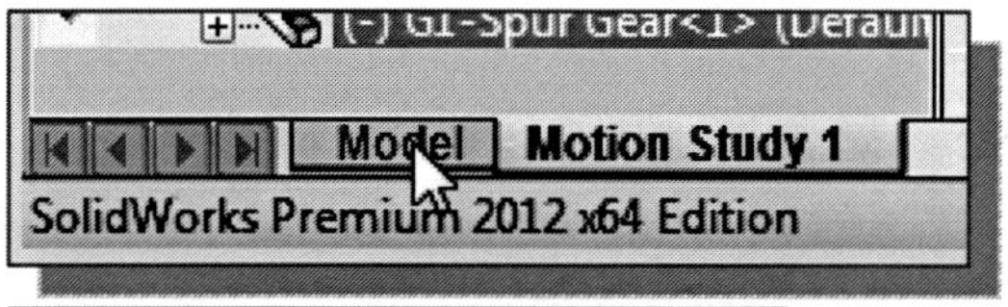

1. Select the **Model** tab at the bottom of the *SolidWorks* window to switch back to the *Assembly Modeling* mode.

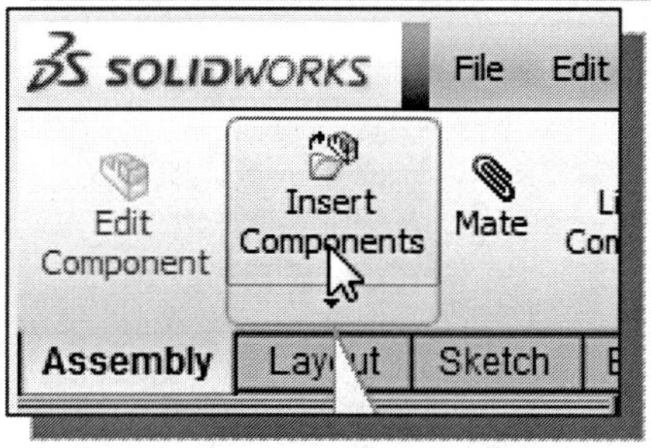

2. In the *Assembly* toolbar, select the **Insert Components** command by left-mouse-clicking the icon.

3. Click **Browse** in the *Property Manager.*

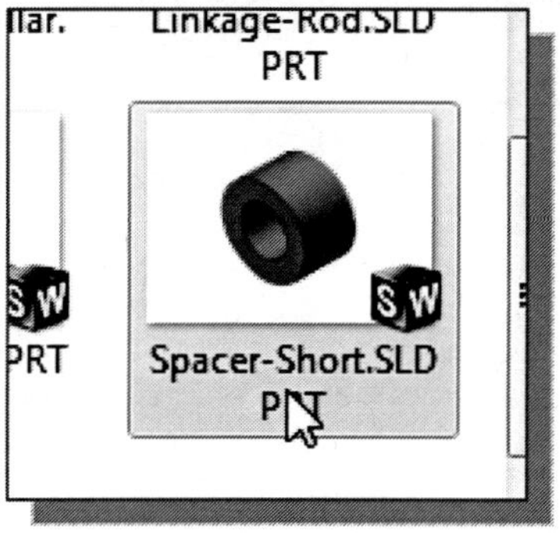

4. Select the ***Spacer-Short*** part in the list window.

5. On your own, place a copy of the selected part on the screen next to the *GearBox*.

6. On your own, apply three constraints to fully assemble the second *Spacer-Short* as shown. (Hint: Apply a **Parallel** constraint on one of the datum planes.)

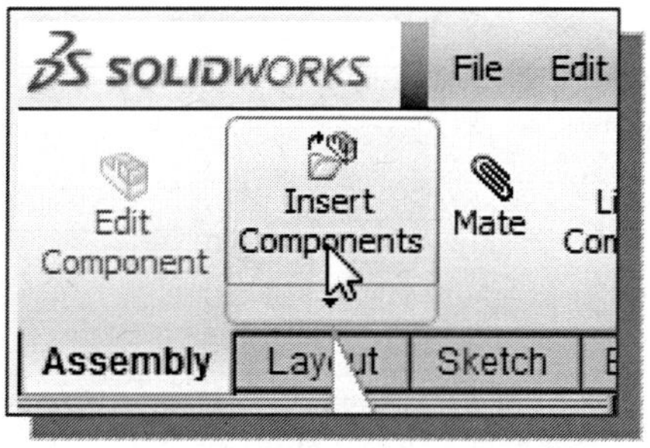

7. In the *Assembly* toolbar, select the **Insert Components** command by left-mouse-clicking the icon.

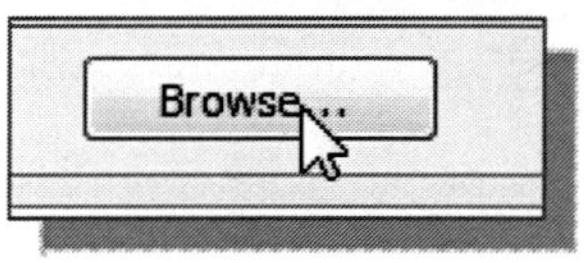

8. Click **Browse** in the *Property Manager.*

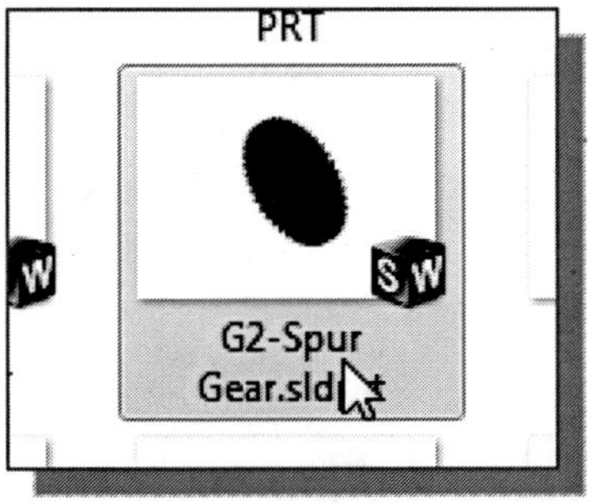

9. Select the ***G2-Spur Gear*** part in the list window.

10. On your own, place a copy of the selected part on the screen next to the *GearBox*.

11. On your own, apply a **Coincident** and a **Concentric** constraint to assemble the *G2-Spur Gear* part so that it is aligned to the *Spacer-Short* part as shown.

12. Adjust the position of the gear by using **drag and drop**.

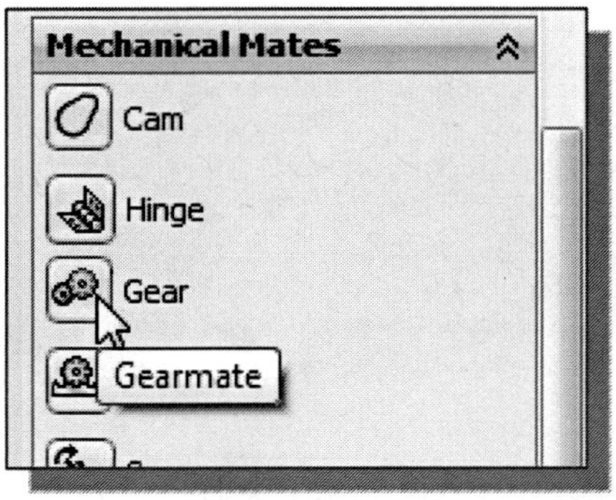

13. In the *Property Manager*, select the ***Mechanical Mates*** panel.

14. Activate the **Gear** icon to apply another **Gearmate**.

15. On your own, select the two mating gears and set the proper teeth number, **12** and **42**, as shown.

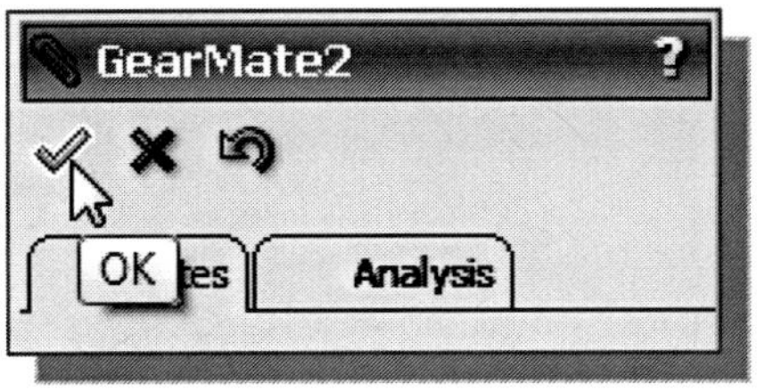

16. Click **OK** to accept the settings.

17. On your own, **drag** the *Pinion* gear in the assembly and confirm all gears are moving correctly.

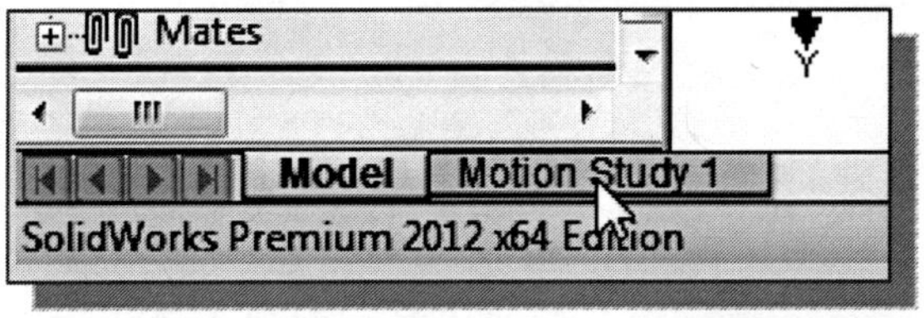

18. Select the **Motion Study 1** tab at the bottom of the *SolidWorks* window.

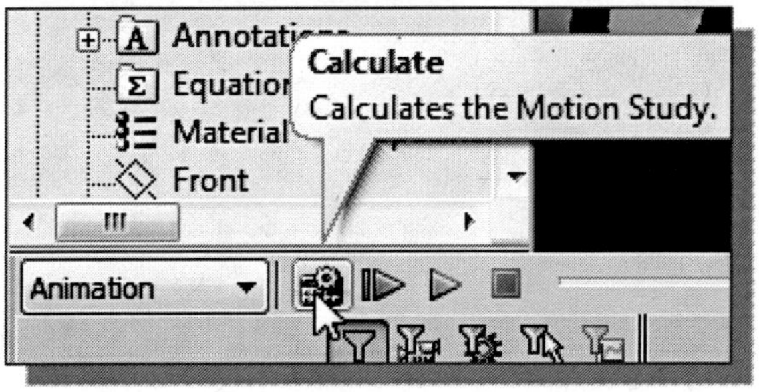

19. Click the **Calculate** command on the *Motion Manager* toolbar to calculate the *Motion Study.*

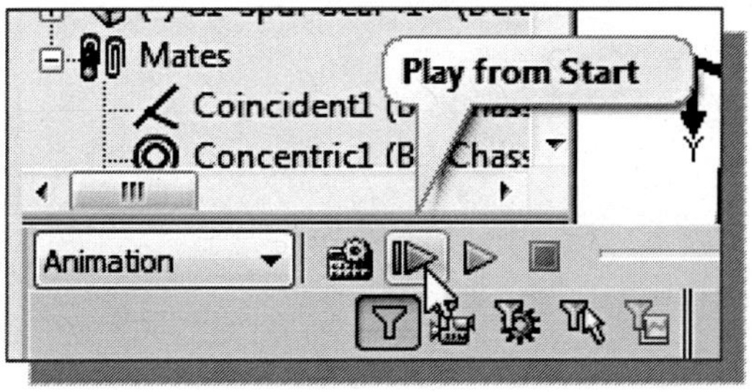

20. Click on the **Play from Start** button to view the animation.

- On your own, confirm the simulation of the assembly is behaving correctly.

Assemble the G3 Gear

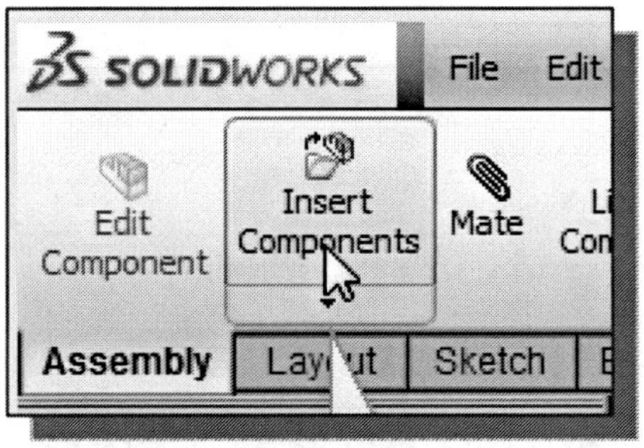

1. In the *Assembly* toolbar, select the **Insert Components** command by left-mouse-clicking the icon.

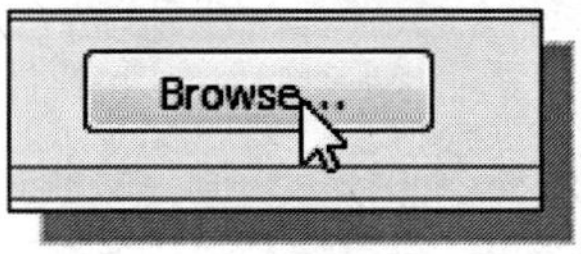

2. Click **Browse** in the *Property Manager.*

3. Select the ***G3-Spur Gear*** part in the list window.

4. On your own, place a copy of the selected part on the screen next to the *GearBox*.

5. On your own, apply a **Coincident** and a **Concentric** constraint to assemble the *G3-Spur Gear* part so that it is aligned to the *G1-Spur Gear* part as shown.

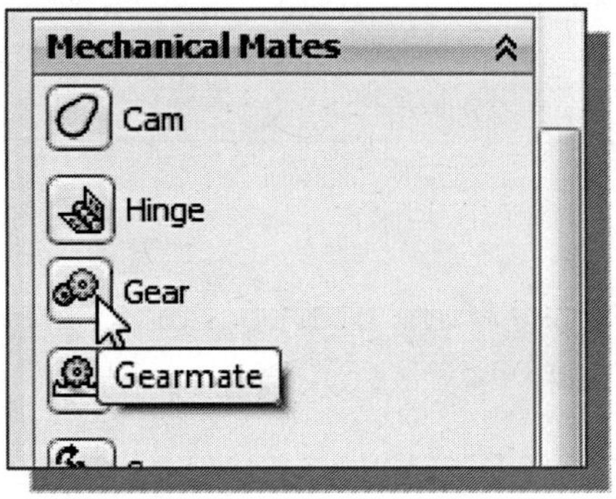

6. In the *Property Manager*, select the ***Mechanical Mates*** panel.

7. Activate the **Gear** icon to apply another **Gearmate**.

8. On your own, select the two mating gears and set the proper teeth number, **12** and **42**, as shown.

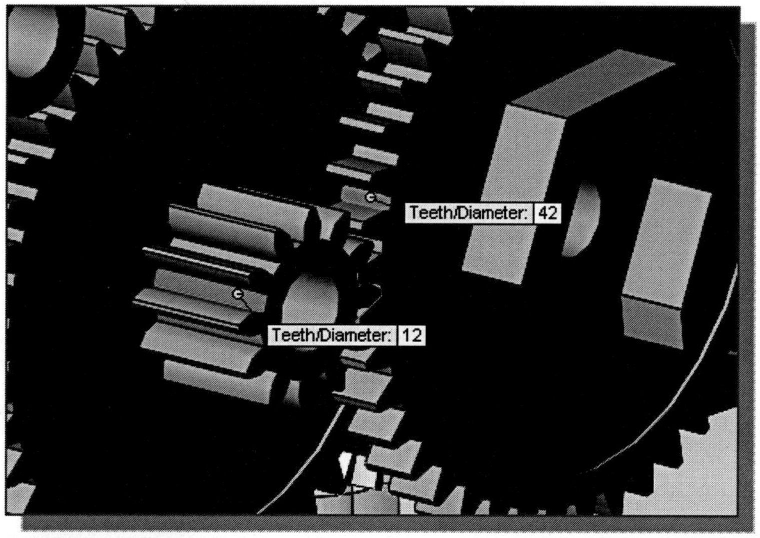

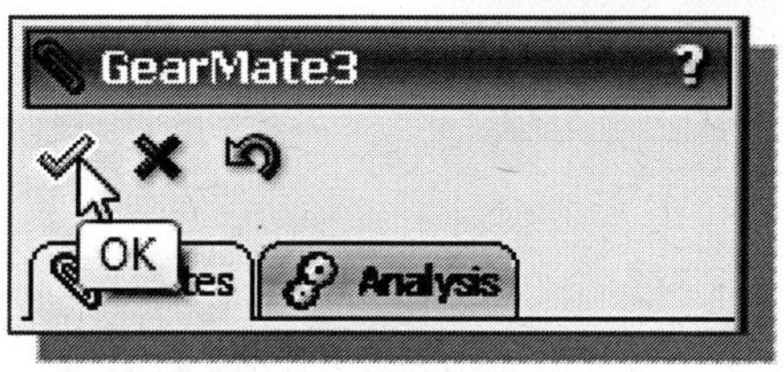

9. Click **OK** to accept the settings.

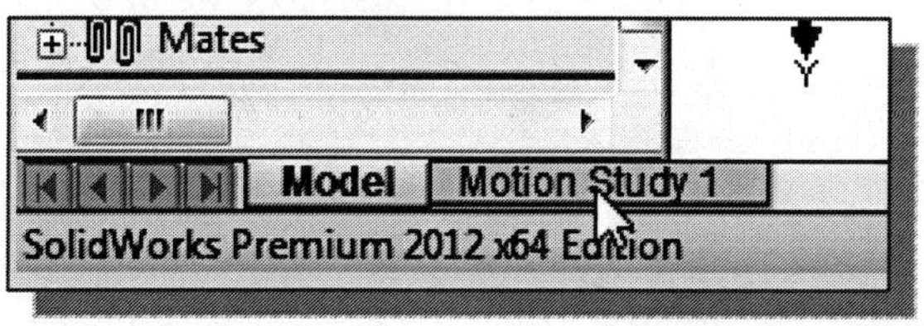

10. Select the **Motion Study 1** tab at the bottom of the *SolidWorks* window.

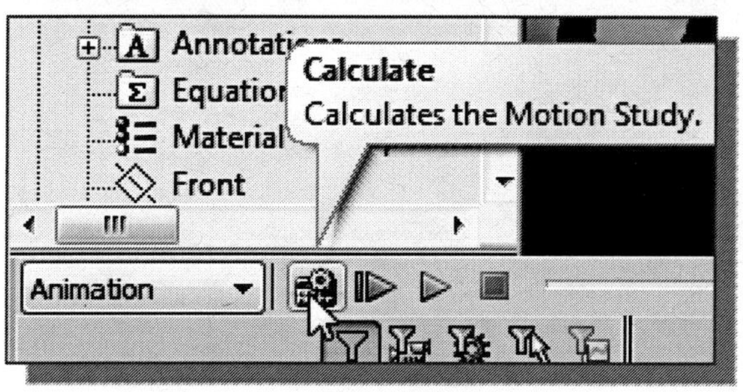

11. Click the **Calculate** command on the *Motion Manager* toolbar to calculate the *Motion Study.*

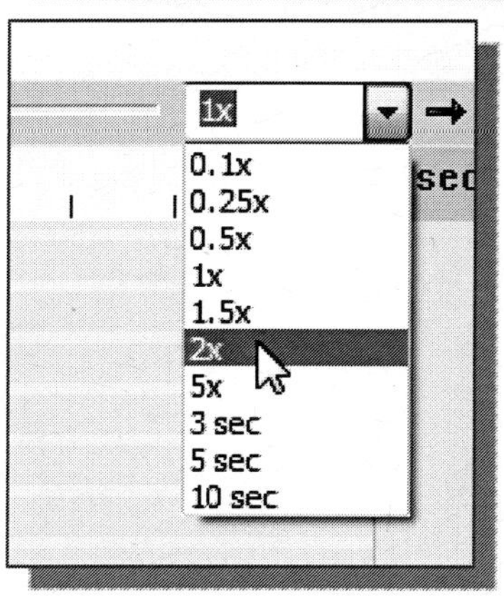

12. Set the playback speed to **2X** in the *Motion Manager* toolbar. This setting allows the adjustment of the playback speed to twice as fast as before.

13. Click on the **Play from Start** button to view the animation.

- On your own, confirm the simulation of the assembly is behaving correctly.

Assemble the Hex Shafts

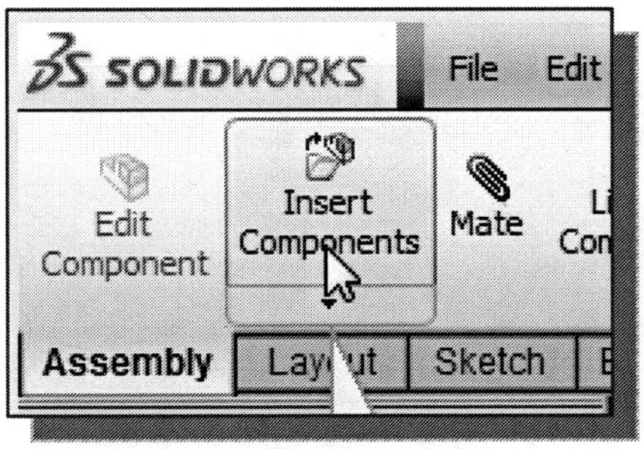

14. In the *Assembly* toolbar, select the **Insert Components** command by left-mouse-clicking the icon.

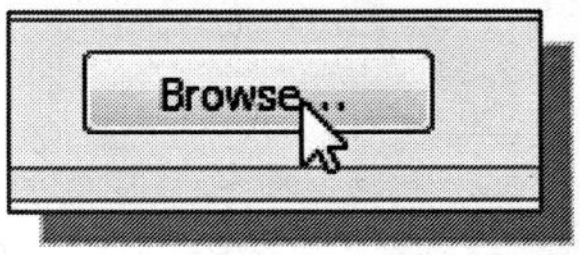

15. Click **Browse** in the *Property Manager*.

16. Select the ***Hex-Shaft-Collar*** part in the list window.

17. On your own, place a copy of the selected part on the screen next to the *GearBox*.

18. On your own, apply three constraints to assemble the *Hex-Shaft-Collar* part next to the *G3-Spur Gear* part, with the longer end of the shaft into the gear, as shown. (Hint: Apply a **Parallel** constraint to the hexagon surfaces.)

- The *Shaft* should be fully constrained so that it moves with the *G3-Spur Gear*.

19. On your own, place a copy of the ***M1-Spacer*** part on the screen next to the *GearBox*.

20. On your own, assemble the ***M1-Spacer*** part next to the ***G2-Spur Gear*** part using two constraints as shown.

21. On your own, assemble the *Hex-Shaft* part aligned to the *G2-Spur Gear* part and the *GearBox-Right* part as shown. (Hint: Use the datum planes that pass through the center of the *Shaft* to aid the assembling of the part.)

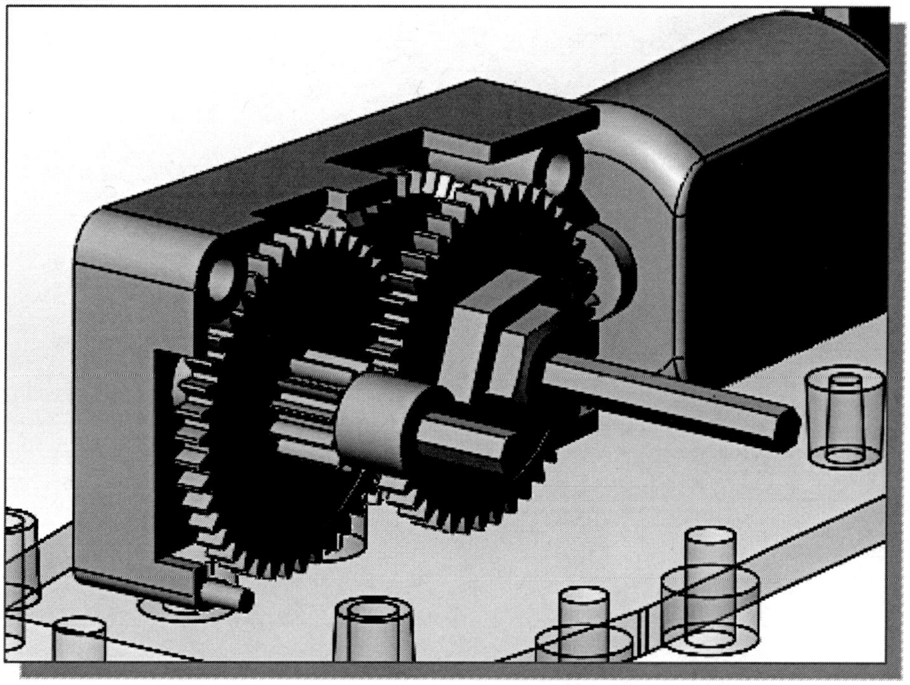

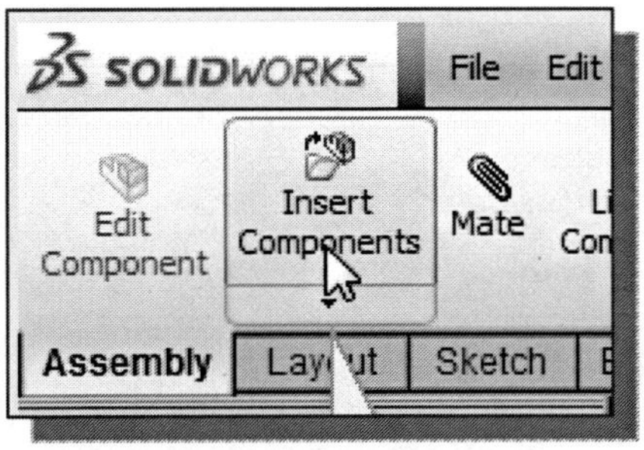

22. In the *Assembly* toolbar, select the **Insert Components** command by left-mouse-clicking the icon.

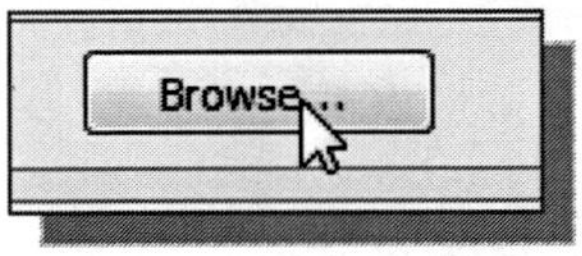

23. Click **Browse** in the *Property Manager*.

24. On your own, assemble the ***GearBox-Left*** part as shown.

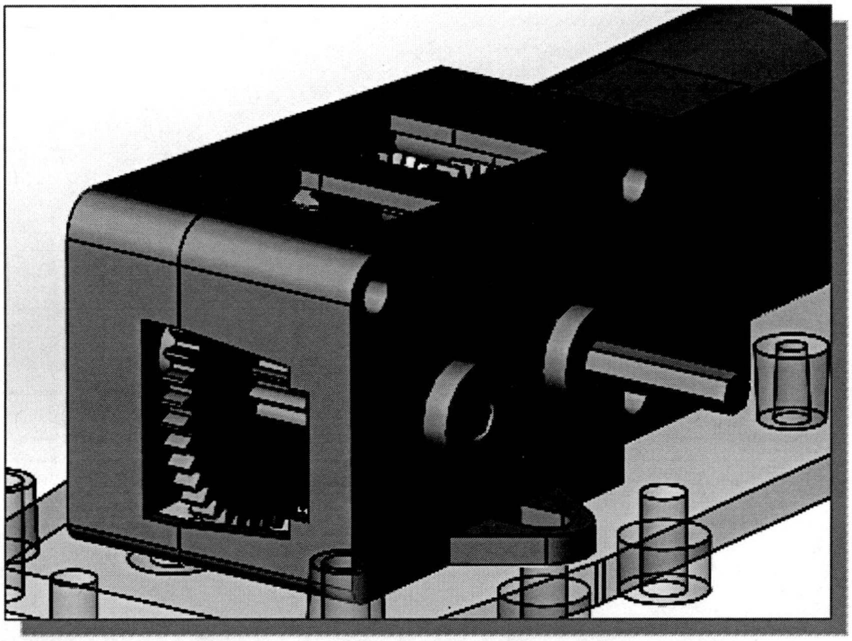

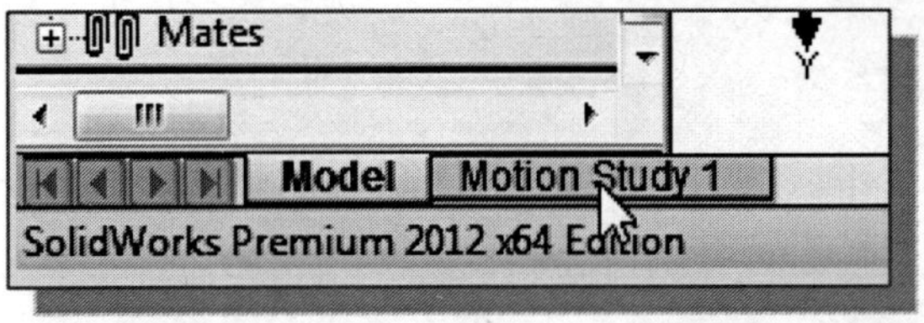

25. Select the **Motion Study 1** tab at the bottom of the *SolidWorks* window.

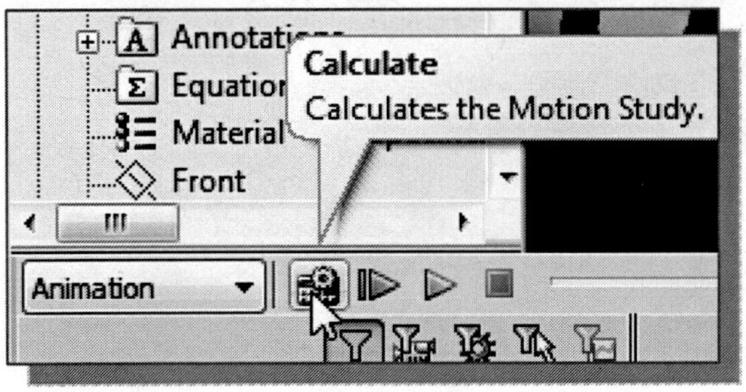

26. Click the **Calculate** command on the *Motion Manager* toolbar to calculate the *Motion Study*.

- On your own, confirm the simulation of the assembly is behaving correctly.

Assemble the Crank Parts

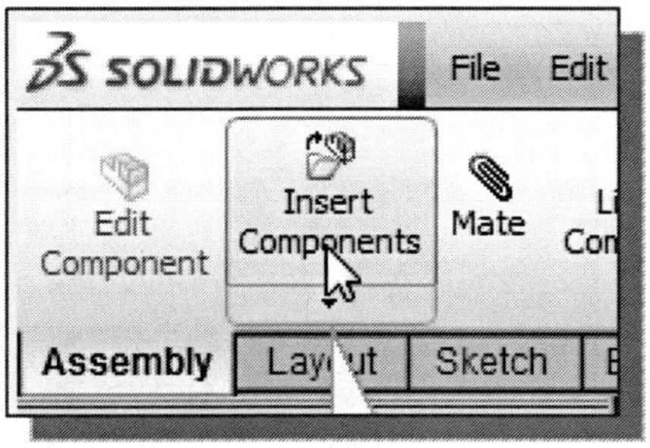

1. In the *Assembly* toolbar, select the **Insert Components** command by left-mouse-clicking the icon.

2. Click **Browse** in the *Property Manager.*

3. Select the ***A9-Crank-Right*** part in the list window.

4. On your own, place a copy of the selected part on the screen next to the *GearBox-Right* part.

5. On your own, first apply a **Coincident** constraint to align the end surface of the *Crank* to the *Hex-Shaft* part as shown.

6. Apply a **Concentric** constraint to align the center axis of the *Crank* to the *GearBox-Right* part as shown.

7. Apply another **Coincident** constraint to align the *Crank* by constraining the corresponding datum plane to the *Hex-Shaft-Collar* part as shown.

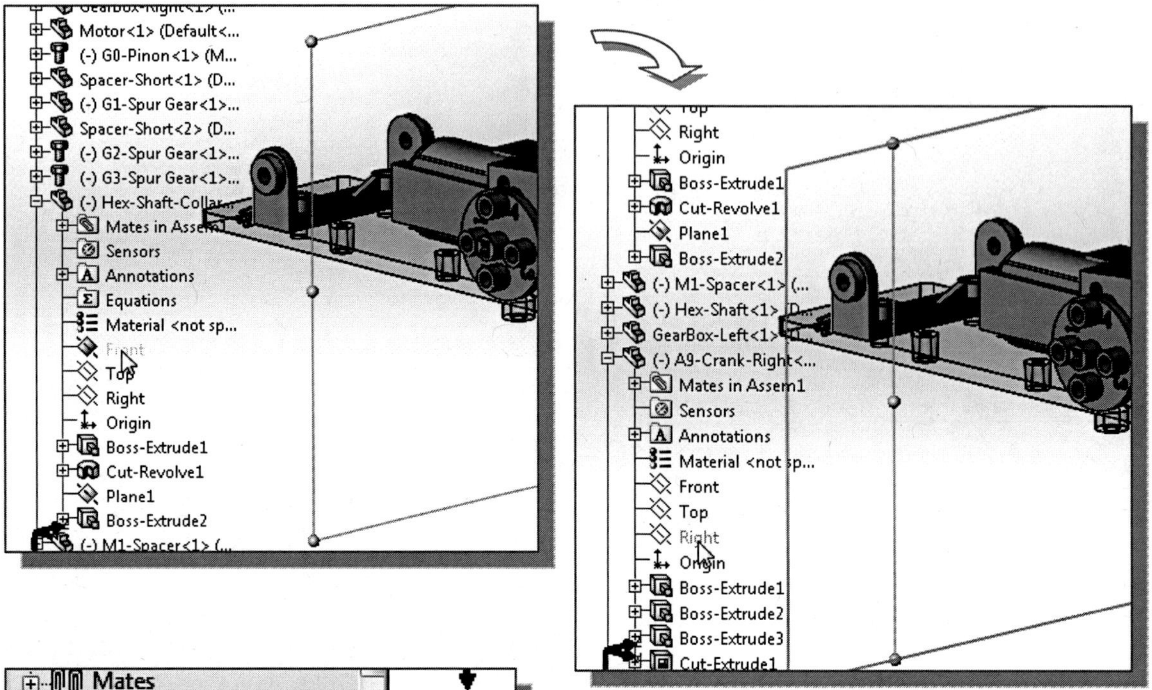

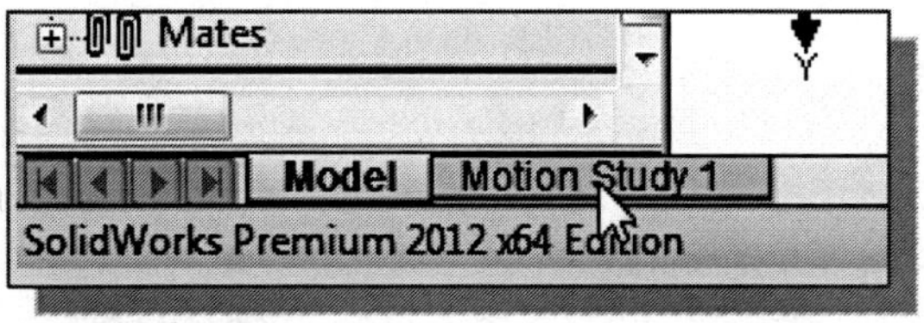

8. Select the **Motion Study 1** tab at the bottom of the *SolidWorks* window.

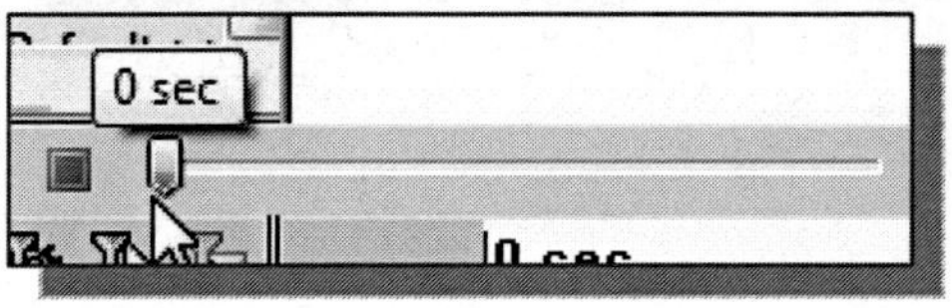

9. Drag the **Time slide bar** back to **0 sec**.

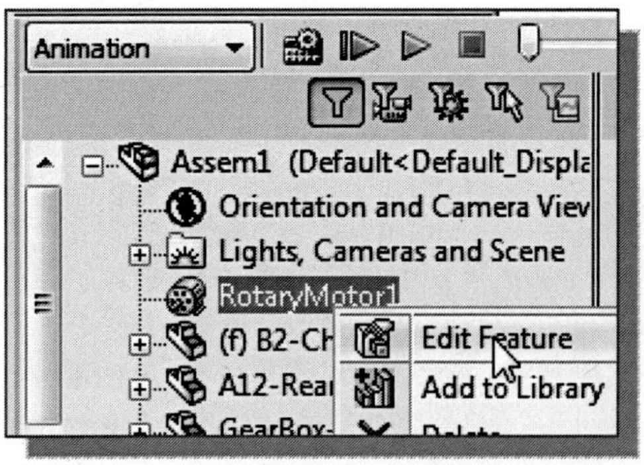

10. On your own, use the **Edit Feature** option on *Rotary Motor* and set the speed to **30 RPM** to match with the gear ratio of the gear box.

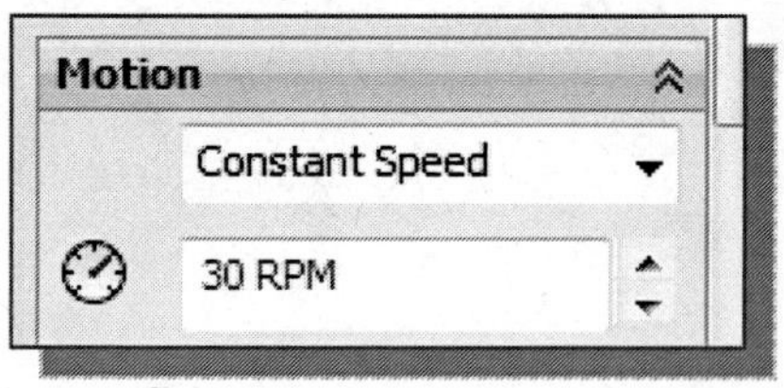

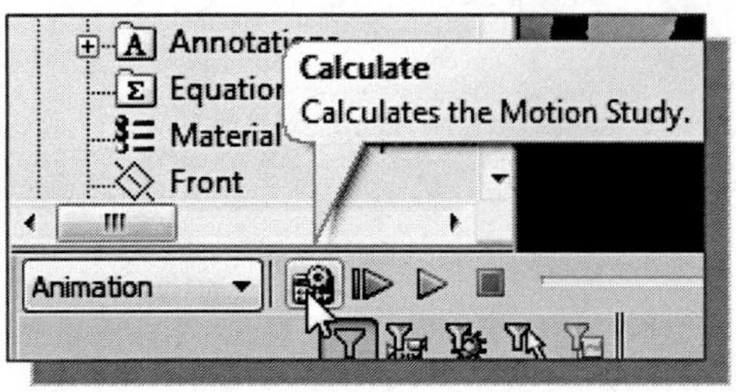

11. Click the **Calculate** command on the *Motion Manager* toolbar to recalculate the **Animation**.

12. Click on the **Play from Start** button to view the animation.

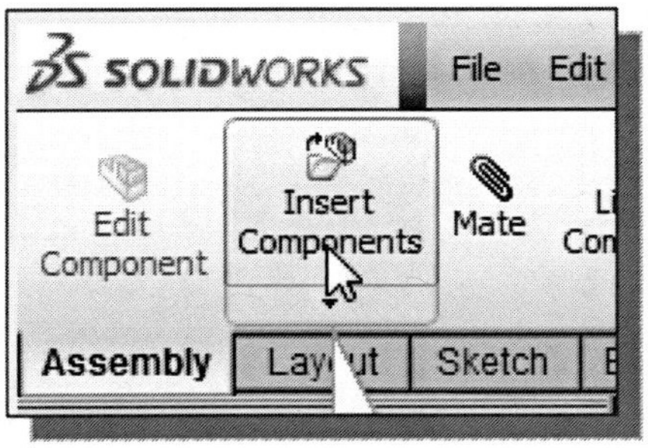

13. In the *Assembly* toolbar, select the **Insert Components** command by left-mouse-clicking the icon.

14. Click **Browse** in the *Property Manager.*

15. Select the ***A10-Crank-Left*** part in the list window.

16. On your own, place a copy of the selected part on the screen next to the *GearBox*.

17. On your own, first apply a **Coincident** constraint to align the end surface of the *Crank* to the *Hex-Shaft* as shown.

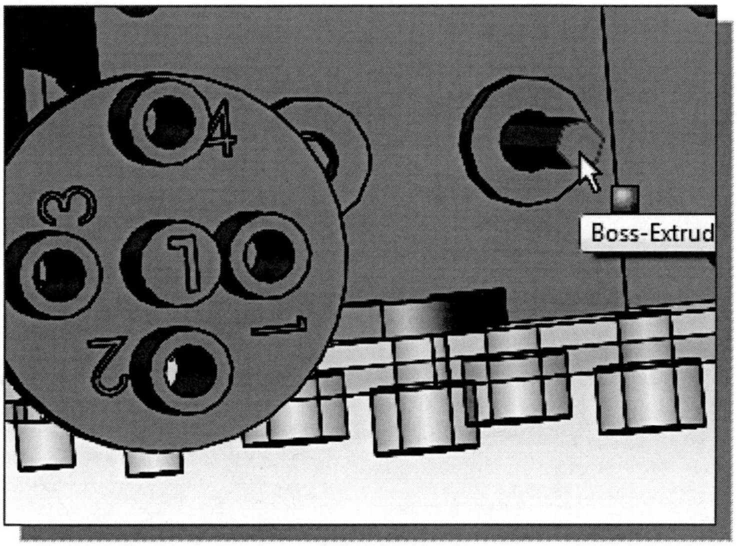

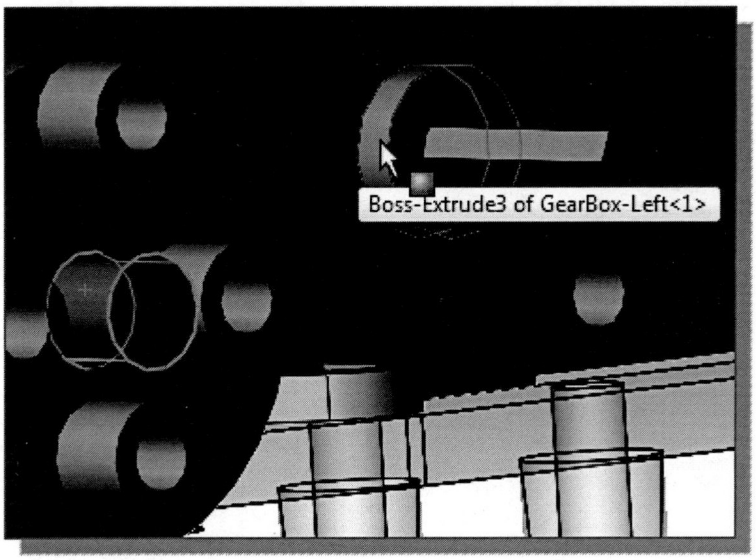

18. Apply a **Concentric** constraint to align the center axis of the *Crank* to the *GearBox-Right* part as shown.

19. Adjust the *Crank*, using **drag and drop**, so that its ***hole No. 1*** is roughly aligned **180 degrees** to the *hole No. 1* on the *A9-Crank-Right* part.

20. Apply another **Coincident** constraint to align the *Crank* by constraining the corresponding datum plane to the *A9-Crank-Right* part as shown.

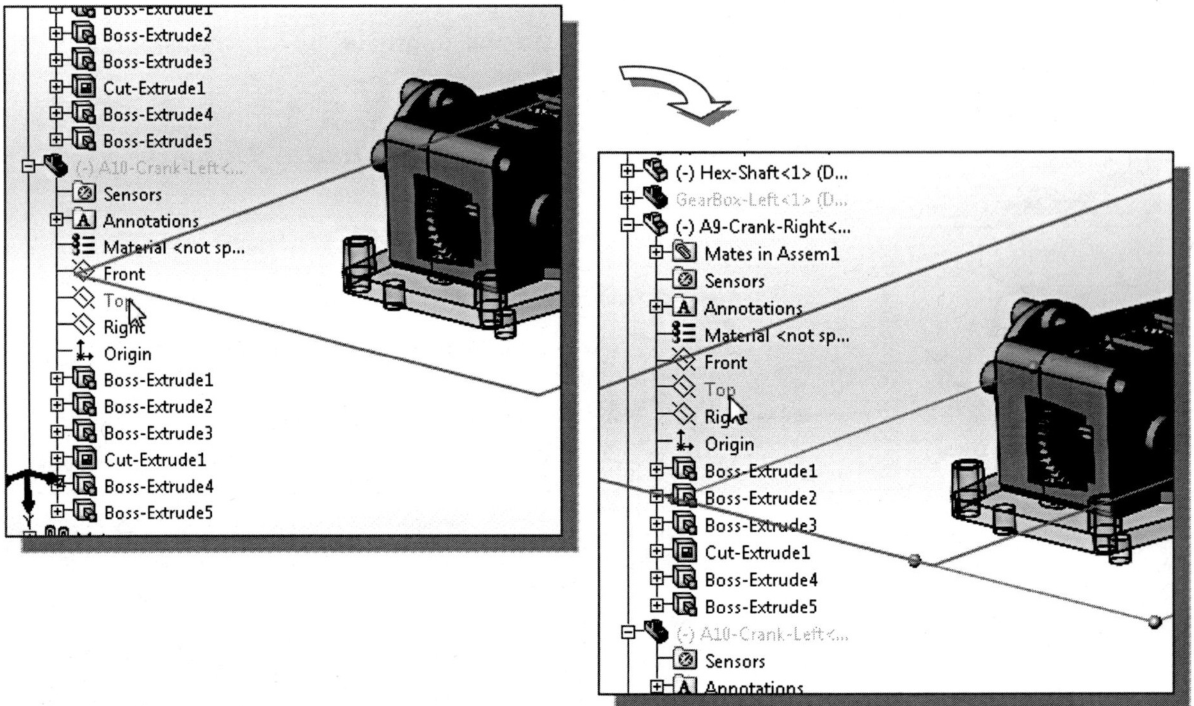

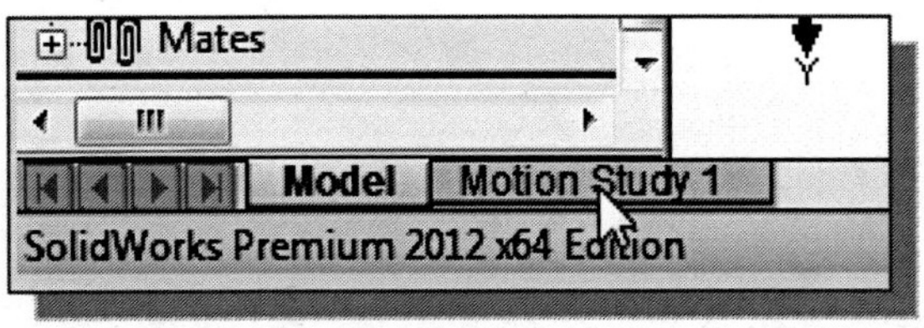

21. Select the **Motion Study 1** tab at the bottom of the *SolidWorks* window.

22. Drag the diamond shaped marker to **20 sec**. This will extend the animation to 20 seconds.

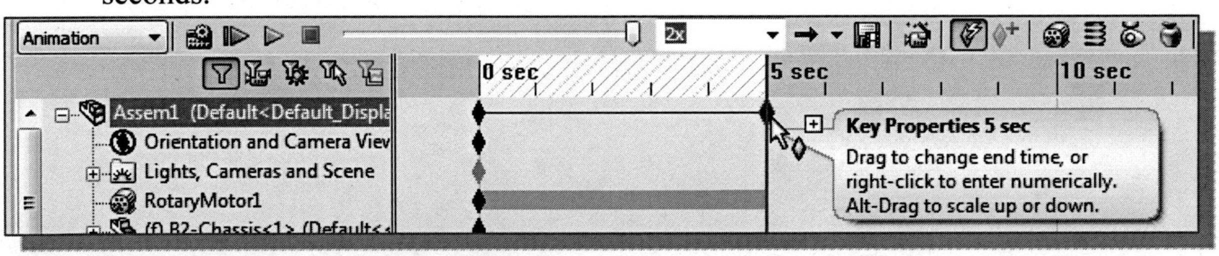

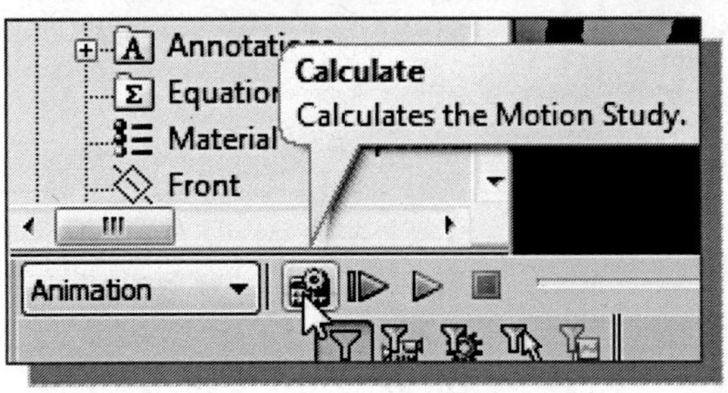

23. Click the **Calculate** command on the *Motion Manager* toolbar to calculate the *Motion Study*

24. Click on the **Play from Start** button to view the animation.

- On your own, confirm the simulation of the assembly is behaving correctly.

Assemble the Rear Shaft and Legs

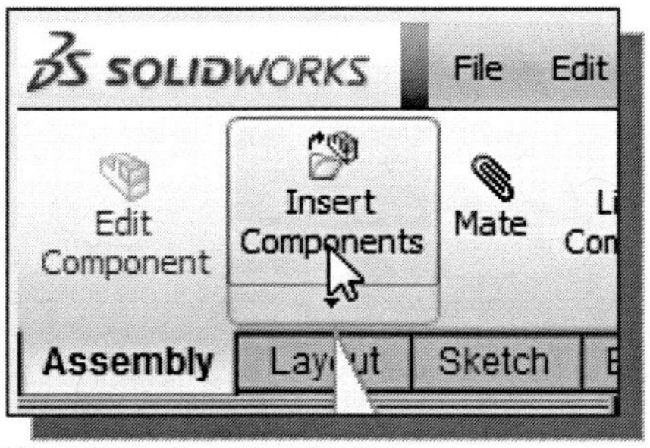

1. In the *Assembly* toolbar, select the **Insert Components** command by left-mouse-clicking the icon.

2. Click **Browse** in the *Property Manager.*

3. Select the ***Shaft-3x80*** part in the list window.

4. On your own, place a copy of the selected part on the screen next to the *GearBox.*

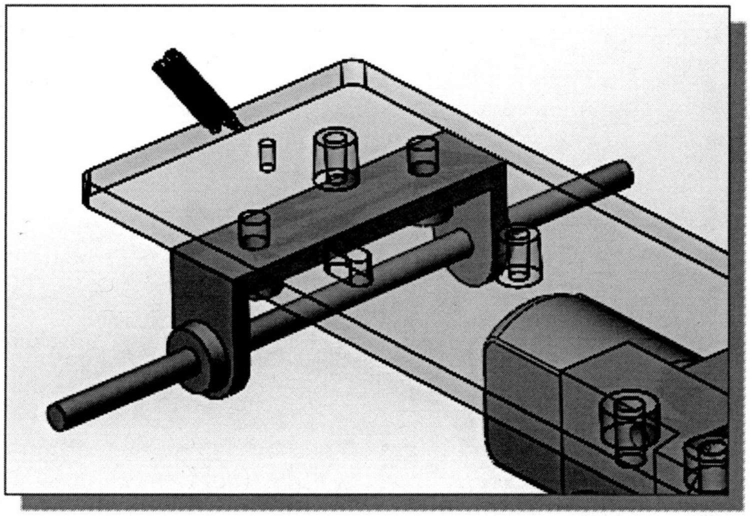

5. On your own, apply the necessary constraints to align the *Shaft* to the *Rear Axle Support* as shown.

6. On your own, assemble two copies of the ***A3-Spacer*** part to the *Rear Axle Support* as shown.

7. On your own, place four copies of the ***Knee-Leg Sub-Assembly*** near the assembly model.

- In *SolidWorks*, a subassembly is treated the same way as a single part during assembling.

8. Assemble one of the rear legs, so that the center axis is aligned to the rear ***Shaft***. Also, apply an **Offset** constraint with an offset distance of **2.0 mm** to the *A3-Spacer* as shown.

9. Assemble the second leg the same way to the other rear end of the ***Shaft***.

10. Assemble the left front leg, with the center hole aligned to ***hole No. 1***, the hole that is nearest to the center axis of the *Crank* model.

11. Also apply an **Offset** constraint with an offset distance of **2.0 mm** to the *A9-Crank* as shown.

12. Assemble the last leg the same way to the other side. (Hint: Also align the center axis to *hole No. 1.*)

13. On your own, use the **constrained move** option and adjust the orientation of the four legs as shown.

Assemble the Linkage-Rods

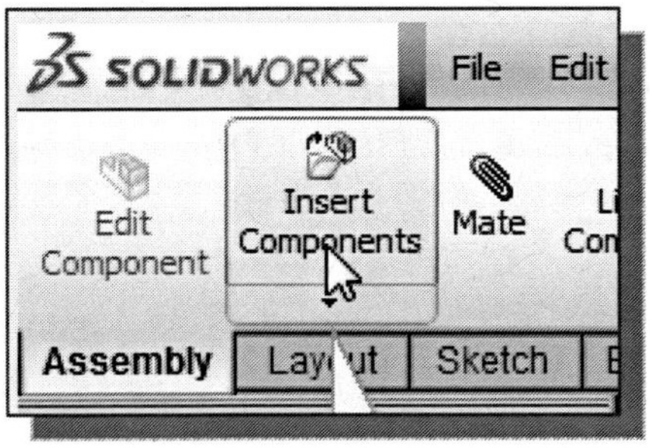

1. In the *Assembly* toolbar, select the **Insert Components** command by left-mouse-clicking the icon.

2. Click **Browse** in the *Property Manager.*

3. Select the ***Linkage-Rod*** part in the list window.

4. On your own, place a copy of the selected part on the screen above the assembly model.

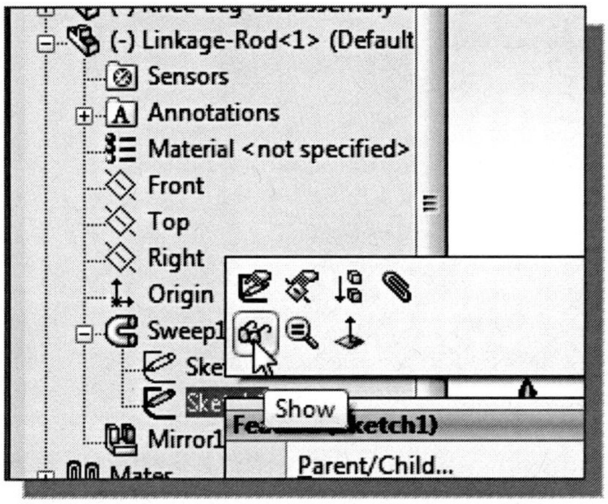

5. In the *Model History Tree*, **right-click** once on the **Sketch1** item under the **Sweep1** feature to bring up the option menu.

6. Click on the **Show** icon to make the selected sketch visible on the screen.

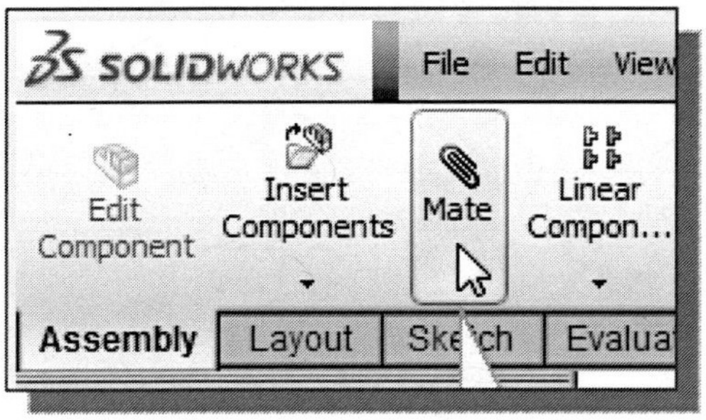

7. In the *Assembly* panel, select the **Mate** command by left-mouse-clicking once on the icon.

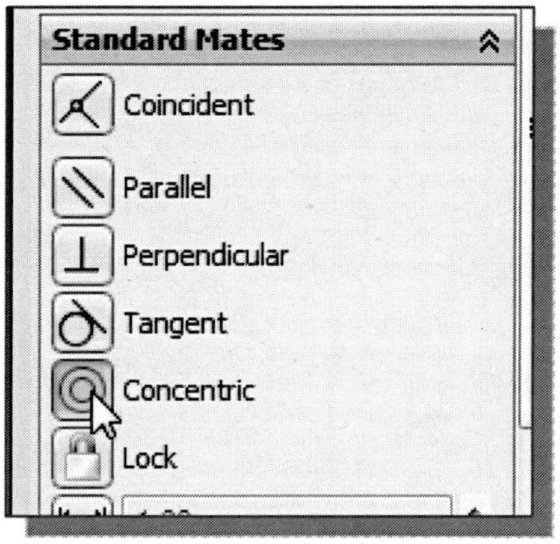

8. In the *Standard Mates* panel, activate the **Concentric** option as shown.

9. Apply a **Concentric** constraint to align the **center point** of the *Linkage-Rod* loop to the **upper axis** on one of the rear legs, so that the center axis on the *Linkage-Rod* is aligned as shown.

- Note the center point in a sketch can be used to align components in an assembly model.

10. On your own, apply an **Offset** constraint with an offset distance of **0.5 mm** to the **Front Plane** of the *Rod* to the inside surface of the *Leg* as shown.

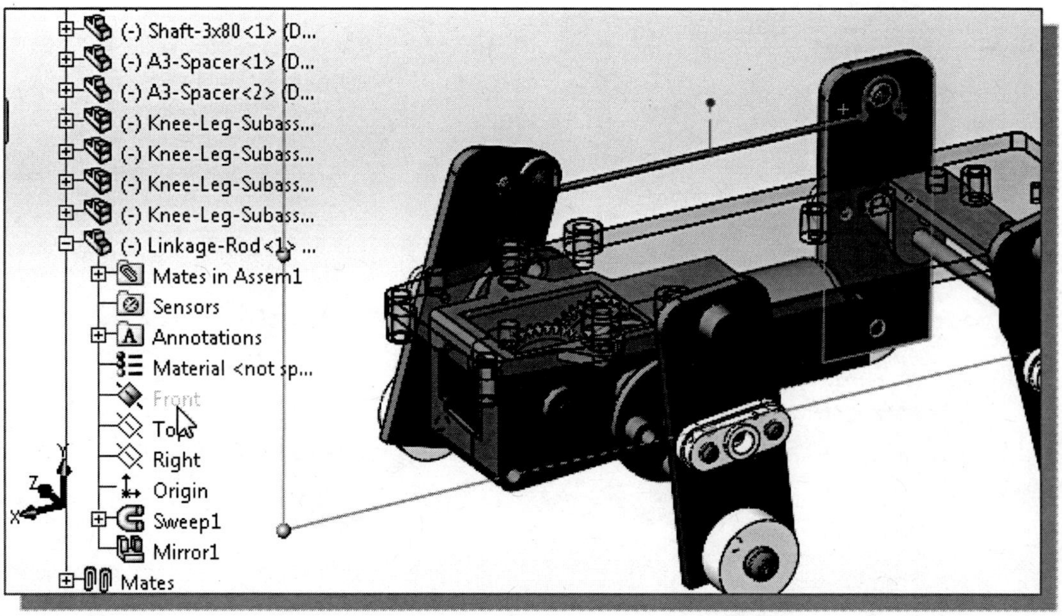

11. For the other end of the *Linkage Rod*, apply another **Concentric** constraint to align the other center point on the *Linkage-Rod* to the center axis of *hole No. 1* on the *Crank* as shown.

12. On your own, repeat the above steps and assemble the other three *Linkage-Rods*.

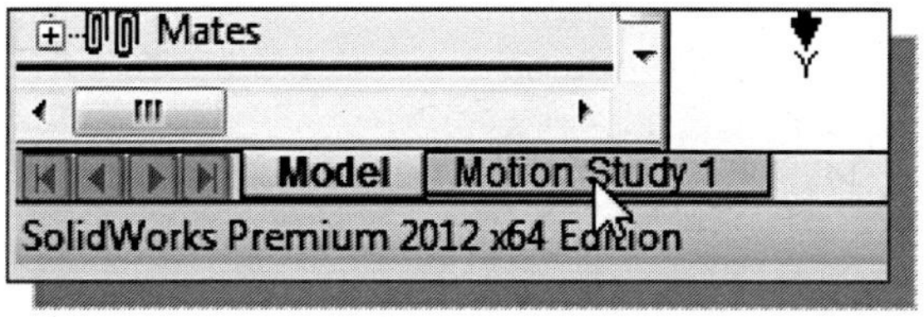

13. Select the **Motion Study 1** tab at the bottom of the *SolidWorks* window.

14. Drag the time slider to **0 sec**. This will reset the animation to the starting position.

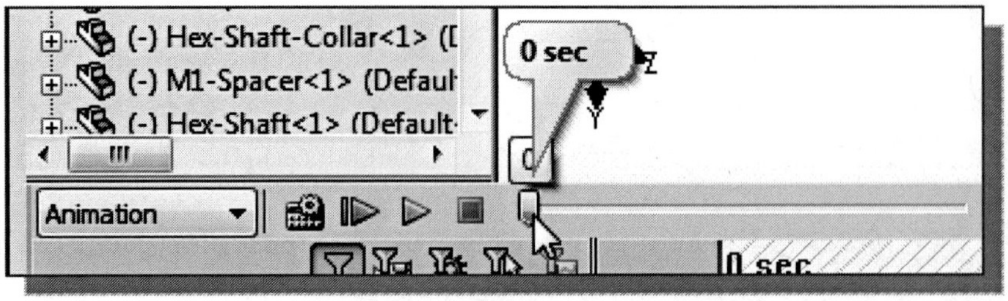

15. On your own, adjust the display, using the dynamic viewing functions, roughly as shown.

16. In the *Animation Model Tree*, move the cursor on the diamond shaped marker of the **Orientation and camera views** item, and note the current orientation is set to **Custom**. Note that *SolidWorks* allows the use of (1) *Motors* and (2) *Key frames* to perform animation and motion analysis.

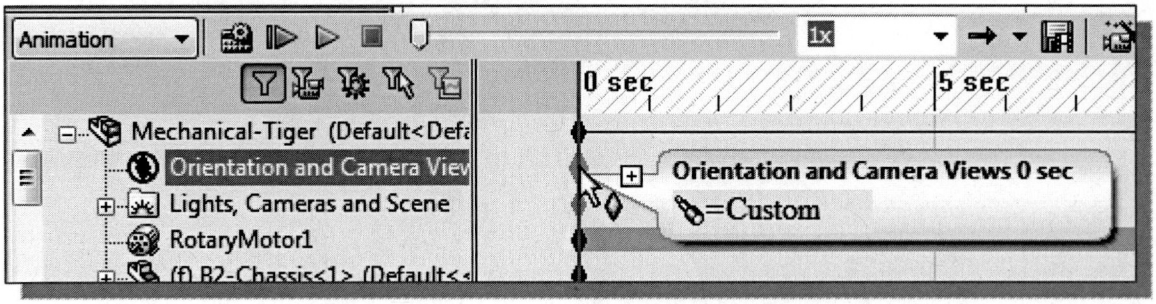

17. **Right-click** once on top of the diamond shaped marker to bring up the option menu.

18. In the option menu, select **Replace Key** to use the current display as the view angle.

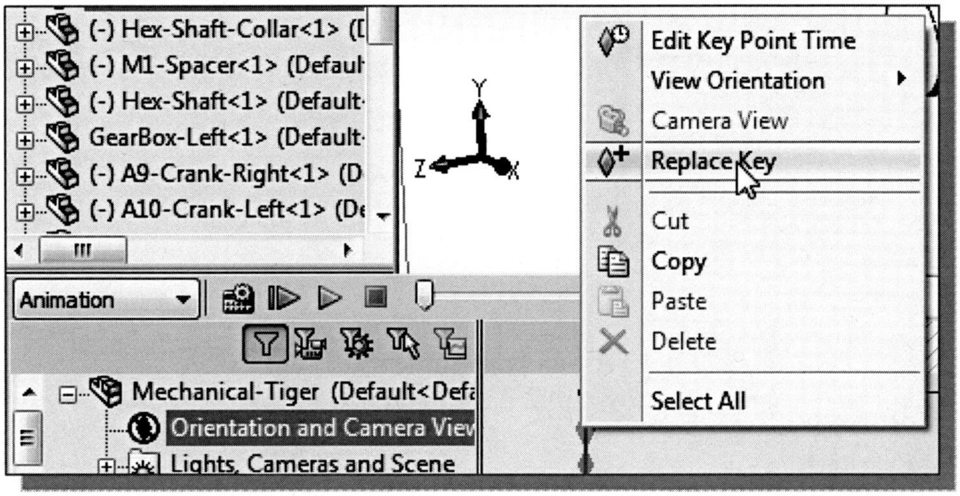

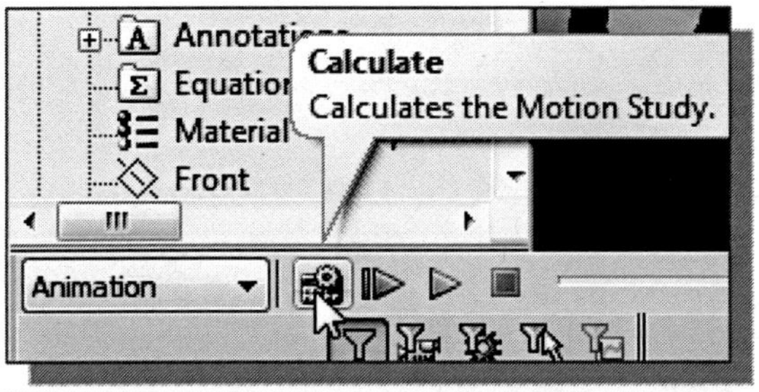

19. Click the **Calculate** command on the *Motion Manager* toolbar to calculate the *Motion Study*.

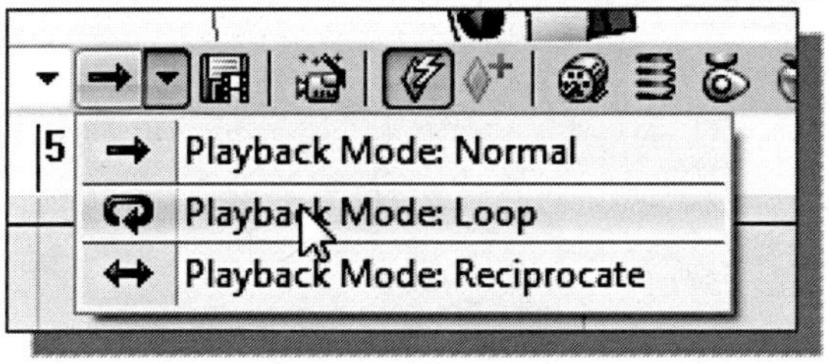

20. Set the *Playback* mode to **Loop** as shown.

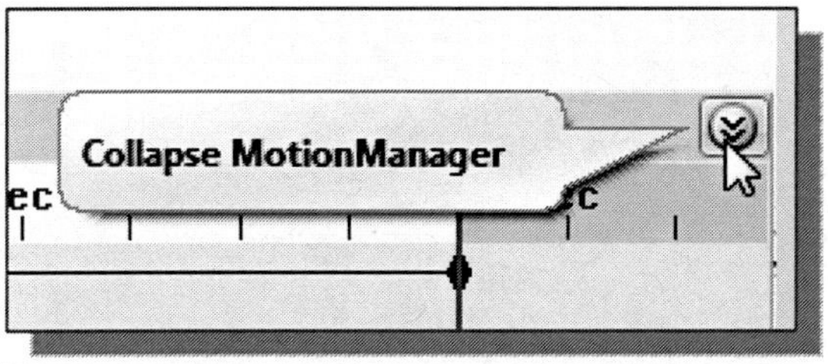

21. Click on **Collapse Motion Manager** to minimize the *Motion Manager*.

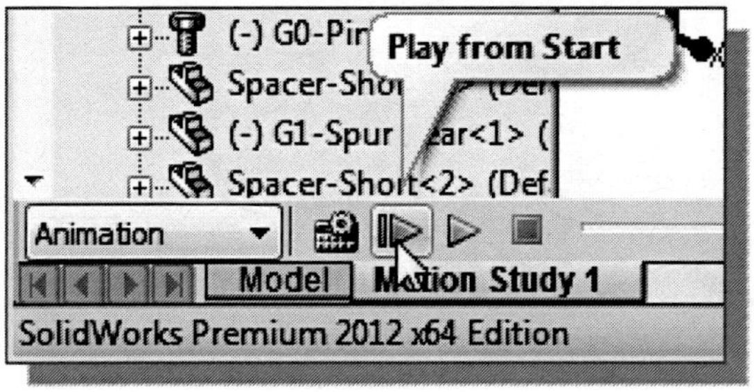

22. Click on the **Play from Start** button to view the animation.

23. Click **Stop** before proceeding to the next section.

Complete the Assembly Model

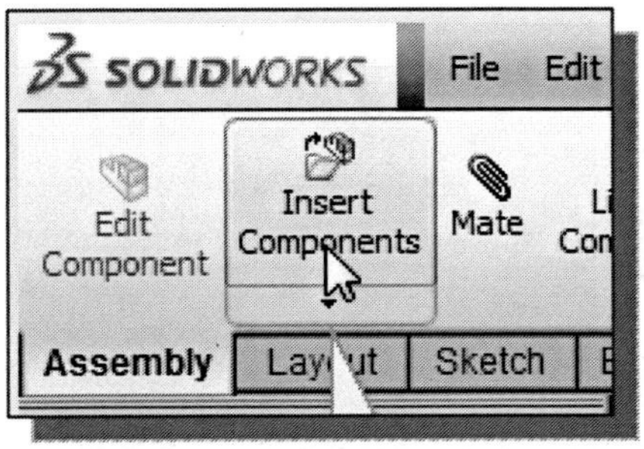

1. In the *Assembly* toolbar, select the **Insert Components** command by left-mouse-clicking the icon.

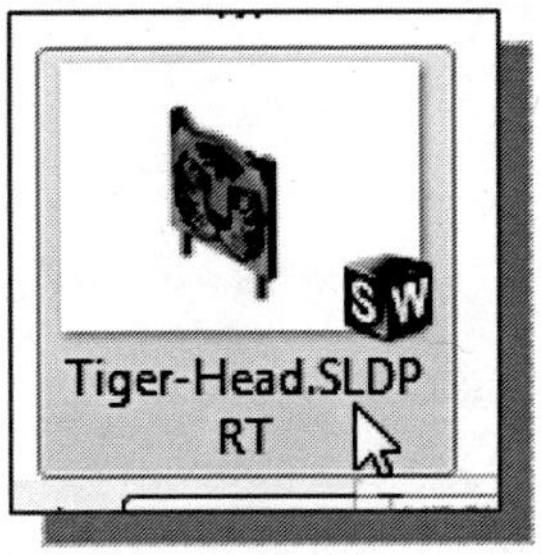

2. On your own, assemble the ***Tiger-Head*** to the assembly model as shown in the figure below.

3. On your own, assemble two copies of the ***Axle-EndCap*** parts and the ***Battery Case*** to the assembly model. (Hint: First adjust the two hole-locations on the *Battery Case* part.)

Record an Animation Movie

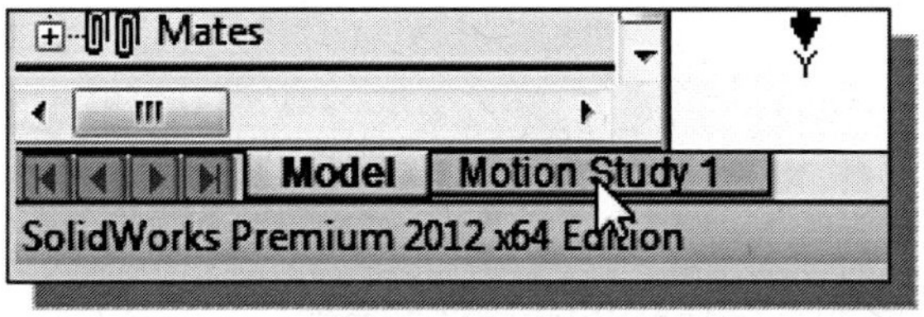

1. Select the **Motion Study 1** tab at the bottom of the *SolidWorks* window.

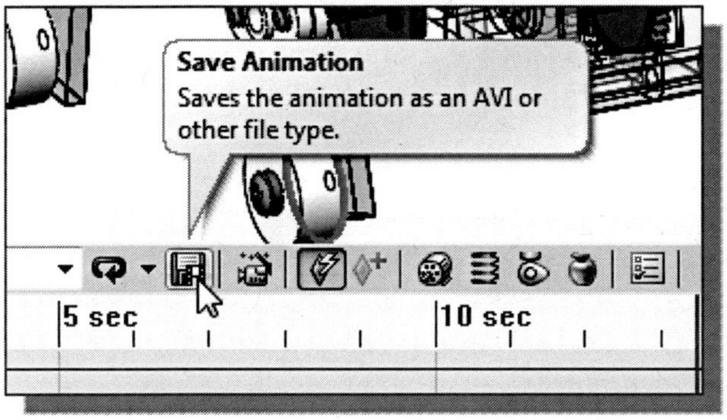

2. The simulation can also be saved as an AVI or other format file. Click the **Save Animation** button on the *Motion Manager* toolbar as shown.

3. Enter ***Mechanical-Tiger*** as the *File name* and click **Save** to accept the filename.

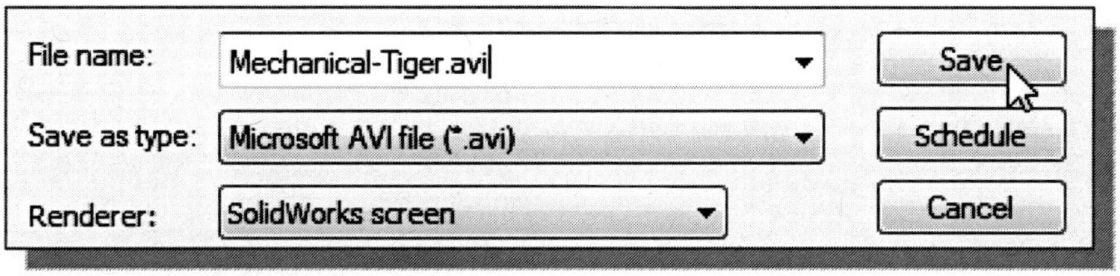

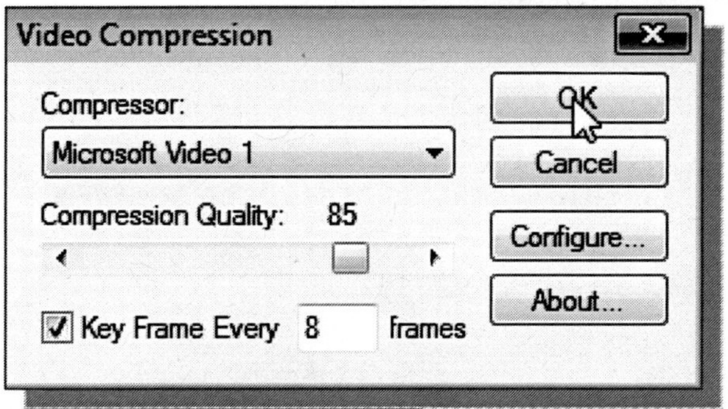

4. Select the *Video Compression* setting to set the quality and speed of the file and click **OK** to proceed.

5. On your own, view the recorded video file.

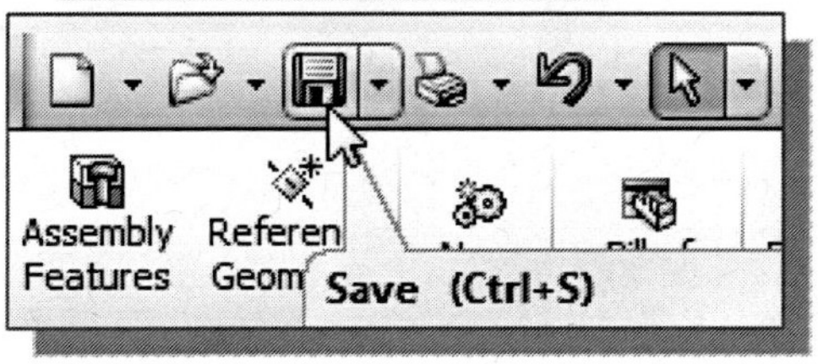

6. In the *Quick Access* menu, click **Save** and save the assembly model using the filename ***Mechanical-Tiger***.

Conclusion

Engineering design includes all activities involved, from the original conception to the finished product. *Engineering design* is the process by which products are created and modified. For many years designers sought ways to describe and analyze three-dimensional designs without building physical models. With advancements in computer technology, the creation of parametric models on computers offers a wide range of benefits. Parametric models are easier to interpret and can be easily altered. Parametric models can be analyzed using finite element analysis software, and simulation of real-life loads can be applied to the models and the results graphically displayed.

Throughout this text, various modeling techniques have been presented. Mastering these techniques will enable you to create intelligent and flexible solid models. The goal is to make use of the tools provided by *SolidWorks* and to successfully capture the **DESIGN INTENT** of the product. In many instances, only one approach to the modeling tasks was presented; you are encouraged to repeat all of the lessons and develop different ways of accomplishing the same tasks. We have only scratched the surface of *SolidWorks's* functionality. The more time you spend using the system, the easier it will be to perform parametric modeling with *SolidWorks*.

Summary of Modeling Considerations

- **Design Intent** – determine the functionality of the design; select features that are central to the design.
- **Order of Features** – consider the parent/child relationships necessary for all features.
- **Dimensional and Geometric Constraints** – the way in which the constraints are applied determines how the components are updated.
- **Relations** – consider the orientation and parametric relationships required between features and in an assembly.

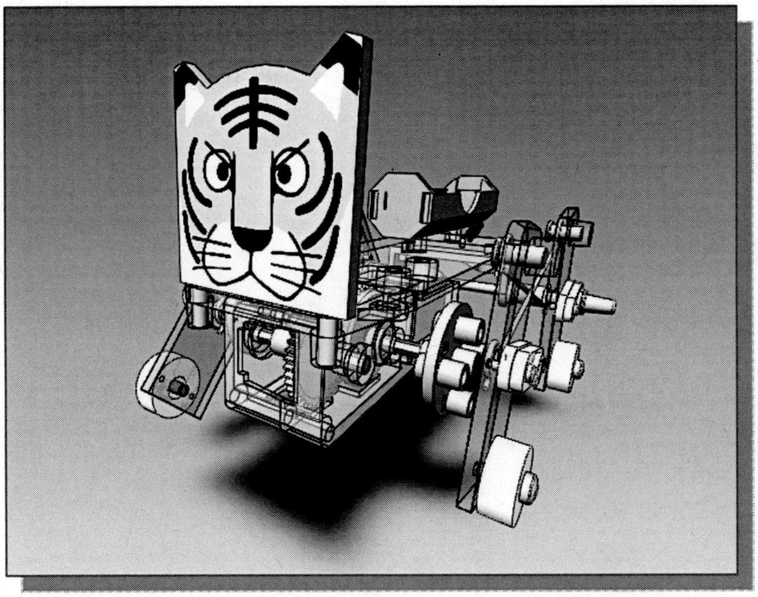

Questions:

1. What is the purpose of using ***assembly relations***?

2. List three of the commonly used ***assembly relations***.

3. Describe the difference between the **Mate** constraint and the **Aligned** constraint.

4. In an assembly, can we place more than one copy of a part? How is it done?

5. How should we determine the assembly order of different parts in an assembly model?

6. Can we perform a constrained move on fully constrained components?

7. Can *SolidWorks* calculate the center of gravity of an assembly model? How do you activate this option?

8. Can assembly relations be temporarily disabled in an assembly model? How?

9. Can *SolidWorks* calculate the weight of an assembly model? How is this done?

Exercises:

1. **Quick Return Mechanism**

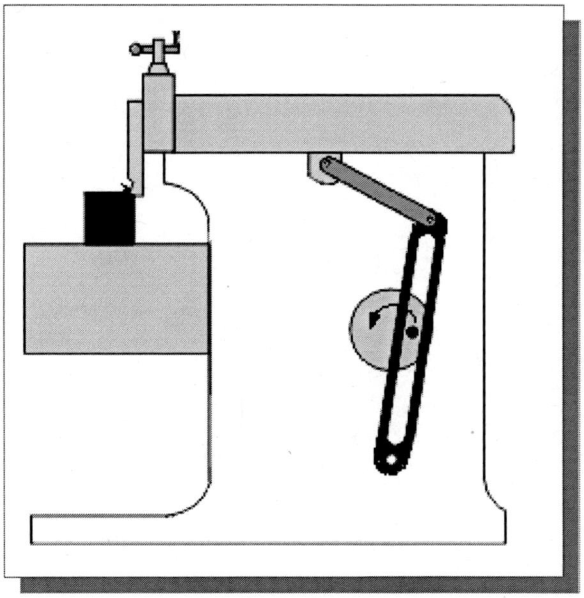

Design and create the necessary parts.

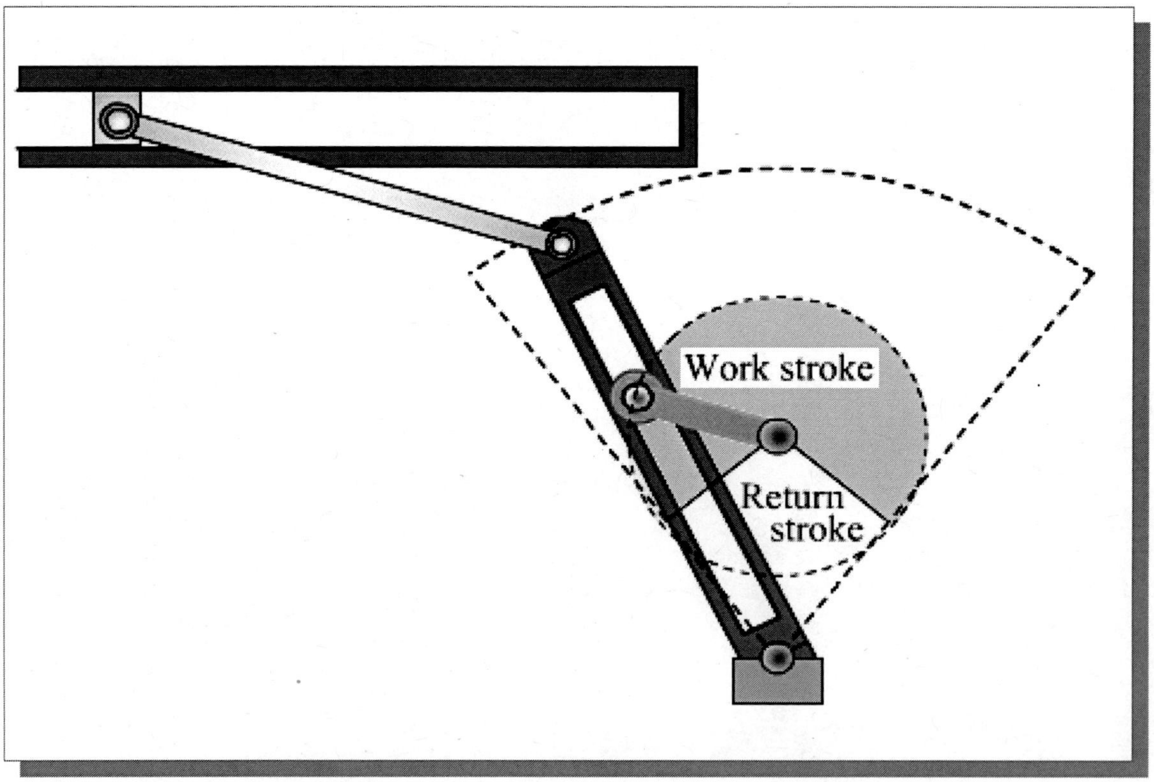

2. **Leveling Assembly** (Create a set of detail and assembly drawings. All dimensions are in mm.)

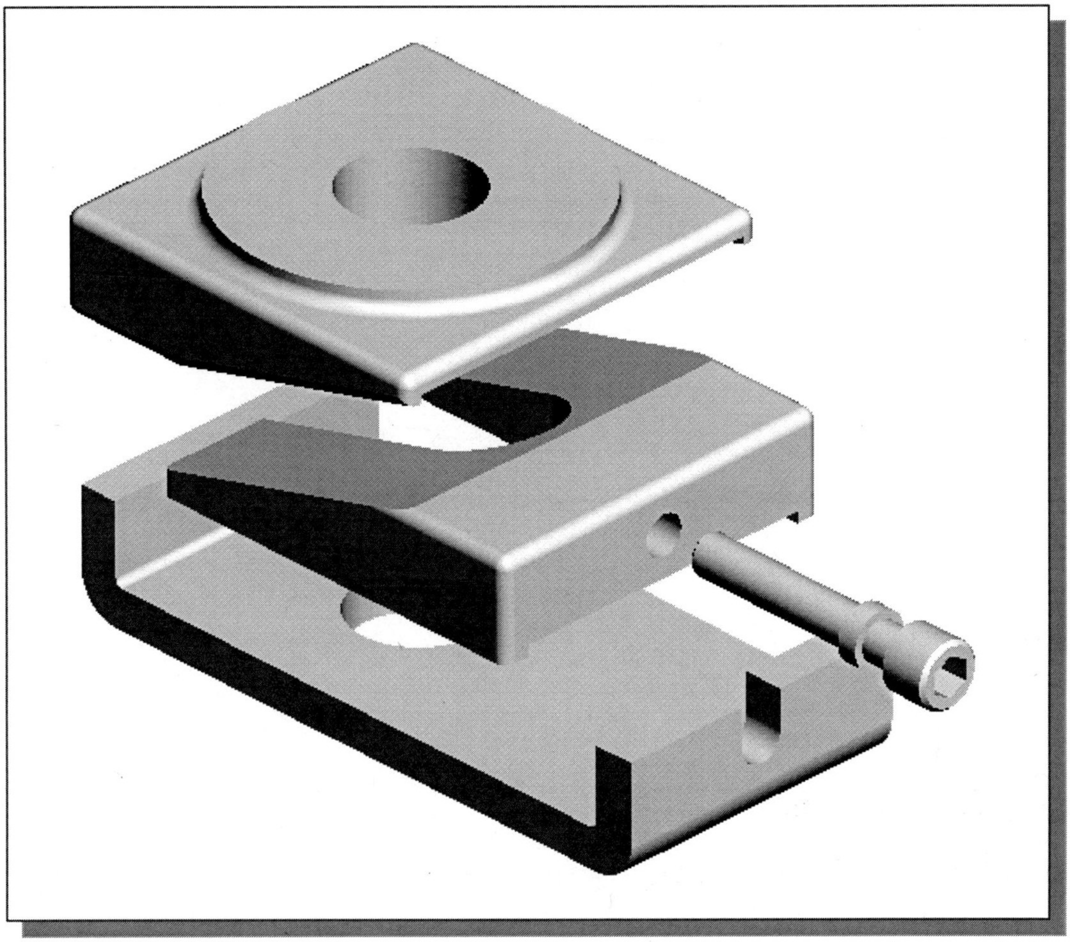

(a) **Base Plate**

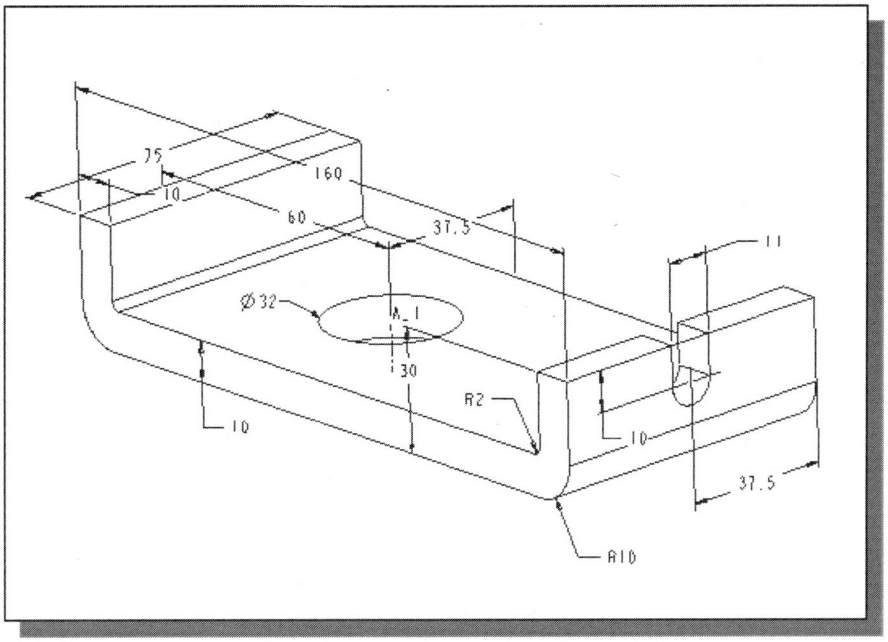

(b) **Sliding Block** (Rounds & Fillets: R3)

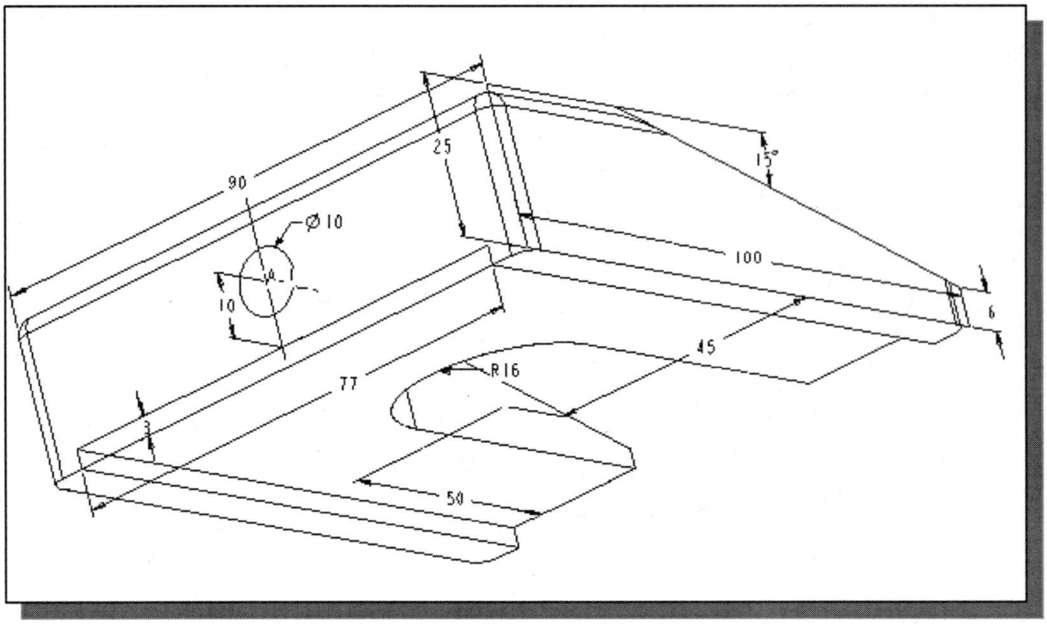

(c) **Lifting Block** (Rounds & Fillets: R3)

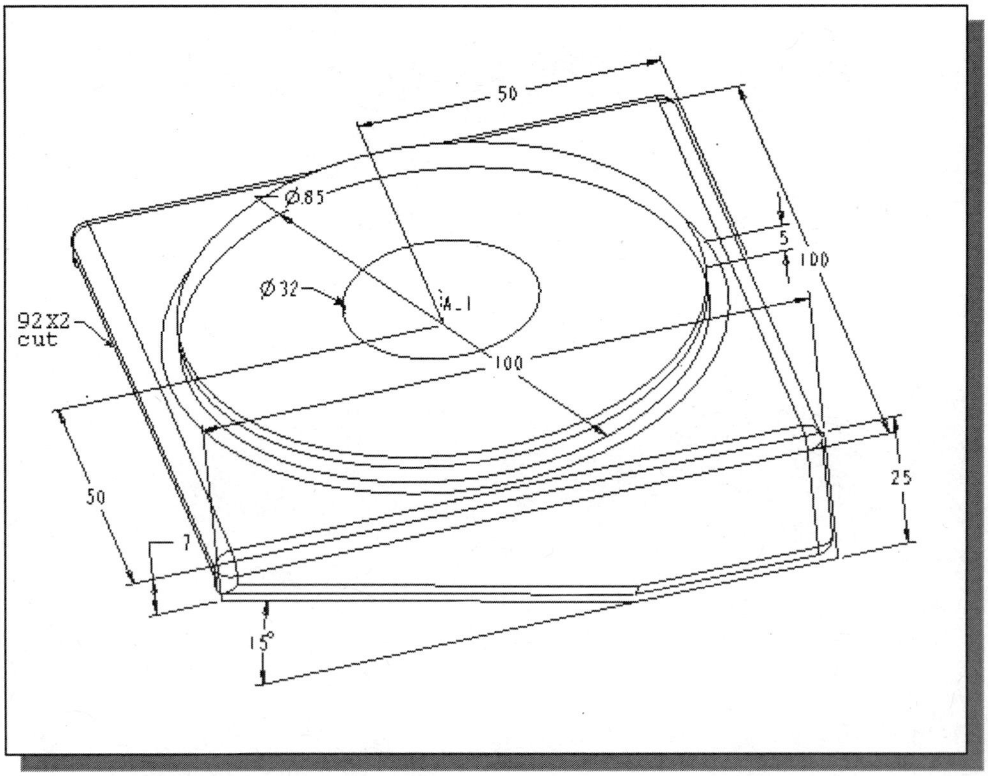

(d) **Adjusting Screw** (M10 X 1.5)

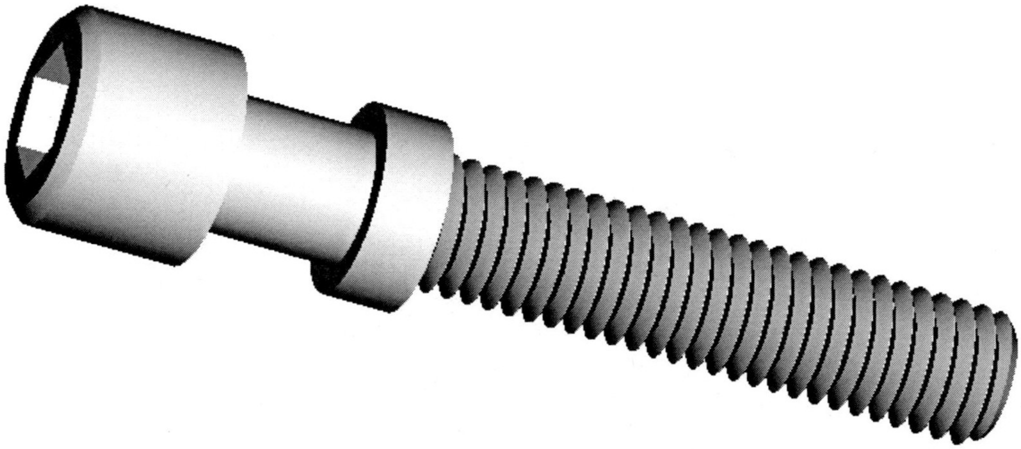

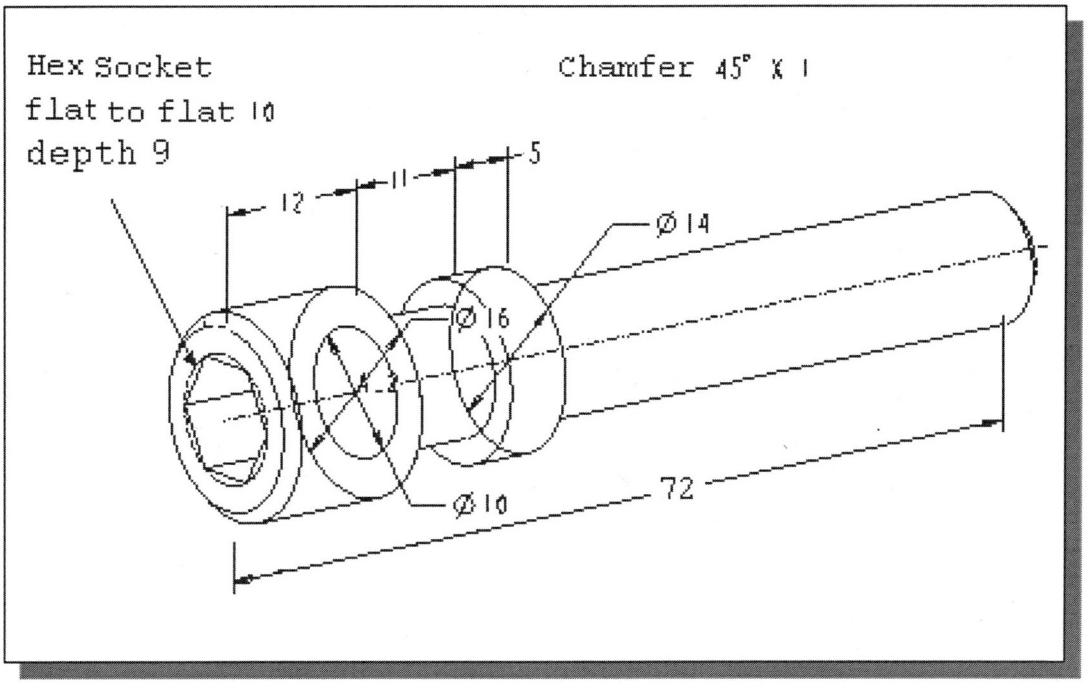

3. **Vise Assembly** (Create a set of detail and assembly drawings. All dimensions are in inches.)

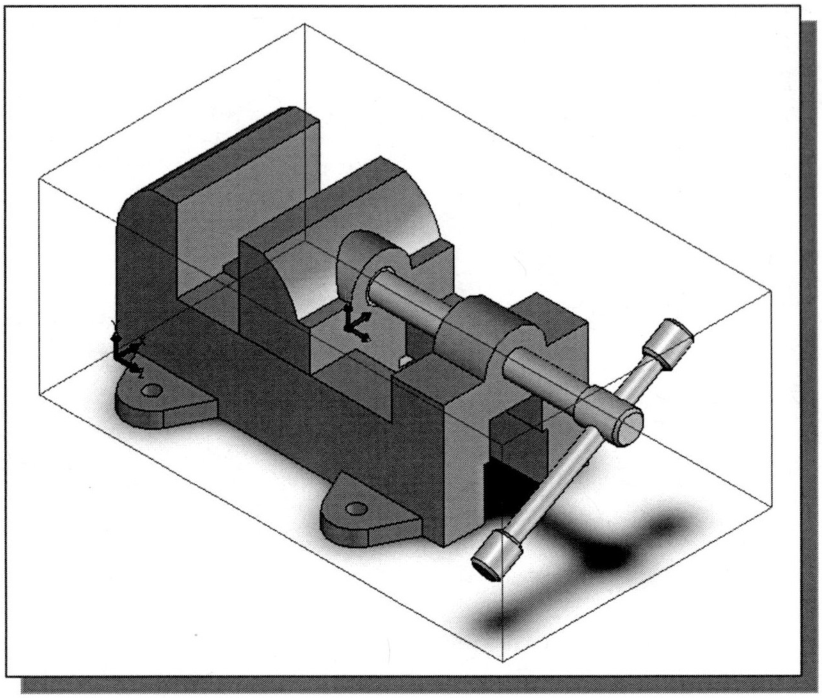

(a) **Base:** The 1.5 inch wide and 1.25 inch wide slots are cut through the entire base. Material: Gray Cast Iron.

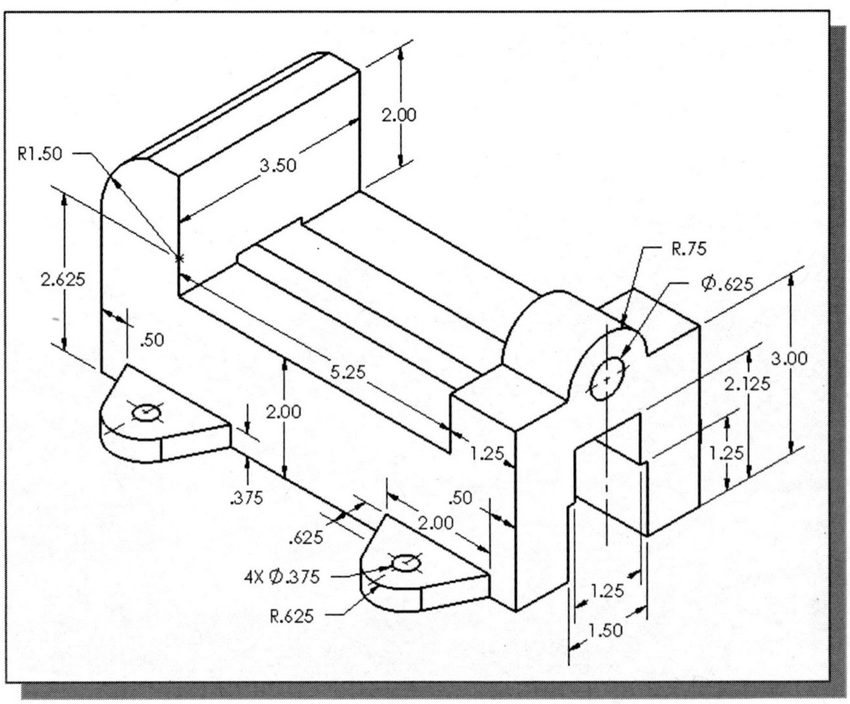

(b) **Jaw:** The shoulder of the jaw rests on the flat surface of the base and the jaw opening is set to 1.5 inches. Material: Gray Cast Iron.

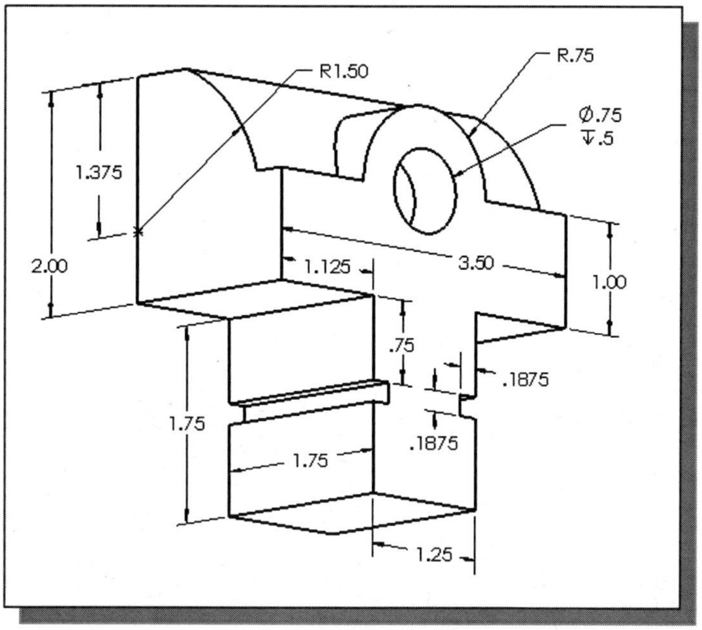

(c) **Key:** 0.1875 inch H x 0.375 inch W x 1.75 inch L. The keys fit into the slots on the jaw with the edge faces Aligned as shown in the sub-assembly to the right. Material: Alloy Steel.

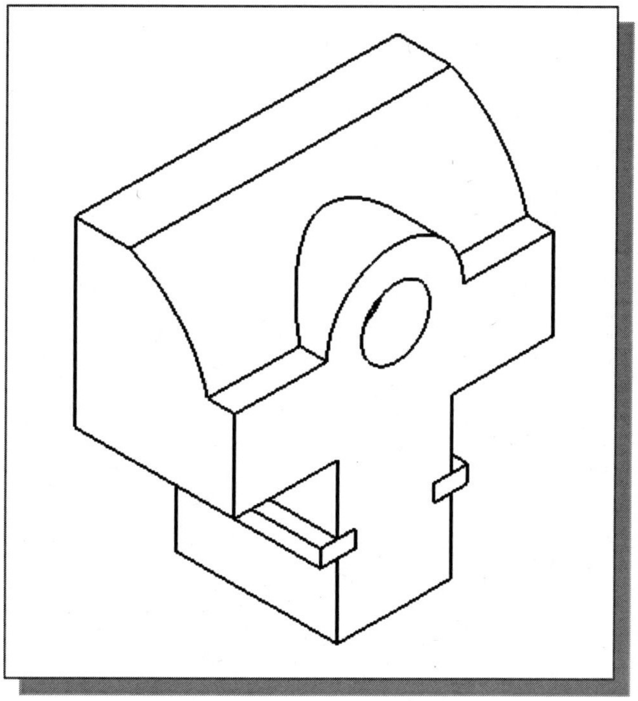

(d) **Screw:** There is one chamfered edge (0.0625 inch x 45°). The flat ∅ 0.75″ edge of the screw is Aligned with the corresponding recessed ∅ 0.75 face on the jaw. Material: Alloy Steel.

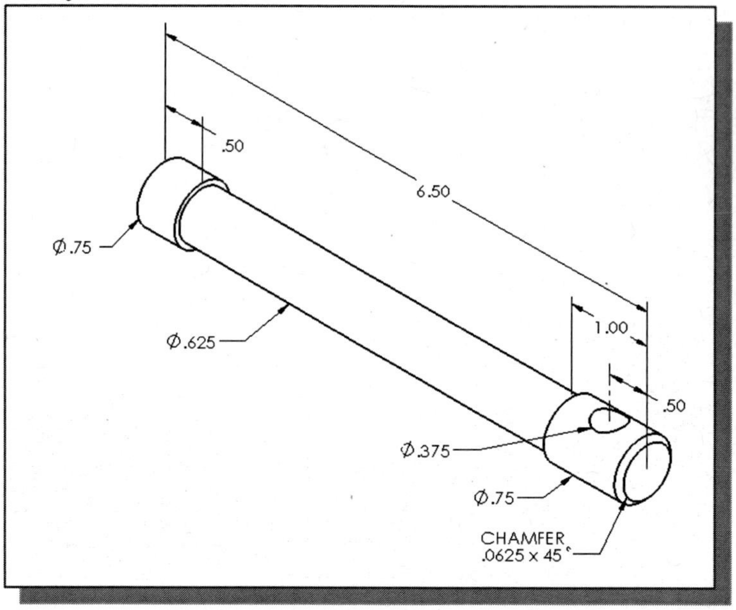

(e) **Handle Rod:** ∅ 0.375″ x 5.0″ L. The handle rod passes through the hole in the screw and is rotated to an angle of 30° with the horizontal as shown in the assembly view. The flat ∅ 0.375″ edges of the handle rod are Aligned with the corresponding recessed ∅ 0.735″ faces on the handle knobs. Material: Alloy Steel.

(f) **Handle Knob:** There are two chamfered edges (0.0625 inch x 45°).The handle knobs are attached to each end of the handle rod. The resulting overall length of the handle with knobs is 5.50″. The handle is aligned with the screw so that the outer edge of the upper knob is 2.0″ from the central axis of the screw. Material: Alloy Steel.

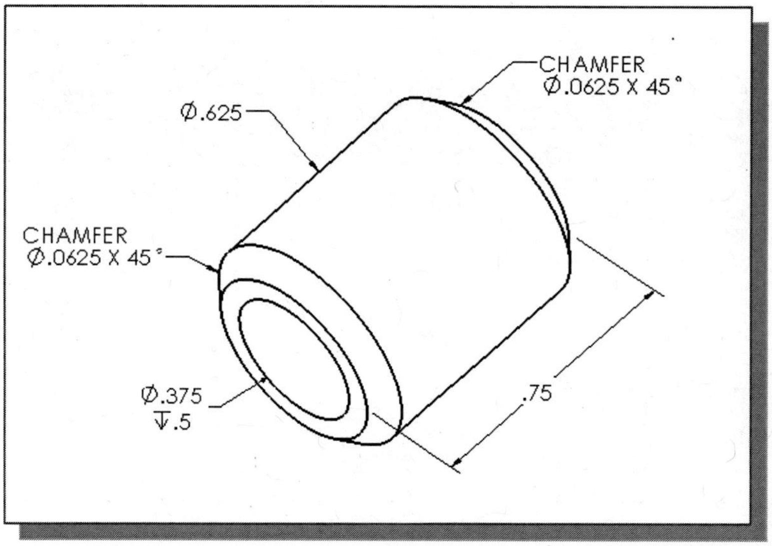

4. **Toggle-Clamp Assembly**
(Create a set of detail and assembly drawings. All dimensions are in inches.)

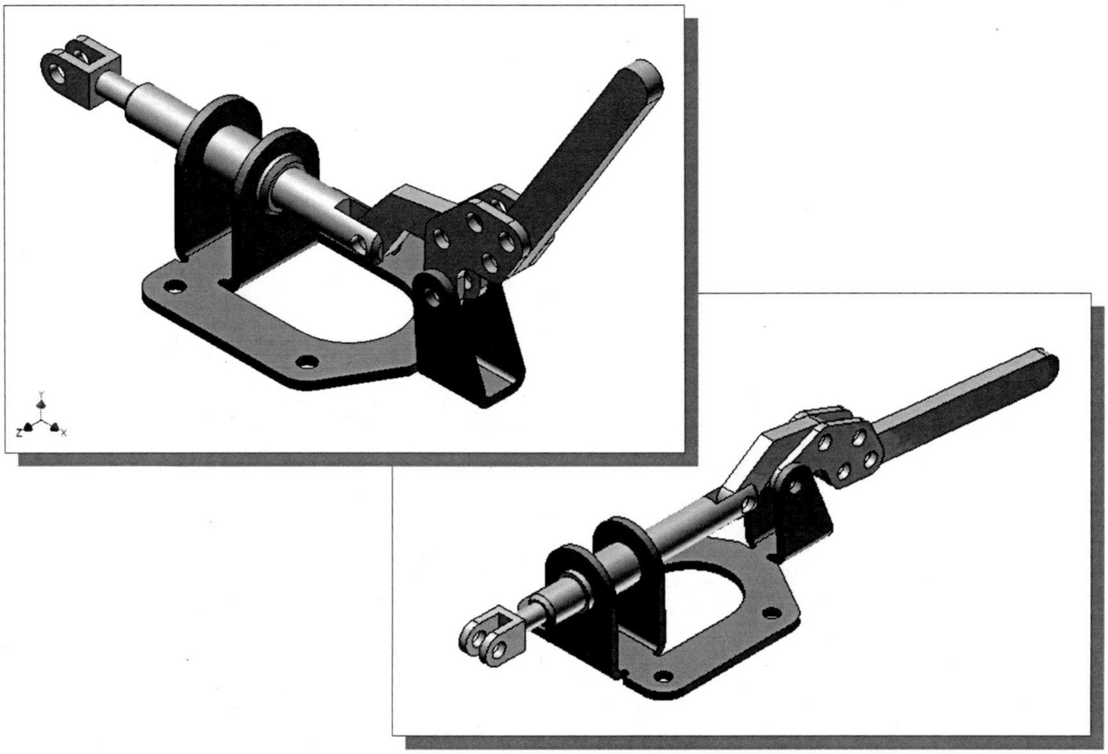

(a) **Sheet Metal Base**

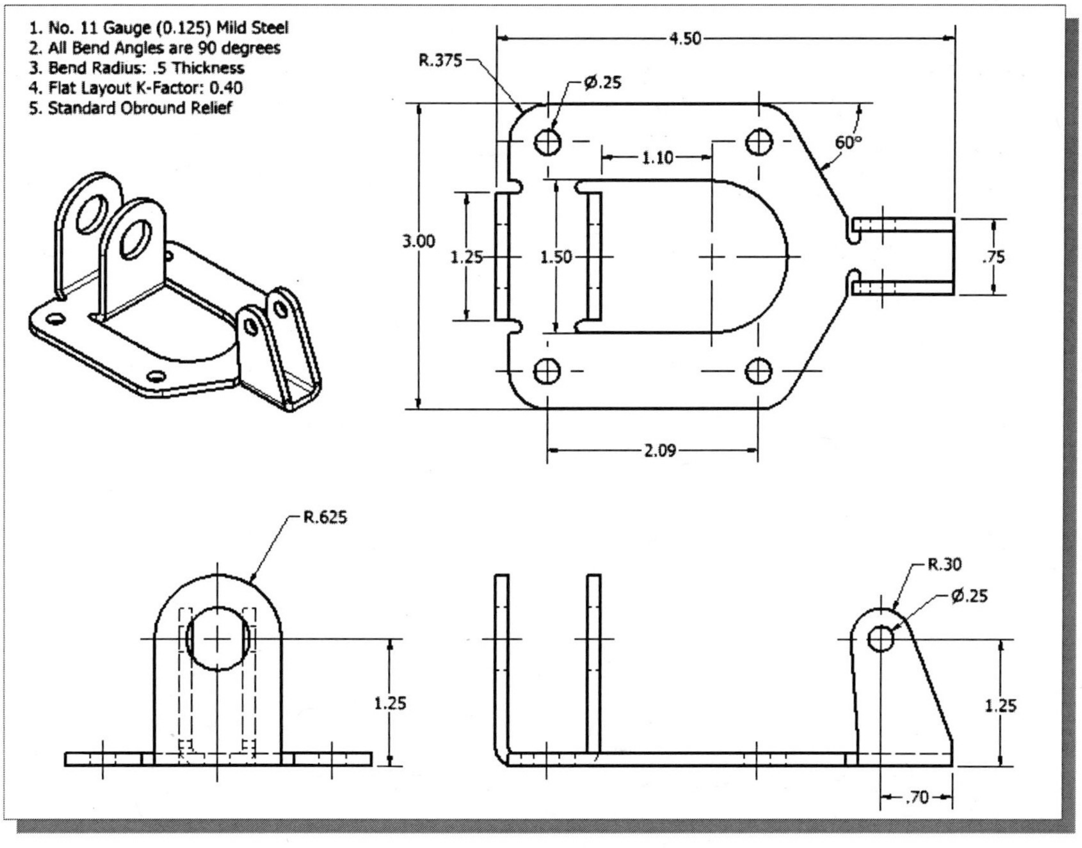

(b) **Connector**

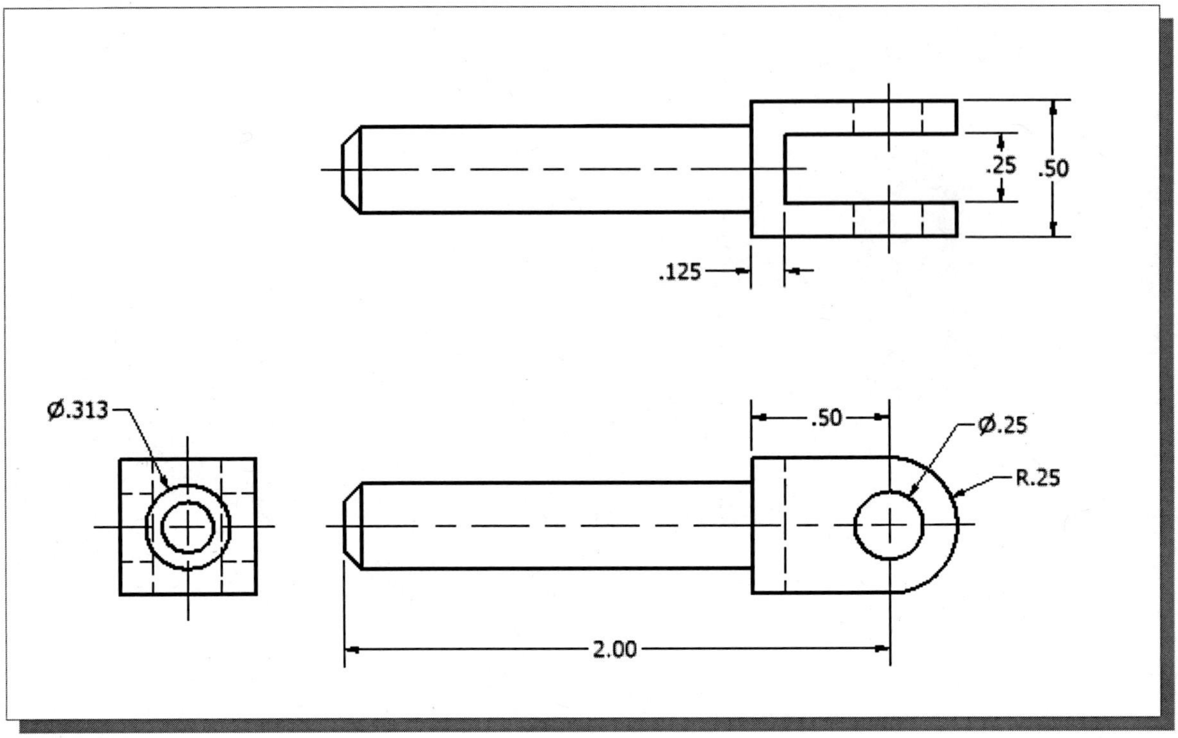

(c) **Handle**

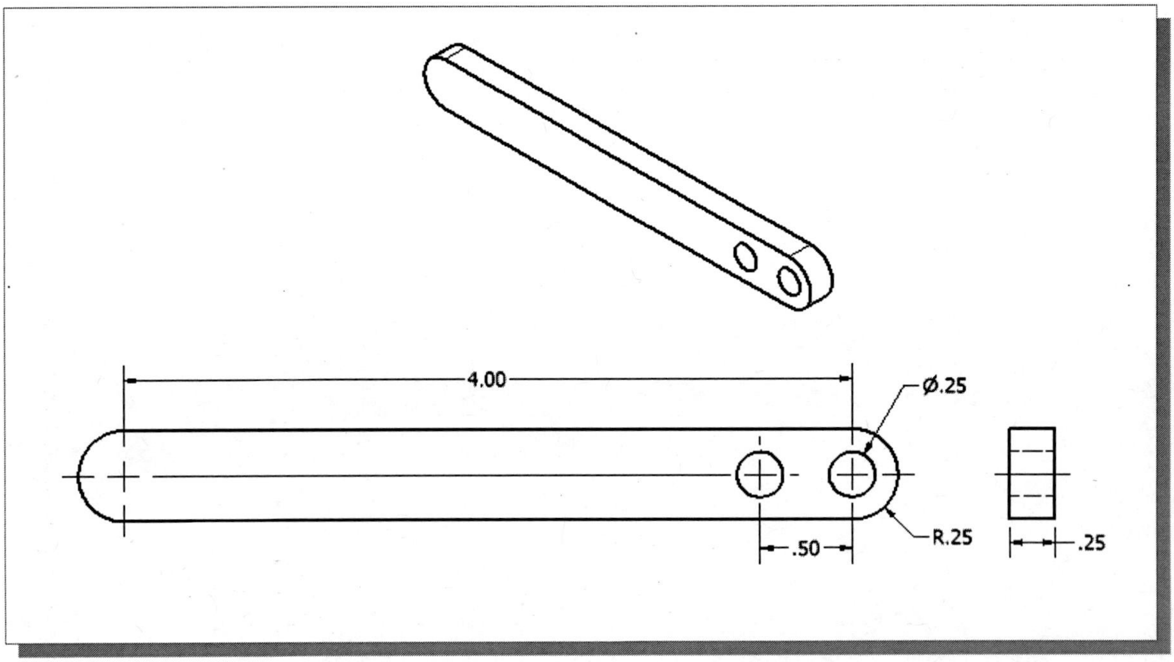

(d) **Joint Plate**

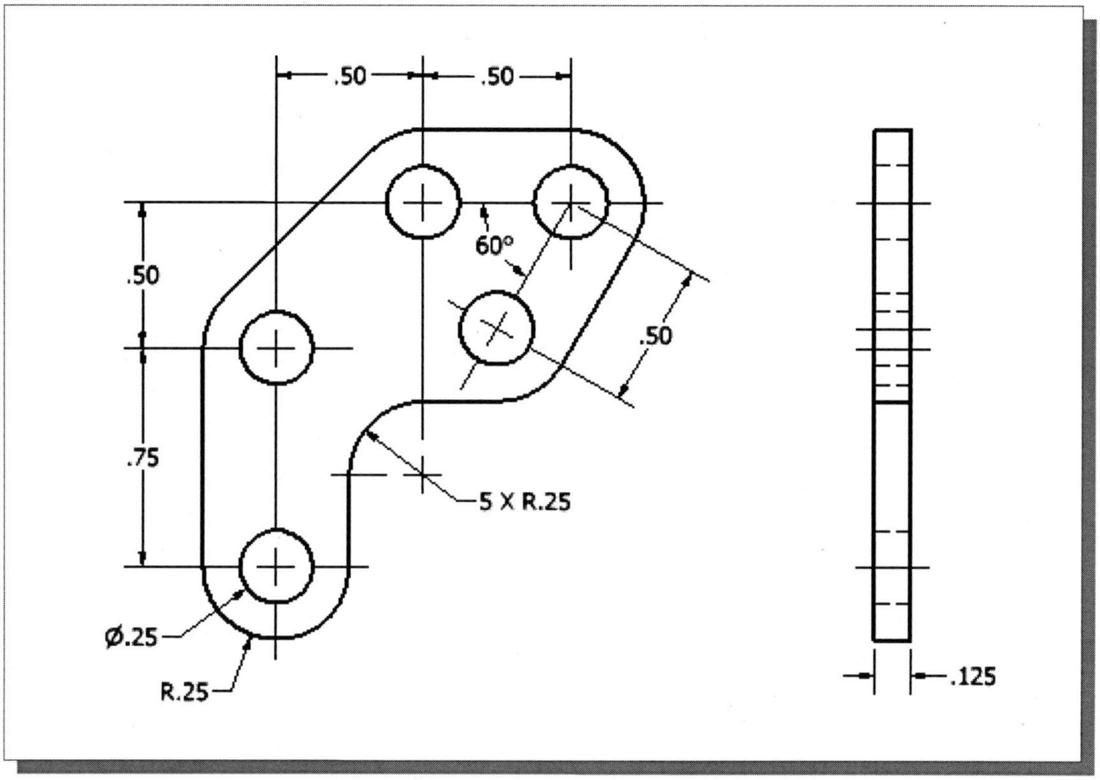

(e) **V-Link**

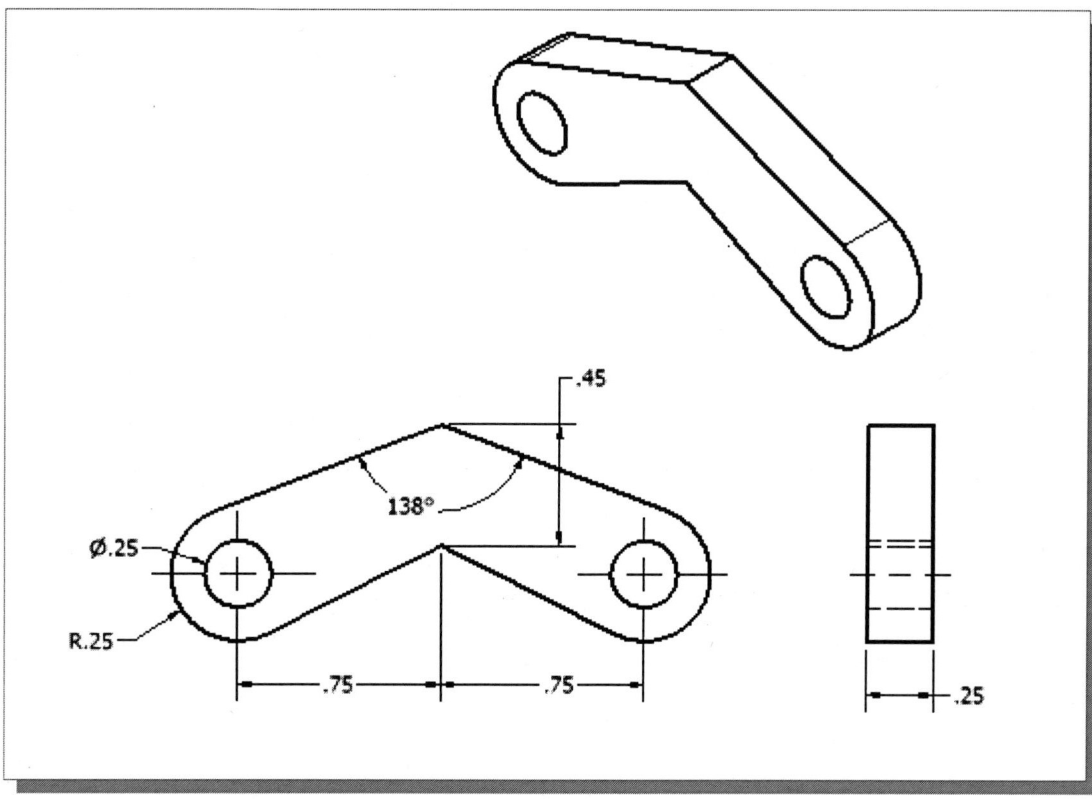

(f) **Rod**

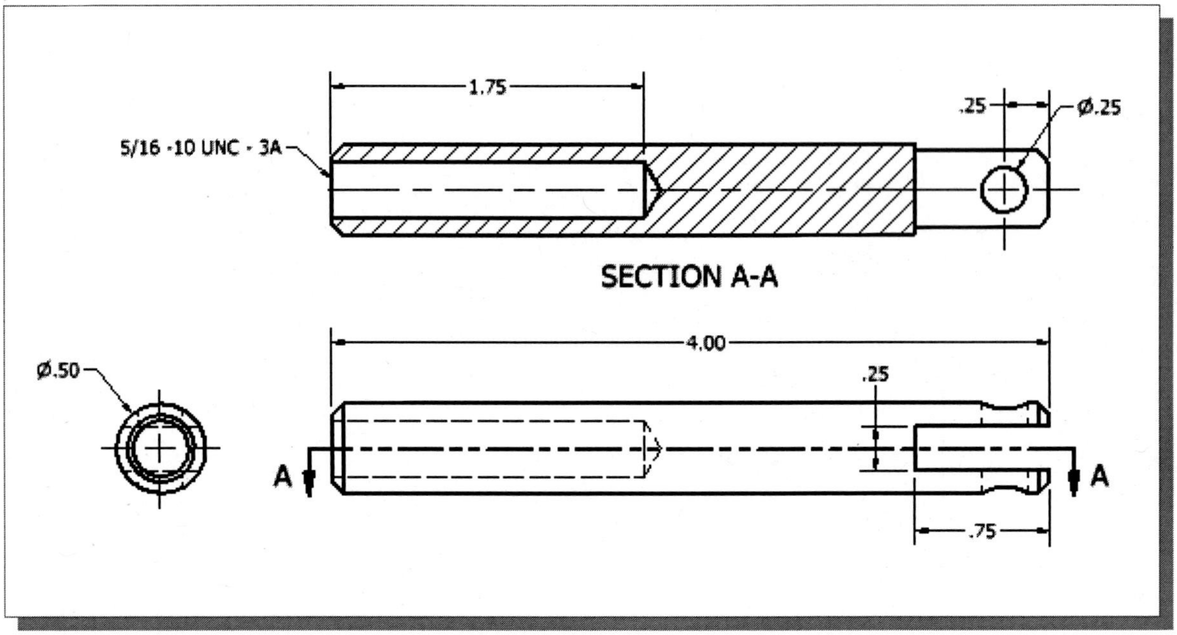

(g) **Bushing**

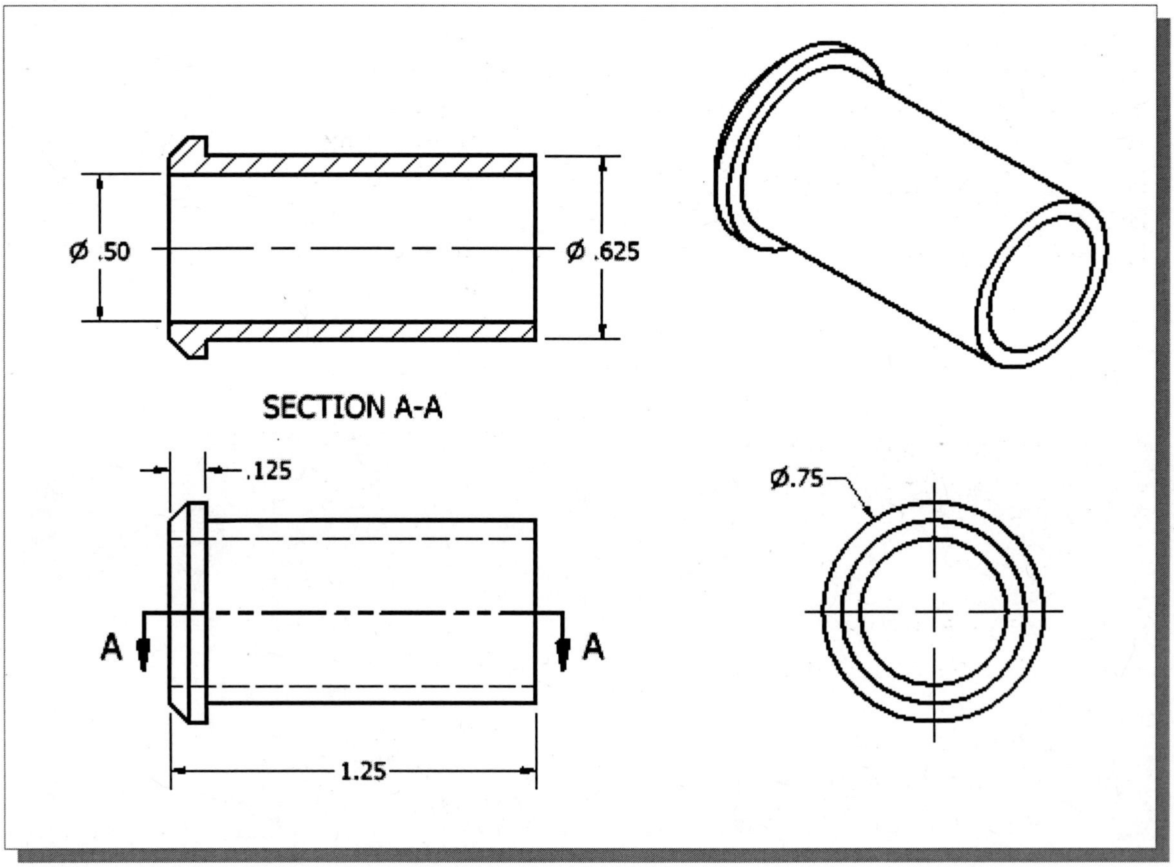

INDEX